1997 - 2002

PARLIAMENTARY
PROFILES

Andrew Roth and Byron

Caricatures by Ed Pentin and Terry Roth

PARLIAMENTARY PROFILES

CONTENTS

©1998 Parliamentary Profile Services Ltd

Address: 34 Somali Road, London NW2 3RL
Telephone: 0171 222 5884 or 0171 435 6673
Fax: 0171 222 5889

Computing Services by Padded Cell Software Ltd, London (info@paddedcell.com)

ISBN

-volume series   0 900582 43 X
A-D   0 900582 44 8
E-K   0 900582 45 6
-R   0 900582 46 4
S-Z   0 900582 47 2

Printed in Great Britain by Cedric Chivers Ltd, Bristol

MPS' RESPONSES: FROM THE SUBLIME TO THE RIDICULOUS

"I'll have to correct your draft profile of me, otherwise my obituaries will be all wrong!" gushed the friendly MP. Although his insight into the dependence of obituarists on these volumes was perceptive, it is not the main driving force for asking MPs to check our profiles for factual accuracy and completeness.

The main inspiration lies in the remembered injunction of an old journalist friend, Ferdinand Kuh, who cycled around wartime Washington, producing revelation after revelation. Asked why he put in so much hard work, he explained: "If you gather 95% of the story, the subject will disgorge the rest!"

Another discipline is British libel law. One learned to respect it when sued on 27 counts by the late former Prime Minister, Harold Wilson, who also tried to keep my 'Sir Harold Wilson - Yorkshire Walter Mitty' out of bookshops. Harold Wilson and his Political Secretary, Marcia Williams (later Baroness Falkender), soon made it clear they would not provide even factual information or checking, as had been readily provided by Enoch Powell for 'Enoch Powell - Tory Tribune'. The Wilson book, when complete, was cleared for libel by a top libel lawyer. After this, no writer likes to spend three years expensively defending himself against libel charges, 26 of which melted quickly under scrutiny. The last one, about which there was confirmation in Mary Wilson's poetry, never reached court.

Draft profiles are thus circulated to provide MPs with a chance to correct genuine mistakes which find their way into the public record, to update information, including telephone numbers and addresses - or to excise them if MPs want only their Westminster address and 'phone to be known, to protect them from threats or cranks. It is difficult, even for litigious MPs, to sue if they have a chance to suggest corrections to our record.

Curiously, the very process of soliciting corrections takes on a strange life of its own, with results ranging from the sublime to the ridiculous. There are no current corrections as juicy as that provided by a former Cabinet Minister who explained that his errant daughter, charged in Bristol as a prostitute, had actually been buying drugs but was clever enough to know that, in comparison, prostitution attracted a relatively derisory fine.

The 'sublime' responses are those carefully-read proofs which come back with corrections, updates, additions and responses to questions plus occasional compliments. The compliments usually refer to the completeness of our researches, including events the MP enjoyed being reminded about but had forgotten.

Among the more 'ridiculous' replies this time is that from the leader of a Northern Ireland party who responded to 2,000 words of his controversial history by sending back the sort of puff-biography his staff might hand out to a friendly young Irish-American journalist.

The prize however must go to the most mocked of new Labour women MPs who crossed through most of her profile, deriding it as "crap" and "rubbish" but insisted on its including the fact that "my husband left me for another woman, without any prior notice, two weeks after I was elected to the House of Commons". She also wanted excised the name of her lover, a TV political editor, well known to the whole Parliamentary Press Gallery. Like MPs, Parliamentary Profiles has learned to expect a small but steady percentage of irrational responses. At least ours are not in purple or green ink.

Our percentage of replies in toto have notched up to four out of five as our authority in the field has strengthened. One of the striking things about non-repliers is how high is the percentage among Labour MPs with a Trotskyist or semi-Trotskyist background. Of course, if you are a Minister in the Blair Government, it is irritating to be reminded that you secured your first candidacy by a Trotskyist putsch in a marginal seat in which you were pushed into third place. Or that you engaged in Trotskyist rants at conference-fringe meetings of 'Red Ted' Knight's former organ, the LABOUR HERALD, allegedly Libyan-financed. This time their ranks are joined by a septuagenarian 'New Trotskyist' who has never been willing anyhow to disclose his inherited wealth until partly forced to do so by new Commons rules.

In contrast, on the Conservative side, there is a new enthusiasm for disclosure, particularly among new bachelor MPs. They are anxious to have published the up-to-date names of their girlfriends. Even those who do not want names unveiled want to underline their heterosexuality. One Tory bachelor objected to a PRIVATE EYE joke about his never having "chased any kind of pussy". This sensitivity is understandable for anyone who, while conversing with the then bachelor, John Biffen, at a Brighton Tory conference had the conversation interrupted by his Tory chairwoman half-whispering in his ear, "Are you married yet?". He soon was.

In contrast, the new wave of a Labour MPs - and some of the '92 vintage - are quite upfront about disclosing that they are normal in the sense of having partners rather than spouses. When Stephen Byers was promoted to the Cabinet, he 'phoned his lady partner after his mother. But, after the July 1998 reshuffle, the gay community claimed that two of the bachelors promoted to the Cabinet belonged in their camp. It all goes to show that MPs are a slice of the human race, albeit a highly selective one.

ANDREW ROTH

Diane (Julie) ABBOTT **Labour** **HACKNEY NORTH & STOKE NEWINGTON '87-**

Majority: 15,627 (47.6%) over Conservative 7-way;

Description: Underprivileged northeast London working class area; has a third of non-whites and only a quarter of owner-occupiers; only slightly gentrified, with one Tory ward; this seat took half of Hackney Central in '83; "the highest unemployment in the southeast" (DA);

Position: On the Foreign Affairs Select Committee '97-; on Labour's NEC '94-; Chairman: Parliamentary Black Caucus '89-, all-party Parliamentary Group on Street Prostitution '94-; Vice Chairman, Black Sections Steering Committee '86-; ex. on Treasury and Civil Service Select Committee '89-97; Secretary: Campaign Group '92-93, Westminster Councillor '82-86; President, Anti-Racist Alliance '94;

Outlook: A leader of the 'ostracised Left'; the colour-and-class-conscious first black woman in the Commons and on Labour's NEC; a highly-charged, highly-intelligent, sarcastic, pugnacious extrovert; can make "a serious and thoughtful contribution" (Tory MP Geoffrey Clifton-Brown); she is unswervingly loyal to the anti-Maastricht hard-Left; was demoted in '97 from the Treasury Select Committee, where she was brutally direct, asking Bank of England Governor Eddie George whether he was "just an inflation nutter"; best at passionate, coherent oratory; tends to overstate and under-prepare; "fearless in the face of opprobrium" (Claudia Fitzherbert, DAILY TELEGRAPH); hard-Left (Campaign Group), semi-Trot (Socialist Action), but anti-Militant (because they are against blacks and women); advocate of female equality and working class control; the only black MP who has remained loyal to black sections; "like a politically active Eartha Kitt", "she may purr her way to the top; but with Leftwing claws like that, she is no pussy cat" (Baroness Falkender); slightly mellowing: "as I get older I realise that real progress is evolutionary and that it happens at a snail's pace"; was formerly highly ambitious, but as someone completely outside the Blair camp, she has lowered her sights to hoping "to be a good constituency MP and a good mother";

History: When a child, local racists forced her parents to leave Paddington for Harrow; she joined the Labour Party '71; she joined Anti-Apartheid, CND and the Campaign for Labour Party Democracy, which backed Tony Benn for Deputy Leadership Sep '81; was elected for her natal ward on Westminster Council May '82; as candidate for women's section of NEC, won 1,382,000 votes Sep '84; vigorously moved motion supporting black sections at annual conference, attacking Militant, Labour Rightwingers and Labour "racists" Oct '84; had conversations with Brent East ward officials about her standing against Ken Livingstone who was seeking to replace its MP, Reg Freeson Nov '84; co-authored, with Trotskyist Sharon Atkin, a paper for a hard Left (LABOUR BRIEFING and Target Labour Government) conference in Birmingham, versions of which claimed: "a Labour Government which really tried to take power from the capitalist class would find itself blocked; a new apparatus would have to be formed...destroying the outlived state machinery"; "we are not interested in reforming the prevailing institutions - of the police, armed services, judiciary and monarchy - through which the ruling class keep us in 'our' place; we are about dismantling them and replacing them with our own machinery of class rule" Jan-Feb '85; confronted Ken Livingstone over premature activities by his supporters in Brent East Feb '85; ran second to Livingstone in selection for Brent East Apr '85; was on all-woman short list for Westminster North May '85; on 'Briefing' slate won 1,426,000 votes for NEC in women's section Sep '85; accused Kinnock of wanting to be Prime Minister at any cost Oct '85; backed absolute support for Scargill in the miners' strike Oct '85; moved motion calling for women's seats on NEC be elected by women alone Oct '85; was selected for safe Hackney, replacing reluctant, aged Ernest Roberts by 42 to 35, after having told selectors "to choose between a selection that looked to the past or one that looked to the future", overcoming resistance from Livingstoneites and LABOUR BRIEFING backers Dec '85; was endorsed by NEC Jan '86; won 654,000 votes in women's section of NEC Sep '86; at the hard-Left LABOUR HERALD conference meeting said Neil Kinnock was purging the Left to "make the party more acceptable to journalists"; warned: "if they came for Militant in the morning, they'll come for the rest of us in the afternoon" Sep '86; again lost conference battle for black sections Oct '86; predicted a "caucus" of black Labour MPs in the next Parliament Oct '86; was elected with 7,678 majority June '87; joined hard-Left Campaign Group June '87; was only one to turn up for first meeting of "black caucus" of Labour MPs June '87; visited Tamils detained on ferry Aug '87; with support of Campaign Group, CLPD and Labour Left Liaison, ran ninth in contest for seven constituency seats on Labour's NEC, with 234,000 votes Sep '87; in her belated Maiden she disparaged Government's Immigration Bill as "born in racism" Nov '87; backed Jeremy Corbyn's right to insist on Commons entry for a formerly imprisoned ex-IRA-sympathising researcher Nov '87; urged "racism awareness training" in Whitehall Dec '87; acclaimed ILEA for its contribution to Hackney's special educational needs Feb '88; belittled 'Action for Cities' as a "PR initiative" Mar '88; said ILEA educated 45% of black children "if you attack education in London you are attacking the educational prospects of nearly half the black children at school" Mar '88; in the USA she described UK as "one of the most fundamentally racist nations on earth" Apr '88; backed Militant Dave Nellist against Speaker's suspension of him Apr '88; co-sponsored Tony Benn's Bill to ban foreign nuclear bases Apr '88; complained that the 38,000 in Hackney on housing benefit would mostly have their benefits cut under Housing Benefit (Changes) Bill Apr '88; accused Zola Budd of being a "walking, talking, running, public relations stunt for Apartheid" Apr '88; accused Commons attendants of maltreating black visitors May '88; said, "we have seen in London a Government bent on a spiteful, wholly ideological holy war against areas whose only fault is they voted Labour" July '88; won 258,000 votes for constituency section of NEC Oct '88; claimed that in almost 7 years she and Sharon Atkin had put the issue of "black self-organisation" on Labour's agenda; welcomed Larry Whitty's attempted compromise proposal on black sections but said she would wait to see if it was "a holding mechanism" or could deliver on "the principle of black self-organisation" Oct '88; voted against Defence Estimates Oct '88; voted against anti-IRA oath in Elected Authorities Bill, instead of abstaining as requested Dec '88; strongly urged Parliamentary oversight of security services Dec '88; voted against Prevention of Terrorism Bill Dec '88; warned that Thames Water was planning to cram 1,100 houses into Stoke Newington reservoir site Feb '89; opposed threat to Rushdie because "censorship is wrong and any calls for censorship by any fundamentalist religious leaders should be resisted" Feb '89; was named to Treasury Select Committee Mar '89; with Bernie Grant and Keith Vaz, launched Black Parliamentary Caucus, imitating that in Washington Mar '89; urged a black Labour candidate be selected for Vauxhall by-election Apr '89; complained about deterioration of London Transport Apr '89; with 49 other CND MPs, reaffirmed their rejection of Neil Kinnock's abandonment of unilateralism May '89; speaking of her former jobs as press officer for Ken Livingstone and Ted Knight, said: "I know what it is like to work for unscrupulous and power-crazy politicians" June '89; received 196,000 votes for NEC Oct '89; complained of under-provision of health care in Hackney Nov '89; complained that "in the headlong pursuit of market values, Conservative

Members are willing to throw away all that is good about British television" Dec '89; complained about the absence of aid to Vietnam Dec '89; disclosed confidential minutes of a secret seminar in the Carlton Club to privatise the NHS Dec '89; criticising Tory MPs for near-racism on Hongkong asylum proposals, claimed they would react differently to South African white immigrants Dec '89; criticised Labour's "studied ambiguity" about immigration from Hongkong Jan '90; in CAMPAIGN GROUP NEWS said "the necessity for exchange controls is obvious" Jan '90; accused Mrs Thatcher of being "Apartheid's fifth columnist" Feb '90; urged reduction of 3rd world debt by 50% as a footnote to Treasury Select Committee report Mar '90; said she would pay her poll tax, although prominent in non-payment campaign Mar '90; astonished colleagues by stating "the London Labour Party is not just an adventure playground for Trotskyists" (GUARDIAN) June '90; after visiting Frankfurt, Berlin and Budapest with Treasury and Civil Service Select Committee, said East Germany and Eastern Europe were ripe for a German takeover "at knockdown prices" June-July '90; claimed Hackney was suffering from the second highest level of teachers' vacancies in the country July '90; voted against Gulf War Sep '90; received 189,000 votes in constituency section of NEC Oct '90; voted for Jonathan Aitken's anti-EEC amendment Dec '90; again voted against Gulf War Jan '91; said that her weekly surgeries were dominated by complaints about damp housing Mar '91; with other hard-Leftists on 'Committee for a Just Peace in the Middle East', opposed restoring the Kuwaiti regime because it had never been elected and treated its women badly Apr '91; urged re-scheduling of Nigeria's debts Apr '91; was on Campaign Group slate for NEC May '91; defended Norman Lamont's £50 tax on mobile phones June '91; urged aid for "good government" of Sierra Leone June '91; claimed Labour had achieved more social and racial integration in London than reached in New York or Washington June '91; with others in Campaign Group complained that Labour's leadership was too timid; called for restoration of full employment, lower ERM parities Sept '91; on hard-Left Campaign Group slate, her constituency section vote dropped from 189,000 to 101,000 Sep '91; held her seat with a 5.56% swing to Labour Apr '92; became Secretary of Campaign Group May '92; dropped to 49,000 votes for NEC's constituency section Sep '92; was rebuked by Labour's Gordon Brown for saying UK had entered the ERM on too high a parity Oct '92; claimed Bank of England only moved against BCCI because New York authorities were about to act and expose their laxity Oct '92; defended Barts hospital against Tomlinson threat Oct '92; visited Germany where she witnessed "the rising tide of racism and anti-Semitism" Oct '92; opposed the Government's Asylum and Immigration Appeals Bill: "Conservative Members cannot understand what it means to come from rural Jamaica or Trinidad - to have saved and come across in one's best suit - only to be treated by immigration officers as some sort of criminal" Nov '92; opposed Maastricht as leading to "a fortress Europe, a xenophobic little Europe" Nov '92; was rated as one of the most rebellious Labour MPs, with 7 rebellious out of a possible nine Feb '93; told Cabinet Secretary Sir Robin Butler that "you were used by Mr [Jonathan] Aitken to give credibility to what remains a very opaque episode" - the payment for Aitken's stay at the Ritz Hotel in Paris Mar '93; voted against 3rd Reading for Maastricht Bill May '93; in wake of murder of black schoolboy, spoke against racial violence May '93; complained of growth of prostitution and kerb-crawling in her constituency May '93; in GUARDIAN letter co-opposed military intervention in Bosnia, for fear of being involved in a "Vietnam-type war in Europe" June '93; introduced Workplace Childcare Bill to provide creches, a Bill she later abandoned June '93; in INDEPENDENT letter co-urged lifting of US trade embargo on Cuba July '93; accused Tory MPs like Winston Churchill of being "most unpleasant and unsavoury" in talking about immigration and asylum matters July '93; complained that fight against drugs in London, "the drug capital of the UK", was being starved of resources July '93; in a DAILY MAIL feature her husband, architect David Thompson, disclosed that their marriage had been a "sham" devised to prevent her from falling into "the black stereotype of having a baby out of wedlock" Sep '93; opposed restoring capital punishment Feb '94; voted to reduce age of homosexual consent to 16, Feb '94; complained about growth of drugs in her constituency Mar '94; urged Margaret Beckett to stand to avoid an all-male contest May '94; voted for Margaret Beckett for Leader and Deputy Leader July '94; was accused of fare dodging July '94; she surprised observers by beating Mo Mowlam to retain her last-place NEC seat with 36,539 votes and, with women's preference, also beating Ken Livingstone who received 47,960 votes Oct '94; co-sponsored Tony Benn's Bill to remove curbs on unions Oct '94; was one of a score of Campaign Groupies who wrote to the GUARDIAN opposing the Criminal Justice Bill as criminalising protest and removing the historic right of silence Oct '94; voted against European Communities (Finance) Bill Nov '94; with three other NEC members, opposed Tony Blair's revised Clause IV document as "full of feel-good phrases and just vague waffle" Nov '94; was elected President of the Anti-Racist Alliance, in succession to Ken Livingstone, but walked out three weeks later in protest against the activities of Marc Wadsworth ("impossible to work with") Oct-Nov '94; on the NEC, voted with Clare Short and Dennis Skinner against the Clause IV reform timetable Dec '94; warned that "if a new Labour government takes off with only wishy-washy ideas, then the civil service will eat them alive" Feb '95; on the NEC, voted against the Blairite version of Clause IV Mar '95; told BBC radio that the new Clause IV was "a lot of tosh"; if the Blair leadership asked for a vote on "the healing qualities of cabbage", it would get it Apr '95; wrote: "elections to the Shadow Cabinet provide a useful corrective to patronage and cronyism" June '95; urged a more intensive anti-drug programme to protect inner-city dwellers like her constituents June '95; with Bernie Grant, refused to attend a meeting on mugging with Sir Paul Condon because he had said that most muggings in London were carried out by black youths July '95; retained her seat on the NEC with an improved vote of 45,653, with the help of pro-female discrimination which enabled her to defeat Jack Straw Oct '95; with other Campaign Groupies, backed a dissident motion to cut Defence expenditure to the average of other West European states Oct '95; attacked anti-black racism in sport Oct '95; on the NEC, with Dennis Skinner, voted against the compromise on the candidacy of semi-Trotskyist Liz Davies Oct '95; on the NEC, with Dennis Skinner, voted against suspending the Leader and Deputy Leader of Walsall Council for having led a "party within a party" Nov '95; attacked Michael Howard's Asylum and Immigration Bill as "cruel", "inhumane", colour-biased and "based on a wholly unquantified, exaggerated and apocalyptic notion of the threat that so-called bogus asylum-seekers present to the British way of life" Dec '95; was "sad" at the abandonment of all-women short-lists because of judicial resistance Jan '96; attacked Clause 8 of the Asylum and Immigration Bill, aimed at barring employment of illegal immigrants, as making employment more difficult for all coloured workers; pointed out that official unemployment was 60% among black males between 18 and 24 Feb '96; with Dennis Skinner voted against Tony Blair's proposal to ballot Labour's membership on an unamendable party manifesto Mar '96; was one of 25 Labour rebels voting against the renewal of the Prevention of Terrorism Act Mar '96; the all-party Parliamentary Group on Street Prostitution which she had chaired was not able to reach agreed radical solutions Mar '96; with Ken Livingstone wrote to the GUARDIAN claiming that child benefit paid to 1m families for older teenagers made the difference between keeping children in school or not Apr '96; accused Tory Minister Ann Widdecombe of "utterly repellent" views on childbirth Apr '96; was one of the rebels against Jack Straw's agreement to co-operate with the Tory anti-terrorist Bill, including new stop-and-search provisions Apr '96; criticised Jack Straw's plans for a "curfew" on wayward youngsters June '96; claimed that "although a quarter of our professional footballers are black, a tiny proportion of regular attenders at football matches are black", showing "the continuing prevalence of racism among football crowds" June '96; led group urging more anti-kerbcrawler powers July '96; voted to reduce MPs' mileage allowance but to base pensions on a salary increased to £43,000 July '96; with Ann Clwyd, resisted John Prescott's appeal not to stand against Harriet Harman for the Shadow Cabinet, accusing Labour Whips of stuffing ballot boxes with the votes of absentee MPs; she claimed Harman had her own "Assisted Places scheme"; was criticised by Chief Whip Donald Dewar for charging the Blair leadership with "strong-arm tactics" July '96; she aligned herself with Denzil Davies, Alan Simpson and other Eurosceptics in opposition to a single European currency, saying: "you will get turmoil if Gordon Brown as Chancellor in a Labour Government has to make £18b worth of spending cuts and has to give way to the European bankers" July '96; warned the NEC it was backing the wrong faction in Hackney July '96; opposed Tom Sawyer's proposal to downgrade the NEC in favour of an unaccountable Policy Forum July '96; wrote to General Secretary Tom Sawyer saying it was a "fatal miscalculation" not to back the Hackney faction urging an inquiry into Hackney Social Services Aug '96; a survey credited her with 30 rebellions since '92, a third as many as Dennis Skinner Sep '96; criticised Gordon Brown for proposing to end child benefit grants for 16-to-18-year-olds Sep '96; retained her NEC seat with votes increased to 54,800 Sep '96; was sharply critical of the Bank of England's failures to prevent financial collapses Nov '96; in the HACKNEY GAZETTE criticised local Homerton Hospital for employing "blonde, blue-eyed girls from Finland, instead of nurses from the Caribbean who know the language and understand British culture and institutions" Nov '96; Marc Wadsworth, of the Anti-Racist Alliance, riposted that the current 'Miss Finland' was "a black Finn like me" Nov '96; complained that EMU was a device for political as well as economic union, and would impose lower social expenditure Nov '96; she was targeted for her pro-choice views by the Pro-life Alliance Party which urged opposition to her by an anti-abortion candidate Feb '97; was sharp in her assault on those who had mis-sold pensions and delayed compensating victims Mar '97; in campaigning for fellow Campaign Groupie Alan Simpson in Nottingham, supported Labour's manifesto, although she had not voted for it on the NEC, "because I felt the words weren't right in some respects, but it is party policy, right?" Apr '97; retained her seat with a 15,627 majority, an increase of of 5,000 on a pro-Labour swing of 8.3% May '97; lost her longtime 'pair' when Jonathan Aitken lost his Thanet South seat after the collapse of his libel action against the GUARDIAN May '97; was the only Labour member of the Treasury Select Committee to oppose Gordon Brown's proposal to give independence to the Bank of England because it was "fundamentally undemocratic" and "we cannot decouple economic management from politics" June '97; she was removed from the Treasury Select Committee and put on the Foreign Affairs Select Committee July '97; retained her seat on Labour's NEC in last place, with 76.772 votes, 8,000 ahead of Peter Mandelson but behind Ken Livingstone and Harriet Harman Sep '97; backed Dennis Skinner in opposing PR for the Euro-elections Oct '97; opposed the Bill giving independence to the Bank of England as "the first step towards Maastricht" and a single currency Nov '97; she denied the claims of Tony Blair's spin doctors that the PM had warned her at the NEC against informing the media of her insistence on Labour's full disclosure of its sources of finances before discussing it in the NEC or PLP Nov '97; was one of the 23 rebels who voted against the cut in lone-parent benefits Dec '97; asked PM Blair to justify cutting benefit for mothers with under-5 children unable to go out to work Dec '97; had adjournment debate on racism in the armed forces Jan '98; contrasted treatment of white Falkland Islanders and black Montserratians Feb '98; said there was no unanimity on a military strike against Iraq in the UN or the Arab world; was one of 23 Leftwing or pacifist MPs who rebelled against endorsing a military strike Feb '98; attacked the closed-list system of PR for Euro-elections as "possibly the worst conceivable system of PR" Mar '98; after she said tuition fees would bar the kids of poor families from attending university - "without access to a grant and free tuition, a working-class black 16-year-old [like me] could never have gone to Cambridge" - complained that Education Secretary David Blunkett heckled her in the Commons "after the style of a comedy-club drunk"; the Deputy Speaker intervened in her support Mar '98; attacked Trevor Phillips as "Mandelson's glove puppet" in his bid for the London mayoralty Mar '98; backed most of the Budget but baited Chancellor Brown on his welfare-to-work programme, asking whether it could succeed in her deprived constituency if there was a recession due to his devolving interest-rate responsibility to the Governor of the Bank of England Apr '98; on the Foreign Affairs Select Committee, gave Foreign Minister Tony Lloyd a hard time over his fumblingly inadequate answers on Sierra Leone; despite Whips' pressures, she repeated this in the Commons May '98; voted against the abolition of student maintenance grants, which she had needed to attend university June '98; was one of 24 Labour rebels who voted against Murdoch-style predatory newspaper pricing July '98;

Born: 27 September 1953, Paddington, London

Family: Daughter, of late Jamaican-born Reginald Abbott, ex-welder (who discouraged her taking A-levels but also told her: "no good coming second; you have to be better than white people"), and late Julia (Mclymont), retired mental hospital worker, who also came from rural Jamaica in '50; her mother's funeral service was at fashionable St Margaret's, Westminster; m May '91 Ghanaian architect David Thompson, who had had three children by differing previous relationships, with attendant court cases for maintenance; he claimed he was bullied by her friends and their communities into marrying her when pregnant: "it was not going to look good if some African guy had got Britain's first black woman MP pregnant and then dumped her"; their son, James Alexander Kojo was born Oct '91, christened in Commons Crypt Dec '91, with her then Tory 'pair' Jonathan Aitken as its godfather; the 'marriage', with separate flats and occasional weekend meetings, terminated after the April 1992 election; "I was paraded on the doorsteps during the last election, but was excluded from her victory celebration; I was just the walk-on part"; in May 1992, she wrote: "I know perfectly well that you never wanted to marry, and for me the relationship has been empty, humiliating and pointless"; the solicitors' letters which began in August 1992 included a demand that he sign a legal agreement barring him from talking to the press, which he refused to sign; the separation was announced in Sep '93;

Education: Harrow County Grammar School for Girls (the only black girl there; teachers found her "very confident and not easily fazed by anything"; gained 10 O-levels and 4 A-levels; played in joint drama society with Michael Portillo, including TS Eliot's 'Murder in the Cathedral'; wore pebble glasses and spent her pocket money on sweets); Newnham College (the first black state school student), Cambridge University (lower second in History);

Occupation: Ex: Press Officer for Lambeth Council Leader, half-black Linda Bellos '86-87; was in Press Office of GLC '84-85; Reporter, for Thames TV and TV-AM (Equality Officer of ACTT) '80-84; National Council for Civil Liberties (where she worked for Cobden Trust against 'sus' laws and on race relations) '79; Trainee Civil Servant in Home Office (denies having worn a see-through blouse; "I was just one token black person in a fundamentally racist institution") '75-78;

Traits: Short; chubby; "she dresses these days in black stretch velvet and looks like an exploding mole" (Matthew Parris, TIMES); attractive Benin head; articulate; ambitious; is regularly restyled in pursuit of current fashion (her suits are "made by one of my favourite designers, Jenny Fletcher-Simms, a black haute couture designer based in Hackney"); "likes her gear cut sprauncy rather than severe" (Alix Coleman, SUNDAY EXPRESS); a fat-fighter ("don't ask me about my measurements; they make me neurotic; it's not impossible to seem slim if you're overweight, but its expensive; I have a short neck, waist and legs and very square shoulders and I've always yearned to be a willowy Somalian woman; I'm always on a diet"; spent four days and £185 slimming at Lord de Saumarez's health hydro to remove her "wobbly bits" June '87 and thereafter, even when pricier; she gave up by May '93 when she signed a motion against diets "because 96% don't work and dieting causes other problems, including low self-esteem, constipation and headaches"); enjoys West Indian Sunday dinner of chicken, rice, red kidney beans, onions and coconut; "Miss Piggy"; "her only truly outsized attribute is the massive chip on her shoulder" (Trevor Leighton, SUNDAY TELEGRAPH); formerly paired with Jonathan Aitken, her ex-boss at TV-AM; "spoiled and self-indulgent" (John Torode, INDEPENDENT); "tempestuous" (EVENING STANDARD); uses "abusive language" (Chris Grant, former aide); "subjected us to a humiliating tirade" (Wood Green Civic Centre); can be "sophisticated and amusing, bringing a welcome gust of humour" (DAILY TELEGRAPH); although "disarmingly jolly", "the language is menacing, the jargon is dire, instantly classifying Miss Abbott as a member of the Surly Tendency" (SUNDAY TELEGRAPH); "gutsy", "angry", "punching the air with her fist, being outrageous, looking for trouble", "always having rows"; "pushy", "cheeky" (Julia Langdon, DAILY MIRROR); says: "life is one perpetual hassle when you're a British black woman", "as a woman you always have to be better than a man to get on in life; as a black woman you have to be better still"; "I've always been a talker, ever since I was three"; her conversation is laced with expletives; highly selective in her human contacts; jokingly described as her "finest half hour" a clothed lovemaking session with a naked man in a Cotswolds field (SHE April '85); a longtime friend of Jeremy Corbyn; "prefers the company of her old friends" (Trevor Leighton, SUNDAY TELEGRAPH); no church-goer ("the Baptists probably think I'm with the Pentecostalists and the Pentecostalists think I'm with the Baptists; and all the time I'm at home ploughing through the SUNDAY TIMES"); admits to procrastination; enjoys watching 'Blind Date' and listening to R&B and soul;

Address: House of Commons, Westminster, London SW1A 0AA; 8 Manor House Place, Palentine Avenue, Stoke Newington, London N16 8XH;
Telephone: 0171 219 5062/4426 (H of C); 0171 275 8414;

'Gerry' (Gerard) ADAMS   **Sinn Fein**   **WEST BELFAST '97-, '83-92**

Majority: 7,909 over SDLP 6-way;
Description: The largely-Catholic slums of west Belfast, expanded into Lisburn in '95 to take in almost 10,000 more voters; the UK's most troubled and war-torn constituency, with some of its worst housing, including the Falls Road; much of its population is unemployed; of late it has been a battlefield between the moderate nationalists in the SDLP and the IRA-linked Provisional Sinn Fein;
Position: President '83-, Vice President '79-83 of the Provisional Sinn Fein; Northern Ireland Assemblyman '82-86
Outlook: Is "the driving and controlling force" of the Sinn Fein and IRA (Sir Hugh Annesley, former RUC Chief Constable); a key to peace through his influence over the IRA's "hard men", having, with Martin McGuinness, ousted the southern old guard from the leadership of both organisations in the '80s; has taken a military-orientated movement into politics while retaining

the bulk of its personnel; "the most thoughtful and intelligent person in the Republican leadership", who "turned Sinn Fein from an insignificant and unconvincing IRA front into a serious grassroots political movement" (David McKittrick, INDEPENDENT); a "brave man" (former Northern Ireland Secretary Peter Brooke) for bringing about the '94-95 ceasefire; "the most capable person in the [Provisional] movement at thinking simultaneously in political and military terms, as well as its most visible and charismatic figure" (Paul Johnson, GUARDIAN); "Gerry Adams insists that he would not dream of going to the IRA with anything less than their terms for a truce - a British withdrawal and a release of IRA prisoners" (David Hearst, GUARDIAN); has served as an honour guard at over 200 IRA funerals since 1971; was allegedly previously the military Chief of the Provisional IRA '76-78; having given up boycotting the Dail and the Northern Ireland Assembly, remains inhibited by the historic IRA dogma of boycotting Westminster;

History: Joined the Fianna, the IRA's youth wing at 16, "which was a great source of heartbreak to my Da" '64; witnessed the notorious Divis riots, when the RUC brutally broke up the election headquarters of the republican candidate in West Belfast; he joined Sinn Fein '64; was part of the "popular uprising" of the northern Catholic working class from '69; at 20 was "one of the first people to volunteer to join the Provisional IRA after the organisation was set up", splitting from the Orthodox IRA Dec '69; following RUC attacks on nationalist areas in Belfast and Londonderry, allegedly became the commander of the Belfast Brigade's 2nd Battalion '71; was photographed in black jacket and beret as part of a guard of honour at an IRA funeral '71; was missed in the internment scoop, but his father and brother were taken Aug '71; after having been on the run as a wanted man, was arrested and imprisoned, first on the prison ship 'Maidstone' Mar '72; at 24, in response to IRA demands that he be included in the talks, was flown to London for secret negotiations with William Whitelaw, the Northern Ireland Secretary June '72; as 'Brownie' in REPUBLICAN NEWS developed the theory of advancing republicanism on two fronts: "the ballot box and the Armalite" '72; allegedly became Adjutant of IRA's Belfast Brigade; allegedly helped plan 'Bloody Friday' July '72; allegedly became Commander of the IRA's Belfast Brigade Mar '73; was captured by the Army, beaten and reinterned July '73; allegedly became Chief of Staff of the Provisional IRA '76; was jailed on charge of Provisional IRA membership, a charge later dropped '78; was jailed for a further 18 months for trying to escape from the Maze; on his release, he allegedly took command of the IRA's newly-formed 'Northern Command' '80; he and other northern Irish 'Young Turks' replaced southerners in the leadership of the IRA-Sinn Fein; argued that the IRA could not win a purely military victory, therefore a political solution had to be found '80; allegedly asked what the impact the death of John Hume would have July '82; was elected to Northern Ireland Assembly, topping the poll in West Belfast Oct '82; was banned from the mainland after the Ballykelly bombing Dec '82; said, "assassination of industrialists has been marginally successful" Mar '83; was arrested during the election June '83; ousted SDLPer Gerry Fitt from his long-held West Belfast seat June '83; reaffirmed his refusal to take his seat in a "foreign Parliament" July '83; he expected arrest after a "supergrass" started spilling the beans Aug '83; placed an IRA beret, belt and gloves on the coffin of an alleged Provo killed by an SASman Dec '83; he denied the veracity of a 'World in Action' telecast accusing him of playing a leading military role in the Belfast Provisional IRA Dec '83; was wounded by a loyalist gunman with three bullets '84; he denied the SUNDAY TIMES' claim that he had taken over as the IRA Chief of Staff Aug '85; he denounced the Anglo-Irish Agreement as containing nothing that would make him urge the IRA to end violence Nov '85; decided on the need for wider support because the IRA alone could not win militarily and Sinn Fein alone could not win politically; he succeeded, at its Dublin conference, in persuading Sinn Fein to end its 60-year-old boycott of the Dail, the Irish Republic's parliament; this change, he claimed, would enable the Provos to cease "being spectators of a struggle in the six counties [of northern Ireland] and become pioneers of republicanism in the 26 counties" of Eire Nov '86; in Oxford Union debate said, "I have never condemned the IRA and I never will; for me to condemn them would be to say I do not understand them" Mar '87; claimed the Anglo-Irish Agreement had not worked because it had not "removed the causes of alienation" and "will not bring about the isolation of Sinn Fein" Apr '87; defended the IRA killing of an informer Apr '87; was accused of "hypocrisy" by Northern Ireland Secretary Tom King when he described the killing of 8 IRAmen in an RUC trap as "murder" May '87; he survived the general election with a halved majority June '87; had a secret meeting with SDLP Leader John Hume Jan '88; tried to calm Catholic youth mobs reacting to cemetery killings of two British corporals, caught by an IRA mob at the funeral of IRA volunteer Kevin Brady, killed by a loyalist Mar '88; after he told a Dublin magazine that another IRA bombing like that at Enniskillen, which killed 11 people, would "undermine the validity of the armed struggle", had another secret meeting with John Hume, allegedly to find a peaceful road to Irish unity to "get our people in from the cold"; missing was Martin McGuinness, the Londonderry Provo leader, whom Adams had described as "the head of the IRA" Mar '88; a senior RUC officer said: "Adams is developing into a political figure as distinct from a subversive general; he has distanced himself from the Provisionals to the extent that he now holds little control over their military activities; Martin McGuinness is the person with the power" Apr '88; he told the OBSERVER that killing British soldiers was "vastly preferable" to killing RUC or UDR members because it yielded more publicity and would "remove the agony" from Northern Ireland June '88; the "Adams faction" was said to be urging that "going political" by taking his seat in Parliament would present Britain with bigger problems than continued terrorism July '88; he was forced to withdraw from the talks with John Hume by the IRA hawks who objected to Hume's suggestion of an all-Ireland conference on a peaceful settlement, including Unionists Aug '88; in a US intelligence report 'Terrorist Group Profiles' released by the Pentagon, he was identified, with Martin McGuinness, as the two leaders of the Provisional IRA Jan '89; hit out at IRA killings of civilians "by mistake" Jan '89; at annual conference in Dublin, admitted that IRA and Sinn Fein alone could not win Irish unity Jan '89; the broadcast ban on the Sinn Fein was ended Apr '89; shared a Sheffield platform with Tony Benn who argued the case for British withdrawal from Ulster June '89; his brother, Sean Patrick, was charged with attempting to murder RUCmen Oct '89; in the wake of the killing of 10 Royal Marines at Deal, he defended the IRA's bombing campaign as "legitimate" Oct '89; the new Northern Ireland Secretary, Peter Brooke, admitted the armed struggle in Ulster was one neither side could win; said there could be talks if the IRA put down its arms Nov '89; described as "cold-blooded murder" the killing of 3 IRA men by an Army under-cover unit Jan '90; blamed "media mischief" for speculating on an IRA cease-fire Mar '90; welcomed the release of the 'Winchester Three' as underlining "how easily and groundlessly Irish people are sentenced to massive terms of imprisonment by the British courts" Apr '90; at the funeral of IRAman Desmond Grew, said: "those of us left to finish the unfinished business, will do so" Oct '90; secret negotiations between the British Government and the Sinn Fein began, at the instigation of MI5 '90; welcomed the IRA's three-day Christmas cease-fire Dec '90; after a fire-bombing campaign, was described by Economy Minister Richard Needham as an "apologist for those who burn jobs" Jan '91; urged Unionists to join in seeking a demilitarised future Feb '92; said, "I regard the IRA as a legitimate organisation, as freedom fighters, but the IRA doesn't tell Sinn Fein what to do and Sinn Fein doesn't tell IRA what to do" Mar '92; was defeated in West Belfast by SDLP's Dr Joe Hendron by 589 votes Apr '92; he briefly shook hands with Irish President Mary Robinson June '93; a grenade attack on his home injured his wife and son June '93; Hume-Adams talks resumed 'in secret', apparently bugged by MI5 Sep

'93; was barred from mainland Britain Oct '93; President Clinton initially refused him a visa for being "involved at the highest level" in IRA's terrorist strategy Nov '93; accurately described secret negotiations with the British Government Nov '93; his demand for an amnesty for jailed terrorists was rejected Dec '93; said he was "disappointed" that the Anglo-Irish Downing Street Declaration offered him a place at the negotiating table only if the IRA gave up violence Dec '93; after President Clinton allowed him a visa - to the dismay of John Major and Ulster Unionists -he paid a two-day visit to the USA, during which the President urged him to embrace the Downing Street declaration; Feb '94; at the Sinn Fein's annual conference in Dublin, said the mortar bombs at Heathrow showed "the causes of the conflict" still remained Feb '94; was given legal aid to fight his ban from mainland Britain Mar '94; John Hume urged the British Government to resume talks with Adams Mar '94; the IRA called a 72-hour ceasefire Apr '94; he called for a full amnesty for all imprisoned terrorists May '94; after years of his persuasion, the IRA began its ceasefire Aug '94; was welcomed in Dublin by Irish PM Albert Reynolds Sep '94; he demanded British "demilitarisation" and direct talks, insisting the IRA would not disarm before a settlement Oct '94; during his Washington visit, he met President Clinton's security adviser Nov '94; was described by Sir Patrick Mayhew as needed to carry those reluctant to see a cease-fire Nov '94; was praised by former Northern Ireland Secretary Peter Brooke as "a brave man" in having urged a ceasefire on the IRA Jan '95; on his St Patrick's Day visit, President Clinton urged the IRA to disarm Mar '95; on the first anniversary of the IRA ceasefire, claimed the British Government was using the decommissioning issue to "try to win a victory through stalemate" Apr '95; visited South Africa to meet President Mandela June '95; accused the UK Government of "strangling the peace process", warning that the IRA "hadn't gone away" Aug '95; said the peace process was "doomed to collapse" if Britain insisted on IRA disarmament before Sinn Fein could enter the talks Sep '95; called for an independent international judicial investigation into all "disputed killings" by British forces, such as the killing of three IRAmen on the Rock Sep '95; agreed the IRA would not give up arms in advance of a settlement but might gradually decommission some after Sinn Fein had been allowed into talks Jan '96; demanded an unconditional date for talks Feb '96; after he warned the White House it might happen, the IRA cease-fire broke down with a bomb in London's Docklands, which he blamed on the British Government's floundering Feb '96; wrote that the IRA leadership had begun its ceasefire on the basis of a "pan-nationalist alliance" of Dublin, the SDLP, Sinn Fein and Irish America to bring about a settlement; in the absence of the settlement, the IRA might begin "another 25 years of war" Mar '96; there was a breakdown in his relations with SDLP Leader John Hume and Irish PM John Bruton Apr '96; in the election to all-party talks, he achieved 53.4% of the vote in Belfast West, twice that of the SDLP, with the Sinn Fein collecting 15.4% of the poll in the Province, its best result May '96; said he was "shocked and saddened" by the Manchester bomb June '96; told Irish radio Sinn Fein wanted to "see an end to the armed struggle"; "we're not involved in it and we do not advocate it" June '96; told President Clinton: "don't ask me to push the IRA over a ceasefire - because I cannot deliver" June '96; declared "the peace process is in tatters" after 48 hours of rioting and intimidation visited on Catholic families after the RUC led Orange paraders through Portadown July '96; led Sinn Fein's newly-elected delegates up to the gates of Belfast's Castle Buildings to demand access to talks, despite the IRA's refusal to proclaim a ceasefire July '96; published his autobiography, Before the Dawn Sep '96; the Commons' Serjeant-at-Arms and the Labour Chief Whip Donald Dewar blocked attempts by Jeremy Corbyn and Tony Benn to host an Adams book launch Sep '96; after the Lisburn bombing, Ireland's PM, John Bruton compared the IRA to the Nazis and urged the Sinn Fein to limit itself to the ballot box Oct '96; he rejected angrily SDLP Leader John Hume's conditions for an electoral pact, including "a complete end to violence" by the IRA and his taking a seat in

Westminster Oct '96; Australia refused him an entry visa Nov '96; President Clinton refused him an American visa Feb '97; said he was "quite surprised" - when he meant angered - by the proposal that the imprisoned IRA suspect Roisin McAliskey might stand for her mother's old seat of Mid-Ulster, which his partner Martin McGuinness was planning to take Mar '97; showed interest in a "new opportunity for peace" after Labour's 'shadow' Northern Ireland Secretary, Mo Mowlam, promised that if there were an immediate ceasefire, maintained by word and deed, Sinn Fein might enter the multi-party talks in June, Mar '97; the Irish PM, John Bruton, said: "a vote for Sinn Fein is a vote of support for the IRA and the IRA's campaign of killing and murder" Apr '97; he carried the coffin of a Catholic father of 10, murdered by Loyalists - as he had done in more than 200 IRA funerals since 1971 Mar '97; he ousted Dr Joe Hendron from altered Belfast West to retake it with a majority of 7,909, a swing of 9.8%; 18,000 names appeared on the electoral register more than once May '97; visited Westminster with fellow SF winner Martin McGuinness, to be told he could have House of Commons stationery, but without pledging allegiance to the Queen, he could not take his seat, speak or vote, despite his election victory May '97; as a reward for the renewed IRA ceasefire, President Clinton granted him a visa Aug '97; he was also invited by Northern Ireland Secretary Mo Mowlam to join the all-party talks Aug '97; in Washington, he promised to "compromise, compromise, compromise, compromise" in all-party talks Sep '97; he accepted the "Mitchell principles", committing Sinn Fein to non-violence, on entering the talks Sep '97; he met PM Tony Blair at Stormont, the first such meeting in 76 years Oct '97; three IRA top hard-liners quit over the peace process Nov '97; he met PM Tony Blair at 10 Downing Street, describing it as "a moment in history" - the first such visit since Michael Collins met David Lloyd George there in 1921; denied the BBC claim that he and Martin McGuinness were members of the IRA's ruling body, the Army Council Dec '97; he was again banned from Parliament by Speaker Boothroyd Dec '97; he saw Tony Blair again Jan '98; an agreement was reached on a Northern Ireland Assembly, elected by PR, new Anglo-Irish cross-border institutions, protection of cultural identity against discrimination, decommissioning of arms, early release of prisoners, reform of the RUC Jan '98; after Sinn Fein was excluded from the talks for two weeks after two suspected IRA killings, he warned that any "partial" or "factional" agreement, excluding Sinn Fein, "won't work"; he would only return to talk after another meeting with Tony Blair Mar '98; conceded there was no imminent likelihood of Irish reunification, but demanded RUC reform and British Army withdrawal Mar '98; the Good Friday Agreement was reached after a hitch when the Ulster Unionists rejected George Mitchell's draft; it took Tony Blair's all-night talks and written assurances to retrieve the situation Apr '98; he won support from Sinn Fein's annual conference in Dublin by 72% to 28%, after he congratulated David Trimble for securing Ulster Unionist backing Apr '98; he and Martin McGuinness saw Tony Blair and Mo Mowlam in private for 30 minutes at Downing Street to discuss the British Army's role Apr '98; Sinn Fein was given the green light by the IRA Army Council to participate in the proposed Northern Ireland Assembly May '98; in the campaign for the Referendum on the Good Friday Agreement, said no republican need have any fears about the Agreement; the Agreement was accepted by 71% to 29%, with 96% of nationalists supporting it May '98; the Sinn Fein Conference agreed to support the Agreement May '98; promised to try to persuade the IRA to reveal the whereabouts of Northern Ireland's "disappeared" victims May '98; was said to have received a cool reception in the US May '98;

Born: 6 October 1948, West Belfast

Family: His maternal grandfather was a personal friend of James Connolly and James Larkin; his paternal grandfather had helped found the Irish Republican Brotherhood, predecessor of the IRA; was the eldest of 10 children of building worker Gerard ("old Gerry") Adams, an

IRA veteran of the 1939 campaign who was shot and wounded by the RUC and imprisoned for five years in the troubled '40s; his mother, a Hannaway, came from Belfast's leading Republican family; his cousin, David Adams, was jailed for 25 years for conspiracy to murder; he was awarded £30,000 against the RUC for injuries received at their hands '95; m '71 Collette (McArdle); 1s Gearoid '73, who trained as a teacher;

Education: St Mary's Grammar (Christian Brothers); left at 17;

Occupation: Author: Before the Dawn (1996, for which he was alleged to have received £100,000 as an advance), Selected Writings (1994), The Street and Other Stories (1992), Cage Eleven (1990), Politics of Irish Freedom (1988), Falls Memories (1982); was a barman '69-73 in Belfast pubs, since when he has collected unemployed benefit of £53.65 weekly;

Traits: Tall; cropped black beard; specs; reconstructed teeth; pipe-smoker; dresses neatly in dark suits; courteous; polite; wary; "complicated and elusive", "cold-blooded, unemotional, articulate and intelligent" (SUNDAY TELEGRAPH); "hard, cold, cliche-ridden and deep" (Sean O'Callaghan, IRA informer); changes abode almost every night; travels in bullet-proof cars; sometimes wears bullet-proof vests; pious Catholic;

Address: 51-53 Falls Road, Belfast 12; Norfolk Gardens, West Belfast;

Telephone: 01232 223214

(Katherine) 'Irene' ADAMS   **Labour**   **PAISLEY NORTH '90-**

Majority: 12,814 (37.5%) over SNP 6-way;

Description: Declining mill town; its cotton industry, employing 10,000 skilled women, died in the early '80s, followed by shipbuilding; Howden's high-tech engineering went in '90; Babcock and Wilcox is the last surviving major engineering works; when Paisley was cut in half in '83, Renfrew was added to this half;

Position: On the Select Committee on Scottish Affairs '97-; ex: on the Commons Catering Committee '91-95; Strathclyde Regional Councillor '79-86, Renfrew District Councillor '74-77, Paisley Town Councillor '71-74;

Outlook: Tough-minded, tough-talking, dynamic, sharp-witted, semi-hard Left widow who succeeded her late Centre-Left husband, Allen Adams; she also lost her friend and neighbour, Gordon McMaster in his 1997 suicide; with him and Norman Godman she was involved in a struggle for the control of Renfrewshire politics with the faction led by Tommy Graham; this led to the infiltration of her constituency party by hostile factionalists, leading to its suspension; a skilful dramatiser of Paisley's loss of industries and of recent inroads by drug gangs; an opponent of 'assisted places' quotas for women MPs; highly-rated by Labour MPs, particularly in Scotland and among MCPs; a home-ruler in the 'Scotland United' faction - with John McAllion, George Galloway and Dennis Canavan - which campaigned for a referendum on Scotland; anti-EC; an opponent of Gulf War '90-91; refused to be used as a stalking mare against Harriet Harman;

History: She joined the Labour Party '65; at 24 became youngest woman councillor when elected to Paisley Town Council, joining her husband May '70; at 25 became youngest JP in Scottish history '72; was elected to Renfrew District Council May '74; "I lost my seat to the SNP when the Labour Party got wiped out in Scottish local government" May '77; she replaced her husband, Allen, on Strathclyde Regional Council at a by-election '79; "I came of the council altogether because I decided that the children were all at an age when they needed more of my time" '86; was selected as Labour candidate for Argyll and Bute '89; when her MP-husband died suddenly of a virus infection, she was both widowed and made jobless, because she had been working as his Secretary-Researcher Sep '90; at her daughters' prompting, decided to contest his seat, resigning as candidate for Argyll and Bute Sep '90; short-listed for Paisley North with John Ryan and John Carty, was selected over them Oct '90; during the campaign urged Scottish Secretary to rule out application by Cleveland Fuels for a local incinerator; said she would not rule out nationalisation of Clydesdale tube works to keep local people employed there; retained seat in by-election with majority reduced to under a third (3,770), the SNP finishing a strong second; said: "nobody remembers who came second, it is winning that counts" Nov '90; her first act as an MP was to add her name to the home-rule plan drawn up by the Scottish Constitutional Convention Dec '90; in her Maiden underlined the problem she had in paying tribute to her predecessor, since he was also her husband; she pointed out that her once strongly industrial constituency - manufacturing cotton, ships and light engineering - was "now just a skeleton of its former self" with "pockets in which there is 40% male unemployment" - "when they come south, young people, middle-aged people and elderly people are forced to languish on the streets of this city" of London - "they find a shop doorway in the Strand with no chance of finding employment and no chance of finding a home" Dec '90; opposed war in Gulf Dec '90, Jan '91; again complained of de-industrialisation of Paisley: "we now make hamburgers instead of ships" - "one of the great difficulties is that because we have lost these work forces through redundancies, we have missed a rung on the evolutionary ladder of converting old skills to fit new technologies" Feb '91; backed Dave Nellist's motion urging cancellation of a Defence Components exhibition and pressing "the staff to be redeployed in non-military work, and for a guarantee to existing defence workers of the safeguarding of their jobs through alternative production which is socially useful" Feb '91; baited John Major with the complaint by Norman Tebbit's secretary that she would be paying almost as much under Heseltine's new council tax for her small Barbican flat as the Heseltine family for its Westminster mansion Apr '91; deplored loss of 14,500 manufacturing jobs in Paisley, a town of 85,000, June '91; after a year as an MP, said manufacturing investment in Paisley had decreased by 12%, and manufacturing output by 5%; urged "a major economic initiative to regenerate its manufacturing base"; "the only jobs that we have been offered are at a toxic waste incinerator" Dec '91; urged an employment boost Feb '92; again retained the seat with her majority only two-thirds back to her late husband's, due to a near-doubling of the SNP vote Apr '92; helped form 'Scotland United' - with John McAllion, George Galloway and Dennis Canavan - to campaign for a referendum on Scottish home rule, in tandem with SNP Apr '92; backed Margaret Beckett for the Deputy Leadership Apr '92; with 15 others, backed failed effort of John McAllion MP to sabotage vote on Maastricht May '92; was one of five Scottish Labour rebels who tried to prevent the removal of the Mace in protest against Government policies on Scottish self-rule; officials moving on them were warned by neighbouring MP Gordon McMaster against tackling her: "go for the two on either side; don't tackle the one in the middle; her son is 6'5" July '92; on the fringe of Labour's annual conference in Brighton denied that the home-rule campaigning organisation, Scotland United, would lead to a breakaway Labour Party in Scotland; she insisted that its SNP, Labour and Liberal Democratic members were united only in their desire to win a multi-option referendum so the Scots could choose their own constitutional future Oct '92; after two deaths, demanded an inquiry into her local ambulance service Feb '93; joined demonstration against extended hours for betting shops Feb '93; complained that Rolls-Royce was shedding a further 500 jobs in her constituency Mar '93; voted against National Lottery Bill Apr '93; voted against 3rd

Reading of Maastricht treaty Bill May '93; complained that rejection of Rosyth for nuclear refits would hit her constituency too because "Babcock Thorn, the major employer at Rosyth, is also the major employer in my constituency", which had already "lost an incredible 89% of its manufacturing base" June '93; with Llin Golding and Gwyneth Dunwoody, formed a new group, Labour Supporters For Real Equality in opposition to 'assisted places' quotas for women candidates July '93; in Shadow Cabinet election, received unexpectedly high vote of 88, 7th runner-up, despite not having stood before, arousing suspicions of support from male chauvinists among Labour MPs anxious to undermine female front-runners Oct '93; again complained about a constituency job loss Apr '94; backed John Prescott for Leader and Deputy Leader June-July '94; opposed penalising constituency parties for failing to send female delegates in alternate years: "it is not easy if you are a woman with a young family; many women are in low-paid work with little employment protection and they cannot take a week off without fear of losing their jobs" Sep '94; she received 57 votes for the Shadow Cabinet Oct '94; she and her children received death threats after urging more police to control local drug gangs Mar '95; she was given police protection after alleging that the council-subsidised FCB security firm, infiltrated by a gang called "the brothers" or "buddies", had connections with a community business project and links with illegal drugs trading; these allegations were discounted by opposing factionalists who pointed out that two councillors in the FCB were her rivals in her imminent re-selection contest, in which she was said to be backed by Militant Apr '95; she left the Commons Catering Committee June '95; received 71 votes in the Shadow Cabinet ballot, more votes than garnered by eight men who later became Blair's ministers Oct '95; joined with other Scottish Labour MPs in attacking abuse of freely-available Temazepan Oct '95; insisted that "devolution is the only option for keeping the Union together" May '96; after Tony Blair said Labour's devolution proposals would be put to referendums, she said she had decided not to resign her frontbench (?) post, to spare the Labour leadership embarrassment June '96; voted to increase MPs' pension base to £43,000 July '97; after John Prescott warned against "rocking the boat" and urged backing the existing Shadow Cabinet (and especially Harriet Harman), Mrs Adams dropped out: "I was going to stand but I thought there was going to be a whole card of candidates; what I was not going to do is stand alone; it would be seen only as a challenge to Harriet Harman, which it never was"; denying she had been strong-armed into standing down, adding: "one of the final deciding factors was when Mr [Ken] Livingstone passed me in the tearoom and told me that he would vote for me if I stood" July '96; came 14th in the ballot for Private Members' Bills Oct '96; the Conservative Government killed off her Witness Protection Bill providing anonymity for witnesses fearing intimidation Jan '97; complained that women were too often expensively imprisoned for minor crimes like defaulting on £100 fines for failing to pay for TV licences Jan '97; again contested Paisley North, expanded to embrace the former car town of Linwood, winning by 12,814 over the SNP in a 5-way contest, on a notional swing of 4.6% from the SNP May '97; she was named to the Select Committee on Scottish Affairs July '97; she was shocked by the suicide of her friend, Paisley South MP Gordon McMaster, with whom she had been elected in 1990's joint by-election; a sufferer from ME, his depression had been deepened by malicious gossip charging both that he was a closet gay and was having an affair with her; she said: "vicious gossips drove Gordon to his death"; "I can assure you they were total untrue and without foundation"; "Gordon always had a deep suspicion that [Deputy Chief Labour Whip] Don Dixon was shielding Tommy Graham; we have to lance this boil once and for all"; Graham countered that she was "milking" McMaster's death for publicity; she urged he be sacked Aug '97; she was one of a group of Leftwing Labour women MPs led by Ann Clwyd whom Princess Diana had expressed an interest in meeting about landmines, in secret Sep '97; an internal Labour inquiry into Tommy Graham found him innocent of hounding Gordon

McMaster into suicide but found that he publicly and privately criticised Mrs Adams in a bitter personal feud Oct '97;
Born: 27 December 1947, Paisley
Family: "My own grandfather took part in the hunger marches south"; d late David Love, and Mary Kyle (Tait); m '68 Allen(der) Steele Adams ("he was my first boyfriend when I was 17"), late MP for Paisley and Paisley North '79-90; 1s 6'5" Allen '77, 2d Barbara, London University '71, Kirsty, Glasgow University '73;
Education: Mossvale Primary, Paisley; Stanely Green High, Paisley ("I couldn't afford to stay on at school past 16; I was the eldest of eight"); later took a diploma in ballet, in order to teach it;
Occupation: Ex: Secretary-Researcher, to her late husband, Allen Adams MP '86-90; previously taught ballet and worked in the Borough Treasurer's office;
Traits: "Elegant honey blonde" (DAILY RECORD); with "subtle glamour" (Teresa Gorman MP); well-spoken verbal tactician with an outspoken sardonic style; showed "courage" (Thomas McAvoy MP) in taking on drug dealers; a smoker; "I don't like London for a start and it (is) a pain in the neck to have to spend so much time there";
Address: House of Commons, Westminster, London SW1A 0AA; 'Oaklands', 26 Hunterhill Road, Paisley PH2 6ST;
Telephone: 0171 219 3564 (H of C); 0141 887 3064 (home); 0141 848 9004 (constituency);

'Nick' (Nicholas) AINGER   **Labour**   **CARMARTHEN WEST & SOUTH PEMBROKESHIRE '97-**

Majority: 9,621 (22.6%) over Conservative 5-way;
Description: This '95-new seat includes the whole of the county town of Carmarthen, the rural fringe on the border between Carmarthenshire and Pembrokeshire and 30,000 voters from south Pembrokeshire, including "little England beyond Wales" (English-speaking Tenby, Saundersfoot and Manorbier) as well as industrial Pembroke Dock;
Former Seat: Pembroke '92-97
Position: PPS, to Ron Davies '97-; on Welsh Select Committee '93-; ex: on Commons Broadcasting Committee '92-94; Dyfed County Councillor (Vice Chairman of Labour Group) '81-93;
Outlook: One of West Wales' most successful 'incomers' from 'away' in the northeast; a former ship's rigger who proved himself by his constructive criticisms of the mishandling of the holed 'Sea Empress' oil tanker pollution incident; an opponent of fox-hunting and a supporter of an elected head of state; a very bright, highly-active and well-regarded local job and environment defender; a full-timer with no sponsorship, no consultancies, who gives his media income to charity; a former Dyfed County Councillor who became the prime instrument for ending Tory ex-MP Nick Bennett's local career; Aneurin Bevan is his hero; a multi-cause groupie (Amnesty, Friends of the Earth, League Against Cruel Sports, Dyfed Wildlife Trust, RSPB, Greenpeace); a TGWU-backed former marine rigger;
History: He joined the Labour Party '79; was elected to Dyfed County Council May '81; formed an action committee to block import of hazardous PCBs from Canada through

Pembroke en route to ReChem plant in Pontypool Aug '89; was endorsed by NEC as Pembroke's Labour candidate with a personal commendation from Neil Kinnock (not an admirer of Nick Bennett) Apr '90; was active in resisting Ministry of Defence plans for a giant £100m 'over-the-horizon' radar base at St Davids Airfield in the Pembrokeshire Coast National Park Apr '90; said: "I have yet to meet a single person who is not outraged by the poll tax; the strength of feeling against it is not going to die down; it is an albatross around the neck of the Tory Government" Apr '90; warned that "people contemplating not paying [the poll tax] must be made aware of the power and penalties involved" May '90; at Welsh Labour Conference criticized health dangers from giant radar beam at St Davids; but spoke of need to retain Royal Naval Armament Depot at Trecwn, North Pembroke: "Trecwn is the best facility of its kind in the country and probably Europe; there will always be a need to store conventional explosives, whatever happens in Eastern Europe, and Trecwn is the place to store them" May '90; warned local health authority against allowing local hospitals to opt out May '90; backed a decommissioning policy for Milford Haven fishermen, criticizing local MP Nick Bennett for forcing them to become victims of "market forces" Apr '91; on a visit by Labour's shadow Welsh Secretary, criticized Nick Bennett and Geraint Howells for "throwing in the towel" over the planned closure in 1996 of Trecwn, the local Royal Naval Armament Depot July '91; after meeting consultants and others at Haverfordwest's Withybush Hospital, said: "we will attempt to find the resources to ensure that the people of Pembrokeshire will have their say in the future of their health service; it is clear that some people who supported the opt-out originally had not realised the whole truth and are now opposed to it" Sep '91; criticized Welsh Office payment of £50,000 to prepare Pembrokeshire Health Authority's trust application as "outrageous" Oct '91; his possible victory was first bruited Feb '92; with Neil Kinnock's backing, pledged to keep open threatened RAF Brawdy air establishment Mar '92; urged a Welsh Assembly Mar '92; narrowly won seat - by 755 votes - the first Labour victor since '66 - overturning Nick Bennett's 5,700 majority with substantial tactical support from local Liberal Democrats Apr '92; in Maiden opposed burning Orimulsion at Pembroke power station without flue gas desulphurisation May '92; warned against massive local damage for small savings in closing RAF Brawdy May '92; was named to Commons Broadcasting Committee June '92; urged more open data on transport of hazardous chemicals through ports and roads of Wales July '92; opposed Sea Fish (Conservation) Bill; complained about Spanish "quota hoppers", based in Milford Haven, who fished in British waters and landed fish in Spain, providing "no benefits to the local economy" July '92; opposed Dyfed's award of school cleaning contracts to low-pay private companies Aug '92; complained about commercialisation of Pembrokeshire NHS Trust Oct '92; opposed end of search-and-rescue flights from RAF Brawdy Nov '92; complained of decline of Milford Haven, once "the hake capital of the world" but now exploited by Spaniards, with "supposedly British-registered vessels...owned by Spanish interests"; locals saw "British quota fish" "loaded by the Spanish crews" "into Spanish lorries driven by Spanish lorry drivers" Dec '92; was named to Welsh Select Committee in place of Jon Owen Jones Jan '93; said that many tankers he had seen coming into Milford Haven over 14 years had been "poorly maintained, poorly crewed and with poor officers" who often could not communicate with their crews because of language differences Jan '93; presented petition from 19,676 people objecting to removal of search-and-rescue helicopters from RAF Brawdy Feb '93; attacked the threat to remove assisted area status from all Pembrokeshire June '93; attacked the Government's plan to franchise Regional Railways in South and West Wales as "a ludicrous, unworkable plan which will cost the taxpayer more and could well see the end of the railway in Pembrokeshire" June '93; he voted for Tony Blair for Leader July '94; the Boundary Commission divided his Pembroke seat in half Oct '94; complained about tolls on Milford Haven's Cleddau Bridge Dec '94; criticised Spanish quota-hoppers Jan '95; in the split of his constituency, he announced he would contest the new Carmarthen West and South Pembrokeshire half Feb '95; since the Royal Welch Fusiliers' base was at Brawdy, he expressed the concern of their families about their 33 hostages detained in Bosnia May '95; accusing John Major of "uncertainty based on indecision", asked the PM whether it was now "the job of the Deputy Prime Minister to make the decisions, or hasn't he decided yet?" July '95; was unanimously selected to contest the new Carmarthen West seat Oct '95; introduced Bill to allow interest payments on overdue bills Dec '95; urged more power for NHS Ombudsman who could not investigate complaint of local family that their mother had died in their family saloon on the M4 after being refused an ambulance home after a heart operation Dec '95; complained, for his potato-growers, that the Government was winding up the Potato Marketing Board but leaving them at the mercy of state-aided Spanish, French, Italian and Greek potato-growers Jan '96; awoke to one of the 20 worst oil pollution incidents ever on his doorstep Feb '96; complained that, with no port radar working, the tanker 'Sea Empress' had been allowed to enter Milford Haven only 80 minutes before low water, even before it was further mishandled, spilling 72,000 tons of crude oil Feb '96; urged Britain, as "a mature democracy", be allowed to elect its head of state Mar '96; urged a wide-ranging inquiry into the mishandling of the holed oil tanker 'Sea Empress' grounded while entering Milford Haven Apr '96; voted against limiting MPs' pay increases to 3%, in favour of cutting their mileage allowances and in favour of basing pensions on annual pay of £43,000 July '96; opposed the incompetent sale of the local Navy armaments depot at Trecwn Aug '96; spoke against the closure of the local Gulf refinery Nov '96; defended the Pembrokeshire Ambulance Service against its second threat within a year Feb '97; was one of 72 candidates blacklisted as an opponent of fox-hunting in THE FIELD Apr '97; was elected for his new seat of Carmarthen West and South Pembrokeshire by an unexpectedly large majority of 9,821 over his Conservative opponent, on a pro-Labour swing of 9.8%; his former Researcher, Jackie Lawrence, won Preseli, the other half of his former constituency on a swing of 11%, May '97; was named PPS to Ron Davies, Welsh Secretary June '97; voted to outlaw fox-hunting June '97; asked "why the price of beef in our supermarkets does not correspond to the low prices in the marts and why they are continuing to import products that could be sourced in Britain" Dec '97;

Born: 24 October 1949, Sheffield

Family: Son, late Richard John Wilkinson Ainger, steel industry foreman, and Marjorie Isabel(Dye); m '76 Sally (Robinson); 1d Sadie '77, who studied at Carmarthen's art college and University of Westminster; her plea for press exclusion because her father was "in the public eye" was ignored by magistrates when she was tried in '96 for speeding, without insurance, MOT or a driving license;

Education: Netherthorpe Grammar School, Staveley, Derbyshire;

Occupation: Ex: Marine Rigger, employed by Marine and Port Services Ltd at super-tanker port of Milford Haven (TGWU Branch Secretary and Senior Shop Steward '78-92) '77-92; previously employed by offshore oil exploration agency, as Ships Agent and Materials Controller (made redundant the day before his daughter was born) '73-77; Building Worker '71-73;

Traits: Tall; lean; balding; bearded; domed head; hyperactive; flexible thinker; a non-practising Anglican; enjoys swimming, the theatre and foreign travel; Sheffield-born, his ambition was to open the bowling for Yorkshire; in '97 had a real ale brewed in his honour, 'Ainger's Delight';

Address: House of Commons, Westminster, London SW1A 0AA; Ferry Lane Works, Ferry Lane, Pembroke Dock SA71 4RE(constituency office);

Telephone: 0171 219 4004 (H of C); 01646 682742 (home); 01646 684404 (constituency office);

Peter (Michael) AINSWORTH   Conservative   **SURREY EAST '92-**

Majority: 15,093 (27.6%) over LibDem 6-way;
Description: Affluent, semi-rural seat with little towns like Oxted, Lingfield, Caterham and Warlingham, stretching to the Kent border; in '95 14,700 voters were added from Horley, near Gatwick Airport;
Position: Shadow Culture Secretary '98-; ex: Deputy Chief Whip '97-98; Assistant Whip '96-97; PPS: to Virginia Bottomley '95-96, to Jonathan Aitken '94-95; on the Select Committees: on Public Service '95-96, on the Environment '93-94; Secretary, all-party Conservation Group '94-??;Secretary: Conservative MPs' Arts and Heritage Committee '92-97?, M25 Parliamentary Action Group '92-97?;
Wandsworth Borough Councillor (Chairman of Conservative Group '90-92, Deputy Chairman, Policy and Finance Committee) '86-94; on Council of Bow Group '84-86;
Outlook: The cautious but able former merchant banker (S G Warburg) unexpectedly promoted to the front bench after quiet service as the Tories's Deputy Chief Whip; "looks like an aggressive and hungry performer" (Gordon Letts, DAILY TELEGRAPH); a pragmatic and functional politician with little interest in ideologies; after cutting his teeth in Wandsworth, he made his initial reputation by blocking the 14-lane highway to Heathrow Airport and his battle for a Hedgerows Bill, frustrated by his own party on behalf of commercial farmers; '92's low-profiled, cautious young successor to Sir Geoffrey (now Lord) Howe; became the 'Campaigning Politician of the Year' because he had shown himself "a remarkably adroit negotiator" (GREEN MAGAZINE) over hedgerow protection; an assiduous defender of the rural environment, as shown by his Hedgerows Bill and battles against the spreading M25; is deft although he did not have to go through the normal preliminary hoop of contesting a hopeless Parliamentary seat; a careful young man who believes in "balance"; a former merchant banker (S G Warburg); well-connected: Paul Channon ex-MP, John Bowis ex-MP, Sir Paul Beresford MP;
History: He became a Conservative as a schoolboy, joining the party in the early '70s; the three-day week was his "most important political influence" '73-74; began canvassing at 18 in Wokingham in '74; at Oxford became President of the Oxford University Monday Club '78; on graduating, became Research Assistant to Sir John Stewart-Clark MEP '79; became a committee member and ward Vice Chairman of Chelsea Conservatives '81; was elected to Bow Group Council '84. to the Editorial Committee of CROSSBOW, and to Chairmanship of Bow Educational Trust '85; moved to Battersea Conservative Association '85; was elected to Wandsworth Borough Council May '86; was elected Deputy Chairman of Wandsworth Borough Council's Policy and Finance Committee and Chairman of its Conservative Group May '90; on the announced retirement of Sir Barney Hayhoe, was shortlisted for Brentford and Isleworth Feb '91; after the announcement of Sir Geoffrey Howe's imminent retirement, was selected for East Surrey Apr '91; retained seat, despite a 2% swing to Liberal Democrats Apr '92; was one of 20 MPs who won ballot for a Private Member's Bill May '92; decided to promote a Hedgerows Bill June '92; signed the EDM calling for "second thoughts" on

Maastricht June '92; made his Maiden speech on the countryside, warning against threat of M25's expansion to 14 lanes June '92; defended the Government's Civil Service Bill against Labour fears that it proposed privatisation of the civil service Nov '92; backed the rents-to-mortgages scheme in Housing and Urban Development Bill as a "simple, cost-effective and relatively low-risk mechanism for council tenants to acquire part or all of their homes"; expressed doubts about the Bill's leasehold enfranchisement because it involved "Government intervention in freely-entered-into contracts", for the benefit of the leaseholder Nov '92; as Secretary of the M25 Parliamentary Action Group deplored "the ridiculous situation where it is extremely difficult to build a house extension in the Southeast, but very easy for the Transport Department to build huge highways in a completely uncoordinated way" Nov '92; in the Standing Committee on Housing and Urban Development Bill tabled an amendment stating that a head lessee could not be the qualifying tenant of more than one flat in a block for the purpose of leasehold enfranchisement; this was accepted Jan '93; on behalf of English Heritage and Historic Houses Association tabled an amendment to Housing and Urban Development Bill to ensure that the Bill did not lead to the forced sale and break-up of important properties of outstanding historic or architectural interest Feb '93; in adjournment speech strongly objected to expansion of M25 by six more lanes Feb '93; despite threats from fellow-Tory Christopher Gill to object, his Government-backed Hedgerows Bill received its 2nd Reading on the nod Feb '93; was named to Environment Select Committee Feb '93; insisted it was "most important that shareholders and corporate management should know and understand each other and should talk to each other regularly on a basis of confidence" Apr '93; denied that "insider trading" was a "victimless crime"; "insider dealing, put simply, is a form of cheating"; "larger and more active City institutions - for example, those handling large pension portfolios - are likely to suffer the most"; he feared that "the well-intentioned measures in Part IV could so impede the flow of reasonable information between companies...that they could reverse the trend to corporate glasnost" Apr '93; again protested widening of M25 and establishment of more link roads Apr '93; Labour MP Tam Dalyell complimented him for his "serious, competent and good-hearted attempt to introduce hedgerow legislation" which "will obviously not reach the statute book"; his Bill was talked out by fellow Tory MPs ("a motley crew of agri-farming apologists" - Robin Page, DAILY TELEGRAPH) because it would have forced landowners to notify their local council before destroying more than 60 feet of hedge May '93; urged "substantial aid" "to help the difficult process of economic transformation" in Yeltsin's Russia May '93; received GREEN MAGAZINE award for the 'Campaigning Politician of the Year' because of his skilful Hedgerows Bill effort June '93; claimed that Tory MPs were divided on more road-building, with more deciding against excessive roadbuilding Dec '93; voted against restoring capital punishment Feb '94; voted to reduce age of homosexual consent to 18 or 16, Feb '94; credited the "lending institutions" with having reduced the "rate of repossessions" of homes in recent months Mar '94; introduced a Contaminated Land Bill to "require those who were responsible for polluting land to be responsible for its restoration and decontamination" Mar '94; was congratulated by Tory MP Peter Thurnham who said he "so ably represents [S G Warburg's] interests in the House" May '94; urged Labour to condemn rail strike as "unnecessary" and bringing "misery and inconvenience to millions of people" June '94; opposed national legislation on dog-fouling, insisting it could be prevented by local statute, properly enforced July '94; backed publicity for the Home Energy Efficiency Scheme to lower fuel bills and stabilise emissions of greenhouse gas Oct '94; was discharged from the Environmental Select Committee Nov '94; pointed out that "many people who report either zero or negative incomes have higher than average spending patterns", including cars, videos and washing machines July '95; was honoured as the 'Country Parliamentarian of the Year' by COUNTRY

LIFE for his campaign against the widening of the M25 Sep '95; urged protection of "the green belt and particularly sites of special scientific interest" Oct '95; his consultancy with the Samuel Warburg Group was widely mentioned Nov '95; was named to the Public Service Select Committee Dec '95; described his constituency: "starts where Croydon stops and goes down to Gatwick, so the northern part is fairly densely populated and the southern part is rural, with the constant pressure on the local environment" Dec '95; welcomed privatisation of railways as improving the management and service while reducing the cost Jan '96; voted to curb MPs' mileage allowances, to keep a 3% cap on MPs' pay increases, and against basing pensions on an increased pay level of £43,000 July '96; entered the Government for the first time as an Assistant Government Whip July '96; was discharged from the Public Service Select Committee July '96; retained Surrey East - altered by the addition of Horley, near Gatwick, from Reigate - by a reduced majority of 15,093 over the Liberal Democrats, an anti-Tory notional swing of only 3.3% May '97; was thought a backer of Peter Lilley for the new Tory Leader June '97; was named the Tories' Deputy Chief Whip by William Hague June '97; he listed no consultancies in the new Register of MPs' outside interests Nov '97; he was promoted Shadow Culture Secretary, to oppose Chris Smith June '98;

Born: 16 November 1956, Hampshire

Family: Son, late Michael Ainsworth, rtd RN Lieutenant Commander and Ludgrove schoolmaster, and Patricia Mary (Bedford); his father was an avid cricketer who played for Worcestershire and coached at Ludgrove m '81 Claire Alison (Burnett), banker at Morgan Grenfell, where she has specialised in debt and structured finance; 1s Benedict '92; 2d Imogen '88, Olivia '90;

Education: Ludgrove School, Wokingham; Bradfield College; Lincoln College, Oxford University (BA Hons in English);

Occupation: Consultant, S G Warburg Group Plc '92-97; Director, JLI Group (food processing group, a Warburg client) '93-97?; Director of Corporate Finance, S G Warburg Securities '89-92; Investment Analyst: Warburg Securities '85-89, Laing and Cruickshank (stockbrokers) '81-85; Research Assistant, Sir John Stewart-Clark, MEP '79-81;

Traits: Curly brown hair; strong chin; dimpled smile; well-organised; politically obsessed; his political hero is William Pitt the Younger;

Address: House of Commons, Westminster, London SW1A 0AA;

Telephone: 0171 219 3567/5078 (H of C);

WADING IN FILES:
Apart from the boiled-down versions which appear in these books and on our computers, we have shelves and shelves full of information built up over our over forty years of existence. Since we are not run by accountants, we are not compelled to purge the best bits by having junior assistant librarians culling our files. If you want to write the biography of ex-MP Sir John Stokes, it will only cost you £30 to see his file. There you will find that he was so pro-Franco during the Spanish civil war, that Balliol put up its own anti-Franco candidate against him for President of the Oxford University Conservative Association. This win was the springboard for Ted Heath's political career. Postwar, having held this position helped him overcome the deep prejudice among Conservative selectors who resisted choosing as the candidate for a winnable seat the son of a carpenter and a housemaid.

'Bob' (Robert) AINSWORTH   **Labour**   **COVENTRY NORTH EAST '92-**

Majority: 22,569 (46.9%) over Conservative 7-way;

Description: Mainly Richard Crossman's old Labour stronghold, then called Coventry East: a compact constituency of over 65,000 electors; terraced houses in the centre, council houses and less expensive private homes on the fringes; its factories produce manmade fibres, machine tools and parts for motor cars; in '95 it gained one ward, Lower Stoke, from former Coventry South East;

Position: Government Whip '97-; ex: Opposition Whip '95-97; on Environment Select Committee '93-95; Vice Chairman: PLP Environment Committee '95-97, Trade and Industry Committee '93-97, West Midlands Labour Group '9?-97, European Secure Vehicle Alliance '??-??; Secretary all-party Chess Group '??-??; Coventry City Councillor (Deputy Leader '88-91, Chairman of Finance '89-92) '84-92;

Outlook: Coventry-centred mainstream trade unionist and former Deputy Leader of Coventry Council; still indignant about injustice to the under-privileged; a former Jaguar sheet metal worker and shop steward; a loyal Labour man who replaced obstreperous, hard-Left John Hughes, a non-poll-tax-paying Campaign Groupie;

History: He joined the Labour Party "following shop-floor influence by fellow workers" '75; "I voted against membership of the Common Market in 1975"; was elected to Coventry City Council May '84; was elected Deputy Leader of the controlling Labour Group on Coventry City Council May '88; was also elected Chairman of the City Council's Finance Committee May '89; at re-selection conference outpointed runner-up Bill Lapworth, TGWU district official, by 39% to 37%; the sitting MP, John Hughes, came third and demanded an inquiry into postal voting in the ballot Dec '89; the NEC refused John Hughes an inquiry after the West Midlands Regional Organiser, Joe Payne, had investigated his complaints Jan '90; John Hughes threatened to sue the Labour Party to insist on an inquiry, alleging 62 postal votes were in the same handwriting, using false addresses Feb '90; the NEC endorsed Bob Ainsworth as the chosen candidate and rejected John Hughes' complaints May '90; John Hughes' further challenge failed in the High Court, with Mr Justice McCullough refusing to grant him leave to apply for judicial review to overturn the decision of the party's National Executive June '90; local magistrates took the first step to force John Hughes to pay his £384 in poll tax Sep '90; Bob Ainsworth resigned as Deputy Leader of Coventry City Council '91; was supported in election campaign by George Park, the retired MP who had preceded John Hughes, '91-92; retained the seat with an almost identical majority, despite John Hughes' candidacy, which attracted 4,000 votes Apr '92; in his Maiden speech warned of US-style threats to inner cities: "if effective action is not taken, we shall see in our country what I call the doughnut effect: cities with great holes in the middle, where people do not go and dare not go"; "security, hope and opportunity must be brought back to citizens living in those areas; current urban policy is, in many cases, exacerbating and increasing the divisions"; the poor in his constituency were living seven years less than the more affluent May '92; worried that a joint application for trust status by two Coventry hospitals would result in the closure of the Coventry and Warwickshire Hospital July '92; complained that the concession of two days to file an asylum appeal in the Asylum and Immigration Appeals Bill was "a concession in name only"; "it cannot be done in two days"; "my blood boils when I read the details of interviews that relatives of my constituents have been put through by employees of Her Majesty's Government when they go to the High Commission in Delhi, Bombay and elsewhere"; "it appears that we are now determined to create...an iron curtain...of our own and to turn our backs on ordinary human beings in desperate circumstances" Nov '92; having been on the Standing Committee of the Trade Union Reform Bill for two months, strongly criticised Government for ending subsidy for trade union postal ballots, having legislated to insist on it: "I readily admit that I never was, and still am not, in favour of compulsory postal ballots"; "well-organised factory branch ballots...are a good, efficient and cheap way for people to participate"; also attacked abolition of wages councils as "a blatant abuse of privilege and power at the expense of the weakest in our society" Feb '93; accused Environment Secretary Michael Howard of trying to "doctor the figures" again to deprive Coventry of the rate support grant to which it was entitled Feb '93; complained of loss of funds for successful project to enable dangerous young motorbike joyriders to ride bikes legally off the road Feb '93; said Coventry had lost 20% of its top-level industrial firms in the first, '79-81 Conservative recession and unemployment had doubled since, Mar '93; backed access to Kashmir by Amnesty International Mar '93; blasted VAT on fuel as breaking an election pledge and aimed at the poorest May '93; complained that the Citizens' Charter was an empty sham since "existing services for mentally handicapped people are to be closed in Coventry", making it impossible for those affected to claim their rights June '93; voted against restoring capital punishment, even for killers of policemen Feb '94; voted to reduce age of homosexual consent to 18 or 16, Feb '94; as a member of the Environment Select Committee, he was passed allegations about how Clare Spottiswoode became Director General of Ofgas May '94; voted for Blair for Leader, Prescott for Deputy Leader July '94; urged a full inquiry into "astonishing" revelations of a "massive security breach by an employee on a short-term contract at BT" Nov '94; in discussions of Commons reforms, his wife wanted him home for longer weekends so that his daughters saw more of him Dec '94; again complained of a "blatant fiddle" of the Revenue Support Grant, as shown by comparing Coventry and Westminster Feb '95; held a debate on Carbon Dioxide Emissions, complaining about too modest targets Feb '95; tabled a motion demanding an audit of Westminster Council after it was disclosed it had provided free or cheap upkeep for flats sold to favoured purchasers Feb '95; in a Parliamentary motion complained of "untrue and defamatory allegations" by Tory MP Sir John Wheeler against a Westminster tenants group Mar '95; was named an Opposition Whip Apr '95; complained about "totally inadequate" inquiries by the Charity Commissioners into Westminster Tories led by Dame Shirley Porter misusing a charity to oppose investigations of gerrymandering May '95; introduced his Motor Vehicle (Proof of Ownership) Bill May '95; complained that the problems of anti-social behaviour on housing estates was made worse by the Government's mishandling of homelessness and its attempts to blame Labour for not agreeing to fight crime on the estates Jan '96; complained to TRIBUNE about its misrepresentations about his role in MSF elections, where he was alleged to be trying to defeat a Leftwing candidate Feb '96; in the wake of the crash of a cattle-exporting freight plane, expressed his doubts about such a trade from Coventry Airport Feb '96; complained about delays caused for Coventry hospitals by the Government's private finance initiative June '96; he supported a 3% limit to MPs' salary increase July '96; he staged another adjournment debate to complain about shortfalls in the Government's energy conservation programme July '96; on a visit to Hongkong, admitted that his colleague, Deputy Chief Whip Nick Brown, had blocked a Bill to aid Hongkong war widows in retaliation for a Tory manoeuvre July '96; again complained about inequities in local government finances Feb '97; he retained his seat by a majority doubled to 22,589, a pro-Labour swing of 12.7% May '97; he was made a

Government Whip in the new Blair Government May '97; visited New York to study the UN Nov '97;
Born: 19 June 1952, Coventry
Family: S Stanley Ewart Ainsworth, ?occupation?, and Monica Pearl, later Mrs D J Scullion; m '74 Gloria Jean (Sandall); 2d;
Education: Foxford Comprehensive School;
Occupation: Ex: Sheet metal worker and fitter at Jaguar Motors, Coventry (Shop Steward for TGWU, then MSF '74-91, Secretary of Joint Stewards '80-91)'71-91;
Traits: Front-combed dark hair; soup-strainer moustache; modest ("unless you are some kind of big-headed twit, you have to accept it takes a while before you can make an impact"); enjoys chess and walking;
Address: House of Commons, Westminster, London SW1A 0AA; 171 Purcell Road, Courthouse Green, Coventry CV6 7LS;
Telephone: 0171 219 4047 (H of C); 01203 664766 (home); 01203 457318 (Dorothy Dalton); 01201 553 6601 (West Midlands office);

Douglas ALEXANDER   **Labour**   **PAISLEY SOUTH '97-**

Majority: 2,731 over SNP 9-way;
Description: The southern half of the solidly Labour town dominated by thread, engineering and motor cars; once held by HH Asquith, Liberals showed strength as recently as the '61 by-election and the '64 general election; the constituency includes the town of Johnstone a few miles to the west, where "the first machine tool foundry in the world was established" (DA); it exchanged a few thousand voters with Paisley North in '95; its recent notoriety has come from the controversies around the suicide of Labour MP Gordon McMaster in the summer of '97;
Outlook: A Buchan-inspired, Brown-encouraged Scots 'New Labour' enthusiast, accused of "reciting the line of the day from Millbank" (Diane Abbott MP); a "confidant of the Chancellor, Gordon Brown" who "set aside a lifetime's support for a Scottish Parliament to run for the Westminster seat" (Lawrence Donegan, GUARDIAN); he narrowly won '97's low-key by-election in Paisley South after losing '95's Perth and Kinross by-election, despite a Blair-led "blitz"; "if New Labour had its own academy for training by-election candidates, then Douglas Alexander would surely be its role model", "very young, very moderate and very very sure of his soundbites" (Toby Helm, DAILY TELEGRAPH);
History: He was influenced in his politics by the frequent visits to his parents' manse by their local MP, Norman Buchan, whose "inspirational conversation and commitment to socialism" made a major impact; he joined the Labour Party at 15, '82; he campaigned for Gordon McMaster in the Paisley South by-election Nov '90; he contested the Perth and Kinross by-election caused by the death of Sir Nicholas Fairbairn; despite two visits by Tony Blair, and a "blitz" which included Gordon Brown and every Scottish Labour MP who could be press-ganged, he lost to the SNP's Roseanna Cunningham by 7,311 votes, but pushed the Tory into 3rd place May '95; he contested the changed seat of Perth, again losing to Roseanna Cunningham, by 3,141 votes May '97; the by-election in Paisley South was a result of the

suicide of Gordon McMaster, its Labour MP, who was depressed in the wake of exposure to organophosphates while a gardener; he left a note accusing neighbouring West Renfrewshire MP Tommy Graham of spreading rumours about his homosexuality July '97; Alexander was short-listed for the by-election by the NEC only with Margaret McCulloch; Alexander was selected as Labour's candidate by the local party, it was alleged, because of his closeness to Gordon Brown, for whom he had written speeches Oct '97; during his by-election campaign he was pleasantly charming while dodging any controversial questions about local sleaze ("it would be injudicious to speak about individuals when an inquiry into serious allegations is under way"); he debated with his SNP opponent Ian Blackford on Scottish TV but concentrated on discussing dangerous fireworks and taxis for the disabled Oct '97; his somewhat muted campaign ("Operation Charm, Dodge and Bore") and accusations of Labour sleaze, succeeded in winning the by-election by an inevitably narrower majority of 2,731 over the SNP, down from Gordon McMaster's 12,750 at the general election, a swing to the SNP of 11% Nov '97; when he signed on, Tory jeerers - who were aiming at the PM - were reproached by Speaker Boothroyd Nov '97; made his Maiden on the National Minimum Wage Bill, much needed by his constituents "to end the centuries-old injustice of poverty pay" Nov '97; was accused by Diane Abbott of "reciting the line of the day from Millbank" Mar '98; asked Scottish Secretary Donald Dewar about the progress toward reducing the number of NHS trusts operating in Scotland Apr '98;

Born: 26 October 1967, Glasgow

Family: Son, of Rev Douglas N Alexander, Church of Scotland minister, and Dr Joyce (nee Garven) Alexander, GP; both of his parents were ousted from their Labour Party offices by Tommy Graham factionalists;

Education: Park Mains High School, Erskine; Lester B Pearson College, Vancouver; Edinburgh University; University of Pennsylvania;

Occupation: Solicitor '94-97; ex: Speechwriter for Gordon Brown '90-91;

Traits: Beaky nose; "his hair neatly gelled, wearing a Mandelson-black suit with Dewar-red tie" (John Arlidge, OBSERVER); "a good-looking, very nice young man" (Anne McGuire MP); "clean-cut" (Auslan Cramb, DAILY TELEGRAPH); "looks more like 19" (Magnus Linklater, TIMES); looks "as out of place among Scots Labour as an insurance clerk on a strikers' picket" (Matthew Parris, TIMES); a Bill Simpson/'Dr Finlay' look-alike;

Address: House of Commons, Westminster, SW1A 0AA;

Telephone: 0171 219 3000;

KEEPING PARLIAMENTARY SECRETS

A rueful MP claimed, with some truth, that the best way to keep something secret is to make a speech about it in the Palace of Westminster. He was commenting on the emptiness of the Press Gallery (except for HANSARD writers and the Press Association). Long gone are the days when serious newspapers carried a full or half-page summarising Parliamentary debate. Of late, Westminster has been used as a source of news stories. In our old-fashioned way, we read HANSARD daily and watch the Commons and Lords on the Parliamentary Channel. Parliamentary debaters are very self-revealing in debate. And we don't mean only Kerry Pollard MP, in whose Maiden he disclosed that until 12 he had to drop his trousers regularly to prove that Kerry was not a girl's name.

Majority: 8,271 over Conservative 5-way;

Description: Formerly the only Tory seat in Sheffield and south Yorkshire; a leafy, mainly middle-class residential area in the city's southwest, stretching from the university area of Broomhill to the edge of the Peak District; contains Sheffield and Hallam universities and houses much of the city's professional and managerial elite; its latest change, the removal of pro-Labour Nether Edge ward, allegedly made it safer for Conservatives;

Position: Spokesman, on Community Relations '97-; on Select Committees: on Information (Chairman '98-) '97-, on Home Affairs '97-98; ex: Bath City Councillor '94-95; Avon County Councillor '93-95;

Outlook: "One of the party's rising stars" (Paddy Ashdown MP); "a future Leader" (Don Foster MP, his mentor); bright, busy and hardworking; so computer-literate that his colleagues on the Information Select Committee insisted he become Chairman; was initially "wary of co-operation with Labour" (NEW STATESMAN); a young, locally-born, Leftwing LibDem who won on his first Parliamentary attempt in the party's 1997 mini-landslide; he also won in his first council attempts in Bath and Avon; a classless-seeming computer manager and Leftwing cause groupie: Liberator, ALDC, Green Liberal Democrats, CPRE, Voting Reform Group, Searchlight, World Development Movement; his key political interests are the NHS (its preservation in public service), the social services, civil rights for disabled people: "all are issues on which I have acted or spoken over several years; I am also very supportive of the constitutional reform agenda, especially a legal framework for the relationship between the citizen and the state" (RA);

History: At school he was against party politics; he joined the LibDems at 25, Sep '91; successfully contested Avon County Council May '93; successfully contested Bath City Council, with the support of his mentor Don Foster May '94; was selected as the LibDem candidate for Tory-held Sheffield-Hallam, which had twice been won by Sir Irvine Patnick, in 1992 by a majority of 6,741 over his LibDem opponent Peter Gold '95; won the seat by a majority of 8,271 (18%) on an astonishing swing of 18.53%, making him "the only opposition MP in the whole of south or west Yorkshire" (RA) May '97; in his Maiden speech, emphasised the problem of youth crime in the Low Edges estate and the need to keep a "high-quality urban environment that people will respect" and enough local policemen May '97; although he had voted to ban handguns, asked about compensation for debts of gun clubs June '97; co-sponsored motion urging complete ban on organophosphates June '97; was named to Select Committee on Home Affairs July '97; opposed resumption of death penalty in Colorado July '97; was named to Information Select Committee Sep? '97; urged "human rights considerations be made more explicit in immigration law" Oct '97; urged a political balance on regional development agency boards, including minority parties Dec '97; urged the Government to pay the full costs of the South Yorkshire SuperTram Jan '98; urged more and better jobs for the young from ethnic minorities Jan '98; complained about rail enquiry lines Feb '98; backed the Sainte-Lague formula as fairer for allocating seats in the PR election for the European Parliament Feb '98; enthused about retaining a genuine regional base in Parliamentary TV coverage Mar '98; urged wider public access to results of police complaints procedures Mar '98; backed the European Parliamentary Elections Bill, recognising "the

Labour Government have been brave to introduce a Bill which appears to damage them in terms of the current electoral situation" Mar '98; was elected Chairman of the Information Select Committee Apr '98; complained about "the low rate of successful prosecutions in rape cases" Apr '98; complained about "the number of mentally disordered offenders who are inappropriately held in prison" May '98; introduced a Bill to compulsorily register dogs May '98; left Home Affairs Select Committee June '98;

Born: 11 February 1966, Sheffield

Family: Son, of John Allan, chauffeur and personnel manager, now retired, and Elizabeth (Beaumont), doctor's receptionist; m '91 Louise (Netley), school supervisory assistant; 1d Rosie '88;

Education: Ecclesall Infants; Ecclesall Junior; Birkdale Prep; Oundle School; Pembroke College, Cambridge University (BA Hons); Bristol Polytechnic (MSc);

Occupation: Ex: Consultancy and Systems Integration Manager (Information Technology) in NHS's Family Health Systems '??-??; previously an archaeologist;

Traits: Short; oval face, with silly-looking light tufted fringe beard and thin moustache; holds his head erect; uses his hands; slight Yorkshire brogue; has a tattoo;

Address: House of Commons, Westminster, London SW1A 0AA; 99 Clarkehouse Road, Sheffield S10 2LN (constituency office);

Telephone: 0171 219 1104/0971(Fax) (H of C); 0114 249 4775 (Fax); 0410 497095 (mobile); 0114 249 4774 (answering service);

Graham (William) ALLEN   Labour   NOTTINGHAM NORTH '87-

Majority: 18,801 (45.4%) over Conservative 5-way;

Description: A heavily working-class part of this East Midlands industrial city, formerly semi-marginal; two-fifths live in council housing;

Position: Government Whip (Vice Chamberlain to HM Household '98-) '97-; ex: Assistant Spokesman: on Transport '95-97, on Home Affairs (Constitution '94-95, Immigration '93-94), Environment (Health and Safety) '92-93, on Social Security '91-92; on Plant Commission on Electoral Systems '93-95; Secretary, Lords and Commons Cricket Club '92-96; on Select Committees on Procedure '90-91, Public Accounts '88-91, on Members' Interests '88-90; on Joint Select Committee on Consolidation Bills '87-91; Chairman, PLP Treasury and Civil Service Committee '90-91; Organiser of PPCs' Liaison '85-87; National Co-ordinator, Trade Union Co-ordinating Committee on Political Fund Ballots '84-86; Tower Hamlets Councillor '82-86;

Outlook: The Commons' top cricketer reduced to climbing the Whip's ladder, after five over-enthusiastic tries in shadow ministerial jobs; "the most reform-minded Member in the House" (Max Davidson, DAILY TELEGRAPH); initially "irritate[d] his elders with constant calls for Parliament to be made more hospitable" (Alastair Campbell, SUNDAY MIRROR); feels "our deferential, hierarchical and semi-feudal values and all its consequent waste just has to go"; is the originator of Labour's proposals for "a plurality of democratically accountable institutions, each checking, restraining and limiting the powers of the others" - the supplementary-vote system for the Commons plus "election to a reformed Lords by regional list, and list-PR for European Parliamentary elections as well"; is a great supporter of a better-armed legislature able to do effective battle against the executive; was a moderniser before it became fashionable; "the great quality of Graham Allen is his relentless radicalism" (Edward Pearce, GUARDIAN); shows great organisational drive; a forceful agitator for pluralism, modernisation of Parliamentary democracy and for US-style separation of powers, Labour campaigning and politicisation of trade unions, with emphasis on a workplace participation; as a strong supporter of 'Charter '88', has presented Bills to set up a Bill of Rights and a written Constitution; initially favoured hopeless broad-Left (Tribune and Campaign Groups) unity; an occasional TRIBUNE columnist; an enthusiast for 'real ale' brewed by small independents and a first-class cricketer; "no man who could remove Gary Sobers twice in a fortnight from the wicket can be bereft of a certain quality" (Tory ex-MP Nicholas Scott); formerly TGWU-sponsored;

History: He was born into a Labour family in Nottingham, his grandfather having been a founding member of the Nottingham Labour Party; his first and only affiliation was to the Labour Party, at 18 '71; was elected to Tower Hamlets Council but failed to secure hopeless GLC seat May '82; was a candidate for post of Labour Party General Secretary Jan-Mar '85; was selected for marginal, Tory-held Nottingham North, won in '83 by Conservative Richard Ottaway from veteran Labour MP William Whitlock by 362 votes Apr '85; created and organised Political Funds Campaign, against current expectations, winning 40 nation-wide trade union votes, which he proclaimed as "Mrs Thatcher's only defeat by the Labour movement" at party conference Sep '85; won shield for recruiting most members for his constituency June '86; with Peter Hain formed PPCs' Liaison, a candidates' pressure group to reform Labour at Westminster by transforming the PLP into a "council-style" Labour Group, to develop Parliamentary socialism and "carry through socialist policies in the teeth of entrenched opposition" while providing MPs with proper facilities Sep '86; retook Nottingham North June '87; attended both Tribune and Campaign Group meetings to emphasise he was not interested in fratricidal Left rivalry June '87; in Maiden pointed out that 10,000 industrial jobs had been lost in Nottingham since 1983, June '87; urged a complete overhaul of Parliamentary democracy to make it more open and democratic July '87; withdrew as impractical his PLP motion urging tighter discipline over Labour MPs' interviews July '87; in his first adjournment speech -urging better MPs' facilities and improved Parliamentary financial accountability procedures - he ridiculed the idea of holding it at 1:30 am July '87; urged pump-priming to increase Northern industrial jobs July '87; was hauled over the coals by Whips after complaining loudly about "public school pranks" which lost a day's debate Nov '87; complained of "philistine" efforts of Nottingham's Conservative council to erect plastic battlements and fibreglass turrets on its castle Nov '87; was the last to sign the Register of Members' Interests as a protest against its inadequacy Dec '87; demanded adequate scrutiny of the £48b Consolidated Fund Bill Dec '87; complained that the poll tax would hurt all organized religions Dec '87; demanded adequate debate of Select Committee reports Dec '87; asked Mrs Thatcher if it was not "the most gutless, sycophantic Cabinet in which she has ever served" Dec '87; was added to Public Accounts Committee Jan '88; in his adjournment debate he urged better treatment of retired elderly in Nottingham and elsewhere Mar '88; lamented the spread of a bee disease Mar '88; on Register of MPs' Interests, was in a minority of one in urging a list of remunerations from all directorships, details of clients of MPs involved in PR firms and a list of all shareholdings Mar '88; demanded Government help to rebuild system-built Bison houses Apr '88; complained of the "lack of direction and conservatism of the PLP" Apr '88; introduced Bill to regulate tenancies of brewery companies June '88; voted against EC money resolution July '88; voted with hard Left on Revolutions of 1688-89 July

'88; at annual conference urged a more active role for the PLP in the formation of policy Oct '88; backed John Prescott for Deputy Leader Oct '88; urged a written constitution, Bill of Rights Dec '88; called for a Legal Affairs Select Committee Mar '89; was first MP to be re-selected under Labour's new OMOV procedure Apr '89; blamed misbehaviour among Labour back-benchers on frustration at the inadequacies of Parliamentary procedures Apr '88; urged much more research on child abuse May '89; complained that failure to build a Channel link was frittering away opportunities for the North May '89; presented a Bill to elect a new House of Lords Oct '89; asked the highest number (634) number of questions by any back-bencher in 1988-89 Parliament Nov '89; complaining that Labour MPs behaved like either "workaholics" or "alcoholics", acting like 200 one-man businessmen, urged more collective activities Nov '89; urged an "informed and participatory democracy" May '90; it was estimated that his continually-printed motions on reforming Commons procedure on its Order Paper had cost £10,000, to which he replied that reformed procedure would save millions May '90; urged a written constitution June '90; urged more open Budget-making Nov '90; again presented a Bill providing for a written constitution Dec '90; presented a Human Rights Bill, replicating the European Convention Dec '90; was named Assistant Spokesman on Social Security after Tony Banks resigned in opposition to Labour's support of Gulf War Jan '91; attacked undermining of SERPS Jan '91; urged a new Budget-making process Mar '91; travelled to Moscow and Kiev with the British-Atlantic Group Mar '91; because he had become an Assistant Spokesman, was retired from Public Accounts Committee Apr '91; urged expansion of women's rights June '91; opposed "coercing" women to give the names of the fathers of their children July '91; in a minority report of Procedure Committee, called for election of Select Committees by secret ballots July '91; urged further democratization of UK and EC Nov '91; urged Government to provide MPs with two staff in Commons and two in constituency Nov '91; was retired from Select Committees on Procedure, Consolidation Bills Dec '91; complained that "the Conservatives' self-regulation in this [pensions] area has left occupational pension funds and their members at the mercy of fraudsters, company raiders and asset-strippers" Jan '92; complained that state pensioners and ordinary taxpayers had subsidized private pensions Mar '92; retained seat with a majority massively increased by 9,087, a swing to Labour of 8.66% in Apr '92; led successful teams which won elections of Leader John Smith and Deputy Leader Margaret Beckett May '92; re-introduced Bills to abolish Lords and for written Constitution and Bill of Rights June '92; successfully moved resolution in PLP to set up a Review Committee to modernise its organisation and procedure July '92; received 29 votes in ballot for Shadow Cabinet, the third lowest July '92; was named by John Smith an Assistant Spokesman on the Constitution on the Home Affairs team July '92; urged an end to union sponsorship of MPs, "a relic of the past, when MPs were not paid" which could be misrepresented Aug '92; announced a Bill to give a majority of MPs the right to recall Parliament Sep '92; at annual conference, urged a Bill of Rights Oct '92; was revealed as the second most assiduous written questioner (272) in the 1991-92 session Oct '92; had an adjournment debate on need for sex offence clinics Nov '92; attacked as the "most obnoxious" part of Asylum and Immigration Appeals Bill the provision scrapping the right of would-be visitors and short-term students to appeal against refusal of entry clearance, "when thousands of unjustified refusals are being brought to light" Jan '93; backed an independent electoral commission to restore missing voters to registers, as in Brent Feb '93; opposed extension of betting hours Feb '93; said that Labour's Plant Committee - of which he was a member - had not reached a "Holy Grail" in electoral reform Mar '93; on Plant Committee, was reported as having voted for SV (Supplementary Vote) system of proportional representation -where voters had a second choice when candidates did not attain 50% or more Apr '93; emphasised that Plant Committee's proposals for the Lords, Commons and Europe had to be understood as three interlocking representative bodies with different electoral systems Apr '93; after two-year battle, succeeded in getting Procedure Committee to modernise the language of petitions to Parliament May '93; urged centralised research on child abuse May '93; introduced Bill to provide UK citizens with the rights and freedoms of the European Convention of Human Rights June '93; criticising the Governments "mean-minded" anti-immigration measures, likely to reduce chances for legitimate asylum seekers July '93; pressed for public inquiries to be included in setting European Parliamentary boundaries July '93; urged reinvigoration of local government, freed from domination from the centre Aug '93; was thought to be the main inspirer of John Smith's "Democratic Agenda" proposals unveiled at annual conference at Brighton Oct '93; again received only 29 votes in ballot for Shadow Cabinet Oct '93; again urged adoption by UK of European Convention Oct '93; as Captain of the Lords and Commons Cricket team, urged PM John Major to give up Parliamentary question time to listen to the Test Match Oct '93; criticised mass Christmas detention of Jamaican visitors as "a bizarre event which is unprecedented in my experience" Dec '93; urging "democratic renewal", blamed public cynicism on Government's devaluing of "the concepts of civic participation and public service in its relentless quest to substitute market solutions for democratic ones" Jan '94; again presented his Bill to give UK citizens the rights of the European Convention Jan '94; outlined a programme for Parliamentary reform: MPs' committees should take evidence on Bills for six weeks before their presentation to the Commons, all Bills should be timetabled, all select committees should be elected, outside employment should be banned for MPs, the Lords should be democratised Jan '94; backed ousting of anti-social tenants by Nottingham City Council Jan '94; voted against restoring capital punishment, for reducing age of permitted gay sex to 16, Feb '94; urged the Commons' chamber be made circular Apr '94; previously pro-Prescott, organised campaign for Blair for Leader June '94; voted for Blair for Leader, Beckett for Deputy Leader July '94; was named by Tony Blair to his National Heritage team as Assistant Spokesman on the Constitution, under Chris Smith Oct '94; said that the monarchy was not included in Labour's constitutional review Oct '94; committed Labour to the European Convention on Human Rights Oct '94; as Assistant Spokesman on Immigration, complained about more backward immigration rules Oct '94; again enthused about wholesale reform of Commons procedures Nov '94; urged PR for all bodies but the Commons Dec '94; defended the BBC against Tory attacks Feb '95; urged an elected second chamber to replace the Lords Feb '95; held an adjournment debate on the Information Super-Highway Mar '95; called a debate on digital television June '95; captained Lords and Commons cricket team tour of South Africa Sep '95; described the accelerated elevation of Lord Cranborne as bringing "both houses into disrepute" Feb '95; enthused about Labour going on line Oct '95; was involved in negotiations with BT and cable companies to cable up all schools Oct '95; was switched to Clare Short's team as an Assistant Spokesman on Transport Oct '95; blamed traffic pollution on "the absence of any coherent strategy from the Department of Transport" Nov '95; blamed the Conservatives for slashing transport funding Jan '96; urged double hulls for oil tankers Feb '96; attacked cuts in the coastguard Mar '96; pledged Labour to a "national transport framework" Apr '96; enthused about the Channel Tunnel Rail Link Apr '96; praised car-sharing in Nottingham's "imaginative and innovative green commuter plan" May '96; voted: to limit MPs' mileage allowances, against a 3% cap on MPs' pay and in favour of basing pensions on £43,000 July '96; complained about the privatisation of NHS dentistry in his constituency July '96; pledged a Labour overhaul of driver testing July '96; urged alternatives to excessive use of cars and road-building July '96; his plan to breathe health into Britain's ailing merchant marine with a £60m package, was shelved on the insistence of the Shadow Chancellor, Gordon Brown Aug '96; was confirmed in the 'final' pre-election reshuffle as an Assistant Spokesman on Frank

Dobson's Environment team Aug '96; highlighted the number of fatal industrial accidents in his constituency Oct '96; warned against the battle over Europe interfering with a safe working environment Nov '96; urged a rebirth of local government, with "an end to capping, the introduction of annual elections, the return of the business rate to the localities, and evolving regional government" Dec '96; proposed penalties for violence or intimidation at work Dec '96; was targeted for defeat by pro-Lifers Feb '97; in anticipation of becoming the father of his first child, asked every Secretary of State "if Ministers are entitled to use child-care facilities" in their departments Jan '97; enthused about police anti-drug talks to schoolchildren Feb '97; urged fairer funding for local councils, pointing out that a Nottingham house worth £40,000 paid more council tax than a Mayfair millionaire Apr '97; won by an enhanced majority of 18,801 over his Conservative opponent, on a pro-Labour swing of 12.4% May '97; was named a Government Whip May '97; in the reshuffle was promoted to No 4 Whip, being given the additional responsibility, as Vice Chamberlain of HM Household, of daily reports to HM the Queen, in succession to Janet Anderson; on his debut, refused to don the formal regalia or walk backward from Speaker Boothroyd July '98;

Born: 11 January 1953, Nottingham

Family: Son, William Allen, miner, and Edna (Holt), textile worker; m '95 Allyson (Stewart), Californian marketing consultant; 1d Grace Madrid '97;

Education: Robert Shaw Primary; Forest Fields Grammar; City of London Poly (President of Union '76) '72-75; Leeds University '77-78;

Occupation: Author: Reinventing Democracy (1996), ex: Sponsored, by TGWU (£600 p a to his constituency, 80% of election expenses) '87-95, by Communication Managers Association (donations to constituency) '88-96; Regional Research and Education Officer, GMB '86-87; Seconded from GLC, ran the Trade Unions' Political Funds campaign '84-86; GLC Senior Officer (where he was a 'progress chaser' responsible for freeing money and ensuring council staff implemented GLC policies) '83-85, Labour Party Researcher '78-83; Warehouseman '71-72;

Traits: Very tall (6ft 4in); parted dark blond hair; "spikey-faced" (Craig Brown, TIMES); "is regarded as rather solemn and relentless" (Andrew Marr, INDEPENDENT); "self-important": "his press releases are usually about Graham Allen" (Paul Routledge, INDEPENDENT ON SUNDAY); forceful speaker; tireless organiser; Humanist; sports all-rounder; excellent cricketer (twice bowled Gary Sobers; was first Labour MP to score a century in 150 years of Westminster cricket); saxophonist; wine enthusiast; oil painter; cook;

Address: House of Commons, Westminster, London SW1A 0AA; 170 Robinswood Road, Aspley, Nottingham, NG8 3LD; 23 Tufton Court, Westminster SW1;

Telephone: 0171 219 4343 (H of C); 01554 792344 (Nottingham home);

ANOREXIA OR OBESITY

Profiles, like politicians, can be very slim or very full-bodied. This can depend on how varied and colourful is the past of the MP concerned, or the quality of the newspapers reporting them. Some politicians are paranoid about disclosing anything beyond the bare minimum and then complain if second-hand information beyond the bare essentials turns out to be less than accurate. Others turn to their libel lawyers as an expensive threat. We adhere to the quaint idea that if people have decided to plunge into the glass fishbowl of politics they are not entitled to wear wetsuits. After all, most wrongdoing has been exposed by the media's investigative journalists, very little by politicians themselves.

David (Anthony Andrew) AMESS   **Conservative**   **SOUTHEND WEST '97-**

Majority: 2,615 (5.6%) over LibDem 6-way;
Description: The more desirable - and Tory - residential half of the resort town at the Essex mouth of the Thames, for 85 years the fiefdom of the Guinness-Channon family; it contains Leigh-on-Sea and Westcliff-on-Sea;
Former Seat: Basildon '83-97
Position: Vice President, Lottery Council '98; Joint Chairman, all-party Fire Safety Group '98-; Vice Chairman: Association of Conservative Clubs '97-, all-party Scout Group '98-; Secretary, Conservative Friends of Israel '97-; ex: PPS: to Michael Portillo '87-97, to Edwina Currie and Lord Skelmersdale '87-88; President, Basildon Dyslexia Association '90-97; Redbridge Borough Councillor (Vice Chairman of Housing) '82-86;

Outlook: The indefatigably partisan former "Basildon Bore" (Andrew Rawnsley, GUARDIAN) now boring for safer Southend West; the cheer-leader of Essex Tory proles and originator of the 'I Love Basildon' campaign, who shrewdly avoided defeat by recognising the significance of the Lib-Lab capture of Basildon's council and the change in Basildon's boundaries; his importance was elevated temporarily by his early and unexpected victory in his marginal seat in the '92 election, which put paid to Labour's hopes; a Thatcherite Rightwinger in Parkinson's 'Conservative Way Forward' group; the hyperactive, naively enthusiastic, bitterly partisan, articulate voice of local ratepayers; was one of the first to call for a poll tax; the Rightwing Cockney and former Redbridge Councillor who deepened his constituency roots temporarily by publicising his tireless local involvement in Basildon; anti-litter; pro-hanging; pro: Israel and Apartheid South Africa; Catholic opponent of abortion and embryo experimentation; "I'm interested in everything and expert in nothing" (DA); "I do not believe in the equality of men and women"; "if I were pressed, I would probably say that I believe that women are superior to men" (DA); "typical of homo essexus": "an industrious backbencher, but with a slightly less developed brain than Tory MPs further up the evolutionary chain"; "he shares his species' primitive beliefs - they still, for instance, worship Mrs Thatcher; and he is an enthusiast for hanging"; but he developed "a ruthlessly simple technique for securing his re-election: he never completed a sentence without mentioning his constituency"; "it has turned the town's MP from a figure of affectionate fun on the Tory backbenches into a revered icon; whenever he rises from his place, a great roar goes up, often accompanied by the football terrace chant, 'Basildon! Basildon'" (Andrew Rawnsley, GUARDIAN);

History: "At the age of 11 I decided that I wanted to be a Member of Parliament"; reacting against Labour's behaviour in Newham, joined the Conservative Party at 16, '69; contested seat on Newham Council May '74; contested GLC seat in Newham NW May '77; became Chairman of Newham NW Conservative Association and Chairman of its Forest Gate ward June '77; contested seat on Newham Council May '78; contested Newham NW against Arthur Lewis May '79; won seat on Redbridge Borough Council May '82; won altered Basildon, (thought to be safely Labour and therefore abandoned by its ex-MP Harvey Proctor), with help of SDP candidate Sue Slipman, who took 25% of vote; was the only victorious Tory without a Tory councillor in his constituency June '83; supported restoration of death penalty saying, "I would pull the lever" (according to PA's Chris Moncrieff) July '83; attacked unions for blocking Youth Training jobs Sep '83; urged removal of Henry Moore statue in front of Parliament Oct '83; urged privileged position for business ratepayers when councils fix rates Dec '83; strongly defended Rates (capping of) Bill in Maiden Speech in which he backed a poll tax as an alternative to rates Jan '84; urged tour operators guarantee safety of hotels they offered Feb '84; opposed further expansion of Basildon Apr '84; warned against dangers of walking into plate glass July '84; attacked Government's £3m subvention to International Planned Parenthood Federation because it accepted abortion Aug '84; urged better protection for Basildon schools because of £1.5m damage by arsonists Nov '84; again attacked abortion Dec '84; co-urged three-tier VAT to avoid increased tax on children clothing and books Jan '85; urged rate-capping Jan '85; voted against big increase in Top People's pay July '85; spoke at SPUC/Pro-Life anti-abortion rally on fringe of Tory Blackpool conference Oct '85; after an adjournment debate, took part in human chain demonstration against moving Basildon Hospital's maternity services to Orsett; he was accused of "hypocrisy" by Labour opponents who alleged move had been forced by Tory Government cuts Dec '85; complained about high cost of local district central heating Apr '86; claimed "research on human embryos cannot supply us with the answers that scientists are rightly seeking for the tragedies of infertility and other inherited disorders" May '86; warned Government: "we are not prepared to see the embryonic human being employed by scientists as guinea pigs" July '86; asked for information on local drug-pushers, which he passed on to Scotland Yard July '86; was one of 48 MPs (all Tories except Enoch Powell and Cyril Smith) who voted for right of parents to withdraw children from any sex education to which they objected Oct '86; supported Kenneth Hind's Unborn Children (Protection) Bill to ban embryo experimentation Oct '86; on eve of visit to Pope, urged more anti-abortion legislation Nov '86; urged more decent and varied housing within Basildon Nov '86; visited Poland Dec '86; again protested concentration of cancer treatment in constituency Mar '87; complained that vote against restoring capital punishment showed that Commons had not done "everything that we could to stop...murder" like that of his cousin's wife a year before Apr '87; in an adjournment debate, fiercely attacked the overspending by Basildon district council, until recently Labour-controlled May '87; doubled his majority June '87; urged better provision for special education for those with learning difficulties like dyslexia, especially in Essex July '87; backed Mrs Thatcher's resistance to stiffened sanctions against South Africa Oct '87; co-sponsored Edward Leigh's Bill to report foreign girls having abortions in Britain to their home GPs Oct '87; deplored dangerous practice of driving while talking on carphones Dec '87; urged a taxi alarm system Jan '88; served on committee considering David Alton's abortion-curbing Bill Feb '88; urged taxis be obliged to handle disabled in wheelchairs Feb '88; enthused about the rate-capping of Basildon Feb '88; again introduced his protective Horses, Ponies and Donkeys Bill, this time successfully Mar-May '88; called for tune for "I Love Basildon", which he later recorded May '88; voting records again showed him to be very assiduous May '88; again urged capital punishment June '88; attacked litter-louts Jan '89; introduced Abortion (Right of Conscience) (Amendment) Bill to require doctors and nurses to give a positive indication of assent before being required to perform or assist at an abortion Feb '89; introduced Bill to give honourary British nationality to Raoul Wallenberg Mar '89; local elections showed a cut in the Tory vote by 11% in his constituency, indicating he might lose his seat May '89; again opposed abortion July '89; visited South Africa as guest of its government Sep-Oct '89; criticised televising of Commons debate on Queen's Speech Nov '89; introduced Adoption (Amendment) Bill to set up statutory controls Jan '90; opposed ordination of divorced men Feb '90; urged surcharging of Basildon's Labour-controlled council after it sent every resident a Valentine's card Mar '90; welcomed capping of Basildon's council Apr '90; opposed abortions as late as 24 weeks and foetus experimentation Apr '90; introduced Dogs Bill to penalise cruel or careless owners or those who kept dangerous dogs Apr '90; visited Israel as guest of its government May-June '90; said it was "appalling" to allow abortion up to time of birth for foetuses of disabled June '90; again opposed televising Commons July '90; said he had not moved his Raoul Wallenberg (Memorial) Bill because Government had agreed to provide land for a memorial July '90; said he would vote to retain Mrs Thatcher as Leader because he owed his seat to her populist policies Nov '90; urged better transport for Basildon Dec '90; criticised timeshare schemes Mar '91; backed the Badgers Bill May '91; disclosed his late-night "anti-vandal" patrols in Basildon May '91; introduced Pet Animals (Amendment) Bill to ban sale of pets to children without parental agreement June '91; led an attack on Sir Bob Reid before media to complain about Fenchurch Street line Nov '91; backed ban on hunting with hounds Feb '92; invited John Major to visit "Basildon - the finest and most exciting town in the country!" Feb '92; called for Basildon to be made a city, as the oldest and largest new town in the country with plans to build a cathedral Mar '92; had many famous visiting supporters, including Mrs Thatcher and fellow East End prole Norman Tebbit, during election campaign; campaigned on 'No More Tax'; TV-watchers knew the Tories had won when he retained his seat with a majority of 1,480 reduced by 1,169 by a swing to Labour of only 1.26% Apr '92; was named PPS to Chief Secretary Michael Portillo Apr '92; in the local elections, Tories swept the board May '92; secured permission from Westminster Council for a bust of Raoul Wallenberg to be placed in Cumberland Place Nov '92; urged a separate frequency for hospital radio Dec '92; introduced Children (Prohibition of Sex Selection) Bill to ban choice of sex at conception Feb '93; having bought Hoover products on their promise of free flights to the USA, was shocked at the subsequent "fiasco" Apr '93; his Children (Prohibition of Sex Selection) Bill was defeated 116 to 86, Apr '93; extensively attacked defeated local Labour councillors Apr '93; complained about "the slaughter of the innocents" in Bosnia Apr '93; complained about Basildon men "moving in and out of relationships with women, producing children and then abandoning those women and the children", thus increasing pressure on housing Apr '93; in Basildon Conservatives lost control, with Essex County Council being split equally among Labour, LibDem and Tories May '93; introduced Voluntary Personal Security Cards Bill to prove identity; it was given a First Reading May '93; strongly urged that no shopworker be forced to work on Sunday against his will Oct '93; introduced Football Matches (Violent and Disorderly Conduct) Bill to restrain hooligans Nov '93; complained about closure of Pitsea Post Office Nov '93; visited as a guest the headquarters in Omaha of First Data Resources, a constituency firm Jan '94; voted in favour of restoring capital punishment, also for killing policemen; voted against homosexual sex at 16, in favour at 18, Feb '94; attacked "the incompetence of the rotten, socialist Essex County Council", "a love affair between the Labour Party and the Liberal Democrats" Mar '94; as the father of five children, he was offered a "do-it-yourself vasectomy kit" by Labour MP Tony Banks to reduce the strain he had imposed on the Basildon midwifery services Mar '94; all the seven Amesses greeted John Major on his Basildon visit Apr '94; introduced Bill to make new drivers display the newness of their qualification Apr '94; the lobbyist Ian Greer offered a meeting with Amess, as PPS to Chief Secretary Michael Portillo, in the film of a pretend Russo-American company set up by Central TV's 'Cooke Report' to trap lobbyists at work; Amess: "I certainly knew nothing of this and Michael Portillo certainly cannot be seen to be compromised" May '94; complained that Fenchurch Street station had been closed for seven weeks June '94; met with tobacco lobbyists to help avoid a ban on tobacco advertising Nov '94; his wife Julia opposed any curb in Commons hours, since he would only spend them on constituency activities Dec '94; lined up in favour of banning fox-hunting Jan '95; resisted turning a beautiful wood in Basildon into a business park Jan '95; voted for the Bill to ban hunting Mar '95; his new Bill urged UK to withdraw from UN fund financing birth control in China May '95; complained that the

Boundary Commission had "raped the town of Basildon" in creating an extra seat in Essex, although they had made his marginal seat slightly safer June '95; since the LibDems and Labour had captured Basildon Council, he succeeded in being selected for safer Southend West on the retirement of Paul Channon, narrowly beating Eleanor Laing; he was jokingly described as being "the only Tory to have moved closer to Europe" July '95; John Prescott described him as "clucking off to become Southend Fried Chicken" in the 'chicken run' of frightened Tories Oct '95; made a powerful speech extolling Raoul Wallenberg Feb '96; on TV agreed to play noughts and crosses with fellow Tory MP David Martin on a young woman's stomach with a marker pen Feb '96; derided Tony Blair's "sanctimonious humbug" Apr '96; introduced Freezing of Human Embryos Bill to ban the practice Apr '96; backed a 3% cap on MPs' wage increases, opposed basing MPs' pensions on £43,000 July '96; exploded incoherently about attacks on him for sending his son to an RC single-sex school 8 miles outside his constituency Oct '96; was tricked by Channel 4 into putting down a question about a non-existent drug Nov '96; his Abortion (Amendment) Bill tried to tighten the grounds for allowing termination Dec '96; a MORI Poll for The SUN showed that "th Tories have sensationally lost the support of Basildon Man and Woman", plunging to half their '92 support Dec '96; declared himself an opponent of a single European currency Apr '97; after a "poisonous, wicked campaign" emanating from his LibDem opponent, retained Southend West with a narrow majority of 2,615 over her, after a 9.1% anti-Tory swing; there were 6 contestants May '97; in his new Maiden, pledged "to establish Southend as the premier seaside resort in the country" May '97; in the Leadership contest was initially a supporter of Peter Lilley June '97; he was one of 8 Tory MPs to back Labour MP Mike Foster's anti-hunting Bill Nov '97;

Born: 26 March 1952, Plaistow, London

Family: Son, late James H V Amess, ex-electrician, and Maud Ethel (Martin), dressmaker; "we were very poor and lived in a small terraced house with no bathroom, an outside toilet and a tin bath hanging on the wall"; his cousin's wife was killed by 52 stab wounds in a multi-story carpark in Worcester in '86; m '83 Julia (Arnold), ex insurance underwriter; 1s David James '84; 4d Katherine Louise '85, Sarah Elizabeth '88, Alexandra Charlotte Clementine '90, Florence Rebecca '91; "I have five children, which is not unusual for Basildon"; "I attended the birth of every one of the children - in fact, I think I could quite easily deliver a baby by now!"; Ann Widdecombe is the godmother of his daughter Alexandra;

Education: St Antony's Junior School, Forest Gate ("I was often in classes of 50 and the teachers still gave us excellent tuition and kept order to a high standard" (DA)); St Bonaventure's Grammar School, Newham ("I was quite bossy and pushy" (DA); he hit one fellow student over the head with a bicycle pump); Bournemouth College of Technology (BSc Econ Hons lower second);

Occupation: Parliamentary Adviser, to Caravan Club '97-; Spokesman (unpaid), for National Association of Hospital Broadcasting Organisations '87-; ex: Chairman: Accountancy Aims Group (specialist employment agency) '90-97, A & G Executive Search and Selection '85-87; Senior Partner, in Accountancy Aids (specialist employment consultancy) '81-87; Senior Consultant, with Executemps Company Agency '79-81; Head of Temporary Department of Accountancy Personnel '76-79; Underwriter with Leslie Godwin Agency '74-76; Teacher '70-71 ("for 18 months I taught at a junior mixed school, St John the Baptist in Bonner Road, Bethnal Green; I specialised in teaching children who were described as ESN");

Traits: Blond hair; long face; strong chin; "he sports a footballer's haircut" and "a split melon grin" (Andrew Rawnsley, GUARDIAN)); "a bizarre pudding bowl haircut even a fourth division footballer might consider unwise" (Quentin Letts, DAILY TELEGRAPH); "foppishly good-looking" (GUARDIAN); "cheeky Cockney chappie" (Nicholas Timmins,

INDEPENDENT); gullible; convivial ("what I'm always impressed by is when some MPs give up alcohol for Lent; that to me is quite astonishing" - DA); "young, smart, upwardly-mobile and distinctly Southern"; has "an Estuary English accent" (Matthew Parris, TIMES); punchy speaker; "ebullient" (Sir David Mitchell ex-MP); "I suspect that Members of Parliament are not, by and large, modest people; you've got to have a high opinion of yourself and you need a vivid imagination to accept the idea that someone pushes you into being a Member of Parliament" (DA); "I am a lifelong supporter of West Ham United and since June 1983 I have been a supporter of Basildon United" (DA); grasshopper conversationalist; ex-dyslexic: "until the age of five I had the nickname of 'Double Dutch'; I had a very bad stutter: I could not make the sounds 'st' or 'th'; the reason that I have no Cockney accent now is that I had to go to a speech therapist for three years"; RC ("confession is very important to me" - DA);
Address: House of Commons, Westminster, London SW1A 0AA;
Telephone: 0171 219 6387/3452/2245 (Fax) (H of C);

Rt Hon Michael (Earl of) ANCRAM DL   Conservative   DEVIZES '92-

Majority: 9,782 (16.3%) over LibDem 6-way;
Description: The largely rural and agricultural seat in northeastern Wiltshire; its suburbanised bit in the Thamesdown area around Swindon, containing Rover and Honda's car factories, was removed in '95 and replaced by Calne from North Wiltshire and Melksham from Westbury;
Former Seat: Edinburgh South '79-87; Berwick and East Lothian Feb-Oct 74;
Position: Deputy Chairman, of the Conservative Party '98-; Deputy Lieutenant, Roxburgh, Ettrick and Lauderdale '90-; ex: Spokesman on the Constitution '97-98; Minister of State '94-97, Under Secretary '93-94, for Northern Ireland; on Public Accounts Committee '92-93; Chairman, Conservative MPs' Constitutional Committee '92-93; Scottish Under-Secretary '83-87; Chairman '80-83, Vice Chairman '75-80, Scottish Conservatives; Chairman, Scottish Conservatives Committee on Local Government '88-89; Vice Chairman, Conservative MPs' Constitutional Committee '79-80; on Select Committee on Energy '79-83; Secretary: Conservative MPs' Horticultural Subcommittee '74, Conservative MPs' Scottish Committee '79-80; Chairman, of Thistle Group (pro-devolution Scottish Tories) '67-69;
Outlook: The man put in charge of rebuilding the Conservative Party after serving as the intellectual leader of the fightback against Labour's devolution; a witty, deft, flexible, urbane, moderate English-accented Scots Roman Catholic aristocrat; as a Catholic he is partly outside the Establishment; "posh, charming - but with a touch of ruthlessness...he seems to embody the charm of the British aristocracy without its snobbishness or aloofness" (Stephen Castle, INDEPENDENT ON SUNDAY); has overcome his two Scottish defeats and departure from politics there and his U-turn into a counter-devolutionary; his active part in introducing the poll tax first to Scotland is partially forgotten; in the mid-'90s was able to move the negotiations forward in Northern Ireland enough to arouse Unionist suspicions, but was crippled by John Major's insistence on decommissioning IRA arms BEFORE admitting the IRA to top talks; was recommended in '96 by Sir Patrick Mayhew as his successor as Northern Ireland Secretary; "a clubbable lawyer with a razor-sharp mind; [was] tipped for Cabinet

position after he performed brilliantly as political affairs Minister under Sir Patrick Mayhew"; "carries his status lightly" (Paul Routledge, INDEPENDENT ON SUNDAY); is suspected of hiding his own opinions behind the briefs of the party's current Leader; "if, on a Monday, he is in Belfast, he argues passionately for devolution; if, on a Tuesday, he is in Glasgow or Cardiff, he argues against political devolution" (Norman Godman MP); has thrived on his own and his party's disasters: he was named Spokesman on the Constitution in '97 after his party had been wiped out in Scotland and Wales; despite the five-year gap in his Parliamentary career was quickly re-promoted in Northern Ireland for his assiduous and sensitive handling of the constitutional parties there; formerly "a genuine Cabinet prospect" (GUARDIAN); the most aristocratic of the 'carpetbaggers' who fled from defeats of Scots Tories; has mildly progressive, spasmodically independent views and an original mind of high quality, with the style of a successful barrister and the discretion of a veteran politician; made his retread reputation on the Public Accounts Committee by his devastating attack on the Wessex Health Authority's mishandling of its £20m computer contract; recently a self-described 'Euro-pragmatic' opposed to a federal superstate; was close to Malcolm Rifkind; a co-founder of 'Thistle' and 'Blue Chip'; was initially pro-devolution and pro-PR for Scotland; recently an advocate of a radical rethink about a renegotiated Union; critical of AGR nuclear power;

History: Contested West Lothian against Tam Dalyell, urging tougher penalties for gun wielders; because he was a Catholic, the local Orange Lodge told him they could not support him June '70; was elected for Berwick and East Lothian, the first Scottish Tory Catholic to be elected to Parliament Feb '74; stopped being an abolitionist and backed hanging for terrorists July '74; lost Berwick Oct '74; supported a Douglas-Home type of mild devolution May '75; insisted Tories still backed a Scottish Assembly; urged use of Assembly for 2nd Readings, Committee and Report stages of Scottish Bills Nov '75; said: "the movement for self-determination...is undeniable" '76; was widely applauded at Tory conference when he attacked Mrs Thatcher's Tory Shadow Cabinet as weak and divided Oct '75; supported PR for Scotland Sep '76; insisted the Labour-preferred Scottish Assembly was "unworkable" Jan '79; was elected for Edinburgh South May '79; backed Corrie's anti-abortion Bill Jan '80; attacked as "irresponsible" Lothian's 43% rate increase Feb '80; was promoted Chairman of Scottish Tories by Mrs Thatcher Apr '80; sought reintroduction of "Emslie provision" which would oblige judges in most cases to specify minimum sentences for murders Apr '80; criticised extent of teacher training cuts Dec '80; opposed construction of Torness nuclear power plant Feb '81; urged Edinburgh be pulled out of Labour-controlled Lothian Regional Council Feb '81; accused Lothian Council of "blackmail" when it asked contractors about political contributions Apr '81; defended Thatcherism as an economic "cure" rather than a "placebo" Aug '82; urged battle against unemployment be given priority over inflation in 'Changing Gear' pamphlet Oct '82; opposed closure of Ravenscraig plant, urging Mrs Thatcher to throw monetarism to the winds for it Nov-Dec '82; on re-election, was promoted Scottish Under Secretary June '83; voted for restoration of death penalty for terrorists and murderers of police July '83; was howled down at Scots Tory conference when he supported rates as the local government Minister May '84; agreed to lower building standards in Scotland Sep '84; responsibility for home affairs was transferred from him to John Mackay, to give Ancram more time for increasing volume of work on poll tax Sep '85; said he hoped to see a major expansion of the ways in which council tenants could take part in managing their homes Oct '85; was quoted as having informed a constituent, "having opposed Torness from its inception in 1974, I can take little comfort from the fact that increasingly the arguments which I put forward are being proved right" by Chernobyl June '86; backed abolition of caning in schools July '86; derided Labour's "scaremongering" on deregulated bus charges Aug '86; in Scottish Office reshuffle, was confirmed in charge of poll tax legislation Sep '86; backed reintroduction of hanging for child-killers Jan '87; denounced Lothian's proposed 34% increase in rates Feb '87; launched campaign to boost council house sales Mar '87; rejected exemption from poll tax for students Mar '87; claimed "the old municipal solutions" to housing were "now thoroughly discredited" Apr '87; finished piloting Scottish poll tax through Parliament May '87; pointed out that the poll tax was introduced as a direct response to demands from within the Conservative Party, demands which became ferocious in 1985, when the regular review of rateable value produced dramatic increases, especially for the better-off May '87; was one of three Scottish Office Ministers to lose their seats when Edinburgh South went to Labour's Nigel Griffiths by a Labour majority of 1,859 instead of his majority of 3,655, a pro-Labour swing of 6% June '87; secured a two-year delay before he had to decide whether to fight Edinburgh South again July '87; again backed mixture of private and public backing for housing Aug '87; urged a rethink for development of Edinburgh Feb '88; urged a streamlining of the Scottish Tory party machine May '88; was mentioned as a possible Tory candidate in Kensington, on death of Sir Brandon Rhys Williams May '88; was named Chairman of Scots Tories' local government reform committee May '88; was first mentioned as Leon Brittan's possible successor at rock-solid Richmond Aug '88; his unpaid management of Waverley Housing Trust, an organization established to manage public sector housing in the Border, was criticized by Labour MP John Home Robertson: "Mr Ancram cannot get himself elected to do any job either at local or national level yet he is able to manipulate his way into a position of power" Oct '88; in wake of SNP's Govan by-election victory, urged a new "true partnership" between Scotland and England Nov '88; complained that his successor, Nigel Griffiths, had dishonoured his pledge on abortion Nov '88; was on by-election shortlist for Epping Forest where he was pipped by Steve Norris Nov '88; said he would not seek the South Edinburgh re-selection because of opposition from Rightwing opponents in the constituency association Jan '89; urged a radical rethink by Scots Tories about relations with England; urged the Union, by now a "jaded concept", be developed as a true partnership with the transfer of UK departments to Scotland, and vice versa, with Scots Ministers in other departments May '89; twitted Scots Liberal Democrats on their support for PR, since they had won only 5% of Scots votes for Euro-Parliament; under PR they would have been without any seats June '89; admitted his local government reform committee was divided over single-tier authorities Nov '89; shortlisted for Windsor and Maidenhead, was pipped by Michael Trend Apr '90; resigned from Scots Conservatives Committee to reform Scottish local government Feb '90; with Alan Duncan was shortlisted for Rutland and Melton; had to promise not to accept his father's title if he succeeded May '90; was finally selected for Devizes in the wake of Sir Charles Morrison's announcement of his impending retirement May '90; declined to sign the candidates' letter backing Mrs Thatcher Nov '90; retained the seat with an almost identical proportion of votes Apr '92; was named to Public Accounts Committee May '92; in his third 'Maiden' backed new diversity in housing as a breaking away "irrevocably from the "soul-destroying and socially-divisive separation between council and owner-occupied housing", welcoming particularly the extension to England of the rent-to-mortgage scheme he had pioneered in Scotland May '92; in CAP debate warned that set-aside could not be maintained for long and organic farmers should be exempt to encourage extensive farming May '92; welcomed Agriculture Minister Gummer's Brussels achievements, but felt they were not enough for 80% of UK wheat-growers June '92; was elected Chairman of the Conservative MPs' Constitutional Affairs Committee July '92; as an "ardent monarchist", insisted "changes have to be made" in the Civil List, overloaded with minor royals: "we are beginning to muddle the extended royal family and the monarchy"; "I think we have to concentrate on the monarchy and the heir"; opposed having the Queen pay taxes Sep '92; co-signed a TIMES letter by Major loyalists Oct '92; said he had been disillusioned when a Scottish Minister by Brussels' tendency to intervene in the "nooks and crannies of our national life", threatening Scottish distillery jobs; he did not want "a European super-state and a European federation"; Maastricht had shown that Europe was not a train on a single track but a tanker that could be turned, however slowly; "I want to be part of the decision-making process" Nov '92; welcomed Autumn Statement's abolition of car tax which helped Rover and Honda in his constituency; also the cracking of Ryrie rule which banned mixing of public and private financing, a reform for which he had long battled Nov '92; as Chairman of Conservative MPs' Constitutional Affairs Committee said: "Disestablishment is something that will need to be looked at in the longer term because there are a number of other religions, let alone Christian ones, which must now be regarded as having a call on the affections of the State" Jan '93; voted against 2nd Reading for Clive Soley's Freedom and Responsibility of the Press Bill Jan '93 ; urged more recycling of paper, particularly at Gartcosh Jan '93; welcomed the Budget but worried about its discrimination against rural areas Mar '93; warned that military intervention in Bosnia "would cause more suffering and bloodshed" Apr '93; defended the monarchy against its press attackers; the monarch was superior to an elected president as "patently above party politics" and could therefore provide "a truly impartial and credible arbiter" when needed May '93; attacked role of "safely-distant American politicians" in criticizing Britain's role in ex-Yugoslavia May '93; expressed doubts about toll roads May '93; replacing Jeremy Hanley, was named Northern Ireland's Under Secretary May '93; was therefore discharged from Public Accounts Committee July '93; said the Shankill Road bombing made "a total mockery of any talk of peace on the part of the Provisional IRA" Oct '93; in the wake of the Hume-Adams talks, was urged by PM John Major to speed up his painstaking separate talks with all the constitutional parties Nov '93; said, "it is generally accepted by the parties that, at this moment, the groundwork to get around a table does not exist" Nov '93; he did most of the day-to-day drafting of the Anglo-Irish Joint Declaration, so hated by Unionists Dec '93; was promoted Minister of State for Northern Ireland, in mini-reshuffle caused by Tim Yeo's love-child resignation, "said by Downing Street to be a reward for his painstaking efforts over the past six months to find common ground among the constitutional parties" (DAILY TELEGRAPH) Jan '94; announced that 8% more Northern Ireland students entered higher education in '93-94, a total of 39% in Ulster as against 31% in Great Britain Jan '94; agreed it was necessary to "take forward in an intensified way" talks with the constitutional parties in Ulster Feb '94; voted to restore capital punishment for killing policemen; voted against homosexual sex at 16, or at 18 Feb '94; admitted that proposed new cross-border bodies would have "some" executive powers Jan '95; met representatives of the Loyalist paramilitaries Mar '95; said serious negotiations required decommissioning of arms May '95; told Sinn Fein that he could not meet them until the IRA began giving up its arms June '95; shook hands with Gerry Adams for the first time June '95; had two secret meetings with Gerry Adams July '95; was made a Privy Counsellor Jan '96; the Northern Ireland Secretary of State, Sir Patrick Mayhew, offered to step down if PM John Major wanted Ancram to replace him June '96; he refused to make concessions to achieve an IRA ceasefire Dec '96; travelled to Washington to counter Sinn Fein propaganda Sep '96; retained his altered seat with a halved majority on a notional 2.1% swing to the LibDems May '97; a close friend of William Hague, backed him for the Leadership from the outset May '97; was named Spokesman on Constitutional Affairs, a notable rebuff for the arch-Unionist adviser to John Major, Viscount Cranborne June '97; described proposals for a Welsh Assembly as "a vast constitutional mess" July '87; described the Scottish White Paper as "dangerous, damaging and dishonest" and leading to the breakup of the UK; tried to delay the Referendum on it July '97; insisted the Conservatives were right to campaign against Scottish devolution and sleaze there Sep '97; said the Welsh referendum could hardly be said to have established "the "settled will of the Welsh people" Oct '97; urged a nonpartisan inquiry into the

'West Lothian question' to overcome the "raw deal" to be suffered by the English May '98; was named Deputy Chairman of the Conservative Party and an early successor to Lord Parkinson as Chairman June '98;

Born: 7 July 1945, London

Family: Son and heir, 12th Marquess of Lothian KCVO DL and Antonella (Newland), "a real Tory matriarch, class and style oozing from every pore"; his father has a life interest in Melbourne Hall, Derbyshire, and its 1,100-acre estate, and their stately home at Monteviot, Jedburgh, with 20,000 acres (EVENING STANDARD) and the fabulous Lothian Collection of paintings; m '75 Lady Jane Fitzalan-Howard, d of 16th Duke of Norfolk, who was mistakenly pursued by the press as the Earl of Caithness's similarly-named ladylove; 2d Clare Therese '79; Mary Cecil '81;

Education: Small French-speaking Swiss school; Ampleforth; Christ Church, Oxford (BA); Edinburgh University (LLB);

Occupation: Edinburgh Advocate '70-; Commercial Farmer: Director: Portzim Ltd (family agricultural firm, in which he is a shareholder) '75-, Nisbet Mill Farm Partnership (family's Jedburgh farm, tenancy of 1,500 acres, raising wheat and beef) '70-, Kirkmains Farm (family's Roxburgh farm, 400 acres) '66-; Shareholder, Stirling Fibre (Holdings) Ltd '92-; ex: Public Relations Consultant: Director, CSM Parliamentary Consultants '87-93; Columnist, on DAILY TELEGRAPH (Northern Edition) '88-92; on Board of Scottish Homes (at £3,750) '88-90; Chairman: Northern Corporate Communications (which promoted Cairngorm Recreation Trust) '89-91, Waverley Housing Trust (unpaid; it took over Scottish Special Housing Association's stock of 1,200 houses in the Borders after his chairmanship, at a cost to the taxpayer of £3.6m, according to the National Audit Office) '89-90; Director: Lilliardsedge Park Partnership (Jedburgh caravan park) '70-83;

Traits: Burly; pleasant-looking; bulbous forehead; witty; clever-clever; multilingual (French and Italian); "popular and personable" (Ian Aitken, GUARDIAN); "a toff right down to his cotton socks; one colleague who shared a hotel room with him on a trip many years ago insists that he was wearing monogrammed underpants" (Stephen Castle, INDEPENDENT ON SUNDAY) "how odd that he should speak in a voice bred and buttered in England, but sing with a Scots accent!" (DAILY RECORD); guitarist (has a 12-string Martin acoustic guitar, a present from his wife); folk singer (with a repertoire ranging from Jacobite ballads to rock and roll); does a Buddy Holly imitation; fast on slalom; skilled skier (was second fastest in Anglo-Swiss ski race at Davos '88; was on team for '93 Anglo-Swiss contest); RC (the first Scots Tory Catholic to be elected to Parliament for a Scottish seat); miscalled "Norman Crumb" by a half-deaf butler; short-story writer ("too intelligent to be Scotland's answer to Jeffrey Archer" - TIMES); ex-smoker (was a "40-a-day man" - DAILY MAIL); suffers from untreated gout;

Address: House of Commons, Westminster, SW1A 0AA;

Telephone: 0171 4435/5072(H of C); 01672 63469;

TAKING US SERIOUSLY

We noticed that politicians began to take us seriously after it became apparent to them that most press profiles and biographies relied on the facts in our four-volume PARLIAMENTARY PROFILES. Our profiles even follow politicians to their graves. We noted one obituarist who relied on us completely, causing us to break out into the famous comic song enjoining American academics to plagiarise.

Donald ANDERSON   **Labour**   **SWANSEA EAST '74(Oct)-**

Majority: 25,569 (66.1%) over Conservative 6-way;
Description: Swansea's safe Labour industrial heartland, including the DVLC;
Former Seat: Monmouth '66-70;
Position: Chairman, Select Committee on Foreign Affairs '97-; on Ecclesiastical Commission '92-; on the Chairmen's Panel '95-; on the Liaison Committee '97-, Leader, UK delegation to the North Atlantic Assembly '97-; on the Parliamentary Assembly of the OSCE '97-; Chairman: Parliamentary Christian Group '90-, National Prayer Breakfast '89-, British-Zimbabwe Parliamentary Group; Vice Chairman: of Executive of IPU and CPA '85-, its Treasurer '93-; Vice Chairman, British-German Parliamentary Group (decorated by West Germans); Deputy Chairman: of Anglo-French and British-Norwegian Parliamentary Groups; Senior Vice President of the Association of European Parliamentarians for Africa '84-; on Executive of Anglo-Austrian Society; ex: Shadow Solicitor-General '94-95; Deputy Spokesman, on Defence and Disarmament '93-94; on Home Affairs Select Committee '92-93; Assistant or Deputy Spokesman on Foreign Affairs '83-92; Assistant Spokesman on Legal Affairs '83-87; Chairman: of Select Committee on Welsh Affairs (member '80-83) '81-83, of Welsh Labour Group (Vice Chairman '68-70) '77-78, Parliamentary Campaign for the Homeless and Rootless (CHAR) '85-90; on Environment Select Committee '79-80; PPS: Sam (later Lord) Silkin '74-79, Roy Hattersley '69-70;
Outlook: Shrewd, thoughtful, loyal, dedicated, anti-racist, pro-EU radical moderate idealist; a Christian socialist and born-again supporter of Welsh devolution; very Methodist on drink, pornography, abortion, Sunday trading; locally-born, locally-rooted defender of DVLA; a formerly RMT-sponsored barrister-politico and ex-diplomat; one of the most serious and well-informed of free-trippers; "one of the most reasonable of men" (Edward Pearce, DAILY TELEGRAPH); pro: family courts;
History: Captured Monmouth from Peter Thorneycroft Mar '66; lost Monmouth June '70; was elected to Kensington and Chelsea Council May '71; campaigned for entry into EEC, insisting it was required for growth Oct '71; was elected for Swansea East Oct '74; warned that investment would stop if UK withdrew from EEC Apr '75; was reprimanded by Welsh Labour Council for his anti-devolution articles and speeches Oct '75; opposed film on Christ's sex life Oct '76; fought to defend Driver and Vehicle Licensing Centre in Swansea Nov '78; claimed Welsh Assembly could do nothing for jobs Jan '79; was accused of betraying his pledge to a Welsh Assembly Feb '79; criticised attacks on ethnic minorities Nov '81; criticised reliability of radar speed traps Mar '82; criticised de-industrialisation of Wales May '82; accused Mrs Thatcher of hiding behind secrecy on Cheltenham spies Oct '82; complained that Security Commission were "too old" to be sufficiently sceptical and worldly wise about GCHQ Nov '82; urged Andropov to release Anatoly Shcharansky Jan '83; was promoted Deputy Foreign Affairs Spokesman Apr '83; as Chairman of Select Committee on Wales, launched their "Water in Wales" report, saying the Welsh sense of grievance on the high cost of water was justifiable May '83; in the wake of the general election defeat wrote: "Let us continue to say that for a country of our resources an independent nuclear capacity is an absurd and incredible status symbol; but 'they' (the Labour voters) do not wish to be

defenceless and we must accept the implications of being under the US umbrella by excising neutralist elements from our programme; we should say firmly that the EEC issue is dead" June '83; backed Hattersley for Leader, Kinnock for Deputy Leader Sep '83; in the 25,000-word Holland-Anderson report on Central America said that the claim "that Nicaragua threatens the United States is about as impressive as a report of impending assault by an ant on an elephant" Jan '84; was the only Labour MP on the Commons committee on 'video nasties' to vote to ban the right of adults to buy porno videos for watching at home Jan '84; again co-pleaded for release of Anatoly Shcharansky Mar '84; visited Chile Sep '84; asked whether departed Soviet "defector" had tricked UK security services Sep '84; was attacked by South African Foreign Minister Pik Botha during his fact-finding visit to the 'Durban Three' there Oct '84; described Britain as "the best collaborator of the Apartheid regime in Europe" Oct '84; travelled to Namibia as guest of Christian charity Mar '85; attacked periodic finger-shaking at South African Ambassador as the limit of British action against Apartheid Mar '85; was re-selected from a shortlist of one July '85; insisted that, because "none of us is interested in the destruction of South Africa's infrastructure", there could have been "ordered change, rather than [the]...revolutionary change...now yawning" had the South African Government "been willing in 1960 to embark on a process of negotiation with the black majority" Oct '85; alleged Britain's Middle East initiatives had ended in a shambles because of unrealistic assumptions about the PLO Oct '85; again complained of shipments of British arms (Chieftain "spare parts") to Iran Dec '85; visited Mexico with IPU Apr '86; warned against UK being taken in by anti-Syrian disinformation of Israel's Mossad May '86; visited South Africa and Zambia with Denis Healey June '86; urged ejection of Syrian Ambassador for complicity in bomb plot Oct '86; was unable to attend the funeral of Mozambique's Samora Machel because Labour Party ran out of cash '86; visited Argentina Oct '86; visited Hongkong Dec '86, China Jan '87; his Housing (Houses in Multiple Occupation) Bill, which sought to provide safe conditions for 2.5m bedsits, was lost Feb '87; visited Nicaragua Apr '87; said that South Africa's President Botha was praying for a Thatcher victory June '87; he asked about the covert supply of British 'Blowpipe' ground-to-air missiles to Afghan rebels June '87; received 36 votes for Shadow Cabinet, without being on any slate July '87; was again named Assistant Spokesman on Foreign Affairs July '87; visited Sri Lanka Oct '87; introduced Bill to limit restrictions on access to local authority housing lists Oct '87; urged Mrs Thatcher to denounce vigilantes in South Africa as well as deploring 'necklacing' and to use shock tactics to force Afrikaners to avoid a bloodbath Nov '87; as Patron of Keep Sunday Special Campaign, sought to exclude Wales from Licensing Bill Dec '87; voted against looser Licensing Bill Feb '88; sought to fight off "ideological experiment" of privatisation of Driver and Vehicle Licensing Centre in his constituency Feb '88; visited Southern Africa as Vice Chairman of Association of West European Parliamentarians for Action Against Apartheid Mar-Apr '88; visited Guatemala with IPU Apr '88; voted against reduction of abortion ceiling from 28 to 26 weeks May '88; visited Algeria at invitation of Polisario Front, Morocco at invitation of its government Aug '88; visited Cyprus at invitation of its House of Representatives Nov '88; spoke against locating a Z-base for berthing and servicing nuclear submarines in Swansea July '89; sought to free 10 Swansea City fans imprisoned in Greece Sep '89; was renamed Assistant Spokesman on Foreign Affairs Nov '89; was one of three MPs monitoring Namibia election for IPU Nov '89; welcomed new environmental consciousness in Wales but deplored deterioration: "as a boy I spent most of my summer bathing on the beach at Swansea Bay and used to collect cockles there with my family; now no one would dare to eat them, even if they were to be found" July '90; was one of 7 MPs who visited Mexico for IPU to discuss action against drug barons Oct '90; wrote that sanctions on South Africa "will be needed for a while yet" Feb '91; visited Moscow and Baltic republics Feb '91; complained about the misdeeds of absentee ground landlords in Swansea Mar '91; complained about "Government's total identification with the white South African Government" July '91; applauded increased arms control and disarmament July '91; again visited South Africa Nov '91; complained that Sunday trading rich retailers were not being harassed like non-payers of poll taxes Nov '91; complained that, whatever Welsh Secretary David Hunt claimed to be doing, it was impossible for his constituents to have collapsing ceilings repaired with a discretionary grant Feb '92; reported to Commons on the efforts to limit the Yugoslav tragedy Mar '92; retained seat with a majority up by 4,144 , a swing of 3.84% to Labour Apr '92; urged reimposition of sports boycott on South Africa unless political impasse was broken June '92; was suspicious of rushed Boundary Commission report June '92; co-sponsored anti-pornography motion July '92; was not included in John Smith's first frontbench team July '92; opposed efforts of Voluntary Euthanasia Society July '92; co-sponsored Obscene Publications (Amendment) Bill Oct '92; attacked "ultimate madness" of privatising Driver Vehicle Licensing Agency "which was put in [my constituency] for regional employment reasons" Oct '92; was named to Home Affairs Select Committee Oct '92; supported Ray Powell's restrictive Shops (Amendment) Bill, accusing Government of conniving at law-breaking to allow Sunday trading by store giants Jan '93; warned the Attorney General, Sir Nicholas Lyell, against entering "a partisan field" on Maastricht advice Feb '93; warned that "failures by an excess of intervention can do immense damage to the international community and to the United Nations" Feb '93; complained that because the Government had "destroyed the instruments of regional planning", they had left themselves "without a framework within which Wales can be planned" Mar '93; warned that all aspects of drug abuse had to be considered together, beginning with preventing young people from starting Apr '93; complained about Government's use of private bailiffs for debt collection May '93; warned the Tory Welsh Secretary, John Redwood, to yield to the consensus of Welsh MPs on the Welsh Language Bill June '93; in the wake of the Asil Nadir case, called for an end to secrecy in party financing Sep '93; high-lighted the links between drugs and crime Oct '93; in John Smith's reshuffle, was restored to the front bench as Deputy Spokesman on Defence Oct '93; complained that because of Government connivance at Sunday law-breaking, "stores like M&S and John Lewis have obeyed the law and lost substantial sums as a result" Dec '93; warned that Defence cuts would make it difficult to regenerate the armed forces Jan '94; retired from Home Affairs Select Committee Feb '94; complained that, after spending £910m on them, newish Upholder-class submarines would be withdrawn from service in '95 to save £25-30m Feb '94; was one of the most active opponents of the 6-hour compromise on Sunday trading Feb '94; with other members of the Houses of Parliament Christian Fellowship, opposed lowering the age of consent for homosexual acts below 21, Feb '94; voted: against restoring capital punishment, in favour of homosexual sex at 18, not 16, as urged by the Parliamentary Christian Fellowship Feb '94; backed Tony Blair for Leader June '94; voted for Blair for Leader, Beckett for Deputy Leader July '94; was a sharp critic of the Tory government's "Treasury-driven" Defence cuts in 'Front Line First', asking Defence Secretary Malcolm Rifkind, "is it Front Line First or bottom line first?" July '94; co-urged retention of a "statutory requirement for a daily act of Christian worship in maintained schools" July '94; was named shadow Solicitor-General in Blair's reshuffle Oct '94; lost his post as Shadow Solicitor General in Tony Blair's reshuffle Oct '95; was named to the Chairmen's Panel Nov '95; told Welsh Secretary William Hague that his proposal for the Welsh Grand Committee to meet in various places in Wales was a "mouse" with the longest gestation period in history - 16 years after Nicholas Edwards had promised a forum for Wales Nov '95; said the campaign against sexual exploitation of children in the 3rd World by perverts was like earlier campaigns against the slave trade Feb '96; as a former divorce lawyer, warned against simplistic thinking about fault in marriage breakdowns Mar '96; baited PM John Major on how much further "appeasement" he had in mind "to placate the patriot across the water", Sir James Goldsmith Apr '96; claimed Lords debates had shown that Home Secretary Michael Howard's sentencing policies had "uniquely managed to array against him and his policies the senior judges in the country and the great majority of practitioners" June '96; voted to cut MPs' mileage allowance and against a 3% cap on MPs' wage rise July '96; was one of 14 pro-EU Labour MPs who co-wrote a pamphlet warning it would be a disaster for Britain to rule out joining a single European currency Sep '96; said he was willing "with some hesitation to accept a complete ban on handguns but wanted more generous compensation for shooting centres which would be bankrupted, like 'Shooters of Swansea' Nov '96; attacked the Eurosceptic demand for another referendum on Europe as an attempt to reverse that of 1975 when, he claimed, "our people voted not for a static Europe but for a dynamic Europe" Dec '96; warned against the possible effect on Ford's Bridgend plant of its decision to transfer production from Halewood to Saarlouis Feb '97; urged more generous funding for further education in Wales Feb '97; was re-elected for Swansea East by the enhanced majority of 25,569, a pro-Labour swing of 6.8% May '97; loyally welcomed the Welsh Assembly as the sole survivor in the Commons of the "gang of six" Welsh counter-devolutionary MPs who had opposed devolution 19 years before July '97; was named Chairman of the Select Committee on Foreign Affairs, instead of Ted Rowlands, considered more independent of the party leadership July '97; was named to the Parliamentary Assembly of the OSCE July '97; loyally defended Foreign Office inquiry against Michael Howard's imperious demands for advance knowledge on Sierra Leone May '98; voted against reducing age of homosexual consent to 16, June '98;

Born: 17 June 1939, Swansea

Family: Grandson of Norwegian ship's carpenter and NUR pioneer; "my great-grandfather worked in the [Swansea] docks, my grandfather worked on the railways in the docks and my father worked as a fitter on the Graigola wharf - the very wharf where the [nuclear submarine] wharf is likely to be established"; is distantly related to Swansea-born Michael Heseltine; son of David Robert Anderson, fitter, who died of an industrial disease, and Eva (Mathias); m '63 Bolivian-born Dorothy (Trotman) PhD; 3s Robert '64, Hugh '67, Geraint '72;

Education: Swansea Grammar School; University College, Swansea (First Class Hons in Modern History and Politics); Inner Temple;

Occupation: Barrister on Southeastern Circuit '69-, but no longer practicing; Consultant, to Royal Society of Chemistry (unremunerated) '84-; on Harris Parliamentary Panel, receiving up to £1,000 a year, donated to charity '94?-; Sponsored, by RMT (£600 to his constituency, 80% of election expenses, £100 in personal expenses) '74-95; during the '97 general election RMT contributed "more than 25% of my election expenses"; ex: Consultant, Directory Publishers Association '91-92, Director of Campaign for a European Political Community '67, Lecturer in Politics at University College, Swansea '64-66, Diplomat '60-64: Third Secretary, Political, British Embassy, Budapest '63-64; Economic Relations Department '62-63, Adviser to UK delegation to Council of Europe, Strasbourg '62; Western Organisations and Planning Department of Foreign Office '60-62;

Traits: Tall; lean; balding, grey; bulging forehead; skeletal face; paunch; genial; chatty; witty; arthritic; Methodist lay preacher; linguist (French, some German and Hungarian); walker; "amiable, rangy, bald and usually sane" (Andrew Brown, INDEPENDENT); former diplomatic ping-pong champion of Budapest;

Address: House of Commons, Westminster, London SW1A 0AA; 8 Marine Walk, Maritime Quarter, Swansea; Lamb Building, Temple, London EC1; 88 Ladbroke Road, London W11;

Telephone: 0171 219 3425 (H of C); 0171 727 2935 (London home); 01792 458333 (Swansea home); Fax: 0171 219 4801 (H of C);

Majority: 10,949 (21.4%) over Conservative 5-way;

Description: Formerly Rossendale, northeast Lancashire's marginal seat; it still includes Rawtenstall, Helmshore, Bacup and part of Ramsbottom; was extended in '83 to include Tory-leaning Darwen in the next valley to the West; in '95 it lost two wards to Hyndburn; has been changing from closed mills to tourist and commuting territory, due largely to the M66; "the constituency contrasts the starkness of an industrial landscape with areas of great natural beauty" with "handsome views across the West Pennine moors" (Janet Anderson);

Position: Under Secretary, Culture, Media and Sports '98-; ex: Whip '97-98, '95-96; Spokesman, on Women's Issues '96-97; PPS, to Margaret Beckett, '92-93; on House of Commons Commission '93-94; Secretary, Tribune Group '93-95; Vice Chairman, Labour Campaign for Electoral Reform '93-97; Coordinator of Industry 2000 Campaign; Co-Founder, 'Emily's List' '93-97; on Steering Committee of Labour Women's Network '89-97; PLP Campaigns Officer '88-90;

Outlook: A rising feminist loyalist apparatchik, music-lover and former Sunday trading lobbyist; although she pioneered registers of sex offenders and anti-stalking legislation, she may have missed a ministerial post in '97 for telling Petronella Wyatt of the DAILY TELEGRAPH that "under Labour women will become more promiscuous"; "on some things I am probably perceived as being quite Leftwing and on others quite Rightwing with some very basic, unshiftable beliefs about social justice and fairness in economic policy"; an electoral reformer; has a sharp eye for the backgrounds of her opponents; a 'man-eater' who succeeded in ousting less-loyal Peter Hain as Secretary of Tribune Group; first did this to David Trippier, her Tory predecessor in the constituency, despite his belief that the Labour Party was "crazy to choose a Londoner as its candidate" (Alexander Chancellor, INDEPENDENT); mainstream soft-Leftist (LCC, CND, Women Against Pit Closures); pro: mandatory re-selection of Labour MPs, sensibly-controlled Sunday trading (former Northern Organiser of Shopping Hours Council), quotas for selection of women candidates, fluoridation of water;

History: Her family were northeastern miners, Methodist by religion and socialist in sympathy; her father was "a lifelong Labour agent"; she was agent for the Labour candidate in school mock elections Feb '66; joined the Labour party at 17, '67; joined the NUS '68; was selected for Tory-held Rossendale and Darwen on 2nd ballot by 22 to 13, from a short-list of four, embracing two women and two men, one of whom thought the seat was in Yorkshire Nov '85; was endorsed by NEC Dec '85; was informed by Robin Cook that she had been "twinned" with Jack Straw in neighbouring, Labour-held Blackburn, not knowing she had been Mr Straw's Personal Assistant and Agent for years Apr '86; complained that local workers were employed at poverty wages under primitive conditions Mar '87; contested Rossendale against David Trippier, halving his majority to 4,982 (8.3%) June '87; claimed northeast Lancashire voters "would like a change", pointing out that Rossendale was "one of those constituencies which Labour has to win in order to have any chance of government" Nov '89; was re-selected for Rossendale and Darwen Mar '90; was active in enlisting support for the Bacup Moors Action Group, which feared wanton destruction of former industrial sites May '91; at annual conference appreciated new emphasis on Europe Oct '91; supported Kevin

Barron at launch of Coalfields Communities Campaign Opencast Charter Dec '91; very narrowly won Rossendale by 120 votes - the smallest Labour majority - overturning Minister David Trippier's 4,982 majority Apr '92; in her Maiden speech urged Government to accept responsibility for Maxwell pensioners since its laws had been inadequate to protect them June '92; co-sponsored motion deploring Norweb's overlarge profits as "unacceptable exploitation" of their electricity customers June '92; led motion opposing Government cuts in grants for Lancashire County Council June '92; was named PPS to Labour's Deputy Leader, Margaret Beckett July '92; claimed the Chancellor's Autumn Statement showed "the gap between what Ministers promise at the election and what they do when they are re-elected", particularly in their near-freeze on nurses' pay and delay of nurse-prescribing Nov '92; complained that Ray Powell's restrictive Shops (Amendment) Bill flew "in the face of public opinion" which was two-thirds "in favour of liberalisation of the law on Sunday opening"; as the former Northern Region Organiser for the Shopping Hours Council and "the mother of three teenage children, I must tell the House that the only time that I get to do my weekly household shop is on Sundays; the same is often true for more than 70% of married women who now work outside the home"; voted against Powell's restrictive Bill Jan '93; backed motion approving 1967 Abortion Act for having saved women from back-street abortionists Apr '93; co-sponsored amendments emasculating Ray Powell's Shops (Amendment) Bill tabled by former Conservative Minister, Dame Angela Rumbold Apr '93; backed one-member one-vote with other Labour women MPs June '93; resigned as PPS to Margaret Beckett, allegedly to pay more attention to her very marginal constituency Oct '93; was fielded as opponent to Peter Hain, Secretary of Tribune Group, who was alleged to have used the post as a platform for damaging attacks on the economic timidity of the Smith leadership Oct '93; was named to House of Commons Commission, replacing Peter Shore Nov '93; defeated Peter Hain by 37 votes to 34; despite canvassing on her behalf by acolytes of Gordon Brown and Peter Mandelson denied that she was acting on behalf of the leadership; Clare Short described her victory as "a sad day for democracy" because it left the soft Left "homeless" Nov '93; lined up Sunday-liberators against Keep Sunday Special would-be saboteurs of 6-hour Sunday trading compromise Feb '94; voted against restoring any capital punishment Feb '94; voted in favour of homosexual sex at 16, Feb '94; she backed Tony Blair June '94; she voted for Blair for Leader, Prescott for Deputy Leader July '94; was campaign manager for Jack Straw in contest for seat on the NEC Aug-Sep '94; she came off the House of Commons Commission Nov '94; backed the Blairite rewriting of Clause IV Dec '94; she was named to the Home Affairs Select Committee Dec '94; she again spoke up for deregulated Sunday trading and easing Sunday opening hours for pubs, volunteering that "the Argyll Group which runs a number of supermarkets, makes a small contribution to the running of my constituency office" Feb '95; complained to Home Secretary Michael Howard about a senior Home Office civil servant, in charge of setting up a multi-million pound computer project, who joined the private company almost certain to win the contract to carry out the work Aug '95; asked questions about jailing of women for defaulting on fines Oct '95; with three other women, was named an Opposition Whip Oct '95; complained about Home Secretary Michael Howard's meddling in the Prison Service Oct '95; complained about the number of women injured by misjudged radiation for cervical cancer Nov '95; was replaced as Secretary of the Tribune Group by Ian Davidson, with its membership having fallen by a half during her two-year stint Nov '95; she was discharged from the Home Affairs Select Committee Nov '95; it was disclosed that a reply to her letter questioning security precautions after the Parkhurst breakout had been censored at the instigation of the Prisons Minister, Ann Widdecombe Dec '95; in a heavily documented speech, highlighted the increases in crime in the constituencies of the Tory MPs who had spoken on crime Dec '95; initially proposed the Sexual Offences Against Children (Registers of Offenders) Bill Mar '96; instead secured the 1st Reading of her Stalking Bill Mar '96; despite her vivid speech, her Stalking Bill failed to secure its 2nd Reading because the Conservative Government said it was "full of flaws" and the Government would introduce its own measure; she accused it of condemning "thousands of people to at least twelve more months of misery" May '96; co-opposed the first-past-the-post electoral system which had "already brought 17 years of anti-consensus government with the Tories" May '96; she voted against a 3% cap on MPs' pay rises and in favour of pensions based on £43,000 July '96; was promoted Spokesman on Women's Issues, replacing Tessa Jowell July '96; urged an end to the "appalling distress" of allowing alleged stalkers and rapists to cross-examine their victims in court Sep '96; in an interview with Petronella Wyatt of the DAILY TELEGRAPH, she said "women like seeing men as sex objects" and insisted, ironically, that "under Labour, women will become more promiscuous; that's an election pledge" Oct '96; led a group of Labour women MPs to Downing Street to demand PM John Major sack Tory MP-candidate David Evans for his crude sexist attack on his Labour woman opponent Mar '97; retained her seat by an enormously enhanced majority of 10,949 over her Tory opponent, on a pro-Labour swing of 10.5% May '97; she was named a Government Whip, with the task of writing a daily report to the Queen May '97; she rocked on her high heels when retreating backward to the Bar of the Commons after delivering the Queen's message June '97; after complaints from new women MPs, complained to the Speaker about sexist remarks by male Tory MPs: "the remarks vary from 'get back to the kitchen' to 'you must be on PMT' or 'you're menopausal'" Oct '97; was promoted to Under Secretary of Culture, Media and Sports July '98;

Born: 6 December 1949, Newcastle-upon-Tyne

Family: Both her grandfathers were miners; daughter, late Tom Anderson, Labour Party Agent, and Ethel (Pearson), small shopkeeper; m '72 Vince Humphreys, solicitor; 2s James '77, David '78; 1d Katie '81;

Education: Newtown Junior School, Trowbridge; Trowbridge Girls High; Kingsfield Comprehensive, Bristol; Kingswood Grammar; Polytechnic of Central London; University of Nantes (Diploma in Modern Languages and Business Studies);

Occupation: Ex: on Parliamentary Panel, of Royal College of Nursing '92-97; Consultant to Safeways (at up to £5,000 a year) '92-97; Northern Regional Officer, Shopping Hours Reform Council '91-92; PLP Campaigns Officer '88-90; Executive, with Central Lobby (lobbyists; campaigned for Airbus Industry, Royal College of Nursing) '87-88; Personal Assistant, to Jack Straw MP '81-87; Personal Assistant to Barbara Castle, in Westminster, Blackburn and Brussels '74-81; "I went for a while to work on the SUNDAY TIMES" '72-74;

Traits: Blonde; blue-eyed; attractive; "her hair is blonde and sleek and her lips are painted a slippery red" (Petronella Wyatt, DAILY TELEGRAPH); articulate; multilingual; "I play the piano, am a great opera buff and get told off by my family for playing music too loud late at night!"; also enjoys swimming and tennis; "a force to be reckoned with" (MAIL ON SUNDAY) after she tried to stop a car rolling out of control; at Barbara Follett's suggestion, purchased a red Windsmoor suit;

Address: House of Commons, Westminster, London SW1A 0AA; 21 Caterham Road, London SE1 5AP; 76 Earnsdale Road, Darwen, Lancs BB3 1HS;

Telephone: 0171 219 6629/5375 (H of C); 877010/0254 704201 (constituency); 0181 297 8524 (home); 01254 703638 (home);

We make up for all the debates missed by the empty Press Gallery

---

          Copyright (C)Parliamentary Profile Services Ltd

James (Norwich) ARBUTHNOT   **Conservative**   **HAMPSHIRE NORTH EAST '97-**

Majority: 14,398 (28.2%) over LibDem 6-way;
Description: Overwhelmingly the over-large former Hampshire East cut back to two-thirds it size, with 2,000 thrown in from Aldershot; its main population centres are fast-growing Fleet on the M3, Whitehill, Liss, Liphook and Hook;
Former Seat: Wanstead & Woodford '87-97
Position: Chief Whip '97-; ex: Minister of State, for Defence Procurement '95-97; Under Secretary, Social Security '94-95; Assistant Whip '92-94; PPS: to Peter Lilley '90-92, to Archie Hamilton '88-90; Kensington and Chelsea Borough Councillor (Deputy Mayor, '83-84, Chairman of Works '82-84, Whip '78-82, Chief Whip '84-86, Vice Chairman of Housing '86-87) '78-87; Jt Deputy Chairman, Chelsea Conservative Association '80-82;

Outlook: Hague's Chief Whip who was once ranked with his boss as a possible future Leader by John Major; a bright Rightwing Chancery Barrister and badly-hurt Lloyd's 'name' from a good Parliamentary stable; found it easier to be super-loyal - and win promotion - under Major than under Thatcher; "I was never enthusiastic about the community charge, to the extent that I did not vote for it"; he abstained instead; under Major he was promoted an Assistant Whip, then an Under Secretary for Social Security and, finally, Minister of State for Defence Procurement; before that he had long been at disposal of the Whips' Office to use dry legal arguments against Labour MPs' Private Members' Bills; is very dry in economics; is an opponent of restrictive practices - even for barristers; his occasional early naivety could win him a "prize for fatuity" (Nick Comfort, DAILY TELEGRAPH) as a soft questioner; used to have ambitions to simplify tax law; before it disappeared, he enjoyed his safe seat of Wanstead and Woodford after being 'blooded' twice in South Wales; after some difficulties, he enjoys another safe seat in Hampshire, unless he is again squeezed out by reapportionment or resurgent LibDems;

History: Although his mother's family was musical and legal, his father's was military (grandfather died at Ypres), banking and Conservative; his father became Dover's Tory MP '50-64, with James canvassing from the age of five; James became Secretary of the Eton Political Society '68; canvassed for other Conservative candidates from his late teens '70; won a seat on the Kensington and Chelsea Borough Council May '78, becoming a Whip Sep '78; he opposed the destruction of the galleries in the Natural History Museum '79; supported wheel clamps in letter to TIMES June '82; as Chairman of Works won agreement with Kensington and Chelsea's dustmen, after threatening to go to private tender, achieving savings of £1m and a cut of one-third in the work force Dec '82; contested Cynon Valley in general election, coming 3rd with 14.2% June '83; again contested Cynon Valley in by-election; after calling for an end to miners' strike came fourth after Ann Clwyd, losing his deposit with 7.4% May '84; failed to be selected for Southgate, Esher and Hendon South Dec '85; was selected for Wanstead and Woodford from a short-list of 30 to succeed retiring Patrick Jenkin Nov '86; urged simplification of the taxation system to make it unnecessary to hire expensive tax lawyers like him July '87; abstained against poll tax Dec '87; voted against 2nd Reading of David Alton's abortion-curbing Bill Jan '88; was first Englishman to serve on a Scottish standing committee -provoking a walkout Jan '88; urged Inland Revenue's discretionary powers be somewhat reduced Mar '88; acclaimed his success on the Kensington and Chelsea

Council in reducing the cost of its rubbish collection Mar '88; was named as being involved in Associated Farmers Plc, a tax-saving BES company Mar '88; thought Nigel Lawson's tax-cutting Budget was "the best Budget I had ever heard" Mar '88; urged barristers be subjected to competition policy Mar '88; said: "the sooner we can achieve regional pay negotiations the better" July '88; his amendment - New Clause 35 - to Finance Bill was described as "a recipe for tax avoidance; it would have exempted gifts or bequests of woodlands from inheritance tax" and "was withdrawn under duress", according to Labour MP Nick Brown; Mr Brown attributed the same fate to Arbuthnot's New Clause 43 which "would have given substantial financial benefit to small family businesses" July '88; opposed Lawrence Cunliffe's Citizens' Compensation Bill because, although "fraught with good intentions", it would not achieve even its limited aims because it would push insurance rates out of the reach of ordinary people Mar '89; was awarded a "prize for fatuity" by DAILY TELEGRAPH's Nick Comfort for saying the OBSERVER had shown "a surprising lack of objectiveness" in supporting the views of its owner, 'Tiny' Rowland, in the Harrod's affair Apr '89; attended Italian conference as guest of German CDU Sep '88; persuaded the Government to drop from its Finance Bill a clause to outlaw Instruments of Variation May '89; again criticized Citizens' Compensation Bill July '89; voted against ordination of divorced men July '89; attended Italian conference as guest of German CDU Sep '89; again voted against ordination of divorced men Feb '90; backed Michael Colvin's Computer Misuse Bill Feb '90; urged Mrs Thatcher to stick to "her courageous line" in keeping Government spending under control Mar '90; was a teller for opponents of amendment by Andrew Bennett to Sexual Offence Bill (on kerb-crawling) May '90; backed a blocking motion on London Underground Bill to help protect a constituent against having his land and business compulsorily purchased July '90; visited Germany as guest of Konrad Adenauer Foundation Sep '90; voted for Mrs Thatcher on the first round, then backed John Major in second round of Leadership contest; on Major's victory was given to understand that, within months, he could expect promotion Nov '90; expressed concern about growth of graffiti Nov '90; wished to see "a tax system which is simply-worded and administered and which everyone can understand" Dec '90; visited Israel as guest of its government Jan '91; sponsored Public Safety Information Bill to compel local authorities to publicise reports of interest to public Feb '91; welcomed council tax as replacement for poll tax for which, he emphasised, he had never voted Mar '91; again tried to amend Finance Bill June '91; urged laser heat cabling to provide fire alarms more rapidly in Underground July '91; opposed compulsory installation of fire alarms in old buildings if unenforceable July '91; complained that London's police were getting too young because more mature officers were transferring out of the 'Met' Oct '91; strongly backed record of London East's TEC Nov '91; was credited with being the second most assiduous MP in the '90-91 session, with 217 votes out of 233; after Labour's Spokesman, Robin Cook, disclosed 86 hospitals were in financial difficulties, Arbuthnot charged that the information had come from an NHS employee who had been recommended for his job by Cook's political adviser Feb '92; retained seat with his majority up by 473, despite a swing to Labour of 3.02%, Apr '92; was promoted an Assistant Whip Apr '92; was targeted as a Lloyd's 'name' by Leftwing Labour MPs seeking a "full public inquiry into insider dealing" May '92; visited Cadenabbia for a conference of German and British MPs, as a guest of the Konrad Adenauer Foundation Sep '92; was alleged to have persuaded Vivian Bendall to vote for Government on Maastricht, instead of abstaining Nov '92; was said to have tried to sabotage Clive Soley's Freedom and Responsibility of the Press Bill by inviting his charges to speak up on Private Member's Bills preceding it Apr '93; complained to Conservative Party's Deputy Chairman that his seat and that of other London Tories were endangered because Central Office had mishandled the operation by allowing boroughs to be paired for boundary redrawing July '93; was rated the Whip with the second best voting record Dec '93; voted for homosexual sex at 18 and for the restoration of capital punishment, for killing policemen as well Feb '94; he was publicised as one of the top 10 of Tory losers at Lloyd's, allegedly facing a possible bill of £500,000 or more Apr '94; in the course of Tony Blair's campaign to become Labour's Leader, Whip Arbuthnot walked up and down the Government benches asking MPs to leave, to deprive Mr Blair of an audience July '94; was named Under Secretary for Social Security July '94; in boundary changes, his Wanstead and Woodford seat disappeared Aug '94; insisted frauds were being excluded from the Social Security system Oct '94; he again ranked second to Dennis Skinner in the frequency of his votes during the year Dec '94; announced benefit claimants would have to show 'smart' cards May '95; resisted a Labour amendment to the Pensions Bill allowing divorcing couples' pensions to be split immediately as a step too far, that would cost the Treasury up to £300m a year June '95; was promoted Minister of State for Defence Procurement in PM John Major's reshuffle, replacing Roger Freeman July '95; was mentioned as hoping for selection for Kensington and Chelsea; he failed to be selected for Cambridgeshire South, which went to Andrew Lansley Sep '95; was selected instead for redrawn Hampshire North East Sep '95; basing an attack on Labour pacifists on a misreading of the Commons' Order Paper, he attacked them for shrinking their declaration for defence cuts from 37 Labour names to 11, when these were in fact additional names Oct '95; he was also corrected by Labour's Dr John Reid when he said NATO was based at Mons, when it was in Brussels; SHAPE was in Mons Oct '95; insisted that the Conservative Government was "at the forefront of international efforts to restrict the export and use of anti-personnel mines" Oct '95; in the EVENING STANDARD Simon Heffer mentioned that John Major thought Arbuthnot might succeed him as Leader, having previously cited Stephen Dorrell and William Hague Nov '95; announced the upgrading of the Tornado F-3, rather than leasing US F-16s Mar '96; his sale of the MOD's 41,000 married quarters for £1.5b to a Japanese bank came under fire from the Royal British Legion; he narrowly averted a back-bench revolt June '96; claimed "the problem is that the Labour Party does not believe in defence" June '96; voted against the 3rd Reading of the Family Law Bill, as modified by an agreement with Labour over wives' equal rights to their ex-husbands' pensions on divorce June '96; in the run-up to the election, was rated as displaying an anti-Brussels tone without specifying his policy on a single European currency Apr '97; won his reconstructed seat by a majority of 14,398 over his LibDem opponent, a notional pro-LibDem swing of 5.4%; there were six contenders May '97; in the contest for the Tory Leadership, he became William Hague's campaign manager May '97; on William Hague's victory, he became his Chief Whip, replacing Europhile Alastair Goodlad July '97; was retained in post in the reshuffle June '98;

Born: 4 August 1952, Deal

Family: He "claims to be descended from King James VI of Scotland, James I of England"; the Arbuthnots have held land in Kincardineshire for nine centuries; his grandfather was a Seaforth Highlander; 2nd son of late Sir John Arbuthnot 1st Bt, Conservative MP for Dover '50-64, and later Chairman of the Folkestone Water Company and Director of the Ecclesiastical Insurance Office, and Margaret Jean (Duff); is the heir to the baronetcy held by his older brother, Sir William; m '84, Emma Louise (Broadbent) barrister; 1s Alexander '86, 3d Katerine '89, Eleanor '92, Alice '98;

Education: Wellesley House, Broadstairs; Eton (Head Boy; was verbally abused there by Charles Moore, later the DAILY TELEGRAPH's editor); Trinity College, Cambridge University (MA);

Occupation: Chancery Barrister, Lincoln's Inn '77-92; Lloyd's Underwriter in Wren MAPA (in '96, in KPH, was estimated to have lost roughly £400,000 in 21 'open' syndicates); Shareholder: in a BES company, Associated Farmers Plc, along with golfer Nick Faldo (according to Labour MP Chris Smith); Owner, of "a property in London SW 10";

Traits: Brown, thinning hair; aquiline, pale, long, thin face; "lanky" (Simon Hoggart, GUARDIAN); an "odd dried-up figure", "whose dessicated reality bears so little resemblance to the handsome adolescent in the official photographs that one can only assume that he is either very ill or very vain"; uses "the absolute minimum of vocal inflection, rhetorical flourish or humour; he is a party election broadcast as delivered by the speaking clock"; "what establishes Mr Arbuthnot as an amusing character is the declaration in the gravest monotone of preposterous statements" (David Aaronovitch, INDEPENDENT); has "a pleasant light baritone, with some nice vibrato in the upper register" but can sound "like a speaking clock" (Max Davidson, DAILY TELEGRAPH); has a "dogged and enthusiastic approach" (Val Elliott, DAILY TELEGRAPH); "a gentleman" (Labour supporter in South Wales); "meticulous" (NEWCASTLE EVENING STAR); "that most proper of young men" (Matthew Parris, TIMES); pedantic (insists: "'access' is a noun, not a verb"); discursive; witty; modest; self-deprecating humour; former aerobatic flyer at Biggin Hill; skier (on '88 Parliamentary team); cyclist (carried briefs in saddlebags); has a new enthusiasm for roller-skating; enjoys guitar-playing; has high standards (he lost his former secretary, Lord Rippon's daughter, Fiona, after he listed 32 items in her job specifications); the placename 'Arbuthnot', in Kincardineshire, was originally Aberbuthenoth, from the Gaelic, meaning "marsh of the silly fellow" according to Labour MP Frank Doran, but actually means "grounds containing a manor-house and through which a stream flows";

Address: House of Commons, Westminster, London SW1A 0AA;

Telephone: 0171 219 4649 (H of C); 0171 352 3974;

Hilary (Jane) ARMSTRONG   **Labour**   **NORTH WEST DURHAM '87-**

Majority: 24,754 (53.4%) over Conservative 4-way;

Description: The largely-rural Wear Valley with some of its shrinking mining population enhanced by steel-stripped Consett voters in the '83 boundary changes; in '95 it took in 6,000 voters from Durham North;

Position: Minister of State for Local Government and Housing '97-; on Labour's NEC (Women's Section)'96- '93-94; on its By-Election Panel '96-; ex: PPS, to John Smith '92-94; Assistant Spokesman, on Local Government '95-97, the Treasury '94-95, on Primary and Pre-School Education '88-92; Chairman, PLP Education Committee '87-88; Vice Chairman, of Tribune Group '92-; on Labour's North Regional Executive Committee '86-, '82-84 and North Regional Woman's Committee '82-; on Parliamentary Panel of NUT '88-, Royal College of Nurses '88?-; Vice President, National Children's Homes '91?-; Treasurer, Methodist Church, Division of Education and Youth '91-; ex: on Select Committee on Education '88-89; Durham County Councillor '85-87; Chairwoman, Northern Regional Council, ASTMS '81-88; Secretary, Sunderland North Labour Party '77-81; MSF-sponsored '88-95;

Outlook: The Local Government Minister with high hopes, strict targets, but little funds initially with which to finance desired improvements; an unflashy, worthily competent lady regionalist and deeply-committed reforming missionary for her area, who resents the northeast being treated as "lobby fodder" by the Labour Party; has long tried to set up a northeastern development authority; has a "relentless, powerhouse defence of the north's industrial well-being" (Simon Beck, NEWCASTLE JOURNAL); allegedly a "Brown protege" and member of the "North East Mafia" (Nicholas Wood and Michael Gove, TIMES); has proved herself a key link with the unions; was "instrumental in securing union support for one-member one-vote reforms in 1993" (TIMES); has the added advantage, as a loyalist moderate, that Tony Blair's Sedgefield is almost her own seat's neighbour in Durham; is a supporter of elected mayors as a way of counter-balancing one-party rule in local government; even before attaining office was active in her area, where Labour almost completely blankets local government, "indulging in some unsubtle arm-twisting in demanding town hall improvements; she has a reputation for integrity and tenacity, yet others on the greasy pole, probably mistakenly, do not generally see her as competition" (James Meikle, GUARDIAN); the late John Smith's former Lady Friday; "Hilary's a good listener" (Labour colleagues, to Michael White, GUARDIAN); "she is sensible, low-heeled and efficient, [and was] the perfect Miss Moneypenny for Mr Smith", with an "ability for back-room persuasion rather than front-room fizzle" (Alice Thomson, TIMES); "a dull Harriet Harman" (John Williams, EVENING STANDARD); a moderate-Left inheritor of father's seat; a Methodist Christian socialist; ex: Anti-Apartheid, CND, MSF-sponsored;

History: "I was born into the Labour Party and remain in it by conviction"; her earliest memories include putting election leaflets into envelopes at the age of eight '53; she was made a target when her father turned her grammar school into a comprehensive: "my English teacher had me kneeling on a coconut mat while he told the rest of the class that my dad was going to be responsible for letting 'the clot into the cream'"; joined the Labour Party at 15, '61; volunteered to help at Patrick Gordon Walker's racially-charged, unsuccessful Leyton by-election Jan '65; campaigned for CND, Anti-Apartheid '66-68; decided to become an MP for the northeast ("I didn't want to be a carpetbagger") '77; became Secretary of Sunderland North Labour Party '77, member of Northern Regional Executive Committee of Labour Party and of Northern Regional Woman's Committee '82; was nominated for Durham County Council for the Crook North ward, displacing an 81-year-old veteran Oct '84; produced ASTMS document 'Securing Our Future: A Regional Policy for the North' Jan '85; was selected for North West Durham from shortlist of five - including David Clelland - on second ballot by 34 to 33, on impending retirement of her father; she was only the second woman selected for a safe seat in the northeast from '50; "it was my father's seat and it was the last one I wanted; I always wanted to be seen as being independent of him and I didn't want to be seen as getting anything off his back" Apr '85; was elected to Durham County Council May '85; at annual Labour conference supported job-creation resolution, emphasising that all mines had closed in NW Durham and the steel industry in Consett had been razed Oct '85; at annual Labour Conference emphasized that local authorities had to be allowed to initiate reindustrialisation, not leave it to Westminster Sep '86; was elected an MP with a trebled majority June '87; in Maiden urged matching resources to needs of her area, where a third of industrial jobs had been lost June '87; complained that previous regional policies had not worked "because it was gifts from afar" July '87; warned Labour Party against treating Northern Region simply as "good voting fodder" Sep '87; retired from Durham County Council Oct '87; complained that the one-third cut in jobs in her constituency was from over-reliance on market forces Nov '87; was elected Chairwoman of PLP Education Committee Dec '87; warned that privatisation of pathology laboratories might lower standards Jan '88; criticised Budget for using greed as basic motivation Mar '88; was promoted an Assistant Spokesman on Pre-School and Primary Education Nov '88; as a Nonconformist accepted the interaction of the personal, political and spiritual aspects of life Feb '89; resisted

Assisted Places Scheme as another example of Tory advocacy of inequality in education July '89; decided to stand for Women's Section of National Executive of Labour Party, with MSF support Aug '89; was 2nd runner-up with 2,638,000 votes Oct '89; urged Labour to react sensitively to the Greens' garnering 15% of the Euro-vote in that month's election Oct '89; co-urged Channel Tunnel links with the north Oct '89; asked Education Minister Angela Rumbold to ban pin-ups in her department Mar '90; visited Israel with British-Israel Parliamentary Group; while there was a guest of its Foreign Affairs Ministry Sep '90; criticized the poll tax as a "fraud on young children" because teaching posts would be cut Sep '90; visited British School in Brussels at invitation of its management board Nov '90; urged a three-day week for Commons with devolution to regional assembly for northeast Dec '90; complained of shortage of speech therapists locally Jan '91; criticized dehumanising conditions at Durham Prison with "virtually no education or work being undertaken by the male prisoners" Feb '91; pointed out that an extra 20,000 nursery places could be funded by money spent on City Technology Colleges Apr '91; urged a more independent teachers' pay review body June '91; was named to Committee on Sittings of Commons July '91; was rated the 10th most active questioner among northeastern MPs Nov '91; attacked privatisation of schools inspectorate Nov '91; after a study tour of New Zealand, advocated out-of-class teaching for children with learning difficulties Dec '91; complained that Government did not accept EC directive to provide every three or four-year-old with a childcare place Dec '91; protested passage of nuclear convoys through her constituency Jan '92; said Labour would provide a nursery education place for 3-and 4-year-olds by year 2000, Feb '92; rejected the Government's idea that it could only educate a few well Mar '92; retained seat with her majority up by 3,825, a swing to Labour of 3.86% Apr '92; nominated Margaret Beckett for Deputy Leadership Apr '92; insisted the northeast, which had voted over 50% for Labour, wanted partnership schemes to replace vanished old industries May '92; received 70 votes in ballot for Labour's Shadow Cabinet, when 104 qualified July '92; was named the PPS to Labour's new Leader, John Smith July '92; spoke up for retention of schools music service in Durham Mar '93; backed one-member one-vote June '93; energetically saved John Smith from defeat at Labour's annual conference by pointing out to her sponsoring union, MSF, a clause which enabled it to switch its vote to support one-member one-vote Sep '93; she was elected to the NEC's Women's Section in 4th place, with 4,986,000 votes Sep '93; published a leaked Cabinet Office draft circulated to Ministers which said there was "little clear evidence" that higher benefit would encourage single women to have children and there was "no evidence" of women becoming pregnant to jump the queue for council housing; it also said there was no direct link between single-parent families and criminality, despite Home Secretary Michael Howard's claims at the Conservative conference; she added: "what this document shows is that the policies ministers espouse will make things even worse; cutting benefits will push more families into poverty and put even more strain on relationships within families" Nov '93; voted against restoring any capital punishment Feb '94; voted for homosexual sex at 16, then at 18, Feb '94; on the death of John Smith, voted for Tony Blair for Leader, Margaret Beckett for Deputy Leader July '94; in the vote for the National Executive, was the runner-up as sixth woman with 10%, 4% short; told that she had lost out because some unions resented her role in backing one-member one-vote the previous year, she replied: "it is a price I am well prepared to pay" Oct '94; received 93 votes - with 97 required - for the Shadow Cabinet, up from 21, partly because of the need to vote for four women; in Blair's first reshuffle, was named to the Treasury team under Gordon Brown Oct '94; she was active in the northeast in getting local support for the rewriting of Clause IV Dec '94; reflected the disappointment in mining areas about the way the nationalised mines had been run: "if we want people to play a part in running our society then we have to make sure that they can do that through forms of influence and power that they feel are relevant to their lives, not a centralised board of the great and the good" Feb '95; moved the motion at the northeast regional TUC and the annual Labour conference to set up a Northern Development Company for the northeast Oct '95; received 80 votes for the Shadow Cabinet - with 107 required; was switched to Deputy Spokesman on Local Government on Frank Dobson's Environment team Oct '95; strongly attacked Tory MPs for not tackling the fact that there had been considerable devolution to unaccountable civil servants in the regions but none to democratic forms of local government Feb '96; deplored the fact that virtually none of the Tory MPs could bring themselves to criticise what went on in Westminster Council, although MPs should not "condone or tolerate corruption and malpractice in any council wherever it happens" May '96; at Blair's request, loyally decided not to stand for the Shadow Cabinet, to avoid the unseating of Harriet Harman July '96; in Tony Blair's 'final' pre-election reshuffle, she was retained as Local Government Spokesman and Frank Dobson's Deputy Aug '96; she was re-elected to the women's section of Labour's NEC, replacing retiring Joan Lestor Oct '96; in her tours of Labour local government strongholds her team "assured councils that compulsory tendering will become voluntary but Armstrong is painstakingly drawing up a regime for setting targets and monitoring standards that could make the Audit Commission's preset collection of performance indicators look soft" (James Meikle, GUARDIAN) Oct '96; on a notional swing of 11.4%, retained enhanced North West Durham with a bigger majority of 24,754 May '97; was named Minister of State for Local Government and Housing under John Prescott in the new Blair-led Government May '97; after she said certain things could not be discussed openly at a Local Government Association conference, its leader, Sir Jeremy Beecham reassured her, "Don't worry, Peter Mandelson isn't here"; she replied, "No, but his tentacles are..." June '97; she was on the by-election panel which picked 'Blairite' Andrew Slaughter as the candidate for the Uxbridge by-election rather than the more Leftwing local council leader David Williams June '97; suffered a five-man Leftwing rebellion when she insisted on capping Oxfordshire and Somerset until new, more flexible legislation was in place July '97; urged more flexible mortgages to coincide with the new uncertainties of employment Sep '97; she came 3rd after Margaret Beckett and Clare Short of five women victors for NEC seats, with 18.6% of the vote Sep '97; urged consideration of cash penalties to inhibit gazumping Mar '98; backed "democratic renewal in local government" Mar '98;

Born: 30 November 1945, Sunderland

Family: D late Ernest Armstrong, MP for North West Durham '64-87 and Second Deputy Speaker '83-87, and Hannah Potter (Lamb), retired school teacher; m '93 Paul Corrigan, former Labour Party official, recently Head of Quality Control in Islington, "a strong man who recognises my strength too"; "he has shown me that holidays are for re-charging batteries rather than fact-finding missions";

Education: Fulwell Junior School, Sunderland; Monkwearmouth Grammar School ("I was made to kneel on a coconut mat in front of an English class while the teacher told us why we should not go comprehensive" - her father was Chairman of the Education Committee, which had so decided); West Ham College of Technology (BSc in Sociology); Birmingham University (Diploma in Social Work);

Occupation: Director, of Project Genesis Ltd (unremunerated; it has examined the feasibility of redeveloping Consett's steelworks site) '91-97?; Vice President, National Children's Homes '91-; ex: Sponsored: by MSF (£1000 to constituency party, supposedly 80% of election expenses) '88-92; on Parliamentary Panel: of NUT (£2,000 per year) '88-92, of Royal College of Nurses (expenses only) '88-92; Secretary/Researcher for her father, Ernest Armstrong MP '86-87; a member of Durham Council '85-87; Lecturer in Community and Youth Work for Sunderland Polytechnic '75-86; Community Worker '73-75; Social Worker '70-73; Deputy

Head, of Murray Girls' High School, Kenya and teacher of English and History while in VSO '67-69;

Traits: Dark blonde hair; pleasant looking; sturdy; has recently slimmed and become more stylish-looking; a strong resemblance to her late father; had long struggle to emerge from his shadow, including refusing a job offered by Durham County Council to work in Newcastle; Methodist (contributed chapter in Christian Socialist book, Reclaiming the Ground); forceful; serious-minded; has an inexorable debating style; likes knitting and the theatre; was Swahili-speaking; likes value for money;

Address: House of Commons, Westminster, London SW1A 0AA; North House, 17 North Terrace, Crook DL15 9AZ;

Telephone: 0171 219 5076 (H of C); 01388 767065 (constituency);

Rt Hon 'Paddy' (Jeremy John Dunham) ASHDOWN   **Liberal Democrat**   **YEOVIL '83-**

Majority: 11,403 (21.1%) over Conservative 7-way;

Description: Yeovil (Westlands) plus Chard, Crewkerne and Ilminster, in a fold of the Somerset hills;

Position: Leader of the Liberal Democrats '88-; ex: Spokesman: on Northern Ireland '88-97, on Education '87-88, on Trade and Industry '83-87; on Members' Interest Select Committee '84-87;

Outlook: The LibDems' whirling dervish Leader into his second decade; is waiting for Tony Blair to reward him with some sort of PR; his ritual Blair-baiting is normally greeted by a groan in the Commons; an able, charismatic, technically literate, ambitious, impetuous, cocky, hyperactive, innovative type always sparking off new ideas, like his '98 demand for a written EU constitution; "the most assured orator of all the party leaders" (Andrew Brown, INDEPENDENT); the doubling of his cohort has given extra weight to his illusion that his party is ready to share power when all that is on offer is minor participation in a Cabinet committee on voting and constitutional reform; the hope of anything more has been destroyed by the size of the Labour majority, six times that expected or planned; his own enlarged high-quality cohort enables him to sink a sharper elbow, often into the side of his cherished ally and dangerous competitor, Tony Blair; he is still more popular with LibDem supporters in the country who elected him than with his MP-colleagues; "realises he has to be adventurous to be noticed"; "his conversation is full of the buzzwords of the new politics" that "can easily degenerate into well-intentioned but meaningless claptrap" (Peter Riddell, TIMES); "he trots around the tragedy in Bosnia, comes back, makes a speech, grabs a headline; sometimes he says 'bomb them' - I'm not sure whom or why; sometimes he says 'more troops', sometimes he says 'less troops'; but it is all just for effect; he is only a political tourist" (Lord (Douglas) Hurd); "the hero of the long march back from fratricidal merger" of the Liberals and Social Democrats (Michael White, GUARDIAN); his party still needs his energy and his conciliation skills; after its '87 electoral disaster it was "Paddy's energy that saved the Liberal Democrats from disappearing down the plughole" (LibDem colleague); "for all his good intentions, he is that most dangerous of political beings, a man in love with unexamined ideas"

(Allan Massie, SUNDAY TELEGRAPH); used to believe that "Westminster and Whitehall are not part of the solution, they are part of the problem"; and that we cannot solve problems without unleashing the power of the community; this has been forgotten, now that Westminster promises constitutional and voting reforms; had a "capacity to drive Mr Major to the brink of his sanity" (Simon Hoggart, GUARDIAN); "has mastered the television medium", "appeals to the otherwise intelligent people who are not politically intelligent" (A N Wilson, EVENING STANDARD); has a tendency to prance on to "the high moral ground" (Sarah Baxter, NEW STATESMAN); "for all his military bearing, his bristling efficiency and his daringly patterned ties, Paddy has yet to develop something more than his strictly one-dimensional television ego, that of Mr Clean marching furiously along the path of righteousness" (Jan Moir, SCOTSMAN); "if prizes were awarded for building bricks without straw, Paddy Ashdown would be a gold medallist" (Peter Kellner, INDEPENDENT); "Rambo of the thinking classes" (SUNDAY TELEGRAPH); "he comes across well on radio, television and in the glossy magazines women read; he talks straight to camera and shows no fear; his stout stand in the Gulf War won much admiration, reminding us he was a military man" (Michael Jones, SUNDAY TIMES); until his '85 softening on Cruise was "the champion of the younger and unilateralist activists" (Peter Riddell, FINANCIAL TIMES); recently a pro-NATO multilateralist, concerned about nuclear safety, military and civil; "a spunky fighter, which is why Tory MPs don't like him" (David McKie, GUARDIAN); has "a background of Buchanesque romance that makes him a dream for the popular media" (Robin Oakley, TIMES); "the only party leader capable of killing Norman Tebbit with one blow while conversing in Mandarin" (Andrew Rawnsley, GUARDIAN);

History: His eyes were opened to the excitement of ideas at 16 by two socialist teachers at Bedford School '57; was a Labour supporter until 'In Place of Strife' convinced him the party was too beholden to the unions '69; on duty as a commando company commander in the Marine Commando in Northern Ireland, he was present at John Hume's arrest shortly after 'Bloody Sunday' '70; decided he was a Liberal '72; joined the Liberal Party '75; he made a "crazy, irresponsible, naive decision" to throw up his diplomatic career to enter Liberal politics '76; was selected for Yeovil, in his wife's home area '76; welcomed Lib-Lab Pact Mar '77; contested Yeovil against John Peyton, improving Liberal vote May '79; at Assembly warned against replacement of British troops by UN troops, insisting religion was only the vehicle of an Irish passion sparked by poverty, alienation and the failure of a corrupt democratic system Sep '79; backed: profit sharing, worker participation Sep '79; at Assembly proclaimed: "in the next war there would be no victory"; opposed Cruise missiles, favoured nuclear-free zones Sep '81; helped persuade Liberal Assembly to defy the leadership and vote for the immediate removal of all Cruise missiles Sep '82; captured Yeovil, Tory-held for over 70 years, defeating David Martin June '83; favoured the final unity of Alliance partners June '83; voted against Defence Estimates July '83; at Assembly warned against motion urging troop withdrawal "as an Irishman, brought up outside Belfast, who had to return to that sad city as a soldier to fight violence and witness death on the streets of my own town" Sep '83; backed nuclear "freeze" Sep '83; supported Cyril Smith's first failed attempt to have a Liberal Deputy Leader Sep '83; showed concern about personal data on PAYE computer Dec '83; introduced Bill for establishment of regional assemblies Dec '83; opposed Royal Ordnance Factories' privatisation, maintaining they were not only a capital asset but also a revenue asset Jan '84; urged the Alliance become a "single organisation dedicated to a single purpose" Mar '84; alleged that the CIA was spying on British firms Apr '84; with Richard Holme published 'First Steps Back from the Brink', a pamphlet urging a radical reappraisal of defence, including 'no first use' and a nuclear 'freeze' June '84; split with SDP in opposing Data Protection Bill, fearing a "Big Brother organisation" June '84; sponsored Bill to limit off-duty immunity for visiting servicemen July '84; sponsored debate on the problems of high technology exports July '84; was hailed as "rising star" at Liberal Assembly but was also accused by some colleagues of "disloyalty, political opportunism" and "irresponsible behaviour" for leading the demand for removal of Cruise and Pershing missiles from the UK forthwith Sep '84; sponsored motion deploring the closure of sub post offices Dec '84; voted against government's fluoridation proposals Jan '85; urged help for small businesses and exemption from some legal requirements Jan '85; supported computer software copyright legislation Feb '85; supported Enoch Powell's Unborn Children (Protection) Bill Feb '85; sponsored debate on gallium arsenide, maintaining that it was "essential and vital for the new super computers of the future" Mar '85; attacked US-imposed restraints on UK high tech industries July '85; said Trident submarines would have to depend on US for their fuel as well as missiles July '85; again urged Government to provide helicopter orders for imperilled Westland July '85; at Liberal conference said it had been wrong to station Cruise in the UK but it had achieved a symbolic rather than a military value, making withdrawal less important; he was tagged "Paddy Climbdown" by a Young Liberal Sep '85; insisted there should be a crash safety review of the nine first-generation Magnox stations or a shutdown Sep '85; aligned with local trade unionists, he strongly opposed Michael Heseltine's effort to link Yeovil firm Westland with European consortium rather than with Sikorski Jan '86; criticised Government for allowing US to bomb Libya illegally from British bases Jan '86; said Liberals did not exclude renationalising BT and British Gas Jan '86; opposed Government's Shops Bill which tried to liberate Sunday trading Apr '86; disclosed that Dungenness A nuclear power station in Kent had been kept running with faulty turbines in previous Feb-Mar, Apr '86; described nuclear power as a "Faustian bargain" exchanging "unlimited power" for "the integrity of our environment" May '86; helped negotiate a peace deal between riot police and hippie convoy May '86; claimed changes in Financial Services Bill had been required by Tories' paymasters in Stock Exchange June '86; at a Liberal-CND meeting warned Dr Owen that attacks on the fragile Alliance compromise proposed by its defence commission could blow the Alliance apart June '86; urged a law on mass trespass which would cope with hippie convoys June '86; demanded disclosures about Hinkley Point shutdowns (in Sept '84 and Sep '85) June '86; again attacked Minister for lying down in front of US Government encroachment on UK firms' rights to export high tech products to Communist states July '86; criticised costly delays of British Approvals Board for Telecommunications July '86; supported David Steel at Eastbourne Assembly, despite heavy reservations on the Owen-Steel proposed Anglo-French nuclear deterrent - had a serious argument with CND's Bruce Kent Sep '86; urged full disclosure of partial meltdown in the Chapelcross nuclear reactor in '67 during production of plutonium for nuclear weapons Oct '86; opposed Government pressure on British Aerospace to take a share in Westland: "what Westland needs is the order, not another partner" Nov '86; demanded a thorough review of safety at the "ancient and crumbling" Magnox nuclear generator, Hinkley Point A Nov '86; backed purchase of Nimrod as furthering British technology Dec '86; asked Government to stop "shilly-shallying" about orders for Westland's military helicopters Dec '86; at Cheltenham, campaigned against GCHQ workers' deprivation of rights Jan '87; was named Education Spokesman of Alliance Jan '87; protested British Government's permitting US inspectors to curb inclusion of American parts in selling on of technology Feb '87; co-protested "shambles" of UK preparations for a Chernobyl-style nuclear accident Apr '87; in wake of Alliance's election setback, he urged an early merger, tightening of the organisation and sharpening of its message - which was interpreted as a challenge to David Steel's leadership June '87; backed David Steel's leadership against post-election attacks by John Pardoe Aug '87; attacked Kenneth Baker's Education Bill as a "deliberate act of destruction" Sep '87; insisted: "unless we have a just society, we will never build a strong economy", adding that: "all other things being equal and fair, the market is the best economic model; but all other things are not equal and the market is very often extremely unfair" Sep '87; urged a ban on BNFL's plan to transport plutonium by air to Japan Feb '88; as a sponsor of Nuclear Weapons Freeze, asked Mrs Thatcher why she wanted more nuclear weapons since USA and USSR could destroy each other 50 times over Mar '88; criticised the Education Reform Bill as the most dangerous in over 20 years Mar '88; ignored the savaging of his bid for the Leadership in a widely-deplored unsigned attack by Beith-backer Alex Carlile May '88; became first elected Leader of Liberal Democrats, defeating Alan Beith with 71.9% of the vote July '88; was guest of BAT for flight to Hague for meeting of Action Committee for Europe Nov '88; was promoted a Privy Councillor Dec '88; criticised forced deportation of Vietnamese from Hongkong Dec '89; voted against war crimes trials of elderly Baltic immigrants Dec '89; voted to support embryo research Apr '90; established a good public identity on the Gulf War Sep '90-Jan '91; the Liberal Democrats took Eastbourne from the Tories at a by-election Oct '90; Ashdown claimed the Eastbourne by-election decided the ouster of Mrs Thatcher Nov '90; favoured allowing Hongkong citizens to come to reside in UK Dec '90; was reassured by new PM, John Major, that machine tools exported to Iraq were not for military purposes Dec '90; his party took previously Tory-safe Ribble Valley Mar '91; Labour MP Mildred Gordon sent him a copy of a racist Focus leaflet distributed by Liberal Democrats in Tower Hamlets Mar '91; said: "Britain should not fear [European] federalism" June '91; promised his party would replace Labour as the progressive force of the '90s, July '91; at party conference time he was rated at +30, while John Major was +25 and Neil Kinnock was -20 Sep '91; his party captured Kincardine Nov '91; over the objections of Sir Russell Johnston, urged a referendum on the Maastricht treaty, which he favoured -without its Social Chapter Nov '91; hounded John Major over mortgage defaults and house repossessions Dec '91; was tagged "Politician of the Year" (Robin Oakley, TIMES) and "Sound Gobbler of the Year" (Andrew Rawnsley, GUARDIAN) for his frequent TV appearances Dec '91; achieved the highest popularity rating of any party leader Jan '92; urged an independent Bank of England Jan '92; was disclosed to have had a five-month-long extra-marital affair with his former secretary, Tricia Howard, five years before - as a result of which his poll rating rose by 13% Feb '92; backed Trident subs with limited firepower Feb '92; opened election campaign with declaration that his party would put 1p on income tax to improve education and would not support a government which turned its back on PR Mar '92; derided Labour's new willingness to consider electoral reform Mar '92; a Cabinet Minister allegedly telephoned the SUN to provide names of three additional Ashdown girlfriends, who did not check out Mar '92; in the election campaign had high media coverage but the party vote sagged to 18% (down almost 5% from Alliance vote in '87) in the last few days under Major's charge that LibDems would "let in Labour" Mar-Apr '92; only secured 20 of expected 30 seats; retained his own seat with majority up by 3,133, a swing of 2.29% to LibDems Apr '92; reshuffled his team comprehensively replacing departed MPs with the newly-arrived ones and demoted Jim Wallace and Deputy Leader Sir Russell Johnston May '92; in Chard speech urged a search for "a viable alternative to Conservatism" May '92; urged more working together by opposition parties June '92; Labour's new Leader, John Smith, ignored his proposal for a "non-socialist alternative to the Conservatives" July '92; insisted UN should have used its power to stop or limit the war in ex-Yugoslavia Aug '92; called for air strikes to prevent Serb shelling of Bosnian towns Sep '92; minimised David Alton's threat not to stand again over LibDems' pro-abortion stand: "he has played no part in either building our party or in campaigning for it for four years now" Sep '92; provided 19 votes to enable John Major to win his Maastricht paving debate by three Nov '92; backed a Maastricht referendum Nov '92; accused John Major of having misled him over military machine tools for Iraq Nov '92; was rated as a good Leader of the Liberal Democrats by 54.5% of those polled Dec '92; urged a graduated UN military intervention in Bosnia to enforce safe havens; endorsed air strikes Dec '92; accused PM Major of reducing UK influence in EC Dec '92; launched a four-month campaign to see how the other, non-political half lives, spending Monday to Wednesday away from Commons Jan '93; his party won the Newbury by-election May '93; was accused by John Major of "developing pomposity into an art form" June '93; Major accused him of "wriggling like an eel" over Maastricht; he accused Major of using the confidence vote on Maastricht to put party unity before EC unity July '93; his party won the Christchurch by-election July '93; warned annual conference the disillusioned might turn to "Ross Perot or worse"; accepted local pacts with Labour; for Liberal Democrats, insisted there was no "glass ceiling" limiting their rise Sep '93; predicted a Tory split in the wake of Euro-elections Oct '93; urged 3p more on income tax for those earning over £25,000 Nov '93; John Major visited his constituency after a BBC poll had shown that the Conservatives had lost 41% of their support in 48 southwest constituencies Nov '93; was sharply attacked by allegedly-racist Liberal Democrats in Tower Hamlets Dec '93; was rebuffed by his party executive in his attempt to install Lord Holme as director of general election campaign, a supporter of closer relations with Labour Dec '93; said the West was preparing to "wash their hands of Bosnia" Dec '93; was disclosed to have been serving as "Postman Paddy" carry messages from Bosnians in UK to relatives in Bosnia Jan '94; asked new Lord Dahrendorf to head a commission on how to develop UK economy in an increasingly globalised world Jan '94; in local government review, argued for Somerset to be divided into three unitary authorities Jan '94; voted against restoring capital punishment, even for killers of policemen Feb '94; voted for homosexual sex at 16, and at 18, Feb '94; again urged EC and UN to "take premeditated and co-ordinated action" against Serb invaders of Bosnia Feb '94; the PM asked him to "stop pretending that there is some easy magical and painless solution to a problem that is so intensely difficult for the commanders on the ground" after he asked PM Major why he had not delivered his promised opening of Tuzla airport Feb '94; voted for a referendum on closer integration with Europe Feb '95; suggested Britain should prepare for war with Serbia over the 300 hostages taken May '95; was irritated with the timing of Tony Blair's conference-eve message saying "that part of the Liberal Democrats that is essentially social democrat has a lot in common with our party" Sep '95; expressed his fear of the "tribalism" shown in Ulster and Bosnia Sep '95; was attacked by a knife-armed drunk in Yeovil Nov '95; in Dublin to see the Taoiseach, urged a "limited cross-Ireland amnesty for Semtex" Dec '95; when PM John Major announced he would not co-operate with the EU until it raised its ban on UK beef, Ashdown said he was caving in to Tory Eurosceptics May '96; urged 50% tax on the 120,000 incomes over £100,000 June '96; PM John Major said he showed "his breathtaking capacity to understand nothing" about the beef ban and culling June '96; in reshuffle demoted Alan Beith from Treasury Spokesman to Home Affairs July '96; in a NEW STATESMAN interview, predicted the breakup of the Conservative and Labour parties after the next election Sep '96; told his Brighton conference the country was hungering for leadership; the press were only interested in whether he would accept a Cabinet post in a Labour government with an inadequate majority; he refused to rule this out, saying Blair had more in common with him than with Leftwingers in his own party; although the LibDems were stuck around 15% in the polls, he did not want to be Labour's "mascot" Sep '96; deriding Blair's "U-turn", opposed a Scottish Parliament without tax-raising abilities Sep '96; co-rejected Brussels' Common Fisheries Policy Sep '96; urged PM John Major to back his own Chancellor, Ken Clarke, on the single European currency Sep '96; welcomed Peter Thurnham, defecting Tory MP, into the LibDems Oct '96; PM John Major rejected his demand, with Tony Blair, for a judicial public inquiry into the Hamilton cash-for-questions affair Oct '96; insisted "people are so fed up with all this [Tory] lying about tax" Nov '96; in response to LibDem rebels against Lib-Lab pacts, wrote in LIBERAL DEMOCRAT NEWS that no pre-election decision would be taken "that limits the decisions we may want to take after it" Nov '96; described Tory Government policies as "crap" Dec '96; denied as a "travesty" the accusation of departing LibDem MP David Alton that he was cosying up to Labour for a Cabinet seat Jan '97; agreed on a five-a-side joint consultative committee led by Robin Cook and Robert Maclennan Feb '97; described as "the most soul-destroying day of my life" the time he had to sack himself and 30 other employees when Morlands collapsed in '81, Mar '97; in the lead-up to the election, Cabinet Secretary Sir Robin Butler sounded him about preliminary positions in possible coalition negotiations Apr '97; retained minimally-altered Yeovil by an enhanced majority of 11,403 on a notional swing of 3.2%; there were 7 contestants May '97; he and Blair congratulated each other on the 'phone on the doubling of LibDem and Labour seats; the 179 Labour majority ruled out any need for LibDem backing, coalitions or Cabinet seats May '97; he baited Blair on keeping Tory ceilings on education May '97; he urged speed on LibDem President, Robert Maclennan MP, engaged in talks with Home Secretary Jack Straw on the formation of an electoral commission to recommend forms of PR, to be submitted to a referendum June '97; he baited Blair on inadequate funds for schools and hospitals June '97; urged a new shakeup in welfare based on personal pensions June '97; attacked Tories for chosing Eurosceptic Hague instead of Europhile Clarke, offering disaffected pro-Europeans "a welcome home with the Liberal Democrats" June '97; discussed constitutional reforms informally with Tony Blair at a refuelling stop on Novosibirsk airport on the way back from the Hongkong handover July '97; welcomed Tony Blair's offers of seats on a consultative Cabinet committee on constitutional change, an offer attacked by Tony Benn July '97; in the planning for annual conference, accepted the need for a more anti-Labour line to preserve LibDem autonomy and prevent a wipeout in looming council elections Sep '97; the first meeting of the consultative Cabinet committee produced agreement on conducting the 1999 Euro-electons under PR and the setting up of an electoral commission Sep '97; Ashdown welcomed Tory defector, Europhile Hugh Dykes, into the LibDems Sep '97; defended Lord [David] Steel for accepting £93,752 for two-days-a-week work for the pro-hunting Countryside Movement Sep '97; said he opposed euthanasia, but his wife Jane backed it Sep '97; reassured his LibDem conference at Eastbourne that he would go on attacking Labour's under-funding of education, health and social services but try to reach agreement on constitutional reforms Sep '97; baited PM Tony Blair over Robinson-exploited offshore trusts Dec '97; set up eight commissions to review his party's policies Feb '98; protested to PM Tony Blair about "the seemingly unstoppable growth in media power and political influence of Mr Rupert Murdoch" Apr '98; urged LibDems to shed their image as Britain's most pro-European party May '98; proposed an EU written constitution to define its powers July '98;

Born: 27 July 1941, New Delhi

Family: He is the great, great, great grandson of Daniel O'Connell; his father's family were soldiers and administrators in India from the time of Clive; son of late Lt Col John Ashdown, ex-Indian Army, a lapsed Roman Catholic from the South of Ireland and Lois (Hudson) a North Ireland Protestant; when the family returned from India in '46 they bought a 1,000-pig farm in Ulster, which foundered in '57; m '61 Jane (Courtenay), interior designer and the daughter of a West Country Tory Councillor; "the complete army wife: loyal, down-to-earth, supportive"; 1s Simon, a rock musician '67, 1d Katharine '65; 1 grandson '97;

Education: County Down Kindergarten (where he imprisoned his headmistress in a cupboard); Garth House (prep school in Northern Ireland); Bedford School (where his father, grandfather and great-grandfather had preceded him and where he was tagged 'Paddy'); Hongkong Language School (Chinese qualification: First Class Interpreter);

Occupation: Shareholder: in Westland Plc ("value is less than £100"); Author, Beyond

Westminster (1994); ex: Dorset Youth Officer '81-83; Executive: in Morlands sheepskins '78-81; Normalair Garrett (Westland Group) '76-78; in Foreign Office '72-76: First Secretary to UK Mission to UN in Geneva '74-76); Marine Officer '59-71 (enlisted at 18, was in Royal Marine Commando, then with Special Boat Squadron in Far East '61-68 [where he became the youngest postwar Commander], in Northern Ireland '69-71);

Traits: Tall; fair; his "greatest political strength is his curly hair"; "retains...a certain boyishness; the suggestion of adventure hangs charmingly about him" (Allan Massie, SUNDAY TELEGRAPH); "his manner is brisk, bold and slightly condescending" (Andrew Alexander, DAILY MAIL); "has five favourite poses: his favourite is staring, commando style, flinty-eyed into the middle distance, hand-to-chin, one finger up the side of his face, three fingers under the jaw, with neck jutting forward"; "there is something about Mr Ashdown which seems to irritate other MPs; perhaps it is the high moral tone with which he lectures ministers for their supposed timidity in the Balkans" (Matthew Parris, TIMES); "not that it's easy to meet his eye, since it always seems to be looking past you to some sunlit upland" (Mark Steyn, EVENING STANDARD); "workaholic political loner, unroped rock climber, information technology freak" "characterized more by restlessness than self-reliance" (INDEPENDENT); "intelligent, industrious, handsome....humane, fit and strong" (SUNDAY TELEGRAPH); the second-fittest MP (after William Hague); "a certain impatience with rules, a desire to get things done and a conviction that he knew, as well if not better than the rule book, how they might be done" (INDEPENDENT); "marathon man" - because of his '92 campaign pace (SUNDAY TELEGRAPH); Irish origins (half-RC, half-Protestant); as a result of his father's bankrupcy, "is paranoid about living within his means": "has never had an overdraft ('I couldn't live with one')" (LIVING, Ian Woodward); former Malay, Dyak and Chinese linguist; tone-deaf but loves classical music (Puccini and Verdi operas); "opera is my greatest passion"; fitness freak (runs most weekends); "never an enthusiastic insider in the Westminster club" (Peter Riddell, TIMES); self-critical: "if I have a strength it is enthusiasm, if I have a weakness, it is impatience"; smokes about four cigarettes of his own a day, then cadges; "I smoke one small cigar a day and four or five cigarettes"; can indulge in "near-Messianic displays" (Robert Hardman, DAILY TELEGRAPH); "I've always done things that seemed impossible: people said I couldn't learn Chinese; they said I couldn't run 30 miles in six hours; this sounds extraordinarily arrogant, but I can't remember a thing upon which I've set my mind that I didn't succeed in doing; I don't have many other gifts, but I do have strong will-power (PA)"; "if ever you get Paddy a little pickled, you see a different side to him; he'll start singing his dirty songs"; "the thing I find most attractive about him is his maleness; he's essentially a man; cooking is a word that doesn't enter into his vocabulary" (Jane Ashdown); has a mongrel called 'Luke'; "I can go for three months on two to three house sleep a night; and I can catnap anywhere for five or 10 minutes and feel refreshed"; "I love all things Chinese except China tea"; "I am 90% vegetarian"; "I'm also a computer nut"; "Jane calls it my alternative train set"; "the Commons is too much like a club; I find it very stuck-up and pompous"; truthful: when his girlfriend-secretary, Tricia Howard, knew disclosure was imminent, he rejected her suggestion that he deny it all; regretfully admits he smacked his kids; takes four ultra-violet sessions a year "to help sooth a minor skin complaint"; Jane Ashdown bans the GUARDIAN from their home "for fear of Paddy having a heart attack; he's thrown it across the kitchen a couple of times in a fit of rage, so we can't have it anywhere near the house"; says his prayers every night; loves skiing; a former schoolboy boxer for Bedford School, "I now hate the sport; my last fight was the night before I met my wife - when we met, I had a black eye";

Address: House of Commons, Westminster, London SW1A 0AA; Vane Cottage, Norton-sub-Hamdon, Somerset TA14 6SG;

Telephone: 0171 219 6339/6226 (H of C); 0193588 491;

'Joe' (Joseph William) ASHTON   **Labour**   **BASSETLAW '68-**

Majority: 17,460 (36.4%) over Conservative 4-way;

Description: A seat centred about the mining town of Worksop, with two working pits feeding three power stations; in '83 it lost some Tory rural areas and marginal East Retford but gained the mining town of Warsop;

Position: On Catering Committee '97-; Chairman, Parliamentary Association Football Committee '92-; ex: on Select Committees: on Modernisation of the Commons '97-98, National Heritage '92-97, on Home Affairs '89-92, on Trade and Industry '87-89, on Members' Interests '79-83; Assistant Spokesman, on Energy, '79-81, Assistant Whip '76-77, PPS: to Tony Benn '74-76, Denis Howell '69-70; Chairman: East Midlands Labour Group '74-75, PLP Industry Group '74-75, PLP Public Building and Works Group '71-74; Vice Chairman, PLP Broadcasting Group '74-76; Select Committee: Members' Salaries '81-82, Nationalized Industries '74-77, Statutory Instruments '68-69; on Steering Committee of Labour Solidarity '81;

Outlook: Bright, shrewd, rooted, realistic, outspoken trad Labour Centrist; recently the quoteworthy commonsensical pillar of select committees; understands and explains how the real world works; also has colloquial talents as a columnist, playwright and novelist who can be entertaining even about his haemorrhoids in New York; his realism derives from his first-hand insights into Northern working class life, including his factory-floor experience as a Sheffield engineer; "one of the liveliest speech-makers" (Hugh Lawrence, SHEFFIELD STAR); "the tabloid MP" who "would love to be Mr Plain Commonsense" (Andrew Rawnsley, GUARDIAN); "if the DAILY MIRROR editorial column were to walk the earth in human form, it would look and sound like Mr Ashton; everything is a disgrace; everything is [the former] Tory government's fault; everything ought to have something done about it; and everything can be expressed in one-line sentences" (Matthew Parris, TIMES); the "voice of the people, commonsense, the North, the vast majority of ordinary men and women, all that is decent, the Working Class, rightminded folk and much, much more" (Craig Brown, TIMES); a pioneer crusader for one-member one-vote and other democratic party reforms; favours voluntary euthanasia; an unpredictable "maverick" (GUARDIAN) with little support among colleagues; "I am Number One supporter of Keep Sunday Special" (JA); still resents his being censured in '74 for blowing the whistle on corrupt MPs; a former Tribune Groupie, later a Hattersley backer; formerly MSF-sponsored;

History: Was elected to Sheffield City Council May '62; won Bassetlaw narrowly over Jim Lester at by-election Oct '68; urged banned-for-bribery players be allowed back into football eventually Jan '69; attacked advertising on local radio May '69; attacked the 'lump' for self-employed building workers as "a national scandal" June '69; wanted more money for British film-makers Feb '70; sponsored Bill to abolish hare-coursing Dec '70; began campaign against "slacking" MPs Feb '71; warned that MPs were paid by outside interests Oct '72; urged Football Betting Levy Board Nov '72; urged Register of MPs' Interests Apr '74; was accused of Breach of Privilege because he alleged there were a few "MPs for hire" citing another MP who took up, for payment, the cause of slag heaps Ashton had refused; he defied pressure to "grovel, apologise, purge your contempt and say you will never do it again"; he was found guilty of a "serious contempt" for whistle-blowing on corrupt MPs Oct '74; voted against Defence Review Dec '74; rebelled against Queen's Civil List increase Feb '75; urged better pay for MPs Mar '75; was sacked by Harold Wilson as Tony Benn's PPS for voting against cuts Mar '76; was campaign manager of Benn-for-Leader effort Mar '76; again opposed cuts July '76; was promoted Assistant Whip Oct '76; opposed mandatory re-selection of Labour MPs at Conference Oct '77; resigned as Whip over Government's mishandling of power strike Nov '77; attacked National Front in broadcast Dec '77; urged simultaneous pay increases to avoid leap-frogging Jan '79; defended Rampton nurse constituents against charges in Yorkshire TV documentary July '79; complained of sackings at Labour Party HQ Nov '79; urged defeated MPs get six-months-plus redundancy Mar '80; was slow handclapped at Conference when he urged one-member one-vote for MPs' selection, accurately warning that, without it, 25 Labour MPs would break away to form SDP Oct '80; said that a poll among constituents had persuaded him to support Michael Foot rather than Peter Shore for Leader Oct '80; received 21 votes for Shadow Cabinet Dec '80; complained that new Labour conference delegates were unrepresentative because often chosen because they could pay their own way Feb '81;joined Steering Committee of moderate Labour Solidarity Feb '81; defended it as a way putting both Right and Left "both on the same platform arguing a case on its merits and gaining support for a cause by argument instead of by backstairs plotting" Mar '81; wrote that "I am always relieved to see the police doing their job", "no matter how inconvenient it is for youths, black or white, to be stopped in the street and questioned" because contemporary young villains tended to victimize the poor and weak instead of robbing from those who could afford it June '81; accused Benn of going against conference decision by calling for nationalization without compensation Nov '81; left Solidarity as "too Rightwing" and "a Denis Healey front organization" Nov '81; complained that quote-happy Labour MPs were played for suckers by media who wanted them to savage one another Feb '82; warned against positive discrimination, writing: "as a socialist I am totally opposed to any form of discrimination whatsoever - except that in favour of the poor against the rich" Mar '82; after the Argentine invasion of the Falklands, urged the Tory Government be allowed to "hang and twist slowly in the wind, like they did at Suez" Apr '82; wrote: "in my experience of well over 30 years in the party I cannot recall one single instance of bias against women" June '82; complained of Left sectarianism on Mullins-captured TRIBUNE Dec '82; supported PLO and "inalienable rights of the Palestinian people to self-determination" Apr '83; warned union leaders to allow their members a vote for Labour Leader before Norman Tebbit imposed it on them July '83; accused Kinnock and Heffer of fearing one-man one-vote July '83; backed Roy Hattersley for Leader, Gwyneth Dunwoody for Deputy Leader Sep '83; resigned as columnist from LABOUR WEEKLY '83; complained about illegal and excessive policing during miners' strike Apr '84; complained that backbenchers from mining constituencies had no chance to put their case in Commons Apr '84; paid tribute to loyalty of striking miners despite "terrible hardship" Sep '84; urged Neil Kinnock to come to terms with breakaway UDM miners, who were strong in Nottinghamshire June '85; declined suggestion that he contest Chief Whip's post because of warring factions among his local miners July '85; urged extra tax on football pools to pay for better segregation at matches July '85; was defeated by 159 to 118 in his Tory-backed 10-minute-rule Bill urging advertisements on BBC to avoid pricing its license fee out of range of poor Jan '85; opposed televising Commons, for fear of turning it into the "Maggie and Neil Show" Nov '85; served as 'minder' to Labour candidate Bill Moore during West Derbyshire by-election May '86; supported Joan Lestor for NEC at AEU delegation Sep '86; secured 2nd

Reading for Bill urging pubs be compelled to set aside a non-smoking area Oct '86; opposed Kenneth Hind's Unborn Children (Protection) Bill Oct '86; in opposing restoration of capital punishment, said that if Myra Hindley had been hanged, she would have caused nowhere near the revulsion she had Jan '87; was furious at impact of London hard Left on Greenwich by-election, saying: "I was told to keep quiet after the Bermondsey by-election; I kept quiet after the miners' strike; I kept quiet during the Militant Tendency row, but I'm not going to keep quiet any longer" Mar '87; welcomed building of new coal-fired station in his constituency Mar '87; strongly opposed physical mistreatment of prisoners Mar '87; resigned as DAILY STAR columnist over their conversion to soft porn Sep '87; complained the Government was soft-pedalling anti-gun legislation because shooting was an upper class pursuit Nov '87; pointed out safety loophole in continuation of foam-stuffed mattresses Jan '88; complained that farmers in the fat South got subsidies but Northern industries got a dab of lipstick and their crutches snatched away Jan '88; voted against televising Commons, partly because it would be "baffling" to viewers Feb '88; complained that his was the only Labour constituency of 18 - the others being rich Tory areas - which did not receive any rate support grant, despite massive unemployment Dec '88; voted, mainly with Tories, against Right of Reply Bill to curb press extremism Apr '89; criticised Mrs Thatcher's football identity card Bill as "an immense, gigantic cock-up of the first order" Oct '89; asked for an assurance that Sky would not be able to buy up all the rights to sporting events and charge viewers for watching them Dec '89; said there was no such thing as a "football industry" because 95% of clubs paid no dividends, made no profits and relied on subsidies from directors and raffles from fans Jan '90; his motion urged registration of lobbyists and PR firms Feb '90; introduced Children and Young Persons (Protection from Tobacco) Bill to bar sale of single cigarettes to children Mar '90; visited Mexico with IPU Group to study anti-narcotic measures Oct '90; suggested handing over 2.5% of gate to local police Nov '90; co-sponsored Andrew Faulds' Children and Young Persons (Protection from Tobacco) Bill Dec '90; urged better retirement pay for under-50s MPs who were defeated after 15 years' service Jan '91; again backed non-smoking areas in pubs Jan '91; introduced Bill to force manufacturers to carry "tested on animals" label on suitable products Jan '91; co-sponsored motion urging introduction of real ale to Westminster's bars Jan '91; attacked random breath-testing as advocated by anti-drinkers: in his rural constituency, after a couple of pints in the village pub "the only thing you would knock down would be a rabbit"; "to say that because one likes a drink one is in favour of drunken driving is like saying that because one likes sex one is in favour of rape" Feb '91; complained about "enormous profits" by funeral directors, who should be compelled to post their prices Apr '91; complained that privatisation of electricity and imports of foreign coal would destroy the links between local coal mines and the three power stations in his constituency Oct '91; complained when Gerald Kaufman made a joke of Foreign Office correspondence being sent to Wandsworth Prison: "there are 3m unemployed and this country is in deep economic crisis, yet all this [tomfoolery] is being shown on television and it is a disgrace" Dec '91; denounced national lottery as a threat to the pools, with their 6000 jobs in Liverpool and their £40m contribution to football Jan '92; disclosed belatedly that Bassetlaw did not receive rate support grant because of the extra rates received from the big power stations in the area Jan '92; retained seat with majority up by 3,133, a swing to Labour of 3.86% Apr '92; congratulated Neil Kinnock, on leaving Labour's leadership, for having "led us out of the wilderness" Apr '92; warned that football fans were being priced out of the grounds May '92; said that the government's policy of letting schools opt out was a flop May '92; urged prosecution of those who knowingly passed on AIDS virus July '92; backed David Mellor against "tabloid tyranny" July '92; Trotskyists in Socialist Organiser group attempted to rig votes in his constituency Oct '92; complained that Germany was able to subsidise its miners more generously Oct '92; cited, during select committee investigation into press freedom and privacy, that a man who glued his buttocks together by using superglue instead of anal cream was made a national laughing stock by press Nov '92; worried about mines safety with privatisation Oct '93; urged a referendum on Maastricht Nov '92; backed protest against National Lottery as damaging football pools Dec '92; urged a press complaints authority where a justified victim could be awarded £5-10,000 Jan '93; when SUN editor Kelvin McKenzie threatened to expose all perverted MPs, he retorted "only those who went to public school, Mr McKenzie, like you did" Jan '93; objected to secrecy surrounding National Lottery since it would require 10,000 outlets with a £7,000 computer in each; urged allowing pools companies to have a level playing field with National Lottery Jan '93; complained that most of those prosecuted for not paying their license fees were women or pensioners Feb '93; said "I do not trust any Government", suggesting the Millennium Fund and National Lottery would be exploited by the Government in power Apr '93; following the bugging of David Mellor's mistress's bedroom, complained that the uncontrolled press, with its modern technology, had become as powerful as the KGB in invading privacy June '93; explained the setbacks for women MPs contesting the 'Shadow Cabinet': "the women got too bossy" Oct '93; again asked BBC's chairman to "do something about the [TV] license fee" Oct '93; voted with Left Eurosceptics against the European Economic Areas Bill Oct '93; urged national inquiry into hospital deaths through sabotaging of equipment Jan '94; voted against bringing back capital punishment Feb '94; voted to allow homosexual sexs at 18, Feb '94; complained there was much less discussion about pits closures - even longlife "core pits" - than Parliamentary boundary shifts Mar '94; backed: Tony Blair for Leader, John Prescott for Deputy Leader June-July '94; urged decriminalisation of non-payment of TV licenses July '94; urged public hearings of breach of privileges and full publication, on the basis of his own unpleasant '74 experiences July '94; on the National Heritage Select Committee accused British film-makers of being elitists who made films for one another, instead of popular 'Carry On' type commercial films Dec '94; complained that electronic surveillance by the press had gotten out of control and should be curbed Apr '95; attacked British publishers for snobbery in refusing to allow books to be discounted in supermarkets Apr '95; criticised National Heritage Secretary Virginia Bottomley for refusing to curb intrusive tabloid journalists July '95; pointed out that £400m had been spent on building all-seat stadia for top football clubs Oct '95; accused National Heritage Secretary Virginia Bottomley of allowing her officials to be "led up the garden path" on the enormous profits made by Camelot on the National Lottery Feb '96; accused the BBC of "complete defiance" of the National Heritage Select Committee over its refusal to disclose the terms of its Lottery results contract with Camelot Mar '96; as a Director of Sheffield Wednesday, complained it was unfair to show its games free on TV while having to pay £10,000 a week to star players Apr '96; complained that police knowledge of known football hooligans could not be published or otherwise exploited to prevent international incidents June '96; complained about aggressive BBC TV license collection from pensioners in holiday caravans July '96; voted to keep high MPs mileage allowance and £9,000 pay increase, with pension based on £43,000 July '96; brokered truce over local disruptive pupil Sep '96; sought to alter fertilisation law on behalf of constituent seeking to have her dead husband's baby Oct '96; retained his seat with a majority doubled to 17,460 on a 9% pro-Labour swing May '97; tried to restore order in first post-election private PLP meeting with Tony Blair May '97; voted to outlaw fox-hunting June '97; was named to the Select Committee on Modernisation of the House June '97; welcomed another inquiry into the Hillsborough Disaster, of which he was an eyewitness June '97; complained about local miners' houses sold to private landlords July '97; complained against BBC's threat to 'Today in Parliament' July '97; helped restore Northern male dishes to Commons menus which, under the influence of new

Labour women, "had got like a Kensington wine bar" Nov '97; introduced Doctor-Assisted Dying Bill, which was rejected by 234 to 89 Dec '97; objected to the 40% threshold in 'Fairness in Work' and the danger of subsequent blacklisting May '98; lost by 40 votes his amendment to keep the age of consent at 18 for those threatened by teachers or others with a duty of care June '98;

Born: 9 October 1933, Sheffield

Family: One grandfather, Paddy Maloney, an Irish Catholic from Sligo, was a DAILY WORKER reader; son of Arthur Ashton, miner then steel smelter, and Nellie, school cleaner; m '57 Margaret Patricia (Lee), former Co-op secretary, from '69 his Commons secretary; 1d Lucy '74;

Education: High Storrs Grammar; Rotherham Technical College;

Occupation: Sponsored: by MSF (£850 p a for constituency, £750 for election expenses) '88-95; Director (unpaid), of Sheffield Wednesday Football Club '90-; Columnist: on HOUSE MAGAZINE '84-, SUNDAY PEOPLE '87-88, on DAILY STAR, '79-87 (resigned over soft porn policy of new editor), LABOUR WEEKLY '72-83, SHEFFIELD STAR '70-75, '79-80; was awarded 'Columnist of the Year' award in '85 by Granada TV's 'What the Papers Say'; Novelist: Grass Roots (1977); Playwright: Majority of One (1981) (staged in Oldham, Nottingham and on radio}; ex: Cost Control Design Engineer at Davy-Ashmore, Sheffield , '56-68;

Traits: Grey, curly hair; engaging smile; Sheffield colloquial speech; "a blokish character who doesn't look as if he could find the washing-up liquid if you gave him a scale map of the kitchen" (Max Davidson, DAILY TELEGRAPH); witty; vivid; provocative; mischievous; contrary; bright-brash; "a naturally funny man" (Ray Connolly, OBSERVER); "he sits behind me and never shuts up; he gives the Speaker a terrible time" (Roy Hattersley MP); was born 200 yards from opening canal scene in "The Full Monty" and started work 300 yards away in the local steelworks; football supporter (7 shares in his life-long love Sheffield Wednesday); proudly prole (cites Sheffield's Foundry Working Men's Club as his, gives recipes for chip butties, tries to organise shrinking band of Labour proles); part Irish Catholic by origin; was a four-day haemorrhoids sufferer in New York; recently has suffered from hereditary gout;

Address: House of Comons, Westminster, London SW1A 0AA; 16 Ranmoor Park Road, Sheffield S10 3GX;

Telephone: 0171 219 4453 (H of C); 01742 301763 (home);

INDIVIDUAL SEARCHES:
The compressed political insights in our books are boiled down from the most comprehensive political files available. Access to our computer and cuttings files is available on Peers as well as MPs, from £35 per Parliamentarian.

TO EACH ACCORDING TO HIS NEED
MPs, journalists and others use these books for differing purposes. In committees, MPs on either side tend to bait each other with embarrassing information culled from our pages - like former MP Ron Brown's "snip" as his wife called it. When one Tory MP goes to another's constituency, he likes to be able to ask about his colleague's children by name. Journalists like to have additional telephone numbers. The biggest all-round use is to mug up on an MP before taking him for a meal, to prove that you know just how fascinating he or she is.

Majority: 2,688 over Conservative 9-way;

Description: The unaltered seat in southern Cornwall based on the working port of Falmouth and the former tin-mining centres of Camborne and Redruth; "probably the lowest-paid constituency in the country" (CA); it has the only local Labour tradition, more recently in local councils, since Dr John Dunwoody was ousted by David Mudd in '70; the difficulty of removing Mudd's successor, Olympic gold medallist Sebastian Coe, centred on the rivalry of his Labour and Liberal Democrat would-be ousters;

Position: On the Select Committee on Education and Employment '97-; Chairman, all-party Water Group '97-; ex: Islington Borough Councillor (Mayor '89-90)'86-92; on Islington Health Authority '86-90;

Outlook: The new MP who fought hard for eight months to try to save Cornwall's (and Europe's) last tin mine, providing "leadership in the campaign to save South Crofty" (Minister Barbara Roche); proud of being a Labour island in a sea of LibDems; with the Labour tide behind her, managed to overtake the greater, earlier activity of her rival anti-Tory, the LibDems' Terrye Jones, and blocked a LibDem clean sweep in Cornwall; the Blairite former Islington Mayor and journalist who was the first selection from an all-women short-list; won selection and election in a town in which her mother, a former hairdressing salon owner, was the current Mayor-Consort; fought her corner locally initially on low wages, unemployment and the high price of water; "a stimulating hybrid of Peter Mandelson and Dawn French" (Robin Stummer, INDEPENDENT ON SUNDAY); as a former researcher for Leftwing MPs Jo Richardson and Judith Hart, may not always have been a moderate;

History: Joined the Labour Party '79; was elected to Islington Borough Council May '86; was made a Freeman of the City of London for her contribution to the reorganisation of local schools '90; selected for hopeless Chesham and Amersham, came 3rd with 10.4% of the vote Apr '92; helped Barbara Follett set up 'Emily's List' to support women politicos in finding seats '93; was the first woman selected from an all-women short-list Dec '94; this selection met with considerable opposition from male aspirants, with two local councillors resigning; Jim Geach, a local county councillor and former Labour candidate for Truro, resigned from the party and threatened a legal action, which collapsed, and then to stand as an Independent candidate; she blamed Conservative policies for the loss of thousands of jobs in the constituency Mar '95; attacked for being a classic example of a shoulder-padded middle-class woman being foisted on a Cornish seat, retorted: "I can speak for the fishermen, the family and economics as well as any former Olympic runner or Labour stalwart; what will make the difference with the [all-women] short-lists is having a mass of women who together can influence the party on issues like hours in the Commons, civilised debate and childcare" May '95; urged a concerted campaign to restore the lifetime benefit for those injured at work, cut from £38.12 a week to £9.90 June '96; launched a defence of Albert Tong, a Camborne-based illegal immigrant of 17 years standing whom Home Office Minister Ann Widdecombe was trying to deport to Hongkong (an attempt which was eventually reversed) June '96; when Labour successfully defended a local by-election, she said: "the LibDems are going backwards while Labour surges forward" July '96; told annual conference that Britain was "crying out" for a national minimum wage: "our traditional industries are in decline, so the low-pay merchants have come to town; if we believed the Tories' claim that low pay attracts jobs, we should be knee-deep in Japanese jobs; surprise, surprise, we are not - and unemployment continues to rise in Carnwall, month after month"; "the Tories' idea of the moral high ground is to leave the market free to pay the lowest amount" Sep '96; with 17 other local candidates, criticised the INDEPENDENT for seeking divisions among candidates, insisting "the Labour Party is a united dynamic party ready to solve the problems this country faces" Oct '96; opposed a local multi-storey car park "on environmental and social grounds" Feb '97; said "I am not in favour of a federal superstate, but I am not happy with us always being a 'no, no,no' nation" Mar '97; the local LibDems distributed a phoney 'MORI Poll' - disavowed by MORI - showing Labour running 3rd with 22% Apr '97; her election efforts were reinforced by the arrival of 20 Labour peers, MEPs and MPs, led by Harriet Harman Apr '97; despite her local Labour rival, Jim Geach, polling 1,691 as 'Independent Labour', she managed to overtake LibDem Terrye Jones and oust the sitting Tory, Olympic champion Seb Coe with a majority of 2,688 , a swing from the Tories of 6.64%; this made her Cornwall's first woman MP since the '20s and Falmouth's first Labour MP since '70, May '97; opposed plans to build a multi-storey car park in Falmouth May '97; co-sponsored motion applauding restoration of union rights at GCHQ May '97; asked about time taken for breast cancer referrals June '97; complained about rail services to Penzance June '97; in her Maiden urged a development agency for Cornwall and a national minimum wage; also raised the crisis in Cornwall Care, the charity to which the LibDem-controlled county council had transferred its homes for the elderly,·which had lost its case before the industrial tribunal after trying to cut staff wages sharply June '97; was named to the Select Committee on Education and Employment July '97; promised support to keep the local MAFF office in Truro, rather than move to Exeter July '97; acclaimed Chancellor Brown's first Budget as giving "new hope to young and long-term unemployed in Falmouth and Camborne" July '97; backed plans for an £8.2m local planetarium Aug '97; she led a delegation to Minister Roche to try to stop the closure of South Crofty, the last Cornish tin mine Sep '97; at annual conference fringe complained of the "shameless tactics" of local LibDems, who had called her "that harridan woman from London" Oct '97; signed European Movement advertisement, 'Europe: A Force for Fairness, Equality and Opportunity for Women' Nov '97; backed a national minimum wage, explaining "the gross domestic product for Cornwall generally is 69% of the national average" Dec '97; asked John Prescott whether planned Regional Development Agency would help Cornwall Dec '97; asked PM Tony Blair whether the new Regional Development Agency would tackle Cornwall's problems, including threatened South Crofty Jan '98; promised a Redruth audience that the Government would retrain sacked tin miners from South Crofty, receiving the reply: "Retraining to do what? Sell ice cream to tourists?" Jan? '98; urged more generous regional selective assistance for Cornwall, having been turned down for funding for South Crofty as not viable; the Minister, Barbara Roche, congratulated her on her hard work in trying to save the mine; in an adjournment debate complained South Crofty's impending closure would end "4,000 years of mining in Cornwall" Feb '98;

Born: 21 September 1955, Sutton, Surrey

Family: Daughter, of Denis Atherton, former DAILY MIRROR journalist, and Pamela (Osborn), hairdressing salon owner and Mayoress of Falmouth '96-98; her Partner is Broderick Ross, a Cornishman living in Falmouth;

Education: Sutton High School; Midhurst Grammar School; North London Polytechnic (BA Hons in Applied Social Studies);

Occupation: Free-lance journalist: recently in a Wiltshire-based agency (NUJ); was a co-founder of EVERYWOMAN; a former Probation Officer; a part-time organiser for

UNISON; a one-time researcher for Leftwing Labour MPs Judith Hart and Jo Richardson;
Traits: Long straight blonde hair; very chubby; large specs; glider pilot; ornithologist; formerly owned a narrow-boat;
Address: House of Commons, Westminster, London SW1A 0AA; 4 Webber Hill, Falmouth, Cornwall TR11 2LY (constituency office); a flat in south London;
Telephone: 0171 219 3000 (H of C); 01326 314440/314415 (Fax) both in her constituency office;

Charlotte ATKINS   **Labour**   **STAFFORDSHIRE-MOORLANDS '97-**

Majority: 10,049 over Conservative 4-way;
Description: A lovely north Staffordshire seat changed in all but name by the addition of pro-Labour Kidgrove's 19,000 voters (from Stoke-on-Trent) and the deletion of 27,000 voters from pro-Tory villages; this almost changes it back to the marginal Labour seat of Leek -named after its old textile town - formerly held by the late Harold [later Lord] Davies; it also marks the retirement of Sir David Knox who took it from him; it borders on ten other constituencies; it has lost its potteries and pits but retains textiles; the headquarters of the Britannia building society;
Position: On: Committee of Selection '97-, Select Committee on Education and Employment '97-, PLP's Parliamentary Committee '97-; Women's Committee of Labour's NEC '93-; ex: Labour Party National Policy Forum '95-97, Wandsworth Borough Councillor (Deputy Leader of its Labour Group '85-86, Chief Whip '83-85) '82-86;
Outlook: Rightward-moving Leftish ex-UNISON lobbyist; loyal, computer-phile enthusiast for raising educational standards; after 20 years of working for unions, has been accepted within the party leadership as "quintessentially one of us" (INDEPENDENT); others rate her a "Kinnockite realist" (RED PEPPER) or "Centre-Left" (NEW STATESMAN); has worked her passage partly by helping women aspirants to win selection through the Labour Women's Network; the daughter of Ron Atkins, the former soft-Left Labour MP for Preston North for nine years; a one-time collaborator with Bennite Chris Mullin in instructing activists on how to dump moderate Labour MPs; was in CND and the Labour Co-ordinating Committee, on the editorial board of The CHARTIST and for two years on the Executive of Liberty (formerly National Council for Civil Liberties);
History: She joined the Labour Party at 16 - the earliest age possible - when her father won Preston North '66; became COHSE Press Officer '80; collaborated with the leading Bennite, Chris Mullin, in the Leftwing activists' manual, 'How to Select or Reselect Your MP', which made life miserable for scores of challenged moderate Labour MPs for the next decade; her contribution was to analyse how Labour MPs had voted on 12 key Commons divisions; the pamphlet was published by the CLPD and the Institute for Workers' Control Oct '81; was elected to Wandsworth Borough Council May '82; became Chief Whip of its Labour Group May '83; became Deputy Leader of its Labour Group May '85; was imposed by the NEC as the Labour candidate for the Eastbourne by-election, in the wake of Ian Gow's assassination by the IRA; the existing candidate, Peter Day, had refused to pay his poll tax; her Labour vote

was squeezed down from 8.8% to 5% (2,308 votes) by the successful Liberal Democrat, David Bellotti Oct '90; as an activist in Labour Women's Network, in EMILY NEWS urged women aspirants to "get networking" since one-member one-vote required them to "get around the constituency and meet as many members as possible and not rely on trade union nominations, thinking that by just getting on the short-list the union support will lead members to vote for them"; "all the evidence points against this"; "members decide to vote for you on the evidence of their experience of you or their friends' views" Oct '94; her own selection for the favourably redrawn seat of Staffordshire-Moorlands - without the intervention of an all-women short-list -provoked the resignation of some local constituency officers '95; prepared UNISON's evidence for the Nolan Committee into Standards in Public Life '95; in a joint letter with 17 other loyal candidates, protested to the INDEPENDENT about its search for divisions, insisting "the Labour Party is a dynamic united party, ready to solve the problems this country faces" Oct '96; in a discussion on Parliamentary lobbyists on BBC-TV said that in her role as Parliamentary Officer of UNISON, "we can get to places where we need to get in" Jan '97; her victory, on a notional swing of 8.7%, made her the seat's first Labour MP since the late Harold [later Lord] Davies 1945-70, May '97; was named to the prestigious Committee of Selection June '97; was also named to the Select Committee on Education and Employment and elected by fellow backbenchers to the Parliamentary Committee of the PLP July '97; in her Maiden, deplored the £2.50 an hour many of her constituents were paid and looked forward to the minimum wage July '97; she ridiculed the "crocodile tears" of Tory MPs deploring the end of tax relief for pensioners taking out health insurance; the £110m spent on this was better used in reducing waiting lists; her own 81-year-old mother, rather than wait a further two years to end "excruciating pain", had to pay to have a hip operation; "my mother did not get any tax relief" July '97; she urged the maintenance of "the principle of free [higher] education for the poorest students" July '97; urged more local availability of abbatoirs July '97; pressed for "a sensibly-set national minimum wage" as "so important to my constituents" and likely to "encourage employers to invest in the skills of their staff and hence help this country to compete" Dec '97; enthused about raising school standards, since "we do not want a generation of our children blighted in the labour market, failed by our education system"; enthusiastically endorsed "the procedures to remove incompetent teachers from the classroom when all other measures to improve performance have failed"; cited one "computer-phobic" teacher who transformed her six-year-old daughter from one "who loved school into one who hated it" Dec '97; urged additional efforts to secure male teachers in primary education Feb '98; congratulated Government on Northern Ireland's step toward lifting the beef ban Mar '98; asked about badgers' role in bovine TB, a serious local affliction May '98;

Born: 24 September 1950, Chelmsford

Family: Daughter of Welsh-born Ron Atkins, former teacher and further education lecturer and Labour MP for Preston North '74-79 '66-70, and Jessie, "a strong dominant figure"; her twin sister Liz, a former Co-op and Labour Party officer, recently Head of Policy for the NSPCC, sought the nomination for Gravesham; she has three half-brothers; m Gus Brain, journalist and former dealer in 18th century English porcelain, "6ft 4in with a beard" (CA); 1d Emma '86 a keen chess-player;

Education: Colchester County High School; LSE (BSc Econ, MA);

Occupation: Parliamentary Officer, for UNISON '92-97; received more than 25% of her '97 election expenses from UNISON, including the post-election five-week loan of a Ford Escort; Press Officer (NUJ), for COHSE/UNISON '80-92; also worked for UCATT and TASS;

Traits: Dark hair in a neat, short practical hair style; straight-faced and serious-looking; has head-prefect good looks; smart; flat classless speech; "brisk to the point of brittleness"

(INDEPENDENT ON SUNDAY)
Address: House of Commons, Westminster, London SW1A 0AA; she has moved into the constituency;
Telephone: 0171 219 3591 (H of C); 01782 866666 (constituency office); 01538 371188 (Leek home);

David (Anthony) ATKINSON   **Conservative**   **BOURNEMOUTH EAST '77-**

Majority: 4,346 (10%) over Liberal Democrat 5-way;
Description: Half of the staid old blue-rinsed Dorset seaside town, stiff with retired folk but very thin on council tenants; in '95 it lost the centre of the town and the East Cliff ward to its neighbour, Bournemouth West;
Position: On the Select Committee on Science and Technology '97-; on the Council of Europe (Leader of Conservative delegation '97-, Chairman of European Democratic Group '98-) and WEU (Chairman of Council's Committee for Relations with European Non-Member Countries '91-) '79-; Vice Chairman: Conservative MPs' Tourism Committee '92-, Conservative MPs' Health Committee '88-; Chairman, International Society for Human Rights UK (Rightwing group founded in West Germany by anti-Soviet emigres) '85-97; President '83-, Chairman '81-83, Christian Solidarity International UK '83-; Vice Chairman '97- Treasurer '81-97, British-Russian Parliamentary Group; ex: PPS to Paul Channon '79-87; Vice Chairman, Conservative MPs' Health and Social Services Committee '87-88; Chairman: All-Party Group on Space Research '81-83, on Environment Select Committee '79 (three weeks); National Chairman, Young Conservatives '70-71;
Outlook: The James Bond of the Christian Right; the former two-dimensional Rightwing cold warrior who has found added dimensions as a leader of the Council of Europe's humanitarian aid efforts -including easily-misunderstood efforts in Eastern Europe, Vietnam and among Palestinian Arabs; "plays a distinguished role in the international efforts to reach a solution" to problems "of Vietnamese migrants to Hongkong" (Alastair Goodlad MP); a pioneer on computer compliance; has long taken an interest in mental health after the suicide of a schizophrenic friend; a quiet, behind-the-scenes, loyal hard-Right PRman; was accused of working for rival sides in Channel Tunnel dispute, he says falsely; a space enthusiast; also a devotee of complementary and alternative medicine; "has been unceasing in his determination to promote the chiropractors' cause" (ex-MP Toby Jessel); formerly waged a lukewarm war for South Africans in Namibia and against Russians (especially over Afghanistan and Christian dissidents), Bulgarians (over Turkish minority) and VATmen; in hard-Right '92 Group' and international Rightwing Christian organisations;
History: Joined Young Conservatives '59; urged Tory Party be made more attractive and efficient Oct '66; as YC Vice Chairman opposed sale of anti-Biafra arms to Nigeria Nov '69; was elected to Southend Borough Council May '69, to Essex County Council May '73; contested: Newham Northwest Feb '74, Basildon Oct '74; was chosen from among 243 as candidate for Bournemouth East after scandal-dogged John Cordle's resignation Sep '77; told Tory conference that closed shop was core of Communist-inspired strategy to establish a

non-Parliamentary base in media Oct '77; won Bournemouth East Nov '77; in Maiden speech extolled small firms which "have not heard of the eight-hour day or the five-day week" Mar '78; attacked "Soviet-style methods" of VATmen May '79; visited Moscow to interview Christian dissidents, one of whom was later arrested June '79; urged Western invasion of Cuba or South Yemen if Soviets did not withdraw from Afghanistan Jan '80; accused VATmen of tapping telephones Feb '80; complained Lords were overturning legislation giving acupuncturists equal rights Feb '80; demanded more spending cuts Mar '80; visited Leningrad to meet free trade union campaigner May '80; urged all aid and equipment for Afghan freedom fighters June '80; warned "all hell would break loose" if IRA hunger-striker died Dec '80; demanded Helsinki Agreement be used to end Soviet abuses of psychiatry Feb '81; claimed private health care had saved taxpayer £86m Feb '81; welcomed Sunday Trading Bill Feb '81; said Soviet intervention could only be stopped by "damaging measures of diplomatic and economic retaliation short of war" Apr '81; relaunched All-Party Group on Space Research after previous year's failure May '81; wanted CBI again to persuade biggest firms to hold down price increases Nov '81; was virtually only Tory MP who liked the Budget Mar '82; warned: the Soviet gas pipeline was converting Western Europe into a neutralized Finland July '82; warned of danger of "cold feet" and another "Suez fiasco" in liberating the Falklands May '82; warned of radiological pollution of Channel coast from French nuclear power stations opposite Oct '82; urged second Thatcher Government should denationalize more Mar '83; visited Taiwan Apr '83; introduced Licensing (Occasional Permission) Bill May '83; voted to restore hanging for all categories of capital crime July '83; urged more privatisation of local government June '84; urged Select Committee inquiry into embryo research and genetic engineering July '85; denied press report he was working as a PRman for both sides of the Channel Tunnel argument, through Good Relations (pro) and Grayling (anti) Dec '85; complained that detente was being exploited by Soviets Dec '85; demanded abolition of totally discredited rates system Jan '86; helped organize London conference on Namibia under auspices of his International Society for Human Rights Mar '86; visited Hong Kong as fully-sponsored guest of Hongkong Government '87; opposed any compromise on uncontrolled Sunday trading Apr '86; accused Eire of trading food for arms for IRA May '86; introduced motion attacking persecution of Turks in Bulgaria July '86; again attacked detente as "a one-way street for the Soviet Union", which was seizing all the advantages of trade, credit and technology transfer while delivering nothing on the human rights issues Nov '86; visited Namibia as regime's guest Dec '86; again complained about Christians imprisoned in Soviet camps Dec '86; complained of unfair US discrimination against UK exports to USSR Jan '87; urged complete withdrawal of Soviet troops from Afghanistan and West's backing for Pakistan's support of Afghan rebels Mar '87; defended Turkish minority in Bulgaria Mar '87; his pro-Namibia International Society for Human Rights tricked pro-SWAPO Labour candidates into supporting pressure against SWAPO May '87; supported Turks in Cyprus July '87; backed Government support for space race Oct '87; urged restoration of corporal and capital punishment Nov '87; urged immediate abolition of national dock labour scheme Nov '87; backed right of cricketers to play anywhere, including South Africa Jan '88; visited Singapore as guest of Singapore Airlines Feb '88; opposed imports of furs from animals trapped with steel-jaw leg-hold traps Feb '88; voted to televise Commons Feb '88; backed anti-abortionists Apr '88; backed free optical and dental examinations July '88; visited Namibia as guest of its South-African-backed regime Oct '88; voted against Government on payment for dental checks Nov '88; introduced Schizophrenia After Care Bill (Lords), as Consultant to National Schizophrenia Fellowship Feb '89; visited Singapore to address Hitachi Executives Seminar Apr '89; was named a Government substitute delegate to Council of Europe Apr '89; criticized Bulgarian treatment of its Turkish minority July '89; warned of the need to quantify the increased cost of supporting elderly in under-financed private sheltered homes, which were numerous in his constituency Oct '89; visited Namibia as guest of its Foundation for Democracy in Namibia Oct-Nov '89; backed Turkish regime in Northern Cyprus Nov '89; wrote report on COCOM for WEU, urging its conditional retention to keep West's 10-year lead over Communist technology Dec '89; wrote report on Baltic States for Council of Europe at behest of Association of Estonians (£250), Lithuanian Association in Great Britain (£250) and Byelorussian Liberation Front (£120) Dec '89; complained that Government had combined in one Bill its NHS proposals as well as those for community care, with resultant underplay of need for specific training in care for mentally ill Dec '89; backed Teresa Gorman's effort to abolish Rent Acts Jan '90; led motion urging continuation of COCOM to limit technology transfer in arms to Soviet Union and Eastern Europe Feb '90; again pleaded the causes of the Baltic states Apr '90; visited Nepal for Christian Solidarity International May '90; urged ban on drinking near football grounds May '90; at behest of British Chiropractic Association, urged NHS recognition of chiropractors June '90; visited Tokyo to lecture to Hitachi Executives' Seminar June '90; backed removal of education from poll tax Nov '90; urged the feeding of the hungry in Russia and help for Palestinian Arabs Dec '90; in the wake of Bournemouth riots, urged chief constables be given right to veto any match Dec '90; introduced new clause to force local authorities to pay small businesses within 30 days Feb '91; again urged recognition of Baltic states' independence Feb '91; defended principle of poll tax, claiming it would have succeeded had it not been so high; "I was one of the 100-odd Conservative Members who advocated the removal of the cost of education to halve the community charge" Mar '91; visited Beaumont, Texas to address Law Day Ceremony as guest of Jefferson County Bar Association May '91; opposed by a German social democrat, was elected Chairman of Council of Europe's Committee for Relations with European Non-Member Countries May '91; was promoted a full delegate to Council of Europe June '91; visited Albania on behalf of Council of Europe Sep '91; backed restoration of county boroughs like Bournemouth Nov '91; urged lifting of COCOM controls on trade with Eastern Europe: "none of them pose any threat to us now" Feb '92; voted for Bill against hunting with hounds Feb '92; visited Angola as leader of Parliamentary delegation to observe peace process there, sponsored by Strategy Network International Feb '92; retained seat with majority of 14,823, up from 14,683, despite minor swing to Liberal Democrats of 0.29% Apr '92; was again named a full delegate to Council of Europe May '92; staged adjournment debate on schizophrenia July '92; against the Tory Whips' wishes, voted for £11,000 increase in MPs' office allowances July '92; visited Nagorno Karabakh to deliver humanitarian aid, sponsored by Christian Solidarity International July-Aug '92; staged debate on "the continued denial of human rights in China" Oct '92; asked about integrating complementary medicine into NHS Dec '92; backed Jim Lester's Bill to enable Britain's local government specialists to help eastern Europe's newly-democratic countries Dec '92; supported Malcolm Moss's Osteopaths Bill, because of his own support for chiropractice Jan '93; joined pro-EC 'Positive Europe Group' Jan '93; visited Hongkong to investigate Vietnamese 'boat people' for Council of Europe Jan '93; in pain from a recent operation, twice voted in his pyjamas to support the Major Government on the key Maastricht votes Mar '93; said he wanted "to see a decentralised, less bureaucratic and widening Community that will embrace EFTA and the new democracies, and a successful and expanding single market without a premature commitment to a single curency" May '93; visited Romania, paid for by Christian Solidarity International; SNI was formed to lobby against South African sanctions and in favour of UNITA June '93; visited USA, paid for by University of South Florida Sep '93; urged "the deployment of space-based missile defences, preferably in co-operation with the Russians" to cope with potential new nuclear aggressors Oct '93; said he opposed ordination of women, like his Roman Catholic church, because "if our Lord had meant there to be women priests - and certainly women bishops will follow - he would have chosen women to be among his Apostles and would have invited them to participate in the Last Supper" Oct '93; urged further liberalisation in Vietnam to allow more 'boat people' to be repatriated Oct '93; again urged need for "a national identity card system" Nov '93; was re-nominated to Council of Europe Dec '93; urged Government to warn Russian people "to avoid the fascist, ultra-nationalist policies of Vladimir Zhirinovsky" Feb '94; voted to restore capital punishment Feb '94; voted to reduce age of homosexual consent to 18, Feb '94; proposed Cardinal Hume be elevated to the Lords June '94; backed David Liddington's Chiropractors Bill, which he would have introduced had he had the opportunity Feb '94; welcomed Bournemouth's return to unitary status July '94; protested prosecution of Christians and Tibetans in China Mar '94; his "lost" research assistant and friends were found in Tony Blair's office Dec '94; voted for anti-hunting Bill Mar '95; introduced Bill to establish Peace and Freedom Day instead of the May Day bank holiday June '95; as one of the National Szhizophrenia Fellowship's consultants said that mental illness was one of the great challenges facing the NHS June '95; enthused about grant-maintained schools Nov '95; asked PM John Major about computer compliance Dec '95; told the Commons of his long involvement in Christian Solidarity International "which campaigns for on behalf of those who are persecuted for being Christian" and which had sent him on "on several missions behind the iron curtain to meet brave campaigners" and which gave him a KGB file describing him "as working at various times for MI5, CIA and Mossad"; then Baroness Thatcher "appointed me to the British delegation to the Council of Europe which provided me with an appropriate platform...from which to publicise the human rights situation which I had seen at first hand in the Soviet Union and its European allies; I did so, in five reports over 10 years"; "I was especially delighted that the Vienna concluding document of the Conference on Security and Co-operation in Europe...which only Caucescu's Romania refused to sign, defined freedom of religion according to the CSI definition that I had recommended"; "it was on the strength of those reports that I was appointed the Rapporteur on Russia, following its application for membership"; however expectations of Soviet democratic advance "were dashed by Russia's conduct in Chechnya a year ago"; "consequently, we suspended dealing with Russsia's application"; (in debate on Russian accession to the Council of Europe) Jan '96; backed David Winnick's Employment Bill to ban discrimination against the older unemployed Feb '96; as Chairman of the Council of Europe's Committee for Relations with European Non-Members, admitted that Romania had made very little progress toward democracy in the three years since it had been admitted Feb '96; as Chairman of the Council of Europe's Committee for Relations with European Non-Members, admitted that Romania had made very little progress toward democracy in the three years since it had been admitted Feb '96; introduced Freezing of Embryos Bill to ban the practice in hospitals where used for in-vitro fertilisation Apr '96; asked about the risks of long-range missiles supplied by North Koreans and possibly China to North African and Middle Eastern pariah states June '96, in an adjournment debate, again raised the question of computer compliance June '96; voted to keep the higher MPs' mileage allowance and £9,000 pay increase July '96; was named to the Assembly of Western European Union Dec '96; signed the 'Europe 97' advertisement of the European Movement Mar '97; asked whether single-currency computers were "millennium compliant" Mar '97; retained Bournemouth East by a reduced majority of 4,346, after a notional anti-Tory swing of 7.2%, with the seat altered by a sixth May '97; backed William Hague for the Tory Leadership June '97; he was named to the Science and Technology Select Committee July '97; re-introduced his Companies (Millennium Computer Compliance) Bill July '97; backed Mike Foster's Bill banning fox-hunting Nov '97; again raised the question of computer compliance Nov '97;backed the Mental Health (Amendment) Bill of Dr Julian Lewis to improve mental health facilities Dec '97; received 1st

Reading of his Millennium Conformity Bill Mar '98; after ten years as the Rapporteur on Palestinians for the Parliamentary Assembly of the Council of Europe, urged the final resettlement of the 3.4m displaced Palestinian Arab refugees Apr '98;

Born: 24 March 1940, Westcliffe, Essex

Family: Son, late Arthur Joseph Atkinson, motor trader, and Joan Margaret (Zink); m '68 Susan Nicola (Pilsworth), CCO worker; 1s Anthony '77; 1d Kathleen '73; divorced '92 but continued "living under the same roof for practical purposes;...no one else involved" (DA);

Education: Alleyn Court School; St George's College, Weybridge; Southend College of Technology; Chelsea College of Automobile and Aeronautical Engineering (First class Diploma);

Occupation: Parliamentary Adviser, to National Schizophrenia Fellowship (unpaid) '92-; ex: Partner, Exponential (public relations firm which has also worked for other firms like Dewe Rogerson, Grayling and Good Relations) '83-90; Parliamentary Consultant, National Schizophrenia Fellowship '88-90; Managing Director: David Graham Studios Ltd (printing and marketing) '72-82; Director: Modus Politics (Parliamentary and Public Affairs Consultancy) '82-85, David Graham Ltd (printing, design, PR and marketing) '72-82; Motor Retailer: in Chalkwell Motor Company (family motor agents and engineers) '62-72;

Traits: Dark but greying; tall-seeming; slender but very well-muscled; brisk; smiler; well-travelled, often with sponsorship; mountaineer; RC; health-preoccupied (benefited from chiropractice); "every Parliament needs one techno-nerd"; "Atkinson is that man" (Matthew Parris, TIMES);

Address: House of Commons, Westminster, London SW1A 0AA;

Telephone: 0171 219 3598/3600 (H of C);

Peter (Landreth) ATKINSON   **Conservative**   **HEXHAM '92-**

Majority: 222 (.5%)13,438 (28.21%) over Labour 5-way;

Description: Northumberland's sole Conservative constituency, made even safer in '83; England's second largest seat, with 1,000 square miles of beautiful country, devoted largely to agriculture and forestry, with prosperous market towns at Hexham and Corbridge; sheep and hill cattle dominate the north, with cereals and dairying in the south; it has the largest man-made forest and Kielder, Britain's largest man-made reservoir; it has factories for Crown Paints and Kleenex;

Position: PPS, to Lord Parkinson '97-; on the Select Committee on Scottish Affairs '92-; ex: PPS to Jeremy Hanley '95-96; on Select Committees on Deregulation '95-97, European Legislation '92-97; Vice Chairman '94-95, Secretary '92-94, Conservative MPs' Agriculture Committee; Suffolk County Councillor '89-92; Wandsworth Borough Councillor '78-82; on Wandsworth Health Authority '82-89;

Outlook: A male version of "Mary, Mary, quite contrary" and the unbridled voice of the constituency's big farmers, the British Field Sports Society and newspaper moguls; a "Rightwing free marketeer" (Rachel Sylvester, DAILY TELEGRAPH) who learned partisanship on the Wandsworth Council; an almost-parody partisan loyalist who was "pleased to be able to assist in defeating junk legislation" from the Labour Opposition, like the Hedgerows Bill and Clive Soley's press responsibility Bill; the former Deputy Director of the British Field Sports Society, recently its paid Consultant; was '92's locally-born last-minute, pre-election substitute for ex-MP Alan Amos, disgraced by a gay outing on Hampstead Heath; from '97 the only surviving Tory MP in the northeast, by a very narrow margin; a former journalist-executive in London and Suffolk who turned public affairs consultant;

History: He was elected as a Conservative to Wandsworth Borough Council, while News Editor of the London EVENING STANDARD May '78; "I was pleased and surprised to be part of the [Wandsworth Tory] team that had to sort out the mess left by Labour", including chairing the Disposal Committee which sold the houses Labour had municipalised; was elected to Suffolk County Council May '89; was selected for Hexham from a short-list of 17 from among 260 applicants to replace the sitting MP, Alan Amos, who had been forced to resign after a police caution for an alleged act of indecency with another man behind Jack Straw's Castle, a gay rendezvous atop Hampstead Heath; said a constituency spokesman: "the aim...was to find the best candidate; we feel fortunate in being able to put forward a candidate who is both a local man [by birth] and a family man"; the candidate followed this up by announcing he would try to sell the family's Suffolk home and move to Hexham: "if Mr Lamont does something about the recession, perhaps it might sell"; it did, within three months Mar '92; retained the seat with an increased majority, largely because the Liberal Democrat candidate declared himself gay, sinking to 3rd place behind Labour Apr '92; in Maiden, half-welcomed Minister of Agriculture John Gummer's achievement in reducing the worst impact of EC's agricultural proposals, although his farmers expected cuts in their income June '92; was elected Secretary of Conservative MPs' Agriculture Committee June '92; with a seat on the Scottish border, was named to Scottish Affairs Select Committee, because not enough Scots Tories were willing to serve; justified his appointment by saying he had a Scottish wife and had spent the past 17 Hogmonays in Scotland: "having destroyed my liver [drinking] in Scotland for a number of years, I think that makes me an honorary Scotsman" July '92; again claimed that BSE was on the wane and dangers were exaggerated by Labour spokesman who were injuring his beef-raising constituents July '92; backed retention of minimum value for horses exported to Continent for meat Nov '92; congratulated Scottish farmers on 44% increase in their livestock settlement, urging them to cross the Border to buy bargains in Hexham's cattle market Dec '92; joined the pro-EC 'Positive Europe Group' Jan '93; voted against 2nd Reading for Clive Soley's Freedom and Responsibility of the Press Bill Jan '93; sought extensively to amend Hedgerows Bill to allow their uprooting to repair ditches, helping to talk it out Mar '93; endorsed workstart Apr '93; in his amendment to Road Traffic Bill, sought new medical assessments for disabled would-be driving instructors Apr '93; criticised Clive Soley's press Bill as "an iniquitous attempt to censor" the press (and later helped talk it out) Apr '93; expressed disappointment at loss of contract bid for by Swan Hunter May '93; complained that regulations of Veterinary Medicines Directorate were "now so complex that each new product costs about £100,000 to license, which has resulted in some well-regarded products disappearing from the market" June '93; having drawn sixth place in the ballot for Private Members' Bills, was "surprised at the onslaught by a posse of single-issue pressure groups and lobbyists who pursued me for at least three weeks to persuade me to legislate against all sorts of things" Nov '93; claimed the nationalisation of the British coal industry had been "nothing more than an unremitting disaster" and that it needed privatisation because British Coal had become "featherbedded, feeble and incompetent"; said it was wrong that British Coal was "through their plans for colliery closures, helping to shape the future of the privatised industry", "while private companies are being frustrated in their efforts to take over pits which British Coal has closed"; amidst ex-miners' laughter, also alleged that, like US mines, private owners would be able to "land coal on the surface for £7 a ton" Jan '94; co-sponsored amendment rebutting Peter Hain's motion criticising Wandsworth for selling empty properties to Conservative supporters Jan '94; as a former Wandsworth councillor, said: "I am angry that families have to live on the Lambeth estate in unacceptable conditions merely because of the idleness, ineptitude and corruption of a bunch of Labour councillors" Jan '94; voted to restore capital punishment, especially for killers of policemen Feb '94; voted against reducing the age of homosexual consent Feb '94; was a Teller against Kevin Barron's Bill to ban tobacco advertising Feb '94; introduced his Bill to allow the Tour de France and similar events to take place in the UK Mar '94; congratulated the Government on changing, in the CAP negotiations, the method of paying premiums on lambs, which was valuable for his hill farmers Mar '94; welcomed the Inshore Fishing (Scotland) Bill because it sought to curb over-fishing for cockles in the Solway Firth, where he enjoyed shooting wildfowl July '94; defended privatised water companies against Labour criticisms July '94; complained the Countryside Commission had "ignored the arguments of farmers and landowners" in proposing an 81-mile walkers' trail along the Hadrian's Wall crossing his constituency Oct '94; was rated the 7th most assiduous voter in '93-94, Dec '94; in the OBSERVER was accused of giving lobbyist Hugh Mckinney facilities as his Researcher Jan '95; favoured continued export of veal calves by filibustering during preceding debate (on protection of Olympic symbols); Eric Martlew, the sponsor of the Protection of Calves (Export) Bill blamed him for "cynical methods" in blocking its 2nd Reading Feb '95; was named to the Deregulation Committee Mar '95; claimed that "many hill farmers in my constituency" would be "seriously damaged" by William Olner's Bill to outlaw the export of live animals under unsuitable conditions Mar '95; insisted that opencast mining was often better than deep mining July '95; predicted the demise of John McFall's Bill to outlaw the hunting of foxes, deer and hares with hounds July '95; backed the Army's demand for an expansion of its local Otterburn training area Jan '96; opposed a ban on advertising dangerous knives as a threat to the "freedom of the press" Jan '96; claimed that the northeastern assembly with tax-raising power desired by many Labour MPs would provoke widespread opposition Feb '96; backed the protection of red squirrels Feb '96; was one of the few who spoke against Paul Flynn's Bill to ban bull bars on four-wheel drives Mar '96; he opposed the banning of advertising of dangerous weapons like commando knives as "going down the slippery slope of restricting freedom of expression" Apr '96; he resigned as PPS to Jeremy Hanley after defying the Government policy on cross-media ownership; he and John Whittingdale (who resigned as PPS to Eric Forth) narrowly failed to halt Government plans to bar newspaper groups with 20% or more of the national readership from bidding for ITV franchises; their amendment to abolish the 20% limit - which barred the DAILY MIRROR - failed on a 14-13 vote during the committee stage of the Broadcasting Bill; he said: "I believe in liberalisation and free trade; I am fundamentally opposed to shutting the MIRROR out of the market" May '96; wrote: "in every respect, Mr Murdoch should be a Tory hero" May '96; backed Agriculture Minister Douglas Hogg on his cattle disposal scheme May '96; backed lower mileage allowance for MPs, but opposed 3% cap on salary increase and backed pensions based on £43,000 July '96; he helped lead the resistance to the tougher ban on handguns after Dunblane Aug '96; he was accused by Labour Spokesman Doug Henderson of violating the new MPs' guidelines in introducing amendments in committee to the legislation banning handguns while a paid Consultant, earning up to £10,000 from the British Field Sports Society, part of the pro-gun lobby, the British Sport Shooting Council Nov '96; urged the establishment of a "modest potato regime" Nov '96; backed Dr Robert Spink's Confiscation of Alcohol Bill as "an assault on yobbery" Jan '97; opposed the London sale by the Forestry Commission of local houses over the heads of local occupants Jan '97; he retained the unaltered seat with the vastly reduced majority of 222 over Labour, down from

13,438, on a pro-Labour swing of 13.9%; his seat was the only one retained by the Tories in the northeast May '97; as "a Consultant to the British Field Sports Society" opposed the new Government's Firearms (Amendment) Bill as threatening a "significant and law-abiding minority - those who practice target shooting at a high level of skill" June '97; was again named to the Select Committee on Scottish Affairs July '97; proclaimed his intention to kill off the "illiberal" Bill to ban fox-hunting sponsored by the new Labour MP Mike Foster on the ground that it would "take away the freedom of a minority group of people" July '97; defended hare-coursing as a matter of "individual rights" Oct '97; opposed ban on unpasteurised milk since "some of my constituents have been drinking green-top milk all their lives with no ill effects" Feb '98;

Born: 19 January 1943, Corbridge, Northumberland
Family: Son, late Major Douglas Wilson Atkinson, of 19th King George's Own Lancers who died in Burma in '45, and Amy (Landreth); m '76 Brione (Darley), Scottish daughter of late RN Commander; 2d Sophie '77, Eleanor '79;
Education: Cheltenham College;
Occupation: PR Consultant, on countryside matters to British Field Sports Society (at £5-10,000) and others, '92-; ex: Deputy Director, British Field Sports Society '87-92; Newspaper Executive: on Board of DEBEN JOURNAL, Suffolk '81-87, Chairman of Southern Free Press Group '81-87, associated with South London Guardian Group '81-87; Journalist: Reporter '61-73, broadcasting writer, Deputy News Editor, News Editor '73-81 on EVENING STANDARD; Reporter on NEWCASTLE JOURNAL '60-61;
Traits: Curly parted white thatch; specs; "genial" (Colin Wright, DAILY TELEGRAPH); hearty, pompous; middle-class speech; a clanger-dropper who likes being the only aggressively loyal partisan on the burning deck; enjoys: shooting, racing and gardening; had a black Labrador named 'Chips', a cocker spaniel called 'Gaff'(dcd), and a neutered cat called 'Woolly' (dcd), replaced by 'Mischief'; considers himself an honorary Scot by liquid intake;
Address: House of Commons, Westminster, London SW1A;
Telephone: 0171 219 4128/6547 (H of C); 01434 603777 (agent Susan Cresswell);

John AUSTIN(-WALKER)   **Labour**   **ERITH & THAMESMEAD '97-**

Majority: 17,424 (41.9%) over Conservative 6-way;
Description: South London working-class seat, redrawn in '95; includes 30,000 from Erith and Crayford and 30,000 from his former Woolwich seat; the area's political history has been complicated by the defection of two local MPs from Labour to the former SDP: James Wellbeloved in Erith and Crayford and John Cartwright in Woolwich, which he represented until '92;
Former Seat: Woolwich '92-97
Position: On the Select Committee on Health '94-; Chairman, all-party Slovenia Group '97-; Vice Chairman: London Group of MPs '92-, all-party Falklands Islands Group '97-, MSF Parliamentary Group '97-; Secretary: all-party Hungary Group '97-, Czech and Slovak Group '97-; Treasurer, all-party Gibraltar Group '97-; on Executive of British Group, Inter-Parliamentary Union and Commonwealth Parliamentary

Association '94-; Treasurer, Parliamentary Human Rights Group '97-; Chairman, all-party Osteoporosis Group '96-; ex: Chairman, Campaign Group '94-95; Secretary: Western Sahara Group '96-97, Albania Group '94-97; Greenwich Borough Councillor (Leader '82-87) '70-94; Chairman: London Ecology Unit, Emergency Planning Information Centre; Vice Chairman: Association of London Authorities '83-87, London Strategy Policy Unit '86-88; Chairman: Association of Community Health Councils '81-83, British Youth Council '69-71, Greenwich MIND '78-82;

Outlook: The Left internationalist defender of southeast London and its services; as fierce a campaigner against local short-changing on employment, NHS and fire services as he is against Turkish or Serbian aggression; pro-European but hostile to a single currency; favoured US military intervention in Bosnia but not in Iraq; "a doughty champion of his constituency interest" (Tory MP Nicholas Soames); the anti-nuclear, pro-Arab former Chairman of the Campaign Group; the dropping of the second half of his double-barrelled name undermines his nickname of 'JAWS'; the former Greenwich Council leader who ended the Parliamentary career of pro-nuclear John Cartwright; was a contributor to the now-defunct semi-Trotskyist LABOUR HERALD run by Ted Knight and Ken Livingstone; MSF stalwart;

History: Joined the Labour Party '59; was Agent to Francis Noel-Baker in Swindon Feb '66, Richard Marsh in Greenwich June '70 and Guy Barnett in Greenwich Feb and Oct '74; was elected to Greenwich Borough Council May '70; became Leader of Greenwich Borough Council in the year it increased rates by 59% '82; was selected for Woolwich to oppose John Cartwright, SDP defector, in succession to Audrey Wise, defeating NUPE official Pete Willsman and Militant-supporter Eddie McParland Mar '85; was one of group of council leaders who criticised Neil Kinnock for having appealed to them not to defy the Government's rate-capping plans; he said: "we are not prepared to cling to office to make Tory cuts"; also warned that if the Government tried to remove Labour councils from office, it had to reckon with trade unions in each area Mar '85; joined with Jack Straw in picketing the offices of London Docklands Corporation to try to stop the 70-acre Canary Wharf project Nov '86; at Labour's local government conference in Leeds, urged priority for reconstituting the GLC before any other metropolitan local government as "essential and crucial" for job creation Feb '87; was defeated by John Cartwright by 1,937 votes June '87; was re-selected for Woolwich Dec '89; urged an inquiry into where the profits from the London Marathon were going (later becoming a Trustee) Mar '91; criticised scale of rent increases in Thamesmead Town, particularly a three-bedroom maisonette which went up from £46.20 a week to £85, saying it was "bizarre" and "divorced from reality" Aug '91; as Bexley's Race Relations Officer, wrote to local MP, Edward Heath, to express concern that European Community law would enable others in Community to vote in England but perhaps diminish the voting rights of Commonwealth citizens; Heath reassured him Aug '91; in poll for the South East Coop's favourite politician, he came third after John Cartwright and Richard Balfe MEP Sep '91; backed Government funding of all adult education courses, even when not job-related Oct '91; urged continued pressure against the East London River Crossing, to try to get the European Commission to make a full environmental impact assessment; "I sought assurances from both John Prescott and Joan Ruddock about ELRC; John has given us a personal pledge that he will carry out a thorough review of all the transport proposals for the area before reaching any conclusion" Oct '91; was associated with Nigel Griffiths in campaign against dangerous toys Nov '91; said it was wrong for homosexual couples to be denied the experience of being able to adopt children Feb '92; demanded a public inquiry into proposals for Thames-side incinerators and power stations Feb '92; narrowly succeeded in ousting John Cartright despite latter's tactical support from Conservative voters Apr '92; in Maiden called attention to growth of unemployment in his constituency and closedown of Woolwich Arsenal, which provided an enormous 75-acre opportunity; as Chairman of the London Ecology Committee, also opposed the driving of an urban motorway through 8,000-year-old Oxleas Wood as part of the East London River Crossing May '92; complained that Greenwich had been given an inadequate grant as compared with Westminster June '92; complained of activities of racist British National Party in neighbouring Bexley June '92; urged the extended Jubilee Line should go as far as Woolwich, with the highest rate of unemployment in London (60%) Aug '92; visited Libya with Bernie Grant and Alan Simpson, as guest of Libyan Ministry of Foreign Affairs Sep '92; co-deplored rise of racism locally Sep '92; as a show of solidarity with the homeless, slept on steps of Greenwich Town Hall with Nick Raynsford and Peter Bottomley Oct '92; proposed ban on smoking in Parliament's dining rooms Oct '92; visited Slovenia Oct '92; visited Dominica, as guest of Dominica Labour Party Nov '92; agreed with Roy Hattersley that Asylum and Immigrations Appeals Bill was "squalid"; "there is a need for a process to deal with asylum applications; it must be based on the 1951 UN Convention on Human Rights and it must contain an automatic right of appeal" Nov '92; as co-author of a report on effects of Libyan sanctions, agreed that Libya should approach the UN and request a relaxation of sanctions on spare parts for air ambulances, while continuing the search for those who had caused Lockerbie air crash Dec '92; led motion urging new US President Clinton to help "implement the resolutions of the Security Council on Bosnia, Cyprus, Israel, the Middle East and Palestine Jan '93; led motion criticising Israeli Tourist Board's use of picture of ex-Palestinian East Jerusalem Dec '92; backed law suit to save Oxleas Wood Jan '93; asked Defence how much radioactive and contaminated soil they had removed from former site of Woolwich Arsenal Feb '93; welcomed 25th anniversary of 1967 Abortion Act Apr '93; with 16 other Labour MPs urged an end to appeasement of Serbian aggressors Apr '93; with 43 others urged President Clinton to intervene militarily in Bosnia May '93; urged legislation to include the specific crime of racial harassment, pointing out that "if four white youths had been killed by four blacks the outcry and white backlash would have been of enormous proportions" May '93; launched a motion on the decline of living standards and services in London May '93; voted against 3rd Reading of Maastricht Bill May '93; visited Jordan, Gaza and West Bank as guest of Labour Middle East Committee, with additional hospitality by PLO and Jordan May-June '93; urged Government to "bring pressure to bear on the Government of Israel to prevent them from frustrating the peace process" June '93; co-opposed US military intervention in Iraq July '93; acclaimed saving of Oxleas Wood as "a great victory for Londoners" July '93; visited Tirana, Albania July '93; voted against Defence Estimates, instead of abstaining Oct '93; visited northwest Turkey with Lord Avebury on behalf of the Parliamentary Human Rights Group, paid for by London Kurdish Community; complained about silencing of Kurds Oct '93; led motion attacking Turkish authorities for raid on Kurdish newspaper Dec '93; complained that the trouble with the local hospital trust was "the incompetence of those who are responsible for managing the health care trust but [also] the total unaccountability of the structure"; "I was replaced on the health authority by a company director...a computer company specialist; on his appointment, he said he knew nothing about the NHS, that he was a friend of the Director of Finance and the Chair of the Health Authority and that he assumed that was why he had been appointed" Jan '94; voted against restoring capital punishment, not even for killers of policemen Feb '94; voted to reduce age of homosexual consent to 18 or 16, Feb '94; backed Bill to ban tobacco advertising Feb '94; asked Foreign Secretary Hurd why Serbs were being allowed to hang on to any of the land they had taken Mar '94; asked for reversal of Tomlinson Report on London hospital closures on basis of new evidence from Professor Jarman Mar '94; strongly backed Dr Roger Berry's Civil Rights (Disabled Persons) Bill Mar '94; complained of having seen "brutal evidence of the destruction and depopulation of [Kurdish] villages" in Turkey Mar '94; urged more civil rights for disabled people, regretting Nick Scott had been the "fall guy" for their failure to advance May '94; backed Margaret Beckett for Leader June '94; voted for Beckett for Leader and Deputy Leader July '94; complained of growth of pollution, including sulphur dioxide, nitrogen dioxide and hydrogen chloride from local industrial processes, even without largest sludge incinerator planned for Belvedere July '94; co-urged defence cuts "to the level of other West European countries" Oct '94; co-opposed Turkish Government's persecution of its Kurdish opponents Oct '94; complained about arrest of Kurdish guerrilla spokesman about to address MPs Nov '94; urged favourable consideration of an East Thames river crossing to link Barking to Thamesmead Nov '94; voted with Left Eurosceptics against the European Communities (Finance) Bill Nov '94; was named to the Health Select Committee, replacing Tessa Jowell Dec '94; opposed "the leadership's attempt to railroad their plans to replace Clause IV through a special conference" Dec '94; backed Winston Churchill's motion urging an end to discrimination against British pensioners overseas Dec '94; condemned bombing of Kurdish paper Dec '94; was selected for the new seat of Erith and Thamesmead, embracing part of his old seat ??? '95; insisted London's Ambulance Service had been in deep crisis since 1991 at least Feb '95; introduced his Rape Victims Compensation Bill Mar '95; said the London Ambulance Service had been "characterised by catastrophe, crisis and chaos since the 1980s" June '95; again bemoaned the shortage of emergency beds in London July '95; with other Campaign Groupies, voted against Defence Estimates, instead of abstaining Oct '95; was one of 21 in the "awkward squad" who voted against procedure changes Nov '95; complained that the distribution of NHS resources hit the most needy Londoners Nov '95; urged redevelopment of the 75-acre derelict Royal Arsenal site, including a Royal Artillery Heritage Museum and industrial regeneration Nov '95; complained that "the incidence of breast cancer in the UK is not particularly high by international standards yet we have the highest recorded rate of mortality in the world" Dec '95; complained about the closure of Shooters Hill Fire Station Feb '96; was one of the 25 Labour MPs, mainly Campaign Groupies, who voted against the renewal of the Prevention of Terrorism Act, instead of abstaining Mar '96; was criticised by Labour Leader Tony Blair as "wrong and foolish" for a speech to Sinn Fein's Dublin annual conference in which he blamed PM John Major for the collapse of the IRA ceasefire Mar '96; after seeing Chief Whip Donald Dewar, issued a statement saying that making the speech from a Sinn Fein platform had been a mistake Mar '96; attended a meeting with Tony Blair to discuss Labour Party discipline May '96; with other Left unilateralists, urged reconsideration of Trident July '96; backed a ban on pro-Nazi skinhead bands in Woolwich pub Oct '96; declined to go to Libya on a trip organised by its lobbying organisation, GJW Dec '96; was described as "pro-European but...hostile to monetary union on the ground that it involves too strict a control of public spending" (Denis MacShane MP) Dec '96; in Dalyell's debate on lifting food and medicine sanctions on Iraq, he added: "there is nothing that Saddam Hussein has done against his Kurdish population that has not been done by the Turkish Government against their Kurdish population" Feb '97; was targeted as pro-abortion by the Prolife Alliance Party Feb '97; was targeted by THE FIELD as anti-hunting Apr '97; was elected for Erith and Thamesmead by a majority of 17,424 over his Tory opponent, a notional swing of 15.3% May '97; introduced a motion to ban smoking in the Palace of Westminster May '97; backed inquiry into murder of Stephen Lawrence May '97; criticised Turkish invasion of Iraqi Kurdistan May '97; introduced motion to seek continuance of road running as a popular sport June '97; voted against cuts in lone-parent benefits Dec '97; accepted congratulations for Greenwich Council, as its former Leader, as having first thought of the Millennium celebration, as part of the regeneration of the Thames gateway Jan '98; introduced Religious Discrimination and Remedies Bill to make discrimination unlawful in employment and provision of services Mar '98; abstained against tuition fees in Higher

Education Bill June '98; was one of 24 Labour rebels voting against Murdoch-style predatory newspaper pricing July '98;
Born: 21 August 1944, Blaby
Family: Son, Stanley George Austin, journeyman electrician, and late Ellen Elizabeth (Day); m '65 Linda Margaret (Walker); 2s Damien '72, Toby '75; 1d Zoe '75; separated '88; divorced '98;
Education: Glyn County Grammar School, Epsom; Goldsmith's College, New Cross; Bristol University (MSc in Policy Studies);
Occupation: Ex: Community Relations Officer, (Director, Bexley Council for Racial Equality) '74-92; Social and Community Worker '72-74; Labour Party Organiser '63-70; Medical Laboratory Technician '61-63;
Traits: Slim; dark, parted hair; greying beard; specs; wide forehead; slim; Humanist; marathon runner (took part in 1989 London Marathon after starting it as Mayor of Greenwich; was also in 1991 and 1993 London Marathons; could not race in 1994 because he fell down a manhole in Kampala; before that ran in Berlin (thrice), Budapest and Siberia); enjoys abseiling from tower blocks for charity; initially retained the hyphenated surname of his separated wife, which enabled him to keep intact his nickname, 'JAWS'; he abandoned the 'Walker' bit in '97;
Address: House of Commons, Westminster, London SW1A 0AA; 27 Bertrand Way, Thamesmead, London SE28 8LL;
Telephone: 0171 219 5195/2706 (Fax) (H of C); 0181 310 8705 (home);

Norman BAKER   **Liberal Democrat**   **LEWES '97-**

Majority: 1,300 over Conservative 5-way;
Description: The slightly shrunken seat embracing Lewes, the historic East Sussex county town and administrative centre, the ferry port of Newhaven and the resort of Seaford plus many villages, some affluent; the '95 boundary changes decanted to Brighton-Kemptown 16,000 voters including those in Tory-leaning Peacehaven, in exchange for suburban Polegate from Eastbourne; until the '97 election it had been a Tory seat for 123 years;
Position: On the LibDem Environment team '97-; on the Environmental Audit Select Committee '97-; Lewes District Councillor (Leader '91-97) '87-; Director: of Newhaven Economic Partnership '95-; ex: East Sussex County Councillor '89-97; President, Tourism Subcommittee in Assembly of European Regions '95-97; on the European Legislation Select Committee '97-98;
Outlook: Hyper-active Aberdeen-born East Sussex professional politician, the first non-Tory MP for Lewes since 1874; hit the Parliamentary scene running, spraying questions in all directions; among the worthiest and busiest of political busybodies; Parliament's most assiduous written questioner; "has made it his business to irritate everyone equally and appears to have succeeded"; "he has exercised his right to ask questions of Ministers with glorious disregard to their opinions of his qualifications as an interrogator and the nature of their answers" (Matthew Engel, GUARDIAN); "a persistent gadfly whose detailed questions are really starting to irritate and inconvenience Ministers" (Quentin Letts, DAILY TELEGRAPH); a fiery campaigner against secrecy; a twitchy-nosed hunter of Peter ("Scarlet Pimpernel")

Mandelson; in his first three months asked more questions than his predecessor, Tim Rathbone, had asked in 23 years; "any comment I could make on Mr Baker's policies, principles, methods or attitudes would be unprintable" (his defeated opponent, ex-MP Tim Rathbone); "Baker bores for Lewes in the way Kelly Holmes runs for England: with total energy and commitment"; "Norman Baker could preside over the [Millennium Dome's] Boredome Zone, asking interminable questions as visitors ran screaming for the exits" (Matthew Parris, TIMES); was initially hurt by Matthew Parris's legpull, but later enjoyed the recognition of becoming an awkward bugger in the style of Tam Dalyell; "would have mae a good headline-writer for The SUN" (LibDem colleague); a campaigner for the environment, economic regeneration, public transport, tourism, agriculture, constitutional reform; a cause groupie in Greenpeace, Amnesty International, Charter 88, Free Tibet;

History: He has "listened to Queen's speeches since I was in short trousers"; he joined the Liberal Party at 24. '81; was elected to Lewes District Council, ousting the Tory Leader from the previously safe Tory Ouse Valley ward by 524 to 312 votes May '87; against the trend, won the East Sussex County Council seat of Telscombe, held for 22 years by Sir John Lovill May '89; was elected Leader of Lewes District Council May '91; was selected as LibDem candidate for Lewes Jan '90; retained a strong second place (34.5%), but only cut the majority of the sitting Tory MP, Tim Rathbone, by 1,500 to 12,175 Apr '92; challenged Tim Rathbone over his clash of interest between serving as a consultant to Eurotunnel and the vulnerability of the ferry port of Newhaven and a tunnel-linked Downland-despoiling dual carriageway; Rathbone gave up his consultancy '94; apart from boundary changes, was helped in election campaign by local 'Labour Supporters for Tactical Voting' and the anti-European campaigns of the Referendum Party and the UK Independence Party, which mostly hurt pro-European Rathbone Apr '97; won the seat on his second effort, with a majority of 1,300, the two anti-Europe parties having taken 2,481 and 256 votes May '97; Baker promised to "work full-time; there will be no outside interests; I will keep in touch" May '97; in his Maiden speech, said the Blair Government's Queen's Speech was the first one he could largely agree with, although he thought it weak on the environment and lacked a Freedom of Information Bill May '97; in his first fortnight asked questions on legal aid, landfill, BSE, price marking, air pollution, and overseas aid May '97; presented the Public Records (Amendment) Bill to improve public access to public records June '97; voted against a total ban on handguns June '97; backed ban on fox-hunting June '97; as LibDem Spokesman sought to amend the Plant Varieties Bill, intervening 24 times to make it more transparent June '97; sought to persuade Peter Mandelson to make himself available for questioning on a regular basis July '97; led a motion opposing the patenting of genetic modifications July '97; led a debate urging a freedom of information Bill July '97; Matthew Parris devoted a whole column to him as a classic reincarnation of what Joseph Chamberlain classified as "the House of Commons bore" July '97; when a local Tory Councillor, Michael Murphy, referred to him as "Storming Norman, a bore of hurricane proportions", Baker dismissed his comments as "sour grapes": "the Tories are still smarting from losing the general election in Lewes" Aug '97; asked for reassurance that the US-controlled listening base at Menwith Hill was "not busying itself with economic sabotage against the UK" Aug '97; at annual conference in Eastbourne, reminded the welcoming LibDem Mayor that "here in Sussex we have the first Liberal Democrat MP to be elected since the 1920s" Sep '97; urged Government to back cuts in vehicle emissions Dec '97; asked about impact on the poorest 10% of withdrawing lone-parent benefit Dec '97; copmplained to Peter Mandelson about his refusal to provide information about the Millennium Dome's finances Jan '98; pressed about disposal of growing mountain of nuclear waste Jan '98; introduced Public Records (Amendment) Bill to cut the 30-year rule on secrecy, citing the still-secret 1935 report on "Taxi-drivers carrying fares without depressing flag" Jan

'98; deplored scarcity of strategic thinking on pricy Millennium Dome Jan '98; elicited annual running costs of C of E church buildings, including Lambeth Palace (£440,000); deplored £13.7m spent on supporting bishops Jan '98; urged tackling of backlog on local school repairs Jan '98; urged ban on recycling of radioactive materials Jan '98; urged Ministers travel to work other than by car Feb '98; complained that CPS's tight constraints curbed prosecution of vandalism Feb '98; asked how many people had MI5 files, how many telephones were tappped Feb '98; complained that crated primates had to fly for up to 58 hours before reaching UK Feb '98; urged at least a sharp cut in the 2.7m experiments on animals authorised annually in the UK Mar '98; opposed transplanting of animal organs to humans Mar '98; complained that rail travel costs had increased by 78% over inflation since '74, Mar '98; introduced Farming of Animals for Fur (Prohibition) Bill Mar '98; objected to cooling the Millennium Dome with HFC gases Mar '98; again asked MoD about US commercial spying from Menwith Hill Apr '98; accused Alastair Campbell of being the "unoffficial 23rd Cabinet Minister" and Downing Street of trying "to keep Mr Murdoch on board and his newspapers on side" Apr '98; urged a moratorium on planting genetically-modified crops in UK Apr '98; complained about difficulty of getting information from Minister Without Portfolio (Peter Mandelson) about his information-co-ordinating role) Apr '98; was discharged from the European Legislation Committee Apr '98; was rated as the top written questioner, with 859 posed in his first year May '98; urged tighter control of genetically-modified organisms (GMOs) May '98; presented a brief for the further development of Newhaven as a ferry port June '98;

Born: 26 July 1957, Aberdeen, Scotland

Family: He declines to provide family details; in Dec '97 he made a jokey New Year's resolution to acquire a girl friend, "very eco-friendly, with principles, who can cope with sombody who is idiosyncratic";

Education: Royal Liberty School, Romford; Royal Holloway College, University of London (BA in German with History);

Occupation: Teacher of English as a foreign language, Portslade '92-97; Eastbourne-based Researcher for David Bellotti MP '91-92; Westminster-based Environmental campaigner servicing all LibDem MPs, especially Simon Hughes '89-90; Manager, of a wine shop in Reigate '84; ran Hornsey railway station '83; London Regional Director, of Our Price record chain '80-83;

Traits: Wide-spaced eyes; dark, receding hair; wily-looking; residual Scots burr; "Stormin' Norman" who "simply crushed the life out of the [Tory] opposition" (SUSSEX EXPRESS); "gangling, awkward and entirely without charisma or self-awareness" (Matthew Engel, GUARDIAN); has a rather bizarre dress sense and looks as if he could do with a good bath; thinks information about his parents is "irrelevant"; also tried to resist inclusion in 1998 WHO'S WHO; plays a rock guitar and collects '60s and '70s rock and roll; enjoys group singing;

Address: House of Commons, Westminster, London SW1A 0AA; 2 Railway Cottages, Beddingham, Lewes BN8 6JP;

Telephone: 0171 219 3000 (H of C); 01273 480281/480287 (Fax);

WEEKLY UPDATES
The weekly shifts in Parliamentary conflicts are analyzed by us in WESTMINSTER CONFIDENTIAL (£50 for 40 issues). A sample issue is available to you on request.

'Tony' (Antony Brian) BALDRY   Conservative   BANBURY '83-

Majority: 4,737 (8.1%) over Labour 7-way;
Description: A lovely area including most of the Cherwell district of northeast Oxfordshire, especially Banbury and Bicester; in '95 it lost two rural wards to Witney;
Position: On the Select Committee on Trade and Industry '97-; ex: Minister of State, Fisheries and Agriculture '95-97; Under Secretary: Foreign and Commonwealth Office '94-95, Environment '90-94, Energy '90; PPS: to John Wakeham '87-89, to Lynda Chalker '85-87; on Select Committee on Employment '83-85; Secretary, Conservative MPs' Employment Committee '84-85; Chairman, Ethiopian Society '85-86; on Conservative Party's Academic Liaison Programme '86-90; on NEC of British Council of the European Movement '73-74; on Executive, European Union of Conservative and Christian Democratic Students '71-72; Research Secretary, Federation of Conservative Students '71-72;
Outlook: A pro-European moderate former middle-ranking Minister sitting out his party's tightened domination by Eurosceptics and Europhobes; an ambitious barrister-director whose assiduity, competence and loyalty were rewarded with office; his passionate Europhilia was tempered by his two years as Fisheries Minister; but he cannot stomach the "not for ten years" isolation enforced by Europhobic blackmail; a split personality: sometimes a pompously middle-class climber, sometimes an engagingly pragmatic 'wet'; an admitted Freemason in the Tory Reform Group and Bow Group; used to back capital punishment;
History: He joined the Conservative Party at 15, '65; became active Young Conservative at Sussex University in response to Left attacks '70-72; won legal action (Baldry v Feintuck) against Sussex University Students Union's payments to Left organisations '72; was founder-member, 'Students for a United Europe', first National Chairman, Young European Democrats '74; was PA: to Maurice Macmillan Feb '74, to Mrs Thatcher ("keeper of the hairspray" - PRIVATE EYE) Oct '74; was appointed to Mrs Thatcher's Private Office when she became Leader Feb '75; was awarded Robert Schuman Silver Medal for contributions to European politics '78; fought Thurrock June '79; was adopted for Banbury, from over 200 applicants, to succeed anti-EEC Neil Marten, March '82; voted to restore hanging for terrorism, for killing police and prison officers July '83; tried to stop attempted blockage of M40 extension July '83; saw no distinction in international law between US invasion of Grenada and Argentine invasion of Falklands Oct '83; urged Africa be enabled to feed itself instead of being provided with "high prestige projects" Dec '83; abstained against housing benefits cuts Jan '84; urged more safety at work Feb '84; rebelled against paving Bill to abolish GLC Apr '84; tried to simplify diversion of footpaths June '84; introduced Bill to force unions like NUM to pay for policing pickets in excess of TUC's permitted six July '84; urged famine help for Ethiopia Oct '84; backed Charter Movement (to democratise Tory Party) Oct '84; visited Ethiopia Nov '84; in debate on sinking of Belgrano, accused Tam Dalyell of having given comfort to the Argentine enemy during their Falklands aggression Feb '85; claimed Thatcherites' "simple prize" of free market offered no solution to economic problems Mar '85; urged ACAS be made responsible for better employee relations Mar '85; urged expansion of community programme Apr '85; declined to join Pym's 'Conservative Centre Forward' group as "a party within a party" May '85; defended large top persons' salary rise July '85; opposed

new Government tax on workplace nurseries July '85; urged better support of church schools July '85; in Tory Reform Group urged Tories to try again to talk to unions July '85; visited Ethiopia for Save the Children Fund and Oxfam '85; welcomed Government's decision not to sell Austin Rover Feb '86; urged reform of wage councils, rather than their abolition Feb '86; said ridiculous Sunday trading laws needed revision Mar '86; urged better choice of schools for middle class parents May '86; urged complete deregulation of Sunday trading with employment safeguards May '86; wrote "No Easy Answers" (on Education) for Tory Reform Group, urging the Tories to do "more than seek to improve the mechanics of middle-class parents' choice of schools" May '96; with Jim Spicer wrote 'Defence Begins at Home' pamphlet urging a new volunteer Home Guard June '86; opposed retaining right to cane July '86; opposed continuation of peremptory challenge for jurymen July '86; defended guaranteed rights of free speech for Rightwingers at universities Oct '86; opposed big rate increases for shire counties Oct '86; defended Teachers' Pay and Conditions Bill Dec '86; voted to restore capital punishment Apr '87; attacked Labour MPs for using order paper to charge MI5 agents with treason against Wilson Government May '87; supported poll tax as curbing spendthrift councils July '87; travelled in USA as its Government's guest Sep '87; defended giving parents primary power to decide their children's education Oct '87; pressed Merlyn Rees to support Douglas Hurd against efforts to reform the Official Secrets Act as William Whitelaw had backed him over Hosenball and Agee deportations Jan '88; urged a memorial for those who had died on the home front in World War II Apr '88; loyally claimed that "the community charge will at last put the community in charge" Apr '88; was reported being a Freemason in Martin Short's 'Inside the Brotherhood', which he had freely volunteered Apr '89; voted against war crimes trials of elderly Baltic immigrants Dec '89; was named Under Secretary for Energy, under John Wakeham, to whom he had been PPS, with responsibility for coal, electricity, nuclear power and energy efficiency Jan '90; said: "the coal industry is now better placed than ever to remain a major supplier of choice in the coming years" Feb '90; said: "when the Conservative Party wins the next election, we will privatise the coal industry - let there be no doubt about that" May '90; refused funds to reduce sulphur emissions from power stations June '90; backed Douglas Hurd for Leader Nov '90; was switched to become Under Secretary for Environment and the Countryside, under fellow-Freemason David Trippier Nov '90; spoke for Nigel Evans, unsuccessful Tory candidate in Ribble Valley Feb '91; announced £12m allocation to local councils for recycling May '91; stoutly defended achievement of privatised water industry June '91; announced benefits for "environmentally beneficial" hedgerows July '91; urged councils to speed their action to eliminate feces of 7.3m dogs Aug '91; he stripped to his trunks and took his children into the sea at Sandsend, near Whitby, which was later found to be polluted by raw sewage, with a bacteria count 200 times the EC limit Aug '91; claimed UK water charges were still among the lowest in Europe, averaging 17p a person per day Sep '91; insisted: "the safety record of the genetic modification sector of the biotechnology industry is good" Oct '91; announced shutdown of Coalite incinerator responsible for polluting Bolsover dairy farms Nov '91; insisted Britain was coping with hazardous waste increasingly well Dec '91; played down threat of pollution from Cornwall's Wheal Jane abandoned tin mine Jan '92; announced 'recycling credits' scheme Jan '92; launched council tenants' Charter Jan '92; ridiculed exaggerated fears of skin cancer from ozone holes Mar '92; retained his seat with majority down from 17,330 to 16,720, a swing of 3.62% to Labour Apr '92; having announced increase for Housing Association build to £2b for two years, backed consultation as part of tenants' rights; "we are fast moving away from the old municipal paternalism" June '92; freely confirmed he was a Freemason July '92; announced new planning guide for farmers Nov '92; accused Labour of exaggerating repossessions Jan '93; again announced impending legislation on illegal camping by new-age Travellers Mar '93;

opening a children's farm in Oxfordshire, "went beyond the normal politicians limit of kissing babies and picked up a piglet name Sybil to cuddle; unfortunately, Sybil chose that moment to lose a deposit of her own" (SUNDAY TIMES) Sep '93; voted against restoring capital punishment, even for killers of policemen Feb '94; voted to reduce age of homosexual consent to 18, Feb '94; in reshuffle, was moved sideways as Under Secretary to Foreign and Commonwealth Office July '94; the OBSERVER disclosed he provided facilities as his Researcher to Roger White of Williamson Tea Holdings Jan '95; attacked Teresa Gorman's Referendum Bill as prsenting an "absurd choice" Feb '95; in PM John Major's reshuffle he was promoted Minister of State for Fisheries under Douglas Hogg July '95; insisted that, as UK's Fisheries Minister, "I hold no brief for the European Union and I certainly hold no brief for the European Commission or the European Parliament"; but it was a distraction to pretend "we could unilaterally abandon the CFP [Common Fisheries Policy]" Nov '95; he claimed a "famous victory" for UK fishermen after Brussels negotiations; they did not agree Dec '95; described as "quite crazy" the European Court judgment allowing Spanish fishermen to sue the British Government for barring them from British waters Mar '96; announced the Cattle Disposal Scheme, into which he had been drafted by Douglas Hogg May '96; told the European Commission there was no chance of a 40% cut in the British fishing fleet until quota hoppers were barred June '96; introduced new fishing vessel decommissioning scheme June '96; welcomed halving of herring quota as an alternative to "complete closure in 1997" July '96; was described as Grand Officer of the Freemasons, in the Masonic Year Book 1996-97 Aug '96; insisted that UK-registered quota-hoppers "should have someone on board who can speak English" Nov '96; claimed victory in keeping quotas virtually unchanged; did not mention he had accepted 'spy in the cabin' satellite surveillance Dec '96; in Brussels, he voted against cuts in quotas Apr '97; in a letter soliciting southwestern voters' support for his party's defence of fishermen, ended "you can only be sure with the Conservatives" Apr '97; his own majority in minimally-altered Banbury fell to a third, with a 4,737 lead over his Labour opponent, down from 16,720, on a 9.9% notional swing to Labour; there were 7 contestants, including two anti-EU parties May '97; claimed Labour had won by accepting "much of Conservative philosophy" and predicted "a short honeymoon" May '97; backed fellow-Europhile Ken Clarke for the Tory Leadership May '97; warned that Treasury would have to finance a more generous decommissioning of fishing vessels July '97; was named to the Select Committee on Trade and Industry July '97;

Born: 10 July 1950, Hillingdon Hospital, Middlesex

Family: Son, Dr Peter Baldry, consultant physician, and Oina (Paterson) ex-nurse; m '79 Catherine (Weir) interior designer; 1s Edward '83, 1d Honor '85; divorced '95; she went off with her financial adviser, Leighton King; he took up with a former Sussex University girlfriend Caroline Noortman;

Education: Leighton Park (Quaker public school), Reading; Sussex University (BA Law);

Occupation: Barrister, Lincoln's Inn '75-; Director: Merchant International Group (advice on emerging markets) '97-, Tileform Plc (roofing contractors) '97-; Parliamentary Adviser: British Constructional Steel Association Ltd (£10-15,000), Construction Industry Council (£1-5,000) '97-; ex: Director: New Opportunity Press (books on employment, jobs and careers) '74-90, Newpoint Publishing Group Ltd '80-90, Ergo Communications Ltd '89-90; Shareholder, Heavy Goods Vehicles Parking Ltd (business venture to set up lorry parks with Tony Brooks, late Roger White, ex-MI5 officer, ex-MP and intelligence officer, and publisher Alexander Macmillan, later Earl of Stockton; stopped trading in '87); Adviser: British Surgical Trades Association '89-90, British Constructional Steelwork Association '89-90;

Traits: Dark; chubby; "below averagely unfit"; friendly; charming; open; "round, bustling, self-confident and/or pompous Baldrick" (Colin Welch, DAILY MAIL); "bumbling before his

time"; "the kind of husband whose wife would not entrust him with the washing up" (Matthew Parris, TIMES); can display his "portentous district attorney manner" (David McKie, GUARDIAN); "a resourceful social climber" (PRIVATE EYE); was a flatmate of Adam Macmillan and partner of Alexander Macmillan, later Earl Stockton; cricketer; Rugby player; in Territorial Army; Freemason in New Welcome Lodge (5139); tagged 'Baldrick' by his civil servants; Gummer-style public clanger-dropper: took his kids into contaminated swimming water, kissed a pig which crapped on him, at Brighton asked a civil servant which department was responsible for the decay of West Pier; "Yours, Minister"; 'Kissed a Pig Which Crapped' will make a very suitable title for any autobiography that I do" (AB);
Address: House of Commons, Westminster, London SW1A 0AA;
Telephone: 0171 219 4476 (H of C);

Mrs 'Jackie' BALLARD   **Liberal Democrat**   **TAUNTON '97-;**

Majority: 2,443 over Conservative 5-way;
Description: The unaltered seat embracing the large county town of Taunton plus four wards of West Somerset District, stretching across Exmoor to the Devon border; has two of the country's three packs of deer hounds and 1,000 dairy farms; the town is increasingly dependent on service jobs due to the decline of local manufacture; Taunton's voters voted for the Liberal Democrats in district, county and Euro elections before '97;
Position: On Select Committee on Catering '97-; LibDem Spokesman on Women's Issues and on Local Government '97-; ex: Somerset County Councillor (Deputy Leader '93-95) '93-97; South Somerset District Councillor (Leader '90-91, Deputy Leader '88-90) '87-91; on Liberal Democrats' Federal Policy Committee '92-95;
Outlook: The first-ever woman MP for this seat, likely to progress in her party because it has fielded so few women; a strongly-rooted local activist on the radical wing of her party, recruited by Paddy Ashdown but no longer one of his admirers; a self-confident tough-talking professional; the late Nancy Seear was one of her heroines; a promoter of devolution, citizens' participation in local government and an enhanced role for women in politics; a lone parent; a strong opponent of capping; pro-EU; a cause-groupie in Charter 88, Liberator, Amnesty International, Friends of the Earth; "fiercely anti-hunting" (NEW STATESMAN), opposing local deer-hunting as well as fox-hunting (favoured by her Tory-leaning farmers);
History: She was born into a non-political family, although her father's cousin was a long-serving Liberal councillor in Scotland; she spent her first ten years there, arriving in Somerset via Monmouth and LSE at 23, '76; she joined the Liberal Party '85; was elected to South Somerset District Council for Yeovil, Paddy Ashdown's constituency May '87; wrote that the new Liberal Democratic Party should have "a Leader who is committed to the values of Liberalism, justice, freedom and democracy and who can get those values across to the electorate; policy proposals should be formulated by think-tanks and accepted or rejected by the members of the party; the new Leader needs to have the ability to recognise people who are intellectually capable of formulating policy and the commonsense and humility to listen to the grassroots" June '88; became Leader of South Somerset District Council May '90; selected

to contest Taunton, polls showed her in the lead right up to the last days, when ex-Tories returned to the fold in fear of a Labour victory nationally; on a 6% swing to the LibDems, she managed to cut the majority of the sitting Conservative MP, David Nicholson, from 10,380 to 3,336, Apr '92; was re-selected to contest Taunton Oct '92; she gave up her post as Deputy Leader of Somerset County Council May '95; delivered a paper on citizen participation in local government at an international conference in Slovakia Nov '95; at annual conference, expressed her concern about young girls begging on the streets of Taunton and the paradox that one in five under-25s were not registered to vote Sep '96; at the invitation of the British Council, spoke in Jordan at a workshop helping potential women Parliamentarians there Nov '96; in the election campaign her leaflets hammered home the need for tactical voting by Labour supporters, who could not win the seat; "only Jackie Ballard or the Conservative can win here"; an OBSERVER-ICM Poll four days before the election was helpful, showing Nicholson on 39%, Ballard on 38% and Labour at 19% Apr '97; won the seat with 43% to Nicholson's 39% and Labour's 13.5% May '97; in her Maiden concentrated on the 2,000 local families in housing need June '97; in the debate on the "fundamentally flawed" Child Support Agency, she concluded that "perhaps the only alternative is to scrap it completely"; she focussed also on the need to assess better the self-employed absent parent June '97; led motion urging a ban on organophosphates June '97; took on her big local hunting lobby: responded to the huge Hyde Park pro-hunting rally by saying, "rural Britain does not need a small minority carrying out a barbaric sport" July '97; asked about "the risk to health from hunt kennels which are assessed to be unsatisfactory under the BSE enforcement programme" July '97; co-sponsored a motion urging a lower council tax banding for mobile homes July '97; with David Heath fought a fruitless battle to reverse capping of Somerset July '97; clashed with pro-hunting lobby when fox-hunting was banned from Exmoor Aug '97; at Eastbourne annual conference, despite backing from Paddy Ashdown, failed to secure adequate backing for allocating to women half the places on all short-lists, but insisted "there was a clear will of conference to improve equality" Sep '97; urged PM Blair to set up a Royal Commission on the use and abuse of drugs Oct '97; with two of the UK's deer-hunting packs in her constituency, strongly backed end of mammal-hunting, as intended in Mike Foster's Bill Nov '97; signed up for European Movement's campaign: 'Europe: A Force for Fairness, Equality and Opportunity for Women' Nov '97; co-sponsored a motion urging Government help with grants to Barnardo's to provide children exported to Australia to "gain details of their natural families" Dec '97; sharply attacked cuts in lone-parent benefits: "those of us who are single parents know that having sole day-to-day responsibility for a child is even harder work and is more expensive" Dec '97; backed deregulation of emergency contraception Jan '98; said women had far "yet to go before the glass ceiling is broken, but the ceiling is being cracked, and progress is being made towards equality" Feb '98; urged "a system of national registration for all child-care workers" Feb '98; again urged a replacement for the Child Support Agency, after wide consultation Feb '98; spoke on inadequacies of NHS dentistry Feb '98; urged EU sanctions against Burma for repressing democrats and Karens May '98; was among the 'top 100' written questioners in her first year, clocking up 146, May '98; put down a motion responding to disparaging TIMES article on Taunton and its people July '98;

Born: 4 January 1953, Dunoon, Scotland

Family: Daughter of Alexander Mackenzie, retired shopkeeper, and Daisy Margaret (Macdonald), retired nurse; m '75 Derek Ballard, quantity surveyor; 1d, Christine '79; divorced '89;

Education: Various Scottish state primary schools; Monmouth School for Girls (where she started a debating society and was "generally rebellious" and "a trouble-maker" (JB); LSE (BSc in Social Psychology);

Occupation: Local Government Adviser with the Association of Liberal Democrat Counciillors (ALDC) (advising LibDem councillors across the country) '94-; Author: 'Beyond Public Question Time' (1995), 'On The Council' (ALDC 1993); ex: Lecturer in Psychology, Computing and Communications in Further Education colleges '81-93, Social Worker in London's East End '74-76;

Traits: Large, square, with no neck; wears her hair short; "bears a striking resemblance to Ann Widdecombe" (TIMES Diary); unphotogenic; good sport; "very tough" (LibDem activist to Simon Hoggart, GUARDIAN); her aggressive manner can be off-putting on first encounter; likes Cajun music, also Celtic rock; is sensitive to the problem of leukaemia (her godson, Harry Burden, died of it at seven);

Address: House of Commons, Westminster, London SW1A 0AA; 71 Greenway Crescent, Taunton, Somerset TA2 6NH;

Telephone: 0171 219 6247 (H of C); 01823 324512 (home); 01823 337874 (constituency); 01823 323075 (Fax);

'Tony' (Anthony Louis) BANKS   **Labour**   **WEST HAM '97-**

Majority: 19,494 (59.7%) over Conservative 6-way;

Description: Altered and renamed East End seat with his smallish former Newham NW expanded by three wards from abolished Newham South; over a fifth of its voters are Afro-Caribbean and almost a fifth Asian; 30% in large new council blocks, 47% owning crumbling houses on Victorian streets; the second most deprived local authority area in the country, with almost 10,000 households without their own bath or inside toilet;

Former Seat: Newham North West '83-97

Position: 'Minister for Sport' (Under Secretary for Culture, Media and Sport '97-; on Select Committee on Procedure '88-; ex: Chairman, Britain-Nicaragua Parliamentary Group '87-97; Delegate to Council of Europe (Alternate '90-92) '92-97; Spokesman, on London '92-93; Chairman, PLP's London Regional Group '87-92, Assistant Spokesman, on Social Security '90-91 (resigned over Gulf War); Whip (London) '87-88 (resigned); last Chairman of GLC '85-86, Chairman, its Arts Committee '81-83, its Councillor for Tooting '81-86, for Hammersmith '70-77;

Outlook: Quick-witted, hyperactive, widely-popular, verbally-incontinent, rooted hard-Left former rebel; he anticipated his unexpected post by saying eleven months earlier: "being Minister for Sport is not so much a job as a sending to heaven without having to die first" (TB); "notorious for his caustic and entertaining tongue" (Leslie Geddes-Brown, DAILY TELEGRAPH); "the lippiest man about the House, rarely misses a chance to jump on a passing bandwagon or grab a passing microphone" (SUNDAY TIMES); "but for all his noise, he is not an empty vessel" (Mike Rowbottom, INDEPENDENT); was rated the top backbencher by fellow MPs in '91; "the quickest heckling gun in the West" (Austin Mitchell MP); "the Left's most effective comedian" (Ian Aitken, GUARDIAN); "beneath the humour there is a serious ambition: to be the first directly-elected Mayor of London" (Emma Tucker, FINANCIAL TIMES); has learned how to exploit the Parliamentary stage while admitting, "I don't think we will ever be allowed to use Parliament to achieve socialism"; formerly the leading bantam cock in Labour's backbench awkward squad; was an assiduous, informed questioner (asked most questions in '83-87 Parliament}; "both an accomplished sniper at the [Tory] Government front bench and the funniest MP in the House"; "contrary to popular prejudice, Mr Banks has his merits, not the least of which is an inability to take himself or much else too seriously" (Andrew Rawnsley, GUARDIAN); favours a democratic federal United States of Europe; once wanted to move to Euro-Parliament from his once-threatened seat; wanted air strikes to curb the Bosnian Serbs; also wanted to decriminalise cannabis; the municipal socialist who led the Commons rearguard action against GLC abolition; "crawling from the wreckage of the GLC, he has survived it better than Ken Livingstone" (TIMES); an art-for-the-people enthusiast; an obsessional animal-lover ("I've been involved in virtually any animal campaign you could mention"); backed 'troops out' of Ulster where he was born; was TGWU-sponsored;

History: His father, an engineer and then a diplomat, was a Labour and trade union activist ; at 20 Tony left the Young Liberals to join the Labour Party, inspired by Harold Wilson's 'white heat' speech '63; was elected to the GLC for Hammersmith May '70; contested hopeless East Grinstead June '70; was elected to Lambeth Borough Council (where he served with Ken Livingstone and John Major ("a fairly competent Chairman of Housing" [TB]) May '71; contested Newcastle North Oct '74; urged abolition of Lords Oct '77; urged abolition of City '77; worried about pro-Tory prejudices of 'Archers' Sep '78; helped launch Labour Co-ordinating Committee Mar '79; contested Watford May '79; met with Tony Benn and other Leftists to try to get rid of James Callaghan as Leader Oct '80; was elected to GLC for Tooting May '81; backed Benn for Deputy Leader Sep '81; was selected for Newham NW but endorsement was delayed by retiring MP Arthur Lewis's protest Nov '82; was endorsed Feb '83; urged Jubilee Gardens be renamed Peace Gardens Feb '83; stopped GLC's Royal Opera House grant and switched much of the arts budget to community-based arts with a pop and ethnic emphasis, closing Festival Hall's champagne wine bar as it was "totally elitist" May '83; won Newham NW despite candidacy of Arthur Lewis, who attacked him as a Militant June '83; offered to resign his seat in favour of defeated Tony Benn, to enable latter to contest Leadership June '83; in his Maiden speech said "the GLC is not going to be seen as some sort of South Bank equivalent of the Belgrano - to be destroyed merely to satisfy the power lust of the Prime Minister"; also condemned the DAILY MAIL, SUN and DAILY EXPRESS as "semi-fascist comics" July '83; rejected MPs' pay increase, demanded doubled allowances July '83; complained that live animals were used to test wounding effects of live ammunition Feb '84; claimed that import of human organs from 3rd World countries was "a form of cannibalism" Feb '84; secured confirmation that live human volunteers were used for chemical warfare experiments at Porton Down Feb '84; urged inquiry into police membership of Freemasons Mar '84; said Arts Council was dominated by white, middle class, male values June '84; was found by the Committee of Privileges to have committed a breach of privilege when he had suggested that the GLC should practice "selective vindictiveness" against London Conservative MPs who voted to cut GLC spending July '84; described MPs' working place as a "legislative slum" July '84; was arrested in street demonstration in front of South African Embassy with Stuart Holland MP July '84; complained that descriptions of striking miners as Scargill-organised "lawless thugs" was a figment of "London-based fat-cat journalists" Sep '84; with Jeremy Corbyn accepted support of Revolutionary Communist Group in unsuccessful challenge to MP Bob Hughes' leadership of Anti-Apartheid Oct '84; there was resistance to his determination to turn the GLC Chairman's post into a political one for its last months Feb '85; expressed concern about great tortoises on fire-threatened Galapagos Islands Mar '85; he split with Ken Livingstone over latter's compromise in accepting forced cuts in GLC spending Mar '85; urged "political will and financial commitment" to reducing football violence Apr '85;

conducted campaign against Department of Environment's extravagance Apr-May '85; in his first two years he asked over 1,500 questions at a cost of £63,560, many of them supplied by GLC officials June '85; raised desperate plight of Newham youth June '85; resisted Edward Leigh's Bill to depoliticise town hall spending July '85; extolled the achievements of the Greater London Enterprise Board July '85; was twice reselected with black section support Jan-Feb '86; was GLC Chairman for its last year, ending Mar '86; attacked the GLC's successor, the London Residuary Body, as "the Government's dumping ground...in a vain attempt to clear up the appalling mess left in London" May '86; urged exclusion of turtle soup and frogs' legs from Westminster menus June '86; raised question of miscarriage of justice in 'Birmingham Six' pub bombing July '86; raised high incidence of death among Falklands penguins, suggesting they were contaminated by sunken nuclear weapons rather than lead concentrations July '86; received 37 votes for Shadow Cabinet, on Campaign Group slate Oct '86; refused to return £50,000 worth of GLC silver, insisting on holding it for its successor authority Nov '86; criticised secretive and one-sided operations of London Residuary Body Dec '86; pressed for a £5,000 cut in salary of Arts Minister Dec '86; asked about tapping of MPs' phones Dec '86; urged a bigger Arts Council budget Jan '87; claimed the few local jobs provided by London Docklands Development Corporation were outweighed by increases in local property costs Jan '87; urged women judges for rape cases Feb '87; spotlighted false or malicious imprisonment cases Mar '87; wore an African National Congress T-shirt in Commons as a "legitimate protest" against Apartheid Apr '87; blocked City of Westminster Bill May '87; since his selection had been disallowed because of black sections participation, he had to be imposed on seat for election May '87; introduced Bill to make voting compulsory May '87; complained his parrot had almost been killed by the lead in Newham water July '87; was again arrested in anti-Apartheid demonstration July '87; received 42 votes for Shadow Cabinet on Campaign Group slate July '87; was named London Whip July '87; visited Panama as its guest Sep '87; supported Campaign Group effort to restore a Commons pass to Jeremy Corbyn's ex-IRA-sympathising research assistant Nov '87; he rejected being awarded SPECTATOR's 'Backbencher of the Year' award because it was a Tory weekly Nov '87; introduced a Bill to ban war toys Dec '87; backed "a properly funded dog warden scheme that is paid for by the license fees that are paid by responsible dog owners" Dec '87; sought an emergency debate on abolition of ILEA Feb '88; sought unsuccessfully to refer a column by Andrew Rawnsley of The GUARDIAN to the Committee of Privileges Mar '88; defended General Noriega, an alleged drug-runner whom he had met, as the intended victim of a US plot to hold on to the Canal Zone Mar '88; resigned as London Whip because he felt Ron Brown had been over-punished by also having the Labour Whip removed May '88; urged MPs be permitted to table an unlimited number of questions, but only one question for oral answer to any one Minister on any one day May '88; co-sponsored Tony Benn's Bill to disestablish the Church of England May '88; introduced Bill to put health warnings on liquor bottles June '88; had been the third most assiduous questioner in the previous year, with 777 questions July '88; was the 4th most popular MP Sep '88; with other Campaign Groupies, voted against Defence Estimates, instead of abstaining Oct '88; received 50 votes for Shadow Cabinet, with 86 votes qualifying Nov '88; with other Campaign Groupies, voted against Prevention of Terrorism Bill, instead of abstaining Dec '88; in a debate on organ transplants, said: "may I put in a bid for Cecil's plonker? one careful owner" Mar '89; introduced Bill for an elected mayor of London Dec '89; said Japanese firms were using UK as a "doormat" to secure entry into EC Apr '89; was on joint committee which urged radical changes in Private Bill procedure Apr '89; was named an alternate Labour delegate to Council of Europe Apr '89; urged Stratford become interchange for Channel Tunnel link May '89; received 62 votes for Shadow Cabinet, with 104 qualifying Nov '89; was found to have been the 3rd most frequent intervener and the 6th most

assiduous questioner in previous two years Nov '89; asked whether British Government would
have approved the Soviet Government treating a country the way the way they approved the
US invasion of Panama Dec '89; complained that Mrs Thatcher was allowing Hongkong to
import ivory again Jan '90; introduced Protection of Badger Setts Bill Jan '90; confessed to
paying the equivalent of his rates bill instead of the poll tax Mar '90; urged sanctions to force a
halt to Japanese whaling Mar '90; was renamed an alternative delegate to Council of Europe
Apr '90; backed an elected London council and directly-elected mayor May '90; voted for
voluntary euthanasia Bill May '90; voted for non-smoking areas May '90; lost his Badgers Bill
because of intervention of Sir Charles Morrison and "the determination and selfishness of the
fox-hunting lobby" June '90; moved a resolution on London homelessness June '90; said: "I
look forward to a socialist United States of Europe" June '90; introduced Bill to abolish
fox-hunting July '90; was rated fifth most popular backbencher Sep '90; received 49 votes for
Shadow Cabinet, with 85 qualifying Oct '90; co-sponsored another Badgers Bill Nov '90; was
named Assistant Spokesman on Social Security Nov '90; signed a Benn-led motion opposing
use of military force against Iraq Dec '90; resigned as Assistant Spokesman on Social Security
to vote with other Campaign Groupies against Gulf War Jan '91; complained that "those
American, British and French pilots who have been risking their lives realise that they are
facing weaponry that was provided by their own countries" Feb '91; introduced Bill to abolish
political honours Apr '91; urged abolition of commercial whaling Apr '92; said PR was a
"fairer system" May '91; was renamed a substitute delegate to Council of Europe June '91;
complained of way Dangerous Dogs Bill was being rushed through June '91; urged a
fixed-term Parliament Oct '91; secured 41 votes for Shadow Cabinet, with 87 qualifying Oct
'91; again had to resign from Social Security team after defying party Whip over the Gulf War
Oct '91; supported armed intervention in Yugoslavia Nov '91; said: "I want a United States of
Europe, with our own independent foreign and defence policies; of course it must be a
democratic federal Europe" Dec '91; criticised televising of Kennedy rape trial Dec '91;
suggested legalising of soft drugs Jan '92; led motion backing ban on ivory trade Jan '92; led
motion opposing culling of badgers Jan '92; led motion opposing "Japanese slaughter of minke
whales" Jan '92; criticised Tony Benn for not caring about dislocation for people in King's
Cross terminal area; still insisted on interchange in Stratford, despite party decision to back
King's Cross Jan '92; suggested sacking the headmistress as well as her persecuting governors
at opted-out local Stratford School, with its return to the local education authority Feb '92;
introduced Bill for fixed-term Parliaments Mar '92; retained seat with majority up from 8,496
to 9,171, a swing to Labour of 2.59% Apr '92; announced he would seek to become an MEP
Apr '92; was elected a Labour representative on the Council of Europe May '92; withdrew his
offer to host Commons launch of autobiography of madame Lindi St Clair June '92; backed
referendum on Maastricht June '92; urged use of WEU military forces against Serb irregulars
shelling Sarajevo July '92; conceded Boundary Commission would probably deprive Newham
of one seat June '92; backed campaign to relocate LSE in County Hall instead of selling latter
to Japanese hotelier June '92; won 42 votes for Shadow Cabinet, with 104 qualifying; was
named Spokesman on London, serving on Labour's Transport and Local Government teams
July '92; nominated anti-EC Bryan Gould for Deputy Leader but voted for pro-EC Margaret
Beckett July '92; signed petition to legalise marihuana July '92; complaining about being a
"successful failure", convulsed TRIBUNE meeting with blue jokes about David Mellor Sep
'92; was rated the 26th most active questioner, with 114 questions in first three months of
session Oct '92; flew to Seattle and Cincinnati as guest of British Airways, Boeing and General
Electric Oct '92; sought to replace anti-EC Bryan Gould on Labour's front bench Oct '92; was
forced by Speaker to retract personal abuse aimed at Health Secretary Virginia Bottomley for
threatening to close ten London hospitals Oct '92; backed Jubilee Line extension Oct '92; came

third -after Ron Davies (78) and George Robinson (77) - with 34 votes in contest to succeed Bryan Gould in Shadow Cabinet Nov '92; launched Labour's 'London Policy Forum' Nov '92; was re-appointed to Procedure Committee Dec '92; reaffirming his devotion to a federal Europe, urged a renegotiated Maastricht treaty to avoid its deflationary impact Dec '92; led motion deploring National Heritage requiring a £15,000 fee from London Marathon for use of Royal Parks Feb '93; discovered the Channel Tunnel rail link was due to go through a tunnel beneath his Victorian house in Forest Gate Apr '93; urged air strikes against the Belgrade Government unless it curbed the Bosnian Serbs Apr '93; introduced Bill to make illegal the hunting of foxes with dogs Apr '93; raised with Labour Leader John Smith whether it was compatible for him to remain Spokesman on London while a Delegate to the Council of Europe; Smith agreed that it was not, but that he should not come off until the next reshuffle (when it was assigned to Frank Dobson); Smith assured him: "You will be a Minister in my next Government" June '93; visited Azores for International Fund for Animal Welfare Aug '93; won 46 votes for the Shadow Cabinet (up from 42) Oct '93; voted against Defence Estimates, instead of abstaining Oct '93; visited Hongkong as guest of its government Nov '93; led a motion urging decriminalisation of cannabis Dec '93; "I gave a cheque to the Fees Office for £8,000, the excess of my office costs" Dec '93; was again named a Delegate to the Council of Europe (which John Smith told him meant he had to give up his post as Spokesman for London) Dec '93; urged having Commons condom machines to save Conservative MPs from embarrassment of further illegitimate children Jan '94; voted against restoring capital punishment, even for killers of policemen Feb '94; voted to reduce age of homosexual consent to 18 or 16, Feb '94; joked that the Church's property losses showed God's disapproval of property speculation Mar '94; favoured decriminalising cannabis, insisting: "I have never in my life taken or used illegal substances such as cannabis" Mar '94; in debate on the Arts, pointed out that they generated £7,465m a year, with net overseas earnings of £1,300m, with employment given to unskilled and semi-skilled as well as creative artists May '94; sought to outlaw discrimination against fat people Mar '94; the Speaker accused him of going "over the top" when he accused Chancellor Clarke of being "a pot-bellied old soak" engaging in "intimidatory begging" June '94; said, "since I was elected, I notice that I have tabled 6,919 questions; if [like two Tory MPs] I had received £1,000 a throw for each of those, I would have netted a cool £7m, which would have meant I could have faxed this speech from Mustique" July '94; voted for Margaret Beckett for Leader July '94; won 42 votes for the Shadow Cabinet, with 97 qualifying Oct '94; back from the Antarctic, sought to defend the functioning of the UK's Faraday station there Feb '95; urged legalisation of cannabis Feb '95; voted against easing of pub licensing Feb '95; urged the promotion of vegetarianism Mar '95; said he would be willing to pay extra taxes to compensate farmers for not exporting veal calves Mar '95; deplored treatment of English football supporters abroad June '95; received 41 votes for the Shadow Cabinet, 107 qualifying Oct '95; signed motion honouring Greece's 1940 anti-Nazi heroism Oct '95; voted against Defence Estimates, instead of abstaining Oct '95; was told that he would be barred from asking questions on animal welfare because his Researcher was financed by the International Fund for Animal Welfare Nov '95; "I very much welcome the concept of a single [European] currency" Dec '95; joked about building congregations by privatising the church, setting up a regulator ("Ofgod, or something like that") and a few consultants Dec '95; attacking local litter, said "I seem to represent some of the dirtiest constituents in the country" Jan '96; opposed guillotine on anti-terrorist legislation Mar '96; made a brilliant ranting attack on Eurosceptic Bill Cash's referendum proposal, "washing over the [Euro]sceptics, taunting them reviling them , showering them with his contempt like so much spittle" (Simon Hoggart, GUARDIAN); Banks ended: "I don't like this...Bill because I don't like being dictated to by a rich greengrocer...who apparently lives in Mexico and pays no taxes in this country" June '96; welcomed President Mandela's speech to Parliamentarians "as someone who was arrested twice outside South Africa House" July '96; complained: "there are far too many policy changes originating from front-benchers in tight media corners with the result that the ground always seems to be moving beneath our feet" July '96; backed a 3% limit on MPs' pay increase July '96; one of seven Labour MPs who defied the leadership and put in for the Shadow Cabinet, receiving 47 votes (149 qualifying) July '96; asked whether he would take the job of Mayor of London, replies: "is the Pope a Catholic?"; in a poll came fifth with 9% support Nov '96; insisted Hongkong's prosperity "is not a triumph of monetarism and rapacious capitalism; it is a triumph of planning and regulation, as well as of energy on the part of the people" Nov '96; baited the Conservative Church Commissioner Sir Michael Alison for allowing hunting on church lands, reminding him of St Luke and the five sparrows Dec '96; insisted it would be "economic lunacy" to leave the EU Dec '96; asked: "other than the public hanging of Tony Benn and Dennis Skinner, what more could Labour do to reassure Middle England of our fitness to govern?" Dec '96; was again named a Delegate to the WEU Assembly Dec '96; sponsored a motion deriding as "vulgar and obscene" the excessive publicity for Galliano and McQueen, the new young British designers of "over-priced and grotesque flights of fancy for hanging on the limbs of the super-rich" Jan '97; suggested South Africa should host the 2006 World Cup Jan '97; retained his altered and renamed seat of West Ham by a doubled majority of 19,494, a notional pro-Labour swing of 15% May '97; was "gobsmacked" by Blair's offer to make him 'Minister for Sport' instead of Tom Pendry May '97; was caught on camera crossing his fingers "for good luck" when taking the oath May '97; was criticised for suggesting fielding a possible United Kingdom football team instead of the existing four nations' teams May '97; said Lord Laurin's active campaigning for the Tories was "not a shrewd career move", causing Laurin to resign as Chairman of the UK Sports Council May '97; replying to the 'Sports for All' debate, said "my role is as the long-stop for those who are cricketers, or as the sweeper for those interested in soccer"; said the location of the national academy of sport was narrowed to three locations June '97; deplored "soft porn" tendency of tabloids to concentrate on women tennis players' shapes and underwear instead of their sports abilities June '97; named David Mellor as head of a football task force because he needed someone with Home Office and Foreign Office experience, who understood how government worked and was happy to say unpopular things about football Sep '97; at Brighton conference's Tribune Rally joked about the Tories having elected "a foetus as a Leader", adding: "I bet a lot of Tory MPs wished they hadn't voted against abortion"; Tony Blair pressed him to apologise for his "tasteless" joke; he had also been cruel about Peter Mandelson, warning Labour listeners who had not voted for him to carry a clove of garlic for protection Oct '97; said that stands could be restored temporarily to football grounds in international matches Oct '97; urged fans hurt during the match against Italy to write to him about their treatment Oct '97; congratulated Michael Fabricant for putting the "camp" into "campanology" May '98; had his wrist slapped for backing a pro-animal motion without noting his researcher was subsidised by a pro-animal body May '98; pushed for more women and ethnic minorities in sports governing councils June '98; criticised Chancellor Brown for taking too big a tax cut from the National Lottery June '98;

Born: 8 April 1943, Belfast

Family: Son, Rene (Rusca) and the late Albert Banks, abattoir worker, engineering fitter in BSA, Sergeant Major in the 8th Army, then a diplomat (First Secretary in the postwar Warsaw Embassy), who was "very active in the Labour Party"; "you didn't cross him; I loved my Dad but I didn't love the beltings he use to give us"; has a sister, Angela, a former beautician; m blonde, attractive Sally (Jones), Carmarthen-born social work team-leader at Newham General Hospital, who is a "keen campanologist";

Education: St John's Primary School, Brixton; Archbishop Tenison's Grammar School, Kennington Oval; rebellious, he was caned and had to make up for failed exams; York University; LSE, University of London (BA);

Occupation: A collector of political memorabilia; formerly Sponsored: by TGWU (£600 to constituency, 80% of election expenses) '88-95; the TGWU contributed "more than 25% of my election expenses at the 1997 general election"; Parliamentary Adviser: to Broadcasting, Entertainment, Cinematographic Trades Union (BECTU) '88-??, to the Musicians' Union '92-??, London Beekeepers' Association (paid in pots of honey)'93-; "I also receive money from the International Fund for Animal Welfare to pay a full-time worker"; Co-Presenter (with Jeffrey Archer), of BBC's 'Behind the Headlines' '91-??; Panelist, on 'Have I Got News for You' '93-??; Co-Author, How To Be a Disorderly MP (planned but not published); ex: Parliamentary Adviser, to Issue Communications Ltd '89-91; Assistant General Secretary, Association of Broadcasting Staff '76-83; Political Advisor to Dame Judith Hart '75; Head of Research, AUEW '69-75; Clerk, in the Cabinet Office '64;

Traits: Short (5'7"); short, bowed legs; slight (10st 11 pounds); "his strong, compact frame gives him the innate athletic ability necessary on the dance floor" (Ruth Gledhill, TIMES); greying, dandyish; trendy hairstyle; "sharp-suited" (Michael Cassell, FINANCIAL TIMES); "compact, eager and vole-like" (David McKie, GUARDIAN); "like a perennial wit at the back of the classroom" (Mike Rowbottom, INDEPENDENT); bright; over-eager; irrepressible; touchy; self-doubting; "an urchin Astaire" (Mark Lawson, INDEPENDENT); "his performance of a cheeky chirpy chappie defies belief" (Martin Ivens, DAILY TELEGRAPH); "all street cheek and quick wit and the nearest Westminster has to Jonathan Ross" (Mark Lawson, TIMES); "Banks's lip, his street-cred suits and street-wise insults bring the flavour of Newham to the corridors of Westminster" (TIMES); "he has the persuasive power of a market trader packing heat" (Charles Nevin, INDEPENDENT ON SUNDAY); "loquacious windbag", "little whippet", "diarrhoetic loquaciousness on every occasion" (Andrew Faulds MP); on himself: "I tend to be too hasty and aggressive"; "sometimes I'm appalled, because I tend to throw myself into situations with more enthusiasm than judgment, and then I regret what happens afterwards, especially if I've said something spiteful or in poor taste; good taste was never one of my qualifications"; "if you ask what I LIKE to do, it's to stay at home and potter about"; "I do my best to be a vegetarian"; "I like sparkling wine; if I could afford it, I would only drink Champagne"; "I'm also a season-ticket holder at Chelsea FC and Saturday afternoon will usually find me there if Chelseas is playing at home; I used to be a footballer"; "I have a parrot and two tortoises"; the parrot, 'Chunky', died; the surviving tortoise is called 'Snotty'; "I was a flight sergeant in the Air Training Corps"; "my wife and I rent a simple but comfortable villa on the Greek island of Symi for three weeks every August"; "Our Tonc"; lapsed Anglican ("I am not a practising communicant, although I have been baptised and confirmed in the Church of England...I was a verger at one time"); has circulation problems from a motorcycle injury; stopped smoking in '66; likes traditional classical music, especially Tchaikovsky; his favourite TV programme is 'Frazier'; his hobby is "18th century political iconography" (TB);

Address: House of Commons, Westminster, SW1A 0AA; 9 Sprowston Road, Forest Gate, London E7 9AD; 306 High Street, Stratford, E15 1AJ;

Telephone: 0171 219 3522 (H of C); 0181 534 7195 (home); 0181 555 0036 (constituency);

These profiles show our monitoring is top-notch; check with us on 0171 222 5884.

'Harry' (Harold) BARNES   Labour   NORTH EAST DERBYSHIRE '87-

Majority: 18,321 (35.2) over Conservative 3-way;
Description: A kidney-shaped seat wrapped around Chesterfield; less dominated than it was by coalmines since the closure of pits and commuters coming in from Chesterfield and Sheffield to gentrify Dronfield and Wingerworth; but its eastern part still has Clay Cross and other mining villages;
Position: On Select Committees: on Northern Ireland '97-, on European Legislation '89-; Vice Chairman, PLP Committees on Northern Ireland '89-, East Midlands '89-; Treasurer '97-, Vice Chairman '93-87 PLP Central Region Group; Joint President '92-, Chairman '90-92, New Dialogue (formerly New Consensus); on British-Irish Inter-Parliamentary Body '97-; ex: on Select Committee on Members' Interests '90-92; Vice Chairman, Sheffield and North Derbyshire Euro-constituency '85-87;

Outlook: Hyperactive, ILP-conditioned, hard-Left Campaign Group nuclear pacifist; a mixed-doctrine member of Labour's core 'awkward squad', second only to Dennis Skinner in the number of his rebellions; formerly anti-EC, then a federalist, then a Eurosceptic again; obsessed with the absence from electoral registers of 3-4m potential voters, mainly former poll-tax dodgers; recently an active co-leader of non-sectarian, anti-violence Irish 'New Dialogue' (formerly 'New Consensus'); an ardent opponent of Gulf War; as a former lecturer, tends to long, diffuse, fact-packed lectures; assiduous voter and questioner until his '98 stroke; locally-resident multi-cause activist (CND, Amnesty, formerly the Institute of Workers Control, Labour Co-ordinating Committee, Campaign for Labour Party Democracy); ex-Sheffield University extramural Lecturer, previously a railway clerk; long active in ILP (recently Independent Labour Publications), largely as contributor to its organ, LABOUR LEADER '75-85; "is living in a complete fantasy world" (Tory ex-Minister Alastair Goodlad); "he follows a very important principle which is never to let the arguments be bedeviled by the facts and always to ensure that one speaks on subjects about which one has not the slightest personal experience" (Tory ex-Minister Steve Norris);

History: He comes from a Durham miners' family in Easington; as a BR railway clerk, did his National Service with Iraq State Railway, where he was shocked by "the mud huts, the mud streets, the open sewers, the flies and the general deprivation" '54-56; on returning he joined the Labour Party at 21, '57; was active in Easington CLP as local election agent to Manny Shinwell and branch secretary and constituency delegate '57-60; was active in Labour and socialist societies at Ruskin College and Hull University '60-65; became active in ILP (Independent Labour Publications) because he saw its surviving rump as as having a "realistic, socialist" approach '75; became member of ILP's National Administrative Council and a member of Editorial Board of its paper, LABOUR LEADER '77; warned against Chris Mullin's proposal for a "coordinated mass refusal by Labour councils to increase rates and rents unreasonably or to slash services", asking: "what happens...when councils are surcharged and have to suffer while they await the return of a Labour government?" Sep '81; wrote critical pamphlet, 'The Public Face of Militant' for ILP, ridiculing its Trotskyist ideas but opposing ban on Militant '82; because the ILP did not favour office-seekers in its limited membership, retired to associate membership, leaving the editorial board of LABOUR LEADER and ILP's National Administrative Council '85; helped set up the Dronfield Miners'

Support Group; was quietly critical of Arthur Scargill's leadership of miners' strike but was inhibited from expressing it because so many of his extramural students were miners '85; although not a miner, was selected for North East Derbyshire in preference to John Dunn, a working miner, NUM nominee and Clay Cross Councillor whom Militant claimed as a supporter Jan '86; was endorsed by NEC June '86; after his election with an almost doubled majority, he hesitated about joining either the Tribune Group or the Campaign Group June-July '87; in his Maiden, urged help for local underground fire July '87; voted with Campaign Group to restore Commons pass to Jeremy Corbyn's ex-IRA-sympathising research assistant Nov '87; joined both the Tribune and Campaign Groups Jan '88; introduced ten-minute-rule Bill on underground fires Jan '88; voted against Licensing Bill to ease drinking hours Feb '88; with Campaign Group backed Dave Nellist against Speaker's ruling suspending him Apr '88; was attacked by Trotskyist LABOUR BRIEFING for "jumping frenetically" over political fence dividing Tribune Group from Campaign Group; he replied that "it was a damned silly place to put a fence in the first place" Apr '88; expressed sympathy for non-sectarian Workers Party of Ireland May '88; voted against money resolution for EC July '88; voted against Defence estimates, instead of abstaining Oct '88; voted against Prevention of Terrorism Bill, instead of abstaining Dec '88; co-sponsored Robin Corbett's Hare Coursing Bill Feb '89; urged selective demonstrations of civil disobedience to demonstrate against poll tax Mar '89; voted against EC on CAP fraud Mar '89; was one of 50 unilateralist Labour MPs who complained about Neil Kinnock's move toward multilateralism May '89; voted against EC broadcasting directive June '89; was named to Select Committee on European Legislation July '89; urged a "major rethink" on Labour's Left Oct '89; was found to have been the 23rd most assiduous questioner in the previous year Nov '89; was named to Members' Interests Select Committee, replacing Graham Allen Dec '89; backed Jonathan Aitken's anti-EC amendment Feb '90; complained that poll tax was cutting electoral rolls by up to 5% Apr '90; warned about side-effects of over-prescribed steroids June '90; with other Campaign Groupies voted against the Gulf War Sep '90; came next to last with 24 votes for Shadow Cabinet, one vote ahead of George Foulkes Oct '90; again protested absentees from electoral roll Nov '90; launched British branch of Irish anti-violence 'New Consensus' group Nov '90; warned that war against Saddam Hussein would make Arab governments collapse, "the Jordanian Government would fall into the arms of Saddam Hussein, war would break out with Israel" Nov '90; voted against Gulf War Nov '90; again voted against Gulf War Dec '90; insisted UN forces be limited to enforcing economic sanctions against Iraq Jan '91; urged President Bush stop carpet-bombing Basra Jan '91; attacked bombing of Iraqi civilian targets from Britain Feb '91; opposed united Ireland and sectarian politicians and terrorists there Mar '91; urged more aid to Kurds Apr '91; supported Ulster Secretary Peter Brooke's talks Apr '91; admitted he had finally paid his poll tax, with interest June '91; with Ken Livingstone unexpectedly called for a "democratic, social and federal Europe" Nov '91; was named to European Standing Committee A Nov '91; co-sponsored motions attacking US role in East Timor and El Salvador Dec '91; claimed up to 1.9m voters were not on electoral register because of poll tax dodging Feb '92; was rated as a top Green voter Mar '92; retained seat with majority up from 3,720 to 6,270, a swing to Labour of 1.97% Apr '92; backed John Prescott for Deputy Leader Apr '92; coming 6th in ballot for Private Members Bills, planned to modernise electoral registration in Representation of the People (Amendment) Bill Apr '92; was again named to Select Committee on European Legislation June '92; debated Boundary Commissions Bill in terms of under-representation of 1.88m poll-tax dodgers June '92; with Kate Hoey and Nick Raynsford launched 'New Democracy' to back offer of Labour candidates for Northern Ireland seats July '92; was rated 15th most active MP in terms of written questions asked in 1991-92, Oct '92; criticised Israel for advertising occupied East Jerusalem as part of Israel Dec '92; introduced

Energy (Fair Competition) Bill to eliminate unfair competition for coal Jan '93; was rated as the most rebellious of Labour MPs Feb '93; introduced his Bill proposing a rolling poll register, allowing additions and deductions to keep it up to date Feb '93; voted against National Lottery Bill Apr '93; voted against 3rd Reading for Maastricht Bill May '93; co-sponsored Robert Parry's motion warning of threat of "possible intervention by the USA against North Korea" Feb '94; voted to reduce age of homosexual consent to 18 or 16, Feb '94; opposed change in local government Feb '94; complained of loss of £1.5b contract to supply water for Malaysia by Biwaters in Clay Cross in his constituency "because of the link between arms and aid" Mar '94; was rated the busiest MP after Dennis Skinner July '94; backed Margaret Beckett for Leadership July '94; urged presence of Labour Party in Northern Ireland as a "non-sectarian political presence", instead of Labour's support of the SDLP Sep '94; urged a complete rethink on Northern Ireland Oct '94; came 4th in ballot for Private Members' Bills Nov '94; urged PM John Major to move powers to national Parliaments and the European Parliament, away from "secret bodies such as the Council of Ministers" Dec '94; Speaker Boothroyd announced his Labour-backed Bill on disability would be allowed to compete with the Government's cheaper, narrower Bill Jan '95; his Civil Rights (Disabled Persons) Bill, a version of Dr Roger Berry's Disability Discrimination Bill which the Government had blocked as too expensive in the previous session, received its 2nd Reading by 175 votes to nil Feb '95; voted for Paddy Ashdown's Bill for a Referendum on any further substantial constitutional change regarding Europe Feb '95; voted against extending pub hours Feb '95; spoke "as a pedestrian" and non-driver about road dangers, evoking the ridicule of Steve Norris Feb '95; urged bringing abortion in Northern Ireland into line with mainland legislation Mar '95; backed diplomatic relations with North Korea Mar '95; accused Government of "shabby maneuvres" to block his superior Civil Rights (Disabled Persons) Bill, which William Hague derided as a "blank cheque" Apr '95; with other hard-Leftists protested attempts to dilute Labour's Clause IV May '95; urged a stronger European Parliament June '95; told the Nolan Committee that he suspected MPs cheated on their car travel expenses June '95; on 50th anniversary of Hiroshima, urged study of unjustified use of A-bomb in 1945, June '95; despite demonstrations by the disabled, the Tory Government blocked his disability Bill by appending 168 wrecking amendments July '95; said he would resist the Tory Government's desire to cripple the power of the Labour-led Derbyshire County Council by carving up the county July '95; estimated that, three years after the end of the poll tax, 3m were still missing from electoral registers Aug '95; accused Sinn Fein of "calculated ambiguity" on decommissioning of IRA arms Aug '95; voted against Defence Estimates, instead of abstaining Oct '95; was part of "awkward squad" on Parliamentary procedure reform Nov '95; introduced Representation of the People (Amendment) Bill to improve electoral registration Nov '95; voted with pacifists and hard Left against Defence Estimates Dec '95; again urged fuller voter registration Dec '95; launching the "white ribbon campaign for peace", described his group as "reforming neutralists" on Ireland, insisting the blame for the end of the ceasefire rested mainly on the IRA Feb '96; was one of 25 Labour MPs who voted against the Prevention of Terrorism Act instead of abstaining Mar '96; said: "I would end royal prerogative powers; if people want a ceremonial head of state with no residual legal powers, that's acceptable to me" Mar '96; was one of 30 Labour MPs who voted against a guillotine on anti-terrorist measures Apr '96; complimented Tony Blair for discussing differences with dissident backbenchers, unlike other Labour leaders May '96; in the wake of the IRA's Manchester bomb, put down a motion with Tory MP Peter Bottomley calling for IRA prisoners to serve longer sentences and murderers released on license to be reincarcerated until the IRA reinstated a "credible and genuine ceasefire" June '96; agreed there should be a referendum before a single European currency was accepted June '96; again insisted that only a "rolling register" could enfranchise the 3-4m disenfranchised by being left off the electoral rolls July '96; voted to curb MPs' car mileage allowances and to cap their salary rise at 3% but to base their pensions on £43,000 July '96; was rated by Hull University researchers as second only to Dennis Skinner as one of "Blair's Bastards", with 75 rebel votes since '92, Sep '96; opposing his Chesterfield neighbour Tony Benn, wrote that "the answer to the Irish question isn't a simple British withdrawal" Oct '96; favoured a handgun ban except for .22 caliber target pistols, which could be dismantled, as recommended by Lord Cullen Nov '96; said his constituency was built on "great seams of coal" but, with the closing of all deep mines in Derbyshire, was now threatened with massive, polluting opencast operations Dec '96; with Tory MP Peter Bottomley urged a new investigation of 1972's 'Bloody Sunday' Jan-Feb '97; voted to disassemble target pistols Feb '97; retained his unaltered seat with a trebled majority of 18, 321 over his Tory opponent, on a pro-Labour swing of 12.3% May '97; asked: since Sinn Fein had allowed a successful candidate to take his seat in the Irish Parliament, also based on partition, why not do this for Westminster? June '97; was one of six Labour MPs who voted against the Firearms (Amendment) Bill on 2nd Reading June '97; was one of five Labour MPs in the revolt against the capping of Somerset and Oxfordshire July '97; urged the new Government to allow MPs to table questions during the 12-week summer recess July '97; urged Gerry Adams to disown IRA's statement that it had "problems" with the Mitchell principles Sep '97; secured unopposed first Reading for Bill giving homeless a vote Nov '97; voted against Labour Government's cuts in lone-parent benefits Dec '97; with 22 other Labour rebels, voted against possible military strike against Iraq Feb '98; with four other Labour MPs, urged PM Tony Blair to allow Labour to organise in Northern Ireland June '98; was forced to retire temporarily from Parliament after a stroke June '98; returned July '98;

Born: 22 July 1936, Easington

Family: Son, Joseph Barnes, miner, and Betsy (Gray) former household servant; m '63 'Ann' Elizabeth (Stephenson), Secretary, Derbyshire County Youth Service; she was a delegate to the Twelfth World Youth Festival, Moscow '85; 1s Richard Stephen '68, 1d Elizabeth Joanne '72;

Education: Easington Colliery Primary; Easington Colliery Grammar; Ryhope Grammar ("left with 4 rather low standard O-levels"); Ruskin College (Diploma); Hull University (BA, joint Hons in Philosophy and Political Studies - Upper Second);

Occupation: Ex: Lecturer at Sheffield University (ASTMS), recently as Director, Mature Students Courses - where he taught Kevin Barron, Terry Patchett, Kevin Hughes and Martin Redmond '68-87; previously Lecturer at North Nottinghamshire Further Education College, Worksop (NATFHE) '65-66; Railway Clerk (TSSA) '52-65;

Traits: Slight; balding, with grey fringe; specs; worried frown; fussy; long-winded; Durham accent; assiduous; thoughtful; late developer; cannot drive; "a little, bald-headed 60-year-old man with glasses and false teeth and whose trousers do not match his jacket", "someone who cannot change a light bulb or plug, or keep his own accounts" (HB); suffered stroke in '98; Humanist;

Address: House of Commons, Westminster, London SW1AA;

Telephone: 0171 219 4521/5013 (H of C); 01246 412588 (home);

Kevin (John) BARRON   **Labour**   **ROTHER VALLEY '83-**

Majority: 23,485 (50.9%) over Conservative 4-way;

Description: Steel and, formerly, coal seat surrounding Rotherham like a red blanket; once dotted with coal communities like Kiveton Park, Thurcroft and Maltby, which made it ultra-safe for Labour until the last mine, Maltby, was closed in 1993;

Position: On the Intelligence and Security Committee '97-; Chairman: PLP Health Committee '97-, PLP Yorkshire Group '87-, all-party groups on Pharmaceutical Industry '97-, Smoking and Health '97-; ex: Assistant Spokesman, on Health '95-97, Health and Safety '93-95 Energy '88-92; PPS, Neil Kinnock '85-88; on Environment Select Committee '92-93; Vice President, Combined Heat and Power Association; Secretary, Parliamentary CND '83-85; on Select Committee on Energy '83-86; Vice Chairman, PLP Health and Social Security Committee '83-86; Treasurer, Tribune Group '90-92?; on Executive, Yorkshire Labour Party '82-83; President of Rotherham TUC '83; Vice Chairman, Rother Valley Labour Party '81-83; formerly NUM then AEEU-sponsored;

Outlook: A quiet wide-ranging soft-Left former Yorkshire miner; recently a campaigner against tobacco advertising and sponsorship and a Clause IV moderniser; previously a Kinnockite frontbencher and former aide and "Mr Scargill's most vocal opponent" (Seumas Milne, GUARDIAN); as such was deprived of NUM sponsorship, after having been Scargill's '81 Presidential campaign manager in Yorkshire; as an MP was originally a Scargillite understudy to Dennis Skinner - until he saw the blinding light in '85; shrewd, balanced energy and health specialist with a deep soft spot for fellow ex-miners and their shrunken industry; "decent and competent but not a driving force" (SUNDAY TIMES); assiduous voter; pro-abortion (in Pro-Choice Alliance); was NUM-sponsored until '92, AEEU-sponsored '93-95;

History: He joined the Labour Party '74; was elected Maltby delegate to NUM's Yorkshire Area Executive '79; was Yorkshire campaign manager in Arthur Scargill's NUM Presidential campaign '81; Scargill announced Barron would be the NUM's candidate for Rother Valley against Peter Hardy MP Apr '81; was selected May '83, elected June '83; supported a motion to back pigeon racing from the Continent June '83; urged the suspension of the sale of arms to Chile and the restoration of human rights there June '83; co-sponsored motion congratulating Greenham Common women and opposing installation of Cruise and Trident missiles July '83; deplored the waste of North Sea oil revenues, favoured the building of more coal-fired power stations and stressed the need to consider the long-term effects before closing collieries July '83; co-sponsored motions: condemning the execution of Baha'ais in Iran, opposing the installation of Cruise and Trident missiles, opposing Project Mercury July '83; co-nominated Michael Meacher for Deputy Leader Aug '83; urged more investment in coal industry Dec '83; asked about "para-military" policing of miners strike Apr '84; supported selective boycott of Merrell Pharmaceuticals until they compensated UK patients injured by Debendox on same level as Americans July '84; was hospitalised after being hit by police baton while trying to pacify strikers at his old Maltby pit Sep '84; tried for emergency debate on withholding of supplementary benefit from striking miners Nov '84; tried to stop Earl of Scarborough taking over Maltby Common for golf course Dec '84; urged an emergency debate on strikebound coal Feb '85; introduced Bill to ensure that mines with workable reserves should be exploited to exhaustion Feb '85; emphasised that three-quarters of those miners charged with violence had been discharged by magistrates Feb '85; urged tighter control of telephone tapping to decrease its use against trade unionists and CNDers Mar '85; urged a public inquiry into policing during the coal strike Mar '85; raised question of Select Committee's report on Coal Board's refusal to re-employ dismissed miners June '85; was reselected from a short-list of one June '85; raised question of professional support for voluntary organisations helping victims of child abuse July '85; complained of "authoritarian" and high-handed action by Campaign Group Treasurer Bob Clay in replying to Kinnock's speech at Labour Conference in name of unconsulted Campaign Groupies Oct '85; resigned from Campaign Group, was named PPS to Neil Kinnock Oct '85; complained of attempt of Tory MPs John Butcher, Jim Pawsey and Iain Mills to block development of South Warwickshire coalfield Mar '86; complained of non-re-employment of Chairman of Rotherham Health Authority because he opposed privatisation Apr '86; opposed Kenneth Hind's Unborn Children (Protection) Bill Oct '86; warned of danger of human error even in Sizewell B PWR station Feb '87; complained of "despair that is in the British coalfields" because of inadequate replacement of lost miners' jobs Mar '87; sought emergency debate on frauds in sale of British Gas shares Apr '87; complained of local youth unemployment May '87; warned that electricity privatisation was a threat to British coalfields July '87; urged more investment in renewable geothermal and solar energy Oct '87; claimed Armilla patrol in Persian Gulf was inadequately protected Nov '87; introduced debate on the deepening crisis in coal communities and inadequacies of Government help Nov '87; warned that a weak dollar could make US coal seem attractive, but that large purchases by UK would drive its price up Dec '87; sought to prevent closure of local Firbeck Hospital Jan '88; claimed "divisive" Tony Benn and Eric Heffer were heading for the same "political wilderness" as the Workers Revolutionary Party Mar '88; was elected Vice Chairman of Tribune Group Nov '88; was named a Deputy Energy Spokesman under Tony Blair Nov '88; warned that National Power and PowerGen, the CEGB's successors, would cut coal use by 15m tones Feb '89; received 13,000 votes in contest for constituency section of NEC, the second lowest Oct '89; with other ex-miner MPs resisted introduction of private Bill to develop Immingham and Felixtowe as coal-importing ports Nov '89; was renamed Deputy Spokesman on Energy, under Frank Dobson, with responsibility for coal, electricity and nuclear industries Nov '89; described Government £5b writeoff of British Coal's debts as "privatisation by the front door" Dec '89; was re-selected for Rother Valley Dec '89; visited Israel as guest of Labour Friends of Israel Jan '90; urged an inquiry into whether NUM funds had been mishandled by Arthur Scargill and Peter Heathfield, as alleged by DAILY MIRROR Mar '90; visited Hongkong as guest of its government Apr '90; backed the 1967 Abortion Act but urged better funding to avoid late abortions Apr '90; complained Government was cutting reduction of sulphur dioxide emissions to avoid putting too big a burden on privatised generators Apr '90; warned that without Government-backed long-term contracts, "the coal industry could free-fall into oblivion" June '90; observed Bulgarian elections on IPU delegation June '90; spoke of difficulties of supporting a victim of Alzheimer's on basis of his late mother-in-law's experience June '90; in wake of Lightman Report said: Scargill's "support is waning all the time" Sep '90; described as a Scargillite "sell-out" the NUM's acceptance of £742,000 instead of a claimed £2m from International Miners Organisation (President: A Scargill) Sep '90; was threatened with loss of NUM membership and sponsorship after he urged Arthur Scargill and Peter Heathfield to resign as the NUM President and General Secretary and seek re-election on the grounds of financial mismanagement of the NUM's funds during the 1984-85 strike, as disclosed by the Lightman report Dec '90; declined to give

Labour's support for development of Killingholme as a gas generator Jan '91; was allowed to refer his union's threat to him to the Committee of Privileges Jan '91; welcomed Coal Mining Subsidence Bill as long overdue Feb '91; urged British Coal to reopen Monktonhall colliery, closed because of excessive PWR development May '91; complained that Government was absorbing EEC RECHAR money intended to retrain redundant miners instead of supplementing it May '91; backed urgent negotiations to avoid post-'93 cuts in British Coal's supplies to electricity generators May '91; with Win Griffiths urged a more efficient use of fuel by Combined Heat and Power Aug '91; complained that "Britain's coal industry has become a symbol for old-fashioned, dirty, strife-ridden industry" but that "privatisation is not the answer" Sep '91; the Committee of Privileges ruled in his favour on the NUM's threat to remove its sponsorship of him Oct-Nov '91; insisted Coal Industry Bill was part of Government preparation for British Coal privatisation Nov '91; it was disclosed that Bob Worcester, the MORI pollster, was registered as his researcher Dec '91; retained his seat with majority up from 15,790 to 17,222, a swing to Labour of 1.08% Apr '92; supported Margaret Beckett for Deputy Leadership Apr '92; warned of impact on mines of approval for 28 gas-fired power stations May '92; was expelled from NUM over his 1990 contacts with Gavin Lightman QC, who reported financial mismanagement during 1984-85 strike by its President, Arthur Scargill June '92; supported effort by Yorkshire miners to reopen Thurcroft colliery near Rotherham June '92; was offered an Assistant Spokesman's post in Environment by John Smith but declined July '92; after long absence with back trouble, spoke in protest at threatened shutdown of Maltby colliery Oct '92; was named to Environment Select Committee Oct '92; failed to win election to the National Policy Forum Feb '93; again protested shutdown of his last local pit, Maltby, where he had worked Apr '93; with 43 other Labour MPs urged President Clinton to intervene militarily against the Serb aggressors in Bosnia May '93; was named Spokesman on Employment (Health and Safety) Oct '93; opposed VAT on fuel, dismissing its impact on the environment Nov '93; drew 3rd place in ballot for Private Members' Bills Nov '93; came off the Environment Select Committee Dec '93; warned that Government's inactivity might force Yorkshire mining towns to miss out on EC money in the RECHAR programme Dec '93; co-defended Diana Scott, energetic local water consumer watchdog Dec '93; welcomed Government's "climb-down" on repeal of Health and Safety legislation Jan '94; sought to amend Sunday Trading legislation to prevent ruthless employers from sacking employees to deprive them of religious conscience protection Feb '94; introduced 2nd Reading of his Bill to ban tobacco advertising and sports sponsorship Feb '94; voted against restoring capital punishment, even for killers of policemen Feb '94; voted to reduce the age of homosexual consent to 18 or 16, Feb '94; more than 100 wrecking amendments, drafted by the tobacco industry and its lobbyists (Ian Greer Associates, Sharpe Pritchard and Co), were put down by Tory MPs to talk out his Tobacco Advertising Bill; the Government was not sympathetic to his Bill, preferring to rely on voluntary agreements with the industry; the Bill was talked out; he described it as a "procedural mugging" of a measure which could help save 10,000 lives a year May '94; complained about risks from job cuts at Health and Safety Executive May '94; was Denis MacShane's 'minder' during the Rotherham by-election May '94; backed Tony Blair for Leadership June '94; voted for Blair for Leader, Prescott for Deputy Leader July '94; was retained as Assistant Spokesman on Employment Oct '94; with Left Eurosceptics voted against the European Communities (Finance) Bill Nov '94; with Helen Liddell - co-leader with him of the about-to-be-launched New Clause IV Campaign - privately warned new Leader Tony Blair that there was a lack of enthusiasm for change within the party Dec '94; in a newsletter sent to all constituency parties, the New Clause IV Campaign urged limiting public ownership to cases justified "on grounds of efficiency and equity" Jan '95; his adjournment debate detailed his long pursuit of housing for an unemployed ex-miner trying to pursue new training as a mental nurse Jan '95; strongly supported the effort of colleague Terry Lewis to strengthen labelling of tobacco dangers Feb '95; as Labour's Spokesman on training, pointed out that large numbers of young trainees left programmes prematurely or without qualifications Feb '95; under pressure from his Whips, dropped his amendment seeking to expel two cash-for-questions Tory MPs, Graham Riddick and David Tredinnick Apr '95; wrote to GUARDIAN complaining that a Disneyland ad featured caterpillars smoking May '95; unsuccessfully sought election as Labour's Chief Whip Sep '95; was low man in Shadow Cabinet election, with 30 votes Oct '95; attacked CAP's £800m annual tobacco subsidy May '96; was named Assistant Spokesman on Health Oct '95; attacked NHS's unlawful relocation expenditures Mar '96; insisted PFI could not make up for Conservative cuts in hospital building Mar '96; voted against Iain Duncan-Smith's Eurosceptic Bill attacking the European Court Apr '96; attacked Scargill's new Socialist Labour Party as providing "a service to the Conservative Party...by splitting the Left-of-Centre votes" May '96; voted against a 3% cap on MPs' pay, in favour of a cut in MPs' mileage allowance and a pension based on £43,000 July '96; asked party Chairman Brian Mawhinney how addicted the Tories were to funding by tobacco manufacturers Aug '96; in Blair's 'final' pre-election Shadow Cabinet reshuffle, retained his place as Assistant Spokesman on Health Aug '96; complained that people in poor housing had to use the NHS 50% more than others Nov '96; spoke on the problems of testing ex-miners with emphysema Nov '96; promised Labour would ban sports sponsorship Nov '96; said Labour Government would have to work closely with the pharmaceutical industry to maintain its prominence Nov '96; was named as a target by the Prolife Alliance Party Feb '97; retained his seat with an enhanced majority of 23,485, a pro-Labour swing of 8.3% May '97; was one of 18 former frontbenchers left out in the cold without initial appointments; PM Tony Blair wanted him to take a party campaign post but this was vetoed by John Prescott May '97; asked about smoking prevalence June '97; asked about tobacco revenues July '97; was named to the Parliamentary Intelligence and Security Committee July '97; said it would be interesting to hear the testimony of defecting MI5man David Shayler Aug '97; with Mike Clapham and Paddy Tipping began a behind-the-scenes lobby to save the shrunken coalmining industry from extinction Nov '97; welcomed Government's reprieve for coalmining industry June '98;

Born: 26 October 1946, Tadcaster

Family: Son, Richard Barron, retired power station attendant, and Edna (Brown); m '69 Carol (McGrath), whose mother Nancy died in '88 of Alzheimer's Disease; 1s Robert '76, 2d Amy '72, Emma '75;

Education: Maltby Craggs Junior; Maltby Secondary Modern; Ruskin College, Oxford;

Occupation: Formerly Sponsored by AEEU (after NUM withdrew its sponsorship because of his opposition to Scargill) '93-95; ex: Coal Miner at Maltby '62-83 (NUM);

Traits: Dark; greying; good-looking; casual stance; Yorkshire accent; straightforward; modest; pleasant; enjoys football, fly-fishing and films; 'I'd Lie For You and That's the Truth' was his favourite single; had serious back trouble in '92, leading to a spinal operation;

Address: House of Commons, Westminster, London SW1A 0AA; 73 Blyth Road, Maltby, Rotherham, South Yorkshire S66 7LF;

Telephone: 0171 219 4432/6306 (H of C); 01709 817992 (home); 01909 568611 (constituency);

Our "MEW MPs of '97" was 2nd on Politico's '98 "Top of the Pops"

John (Dominic) BATTLE   **Labour**   **LEEDS WEST '87-**

Majority: 19,771   (49.2%)   over   Conservative 6-way;

Description: An inner-city working-class seat divided by the river, made up of separate 'villages'; in tightly knit and distinctive Armley and Bramley wards, Labour and Liberals fight it out, Wortley is three-sided and Kirkstall is a Labour stronghold;

Position: Minister of State, for Trade and Industry (Energy and Science) '97-; ex: Deputy Spokesman, Trade and Industry (Energy) '95-97; Spokesman, on Science '94-95; Deputy Spokesmen, on Environment (Housing) '92-94; Whip (Treasury) '89-91; on Select Committees: on Broadcasting '95-97, Environment '91-92, on Environment '91-92; Leeds City Councillor (Chairman: Employment '81-83, Housing '83-87) '80-87;

Outlook: Labour's Minister of State for Science, Energy and Industry, who has successively grown into new responsibilities; one of the rare politicians who is both computer-literate and reads poetry; took over as Spokesman on Science from Dr Lewis Moonie; previously, as Housing Spokesman, made 180 visits to housebuilders, City lenders and tenants' groups; as a poverty-hating radical Catholic, initially an aspirant priest, he comes from a different and wider philosphical base from most Nonconformist Labour politicians in his area, with links to the Catholic 'Justice and Peace Movement'; has a wide-ranging intelligence linked to an engaging personality; a non-sectarian broad Left conviction politician with a warm heart and vivid tongue for the poor at home and abroad; "I believe him to be a decent man" (Tory MP Sir George Young); was fairly hard-Left, especially on defence, opposing nuclear weapons and the Gulf War; a former Leeds Councillor who retook previously safe-Labour Leeds West from Liberals' Michael Meadowcroft; anti-abortion (as an RC), was on the MSF Parliamentary Committee;

History: He joined the Labour Party '74; was elected for Hunslet to Leeds City Council May '80; contested then safe-Tory Leeds North West against Dr Keith Hampson, coming third with 22.2% of vote June '83; as Leeds North West delegate at annual conference, moved composite motion urging a major house-building campaign, with "more sensitive housing management" in the public sector Oct '84; was selected as candidate for Leeds West Nov '85, endorsed by NEC Jan '86; dismissed Liberal Leader David Steel's castigation of him as one of hard-Left "101 damnations" as "libellous" and "low-grade political smearing" May '87; ousted Michael Meadowcroft June '87; challenged the wisdom of Home Secretary Douglas Hurd in spending £3m on new prison officers' uniforms, insisting priority should be given to improved conditions in jails like Armley in his constituency July '87; in his Maiden speech attacking the "unjust" Local Government Bill, deplored his constituency's "hopelessness and resentment" due to an absence of jobs, except for a handful of very poorly-paid ones July '87; supported the Campaign Group move to restore the Commons pass to Jeremy Corbyn's ex-IRA-sympathising research assistant Nov '87; supported Tony Benn motion claiming Northern Ireland crisis "stems primarily from the long-standing British occupation of that country and the partition imposed by force in 1921" Nov '87; although most of his constituency activists were against it, as a Catholic voted for 2nd Reading of David Alton's abortion-curbing Bill Jan '88; urged Tories to see Little Dorritt film because of Government's recreation of Dickensian poverty Feb '88; criticised new powers for auditors to block local government expenditure in advance Mar '88; launched adjournment debate on 'Poverty and Low Pay', rejecting Government claim that the poverty line was indefinable Mar '88; voted against 26-week ceiling for abortion May '88; attacked the Budget's encouragement to private landlords under Business Expansion Schemes as "a pocket-liner" which would not "improve the housing stock" in areas like Leeds May '88; introduced Bill urging a statutory minimum wage May '88; urged repair of all unfit housing in Leeds, private as well as public June '88; after discovering concentrated local deaths from mesothelioma (a form of absestosis), urged inquiry into lethal asbestos pollution from former J W Roberts plant in Armley in his constituency Nov '88; warned against making repossessions easier Nov '88; voted against extending Prevention of Terrorism Bill, instead of abstaining Dec '88; voted against loyalty oath for Northern Ireland councillors, instead of abstaining Dec '88; co-sponsored Andrew Smith's Bill to force local authorities to make public fire safety information Dec '88; reaffirmed, with 49 other unilateralists, Labour's rejection of nuclear deterrence May '89; warned that new Social Security Bill would force unemployed to take low-paid jobs because they would not receive benefits if they rejected them May '89; complained that his constituents on social security could not pay their basic bills May '89; expressed doubts about Business Expansion schemes May '89; complained of forced increase in council rents under Local Government and Housing Bill June '89; urged Labour to back more 'green' issues June '89; warned the Government was deliberately exaggerating the numbers who would benefit by the mobility allowance July '89; warned that £2m in social security budget was unspent because managers were terrified to overspend their budgets July '89; was named Treasury Whip Dec '89; backed fundraising campaign of MORNING STAR to maintain "diverse editorial opinion" Feb '90; urged more spending on homelessness Feb '90; contrasted Nigel Lawson's second part-time job at £40,000 with difficulties of needy constituents trying to get a few more pounds out of DHSS Feb '90; said Budget was hard on those on low pay who paid taxes Mar '90; opposed embryo research Apr '90; insisted that football hooligan disorders in Bournemouth were not the action of true Leeds United supporters but of "a few who hitch a ride on Leeds United" May '90; complained he could secure no information about toxic emissions from aircraft, especially military June '90; deplored inadequacy of increasing child benefit by only £1 for first-born since a packet of 10 disposable nappies cost £1.24, or a pair of shoes for a five-year-old cost £15 July '90; emphasised that statutory sick pay was being cut for low-paid Nov '90; was one of 17 Labour MPs, mainly hard-Left, who urged in the GUARDIAN a "peaceful negotiated settlement to the crisis in the Gulf" Nov '90; pointed out that many parts of 'developing world' were going backward Dec '90; as part of 'Christians for Labour', appealed in CATHOLIC HERALD for support for Labour Party Dec '90; signed motion opposing the Gulf War; abstained in vote on Gulf War, resigning as Whip, saying he could not advise colleagues to vote for something in which he did not believe Dec '90-Jan '91; favoured limiting abortion to under 18 weeks Mar '91; backed higher taxes on top 5% of taxpayers; complained that the Tories' anti-tax campaign was designed "to undermine the idea that the rich should pay a larger proportion of income than the poor" May '91; was named to Environment Select Committee in succession to Kim Howells May '91; pointed to rash of suicides in local Armley Jail July '91; opposed penalising of mothers who did not name the non-contributing father of their children July '91; urged early identification of youngsters tending to steal cars Dec '91; retained his seat with majority up from 4,692 to 13,828, a swing from Conservatives to Labour of 4.46% Apr '92; backed Margaret Beckett for Deputy Leader Apr '92; was renamed to Environment Select Committee July '92; urged early Government help, complaining that local asbestosis sufferers were dying off before their law suits could be heard July '92; was named Housing and Local Government Spokesman, as Labour's No 2 in Environment team under Jack Straw; this made obligatory his departure from Environment

Select Committee July '92; opposed draft Euthanasia Bill in Alton-led motion Sep '92; was rated 30th most assiduous poser of written Parliamentary questions Oct '92; co-protested against continuing military coup in Haiti Oct '92; after Michael Heseltine had sneered that Leeds City Council had bought coal from Colombia, pointed out it had been forced by compulsory competitive tendering in Government's 1988 Local Government Act to accept cheapest bid and local company had undercut British Coal by £600,000 a year Oct '92; said families were suffering from the worst housing crisis since World War II: "many people now believe they live simply a pay cheque away from redundancy" Nov '92; protested that under the Housing and Urban Development Bill tenants would "lose the right to veto any change in the management of their homes" Dec '92; warned that secondary lenders like double-glazers were overtaking banks and building societies in applications for repossessions Jan '93; claimed London was absorbing too much of Rough Sleepers Initiative, since two-thirds of street sleepers were in the provinces Jan '93; attacked the Leasehold Bill, scaled down to meet backbench Tory objections, as having the impact of "a damp squib on a dull day" June '93; attacked the "corrosive rhetoric of apocolyptic pessimism and cynical nihilism" which induced "paralysis and impotence" July '93; urged Government to do more, not less, for the homeless Dec '93; derided as a "pig in a poke" Sir George Young's new effort to sell council and housing association homes Oct '93; voted against restoration of capital punishment, even for those killing policemen Feb '94; voted to reduce age of homosexual consent to 18 or 16, Feb '94; criticised squeeze on housing associations' tenants Mar '94; backed Margaret Beckett for the Leadership June '94; voted for Margaret Beckett for Leader and Deputy Leader July '94; Tony Blair named him to the team of Ann Taylor, shadow Leader of the House, asking him to switch his speciality from Housing to Science Oct '94; was praised by a previous Science Spokesman, Dr Jeremy Bray as "a diligent visitor to every kind of scientific establishment in the private and public sectors and...well-respected by the research community as an observer of the field of science; he speaks with real authority of feeling in the science community"; was added to the Select Committee on Broacasting, replacing Nick Brown Jan '95; voted against extending pub licensing hours Feb '95; urged the establishment of an Office of Science and Technology, to co-ordinate Education, Trade and Industry and Transport Mar '95; was named an Assistant Spokesman on Trade and Industry (Science) under Margaret Beckett Oct '95; led for Labour in debate on Science and Technology, in the absence of Margaret Beckett, the new Shadow Spokesman on Trade and Industry, on the morrow her appointment; he invited Tory Ministers to congratulate Professor Emeritus Joseph Rotblat on his Nobel Peace Prize, without any response Oct '95; again pressed the Government to finance a survey of the homes in Armley, near Leeds, contaminated by asbestos Dec '95; urged the halting of the privatisation of the newer nuclear power plants in British Energy at least until uncertainties over funding decommissioning were cleared up Mar '96; attacked nuclear privatisation as a "massive short-changing con" when a hidden £6.9m "sweetener" was disclosed June '96; complained that British Energy should "stand on it its own two feet, in free and fair competition with other power generators" instead of being given preferred status June '96; attacked Tory Government for its "incoherent" approach to takeovers and mergers July '96; in the last pre-election reshuffle, was confirmed on the Trade and Industry team under Margaret Beckett Aug '96; suggested at Labour's annual conference that it might be sensible to merge the gas and electricity regulators Oct '96; when the American-owned CE Electric moved to take over Northern Electric, he said: "if this bid is succcessful, it will mean that four of the 12 regional electricty companies in England and Wales will be owned by US-based corporations'; Labour is not opposed in principle to foreign takeovers but it is essential that these companies do not move beyond the reach of the regulator when they are taken over" Oct '96; attacked the National Grid for dipping into its pensions surplus Jan '97; said the new Labour Government would curb the "dash for gas" electricity generators Feb '97; urged utility chiefs to work with Labour on the windfall tax instead of "using megaphone diplomacy in favour of the Conservative propaganda machine" Mar '97; retained Leeds West with an enhanced majority of 19,771, a pro-Labour swing of 10.1% May '97; on Labour's victory, was named Minister of State, with responsibilities for Industry, Energy and Science May '97; in debate on the 'Information Society' predicted: "within the next generation, every book ever written, every symphony ever composed, every film ever made, every painting ever painted will be, with the click of a mouse, within the reach of all children", adding: "the challenge of the new technologies will be to harness their potential for the benefit of all" July '97; pressed European Commission to tackle unfair competition from state-subsidised Euopean coal pits Aug '97; announced a complete review of the 'pool', the controversial electricity trading market, by Professor Stephen Littlechild, in response to widespread complaints Oct '97; introduced Wireless Telegraphy Bill to manage the radio spectrum by charging for the right to use certain waves by mobile phone, pager, cab or other radio-based services Oct '97; said that there was "no quick fix" for the coal industry now that it and its customers and competitors were all in the private sector and thus outside Government control; told protesting miners that renationalising the pits was "not an option" Nov '97; met the heads of 14 electricity providers to speed the introduction of competition in the electricity market Jan '98; with Scottish Secretary Donald Dewar, announced the impending shutdown of reprocessing at Dounreay June '98; after ten frustrating trips for No 10 approval, was able to introduce his White Paper on future energy competition June '98;

Born: 26 April 1951, Bradford

Family: Son, John Battle, electrician, and late Audrey (Rathbone), teacher; eldest of 8 children; m '77 Mary (Meenan) mathematician/engineer; 1s Joseph '78, 2d Anna '82, Clare '83;,

Education: St Paulinus, Dewsbury; Upholland College, Liverpool (where he studied for the Catholic priesthood); Leeds University (BA Eng as a mature student; he also studied William Empson and the World War I poets);

Occupation: Ex: National Co-ordinator, Church Action on Poverty (ecumenical), based in Manchester, (ASTMS/MSF) '83-87; Research Officer, for Leeds MEP Derek Enright '79-83; worked in a mental hospital; worked on building sites;

Traits: Very tall; slim; dark-greying; bearded; long face; specs; "reminds me of an Assistant Physics-with-Chemistry (and special Maths) teacher in a struggling comprehensive" (Matthew Parris, TIMES); warm-hearted worker-priest or street politician type; one of the first MPs with an e-mail address, he still reads poetry; normally talkative; but he once retreated to a silent Trappist monastery; he still loves silence: "my personal resolution is to try to observe a few minutes silence every day";

Address: House of Commons, Westminster, London SW1A 0AA; 26 Victoria Park Avenue, Leeds, L55 3DG;

Telephone: 0171 219 4201/5954/4286(Fax) (H of C); 01132 310258 (constituency office); 01532 789094 (home);

WE'RE GETTING FATTER
MPs profiles tend to get fatter, like the papier mache masks we made in our youth by adding to a clay portrait model soggy strips of newsprint soaked in flour and water. Just as you can build up a strong papier mache mask, so too we hope we have transformed a dimly lit outline form into sharp features plus a few warts.

Hugh BAYLEY   **Labour**   **YORK '92-**

Majority: 20,523 (35.2%) over Conservative 7-way;
Description: An unaltered historic, formerly-marginal city; its historic centre makes it a tourist Mecca; it is also a railway centre and a base for confectionery manufacture (Nestle-Rowntree, Terry and Craven) which provides a third of its manufacturing jobs; it has 1,600 bioscientists working in private laboratories, the Government and the University of York; it also houses General Accident Insurance; the city has attracted public sector relocations like MAFF and the Land Registry;
Position: PPS to Frank Dobson '97-; Delegate to the North Atlantic Assembly '97-; on the Executive, UK Branch, of the IPU and CPA '97-; Chairman, all-party International Development Group '97-; Vice Chairman, PLP International Development Committee '97-; Chairman, for Yorkshire of the Fabian Society '88-; ex: on Health Select Committee '92-97; Vice Chairman, PLP's Environmental Protection Group '93-96; Campaigns Officer, PLP's Yorkshire Group '93-97; on NALGO Parliamentary Group '92-97; on National Committee, Anti-Apartheid Movement '73-87; on York Health Authority '88-90; York Council for Voluntary Service '7?-92; Camden Councillor (Chairman: Employment Committee '81-82, Labour Group '82-85) '80-86; Chairman, St Pancras North Constituency Labour Party '82-83; on Executive, Labour Co-ordinating Committee '89-91; RMT-Sponsored until '95;
Outlook: A middle-class Fabian health economist who has found a sensible niche as PPS to Labour's Health Secretary; formerly a "big hitter" on the Health Select Committee; an internationalist and a productive writer on social work, particularly on care for the elderly; a hyperactive, creatively ingenious, multi-cause soft-Leftwinger; worthy rather than exciting; speaks only from considerable and detailed knowledge; a railway enthusiast, formerly RMT-sponsored, is also an assiduous defender of York's railway heritage; the belated retaker of marginal York, who returned to achieve it and finally made it rock-safe; had extensive organisational experience in Camden, Dobson's home turf; one of the rare surviving public-school socialists (Haileybury, like Attlee); "I speak...as someone who set up and built up a small business; I see no contradiction between doing that and being a socialist" (HB);
History: He first became politically active at Bristol University, where he was an Anti-Apartheid activist and President of the Union '72; as Vice President of the NUS, initiated and organised the first national student rent strike, which achieved reductions in student residence fees '74; joined the Labour Party '75; as a NALGO National Officer, organised an early campaign against NHS privatisation, culminating in the two-week High Court case, Health Computing Ltd v John Meek, which put the company out of business '80; won Chalk Farm in Camden Council by-election '80; chaired the Camden Employment Committee which introduced pioneering employment creation schemes '81; again won Chalk Farm seat on Camden Council May '82; proposed renaming a Camden road Mandela Street '83; was a founder-Secretary of the London Labour Co-ordinating Committee '82; succeeded in four-year campaign to take Arlington House (privately-owned 1066-bed hostel) into council ownership '83; set up International Broadcasting Trust, an independent broadcasting organisation owned and controlled by 70 voluntary bodies, including trade unions, Oxfam and WEA '84; was selected for York, defeating its already-ailing ex-MP Alex Lyons, and local

Councillor Rodney Hills Dec '85; at annual Labour conference, urged more aid for 3rd World, which should not have been left for Bob Geldof, insisting "socialism is nothing it if is not internationalist"; socialists should organise a fundamental shift in power to the poor countries Oct '86; said that Labour's plan for a Yorkshire and Humberside Development Agency, controlled locally, was essential to improve job prospects in York May '87; attacked by Alliance for being one of the hard-Left "101 damnations", called this a "pack of lies", pointing out that he had been persistently attacked by the hard-Left when on Camden Council for voting in favour of staying within the law on rates; he had also been attacked by the the Trotskyist 'London Labour Briefing' for his support of Neil Kinnock and mainstream Labour policies May '87; at York reduced Conservative majority by 3,500 from previous 3,647 to 147 June '87; at Labour's annual conference, complained that, under Mrs Thatcher, the local railway system had been "run into the ground" in York: "first 350 redundancies were announced at the carriage works, then 50 redundancies at the regional headquarters in York; then they closed Clifton Wash Sheds , a depot built at a cost of £6m only six years ago; then British Rail lost its freight to Rowntrees, so they decided to close the entire freight operation out of York and the marshalling yard that went with it" Sep '87; warned of the danger of the infective agent in BSE jumping from cattle to humans Mar '89; in local elections, Labour had a lead of 28% May '90; was sacked from York Health Authority after securing a majority against hospital opt-out '90; was re-selected for York June '90; in local council elections, Labour had a lead of 17% May '91; insisted that Labour's minimum wage policy was essential locally because "North Yorkshire has a higher proportion of low-paid workers than any other county in England; therefore, there would be more gainers from a minimum wage in York" Sep '91; during the election campaign, Tories distributed a cutting from his Camden Councillor days, when he presented his local library with a facsimile from East Germany of Marx's Communist Manifesto; his reply: "Yes, I did give Camden that facsimile; Marx had lived in Camden, written the manifesto in Camden; Dick Turpin was hanged in York; if I came across his letters from jail, I would offer them to the local museum; would that make me a supporter of highway robbery? I was not, and am not now, a Marxist, a communist, a member of the Socialist Workers [or] Militant; all these are irrelevant, like this silliness" Mar '92; retook York from Conal Gregory by 6,342 votes, a pro-Labour swing of 5%, Apr '92; voted with Government on King's Cross Railways (No 2) Bill, with a few other Labour MPs June '92; complained that elderly were being squeezed out of public sector homes; warned that cost of residential homes was outstripping resources of many of their residents July '92; to gather information against privatisation, spoke to Amtrak officials when he visited USA with British-American Parliamentary Group which financed it together with US Information Service Sep '92; complained of absence from 'The Health of the Nation' White Paper of any analysis of impact of poor housing, poverty and unemployment and inadequate disease prevention, such as a smoking ban Oct '92; was named to Health Select Committee Oct '92; expressed concern that York would lose many jobs through rail privatisation, as well as contracts for rail car builders ABB (formerly BREL) Oct '92; urged more funds for live music, especially jazz Nov '92; expressed concern that Citizen's Charter commitments had been watered down and mostly not delivered Nov '92; as spokesman for the all-party Jazz Group, urged change in Licensing Act 1964 to allow more than two live musicians in a licensed pub Nov '92; expressed concern about the continued manufacture of railway locomotives and rolling stock in York and the UK Nov '92; accused the Health Select Committee of having failed to include in its report vital evidence from the BMA which said a competitive market threatened the stability and integration of the NHS Dec '92; observed Serbian elections Dec '92; urged a US-style statutory limit on railway hours worked, since the Clapham disaster had been blamed on an overtired electrician's wiring Jan '93; introduced Bill to ban tobacco advertising except at point of sale, receiving a 1st Reading by 206 to 61 Jan '92; opposed Virginia Bottomley's effort to merge five district health authorities in North Yorkshire into one Sep '92; was named to Standing Committee on Railways Bill Feb '93; claimed that local Labour council taxes were lower than Tory or LibDem council taxes Apr '93; was one of 17 Labour MPs who backed Baroness Thatcher in co-urging military intervention against Serbian aggressors in Bosnia Apr '93; claimed rail privatisation would deal York an economic body blow with up to 3800 jobs at risk May '93; again accused Transport Secretary MacGregor of frightening railway pensioners by his proposal to "appropriate" part of the pension fund to pay pensioners, which he had "lodged in every public library in my constituency" May '93; tried unsuccessfully to adjourn Commons over 896 sackings at railcoach builders ABB Transportation Ltd in York, Derby and Crewe June '93; visited Bonn for European Parliamentarians Conference, paid for by the Society for International Development Sep '93; voted with Left Eurosceptics Oct '93; in debate on Railways Bill again lengthily defended rail pensioners against Government's manipulations Nov '93; complained that, despite promises, the Government was not defending hedgerows Dec '93; warned that saving on contraceptives would lead to a rise in teen-age pregnancies Dec '93; was elected Campaigns Officer of the PLP's Yorkshire Group Dec '93; complained of heavy impact of revaluation on York, "higher than anywhere else" Jan '94; urged registration of second-hand dealers at car-boot sales Jan '94; objected to taxpayer having to pay over £44,000 for Ministers' Christmas cards Feb '94; complained of lavish expenditure on specially-woven carpet for York-based Government educational quango Feb '94; complained that Government did not want to protect future shopworkers who did not want to work on Sundays Feb '94; voted to abolish capital punishment Feb '94; voted to reduce age of homosexual consent to 18 or 16, Feb '94; urged emergency expenditure to keep alive the York-based ABB carriageworks Mar '94; led motion and made speech deploring misuse of overseas aid on tax havens like British Virgin Islands June '94; backed Tony Blair for the Leadership, Margaret Beckett for the Deputy Leadership June '94; voted for Blair for Leader, Prescott for Deputy July '94; urged smaller satellite towns rather than concentrate on a 'super-village' to absorb York's excess housing demand Aug '94; having visited the Tornado and Jaguar detachments based at Gioia in Italy, urged the RAF be given "whatever material resources it needs" for its Bosnia commitment Nov '94; complained of growing inequities within the NHS Dec '94; complained that £20m in overseas contracts had gone to companies to which former Tory Ministers were linked Dec '94; complained that local opinion was overwhelmingly opposed to the Government's proposals for local government boundaries in York Feb '95; again complained of the decimation of local skilled rail jobs Feb '95; complained, with the endorsement of Cabinet Secretary Sir Robin Butler, about Virginia Bottomley's party conference speech on GP fund-holding being publicised in Government-financed PURCHASING IN PRACTICE Mar '95; after a trip to Japan as its Government's guest, disclosed Japan, as its second biggest customer, would oppose the simple privatisation of the Crown Agents June '95; his 'The Nation's Health' Fabian pamphlet urged socially equitable treatment and concentration only on demonstrably effective medical treatments June '95; introduced Railway Communities (Job Creation) Bill to encourage alternative job opportunities July '95; deplored the closure of the ABB carriageworks in York, despite a £50m investment based on false Government promises Oct '95; urged new laws to protect private NHS files which could be bought for £150 each Nov '95; asked PM John Major for an independent inquiry into BSE; Major denied any link with CJD Dec '95; said Labour would only be credible if its leadership committed it to higher NHS spending Jan '96; complained the privatised railways were inefficient, uncompetitive monopolies Apr '96; said Londoners were receiving more than their fair share of Lottery grants July '96; after a trip to the Lebanon, urged the Government to provide aid to its 40,000 refugees, without abandoning

Israel or the peace process Apr '96; blamed the increase in RAF crashes on cheap maintenance and inadequate training time June '96; after visiting Japan with the Health Select Committee to study care of the elderly, wrote that US-style private insurance schemes were only suitable for the affluent elderly June '96; backed cuts in MPs' mileages and capping their increases at 3% - "Parliament's standing has never been lower" but pensions at £43,000 July '96; admitted he was conned into signing a passport application for an American alleged rapist July '96; on Commons Library figures, was the first to disclose that the Conservative Government had taken more money in taxes in every year since 1979, July '96; erroneously charged Steve Norris with having moved "from the boudoir of the Department of Transport to the profitable and sweet embrace of Capital City Bus" which he had privatised Nov '96; urged a rerun of the franchising of Regional Railways North East when the winner was shown to have been provided with financial information three months fresher than its competitors Jan '97; introduced Overseas Development Co-operation Bill to ensure ODA money was better spent on poor people in poor countries, not on inducing arms purchases by Malaysia and Indonesia by financing dubious aid projects Jan '97; was reproached by Speaker Boothroyd for accusing Tory Home Minister David Maclean of "lying" about Labour's attitude toward crime detection Jan '97; was targetted by Prolife Alliance Party Feb '97; attacked Health Secretary Stephen Dorrell's insurance scheme to help elderly middle-class pensioners keep their homes as doing "nothing for the poorer pensioners" Mar '97; retained his seat with a trebled majority of 20,523, a pro-Labour swing of 12.6% May '97; was named PPS to Health Secretary Frank Dobson May '97; raised the faulty justice accorded to a murdered local stonemason May '97; backed the outlawing of fox-hunting June '97; rejoiced at the reopening of the local carriageworks with the investment of US money July '97; endorsed the inquiry into the origins of BSE, having warned nearly nine years before of the possibility of an infective agent jumping species Dec '97; told of a large local printworks, saved from closure by a massive Dutch contract, demonstrating "that Britain benefits from involvement in the European Union" Jan '98; introduced Bill to outlaw international bribery Feb '98; held adjournment debate to resist transfer Army's North of England command from York to Edinburgh Apr '98; blunted Tory attack on handling of Sierra Leone May '98; insisted that first-past-the-post was "an 18th century system" and the referendum on the Jenkins Commission proposal would allow its replacement of something more suitable June '98;
Born: 9 January 1952, Oxford
Family: Son, Michael Bayley, architect, and Pauline (Oppenheimer) secretary; m '84 Fenella (Jeffers) researcher; 1s Benjamin '85; 1d Eleanor '87;
Education: Haileybury Junior; Haileybury; Bristol University '70-74 (BSc; President of Union); York University '74-76 (BPhil);
Occupation: Author and co-Author: 'Care of Elderly in Lincolnshire' (1989), Changes in the Dependence of Residents' (1989), 'The Dependency of Elderly People' (1990), 'Future Role of the District Health Authority' (1990), 'North Lincolnshire Health Authority' (1991); 'The Nation's Health' (1995); on Parliamentary Panels of Harris and Business Planning and Research International (at up to £1,000 each: "I complete up to eight questionnaires about my opinions"; "I do not meet or act for any [of their] clients") '95-; Director (unpaid), Foundation for Traditional Chinese Medicine (a registered charity) '93-97; Patron (unpaid), of Ecology Building Society '93-97; ex: Sponsored, by RMT (£750 p a for constituency, 80% of election expenses)'93-95; Research Fellow, in Health Economics, at York University '87-92; Lecturer, in Social Policy, York University (AUT) '86-87; General Secretary, International Broadcasting Trust (TV production company specialising in programmes about the 3rd World; ACTT) '82-86; National Officer, NALGO '77-82; District Officer, NALGO '75-77; [he considered in '94 that he could have been earning £50,000 if he had remained in TV production; since he still

considered York a marginal seat, "I have to face the fact that I might cease to be an MP before the kids are grown up and my financial circumstances may change substantially" Feb '94;]

Traits: Slim; light brown, parted, front-combed hair; "with strict haircut, expensive overcoat and soft-voiced compassion and fiscal pragmatism, Mr Bayley looks the model of the modern Labour candidate" (Mark Lawson, INDEPENDENT); forceful shouter (at conference); lover of live music, especially jazz;

Address: House of Commons, Westminster, London SW1A 0AA; 9 Holly Terrace, York YO10 4DS; 59 Holgate Road, York YO24 4AA;

Telephone: 0171 219 5100 (H of C); 01904 623713 (home);

(Christopher) Nigel BEARD   **Labour**   **BEXLEYHEATH & CRAYFORD '97-**

Majority: 3,415 over Conservative 6-way;

Description: A new seat combining parts of old safe-Tory Bexleyheath and marginal old Erith and Crayford; it is the London constituency that is the furthest east on the south bank of the Thames; it was considered safe enough for Tories for ex-Tory MP David Evennett to fight to represent it; on a '92-type division of the vote, it was expected to provide a 12,000 Conservative majority;

Position: On the Select Committee on Science and Technology '97-, Ecclesiastical Committee '97-; ex: on Labour Party National Constitutional Committee '94-98; on the Board, Royal Marsden Hospital '82-90, SW Thames Regional Health Authority '78-86; Chairman, Woking Constituency Labour Party '81-82; on the Political Committee of CWS, Labour's Southern Region Executive;

Outlook: The seniormost member of Labour's 1997 intake, an industrial intellectual straight from the laboratories of big business (ICI-Zeneca); a former election-time "hobby politician" who was unexpectedly successful on his fourth effort; has "considerable knowledge of medical research and the NHS" (Health Under Secretary Paul Boateng); a veteran Research and Development manager, most recently at Zeneca; self-described as "fairly consistently New Labour"; a top planner, originally for the MoD, then GLC, recently for Zeneca; apart from his Maiden, initially played a minimal role in the Commons, while extricating himself from his Zeneca commitments; posed few written questions, only six in his first year, until he got into his stride; a Fabian who wants wider and deeper industrial democracy, Government support in establishing high-technology industries, Marshall-Plan-type economic aid for the ex-USSR, EU control of the arms trade, legal and electoral reform;

History: His family background was Tory, although his father, a BR goods porter, was an NUR activist; he joined the Labour Party at 27, '63; campaigned for consistent and predictable levels of Government funding for inner-city renewal, especially in the East End '74-79; contested hopeless Woking May '79; was selected for Portsmouth North by 15 to 10 from a short-list of four Oct '82; spoke at a meeting with Ken Livingstone and Ted Knight sponsored by their Trotkyist LABOUR HERALD Feb '83; unsuccessfully fought Portsmouth North June '83; as a Co-op nominee, was beaten by Russsell Profitt in selection for marginal Lewisham East, when its constituency party defied the NEC and held an unofficial selection conference including an illicit 'black caucus' May '85; was selected to retake Tory-held marginal Erith and

Crayford Feb '90; backed higher pensions Dec '90; complained of an 48% increase in unemployment in the constituency in the previous year Mar '91; increased the Labour vote by 6,000, but lost by 2,339 votes (5%) Apr '92; was re-selected for overlapping Bexleyheath and Crayford July '95; as the 22nd least-expected new Labour MP, quite unexpectedly won the seat, by a majority of 3,415 after a notional swing to Labour of 15%, ending the 14-year Commons career of David Evennett May '97; in his impressive Maiden underlined the loss of his seat's engineering industries during the two previous decades, emphasising: "we have to regenerate opportunities for people to use their skills and talents to the full; unless we do that, we shall not raise the long-term rate of economic growth of the country as a whole"; "a greater proportion of small and medium-sized companies need to be based on high technology so that they can compete internationally" July '97; was named to the Select Committee on Science and Technology July '97; urged a wholly new defence strategy, based on current and future realities; he ridiculed the idea that Britain could usefully use "even half of the 232 [Eurofighter] aircraft that we are committed to purchase" or needed to plan for "tank battles across the north German plains" Oct '97; complained about the erosion in past years of "the capital foundation, the equipment and the infrastructure of research in universities" Nov '97; urged the alleviation of public anxiety about the applications of biotechnology Dec '97; asked about "developing a means of diagnosing BSE before the symptoms become obvious" Dec '97; spoke knowledgeably about the use of flexible small companies in the end product of scientific research, technical development and marketing of new products; urged consideration of launch aid for the early stages of commercialisation, "an expensive and risky business" Dec '97; pointed out that the Governmenty's winter payments, two thirds to women pensioners, partly overcame the inequalities suffered by women pensioners Jan '98; co-sponsored motion deploring the threat to community pharmacies in ending resale price maintenance for over-the-counter sales of patent medicines Jan '98; welcomed the rebuilding of the Queen Elizabeth Hospital in Greenwich Feb '98; joined complaints about threatened closure of Shooters Hill fire station Mar '98; urged the representation on companies' boards of its employees with "scientific, technological, design, commercial and managerial abilities" Mar '98; complained about current arrangements for compensation for medical accidents or negligence Apr '98; largely backing the Competition Bill, said its role was "to arrest the natural tendency towards the erosion of competiton while leaving adequate scope for businesses to adapt to changing circumstances"; he complained about the disappearance of any "redress available to a third party who has suffered from the anti-competitive behaviour of another company"; he opposed Lord McNally's anti-Murdoch amendment as "redundant"; May '98; was rated as one of the 'Bottom 100' written questioners, having posed only six in his first year May '98;

Born: 10 October 1936, Leeds

Family: Only son of Albert Leonard Beard, BR goods porter and NUR activist, and Irene (Bowes); m '69 Jennifer Anne (Cotton), teacher; 1s Daniel '71, 1d Jessica '73;

Education: Temple Street Junior, Castleford; Castleford Grammar School, Yorkshire; University College, London University (BSc [Hons] in Special Physics); London Business School; FRSA;

Occupation: Author: The Practical Use of Linear Programming in Planning and Analysis (HMSO 1974); ex: Senior Manager, for Research and Development, of Zeneca (GMB) '93-97; Senior Consultant, to ICI, on New Business and New Technology '79-93; Director, of London Docklands Development Team '74-79; Chief Planner, for Strategy, GLC '73-74; Superintendent of Studies, Army Land Operations in the Defence of Europe '68-72; Scientific Officer, later Principal Scientific Officer, in the Defence Operational Analysis Establishment '61-68; Market Researcher, Esso Petroleum '61; Physicist, with English Electric's Atomic

Power Division, working on design of Hinckley Point '59-61; Assistant Mathematics Master, Tadcaster Grammar School '58-59;
Traits: Serious-looking; high forehead; parted hair; hooded eyes; enjoys: theatre, music, contemporary painting;
Address: House of Commons, Westminster, London SW1A 0AA; 50 Peareswood Road, Slade Green, Erith, Kent DA8 2HR;
Telephone: 0171 219 5061 (H of C); 01322 332261(home);

Rt Hon Margaret (Jackson) BECKETT   **Labour**   **DERBY SOUTH '83-**

Majority: 16,106 (31.1%) over Conservative 5-way;
Description: Railway works, Rolls-Royce aero factory and old grounds of Derby County Football Club, surrounded by dingy housing; in '95 the Tory-leaning Mickleover ward was added from South Derbyshire to this once-marginal seat;
Former Seat: Lincoln Oct '74-79;
Position: President of the Council and Leader of the Commons '98-; Chairman, Commons Modernisation Committee '98-; ex:President of the Board of Trade '97-98; on Labour's NEC '89-98, '87 (July-Sep), '85-86, '80-81; in Shadow Cabinet '88-97; Spokesman on Trade and Industry '95-97; Health Spokesman
'94-95; Labour Leader May-July '94, Deputy Leader '92-94; Shadow Leader of Commons and Campaign Co-ordinator '92-94; on Plant Commission '90-93; Shadow Chief Secretary '89-92; Assistant Spokesman, Social Security '84-89; Under Secretary, for Education '76-79, Assistant Whip '75-76, PPS to Judith Hart '74-75;
Outlook: Labour's best and most experienced female brain; "tough, competent, inscrutable" (TIMES), has moved out from the hard-Left to establish sometimes-strained links with Gordon Brown and Tony Blair; a strong supporter of Labour's union links; is cautiously determined to increase Britain's competitiveness long-term by adequate investment in research and training; "under-appreciated", "a grown-up Parliamentarian" with "a long pedigree on the Left of her party" who "is a more-convincing friend of the huddled masses than many Cabinet Ministers" (Quentin Letts, DAILY TELEGRAPH); she was never "taken seriously as a possible Leader of the Labour Party and it obviously hurts"; "she has suffered from being seen as an apparatchik, a manager rather than a visionary" (Peter Riddell, TIMES); has recently been obscured from sight mainly by Chancellor Brown, although she has remained loyal to his tight-money vision; there has been little payoff for Tony Blair's promise in November 1996 that she would be recalled from TV exile because she was the public's second most popular Labour woman after Claire Short; she has also been under-rated by much of the party and the media because she has a logical, numerate, technocratic mind ("like a steel trap" - Leo Beckett) but a tightly-controlled warmth; fights her ideological corner without leaking or spin-doctorin; despite her identification with the old Left, was the late John Smith's politically fickle but highly competent chosen lady Deputy who gambled all and lost the '94 contest for Leader and Deputy Leader; "possibly the Labour politician who has travelled furthest both personally and politically in recent years" (Nicholas Timmins, INDEPENDENT); "she has always been a pragmatist who has tried to stay attuned to the mood of the Labour Party"; she

"has moved from Left to Right with the rest of the Labour Party but has gone to unusual lengths to remain on good terms with everyone" (Sarah Baxter, SUNDAY TIMES); a firm party loyalist who has worked hard behind the scenes ("I hope I am a good servant of the party" - MB); a "team player" who tries "to take decisions on their merits" (MB); one of Labour's "toughest frontbench speakers", "assiduous in mastering the details of her brief" (Colin Brown, INDEPENDENT); "lucid, coherent, sharp-minded and impactive" (Edward Pearce, EVENING STANDARD); "hard-working and good on detail, if far from universally liked within the party" (Michael Cassell, FINANCIAL TIMES); a 'moderniser who has emerged from the semi-hard Left; "is no longer on the Left by any definition but her own", but "she has been able to move steadily Rightwards while maintaining old links"; she long remained a member of CND and the Common Market Safeguards Committee; was"among the most steadfast opponents of electoral reform on the Plant Commission" (Sarah Baxter, NEW STATESMAN); still insists that "my roots tend to be in the Left of the party"; "the conversion of Margaret Beckett from hard-Left trouble-maker into strict keeper of the public spending purse [was] remarkable" (INDEPENDENT); shows "hard-nosed scepticism which mingles with the politician's natural prudence" (Michael White, GUARDIAN) in '89-92 was "a political tough guy whose draconian grip on the spending promises of her Shadow Cabinet colleagues succeeded - for a while - in preventing the Conservatives making hay with Labour's tax-and-spending campaign" (GUARDIAN); in '84-89 was a very able, hardworking, effective but under-noticed frontbencher on social services ("on top of the subject" - David Hencke, GUARDIAN); anti: fox-hunting, Militant-purging, PR; pro: positive discrimination; formerly TGWU-sponsored, UNISON-helped;

History: Her childhood was dominated by poverty caused by the illness and death of her carpenter father; "I went to college and I became a member of the Labour Club - largely I must admit because my then boyfriend was the Secretary" '63; in reaction to the Sharpville massacre and Apartheid, joined the Labour Party '64; contested Swinton municipal elections May '68; contested Lincoln against premature SDP-defector Dick Taverne, cutting his majority to one-tenth that of the '73 by-election Feb '74; was appointed Political Adviser to Judith Hart Mar '74; captured Lincoln from Dick Taverne by 984 votes Oct '74; joined Tribune Group Nov '74; was appointed Assistant Whip, for a period writing reports on Commons for the Queen Jan '75; voted against staying in the EEC June '75; to the surprise of Leftwingers, accepted post of Under Secretary for Education in place of Joan Lestor, who resigned in protest against cuts Mar '76; contested women's section of NEC winning 264,000 votes Oct '76 and 245,000 votes Oct '77; lost Lincoln to Conservative Kenneth Carlisle May '79; won seat on NEC Oct '80; failed to secure candidacy for Warrington June '81; after losing her seat on the NEC, she lashed out at a conference-fringe Tribune Rally against Neil Kinnock and other soft-Left MPs who had abstained against Tony Benn's candidacy for Deputy Leader, provoking fierce personal arguments with Stan Orme and Joan Lestor Sep '81; was selected for Derby South to succeed retiring Walter Johnson Nov '81, NEC-endorsed Dec '81; on CLPD slate, unsuccessfully contested Women's Section of NEC Oct '82; narrowly won Derby South, joining both the Tribune and Campaign Groups of Labour MPs June '83; again contested NEC unsuccessfully, winning 2.2m votes Oct '83; backed Michael Meacher for Deputy Leader, Neil Kinnock for Leader Oct '83; on Campaign Group slate for Shadow Cabinet, won 27 votes Oct '83; on Campaign Group slate for Deputy Chief Whip, won 34 votes Nov '83; promoted Assistant Spokesman on Social Security, replacing Frank Field, was sacked for voting with Campaign Group against Government on GCHQ Mar '84; despite Neil Kinnock's appeal for moratorium on comment on miners' strike, supported a Campaign Group statement of full support for Arthur Scargill's strategy and campaign May '84; on hard-Left Campaign Group slate for Women's Section of NEC, failed with 1,985,000 votes Oct '84; on

Campaign Group slate for Shadow Cabinet, won 35 votes Nov '84; on Briefing's slate for Women's Section of NEC, succeeded with 3,591,00 votes, ousting Rightwinger Ann Davis Sept '85; on joint Tribune and Campaign Groups' slate for Shadow Cabinet, won 58 votes Oct '85; signed minority report of Labour's Liverpool inquiry, opposing expulsion of Derek Hatton and other Militant sympathisers Feb '86; expressed "about the unscrupulous over-selling of personal pensions" Feb '86; described as "outrageous" Government decision to extend disqualification to 13 weeks of dole for those leaving a job without good cause Apr '86; urged NEC to postpone Militant expulsions Apr '86; co-described Militant's views as "often reactionary and outdated" and Rightwing (on blacks' and women's rights) May '86; with 3,101,00 votes she lost her seat on NEC to pro-Kinnock Diana Jeuda Sep '86; attacked the situation where the middle class got smear tests while the working class got cancer Oct '86; on Campaign Group slate for Shadow Cabinet, won 42 votes Oct '86; again joined both soft-Left Tribune Group and hard-Left Campaign Group July '87; rejoined the NEC as the runner-up when Betty Boothroyd retired to become Deputy Speaker July '87; on Campaign Group slate for Shadow Cabinet, won 66 votes July '87; irritated the TGWU, her sponsoring union, by voting with the hard Left in opposing one-member one-vote on the NEC Sep '87; failed (with 3,064,000 votes) to retake an NEC seat, with Ann Davis and Joan Lestor making comebacks Sep '87; made a powerful last speech from the platform urging priority for the child victims of abuse, emphasising that they tended to blame themselves, becoming alienated drug-users or prostitutes Sep '87; accepted televising of Commons although "cameras love beautiful people" Feb '88; with Jo Richardson and Clare Short, resigned from Campaign Group over its decision again to back Benn's challenge to Kinnock's leadership, which she had opposed Mar '88; backed Chief Inspector, victimised for campaign against Freemasonry May '88; attacked new Social Fund because the "grants are so restrictive that local DHSS offices are simply not able to pay out the money that is desperately needed" July '88; on Campaign Group slate for Women's Section of NEC, won her place with 3,590,000 votes Oct '88; supported John Prescott against Roy Hattersley for Deputy Leadership Oct-Nov '88; with 71 votes for Shadow Cabinet, was 2nd runner-up, behind Martin O'Neill Nov '88; complained Government was saving £6b a year from breaking the link between pension levels and average earnings Dec '88; successfully called for Tory rebels to join with Labour to give justice to pre-1973 war widows Mar '89; on NEC voted with Left minority against Kinnock's abandonment of unilateralism May '89; was elected to Women's Section of NEC, with 3,786,000 votes Oct '89; with the backing of Tribune Group and 'Supper Club' of semi-hard Leftwingers, won 106 votes, in 17th place, qualifying her for enlarged Shadow Cabinet; was named Shadow Chief Secretary; Norman Tebbit said it was like "putting a vixen in the hen house to guard the chickens" Nov '89; helped commit party only to higher child benefits and pensions Feb '90; promised to restore attractiveness of SERPS (State Earnings Related Pension Scheme) which the Tories had devalued to encourage people into private personal pension schemes Apr '90; claimed average family had lost more through VAT and National Insurance rises than it had gained through Tory tax cuts June '90; in new mini-manifesto, 'Looking to the Future', pared down party's expenditure commitments June '90; voted with hard Left on NEC against Kinnock's caution on defence cuts Sep '90; was re-elected to Women's Section of NEC with 4,895,000 votes; warned: "we cannot speedily restore all of the damage" Oct '90; was named to the Plant Commission on electoral reform Oct '90; soared to 3rd place on Shadow Cabinet with 133 votes Oct '90; was publicised as having been a member of the semi-hard Left 'Supper Club' which had been meeting in the Westminster Arms Feb '91; pledged Labour to restore child benefit to its 1987 value in real terms Mar '91; toured City boardrooms with 'shadow Chancellor' John Smith, telling directors: "We don't want to repeat the mistakes of 1974-79; it wouldn't be politically sensible to have a great blowout and then spend the years up to the next election reigning back; you can at least believe that, in our own self-interest, we won't be getting ourselves in a position that we have to hand it all back to the Conservatives" Jan-May '91; improved her reputation in head-to-head clash with David Mellor, then Chief Secretary May '91; was dubbed "class traitor of the month" by Trotskyist LABOUR BRIEFING May '91; was found to be marginally more popular than her opponent, Chief Secretary David Mellor, by 33% to 31% May '91; said Labour's taxation policies would increase burden only on "the wealthiest 5% in the country" May '91; insisted Labour would not spend more than the economy could afford, but would "put every penny the economy can afford into investment and into public services" May '91; warned Labour conference the party would have to "move steadily and with caution" if it attained office because of "the scale of the problems, the fragility of the economy and the constraints of the unfettered competition we shall so quickly face in the single European market" Sep '91; was re-elected, top, to Women's Section of NEC with 5,405,000 votes Sep '91; came 6th with 134 votes for Shadow Cabinet Oct '91; with Chris Smith, decided a Labour Government would split Treasury accounts for the first time to show capital and revenue spending separately Oct '91; was jokily rated "1991's Least Promising Frontbencher" by GUARDIAN's Andrew Rawnsley because of her "when resources allow" refrain Dec '91; insisted that 96% of families would be better off under Labour's tax and national insurance package Jan '92; toured EC with John Smith and Tony Blair talking up their ideas for EC-wide supply-side policies on investment and training Jan '92; warned against public borrowing of even 5% of national income, as advocated by Major Feb '92; accused Government of a "buy now, pay later" Budget Mar '92; retained her seat with majority up from 1,516 to 6,936, a swing to Labour of 5.35% Apr '92; after initial hesitation, decided to contest Deputy Leadership, in partnership with John Smith; was nominated by 89 MPs, including Ann Clwyd, who withdrew; said: "we need to widen our appeal still further to convince our fellow-citizens where self-interest and common interest go hand-in-hand, that morality and efficiency need not conflict"; "my roots tend to be in the Left of the party"; as a belated supporter of one-person, one-vote, objected to her sponsor, the TGWU, not going for balloting of its membership Apr '92; in interview with David Frost, defended her Euro-scepticism and CND membership: "I've not allowed my membership of CND to lapse because I joined it because I wanted to see nuclear disarmament by whatever means and CND was the only organisation then really working for it; that's why I've stayed in it"; also said Neil Kinnock had been "probably more right than I was" over expulsion of Militants May '92; launched a 'Modernisation Manifesto' calling for re-establishing trust for Labour, largely by ending its traditional macho image"; also proposed state funding for political parties and a poverty census May '92; said: "one member, one vote is the way ahead" but urged retention of block vote for leadership election and policy formulation May '92; was reticent about what percentage of her expensive campaign's financing came from unions May '92; after cautious, low-key campaign, won Deputy Leadership by 57.3% to 28.2% for John Prescott and 14.5% for Bryan Gould July '92; was named Shadow Leader of the Commons and Campaigns Co-ordinator July '92; was named to the Review Group on union-party relations, including the abolition of the block vote July '92; opposed a Maastricht referendum because "the vast majority of those who are calling for a referendum are doing so because of their basic opposition to our membership of the European Community" Sep '92; John Smith was alleged to have joked to his colleagues that his deputy was living proof that the rehabilitation of offenders actually worked Sep '92; was named to Commons Commission Oct '92; said the country would not forgive the Liberal Democrats if they propped up the Major Government on Maastricht Nov '92; abstained against year-long freeze on MPs' pay as designed "to create an illusion of fairness" Nov '92; on Review Group was said "to favour more union influence than Mr Smith" (SUNDAY TELEGRAPH) Nov '92; said Major was the "most unpopular

Prime Minister in history" Dec '92; visited USA in wake of Bill Clinton's victory Dec '92; came under attack from John Prescott as a Clinton-emulating 'moderniser' when she introduced Clinton adviser Stan Greenberg to Shadow Cabinet Jan '93; was elevated to the Privy Council Feb '93; on Plant Commission was the firmest defender of the existing first-past-the-post ballot for the Commons Mar '93; complained of Government inactivity over loss of 5,000 skilled jobs at Rolls-Royce Mar '93; her seat was made more marginal by plan to transfer into it 8,000 mainly Tory middle-class people from Edwina Currie's neighbouring Derbyshire South Mar '93; as a supporter of first-past-the-post, was in a minority on the Plant Commission, which narrowly backed a supplementary vote system Apr '93; after advances by Labour and Liberal Democrats in county council elections - of which she had been in command - opposed any deals with Liberal Democrats May '93; made a slashing attack on the Conservative Party's undeclared funding by businessmen, including foreigners; said Labour would make public all donations over £5-10,000, ban donations by foreigners and return any tainted money June '93; urged an "agreed settlement" between those backing one-member one-vote and reluctant union leaders like Bill Morris of her sponsoring union, the TGWU July '93; with Jack Straw, agreed to nip Liberal Democrats' revival in the bud Aug '93; refused initially to support John Smith's version of one-member one-vote, preferring an agreement with union leaders; was finally pushed into saying, "I fully support John Smith on one-member one-vote, as I support his leadership"; because of her lukewarm attitude, John Smith had to call in John Prescott to do his crucial rabble-rousing speech in favour of one-member one-vote Sep '93; she lost her PPS, Janet Anderson, a strong supporter of one-member one-vote Oct '93; rebutting doubts about her survival, John Smith said: "we have just re-elected both myself and Margaret as Deputy Leader at the conference; there is no vacancy for either of these posts" Oct '93; expressed concern about operations of Child Support Agency Oct '93; voted against restoring capital punishment, even for cop-killers Feb '94; backed reduction of homosexual age of consent, either to 18 or 16, Feb '94; told the PLP the party would make the Euro-elections a referendum on the Major Government: "we will denounce tax increases day by day" Mar '94; after sudden death of John Smith, she became Labour's first woman Leader May '94; she "was clearly upset when, in the days after Mr Smith's death, she was virtually written out of the script" (Peter Riddell, TIMES); INDEPENDENT ON SUNDAY gave 16-1 odds against her being elected Leader May '94; threw her hat into the ring - yielding up her Deputy Leader's post - to contest both the Leadership and Deputy Leadership, offering "a degree of continuity and stabiility" June '94; challenged the Blairite reformers by insisting it would be madness to change the party constitution further "at this stage in the electoral cycle" June '94; in the count for Leader, she came third after Tony Blair and John Prescott (57%/24%/19%); in the count for Deputy Leader, she came second to Prescott (56.5%/43.5%) July '94; she decided to contest both the NEC and the Shadow Cabinet, hoping for Tony Blair's former Home Office portfolio July '94; secured the highest percentage (18.77%) for the Women's section of Labour's NEC Sep-Oct '94; having secured the second highest number of votes (170) for the Shadow Cabinet, she accepted the Health portfolio Oct '94; attacked Virginia Bottomley for her "gradual destruction of London's health care" Jan '95; arguments about its contents allegedly delayed her policy paper on the NHS, with Blairites allegedly urging a softening of opposition to Conservative changes and private health care Mar '95; said Tory reforms had increased accountants by 49% but nurses had dropped by 37,000 Apr '95; she and Blair negotiated a compromise in which there would be no pledge to increase financing, the NHS internal market would be effectively dismantled, GP fundholding would be replaced by co-operative purchaser agencies; Labour's National Policy Forum endorsed their compromise June '95; described the Private Finance Initiative as "totally unacceptable" and "the thin edge of privatisation" '95; on the NEC, abstained from voting to end the Leeds candidacy of the semi-Trotskyist Liz Davies Sep '95; having polled the highest total in the Shadow Cabinet election (187), Blair offered her the Trade and Industry portfolio she accepted, including scientific policy and the information super highway; she was given a 7-person team under her; Harriet Harman had asked for Social Security but accepted Health, Beckett's previous portfolio Oct '95; urged an end to nuclear privatisation, claiming it would be costly for the Government to finance the abandoned obligations Jan '96; spoke against privatisation of the Royal Mail and Parcelforce, urging they be allowed more commercial freedom, like the BBC Feb '96; accused T&I of being the worst department in late payments Feb '96; in replying for Labour on the Scott Report, insisted that a Government which had nothing to hide did not limit to only a few hours the Opposition's access to the Report before its publication and debate Feb '96; wrote that everyone should be enabled to have access to the Information Super Highway Feb '96; in the run-up to the unwanted-by-Blair Shadow Cabinet election, Tony Blair allegedly gave support to "people he loathes to ensure Labour goes into the general election with a united campaigning team", according to Michael White and David Hencke of the GUARDIAN; quoting a "senior Labour spokesman speaking privately", they wrote that Beckett was "detested" by Blair but "supported through gritted teeth" July '96; she again topped the poll for the Shadow Cabinet with 251 votes - 102 more than received by the last in, Harriet Harman, for whom the leadership apparatus worked very hard July '96; voted to reduce MPs' mileage allowances but to increase their pay and pensions July '96; was retained as Shadow President of the Board of Trade in the 'final' Shadow Cabinet reshuffle Aug '96; a private Labour poll showed the public found her the second most attractive Labour woman after Clare Short Nov '96; Tony Blair told her she would be recalled from TV exile and given more prominence to help boost Labour's appeal to older women Nov '96; did a restrained but savagely effective job in destroying Tory Government claims for its Budget Dec '96; after the Red Book became available, she accepted that the £1.5b in receipts for privatising the national air safety board would require further Labour consideration of how to replace it Mar '97; during the election campaign, pressmen noted that their efforts to ask her questions were blocked by replies from Gordon Brown Apr '97; retained her somewhat altered seat with an enhanced majority of 16,106 over Conservative opponent, on a notional swing of 11.8% May '97; on taking office as President of the Board of Trade, increased the 700 mgw gas-electricity station being built at Stone Bridge Lincolnshire by 90 mgw May '97; she won a battle with David Blunkett (Education and Employment), that the Low Pay Commission would come under her department May '97; referred the takeover of Scottish Rail and West Midlands by National Express to the MMC May '97; visited Japan on trade and inward investment mission May '97; saw TUC General Secretary John Monks after announcing that unions would be involved in promoting industrial competitiveness June '97; ruled against Bass's takeover of Carlsberg-Tetley June '97; she announced that the regulation of utility prices would be made fair and transparent both to consumers and shareholders June '97; wrote to John Redwood that Lord Simon had "placed the generality of his shares in a blind trust" but had not disposed of his BP shares, which would be reconsidered in six months' time July '97; again insisted that, despite John Redwood's obsessive challenges, Lord Simon had followed proper procedures in resolving possible clashes of interest as a former Chairman of BP; John Redwood was being fed, allegedly, by anti-Labour former colleagues in BP July '97; challenged alleged price-fixing by Dixon's and Curry's in electrical goods July '97; after she announced the eight members of the Low Pay Commission, she was accused by Conservatives of packing it with trade unionists and pro-union academics July '97; defended Lord Simon: "it seems to me that what [Tory] Opposition members really resent is that he is a brilliant businessman who has taken up a post in a Labour Government for no pay - which is not of course the standard to which they are accustomed" July '97; referred the attempted takeover of Energy Group by Pacificorp to the MMC Aug '97; she continued to be attacked by John Redwood for allegedly misleading the Commons over Lord Simon's shareholdings Aug '97; in her new Competition Bill she proposed to crack down on anti-competitive practices; the MMC would be changed into the Competition Commission with tough punishment for those who violated its rules Aug '97; wrote to John Redwood that the £411 in P&O shares inherited by her junior Minister Nigel Griffiths had not delayed consideration of the merger by P&O and Stena, because he had ruled himself out of considering the case Sep '97; in Cabinet was alleged to have complained against Chancellor Brown's briefing about an impending civil service pay freeze without Cabinet authorisation Sep '97; she asked the Chairman of the Low Pay Commission to consider at what age the full minimum wage should be paid Sep '97; she came top in the vote for women on Labour's NEC with 20.71%, ahead of Clare Short and Hilary Armstrong Sep '97; was extensively criticised by Tory MPs for taking a delayed holiday in a caravan Nov '97; was the first Labour President of the Board of Trade to address a CBI conference Nov '97; she said her original Euroscepticism had been changed by "two referendums and the experience of the British people who clearly chose by a democratic decision to remain in the European Union; in my view it is now the case that all our interests are irrevocably bound up with our membership of that body" Dec '97; appointed Derek Morris as head of the Monopolies Commission and its successor, the Competition Commission Jan '98; was said to be set to lift early the Tories' ban on BT using its network to provide entertainment Jan '98; wound up her office's blind trust Apr '98; ended price-fixing for electrical goods May '98; unveiled the Blair-supervised compromise between the TUC and CBI on workplace conditions, the "Fairness at Work" White Paper with its disputed 40% minimum turnout for union recognition votes May '98; was said to be locked in Cabinet debate against Chancellor Brown's and PM Blair's insistence on lower minimum wage for young starters June '98; introduced the Energy Review for consultation, aimed at securing "diverse and sustainable supplies of energy at competititive prices"; a "level playing field" would be achieved by slowing further consents for gas-fired generators and encouraging contracts for competitive coal to be burned in generators with desulphurised flues June '98; was said to be "spitting blood" because Chancellor Gordon Brown had forced her to accept a National Minimum Wage of £3.20 for those between 18 and 20, June '98; replaced by Peter Mandelson, she was reshuffled into Leader of the Commons July '98;

Born: 15 January 1943, Ashton-under-Lyne

Family: Daughter, late Cyril Jackson, Leftwing carpenter, a Congregationalist who became an invalid when she was three and died when she was 12, and Winifred (Quirke), Irish Roman Catholic infant-school teacher; one of Margaret's two sisters became a consultant psychiatrist, the other a nun, then a teacher; m '79 supportive 'Leo'/Lionel Beckett, ex-fitter, recently her office manager; 2 stepsons; 5 stepgrandchildren;

Education: St Mary's, Ashton-under-Lyne; Notre Dame Prep; Notre Dame High School, Norwich (head girl at this RC convent school); John Dalton Polytechnic, Manchester; Manchester College of Science and Technology (sandwich course);

Occupation: Formerly TGWU-sponsored (£600 a year to constituency party, £3,000 for election expenses) '83-95; was also provided with a researcher by UNISON '94-95; has had office support services financed by the Margaret Beckett Research and Administration Trust (a blind trust) '96-98; ex: Principal Researcher, Granada TV '79-83; Political Adviser, to Judith Hart, Minister for Overseas Development '74; Research Assistant, Labour Party '70-74; Experimental Officer, Department of Metallurgy, Manchester University '66-70; Student Apprentice, in metallurgy, at AEI, Manchester (as one of 20 women among 2,400 apprentices) '61-66;

Traits: Looks like a smaller, working-class Princess Anne - "a Princess Anne without horses"

(John Williams, EVENING STANDARD); blonde; toothy; "slim, angular" (Joanne Robertson, SCOTSMAN); "smart, businesslike figure" (INDEPENDENT); "hard-working, sharp, even acid-tongued" (GUARDIAN); "her disappoving stare is a refinement of the Medusa" (Quentin Letts, DAILY TELEGRAPH); "I've been called horsy and compared to Princess Anne; I feel sorry for her over that; she's younger than me and she has good hair; if I could change one thing, it would be my hair; it's impossible; there's a constant battle" (MB); "was never, in appearance or inclination, the prototype of the New Labour woman; where New Labour woman got the Barbara Follett makeover, she stuck with the Princess Royal tailoring; where New Labour woman shopped for peppers in Riberae market, she went caravanning in Yorkshire" (Mary Riddell, TIMES); "scrupulously courteous" (Charis Gresser, DAILY TELEGRAPH); "she's very cool, very encyclopaedic, her style is not broad-brush, it's sort of hairline-detailed" (Paul Flynn MP); "does a fine line in sneering putdowns" (Derek Brown, GUARDIAN); "brisk and bristly" (MAIL ON SUNDAY); "there is nothing about the way Mrs Beckett looks or the tone of her voice to frighten the horses...from the neat middle-market, middle-class clothes to the carefully back-brushed and spray-detained hair she conveys safety and competence" (Nesta Wyn Ellis, MAIL ON SUNDAY); "small, intense, plain-speaking, tough and toothy" (OBSERVER); "collected, careful, occasionally acerbic" (Kirsty Milne, OBSERVER); "careful, controlled, passionless and humourless, her lips pursed at her own prudence" (Andrew Rawnsley, GUARDIAN); "one of the best turned-out among the [Labour] women" (Nicola Tyrer, DAILY TELEGRAPH); "a tense and somehow lonely figure dressed in soft sludgy colours" (Melanie Phillips, GUARDIAN); "headmistressy" (Geraldine Bedell, INDEPENDENT ON SUNDAY); has a "matter-of-fact, business-like tone that detractors say can border on bossy" (Sue Heal, OBSERVER); has a manner "like a rather prim and terrifying aunt" (INDEPENDENT ON SUNDAY); "at social functions I am happiest being the quiet mouse in the corner"; "I think I am basically lazy so I enjoy functioning under pressure; otherwise, I'd stop altogether"; "I am a terrible pessimist; I always expect the worst, on the basis that then hopefully at least I won't be disappointed or taken by surprise"; "I am an obsessional like my father; I am alway making lists, but can put things behind me when they are done; I also have my mother's explosive Irish temperament; if someone interrupts me when I am under intense pressure, I can blow up for an instant"; "I hate having my photograph taken; I am conscious of the fact the television likes beautiful people and I don't happen to be one of them; but I can live with that"; competent; hardworking; witty; she suffered an impoverished and very isolated childhood: "I lived in the ghetto of my Catholic childhood" (MB); lapsed Catholic; likes telling interviewers that she and her beloved husband are "boring", citing their preference for caravanning; eating out, she likes tandoori mixed grill; "if I cook it is something like ratatouille; that 's about as exotic as I get";

Address: House of Commons, Westminster, London SW1A 0AA; 102 Village Street, Normanton, Derby DE3 8DF; her official flat in Admiralty House, Whitehall; has her own flat at Millbank Court SW1;

Telephone: 0171 219 3584/5135/6662; Fax: 0171 219 4780 (H of C); 0171 834 0583 (London flat); 01332 774856 (Derby home); 01332 45636 (constituency);

We reach the uncovered parts of MPs the press no longer notice, because the correspondents leave the Press Gallery too early.

Anne BEGG **Labour**

Majority: 3,365 over Liberal Democrat 5-way;
Description: A completely redrawn three-way marginal on both sides of the Dee; made up of half of old Aberdeen South, a Con-Lab marginal, and 27,000 voters from old Kincardine & Deeside, a Con-LibDem marginal; "a beautiful city: when the sun shines, it positively sparkles with the light reflected off the grey granite" (AB)
Position: On the Select Committee on Scottish Affairs '97-; Secretary: all-party BBC Group '97-, EIS Parliamentary Association '97-; ex: Teacher Member of General Teaching Council '95-97; on Board of Scottish PHAB (Physically Handicapped, Able-Bodied) '94-97; on National Council of Educational Institute of Scotland '90-95;

Outlook: Britain's first permanently wheelchair-using MP; the only MP who knew her wheelchair would place her at the front bench if elected; a Blair-loyal, pro-EU newcomer; "I believe work for people of working age is important" (AB): a strong home-ruler who has decided to stay in Westminster; overcame the electoral disability of starting from third place;

History: When an impoverished student she was helped by her Tory constituency MP, Iain Sproat, with an enormous 'phone bill unfairly assigned to her and other poor students '70; despite this, she joined the Labour Party '83; was named the 'Disabled Scot of the Year' '88; was selected from an all-women short-list to contest redrawn Aberdeen South, joking to her selection meeting that, with her wheelchair, she would go straight to the front bench if Labour won '95; at Labour's annual conference in Brighton, she was warmly applauded when introduced as "the next MP for Aberdeen South"; in her speech, she deplored people having to sleep rough in Aberdeen Oct '96; was included in Tony Blair's cavalcade during his visit to the constituency Mar '97; in the election campaign complained her Tory opponent, Scottish Minister Raymond Robertson, always dodged any head-to-head debate, warning him: "you can run, but you can't hide!" Apr '97; was helped electorally by the OBSERVER-ICM poll which showed her ahead of the LibDem as well as the Conservative four days before polling: Labour 35%, Tory 27%, LibDem 24%, Apr '97; with a majority of 3,365, defeated the LibDem and the Scottish Tory Minister Raymond Robertson, who was pushed into third place May '97; supported Scottish devolution in a charming Maiden speech May '97; was named to Select Committee on Scottish Affairs July '97; applauded the fact that the Scottish Parliament would be "elected by a form of proportional representation, which is of supreme importance to people in the northeast of Scotland" July '97; led a motion criticising Air UK for its "discriminatory and insulting" behaviour toward disabled passengers July '97; signed European Movement's advertisement, 'Europe: A Force for Fairness, Equality and Opportunity for Women' Nov '97; hailed the Scotland Bill setting up a devolved Scottish Parliament as historic but warned that "as Scottish Parliament will not help Scotland win the World Cup" Jan '98; a filmed chronicle of her first six months as an MP was shown on BBC2 Jan '98; after she urged disabled people to work if they could, rather than rely on benefits, she received hate mail Feb '98; some campaigners for the disabled were said to be angry that the Commons had voted her an increase of up to £20,000 in allowances to make it easier to do her MP's job Mar '98; urged companies to support high-quality child care May '98; was one of three names pre-printed by Chief Whip Nick Brown - at the instigation of PM Tony Blair - for MPs' nominations to

Copyright (C)Parliamentary Profile Services Ltd

Labour's new NEC June '98;
Born: 6 December 1955, Brechin
Family: Daughter, of David Begg MBE, retired orthotist (hospital technician), and Margaret Catherine (Ross) retired nurse; unmarried ("too independent" [AB])
Education: Brechin High School; Aberdeen University; Aberdeen College of Education;
Occupation: Principal Teacher of English, in Arbroath Academy '91-97; Teacher in comprehensive (EIS) '78-91; she had to fight for three years before she was allowed to teach because it was claimed that it was against the General Teaching Council's medical regulations to have a disabled person as a teacher;
Traits: Pretty; longish dark-brown centre-parted hair; toothy; alternately smiling or serious-looking; dogged ("when somebody says 'no' it spurs me on"); optimistic ("I always see the glass as half-full"); "an attractive woman" who "radiates confidence" and "describes her life philosophy as eternally optimistic" (Sarah Villiers, MAIL ON SUNDAY); finds her MP's job as less stressful than teaching 15-16-year-olds; has Gaucher's Disease, an enzyme deficiency in the blood, making her bones soft and easily broken; it takes her an hour to get out of bed in the morning;
Address: House of Commons, Westminster, London SW1A 0AA; 26 Faulds Gate, Kincorth, Aberdeen AB12 5QS;
Telephone: 0171 219 3000 (H of C); 01224 624770 (constituency);

(John) Roy BEGGS   **Ulster Unionist**   **EAST ANTRIM '83-**

Majority: 6,389 (18.6%) over Alliance 9-way;
Description: The coastal, eastern end of the province, comprising the Larne and Carrickfergus district council areas; partly because of closure of ICI and Courtaulds in Carrickfergus it is largely agricultural, with some engineering industry in the busy port of Larne; in '95 it lost five wards in Newtonabbey to expanded Belfast North;
Position: On Public Accounts Commission '87-, '83-85; UU Spokesman on Education, Employment and National Heritage; Larne Borough Councillor (ex-Mayor '78-83) '73-; on North East Education and Library Board (Chairman '85-87, Vice Chairman '81-85) '73-; ex: North Antrim member of Northern Ireland Assembly (Chairman its Economic Development Committee '82-84) '82-86;
Outlook: A constituency-rooted Protestant Ulsterman, initially a Paisleyite and still a hard-liner, fervently Unionist enough to oppose the Good Friday Agreement and the consequent Northern Ireland Bill and to be arrested and fined for inciting an Orange Order blockading crowd; a vehement but not overly articulate local councillor and former local educator, widely active on local issues; a strong defender of local beef farmers; socially caring (defended better rights for pregnant women workers and opposed end of wages councils); pro: caning, death penalty, internment; strongly anti-EU; anti-smoking; religious ("I accept God's word as my guide for life");
History: He was elected to Larne Borough Council, originally as a DUP Paisleyite '73; became Larne's Mayor '78; was elected to Northern Ireland Assembly for North Antrim '82; was narrowly elected - by 367 votes - for East Antrim over his DUP (Paisleyite) rival June '83;

supported the restoration of the death penalty in all categories July '83; supported devolution of local government executive functions to Northern Ireland Assembly July '83; urged training of more skilled boners for Northern Ireland meat industry Dec '83; backed retention of Irish Rangers' barracks at Ballymena - to which he had taken his pupils - so as "not to encourage further slaughter of innocents and more violence in Northern Ireland by retreating further from Ulster" Mar '84; opposed effort of Northern Ireland Housing Executive to rebuild in his constituency "in areas influenced by terrorists and paramilitary groups" Aug '84; claimed teachers would be "left very isolated" if caning were outlawed Nov '84; co-sponsored anti-PLO motion Jan '85; protested the effort to end Protestant over-representation in Ulster's civil service by activities of Equal Opportunities Monitoring Unit including officials being "arbitrarily categorised" by their schools Feb '85; opposed closure of gas industry in Northern Ireland July '85; as a pillar of Consumer Credit Association warned against using "unscrupulous moneylenders" Aug '85; protested establishment of Belfast-based Secretariat under Anglo-Irish Agreement as "the greatest possible insult to the loyal citizens of the Province" and "an immediate encouragement to further murder and bombing, because the gunmen and the bombers will recognise that they have brought this about and will proceed further" Nov '85; resigned seat over Anglo-Irish Agreement Dec '85; was re-elected to seat by majority of 24,981 over sole Alliance opponent Jan '86; walked out of Commons in joint demonstration with Ken Maginnis when Northern Ireland Secretary Tom King spoke Jan '86; in absence of DUP opponent, was handsomely re-elected June '87; having demanded better Irish pursuit of terrorists for years, asked Northern Ireland Secretary to protest Garda's "incursions" into Ulster in pursuit of them Oct '87; opposed appointing "those disposed sexually to interfere with handicapped children" to "positions in connection with children's welfare or education" Nov '87; used Parliamentary privilege to accuse Charles Caulfield, a Sinn Fein member, of having been responsible for killing 11 people in Enniskillen on Remembrance Day Dec '87; voted against poll tax Dec '87; was imprisoned for 7 days for refusing to pay a £20 fine for taking part in a prohibited procession Jan '88; attacked action of Students' Union at Queen's University, Belfast, in sending a letter of condolence to the family of IRA gunwoman Mairead Farrell, killed in Gibraltar Mar '88; shouted at Northern Ireland Secretary Tom King "you were willing to sacrifice loyalists" during his description of funeral killings Mar '88; opposed privatising services at Northern Ireland museums for fear of "the risk of bogus firms with paramilitary connections seeking to tender for contracts" Apr '88; again raised problem of poll tax on Ulster students studying on mainland, as well as their travel expenses May '88; urged restoration of the death penalty as "the only appropriate punishment for murder" June '88; insisted planned privatisation of Short Brothers, Ulster's state-owned aerospace company, would be seen as part of a "phased British economic withdrawal from Northern Ireland" July '88; complained about cuts in support for 16-18-year-olds at school, insisting "young people stay at school after the age of 16 because they have no other choice; there are no jobs for them"; their poor parents "cannot afford to support their able children so that they can escape from the poverty trap" Nov '88; criticised damage done to Ulster's egg exporters by Mrs Currie's "half-baked, half-boiled, irrational statement" about salmonella, despite absence of salmonella from Northern Ireland Dec '88; complained about "disgraceful handling of privatisation in Northern Ireland" Dec '88; urged that during election campaigns there should be a ban on exhortations to violence Jan '89; his attempt to sabotage the Fair Employment (Northern Ireland) Bill, by demanding statistical impossibilities, was defeated Feb '89; voted against Speaker's exclusion of provocative SNPer Jim Sillars Mar '89; claimed that through monitoring of Protestant-Catholic balance "sectarianism has been directly introduced in the workplace" in Ulster May '89; expressed fear that too harsh applications of fair employment principles to appease Washington might frighten employers "who have been fair employers [into] blatantly discriminating against Protestants to raise the number of other groups" June '89; expressed concern about Northern Ireland Secretary Peter Brooke's remark that it might not be possible to defeat the Provisional IRA militarily Nov '89; complained that "the proposed student loans scheme, together with freezing parental contributions and grant in cash terms from 1990-91 will cause unnecessary hardship for students in Northern Ireland and in other areas of high unemployment and deprivation" Dec '89; opposed slight concern about fuller Government subsidies for "integrated" or non-sectarian schools; "I am a member of the governing body of a voluntary grammar school which has a high proportion of Roman Catholic pupils; the matter has never come up because the religion of those pupils is nobody's business but their own" Dec '89; signed motion backing Turks in Northern Cyprus Jan '90; with other Ulster Unionists and hard-line anti-Marketeers, voted against European Community legislation Jan '90; voted against European Community agricultural proposals Feb '90; voted against payment for dental tests Nov '88; opposed ordination of divorced men Feb '90; urged Mrs Thatcher to realign through Northern Ireland a pipeline planned to carry gas to the Irish Republic Apr '90; with the experience of four children and more ponies, opposed too bureaucratic safety rules in Horses Bill Apr '90; again protested use of Order in Council procedure to legislate for Northern Ireland May '90; voted for ban on smoking in public places May '90; congratulated Agriculture Minister John Gummer for his robust defence of the Ulster beef industry June '90; urged investigation of jiggery-pokery in Northern Ireland Conservancy Board July '90; co-sponsored Biffen-led anti-EC motion opposing "a European Central Bank, permanently locked exchange rates and a single European currency" Nov '90; urged a national identity card Feb '91; opposed the "disaster" of privatisation of Northern Ireland Electricity, saying that Northern Ireland Secretary Peter Brooke was "the only person who believes that the proposals will bring competition to Northern Ireland Mar '91; expressed concern about retention in Northern Ireland Electricity of Anthony Hadfield, after he had been sacked for being its only pro-privatisation top executive: "one wonders just what is going on" May '91; urged more Government-sponsored economic development to create jobs in Larne and Newtonabbey in his constituency, which had suffered a disproportionate number of Ulster's job losses in its bigger factories like ICI, Courtaulds, Carreras and Northern Telecom July '91; accused Government of "dogmatic ideology" in inflicting its privatising of electricity Jan '92; said: "no one is convinced that these proposals [for privatisation] will lead to cheaper electricity for domestic consumers or industry and commerce; the only parties likely to benefit in the long run will be the largest industrial users" Mar '92; retained seat with majority down from 15,360 to 7,422, as a result of addition of DUP and Conservative candidates Apr '92; signed anti-EC motion urging delay in Maastricht while EC borders were extended and a "fully competitive common market" was established June '92; warned that farmers were abandoning carcasses of diseased animals by the roadside since the end of subsidy for their disposal June '92; complained that some Northern Ireland officials were regarding potential overseas investors as "yet another De Lorean" June '92; urged higher priority be given the A8 Belfast-Larne road, "the natural Euro-route", rather than the Newry-Dublin road upgrading, inspired by "the Anglo-Irish Agreement" June '92; signed motion opposing euthanasia Sep '92; visited Turkish North Cyprus as a guest of its regime Sep '92; with other Ulster Unionists, voted against Government on coal closures, despite being promised an energy policy for Northern Ireland in Heseltine's coal review Oct '92; welcomed better protection for pregnant women workers in Employment Rights Bill, but opposed end of wages councils Nov '92; visited Gibraltar as guest of its government Jan '93; was one of 44 signatories to a motion urging the Foreign Secretary to meet the Turkish Cypriot leader Rauf Denktash Feb '93; co-sponsored David Amess's Bill to establish voluntary personal security cards May '93; urged "adequate levels of Government support for research and development, launch aid and other investments" plus a "national plan to maintain the UK's technological advantage" in support of privatised plane-builders, Shorts of Belfast Dec '93; expressed concern that "Northern Ireland's young people have the opportunity to realise their full academic potential without the burden of too-heavy [student] loans" Jan '94; asked the PM whether he would stand by the Downing Street declaration and expect the "Sinn Fein-IRA to cease their campaign completely and indicate that they will lay down their guns so that they can enter the democratic process" Jan '94; voted to restore capital punishment, especially for killers of policemen Feb '94; voted against reducing age of homosexual consent from 21, Feb '94; opposed the privatisation of Belfast harbour, which "would bring with it serious disadvantages to the Northern Ireland economy as a whole" June '94; urged the "selective internment of the [IRA] 'Godfathers'" July '94; called on the Government to scrap its plans to privatise the Post Office and instead give a publicly-owned Post Office greater commercial freedom July '94; urged Northern Ireland Secretary Sir Patrick Mayhew to inform the Irish PM about the "widespread distrust and suspicion about corruption" in the Republic Dec '94; with five other Ulster Unionists, saved the Government from an embarassing defeat over an EU fishing deal, which would have allowed 40 Spanish trawlers into the 'Irish Box' Jan '95; while Northern Ireland Secretary Sir Patrick Mayhew was negotiating with the Irish Foreign Secretary, Beggs said: "we feel we have not only been deceived but we have been betrayed" by the "capitulation to pan-nationalism and to IRA thugs", challenging the integrity of John Major and Michael Ancram as well Feb '95; urged separate psychiatric treatment for children Feb '95; voted against easing licensing laws Feb '95; was arrested for inciting an Orange Order mob to block a road outside Larne; he said he had been informed by the protesters that their blockade would remain until the Portadown issue was resolved July '95; said: "we resent the political decision made some time ago to pour money into the Belfast-Dublin road" instead of the Larne road Feb '96; after a free trip to Saudi Arabia on a multi-party delegation, commented: "the high standard of education, health care and economic prosperity of Saudi Arabia was in evidence throughout Riyadh" Mar '96; he was fined £1,350 for inciting an Orange Order mob to block a road outside Larne the previous July, Mar '96; backed the Bill of Eurosceptic Iain Duncan-Smith to curb the European Court Apr '96; his motion on how to get beef from BSE-free naturally-fed herds in Ulster and Scotland into Europe chalked up some 80 cross-party signatures Apr-May '96; during polling, asked why there were only two pencils, attached to 20 feet of string for eight polling booths May '96; again urged the upgrading of the road to Larne June '96; backed Ashdown's motion for a referendum on major European changes June '96; opposed putting a 3% cap on MPs' wage increases, backed a cut in MPs' mileage allowance, favoured pensions based on pay increased to £43,000 July '96; attacked the Conservative Government for the "immense damage" done "to the stability and security of the education service in Northern Ireland through the stubborn decision...to destroy five successful area boards that have served Northern Ireland so well" Oct '96; complained about slowness of Agriculture Minister Douglas Hogg in submitting detailed working papers to the European Commission to enable BSE-free Northern Ireland cattle to avoid the ban on other British cattle Nov '96; voted in favour of caning Jan '97; voted to disassemble .22 calibre target pistols, instead of banning them Feb '97; warned the Conservative Scottish Secretary Michael Forsyth that if he did not approve the electricity interconnector between Scotland and Northern Ireland he would "bear responsibility for sabotaging a link between Scotland and Northern Ireland and, in fact, imposing a huge burden on electricity consumers in Northern Ireland" Feb '97; complained that in Northern Ireland "surgery was on offer and was being sold to patients in the Republic of Ireland while British citizens who have paid taxes and national insurance were left on waiting lists because health authorities and fundholders could not pay for the operations to which their patients were entitled" Mar '97; retained his altered seat with a majority of 6,389 May '97; deplored the tendency of too many of his young people to seek higher education in Great Britain and to remain there June '97; said, "I believe that access to loan funds is no substitute for grants to students" seeking higher education July '97; seeking funds to match the £2.5m offered by the Millennium Fund to develop a local spectacular sea cliff path, was warned by PM Tony Blair that there were "public finance constraints" Oct '97; opposed the acceptance of the Good Friday Agreement May '98; with 9 other hard-liners, voted against 3rd Reading of Northern Ireland Bill putting it into effect July '98;

Born: 20 February 1936, Belfast

Family: Son, John Beggs, farmer, and Amelia (Farr); m '59 Wilma (Lorimer), secretary; 2s Samuel '60, Roy '62, 2d Elizabeth '61, Margaret '65;

Education: Ballyclare Primary; Ballyclare High; Stranmillis Training College, Belfast (Dip Ed);

Occupation: Director, Larne Enterprise Development Company (LEDCOM) (unremunerated) '86-; on North Eastern Education and Library Board; Farmer: one farm in Larne and another at Ballyclare, acquired in '86, with total of 60 acres; ex: Partner, Central Coachworks, Larne '83-86; Vice Principal, of Larne High School '78-83; Assistant Teacher, in Science Department '57-78 (NAS/UWT);

Traits: Tall; lean; balding; grey; dark eyebrows; specs; snub-nosed; inarticulate (reads questions); advocates raw eggs and brandy as a pick-me-up;

Address: House of Commons, Westminster, London SW1A 0AA; 9 Carnduff Road, Ballyvernstown, Larne, Co Antrim, N Ireland;

Telephone: 0171 219 6305 (H of C); 01574 3258;

Rt Hon Alan (James) BEITH   **Liberal Democrat**   **BERWICK-upon-TWEED '73-**

Majority: 8,042 (19.2%) over Labour 5-way;

Description: England's vast (about 1,000 sq miles), rural, almost feudal northernmost constituency: it has tourism (Cheviot Hills and North Northumberland coastline), agriculture (15%%)), fishing and mining; received 10,000 voters from Morpeth in '83 boundary changes;

Position: Deputy LibDem Leader '92-; Spokesman on Home Affairs '94-; on Parliamentary Intelligence and Security Committee '94-, on House of Commons Commission '79-; ex: on Treasury and Civil Service Select Committee '87-94; on Committee on Sittings of Commons '91-97; Treasury Spokesman '87-94; on Committee of Privileges '86-92; Deputy Leader, of Liberals '85-88; Spokesman on Foreign and Commonwealth Affairs '85-87, on Constitutional and Parliamentary Affairs '83-87, on Education and Fisheries '76-83; Northern Ireland '82, '74-76, Home Office '73-76; Chief Whip '76-85; Committee on Procedure '84-88, '75-79; Committee of Selection '77-85; WEU and Council of Europe, '76-; General Advisory Council of BBC '74-84;

Outlook: Shrewd, sensible, worthy, realistic, hard-working, well-informed. conscientious deputy headmaster type in the Centre-Right of the mainstream of LibDem politics; unlike Ashdown, does not "see the Labour Party and the Liberal Democrats coming together"; a

Eurofanatic enthusiast for ERM (even narrow band), EMU and European Central Bank; as an uptight Methodist, his "low point was...contending as Chief Whip with the problems of the Jeremy Thorpe case" (AB); was demoted in '94 from shadowing Treasury to Home Affairs; was defeated in '88 as a less charismatic alternative to Paddy Ashdown; was "the safety-first candidate: strong on judgement, effective in the Commons, but lacking charisma" (Robin Oakley, TIMES); "his politics are cautious, conservative and his platform performance donnish" (Matthew Parris, TIMES); can be "reliable but dull" or "a master of Parliamentary guile" (Simon Beck, NEWCASTLE JOURNAL); caring, puritanical Methodist lay preacher; active in his constituency, long rooted in North; anti: Sunday trading, abortion, embryo experimentation, porn, drink, tobacco, fluoride, Trident, nuclear power; pro: NATO, PR, Israel, Pro-Life;

History: "There was no political tradition in my family at all; my parents came from a working-class Conservative tradition, not drawn to the Labour movement and not involved in politics at all, although my grandfather, whom I never knew, was a councillor"; Alan was elected as a Liberal to Tynedale District Council, then to Corbridge Parish Council May '70; contested Berwick winning 22% of the vote June '70; urged a regional policy Sep '73; on Lord Lambton's call-girl-inspired resignation, won Berwick by a 57-vote majority in by-election Nov '73; retained it by 443 in Feb '74, by 73 in Oct '74; attacked Alternative Vote as inferior as a PR system to the Single Transferable Vote Apr '74; said Price sisters should be allowed to starve themselves to death May '74; claimed MPs' expenses were inadequate June '74; urged 12-mile offshore fishing preserve for fishermen Oct '74; welcomed compulsory Register of MPs' interests '75; was concerned about impact of smoking on non-smokers May '75; urged ban on cigarette advertising July '75; sought to introduce Bill of Rights July '75; urged end of Ulster's detention without trial '75; was promoted Chief Whip in succession to Cyril Smith Mar '76; presided over election of Jeremy Thorpe's successor, backing David Steel May-June '76; fought Ken Clarke's effort to ease pub licensing curbs June '76; amended Methodist Church Bill Oct '76; warned of churches' economic crisis Dec '76; opposed manner of deportation of ex-CIA agent Philip Agee Jan '77; backed Bill to curb abortion May '77; introduced Bill to give UK exclusive 50-mile fishing zone May '77; urged tighter laws against child pornography Nov '77; wanted continuation of Lib-Lab Pact Dec '77; attacked false split between polys and universities Mar '78; defended compulsory student unions July '78; urged statutory pay policy Oct '78; sought more school information for parents Mar '79; predicted Liberals would be in a "special position" in the next Parliament Apr '79; backed Indecent Displays Bill July '79; attacked Mrs Thatcher's spending cuts Sep '79; opposed "continuous drinking" Nov '79; backed curbing of abortion under David Steel's 1967 Abortion Act, Jan '80; fiercely attacked bus charges in new Education Bill Feb '80; co-sponsored bill to limit licensing hours Apr '80; opposed porno films for mentally ill June '80; led Liberal attack on Trident deal Aug '80; insisted Liberals must support NATO to defend freedom Sep '80; dissented from Steel's pro-Arab position on Palestine Dec '80; favoured Liberal-SDP alliance if each fought equal number of Labour and Tory seats Feb '81; his Bill of Rights was talked out May '81; in defeated minority, favoured Cruise missile Sep '81; opposed cuts in lecturers Nov '81; complained about bigger fees and fewer overseas students Nov '81; prodded Mrs Thatcher on spies at Cheltenham July '82; opposed increase in candidates' deposits Apr '83; opposed Defence Estimates July '83; favoured retention of Leader's veto Sep '83; tried to annul Education Fees Regulations because Government had broken its promise not to charge foreign refugee students in UK Nov '83; called for withdrawal of guns from nuclear police Nov '83; urged cancellation of Trident, strengthening of conventional forces Dec '83; opposed increase in candidates' deposits Jan '84; complained of striking Durham miners' invasion of Northumberland to confront working miners Mar '84; tried for emergency debate on "horrifying incompetence" of security services displayed in Bettaney case Apr '84; spoke against nuclear power station at Druridge Bay June '84; complained that not enough opera made it over Hadrian's Wall June '84; opposed increased MPs' mileage allowance based on engine size July '84; voted for Trade Union Bill amendment to stop malpractice in workplace ballots July '84; urged end of miners' strike by removing Scargill and MacGregor from negotiations Sep '84; warned that rural bus services would be cut by deregulation Oct '84; visited Zimbabwe Dec '84; was a principal backer of Enoch Powell's Bill to oppose embryo experimentation Dec '84; Mrs Thatcher again rejected David Steel's appeal to make Beith a Privy Councillor Dec '84; voted against fluoridation Jan '85; was active in campaign to incorporate in UK law the European Convention on Human Rights Jan-Feb '85; urged a list of exceptions to Government's cost-cutting limited list of drugs Mar '85; introduced Bill to give workers the right to opt in to political deductions rather than be forced to opt out Mar '85; urged freedom to support strike-breaking Apr '85; attacked Tories' three-line Whip in support of Sunday trading May '85; defended British School of Motoring donation to Liberals May '85; became Deputy Leader July '85; urged sanctions against South Africa Sep '85; said Labour's anti-Militant posture was a "phoney war" concealing a big Leftward shift Nov '85; backed televising Commons Nov '85; urged suspension of reprocessing at Sellafield until experts had checked Feb '86; voted against 2nd Reading of Bill to curb scientific experiments on animals Feb '86; insisted regional investment was more important than tax cuts Mar '86; warned against possible closure of three or four universities Apr '86; on IPU Soviet trip May '86; attacked US willingness to sacrifice SALT treaty June '86; stressed Liberals' anti-nuclear policy (in contrast to David Owen's pro-Polaris statement in Bonn) June '86; condemned Nicaragua's anti-Liberal actions July '86; urged Sir Geoffrey Howe to resign in protest against Mrs Thatcher's anti-sanctions posture July '86; opposed SDI and favoured nuclear 'freeze' Sep '86; supported Kenneth Hind's Unborn Children (Protection) Bill Oct '86; urged free equipment for parents of diabetic children Oct '86; renewed his '79 call for Parliamentary oversight of security services Dec '86; was named joint Alliance spokesman on Foreign Affairs for election campaign Jan '87; visited West Germany as its guest Jan '87; challenged Government to deny its involvement in Contra arms Mar '87; criticised CAP as "out of control" Apr '87; received a contribution of £500 from lobbyist Ian Greer Apr '87; after election disappointment called for Liberal-SDP merger on grounds that "voters prefer the respectability of marriage" June '87; urged reduction in divorce on demand June '87; was one of 14 signatories - with Cyril Smith - of Pro-Life allegations on premature babies Aug '87; was one of 8 elected by Liberal Assembly to negotiate merger with SDP Sep '87; with Cyril Smith backed David Alton's abortion-curbing Bill Oct '87; visited Hong Kong as guest of Hong Kong Government '87-88; although he privately made his objections known, he was damaged by his public silence on the Steel-Maclennan draft joint policy document authored by Maclennan's Euro-fanatic research assistants Jan '88; voted against more liberal Licensing Bill Feb '88; complained that absence of Religious Education from the core curriculum would "marginalise" it Mar '88; criticised the Budget as sheer barefaced injustice Mar '88; disavowed Alex Carlile's mudslinging attack on the personal qualities of Paddy Ashdown, his rival for Leadership of the Liberal Democrats May '88; was defeated in contest for Liberal Democrats Leadership, receiving 28.1% of the vote, as a result of his "lack of sparkle and non-libertarian attitude on social issues" like abortion (John Carvel, GUARDIAN) July '88; was named Liberal Democrats' Treasury Spokesman Sep '88; backed televising the Commons Nov '89; visited Zimbabwe for discussions on developing African democracy Dec '89; voted against smoking in public places May '90; was given additional responsibilities of speaking for Liberal Democrats on the poll tax and Liberals' own local income tax July '90; attended Warsaw conference as guest of European Liberal, Democrat and Reform Parties Group in European

Parliament Nov '90; was named to Committee on Sittings of Commons July '91; attended two-day conference in Stockholm as guest of European Liberal, Democrat and Reform Parties' Group in European Parliament July '91; urged £6b in additional borrowing to stop Britain sliding into a slump and 1p on basic tax rate for educational improvements Mar '92; retained his seat with the majority down from 9,503 to 5,043, a swing of 5.5% from Liberal Democrats to Conservatives Apr '92; was renamed Liberal Democrats' Treasury Spokesman May '92; became Privy Counsellor June '92; was re-named to Treasury and Civil Service Select Committee July '92; opposed returning Berwick-upon-Tweed to Scotland as "disruptive", after 15 changes in several centuries July '92; opposed euthanasia July '92; opposed devaluation July '92; was attacked at Liberal Democrats' annual conference for his "fundamentally flawed" defence of a European Central Bank, enthusiasm for entering the ERM's narrow band, his opposition to devaluation and defence of European Monetary Union; he denied the pound was over-valued, only perhaps against the dollar, urging Mr Lamont to resist calls for devaluation Sep '92; tagging the Treasury's departure from ERM as akin to "bungee jumping", demanded resignation of "discredited and incompetent" Government's over 'Black Wednesday'; urged early re-entry into ERM Sep '92; complained that, in devaluing, Norman Lamont had become a member of the Cambridge group of economists Nov '92; deplored Bank of England's slack behaviour over BCCI's "massive fraud" Nov '92; alleged the French had delayed the German request for a currency realignment within ERM Nov '92; as Spokesman of the Commons Commission, refused to disclose which MPs were sponsoring commercial events in its dining rooms Nov '92; urged Norman Lamont's replacement as Chancellor Dec '92; opposed increasing taxes in the Budget Mar '93; attacked Tory plans to increase VAT on domestic fuel and increase National Insurance contributions, depite contrary pledges Apr '93; visited Germany, paid for by Goethe Institute Oct '93; voted for a less than 2.7% increase in MPs' pay Nov '93; came second in the ballot for Private Members' Bills Nov '93; his Bill to press councils to survey energy-saving in its homes acquired wide support but was resisted by the Government and Environment Secretary John Gummer Feb '94; opposed restoration of capital punishment, even for killers of policemen Feb '94; backed reduction of age of homosexual consent to 18 or 16, Feb '94; was optimistic that many of those mis-sold pensions by household-name insurance companies would get their money back Mar '94; said a single European currency would mean lower interest rates and stable prices Apr '94; his energy-saving Bill was talked out by Tory Minister Tony Baldry Apr '94; fought against allowing DIY shops and garden centres unlimited hours to trade on Sundays June '94; after seven years as Treasury Spokesman, was down-shifted to Home Affairs by Paddy Ashdown in his reshuffle on Tony Blair's enthronement and David Steel's departure from the front bench July '94; urged 60% income tax rate on those earning over £100,000 to provide another £5 a week increase in child benefit Aug '94; after he warned the LibDem conference against decriminalising "recreational" drugs, it voted by 426 to 375 in favour of a Royal Commission on decriminalising cannabis Sep '94; deplored the impact on drug smuggling of the cutting of 4,000 Customs and Excise jobs Nov '94; was discharged from the Treasury and Civil Service Select Committee Nov '94; was named to the Intelligence and Security Committee Dec '94; on behalf of the House of Commons Commission, presented the alternatives for child care for those working in the Commons Jan '95; voted against easing licensing hours Feb '95; the new Register of MPs' Interests showed him as a Consultant to a medical PR company with 13 drug company clients Feb '95; voted for John McFall's Bill to ban fox-hunting Mar '95; complained that the new Commons procedures, which tried to avoid heavy debates on Thursdays, meant many MPs were leaving for their constituencies on Wenesdy night Mar '95; said he would be happy to see the abolition of border controls, but this would mean that "anyone could be stopped in the street at any time to show an identity card" Apr '95; asked PM John Major about job losses associated wit the "dreadful chaos of rail privatisation" May '95; again opposed decriminalising cannabis June '95; after Labour's unpleasant campaigning in the bruising Littleborough and Saddleworth by-election said that Labour no longer knew where it was going July '95; said the Major Government was deeply irresponsible in handing over prisons and security to unregulated private companies Sep '95; was asked to take charge of formulating a costed election manifesto, with Alex Carlile taking over much of his Home Office responsibilities Nov '95; urged better funding for Northumberland schools Nov '95; tried to amend the Security Services Bill to make more precise how MI5 could help the police in fighting organised crime Jan '96; backed a regulatory system for the private security system Feb '96 spoke up in defence of his declining fishing fleet in Northumberland ports Mar '96; opposed passage of authoritarian Prevention of Terrorism Bill after only six hours' debate Apr '96; deplored the "delay, difficulty and confusion" attending the cattle cull in his constituency May '96; urged a principled debate on whether MI5 should deal with organised crime; reassured Brighton's homegoing LibDem delegates "with Liberal Democrats you know where you are" Sep '96; welcomed the Tories plan for an anti-stalking Bill and a paedophile register, but deplored the dropping of the Bill to curb sex tourism Oct '96; asked PM John Major whether he was going to cut war pensions Dec '96; criticised "cosy alliance" whereby Jack Straw forced Michael Howard to accept bugging by police had to be authorised by a Home Office commissioner; he preferred a circuit judge Feb '97; supported law peers' resistance to being deprived of discretion in sentencing Mar '97; was cleared by Sir Gordon Downey about charges of having received a contribution of £500 from lobbyist Ian Greer in 1987, Mar '97; insisted "zero tolerance" was a "misleading phrase" Apr '97; he predicted the LibDems would win just over 30 seats; he retained his seat with his majority up by 3,000 to 8,042 over his Labour opponent who forced the Conservative into third place May '97; insisted funds were urgently needed to provide 3,000 more policemen May '97; he was one of the five LibDem MPs on the inside of the negotiations with the Labour leadership on participation in a Cabinet committee on constitutional reform June-July '97; was again named to the Parliamentary Intelligence and Security Committee July '97; voted against Mike Foster's anti-hunting Bill Nov '97; said most security services' files were "completely redundant" but "there has to be some secrecy to protect current inquiries and sources" June '98;

Born: 20 April 1943, Poynton, Cheshire

Family: His great-grandfather, a handloom weaver in Paisley, "moved to Glasgow to find work when industrial change put all handloom weavers out of work in the 19th century"; son, late James Beith, textile factory packer, and Joan (Harty); m '65 late Barbara Jean (Ward), teacher, died of cancer '98; 1s Christopher '76; 1d Caroline '80 (both adopted, one diabetic);

Education: King's School, Macclesfield; Balliol and Nuffield Colleges, Oxford University (B Lit, MA Oxon);

Occupation: Adviser, Association of University Teachers '82-; Consultant, to Magellan Medical Communications Ltd (medical PR company; its clients: Pharmaceutical Contraceptive Group, Schering Healthcare, Wyeth Laboratories, Organon, Cilag, Roussel Laboratories, Smith and Nephew, Parke-Davis) '92-; Broadcaster/Lecturer; Author: The Case for the Liberal Party and the Alliance, (1983); Co-Author: Faith and Politics (1987); ex: Lecturer, Department of Politics, Newcastle University '66-73;

Traits: Owlish; "looks like the kind of bank manager we had when we had proper bank managers" (Simon Hoggart, GUARDIAN); a waddling bustler; "walks like Charlie Chaplin" (NEWCASTLE JOURNAL); "a small, cuddly man with spectacles", a result of mating "an owl and a penguin" and crossing "a waddle with a shuffle": "if you try to imagine an owl-guin in glasses, walking with a kind of wuffle and wearing an expression of surprised wisdom, then you have Mr Beith", usually in "his funeral director's suit" speaking in a "schoolmasterly

drone" (Matthew Parris, TIMES); earnest; mild; genial; "dogged and diligent but has a limp and unpercussive personality" (SUNDAY TELEGRAPH); "does not sparkle but sometimes shines"; "when they went to the bar for charisma, Alan got the orange juice" (Liberal colleague); "excessively worthy and, in the end, rather dull" (GUARDIAN); a Methodist lay preacher; near-teetotal (drinks a daily glass of red wine for his health); linguist (Norwegian, Welsh - from a boyhood stay); fine cornet trumpet player who enjoys trad jazz and choral singing;
Address: House of Commons, Westminster, London SW1A 0AA; 28 Castle Terrace, Berwick-upon-Tweed;
Telephone: 0171 219 3540 (H of C); 01665 60290;

Martin BELL   **Independent**   **TATTON '97-**

Majority: 11,077 over Conservative 10-way;
Description: Until the '97 election, this was rated the fifth safest Conservative seat, after the '95 removal of Labour-leaning industrial Northwich and the addition of Alderley Edge, a favourite Cheshire commuting area for well-off executives;
Position: On Select Committee on Standards and Privileges '97-;
Outlook: The first Independent MP since 1950, "proving there is a role for an Independent in the Commons" (Matthew Parris, TIMES); the '97 election's most curious accidental fusion, created by the impact of his own first-rate reputation as a shrapnel-wounded BBC war correspondent on local disgust with the lying, sleaze-ridden sitting Tory MP, Neil Hamilton; an un-saintly idealist ("I wear an OFF-white suit because I am NOT a saint"); was more a Labour-supported candidate than he initially admitted; thinks he still "has a chance to make a difference"; is a mild Eurosceptic who doesn't disagree with the single European currency in principle; his desire to carve out a new role may be motivated in part by his aversion to being squeezed out of the Birtian BBC into unproductive premature retirement; "a loner" (BBC producer David Akerman); "a genuinely non-party animal", "strong on defence and welfare" (Oliver Kamm, his nephew and campign aide); "a conservative with a small 'c'" (John Sweeney, OBSERVER); believes Richard III was maligned by "the greatest of all spin-doctors, W Shakespeare";
History: As Head Boy at Taverham Hall prep school, he was the winning Liberal candidate in the October '51 mock election, chosen because his father wrote Liberal opinion pieces for the EASTERN DAILY PRESS; he joined Cambridge University's Marxist Society "to find out what it was like"; "I seemed to be the only one at King's College who was not a member" '60; joined the Young Liberals '60; quit the Young Liberals on joining the BBC '62; spent 30 years developing his reputation as an honest BBC-TV reporter/war correspondent, culminating in his being wounded by shrapnel in Sarajevo, while reporting the Bosnian civil war Aug '92; blamed the civil war on the British Government for having traded opt-outs on Maastricht for German-desired recognition of breakaway ex-Yugoslav republic of Croatia in Dec '91; was one of two war correspondents to testify to the War Crimes Tribunal in Brussels; came into conflict with the BBC over its requirement for neutral reporting: "you don't report genocide in the same terms as a flower show" July '96; initially at the suggestion of photographer Tom

Stoddart, partner of Labour MP Kate Hoey, emerged as the all-party Independent anti-sleaze candidate to oppose the discredited Tory MP Neil Hamilton, with Labour and LibDem candidates standing down in his favour Apr '97; his first press conference was aggressively gate-crashed by Neil Hamilton and his formidable wife, Christine Apr '97; virtually all Conservative newspapers and journalists were hostile to Bell's candidacy Apr '97; gave his opponent, Neil Hamilton, a detailed list of the lies and corruption to which he had already confessed Apr '97; had to drop "Anti-Corruption" from his nomination papers to avoid a legal challenge from Neil Hamilton Apr '97; his campaign was helped by the OBSERVER-ICM Poll which predicted he would take 50% and Hamilton 39%, Apr '97; won the seat by a sensational majority of 11,077 May '97; in his Maiden speech, paid tribute to Neil Hamilton "for the effect that he had, whether deliberately or not, in reviving the spirit of democracy in Tatton"; insisted: "good and evil are not abstractions, but actual forces in the world, and that the difference that an individual can make is greater now than it was in the more predictable world of the old cold war"; he called for the banning of anti-personnel mines, duly announced by PM Tony Blair the next day May '97; in his first constituency problem-visit, backed the right of protesters against Manchester Airport's second runway to protest peacefully and also the right of bailiffs to evict peacefully May '97; as a member of the all-party Land Mines Group, regretted Princess Diana's withdrawal from a planned Commons meeting, forced by Conservative criticism June '97; he criticised the 20% pay rise of John Birt as damaging BBC staff morale July '97; urged a "clear-eyed as well as compassionate" approach to foreign aid; "never again must we push food aid into an active war zone where we and the agencies associated with us do not control the secondary distribution" because "we prolong rather than shorten the conflict because we are feeding the front-line troops" July '97; when Sir Gordon Downey's report concluded that Neil Hamilton had "received cash payments directly from [Mohamed] al-Fayed", Bell said this vindicated his decision to stand in Tatton July '97; again sided with protesters against a second runway for Manchester Airport July '97; after BBC Director General John Birt accepted an 18% pay increase, asked: "have we turned back the culture of greed in our politics only to have it seep into our public broadcasting?";"How many Giorgio Armani suits can one man wear?" Aug '97 admitted that Alastair Campbell had composed much of his first election address Sep '97; claimed that Britain's was the "best little army in the world" but had "to change as fast as circumstances are changing" Oct '97; admitted that the Commons appeals procedure after 'sleaze' investigations had not worked in the case of ex-MP Neil Hamilton, who had become "my constituent"; "I want to do what I can to help my constituent; he has no further appeal left in the system"; "I think the committee has to review the appeals procedure" Nov '97; after Rupert Murdoch refused to ban purchases of paparazzi photos pledged himself never again to buy a Murdoch paper Nov '97; after disclosures about Labour's having received a donation of £1m from 'Formula One' chief Bernie Ecclestone before softening the conditions on sponsorship, warned the PM: "the perception of wrong-doing can be as damaging to public confidence as the wrong-doing itself", adding: "have we slain one dragon only to have another take its place, with a [New Labour] red rose in its mouth?" Nov '97; was nominated to the Commons Select Committee on Standards and Privileges by Conservative Leader William Hague, to replace Ann Widdecombe; Hague rejected the protest of Douglas Hogg Nov '97; launched a campaign to free two Scots Guardsmen jailed for the murder of a Catholic teenager in Belfast Dec '97; spoke up for arrested British Major, Milos Stankovic MBE, the son of a Serbian Chetnik Dec '97; after it was disclosed that the Labour and Liberal Democratic parties had shared payment for the legal opinion on his designation as an Independent or Independent Anti-Sleaze candidate, he repaid the £9,400 expended, although he had not known about the payment; the OBSERVER suggested that New Labour released the information to dent his image because of his sideswipe against Blair over Bernie Ecclestone Jan '98; spoke up for imprisoned Guardsmen Fisher and Wright in the Commons Feb '98; expressed reservations about another military attack on Iraq: "as one who was in the front line last time may I ask for the [Defence] Secretary of State's personal assurance that no similar action will be contemplated without the same sort of coalition of opinion at home and support in the Arab world and in the United Nations at large?" Feb '98; attended burning beacon in Grosvenor Gardens to celebrate the Countryside Alliance's campaign in support of fox-hunting Feb '98; led demonstration protesting cancellation of £22m bypass linking the A34 to the M6 Mar '98; urged PM Blair for "a Whips' ceasefire" to allow MPs to ask "questions they wish to ask rather than those they have been encouraged or instructed by others to ask" Mar '98; warned that broader sanctions on the Serbs had rewarded "the blackmarketeers and racketeers" and punished and sometimes killed "the poor, the weak and the old" Mar '98; was thought to be the only man who could retain Tatton against Seb Coe, the new Tory candidate July '98;

Born: 31 August 1938, Beccles, Suffolk

Family: Grandson, of Robert Bell, News Editor of the OBSERVER; son, of Adrian Hanbury Bell, Liberal-inclined farmer and writer who was the compiler of the first TIMES crossword, and Marjorie (Gibson); m 1st '71 Nelly Lucienne (Gourdon); 2d: Melissa, his campaign manager (who later married ex-Major Peter Bracken, a Labour helper) '72, Catherine '74; divorced '81; m 2nd '85 Rebecca Sobel, American TV reporter; this marriage was "four years of pure disaster" (MB); divorced '88; m 3rd Fiona (Goddard) daughter of a hostile Tory farmer; in '98 he had a "lovely and emotional" reunion with Jessica Sobel, his former stepdaughter, who had written a book about her period as a prostitute, porn star and drug addict; "Martin was the only real father figure I've ever known," she told the DAILY MAIL

Education: Taverham Hall prep school (Head Boy); The Leys School, Cambridge (Scholarship Boy); King's College, Cambridge University (First Class Hons in English); received an honorary doctorate from the University of North London '97;

Occupation: Columnist, in the MANCHESTER EVENING NEWS (at £1,320 a year) '97-; Author: In Harms Way (1995); ex: BBC-TV Newsman '62-97, successively as Trainee '62-65, Reporter, '65-77, Diplomatic Correspondent '77-78, Chief Washington Correspondent '78-89, Berlin Correspondent '89-93; Bosnian and East European Correspondent '93-94, Pool TV Reporter with 7th Armoured Brigade in Gulf War '91; honoured as Royal Television Reporter of the Year '77, TV Journalist of the Year '92, OBE '92;

Traits: Medium height; grey hair; deep-set eyes; staccato speech; a crumpled face like a middle-aged Russian; has a bear-like shambling gate; walks with a limp from his shrapnel wound; had a hip replacement op in '98; dour; dogged; no small talk; "has a reputation for shuffling past people, looking at his feet and rarely exchanging a word" (Helena de Bertodano, SUNDAY TELEGRAPH); self-consciously righteous; wears crumpled off-white or cream suits as a uniform; "stands around looking lugubrious like a little boy lost" (disaffected campaign helper); "that rare breed, an old-fashioned patriot, the sort of person whose eyes would go moist at the sound of Elgar" (former war correspondent colleague); "the trouble with you, Corporal Bell," said Captain Pat Hopper, during his National Service, "is that you think too much"; in Bosnia "he was never the kind of person who would send his cameraman where he was not prepared to go himself" (fellow TV newsman); his toothbrushes are always yellow and his socks are always green; "I always take a dark blue Globetrotter suitcase; I've had six of them in my careeer; I'm actually very superstitious and pessimistic when I travel; but pessimists travel happily, as their worst fears are never realised, while optimists are usually disappointed" (MB); "I'm very impatient; I can't stand unpunctuality" (MB); likes to dine at Hampstead's La Gaffe which he describes as "like a home from home"; there he always eats either the scampi al funghetto or the fegato alla Veneziano; as a young man he swam for

Suffolk; had hip operation '98;
Address: House of Commons, Westminster, London SW1A 0AA; Denman Drive, Hampstead Garden Suburb NW11; Great Budworth, near Northwich, Cheshire; **Telephone:** 0171 219 3000 (H of C);

Stuart BELL	Labour	MIDDLESBROUGH '83-

Majority: 25,018 (54.3%) over Conservative 4-way;
Description: Most of the steel city between the Cleveland hills and the River Tees; two ICI plants, BSC, and manufacturers of containers and oil rigs;
Position: Second Church Estates Commissioner '97-; on Interim Steering Committee, British-Irish Inter-Parliamentary Body '90-; ex: Assistant Spokesman, on Trade and Industry (recently Corporate Affairs) '92-97; Assistant Spokesman on Northern Ireland '84-87; Secretary, Solidarity Group '84-87; PPS, Roy Hattersley '83-84; Vice Chairman, PLP Home Affairs Committee '83-84; Newcastle Councillor '80-83;

Outlook: The very able, multi-sided, courageous, but overly sectarian-provocative Rightwing Fabian immoderate who stumbled or was tripped as Labour entered office in 1997; instead of becoming a junior Minister in Trade and Industry, as expected, was fobbed off with answering for the Church of England, or "God's Shop Steward" (Lord [Don] Dixon), "our conduit to the Almighty" (Paul Flynn MP), an unpaid post he initially delayed accepting; by the end of his first year in office he proclaimed himself to the DAILY TELEGRAPH as wary of an "unstoppable tide" of Blairite reform which might say "disestablish the Church" or "get the Bishops out of the Lords"; a pro-European Francophile, long close to Roy Hattersley, later to John Smith; he had curbed his natural exhuberance in a five-year stint as an Opposition Spokesman on Corporate Affairs, mostly making highly-competent but low-key frontbench speeches; this stemmed from the late John Smith's decision in 1992 to give him another chance on the Front Bench to show his ability to be "responsible" after his battering in the Cleveland sex-abuse uproar; there he was credited with having provoked the Butler-Sloss Inquiry; he was criticised by the Lord Justice herself of "intemperate and inflammatory remarks", but was "notably brave, a publicist certainly, but not a publicist on his own account" (B-S); "happy to have both sociology graduates and authoritarian paediatricians spit"; "the Left does not like him because he combines two unusual strands of background: the old County Durham working-class Rightwing (he [was] Secretary of the Solidarity Group) and a degree of sheer, single-handed personal achievement which brings out all the envy, malice and uncharity to be found loitering at street corners in Labour territory"; "to the envy he already attracts, he has added resentment for pillorying a progressive cause" (Edward Pearce, SUNDAY TIMES); was "kamikaze of the year" (Michael White, GUARDIAN); "a bit of a hatchet man and rent-a-quote [regarding] the loony Left" (GUARDIAN); a "jumped-up fool" according to Clare Short, whom he sued for libel but with whom he settled; a zealous defender of Tees and Hartlepool Port Authority against depredations; a compulsive novel-writer, not always of steamy Parisian ones; an Adviser to the US pharmaceutical giant, Merck, Sharp and Dohme; was also GMB-sponsored;

History: His miner-father was not political but just hated Churchill for setting the troops on the striking Welsh miners; Stuart joined the Labour Party '64, but went off to France for over a decade; returned, he contested hopeless Hexham as a pro-European May '79; was elected to Newcastle City Council May '80; there, on its Education Committee, he saw how cuts hurt schools and books, "and how arithmetic, reading and writing were affected"; was selected for Middlesbrough as a pro-European multilateralist Feb '81; in a Fabian pamphlet, urged an elected Senate to replace Lords Sep '81; urged transformation of Law Lords into a Supreme Court, with a greater quota of liberals Mar '82; was endorsed by NEC for Middlesbrough Nov '82, elected June '83; threatened Bill to force tell-all policeman to pay three times their "blood money" to victims of Ripper types June '83; co-nominated Roy Hattersley for Leader Sep '83; he reacted angrily to NIREX's choice of Billingham as a nuclear dump Oct '83; demanded review of DHSS fitness-for-work regulations after death of constituent Oct '83; warned that, despite more police, there were more crimes, partly because victims were losing confidence in police Nov '83; was part of cross-party delegation demanding of William Waldegrave that he change criteria for choosing nuclear waste dump sites Dec '83; expressed Michael Bettaney's fears of an unfair trial after the ex-MI5man had written to him from jail Mar '84; claimed UK's Lebanon contingent was "a gesture to the US" Mar '84; was part of cross-party attack on Government's extension of time in custody without charge to 96 hours; opposed policemen in plain clothes acting as agents provocateurs in sex offence cases; opposed police power to establish road-blocks May '84; declaring himself to be a Lloyd's underwriter, insisted the City needed more than self-regulation July '84; as Secretary of Labour Solidarity declared war on Left, expressed determination run a full slate for Shadow Cabinet Oct '84; with George Robertson and Jack Straw backed Jack Cunningham's repudiation of Labour local authorities who resisted rate-capping Nov '84; was promoted Assistant Spokesman on Northern Ireland, in succession to Clive Soley, as a reward for effective harrying of Tory Ministers Nov '84; called for end to 'supergrass' system Nov '84; in debate on De Lorean car project said there was nothing lunatic about the project's conception, especially job creation May '85; was re-selected from a shortlist of one June '85; complained of Government's shutdown of Ulster's gas industry, with its loss of 1,000 jobs June '85; urged ban on Orange Order parades in Catholic areas of Ulster, adding: "troops out must be a final rather than an early stage in the procedure towards a united Ireland" July '85; at annual conference said Labour wanted Irish unity via acquiescence, not via the wrong end of an Armalite Sep '85; Norman Hogg blamed him for his defeat as candidate for Chief Whip after Bell had attacked Campaign Group's questionnaire to candidates as trying to put the winner into a "Stalinist straitjacket" Oct '85; was criticised by Leftwinger David Winnick for implying Kinnock could only work with a Rightwing Shadow Cabinet Oct '85; predicted that UDM would be recognised by TUC and nobody would be expelled from Labour Party for belonging to it Oct '85; welcomed Anglo-Irish Agreement as death-knell of Unionist veto Nov '85; was part of delegation to Paul Channon complaining of loss of 3,500 jobs in shipbuilding May '86; warned that an independent Ulster would rapidly "acquire the characteristics of the Lebanon...unable to stand on its own two feet, unloved by all, supported by none" July '86; urged a wider post-Militant witch hunt Aug '86; shared platform with convicted IRA bomber in meeting in which IRA violence was attacked Sep '86; toured constituencies to explain Labour's support for Anglo-Irish Agreement and keeping British troops in Ulster Sep '86; contested constituency section of NEC, securing inadequate 232,000 votes Oct '86; infuriated Left by campaigning for a Solidarity-dominated Shadow Cabinet able to work with Kinnock Oct '86; toured Ulster with Labour's senior Spokesman, Peter Archer, seeing Sinn Fein councillors among others Jan '87; attacked Government for allowing massive swindles on Ulster building sites Feb '87; it was suggested that, in a hung parliament, he did not object to a coalition with Ulster Unionists based on reviewing the Anglo-Irish Agreement, eliciting Clare Short's tag of "jumped up fool" - for which she later apologised Mar '87; increased his majority by over 5,000 votes June '87; urged inquiry into local sex abuse allegations June '87; urged purge of "illegitimate Left" June '87; contested Shadow Cabinet, coming bottom of poll with 26 votes July '87; resigned from his Front Bench job as junior Spokesman on Northern Ireland to concentrate on alleged child abuse locally; his call for the suspension of two Cleveland doctors and a select committee helped produce judicial inquiry, although he was criticised by other local Labour MPs for over-siding with accused parents July '87; in view of his involvement in sex abuse in Cleveland, decided not to stand for NEC July '87; talked of replacing Solidarity with Centre Unity Group, which never took off July '87; was accused by fellow local Labour MPs of breaking an agreement not to go public until judicial inquiry had ruled; he denied any such agreement existed Aug '87; his constituency party supported him over child abuse Sep '87; Social Services Inspectorate found no evidence that a consultant and social service workers had colluded against inspectors in their investigation of the handling of child abuse in Cleveland Sep '87; at annual conference was hissed and criticised for "unjustified and personal attacks" on doctors and social workers and "knee-jerk reaction" (Clare Short) Sep '87; he repeated that "child sex abuse is a heinous and evil crime" but pointed out that there had been no prosecutions in Cleveland and yet parents had been parted from their children without being allowed to see them for weeks and months Oct '87; at Cleveland inquiry charged there had been "a clear conspiracy" by the two sex-abuse doctors Higgs and Wyatt and Mrs Sue Richardson with the knowledge of Social Service Director Mike Bishop in the interest of "empire-building" Dec '87; voted for 2nd Reading of David Alton's abortion-curbing Bill Jan '88; TRIBUNE accused him of losing a council by-election to the Liberals by imposing his own candidates as Vice Chairman, Treasurer and Membership Secretary of the Middlesbrough Constituency Labour Party Feb '88; urged an investigation of freelance social worker agencies involved in sex-abuse cases Feb '88; condemned "Parliamentary hooliganism" of the Campaign Group at end of Budget speech Mar '88; voted against an abortion ceiling of 26 weeks May '88; the Inquiry led by Lord Justice Butler-Sloss found his "intemperate and inflammatory remarks" "had a part in exacerbating an already very difficult and sensitive situation" and complained that he declined "to withdraw or modify allegations which could not be substantiated"; it also pointed out that some of the parents he had defended had sexually abused their children; the report did not admit that, without his accusations, the Inquiry might never have been held; he welcomed the report's expressions of regret for innocent families "who through no fault of their own were caught up in this horrible vortex which swooped them all up and almost destroyed their lives; for months they have said no one has listened, no one has said 'sorry'" July '88; psychiatrist Anthony Clare, in reviewing Bell's book, When Salem Came to the Boro, said that he, "as a local politician" was overly "harsh about many of the key figures in the drama" while "the abuser either is frankly ignored on the questionable grounds that there are not too many of them, or is acknowledged but with scant interest and little reflection" July '88; a group of consultant paediatricians wrote to the GUARDIAN to criticise his wild accusations about "empire-building", his charges about professionals "looking for child fodder" and his "intemperate and inflammatory remarks made on television or to newspaper reporters which had a part in exacerbating an already very difficult and sensitive situation" Feb '89; in a reply letter, Bell pointed out that the children involved, all of whom had repeatedly denied being abused, were asking their parents whether they would be taken away again; he pointed out that the paediatricians were challenging his right to free speech: "in the past, it was the prerogative of kings and 0emperors to shoot the messenger; it now appears to have passed to paediatricians" Feb '89; was one of six Commons barristers who supported Lord Mackay's reforms of the legal system Mar '89; voted with anti-Market MPs against agreeing to an EC Court of Auditors until a report had been received on CAP surpluses Mar '89; staged an adjournment debate on the role of consultants within the NHS Mar '89; said child protection in Cleveland was now among the best in the country May '89; his critics among local Labour people took over county council leadership in Cleveland May '89; co-urged improved rail links with Channel Tunnel for northeast Oct '89; complained at fringe meeting of annual conference that Labour's policy on abortion gave right to terminate only to women, even if husbands wanted the babies Oct '89; raised the risk of privatising Tees and Hartlepool Port Authority Dec '89; was named to Interim Steering Committee of British-Irish Parliamentary Body Feb '90; when Tory MP Lloyd's 'names' were attacked by Labour MPs, he was one of the Labour consultants asked by Tories to reveal his remuneration from Merck Sharpe and Dohme Feb '90; was re-selected for Middlesbrough with 71% against 26% for Ann Holmes, despite anonymous letters saying he was anti-women, anti-unions, and a pornographer; the police had been called in because membership lists had been stolen to circulate these defamatory letters June '90; in response to lobbyists questions about whether a new Labour Government would rescue Eurotunnel, said: "it is a market creation and there should be a market solution" June '90; attacked inclusion in Finance Bill of reference to "harbour authority", which would enable the Treasury to grab half of Tees and Hartlepool port's assets July '90; again attacked Treasury's attempt to grab half of Tees and Hartlepool Port Authority's assets Oct '90; on Iraq's invasion of Kuwait, urged that "sanctions should be given time to work and, secondly, that a UN resolution will be required for military action" Nov '90; rebutted an attack on him, in a letter to Neil Kinnock, which accused him of "a relentless vendetta against child care professionals in this county" Nov '90; paid tribute ("a personal appreciation") to Mrs Thatcher's role, after consulting him, in calling for a judicial inquiry to solve Cleveland child-abuse crisis: "she was instrumental in ensuring that the Children Bill was part of the legislative programme for 1989" Nov '90; urged an immediate election Dec '90; attacked the use of an expensive and "corrupt" private Bill procedure to privatise Tees and Hartlepool Port Authority Jan '91; accused Teesside Port chief John Hackney of being prepared to renege on promises to employees Feb '91; urged liberation of Kuwait rather than Soviet compromise plan Feb '91; visited Israel during Gulf War '91; received substantial libel damages from SUNDAY MIRROR for charging he had concealed his authorship of his steamy 'Paris '69' novel Mar '91; attacked Government for having squeezed money to local government and local education, which he had experienced on Newcastle City Council: "over the years we saw how things unravelled and how arithmetic, reading and writing were affected" Mar '91; urged an early settlement with 28 families suing over removal of their 121 children June '91; expressed concern that ICI was running up a bill of £1m a week to fight takeover by Hanson Aug '91; warned against involvement in ex-Yugoslavia's civil war Aug '91; complained that up to a thousand crimes were committed annually in Cleveland by a hard core of 150 youngsters, giving council estate dwellers a very hard time Sep '91; was a sponsor of Energy Labelling Conference '91; was rated as one of the rarest questioners among northeast MPs Nov '91; said: "we must link the free market with the provision of proper social and working conditions" Nov '91; made another powerful attack on the privatisation of the trust port of Tees and Hartlepool; in his lengthy indictment he laid bare the £55m which would go to the Treasury, and the criminal family background of directors of the port authority's successor, Humberside Holdings, with its trail of bankrupt companies Feb '92; in Budget debate deplored "the novel approach that we can borrow money to reduce taxation and the claim is that somehow that will spark a consumer boom" Mar '92; retained seat with majority up from 14,958 to 15,784, a swing to Labour of 1.86% Apr '92; insisted that the EC's single market required social cohesion, and therefore the social chapter May '92; contested Shadow Cabinet July '92; was named an Assistant Spokesman on Robin Cook's Trade and Industry team July '92; insisted MPs needed better pay for their office staff to cope with much bigger loads, particularly in correspondence July '92; in response to Bell's question, PM John Major denied the Bundesbank claim that Britain had been offered realignment within the ERM before being expelled the month before Oct '92; asked Trade and Industry Secretary Michael Heseltine about progress on GATT Oct '92; complained that, despite approaching onset of the Single Market, UK was losing its share of world insurance market Nov '92; speaking for Labour, supported Ray Powell's restrictive Shops (Amendment) Bill to limit Sunday trading because the alternative was the Government's plan for deregulation "with no employee protection" Jan '93; urged the Government to curb the costs of the liquidators of BCCI, running at £640,000 a week Mar '93; promised Labour would protect investors against merchant bankers, lawyers and accountants who were practicing the "black art" of creative accounting Mar '93; wrote a homage to the French and France, where he spent his twenties May '93; unveiled Labour's plan for an American-style Securities and Exchange Commission July '93; as Secretary of the Parliamentary Labour First-Past-the-Post Group, welcomed the TGWU's decision to oppose PR July '93; won 75 votes in the Shadow Cabinet election (up from 60), Oct '93; voted to reduce age of homosexual consent to 18, Feb '94; after the death of John Smith, nominated Margaret Beckettl for Deputy Leader June '94; voted for Tony Blair for Leader, Margaret Beckett for Deputy Leader July '94; had an adjournment debate attacking the Cleveland County Council's handling of local government reorganisation July '94; wrote a significant letter to the TIMES, urging a thorough-going Hattersley-type constitutional reform: "the future of the monarchy is not in doubt, for the Queen is part of our constitution, with the Commons and the Lords; the succession, however, must be resolved and resolved quickly; if Charles wishes to remain heir to the throne and there is no reconciliatiion with Diana he should become, as he appears to wish, not the head of one Church, but the repository, if that is the right word, of a variety of religions and cultures in our society; this seems to require the disestablishment of the Church and the abolition of the House of Lords, where 26 archbishops and bishops sit as part of the Establishment; if the Church of England is to be disestablished, the House of Lords must be replaced by an elected second chamber, elected by a system of proportional representation, with revising and limited delaying powers so that it does not come into conflict with the Commons" Sep '94; promised that a Labour Government would extend employee share-ownership and put workers on the boards of their companies, Euro-style Sep '94; tried to stoke up the question of "cash for questions" sleaze; on the eve of the big GUARDAN scoop about Harrods-owner Mohammed al-Fayed having paid Neil Hamilton and Tim Smith via lobbyist Ian Greer, he disclosed the story in the Commons under the cloak of privilege, to try to nail John Major to his promise to clean up corruption; predicted: "the sleaze of the 1980s will continue to engulf John Major; there are many more examples which may yet come out; he will never be able to clear up what happened in the Thatcher years" Oct '94; he received 67 votes in the Shadow Cabinet election, with 97 required Oct '94; the new Leader, Tony Blair, kept him in the Trade and Industry team, then under Jack Cunningham Oct '94; in commemorating Yitzhak Rabin's murder, he recalled meeting him in 1991 when Rabin told him of visiting Elsinore, where he elicited from his Danish hosts that the castle had had to survive a 100-year-long war with the Swedes Nov '94; with Peter Mandelson refused to vote against the Government's decision to abolish Cleveland County Councl Jan '95; opposed the screening of a semi-documentary on the Scottish sex-abuse seizures: "rehashing events which were nightmares for all the families concerned will do no good whatsoever for them or their children" Mar '95; he did not vote for the Labour amendment which would have required MPs to register their contracts for Parliamentary services to outside interests (like his with Merck, Sharp & Dohme July '95; in the election to the Shadow Cabinet, he secured 82 votes, with 107 needed Oct '95; he retained his place on the Trade and Industry team, now headed by Margaret Beckett Oct '95; underlined that UK was importing £110 worth of goods for every £100 it sent overseas Dec '95; pointed out in TRIBUNE that common ownership could be redefined by a Labour Government since "at least 35% of British stock is held by UK pension funds and something like 75% is held by institutions overall" Mar '96; said: "I don't think the monarchy, living in five palaces and five castles, can be considered close to the people" Mar '96; voted against a 3% cap on MPs' salaries, but in favour of a 26% increase in pay and pension rates July '96; his place on the Trade and Industry team was confirmed in Tony Blair's last pre-election reshuffle Aug '96; promised a new Companies Act Sep '96; as shadow 'Minister for Trade and Corporate Affairs' reassured the Share-Link Private Investors Conference that Labour had no plans to change Tessas or PEPs Oct '96; in a wind-up speech standing in for Margaret Beckett, twitted the Conservatives for trying to discuss 'Trade and Inward Investment' without once mentioning the single European currency Dec '96; opposed as "scandalous muckraking" the local screening of a documentary re-examining the Cleveland sex-abuse case Apr '97; in his 'Strategy for Exports' predicted that a Labour Government would use ambassadors to boost exports Apr '97; retained his altered seat in Middlesbrough with an enhanced majority of 25,018 over his Conservative opponent, on an 11.5% pro-Laboour notional swing May '97; unexpectedly, was not named a Minister on Labour's Trade and Industry team; although a member of the Christian Socialist Movement, he rejected initially the unpaid post of 2nd Church Estates Commissioner, which deals with Church assets May '97; after it had been hawked around, including to one new Roman Catholic MP, Bell was belatedly named 2nd Church Estates Commissioner, possibly after being promised future promotion June '97; at the Durham Miner's Gala, Lord (Don) Dixon referred to him as "God's Shop Steward" July '97; told the Commons that "we want to maintain the establishmen of the Church [of England] but we also want to see an inclusive Second Chamber and to look at the quesion of how other faiths can play their part" Jan '98; made powerful speech in defence of retaining first-past-the-post as an electoral system, rejecting the alleged benefits of PR June '98; voted against reducing age of homosexual consent from 18 to 16, June '98; saw through Parliament the National Institutions Measure, cutting the Church Commissioners from 95 to 33 and establishing an Archbishops' Council June-July '98; in a lengthy interview with the DAILY TELEGRAPH' Churches Correspondent, Victoria Combe, he suggested that the Church might have to be protected from an "unstopppable tide of change" after the next election: "siren voices will say, 'disestablish the Church', 'get the Bishops out of the Lords'" July '98;

Born: 16 May 1938, High Spen, County Durham

Family: Son, late Ernest Bell, a miner for 51 years, and late Margaret Rose (Lintern); m 1st '60 Margaret (Bruce) whom he met at a pit village dance; 1s Ian '63, 1d Yvonne '65; m 2nd '80 Margaret (Allan), who is his constituency secretary; 1s Malcolm Stuart '81;

Education: Hookergate Grammar School, County Durham; Pitmans College (with the intention of becoming a Hansard reporter); Council of Legal Education; Gray's Inn;

Occupation: Barrister '70-; headed a Parisian international law firm '70-77; subsequently set up barrister's chambers in Middlesbrough '81, London '84; Adviser, to Ernst and Young (accountants; "remuneration for Parliamentary services as part of a wider agreement": £10-15,000) '97-; Sponsored by GMB (£600 p a to constituency party, 80% of election expenses) '93-95; "a contribution of more than 25% of my election expenses at the 1997 general election"; on Conciliation Board of European Space Agency '88-; Author: Paris '69 (steamy novel; 1973), Days that Used to Be (novel; 1977), Valuation for US Customs Purposes (1981), When Salem Came to the Boro (the Cleveland events; (1988); Annotation of the Children Act (1989); Journalist: ACCOUNTANCY AGE (regular article £1-5,000 annually) '97-; Columnist on NEWCASTLE EVENING GAZETTE '90-;, on BLAYDON

COURIER '56, DAILY TELEGRAPH night copy-taker '57; ex: Adviser, to Merck, Sharp and Dohme (giant US pharmaceutical firm) '87-97?; Lloyd's Underwriter '84-87 (retired in '85); Secretary, to international lawyer in Paris '59-66; Lloyd's Shorthand Typist '58; Colliery Clerk, Chopwell '55,
Traits: Tall; slim; curly sandy hair; jokey-genial; fast driver (fined and endorsed '86); French-speaking ("I learned my French in Cavaillon, the melon country, in the heart of Provence"); "a committed Anglican although, like the Prime Minister, he worships in a Roman Catholic church in Middlesbrough with his wife and son, who are both Catholics" (Victoria Combe, DAILY TELEGRAPH); has "courage" (Auberon Waugh, SUNDAY TELEGRAPH); "tough-minded and humane" (George Brock, TIMES); "perfectly affable, but for some reason he makes people's flesh creep" (GUARDIAN); "too articulate, too talented and too wealthy" (Atticus, SUNDAY TIMES); says he is no longer rich but was lucky to get out of Lloyd's in good time; jogger; asthmatic; when a young journalist in Newcastle, his pub-crawling colleagues complained he chatted up their birds when they went to the loo; his youthful sexual preoccupations were reflected in vivid descriptions in his novel, 'Paris '69'; he received substantial libel damages from the SUNDAY MIRROR for alleging he was ashamed of it and concealed it;
Address: House of Commons, Westminster, London SW1A 0AA; 38 The Avenue, Linthorpe, Middlesbrough, Cleveland TS5 6PD;
Telephone: 0171 219 3577/6634 (H of C); 01642 85011902 (constituency; 0171 834 1677 (London home);

Rt Hon 'Tony' (Anthony Wedgwood) BENN   Labour   CHESTERFIELD '84-

Majority: 5,775 (11.2%) over LibDem 4-way;
Description: Declining coal centre with steel overflow from Sheffield and massive chemical-steel complex at Staveley; in '83 it lost 10,000 voters to North East Derbyshire;
Former Seat: Bristol South East '50-60, '63-83;
Position: On Select Committee on Privileges '84-; on Executive, Campaign Group (President '87-) '85-; ex: on Labour's National Executive Committee (Chairman '71-72) '62-93, '59-60; Energy Secretary '75-79; Industry Secretary '74-75; Minister of: Technology '66-70, including Power from '69, Aviation from '67; Postmaster General '64-66; Spokesman, Trade and Industry '70-74, Transport '59-60;
Outlook: The ageing radical guru of the hard-Left Campaign Group, self-described as a "prophet of righteousness"; his Chesterfield voters are becoming less impressed; at his persuasive best is the most articulate Parliamentarian; a senior politician who has moved from Right-of-Centre in Labour's mainstream to the marginalised hard-Left, discarding en route close former friends like Peter Shore; Michael Foot judged that he had transmuted himself from a mainstreamer with "a marvelous combination of wit, persuasive power, deep radical instincts, and a zest for politics" into Citizen Benn, a self-righteous, calculating and unctuous outsider; "like my father, I grow more Left as I grow older" ; "I haven't yet decided what I want to do when I grow up" (AWB); "he immatures with age" (Harold Wilson); "no political

judgement" (Hugh Gaitskell); can alternate between the primitive assessments of an adolescent who has just read his first Marxist tract and the sophisticated critiques of a mature politician about the operations of the British Establishment: "my contribution to the Labour Party is that I know the British Establishment inside out and what they're up to" (AWB); his hyper-sensitivity about being born into the comforts of the Establishment prevented him from declaring even part of his inherited wealth until forced to by new Commons regulations; partly out of guilt about his privileged background, he has idealised and idolised the working class in a way which embarrassed genuinely proletarian colleagues like the late Eric Heffer and led him to under-estimate the extent to which Conservative offers of council houses and low taxes were fragmenting the old organised working class; "it was Tony Benn's 'total incapacity to understand the march of modern history', which ensured that, when he came close to capturing the party machine [in the early '80s], he came close to destroying the Labour Party as a force in 20th century British politics" (Lord [Denis] Healey); "why is it that every time Tony proposes anything to unite the party I have sleepless nights?" (Dr John Reid MP); "a downwardly mobile populist of the Left, increasingly convinced of his own personal mission to ensure 'a fundamental and irreversible shift in the balance of power and wealth in favour of working people and their families'" who "also discovered that he evoked in them a respect and attention quite unlike the amused scepticism shown towards him by the chattering classes among whom he had grown up" (Lord [Bill] Rodgers); "like Gladstone, his ambitions may have been cloaked in principle, but Benn has been as concerned with personal advance as any MP" (Peter Riddell, TIMES); a first-rate diarist who has recently peddled his diaries, tapes and videos of his Commons speeches; "I can vouch for his candour...I am struck by the factual accuracy" (Tam Dalyell MP); sees himself, out of office, as a "prophet of righteousness" but identifies his ambition for himself with promoting his causes; with Margaret Thatcher is "one of the last two examples of the Nonconformist conscience active in British politics"; "they are as one in their moral earnestness, their absolute belief in right and wrong, their confidence of their own virtue" (Allan Massie, DAILY TELEGRAPH); "Tony's greatest failing is perhaps his tendency to go over the top; he is hot on conspiracy" (Sir Julian Critchley ex-MP); as his support and influence decline, his output increases of radical new initiatives and far-reaching Bills with no hope of success; "I have got built into me, through my upbringing or whatever, a tremendously strong inner voice saying what I should do at any one moment" (AWB); all that remains is a brilliant ability to communicate and an unsurpassed insight into Britain's less-than-democratic structure, learned as a longtime Minister who also had to fight the Establishment to return to the Commons despite his inheritance of a peerage; now a republican opponent of the monarchy and Crown prerogatives; a principled opponent of the Maastricht treaty; clear on the constitutional and libertarian reforms desired but vague on the economic organisation of the socialism he craves; "one of the most intriguing, provoking, paradoxical and entertaining figures in British politics" (George Hill, TIMES); "one of the two or three most compelling political performers in the country" (Jim Naughtie); "Old Testament prophet" (Harold Wilson); a "Powell of the Left" who has transmuted old friends into enemies and found tolerance recently largely among Campaign Groupies, Scargillites, Trotskyists and Communists; "in the past you could always say for him that at least he was a great democrat; but now he's boxed himself in with a lot of people who have only the most superficial attachment to democracy; he does have a weakness for adoring audiences, and he can still find them and persuade himself that he can appeal to a great body of support in the country over the heads of the party and the media" (Labour front-bencher to George Hill, TIMES); "he has got this great public relations sense but he is no serious thinker" (late RHS Crossman); "powerful, persuasive, perverse" (Terry Coleman); "you never know what he will say next" (Jim Naughtie); "the Joe Bugner of British politics: a heavyweight who always came close but never managed to land the finishing blow" (Ben Preston, BRISTOL EVENING POST); "I've been a spent force all my life" (AWB); a personality split between a self-mocking, sophisticated, articulate administrator and a gimlet-eyed zealot spotting capitalist and Rightwing Labour conspiracies; a Leftwing Queen's Scout in his own hairshirt; "a bit cracked" (late Tony Crosland);

History: The son of a Labour MP and peer, Viscount Stansgate, he joined Labour Party at 18, '43; was selected for Bristol South East at 25 after intervention with locals by his ex-tutor, Tony Crosland '50; was elected for Bristol South East on retirement of Sir Stafford Cripps Dec '50; as a Centre-Rightist then, criticised the Bevanite rebellion which began Apr '51; moved adjournment of Commons on deposing of Seretse Khama Feb '52; joined H-Bomb National Committee Apr '54; led agitation against deportation of US Leftist Dr Cort June '54; backed Indian pressure to ban Marshall Islands atomic testing Aug '54; led movement to suspend capital punishment Feb '55; his Bill to renounce succession to father's title was rejected by Lords Feb '55; backed Silverman Bill to end capital punishment Nov '55; voted for Hugh Gaitskell for Leader and not Aneurin Bevan Dec '55; with Victor Yates, led 100 Labour MPs who welcomed UK withdrawal from Egyptian invasion, deplored Russian violence in Hungary and urged reliance on UN Dec '56; was joint founder of Movement for Colonial Freedom; moved first censure of Speaker in 30 years for refusing his adjournment over UK attack in Oman July '57; introduced Human Rights Bill Dec '57; urged withdrawal of UK troops from Malaysia, opposed nuclear arms for West Germany Mar '58; urged televising of Parliament June '58; was proposed as Morgan Phillips' successor as party General Secretary May '59; moved up from twenty-second to sixteenth place in Shadow Cabinet Nov '59; was elected to National Executive Nov '59; was named Transport Spokesman Nov '59; introduced Bill to allow designation of traffic control zones Dec '59; urged world government become part of Labour policy Jan '60; resigned from NEC after having failed to play a conciliatory role over unilateralism at Scarborough Oct '60; was compelled to resign his seat on his father's death Nov '60; the Peerage (Renunciation) Bill was introduced Mar '61; won by-election after having disclaimed viscountcy but was prevented by the Government from taking seat, or addressing Parliament from Bar of the Commons May '61; was fourth in ballot for NEC Oct '62; after three years' battle succeeded in securing an Act to make disclaimer legally enforceable July '63; was first peer to renounce his peerage Aug '63; after Tory MP Malcolm St Clair stepped down as promised, was re-elected Aug '63; named Postmaster General Oct '64; came second for constituency section of NEC Dec '64; launched GIRO '64-65; was named Minister of Technology Mar '66; according to Tony Crosland, Benn welcomed Labour's defeat in June '70 because only in Opposition could he take a leading role in moving it Leftward; proposed Labour leaders be endorsed by conference Nov '71; was named Industry Secretary Mar '74; was leading advocate of Government funds for co-operatives at Meriden motorcycles, Kirkby and SCOTTISH DAILY NEWS '74-75; Wilson demoted him from Industry to Energy - releasing the information from Jamaica via the DAILY TELEGRAPH June '75; in battle over whether to accept IMF conditions for loans, Benn resisted initially, preferring to retreat to wartime-style siege conditions Nov-Dec '76; sold first tranche of BP shares '76; generously supported coalmining, but held back atomic development, and negotiated very secretly with the oil companies '76-79; was re-elected to Fabian Council, soming second with 871 votes Nov '78; warned that democracy was threatened by advancing technology in the military and security services Feb '79; decided not to contest Shadow Cabinet May '79; finally joined Tribune Group (as part of his strategy for appealing to constituency activists rather than fellow-MPs) Oct '79; reluctantly decided not to stand against Michael Foot for Leader Oct '80; was runner-up in election for Shadow Cabinet Dec '80; opposed action against Militant Dec '80; as runner-up, rejoined Labour's NEC on resignation to join SDP Jan '81; clashed with Michael Foot, accusing him of being soft on SDP; Foot accused him of caucusing with Campaign Group before NEC meetings Jan '81; secured the backing of the hard Left to contest the Deputy Leadership against Denis Healey, ignoring soft Left protests, including Leader Michael Foot Apr '81; voted against Defence Estimates, despite Shadow Cabinet decision to abstain June '81; on NEC supported removal of nuclear weapons from UK July '81; was very narrowly defeated (.5%) by Healey - the percentage accounted for by Rightwing MPs who later joined the SDP Sep '81; told Trotskyists in LABOUR HERALD-LONDON LABOUR BRIEFING meeting that Labour was under attack by Pentagon, Brussels, IMF, House of Lords, SDP Dec '81; on NEC endorsed candidacy of Peter Tatchell Dec '81; on NEC tried to convert Labour to "command economics" '81-82; on NEC urged immediate ceasefire in Falklands May '82; voted against Northern Ireland (Emergency Provisions) Bill June '82; failed to win a place on the Shadow Cabinet Oct '82; urged united Ireland and UK withdrawal from Northern Ireland Dec '82; on NEC voted against making Militant Tendency supporters ineligible for Labour Party membership Dec '82; after boundary changes, was defeated by Michael Cocks in winnable Bristol South as a result of a union-packed selection conference May '83; unsuccessfully contested redrawn, marginal Bristol East after 32 years as a Bristol-area MP June '83; refused Tony Banks' generous offer of his safe Newham North West seat to make him elegible to contest Leadership June '83; was proclaimed a member of Campaign Group Sep '83; moved resolution for a united Ireland Oct '83; was voted top of NEC's constituency section with 554,000 votes Oct '83; in wake of Grenada invasion, warned in TRIBUNE that US might seize control of UK if it acted against US interests Nov '83; on the resignation of Eric Varley was selected for Chesterfield Feb '84, elected Mar '84; on NEC opposed expulsion of Blackburn Six Militants Apr '84; tried to adjourn Commons over police harassment of miners May '84; urged gays to make common cause with miners because of shared police harassment June '84; on NEC opposed changes in selection of candidates July, Sep '84; defended the "right to revolt" against oncoming totalitarianism Sep '84; again topped the constituency poll for NEC Oct '84; won 60 votes for Shadow Cabinet, second runner-up below Brynmor John Oct '84; urged consideration of general strike in support of miners, "the ultimate weapon of self defence" in semi-Trotskyist LABOUR HERALD Dec '84; said he would not challenge Neil Kinnock for the Leadership Jan '85; urged new Reform Bill to end Commons' "growing powerlessness" May '85; introduced Bill to nationalise land over £250,000 in value May '85; failed to be nominated for NEC by Labour Co-ordinating Committee May '85; presented Bill to abolish Lords and repeal Official Secrets Act May '85; introduced Bill to have workers elected to boards of plcs July '86; came second behind David Blunkett for the constituency section of the NEC with 490,000 votes Sep '86; was again unsuccessful on Campaign Group slate for Shadow Cabinet July '87; at Durham miners' gala called for an "enormous struggle, mainly waged outside Parliament" July '87; in WORLD MARXIST REVIEW sought European peace through East-West treaties, remerging of trade union federations Aug '87; submitted proposals to NEC for withdrawal from NATO, phasing out of nuclear power, abolition of Lords, democratisation of magistracy and supervision of judiciary Sep '87; came second to David Blunkett with 439,000 votes in election to constituency section of NEC, where he now had only three other supporters Sep '87; was principal sponsor of 'Socialist Conference', including Communists and Trotskyists, at Chesterfield, predicting street riots and nuclear meltdowns in wake of stock market crash Oct '87; claimed that figures of Soviet military preponderance were often exaggerated in Cabinet documents Oct '87; sponsored motion "for Britain...to withdraw all its troops within the lifetime of this Parliament" from Ulster Nov '87; visited Moscow, urging reinstatement of Anglo-Soviet Treaty Nov '87; accused Neil Kinnock of "consistent failure" to support the socialist struggle outside Parliament, while watering down Labour's basic policies

Jan '88; defying the Official Secrets Act, he published a classified report advising Ministers on how to perform their duties Jan '88; introduced Bill to terminate Her Majesty's jurisdiction over Northern Ireland Mar '88; decided to challenge Neil Kinnock for the Leadership, with Eric Heffer challenging Roy Hattersley for the Deputy Leadership, provoking the resignation of six Campaign Groupies, including Margaret Beckett Mar '88; supported Dave Nellist against Speaker's order for him to withdraw Apr '88; introduced Bill to ban religioius persecution Apr '88; introduced Bill to ban foreign nuclear, chemical and biological weapons bases from Britain Apr '88; with Sinn Feiners on the platform denounced Gibraltar killings of three IRA gunpersons as "summary execution" Apr '88; opposed suspension of Ron Brown Apr '88; introduced Bill to end EC control over UK legislation May '88; introduced Bill to disestablish the Church of England May '88; opposed further PLP punishment for Ron Brown May '88; at Burford celebration compared Ron Brown to the Levellers May '88; attacked Kinnock's retreat from unilateralism June '88; with backing of Campaign Group, urged twelve-point statement of basic rights, including replacement of Crown Prerogative by statute law July '88; voted against EC money resolution July '88; at annual conference, in contest for Leadership, received 11.37% (5.872% from constituency parties, 5.15% from PLP, .34% from unions) to 88.63% for Neil Kinnock; in constest for constituency section of NEC, came second with 416,000 votes Oct '88; alleged Labour would win only when it brought the Left into the Leadership Oct '88; voted against Defence Estimates, instead of abstaining Oct '88; in election for Shadow Cabinet, received 56 votes, with 86 qualifying Nov '88; visited Cologne as guest of German Green Party Nov '88; voted against Prevention of Terrorism Bill, instead of abstaining Dec '88; voted against loyalty oaths in Northern Ireland, instead of abstaining Dec '88; claimed Official Secrets Bill was designed "deliberately to conceal from the electors information that they need to exercise their democratic functions Dec '88; visited Toulouse for Concorde celebration, paid for by British Aerospace Mar '89; on Labour's NEC voted against document rejecting unilateralism May '89; was re-named to Privileges Committee June '89; gave Subhas Chandra Bose lecture in Calcutta as guest of Netaji Research Bureau Sep '89; urged full recognition of the Soviet-imposed Afghan regime ??? '89; introduced Bill to secure equality before the law on sexual behaviour Oct '89; in election for Shadow Cabinet, received 55 votes, with 86 qualifying Nov '89; was reselected for Chesterfield with 69% against 19% for nearest challenger Jan '90; supported Militant-run 'Anti Poll Tax Federation Mar '90; forwarded warning of BCCI corruption from staff to Employment Secretary Michael Howard June '90; in special session of Commons, voted against the Gulf War, predicting it "could cost the lives of tens of thousands of soldiers and civilians" Sep '90; came fifth, with 352,000 votes, in contest for constituency section of Labour's NEC Sep '90; discreetly allied himself with Edward Heath to oppose the Government and Labour leadership over impending war against Saddam Hussein Sep '90; in election for Shadow cabinet received 43 votes, 85 qualifying Oct '90; led vote against war in Gulf Dec '90; predicted Gulf War would be "the greatest environmental catastrophe since the atom bombs" Dec '90; voted against mandate for military attack on Iraqi forces, urging a "peaceful freeing of Kuwait, based on economic sanctions" Jan '91; was involved in Committee to Stop War in the Gulf; claimed the extent of the opposition to war in the Gulf was being muffled by Labour leaders Feb '91; introduced a Commonwealth of Britain Bill to establish a democratic, federal and secular republic May '91; came sixth, with 343,000 votes, in contest for 7-place constituency section on Labour's NEC Sep '91; in hard-Left 'Programme for Action' co-urged devaluation, a new core of state-owned companies, £7b cut in military expenditure Sep '91; on NEC, opposed suspension of Militant Dave Nellist Sep '91; co-sponsored motion urging sharp defence cuts with withdrawal of US forces from UK Oct '91; in election to Shadow Cabinet received 39 votes, with 107 qualifying Oct '91; opposed Maastricht concessions to an "unelected Commission or Central Bank"

Oct-Nov '91; at Manchester constitutional conference, urged end of monarchy Nov '91; in discussion of Citizens Charter, insisted: "we in this country are not citizens, we are subjects of the Crown" Nov '91; claimed "the war against Iraq was really about the determination of the United States to control the oil there and to assert its military ascendency over its client states" Dec '91; introduced Commonwealth of Europe Bill Dec '91; restated his intention of campaigning as an anti-nuclear candidate Jan '92; predicted: "far from pulling out of the recession, Britain and the western world may be falling into a major slump comparable to that which occurred in the 1930s" Jan '92; backed Wild Animals (Protection) Bill and end of fox-hunting Feb '92; said he felt "hounded" as a pipesmoker but opposed banning all tobacco advertising, preferring to "discourage people" Feb '92; with Dennis Skinner voted against support for Maastricht treaty being included in Labour's manifesto Mar '92; during campaign repeatedly predicted post-election "rioting" because issues were being dodged Mar-Apr '92; in his 16th election battle, retained his seat with majority down from 8,577 to 6,414, a swing to Liberal Democrats of 2.22% Apr '92; blamed Labour's defeat on its being too Rightwing Apr '92; co-urged UN control of Sarajevo airport and effective protection for food convoys May '92; voted against Maastricht ratification May '92; urged NEC to prepare for next election by supporting "full employment, a big house-building programme, a free NHS and better care for the disabled, lifelong and equal education for everyone, higher pensions and dignity for all retired men and women..." June '92; applauded Danish referendum rejection of Maastricht as a blow for people against EC bureaucrats June '92; as an alternative to the EC, introduced a Bill for a European Commonwealth, including eastern Europe June '92; was prevented by PLP from putting a motion for a Maastricht referendum June '92; in election for Shadow Cabinet, received 47 votes, with 104 qualifying July '92; demanded recall of Parliament if armed forces were sent to Yugoslavia July '92; complained about tritium leak from Bradlwell nuclear power sation, seven miles from his inherited farmhouse at Stansgate Abbey Aug '92; was jointly "appalled" at US threats of renewed war against Saddam Hussein Aug '92; introduced Bill for Maastricht referendum, after Commons' "totally unrealistic debate" after ERM ejection Sep '92; after defeat of ally Dennis Skinner, survived in last place on NEC with 354,000 votes Sep '92; failed to win Labour's annual conference for a referendum on Maastricht Sep '92; attacked pit closures, saying that if market forces had been "applied to the farming industry, half the farms in Britain would have closed years ago; we couild get cheaper food from New Zealand and Australia" Oct '92; presided over day-long meeting of 'Socialist Movement' at Chesterfield, addressed by semi-Trostskyist Jeremy Corbyn and expelled Militant Dave Nellist; Benn criticized Labour's expulsion of "many good socialists" Oct '92; backed ordination of women, one of his mother's causes Oct '92; insisted the war against Saddam Hussein had been "a war for profit, oil and control of the region" by Ministers who had been "selling weapons to Saddam Hussein who was repressing Kurds and Shi'ites before and after the war"; insisted the Commons should investigate this, not Lord Justice Scott Nov '92; demanded right to discuss referendum on Maastricht; attacked the Maastricht treaty as further emasculating Parliament; it was "a pathway to the feudal past" Dec '92; revived his Commonwealth of Britain Bill which also hoped to replace the Queen by a President Dec '92; joined Tory and Liberal Democratic Euro-sceptic MPs in pro-referendum-on-Maastricht rally Jan '93; warned against bombing Bosnia Jan '93; was one of 21 Labour MPs who voted against possibility of further anti-Iraqi action in Gulf Jan '93; was tagged as having voted six times against Maastricht in defiance of the Labour Whips, with nine as the maximum Feb '93; his motion to criticise the Deputy Speaker, Michael Morris, as "profoundly mistaken" for refusing a vote on whether Britain should opt out of Maastricht's Social Chapter. was heavily defeated Apr '93; again strongly warned against military involvement in Bosnia May '93; led motion backed by Campaign Group calling for basic constitutional reform, including the abolition of the monarchy and the

House of Lords and the disestablishment of the Church of England May '93; voted against 3rd Reading of Maastricht treaty Bill May '93; decried Tony Blair and Gordon Brown as "Victorian Liberals" and claimed that John Smith was preparing Labour for joining "with Mr Ashdown in some nice American Democratic Party" and "finally expunge any ideas that it is a socialist party" Sep '93; lost his seat on the National Executive, his vote having declined from 354,000 to 269,000 - after which he was accorded a standing ovation Oct '93; protested against Home Secretary Michael Howard's refusal to allow Sinn Fein leader Gerry Adams to enter Britain to adress a Westminster meeting, "to prevent MPs and the Lobby from hearing his proposals for peace" (AWB) Oct '93; again backed ordination of women, the campaign for which his mother had pioneered as "a member of the League of Church Militant in 1920" Oct '93; co-sponsored Campaign Group's motion against the Defence Estimates Oct '93; introduced a Bill to enable the police to join a union and affiliate to the TUC Nov '93; for the first time, registered his shareholding in United Newspapers; the requirement was for a shareholding of greater than 1% of issued share capital or over £25,000 in value Jan '94; co-warned againt "threats of punitive military action" in Bosnia Feb '94; voted against restoring capital punishment, even for killers of policemen Feb '94; voted to reduce age of homosexual consent to 18 or 16, Feb '94; voted for Prescott for Leader, Beckett for Deputy Leader July '94; decided not to stand again for Labour's National Executive July '94; presented a Bill to deregulate trade unions Oct '94; voted against Eurpean Communities (Finance) Bill Nov '94; made public the confidential proceedings of the Committee on Privileges on the "cash for questions" affair Nov '94; in his TRIBUNE column, predicted: "this year, the Labour Party could, if we are not very careful, be virtually dismantled by defeault, disengaged from the trade unions, persuaded to repudiate socialism and to commititself, formally, to the maintenance of world capitalism, now run by the International Monetary Fund and the Brussels Commission" Jan '95; backed Ashdown's Bill for a Referendum on major European changes Feb '95; voted against easing licensing hours Feb '95; insisted the UN could not be both humanitarian and unleash air strikes in Bosnia May '95; led amendment to cut Defence spending "to the average level of other West European countries" Oct '95; warned against transferring "the right to tax, to borrow and to spend" to any authority "not accountable to the British electorate" Mar '96; voted against Prevention of Terrorism Bill instead of abstaining Apr '96?; backed cuts in MPs' mileage allowances July '96; voted for Bill Cash Bill urging Referendum on Euro-federalism July '96; led letter against Trident July '96; was rated the 14th most active of the hard-Left rebels against the Labour leadership, with 37 rebellions from 1992, Sep '96; led motion against the bugging allowed by the Police Bill Jan '97; voted against the Police Bill because of its indiscriminate intelligence-seeking, such as used against him, even when he was a Cabinet Minister Fab '97; retained his seat with a reduced majority of 5,775 over his LibDem opponent, who managed to secure a 0.1% swing against him, virtually unprecedented among Labour candidates May '97; accompanied elected Sinn Feiners Gerry Adams and Martin McGuinness on their Westminster tour and challenged Speaker Betty Boothroyd's ruling that they could not take their seats without swearing allegiance to the Queen May '97; voted to ban fox-hunting June '97; said he would not vote for the Committee on Standards report on Neil Hamilton because he had not broken the law, although what he had done was "totally disreputable" July '97; again urged the Government to give up its jurisdiction over Northern Ireland and withdraw British troops July '97; voted for LibDem amendment against capping Somerset and Oxfordshire July '97; challenged PM Tony Blair over the propriety of allowing LibDems into a Cabinet Committee without a Parliamentary statement; he then attacked this LibDem alliance as "the beginning of the end of the Labour Party" July '97; when he attacked the 1967 Labour Government for having arrested 4,000 Hongkong demonstrators, Gerald Kaufman MP asked why, since he was a member of that Government, he had not resigned July

'97; in an OBSERVER article accused Tony Blair of abandoning socialism for a merger with the Liberal Democrats in a wholly new party July '97; in an interview with the semi-Trotskyist LABOUR LEFT BRIEFING said Tony Blair was trying to change the party into something new and non-socialist Sep '97; he joked at the Brighton annual conference that Labour had replaced OMOV (One-Member One-Vote - which he had opposed) with OLAV (One Leader All Votes) Oct '97; voted against Government's cuts in lone-parent benefits Dec '97; devised a new oath for MPs which could enable Sinn Feiners to take their seats Jan '98; voted against abolition of student maintenance grants June '98;

Born: 3 April 1925, London

Family: His great-great grandfather was a master quiltmaker in Manchester; his son, the Rev Julius Benn, ran away at 13 to Liverpool when his father remarried; the family reached Stepney in 1850; "my grandfather, John, went to work in his mother's boots at the age of 11", becoming a member of the first London County Council and a Liberal MP; the late Margaret Rutherford was his first cousin, once removed; her father, Tony's great-great-uncle, murdered his father by striking him with a chamber pot; Tony is the elder surviving son of 1st Viscount Stansgate, formerly Liberal MP (Leith '18-27), then Labour MP (Aberdeen '28-31, Gorton '37-42), Secretary of State for India '29-31, elevated to peerage '42 as part of wartime coalition Government, Air Secretary '45-46; Tony's mother, the late Viscountess Stansgate, Margaret Eadie (Holmes), was a leading Congregationalist, first President of the Congregational Federation, pioneer suffragette and campaigner for ordination of women, and active on the Council for Christians and Jews; m '49 Caroline (Middleton De Camp), a Leftist from a wealthy Cincinnatti legal family; 3s Stephen '51 (ex-ILEA, married to Nita Clarke), Hilary '53 (Ealing councillor), Joshua '58, 1d Melissa '57 (journalist);

Education: Westminster; New College, Oxford (President of Union '47);

Occupation: Writer/Broadcaster; Author: The Privy Council as a Second Chamber (1957), The Regeneration of Britain (1964), The New Politics (1970), Speeches (1974), Arguments for Socialism (1979), Arguments for Democracy (1981), The Sizewell Syndrome (1984), Writings on the Wall (1984), Out of the Wilderness -Diaries 1963-67 (1987), Fighting Back (1988), Office Without Power - Diaries 1968-72 (1988), Against the Tide - Diaries 1973-76 (1989), Conflicts of Interests - Diaries 1977-80 (1990), A Future for Socialism (1991), The End of an Era - Diaries 1980-90 (1992). Years of Hope, 1940-62 (1994); Shareholder, with over 1% or over £25,000 in United Newspapers/United Media '93-; former Shareholder, with 88,674 shares in family firm of Benn Brothers, for which he worked as a salesman in '47; these were convertible into 65,000 Extel shares after '85 takeover, then into United Newspaper, then United Media shares, which he declared for the first time under new Commons rules; Owner-Occupier: house in Holland Park, Stansgate Abbey Farm, Essex (formerly his mother's residence); ex: Producer, BBC North American Service '49-50; Mrs Benn comes from a very wealthy Cincinnatti family; her "grandmother...left something like £300,000 in 1974 in trust for her daughter's four children" (John Junor, SUNDAY EXPRESS); Mr Benn says the above financial descriptions are "wrong" and claims many other errors in this profile but has consistently declined to correct them;

Traits: Grey parted hair; long jaw; grey complexion; "ashen faced" (Craig Brown, TIMES); "swivel-eyed" (Michael Lord, BRISTOL EVENING POST); "intense eyes staring round the audience and a thin smile playing on his lips" (Jamie Dettmer, SUNDAY TELEGRAPH); "the startled stare and the off-stage gaze" (Mark Lawson, INDEPENDENT); an absent-minded professor with a "lovely wuffly Children's Hour voice" and "a deep vein of paranoia"; "he seems to believe that anyone who is not 100% for him is against him" (Lynn Barber, INDEPENDENT ON SUNDAY); intense; self-isolating; "safe in his messianic world" (Ian Aitken, GUARDIAN); prefers talking to the converted or convertible; has used tape recorders

and recently an electromagnet to protect himself against media distortion; has "charm, courtesy, intelligence and oratorical ability", "a fundamental decency and seriousness" (Allan Massie, DAILY TELEGRAPH); "Benn's wit is one of his under-appreciated qualities" (Michael White, GUARDIAN); "a man of stubborn courage, humour and warmth", "a questioning figure, a rejector of orthodoxies", with "childlike ambitions" (Ben Pimlott, EVENING STANDARD); "naivete...strong destructive propensity...disproportion between his superb gifts of expression and his limited stores of either common sense or of intellectual sinew" (Lord (Roy) Jenkins); "he has an imperviousness which only the most immaculately self-righteous ever achieve" (George Hill, TIMES); "there is something manic about him, but he has the persuasiveness of someone who has worked it all out to his satisfaction; he has these extraordinary theories into which he can fit all the facts, and this gives him a great flow, like a huge river which is unmistakably coming from somewhere and going somewhere; but the longer you listen, the more you realise he is trying to push water up hill" (Michael Heseltine MP); "his ideological self-righteousness is lightened by a mischievous sense of houmour" (John Torode, INDEPENDENT ON SUNDAY); prefers cardigans and trade union ties; pipe-smoker (Pipesmoker of the Year '92); drinks a pint mug of tea hourly, recently made of instant tea ("I'm an addict!"); always a teetotaller (like his father and grandparents); since '80 a vegetarian; has an unsteadiness of gait and hearing trouble in wake of '81 nervous illness (diagnosed as Guillain-Barre Syndrome); ex-flier (RAFVR Pilot Officer '43-45 and Sub-Lieutenant RNVR '45-46); "Wedgie"; "Bennatollah" (PRIVATE EYE); "Jimmie" (family nickname); his greatest extravagance: "office equipment of all kinds and any labour-saving devices"; a Metyclean office equipment shop "is one of my favourite ports of call when things are going wrong"; is most depressed by "the disapproval of friends"; is kept awake by "anxiety at night and cramp in the morning"; "I just can't cope with financial matters";
Address: House of Commons, Westminster, London SW1A 0AA; 12 Holland Park Avenue, London W113 4QU;
Telephone: 0171 219 6443 (H of C); 0171 229 0779 (secretary); 01246 239077 (constituency office); Fax: 0171 219 6155;

Andrew (Francis) BENNETT   Labour   **DENTON & REDDISH '83-**

Majority: 20,311 (44.1%) over Conservative 5-way;
Description: Created in '83 from parts of his old Stockport North in southeast Greater Manchester; it is afflicted with poor housing and heavy unemployment; in '95 Labour-leaning Brinnington was moved back into Stockport; in exchange Dukinfield arrived from Stalybridge and Hyde;
Former Seat: Stockport North '74-83;
Position: Joint Chairman, Select Committee on Environment, Transport and Regional Affairs '97-; Secretary, PLP Civil Liberties Group '78-; President Ramblers Association '98-; Vice President, Peak and Northern Footpaths Society '95-; ex: Spokesman, on Higher and Further Education '83-88; on Select Committees: Statutory Instruments (Joint Committee '92-97; Chairman of both '93-97, '83-87) '75-97, on the Environment (Chairman '94-97) '92-97, on Information '92-97, on Sittings of the Commons '92, MPs' Interests '79-83,

Social Services '89-92, '79-83, Liaison '83-87, Domestic Violence '83-87; Chairman, Labour Health and Social Security Group '81-83; Secretary, Northwestern Labour Group '83-84; **Outlook:** Low-profiled but assiduous, socially-concerned, quietly effective Leftwinger; "an experienced and capable Parliamentarian" (ex-MP David Mellor); a civil libertarian sensitive to the rights of British Ramblers and Irish dissidents; a constituency-rooted defender of decent housing and the financing of foster care and other social benefits; a unilateralist opponent of high defence costs; a leading tactician on procedure ("can run rings...around many...Members when it comes to procedural matters" - Peter Snape MP); a specialist in Private Bill procedure who can block them to extract concessions (has "blackmailed various organisations, including British Rail, with the amount of time that we would take in the House unless they did something to improve the position of our constituents" -AFB); peacenik (attended World Peace Council '77, '79, '81, opposed Gulf War '90-91); Ramblers' spokesman: critic of path-blocking farmers and their bulls, arbitrary policemen and stray dogs; "a sly, if slightly cranky, bio-boffin" (Robert Hardman, DAILY TELEGRAPH); "is the sort of endangered Labour Leftwinger whom biodiversity treaties should protect: he believes in Ramblers, creches and beards; you can almost hear the sandals in his voice"; but "it is alway hard to take seriously a small man with a large beard and a falsetto voice" (Matthew Parris, TIMES);

History: He joined the Labour Party '57; was elected to Oldham Borough Council May '64; contested hopeless Knutsford June '70; won Tory-held Stockport North Feb '74; made Maiden speech on "appalling" housing conditions there Mar '74; demanded retention of better Ordnance Survey maps for Ramblers Apr '74; urged better allowances for foster children June '74; complained about "unfair" treatment of Irish terrorist suspects May '75; urged Children's Charter instead of child-snatchers' license June '75; voted against Prevention of Terrorism Bill Nov '75; defeated Government with amendment putting 3-month limit on dealing with complaints against police Feb '76; urged more generous payment for foster parents Jan '77; claimed "granny bashing" was result of having to look after difficult aged relatives May '77; urged a more independent Register of MPs' Interests Nov '77; pushed Bill to give rebates on water bills July '78; tried to ban school caning Jan '79; attacked too-wide application of anti-terrorism Act Mar '79; complained Tornado aircraft were over-sophisticated Oct '79; in protest against council rent increases organized picket to keep Black Rod out of Commons, delaying session's end Nov '80; criticized court's attack on National Council for Civil Liberties Nov '80; called for inquiry into "appalling" Liverpool school canings Jan '81; attacked curbs on Manchester street parades Apr '81; complained about heavy standing charges for minimal users of gas and electricity Jan '82; supported dog-curb Bill Feb '82; pushed Walkers Charter for Ramblers and other access-seekers Apr '82; introduced Falkland Islanders (British Citizenship) Bill to dramatize Government's previous neglect May '82; alleged police harassment of young males, especially blacks Nov '82; urged 11-point Charter of Human Rights Nov '82; warned police were using hidden video cameras Jan '83; delayed British Railways Bill to secure guarantees about two Stockport railway stations Mar '83; worried about police identity parades Mar '83; criticized Oxford's 'Operation Major' against social security fraud Feb '83; on boundary changes was selected for safe-Labour Denton and Reddish Apr '83; attacked baby seal culling Feb '83; complained of arbitrary exercise of power by Manchester's Chief Constable May '83; voted against Defence Estimates July '83; urged higher student grants Oct '84; visited Ethiopia as guest of its government Nov '84; backed more generous aid for Ethiopia Jan '85; was fourth most assiduous committeeman in '84-85; led Labour team on Bill to ban corporal punishment received 17 votes for Shadow Cabinet Oct '86; opposed Kenneth Hind's Unborn Children (Protection) Bill Oct '86; insisted a Freedom of Information Act could be more helpful than a Bill of Rights, partly because judges would enforce latter Feb '87; led Labour campaign for better nursery education Mar '87; asked how many people had been injured or sickened by dogs June '87; tried to amend Felixtowe Dock Bill to protect areas of wildlife interest July '87; came third in election for Deputy Chief Whip with 32 votes (with 102 for Don Dixon, 69 for Peter Snape) July '87; resisted Greater Manchester's Light Railway project until he received reassurances about constituency services Nov '87; complained of rundown of BR services to Northwest Jan '88; warned that parents at opted-out schools might be pressured into contributions Jan '88; warned against back-door introduction of student loans instead of grants Mar '88; voted against Prevention of Terrorism Bill instead of abstaining Dec '88; criticized retention of independent nuclear deterrent, partly because its command, control and communications had not kept up with these weapons Feb '89; was named to Social Services Select Committee Mar '89; on Water Bill recalled that he had rambled every weekend for 10 years as a youngster and had been upbraided for "brewing up with a Primus stove" by the waterside Mar '89; urged planning inquiries instead of private Bill procedure for major changes requested by railways or canal authorities Apr '89; with 49 other unilateralists, rejected Neil Kinnock's abandonment of their cause May '89; strongly resisted London Regional Transport Bill because LRT had not kept promise to retain an alternative to mechanical ticket barriers June '89; in response to his complaint, LRT abandoned Sherwood's as their Parliamentary Agent July '89; deplored Government's failure to exploit new armament-curbing opportunities Oct '89; said Government's student loan scheme was "attractive to nobody" and particularly not to working-class students Oct '89; co-sponsored amendment to Queen's Speech urging restoration and expansion of civil liberties Nov '89; opposed almost all twenty private Bills to express his distaste for their timewasting procedures Nov '89; when he asked about arms diversification, Douglas Hogg pointed out there were six arms-producing factories in his constituency Nov '89; urged a Walkers Charter to improve accesss to mountain and moorland Nov '89; urged more aid for Ethiopia Dec '89; voted against War Crimes Bill Dec '89; opposed reorganization of National Conservancy Council and Countryside Commission Jan '90; railed against excess packaging by unpacking a new shirt in committee Feb '90; backed Edward Leigh's Rights of Way Bil, urging retention of footpaths as a "historical record" which "reminds people of old mills, chapels and other buildings which have perhaps almost disapppeared" Feb '90; voted for curb on EC's CAP programme Feb '90; asked about experimental trial of ELF transmitter for contract with submarine Feb '90; again voted against War Crimes Bill Mar '90; accused Tory Whips of trying a "crude filibuster" against part of Consumer Guarantees Bill Mar '90; questioned British control over Cruise missiles from US submarines in British waters Mar '90; complained he was not able to secure Government information on the discharge of contaminants in Scottish waters from nuclear-powered submarines, and having to rely on environmental lobby groups for his information Apr '90; urged clearing of Welsh footpaths of barbed wire and felled trees May '90; voted to ban smoking from public places May '90; as a civil libertarian, helped Ken Livingstone resist William Shelton's Bill against kerb-crawling after the word "persistently" was removed and no guarantees were given about adequate policing May '90; warned Tories against filibustering against Protection of Badger Setts Bill July '90; criticized Government's "crazy" students loans scheme July '90; proposed Commons again have morning sittings July '90; as "one of the few people on Opposition benches who greatly regret the Government's intention to reintroduce the war crimes legislation" felt "forgiveness is far more important than revenge" Nov '90; complained that Tameside authorities were being frightened into cutting expenditure when it needed more to protect elderly and children at risk Dec '90; was named to the Social Security Select Committee Dec '90; pointed out that with two Polaris submarines "no long seaworthy" and the other two on the Clyde, the PM was "the first Prime Minister for 20 years not have had a nuclear deterrent at his fingertips" Dec '90; voted against/ opposed war in the Gulf Dec '90, Jan '91; complained that confidential census material was being sold and decifered, producing unwanted junk mail Mar '91; complained about mislabelling of products allegedly friendly to the environmennt Mar '91; again complained about retaining ex-Strangeways prisoners in Greater Manchester police cells Mar '91; pleaded with social workers "to be aware of the continued retelling of such [satanic ritual] myths" throughout the ages Mar '91; "as an ex-geography teacher I find it unpalatable the attempt to impose a national curriculum...I suggest that my geography lessons were interesting and exciting to pupils because I could teach them about things with which I was familiar and understood" Apr '91; insisted Defence Secretary Tom King's 'Options for Change' had not caught up with end of 'cold war'; urged cancellation of whole Trident system June '91; strongly backed dog registration June '91; attacked North West Water's "disgusting record since privatization" including increased illegal discharges of sewage June '91; disconcertingly asked John Major "why hasn't a minimum wage caused difficulties in West Germany?" June '91; complained that BR had not accepted Tameside's plans for a Euro-terminal at Guide Bridge July '91; was named to Committee on Sittings of Commons July '91; was named to Information Committee of Commons Nov '91; urged allowing sick MPs to vote by proxy if they had a note from their own doctor and a consultant Dec '91; opposed 2nd Reading for Prison Security Bill because of shortage of prison accommodation, particularly in Manchester area in wake of Strangeways riot Dec '91; with Campaign Groupies opposed nuclear defence Jan '92; welcomed new Mark 2 Police National Computer but warned against its abuse by including unfounded suspicions Feb '92; urged further community colleges like those in Leicestershire and Cambridgeshire Feb '92; urged shifting of public inquiries to areas affected Feb '92; introduced Bill to ban convictions on basis of uncorroborated confession Feb '92; retained seat with majority up from 8,250 to 12,084, a swing to Labour of 3.64% Apr '92; was named to Joint Committee (with Lords) on Statutory Instruments June '92; was named to Environment Select Committee July '92; urged earlier hours for Commons July '92; again urged better access to countryside July '92; again raised question of inaccurate 'ecolabelling' for environmentally-friendly products Nov '92; put down a motion sharply criticizing former Home Secretary David Waddington and his predecessors for their mishandling of Strangeways Prison riots Nov '92; warned that mines shutdown would damage those making mining equipment like Oldham Batteries in his constituency Dec '92; urged a more scientific study of coastal defences to ensure that efforts were not counter-effective Dec '92; urged better street lighting to reduce public fears Dec '92; was rated an anti-Maastricht rebel on five votes Feb '93; complainedthjat local magistrates in Stockport did not "reflect the social composition of the whole of Stockport but appears to reflect the membership of the Conservative Party and ofsecret societies, such as the Masons, rather than a proper cross-section" Feb '93; voted against 3rd Reading of Maastricht Bill May '93; opposed allowing British Waterways Bill to proceed unless "the concessions given today and in writing by the Board are contained in the Bill"; "people outside are worried that they might lose the right to go along towpaths"; "I hope we will be given undertakings that there will be no...piecemeal selling off of canal sections" May '93; visited Germany to study environmental legislation, as guest of BASF Sep '93; voted against Defence Estimates, instead of abstaining Oct '93; objected to the revival motion for the British Waterways Bill, to which he had been objecting on behalf of constituents since '91, without the BWB speedily meeting their objections; he pressed for more concern about heavier burdens on poorer northern canal users without permanent moorings Jan '94; complained that Tameside Council was running its homes unsatisfactorily, as experienced by the Tameside Community Care Trust, of which he was a Trustee Jan '94; was attacked by Tory MPs for misdeeds of Tameside Council Feb '94; voted against restoring capital punishment, even for killers of policemen Feb '94; voted to reduce age of homosexual consent to 18 or 16, Feb '94; introduced a Bill to prevent newspapers using computlers to alter the pictures they print Mar '94; made a fierce attack on Charles Hendry for his "despicable" attack on Shelter "for exercising the right to free speech" in opposing cuts in housing association grants Mar '94; in ten-minute-rule Bill tried to control computer phoneying of pictures Mar '94; tried to object to British Rail Order, but his objection was refused by Speaker Boothroyd Mar '94; opposed the Criminal Justice and Public Order Bill for threatening ramblers while aimed at hunt saboteurs Apr '94; backed John Prescott for Leader June '94; voted for Prescott for Leader and Deputy Leader July '94; was nominated to the Standing Orders Committee July '94; opposed increase in cost of Ordnance Survey maps July '94; urged a £5 dog license July '94; with other Campaign Groupies, demanded cuts in Defence expenditure Oct '94; on the appointment of Robert Jones to Ministerial office, became Chairman of the Environment Select Committee Nov '94; complained about the impact on his "disorganised" constituents of the Government's desire to remove the right to silence when charged Oct '94; vpted against the EC financing Bill Nov '94; complained that the Child Support Agency did not take travel costs into account when assessing net income Dec '94; demanded full information about the costs and benefits of the Anglo-American Mutual Defence Agreement Dec '94; voted for Ashdown's Bill for a Referendum on major European changes Feb '95; as Chairman of the Environment Select Committee, called for a dramatic cut in road pollution Apr '95; spoke at Ramblers' meeting demanding acccess to 'forbidden' Forest of Rowland Sep '95; with fellow Campaign Groupies voted against the Defence Estimates, instead of abstaining Oct '95; welcomed the procedural reform allowing MPs to leave at 7 PM on Thursdays but "we must be very careful that we do not change the nature of the whole of Thursday" Nov '95; voted against a Parliamentary Commissioner for Standards Nov '95; with the 'awkward squad' voted against procedure changes Nov '95; insisted the housing problem could only be solved by spending substantially more money Jan '96; met as a member of PLP's Review Committee to establish a new disciplinary code for Labour MPs Jan '96; was one of 25 rebel Labour MPs who voted against renewing the Prevention of Terrorism Act Mar '96; was one of 30 rebel Leftwing MPs who voted against a guillotine on the renewal of the Prevention of Terrorism Act Apr '96; pressed for reduction of smog-producing volatile organic compounds Apr '96; complained about the difficulty of restoring the right of access that the Lords had removed from the Bodmin Moor Commons Bill May '96; in introducing the report on Housing of the Environment Select Committee, criticised his own Stockport Council for putting alocolics, druggies and psychotics into bedsits next to elderly people; urged more livable high-density flats July '96; voted to curb MP's mileage allowances, against a 3% cap on their pay rises and in favour of pensions based on £43,000 July '96; he was found to be the 13th most active rebel among Labour MPs, with 38 defiances of the Whip since 1992, Sep '96; it was disclosed that the PLP's Review Committee would discipline Labour MPs for bringing "the party into disrepute" Nov '96; he sympathised with the 3rd World in reporting for the Environment Select Committee on the interaction between world trade and the environment Dec '96; retained altered Denton and Reddish with a majority enhanced to 20,311 over his Conservative opponent on a notional swing of 12.5% May '97; again pressed for urgent reform of the private Bill procedure June '97; was named Joint Chairman of the expanded Select Committee of Environment, Transport and Regional Affairs chairing Environment with Gwyneth Dunwoody chairing Transport July '97; abstained against the cut in lone-parent benefits Dec '97; opposed threatened use of force against Iraq Feb '98; welcomed the "slightly timid" recommendations of the Commons' Modernisation Committee; he thought the Serjeant at Arms could dispense with his sword, to avoid tripping over it June '98;

Born: 9 March 1939, Manchester

Family: Son, William Bennett, local government officer, and Elma (Francis); m '61 'Gill'/Gillian (Lawley) PhD; 2s Matthew '66, Lee '68 (fostered), 1d Kate '64;

Education: Kings Road Primary, Stretford; Hulme Grammar School, Manchester; Birmingham University (BSocSc);
Occupation: Lecturer/Broadcaster; Trustee (unpaid), of Tameside Community Care Trust (a charitable trust which is the majority shareholder in Tameside Enterprise Ltd which provides residential care for the elderly) '90-; Part-Owner, North Wales holiday cottage '88-; ex-Teacher: Head of Geography Department, Roch Valley Comprehensive School, near Rochdale '69-74; Mooreclose, Middleton '61-69 (NUT);
Traits: Greying dark hair; greying full beard; specs; "squeaky" voice; "a small man with a large beard and a falsetto voice" (Matthew Parris, TIMES); his "penetrating counter-tenor emerges oddly from a luxuriant beard" (Colin Welch, DAILY MAIL); dark-coloured shirts; soft-spoken; persistent; word-blind; computer buff; photographer; fell-walker until he developed an arthritic hip; as a child was a wartime evacuee to North Wales' Ceriog Valley, from which his love of rural nature derives;
Address: House of Commons, Westminster, London SW1A 0AA; 28 Brownsville Road, Heaton Moor, Stockport, Cheshire SK4 4PF; "when I am in London I stay in a set of deck access flats in the Barbican";
Telephone: 0171 219 4155/6593 (H of C); 0161 432 2953 (home); 0161 320 1504/ 0161 320 1503 (Fax)(constituency); E-mail: bennett.andrew@pop3.poptel.org.uk

'Joe' (Joseph Edward) BENTON Labour BOOTLE '90(Nov)-

Majority: 28,421 (74.4%) over Conservative 6-way;
Description: The tough inner-city Merseyside dockside area, with older terraced property and a large postwar council estate at Netherton; in '83 it was extended to Seaforth, but lost it back to Crosby in '95; one of Labour's safest seats;
Position: On Select Committee on Education and Employment '97-; ex: Whip '94-97; on Chairmen's Panel '93-95; on Energy Select Committee '91-92; on the 3rd Standing Committee on Statutory Instruments '93; Sefton Borough Councillor (its Leader '85-90) '70-90;
Outlook: Low-profiled local working-class Merseyside Catholic moderate; believes in "the framework of a Christian state"; interprets this to mean co-sponsoring Bills against abortion by fellow-Catholics, whether Tory or LibDem; insists "I am not a dinosaur"; Sefton Borough Council's former Leader; a rare one-note voice always demanding a better shake for the Merseyside; a veteran of twenty years in local government on the Merseyside; deeply rooted, warm-hearted, old-school; "although nervous and cautious at press conferences," he "is clearly at ease on the stump"; "displays a taxi-driver's knowledge of the streets in the area" (Robert Shrimsley, DAILY TELEGRAPH); was slow to make his views known in the Commons initially, except on local government and its financing; anti: abortion, frozen embryos, National Lottery; was NCC-sponsored;
History: His family were Labour; he was a Labour supporter at school; was elected to Sefton Borough Council (which includes Bootle) May '70; tried to secure selection for Bootle, but was outstripped by genial, articulate Allan Roberts May '78; on Labour winning a majority, became Leader of Sefton Borough Council May '85; again tried to secure selection for Bootle,

but was outpointed by Mike Carr Apr '90; was selected after sudden death of Mike Carr only eight weeks after he had replaced Allan Roberts as Bootle's MP Sep '90; retained Bootle at the by-election, with the majority down by a fifth Nov '90; expressed disappointment at Michael Heseltine's announcement of a review of local taxation, including a replacement of poll tax and especially the Heseltine-imposed cut of £10m in Sefton Borough Council's funds, including £5m from its education budget and his taking 100 policemen off the beat; "I recognise that there will always be difficulty and debate over how local government is funded - that has been the case for 20 years, and, no matter what alternatives are produced, they will never satisfy everyone"; objected to Heseltine's suggestions about "profligacy" of all Labour local governments: "my local authority, Sefton Borough Council, would be called mean by some; I prefer to call it stringent and careful"; "its spending practices have earned the praise of several Conservative Secretaries of State of the Environment in the past" Jan '91; spoke forcefully about the injustices of the poll tax, citing four sad cases from his surgery; "I always say to people, 'you should pay your poll tax'"; "however the Government must understand that many people cannot pay their poll tax and Ministers must make a distinction between those who will not pay and people...who face tremendous hardship" Feb '91; served on Severn Bridges Bill committee '91; was named to Select Committee on Energy, replacing Eric Illsley July '91; retained seat with majority up from 19,465 to 29,442, a swing to Labour of 5.91% Apr '92; lost his place on Energy Select Committee with its absorption into Trade and Industry Select Committee Apr '92; backed David Alton's motion opposing euthanasia July '92; in Labour's Leadership election, nominated John Prescott for Deputy Leader but voted for Bryan Gould July '92; was named to Chairmen's Panel Feb '93; voted against National Lottery Bill, because of Liverpool's pools industry Apr '93; co-sponsored anti-abortion motion deploring 3.7m unborn children "killed" in 25 years under 1967 Abortion Act Apr '93; served as Chairman of Third Standing Committee on Statutory Instruments in respect of High Court and County Courts Jurisdiction (Amendment) Order 1993, May '93; during 1993 he asked only one question Oct '94; voted against restoring capital punishment, even for killing policemen Feb '94; voted again lowering age of homosexual consent Feb '94; backed Tony Blair for Leader June '94; voted for Blair for Leader, Prescott for Deputy July '94; was named a Labour Whip June '94; demanded to know why the Liverpool School of Tropical Medicine had not received money from the National Lottery (against which he had voted) Dec '94; he demanded housing for the 7,000 on Sefton's housing list June '95; co-sponsored Freezing of Human Embryos Bill introduced by Tory fellow-Catholic David Amess Apr '96; voted for a 3% cap on MPs' salary rises, but the pension base to be increased to £43,000 July '96; was included as a Whip in the 'final' pre-election reshuffle July '96; co-sponsored Abortion (Amendment) Bill introduced by Tory fellow-Catholic David Amess Dec '96; cited three horrendous cases of maltreatment of seriously-ill constituents at Fazakerley Hospital Jan '97; was the Labour Whip who checked the incorrect figures of Tory Whip Antony Coombs who said Labour won by 273 to 272 to defeat the expansion of grant-maintained schools; in fact it was a 272 to 272 tie Jan '97; retained his altered Bootle seat with a 28,421 majority over his Tory opponent, on a 6% pro-Labour notional swing May '97; he was dropped as a Whip but named to the Select Committee on Education and Employment July '97; complained about the closure of the Crosby Coastguard station Nov '97;

Born: 28 September 1933, Bootle

Family: S late Thomas Edward Benton, dock labourer, and late Agnes Maria (Smullen); m '59 Doris Irene (Wynne), ex-hairdresser; 4d Helen Maria (now McDermott) '60, Catharine Elizabeth (now Howard) '61, Margaret Mary '63, Marie Louise '68;

Education: St Monica's Roman Catholic School, Bootle; Bootle Technical College;

Occupation: Sponsored, by National Communications Union (80% of election expenses)

'92-95; the renamed Communication Workers Union made "a contribution of more than 25% of my election expenses in the 1997 general election"; ex: Personnel Officer at Girobank '82-90; previously Manager, Clerk at Pacific Steam Navigation (which collapsed) '??-81?, Engineer '50-??; Apprentice Fitter and Turner '49;

Traits: White-haired; pleasant smile; "soft-spoken", "most relaxed when talking to voters, particularly the older ones who share his memories" (Robert Shrimsley, DAILY TELEGRAPH); Roman Catholic; was in RAF '55;

Address: House of Commons, Westminster, London SW1A 0AA; 3 Warwick Road, Bootle, Merseyside L20 9BY;

Telephone: 0171 219 6973 (H of C); 0151 933 8432 (constituency secretary); 0151 922 1304 (home);

John BERCOW   **Conservative**   **BUCKINGHAM '97-**

Majority: 12,386 over Labour 4-way;

Description: A solidly Conservative county seat, including Buckinghamshire's small county town and a large tract of the county south of Milton Keynes; part agricultural, part affluent suburbia; in the '90 split of MK into two constituencies, the new town took away bits around the pro-Labour old railway town of Wolverton; in the '95 boundary revision Buckingham acquired Aston Clinton ward from Aylesbury; the seat attracts oddities: the country's first private university, Robert Maxwell and George Walden;

Position: Assistant Spokesman, on Trade and Industry '98-; on Select Committee on Welsh Affairs '97-; ex: Special Adviser: to Virginia Bottomley '95-96, to Jonathan Aitken '95; Lambeth Borough Councillor (Deputy Leader of Conservative Group '87-89) '86-90; National Chairman, Federation of Conservative Students '86-87; Chairman, Essex University Conservatives '84-85; former Secretary, Monday Club's Race and Repatriation Committee '81-83;

Outlook: A very Eurosceptic Thatcherite replacement for quirky 'One Nation' Tory MP George Walden; a jack-in-the-box who hardly lets a day pass without interventions; the political son Norman Tebbit never had ("Tebbit the Younger" - Ian McCartney MP); only his hair is parted in the centre; one of the ambitious, driven Rightwing figures, formerly floating between the "barmy Right" (initially in the Monday Club) and the acceptable face of the Tebbit-Thatcher Right; in the Thatcherite 'Conservative Way Forward', Freedom Association; well-networked; admits to having been the beneficiary of a network of ex-FCS activists; has a talent for abandoning sinking ships in favour of others floating in his desired direction; a punchy speaker with no need for notes; an "elegant master of intrigue and Thatcherite phrase-maker" (TATLER); "a tremendous street fighter" (Lord Parkinson); with "the oratorical equipment to be the Tories' answer to Arthur Scargill" (TODAY); like Tory ex-MP David Shaw, is "nasty and ineffectual in equal quantities" (PM Tony Blair); "only a baby" (Labour MP Dennis Skinner); "childish" (Labour MP Audrey Wise); "needs to calm down a little, but he knows how to get under Labour hides" (Quentin Letts, DAILY TELEGRAPH); formerly dependent on the tolerance of big names, he has - after many disappointments - successfully found a safe Tory seat and odd appearances on the front bench;

History: He became consciously a Conservative at 15, '78; joined Hendon YCs and Finchley YCs '80; became Secretary of the Monday Club at 18, Sep '81; became Secretary of its Immigration and Repatriation Committee, run by Powellite Tory MP, Harvey Proctor Sep '81; recorded its minutes which, according to PRIVATE EYE, read: "it was formally agreed that the policy of the Committee should be an end to New Commonwealth and Pakistani immigration; a properly financed scheme of voluntary repatriation, the repeal of the Race Relations Act, and the abolition of the Commission for Racial Equality; particular emphasis on repatriation" '83; he resigned as Secretary of the Monday Club at 29, Feb '83; resigned from the Monday Club because the views of its racialists were "unpalatable" Feb '84; became Chairman of the Essex University Conservative Association '84; was elected to Lambeth Borough Council at 23, May '86; became National Chairman of the ultra-Right-dominated Federation of Conservative Students, a year after it had disgraced itself by riotous vandalism at Loughborough Apr '86; was outvoted by 16 to 1 when, in a damage limitation exercise, he attempted to censure Harry Phibbs, editor of its NEW AGENDA, for having published an interview with Count Nicolai Tolstoy stigmatising Harold Macmillan as a "war criminal" Sep '86; after the disbandment of the FCS by the Chairman of the Conservative Party, Norman Tebbit, became his National Student Director of its sanitised replacement, the Conservative Collegiate Forum, to which a £30,000 subsidy was transferred Oct '86; he became the youngest-ever Deputy Leader of Lambeth's Conservative Group Oct '87; contested the hopeless seat of Motherwell South against Labour's Dr Jeremy Bray, reducing the Tories' vote from 20% to 14.5% and their position from second to third June '87; he did not contest his seat on Lambeth Borough Council May '90; he organised 125 Conservative candidates in support of embattled Margaret Thatcher, then backed John Major Nov '90; said he found Edward Heath's pro-European views "irritating, not to say obnoxious" Oct '91; contested the Labour marginal of Bristol South against Dawn Primarolo, whom he denounced as "an extremist implanted by the Labour Left"; her majority went up from 1,500 to 9,000 Apr '92; after working as a lobbyist, became Special Adviser to Jonathan Aitken, Chief Secretary to the Treasury Mar '95; on Aitken's forced resignation from the Cabinet, became Special Adviser to Virginia Bottomley, National Heritage Secretary Aug '95; having failed in a hopeless and a marginal seat, he pursued safe ones, at first unavailingly: Bedfordshire North East (close runner-up to Attorney General Sir Nicholas Lyell Sep '95), Hampshire North West, Worthing West (pipped by Peter Bottomley Feb '96); dramatically, he commuted by helicopter between two occurring on the same day: Surrey Heath and Buckingham where, he recalled: "I rushed onto the stage with seconds to spare and made a joke about how I had arrived; I don't think it did me any harm; I had put my money where my mouth is; I hope people think of me as resourceful and not as someone who is enormously wealthy and flash"; even before he had been selected over David Rutley and Howard Flight, he told fellow helicopter-traveller, friend Julian Lewis, that hiring the helicopter was "the best £1,000 I've ever spent" Feb '96; replied to call from Brian Wilson for him to apologise for the abuse heaped on "Communist terrorist" Nelson Mandela by the FCS when he was its Chairman by demanding Wilson apologise for his "support for the Marxist government of Nicaragua and the pro-Castro UK-Cuba Association and unilateral nuclear disarmament" July '96; backed nursery school and university vouchers Sep '96; named as one of 16 prospective Tory candidates working for lobbying companies, insisted: "I intend to take a Parliamentary salary and no consultancies and directorships whatsoever" Oct '96; replying to the DAILY TELEGRAPH's inquiry, said he would put his opposition to a single European currency in his election manifesto Dec '96; retained Buckingham with a majority of 12,386, down 8,000 after an anti-Conservative swing of 10.58%, May '97; defending quangos, claimed that "election is not the only source of legitimacy" May '97; dubbed Labour and LibDem MPs as "abstract rationalists who want to meddle with Parliamentary practice" May '97; in the Tory Leadership contest, first joined the campaign team of Peter Lilley May '97; after John Redwood's defeat, said he would consult him before deciding between Clarke and Hague June '97; his Maiden was mainly a panegyric to Baroness Thatcher July '97; was named to the Select Committee on Welsh Affairs July '97; with the support of 52 Tory colleagues, called for the resignation of Lord Simon, the European Competitiveness Minister, over his alleged failure to disclose his interest in BP shares July '97; was part of the Redwood-inspired pack in hot pursuit of Lord Simon for not divesting himself of BP shares July '97; was warned by Speaker Boothroyd that he would "be out in a moment" if he continued his boisterous behaviour July '97; PM Tony Blair snapped that Bercow reminded him of former MP David Shaw, "whose hallmark was to be nasty and ineffectual in equal quantities" Jan '98; urged more exclusion of disruptive students Mar '98; opposed legally-binding home-school agreements Mar '98; asked 60 questions about Ministerial spending, costing an estimated £6,000 Mar '98; tried to amend National Minimum Wage Bill Mar '98; claimed that Lord [Norman] Tebbit "made the greatest contribution in the 20th century to British trade unions" Apr '98; was rated one of the 'Top 100' written questioners, with 165 posed in his first year May '98;

Born: 19 January 1963, Edgware

Family: Son, of late Charles Bercow, car salesman and minicab driver, and Brenda (Bailey), formerly a legal secretary, recently a mature student at Middlesex University; has a girlfriend, Stephanie Gray;

Education: Finchley Manorhill School '74-81; Essex University (BA First-class Hons in Politics) '82-85;

Occupation: Ex: Free-lance Political Consultant (worked with Westminster Strategy) '96-97; Public Affairs Consultant '88-95 with Rowland Sallingbury Casey (a subsidiary of Saatchi & Saatchi); he was a Director '94-95; he acquired a redundancy package from this firm although he quickly become Special Adviser to Jonathan Aitken; he repaid 10% of his redundancy package '95; Credit Analyst, Hambros Bank '87-88;

Traits: Shortish ("just because I am a little chap, it doesn't mean I haven't got a big ambition"); upturned head; centrally-parted spikey hair; mobile mouth; short arms; clear deliberate enunciation; confident; fluent; "sits in an extraordinary position with his arms braced against the bench underneath him and his shoulders hunched forward, so that he seems both slumped and poised for action at the same time" (Simon Hoggart, GUARDIAN) sallow-skinned; Mediterranean appearance; Jewish; combative ("a tub-thumping public speaker"; "he's quick, he's sharp, he's bright and he knows his own mind" (Lord [Norman] Tebbit); driven; "excitable" (Paul Routledge, INDEPENDENT ON SUNDAY); "charming but scary" (NEW STATESMAN); tennis coach;

Address: House of Commons, Westminster, London SW1A 0AA; 31 Marsham Court, Marsham Street, London SW1P 4JY;

Telephone: 0171 219 3000/0981(Fax) (H of C); 0171 828 5620 (home)

BULGING EX-MP FILES

Because of the unprecedented retirements before the 1 May 1997 election and the major massacre of Conservative MPs on the day, our computer and paper files on former MPs are bulging to an unprecedented degree. These are kept up to date, partly because defeated ex-MPs may come back. We also update these files as the base of the obituaries in at least two of the broadsheets.

Sir (Alexander) Paul BERESFORD   Conservative   **MOLE VALLEY '92-**

Majority: 10,221 (18.7%%) over LibDem 7-way;
Description: The seat linking the Surrey towns of Dorking and Leatherhead, embracing Box Hill and Leith Hill; in '95 Ashtead was moved to Epsom and Ewell and Send, Effingham, the Chandons and the Horsleys came in from Esher, moving the geographical centre of gravity a few miles to the west without altering its Right-leaning political centre of gravity;
Position: Ex: Under Secretary, Environment '94-97; on Education Select Committee '92-94; Vice Chairman, Conservative MPs' Housing Improvement Subcommittee '92-94; Secretary, Conservative MPs' Inner Cities and Urban Committee '92-94; Leader of Wandsworth Borough Council '83-92; on Audit Commission '91-92;

Outlook: New Zealand's best-known dentist again able to devote more time to his dental practice; the relocated reincarnation of Wandsworth's once-efficient Rightwing pioneer of privatisation of local government services; his clumsy inarticulacy in junior office made it difficult for him to live up to his former reputation as the Leader of the Tory flagship or win William Hague's favour; he had tried, with little success, to compel local government "to produce better services for less cost", as he had in Wandsworth; in contrast to his noisiness as its much-publicised Tory Leader, affected a low profile in the Commons until a few months before his '94 promotion; believes "less government is better government, so long as the interests of those in need and the environment are protected"; "earned the undying gratitude of Mrs Thatcher by setting a poll tax of four pence" (GUARDIAN) for the Tories' flagship authority; in Wandsworth, was "the thinking man's Terry Dicks, an abrasive Thatcherite, ever ready to anathemise Leftwingers and pour scorn upon his wet and ineffectual Conservative colleagues on Wandsworth Borough Council" (PRIVATE EYE); "chivalry...is something that my accent usually finds difficult" (PB)

History: In response to four years of Labour's "spendthrift" spending locally, he stood for and was elected to Wandworth Borough Council May '78; was elected Leader of Wandsworth Borough Council, succeeding Christopher Chope May '83; Wandsworth started selling vacant properties ??? '83; failed to win nomination for the Kensington by-election, for which Dudley Fishburn was selected June '88; announced he would step down as Wandsworth's Tory Leader, but reversed this decision '89; was knighted Jan '90; had his proudest hour when Wandsworth returned a Tory majority, in defiance of national opinion polls Apr '90; failed to be selected as a candidate at Hertsmere, where he was pipped by veteran by-election loser James Clappison, who was less enthusiastic about the poll tax; "Hertsmere is a very nice area with very nice people, but they didn't want me; they wanted a different type of person from the one before, [Cecil Parkinson, who was] a successful high-profile Minister" Mar '91; was selected as John Moore's successor at Croydon Central Mar '91; gave Conservative Party's broadcast on Channel 4's 'Comment' programme Apr '91; was appointed to Audit Commission by Cabinet Ministers Michael Heseltine, William Waldegrave and David Hunt (although he would have to resign on becoming an MP) May '91; after being asked to advise John Major on the Citizens Charter, his office was alleged by Labour MP Jack Cunningham to have approached Labour-run councils in York and Islington "to find out about their policies for implementing quality services" June '91; promised to "send a fiver" to Battersea Power Station

Community Group if successful in their application to Merton Council for planning permission to turn his house in Raynes Park into a theme park "to rival Euro-Disney", in protest against Wandsworth Council's alleged neglect of its responsibility for the conversion of Battersea Power Station into a theme park June '91; after Chris Patten floated the idea of "a voice for London", Sir Paul snapped: "I'm opposed to a mayor, a GLC-type body or even a Minister for London - they will not work and they're very expensive" Oct '91; was invited to Moscow by a Yeltsin aide to advise on sale of council houses and competitive tendering Oct '91; his Wandsworth Council again set a zero poll tax, which he attributed to "efficiency, quality and value for money" Dec '91; retained Croydon Central for the Conservatives by 9,650 votes, a 4% swing to Labour Apr '92; after his resignation as Wandsworth Council Leader, he facilitated the succession of his friend Eddie Lister, at the expense of Cathy Tracey, wife of Tory MP Dick Tracey May '92; in his Maiden speech welcomed council tax and insisted that 1,000-year-old Croydon was more than a mini-Manhattan and that John Moore had served it well July '92; was said to resent the hard discipline of Tory Whips July '92; with 12 other new Tory MPs, publicly backed John Major over Maastricht, on eve of key vote Nov '92; backed Local Government Bill which enabled councils to help developing countries, including new East European regimes; while Wandsworth's Leader, he had trvelled to Moscow, Warsaw and Gdansk and found an "appalling lack of even basic government structures", but had been limited in his ability to help "because of the restrictions imposed by the current legal framework" in Britain; with new legislation it would be even easier to imitate Wandsworth, which had earned £100,000 a year helping others with its skills, and export expertise even to developed countries, providing substantial overseas earnings Dec '92; accused "corrupt and incompetent" Lambeth of a "whitewash" in its review of local corruption; urged the strengthening of the Audit Commisson - on which he had served - to enable it to "move into councils such as Lambeth" Jan '93; voted against Ray Powell's restrictive Shop's (Amendment) Bill to restrict Sunday trading Jan '93; when his former sister Tory authority, Westminster, was being criticised, complained that "in cases of gross incompetence or considerable incompetence by a local authority, in the armoury of the district auditor and the Audit Commission they can only place a report and a recommendation, and that many millions of pounds of council taxpayers' money is being wasted"; instead, urged "firming up the powers of the Audit Commission for the sake of many residents in [Labour-governed] areas such as Lambeth, Southwark, Islington and many of the imcompetent Labour authorities where he is powerless effectively to act" Jan '94; with the Boundary Commission recommending the reduction of Croydon's seats from four to three, he was considered to be safe, until the former Croydon North East MP, Lord (Bernard) Weatherill came out for his own successor, David Congdon; "it does look like David Congdon and I will be competing for the one seat," Sir Paul told the EVENING STANDARD Jan '94; in a lengthy speech on housing, again contrasted Wandsworth's "low cost, high-quality management" with the incompetence of its Labour neighbours Jan '94; opposed restoring capital punishment, even for killers of policemen Feb '94; opposed lowering age of homosexual consent below 21, Feb '94; complained that Labour still insisted on throwing more money at inner-city regeneration, when the real issue was efficient use of funds available; Wandsworth had collected its tax and spent its money on street-cleaning, refuge collection and housing at a fraction of the cost in adjoining inner-city Labour authorities June '94; in reshuffle, was promoted Under Secretary for the Environment, with responsibility for London, but was still drilling teeth the next day July '94; was allowed to "keep his hand in" dentistry by the Cabinet Secretary, Sir Robin Butler July '94; was discharged from the Education Selection Committee Oct '94; was disclosed to have had a lobbyist, Paul Green of Charles Barker, as his Researcher Jan '95; offered to pull Dennis Skinner's teeth without an anaesthetic Jan '95; claimed that "no other capital city that I have seen run as well as London" to the derision of the EVENING STANDARD which accused him of not realising "what an ass he sounds" Feb '95; told Labour MP Alan Milburn to "stop whingeing" Feb '95; his former Wandsworth Council policy of selling vacant homes rather than use them for the homeless was criticised by the District Auditor Mar '95; the Boundary Commission reduced the number of seats in Croydon from four to three ??? '95; opposed an elected authority for London as expensive and bureaucratic Mar '95; was beaten for selection for Croydon Central by fellow -Tory MP David Congdon July '95; was knocked out of consideration as candidate for Maidenhead, which went to Theresa May Oct '95; made it on to the short-list for Mole Valley when his unloved 'wet' rival, Sir George Young withdrew on winning Hampshire North West Nov '95; introduced Rating (Caravans and Boats) Bill to make them subject to non-domestic rates rather than council tax Dec '95; he finally was selected for Mole Valley, vacated by Kenneth Baker Dec? '95; refused to celebrate the 25th anniversary of David Mellor's selection as Putney's MP Mar '96; it was alleged by Patricia Kirwan, the Tory whistle-blower on Westminster council, that Dame Shirley Porter started on her designated sales policy after a breakfast session with Beresford May '96; voted for a cut in MPs' mileage allowances, a 3% cap on MPs' salary increase but a £43,000 pension base July '96; urged Liverpool to stop its expenditure on parks and roads when it went £5m into the red Aug '96; an opinion poll found him likely to lose Croydon Central Nov '96; Wandsworth, of which he had been Tory Leader, was found guilty of unlawful sale of council homes Dec '96; after secret papers were passed to him by John Marshall MP, he ruled that Barnet had breached Government regulations by awarding its refuse contract to its in-house binmen, TeamBarnet, instead of an outside bidder whose offer was £500,000 cheaper Mar '97; was elected for his new seat, one-third altered Mole Valley by a majority of 10,221 over his LibDem opponent, an anti-Tory notional swing of 7% May '97; in what was "in effect a [second] Maiden speech", he praised the achievements of his predecessor, Kenneth Baker June '97; he backed Kenneth Clarke in the Leadership stakes and was left off William Hague's front-bench team July '97;

Born: 6 April 1946, New Zealand

Family: Son, Joan and Raymond Beresford, New Zealand dentist and son of a dentist; m 1st a New Zealander who returned home; m 2nd Julie (Haynes); 3s, 1d;

Education: Richmond Primary School, Richmond, Nelson, New Zealand; Waimea College, Richmond, where he played Rugby; Otago University, Dunedin; Eastman Dental Hospital, London University;

Occupation: Dental Surgeon, on Park Lane '??-94; Author: The Good Council Guide (1991); on Audit Commission '91-92;

Traits: Efficient; semi-articulate; "could not be more 1980s if he tried; in decades to come, museum designers will place his beaming image next to a little model of the Escort XR31, a Next suit and a record by Wham!" (EVENING STANDARD); "I'm a New Zealander; I don't know what the word 'philosophy' means"; is said to retain the aggressiveness of a New Zealand Rugby player, verbally and otherwise ("one man who was foolish enough to goose Beresford's wife found himself nursing a broken jaw" - PRIVATE EYE); enjoys sport, photography and home renovation;

Address: House of Commons, Westminster, London SW1A 0AA; Flat 21, 140 Park Lane, W1Y 3AA; 120 Coombe Lane, SW20 0QY;

Telephone: 0171 219 5139/5018 (H of C);

'Gerry' (Gerald Edward) BERMINGHAM   **Labour**   **ST HELENS SOUTH '83-**

Majority: 23,739 (53.6) over Conservative 5-way;
Description: A seat made up in '83 of bits of old Huyton, Widnes and St Helens; has its glass industry (Pilkington), coal, engineering;
Position: Chairman, all-party Music Appreciation Group '97-; Treasurer, all-party Space Parliamentary Committee '89-; Vice President, League Against Cruel Sports '87-; ex: on Home Affairs Select Committee '83-97; Chairman '87-92, Vice Chairman '85-87, PLP Home Affairs Committee; Sheffield City Councillor '80-82, '75-79;
Outlook: A soft-spoken soft-Left Dublin-born Catholic pro-European who has survived a colourful history; an assiduous and realistic would-be legal and prison reformer who operates on the basis of his 30 years' experience in the courts; one of the few MPs still practicing at the criminal Bar, with barrister-type Commons attendance; a civil libertarian and defender of the remanded and mentally ill; a strong believer in freedom of the press, an opponent of any form of censorship; a "southern Irishman, born and bred" (GB), he knows the dangers of trying to tell the Irish what to do; is an opponent of PR on regional lists for Euro-elections; is also an enemy of the Boundary Commission's arbitrary constituency-making; a realistic behind-the-scenes manoeuvrer rather than a tub-thumping orator, reserving his theatricals for the courtroom; belonged to both Tribune Group and Campaign Group; is really soft-Left, but used to pretend to be hard-Left, because of extremists in his constituency party; even visited Libya and Bulgaria ("does he believe that if he goes on a grand tour of all the most oppressive Leftwing hell-holes in the world, the Trots of the St Helens Labour Party will relent and allow him to keep his seat after all?" - SUNDAY EXPRESS); those extremists who deselected him were vetoed by the NEC; was GMB-sponsored;
History: He joined the Labour Party '60; as a local 'poor man's lawyer', was elected to Sheffield City Council May '75; contested Southeast Derbyshire May '79; was selected for St Helens as the successor to Leslie Spriggs, defeating Doug Hoyle June '81; selected for redrawm St Helens South, won it June '83; demanded better bail opportunities for imprisoned June '83; joined both hard-Left Campaign Group and soft-Left Tribune Group to protect his back from local hard-Left July '83; consequently voted for Heffer for Leader, Meacher for Deputy Leader Oct '83; opposed proscription of Sinn Fein as negating democratic liberty and not helping solve the Irish problem Oct '83; opposed corporal punishment Oct '83; introduced Bill to shorten trial delays and limit imprisonment without bail Nov '83; backed Pearson Commission's recommendations that Government should pay full compensation to families of vaccine-damaged children Dec '83; resisted constituency calls for his resignation about allegations of an affair with a divorcee Dec '83; after distribution of dossiers on his "sexual frolics", his constituency officers terminated contacts with him Feb '84; asked about complaints about benzodiazepine drugs Feb '84; played an active part in committee on Police Bill Mar '84; introduced Bill to prevent jailing for fine defaulters Mar '84; the Vice Chairman of his constituency party was accused of sending him obscene literature Mar '84; saw no justification for 96-hour police detention, believing 48 hours enough May '84; in debate on investor protection urged ability of investors to sue insurance brokers for bad advice July '84; his paternity trial was adjourned when the baby who was allegedly his was claimed to be too ill

to provide a blood sample to compare with Bermingham's rare blood type; Bermingham was alleged to have admitted to having sex with the nurse involved and to have contributed £1,000 when she said she was pregnant July '84; visited Libya in Liberation party, with Ron Brown MP, Bob Parry MP and Eddie Loyden MP Aug '84; opposed military co-operation with Chile Nov '84; called for levy on TV films to finance UK film industry Dec '84; introduced Bill to allow public entry to water authority meetings Dec '84; opposed TSB Bill, insisting Government was trying to sell something it did not own Jan '85; was a leader of unsuccessful cross-party group trying to stop abolition of National Film Finance Corporation Feb '85; his water authority Bill failed to get 2nd Reading Feb '85; opposed Fluoridation Bill, preferring to leave it to local water and health authorities Mar '85; was one of four Labour MPs on Home Affairs Select Committee expressing unease about lack of control over Special Branch May '85; described EEC's CAP as "bureaucratic madness and a waste of money" June '85; visited Libya with Ron Brown in an effort to free British prisoners - succeeded with two Aug '85; because of irregularities, his constituency party was taken over and its reselection process frozen Dec '85; opposed new US nuclear test Mar '86; signed Benn-Heffer-Corbyn motion attacking US bombing of Libya from UK bases Apr '86; complained about death of constituent in Broadmoor and uncontrolled administration of heavy sedatives there May '86; introduced Bill to compensate those remanded in custody and subsequently found innocent June '86; raised question of maltreatment of 'Birmingham Six' alleged bombers July '86; a report on his constituency confirmed charges of irregularities, and "very considerable manipulation and malpractice" including rigging of votes by a "small, tightly-knit group of individuals" Sep '86; two constituency parties (his and John Evans') were suspended by Labour's NEC together with District Labour Party Oct '86; complained that UK prisons had become "the cesspit of Europe" Nov '86; on the Home Affairs Select Committee supported efforts to import the 'Massachusetts system' of spotting and reforming young delinquents before they committed serious crimes '86; defended right to challenge jurors Nov '86; defended Pilkington Brothers against BTR's attempted takeover Dec '86; his candidacy was imposed on his constituency by the NEC May '87; increased his majority by over 4,000 June '87; urged a Royal Commission into prisons July '87; signed Campaign Group letter against Walworth Road cuts Aug '87; was concerned about deteriorating staffing for Crown Prosecution Service Aug '87; called for "creative" community service to cope with offenders like Lester Piggott Oct '87; his constituency party was re-formed, with normal relations restored Oct '87; urged heavier investment in European space programme to avoid losing scientists Oct '87; asked: "why do we appear to be the most criminal country in Europe? why do we incarcerate more people for longer periods, in quite appalling conditions, than any other country in the civilized world?" Jan '88; showed interest in investigating Freemasonry in police Feb '88; spotlighted inadequacy of prison service Feb '88; with other Campaign Groupies, backed Dave Nellist against Speaker's suspension Apr '88; was concerned about dangers of discrepancies between videoing children just after a crime and during a later trial June '88; again deplored the elimination of jury challenges June '88; voted against money resolution for European Communities July '88; asked about disparities between bail for black and white accused July '88; co-nominated Tony Benn and Eric Heffer for Labour's Leader and Deputy Leader against Neil Kinnock and Roy Hattersley July '88; attacked "absolute insanity" of Ivor Stanbrook's proposal to transfer Ulster's republicans into Eire; it had "all the smell of the Final Solution" Nov '88; voted against imposing loyalty oaths on Northern Ireland councillors Dec '88; attacked Government's "addled" views on salmonella in eggs Dec '88; ridiculed Government's pretence that only state secrets had to be kept, since doctors and lawyers also had to keep clients' secrets Jan '89; co-sponsored Robin Corbett's Hare Coursing Bill Feb '89; blamed Tories for having missed the opportunities of expanding TV, satellite and terrestrial Feb '89; co-rejected Neil Kinnock's rejection of unilateralism May '89; deplored making a decision on football identity cards before Mr Justice Taylor reported on Hillsborough disaster June '89; urged educational programmes against drugs July '89; his constituency de-selected him, nominating far-Leftwinger Brian Green instead by 55% to 39%, making him the first casualty of the new electoral college system Oct '89; the NEC ordered a re-run of his constituency selection process because of "prima facie evidence of irregularities" such as vote-tampering Jan '90; backed War Crimes Bill because "justice is timeless" Mar '90; voted against embryo research, like most Parliamentary Roman Catholics Apr '90; warned against depriving local solicitors of conveyancing, since it had "carried many a private practice through the winter" Apr '90; voted to limit abortion to 20 weeks May '90; backed tax concessions on workplace nurseries, insisting many mothers found it impossible to work because of the existing tax regime May '90; complained that grants for local government discriminated against St Helens because they were nine years out of date; since then industrial employment had declined sharply July '90; succeeded in being re-selected, winning 73% of votes, against St Helens' council leader Marie Rimmer and ex-MP Frank White July '90; urged reparation for barristers unfairly criticised by judges in court July '90; complained that the Crown Prosecution Service was "being starved of funds and therefore cannot brief competently", sending briefs to the under-qualified July '90; his lawyer alleged there had been an attempt to kill him by loosening the wheel nuts on his car Sep '90; complained that new Criminal Justice Bill was "a tragedy" which did "not address the the real issue, which is not whether we have longer or harsher sentences or whether we attack parole or regrade juvenile crime, but how we attack crime itself"; was worried about young people who killed themselves in prison; favoured taking delinquents out of the system and putting them back once they have been rehabilitated Nov '90; backed motion backing sanctions but opposing a war in the Gulf Jan '91; in 'Birmingham Six' debate urged: "anyone arrested should have the automatic right of access to a solicitor" Mar '91; defended War Crimes Bill, asking: "why should we have a statute of limitations for war criminals?" Mar '91; complained that he had lost 3,000 voters from electoral register as a result of poll-tax-dodging Apr '91; backed Home Affairs Select Committee's urging bookies contribute a further £20m towards racing's coffers May '91; complained that because of shortage of judges there were "hurried judgements, strain and people who are not quite up to it being asked to perform functions and duties for which they are not yet ready" July '91; was listed by Conservatives as a "Militant sympathiser" (for which they apologised) Aug '91; backed campaign against export of Irish greyhounds to Spain under appalling conditions Oct '91; complained that St Helens had lost its three pits and workers at Pilkington's had been halved Nov '91; after a murderer absconded on a home visit after 23 years in jail, Bermingham said: "if there is any case where you coulld say to a man on the run, 'don't give yourself up', this is surely it" Feb '92; retained seat with majority up from 13,801 to 18,209, a swing of 4.34% to Labour Apr '92; complained about activities of Boundary Commission who got things "wrong because it used counties as skins and divided the constituencies into them, rounding up or rounding down, depending on how it felt"; also claimed that Commission arbitrarily split cities and added rural areas, thus making a Labour seat into two Conservative ones June '92; was again named to Home Affairs Select Committee July '92; was only Labour MP willing to back fellow-barrister Rightwing Tory Sir Ivan Lawrence for Chairman of the Home Affairs Select Committee July '92; as a racing fan, backed the idea of having a betting shop in the Palace of Westminster Sep '92; in discussing the arms-to-Iraq trial, deplored the failure of the DPP to disclose facts to the defence as "a disgrace and a shame on our society" and should be ended so that "innocent people can never again be put at risk before the courts of our land" Nov '92; visited Sicilian conference on establishing an International Criminal Court under the aegis of the UN Dec '92; to cut cost of legal aid, urged end of VAT and earlier guilty pleas Mar '93; voted for Peter Shore's

amendment against EC Budget Dec '93; co-complained about over-crowded jails Jan '94; voted against restoring capital punishment, even for killing policemen Feb '94; voted against reducing the age of homosexual consent below 21, Feb '94; criticised as a "disgrace" the effort of the Home Secretary to reduce payments for criminal injuries in the Criminal Justice and Public Order Bill, adding: "a civilised society tends to look after the victim" Mar '94; attacked minicab touts Mar '94; deplored police amalgamation efforts in Police and Magistrates' Courts Bill, since in the amalgamations he had observed in South Yorkshire "there was no evidence of increased efficiency as the force grew in size"; also criticised reduction in the number of ranks because it would "create a career blockage"; "nobody will do a more difficult job without getting paid for it"; "I want anyone accused of anything in any court or disciplinary tribunal to be allowed to choose his or her representative" Apr '94; urged police to start recording battered husbands Apr '94; voted for Jim Paice's clause to remove the ban on licensed betting offices being open to the public on Sunday May '94; backed Tony Blair for Leader June '94; voted for Blair for Leader, Prescott for Deputy Leader July '94; was sued for slander by a fellow barrister about remarks in the chambers of Lord Richard Aug '94; protested Home Secretary Michael Howard's curbing home leave for 40,000 prisoners because of the few who broke conditions Nov '94; pointed out to Home Secretary Michael Howard that the Home Affairs Select Committee had warned him long before the breakout of the need for electronic search equipment in Brixton Prison Dec '94; tried to bar spying by companies on their employees Feb '95; urged Continental-style licensing hours Apr '95; described the CSA as incompetent, "obstructive and rude" Nov '95; attacked as "stupid" cutting adrift youngsters leaving care at 16; he urged sheltered accommodation Dec '95; criticised self-assessment in the Finance Bill because of the difficulties of applying it to lawyers like himself who were assessed on money they received months or years later Jan '96; warned that there had to be national funding if national police intelligence was to be followed up, otherwise "things fall apart" Jan '96; wrote to Tony Blair to urge a fully independent review body to fix MPs' pay levels Jan '96; in his first speech on Ireland in 13 years, urged an independent chairman for the Forum proposed Apr '96; backed changes in the Child Support Agency because all MPs "have a postbag full of complaints about the CSA, about the arbitrary way it performs" June '96; said he always turned down 'freebies' July '96; voted for a curb on MPs' mileage allowances, against a 3% cap on MPs' salary increases and for a pension based on £43,000 July '96; voted for the ban on handguns July '96; on the Home Affairs Select Committee, opposed a "McCarthyite" attempts to force senior police officers to declare Freemason affiliations Jan '97; complained about the Tory Government's having abandoned the Merseyside and its unemployed, wiping out its mining industry, seeing its glass industry shrink, with Ford's Halewood plant the next on the list Feb '97; retained his virtually unaltered seat with a majority of 23,739 on a pro-Labour swing of 8.5% May '97; as a pro-European, attacked Eurosceptic Tory MP Bill Cash for ranting and raving against the EU, "with no constructive policies"; complained that the Tories had not enabled his impoverished constituency to claim any of the £350m in RECHAR money or £750m in Objective 1 money by matching it; again urged adoption of the 'Massachusetts system' of spotting young delinquents before they became criminals, citing a 10-year-old who had been spotted by her headmistress when he was a young teacher, whom he defended on murder charge 14 years later May '97; voted to outlaw fox-hunting June '97; suffered a double heart-attack July '97; was elected Chairman of the all-party Music Appreciation Group July '97; resisted as "suicidal" the adoption of PR for Euro-elections because it would cost Labour half its Euro-seats Oct '97; in the debate on the Bill prescribing PR for Euro-elections, asked which of several MEPs in a regional list St Helens could ask for assistance in obtaining inward grants Nov '97;
Born: 20 August 1940, Dublin, Eire

Family: "I was born and bred in Ireland; I come from a family with long roots in Ireland"; son, late Patrick Xavier Bermingham, Medical Officer of Health, and Eva Terrescena (Robinson); m 1st '64 Joan (Baldock), lawyer; 2s Henry '71, James '72; m 2nd '78 Judith (Barnes), solicitor, a member of the Crown Prosecution Service; divorced '98; m 3rd '98;

Education: St John's, Alton; Cotton College; Wellingborough Grammar; Sheffield University;

Occupation: Barrister (Grays Inn) with a successful criminal practice '85-; Sponsored: by GMB ("£300 a year to constituency party and a small contribution to election expenses" '90-95; GMB also made "a contribution of more than 25% of my election expenses at the 1997 general election"; ex: Solicitor '67-84: former Senior Partner in Sheffield firm, Irwin Mitchell and Company til '84; Shareholder: in Archimedes Investment Trust '84-85; Teacher '64; Lecturer in early '60s;

Traits: Slight; light brown hair; cocked small head (the Parliamentary topper sank so low that Deputy Speaker could not recognise him Apr '84); soft-spoken; persuasive; diffident; looks mildly puzzled; "wheedling manner", "quick-witted", "sharp-tongued" (Matthew Parris, TIMES); "perky wag" (HOUSE MAGAZINE); "uxorious" (GUARDIAN); "I am always a calm man" (GB); had heart attack '98; enjoys racing;

Address: House of Commons, Westminster, London SW1A 0AA; 10 Devonshire Drive, Sheffield S17 3PJ; 51B Junction Lane, St Helens, Merseyside WA9 3JN;

Telephone: 0171 219 3502/6216 (H of C); 0744 810083 (constituency);

Dr Roger (Leslie) BERRY   **Labour**   **KINGSWOOD '92-**

Majority: 14,253 (23.8%) over Conservative 7-way;

Description: A formerly-marginal Bristol seat containing parts of the old Cripps-Benn safe-Labour seat, Bristol South East; "half in and half out of Bristol"; "residents hate being called Bristolians and identify strongly with the pattern of old mining villages" (GUARDIAN); in '95 it lost 17,000 voters in Labour-leaning wards St George East and West and gained 19,000 from parts of Tory-leaning Kingswood;

Position: On Select Committee on Trade and Industry '95-; Chairman: PLP's South and West Group '97-, Full Employment Forum '94-; Secretary: all-party Disablement Group '94-; Vice President, Bristol Action for Southern Africa; ex: Avon County Councillor (Leader of Labour Group '86-92, Deputy Leader of Council '85-86; Chairman, Finance Committee '83-86) '81-93;

Outlook: The witty, energetic, deft Leftwing Keynesian academic economist sidelined to a select committee; made himself unusable in the Blair Government by sticking to his Keynesian tax-increasing alternative to Gordon Brown's tax-capping monetarism and his conviction that a single European currency would mean deflation and more unemployment and social division; he admits that his ideas about increased government spending to create jobs is, as President Johnson said to J K Galbraith, "like pissing down your leg, it seems hot to you but it never does to anyone else"; he initially won Labour applause in 1992-94 by becoming the skilful defender of disabled rights; has an ironic, populist attacking style which he adapted skilfuly to the Commons, helping to isolate the Tory Government on disabled rights; later showed his constituency skills by retaining his narrowly-won marginal seat even after the heavy depredations of the Boundary Commission in '95; clearly enjoys campaigning; tends to run a "dedicated and fast-moving campaign" (BRISTOL EVENING POST); was a former team-mate of Peter Hain but was left behind by Hain's ambitious opportunism; was a former admirer of Ken Livingstone, whom he outgrew; a self-confessed "neo-Keynesian" or "reconstructed Keynesian" who can make Leftwing Keynesianism seem fun; anti-nuclear as well as anti-Maastricht;

History: He initially joined the Young Liberals; joined the Labour Party in '74; was an admirer of Ken Livingstone '80; was elected an Avon County Councillor May '81; contested Weston-super-Mare, coming 3rd with 11.1% of vote June '83; was the first Labour candidate selected to fight Euro-elections, for Bristol Nov '83; contested Bristol in Euro-election June '84; was elected Deputy Leader of Labour Group on Avon County Council May '85; selected for marginal Kingswood by 29 to 17 to 10 from a shortlist of four July '85; was endorsed by NEC Sep '85; warned that denationalisation of British Gas might endanger elderly needing cheap heating Jan '86; attacked deterioration of women's lives under Thatcher Government May '86; criticised as "cynical and cosmetic" Health Secretary Norman Fowler's Tory conference speech, offering no comfort for thousands on hospital waiting lists Oct '86; claimed the true dole figures were almost twice those official admitted Oct '86; attacked as disastrous the deregulation of bus networks, promising Labour would "end the chaos" Dec '86; deplored cuts in library service Jan '87; on behalf of Avon's Labour Group put forward a package to improve services and create local jobs, eliciting SDP response that he was "irresponsible", gambling with Avon's services Jan '87; complained that crime had increased by a third under the Tories Mar '87; was accused by Tory MP Rob Hayward of having attended, four years before, a meeting at which a Sinn Fein speaker was featured Apr '87; launched campaign with pledge to create 1,180 jobs locally May '87; contested Kingswood, coming 2nd behind Rob Hayward, who doubled his majority June '87; was re-selected for Kingswood, saying: "Kingswood is one of the seats that we need to win to defeat the Conservatives" Sep '89; thought the Government entered the ERM at too high a rate against the Deutschmark Oct '90; Kingswood Borough Council turned Labour for the first time May '91; was found by GUARDIAN reporter "skipping in the rain, singing 'Happy Days Are Here Again' Mar '92; retook Kingswood, ousting Rob Hayward by 2,370 votes, a 5.7% swing to Labour Apr '92; in Maiden urged more investment in manufacturing because local unemployment had trebled in previous two years because of layoffs in Rolls-Royce Aero-Engines, British Aerospace and others June '92; sponsored Chronically Sick and Disabled Persons (Amendment) Bill June '92; voted against 2nd Reading of Maastricht Bill June '92; co-authored Tribune Group pamphlet 'The Left and Europe', with Peter Hain, Derek Fatchett and George Howarth, which warned that Maastricht was "monetarist and deflationary" and leading toward a "bankers' Europe" Nov '92; warned repeatedly that Maastricht treaty would enforce deflation Jan '93; tabled a motion at PLP opposing an independent European central bank, but was defeated by 112 to 46 when John Smith's made it an issue of confidence Feb '93; a Tory Whip shouted "object!" to kill his Private Member's Bill, the Chronically Sick and Disabled Persons (Amendment) Bill to provide day services and respite services Feb '93; in debate on disabled rights, pointed out that his 1992 early day motion 330 had attacted 288 signature "the largest number of signatures lent to any of the 1,500 early day motions tabled this session"; pointed out that the 2nd Reading of Alf Morris' Civil Rights (Disabled Persons) Bill had been talked out by his Tory predecessor, Rob Hayward, which had helped defeat him Feb '93; at Tribune Group moved resolution urging a £10b increase in public investment to curb unemployment Mar '93; insisted: "if on an a wet Tuesday, the Chancellor can borrow £7b to prop up an over-valued pound, we can borrow £10-15b to invest in the economy and to create jobs" Mar '93; with Dr Lynne Jones, joined Bryan Gould's Full Employment Forum Mar '93; voted against 3rd Reading for Maastricht Bill May '93; with 43 other Labour MPs, urged President Clinton to intervene militarily against Serbian aggressors in Bosnia May '93; co-authored with Peter Hain a Tribune Group pamphlet, 'Labour and the Economy', urging a £10-15n increase in public investment, which was attacked by Gordon Brown and other monetarist 'modernisers' July '93; co-authored with Peter Hain the anti-Maastricht Tribune Group pamphlet 'Labour and Europe', which attracted the criticism of Labour's Europhiles Nov '93; co-urged UK to stop pressuring Non-Aligned Movement of 110 UN states to stop their efforts to make nuclear weapons illegal Nov '93; in debate on the economy, said: "being a bit of a reconstructed Keynesian, I have to say that if one devalues the pound by 15%, if one halves nominal interest rates and if one allows the public sector borrowing requirement to rise from a predicted £27m last year to £50b this year, it would be astonishing if there were not some signs of the economy being turned around"; "devaluation and low interest rates were forced on the Government by Sterling's ejection from the ERM" Nov '93; won 7th place in the ballot for Private Members' Bills Nov '93; chose to relaunch Alf Morris's Civil Rights (Disabled Persons) Bill to make illegal discrimination on the grounds of disability Dec '93; as a result of a last-minute doubling of the membership of the PLP's Treasury Committee, was beaten by 39 to 30 in his bid to oust Peter Mandelson as its Secretary Jan '94; voted against restoring capital punishment, even for killers of policemen Feb '94; voted to reduce age of homosexual consent to 18 or 16, Feb '94; his disabled rights Bill received its 2nd Reading by 231 to nil Mar '94, after which PM John Major said "I hope that the Bill will go into Committee for detailed examination of its provisions", giving the impression that Government objections to the Bill had been withdrawn; the PM then said "what we need to do in committee and thereafter is to look at the practical implications of the Bill" Apr '94; Dr Berry became Chairman of the Full Employment Forum, in succession to departing Bryan Gould Apr '94; supporters of his disabled rights Bill tabled "between 20 and 30 amendments that were designed specifically to address the concerns raised by the Government and by representatives of several organisations"; to take care of Government concern that the Disability Rights Commission might assume policy-making functions, these functions were assigned to the Secretary of State, with Parliamentary approval required; to assuage Government worries about costs, provision was made to phase in the Bill's provisions, with Parliamentary approval required; the Minister approved all but one amendment Apr '94; Dr Berry protested that the Government was belatedly providing assistance to Tory MPs like Lady Olga Maitland to put down wrecking amendments May '94; on the basis of these amendments the Bill was talked out by Lady Olga, Minister Nicholas Scott and others May '94; the Minister for the Disabled, Nicholas Scott, his reputation battered, had to apologise for pretending that the Government was not behind the wrecking amendments June '94; having nominated John Prescott for Leader and Margaret Beckett for Deputy Leader, said he migtht switch his vote July '94; described as "absurd" the Labour leadership's claim to believe in full employment while rejecting Keynesian economics Sep '94; released an alternative new Clause IV, including full employment Nov '94; was named SPECTATOR's 'Backbencher of the Year' for hia campaign for a disability Bill Nov '94; in his TRIBUNE column asked why full employment was not included in the redrafted Clause IV Feb '95; co-urged the inclusion of full employment in the revised Clause IV Mar '95; in his TRIBUNE column wrote that many of the million jobs he wanted to create could come in "housing, education and training, health, community care, public transport, energy conservation and environmental improvement", with the £10b needed coming from half of the £6b set aside from council house sales, £3b from higher taxes on those on the highest incomes and £4b from extra borrowing"; this argument was detailed in a Full

Employment Forum pamphlet co-authored with Cambridge economist, Michael Kitson and Jonathan Michie, 'Towards Full Employment, The First Million Jobs' Apr '95; was re-selected for Kingswood, which had been converted into a Tory marginal by the Boundary Commission which transferred two Labour-leaning wards to Bristol and added 20,000 Tory-leaning rural and suburban voters from Wansdyke, theoretically ending his tenure June '95; in his TRIBUNE column welcomed new book by ex-MP Stuart Holland and MEP Ken Coates, Full Employment for Europe, which demonstrated that the Maastrich Treaty got Europe's economics wrong and applying it would increase unemployment by 1m Oct '95; cross-examined Shadow Chancellor Gordon Brown in the PLP on projected youth benefit cuts, securing the commitment that penalties would not apply until young people had refused places on all four work and training options Nov '95; in a Fabian pamphlet 'Against a Single Currency' warned that the advantages of a single European currency were more than offset by the threat of Europe-wide deflation and the absence of mechanisms or resources to make the large budgetary transfers between member states to compensate for the loss of the ability to devalue Nov '95; explained how dangerous arms got to Iraq: porocedures appeared to be founded "on the bizarre assumption that people who were going to breach the guidelines were going to tell the truth" Dec '95; explained to those puzzled by his liking for some EU initiatives but his distaste for "the deflationary economics of Maastricht": "that is like saying that if one likes stand-up comedy, one must like Bernard Manning; the opposite is the case" Mar '96; pushing his alternative strategy on the fringe of the TUC conference in Blackpool, complained that the European debate was the only place where the Labour Left could make its arguments about tax, public spending and the Welfare State Sep '96; complained that the Coal Authority's records of disused mineshafts in the old Bristol coalfield were "incomplete and sometimes unreliable", causing difficulties for local solicitors and estate agents Nov '96; virtually the only Labour MP-economist still urging higher taxes on the rich, he pointed out that Labour's "strategy rests on getting people off the dole very quickly and, therefore, getting down the social security bill very quickly; that is how the circle is squared; I very much hope that is possible" Jan '97; in a NEW STATESMAN article claimed "the economic benefits from a single [European] currency are hard to find"; the Maastricht terms were "a recipe for deflation and even more unemployment, social division and poverty in Europe" Feb '97; retained his half-altered seat of Kingswood despite its drastic negative alterations by the Boundary Commission; achieved a 14,253 majority over his Tory opponent on a 14.5% notional swing; there were 7 contestants May '97; was named to the Select Committee on Trade and Industry July '97;

Born: 4 July 1948, Huddersfield

Family: Son, Sydney Berry, retired french polisher, and Mary Joyce (Walker); m '85 Amanda (Thyer), training supervisor; dvd '91; m 2nd '96 Alison (Delyth) Head of Education;

Education: Dalton County Primary School, Huddersfield; Huddersfield New College; Bristol University (BSc); Sussex University (PhD);

Occupation: Political Adviser, to Communications Managers Association (at £2,000) '97-; Panellist, for Harris (at less than £1,000) '94-; ex: Lecturer, in Economics: Bristol University (AUT) '78-92, University of Papua New Guinea '74-78, Sussex University Institute of Development Studies '73-74;

Traits: Dark blond hair; specs; light-hearted; bubbly; self-mocking sense of humour; "ebullient" (GUARDIAN);

Address: House of Commons, Westminster, London SW1A 0AA; 9 Manor Road, Bristol, BS16 2JD;

Telephone: 0171 219 4106 (H of C); 01272 654889 (home); 0117 9561837 (constituency);

Majority: 3,844 over Conservative 7-way;
Description: The unaltered major middle-class residential area in West Yorkshire's principal city; its safety for the Tories was helped in '83 by the inclusion of commuting villages and in '92 by the even split between their rival opponents; the Tories' disadvantage lay in the very large number - fully 35,000 - of university students within its boundaries, leading to its former Tory MP, Dr Keith Hampson, advocating an election during their absence at Christmas or Easter;
Position: Ex: Chairman, of Leeds North West Constituency Labour Party '91-95; West Yorkshire County Councillor '81-86; formerly on National Executive Committee of National Council for Civil Liberties (later called Liberty);
Outlook: A traditional Left working-class ex-councillor, who succeeded in the task of ousting Keith Hampson from the Tories' safest seat in Leeds; a life-long political activist, he was a friend of the late Marxist historian, E P Thomson, with whom he was linked in the emergence of the New Left in the '60s; was active in CND, anti-racist groups and Humanist organisations; is said to work on two levels: as an ideological near-Marxist, or a practical political fixer who could chair effectively the Police Committee on West Yorkshire County Council; an ethical socialist; as a 60-year-old grandfather, is somewhat old-fashioned; he is the second oldest of the Labour candidates fielded and, unexpectedly, elected;
History: As a young electrician he joined the old Electrical Trades Union (ETU) '50; as a non-Communist Leftwinger, resisted the ballot-rigging of its Communist leadership; joined the Labour Party '60; was elected Branch Secretary of the Leeds ETU as an anti-Communist '62; when the ETU's Communist leadership was replaced by by that of the authoritarian Rightwinger, Frank Chapple, in '66, he was equally out of favour; he stood for election as General Secretary of the EETPU against Frank Chapple '77; was then blacklisted by the EETPU, compelling him to work for Leeds City Council; was elected to West Yorkshire County Council May '81; as Chairman of West Yorkshire's Police Committee visited 113 picket lines during the miners' strike '84-85; was elected Chairman of the Leeds North West Constituency Labour Party '91; was selected to contest "hopeless" Leeds North West, the city's safest Tory seat '95; unexpectedly won the seat, moving from third place to first, with a majority of 3,844 over Keith Hampson, a Tory MP for 23 years, as a result of an 11.77% swing to Labour May '97; in his Maiden, emphasised how difficult it had been to ascertain the fate of threatened Wharfedale Hospital June '97; was a co-sponsor of a Campaign Group motion opposing any cut in lone-parent benefit July '97; voted against the cut in sole-parent benefits Dec '97; supported the Road Traffic Reduction Bill, partly because of the impact of traffic on asthma, which afflicted five of his grandchildren Jan '98; in the debate on Trade Union Recognition, contradicted the Tory view: "the villainy inside the ranks [of the Electrical Trades Union] was exposed not by Lord Wyatt, but by people such as myself, rank-and-file shop stewards"; he questioned "the virtues of the postal ballot"; "postal ballots can be manipulated, and I was a victim of such manipulation: 1,800 ballot papers ended up at the address of one employer, so that the members of the trade union could vote in the comfort of the employer's offices" Apr '98; was rated as one of the 'Bottom 100' written questioners, having posed only six in his first year May '98; was one of 24 Labour rebels voting against

Murdoch-style newspaper predatory pricing July '98;
Born: 18 December 1937, Leeds
Family: Son, of Fred Best, lorry driver, and Marie (Hogg); m Mary (Glyn); 2s; 2d; 7 grandchildren ("five of my seven grandchildren suffer from asthma to varying extents");
Education: Meanwood County Secondary School; a Technical College;
Occupation: Electrical Technician, recently at Leeds Education Craft Centre; formerly a full-time trade union official for 13 years and an electrician from youth; UNISON/TGWU/EPIU;
Traits: Bald; grizzled grey beard; an active Humanist who has officiated at weddings, naming ceremonies and funerals;
Address: House of Commons, Westminster, London SW1A 0AA; 63 St Michael's Lane, Leeds LS6 3BR;
Telephone: 0171 219 3000 (H of C); 0113 275 5692 (home);

Clive (James Charles) BETTS   **Labour**   **ATTERCLIFFE, Sheffield '92-**

Majority: 21,818 (49.2%) over Conservative 4-way;
Description: Southeastern corner of Sheffield; an industrial working class area, almost two-thirds of owner-occupiers; a mixture of older terraced houses oft overshadowed by steelworks, first war residental areas and extensive recent developments;
Position: Whip (Lord Commissioner) '98-, Assistant Whip '96-98; ex: on Treasury Select Committee '95-96; Chairman '95-96, Vice Chairman '93-95, Secretary '95-97, PLP Treasury Committee; Chairman, South Yorkshire Pension Authority '89-92; Sheffield City Councillor (Leader '87-92, Deputy Leader '86-87, Finance Committee Chairman '86-88, Housing Committee Chairman '80-86) '76-92; Deputy Chairman '88-91, Housing Chairman '85-89, Association of Metropolitan Councils;
Outlook: The former Sheffield Council Leader who, after 18 years of trying, seemed to make a soft landing in the Commons; the quiet-spoken, low-profiled, pro-EU economist hidden in the Whips' Office since '96, possibly because he was a Tory target for Sheffield's heavy spending; before that concentrated on fighting for fair financing for Sheffield; recently a mainstream Blair loyalist, formerly Sheffield's post-Blunkett council Leader; according to former Tory MP, Sheffield-educated Sebastian Coe, this is "a terrific transformation" for one who also "used the city [of Sheffield] very much as a Stalinist experiment en route to greater things in this place"; that background gave him the expertise to bait the Tory Government on allegations about Westminster Council while making him the target of John Gummer's gibes about his responsibility for Sheffield's "excessive" expenditures; "led Sheffield Council when it lost the £10m on the World Student Games" (Tory MP Michael Howard); in fact, he was the originator of the 'New Realism' partnership between the dominant Labour leadership of Sheffield's City Council and its business community, particularly after the post-'85 squeeze on its resources; "belongs firmly to the cerebral school of Sheffield Labour politics; it does not have many other adherents"; "a deep thinker and enthusiastic administrator"; but lacks David Blunkett's "charismatic flair for publicity" (Philp Andrews, ROTHERHAM STAR); a former

local government officer who attempted to "root out inefficiency within the Town Hall's 30,000 work force as one way of fighting cash shortages" (John Spencer, SHEFFIELD STAR); "I have always regarded myself as being on the Left of the party, committed to public expenditure and the rights of people to control their own destiny through the democratic process" (CB); was TGWU-sponsored;

History: He joined the Labour Party at 19, '69; at 24 contested hopeless Hallam, Sheffield against incumbent MP John Osborne Oct '74; was elected to Sheffield City Council at 29 as one of its youngest members for Firth Park, "the area in which I was brought up" May '76; contested hopeless Louth against Michael Brotherton, coming third June '79; wrote to LABOUR WEEKLY opposing special representation of Labour MPs on party's committee of inquiry Nov '79; after becoming Chairman of Housing, "fought long and acrimonious battles with the Government over the sale of council houses" from '80; was defeated in selection contest for Brightside by David Blunkett June '85; was defeated in re-selection contest for Hillsborough against sitting MP Martin Flannery by 42 to 28 June '85; was defeated in selection for North East Derbyshire by Harry Barnes Jan '86; became Deputy Leader of Sheffield Council on retirement of Alan Billings July '86; became Leader of Sheffield City Council on election to Parliament of David Blunkett; congratulated Sheffield on winning for Sheffield, at a cost of £300,000 the bid to host the 1991 World Student Games, on which over £10m was to be lost; began basic change of approach, with the main aim being "to give people value for money, whether they are ratepayers or council departments doing work for each other" June '87; was applauded after addressing Cutlers' Feast, saying: "what we have learnt is that by compromising, we can get a considerable percentage of what we want; we're working together, not fighting together" Apr '88; said: "if people want to sit cosily in their offices they shouldn't be working for Sheffield Council" July '88; expressed his indignation about Government's refusal to finance Sheffield's 'Supertram' for at least a year, as a "major blow to the people of Sheffield" Nov '89; was selected for safe Attercliffe, after the announced impending retirement of Pat Duffy, by a majority of 52% over 42% for ex-MP Ken Woolmer Apr '90; at a party conference fringe meeting, warned that Labour councils like those in South Yorkshire must drop their commitment to avoiding cuts in jobs and services if they were to survive and move forward; "the slogan of no cuts in jobs and services does not really do anything more than defend a status quo and says nothing about priorities, about quality, about deficiencies in the way we deliver services; we have to make changes and whatever money we get from a [future] Labour Government, it will be inadequate of us to say we will just carrry on doing the same old thing adding the money on top of our budgets just to deliver more of the same" Oct '90; again curbed Sheffield's budget, under Government threat of capping, just enough to keep it legal, particularly if a Labour Government were elected '91-92; retained Attercliffe with a majority of 15,480, a 2% swing to Tories Apr '92; in Maiden pointed out that he was starting a new job at 42 when sacked constituents of that age thought they would never work again; unemployment in the constituency had gone up 2.5 times in previous 20 years May '92; complained that council grants were based on 1981 census data, 11 years out of date May '92; pointed out that, as Chairman of the South Yorkshire Pension Authority, small firms had applied in their hundreds for venture capital investment when "no other financial institutions were willing to invest in them" June '92; insisted that a "right to rent" was as important for some people as the Government's "right to buy" slogan for council houses; Sheffield had £21m from sales of capital assets in 1992 it was not allowed to spend on new council building; it now took five times as long to get a desirable council house to rent and homelessness had increased there ten-fold since 1979, June '92; sponsored motion urging more democratic accountability in EC June '92; in Finance Bill debate expressed concern that reimposition of stamp duty "now will send the housebuilding industry into yet further decline";

compared the "disgrace" of spending £2.5b on Canary Wharf as a monument to Thatcherism, compared with only £50m for Sheffield's development corporation over five years July '92; suggested only "premium pay" for shopworkers would allow full Sunday trading Sep '92; insisted that, apart from Sheffield, Britain's sporting facilities were inadequate: "in Belgrade there are more Olympic-standard swimming pools than there are in Britain" Oct '92; in BCCI debate disclosed that Sheffield had been urged to invest its funds with BCCI but, on investigation, discovered it was not safe; Sheffield had made the right decision because, as a large authority, it had banking specialists and City contacts Nov '92; with three other Labour MPs, called for a Parliamentary ban on the EVENING STANDARD for publishing details of Chancellor Norman Lamont's Access payments as an "outrageous breach of privacy" Nov '92; complained about the Government's termination of its urban programme and its replacement by the shrunken urban partnership scheme; Sheffield had been largest beneficiary, receiving £5.894m and had received 51 pages of guidance for 1993-94; "its removal will only make unemployment worse" Dec '92; voted against Ray Powell's Shops (Amendment) Bill to restrict Sunday trading Jan '93; urged improved communications betwen Sheffield and Manchester Feb '93; with 43 other Labour MPs, urged Preident Clinton to military interention against Serb aggressors in Bosnia May '93; was elected co-Vice Chairman of PLP's Treasury Committee Nov '93; told the PM his Government "must specifically have approved all the subsidies for the cash incentive scheme under which Westminster [Council] emptied its houses and that the Government must also have given a specific consent to the disposal of all properties for which a general consent did not exist under the Housing Act 1985" Jan '94; voted against restoring capital punishment, even for killers of policemen Feb '94; voted to reduce age of homosexual consent to 16, Feb '94; asked the Environment Secretary "what his Department knew about the cash incentive scheme in Westminster? was not that scheme approved by his Department? were not the subsidies for that scheme paid by his Department? was not the monitoring of the scheme carried out by his Department?" Feb '94; complained that Sheffield's raised cap was limited to £3m May '94; was a Denis MacShane 'minder' in the Rotherham by-election May '94; backed Blair for Leader June '94; again called for more spending on housing Nov '94; when he again asked the Environment Secretary for more generous financing for Sheffield, John Gummer blamed him fo having "left behind a mess there" Dec '94; led motion urging war pensions be ignored for benefit purposes Jan '95; complained that Tory Britain was the next to lowest spender on housing June '95; complained that Sheffield, "a low-spending authority", was being penalised because of a fortuitious court judgment misunderstood by Environment Secretary John Gummer June '95; pointed out that death rates among the poor were rising for the first time in 50 years Nov '95; urged help for schools built under the defective Derwent system Nov '95; was named to the Treasury Select Committee Nov '95; complained that the Tory Government had been too slow in accepting responsibility for the "scandal" of mis-selling of personal pensions and changing the faulty legislation Jan '96; complained that only a quarter was being spent on housebuilding, compared with '79, Jan '96; attacked the inadequate increases to finance local government Jan '96; again urged more money for Sheffield housing Apr '96; on the basis of the district auditor's report, rubbed the Westminster housing gerrymandering scandal into Tory MPs' wounds May '96; was named an Assistant Whip as a "loyal mainstreamer" (INDEPENDENT) Aug '96; co-wrote the pro-EU pamphlet 'Jobs, Growth and Security' in which 14 Labour MPs laid out the arguments for joining a single European currency Sep '96; played for the Europhile team under Sir Nicholas Scott against the Eurosceptics captained by John Redwood in a cricket match staged by the SUNDAY EXPRESS and the European Movement Sep '96; in HOUSE MAGAZINE insisted Britain's economy was still "built on sand" and required long-term investment and skills training Nov '96; was discharged from the Treasury Select Committee Nov '96; pointed out that industrial production was only 2% higher than in '90, before the recession; recovery in exports was based on '92's massive devaluation Dec '96; as the Duty Whip, counted the ambulance-transported MPs in a close vote Jan '97; retained his safe, unaltered seat by a bigger majority of 21,818 (49.2%) on a 9% swing May '97; was named an Assistant Government Whip May '97; was promoted a full Government Whip (Lord Commissioner) July '98;

Born: 13 January 1950, Sheffield

Family: Son, late Harold Betts, glass-beveller and brilliant-cutter, and late Nellie (Ellis), personnel manager;

Education: Longley School, Sheffield; King Edward VII School, Sheffield; Pembroke College, Cambridge (BA Econ);

Occupation: Sponsored, by TGWU (£600 p a to constituency, 80% of election expenses) '92-95; ex: Director (unremunerated), Hallamshire Investments, '89-93; Leader, Sheffield Council '87-92; Director, Universiade GB Ltd (company for World Student Games; wound up) '87-92; Local Government Economist, with South Yorkshire County Council, then Rotherham Council '86-91;

Traits: Parted front-combed brown hair; snub nose; pouched eyes, usually looking down; shy and self-contained; "his most conspicuous characteristics are caution and commitment" (Philip Andrews, ROTHERHAM STAR); "his right hand waves sheafs of paper, his left hand is anchored in his pocket and his voice rings loudly" while he "rocks on his heels before leaning urgently forward, like a man pushing a vacuum cleaner through dense jungle" (SHEFFIELD STAR); likes cricket and squash, real ale; supports Shefffield Wednesday;

Address: House of Commons, Westminster, London SW1A 0AA; 1 Plumbley Hall Mews, Mosborough, Sheffield S19 5BF; London flat;

Telephone: 0171 219 3588 (H of C); 01742 734444 (Sheffield office);

'Liz' (Elizabeth) BLACKMAN　　　　　　**Labour**　　　　　　**EREWASH '97-**

Majority: 9,135 over Conservative 5-way;

Description: A very slightly altered Derbyshire seat between Derby and Nottingham, better known earlier as South East Derbyshire and Ilkeston; the increase in owner-occupied estates and the decline of mining have changed it from the native area written about by D H Lawrence, who restyled Ilkeston as 'Keston';

Position: On the Select Committee on Treasury Affairs '97-; Broxtowe Borough Councillor (Deputy Leader '95-97) '91-;

Outlook: A fast-climbing woman professional; after loyal back bench support for Gordon Brown's Budget strategy, was rewarded with a place on the Treasury Select Committee, replacing less-loyal Diane Abbott;

was a first-time candidate from an all-women short-list who was able to capitalise on her status as Deputy Leader of Broxtowe Council and head of the upper school of a highly-regarded local comprehensive; "I try to give my best in all areas of my life - as a parent, [and formerly] as a full-time teacher, Deputy Leader of the council and as a candidate; I believe in full commitment"; had the experience of negotiating a private-public regeneration of a local former mining community; thinks women MPs can stop male MPs "behaving like a bunch of badly-behaved schoolboys"; a member of the Fabians, the Socialist Environmental Association and NAS-UWT;

History: She joined the Labour Party at 39, '89; was elected to Broxtowe Borough Council, becoming Deputy Leader of its Labour Group May '91; became Deputy Leader of Broxtowe Borough Council when it was won by Labour May '95; was selected to contest Erewash against its sitting Tory MP -Minister Angela Knight - before the practice was ruled illegal in Jan '96; emphasised education during the campaign: "I'd like to see a tangible improvement in education, with support staff to help deliver the best standards" Apr '97; won the seat from Angela Knight with a majority of 9,135 (15.14%) as the result of a pro-Labour swing of 12.08%, May '97; asked Education Secretary David Blunkett how he proposed to help teachers "confronted by persistent poor behaviour on the part of a small number of pupils" June '97; urged Lottery distribution be made more widely acceptable to her region June '97; complained about inadequate payout by Nationwide to shareholders with learning difficulties June '97; urged women be encouraged more to have breasts screened for cancer June '97; urged police grants be more fairly distributed June '97; urged lorry drivers be banned immediately from driving if they exceeded permitted driving hours July '97; led motion urging the Government to be "tough on road crime" July '97; co-sponsored motion attacking mis-selling of pensions under the Tories July '97; urged care in expanding membership of NATO July '97; repeatedly and vehemently defended the Budget changes as underpinned by Labour values on fairness July '97; emphasised that while the welfare-to-work programme might be temporary, the working skills imparted had an "air of permanence" July '97; objected to majority of taxpayers having to pay twice, once for their own NHS care and again for tax relief for those pensioners who took out private medical insurance July '97; was named to the Select Committee on Treasury Affairs, while Diana Abbott was transferred out to Foreign Affairs July '97; insisted Labour would act on tax avoidance but the Tories were just anxious to exploit the position of Paymaster General Geoffrey Robertson, who had broken no rules Jan '98;

Born: 28 September 1949, Carlisle

Family: She is married, with two children;

Education: Carlisle County High School for Girls; Prince Henry's Grammar School, Otley; Clifton College of Further Education, Nottingham (B Ed);

Occupation: Teacher '72-97; her last post was as Head of the Upper School of Bramcote Park Comprehensive School ("which achieves some of the best results in Nottinghamshire" [EB])

Traits: Dark hair with front-combed fringe; hollow cheeks; pleasant-looking; energetic; fully-committed;

Address: House of Commons, Westminster, London SW1A 0AA;

Telephone: 0171 219 3000 (H of C);

EXPLOSIONS

Sometimes an explosion unveils those who rely on our volumes. After the 1994 explosion damaged the Israeli Embassy in London, an eagle-eyed Welsh fan of ours scanned one of the pictures of its damaged interior and spotted a set of these volumes. A similar photograph of the interiors of other embassies would often show the same - foreign diplomats have been among the most enthusiastic about our interest in the positions of MPs on crises abroad, such as the deep split in the Commons over former Yugoslavia.

Rt Hon 'Tony' (Anthony Charles Lynton) BLAIR   Labour   SEDGEFIELD '83-

Majority: 25,143 (53.4%) over Conservative 5-way;

Description: Spennymoor plus old mining villages in southeast Durham surrounding Darlington; a seat recreated after its '74 abolition;

Position: Prime Minister '97-; Leader of PLP '94-; on Labour's NEC '92-, Shadow Cabinet '88-97; ex: Spokesman: on Home Office '92-94, on Employment '89-92, on Energy '88-89; Deputy Spokesman, on Trade and Industry '87-88; Assistant Spokesman, on the Treasury '84-87;

Outlook: The Labour Leader and PM who changed his party more than anyone thought possible, swinging it from Left-of-Centre to dead Centre, winning over 2m ex-Tory voters en route; he then reasserted his authority by his '98 reshuffle, showing himself the "least sentimental" (Andrew Rawnsley, OBSERVER) of political butchers, while retaining a soft spot for promoting Peter Mandelson; a very persuasive Scots-born, Durham-educated, pragmatic London barrister; has "a remarkable ability to quickly identify the relevant facts, define the issues to which answers had to be found and then come to an overall conclusion; with the possible exception of one other person, Tony is the fastest gun on paper I know" (Lord ['Derry'] Irvine, Lord Chancellor and former head of his chambers); "like Thatcher, he snatched the Leadership from under the nose of an apparently better-qualified rival (William Whitelaw in her case, Gordon Brown in his) and did so in large part through sheer willpower, born of an almost messianic belief that he alone knew what had to be done" (Robert Harris, SUNDAY TIMES); has brushed aside internal dissent with a ruthlessness that suggests Margaret Thatcher in her prime; at the same time has has seemed remote from his top colleagues, without "direct knowledge of how his Ministers are performing" (Peter Riddell, TIMES); "John Major believe[d] Tony Blair to be the Labour front bencher from whom the Tories would have most to fear" as Labour's "most formidable debater and quickest and most dangerous mind" ('Black Dog', MAIL ON SUNDAY); this fear was realised when, during his prolonged "honeymoon", he established a historic lead of a third over the Tories and reduced Liberal Democratic support by a third; his popularity persisted despite Parliamentary complaints that he spent too little time in the Commons and dodged questions while there; said proudly, "I don't carry any baggage of an ideological kind"; believed that voters "need to be sure is that if they vote Labour, then they're getting a government that is going to improve their prosperity, increase their individual aspirations, but do it within a strong and fair community" (TB); from the beginning showed a genius for reaching out to formerly Tory-voting Middle England while showing the insensitivity of a tone-deaf orchestra leader to trade unionists and Leftish activists in his own party; "a politician for the television age, generally smiling and appearing as the reasonable human face of the Labour Party" (Peter Riddell, TIMES); part of the new stream of Labour thinkers who believe efficiency and social justice are partners, not alternatives, and that Labour must change and adapt to win; "the trick is to speak out on new approaches for the Labour Party without leaving people behind" (TB); believes in "a new concept of the public interest standing up for the individual" with "both state and market subject to the public interest"; closer to Washington than to Brussels; a US-style 'new dealer' rather than a social democrat and certainly not a socialist; wants to shed union influence; "the main proponent of a total break with the unions, by scrapping their voting rights in leadership elections and constituency selections of prospective Parliamentary candidates" (Michael Prescott, SUNDAY TIMES); "Blair's own former sponsoring union, the TGWU, and the GMB are highly suspicious of his 'modernising' programme; they also blamed him for having pushed Smith into risking his leadership at the [1993] Labour conference over the adoption of one-member one-vote for the selection of Parliamentary candidates" (Sarah Baxter, EVENING STANDARD); union leaders think him "a container-grown politician, a man with few roots and fewer branches in the party" (Anthony Bevins, OBSERVER); formerly one of the late John Smith's two Euro-friendly modernising lieutenants; overtook his rival-friend, Gordon Brown, as Smith's heir-apparent in '93; "that rare breed: a Labour MP who not only understands money but enjoys talking about it" (Sarah Barclay, LONDON DAILY NEWS); "his detractors say he is too fond of cultivating the media" (Dennis Barker, GUARDIAN); "ask him for a 15-second soundbite and he'll come in just over 14; this knack is regarded in the business as more useful than actually having something to say" (John Williams, EVENING STANDARD);

History: He tried, at 9, to start a civics society at Durham Choristers School but was discouraged by 12-year-old James Fenton '62; he stood as a Conservative at Durham Choristers School at 11, winning by 62 votes to 26 for his Labour opponent and 24 for the Liberal student '64; he showed no interest in politics as such at Oxford, rather in Christian social idealism; he joined the Labour Party at 22, out of "growing concern at the unrest that sectarian elements from the ultra-Left [were] causing" (TB) '75; joined the chambers of 'Derry' [later Lord] Irvine, a Labour supporter, where he met his future wife, Cherie Booth '76; was one of 17 who applied for selection for Middlesbrough, but failed to make the short-list Dec '80; in debate in Hackney South party, favoured electing Leader by one-member one-vote Nov '80; defeated a hard-Left Branch Secretary by 17 votes to 15 Feb '81; joined Centre-Right 'Labour Solidarity' Sep '81; failed to make short-list for Thornaby Nov '81; was ambivalent on the Falklands crisis, supporting the sending of the task force but urging a negotiated settlement, saying the promise of self-determination for the Falklands could lead to full-scale conflict - he was not sure that it was necessary to deprive Argentinians of the spoils of war, including sovereignty May '82; contested the by-election of Beaconsfield, running third with 10% of vote, a drop of 10% since the '79 general election; was not helped by his supporting speaker, Peter Shore, saying "we don't need any more barristers" (like Mrs Thatcher and Sir Geoffrey Howe) May '82; warned against picking on trade unionists for redundancies Aug '82; in a lecture in Perth, Australia, said the growth of unemployment required more than "the mild economic tinkering proposed by the Social Democrats" Oct '82; after the closed short-list was unexpectedly opened for him - after a dead-heat between two trade union candidates - won safe Sedgefield selection against Leftwing ex-MPs Reg Race and Les Huckfield with the help of a favourable quote from Michael Foot; moderates Joel [later Lord] Barnett, David Watkins and Sid Weighell did not make the short-list May '83; won Sedgefield, supported in his campaign by the late Pat ("Coronation Street") Phoenix, his father-in-law's love May '83; was controversial in his Maiden speech: with over 40% unemployment in constituency he said "to close Fishburn [cokeworks] is an act of economic madness multiplied by social disregard on an unbelievable scale", "a blind allegiance to dogma" July '83; attacked Norman Tebbit's plan to redistribute regional aid as a "fraud" to mask cuts Dec '83; protested against nuclear dumping at Billingham Dec '83; criticized police for using "arbitrary emergency powers" to erect roadblocks against striking miners Mar '84; claimed a castle in his constituency had been renovated on profits from "bed and breakfast" hotels for homeless Mar '84; complained about special bail conditions imposed on miners May '84; said uncertainty over imposition of VAT on children's shoes was damaging industry Nov '84; his promotion to Assistant Spokesman on Treasury was hailed as the fastest promotion since Dr David Owen's in '68, Nov '84; attacked

Government for "deception" and "incompetence" in claiming that GLC's abolition would save lots of money Dec '84; was reselected unopposed Mar '85; opposed increased taxes on tobacco and alcohol Feb '85; demanded an independent inquiry into Bank of England's rescue of Johnson Matthey Bank Oct '85; backed televising of Commons Nov '85; opposed Alliance proposal that UK join the EMS, saying it was "essentially a Deutschmark block" which would put "Herr Pohl of the Bundesbank in 11 Downing Street" Jan '86; embarrassed the Government by producing an EC report critical of UK economic policy, countersigned by UK Minister Mar '87; disclosed that 25% of TSB small shareholders had sold their shares in five months since privatization Mar '87; his majority went up by 5,000, helped by Alliance collapse in Northeast June '87; urged Labour to argue that efficiency and social justice were partners, not alternatives June '87; claimed privatized British Airways had been deliberately undervalued, costing the taxpayer £300m July '87; was named City Spokesman, as Deputy to Bryan Gould in Trade and Industry July '87; was described as a "prominent loyalist supporter of [Jack] Cunningham in new mood to keep Left (and London Left in particular) down in the party" (Bruce Anderson, SUNDAY TELEGRAPH) July '87; in first try was second runner-up in Shadow Cabinet poll with 71 votes on the Tribune Group slate, behind Barry Jones July '87; urged Government to halt privatization of electriciy and water because there was a lack of proper safeguards for consumers Sep '87; said the Spycatcher prosecution made the case for a Bill of Rights Sep '87; on the share collapse said: "the City whizz-kids, with salaries only fractionally less than their greed, now seem not only morally dubious, but incompetent; they failed miserably, proving themselves utterly unfit to have such power" Oct '87; investigating the Stock Market crash for the Shadow Cabinet, concluded the Stock Exchange had given small investors a "third class service" Nov-Dec '87; blamed government for acceding to manufacturers' pressure to allow continued production of combustion-dangerous furniture Dec '87; attacked effective end of regional aid after 25 bipartisan years Jan '88; declined to support David Alton's abortion-curbing Bill Jan '88; described Government's policy on monopolies as "frankly pathetic", urging reference of Nestle's bid for Rowntree to the Monopolies and Mergers Commission" Apr '88; after his complaint, IBA agreed to consult Opposition about Government's "political" advertising May '88; warned against letting "market forces rule" over Nestle takeover of Rowntree, and big business dominating the internal market May '88; ably exploited Government's inactivity in Barlow Clowes financial scandal, seriously denting Lord Young's reputation Oct '88; published list of 17 cases of insider trading Nov '88; was first elected to Shadow Cabinet, in 9th place with 111 votes; was named Spokesman on Energy Nov '88; after his claim that tax to subsidize nuclear power would add 25% to bills, Cecil Parkinson delayed its imposition Dec '88; free-tripped to Hongkong as guest of its government '89; accused aspirant electricity tycoons of putting assured profits before security of supply; tried to amend electricity privatization to impose obligations to promote energy conservation Jan '89; denied Government claim that electricity privatization would ensure competition and keep consumers satisfied Feb '89; on the last day of the electricy privatization Bill, during which he had demanded cost of decommissioning, Cecil Parkinson pulled the eight ageing Magnox nuclear power stations out of the projected sell-off July '89; denounced Cecil Parkinson's "chaotic privatization" of electricity; claimed nuclear decommissioning could cost £7b Oct '89; urged Channel Tunnel links with north Oct '89; on the Tribune Group slate, was elected to Shadow Cabinet 4th, with 138 votes; was named Spokesman on Employment, replacing more Leftwing Michael Meacher, with the task of ending Labour's embarrassment over its union ties Nov '89; welcomed EC's Social Charter Nov '89; abandoned Labour's support of pre-entry closed shop to wrongfoot the Tories; "was poked in the stomach and verbally slapped around by a lheavy mob of printers' leaders" -Andrew Rawnsley, OBSERVER Dec '89; failed to secure ban on blacklisting in Employment Bill Feb '90; visited

European Commission in Brussels as guest of British Labour Group Feb '90; in his draft on industrial relations for the Policy Review, insisted on a statutory code of practice "in which there will be a limit on numbers and where secondary picketing will be permitted only where the second employer is directly assisting the first employer to frustrate the dispute" Apr '90; visited India as guest of its Government Apr '90; with Eddie Haigh of TGWU, completed an industrial law package with clear limits on secondary picketing, an end to the closed shop, an industrial court and a new emphasisis on individual rights at work; denied it was a "strikers' charter" May '90; visited European Commission as guest of British Labour Group July '90; complained that UK was "near the bottom of the league for the rights of women in employment in Europe" July '90; visited Paris as guest of its Government Oct '90; claimed Labour was no longer in hock to unions Oct '90; came 8th for Shadow Cabinet with 114 votes Oct '90; thought Tories had made a mistake in dumping Mrs Thatcher, because she had "a sense of direction" Nov '90; visited Australia as guest of its Government Dec '90; urged the young have a legal right to job training Jan '91; visited Germany as guest of Friedrich Ebert Stiftung Apr '91; a Gallup survey for SUNDAY TELEGRAPH found him more popular with the public than his opponent, Michael Howard, by 37% to 24% May '91; visited Brussels as guest of European Parliamentary Labour Party May '91; proposed union trials be transferred to industrial court which could not sequester union's assets June '91; accused Government of planning to strip away protection for 2.5m lowest paid by abolishing wages councils June '91; claimed Government were breaking "their promise to young people that there will be a Youth Training place for them" July '91; said Labour's union law reforms would keep six as limit of pickets July '91; opposed TUC boycott of new temporary work scheme for unemployed Sep '91; published leaked letter in which Treasury was seeking £1b cuts in training over 3 years Sep '91; came 8th for Shadow Cabinet with 132 votes Oct '91; dismissed as a "gimmick" designed to "fiddle" the jobless figures the Government's proposals to put 26,000 youths on temporary work schemes Oct '91; wrote to 82 chairmen to reassure them that Labour would not give unions joint control of TECs Nov '91; accused Employment Secretary Michael Howard of misrepresenting EC Social Chapter's impact on Britain Dec '91; attacked cuts in training places; claimed there was the need for "a new agenda which is about training, skills, dealing with low pay, better opportunities for women and partnership in the workplace; the individual should be subject to the full rigours of the market but should be protected by certain rules against unfair treatment" Jan '92; visited Bonn and Brussels funded by Friedrich Ebert Foundation and Rowntree Trust Feb '92; insisted full employment was still a Labour target; conceded £3.40 minimum wage might not be introduced in Labour's first year in office Mar '92; retained seat with majority up from 13,058 to 14,859, a swing to Labour of 1.71% Apr '92; with Gordon Brown, was persuaded by John Smith not to enter contest for Deputy Leadership, and backed Margaret Beckett for the job; said the new political agenda must be "without no-go areas, without preconceptions, or preconditions"; insisted the party had to bridge a "gulf" before the next election; the issue was not "change or no change" but "what type of change"; "we are not struggling with a pendulum that is obstinately refusing to swing, but a tide of history on which we are trying to regain our balance and direction"; helped prepare John Smith's successful leadership manifesto Apr '92; attributed Labour's defeat to "residual fears" among the electorate, agreeing with Jack Straw that Clause IV would have to be revised May '92; indicated he would like to be Spokesman on Trade or Home Affairs June '92; received 150 votes for John Smith's new Shadow Cabinet, placing him 2nd; was named Home Office spokesman July '92; urged Government to bar Italian and French fascist leaders from attending Conservative Party conference Sep '92; won a place on NEC in first attempt, with 387,000 votes (6th), displacing Dennis Skinner; with Gordon Brown was attacked by Trotskyist LABOUR BRIEFING as "Class Traitors of the Month" Sep '92; criticized

Metropolitan Police for solving only one in ten burglaries Oct '92; attacked the reintroduced Asylum Bill as "arbitrary in its justice" and "shabby and mean in its implementation" Nov '92; urged consulting the whole Labour Party membership about its future Jan '93; visiting the USA as guest of US-EEC Association, admitted that the "early assumption of inevitability" in EC integration had disappeared; agreed that "the citizens of Europe now require persuasion" to "demonstrate how a more integrated Europe is not simply good for commerce or trade but will help us towards a better, more prosperous, more peaceful Continent"; "a stronger and more coherent European Community, with a common sense of direction and purpose, is far better able to play a part in the reconstruction of the economies of Eastern Europe...than a weak and uncertain one" Jan '93; called for a "fundamental recasting" of Labour's relations with unions Jan '93; deplored waste of £30m in moving prison service headquarters from London to Derby Jan '93; urged Labour to seize the initiative on law and order; warned of "moral chaos" and the need to teach "the value of what is right and wrong" Feb '93; was backed by DAILY TELEGRAPH in his insistence Feb '93; was singled out as the leading target for Tories as he overtook Gordon Brown as Labour's "golden boy" and "heir apparent" Feb '93; expressed doubt about allowing MI5 to get involved in fighting drugs or organised crime Feb '93; said, "if you bring up people in poor conditions, if there is poor education, bad housing and lack of employment and training opportunities, then crime is more likely to flourish; it doesn't excuse it, but that is simply the reality of the situation" Feb '93; reinforced demand for an independent tribunal to investigate miscarriages of justice Apr '93; union leaders threatened they would block his hope to become party leader if he kept chopping at their power in the party May '93; was admonished by GMB leader John Edmonds after insisting that "one-member one-vote should be the guiding principle of the modern Labour Party's democracy"; "trade unionists should continue to play a role in the Labour Party, but on the basis of individual participation" June '93; was criticized by Labour activists for his "lukewarm commitment to equality" Sep '93; in NEW STATESMAN poll of union general secretaries, slipped from 3rd to 6th place (while Gordon Brown slipped from 1st to 4th Sep '93; came 6th in Shadow Cabinet elections Oct '93; in Arnold Goodman lecture claimed modernising was about retrieving Labour's most basic beliefs in community values, not just outdated economic or class ideas ??? '93; signed letter urging support for Edwina Currie's proposal to reduce age for homosexual consent to 16, Jan '94; voted to reduce age for homosexual consent to 18 or 16 Feb '94; insisted the issue about the age of consent was equality between heterosexuals and homosexuals Feb '94; voted against restoring capital punishment, even for killing policemen, saying: "the most powerful argument is the risk we will kill the innocent" Feb '94; jeered at retreat forced by Tory peers on Michael Howard on controlling police authorities and magistrates courts as "a humiliating retreat forced on the Home Secretary through pressure, not a genuine change of heart" Feb '94; complained that the Government did not have a coherent strategy for dealing with the links between drugs and crime Mar '94; agreed with Lord Ackner that Home Secretary Michael Howard's proposals to reduce compensation to victims of violent crime were unlawful Mar '94; said Labour was not against tough anti-terrorist laws but objected to Home Secretary banning Ulstermen from mainland Britain and detaining suspects for up to seven days without a court ruling Mar '94; with possibly 200,000 such incidents a year, said Labour would seek legislation to make racial harassment a criminal offence Mar '94; was opposed by Left in urging abstention on Criminal Justice and Public Order Bill, to avoid being accused of being "soft on crime" Mar '94; backed Chris Mullin's Bill to establish a tribunal to investigate miscarriages of justice Mar '94; in debate on Criminal Justice Bill, defended the right to silence Apr '94; complained that Home Secretary relied too much on heavy sentencing when only one in 50 crimes resulted in a conviction Apr '94; supported deregulation of Sunday trading May '94; with the death of

Labour Leader John Smith, opinion polls showed him well ahead of other contestants for the succession: he had 32% against 19% for second-place John Prescott (MORI-SUNDAY TIMES); bookies made him 2-5 or 1-4 May '94; after an Islington lunch with his friend-rival, Gordon Brown, Brown announced he would not be standing for the Leadership against him, allegedly after being assured he would remain 'shadow Chancellor' if Blair won, and Chancellor of the Exchequer if Labour won the next election June '94; announced his candidacy after John Prescott, Margaret Beckett and Denzil Davies had thrown their hats in the ring June '94; after Davies had been forced to withdraw for lack of support, the only question in most minds was: who would be his deputy July '94; came out in favour of a constructive attitude to the EC and a single European currency when the time is ripe July '94; won handsomely in all three sections of the Labour electorate: by 60.5% among MPs, by 58.2% among Labour Party members, and by 52.3% of trade unionists July '94; named his defeated opponent, Margaret Beckett, Health Spokesman, suggesting he wanted to undo Tory NHS "reforms" July '94; three of the 'Gang of Four' - the Labour defectors who established the SDP in '81 - came out in his support July-Aug '94; the Gallup Poll recorded an unprecedented 56.5% support for Labour under his leadership, 23% for the Conservatives, and 14.5% for the Liberal Democrats; 45% favoured him as Prime Minister, as against 15% for John Major and Paddy Ashdown Aug '94; made it clear to the TUC that he wanted a new arms-length relationship with the unions Sep'94; warned: "the geratest single danger in Left-of-Centre politics is that you end up mistaking the politics of pressure groups for the politics of the people as a whole" Sep '94; said he thought the first-past-the-post system of voting was "fair" and he would "have to be convinced" that PR was more fair Sep '94; having eased out Larry Whitty as General Secretary, and rejected a national minimum wage decided on "New Labour, New Britain" as the slogan to relaunch annual conference at Blackpool; his well-received wind-up speech was revealed by his acolytes as promising revision of Clause IV Oct '94; the NEC agreed to rewrite Clause IV Nov '94; challenged the PM over Tory divisions on Europe Nov '94; his decision to send his older son to a grant-aided Roman Catholic school deeply upset Labour activists and teachers Dec '94; having taunted John Major over splits in the Tory Party, the PM taunted him back over Labour divisions; he retorted this was giving the PM "good practice; one day we will move over there and let you ask questions" Feb '95; embarrassed Paddy Ashdown with promises of closer collaboration Sep '95; as part of a move from pro-republicanism, replaced 'green' Kevin McNamara with more neutral Mo Mowlam as Spokesman on Northern Ireland Sep '95; was belatedly informed by Harriet Harman that she had decided to send her child to a selective school Dec '95; was surprised and almost overwhelmed by the indignation among Labour activists over Harman's decision, which had been muted in his case; "Mr Blair had to protect Ms Harman by hurling his leadership in front of her frail body" (Simon Hoggart, GUARDIAN) Jan '96; succeeded in having the revised version of Clause IV overwhelmingly accepted Mar '96; taunted the PM on having had four Cabinet Minister vote against him on the Lord Chancellor's Bill Apr '96; warned John Major against his policy of non-co-operation in the EU over BSE because he showed no way of carrying out his threats May '96; said a future Labour government would not cut Defence expenditure further or get rid of nuclear weapons June '96; demanded to know when British beef would be admitted into the EU June '96; was reluctantly persuaded into having another pre-election contest for the Shadow Cabinet, on the basis that John Prescott and others would back the status quo, to keep Harriet Harman in post (which they narrowly achieved by persuading more popular non-members not to stand) June-July '96; was persuaded by Jack Straw of the usefulness of a referendum on Scottish home rule, which did not sit well with most of the Scottish Labour Party June-July '96; agreed with Gordon Brown to avoid any tax increase commitments apart from a one-off windfall tax on public utility super-profits July '96;

demoted Clare Short from Transport -where she favoured renationalisation - to Overseas Development July '96; was warned by Clare Short to slow the rate of his changes to the Labour Party, complaining about the "dark forces" (Mandelson) behind him Aug '96; came out for "zero tolerance" for street crime Jan '97; restated Labour's more cautious line about convergence and a single European currency, as crafted by Eurosceptic Robin Cook Mar '97; caused a 'wobble' among his colleagues when he suggested that Labour might privatise air traffic control when more cautious colleagues said only that a Labour government would have to consider the £1.5b "hole" in Government finances from planned receipts for its sale Apr '97; as Labour kept its roughly 20% lead, the main burden of the Tory attack was on his personal "hypocrisy" for changing his views and sending his sons to a grant-aided school Apr '97; he retained his seat with a 9.6% swing and his party won an unexpectedly overwhelming majority: Labour MPs doubled and Tory MPs halved, with a Labour majority of 179 in the Commons; he replied in The SUN to attacks on him by Roy Hattersley for his disinterest in equality and Tony Benn for his naming LibDems to a Cabinet committee: "people like them were in charge of the party for almost 20 years while we were losing general elections; the Labour Party of the early '80s has largely gone - and a good thing too; it was dying on its feet and we had to bring it back in touch with people like the readers of The SUN" July '97; he and Princess Diana met in Chequers July '97; when Princess Diana died, in contrast to the leaden-footed new Tory Leader, William Hague, he announced he was "utterly devastated" and helped organise a national public funeral for "the people's princess" Sep '97; brutally urged the TUC to modernise and "get into the real world"; "we will not go back to the days of industrial warfare, strikes without ballots, mass and flying pickets, secondary action" Sep '97; the SUNDAY TIMES claimed the Blairs would send their 9-year-old daughter Katheryn to Lady Margaret School, a fast-improving C of E school which chose its intake by examination Nov '97; at the NEC gave Diane Abbott a stunning personal rebuke for asking for more openness about contributions to the party, like Bernie Ecclestone's £1m, demanding she criticise in the PLP or NEC, instead of on TV Nov '97; announced a surprise 3-month extension of coal contracts to defer pit closures Dec '97; a semi-authorised biography of Gordon Brown by Paul Routledge disclosed his Chancellor was still moping over his being pipped at the post for Leader Jan '98; made an impassioned plea to be given time to deliver on his radical welfare programme Jan '98; delivered on the TUC-CBI compromise on 'Fairness at Work' May '98; after three visits to Northern Ireland and handwritten pledges, delivered on the Good Friday Agreement with an historic 71% vote on an unprecedented 83% turnout May '98; telephoned Presidents Clinton and Yeltsin to urge use of force to stop Serb suppression of ethnic Albanians in Kosovo June '98; ended his six-month presidency of the EU June '98; reasserted his authority in a reshuffle, sacking Harriet Harman, David Clark, Frank Field and Gavin Strang, promoting Peter Mandelson and redeploying threatening 'Brownies' July '98; pledged a partly-elected reformed new House of Lords July '98; switched Freedom of Information legislation to the Home Office July '98;
Born: 6 May 1953, Edinburgh
Family: His real paternal grand parents were in show business: Charles Parsons/Jimmy Lynton, music hall artiste, and Cecilia Ridgeway, dancer-actress, who married three years after young Leo was born in Filey; his adoptive paternal grandfather, James Blair, was a rigger in a Govan shipyard, his Leftwing adoptive grandmother, Mary Blair, came from a family of Scottish butchers; having fostered young Leo from the age of three months, she blocked off all contact with his real parents, claiming he died in World War II; son of Leo Blair, a Young Communist initially, then a Conservative with Parliamentary aspirations until his stroke; became a Law Lecturer in Durham University, later Chairman of the Industrial Tribunal, and late Hazel (McLeay), a Donegal Protestant, who died of thyroid cancer; m '80 Cherie (Booth),

wary Liverpool barrister, Labour candidate for Thanet North '83, daughter of actor Anthony ('Till Death Us Do Part') Booth, the love and later husband of late Pat ('Coronation Street') Phoenix; 2s: Euan '84, Nicholas '86, who both attend Oratory School; 1d Kathryn '88;

Education: Durham Cathedral School; Fettes College, Edinburgh (the grandest and then the strictest Scottish public school, where he failed to become a prefect because he was 'troublesome'; "I was homesick from the beginning and not very happy for the first few years" (TB); "he was intensely argumentative and every school rule was questioned; he could uphold his side of the debate about the rights and wrongs of everything better than any boy in the school" - Dr Eric Anderson, his housemaster, later headmaster of Eton, who tried to keep his hair short and keep verbs in his sentences); St John's College, Oxford University (where he produced revues and played guitar in a rock group called Ugly Rumours with Mark Ellen, later presenter of the Old Grey Whistle Test);

Occupation: Barrister, Lincoln's Inn, recently inactive but formerly in Lord Irvine's chambers (specialised in industrial and trade union law - especially unfair dismissals) '76-; formerly Sponsored by the TGWU (£1,200 for his constituency; £3,000 in election expenses) '83-95; Columnist, formerly for The TIMES '87-88; ex: Owner, of five-bedroom house in Victoria Crescent, Islington, sold for £615,000, £240,000 more than its purchase price;

Traits: Tall (6'); slim (13 stone); good-looking; fresh-faced; somewhat boyish; "photogenic" (Godfrey Barker, DAILY TELEGRAPH); thin tenor voice; graceful; smooth; courteous; precise; "as unlike a horny-handed son of toil as is possible" (Dennis Barker, GUARDIAN); "to look at him is to see only conviction and eagerness" (Barbara Amiel, SUNDAY TIMES); "a man whose tongue is as sharp as his suit" (Robert Hardman, DAILY TELEGRAPH); "rising Boy Scout; handsome, smooth and articulate public school chap who will go far" (Austin Mitchell MP); has "the unbreakable self-asssurance of one who knows he is a member of a class born to rule" (Andrew Rawnsley, GUARDIAN); "the lightest of touches, and complete self-confidence" and "a certain swagger" (Matthew Parris, TIMES); "Matthew Arnold's notion of 'sweetness and light' assembled in a nice dark suit" (Edward Pearce, EVENING STANDARD); "dangerously yuppyish" (GUARDIAN); "smiles often enough to irk opponents" (EVENING STANDARD); "behind the Archie Andrews grin is a keen intelligence" (TIMES); "has become one of his party's most accomplished wordsmiths, a highly-skilled craftsman of the sound-bite, an artisan of alliteration" (Andrew Rawnsley, GUARDIAN); has "the knack of unforced reasonableness; he talks, with attractive intimacy, as if delivering a fireside chat by the light of burning manifestoes"; "can sound as if he has thought more and, and more carefully, than his opponent; he sounds as if he is making more sense" (Andrew Brown, INDEPENDENT); control freak; "astonishingly ambitious" (OBSERVER); "cagey"; "committed Christian" (FINANCIAL TIMES); is High Church Anglican but attends mass with his Catholic wife and children, who attend Catholic schools; loves fish and chips; no longer smokes as a result of contract with wife ("I had my last cigarette at 1.45pm and we married at two"); attended birth of two of his children; plays squash and tennis; swimmer (on Commons charity team '91); is a great fan of the Renaissance artist, Piero della Francesca;

Address: House of Commons, Westminster, London SW1A 0AA; Sedgefield CLP, Trimdon Colliery, Trimdon Station, Co Durham;

Telephone: 0171 219 4410 (H of C); 01429 882202 (constituency);

We help you distinguish clones from rebels

Hazel (Anne) BLEARS   **Labour**   **SALFORD '97-**

Majority: 17,069 over Conservative 5-way;
Description: Manchester's shrinking Siamese twin city beyond the Irwell; a solidly working-class, Labour-voting area; the home of 'Coronation Street' and its begetter, Granada TV; the ninth least healthy constituency in the country;
Position: PPS, to Alan Milburn '98-; on Executive, North West Regional Labour Party '91-; North West representative on National Policy Forum '93-; ex: on Select Committee on European Legislation '97-98; Chairman, Salford Community Health Council '93-97; Salford City Councillor '84-92; Chairman, Bury & Radcliffe CLP, Vice Chairman, Eccles CLP, Campaigns Co-ordinator for Salford CLP;

Outlook: The former Leftwing tigress turned Blairite pussycat; the first woman MP for the city in which she was "born and bred"; an ambitious woman, formerly close to John Prescott and the TGWU, which used to sponsor her; a hyper-intense formerly-Left activist with roots in almost every Left, libertarian or working-class organisation in the area and nationally: Society of Labour Lawyers, NCCL (now Liberty), Legal Action Group, Co-operative Party, Amnesty International, Salford Relate, Greater Manchester Low Pay Unit; Trustee of the Working Class Museum and Library; was in CND; initially moved from hard-Left to Kinnockite; was still Left enough to have opposed the revision of Clause IV; is deviant as a Leftist as a "passionate adherent of constitutional reform" (HB) - including 'Partnership in Power' - and a believer in the practical improvements to be gained from closer European integration; would now like to see herself as an "intensely practical person rather than an organisational apparatchik" (HB) which was her image; favours use of art in industry;
History: She joined the Labour Party '78; was elected to Salford City Council May '84; was selected from a short-list of two women to fight the then-safe Tory seat of Tatton against Neil Hamilton Nov '85; she came 3rd in Tatton, but upped the Labour vote by 3%, from 18% in '83 to 21%, June '87; was selected to contest key marginal, Bury South Feb '90; was accused of leaking details of possible routes of the M62 through the constituency Dec '90; unexpectedly failed to win Bury South from David Sumberg by 788 votes on a low swing of 1.8%, perhaps because her Tory opponent frightened its large Jewish minority with the allegation that her support of CND aligned her with opponents of the Gulf War and so threatened Israel May '92; was selected for Salford, to follow retiring Stan Orme, first from an all-women short-list, then - after the court ruled all-women short-lists illegal - from a mixed short-list; she was supported by the local "TGWU Mafia", other unions, 7 out of 8 party branches and 75% of the votes Mar'96; opposed the revision of Clause IV '95; was elected with a majority of 17,069 (51.53%), a notional swing to Labour of 9.45%, May '97; in her over-loaded Maiden speech welcomed the radical overhaul of the youth justice system May '97; was named to the Select Committee on European Legislation July '97; spoke loyally in favour of the Blairite party reconstruction, 'Partnership in Power' at Brighton conference Sep '97; signed the European Movement's advertisement, 'Europe: A Force for Fairness, Equality and Opportunity for Women' Nov '97; co-sponsored motion deploring the overseas fund-raising for the Conservative Party of Ronald Walker CBE Nov '97; strongly supported the Civil Justice and Legal Aid Bill as enabling "us to encourage and reward lawyers who are genuinely committed to improving access to our legal system" Nov '97; called attention to the Salford Health Action

Group which, "despite its unfortunate acronym" (SHAG), "is working tremendously hard to improve the health of the people" Dec '97; was named PPS to Alan Milburn, replacing Mick Clapham, who had resigned after abstaining against cuts in lone-parent benefits Dec '97; polled 152votes after filing the 6th of nine places in the PLP's representation on Labour's National POlicy Forum Jan '98; as a PPS, left the Select Committee on European Legislation Feb '98; asked PM Tony Blair whether "this Labour Government will tackle the desperation in our inner-city caused by the Tories?" Feb '98; urged Home Office to involve local businesses in fighting crime because "in cities such as Salford it is crucial that businesses, which are the key to economic regeneration, feel safe and protected" Mar '98; welcomed the Crime and Disorder Bill as likely to cut the overwhelming burden of crime in Salford; "my communities are under seige and in crisis"; "in the past four weeks in the police F division, we have had 180 burglaries of dwellings and 168 burglaries of business premises; we have had 255 vehicles stolen, and 207 thefts from vehicles"; "the detection rate in Greater Manchester...is appalling" Apr '98;

Born: 14 May 1956, Salford

Family: Daughter of Arthur Blears, maintenance fitter and AEU shop steward, and Dorothy (Leighton), secretary; m '89 Michael Halsall, solicitor;

Education: Cromwell Road Junior School, Swinton; Wardley Grammar; Eccles VIth Form College; Trent Polytechnic (2:1 BA Law Hons); Chester College of Law (Law Society Finals);

Occupation: Solicitor '85-: Principal Solicitor, with Manchester City Council '85-97; was initially in private practice, and then with Wigan and Rossendale Council '80-81;

Traits: Puckish-looking; brown hair, frequently restyled; small eyes; "snappily dressed" (ECONOMIST); cheerful; vivacious; perky; good sense of humour; fast-talker; gets high on attending small political meetings; loves cats (Russian blues); fell-walker; won a gold medal for tap-dancing; was also a ballerina; enjoys cinema and motor cycling; her motorbike was stolen Feb '98; tends to repeat, "I have to say";

Address: House of Commons, Westminster, London SWIA 0AA; Dolphin Square; 46 Victoria Road, Salford M6 8EY;

Telephone: 0171 219 6595 (H of C);

'Bob' (Robert John) BLIZZARD   Labour   WAVENEY '97-

Majority: 12,093 over Conservative 4-way;

Description: Now largely the Suffolk fishing, cargo and industrial port of Lowestoft - its former name - and the market towns of Beccles and Bungay and their rural hinterlands, on Britain's most easterly coast; Lowestoft suffers from heavy unemployment, poor transport links and unrestored derelict industrial land; the seat's loss of 10,000 Tory-leaning voters in Halesworth and Southwold in the '95 boundary change was thought to make it marginal;

Position: On Select Committee on Environmental Audit '97-; Vice Chairman: PLP Environment, Transport and Regions Committee '97-; Chairman, all-party Britain-Brazil Group '97-; Waveney District Councillor (Leader '91-) '87-; Vice Chairman, Standing Conference of East Anglian Local Authorities;

Outlook: Loyal, extremely-practical local improver; a typical class-of-'97 beneficiary of

Labour's one-member one-vote system of selection: a local council leader and teacher; is more pro-European than his anti-Maastricht predecessor, Tory David Porter, having secured access to European structural funds for job creation; also set up 'Lowestoft 2000', a partnership with town businesses to promote Lowestoft for inward investment and tourism; interested in education, health, employment, transport and local government;

History: He joined the Labour Party '83; was elected to Waveney District Council May '87; was elected Leader of the Council May '91; was selected to contest Waveney as the Labour candidate Dec '95; at annual conference, spoke out for cuts in administration in NHS trusts Sep '96; retook Waveney for Labour after 38 years, with a 12,453 majority over the Tory Maastricht critic David Porter, as a result of a pro-Labour notional swing of 14.63%, May '97; made a good-natured Maiden, in which he emphasised that, after 25 years of teaching, he was convinced that class size was crucial June '97; expressed solidarity with jailed Indonesian union leader June '97; urged inclusion of those recovering from mental illness in Labour's welfare-to-work programme June '97; urged changes in law to prevent gazumping June '97; complained to Tory MP wanting only non-council housing initiatives that his council had built its own houses while working with the private sector; "for ever £1m released under this [Local Government Finance] Bill, about 250 of those homes [with] no central heating [and double glazing] can be fitted with double glazing and central heating; that will be good for energy efficiency, jobs and business" June '97; expressed concern that BSE incinerators would "destroy business confidence" locally June '97; in an adjournment debate complained convincingly that his area was starved of economic development because of its horrendously inadequate transport infrastructure June '97; applauded the end of two-tier access to NHS hospitals July '97; co-sponsored motion applauding patenting of genetic advances July '97; backed action against quota-hoppers, complaining: "in Lowestoft, there is a trawler - which is a Lowestoft trawler with a Lowestoft company - that purely and simply is a quota-hopper; it does not land any fish in the port of Lowestoft, although it is registered there" July '97; criticised excessive paperwork in benefits system, including the "33-page questionnaire" that the disabled had to complete July '97; welcomed the New Deal because it would be targeted precisely at the pockets of unemployment within relatively prosperous areas July '97; joined the 29-Member Labour Seaside Group to secure special consideration for their problems Dec '97; claimed the new Labour Government had begun to establish a better relationship with Lowestoft's fewer fishermen, despite the"terrible inheritance from the previous Government" which had signed up to the Common Fisheries Policy and failed to address the quota-hopping issue; "this Government have achieved more in a few months than the Tories achieved in years" Dec '97; complained that much of the beer drunk at Christmas would be smuggled, with French beer making up 5%, brought in by nearly 100,000 bootleggers' vans Dec '97; urged improvements in the Child Support Agency Dec '97; urged the new Regional Development Agencies correct the disparities in their regions, like "large areas of derelict inudstrial land that are in need of regeneration" in his constituency Dec '97; warned about the threat to community pharmacists from pharmacies in out-of-town supermarkets Jan '98; urged "a far more positive attitude to the single European currency" to help farmers Jan '98; as an ex-teacher, said teachers were unhappy not only because of poor pay and bad buildings, but because they had had so much unnecessary bureaucratic paperwork imposed on them and because of the absence of new challenges: "after 25 years, I still spent one or two break times a week standing outside the toilets"; "I used to wonder whether I really needed a university degre and a postgraduate qualification to stand outside the toilets for up to half an hour each week" Feb '98; urged the PM to visit Brazil, "the seventh largest economy in the world" Feb '98; urged Community Health Councils retain "a key role in the Health Service" Feb '98; said his Regional Development Agency would be judged by how far it could reduce Lowestoft's high

unemployment levels Mar '98; urged "sustainable increases in expenditure" on the NHS, so that free eye and dental checks could be restored Mar '98; loyally welcomed the local launching of the 'New Deal', claiming that local firms Sanyo, Bird's Eye and Shell were "fully involved" Mar '98; urged calling on local doctors to protect the disabled "when it appears that their benefit may be reduced or disappear under...the Benefit Integrity Project" Mar '98; claimed that heads of grant-maintained schools, explaining why they chose that status, confessed "I did it for the [extra] money" Mar '98; defended banning beef on the bone, to avoid "repeating the same old mistakes that the previous Government made" Apr '98; urged starting education against drugs much earlier Apr '98; welcomed extra £3.5m for Suffolk Health Authority Apr '98; complained about the murder of a constituent in Nigeria May '98;
Born: 31 May 1950, Bury St Edmunds
Family: So i, Arthur Blizzard, sign-writer, and Joan; married, with two children;
Education: Culford School, Bury St Edmunds; Birmingham University (BA Hons 2:1); Postgraduate qualification:
Occupation Was mulitply-sponsored in the general election with five unions jointly contributing £6.350 of his £9,064 expenditure, Apr-May '97; ex: Head of English, at Lynn Grove High School, Norfolk, which had 70% A-C passes in English and 80% in English literature) (NUT) '72-97; taught elsewhere '72-86;
Traits: Burly; portly; protruding chin; medium-brown greying parted hair; a vigorous speaker; "perky and confident", "big", "malco-ordinated", "gallops awkwardly", "like a day-old heifer bumping into things" (A A Gill, SUNDAY TIMES); enjoys walking, skiiing, listening to jazz;
Address: House of Commons, Westminster, London SW1A 0AA; 619 London Road South, Lowestoft, Suffolk NR33 0BA;
Telephone: 0171 219 3000 (H of C); 01502 514913;

Rt Hon David BLUNKETT   Labour   **BRIGHTSIDE, Sheffield '87-**

Majority: 19,954 (58.9%) over Conservative 6-way;
Description: The council-house-dominated northeast of Sheffield, with high unemployment and multiple deprivation; one of Labour's strongholds;
Position: Secretary of State for Education and Employment '97-; on Labour's NEC (party Chairman '93-94, Chairman of its Local Government Committee '84-92) '83-98; Trustee, Miners' Solidarity Fund '85-; ex: Spokesman: on Education and Employment '95-97, on Education '94-95, on Health '92-94; in Shadow Cabinet '92-97; ex: Assistant Spokesman, on Local Government '88-92; Vice Chairman, PLP Environment Committee '87-88; Deputy Chairman, Association of Metropolitan Authorities '84-87; Leader, Sheffield City Labour Group and Sheffield City Council '80-87; formerly UNISON/NUPE-sponsored;
Outlook: "A leading municipal socialist of the early '80s who basks in Mr Blair's warm approval" (Michael White, GUARDIAN); the rooted working-class modernising meritocrat who "wants to redeem state education by a political counter-attack on bad teaching, low standards, poor discipline and failed teaching methods" (Andrew Marr, INDEPENDENT);

links traditional Labour and 'New Labour', trying to keep a foot in every camp moving his way; a passionate but pragmatic exponent of the belief that "tolerating mediocrity and excusing failure is unacceptable, passing as it does, disadvantage from one generation to the next, reinforcing the gap between rich and poor and widening the gulf betwen those who succeed and those who fail" (DB); refuses to be distracted from raising standards by inherited problems of structure; accepts that "private education will remain" but "we cannot cling as a nation to the elitist notions which have reinforced privilege in the past; a meritocracy demands the highest possible standards for all and not the 'excape hatch' for the few" (DB); "infinitely adaptable" (Hugh Macpherson, TRIBUNE); "is his own man; he will not shave off that beard, not even for Peter Mandelson" (Michael White, GUARDIAN); "one of the few genuine orators in contemporary British politics" (John Carvel, GUARDIAN); Eurosceptic (was campaign manager for Bryan Gould in '92); a belated arrival in the Shadow Cabinet; in '92 was initially less impressive as Health Spokesman than his harder-hitting predecessor, Robin Cook; was slow to wrongfoot Virginia Bottomley; but by mid-'93 became "a worthy inheritor from Gerald Kaufman of the most acid tongue on the Labour front bench" (Andrew Rawnsley, GUARDIAN); previously the exponent of municipal socialism, including cheap fares for the 'Socialist Republic of South Yorkshire'; the voice of progressive but realistic northern local government innovators; he long headed the constituency section votes on NEC; he "commands an extraordinary level of support in the party at grassroots level" (John Carvel, GUARDIAN); believes "you have to identify with the people in whose interests you claim you're working" (DB); "an instinctive backstairs conciliator and amender of contentious motions in the interests of party unity, he is an honest broker in the NEC, a bridgehead to the party in the constituencies" (Patrick Wintour, GUARDIAN); "very good at skating on thin ice" (Neil Kinnock); was a key figure in Labour's review of local government policy; was a successful baiter of the Tory "shambles" on the poll tax; also a long-standing reformer of party organisation; an anti-factionalist, formerly in the semi-hard or 'firm' Left (was in the 'Supper Club'); "I agree with Tony Benn on some things and disagree with him on others"; tried to commit Labour to an early removal of nuclear weapons; tried to imbed Kinnock in the broad Left rather than lose him to the Centre-Right; a many-road advocate of social ownership rather than old-style nationalisation; "has always been a courageous and honest man who tackles problems head-on"; "an original thinker, he is responsible for placing at the centre of Labour's agenda the issue of the quality of public services, developing local government democracy and ideas of citizenship; he is a good conciliator, partly because he is very intuitive and understands people and has a very good ear for the middle ground of the party" (Joy Copley, SCOTSMAN); "he sees the realities as sharply as anyone" (TIMES); Britain's third blind MP (after Henry Fawcett and Sir Ian Fraser); anti-fluoride; was UNISON-sponsored;
History: His grandfather read the DAILY HERALD but none of his family were Labour Party members; his father died in a works accident when David was 12 and for two years the family lived largely on bread and dripping; he joined the Labour Party as a moderate at 16 in Shropshire '63; was elected to Sheffield City Council for Southey Green ward as the youngest-ever councillor at 22; "I came in as an angry young man on the Right of the political scene" May '70; at 25 was elected a South Yorkshire County Councillor Apr '73; contested hopeless Hallam, Sheffield, coming second with 27.2% of the vote Feb '74; became Chairman of Sheffield's Family and Community Services Committee May '76; failed by one vote to be selected as candidate for by-election in safe Penistone - in which he lived - on Jack Mendelson's death June '78; deplored bickering among Labour's leading figures Nov '79; was elected Leader of Sheffield's Labour Group and City Council; "I was the middle-of-the-road candidate" '80; exploded when Denis Healey, AEU President Terry Duffy and others attacked semi-hard Leftwinger Richard Caborn MEP after he replaced moderate Fred (later Lord)

Mulley as candidate for Sheffield Park; Healey accused Caborn of having "lived high off the hog" in Brussels, to which Blunkett retorted: "as Caborn has donated most of his income and in every other possible way placed his resources at the disposal of the Labour Party in Sheffield, it ill befits a serious politician to launch such petty, ill-informed and hypocritical attacks" Mar '82; was elected to the NEC's constituency section on his first attempt with 322,000 votes, the first non-MP to do so since Harold Laski, 40 years before Oct '83; claimed local government was the new seedbed for socialism Oct '83; at the NEC tried to deflect efforts to expel Militants into a definition of democratic socialism Jan '84; urged a common stand against rate-capping Feb '84; was elected Deputy Chairman of the AMA June '84; at Sheffield conference of rate-capped Labour authorities helped achieve agreement on delaying making a rate, hoping to pressure the Government to return grants July '84; at annual conference urged a better regional structure, more campaigning, more industrial democracy and more municipal socialism Oct '84; as Chairman of Labour's Local Government Information Unit, conducted an orderly retreat, setting a rate in May '85; was criticised by his Sheffield Tory opponent for defying the Government over rate-capping; was selected as candidate for super-safe Brightside, Sheffield as hard-Left Joan Maynard's successor on the third ballot by 33 to 25 June '85; topped the poll for the NEC's constituency section, toppling Tony Benn Oct '85; received a standing ovation at Bournemouth conference when he seemed to offer Militant-dominated Liverpool City Council and others a road back from the perdition threatened by Neil Kinnock Oct '85; at a TRIBUNE meeting claimed that, had Neil Kinnock consulted him on the Liverpool Militants, he might have helped avoid the impression that Kinnock's fury was directed against the broad Left of the party Oct '85; was involved in behind-the-scenes efforts to get the Militant-led Liverpool City Council to retreat from its confrontation on illegal expenditure; by persuading it to open its books to the AMA and Treasurers from three leading Labour authorities, he avoided a major split Oct-Nov '85; attacked both those "in the party desperate to get rid of the Militant Tendency at all costs, and others equally desperate to cover up for them and act as apologists for their every action" Jan '86; only narrowly won a vote to exclude from the Sheffield Labour Group, a Militant councillor who had been expelled by the party nationally, despite threatening to resign if he lost Jan '86; voted for an NEC inquiry into Liverpool Militants Feb '86; criticised the walkout from the NEC of its seven hard-Left members over Liverpool Militants as damaging a "unified, purposeful and responsible Labour Party" Mar '86; deplored the end of South Yorkshire's pioneering cheap bus fares Apr '86; helped end Sheffield City Council's five-year 'cold war' with the Sheffield business community Apr '86; on the NEC voted for the expulsion of Derek Hatton but not for that of Carol Darton June '86; admitted that an increase in basic rate of income tax would be required to pay for Labour's programme - bringing him under fire from Roy Hattersley Sep '86; the hard Left failed to topple him from top place in the NEC's constituency section, though his vote was reduced to 499,000 Sep '86; supported a many-road approach to social ownership, including municipal enterprises Oct '86; conceded Mrs Thatcher could win a third term Feb '87; having persuaded Neil Kinnock not to expel Linda Bellos, Lambeth's half-black semi-Trotskyist Leader, urged black Labour candidates to bury the hatchet on black sections and concentrate on campaigning Apr '87; accused Norman Tebbit of having a "secret agenda" including the privatization of water Apr '87; supported the removal of Kinnock-baiting Trotskyist Sharon Atkins as a candidate (but in '88 opposed her expulsion from the party) Apr '87; retained Brightside for Labour with a majority enhanced by almost 9,000 June '87; made an "outstanding" (TIMES) Maiden defending Britain as a "pluralistic democracy" against centralization and the citizenship rights of those who worked as against those who owned property June '87; having failed to win a place on the Tribune Group's slate of candidates for the Shadow Cabinet, decided not to contest the election June '87; retained his NEC seat with poll-topping 466,000 votes Sep '87; attacked promised sell-off of water boards as "probably the most disgraceful act of a Government intent on turning Britain into an auctioneer's paradise" Oct '87; in a paper for Tony Benn's Chesterfield Conference urged Labour to protect workers against technology's changes in working life Oct '87; urged a property tax combined with a local income tax as an alternative to poll tax Oct '87; in FINANCIAL TIMES insisted Sheffield preferred its own locally-agreed urban renewal efforts to those imposed from outside Dec '87; on NEC sought compromise investigation of Militant infiltration of Bermondsey CLP rather than its suspension Jan '88; complained of impact of poll tax on young volunteers working away from home Jan '88; warned Tony Benn and Eric Heffer against challenging Neil Kinnock because it might humiliate them and give him a position of "omnipotence" Feb '88; complained about not being able to debate the hundred-fold increase in concessionary TV licenses May '88; expressed fears that Kinnock might water down his unilateralist position May '88; supported John Prescott's candidacy for Deputy Leader July-Sep '88; as a result of two serious illnesses and a major gall bladder operation, was disclosed to have been Labour's poorest voter in the previous year Oct '88; was top of constituency section of NEC with 483,000 votes Oct '88; on Tribune slate in election for Shadow Cabinet, received 58 votes, sixth runner-up Nov '88; backed Sheffield's ban on fluoridation of water Feb '89; on NEC failed, by 16 votes to 9, to have his amendment added to Labour's defence document: that nuclear weapons be removed from British soil "by the end of the lifetime of a normal Parliament"; voted against document as a whole with Tony Benn, Ken Livingstone, Dennis Skinner, Margaret Beckett and Jo Richardson May '89; again came top of NEC's constituency section, receiving 485,000 votes Oct '89; at Brighton warned it would be "naive" or "dishonest" to urge non-payment of poll tax Oct '89; in his first attempt, was placed 3rd on Tribune slate for Shadow Cabinet Oct '89; received 63 votes for Shadow Cabinet, the 5th runner-up Nov '89; was named an Assistant Spokesman, on Local Government Nov '89; his plan for poll tax replacement - a property tax plus a local income tax - was vetoed by his boss, Bryan Gould Dec '89; accurately predicted that poll tax figures would be much higher than Government anticipated Jan '90; with Bryan Gould, committed Labour to a much-criticised poll tax alternative, a property tax linked with ability to pay Feb '90; launched Labour's 'fair rates' alternative to poll tax, including revaluation of rateable value and rebates; he was said to have urged a low basic charge, increasing on a sliding scale for those on higher incomes July '90; again came top of the NEC's constituency section with 499,00 votes Oct '90; was one of six semi-hard Left frontbenchers who voted to cut defence expenditures to West European averages Oct '90; received 51 votes for Shadow Cabinet, the 8th runner-up Oct '90; urged a new devolutionary settlement both internally and in relations with Europe Nov '90; complained Government policy was denying many millions of much-need regional assistance from the EC Feb '91; claimed the first two years of the poll tax had cost £14b; wrote that the Tories were giving up the poll tax "to save their own political skins" Mar '91; asked: "how can it be right to give an automatic discount to someone living alone who earns £30,000 or £40,000 or more, while a pensioner couple living next door have to pay the full amount?" Apr '91; successfully complained against allowing Detta O'Cathain, an employee of City of London, to sit as a Tory peer, since political activity by senior local government employees had been barred by Government's own Act May '91; urged Liverpool's Labour leaders to stand firm against Militant and institute needed job cuts June '91; welcomed Peter Kilfoyle's Walton victory as laying "the ghost of the Militant Tendency" July '91; predicted that, without the abolition of the discredited 20% rule, poll tax non-collection would continue to grow July '91; complained that fear of poll tax was shrivelling electoral registration Aug '91; during the NEC's interrogation of David Nellist, devised the form of words which gave Nellist his unseized opportunity to say he would give up supporting Militant, which had revealed itself as a separate party at the Walton by-election Sep '91; again topped voted for constituency section of NEC with 480,000 votes Sep '91; took his turn in chairing Labour's conference at Brighton, calling on Glenda Jackson as "the delegate in the grey suit with a red jumper" Oct '91; decided not to stand for Shadow Cabinet, to avoid knocking off Jo Richardson Oct '91; claimed Tory NHS reforms were producing "a fragmented 'illness service'" Oct '91; in TIMES letter, urged that, under the doctrine of 'subsidiarity', power should devolve down to Britain's regions as well as upwards towards Brussels Nov '91; attacked private landlords for charging rates while tenants had to pay poll tax Nov '91; opposed a simple 'pro' or 'anti' position on EC: "Labour's job should be to define what is appropriate for each particular level of representative government" Dec '91; apologized to Disney Corporation for describing Tories' council tax as "a Mickey Mouse valuation system" Dec '91; promised to purge Government of Thatcherite senior civil servants Feb '82; retained seat with majority down from 24,191 to 22,681, a swing to Conservatives of 0.26%, mainly from Liberal Democrats Apr '92; blamed election loss on "too many decisions being taken not by politicians whose background and experience were responsible for their promotion but by those employed outside the Walworth Road structure to communicate Labour's case to the electorate" Apr '92; backed Bryan Gould for Leadership, becoming his campaign manager; was the first to realize Gould would be defeated crushingly; Apr '92; urged Labour to "return to its historic role as representative of 'the little man and woman' including the self-employed and those running or working in small businesses" May '92; backed retention of pro-nationalisation Clause IV (4) in Labour's constitution May '92; warned against Labour seeming to tolerate "anti-social behaviour" and "freeloaders" June '92; blamed Labour's election loss on its Shadow Communications for policies which were both "unacceptable and out of the hands of the politicians who should have been running strategy" June '92; on NEC, backed immediate end of union vote in choosing Parliamentary candidates June '92; in contest for John Smith's Shadow Cabinet, made it for the first time with 112 votes (15th); the only Shadow Cabinet member not to have backed John Smith, was named Health Spokesman July '92; attacked failure of BR to protect non-smokers July '92; urged Labour to adapt to its "new political constituency" July '92; disclosed he would adapt rather than reject Conservative NHS reforms Sep '92; with Bryan Gould and Michael Meacher, failed in PLP to persuade Gordon Brown to accept his amendment saying Labour "does not rule out a realignment of currencies," before 'black Wednesday' Sep '92; at NEC was defeated in effort to have Tony Benn's call for a referendum on Maastricht deferred; was able to secure nine amendments to NEC's European statement Sep '92; after French referendum urged "a breathing space while both the ERM and Maastricht are considered afresh in a timescale determined by the interests of Britain" Sep '92; SOCIALIST ORGANISER Trotskyists infiltrated into his constituency faked votes for NEC constituency section to favour Campaign Group Sep '92; failed to dissuade Bryan Gould from resigning from Shadow Cabinet Sept '92; emphasising need for more preventive medicine, attacked Health Secretary Bottomley as "Golden Virginia" for refusing to ban cigarette ads Sep '92; retained his NEC seat with 531,000 votes, coming second after Neil Kinnock Sep '92; urged resignation of Chairman of West Midlands Regional Health Authority for costly mismanagement of private contracts Oct '92; opposed a "bankers' Europe" Nov '92; backed one-member one-vote Dec '92; put Euro-sceptic case to PLP Dec '92; warned against being distracted by PR from need for decentralization and continued constituency link Dec '92; urged a "radical and visionary" programme to capture voters and avoid splits between Labour's Clinton-admiring "modernizers" and traditionalists; urged Labour to shed its image as the creator of the dependency culture to win the trust of the aspiring classes Jan '93; admitted he could not fully turn back the clock on NHS reforms after next election Jan '93; complained about the "breathtaking" scale of "the improper use of

[NHS] funds in both Wessex and the West Midlands" Feb '93; referred to Health Secretary Virginia Bottomley's "special understanding of the feelings and emotions of unmarried mothers" in urging better family planning July '93; urged a points system for council housing which would reward responsible couples with a stable relationship before having children July '93; won 531,000 votes for constituency section of NEC, down from 549,000 Sep '93; became Chairman of the Labour Party for a year from Oct '93; voted against restoring capital punishment, even for killers of policemen Feb '94; voted to reduce age of homosexual consent to 18, not 16, Feb '94; as party Chairman, urged Bryan Gould to resign before he took over as Vice Chancellor in New Zealand in September, to enable the Dagenham by-election to be fought with that of nearby Newham North East Feb '94; was the sixth most assiduous provoker of written answers, receiving 474 in the year to Feb '94, Apr '94; lost the battle over spending pledges in his draft health paper after a row with Gordon Brown's Treasury team in Labour's National Policy Committee chaired by John Smith May '94; complained that Britain had become the "sick man of Europe" in that British workers averaged 7.4 days off with illness, while Germans only lost 3.7 days because of more preventive medicine June '94; his new guide-dog, Lucy, made her first appearance in the Commons June '94; voted for Blair for Leader, Prescott for Deputy Leader July '94; came second to Robin Cook in ballot for Constituency section of NEC, with 80,150 votes Oct '94; came 15th in Shadow Cabinet ballot, with 100 votes Oct '94; was named Labour's Education Spokesman or 'Shadow Education Secretary', replacing Ann Taylor Oct '94; he backed school league tables in a more informative 'added value' form Nov '94; said, "we want to see the opening up of education as a central tool of the next Labour Government in implementing our economic and social policies" Nov '94; in NEC discussions of Clause IV revisions, he stressed "a fair distribution of opportunity, income and power is an important objective which socialists have always pursued" Nov '94; in a GUARDIAN interview insisted he would be "tough as well as tender" in raising educational standards and show that Labour was serious about changing a system which was failing a third of its pupils; said he was willing to consider taxing those who benefited from higher education Dec '94; he had to field Labour activists' protests about Tony Blair's sending his elder son to grant-maintained London Oratory Dec '94; he was forced by Tony Blair to recant after he hinted Labour might impose VAT on private school fees Jan '95; in the GUARDIAN warned that "the patronising benevolence of some towards under-achievement has reinforced inequality" Jan '95; urged the Labour Party to develop a flexible partnership with the 1,000 grant-maintained schools whose creation it had opposed Feb '95; refused Tory MPs' invitations to him to comment on Harriet Harman's decision to send her child to a Bromley selective school Mar '95; teachers' unions were dismayed at his "fresh start" for failed school, including plans to reopen them with a new head and staff Apr '95; attacked for "stealing Tory clothes on standards, replied, "if the Labour Party has not been seen as being totally committed to raising standards and bettering opportunities, then its my job to do something about it; if standards, discipline and high expectations are considered Rightwing, then I plead guilty; but I don't consider them to be" Apr '95; after complaining that poor kids got a raw deal from the schools, 30 SWP teachers harassed him at the annual NUT conference Apr '95; with Tony Blair crafted a compromise on the Left demand for the abolition of grant-maintained schools by renaming them "foundation schools" and re-establishing a connection with local education authorities June '95; was counted a member of the new semi-hard Left group, 'What's Left', with Robin Cook, Clare Short and Michael Meacher July '95; came 3rd after Robin Cook and Gordon Brown in vote for Constituency section of NEC, with 75,984 votes Oct '95; under attack at conference by Roy Hattersley for accepting a two-tier system in not pledging to abolish grant-maintained schools, told him that "those who did not come up with solutions should not turn on those who have", insisting: "no selection

either by examination or interview under a Labour Government" Oct '95; came 11th in the ballot for the Shadow Cabinet, with 132 votes Oct '95; promised more homework and less TV to Britain's schoolchildren Oct '95; promised that every school in England and Wales would receive a development plan with targets for improvement based on their previous performance Nov '95; was rated the third most-admired member of their party by Labour MPs Dec '95; was pressed to clarify Labour's policy on grammar schools Jan '96; voted against 3% cap on MPs' pay rise, in favour of basing pensions on £43,000 July '96; came 17th in Shadow Cabine poll, with 175 votes July '96; was confirmed as 'Shadow Education Secretary' in Tony Blair's 'final' pre-election reshuffle Aug '96; disclosed he had given his deputy, Stephen Byers, a "dressing down" for saying Labour was going to break away from the trade union movement Sep '96; "Labour opposes a return to the 11-plus, which failed four in five youngsters" Oct '96; was not informed until later of Blair's insistence to Gordon Brown that Labour would not increase income tax to 50% on those earning £100,000 or more Dec '96; promised classes in parenting to expectant mothers Jan '97; to reassure worried middle-class parents involved in the crucial Wirral South by-election, said: "our policy is about levelling up, not levelling down; grammar schools are not the issue for the next Labour Government"; "we will not wage wars on grammar schools" Jan '97; retained his safe seat of Brightside by a decreased majority of 19,954 May '97; was named Secretary of State for Education and Employment and made a Privy Councillor; offered his department staff a "new partnership" May '97; astonished the educational world by teaming up Tim Brighouse and Chris Woodhead as joint heads of his educational task force May '97; his "naming and shaming" - an SWP phrase - of 15 failing schools disconcerted the teachers' unions May '97; his White Paper established a General Teaching Council and set high achievement targets for heads, teachers and schools July '97; in the vote for Constituency section of NEC came second to Robin Cook with 106,601 votes Sep '97; Lord (Roy) Hattersley accused him of betraying an implied promise to abolish grammar schools Nov '97; set daily homework targets Apr '98; unveiled his strategy of inviting in Tory MPs to discuss education: "if we include them all we can take over as the natural party of government" Apr '98; was said to have decided to spend any extra money squeezed out of the Treasury on further education Apr '98; warned failing schools they would be given two years to improve, after which they would be closed or have radical management changes imposed June '98; after minor concessions to critics of tuition fees, indicated his fury with hard-Left rebels against his Teaching and Higher Education Bill on its 3rd Reading June '98;
Born: 6 June 1947, Sheffield
Family: His grandfather was a DAILY HERALD reader; son, late Arthur Blunkett, Gas Board foreman who died in works accident when David was twelve, and late Doris Matilda Elizabeth, factory worker, whose hair turned white when she discovered David was born blind; m '70 Ruth (Mitchell), teacher and magistrate; separated Mar '88 after she asked him to leave home, saying: "as we grew into middle age together we began to realise that we were no longer compatible"; they were later divorced; 3s Alastair '77, Hugh '80, Andrew '82;
Education: Sheffield School for the Blind (from the age of four); Royal Normal College for the Blind, Shrewsbury (where he was offered training to become a piano tuner, or a capstan-lathe operator in a sheltered workshop, or a commercial course for Braille typing and shorthand - which he chose; he led a revolt against being fed sausages four times a week); Shrewsbury Technical College (night school to get O-levels and A-levels); Richmond College, Sheffield (night school and day release; National Certificate in Business Studies); Sheffield University (Professor Bernard Crick was his Tutor; Hons in Political Theory and Institutions); Huddersfield College of Education (Post Graduate Certificate in Further Education Teaching);
Occupation: Author: On A Clear Day (memoir; 1995), Democracy in Crisis (with Keith Jackson) (1987);; ex: Adviser, to Chartered Society of Physiotherapists (unpaid) '88-97;

Sponsored, by UNISON (formerly NUPE; £600 to constituency party, 40% of election expenses) '87-95; "he receives a special needs allowance to help run his Westminster office of two researchers, two secretaries and the occasional student volunteer and one full-timer in Sheffield - which is about double the staff of most MPs" (Joy Copley, SCOTSMAN); this was partly financed by NALGO and IRSF; ex: Tutor, Barnsley College of Technology '74-87; Clerk and Shop Steward, East Midlands Gas Board '67-69;

Traits: Bearded; front-combed brown hair; blind ("I can distinguish between light and dark"; "I count not being able to see as an inconvenience rather than a disability" [DB]); "the massive personal resilience and drive necessary to achieve so much against the odds is a triumph of will-power and individuality" (John Carvel, GUARDIAN); "in full flood he has the old-fashioned orator's trick of holding a cupped hand to his breast" (Martyn Harris, DAILY TELEGRAPH); "beneath the relaxed exterior, he is slightly prickly" (Helena de Bertodano, SUNDAY TELEGRAPH); there is "a suggestion of prickliness beneath Mr Blunkett's lupine charm" (SUNDAY TELEGRAPH); "has a phenomenal memory" (INDEPENDENT); reinforces his memory during question time by reading his Braille notes; "all his work is done under daunting handicap; he often listens late into the night to cassettes of papers, newspaper cuttings, correspondence and Hansard" (Patrick Wintour, GUARDIAN); he is expensively provided with imperfect equipment which electronically scans Hansard and converts it into Braille; does much of his own cooking, and not longer has difficulty with potato-peeling; had guide dog 'Offa', an Alsatian-Labrador cross, the successor to 'Ted'; Offa's '94 sucessor was Lucy, a Labrador/Retriever cross; "people come up and capture me and I can't use as an excuse that I have just seen someone walk in, or I must go to the toilet; they alway volunteer to take me" (DB); "has a slightly paranoid streak, very sensitive, an extension of his blindness; he had to be consulted; if you tracked him down and went through what Kinnock had in mind, he was fine; but if you missed him - for whatever reason -and reached him only the night before a meeting, he could be very shirty" (ex-staffer of Neil Kinnock [Charles Clarke?]); "a careful, courteous man, his niceness is genuine; but an innocent abroad he is not" (TIMES); "a superb exponent of injured innocence" (Lord Hattersley); "thoughtful and sometimes over-sensitive" (GUARDIAN); "can also be brusque, impatient, intolerant and aggressive" (Angela Levin, MAIL ON SUNDAY); can have a short fuse and get very upset if he does not get his own way; admits he is sometimes "full of myself"; "I detest inefficiency and incompetence; I am a Yorkshireman; I like to be able to say what I think, get it over with and forget it; I don't bear grudges"; "the Methodist work ethic is very strong in me and when I relax I feel I ought to be doing something"; Methodist (METHODIST RECORDER); is health-sensitive ("I come in on the District Line and wherever you sit or stand you seem to be within range of someone sneezing; I'd like to see the full weight of the justice system brought down on those who persistently sneeze without using a tissue"; "what we need are strict laws to protect people from passive smoking" [DB]); enjoys music, sailing, loves poetry; a walker; "I love holidays in this country, enjoying the sounds of nature and wildlife and [could] often be found in the Lake District"; as a young man spent most Saturdays at Sheffield Wednesday football matches;

Address: House of Commons, Westminster, London SW1A 0AA; 4th Floor, Palatine Chambers, Pinstone Street, Sheffield S1 2HN;

Telephone: 0171 219 4043 (H of C); 0114 735987 (Sheffield office);

Crispin BLUNT   **Conservative**   **REIGATE '97-**

Majority: 7,741 over Labour 6-way;

Description: The safely-Tory commuter conurbation of Reigate-Redhill which in '95 lost Horley to East Surrey but gained Banstead from Epsom and Ewell; its more dramatic '97 loss was the premature political suicide of its sitting Thatcherite Tory MP, Sir George Gardiner, sacked by his long-suffering constituency association for intemperate and disloyal remarks about John Major;

Position: On Select Committee on Defence '97-; ex: Special Adviser to Malcolm Rifkind as Defence Secretary '93-95 and Foreign Secretary '95-97;

Outlook: Well-connected mainstream Right-moving loyalist; a General's son and former Captain in the Royal Hussars, he treats Labour Ministers as though they are muddled-brained Other Ranks who mistakenly think they are in command; can on occasion deliver an analysis as if still a backroom adviser to a Defence Minister; still believes Britain can again become "the richest major nation in the world" through "policies that encourage wealth creation, free trade, strong defence, a Europe of nation states, continuing reduction of the public sector" (CB); was initially thought pro-European as a Heseltine supporter, but has become "a latter-day Eurosceptic" (Simon Sebag Montefiore, SUNDAY TIMES) with his former boss, Sir Malcolm Rifkind;

History: He gave in his resignation notice from the Army July '89; was selected from 65 candidates to fight the Labour-held marginal, West Bromwich East, against Peter Snape Aug '89; backed Michael Heseltine in his Leadership bid Nov '90; Peter Snape's majority over him trebled from 983 in '87 to 2,813 Apr '92; was named Special Adviser to Defence Secretary Malcolm Rifkind Feb '93; continued this role when Malcolm Rifkind transferred to the Foreign Office July '95; in the wake of the de-selection of Reigate's Europhobic Thatcherite Sir George Gardiner for his disloyal - "get off the fence" - remarks about PM John Major, was selected over former Tory MPs Tony Favell and Chris Butler as Sir George's replacement, despite his remark that "if you put up a donkey as a Conservative in Reigate it would win" Feb '97; Sir George followed up by announcing he would contest the seat as a Referendum Party candidate Mar '97; when polled by the DAILY TELEGRAPH, said he was against a single European currency Apr '97; retained Reigate for the Conservatives with a shrunken majority of 7,741 (down from 16,940); this came partly from a swing to Labour of 11.98%; Sir George came fourth with 3,352 (6.9%) May '97; asked about minimum mandatory sentences for career burglars and dealers in hard drugs May '97; warned about the dangers of a minimum wage for the tourist industry June '97; complained about Clare Short's "complete fixation with the eradication of poverty" at the expense of sustainable economic development and in isolation from other Government departments July '97; backed the amendment of Julian Lewis that nuclear disarmament could only work if accompanied by conventional disarmament July '97; attacked the Budget's "smash and grab raid on private pensions" July '97; was named to the Select Committee on Defence July '97; when he complained that Labour's "soundbite diplomacy" had lost British arms manufacturers contracts in Malaysia and Turkey, Minister Derek Fatchett said of him, "he would sell to anyone, anywhere, at any time and would take no account of the regime and have no regard for human rights" Oct '97; warned that conceding to the French on "progressive framing of a common defence policy" for the EU would provoke trouble with the Russians if the Baltic states joined Nov '97; asked PM Tony Blair why he had not warned the British electorate that "he aspired to be not so much the Queen's First Minister, as the nation's first nanny" in controlling beef on the bone and target shooting Dec '97; claimed that the Lord Chancellor had intervened, giving "blatant political advice", to prevent a court-martial of Major Eric Joyce for his open criticism of racism and class discrimination in the Army, on the grounds that Joyce could appeal under the European Convention on Human Rights Jan '98; claimed the Labour Government had "dropped the ball" in not securing at Amsterdam guarantees of subsidiarity "with real teeth" Jan '98; attacked the Labour Government for supporting the Treaty of Amsterdam because it had "served to undermine the competitive advantages that the Conservative Government carved out" for the UK by accepting the Social Chapter Jan '98; after his perceived obstreperous behaviour on the subject of Robin Cook's then mistress, was threatened by Speaker Boothroyd: "I shall send you out for the rest of the day" Jan '98; suggested the only achievable target for military action in Iraq was bombing "the sites to which the inspectors have been denied access" since Saddam could only be removed expensively by "hundreds of thousands" of ground troops Feb '98; opposed the "over-correction" of trying to license child labour in things like newspaper delivery because local authorities were incapable of managing a licensing system Feb '98; suggested "a system of specialist jurors with financial qualifications" for complex financial court cases Mar '98; attacked "eccentric" Lord Gilbert, Minister for Defence Procurement, for having "spurned" an official Malaysian Rolls-Royce in favour of a private rented Fiat Punto when arriving a day early for a maritime exhibition Apr '98; urged that "if we have to swallow our distaste at the early release of terrorist murderers to sustain the [Good Friday] Agreement, Guardsmen Fisher and Wright should be released without delay" Apr '98; urged early action over Kosovo "rather than wait for violence to happen" Apr '98; since "my constituency is next to Gatwick Airport" backed the continuation of duty-free trade May '98; co-sponsored all-party motion celebrating the 30th anniversary of the Abortion Act taking effect May '98; Foreign Secretary Robin Cook threatened to sue him for libel if he made, outside the Commons, the allegation that he had improperly delayed the Customs investigation of the Sandline gun-running May '98;

Born: 15 July 1960,

Family: Son, of Major General Peter Blunt, retired soldier and company director, and Adrienne (Richardson); m '90 Victoria (Jenkins); 1s 'Freddie'/Frederick '94, 1d Claudia '92;

Education: Wellington College '73-78; Royal Military Academy, Sandhurst (Queen's Medal) '79-80; Durham University (in-Service degree of BA in Politics; President of the Union) '81-84; Cranfield School of Management (MBA) '90-91;

Occupation: Formerly Special Adviser to Malcolm Rifkind, when Foreign Secretary '95-97, Defence Secretary '93-95; Political Consultant: with PI Political Consultants '93, self-employed '91-92; Army Officer '79-90, reaching the rank of Captain in the Armoured Reconnaissance Regiment, 13th/18th Royal Hussars (Queen Mary's Own), serving in Cyprus and Germany;

Traits: Slim; dark receding parted hair; bulging forehead; good teeth; gently-spoken; "crisply-suited" (TIMES); "charming and decent" but "not universally loved by civil servants, hence the FCO nickname 'Blunt, Whitehall's best-known typographical error'" (SUNDAY TELEGRAPH); "his nickname as Crippen need not be taken too seriously" (Kenneth Rose, SUNDAY TELEGRAPH); "confident, erudite, expert and incisive" (David Davis MP); "cannot hear or his brain is unable to receive information"; "out of tune with the mood of the country" (Clare Short MP); enjoys bridge and cricket (was the captain of his side in the Army) and historical novels;

Address: House of Commons, Westminster, London SW1A 0AA; 35 Fernhurst Road,

Fulham, London SW6 7JN;
Telephone: 0171 219 3000 (H of C); 0171 731 1785 (home)

Paul (Yaw) BOATENG   **Labour**   **BRENT SOUTH '87-**

Majority: 19,981 (57.1%) over Conservative 7-way;
Description: The Southern strip of Brent, from Alperton in the West to Kensal Rise in the East, to Wembley in the North; over half (55%) non-white, with the country's largest concentration of West Indians, largely around the Park Royal industrial estate; in '95 5,000 voters were added from Brent North
Position: Under Secretary, for Social Care and Mental Health '97-; ex: Spokesman, on Lord Chancellor's Department '92-97; Assistant Spokesman, on Treasury and Economic Affairs '89-92; on Environment Select Committee '87-89; Chairman, Afro-Caribbean Education Resources Project '78-81; on Labour's Joint Committee on Crime and Policing '84-86; GLC Councillor for Walthamstow, Chairman of GLC Police Committee and Vice Chairman of its Minorities Committee '81-86; Chairman, Westminster Community Relations Council '79-81; on Executive, of NCCL,'80-86;
Outlook: Britain's first half-black Minister in an unexpected department, possibly as a result of a falling out with Lord Irvine; as the chief architect of Labour's 1995 policy document on the legal profession, he was expected to play an important role under the new Lord Chancellor; this was a widely-expected reward, particularly after his long ordeal on the Family Law Bill; an ambitious, intelligent, deft, flexible, articulate, witty, formerly-radical lawyer of mixed Scottish and Ghanaian descent; a Christian Socialist; a successful London lawyer (recently a barrister, initially a solicitor); "probably the most able of Britain's black politicians" (Nicholas Timmins, TIMES); "there is a wonderful arrogance about him; he doesn't feel inferior to anybody; you see this huge smile and behind it you know the guy's deadly; he has a backbone of steel that other people don't have" (black activist Darcus Howe); "I have always held the view that excellence is never the enemy of equality" (PB); has run the gamut from a police-bashing solicitor with Trotskyist support to a defender of Lloyd's 'names' against unfair attacks; "a sheep who used to dress in wolf's clothing to keep up with fashions when he joined Ken Livingstone's guard at the Greater London Council" (Joe Joseph, TIMES); has eschewed identification with black ghettoes at home while speaking for British blacks at international conferences; effective constituency MP; a softened-by-election former hard-Left black spokesman for London's Livingstoneite cabal; ex-supporter of a "mass campaigning party" and proponent of tight political control of the police when linked to semi-Trotskyist 'Target Labour Government' or close to the defunct semi-Trotskyist LABOUR HERALD and its causes; until his election, was a multi-front Leftwinger: has recently shown a desire to shine as an individual: "one of the major problems of an MP who is black is to be recognised simply as a Member of Parliament who is black rather than a black Member of Parliament; the idea that one is going into Parliament to represent black people is absolute baloney but you constantly have to state that is not the case (PB)"; "has shifted away from the loony Left and, still more important, has distanced himself from the self-consciously 'black' politicians" (SUNDAY

TELEGRAPH); anti-smoking; formerly GMB-sponsored;

History: Arrived back in the UK at 14 with his Scottish mother, after having to flee with her and his sister from Ghana after his Ghanaian Cabinet Minister father had been arrested in a military coup '66; his first affiliation, at 15, was to the Labour Party Young Socialists '66; at their conference moved an anti-racist motion '69; he became politically active in Lambeth; became legal adviser to "Scrap Sus Campaign", to end police right to stop and search young blacks on suspicion of theft or drugs '77; attended the World Festival of Youth in Cuba '78; at 29 was elected to the GLC for Walthamstow, becoming Chairman of its Police Committee (campaigned for "accountability of the Metropolitan Police") and Vice Chairman, of its Ethnic Minorities Committee May '81; backed Tony Benn for Deputy Leader Sep '81; was criticised by Rudy Narayan, another black civil rights lawyer, for his "irresponsible" and "relentless stream of anti-police propaganda" as an activist in the 'Scrap Sus Campaign' '81-82; was defeated in his effort to replace John Fraser as Labour candidate for Norwood by 33 to 10 Dec '81; wrote and presented a Radio 4 talk on Marcus Harvey and the Rastafarians, describing their view that addiction to marijuana was "an aid to meditation and reasoning whereby revelation may be obtained" Jan '82; sought to replace Sidney Bidwell in Southall '82; was unsuccessful in effort to be adopted for Islington South '82; with local hard-Left support, succeeded in ousting ex-MP Robin Corbett as Labour candidate for Hemel Hempstead July '82; at semi-Trotskyist LABOUR HERALD meeting complained he was the "focus of a witch-hunt" as Hemel's candidate Sep '82; survived appeal by Corbett's supporters to Labour's NEC over alleged vote manipulation Nov '82; opposed publication of racial origins of muggers Jan '83; chaired conference on 'Policing by Coercion' Jan '83; urged Metropolitan Police be brought under GLC control Jan '83; apologised after GLC Tories complained he had not disclosed he was representing Roach family when he secured grant to investigate how Roach died in a police station Feb '83; after intervention by Michael Foot, dropped £53,000 grant for 'Troops Out' movement Feb '83; said public confidence in police was breaking down Feb '83; came third with 22.3% of the vote for West Hertfordshire (ex: Hemel Hempstead), considered a Labour marginal, the worst loss of votes by a black Labour candidate June '83; at semi-Trotskyist LABOUR HERALD meeting warned that Left had to be sure "we are not betrayed in the future", insisting that the Left had to "have the guts to support all workers who have the guts to fight Thatcher" Oct '83; attacked Government's use of "draconian powers" to ban Stokely Carmichael/Kwame Ture Jan '84; complained that London police were the country's most expensive, with the lowest clear-up rate Feb '84; claimed the black community was abstaining from voting July '84; was accused by GLC Tories of "exorbitant" use of official cars Sep '84; his name was again put forward in Southall May '85; was selected by 31 votes to 12 for Brent South on retirement of Laurie Pavitt, without black sections involvement, defeating Sharon Atkin and Keith Vaz on an all-black shortlist for the seat with the highest proportion of non-whites in the country; was the first candidate of part-African origins to be selected for a safe seat June '85; the Methodist Conference attacked the SUNDAY TELEGRAPH for its "shameful" attack on Boateng and welcomed his contribution to Methodism June '85; failed to win the following year's Vice Presidency of the Methodist Conference as nominee of the Alliance of Radical Methodists July '85; was the lawyer representing Cherry Groce during trial of police inspector who shot her Jan '87; was one of four black Labour candidates who resisted the blandishments of black Trotskyists led by Sharon Atkin, insisting that "as Parliamentary candidates, our overriding interest is getting Labour into power" Apr '87; retained Brent South with a drop of 2,500 in majority, second only to Bernie Grant in loss of votes by a black Labour candidate; on his election-night said: "we can never be free in Brent until South Africa is free too; today Brent South, tomorrow Soweto!" June '87; co-urged rehabilitation of those purged in Soviet trials of late '30s June '87;

in his fiercely eloquent Maiden he accused Conservatives of treating the inner cities as "another country", "closing the shutters on housing in London" June '87; failed to turn up for first meeting of "black caucus" of black Labour MPs June '87; joined both soft-Left Tribune Group and hard-Left Campaign Group July '87; warned that Labour had to capture the imagination of the "children of Thatcherism" July '87; urged an end to all racial harassment July '87; with Bernie Grant complained of police saturation of All Saints Road area of Notting Hill in pursuit of drug dealing July '87; at Shelter conference in Nottingham infuriated the hard-Left when he "reserved the best polemic for attacks on direct labour organisations and those people in the housing campaign world who still behave as though the working class don't want their own homes" (NEW SOCIETY) Sep '87; addressed Amsterdam Conference on Racism in Europe, sponsored by International Alert Oct '87; spoke in Montreal on 'Nuremburg 40 Years On', sponsored by all-party War Crimes Group Nov '87; made keynote address to Bermuda Progressive Labour Party, at their invitation Nov '87; complained that blacks were over-represented in mental institutions Nov '87; was one of 43 MPs, mainly Campaign Groupies, voting for right of MPs to have any research assistants they wanted, including former Sinn Feiners Nov '87; in debate on South Africa, urged support for sanctions proposals of Commonwealth Eminent Persons Group and churches as offering "the last non-violent solution" Nov '87; attended Brussels executive meeting of European Commission on Human Rights in Syria, at their invitation Dec '87; as a prank, attended GLC pantomime shown on 'Newsnight' during which he pulled back his gown to reveal a bulging jockstrap; a blown-up photo was published in the NEWS OF THE WORLD Feb '88; did not attend Manchester conference of 'black sections', having cut off relations with them as "needlessly divisive" Mar '88; attended Lusaka-Harare conference on Sanctions and Developments in the Southern Africa Region, sponsored by Association of West European Parliamentarians Against Apartheid Mar '88; attended SANE/FREEZE conference in Atlanta and Washington on 'INF and Beyond' conference, also meeting Loretta Scott King and Jesse Jackson Apr '88; said: "there is something peculiarly unpleasant about the sight of Conservative Members in hot pursuit of those whom they would classify as the undeserving and intransigent poor" Apr '88; criticised Norman Tebbit for his "outrageous attack on the frontline states"; unsuccessfully urged Mrs Thatcher to disavow Norman Tebbit's speech to South African Club Apr '88; with Ken Livingstone, opposed merger of Brent and Paddington Health Authorities May '88; was attacked as a "pseudo bourgeois black" by Femi Assegai, wife of black activist Kuba Assegai, after she spearheaded expulsion from Brent 'Black Section' of Boateng's wife Jane, described as a "coconut" (brown on the outside but white inside) June '88; insisted that "the real divide in our society is between...those who have faith and those who have not" July '88; accused Home Secretary Kenneth Baker of sitting on a "volcano of pus which every now and again is bound to explode on the Conservative benches" for introducing more immigration controls July '88; voted against Prevention of Terrorism Bill, instead of abstaining Dec '88; attended Congressional Induction Course at Harvard School of Political Science, sponsored by Hanson Trust Dec '88; instead of abstaining, voted against loyalty oaths for Ulster councillors Dec '88; urged revision of leasing regulation to allow councils to enter into contracts for bed and breakfast accomodation Feb '89; was widely admired for "hugely entertaining and percipient speeches" (TIMES) against Water Bill Mar '89; made keynote speech to Barbados Bar Association Mar '89; observed and reported on UNTAG in Namibia and Zimbabwe for Associatiion of West European Parliamentarians Against Apartheid Apr '89; voted against a Press Commission in Right of Reply Bill Apr '89; addressed meeting on Namibia in Hague City Hall, sponsored by the Holland Committee on Africa Apr '89; addressed Council on Namibia, sponsored by Association of West European Parliamentarians Against Apartheid Apr '89; discussed Namibia and South Africa in Bonn, sponsored by Friederich Ebert Foundation June

'89; in immigration debate attacked as "vile and venomous" suggestion by Thurrock MP Tim Janman that "the birth of a black child in this country is somehow a cause of concern" June '89; attended Rome seminar on Environmental Impact of Air Transport, sponsored by Air Europe June '89; complained that managers of Thames Water were spending all their time on privatisation July '89; co-sponsored London Squares Preservation (Amendment) Bill of Dudley Fishburn Oct '89; spoke in Hamburg on 'Africa, Europe and 1992', sponsored by Africa Cultural Centre of Hamburg Nov '89; was promoted Assistant Spokesman on Treasury Affairs as fourth man on Labour's Economic Affairs team, and the first half-black on Labour's front bench Nov '89; visited Moscow as member of all-party monitoring group on the Helsinki Accords sponsored y the Student Campaign for Soviet Jewry Feb '90; urged increased tax allowances for provision of nursery places May '90; voted with 30 other anti-smokers for a clause banning smoking in public areas May '90; attended Anglo-Polish Seminar on Marine Insurance in Gdansk, sponsored by Mediterranean Average Adjusting Company of London Oct '90; defended Lloyd's as "a major international institution that is widely respected and...needs support and encouragement at this time"; hinted at support for calls for Lloyd's members to be treated as companies so that they could offset trading losses against capital gains, without giving them special treatment June '91; welcomed Justice Bingham's appointment to head BCCI inquiry July '91; promised Labour would bring in a statutory banking code July '91; was replaced by hard-Left extrovert Tony Banks on BBC TV's 'Behind the Headlines' programme for having become too moderate, after seeming to defend Lloyd's 'names' who had fallen on hard times Oct '91; visited South Africa with John Morris to assess human rights there Oct '91; reaffirmed Labour's intention of maintaining London's position as the financial hub of Europe Nov '91; was in the running for "Class Traitor of the Year" contest run by his former Trotskyist friends on LONDON LABOUR BRIEFING Nov '91; described banks' 'code of practice' as too little, too late Dec '91; attacked the Asylum Bill as "a squalid, unworthy Bill; it is discriminatory both in its intent and in its effect" Jan '92; retained seat with majority up from 7,931 to 9,705, a swing to Labour of 3.77% Apr '92; backed Margaret Beckett for Deputy Leader Apr '92; complained about inadequate supervision of financial services which had resulted in "wholly unsuitable home income plans"; urged strengthening of IMRO so that it could avoid its failures, as in the Maxwell pensions case July '92; was named Spokesman on Lord Chancellor's Department by new Leader, John Smith, the first half-black to achieve this July '92; received 18,000 votes for constituency section of Labour's NEC Sep '92; visited South Africa to attend Britain-South Africa Conference, as its guest Sep '92; suggested that if Norman Lamont needed legal help at public expense to curb press excesses about his sado-masochist lady tenant, "then there are considerably cheaper solicitors he might go to", instead of Peter Carter-Ruck Oct '92; co-deplored overturning of elected Haitian government Oct '92; warned Lord Chancellor against denying legal aid to divorcees until they submitted to conciliation Nov '92; addressed a lobby of protesters against Asylum Bill Nov '92; spoke in defence of Camden's law centres Nov '92; complained that Lord Mackay's Court Charter represented a "missed opportunity" Nov '92; complained about elderly, out-of-touch judges Dec '92; urged a judicial appointments commission and contributory pensions for judges Dec '92; was thought to be at risk from activities of Boundary Commission Dec '92; complained that the increase in the number of judges appointed to the Court of Appeal was inadequate Feb '93; described failure to appoint younger judges as a "missed opportunity" Feb '93; contributed to book of essays on Christian socialism, Reclaiming the Ground Mar '93; opposed new legal aid restrictions Mar '93; attended Swedish seminar on EC and South Africa, as guest of Association of Western European Parliamentarians for Southern Africa May '93; attended conference on Development and Democratisation - European South African Partnership, as guest of Association of Western European Parliamentarians for Southern

Africa Oct '93; asked, was it "not worrying that one day last month 24 courts in the southeast of England were closed for want of work?" Nov '93; unwittingly helped speed payments to claimants fraudster Dec '93; voted against restoring capital punishment, even for killers of policemen Feb '94; voted to reduce age of homosexual consent to 18 or 16, Feb '94; he backed Blair to succeed deceased John Smith June '94; voted for Blair for Leader, Beckett for Deputy July '94; he helped "fast-track" the Law of Property (Miscellaneous Provisions) Bill, based on Law Commission recommendations Oct '94; he was confirmed as Commons deputy to the 'shadow Lord Chancellor' in Tony Blair's first Shadow Cabinet reshuffle Oct '94; backed the Blair-sought revision of Clause IV Dec '94; when he decided to send his 9-year-old son Ben to Hampstead's Devonshire House, a £4.500-a-year prep school, the NEW STATESMAN suggested Labour replace 'The Red Flag' with 'The Eton Boateng Song' Jan '95; in a debate with Tony Benn, pointed out that Labour could do nothing unless it became electable by supporting a mixed econmy Feb '95; he was the chief architect of Labour's final, toned-down document on the legal profession, including new ways of making judges more representative; "monitoring of judges' performance was one of the recommendations of the Royal Commission and we are going to introduce it" he said July '95; urged the scrapping of the legal aid's green form, exploited by unscrupulous solicitors Aug '95; Labour's law reforms, proposed by him for its manifesto, were sharply criticised by John Morris QC, the 'Shadow Attorney General', including its abandonment of a plan for a new Minister of Justice to replace the Lord Chancellor Aug '95; Boateng was retained as the Commons deputy to the Lord Chancellor in the Labour Shadow Cabinet reshuffle Oct '95; attacked the "scandalous" situation in Tory-captured Brent, demanding an immediate audit Dec '95; urged Tory party Chairman Dr Brian Mawhinney to investigate "incompetent" sleaze-ridden Conservative-controlled Brent Council Feb '96; initially played an emollient role on the Tory Government's Family Law Bill, recalling his early days as an articled clerk: "there is not an estate sin south London around which I have not been chased by a wife batterer or partner"; "we want the scourge of domestic violence...dealt with in this Bill" Mar '96; was said to feel that too many concessions on the Family Law Bill had been made to the Tory "moral majoritarians"; described the Bill as a "legislative Frankenstein" May '96; urged a joint committee of both Houses of Parliament to discuss allowing Parliamentarians to sue the media May '96; complained about the Government's rushing through a clause to modify the 300-year-old Bill of Rights to enable Tory MP Neil Hamilton to sue The GUARDIAN June '96; urged an amendment to the Family Law Bill to improve the handling of domestic violence; also claimed a "tremendous victory" over pension-splitting in the Bill June '96; having secured a last-minute concession on split pensions - and having had the riot act read to him by Tony Blair - agreed to back the Family Law Bill July '96; voted against a 3% limit on MPs' pay raise July '96; retained his place as Lord Chancellor's Commons deputy in Tony Blair's 'final' pre-election Shadow Cabinet reshuffle Aug '96; promised a Labour Lord Chancellor would reform the legal aid system, perhaps barring criminals from benefiting Jan '97; was criticised by his former partner Benedict Birnberg for attacking lawyers who had "hijqcked" the legal aid system: "as someone whose careeer has been built upon legally-aided criminal defence work, he of all people know that there are no legal aid fat cats; and as one who made his political reputation opposing the old "sus" laws, he is the last person one would expect to come up with a superficial judicial "lifestyle" test for mulcting the allegedly ill-gotten gains of convicted criminals to pay for their defence, let alone mouthing the mantra of 'zero tolerance'" Jan '97; despite his large family, was targeted by the Prolife Alliance Party Feb '97; criticised the Labour pledge not to increase income tax, saying resources were needed for better housing to save marriages Feb '97; again won slightly altered Brent South, this time with a doubled majority of 19,691, a swing of 15.3% May '97; although expected to become Parliamentary

Secretary to the Lord Chancellor, was unexpectedly named Under Secretary for Social Care and Mental Health, with Geoff Hoon being given the job of underpinning Lord Irvine, whom he had long been assisting May '97; a letter to the GUARDIAN chided the paper for ignoring his appointment "as the first black minister of Her Majesty's Government" May '97; launched an inquiry into Broadmoor-type hospitals for the criminally insane June '97; pledged change in law which allowed children to be placed in homes controlled by convicted child offenders July '97; he froze the closure of psychiatric hospitals to ensure that substitute community care facilities were adequate Sep '97; he spoke about fears prevailing in the black community about their more frequent commitment for psychiatric care Sep '97;

Born: 14 June 1951, Hackney

Family: His Scottish grandfather's name was Robert Wallace Burns McCombie; son of Kwaku Boateng, barrister and Christian evangelist, and formerly imprisoned as an ex-Cabinet Minister in Kwame Nkruma's Government in Ghana '61-66, and his Scottish wife, Eleanor (McCombie), Quaker teacher and granddaughter of an LCC Councillor, daughter of a self-educated trade unionist and "life-long socialist" (PB); his father, on release from prison, remained in Accra, while his mother remained in UK, without divorcing; his sister, Rosemary, formerly a teacher in South London, has recently worked for BBC-TV's African and Caribbean unit in Birmingham; m '80 Janet (Alleyne), a "ravishing", "real Evita in the making" (Julie Burchill, MAIL ON SUNDAY), controversial young black social worker and Lambeth Borough Councillor (former Chairman of its Social Services Committee); 2s Benjamin '84, Seth '87; 4d Mirabelle '80, Beth '82, Charlotte '83; ???? '8?; a number have had private educations; one daughter at Watford Grammar School for Girls, an opted-out school, a son to Devonshire House prep school;

Education: Ghana International School; Accra Academy; Apsley Grammar School, Hemel Hempstead (head boy); Bristol University (LLB); College of Law; Grays Inn;

Occupation: Barrister, Grays Inn '89-; Director (unpaid): English National Opera Company '90-, Cities in Schools Ltd (registered charity) '91-; formerly Sponsored: by GMB (£600 p a to his constituency and 80% of election expenses) '90-95; ex: Solicitor: Partner in B N Birnberg and Co '79-87; Paddington Law Centre '76-79; had earlier stint with Birnberg ("the great radical lawyer of the 1960s and 1970s" [PB]) '76;

Traits: Slight; cafe-au-lait complexion ("the Sydney Poitier of the party" - Julie Burchill, MAIL ON SUNDAY); "the prissy, smart-Alec tones of the middle-class revolutionary" (Cross-Bencher, SUNDAY EXPRESS); "always a snappy dresser", his formerly "rare appearances in the Chamber seem[ed] mainly for the purpose of presenting his new initiatives in designer clothing for the approval of the House" (Craig Brown, TIMES); went through a "Terence Trent d'Arby phase, wearing baggy, Paul-Smith-type suits and styling his hair in a '50s coif" (SUNDAY EXPRESS); by '91 was wearing a Berwin wool suit "in trendy olive, spiked with a purple stripe" (DAILY TELEGRAPH); vivid phrase-maker; "there is a wonderful arrogance about him; he doesn't feel inferior to anybody" (Darcus Howe); "personable, enthusiastic, humorous and is not embarrassed to confess that he enjoys politics" (Joe Joseph, TIMES); "sharp-witted, urbane and smooth" (SCOTSMAN); flexible speaker, capable of being mild as a Methodist, cliche-ridden as a delegate, or paranoid Trotskyist at meetings of LABOUR HERALD (now defunct); "blessed with the fluency, opportunism and charm essential for the career activist" (SUNDAY TIMES); self-dramatising; exhibitionist (he was featured in the NEWS OF THE WORLD after appearing at a GLC pantomime in a jockstrap and judge's gown); opera buff (on English National Opera board); Methodist lay preacher (delegate to World Conference of Churches '85, Vice Moderator of their programme to combat racism '84-); likes to eat in Christopher's, B Smith's, Le Palace du Jardin or Bright Rising Star;

Address: House of Commons, Westminster, London SW1A 0AA;
Telephone: 0171 219 5112/6816 (H of C); 0171 403 3166 (office);

Sir Richard (Bernard Frank Stewart) BODY   Conservative   **BOSTON and SKEGNESS '97-**

Majority: 647 (1.4%) over Labour 3-way;
Description: A new, largely agricultural seat apart from the seaside town of Skegness; two-thirds comes from his former Holland with Boston, one-third from abolished East Lindsey;
Former Seat: Holland   with   Boston   '66-97, Billericay '55-59;
Position: On Select Committee on Consolidation of Bills '79-; Chairman: all-party Humane Research Group, all-party Trade Group; Secretary, all-party ANZAC Group '83-; President, Cobden Club '81-; Vice President: Small Farmers' Association '85-, Selsdon Group; ex: Chairman: Select Committee on Agriculture (member '79-87) '86-87, 'Get Britain Out'
'75; Vice Chairman, Conservative MPs' Horticulture Subcommittee '70, its Secretary '66-70; Secretary: Conservative MPs' Trade Committee '70-71, Home Affairs Committee '57-59; on Liaison Committee '86-87;
Outlook: An obsessive and stubborn rebel, but not "barmy" as claimed by John Major: an irreconcilable anti-Marketeer and CAP critic since '71; has long campaigned against factory farming, formerly as 'Old Muckspreader' in PRIVATE EYE ; "the scourge of big farmers and the National Farmers' Union (Richard Ford, TIMES); has several causes as a Rightwing nationalist, monetarist, free trader and believer in less-intensive, traditional farming; his "Quaker conscience revolts against modern on-the-make Toryism" (David Ward, GUARDIAN); has "spared no effort turning in a near-faultless performance as a constituency MP" (Patricia Wynn Davies, INDEPENDENT); "he is a principled, at times obsessive and terrifically obstinate man...I do know that Richard Body has often turned out to be right" (Matthew Parris, TIMES); "notoriously maverick" (Martin Fletcher, TIMES); anti: EC/EU (Chairman Open Seas Forum '70-), nuclear weapons, farm subsidies (especially to big farmers), fluoridation, farm chemicals, corruption (shopped a fellow Tory he suspected of being in league with a Mafia gambling boss); pro: organic farming, old breeds of pigs and cattle, animal welfare; "a backbencher after my own heart" (late Lord Bruce-Gardyne); "a proper Englishman", "not mealy-mouthed...not afraid to go over the top...a hero to those who hate modern agriculture" (Richard North, INDEPENDENT);
History: Founded one of first Young Conservative branches '45; contested: Rotherham Jan '50, Abertillery by-election Dec '50, Leek Oct '51; was elected for Billericay Oct '55; urged UK to be at the Messina Conference where the Treaty of Rome was signed '56; said local authority children's officers seldom seemed anxious to release children from homes Feb '58; voted against Tory government's Children's Bill July '58; suggested corruption in Basildon New Town Dec '58; "to my shame" wrote a pamphlet advocating guaranteed prices, government subsidies and import levies to provide farmers with security '66; introduced Bill to secure humane conditions for animals, backed by Anti-Vivisection Society Feb '67; claimed barristers were "pretty slap-happy" when handling divorce suits June '67; introduced Bill to forbid animal

experiments without anaesthetic Jan '68; said incomes policy was "unnecessary, unworkable and unjust" Feb '68; introduced Bill to compel giving market value for land acquired compulsorily Apr '68; complained of ponies being shipped for slaughter to Holland Feb '69; his Bill to enforce reasonable alternative to vivisection was passed June '71; voted against entering EEC Oct '71; warned of "long term dangers" of EEC entry Feb '72; promised to ignore wage freeze Nov '72; worried about the impact of the EEC on West Indian cane sugar; said Heath's prices and incomes policy was doomed to failure Jan '73; claimed people were eating less meat than under wartime rationing Mar '73; agreed with Enoch Powell's doubts about Edward Heath's "mental and emotional stability" Dec '73; urged probe of whether CIA was backing European Movement May '75; got out of beef-farming "becuse I realised that there were considerable dangers in [feeding] compounds" because British feed manufacturers resorted to includfing offal, in competition with French suppliers '75; urged end of all farm subsidies Jan '76; suggested higher tax on sex films Nov '76; opposed aerial sprays Jan '80; claimed living standards were declining because of transfer of resources to EEC July '80; opposed dumping of sugar Aug '82; claimed that consumers had been milked for farmers to tune of £40,000,000m between '46 and '82, Dec '82; in FREE NATION complained that British people had lost right to opt for cheaper agricultural imports Oct '83; voted against Government on European Budget Dec '83; accused City syndicates of turning forests into tax havens Feb '84; backed right of Rugby Union to tour South Africa Feb '84; in RAMBLER urged "getting agriculture down to a lower gear" to avoid destruction of landscape and wildlife in pursuit of food self-sufficiency Apr '84; complained of cheap export of EEC wine to USSR May '84; voted to toughen voting provisions in Trade Union Bill July '84; urged better treatment of farmworkers July '84; voted against Stansted expansion Jan '85; voted against fluoridation Jan '85; was one of 10 Tory MPs who voted against Government on supplementary payment to EEC Jan '85; disclosed that the UK's 10,000 largest farmers took half the agricultural subsidy Mar '85; co-sponsored briefing by British Psychological Society on devastating psychological effects of nuclear war Mar '85; deplored insufficient availability of information on health impact of pesticides June '85; was one of 16 Tories voting against increased contributions to EEC Oct '85; was only Tory MP initially to back Freeze (on nuclear weapons) campaign Nov '85; found Michael Heseltine's Westland behaviour "unedifying" Jan '86; went on Loyalist march in South Down in support of Enoch Powell at by-election Jan '86; voted against extra payment to EEC budget Feb '86; on death of John Spence, was elected Chairman of Agriculture Select Committee over Government opposition Mar '86; was alleged to be the anonymous source for libellous attack in PRIVATE EYE on fellow Tory MP and childhood neighbour, Sir Frederick Bennett Mar '86; voted against Government on Shops Bill to free Sunday trading Apr '86; in radio interview accused Government of being caught off guard on risks to agriculture from Chernobyl fallout May '86; co-signed Nuclear Freeze anniversary letter Nov '86; accused NFU and farm chemical companies of massive cover-up on nitrate pollution of drinking water Nov '86; attacked as "mistaken" the decision of fellow Quakers to refuse to pay taxes for defence May '87; he attacked MAFF handling of "golden helmshake" for small fishermen May '87; increased his majority by 6,000 through fall in Liberal vote June '87; criticized use of dangerous artificial dye in expensive salmon July '87; produced final report as Chairman of Agriculture Select Committee which censured the pesticides industry and MAFF about secrecy surrounding health hazards, despite opposition of most Tory MPs on it July '87; co-sponsored the Environment and Safety Information Bill launched by Labour MP Chris Smith and the Friends of the Earth Oct '87; was one of 12 Tory MPs who voted against Government Bill to give local authorities the power to withhold contracts from companies which discriminated on grounds of race Dec '87; voted against a three-line whip in support of Richard Shepherd's attempted reform of the Official Secrets Act Jan '88; opposed charges on eye and teeth tests Apr '88; again voted against money for EC July '88; again voted against money for EC Oct '88; was one of 18 Tory MPs who voted for amendment to Official Secrets Bill to allow public interest defence for 'whistleblowers' Feb '89; co-sponsored anti-EC motion July 89; voted against War Crimes Bill to try elderly immigrants from the Baltic Dec '89; co-sponsored anti-EC motion on butter dumping Dec '89; voted for Teresa Gorman's Bill to repeal Rent Acts Jan '90; backed providing Australia with one of the two originals of their Constitutional Act Feb '90; co-sponsored anti-EC motion July '90; voted against joining ERM with ten other Tory MPs Oct '90; was one of 44 Tory MPs who voted against Government on dog registration Oct '90; again urged less pesticides and more organic farming Oct '90; his Welfare of Animals at Slaughter was presented Dec '90; voted for Jonathan Aitken's anti-EC amendment Dec '90; his Pig Husbandry Bill to outlaw the use of pig stalls and tethers within five years received an unopposed 2nd Reading Jan '91; addressing the annual conference of Country Landowners Association, opposed guaranteed prices and pesticides and CAP Feb '91; again opposed War Crimes Bill Mar '91; backed motion calling for resignation of Lord Chief Justice Lord Lane for refusing to free 'Birmingham Six' Mar '91; withdrew his Pig Husbandry Bill and then withdrew his withdrawal, to wash out hostile amendments by Edwina Currie, John Townend and Richard Holt Apr-May '91; ceased being a Vice President of Natonal Anti-Vivisection Society May '91; blamed CAP's guaranteed prices for rapid decline of British agriculture July '91; co-sponsored Jonathan Aitken's motion to "consider the development of a more meaningful relationship with the EC which would preserve essential national sovereignty" Dec '91; opposed the Wild Animals (Protection) Bill, saying "I would never permit the shooting of foxes" because too few were killed cleanly; he favoured the use of hounds as the most humane means Feb '92; opposed voting £450m for European Commission because the "Community has illegally spent that sum of money; it therefore follows that we are seeking to condone something that is illegal" Feb '92; was one of 25 Tory rebels who supported a referendum before Maastricht treaty took effect Feb '92; retained seat with majority down from 17,595 to 13,831, a swing to Labour of 5.59% Apr '92; was one of 12 'conspirators' to meet to plot their anti-Maastricht campaign at the Carlton Club May '92; was one of 22 Tory MPs who voted against 2nd Reading of Maastricht ratification May '92; the first Tory MP to visit Denmark to back the 'nej' campaign, backed "fresh start" motion to renegotiate Maastricht after Danish referendum rejection June '92; urged a "fair" referendum on Maastricht for UK June '92; introduced mock motion celebrating 50th anniversary of the Nazi effort to make "the Reichsmark the single currency of Europe" July '92; celebrating departure from ERM, backed motion to keep UK out of ERM after 'black Wednesday' Sep '92; urged Government to express "contrition and compassion" on mines closures, adding: "I did not join the Conservative Party to see this sort of behaviour"; abstained on Government's three-month moratorium on closures Oct '92; was one of 26 Tory MPs who voted against Government on paving debate on Maastricht treaty ratification Nov '92; visited Gibraltar, at invitation of its government Jan '93; filibustered on Maastricht ratification Jan '93; introduced Gangmaster Bill to require their licensing Mar '93; voted with Labour to curb debate on Maastricht ratification Mar '93; was one of 26 Tory rebels who defeated Government in requiring Government to choose members of EC Committee of the Regions from elected local councillors Mar '93; on a misunderstanding, initially co-sponsored Tony Benn's motion criticising Deputy Speaker Michael Morris for not allowing Labour's Amendment 27 on Social Chapter to be debated Apr '93; abstained from supporting pro-Maastricht Tory candidate, Julian Davidson, in by-election in Newbury, where Body lived Apr '93; introduced Bill to prohibit sale at auction markets of lambs under 28 days of age Apr '93; was reported to Speaker by pro-Maastricht fellow Tory MP, Keith Hampson, for sending out anti-Maastricht propaganda on Commons writing paper May '93; filibustered on Maastricht treaty ratification, twitting SNP on its deal on EC Committee of the Regions May '93; voted against 3rd Reading of Maastricht Bill May '93; was recorded as having rebelled 30 times against the Bill, absented himself 28 times and supported the Government 4 times by May '93; after suffering big losses himself, said a "clear majority" of his Lloyd's colleagues now believed it should be brought within the City's regulatory system June '93; was one of 15 Tory MPs who voted against Government on Social Chapter July '93; during PM's Japan visit, Major said: "when I hear the name of Richard Body, I hear the sound of white coats flapping" Sep '93; incensed by Major's sneer, was said to be considering resigning his seat to write books - thus forcing an unwanted by-election Oct '93; was dissuaded from resigning saying he would stay on for a further year at least; "I am very fond of my constituents; I don't know if I want to be a nuisance to them by causing a by-election" Nov '93; said he was being urged to stand for the European Parliament Jan '94; claimed the House [of Commons] was deceived by Lloyd's when we considered the Lloyd's Bill" to make it think outside regulation was unnecessary; "we were deceived factually" Jan '94; the Commons Register of Members' Interests was published without his giving the numbers of his Lloyd's syndicates, as requested Jan '94; voted to reduce age of homosexual consent to 18, Feb '94; "after 20 years at the criminal bar", congratulated Labour MP Chris Mullin for urging an independent body to review possible judicial injustices: "over the past two decades there have been far too many injustices that have not been put right by the Court of Appeal because of its procedures and various inhibitions" May '94; he was one of 11 Tory MPs, all Lloyd's 'names' cited by the Select Committee on Members' Interests for being in breach of the rule that they had to disclose their Lloyd's syndicates June '94; resigned the Tory Whip before eight anti-federalist collagues lost theirs over refusing to vote to increase UK's contribution to the EU Nov '94; with other Whipless rebels backed trawlermen campaigning against the EU's Common Fisheries Policy; also urged UK's withdrawal from the CFP Jan '95; backed motion against European single currency Feb '95; with three other unWhipped rebels, voted with Government on Maastricht, when other five abstained Mar '95; was selected by the new Boston and Skegness Conservative Association Oct '95; resumed the Tory Whip after 14 months, just after Emma Nicholson left for the LibDems, leaving the Tories with a majority of only three Jan '96; said Brussels should pay for UK beef slaughtered in BSE-control programme Mar '96; backed a Referendum on any federalist move, including a single European currency June '96; opposed spending public money on agricultural research to increase output even further June '96; voted against 3% cap on MPs' pay rises, in favour of a £43,000 base for pensions July '96; with other formerly unWhipped rebels, formed Conservatives Against Federal Europe (CAFE) on eve of Tory conference Sep '96; was one of the 30 Tory rebels on Michal Howard's Firearms (Amendment) Bill, even after Howard doubled compensation for handguns handed in Nov '96; accused Labour Spokesman Gavin Strang of "humbug" for criticising Tory fisheries policy when the Labour Government had failed to veto the Common Fisheries Policy in 1976; he voted with the Tory Government Dec '96; was unanimously selected for the new seat of Boston and Skegness while still Whipless, the first time this ever happened; told the DAILY TELEGRAPH he would oppose ever entering a single European currency Dec '96; co-sponsored Teresa Gorman's UK Membership of the European Union (Referendum) Bill Jan '97; voted to dis-assemble target guns rather than ban them Feb '97; announced he would stand as a "Conservative Against a Federal Europe" Apr '97; narrowly retained his new seat of Boston and Skegness, made up two-thirds of his old Holland with Boston seat; held it with a majority of 647 votes, on a pro-Labour swing of 10.8% May '97; worried about new-style gangmasters organising casual agricultural workers in South Lincolnshire, many of whom had criminal records and were responsible for massive fraud May '97; supported Michael Howard for Tory Leader, then Kenneth Clarke June '97; as a "master of a pack of drag hounds" for 25 years, did not think that they could be expanded enough to replace fox-hunting, as desired by the backers of the anti-foxhunting Wild Mammals Bill; "the drag hounds hunt just one day a week; the packs of fox hounds always two or three days a week, over a slightly longer season, giving a ratio . of 1:20"; drag-hunting had to be on grassland: "over the past 25 years, I have never been able to persuade a farmer to allow 30 or 40 horses to gallop over his precious winter wheat"; shooting foxes was also not a substitute because most of those wounded died horribly of gangrene Nov '97; his publication WORLD REVIEW was threatened with closure Apr '98; was one of 18 Tory MPs who backed 16 as age of homosexual consent June '98;

Born: 18 May 1927, Berkshire

Family: His family has been in Berkshire since the Civil War; "proud of being a kinsman of Jethro Tull", agricultural inventor (SUNDAY TELEGRAPH); son. Lt Col Bernard Richard Body and Daphne (Corbett); m '59 Marion (Graham); 1s Bernard Richard '62; 1d Jane Marion '60;

Education: Reading School; Middle Temple;

Occupation: Barrister '49-, retired '70; Underwriter in six Lloyd's syndicates, from which he has suffered heavily '79-; Editor, World Review '96-; Author: The Breakdown of Europe (1997), Our Food, Our Land (1991), Europe of Many Circles (1990), Red or Green for Farmers (1987), Farming in the Clouds (1984), Agriculture: The Triumph and the Shame (1982), Freedom and Stability in the World Economy (1976), The Architect and the Law (1954), Destiny or Delusion (contributor; 1951); Columnist (reputedly the original "Old Muckspreader" in PRIVATE EYE) '86; Director and Shareholder: New European Publications Ltd '86-; ex: Farmer/Stockbreeder, at Pound Green Farm, Grazeley, Berkshire, now mostly let but where his wife raised Old English Longhorns until '91; was Livestock Judge in Royal Show '83; he used to raise prize pigs '60-75: "starting with Saddlebacks...he went on to Large Whites and later experimented with Berkshires" which he exported to numerous countries abroad (Duff Hart-Davis, COUNTRY LIVING);

Traits: "Tall and slightly stooped, with a rumpled face strongly reminiscent of the gentle [bloodhound] giants that loll about his farmyard, he is also highly articulate, both in speech and on paper; and although he believes passionately in the causes for which he campaigns, he has a disarming habit of exploding with laughter at his own tendency to launch into speeches in the course of ordinary conversation" (Duff Hart-Davis, COUNTRY LIVING); twinkling eye; crooked smile; hunched; sharp; enjoys polemics; erratic; Quaker; failing eyesight (no longer drives); "courtly" (DAILY MAIL); "has bred and kept hounds for 20 years and his favourite recreation is to lay a trail for them himself or to hunt them at his wife Maron or any other volunteers willing to act as quarry; 'it's a sort of madness, I suppose,' he says cheerfully, 'but a harmless one'" (Duff Hart-Davis, COUNTRY LIVING); "I am the only Member present who has been a master of drag hounds that hunted human quarry" (RB);

Address: House of Commons, Westminster, London SW1A 0AA; Jewells House, Stanford Dingley, nr Reading RG7 6LX;

Telephone: 0171 219 4100/6498 (H of C); 01734 744 295;

With all the destabilizing constituency changes, we think it necessary to try to have accurate seat descriptions. Some newspapers (like the SCOTSMAN and GLASGOW HERALD), some MPs, and especially The Almanac of British Politics by Robert Waller and Byron Criddle (Routledge), have been particularly helpful.

Rt Hon Betty BOOTHROYD   Labour   **WEST BROMWICH WEST '74 (Feb)-**

Majority: 15,423 (42%) over Labour Change 3-way;
Description: Old Black Country engineering and metalworking seat, five miles from Birmingham; a study in urban blight and industrial smells; expanded in '95 to embrace Tory-leaning Oldbury and Tividale from splintered Warley West;
Former Seat: West Bromwich '73-74 (Feb);
Position: Speaker '92-; Chairman, of House of Commons Commission '92-; on: Executive Committee, Commonwealth Parliamentary Association '74-; Chancellor, of Open University '94-; ex: Third Deputy Speaker (Second Deputy Chairman of Ways and Means) '87-92; on Labour's NEC (Women's Section) '81-87; Chairman's Panel '79-87; House of Commons Commission '83-87; Assistant Whip '74-75; on Select Committees on: Foreign Affairs '79-81, Public Accounts '78, Broadcasting '78, Abortion '76-77, European Assembly '75-77; Vice Chairman, British-Sri Lanka Parliamentary Group '78-87; Hammersmith Borough Councillor '65-68;

Outlook: Britain's very able first lady Speaker, battling against Blairite 'reforms' which she fears might downgrade the Commons; "she combines the glamour of a diva, the bearing of a kindergarten head and the lip of a barmaid"; "she combines a quick mind, an experienced chairman's judgement and an artful femininity in a most judicious blend" (Matthew Parris, TIMES); "has proved herself a formidable presence" (EVENING STANDARD), deploying her "wit, authority and commonsense" (GUARDIAN); was at one time besieged by both the KGB and MI5; a middlebrow, pro-EC Labour Rightwinger rooted in the northern industrial working class; an excellent constituency MP; "I am a tremendous loyalist and always believe you have got to support a Leader" (BB); "has never been, or even promised to be, a leading political figure; she is more a doughty fighter than a leader: intelligent and well-informed rather than intellectual"; "is popular with all but the most ideological on both the Labour and Tory benches" (Peter Riddell, TIMES); "is agreed to have shown admirable decisiveness" (EVENING STANDARD) on Maastricht; but let Michael Mates off after repeated warnings; "she has a clean, short-lived anger, a lot of good humour and a brisk generosity" (Edward Pearce, NEW STATESMAN); "she is a showman, the job doesn't embarrass her, and she is as hard as nails" (senior Tory MP); "a velvet fist concealed in an iron glove" (Andrew Rawnsley, GUARDIAN): has imposed stricter discipline on Commons ("Betty is so strict she won't call you unless you've been there from the start of the session"); uses a simulated yawn to shorten long-winded speeches and has taken to concluding the PM's question time with the barmaid-like catchphrase, "time's up!"; formerly GMB-sponsored darling of union bosses on the NEC; Militant-basher, price-controller, abortion-backer, job-promoter; an "uncompromising Rightwinger" (GUARDIAN); "a hammer of the Left who comes gift-wrapped and smelling of roses compared to the terrible Edith Summerskill" (Alan Watkins, OBSERVER);

History: "I always say I came out of the womb into the Labour movement"; "my parents were both trades unionists and our home was given over to meetings, to commmittee rooms, to elections"; "if you were born among those 'satanic mills', then you have to want to bring about change, to improve the quality of life for people living in that kind of environment"; joined Labour League of Youth at 16, '45; rose to its National Consultative Committee;

Copyright (C)Parliamentary Profile Services Ltd

contested Dewsbury Borough Council at 21, '50; visited USSR, China and Vietnam with Labour MPs '57; was elected to Hammersmith Borough Council May '65; contested: Leicester SE by-election Nov '57, Peterborough Oct '59; she told MI5 that a KGBman, Anatoli Strelnikov was inviting her out and urging her to spy on the Labour Party; when she refused to spy on four Leftwing Labour MPs for MI5, its chief Sir Roger Hollis informed PM Harold Wilson that she was having an affair with Strelnikov and had her banned on security grounds form the Foreign Office, where here employer Lord Walston was Minister of State '64-65; she lost: Silverman-held Nelson and Colne at by-election June '68, Rossendale (after nosing out ex-MP Trevor Park) June '70: urged more flexible youth training Oct '72; was elected for West Bromwich May '73; was appointed Assistant Whip for West Midlands, with Chief Whip Bob Mellish telling her, "keep your trap shut, girl, and you will get on" Oct '74; an early pro-Marketeer, supported joining Socialist group in European Assembly when anti-Marketeers wished to remain isolated June '75; resigned as Assistant Whip to concentrate on European Assembly Nov '75; resigned from Abortion (Amendment) Bill Select Committee to avoid watering down 1967 Abortion Act Jan '77; was on Rightwing slate for NEC July '77; voted against devolution Jan '78; complained about rise in whisky prices Jan '78; urged bulldozing of "eyesores around the Black Country" May '78; urged Labour to have a radical policy without getting "too far ahead of public opinion"; urged a society organized on the basis of consumer democracy Mar '80; said import controls had to be considered June '80; backed preference for UK-made products Nov '80; was promoted to NEC on defection to SDP of Shirley Williams Feb '81; her re-selection on short-list of one -excluding a Leftwing rival - was rejected by NEC's Organization Subcommittee May '81; was again re-selected June '81; protested threat to close gas showrooms June '81; urged inquiry into leap-frogging petrol prices Aug '81; voted against unilateralism on NEC July '81; backed Denis Healey for Deputy Leader against Tony Benn Sep '81; became member of NEC's Organization Subcommittee Oct '81; was in minority urging investigation by NEC of Militant Tendency Nov '81; voted against endorsing Trotskyist Pat Wall as Labour candidate Feb '82; introduced private Bill to control prices Feb '82; on NEC voted against allowing Militant to affiliate to Labour Party Dec '82; accised Dr Gerald Vaughan of "a grave injustice" in attacking Joan Ruddock, then head of Reading's Citizens' Advice Bureau, because "the demand for advice and guidance is greatly increasing" because of the "strains of unemployment and financial hardship" Apr '83; said selection of Michael Foot had been a "disaster" and that new Leader, Neil Kinnock, must rid party of "headbangers...and extremists and Militants" June '83; came first in women's section of NEC with 4.8m votes Oct '83; said "every male chauvinist was some woman's son" Dec '83; was on Leftwing hitlist Apr '84; on NEC voted for expulsion of 'Blackburn Six' Militants May '84; tried to have re-selection of MPs by whole membership July '84; replying to conference for NEC, urged right of reply to all press distortions Oct '84; on NEC voted for Neville Hough, not Dennis Skinner, as Vice Chairman Oct '84; backed Neil Kinnock's castigation of Tony Benn and Eric Heffer for forcing suspension of Commons on miners' strike Jan '85; was re-selected unopposed by 36 to one Apr '85; had adjournment debate on need to include local Smith Houses in Housing Defects Act June '85; on NEC voted against Eric Heffer's compromise proposal that ethnic minorities be allowed to form affiliated groups with representation on NEC July '85; succeeded in getting Government to include Smith Houses in Housing Defects Act Nov '85; was on NEC inquiry into Liverpool Militants Dec '85; led constituency delegation to Environment Secretary over mining subsidence Feb '86; refused to participate in shadow elections for NEC by Labour Women's Conference, in effort to see who would be elected without union block votes Apr '86; urged local council to investigate "phantom tenants" fiddle Jan '87; had adjournment debate on West German barriers to constituency electrical exports Feb '87; on NEC voted against black sections Mar '87; denied buying 800

BT shares, saying her goddaughter had bought them with money she provided Mar '87; was re-selected Apr '89; favoured dog registration May '89; was re-elected with 1,000-vote drop in majority, but still over 50% of the vote June '87; was voted a Deputy Speaker - the second Labour MP and second woman - by acclamation July '87; when a Member asked her how she wanted to be addressed, she replied: "Call me Madam!" July '87; consequently did not stand for Women's Section of NEC Sep '87; was supported by Speaker in disputed decision Nov '88; three Liberal Democrats stormed out when she insisted on 10-minute limits on speeches Dec '88; insisted on being called "Madam Deputy Speaker" July '89; a plan to block her promotion to Speaker was launched by 'top Tories', one of whom claimed: "Betty Boothroyd is far too partisan in the chair and frankly is loathed by the Conservative Party" (MAIL ON SUNDAY) July '89; she was again mentioned as a possible candidate for Speaker, the other Labour possible being Harold Walker Mar '91; retained seat with majority up from 5,253 to 7,830, a swing to Labour of 2.99% Apr '92; was elected the first woman Speaker in the first contested election in over 40 years; despite a telephone canvassing campaign by Conservative Whips to find a single 'stop Betty' candidate, she had four possible Tory opponents (Peter Brooke, Giles Shaw, Janet Fookes, Terence Higgins); Roy Hattersley spread incorrect rumour that Harold Walker did not wish to be considered for Speaker; she was proposed for Speaker by former Tory Commons Leader John Biffen and elected with the support of many other Tory MPs Apr '92; was elected the 155th Speaker by 372 to 238 for Peter Brooke, with 74 Tory MPs voting for her Apr '92; was named a Privy Councillor June '92; expelled Dennis Skinner from Commons when he refused to withdraw remarks that John Gummer was a "wart" and a "little squirt" July '92; was unanimously chosen 'Parliamentarian of the Year' by SPECTATOR as "the first new Speaker in modern times to show immediately that she is the right man for the job" Nov '92; suspended Commons over Scottish protest against self-governing hospital trusts Dec '92; warned Ann Clwyd not to park in Ministers' places in Palace of Westminster, threatening to have her wheelclamped Jan '93; blamed sex discrimination by male-dominated selection committees for shortage of women MPs Feb '93; she frustrated a planned dialogue between Tory MP Marion Roe and Minister Ann Widdicombe on how much better pensioners' lives were under the Tories by switching off Widdecombe's mike when she tried to answer an unrelated second question Mar '93; executed a mock yawn in criticism of long-winded reply by Tory Minister Neil Hamilton Apr '93; criticized Virginia Bottomley for putting in an important written statement into HANSARD without a question being asked May '93; ruled that a separate vote could be taken on the Social Chapter of the Maastricht treaty, although it had been rejected by her deputy, Michael Morris May '93; after repeatedly trying to stop resigned Minister Michael Mates from discussing subjects which might be sub judice prevent a fair trial for Asil Nadir, allowed him to bulldoze her June '93; following precedent, used her casting vote to support the Government side in what was (falsely) thought to be a tied vote on the Social Chapter of the Maastricht treaty July '93; visited Cyprus as a guest of Calypso Hotels Ltd Sep '93; was the target of a hostile whispering campaign allegedly originating in the Tory Whips' Office Dec '93; decided not to give priority to a privilege complaint against Disabled Minister Nicholas Scott after he apologised for mistakenly saying the Government had not not helped Tory MPs trying to wreck Dr Berry's disabled rights Bill May '94; forced Rod Richards to apologise to her and the House for calling Peter Hain a "liar" - and her as well because he did not speak indirectly July '94; forced Peter Hain to apologise for failing to give Tory MPs who were Lloyd's 'names' due notice he would name them July '94; promised to take action against Tory "yobbos" being incited to disrupt Tony Blair's speeches by Tory Party Deputy Chairman John Maples Nov '94; suspended the passes of two drunken Tory researchers who invaded the offices of Opposition Leader Tony Blair Dec '94; returned in time despite being marooned in mud in a Moroccan rainstorm Apr '95; turned down a private notice question to

Virginia Bottomley on the planned closure of Barts by Peter Brooke on the grounds that it was too narrowly drawn Apr '95; she deplored "personal attacks" by Tory MP David Shaw on Labour MPs Glenda Jackson and Margaret Hodge Oct, Nov '95; rebuked Tory MP Rod Richards for criticising Tony Blair for sending his son to Oratory School Dec '95; when Tory MPs led by Alan Duncan were alleged to be monitoring her behaviour to try to prove bias, she ruled: "if there is any criticism of the Chair, there has to be a motion put on the order paper and it will be debated immediately" Dec '95; urged Opposition spokesman be provided with Government statements in plenty of time Feb '96; again banned launching of a Gerry Adams book in the Commons, sponsored by Jeremy Corbyn Sep '96; when The GUARDIAN disclosed that Paymaster-General David Willets had, when a Whip, canvassed ways of playing down the cash-for-questions charges against Neil Hamilton in discussions with Sir Geoffrey Johnson-Smith, then Chairman of the Select Committee on Members' Interests, she announced the charge was serious enough to warrant a discussion on the floor of the Commons, including a vote to refer it to the Select Committee on Standards and Privileges: "the reputation of the House as a whole has ben called into question" Oct '96; encouraged providing resources for a full investigation of sleaze allegations Oct '96; she urged media to ban generalised statements of 'cash for questions' sleaze to protect Parliament's remaining reputation Jan '97; banned bleepers and electronic prompters from the Commons chamber Mar '97; retained her seat with a doubled majority of 15,423, because the Tories and LibDems did not stand against her May '97; was re-elected Speaker unopposed, on the nomination of Gwyneth Dunwoody May '97; she announced that, under the Parliamentary Oaths Act 1866, those elected as MPs who did not take the oath of allegiance to the Queen could not sit as MPs or enjoy the facilities of the Commons (thus barring Sinn Feiners Gerry Adams and Martin McGuinnes) May '97; defended freedom of speech for MPs when Llew Smith claimed to be threatened by Welsh Secretary Ron Davies for voicing his opposition to devolution June '97; she urged the continuation of 'Yesterday in Parliament' July '97; was given pride of place in Delhi at India's celebration of its 50th anniversary of independence Aug '97; berated MPs for cheering arrivals of their party leaders at PM's question time Feb '98; celebrated her 25th anniversary as an MP May '98; complained to Leader of the Commons Ann Taylor that some of her proposed reforms were downgrading the Commons by reducing it to a four-days-a-week chamber July '98;

Born: 8 October 1929, Dewsbury, Yorkshire

Family: Only child of late Archibald Boothroyd, oft-unemployed textile worker who did not approve of her early dancing career: "my father thought it wasn't a career for a good working-class girl", and supportive late Mary (Butterfield), weaver; "I regret not having married and not having a family" (BB);

Education: Council schools, Dewsbury; dance classes at Temperance Hall, Dewsbury; Dewsbury Technical College of Commerce and Art;

Occupation: Formerly Sponsored by GMB (£420 for constituency, £219 toward election costs '79) '78-92; ex: Director, Thorn Lighting '80-82; Secretary: at Transport House '52, to Sir Geoffrey de Freitas '52-60, Barbara Castle '52-58, US Congressman '60-62, Lord Walston '62-73; Professional Dancer '45-48 (in West End pantomime as a Tiller Girl at 17); Secretary in Dewsbury '45; Singer and Dancer, with Swing Stars Band, '43-45;

Traits: Pretty ("a touch of Coronation Street's Elsie Tanner"); "can still stop a man's heart at 30 paces" ('Cross-Bencher', SUNDAY EXPRESS); buxom; shapely limbs; grey, curly hair; friendly; Yorkshire accent; "no-nonsense approach" (Sheila Gunn, TIMES); "one of those who have started out with the advantage of flat Northern voices and have developed a person-to-person style of plain talking to disguise their femininity" (late Margaret van Hattem, FINANCIAL TIMES); has a "Yorkshire-born cross of wit and practicality, blending discipline and jocularity" (Graham Brough, YORKSHIRE POST); "subtlety is not her game; she has

taken to placing her hand over her mouth and miming ostentatious yawns" "to curb long-winded ministerial replies" (DAILY TELEGRAPH); "gives the impression that she knows who is being naughty and that they should stop it, because she might have been a bit naughty herself in the past; there is nothing of the prim spinster about her - rather the opposite; her liveliness, indeed garrulousness in conversation, put off a number of the more traditional Tory MPs, who were worried that she might not be dignified enough for the post" (Peter Riddell, TIMES); "I have an inclination to be school-marmish in the old-fashioned sense" (BB); enjoys "large gins and large diamonds" ('Cross-Bencher', SUNDAY EXPRESS); "is known for her dressiness"; "her naturally regal demeanour has been enhanced by the specially-created robe she had made for her by Hardy Amies" (Jessica Davies, DAILY MAIL); "one thing my father taught me was always to put my shoes away with paper in them as we couldn't afford shoe-trees, so however late it is I put trees in...and I always hang my clothes up"; as Deputy Speaker: "I never wear the same outfit two days running; I really enjoy clothes; I have at least a dozen outfits, and come back to them once every ten to fourteen days; I feel a different person in different clothes, it does my morale good; they're all classic; which I wear depends on what I'm doing; I have them made, as I'm what you might call pleasantly plump"; "I haven't found it too much of a strain on my voice - it's like a foghorn; smoking - about a packet a day - has given me this lovely deep voice!"; "I'm a Christian but not a practising one"; "I love holidays, especially islands; my two favourite places are Sri Lanka and Cyprus" (BB, SUNDAY TIMES); still a graceful social dancer (Sir Marcus Fox and she attended dance classes together as teenagers in Dewsbury); an enthusiast for scrabble, exotic places, and hang-gliding there; has "the endearing idiosyncrasy of calling everyone 'luv'" (Frances Edmonds, MAIL ON SUNDAY);
Address: Speaker's House, House of Commons, Westminster SW1A 0AA; 14th century cottage in Herts;
Telephone: 0171 219 4136/4111/6293 (H of C);

David BORROW   **Labour**   **SOUTH RIBBLE '97-**

Majority: 5,084 over Conservative 6-way;
Description: Altered marginal seat hugging the south bank of the River Ribble, over the water from Preston; contains the Labour-leaning town of Leyland (Leyland Trucks) and the Tory-leaning suburbs southwest of Preston; bits and pieces have been traded to Preston and from West Lancashire, without altering the assessment of this one-third rural constituency as a Tory marginal which, after all, they had held since its creation in '83;
Position: Preston Borough Councillor (Leader '95-97, '92-94) '87-; Chairman, Preston Constituency Labour Party '90-97;
Outlook: Bright, able, modernising newcomer who came out of the closet after a year; a longtime supporter of "dynamic" constitutional change, including a regional assembly for the Northwest; the replacement candidate who unexpectedly defeated John Major's friend and former Minister, the jaunty lightweight Robert Atkins; a strong backer of the locally-produced Eurofighter; a mainstream Labour type who has had to battle with the hard-Left dominating Preston Council: was ousted by Valerie Wise in '94, but

returned in '95; is interested in electoral and constitutional reform, British Aerospace, local government finance; a member of the Fabian Society, the Co-operative Party and the Labour Campaign for Electoral Reform;
History: Joined the Labour Party at 18, '70; became Secretary, Treasurer and Chairman of the Labour Club at Lanchester Poly '70-73; was elected to Preston Borough Council May '87; was elected Chairman of Preston CLP '90; became Leader of Preston Borough Council May '92; was ousted from the Leadership by hard-Leftwinger Valerie Wise May '94; was restored to the Leadership Nov '95; was runner-up to Dennis Golden when the latter was selected as the Labour candidate for South Ribble Jan '96; was selected to replace Dennis Golden - who was dying of a brain tumour - to oppose the sitting Tory MP, Robert Atkins Feb '97; having seen the Labour victory in the Wirral South by-election, was reassured that his victory at South Ribble was likely; was elected with a majority of 5,084 after a pro-Labour notional swing of 12.11% May '97; backed outlawing of fox-hunting June '97; expressed solidarity with jailed Indonesian union leader June '97; in his Maiden welcomed the Budget as possibly ending the contrast between the ability of his generation to walk into secure jobs and the stark prospects of the young in the '90s, July '97; urged crime prevention be based on more accurate crime statistics July '97; strongly defended the commitment to the Eurofighter produced locally at Warton: "it is essential that Britain retains the capability to produce defence equipment at the cutting edge of technology, rather than becoming entirely dependent on the United States as a monopoly supplier" July '97; led the motion which erroneously criticised John Redwood for having dealt with matters involving BA while a Minister when his wife was BA's Company Secretary July '97; welcomed confirmation of Eurofighter contract; emphasised the civilian spin-off from military contracts, as in his local Leyland Trucks, which also produced military trucks Dec '97; pushed for an early change to PR, preferably at the next election Dec '97; on the signing of the Eurofighter agreement, again urged more co-ordinated defence and industrial policies Jan '98; said, "I support strong unitary local government, elected assemblies with revenue raising powers, a change in the electoral system and a change in the method of decision-making in Europe; decision-making in Europe should be open and it should be accountable through elected members from each member state, not determined by the Council of Ministers" Jan '98; complained of local emphasis on building only executive homes, with no mix with low-cost rented properties Feb '98; urged local transport be networked to allow access to job centres and hospitals May '98; backed the Competition Bill but feared the abolition of Resale Price Maintenance would endanger community pharmacies needed in the rural third of his constituency May '98; informed his local newspaper that he was gay June '98;
Born: 2 August 1952, Huddersfield
Family: Son, of James Borrow, ICI fitter, then training manager, and Nancy (Crawshaw), shorthand typist;
Education: Mirfield Grammar School; Lanchester Polytechnic (BA); Coventry Polytechnic; IRVTech;
Occupation: Ex: Clerk to Merseyside Valuation Tribunal (UNISON) '83-97;
Traits: Rectangular face; regular features; shrewd; can speak without notes; slightly funereal manner; gay;
Address: House of Commons, Westminster, London SW1A 0AA; 117 Garstang Road, Preston PR2 3EB;
Telephone: 0171 219 4126 (H of C); 0181 345 6789; 8800 35 (pager); 01772 787792 (home); 01772 454727 (constituency office);

Tim(othy Eric) BOSWELL **Conservative** **DAVENTRY '87-**

Majority: 7,378 (11.9%) over Labour 6-way;
Description: The expanding overspill town of Daventry (plus Towcester and Brackley), imbedded in the traditional Tory farmland of South Northamptonshire, with his own "lovely village of Aynho, with its unique and distinctive apricot trees" at its southern tip; in '83 it lost a third of its voters to Kettering and Northampton South; in '95 it regained 6,600 voters from Northampton South and lost 3,500 to Kettering;
Position: Deputy Spokesman '98-, Assistant Spokesmen '97-98 on Trade and Industry '97-, on the Treasury '97 (July-Dec); ex: Parliamentary Secretary for Agriculture '95-97, Under Secretary, Further and Higher Education '92-95; Whip (Lord Commissioner) '92, Assistant Whip '90-92; PPS, to Peter Lilley '89-90; Conservative Party Liaison Officer to European Democratic Union '90-92; Secretary, Conservative MPs' Agriculture Committee '86-89; on Select Committee on Agriculture '87-89; Agricultural and Food Research Council '88-90; President '84-90, on Council '66-90 of Perry Foundation for Agricultural Research; Chairman, all-party Charity Law Review Panel '88-90; Chairman '79-83, Treasurer '76-79, Daventry Conservative Association; Head, Economic Section, Conservative Research Department '70-73;
Outlook: A pleasant, civilised, low-profiled, not-overly-partisan 'One Nation' type, in sharp contrast to his aggressively partisan boss, John Redwood; a possible future Agriculture Minister should the Conservatives win power again; a thoughtful, well-off local farmer and loyal refugee from Smith Square; a farmer and agricultural economist slowly making his way up the ladder without sinking his elbows into colleagues' ribs; came belatedly into his safe-seat inheritance because he allowed Reg (latterly Lord) Prentice to usurp his seat; retains the personality of a backroom boy rather than a hardened politician at ease in the knee-in-the-groin limelight; a long-time pro-Marketeer, latterly pro-ERM, who has served as the Conservative Party's Liaison Officer on the European Committee of the European Democratic Union; formerly an assiduous free-tripper; was an important voice of local farmers (County NFU Chairman '83);
History: He comes from a Conservative farming family; he was a Conservative at school and university; supported UK entry into the EEC from '57; spent seven years in Conservative Research Department as an Agriculture specialist '66-70, as its Head of Economics '70-73; the first time he briefed Tory MPs on a Budget was during the passage of Chancellor Roy Jenkins' Finance Bill Mar '68; was selected for marginal Rugby '73; contested Rugby against William Price, coming second with 37.4% Feb '74; was shortlisted for safe-Tory Daventry against then-Tory Roland Freeman before Labour defector Reg Prentice was foisted on the constituency Jan '79; was adopted for Daventry in succession to Reg Prentice, who was to retire due to ill health Nov '86; won the seat June '87; in his Maiden on the Finance Bill urged fresh thinking on farm economics and more emphasis on the investment of public and private money in better training and re-skilling of inner city inhabitants willing "to work to better themselves" July '87; urged EEC food aid again be distributed by the charities (which they later refused), but warned that it "could not make more than the tiniest dent in the huge amounts of surplus food that have accumulated under the CAP" Nov '87; warned that social security was "now a gigantic business" taking one-third of the Budget and likely to increase,

Copyright (C)Parliamentary Profile Services Ltd

without precedent-setting exceptions, like payouts to haemophiliacs infected with the AIDS virus by Government-provided clotting agents Nov '87; voted for 2nd Reading of David Alton's abortion-curbing Bill Jan '88; urged revaluing of green pound to help farmers Feb '88; visited New Zealand with Agriculture Select Committee Feb? '88; backed televising of Commons Feb '88; although alleged to have "only gently prodded" the Government on paying up for storm damage to trees, insisted he was "more than mildly critical" Mar '88; voted against Gale amendment to restore capital punishment June '88; was accused by Labour MP Nicholas Brown of tabling an amendment to Finance Bill for Country Landowners Association to give farmers transitional relief on woodlands July '88; visited Cadenabbia, Italy, on invitation of Konrad Adenauer Foundation Sep '88; attended Harvard University conference as guest of British-American Parliamentary Group and Hanson Plc Dec '88; co-warned Government to help egg producers to avoid their suing Edwina Currie over her "reckless and uninformed" accusations about salmonella in eggs Dec '88; backed Government's £19m scheme to help cure salmonella in eggs Jan '89; urged public and private science research councils to work together Feb '89; said that if the European Commission nosed about in intervention stores in UK, the worst they would encounter would be the MAFF; but if they tried it in Italy, they would run up against the Mafia Mar '89; urged better local street lighting to deter criminals Apr '89; warned: stricter gun laws would hit legal users without stopping guns changing hands on the black market May '89; backed abolition of dock labour scheme, insisting on need for efficient low-cost docks because UK farmers now exported their grain May '89; defended slimming down of food research June '89; deplored the French Revolution July '89; urged training ex-Communist countries in "technical processes of democracy" July '89; visited Warsaw for international conference of young Parliamentarians as guest of Polish MPs Aug '89; atttended conference at Lake Como as guest of Konrad Adenauer Foundation Sep '89; was named PPS to Peter Lilley, then Financial Secretary to Treasury Oct '89; attended Anglo-Hungarian Round Table meeting as guest of Great Britain-East Europe Centre Oct-Nov '89; came off Agriculture Select Committee Nov '89; urged food aid for Poland: "it is no good being a free Pole this winter if one is also a dead Pole" Dec '89; urged need for flexibility in controlling charities Dec '89; supported converting hospitals into self-governing trusts Jan '90; visited Bonn on invitation of German Government to participate in a conference of mixed EC academics and politicians, as Liaison Officer of Conservative Party on the European Committee of the European Democratic Union Feb '90; complaining of declining farm incomes, urged reform of CAP Feb '90; as a layman on the Agricultural and Food Research Council urged a thoroughgoing but cautious approach to BSE, including carcass incineration May '90; chaired Parliamentary Panel on Charity Law which "viewed with alarm" the brainwashing activities of some religious cults June '90; asked Mrs Thatcher a stooge question about her Government's achievements, receiving a 7-column reply June '90; urged increase in proportion of pupils staying on for A-levels to match their Continental counterparts July '90; was named an Assistant Government Whip July '90; supported fight against closing local hospital wards Sep '90; visited Berlin for conference as guest of Konrad Adenauer Foundation Sep '90; unlike Tony Marlow, was sceptical that Tory by-election setbacks would produce a Leadership contest Nov '90; after Mrs Thatcher resigned, said: "everyone is shocked here because it is the end of a very long political era" Nov '90; visited Dresden to attend Konigswinter Conference as guest of British-German Foundation Mar '91; was "tipped for promotion" (Philip Stephens, FINANCIAL TIMES) July '91; visited Stuttgart and Prague as guest of Konrad Adenauer Foundation Sep '91; as a Whip was among the top ten voters in the '90-91 session Nov '91; retained seat with majority increased to 20,274, despite a 1.66% swing to Labour Apr '92; was named a Government Whip, or Lord Commissioner Apr '92; read the Riot Act to new MPs about turning up to support the party on Government business

May '92; was promoted Under Secretary for Further and Higher Education on resignation, for health reasons, of Nigel Forman Dec '92; welcomed expansion to 28% of proportion of young people entering higher education but urged "a genuine commitment to quality management" to "guarantee high standards" Jan '93; in review of higher education, stressed that "by 1992 we had already reached participation rates that we had projected in our White Paper would not be reached until 1994 or 1995" and that "the growth in student numbers has not been at the expense of quality" Feb '93; tried to reassure universities that funding would reward universities with good departments, without political interference Feb '93; disclosed that there were 6m illiterates in UK Feb '93; published a new guide to financial help for students May '93; announced an extra £2m in Access funds to help hard-up students; said university tuition fees were not being contemplated; unles they were linked with bursaries, "they could be regressive" June '93; with the backing of Education Secretary John Patten, tried to wrest the £850m Youth Training scheme from the Employment Department, against the resistance of Employment Secretary David Hunt Sep '93; was alleged to have received over £22,000 from EC for restraining grain production on his 450-acre farm Nov '93; promised reform of student unions, to prevent their spending state funds on political campaigns Nov '93; said he wanted half of all 16 and 17-year-olds to take GNVQs, the vocational A-levels Jan '94; voted against restoring capital punishment, even for killers of policemen Feb '94; voted to reduce age of homosexual consent to 18, but not to 16, Feb '94; wrote to GUARDIAN proudly pointing out that higher education had doubled to 1m full-timers in five years, with per capita costs being cut without losing world-class quality May '94; asked Coopers and Lybrand to investigate "uncorroborated allegations against certain executives" in the state-owned Student Loans Company Nov '94; said student body had increased from 718,000 in 1982-83 to 1,201,000 in 1992-93, Nov '94; despite one inspector's derisory comments on GNVQs, insisted inspectors' verdicts had been "reassuring" Nov '94; with repayments lagging badly, urged a longer repayment period for the Government-owned Student Loan Company Dec '94; his Researcher, Adam Atkinson, was registered as also working as a lobbyist for Union Railways Jan '95; promised £120,000 over two years to UCCA's drive against fraudulent grant applications Jan '95; in the reshuffle was named Parliamentary Secretary at MAFF, responsible fo its 'green' problems July '95; disclosed that £900m had been spent in 1995 on the CAP's tobacco regime July '95; disclosed that the EC had paid farmers £439m for nearly 3m tonnes of fruit and vegetables that were destroyed to keep up prices Aug '95; said the Ramblers had not replied to his invitation to complain about where the Government's land-access scheme was not working satisfactorily Dec '95; gave notice of the revocation in 17 months of the Potato Marketing Scheme Jan '96; said, "I have never had a single case of BSE in my own [beef] herd" of 70 Mar '96; said BSE was "not a risk in the normal sense of the word" for cows' milk May '96; voted for 3% cap on MPs' salary rises, and against basing MPs' pensions on £43,000 July '96; as a shooter was considered a potential rebel over the Major Government's gun-control legislation Aug '96; disclosed that a contingency planning team was examining potential unemployment as a result of the BSE crisis Oct '96; retained his altered seat with a third of his previous majority May '97; supported Kenneth Clarke for Tory Leader June '97; opposed building a second prison at Onley in his constituency, preferring non-incarceration for less dangerous criminals June '97; as one who had aspired to become a plant breeder, and had been an Agriculture minister, backed the Plant Varieties Bill to protect plant breeders; he admitted that, as a wheat-grower, he saved his Riband-variety seeds June '97; was named Assistant Spokesman (or 'shadow Financial Secretary') on Hague's Treasury team, June '97; insisted Labour's abolition of the Assisted Places Scheme would save little June '97; complained that mortgage-payers were hit thrice in the Finance Bill July '97; because of an embarrassing conflict-of-interest disclosure about Michael Fallon, Boswell gave up his Treasury post to him, to become Assistant Spokesman on Trade and Industry Dec '97; claimed that the Tories had done much better out of Toyota investments in the UK than Labour Dec '97; expressed disappointment that Upper Heyford, in his constituency, had not been awarded a sports establishment Jan 98; in the wake of a NEWS OF THE WORLD claim that his youngest daughter had been a £300-a-time call girl, stated: "We love her very much; we will support her in getting on with her life" Feb '98; in the reshuffle, became No 2 to John Redwood June '98; was one of 18 Tory MPs voting for 16 as homosexual age of consent June '98;

Born: 2 December 1942, Brentwood, Essex

Family: Son of late Eric New Boswell, farmer, and Joan (Jones); m '69 Helen (Delahay Rees), Welsh teacher whose grandfather was a docker for 40 years in South Wales; 3d Victoria, 71, who read English at the Royal Holloway and Law at Cambridge, where she was a CUCA activist '91-95, Emily, '75, read Theology at Worcester College and was an OUCA activist '95, Caroline, '78 read History of Art at UCL and attracted the attention of the NEWS OF THE WORLD for moonlighting in sex '98;

Education: Wells House, Malvern '51-56; Marlborough College '56-61 ("I have no science O-levels"); New College, Oxford (read Classical Greats followed by Diploma in Agricultural Economics) '61-66; served as alternate on New College's 'University Challenge' team '65;

Occupation: Farmer '74-, on 480-acre family farm at Lower Aynho Grounds, Croughton, Northamptonshire, managing it until '87; in '96 it had 70 beef cattle; since '92 it has received an estimated £35,000 payout for not growing wheat; ex: Special Policy Adviser to Ministry of Agriculture '84-86; Head of Economic Section, Conservative Research Department '70-73, Agriculture specialist there '66-70;

Traits: Chubby face; specs; parted curly dark hair; soft-edged discursive speaker; farm-rich; owns two shotguns; enjoys shooting, snooker, poetry; a caring parent;

Address: House of Commons, Westminster, London SW1A 0AA; Lower Aynho Grounds, Banbury, Oxfordshire, OX17 3BW; Westminster flat;

Telephone: 0171 219 3520/3546/6222 (H of C); 01869 810224;

Peter (James) BOTTOMLEY   **Conservative**   **WORTHING WEST '97-**

Majority: 7,713 (15%) over LibDem 5-way;

Description: A new safe Conservative seat on the Sussex coast created in '95, three-quarters from the western half of Worthing's seafront plus Rustington, East Preston and Ferring from splintered Shoreham; stiff with comfortably or respectably retired Tory pensioners;

Former Seat: Eltham '83-97, Woolwich West '75-83;

Position: On Select Committee on Standards and Privileges '97-; President, British-Irish New Consensus '92-; ex: Under Secretary: for Northern Ireland '89-90, for Transport '86-89, for Employment '84-86; PPS: to Peter Brooke '90, to Norman Fowler '83-84, to Cranley Onslow '82-83; on Select Committees: on Transport '92-97, Violence in the Family '76, Overseas Development '78-79; Vice Chairman, Conservative MPs' Media Committee '92-97; Secretary: Conservative MPs' Foreign Affairs Committee '79-81, Health and Social Services Committee '77-79; on Committee on Unopposed Bills (Panel) '9?-9?; President, Conservative Trade Unionists '78-80; Vice President, Federation of Conservative Students '80-82; Chairman: Church of England Children's Society '83-84, British-Uganda Parliamentary Group '79-82, all-party Shelter Group '79-83, British Union of Family Organisations '73-80; Founder Chairman of Family Forum '80-82; Vice Chairman, all-party UN Group '81-83; Secretary, all-party Right to Fuel Group '79-83; Treasurer, British-Zambian Parliamentary Group '83-84;

Outlook: The safely transported candidate-saint of the pro-European Tory 'wets'; the errant, quixotic, unpredictable, intelligent, libertarian Leftist; can alternate between an informed mature 'wet' and a simple partisan; was shrewd enough to flee threatened marginal Eltham for a new safe-Tory seat on the Sussex 'Costa Geriatrica' before the '97 Labour flood; is a considerable expert on the press, a principled crusader for peace in Northern Ireland and a refusenik against the Tory Government's abolition of wages councils, although wealthy by inheritance; "has acquired a justified reputation as a man zealous in the cause of righteousness" (Ian Aitken, GUARDIAN); "they say that I usually have five ideas, four of which are good and one of which is mad; the trouble is they think I don't know which one it is" (PB); "an impeccably perverse character" (EVENING STANDARD); his crusade against drink driving cut the numbers killed between '87 and '93 by 2,000; "his acid remarks about anti-social drivers have not endeared him to Tories" (Matthew Parris, TIMES); until he too was sacked, was the only rival to Mrs Currie as a publicity-hungry junior Minister; worried more 'tolerant' senior Tories by "his increasingly hysterical campaign against drinking and driving" ('Cross-Bencher', SUNDAY EXPRESS); "madman" (bibulous Auberon Waugh); "vociferous, unpopular, publicity-hungry" (SUNDAY TIMES); a strong supporter of the EC ; supported ordination of women; before office was the highly rebellious, individualistic, unpredictable and socially-conscious anti-racist Leftish Tory who spent "nine years as a mildly revolting backbencher" (his words); believes that "a Conservative puts country first, constituency second and party next"; was skilled at winning and consolidating his former constituency until it became hopeless; eager-beaver; was intermittently disliked by Mrs Thatcher; behind the scenes he was Virginia Bottomley's chief supporter as a Health Secretary under fire: "he protects her, defends her, advises her without a trace of bitterness or envy; she needs him" (mutual friends); "I am on record as stating that my wife is a better politician than myself; she DESERVES to be more successful" (PB); member of Bow Group and Tory Reform Group as well as Monday Club at one time;

History: He joined the Conservatives at 28, '72; contested Vauxhall in GLC election May '73; contested Woolwich West Feb and Oct '74; campaigned for an incomes policy which was by then against Tory policy and that of his union - the TGWU; won by-election, first to be secured from Labour by Tories June '75; told Mrs Thatcher at their first meeting that he was anti-Smith in Rhodesia July '75; urged Britain to abandon Ian Smith for Zimbabwe's black nationalists Mar '76; urged more funding for NHS Oct '76; lost popularity with Chief Whip when he acted as teller for John Stonehouse after Tories had promised Labour there would be no vote Mar-Apr '76; forced vote on child benefit order July '76; urged full implementation of child benefit scheme Mar '77; illustrated declining school standards by citing Starsky and Hutch Mar '77; attacked DAILY MAIL for false allegation of BL "slush fund" May '77; urged London rates cut to help small businesses June '77; in Tory Reform Group pamphlet, urged a UK resettlement fund for Europeans wishing to leave Rhodesia/Zimbabwe Aug '77; as CPAG supporter, urged child benefit increases Mar '78; visited El Salvador to investigate atrocities Dec '78; as President of the Conservative Trade Unions claimed during the election campaign that workers could trust the Tories May '79; wrote letter supporting proportional representation Apr '79; opposed increases in fees for overseas students Dec '79; abstained from supporting Government on tougher immigration rules Dec '79 and Mar '80; urged patience with Mugabe Government Mar '80; rebelled over child benefits Apr '80; labeled as "false" claim of El Salvador Government that killing of Archbishop Romero was done by others than security forces Apr '80; dissented over Iranian sanctions May '80; introduced Bill to give private tenants same right to buy as council tenants June '80; his letter, sent from South Africa, was intercepted by authorities Sep '81; voiced concern about mounting racialist attacks in UK Oct '81; urged Mrs Thatcher to meet Russian peace group Nov '81; said those cricketers who decided not to go to South Africa were making a "significant gesture" Mar '82; rebelled against Government on cut in unemployment benefit Apr '82; warned nurses against support from higher-paid unionists Sep '82; again urged increase in child benefit Oct '82; argued against cuts in pensioners' benefits Nov '82; urged abolition of GLC without regional replacement Feb '83; warned Whips against pandering to Rightwing rebels on immigration Feb '83; told employers it was cheaper to back higher child benefit and lower wage increases May '83; as a cyclist backed Cycle Tracks Bill Mar '84; signed all-party plea for Shcharansky Mar '84; was promoted Under Secretary for Employment Sep '84; announced that 29% of textile and clothing manufacturing employers were underpaying but Government had no intention of prosecuting Feb '85; voted for Enoch Powell's Bill banning scientific research on human embryos while his MP wife, Virginia, voted against May '85; took part in consultation on wages councils, finding no pressure to end them '85; challenged union general secretaries to disclose what steps they had taken to inform their members of their right to contract out of the political levy Aug '85; attacked Ron Todd for using his 1.25m votes in Labour conference to support Arthur Scargill without consulting his members Oct '85; urged company chairmen to take a personal interest in hiring more young people of Afro-Caribbean or Asian origins Dec '85; on BBC's 'Today' programme insisted that better training was part of the answer to ethnic unemployment, pointing out the programme itself had no black faces Dec '85; was switched to more public role as Under Secretary for Transport ('Minister for Roads and Traffic') Jan '86; was impressed by Auberon Waugh's dirge about his sister's death in a car accident Feb '86; urged drunken drivers be treated like muggers Feb '86; brought out a brochure lauding the completion of the crammed and controversial M25 Sep '86; with stronger Labour vote lost 1100 votes from majority while increasing his vote June '87; defended car clamp as deterring many others from parking illegally June '87; toughened regulations for coach strength July '87; defended two-lane Oxford-Birmingham link as saving enough money to build extra village bypasses and avoid covering the countryside with cement and macadam Aug '87; promised fewer cones and delays due to road repairs Aug '87; foretold heavier insurance costs for drunken drivers Nov '87; the Chancellor's outburst after his wife, Therese Lawson, had been arrested for drunken driving, was an embarrassment Dec '87; complained of whispering campaign against Dr Runcie, then Archbishop of Canterbury Dec '87; warned that "drinking and driving is the equivalent of a King's Cross (disaster) every fortnight" Dec '87; warned that owners might become liable for their cars' offences Dec '87; faced BR's Channel Tunnel link through his constituency Jan '88; said John Gummer's attack on Artchbishop of York made the Synod seem like "Parliament on a bad day" Feb '88; backed Stephen Day's Bill to make rear seatbelts in cars compulsory for children Feb '88; opposed restoring capital punishment June '88; promised to replace 1,200 trees felled for Okehampton bypass by 100,000 new trees July '88; 'Cross-Bencher' in the SUNDAY EXPRESS accurately predicted: "the day may dawn when just one Ministerial car pulls up outside the Bottomley household, to sweep Virginia off to some vital Cabinet meeting; Peter, perhaps relegated to the back-benches, will wave her off before finishing the breakfast washing-up and getting on his bike to pedal to the Commons" July '88; opposed danger of allowing drivers with a drink problem to get back their licenses automatically July '88; flew to Japan to find out how they cut deaths of motorcyclists Aug '88;

criticized Consumers' Association for scaremongering about dangers of unstable mini-jeeps Sep '88; objected to Social Security Minister John Moore's freezing of child benefit Dec '88; cast the only vote against John Browne's Protection of Privacy Bill Jan '89; was falsely accused by MAIL ON SUNDAY of receiving preferential treatment for protecting his house from a nearby bypass Feb '89; introduced 2nd Reading of Road Traffic Bill, designed to reduce road casualty figures further Apr '89; beat off European Commission proposals that would have eliminated volunteer mini-bus drivers Apr '89; was falsely accused by MAIL ON SUNDAY of obtaining preferential treatment for constituent accused of misconduct in children's home May '89; the Press Commission disallowed his complaint that the HAMPSTEAD AND HIGHGATE EXPRESS headlined his speech as "Bumley's tirade", using the disparaging nickname given him by Nicholas Ridley June '89; appproved insurance industry's decision not to pay out to injured drunken drivers June '89; PRIVATE EYE claimed he was being "blacked" by Government drivers - fellow members of the TGWU - for criticising them and insisting on driving himself; was named Under Secretary for Northern Ireland and given responsibility for Agriculture and Environment, including Transport by Northern Ireland Secretary Peter Brooke July '89; the MAIL ON SUNDAY apologised over its libellous story in May, Sep '89; tried to temper Tory anger against social analysis of Dr Runcie, then Archbishop of Canterbury Oct '89; voted against War Crimes Bill Dec '89; was first Minister to sign up as a member of Conservative Party in Northern Ireland Jan '90; said Northern Ireland's food was more natural and healthy May '90; supported Conservative candidate in by-election for Upper Bann May '90; toured Belfast in wheelchair to test accessibility for the disabled, clashing with storeowner who claimed he could not afford lift to basement June '90; was sacked by Mrs Thatcher as Northern Ireland Under Secretary, because "there is one Minister too many in Northern Ireland" according to him; but "his eccentricity and obsessions created hostility" according to the DAILY TELEGRAPH's correspondent, particularly his partial vegetarianism and his crusades against drunken driving and for the disabled July '90; pointed out that the tax allowances enjoyed by a married man with a large mortgage were worth as much as 12 child benefits July '90; after being sacked, was demonstratively named PPS to Northern Ireland Secretary Peter Brooke Sep '90; tried to be elected to Synod for Southwark but failed; urged national religious broadcasting rather than specifically religous stations Oct '90; backed Mrs Thatcher's proposal to give families an extra £1 a week for eldest child Oct '90; opposed dog registration Oct '90; received apologies and damages from NEWS OF THE WORLD Oct '90; stepped down as PPS to Peter Brooke Nov '90; joined protest against four-lane motorway through Oxleas Wood Nov '90; opposed a contest for the Leadership but expressed disgust at the way the SUN was maligning Michael Heseltine's leading supporters Nov '90; said: "the consequences of smoking are appalling"; "we shall have to squeeze the tobacco companies out of sponsoring sport" Nov '90; demanded BR introduce automatic safety controls after rail crash Jan '91; was named to European Standing Committee B Jan '91; again warned of threat to Oxleas Wood Jan '91; was still in the Monday Club when it was alleged to have been taken over by racists and near-fascists Feb '91; said: "there is no driving force on this earth as powerful as the ambitions and aspirations of the urban working class" Feb '91; opposed random breath testing because police already could "lawfully stop drivers at random or for any cause and may then require an alcohol test" Feb '91; sought to delay the War Crimes Bill as retrospective and depriving defendants of "the normal safeguards of a fair trial" Mar '91; served as observer of national elections at invitation of El Salvador Government Mar '91; claimed David Owen's endorsement of Tories would give them "half a million votes which would translate into 20 or 30 seats" Apr '91; led Parliamentary motion claiming that "many who voted to avoid the alteration of even a word or a comma in the War Crimes Bill did so with a heavy heart, and wonders why the Labour Party suspended its usual critical judgement of the Government" May '91; said Eltham would be better off in Bromley or Bexley, rather than Labour-controlled Greenwich May '91; took edge off Sir George Gardiner's attacks on overseas political involvements by British charities by pointing out that Christian Aid had been able to correct a "mistake" over attacks on Apartheid when he was a Trustee June '91; backed phasing out of mortgage tax relief at higher rate and also personal allowances July '91; backed civil liberties in El Salvador July '91; opposed double taxation on Woolwich Building Society July '91; settled the last of three libel actions he had fought against MAIL ON SUNDAY, NEWS OF THE WORLD and DAILY EXPRESS Oct '91; complained that Greenwich Council did not pursue poll tax payments from defaulting Labour councillors Oct '91; urged "an authoritative forum of MPs for London" Oct '91; was named to European Standing Committee B Nov '91; began supporting 'New Consensus' movement in Northern Ireland Dec '91; with Labour MP, Harry Barnes, hia collaborator in 'New Consensus', launched campaign to establish innocence of those killed by troops on 'Bloody Sunday' in '72 Londonderry shooting Jan '92; opposed National Lottery Bill because problems of raising £750m extra for culture and charities had not been thought through Jan '92; urged tougher rules against drinking by train drivers Mar '92; retained seat with majority down from 6,460 to 1,666, a swing of 5.73% to Labour Apr '92; expressed concern about increasing "the size of a student village from 300 to 2,000 bedrooms" in his marginal constituency June '92; waxed indignant about 'double' taxation levied on Woolwich Building Society June '92; tabled motions against censoring the press June '92; again spoke on Woolwich Building Society taxes July '92; was named to Select Committee on Transport July '92; asked Press Complaints Commission whether INDEPENDENT had breached its code of conduct on intrusions into private lives in disclosing unnecessary details about the Bottomley's first child, born three months before their marriage July '92; described Britain's exit from ERM as "a serious consequence of silly French play with referendums" Sep '92; supported ordination of women Oct '92; opposed end of wages councils because, even if low-paid dropped their wages by a fifth, there would only be an increase of one percent in employment Nov '92; when he suggested MPs froze their pay until unemployment dropped, the INDEPENDENT commented that "the Bottomley household is already pulling in some £81,000 in Parliamentary salaries, so things shouldn't be too tough" Nov '92; questioned Murdoch domination of media Dec '92; complained that nuclear industry was being held to ridiculous safety requirements Dec '92; opposed giving National Lottery advantages over pools Dec '92; opposed imposing probationary restrictions on new young drivers as hard to enforce Jan '93; welcomed John Major's statement that people killed on 'Bloody Sunday' in Londonderry in 1972 had been innocent Jan '93; resisted Government requirement to renew union check-off arrangements every three years Feb '93; again opposed abolition of wages councils Feb '93; welcomed possible choice of Irish-American Tom Foley as Presidential envoy to Northern Ireland Feb '93; complained that Clive Soley thought he was being used by Murdoch newspapers in opposing Soley's press Bill Apr '93; sought to extend ability of disabled to become driving instructors Apr '93; strongly supported Maastricht treaty Apr '93; urged action against racist organisations after a black youth was killed in his constituency: "I am clear that if this had been the third white youth to be killed, there would have been widespread press calls for effective action" May '93; welcomed end of road through Eltham and Oxleas Wood May '93; voted against Ray Powell's restrictive Shops (Amendment) Bill May '93; opposed Clive Soley's moderate shackling of press: "the price of an open free society is the acceptance of casualties" July '93; co-sponsored Bill to provide pardons for soldiers executed for cowardice in World War I, Oct '93; voted for lesser increase in MPs' pay Nov '93; voted against restoring capital punishment, even for killers of policemen Feb '94; voted to reduce age of homosexual consent to 18 or 16, Feb '94; blamed failure to solve signalmen's strike not on the clumsiness of Railtrack but on RMT sponsorship of Labour MPs July '94; chided The GUARDIAN for an unbalanced story on dentistry Nov '94; defended the Public Interest Immunity Certificate system as a "judge-created system...to allow the release to the judge and, if relevant, to the defence of documents which would normally be withheld" June '95; his changed constituency was shown as Labour's 14th target, with only a 1.43% swing needed to take it Aug '95; opposed dilution of Lord Mackay's divorce proposals as signalling the party had lurched too far to the Right Nov '95; was named to European Standing Committee B Nov '95; he beat George Carman QC, winning £40,000 from the SUNDAY EXPRESS, who also payed £250,000 costs after an eight-day trial, over a story headlined "The Final Betrayal" which attacked him, as a leader of the peace group, New Dialogue, for appearing on the same platform as Sinn Fein leader Martin McGuinness Dec '95; his adjournment debate on the cost of libel cases showed how Robert Maxwell and BCCI used the law to ban publication of critical information; he also urged immediate correction of wrong stories Feb '96; on the 'chicken run' from threatened Eltham, was selected for redrawn Worthing West which, on a 1992-style vote should have provided him with a 20,000 majority Feb '96; voted against Iain Duncan-Smith's Bill to curb the European Court Apr '96; was Teller in vote against putting a 3% cap on MPs' salary increase and for reduced mileage allowances July '96; he (and Patrick Cormack) abstained when the Tory Government reversed a Lords amendment to give asylum seekers three days grace to lodge a claim for refugee status before they lost their chance to claim welfare benefits July '96; co-urged the reselection of Tory MP Michael Stephen after his constituency disappeared Sep '96; told the DAILY TELEGRAPH that he backed negotiating on the single European currency on the existing 'wait-and-see' basis Dec '96; with Harry Barnes, again urged a new inquiry into 'Bloody Sunday' Jan '97; retained new Worthing West by a majority of 7,713, after a notional swing of 9.8% to the second-place LibDems May '97; he described John Redwood as unelectable, backing William Hague for the Tory Leadership May-June '97; was named to the Select Committee on Standards and Privileges June '97; challenged Margaret Beckett on low pay June '98; was one of 18 Tory MPs voting for 16 as age of homosexual consent June '98;

Born: 30 July 1944, A41 at Newport, Shropshire

Family: Son, Sir James Bottomley, KCMG, ex-UK Ambassador (to South Africa, UN and Geneva), and Barbara Evelyn (Vardon); m '67 Virginia (Garnett), psychiatric social worker who became MP for SW Surrey in '84; "they met when she was 12 and he 16 at her aunt Pauline's Putney home; "in 1967, when Virginia was 19, still an undergraduate [at Essex], they produced their first child Joshua and married three months later" (INDEPENDENT); 1s Joshua '67, 2d Cecilia '69, Adela '82;

Education: Mixed comprehensive in Washington DC, where his father was in the British Embassy; Westminster School; Trinity College, Cambridge University;

Occupation: Adviser, to International Fund for Animal Welfare '91-; Owner: old house in Milford, Surrey; ex: Personnel Adviser/Director to Ralli (Bowater and Cargill) '79-83; Managing Director: Signs Department Ltd (subsidiary of Mills and Allen) '73-75, Vending Centre Holdings '69-71; Marketing Consultant '71-73; Industrial Relations Officer, BSC '68-69; Salesman, of computer peripherals for Friden Ltd; Lorry Driver, for Wall's '66; Station Porter at Victoria, Barker at Battersea Funfair; Street Cleaner, in Westminster; Transport Driver, in Tasmania, delivering new Holdens from Hobart to Queenstown '63;

Traits: Tall; thinnish; gangling; prominent nose; parted hair; friendly zeal; quixotic solitary; original thinker; "polite and prim" (Colin Welch, DAILY MAIL); "with his little round glasses, schoolboy parting and cheeky smile", "looks like a go-ahead vicar from a seaside postcard; here, you would have thought, is a man who would happily lend you his bicycle clips, and might well inform an inquiring stranger of the prettiest route to the village green"; "little-lad haircut", "all-black digital watch, John Lennon glasses", "smiles more often and less slyly than most of his colleagues", "tendency to bite his nails and to lace up his shoes while facing urgent cross-questions", "a twinge of loopiness" (Craig Brown, TIMES); "holier-than-thou manner" (Chris Moncrieff, EVENING STAR); "obviously insane, or at any rate deranged" (Auberon Waugh, SPECTATOR); "a partial vegetarian...I make an exception for Bovril and...I enjoy Marmite as well" (PB); "I don't eat fish" (PB); has a "Cromwellian, puritanical streak; he once sent out for low-alcohol beer with his Cellnet phone from a restaurant table because there wasn't any on the menu" (fellow MP); courageous; "irrepressible" (EVENING STANDARD); climber (walked up a small mountain in Tanzania with Sherpa Tenzing '63); cyclist; swimmer (ex Parliamentary swimming champion '80, '81, '84, '85, '86, beaten by Jim Spicer in '82, '83, '87; "I swim once a year in the Commons and Lords Gala, which I liked because it meant I could introduce myself as the 'fastest wet in Westminster'" [PB]); sometimes wins the Commons v Lords dinghy sailing race; the only politician in 70 years to be awarded the Castrol/Motor Industry Gold Medal; footballer; wears NHS specs and TGWU tie; had back trouble in '87; is genuinely caring (an Asian family from Uganda lived with the Bottomleys for 18 months); "Peter was a lonely boy, and he'd come with his rucksack and camp in our garden; he was part of the family" (Peggy Jay, Virginia's aunt); "I have mixed Yorkshire and Northern Ireland blood in me" (PB);

Address: House of Commons, Westminster, London SW1A 0AA; moved from Lansdowne Gardens, Lambeth, to their Georgian house in Smith Square, Westminster in '91, purchased from his inheritance from his grandmother; lives near Penelope Keith in Milford, Surrey;

Telephone: 0171 219 5060 (H of C); 01903 235168 (constituency);

Rt Hon Virginia (Hilda Brunette) BOTTOMLEY   Conservative   **SOUTH WEST SURREY '84-**

Majority: 2,694 (4.8%) over Liberal Democrat 6-way;

Description: An affluent, normally safe-Tory seat, reshaped from Farnham in '83; attractive countryside and residential areas encasing Farnham, Godalming and super-posh Haslemere (more first-class rail commuters to London than any other town in the UK); two-thirds owner-occupiers in above-average houses; 22% OAPs; some industry including British Aerospace and ICI;

Position: On Select Committee on Foreign Affairs '97-; Vice Chairman, all-party Music Appreciation Group '97-; Patron, Tory Reform Group '??-; Governor, Ditchley Foundation '91-; ex: National Heritage Secretary '95-97; Health Secretary '92-95; Minister of Health '89-92; Under Secretary, Environment '88-89; PPS: Sir Geoffrey Howe '87-88, Chris Patten '85-87; Secretary, Conservative MPs' Employment Committee '85; Joint Chairman, Women's National Commission '91-92; Chairwoman, Children's Society Advisory Panel on Penal Custody '86-88; Vice Chairwoman: National Council of Carers and their Elderly Dependents '82-88; Vice President, Women and Families for Defence '83-88; Secretary, All-Party Social Sciences Policy Committee '85-88; on Medical Research Council '87-88;

Outlook: The dedicated politician who continued to lead with her chin from the backbenches

after most ex-Ministers who survived the May 1997 Labour flood had retreated to boardroom bunkers; the unexpected originator of 'Cool Britannia'; still bears the scars of having tried to apply mechanically and without sensitivity the business-efficiency 'reforms' devised by her predecessors as Health Secretary John Moore and Kenneth Clarke; in three years as Health Secretary she managed to alienate virtually all the health professionals while losing the confidence of the public; her vulnerability increased once she lost the much-needed underpinning of her official advisers, who provided her with floods of oft-misleading figures with which she tried to drown questioners about the NHS when Health Secretary; when down-graded to National Heritage, she embraced the National Heritage "with all the unbridled enthusiasm of an atheist discovering there is a God" (Ginny Dougary, TIMES); "she has, at her best, the terrifying self-assurance of the English middle-class woman being reasonable" (Andrew Brown, INDEPENDENT), showing a steely determination behind English rose good looks; "a bit pious, in the way of bossy head girls" (Julia Langdon, DAILY TELEGRAPH); "there is a kind of Victorian maternalism about her; she's a sort of grown-up prefect; she'll do it decently, do it with a slightly pained smile, but you're going to have good done to you whether you like it or not and there's more than a touch of condescension about it, an attitude of knowing better than ordinary people" (senior Health civil servant, quoted by Graham Turner, SUNDAY TELEGRAPH); "my style is to get there by stealth; I shall deliver results not by talking radical but by achieving change" (VB); was an officials' minister who needed a lot of briefing but then provided an articulate voice and firm support; also has a strong streak of earthy common sense; a former psychiatric social worker; considers herself a 'One Nation' Tory; was not trusted by Mrs Thatcher, who resisted Norman Fowler's early pressure for her promotion; was somewhat schizophrenic, alternately a 'Bimbo' and a 'Rambo': sensible on social welfare, (abortion, and not jailing young offenders), but spasmodically Rightwing (Ross McWhirter Memorial Trust; loved the Bomb equally but more intelligently than Lady Olga Maitland); although thought of as "some kind of political Mary Poppins," she has "behaved more like a rottweiler than the hospital almoner she so perfectly resembles" (Ian Aitken, GUARDIAN); "whatever I do, I work enormously hard; I listen, I consult widely; I want to know what people are saying; but having made my decision, I stick to it" (VB); "undoubtedly one of nature's nannies" (Andrew Rawnsley, GUARDIAN); a "do-gooder" who has "a meddling, puritanical streak", and is "gently fanatical and benevolently intolerant" (Colin Welch, DAILY MAIL); a hardworking constituency MP; the female half of one of the Commons' husband-and-wife team; not as intelligent as Peter, but a more skilful politician;
History: She stood as a Labour candidate in a mock election in Putney School; she canvassed for her aunt, Peggy Jay, a Labour GLC candidate; stayed aloof from tumultuous student politics at Essex University, producing her first child in her second year '67; under the influence of her young husband, Peter Bottomley, she became a Tory, to the dismay of her aunt, Peggy Jay; while at the Child Poverty Action Group "it dawned on me that the Labour Party was dominated by the trade unions, who were bully-boys; I believed in helping those who couldn't help themselves and, almost by definition, those people were unlikely to be trade union members" '71-73; later in the '70s her political activities were largely in support of her husband's career; failed to be selected as candidate for Richmond Nov '81; was selected from among 114 candidates for the Isle of Wight, partly because of her family connections there stretching back four generations, partly because she said she would have favoured restoration of hanging for murderers of the police and prison warders July '82; fiercely contested the Isle of Wight, under the slogan 'Turn Wight Blue', claiming its Liberal council made it the South Coast's "black spot" May-June '83; was inconsolable when, despite an eve-of-poll visit by Mrs Thatcher and nearly 35,000 votes, Stephen Ross's Liberal majority increased; crying on the ferry to the mainland, was consoled by Ross June '83; was a founder-member of Tories'

anti-CND 'Women and Families for Defence', becoming its Vice President '83; was selected from among 300 candidates for South West Surrey in the wake of Maurice Macmillan's death, beating ex-MP Iain Sproat and MEP Stanley Johnson Apr '84; promised to fight against cuts in local care within a more efficient NHS Apr '84; narrowly retained the seat, with a drop of almost 10,000 Tory voters, and a majority one-fifth that of Maurice Macmillan (later recouped) May '84; in her Maiden she deplored Russia's brutally repressive system, gave an orthodox defence of NATO and urged better harmonisation in defence procurement June '84; opposed increased contributions from affluent parents to students' grants Nov '84; urged better protection for the elderly from inflation and crime Nov '84; unlike her husband, opposed Enoch Powell's Unborn Children (Protection) Bill Jan '85; co-proposed restoring an additional VAT rate of 25% for luxury goods Jan '85; as a member of Tim Yeo's dampish 'Third Term Group', urged reduction in National Insurance for lower-paid Mar '85; co-urged an end to controls on future private tenancies and "thereby encourage landlords to make available property for letting at market rents" May '85; complained of the "scenes of violence, intimidation and disruption" in Lambeth Council June '85; co-urged Mrs Thatcher to avoid excessive housing development in rural areas July '85; in an adjournment debate on child abuse, warned that a child died every week at the hands of parents or guardians July '85; joined with women Labour MPs to deplore use of Commons facilities to promote Mecca's 'Miss World' contest Nov '85; was named PPS to Chris Patten Dec '85; in adjournment debate objected to use of Stockstone Quarry in her constituency as a London rubbish dump May '86; backed the Channel Tunnel Nov '86; urged Australian-type family courts Dec '86; again urged a code of practice for the prison service Dec '86; again backed Winston Churchill's Bill to allow sufferers from services' negligence to recover damages Feb '87; restored the Tory majority to its 1983 figure June '87; thinking her too 'wet', Mrs Thatcher blocked her promotion when Norman Fowler wanted her in Environment June '87; in a Crime Prevention debate expressed her concern about the extreme youth of most offenders, their illiteracy and lack of training and the large percentage of those who re-offended Nov '87; in an adjournment debate urged recognition and better funding for the Institute of Oceanographic Sciences Deacon Laboratory in her constituency Dec '87; visited Hongkong as guest of its government '87; introduced Bill to compel parent or guardian to produce a child for medical examination within three days if a social worker or health visitor thought it at risk Jan '88; voted against David Alton's abortion-curbing Bill Jan '88; as a Director of Mid-Southern Water Company, backed water metering Feb '88; supported 26-week ceiling for abortion as amendment to Alton's Bill May '88; again opposed jailing young offenders May '88; backed electronic tagging May '88; first entered the Government as Under Secretary for the Environment, after Mrs Thatcher relented under pressure to promote more women July '88; refused to allow a container ship to dump its load of toxic waste in the UK Aug '88; promised tougher anti-pollution measures; backed switch to unleaded petrol Oct '88; said Cleveland County council could not stop import of highly toxic chemicals Nov '88; warned: threat to ozone was greater than feared Nov '88; was accused of likely to "go down in history as one of the great poisoners" because of the sewage dumped in the sea Dec '88; sought to create an anti-litter climate of opinion Feb '89; backed Joan Ruddock's Bill to control fly-tippers Feb '89; when Michael Heseltine criticized her chief, Nicholas Ridley, for his poor environmental record, Ridley replied that since "Mrs Virginia Bottomley seldom has her green wellies off, I cannot always have them on" July '89; backed green labelling Aug '89; criticized "yuppies in four-wheel-drive vehicles" who cut muddy swathes through the countryside Sep '89; was promoted Minister of State for Health under Ken Clarke, replacing David Mellor, with the task of carrying through NHS changes Oct '89; warned that nobody could afford to be complacent about AIDS Nov '89; backed embryo research Nov '89; clashed with striking

Surrey ambulancemen Dec '89; announced renewed funding for family planning organizations Apr '90; backed multi-disciplinary approach to child abuse cases, incorporating Cleveland experience June '90; opposed "alarmist myths" of anti-abortionists trying to curb embryo research; made clear her personal support for amendment allowing women abortions if one medical practitioner certified the pregnancy had not exceeded 12 weeks June '90; insisted: "the child's best interests should be the paramount consideration" in inter-country adoption Oct '90; supported Douglas Hurd in Conservative leadership contest partly because he knew how to use his great experience to inform his judgement Nov '90; announced deal to cut hours of junior hospital doctors and increase number of consultants Dec '90; complained that although equal numbers qualified from medical schools, women filled only 15% of consultants' posts and only 3% of surgical posts Jan '91; said the Government would not prevent virgins from having babies by artificial insemination Mar '91; warned social workers to look for "bruises and beatings rather than ghosties and ghoulies" in abuse cases Apr '91; urged a balance between plight of Romanian orphans and frustrations of British couples wanting to give them a home May '91; becoming aggressive suddenly, accused Robin Cook of "scaring, not caring" ("it was like hearing Julie Andrews swearing" - Andrew Rawnsley, GUARDIAN; "if I were Mr Waldegrave, I would keep a close watch on my deputy" - Ian Aitken, GUARDIAN) May '91; attacked Staffordshire social service department for its "pin-down" regime in children's homes June '91; opposed dawn raids to seize children involved in suspected sexual abuse cases unless there was a danger to life June '91; supported advance clearance for Romanian orphans arriving for adoption Aug '91; successfully sought delay in application of 1989 Children's Act to allow local social services time to prepare Oct '91; announced Government's decision not to extend compensation to non-haemophiliacs who had contracted AIDS through NHS-provided blood plasma Nov '91; criticized "out of sight, out of mind" children's homes where residents were abused Nov '91; claimed £100m had been saved by charging for eye tests Nov '91; announced 10% increase in prescription charges Feb '92; promised £6m cash injection for community care services Mar '92; retained seat with majority up from 14,343 to 14,975, with no significant swing Apr '92; on the day before she replaced her boss, William Waldegrave as Secretary of State, told Robin Day she wanted to remain Minister of State for Health; this was seen as her advance admission that, she was promoted to Cabient, it would be mainly because she was a woman Apr '92; told the DAILY TELEGRAPH: "the NHS is not for profit; it is not for sale; it will continue to be true to its founding principles, available to all and free at the point of delivery" Apr '92; indicated she would shut some London NHS hospitals if market in health care proved them uneconomic Apr '92; insisted that on-call hours and working hours of junior hospital doctors were already coming down May '92; with PM's backing, won Cabinet battle to limit cut in dentists' payment to 7%, instead of the 23% cut desired by Chief Secretary Michael Portillo; also won battle to ring-fence community care funds June '92; urged Family Health Services Authorities to hire salaried dentists if self-employed dentists struck against cuts June '92; promised to introduce new official mechanisms for NHS whistle-blowers, who would be constrained to restrict their complaints to these channels June '92; refused to allow GPs to relinquish their 24-hours-a-day obligation to their patients June '92; published 'Health of the Nation' white paper, emphasizing that nearly 160,000 people had been out of work on any day during previous year from smoking or excessive alcohol; but she sought no curb on tobacco advertising July '92; when she expressed concern about school-age pregnancies, the INDEPENDENT disclosed that she had given birth to their first child at 19, three months before her marriage to Peter Bottomley July '92; although her grandfather had trained at Barts, she accepted Tomlinson Report recommending closing of four of London's teaching hospitals and increase in its primary health care Oct '92; to general amazement, claimed the Tories had had a share in creating the NHS Oct '92; urged more HIV testing among pregnant women in inner cities Dec '92; criticized as irresponsible budget-holding GPs who refused to return windfall over-payments in their budgets Dec '92; in wake of lion's mauling of schizophrenic, urged consideration of forced treatment of mentally ill Jan '93; ordered use of TV to promote organ donation Jan '93; under pressure from former Health Secretaries in Cabinet, agreed to slim down NHS regional bureaucracies by 5,000 Feb '93; resisted Home Secretary Kenneth Clarke on re-establishing discredited approved schools Feb '93; after surviving the Great Plague, the fire of London and the Blitz, St Bartholomew's hospital surrendered to her and accepted merger with the Royal London Hospital or a slimmed-down centre of specialist units Feb '93; after an adverse inquiry report and the resignation of its Chairman, she ordered a review of London Ambulance Service Feb '93; clashed with her junior Minister, Dr Brian Mawhinney, over her wish to have inner city doctors compete for funds to improve their practices Feb '93; said: "if better, more cost-efffective patient care means drawing on private sector skills, private sector disciplines, private sector investments, let it be" Feb '93; tried to overcome slowdown of operations in hospitals running out of finance: "there can be no question of patients requiring urgent investigation or treatment having it delayed because they come forward towards the end of this financial year" Feb '93; reasserted need for health workers to inform superiors if they were HIV-positive Mar '93; admitted that internal market was setting priorities through choices by GPs and district health authorities Mar '93; said cot deaths had been cut by 60% by campaigning for laying babies on their backs Mar '93; stopped a make-up class for NHS's lady managers Mar '93; cut funding for AIDS charity, the Terrence Higgins Trust Apr '93; visited Russia and Kazakhistan with contract-seeking British health care entrepreneurs Apr '93; ordered a top-to-bottom review of NHS's market-orientated reforms May '93; was criticized by Speaker Betty Boothroyd for attempting to hide 13% increase in prescription charges in a written answer for which no question had been laid May '93; was sharply criticised for endangering London Tories by former Cabinet colleague David Mellor, flaying the planned "insanity" of closing up to nine London hospitals and merging others July '93; was voted the most "insincere" of British politicians in Gallup Poll, with an insincerity rating of 59% Sep '93 voted against restoring capital punishment for killers of policemen Feb '94; voted to reduce the age of homosexual consent to 18, but not to 16 Feb '94; presented her plans to curb and merge London hospitals as "changes to strengthen the Health Service in London" Feb '94; the EVENING STANDARD resumed its campaign against her "rationalisation" of London's hospitals, citing Professor Jarman's statistics to prove that London was not over-provided with hospitals or hospital beds Mar '94; in view of her unpopularity with both the public and the professionals, there was some surprise that she survived the reshuffle, unlike John Patten, when she was suspected of being willing to be out of the NHS firing line July '94; was suspected of having shelved a report by York University medical economists recommending shifting a large share of the NHS budget from the shire counties to the cities July '94; was accused by Labour Spokesman Margaret Beckett of "demented and feverish activity", pretending the NHS was safely afloat when "all that we see are survivors trying to cope in the 485 separate leakiny liveboats of the individual health businesses" Dec '94; her daughter was found to be working as a junior doctor at St Thomas's just the unacceptably long hours her mother had promised to end when the junior Health Minister Jan '95; was disclosed to have recommended hospital trusts to appoint 419 company secretaries at a cost of £12m Aug '95; she was sharply attacked by London Tory MPs led by Peter Brooke for trying to disclose London hospital closures, including Barts, in a written answer; in a 'Today' interview the next morning, Peter Bottomley - who had been her only defender the previous afternoon, insisted "she is a person who does the thing she thinks is right and nothing will get her to do what she thinks is wrong" Apr '95; narrowly avoided a nurses' strike by promising a 3% pay increae

June '95; she celebrated her last day as Health Secretary with "a riot of mixed metaphor"; "her vocabulary soared to new heights of gobbledegook, her prose plumbed new depths of banality, her cliches were fabulous" (Matthew Parris, TIMES); she was transferred into the quieter pastures as National Heritage Secretary July '95; she expressed concern that Lord Gowrie, the Arts Council Chairman, was giving too much cash to elitist, highbrow organisations Aug '95; she insisted on retaining the National Lottery unchanged, despite its £1m profits weekly for its operators because of the glory its reflected on its Conservative creators, calling it "John Major's National Lottery" Oct '95; was embroiled with a cross-party alliance of peers over her refusal to curb Murdoch's Sky Sports on exclusive access to listed events Feb '96; after the Arts Council received another £3m, criticised its Chairman, Lord Gowrie, for "his whingeing that the arts faced an apocalypse' Mar '96; party Chairman Brian Mawhinney, her former subordinate, urged PM John Major to drop her from the Cabinet Apr '96; voted for a 3% cap on MPs' pay increase and lower MPs' mileage allowances but for pensions based on £43,000 July '96; co-complained, with five other Cabinet Ministers, that she was being undermined by the "heavy-handed" campaigning tactics of party Chairman Brian Mawhinney Nov '96; said, "our fashion music and culture...make Cool Britannia an obvious choice for visitors" Nov '96; her Labour opposite number, Jack Cunningham, refused to agree a statement with her which would underwrite the Millennium project, whose cost might reach £1b Dec '96; she turned down the Cardiff Opera House (for which she was later attacked by former Tory Cabinet Minister Lord Crickhowell for "a lack of vision, leadership and courage") Dec '96; was accused by Labour Spokesman Jack Cunningham of withdrawing from the Eurimages scheme, "thereby excluding our film-makers and film industry from access to European funds" Dec '96; complained to BBC about 'Only Fools and Horses' showing a character reading the pro-Labour DAILY MIRROR Dec '96; she urged a TV ban on gratuitious sex and violence Dec '96; she was left out of Tory TV programmes for the duration of the election campaign Jan '97; she expressed her doubts about Michael Howard's policies of long incarceration for the young Apr '97; she narrowly held her previously-safe South West Surrey seat, with her majority reduced by five-sixths to 2,694, on a 10.1% swing to the Liberal Democrats May '97; urged a delay in the election of a new Tory Leader May '97; accused Labour of a "transparent smash-and-grab raid" on National Lottery funds May '97; backed Kenneth Clarke for Tory Leader June '97; retired to the backbenches "voluntarily", according to new Leader William Hague July '97; opposed the minimum wage and the EU's Social Chapter July '97; was named to Select Committee on Foreign Affairs July '97; attacked as "disgraceful and deplorable" Labour's "six months of shenanagins" over the Greenwich Millennium July '97; spoke of plans in her constituency for a new hospital in Farnham Dec '97;

Born: 12 March 1948, Dunoon, Scotland

Family: "She comes from one of the most remarkable and closely knit family networks in Britain, remarkable both for its connections and its earnest good works" (Graham Turner, SUNDAY TELEGRAPH); her great-great grandfather was the Palmer of Huntley and Palmer's biscuits; her paternal grandfather, Maxwell Garnett, was the hero of E M Forster's homosexual novel, Maurice, and became Principal of Manchester University's Institute of Science and Technology; her maternal grandfather, Rex Rutherford-Smith, was a Barts-trained doctor; her great-uncle, Lewis Richardson, was the father of long-range weather forecasting; daughter of late John Garnett CBE, Conservative ex-Chairman, of West Lambeth Health Authority and ex-Director of the Industrial Society, and Barbara (Rutherford-Smith), former teacher and then ILEA member; her father, who later married Julia Cleverdon, two years younger than Virginia, was the brother of Labour-supporting Peggy Jay, ex-wife of late Lord (Douglas) Jay; she is thus a cousin of Peter Jay; her brother, William Garnett, is Paddy Ashdown's solicitor; m '67 Peter Bottomley MP (whom she met when she was 12 and he was

16; "he protects her, defends her, advises her without a trace of bitterness or envy; she needs him" - friend); 1s Joshua, in the City, '67, 2d Cecilia, doctor, '69, Adela, was at £14,000-a-year King's School, Canterbury, '82;

Education: Putney High School (fee-paying all-girls school); Essex University (BA; Upper Second); LSE (MSc in Social Administration);

Occupation: Ex: Director, Mid Southern Water Company '87-88; Columnist, in TIMES '88; Psychiatric Social Worker, in Brixton and Camberwell Child Guidance units '73-84; Researcher, at £12 a week, with Child Poverty Action Group ("she did a pioneering study on the living standards of poor families, and it was well done" - Frank Field MP) '71-73; Lecturer in ILEA Further Education College '71-73;

Traits: A power-dresser who uses sharp colour contrasts well; "tall, fair and blue-eyed, with cheeks that dimple easily into laughter" (DAILY TELEGRAPH); "English rose good looks" (Julia Langdon, GUARDIAN); can look "pink and wholesome while displaying the occasional sharpish thorn" (Ian Aitken, GUARDIAN); "widely fancied for her unthreatening English rose good looks, clear-cut speaking voice and her general air of niceness" (INDEPENDENT); hyper-active ("like Mary Poppins on crack" - Labour MP; "she may still look like Julie Andrews, but it is Mary Poppins on steroids, in Doc Martens, and with knuckledusters" - Andrew Rawnsley, GUARDIAN); publicity-mad (there's a saying on BBC's 'Today' programme that if anyone 'phones before 7am, it is on her behalf); "I simply never leak to the press and I never say destructive things about my colleagues and I never crow about my victories" (VB);"diligent, pleasant, efficient" but "once she steps outside of her well-mastered brief she begins to panic" (INDEPENDENT); "very likeable"; "I can laugh at myself now; I think I'm faintly ridiculous with this deeply embarrassing genetic disorder [of over-enthusiasm] and I do not think that human beings should be like me - so cause-related and campaigning; I regard it as an unhealthy syndrome" (VB); "people will do things for her because she makes them feel she's on their side" (Frank Field MP); can be "skittish" (Colin Welch, DAILY MAIL); "slender and fair, she is attractive...and she is tough" (Kenneth Clarke, DAILY TELEGRAPH); "a subcutaneous sharpness and an edge that can turn the gentle smile very wintry indeed if she is displeased" (Catherine Stott, DAILY TELEGRAPH); "a nanny in Sloane Ranger's clothing" (Colin Welch, DAILY MAIL); "just the touch of the Angela Brazil heroine about her" (Edward Pearce, DAILY TELEGRAPH); "the Julie Andrews look, with its hint of higher inspiration", she "combines smugness with insecurity" (Martyn Harris, DAILY TELEGRAPH); "Goody Two-Shoes"; "Nurse Matilda"; Head Girl"; "Big Sister"; "she has the manner of a young Barbara Woodhouse" (Martin Kettle, SUNDAY TIMES), with "charmlessness, humourlessness, smugness, complacency, inflexibility and a lack of intellectual grip" (Simon Heffer, DAILY TELEGRAPH); "for a politician who provokes such fierce emotion in others, she can seem curiously emotionless" (OBSERVER); questioning her is like "throwing beanbags at a plateglass window; questions seem to slither away in front of you, flopping onto the floor" (unnamed journalist, also unnamed Health civil servant): caring (ex-Magistrate and Chairman of Lambeth Juvenile Court; has quietly had homeless Ugand Asians in her home); "what keeps me sane, my feet on the ground, is belonging to a noisy, affectionate family full of chiefs and precious few Indians" (VB); every Easter Monday her enlarged family makes a long pilgrimage to its family compound on the Isle of Wight; in '92, with her two brothers and her sister rowed 22 miles from Kew to Poplar to raise money for the Save the Chrildren Fund in Somalia; "is totally competent and has a male steeliness while retaining all feminine qualities" (a selection committee member); "like a lady almoner at a rather grand teaching hospital" (Health Department expert); "interviewing Virginia is like throwing bean bags at a plate-glass window: quesions seem to slither away in front of you, flopping on to the floor" (Geraldine Bedell, INDEPENDENT ON SUNDAY); "I am not a good cook - the domestic arts are not my forte - but I have an ability to communicate"; Professor Peter Townsend, husband of Labour MP Jean Corston, was her tutor at Essex and LSE; a "simple Christian" in C of E ("I'd rather not eat on Sunday than not go to church" - VB); after her debut at the dispatch box in shocking pink, a colleague said: "I have seen the fuscia, and it works!";

Address: House of Commons, Westminster, SW1A 0AA; "one of the lovely Georgian houses in Smith Square, bought with the inheritance left to Peter when his grandmother died" (Ginny Dougary, TIMES); a £500,000 manor house in Milford, Surrey; Penelope Keith lives nearby; an inherited holiday home, Stone House, at Horestone Point, Seagrove Bay, near Seaview on the Isle of Wight;

Telephone: 0171 219 6499 (H of C);

Keith (John Charles) BRADLEY   Labour   MANCHESTER-WITHINGTON '87-

Majority: 18,581 (42.2%) over Conservative 8-way;

Description: The former last Tory 'golden redoubt' in Manchester; its relative affluence was being eaten into by multiple occupancy of its big houses and the growth of council housing until the '83 addition of Chorlton-cum-Hardy; the continued onward-march of multiple occupancies restored marginality by '87; has an ageing population relying on state pensions, many public sector workers, especially in local NHS hospitals, with many unemployed;

Position: Deputy Chief Whip (Treasurer of HM Household) '98-; ex: Under Secretary for Social Security '97-98; Deputy Spokesman, on Transport '96-97; Deputy Spokesman '92-96, Assistant Spokesman '91-92 on Social Security; Campaigns Officer, of PLP's North West Group '93; on Agriculture Select Committee '89-92; Manchester City Councillor (Chairman: Environment and Consumer Services, Vice Chairman, Anti-Poverty) '84-88; Director (for City Council): of Manchester Ship Canal '84-88, Manchester Airport Plc '84-88; Secretary, Withington Co-operative Party '85-88;

Outlook: The unexpected new Deputyy Chief Whip; a clear-minded, persuasive but low-key Mancunian former NHS administrator who emerged as an able, balanced but low-profiled Social Security junior Minister after long service as a Spokesman in the field; this came after having first won and then hugely improved his position in a once-marginal seat; his relatively moderate, reformist formulations on domestic affairs contrast with semi-hard Left positions on Irish and foreign affairs (the Gulf war, the US role in Vietnam and Indonesia); in Manchester an NHS-orientated, housing-preoccupied Leftwinger; anti: nuclear weapons, war in the Gulf; before becoming an MP, he voted with the controlling Leftwing group on Manchester City Council but insisted he was "100% behind Neil Kinnock";

History: He joined the Labour Party '73; replacing Frances Done, was selected for marginal Withington; under its former Tory MP, Fred Silvester, it had held out as the last Tory seat in Manchester but was considered Labour's second most winnable seat in the northwest Sep '85; Bradley's hopes were dented when, in the local government elections, Labour came second in total votes in the Withington area and lost seats to both the Alliance and the Tories May '87; the first serious sign that Withington might be lost by its sitting Tory MP came in a MORI poll for 'Granada Reports', which gave Bradley a 15% lead May '87; apart from unemployment and pensioners' problems, he campaigned hard on health matters, saying: "we're concerned with the state of Withington Hospital" May '87; Bradley's capture of Withington was seen as a hardening of the contrast between Labour advances in the North and Tory consolidation in the Midlands and the South June '87; warned that the new Housing Benefit regulations would "again cause misery and chaos", as previous regulations had in 1982-83, Nov '87; warned that the Government's Housing Bill would increase the number of homeless in Manchester Nov '87; co-urged consideration of selective economic sanctions against Israel in wake of Mossad's Abu Jihad execution Apr '88; asked Defence Secretary George Younger whether "the combination of more nuclear-capable aircraft, more air-to-surface missiles and more United States nuclear-capable strike aircraft" were "merely a replacement for the INF weapon cuts" May '88; complained that Manchester's housing investment expenditure had been cut from £129.6m to £28.8m, when it needed a minimum of £600m spent over five years to repair existing defects May '88; co-sponsored Bill to provide an elected North West Regional Assembly Oct '88; reaffirmed his support for CND after Neil Kinnock left the unilateralist fold Oct '88; urged Mrs Thatcher to back a special benefit allowance for teenagers leaving local care Dec '88; voted against Prevention of Terrorism Bill Dec '88; backed 'greening' of Labour June '89; described the Government's Water Bill as a "polluters' charter": "the new water companies want the assets, the land and the juicy contracts but they do not want the liabilities" of meeting new water standards July '89; deplored cuts in health resource allocations to South Manchester Dec '89; was named to Agriculture Select Committee, replacing Elliot Morley Dec '89; voted against agricultural funds for EC, with hard-Left and Ulster unionists Feb '90; backed MORNING STAR to preserve "diverse editorial opinion" Feb '90; urged more paramedic training for ambulance workers Feb '90; attended "absurd" Corfu trial of two Greeks who were released by Appeal Court after having killed a constituent and his Dutch friend May '90; claimed eye tests had declined by 30% locally as a result of fees imposed by Government June '90; opposed use of military force to oust Iraqi invaders from Kuwait Jan '91; tried for emergency debate on refusal of local district health authority to pay surcharge needed to get cancer patients treated at local Christie Hospital Mar '91; complained about the "fiddle" in hospital waiting lists and the "sour taste left in the mouths of local people as a result of the opt-out of Christie Hospital" Apr '91; complained about housing cuts for Manchester and private landords who "ripped off the housing benefit system and tried to increase the rent at the expense of public subsidy" July '91; was promoted an Assistant Spokesman on Social Security, under Michael Meacher, to replace Tony Banks, who resigned for defying the party Whip over the Gulf War Oct '91; co-sponsored motion blaming USA for Indonesian aggression against East Timor Dec '91; co-sponsored motion criticising US's continued "punitive economic blockade against Vietnam" Dec '91; urged Government to close the gap between income support and charges in private retirement homes Dec '91; having been made an Assistant Spokesman on Social Security, yielded his seat on Agriculture Select Committee to Gavin Strang Feb '92; pledged Labour to provide 100% help with mortgage repayment for claimants on income support Feb '92; led the local campaign against Christie Hospital's opting for trust status Mar '92; retained seat with his majority up from 3,391 to 9,735, a swing to Labour of 7.33%, one of the largest in the country Apr '92; having nominated Bryan Gould, voted for John Smith July '92; was named Deputy Spokesman on Social Security, under Donald Dewar July '92; opposed closure of local Withington Hospital Nov '92; warned that the winding up of the old Independent Living Fund would shut off a whole section of disabled people from help Nov '92; expressed concern about the speed with which the old Independent Living Fund for the disabled was being wound up and the exclusions from its successsor fund Mar '93; visited Israel, paid for by Labour Friends of Israel May-June '93; sharply attacked

Social Security Secretary Peter Lilley for excluding the terminally ill from the new Independent Living Fund June '93; criticised Government's plan to tax invalidity benefits July '93; insisted "the Labour Party is as committed as any other party or the Government to rooting out fraud" in social security payments; pointed out that local authorities had been working with the Benefits Agency to crack down on organised fraud, "often organised by unscrupulous landlords who make bogus multiple claims for housing benefit on behalf of individual tenants who do not exist"; urged the Government to pay at least as much attention to £4b in tax evasion as £1b in social security fraud July '93; complained that the Government were curbing spending on the disabled as scapegoats for their financial incompetence Jan '94; voted against restoring capital punishment, even for killers of policemen Feb '94; voted to reduce age of homosexual consent to 18 or 16, Feb '94; welcomed the improvement in maternity pay, maternity allowance and maternity leave which had been "forced on the Government by an EC directive requiring that our maternity benefits be brought into line with those of other European countries" Apr '94; welcomed Lords amendment to Social Security Bill for limiting the Government's curbs on disability spending June '94; voted for Blair as Leader, Prescott as Deputy Leader July '94; was retained as Deputy Spokesman on Social Security under Donald Dewar Oct '94; warned that the Government was trying to offload its Industrial Injuries Scheme on to private employers Nov '94; urged constructive advice rather than drastic penalties to persuade jobless to dress appropriately for interviews Dec '94; complained of the cruelty of the tests for incapacity benefit Feb '95; warned that an estimated 190,000 disabled people would come off invalidity benefit and an additional 55,000 would fail to qualify for incapacity benefit in the first year of the Jobseekers' Allowanc Mar '95; was retained as Deputy Spokesman on Social Security under Chris Smith Oct '95; blamed Tory government's poor administration for the delays in dealing with asylum cases Jan '96; decried the incompetence of the South Manchester University Hospitals Trust for long failing to detect serious accountancy miscalculations Feb '96; celebrated departure of last Manchester Tory councillor and Manchester United's victory May '96; criticised Government's effort to limit housing benefit for young unemployed to persuade them to take low-paid jobs June '96; voted to curb MPs' mileage allowannces, against a 3% cap on MPs' pay rise and to base Parliamentary pensions on pay of £43,000 July '96; attacked as "extremely mean-minded and mean-spirited" the Government's cut of £50 a week in family credit from thousands of low-paid families July '96; in the 'final' pre-election reshuffle was shifted to Deputy Spokesman on Transport, under Andrew Smith Aug '96; made a scorching attack on rail privatisation, promising a Labour government would establish a strategic authority to deal with the fragmentation of the rail structure Nov '96; told an air traffic controller that Labour was "completely opposed to the privatisation of the National Air Traffic Control Services" Feb '97; was targeted by the Prolife Alliance Party Feb '97; retained his seat with a doubled majority on a 10.4% pro-Labour swing May '97; was named Under Secretary for Social Security, possibly to make way for Frank Field as Minister of State; he was given responsibility for poverty, income-related benefits and green issues May '97; sacrificed his beard to the dictum of focus groups that facial hair was a "turn-off" Oct '97; was promoted Deputy Chief Whip under new Chief Whip, Ann Taylor July '98;

Born: 17 May 1950, Erdington, Birmingham

Family: Son, John Bradley, company secretary, and Beatrice (Chamberlain); married; 2s '87, '96; 1d '90;

Education: Bishop Vesey's Grammar School, Sutton Coldfield; Manchester Polytechnic ('73-76, BA Hons in Social Sciences); York University ('76-78, MPhil);

Occupation: Ex: Health Service Administrator with North West Regional Health Authority (NALGO) '81-87;

Traits: Dark hair; no longer bearded; specs; quiet; calm; discreet (does not reveal the names of his wife or children); restrained; cricketer; also on all-party Football Committee; after his Ford Sierra's windows and carphone had been smashed, complained that his sugar-free gum was stolen but not his Tina Turner and Dire Straits tapes: "I'm a bit miffed that they admired my taste in chewing gum more than my taste in music"; a Manchester United fan;
Address: House of Commons, Westminster, London SW1A 0AA; 12 Meadow Bank, Chorltonville, Manchester M21 8FP;
Telephone: 0171 219 5124 (H of C); 0161 446 2047 (constituency);

Peter BRADLEY   **Labour**   **THE WREKIN '97-**

Majority: 3,025 over Conservative 3-way;
Description: The name was retained in '95 despite the removal of much of Telford new town to a seat named Telford; the remains, the northern part of Telford, plus bits of Ludlow and North Shropshire, were thought to portend a new Conservative seat and the return of a controversial former Conservative MP; the voters thought otherwise;
Position: On Select Committee on Public Administration '97-; Chairman, PLP's Rural Group '97-; ex: Westminster City Councillor (Deputy Leader its Labour Group '90-96) '86-96; Political Secretary, Paole Zion '81-83;
Outlook: A newcomer trying to prevent the Countryside Alliance from using hunting to hijack to rural agenda for the Tories; a Labour loyalist with strong anti-Establishment instincts; the public affairs consultant who removed the threat of the "Return of the Hangman", Peter Bruinvels, to the Commons; as a Westminster Councillor was a leader of the campaign to force the Council to re-acquire its three cemeteries sold for 15p and of the Westminster Objectors who insisted in '89 on an investigation into political corruption there, particularly the 'homes for votes' plot to sell council houses in marginal wards to presumed Tories; he was "staggered" at the "stench of corruption" uncovered, which still lingers in his nostrils;
History: His father was (and is) "staunch Labour"; he himself supported Labour in his public school and joined the Labour Party at 26, '79; became Political Secretary of Labour-affiliated Paole Zion '81; was elected to Westminster City Council May '86; as a leader of the Westminster Objectors, urged the Auditor to investigate a Tory 'homes for votes' plot '89; was elected Deputy Leader of the Labour Group on Westminster City Council May '90; supported all-women short-lists as he could see no better way of getting more women into Parliament Apr '95; was selected for the revised version of The Wrekin, when the sitting Labour MP, Bruce Grocott, was selected for new and safer Telford, formed of the bulk of the old Wrekin constituency; The Wrekin, as redrawn, was considered as likely to be a Tory seat, to be won by ultra-Right ex-Tory MP Peter Bruinvels; Labour did not agree; when the Magill Report into Westminster's 'homes for votes' conspiracy was published, Bradley was made the subject of a sustained and scurrilous muck-raking attack by Tory MP David Shaw, alleging he had not disclosed the clients of his PR firm in the Westminster Council's register of interests; Bradley had already received libel recompense for similar charges planted in the TIMES; Bruce Grocott challenged Shaw to repeat his charges outside the House May '96; Bradley won The

Wrekin by a majority of 3,025 over Peter Bruinvels, on a pro-Labour notional swing of 11.27% May '97; in his Maiden, welcomed the phased release of council funds to help ease "a housing crisis of monumental proportions"; it was particularly difficult in his constituency "because The Wrekin is the nation's low-pay capital", with 3,500 earning under £2 an hour June '97; co-sponsored motion urging a public inquiry into the functioning of Westminster City Council June '97; urged collection of statistics on Erb's Palsy July '97; was named to Select Committee on Public Administration July '97; criticised Lord Rees-Mogg for his "black propaganda" in favour of Dame Shirley Porter Sep '97; set up the 80-strong Rural Group of Labour MPs to develop an agenda for rural and semi-rural communities, becoming its Chairman Nov '97; enthused about Dr David Clark's White Paper on open government Dec '97; co-sponsored motion condemning John Major for refusing to criticise Dame Shirley Porter after the High Court had judged her guilty of wilful misconduct resulting in a loss to Westminster City Council of £27m Jan '98; in a lengthy speech asked for a Government inquiry into "the Conservative Government's record in aiding and abetting the corruption at Westminster City Council", citing Dame Shirley Porter's '87 letter to Mrs Thatcher explaining her strategy for preventing Westminster from falling into Labour hands Jan '98; accused the Conservative Government of having staffed quangos "from the 19th hole" Feb '98; pressed Home Secretary Jack Straw to enforce reparation orders on young offenders to "put the victim back at the centre of our judicial system" Feb '98; attacked the Countryside Alliance's preoccupation with foxhunting: "killing foxes - even if that is what rural communities want (and it isn't) - will not bring back buses to country lanes" Feb '98; signed a motion for a new Department for Rural Affairs to stimulate the debate on overcoming rural neglect, particularly in transport Mar '98; was credited with having helped secure the Chancellor's £150m Budget commitment to rural bus services Mar '98; complained that the War Pensions Agency was considered "the enemy within" by "many former prisoners of war and civilian internees" Apr '98; led motion backing David Clark's Freedom of Information White Paper May '98; led motion attacking Sevent-Trent for over-high price hikes May '98; led motion criticising imprisonment of Tibetan nationalist nun June '98;
Born: 12 April 1953, Birmingham
Family: Son, of Fred Bradley, technical translator, and Gertrude (Zunz); his partner is Annie Hart, former nursery school teacher; twin sons, Tom and Jess '97;
Education: New College Prep School, Oxford; Abingdon School; Sussex University (BA Hons); Occidental College, Los Angeles;
Occupation: Ex: Director: of Millbank Consultants (public affairs consultants) '93-97; previously of Good Relations (PR) '85-93; Research Director, for Centre for Contemporary Studies '79-83 (MSF);
Traits: Thinning brown hair; specs; keen sportsman, especially cricket (member of Warwickshire CCC); Aston Villa supporter; Jewish by origin;
Address: House of Commons, Westminster, London SW1A 0AA; 80 Cambridge Street, London SW1V 4QQ;
Telephone: 0171 219 4112 (H of C); 01952 240010 (constituency);

WEEKLY UPDATES
The weekly shifts in Parliamentary conflicts are analyzed by us in WESTMINSTER CONFIDENTIAL (£50 for 40 issues). A sample issue is available to you on request.

Ben(jamin) BRADSHAW   **Labour**   **EXETER '97-**

Majority: 11,705 over Conservative 7-way;
Description: Devon's still unaltered historic county town and commercial centre; it has leant to the Conservatives but gone Labour at its high tides, as in '66 and '97; initially the latter seemed unlikely in view of furious controversy among local Labour activists about the culpability in a South African resistance tragedy of their then candidate; curiously, afterwards the tide probably may have risen higher in '97 because of the clash between an attractive self-proclaimed homosexual and an unpleasant homophobe;
Position: On Select Committee on European Legislation '97-; on Ecclesiastical Committee '97-; Secretary: Labour Movement for Europe '97-,

all-party Cycling Group '97-;
Outlook: Loyal young Blairite regionalist and pro-European; a would-be Commons reformer whose preference for clapping instead of "hear-hear" has been rejected; a bit self-absorbed in his determination not to be pigeon-holed as a gay crusader; otherwise an assiduous self-publicist; "trying too hard" (DAILY TELEGRAPH); the former local reporter and rising star of the BBC who was the hands-down election victor despite two obstacles: he was chosen belatedly after the previous veteran Labour candidate, John Lloyd, was forced to step down after late revelations about his role in refusing to try to save the life of a friend in the South African resistance movement; his other alleged disability was that he was openly gay and was opposed by a primitive Rightwing 'Christian' Tory doctor and homophobe, Dr Adrian Rogers, who described homosexuality as "sterile, God-forsaken and disease-ridden"; Bradshaw preferred to campaign on the NHS, jobs and the environment: "Exeter is a nice, clean, green place; my ambition is to make it greener still and for it to become the green capital of Britain"; in the Christian Socialist Movement, Labour Campaign for Electoral Reform, Amnesty, Campaign for Real Ale;
History: After reporting a speech by John Lloyd, a local Labour barrister-councillor, he joined the Labour Party '84; Lloyd succeeded in making Exeter a Con-Lab marginal, losing to its popular Tory MP, Sir John Hannam, by only 3,045 votes (4.9%) Apr '92; Bradshaw was selected from a short-list of five as the replacement for John Lloyd as candidate for Exeter after the latter was disqualified by Labour's NEC in the light of fuller information from his executed friend's widow; Bradshaw had told his selection conference he was gay but would not make a big thing of it Sep '96; his strange Tory opponent, Dr Adrian Rogers, leader of the one-man Conservative Family Campaign, insisted on making an issue of it, referring to him as "Bent Ben"; Bradshaw admitted Dr Rogers was "my greatest asset"; Bradshaw urged local LibDems to accept Lord [Bill] Rogers' suggestion that they vote tactically in such Con-Lab marginals Sep '96; the complaint of the Exeter Labour Party about John Lloyd's de-selection was kept off the agenda at annual conference; Bradshaw loyally hailed Tony Blair's conference speech as "the speech of the next Prime Minister - one of the greatest Prime Ministers this country has ever seen" Oct '96; urged a more pro-European policy, to the benefit of the southwest and Exeter Mar '97; urged a seven-county south west regional development body, with a Devon-Cornwall sub-region within that Apr '97; his Tory opponent, Dr Adrian Rogers, stigmatised him as "a media man, a homosexual, he likes Europe, he studied German, he lived in Berlin, he rides a bike, he's everything about society which is wrong" Apr '97; Bradshaw

regained marginal Exeter for Labour by the massive majority of 11,705 after a swing to Labour of 11.91%; Dr Rogers lost 8,000 of the '92 Tory vote; the LibDems, otherwise strong in the southwest, lost 1,000 of their supporters to tactical voting May '97; said, "I will be fighting hard to ensure the money which Exeter City Council has from council house sales is spent tackling housing problems locally" May '97; when he clapped PM Tony Blair's first entry into the Commons, his neighbour Gwyneth Dunwoody sank her elbow into his ribs to show it was not allowed May '97; successfully took to the High Court the LibDem complaint that his party had printed a leaflet without its name, inviting people to meet him at a coffee morning that raised £11, June '97; introduced his adopted Pesticides Bill June '97; co-sponsored motion backing fight against prescription fraud June '97; his Maiden was a model of loyal support for the Budget July '97; was elected Secretary of the all-party Cycling Group July '97; was named to the Select Committee on European Legislation July '97; obtained a Commons' spouse's pass for his male partner, Neal Dalgleish July '97; counter-attacked against Roy Hattersley's diatribe against pious cyclists, insisting cyclists "cut congestion, cut pollution and cut costs to the NHS by staying fit" July '97; avoided attending 'Gay Night' at Labour's annual conference because "to allow myself to become appropriated as a gay crusader would lessen my effectiveness as an MP" Sep '97; urged Culture Secretary Chris Smith to "clear out some of some of those old Tory Governors" on the BBC, who helped make "a decision to compete with the Murdochs and CNNs of this world" instead of "doing what [the BBC] does best: excellence, quality and diversity" Sep '97; enthused about Chancellor Brown's declaration in principle for entering the single European currency; with ten other pro-European Labour MPs, urged Brown to join the Euro as soon as "practically possible" Oct '97; co-urged further Parliamentary reforms: "there are people in this Chamber who have to sit here in diamante buckle shoes, wearing swords, and people who have to sit here in wigs; they may like that - and I just want us to be aware of the kind of image that we are projecting to the outside" Nov '97; his application to join the Royal Marines in its Parliamentary Scheme was approved; told THE PINK PAPER: "It will give me the opportunity to hear for myself what those in the front line think of the ban on gays in the armed forces" Jan '98; urged reform of Parliamentary hours, to make it less like "a gentleman's club" Feb '98; claimed the extra winter fuel payments had helped poor pensioners more than if the link between pensions and average earnings had been restored Feb '98; he contrasted the heavy cuts and increased taxes of the LibDem-controlled Devon County Council with the "zero increase in council tax" in Labour-controlled Exeter Feb '98; complained about local "booze cruises": under-age drinking aboard ships Mar '98; urged more predictable recesses Mar '98; pointed out the NFU favoured the Euro, making it "absolutely ludicrous for the Conservative Party to claim to be the friend of the farmer when it is still viscerally opposed to the single European currency" Mar '98; urged the representation of the tourist industry on the Southwest Regional Development Agency Mar '98; succeeded in getting through its 3rd Reading, his adopted Pesticides Bill, which had been around for some time Mar '98; urged NATO deployment on Albania's border with Kosovo Apr '98; when Yeovil's MP Paddy Ashdown complained too little had been done for education, Bradshaw countered that there was "widespread delight in the southwest at the extra Government money for schools, including brand new schools in my constituency and in Torridge and West Devon" Apr '98; expressed dissatisfaction about being pestered by Ministerial aides in search of compliant MPs to ask stooge questions: "it's an insult to our intelligence and very intrusive; I find I am only safe now in my office" May '98; urged Europe to send a mediator to Kosovo, rather than "wait for the Americans to take the lead" May '98; his Pesticides Act received Royal Assent July '98;

Born: 30 August 1960, London

Family: Son, of late Rev Peter Bradshaw, Anglican vicar and Daphne (Murphy); his Partner

is Neal Dalgleish;
Education: Thorpe St Andrew School, Norwich; Sussex University (BA Hons);
Occupation: Journalist: on BBC '86-97: BBC Radio Devon (three years), 'The World at One', 'The World This Weekend'; awards as 'Consumer Journalist of the Year, for coverage of the East German revolution, the fall of the Berlin Wall; EXETER EXPRESS & ECHO (NUJ) '84-86;
Traits: Good-looking ("a veritable Hugh Grant look-alike" -Clare Garner, INDEPENDENT; "gorgeous-looking" - Margaret Hodge MP); blond; centre-parted hair; bags under his eyes; pointed chin; "a leggy, fresh-faced, floppy-haired young man with a quick mind, a pleasant manner, a ready smile, a vaunting ambition, unlimited energy, a merry laugh and a strategic sense of humour-failure whenever humour looks risky" (Matthew Parris, TIMES); a "fairly devout" [BB] practicing Anglican who has preached in Westminster Abbey; considers himself a Labour MP, not a gay MP; was reproached by Speaker Boothroyd when a Tory MP complained about his running around in his socks, his shoes having got wet; criticised for draping his drenched under-pants on Commons radiators, protested: "they are a pair of Calvin Kleins!"; enjoys cooking, tennis, music, the theatre and cycling ("cycling is about freedom, and getting places" [BB]);
Address: House of Commons, Westminster, London SW1A 0AA;
Telephone: 0171 219 6597 (H of C); 01392 424464 (constituency office); email: bradshawb@parliament.wh;

Graham (Stuart) BRADY   Conservative   **ALTRINCHAM & SALE WEST '97-**

Majority: 1,505 over Labour 7-way;
Description: A redrawn seat in the southern Manchester suburbs; with Cheadle is one of the two in the Greater Manchester area to remain Tory, as part of Cheshire's middle-class suburban belt; it has lost eastern Sale to Wythenshawe but gained the equivalent from former Davyhulme;
Position: On Select Committee on Education and Employment '97-; Secretary, Conservative MPs' Education and Employment Committee '97-; ex: Vice Chairman, East Berkshire Conservative Association '92-95; Chairman, Northern Area Conservative Collegiate Forum '88-89; Chairman, Durham University Conservative Association '87-88;
Outlook: At almost 30 he was the Tories' youngest new MP, as the successor to retired Sir Fergus Montgomery; a lucky middle-brow PRman selected and elected for one of the few remaining safeish Tory seats in the north; a simple loyalist who has had great difficulty in adjusting to the idea that the Tories lost control of Trafford in '95 and of the Commons in '97; a locally-born and locally-raised Rightish Eurosceptic who finds it "hard to stomach that the European Court can overturn democratic decisions taken by a British Government"; an obsessed defender of his local grammar schools, grant-maintained schools and the Assisted Places Scheme; favours: employee share ownership, town centre residential development and tough sentencing; is hostile to collective bargaining and public sector strikes;
History: He came from a Conservative but politically inactive family; he joined the Conservatives in Timperley at 16 to defend the status of his own threatened Altrincham

Grammar School '83; was elected Chairman of the Durham University Conservative Association, following Piers Merchant '87; became Chairman of the Northern Area of Norman Tebbit's neutered Collegiate Forum '88; was an unsuccessful candidate for Bowburn and Coxhoe, in the Durham County Council election May '89; published a Centre for Policy Studies pamphlet 'Towards an Employees' Charter and Away from Collective Bargaining', which opposed public sector strikes '91; made a "well-received" (GB) speech on Ulster at annual conference Oct '94; although expected, because part of Davyhulme went into redrawn Altrincham and Sale West, Winston Churchill MP did not apply for selection; Brady was chosen as a local son in his first contest to replace retiring Sir Fergus Montgomery in redrawn Altrincham & Sale West, making him one of the youngest candidates for a winnable seat Oct '95; was one of the 14 candidates for winnable seats who declared in a DAILY TELEGRAPH poll that he would say in his election address that he opposed Britain ever joining a single European currency Dec '96; opposed the Euro Apr '97; retained Altrincham & Sale West by 1,505 votes, a tenth of the majority expected in terms of the previous general election May '97; in the Tory Leadership contest, joined the campaign team of Michael Howard May-June '97; urged Education Secretary David Blunkett to "approve outstanding applications for grant-maintained status" May '97; his Maiden was in defence of the threatened Assisted Places Scheme June '97; warned that subsidised jobs for the young unemployed would displace others June '97; asked Minister to "join me in applauding North West Water for its investment in combating leaks" and to cancel the windfall tax of that wildly profitable and unpopular company July '97; urged "a guarantee that my grammar schools are safe" July '97; was named to Select Committee on Education and Employment July '97; co-sponsored motion to cut Betting Duty and make a measured deregulation of betting and racecourses Jan '98; opposed further integration within the EU Jan '98; opposed Regional Development Agency for northwest Jan '98; warned against too-rapid training of child-carers Feb '98; pressed for pupils to be allowed to finish their Assisted Places Scheme educations Feb '98; complained that the Government's change in Standard Spending Assessment would deprive Trafford Borough of £700,000 Mar '98; defended grant-maintained schools against the Labour Government's efforts to reshape them in the School Standards and Framework Bill Mar '98; complained that Trafford Borough Council, Labour-controlled for the first time in history, was trying to end funding for local Catholic children at St Bede's, an independent Catholic grammar school Mar '98; complained that petrol tax increases would cost "a typical unskilled manual worker" £66 more a year Apr '98; pressed PM Tony Blair for more financial support for the Christie Hospital, the northwest's "premier centre for cancer treatment" Apr '98; complained that allowing Belgium and Italy into the Euro meant "it will be a soft currency and that the value of Sterling will be forced up still further" Apr '98; was one of 18 Tory MPs voting for 16 as age of homosexual consent June '98;

Born: 20 May 1967, Salford, Manchester

Family: Son, of John Brady, accountant, and Maureen (Birch), medical secretary; m '92 Victoria (Lowther), TV reporter; 1s William '98, 1d Catherine '93;

Education: Heyes Lane Primary School, Timperley, Cheshire; Altrincham Grammar School (Deputy Head Boy); Durham University (BA Law);

Occupation: Panellist: for Harris, MORI, BPRI (at £3,000?) '97-; ex: Public Affairs Director, of Waterfront Partnership (a transport and strategic PR consultancy) '92-97; Assistant Director of Publications, Centre for Policy Studies '90-92; Trainee, with Shandwick Plc (public relations; a source there says he was sacked as unpromising; he insists he left "from choice")'89-90;

Traits: Very tall; boyish-looking; toothy smile; dark brown parted hair; his "irresistible combination of hair, muscles and teeth puts one in mind of Prince Andrew at his most virile"

(David Aaronovitch, INDEPENDENT); "my family resembles a circus trekking up and down the M6 with child and dog and luggage; it is quite a show to keep on the road" (GB); given £100 to spend on items of personal hygeine, he had difficulty in spending it: "my normal routine is minimal; I use Gillette shaving cream and a bit of Hugo Boss deodorant; I hardly even bother with aftershave"; "all that Clinique and Calvin Klein stuff is too girly; I would never use it in a million years"; he was attracted to Dunhill products: "a nice bit of soap - and a good English brand; you could say it's a Tory brand; a bit old-fashioned but reliable and not too expensive";

Address: House of Commons, Westminster, London SW1A 0AA; Thatcher House, Delahays Farm, Green Lane, Timperley, Altrincham, Cheshire WA15 8QW (constituency office);
Telephone: 0171 219 3000 (H of C); 0161 904 8828 (constituency phone); 0161 904 8868 (constituency Fax);

'Tom' (Thomas) BRAKE   **Liberal Democrat**   **CARSHALTON**
                                                                   & WALLINGTON '97-

Majority: 2,267 over Conservative 7-way;
Description: A previously safe-Tory seat in the LibDem-controlled borough of Sutton, despite its 40,000 houses in the St Helier estate, built as a garden city in the '30s; before '97 it had never before been out of Conservative hands in this century; the '97 result was anticipated by the May '94 local council elections, when the Tories lost every council seat but one in this constituency;
Position: On the Select Committee on Environment, Transport and Regional Affairs '97-; on LibDem MPs' Environment Team '97-; Spokesman for London on the Transport, Environment and Strategic Planning Team of London LibDem MPs '97-; ex: Sutton Borough Councillor (Vice Chairman, Policy Committee) '94-98; Hackney Borough Councillor '88-90; was on the LibDem Environment Working Group;
Outlook: One of the six thoughtful and enthusiastic new LibDem "thirty-something" MPs; quiet and sensible but rather ineffective initially in the Commons and party; a young computer buff who loves fighting elections and won at his second attempt at this Tory stronghold; backs most LibDem policies (pro: Europe, market economy and positive action to improve the environment) but opposes their decision to allow non-elected representatives in a reformed second Chamber; is a member of Greenpeace, Friends of the Earth, Oxfam, Amnesty International;
History: His family was non-political; he joined the Liberals '83; was elected to Hackney Borough Council Feb '88; left Hackney for Carshalton after he had been selected to contest the latter, giving up his Hackney Council seat Nov '90; he cut the 14,000 majority of Carshalton's 'One Nation' Tory MP, Nigel Forman, by 4,500 votes Apr '92; was elected to Sutton Borough Council May '94; at annual conference endorsed the importance of closed-circuit TV on local estates Sep '96; again contested Carshalton and, to the surprise of Nigel Forman, ousted him by a majority of 2,267 on a 11.76 swing, part of a LibDem sweep through London's southwestern suburbs from Carshalton to Twickenham May '97; was named to the LibDems' Environment Team May '97; in his Maiden did not see how the £100m

supposed to be saved by the abolition of the Assisted Places Scheme could do enough for the massive needs of education, on which the LibDems had pledged an extra £2b each year June '97; in the debate on the London Underground urged the Labour Government to "consider setting up a public interest company which would be free to borrow money on the markets", "outside PSBR" as in the USA; he also suggested "the option of a tax on non-residential parking spaces in London" and road-pricing June '97; co-sponsored motion urging the saving of network cards for rail users July '97; co-sponsored motion urging UK exploitation of "substantial world-wide market opportunities" for "environmental technologies and services" July '97; co-sponsored motion urging patenting of genetic advances July '97; sought to protect the Accident and Emergency unit at St Helier, "the local hospital at which our first child was born two weeks ago" July '97; called for a switch from domestic air travel to rail travel Sep '97; warned against assuming the '91 figure that 4.4m homes were still needed Nov '97; complained that the Government were "hitting the poorest hardest" by not allowing carers to claim more than a month's back allowance Dec '97; backed licensing of minicabs as part of an integrated transport policy, with drivers who knew the direct route Jan '98; attacked the Tories' Denial of Responsibility syndrome, for forgetting their responsibility of the neglect of the London Underground, indicated by their attempt to sell it for £600m when it "had property assets valued at up to £13b" Jan '98; demanded that the Franchise Director force Connex South Central to tackle overcrowding, from which "I am a regular sufferer" Feb '98; insisting that "the volunteers who run the Bluebell Railway could have run the railways better than the previous Administration", supported tightening the powers of the Rail Regulator and the proposed moratorium on sale of railway land Mar '98; urged the completion of the high-speed link to the Channel Tunnel Mar '98; backed the Road Traffic Reduction Bill because traffic pollution was the "trigger for asthma" Apr '98; was rated as one of the 'Top 100' in written questions, chalking up 193 in his first year May '98;

Born: 6 May 1962, Melton Mowbray

Family: Son, of Michael Brake, IT Manager, and Judith (Pape) teacher; separated; his Partner is Candida Goulden, a former LibDem party researcher he made pregnant and then moved in with; 1c '97;

Education: Lycee International (for ten years), Paris; Imperial College, London (BSc Physics);

Occupation: Computer software consultant;

Traits: Tall; lean; young-looking; thin face; brown hair; dark eyebrows; straight-faced good looks; "a smoothie who rather fancies himself and has broken a few hearts in his time" (LibDem colleague); London accent; cyclist; runner; French-speaker;

Address: House of Commons, Westminster, London SW1A 0AA; 62 Gordon Road, Carshalton, Surrey SM5 3RE;

Telephone: 0171 219 3000 (H of C); 0181 255 8155 (constituency); 0181 647 9329 (home);

PROFILERS AS BARBERS

When we started illustrating our volumes, we never anticipated outdated MPs' photographs would force us to double as barbers. In every volume ever published we have incurred cries of "I no longer have a moustache!" or "I have shaved my beard" or "I haven't worn my hair that long for five years". There is nothing more dismaying than telling your artist how good his sketch was and then seeing the woman MP portrayed with hair five inches shorter two hours later.

Dr Peter BRAND   **Liberal Democrat**

Majority: 6,406 over Conservative 9-way; **Description:** The longtime Con-LibDem marginal, with a tradition of long stints: Stephen Ross '74-87, Barry Field '87-97; a quiet south coast holiday and retirement island; has 100,000 electors and sixty miles of coastline; is only reachable by ferry, whose delays impede further development of its industry, now including helicopters (Westland) and electronics (Plessey); Parkhurst and two other prisons also provide jobs; has lowest average GDP of any county; **Position:** On Select Committee on Health '97-; on LibDem Health team '97-; Isle of Wight Unitary Councillor '95-; ex: Isle of Wight Councillor (Deputy Leader '89-93) '85-95; Chairman: Isle of Wight Liberal Democrat Political Committee, LibDems' Health Policy Working Group '94-95, Community Care Working Group '93-94; Chairman, British Medical Association for Isle of Wight '80-84;

Outlook: Witty, intelligent, socially-conscious local GP, LibDem policy formulator and former local BMA Chairman; has a touch of Dutch arrogance and the ability to get the wrong end of the stick, then refusing to let go or turn it around; he long targeted this seat, surviving the disloyal, fratricidal and insane Isle of Wight local party; on the Isle of Wight Health Authority he opposed the setting up of competing health trusts; pushed hard for the integration of health authorities and the maintenance of community hospitals; also for better provision for community care, to allow the elderly and disabled to lead a fuller life in their homes; opposed compulsory water metering without protection for large families living on state benefits; before reaching the Commons had a leading role in formulating LibDems' health and community care policies; with many elderly patients, tends to concentrate on their nursing needs and opposes the concentration of the NHS on acute care; has long campaigned against dumping sewage off the coast; in Amnesty International; comes over well on regional TV;

History: He came from a Left-of-Centre Dutch family; at school as Captain, he avoided politics, but successfully bet the local South Gloucestershire Tory MP, Fred Corfield, his majority would fall Oct '64; was elected for Brading to the Isle of Wight County Council as an Independent May '85, joining the Liberals Nov '85; became Deputy Leader of the LibDem Group May '89; contested Isle of Wight - one of the LibDems' target Parliamentary seats -against Barry Field, cutting the majority from 6,442, losing by 1,827 (2.3%) Apr '92; became a member of the LibDems' Community Care Working Party '93; joined the LibDems' Health Policy Group '94; was elected to the Isle of Wight Unitary Authority May '95; at annual LibDem conference, insisted on people getting "their medical and nursing needs free of charge"; warned against the NHS over-concentrating on acute care Sep '96; was criticised by PRIVATE EYE for having been Chairman of IsleCare, which had been found guilty by local magistrates of "a very serious breach" of regulations by failing to provide adequate night staff; said: "we have sacked the manager" Oct'96; was elected by a majority of 6,406 over Andrew Turner, the Tory candidate who replaced ailing Barry Field May '97; denounced "insanitary" Commons voting conditions June '97; co-sponsored motion urging improved procedure for complaints against solicitors July '97; was named to Select Committee on Health July '97; having had experience in buying in private services for his surgeries, was unhappy about the unclear definitions in Labour's Bill to reactivate PFI for hospitals, fearing "a form of cosy

241

commissioning and delivery by favoured friends" July '97; co-sponsored motion urging a sympathetic review of laws on gays and lesbians July '97; co-sponsored motion opposing segregation of disabled children in schools July '97; in humorous LibDem conference speech said, that since wombs were no longer necessarily involved, clinical care should be from "the sperm to the worm" instead of from "the womb to the tomb" Sep '97; attacked inequalities in health, or "a lottery by postcode"; welcomed Labour Government's recognition of "the important link between poverty and ill health" Feb '98; complained about cuts in school nursing services Mar '98; co-sponsored all-party motion urging much better out-of-hours medical treatment Mar '98; urged tighter regulation of slimming clinics and cosmetic surgery clinics Apr '98; co-sponsored motion demanding compensation for former POWs May '98; urged more widespread water fluoridation May '98; insisted that it was a political decision as to how much was spent on how many people securing infertility treatment May '98;

Born: 16 May 1947, Zaandam, Netherlands

Family: Son, of Louis Brand, shipbuilder, and Ans (Fredericks), teacher; m '72 Jane (Attlee, great niece of Clement Attlee, PM '45-51) GP; 2s: Edmund '76, Jonathan '78;

Education: Thornbury Grammar School, Gloucestershire (School Captain); Birmingham University Medical School; MRCS, LRCP, DObst,RCOG, MRCGP; "I was destined to become a paediatrician, but moved sideways to become a holistic family doctor in general practice";

Occupation: General Practitioner '71-; ex: Chairman of IsleCare (a non-profit company set up to run 21 residential old people's homes formerly owned by the council; unpaid) '93-96; Director, The Mount, Wadhurst, East Sussex (special needs school) '70-76;

Traits: Greying, thinning blond parted hair; slitty eyes; intelligent; witty; Dutch-speaking; enjoys restoring old houses and sailing (Brading Haven Yacht Club, Island Sailing Club, Royal Yacht Association);

Address: House of Commons, Westminster, London SW1A 0AA; the-commons.com/peter-brand; Beechgrove, The Mall, Brading, Isle of Wight PO36 0DE; 30 Quay Street, Newport, Isle of Wight PO30 5BA (constituency office);

Telephone: 0171 219 4404 (H of C); 01983 407368 (home); 01983 406277 (Fax); 01983 524427/01983 525819 (Fax); islandmp@cix.co.ukww (constituency office);

Julian (William Hendy) BRAZIER TD   Conservative   CANTERBURY '87-

Majority: 10,805 (18.39%) over Liberal Democrat 5-way;

Description: The 2,000-year-old Kentish city, like a second Vatican with its Canterbury Cathedral, mother church of Anglicanism, together with the historic fishing town of Whitstable and a number of lovely villages set in the heart of the garden of England; it has the second highest proportion of pensioners in the country; in '95 3,000 voters were lost to Faversham & Mid-Kent;

Position: On the Defence Select Committee '97-; Vice Chairman '93-, '88-90, Secretary '87-88, Conservative MPs' Defence Committee; Secretary, Parliamentary Maritime Group '87-; Chairman, Conservative Family Campaign '95-; ex: PPS: Gillian Shephard '90-93;

Outlook: Dedicated, caring, loyal, hyperactive traditional young Rightwing Catholic TA Reservist; a Redwood-backing Eurosceptic; intense, conscientious, transparently honest and only occasionally cranky; one of those "fearless men with that faintly nutty quality without which it is hard to be noticed on the modern backbench" (Matthew Parris, TIMES); heavy on defence, monetarist economics, Christian values (the undivorced family and law and order, including selective return of capital punishment); "I feel very strongly about the breakdown in national discipline" (JB); "an uncomplicated Thatcherite" (Stephen Goodwin, INDEPENDENT); can be persuasive ("it is almost unprecedented for a colleague in his position to change so much in so short a period; it involved two, and possibly three Ministries; I witnessed the way that he went about it, not least in my office, but he was perfectly amenable and agreeable in the way that he put forward his arguments" - ex-Minister John Butcher MP); anti: child abusers, intervention in Bosnia, the Channel Tunnel initially, abortion and embryo experimentation (as an RC); "truly dedicated" (John Wilkinson MP); can display "visible loopiness", "by no means unreminiscent of Don Quixote" (Craig Brown, TIMES); listing "parachuting as one of his hobbies, his contributions to Parliamentary debate...have sometimes suggested that he has too often landed on his head" (Andrew Rawnsley, OBSERVER); "has the enthusiasm of a character from Enid Blyton" (Quentin Letts, DAILY TELEGRAPH);

History: His preoccupation with the Soviet menace began in boyhood, conditioned by his family's military background; his conversion to monetarism was affected by Nicholas Ridley when he presided over Ridley's speech as President and Treasurer, of the Oxford University Conservative Association Nov '74; served 10 years with the TA including six with Airborne Forces, reaching the rank of Captain, from '72; was selected as candidate for Berwick-upon-Tweed July '82; was loudly applauded when he demanded heavier sentences for violent crimes at Tory annual conference Oct '82; complained that too many light sentences in Northumberland had increased crimes of violence and burglaries June '83; contested Berwick-upon-Tweed, coming second to Alan Beith with 33% of the vote June '83; defended Thatcher Government's re-equipment of RAF and selection of Trident Oct '84; was selected for Canterbury, succeeding David Crouch May '86; insisted that Channel Tunnel would be "an expensive catastrophe" Oct '86; with Dover's David Shaw expressed doubts about soundness of Channel Tunnel company's predictions Apr '87; retained seat with slightly reduced majority June '87; in Maiden welcomed NATO collaboration in procurement and spoke well of uncontrolled project managers June '87; attacked Channel Tunnel's "wretched, half-cocked financial package that is being put together in the City" July '87; served as a teller against the Channel Tunnel being rushed through July '87; welcomed the portable pensions part of the Finance Bill as solving the problems of those who change jobs often July '87; as a fellow Catholic, supported Edward Leigh's Bill to inform the home doctors of foreign girls who come to Britain for their abortions Oct '87; complained that high fliers among junior officers were resigning in protest against "the present organisational structure within the Ministry of Defence" Oct '87; sponsored a motion to penalise parties whose members have been suspended from Commons Nov '87; insisted that Soviet forces should leave Afghanistan without any conditions Dec '87; belatedly accepted the Channel Tunnel, saying "as it is going ahead I have to work with Euro-Tunnel for the best deal for East Kent that I can get" Feb '88; supported local school's pupil exchange with Soviet school Mar '88; tried to defend two local 400-year-old coppice woods Mar '88; introduced Bill to give Service families a better chance of owning their own homes Apr '88; co-urged more time for abortion-curbing Alton Bill May '88; urged floating off of Ministry of Defence research establishments May '88; in response to his pressure, Minister Colin Moynihan brought in tree preservation orders June '88; ex-Minister John Butcher paid tribute to the way he had pressed to modify patent law by urging compensation when Crown seized design rights outside emergency situations July '88;

visited South African coal mines as their guest Sep '88; visited East and West Germany as guest of Konrad Adenauer Foundation Sep '88; introduced Bill to establish a housing savings scheme for armed forces Jan '89; told Mrs Thatcher that "we enjoy so much growth and prosperity" because of her "clear long-term aims" Jan '89; urged a changed route to the Channel Mar '89; again complained of difficulties of serving soldiers in securing home ownership Mar '89; a Parachute Regiment reservist himself, said the main problem was the turnover of territorials May '89; in the Finance Bill debate proposed an amendment which would have given Servicemen mortgage benefits without their having to buy a house until retirement from the forces June '89; staged adjournment debate on the Lebanon July '89; denied Conservatives were in turmoil over Nigel Lawson's resignation Oct '89; introduced Bill to allow councils and housing associations to terminate tenancies of violent tenants who forced out wives and children, to be rehoused elsewhere Nov '89; defended General Aoun "as the last centre of resistance to [Syrian President] Assad's Gestapo" Nov '89; voted to repeal Rent Acts Jan '90; visited Lebanon as guest of General Aoun's regime Jan-Feb '90; complained that his party agent had been assaulted by 60 Leftwing activists Mar '90; worried that improved economic standards had not led to decline in indices of divorce, illegitimacy, wickedness and misery Mar '90; opposed tax relief on child care facilities, preferring tax allowances for working fathers Mar '90; was an anti-abortion teller for David Alton's abortion-curbing Bill Apr '90; although his wife had undergone In Vitro Fertilisation to produce their twins, he opposed the Human Fertilisation and Embryology Bill because it allowed "destructive embryo experimentation" Apr '90; failed to introduce Bill to prevent parents from evicting an umarried pregnant daughter if they had room for her June '90; successfully campaigned for changes in comppensation for reservists injured while serving Jun '90; visited Australian Reserve Army as their local guest Aug '90; visited Poland as guest of Jagellonian Trust Sep '90; supported Douglas Hurd in contest for Leadership Nov '90; was named PPS to Gillian Shephard when Minister of State in Treasury Dec '90; his Bow Group pamphlet, 'The Savings Trap', urged the end of taking people's savings into account when benefits were considered Dec '90; in Bow Group pamphlet, 'Sharpening the Sword', urged wider use of reservists, like US National Guard, particularly when Regulars were being run down June '91; urged retention of death penalty for wartime deserters June '91; complained that defence cuts were leaving forces with too many chiefs and not enough Indians July '91; urged closing of one or two RN bases to provide savings to fund the infantry needed Oct '91; backed TASM (Tactical Air-to-Surface Missiles) as well as Trident Jan '92; urged a register of child-molesters, pointing to Kent's increasing child abuse, reaching 4% of children, but with few convictions of abusers because of the courts' hostile atmosphere for child witnesses; backed NSPCC's campaign on child witness arrangements Feb '92; retained seat with majority down from 14,891 to 10,805, a swing to Liberal Democrats of 4.04% Apr '92; opposed hounding Americans over 'friendly fire' deaths of British soldiers since 16 British marines had been killed by our own fire at Suez May '92; urged a debate before British troops were committed to Yugoslavia July '92; thought monetary conditions were still too tight and property prices might fall further; urged cut in cost of higher education by having undergraduates study at local universities Nov '92; opposed use of shrinking British Army to impose impossible boundaries on wartorn Bosnia, where Serbian reaction, he claimed, was as result of historic Moslem atrocities Dec '92 co-sponsored conversion to Catholicism of Ann Widdecombe Apr '93; introduced Bill to restore the power of courts to take full account of a criminal's previous convictions Apr '93; urged a Cyprus-style "ethnic partition" for Bosnia May '93; the council election results suggested his seat was vulnerable by the Liberal Democrats May '93; said the worst form of industrial ownership was "the faceless pension fund" which took no real interest in companies, only in their short-term profits June '93; said, "I firmly

believe that it is in the armed forces' interests that homosexuals should not serve in their ranks" June '93; was one of a dozen Tory MPs who joined to fight defence cuts for going "too far, too fast" July '93; visited USA for lecture tour on invitation of Louisiana-London Churchillian Trust Sep '93; was one of 14 Rightwing Tory loyalists who threatened to rebel if Defence cuts proceded Oct '93; was nominated to First Standing Committee on Statutory Instruments Nov '93; urged the scrapping of the Royal Yacht Jan '94; voted to restore capital punishment, especially for killers of policemen Feb '94; voted against reducing age of homosexual consent from 21, Feb '94; introduced Bill to reform insolvency law Apr '94; opposed Defence cuts Apr '94; dilated on his constituents' problems with the Child Support Agency July '94; claimed "we really have beaten inflation in the short term" July '94; opposed a Bill specifically to bar racial harassment because it would focus attention on the ethnic content of the jury; in his own and constituents' experience, antipathy to Jamaicans was not because they were black but because so many were drug dealers July '94; welcomed more sympathetic handling of child witnesses in abuse cases Dec '94; he was disclosed to have a lobbyist as his Researcher: Charles Walker of PLS Jan '95; signed Kenneth Baker's motion against a single European currency Feb '95; in the wake of the Clegg case, raised the problem of the unsatisfactory rules of engagement for soldiers serving in Northern Ireland; urged release of Private Clegg on license Feb '95; his amendment to merely reprimand the two 'cash-for-question' Tory MPs was withdrawn together with Kevin Barron's urging their expulson Apr '95; introduced Bill to allow police to use private solicitors to prosecute in magistrates' courts June '95; introduced Victim Consultation Bill to give victims a chance to plead aggravation instead of mitigation on appeal June '95; was on John Redwood's campaign team against John Major in Leadership contest July '95; emphasised personnel shortages in Forces Oct '95; helped persuade the Lord Chancellor to put on ice a Bill which gave lady partners rights to a shared home Oct '95; warned against increased turnover in Territorials if reforms were set by Regular officers Nov '95; he introduced his Marriage Ceremony (Prescribed Words) Bill to give more verbal flexibility Jan '96; his Bill was passed Mar '96; voted for Iain Duncan-Smith's Bill to curb the European Court Apr '96; tried to amend Reserve Forces Bill to create a Director General for the Reserves; the Government agreed to a reservist Direcor on a non-statutory basis May '96; backed the Government's messy Family Law Bill as "an enormous improvement" May '96; opposed the Government's sale of Service housing estates June '96; voted for the Bill Cash Referendum Bill June '96; abstained on sale of Service homes to a Japanese bank July '96; voted for 3% cap on MPs' pay July '96; was SPECTATOR's joint 'Backbencher of the Year' with Paul Flynn Nov '96; broke his 'pair' on the fisheries vote, having to apologise to Rhodri Morgan, his 'pair' Dec '96; opposed entering a single European currency during the next Parliament Dec '96; backed caning Jan '97 opposed the extension of NATO to countries for which "we are not willing to go to war" Feb '97; he retained his seat with a sharply reduced majority of 3,964 a notional swing of 13.8% to Labour May '97; again backed John Redwood for Leader May '97; backed Clarke after Redwood's deal with him June '97; was named to the Defence Select Committee July '97; his Film Classification, Accountability and Openness Bill sought to control excess violence and sex July '97; again defended the TA, including an article in the DAILY TELEGRAPH Apr-May '98; sharply criticised inadequacy of provision for Reservists in Labour's Strategic Defence Review July '98;
Born: 24 July 1953, Dartford, Kent
Family: Grandson of Clifford Brazier, founder-manager of Britain's largest cement works, who set up the Kent Fortress Royal Engineers, a specialist Territorial Army Unit which raided German-occupied France; s Lieutenant Colonel Peter Hendy Brazier RE Rtd who served in Palestine in 1947 and participated in Suez landings in 1956, and Patricia Audrey Helen (Stubbs), granddaughter of Bishop William Stubbs; m '84 Katharine Elizabeth (Blagden), Irish

Protestant daughter of Brigadier P M Blagden; after lengthy and expensive IVF treatment they had twins: William and Alexander '90; she discovered she was pregnant again on election day 9 April 1992, producing John '92;
Education: Dragon School, Oxford; Wellington College; Brasenose College, Oxford (Open Scholarship in Maths; MA); London Business School;
Occupation: Freelance Journalist/Broadcaster/Lecturer '87-; ex: Management Consultant: serving H B Maynard International Consultants, who worked for HAR (Greek state oil refining company) '87-90; Project Manager, H B Maynard (management consultants, who posted him to Aldermaston briefly) '84-87; Aide: to Chief Executive, Charter Consolidated Plc (mining and industrial company); served 13 years in TA, finally serving in 5 (Home Service Force) Company, 10th Battalion, the Parachute Regiment '90-92; held a short service limited commission with the Royal Engineers;
Traits: Very tall (6'4"); "a tall, spare man, he retains the fitness of his ten parachuting years by running two or three times a week on a six-mile circuit of the lanes near his 17th century farmhouse in the Kent village of Chartham"; displays "almost boyish enthusiasm"; has "a voice with a pitch and volume which would annoy you intensely were it coming from a nearby dinner table" (Stephen Goodwin, INDEPENDENT); "looks as if he would have fainted on a hot day on the parade-ground" (Matthew Parris, TIMES); engaging; "lean, overlong body and crazed expression"; "loopy and lanky...gives every impression of being round the bend...with a voice that doesn't seem to realise its own volume and with an over-enthusiastic gleam in his eyes" (Craig Brown, TIMES); "a fidgety orator, he bounces about on his toes like the urban jogger who must remain on the move while waiting at a pedestrian crossing" (Quentin Letts, DAILY TELEGRAPH); marathon runner; parachutist (30 jumps); traveller (has visited 50 countries); ex: sports car driver; enjoys: running (won the Bramley apple-and-spoon race '95), sailing, the theatre, the sciences; idolizes Sir Thomas More;
Address: House of Commons, Westminster, London SW1A 0AA; 9 Hawks Lane, Canterbury, Kent;
Telephone: 0171 219 5673/5178 (H of C);

Colin BREED   **Liberal Democrat**   **CORNWALL SOUTH EAST '97-**

Majority: 6,480 over Conservative 7-way;
Description: A traditional Tory-LibDem marginal which, after '74, remained in Tory hands so long as its MP was the 'One Nation' regionalist Tory, Sir Robert Hicks, who retired in '97; just over the dividing line of the Tamar from Plymouth, it embraces Liskeard, seaside resorts like Polperro, Fowey, Lostwithiel and East and West Looe plus Saltash and Torpoint;
Position: Spokesman on Competition, on LibDems DTI team '97-; on Select Committee on European Legislation '98-; Chairman, LibDems' South West MPs' Group '97-; Saltash Town Councillor (Mayor '95-96, '89-90) '82-; ex: Caradon District Councillor '82-93;
Outlook: A jolly, agreeable, ambitious London-born conservative businessman who has retaken the seat after 23 years; deals competently with his portfolio but aspires to supplant his DTI team leader David Chidgey; a local Saltash-based councillor who has campaigned against

Cornwall's neglect and opposed a second Tamar bridge; has benefited from the retirement of Sir Robert Hicks, his replacement by a typically unsuitable Tory succccessor and the general rise of the LibDem tide in the Westcountry; crusades against high and unfair water charges; **History:** Joined the Liberal Party '66; was elected to both Caradon District Council and Saltash Town Council May '82; became Mayor of Saltash May '89; became Agent to the LibDem candidate for Cornwall South East, Robin Teverson (later an MEP), who made no headway against the sitting Tory MP Robert Hicks Mar-Apr '92; was selected as the LibDem candidate for Cornwall South East Mar '94; again became Mayor of Saltash May '95; opposed the conversion of a store in Saltash to a JobCentre June '96; campaigned against reducing help for the elderly in local hospital July '96; urged the renationalisation of Devonport naval dockyard July '96; attacked Government delay in deciding to set up a business and science park in Saltash July '96; said Olympics sportsmen needed professional-level support instead of competing as "brave amateurs" Aug '96; at annual conference emphasised the problems of youth offenders in small towns Sep '96; campaigned on the neglect of Cornwall, including tourism, cost of water, poor road and rail links, high unemployment Apr '97; opposed any further reduction in the age of consent for homosexuals or same-sex marriages Apr '97; to squeeze the Labour vote, his literature said, "Only local man Colin Breed or the Conservative from London can win this election" Apr '97; was backed by the actor Edward Woodward Apr'97; captured the seat by a majority of 6,480 on the biggest Cornish swing to the LibDems (12%), May '97; complained about security restrictions at the Liskeard count May '97; co-sponsored motion celebrating the 500th anniversary of the rebellious Cornish march on the London of Henry VII June '97; co-sponsored motion urging a development agency for Cornwall, to block the poaching of jobs from those for Wales, Scotland and the north June '97; in his Maiden welcomed the £40m in Lottery money for the creation of the Eden Botanical Institute in his constituency June '97; expressed solidarity with jailed Indonesian union leader June '97; complained of the decline in small shops in Cornwall under pressure from out-of-town shopping centres and tax-favoured charity shops July '97; introduced a Bill to prohibit the use by water companies of rateable values as the basis of their charges July '97; urged careful management of radio spectrum Oct '97; expressed concern about closing local community hospitals Jan '98; asked PM Blair about threatened local hospitals Feb '98; asked for reassurance that NHS trust mergers would not result in closures of hospitals or beds Mar '98; urged control of spectrum reallocation in Wireless Telegraphy Bill Mar '98; warned that Regional Development Agencies would have to address local rural poverty Apr '98; complained about impact of high pound on making imports cheaper Apr '98; urged more funds for council housing Mar '98; complained that drug-taking pupils were treated more softly by police than by school authorities who excluded them Apr '98; was added to Select Committee on European Legislation, replacing fellow LibDem MP Norman Baker Apr '98; urged Labour Government to take tougher decisions on the Competition Bill May '98; co-sponsored motion urging registration of those working with children and young people May '98; co-sponsored motion criticising supermarkets for high profits on beef when farmers were suffering losses May '98;
Born: 4 May 1947, London
Family: Son, of Alfred Breed, chef, and Edith (Smith); m '68 Janet (Courtiour) bank official; 1s Matthew '75, 1d Esther '72;
Education: Primary school in Wandsworth; Torquay Grammar School; Associate, Chartered Institute of Bankers (ACIB);
Occupation: Owner-Director, of Gemini Abrasives Ltd (regional distribution company) '92-; Chairman, Wesley Housing and Benevolent Trust; ex: Stockbroker '91-92; Managing Director, of Dartington & Company Group Plc (regional merchant bank) '81-91; Midland

Bank employee '64-81;
Traits: Chubby; greying light brown front-combed hair; trim beard; mild-looking; Methodist lay preacher; golfer;
Address: House of Commons, Westminster, London SW1A 0AA; 10 Dunheved Road, Saltash, Cornwall PL12 4BW;
Telephone: 0171 219 4594 (H of C); 01752 845516 (home); 01752 840820 (Fax);

Helen (Rosemary) BRINTON   Labour   **PETERBOROUGH '97-**

Majority: 7,323 over Conservative 7-way;
Description: A cathedral city on the edge of the Fens, swollen by accepting London overspill; a once-marginal seat - held by Tories by 3 votes in '66, then held by Labour '74-79; was made marginal again in '83 and '95, causing Dr Brian Mawhinney to flee, just in time;
Position: On Select Committee on Environmental Audit '98-; ex: Secretary, Full Employment Forum (Gouldite pro-Keynesian body) '93-97; Secretary: Kent County Labour Party '89-95, Chairman: North Yorkshire County Labour Party '85-88, Harrogate Constituency Labour Party '86-88;
Outlook: Labour's most-mocked newcomer; obsessively loyal Blairite ("I can't read The GUARDIAN any more; I open it and feel sick" [HB]); a constituency worshipper of the "I love Basildon" intensity; "is trying too hard" (DAILY TELEGRAPH); the former Centre-Left Eurosceptic Keynesian, transformed into a Blair-Mandelson worshipper; "I am certainly 'New Labour' but certainly NOT a 'luvvie'"; the first new MP to become the butt of newspaper diarists' humour, describing her as "android"; she considers many national pressmen as "piranhas"; her friend, Paul Routledge, formerly on the INDEPENDENT ON SUNDAY, described her as belonging to the "I Ring the Local Paper Three Times a Day Tendency"; insists she is "totally without ideological baggage"; but in '92 ran 'Women for Gould' and the next year became National Secretary of his Full Employment Forum; is still strong on animal welfare, particularly against fox-hunting; belongs to the Co-operative Party, Fabian Society, Labour Women's Network, Labour Housing Group, Labour Planning Group;
History: Both her parents were Labour Party members; she joined the Harrogate Labour Party '84; in letter to TRIBUNE complained about "long and demoralising struggle" for women candidates who had to worry about "the correct height of heel, style of suit, shade of tights, absence or presence of a belt and suitable but not flashy jewellry" as well as "carefully loaded questions not asked to male candidates such as 'will your commitments allow you to move to the constituency'" Mar '90; as Labour's Faversham candidate, campaigned against under-priced sale of local houses by London Residuary Body June '91; defended the singing of 'We Are the Champions' as showing John Smith and company "letting their hair down" at the end of Labour's annual conference Oct '91; attacked TRIBUNE for giving space to Lindi St Clair of the sado-masochist 'Corrective Party' instead of an explanation of Maastricht opt-outs Dec '91; campaigned for Kevin McNamara's Wild Mammals Protection Bill to ban fox-hunting Feb '92; succeeded in over-taking the LibDems in coming second in Faversham Apr '92; complained that "Labour has lost touch and we cannot go forward unless we recognise this";

objected to Labour's failed use of a local NHS inadequacy (the 'War of Jennifer's Ear'), without consulting her or the local party about a case which "should not have been touched with a bargepole" May '92; with Leftwingers Dr Roger Berry and Dr Lynne Jones, was a co-founder of Bryan Gould's Keynesian 'Full Employment Forum', which was implicitly critical of shadow Chancellor Gordon Brown's monetarism Mar '93; unexpectedly, became Kent Co-ordinator for Blair's Leadership campaign (four years after Blair had said to her in '90: "it is so great to meet a PPC of such QUALITY") June '94; was selected from an all-women's short-list for the altered key marginal of Peterborough, from which the Conservative Party Chairman, Dr Brian Mawhinney, had fled July '95; did not oppose Blair's abandonment of all-women's short-lists, even before it was declared illegal, insisting "it is not a talking point" Aug '95; won Peterborough with a majority of 7,323 over Jacqueline Foster, a notional swing of 13.41%; "she thought she had won because she was such a wonderful person; most normal people would realise that Tony Blair and the Labour Party had won" (her agent, Mary Rainey) May '97; in her Maiden, enthused about Peterborough's efforts to improve its environment May '97; on her 'Newsnight' debut she wound up with "we're all speaking with one voice, and that is Peter Mandelson's great achievement" May '97; "the degree of Blair worship is now measured in 'Brintons'" wrote the FINANCIAL TIMES Diary, quoting a backbencher: "Helen, who has a Mandelsonian chip wired into her brain, is the sole 10-carat Brinton" June '97; the GUARDIAN Diarist, Matthew Norman, took to referring to her as an "android" June '97; she fell out with her local Agent, Mary Rainey, who later became Mayor of Peterborough June '97; the SUNDAY TIMES quoted her as telling a local paper that it "would be nice to have a valet", then itself added: "whoever heard of an android that needed a valet?" July '97; co-sponsored a motion urging better protection of water meadows July '97; led motion urging US-style fortification of flour with folic acid to avoid spina bifida Oct '97; led motion urging accommodation for young homeless to enable them to take advantage of "high quality training and employment" Oct '97; co-sponsored a motion opposing fur-farming Nov '97; complained to ITV chief Richard Eyre about "Channel 4's obsession with sex", being told the channel was "totally independent of ITV" Nov '97; asked about need for dispersed forms of solar energy conversion Nov '97; urged businesses to adopt environmentally friendly practices Nov '97; "as a former English teacher", enthused about summer literacy classes Dec '97; asked John Prescott for better funding for Energy Saving Trust and her local Energy Advice Centre Dec '97; was named to Select Committee on Environmental Audit Jan '98; led a motion congratulating Government on converting part of its car fleet to liquid petroleum gas Jan '98; enthused about the Government's reversal of the cuts in the Energy Saving Trust Feb '98; urged better testing and information for women taking the Pill Mar '98; welcomed Government's intention to set up a compact with voluntary organisations Mar '98; led a motion for car-free play zones Mar '98; did not move her Private Members' Bill on car-free play zones, on which Friends of the Earth had worked for six months, after being assured of other arrangements Mar '98; urged more work on impact of dyslexia as leading to alienation and social exclusion Mar '98; backed higher petrol tax as civilising the car Apr '98; was named to the Standing Committee on the Crime and Disorder Bill Apr '98; denied having said, "I'll be Home Secretary by the end of this Parliament and Prime Minister in the next" (according to a colleague of Paul Routledge, INDEPENDENT ON SUNDAY) Apr '98; in TV documentary indicated her nervousness by saying she had repeated "a million times" the phrase "as the MP for Peterborough" before asking for her Commons pass the year before May '98; urged community sentencing and electronic tagging as alternatives to prison May '98;

Born: 23 December 1947, Derby

Family: Daughter, of George Henry Dyche, teacher, and Phyllis May (James) teacher; m '79, Ian Richard Thomas Brinton, teacher; "I wouldn't have married him if he'd been into politics, for God's sake"; "he enjoys doing his own thing - he digs the allotment"; 1s Hal Ian '85; 1d Gwendolen '82; "my husband left me for another woman, without ANY prior notice, two weeks after I was elected to the House of Commons" May '97; her boyfriend is the Meridian TV political editor, Alan Clark;

Education: Avalton and Boulton County Primary School, Derby; Spondon Park Grammar Scchool; Bristol University (BA Hons English Literature, MA in Medieval Literature; PGCE)
Occupation: Ex: Teacher of English in Rochester Girls' Grammar School '93-97; Free-lance Examiner for GCE and A-level English with Cambridge Board and others; (NUT/TGWU)
Traits: Straight blonde hair and fringe (shortened from shoulder-length); thin face; toothy; naive-seeming; aggressive (has a "vigorous approach to matters about which she feels strongly" - John Prescott MP); "hyper-active, with an annoyingly earnest manner" (Leftwing journalist); "robotic" (Quentin Letts, DAILY TELEGRAPH); "spine-chilling" (GUARDIAN diarist); can show "rudeness" and "arrogance" (her former Agent, Mary Rainey); accident-prone, especially on trains; cannot drive; her favourite phrase: "I have a job to do";
Address: House of Commons, Westminster, London SW1A 0AA;
Telephone: 0171 219 4469(H of C);

Rt Hon Peter (Leonard) BROOKE   Conservative   CITIES

OF LONDON & WESTMINSTER '77-

Majority: 4,881 (12.2%) over Labour 10-way;
Description: The elite constituency with the City and Westminster, Mayfair and Belgravia, expanded in 1983 by 20,000 voters from the southern part of abolished St Marylebone; in '95 a further 10,000 were added from the abolished Westminster North seat;
Former Seat: City of London & Westminster South '77-97;
Position: Chairman, Select Committee on Northern Ireland '97-; ex: National Heritage Secretary '92-94, Northern Ireland Secretary '89-92; Conservative Party Chairman and Paymaster General '87-89; Minister of State, Treasury '85-87; Under Secretary, Education '83-85, Whip '81-83, Assistant Whip '79-81;

Outlook: The former Cabinet Minister who occasionally flowers on the backbench as a fount of linked historical anecdotes; an honest man untainted by the mud thrown at his local councillors; the orthodox, prewar-style scion of traditional Hampstead Tories; "a not very political politician" (PB); "is markedly lacking in ideology"; "seems incapable of disliking his political opponents"; has "few if any serious political enemies"; "a loyalist of unfailing courtesy, he is as fluent in classical allusions as he is in the arcana of cricket statistics" (David Hughes, SUNDAY TIMES); "the epitome of the old-style English ruling class, affable, diffident, decent and intelligent"; "he has the amiable and drily witty, almost pedantic, style of educated Englishmen of his background (Marlborough, Balliol, the MCC and traditional Anglicanism)" (Peter Riddell, TIMES); "a decent bat on a sticky wicket" (Robert Harris, OBSERVER); "thorough, methodical and persistent", "not easily deflected" (Bruce Anderson, SUNDAY TELEGRAPH); can display "a sort of genial incoherence" (Matthew Parris, TIMES); strongly anti-pornographic; "every Tory MP's favourite maiden aunt" (DAILY

TELEGRAPH); "patently an honest and decent man", "much more resourceful than he looks on TV - not a medium which shows the Old Tory Establishment at its best" (Michael White, GUARDIAN); a decent old-fashioned consensus loyalist ("a superior version of Willie Whitelaw" - Ministerial colleague); "he has an awesomely detailed feeling for the past"; "standing alongside John Major, Mr Brooke appears capable of making even the grey man from Brixton look like an ambition-crazed zealot" (Phil Murphy, YORKSHIRE POST); "admired for his wit, patience and courtesy" (FINANCIAL TIMES); "he has a highly developed intellectual honesty" (knowledgeable civil servant); his first top post was as Conservative Party Chairman; there he "helped to heal some of the wounded egos left by Norman Tebbit's abrasive reign at Central Office, but did little to streamline the party machine" (Donald Macintyre, SUNDAY CORRESPONDENT); "his brain is connected to his mouth in a very candid way" (Conservative official); was initially in the Cabinet as Northern Ireland Secretary; there he "impressed senior officials with an astuteness behind the languid charm" (David Lister, INDEPENDENT ON SUNDAY); "supported hanging for terrorists until the hunger strikes, but is now an abolitionist" (Donald Macintyre); in Northern Ireland he was "more subtle, patient and immune to the provocations - and gaffes - which go with the turf than was Tom King" (Michael White, GUARDIAN); his stint there was "characterised by a general sureness of touch, occasionally punctuated by lapses"; "many observers, however, were initially unimpressed by his bumbling manner, and his early diffidence was much mocked", but he "built a new reputation as a steady and skillful political operator"; "his apparently inexhaustible patience took it much further than many expected" (David McKittrick, INDEPENDENT): he "handled it as reasonably well as he could in the circumstances; he didn't raise expectations too high; he did his job, effectively trying to manoeuvre people into position" (Kevin McNamara MP); he was a warm-up man who likened himself to a sheepdog, gently nudging and pushing the factions together, but when it came to the crunch, he could not quite cut the mustard, but prepared the way for his successor; despite their joint enthusiasm for cricket, he [did] not appear to get on automatically with Mr Major" (Ralph Atkins, FINANCIAL TIMES); was later recalled to Cabinet to become an unlikely-seeming 'Minister for Fun' (Heritage) who stood in after the abrupt departure of his sex-stained predecessor, David Mellor; a cultured man with a family interest in the visual arts; "at Heritage he...held the line against Tory ideologues intent on dismantling the BBC" (Stephen Bates, GUARDIAN); "it was he who master-minded the introduction of the Lottery" (Toby Jessel MP); "I was not the architect of the National Lottery"; "I can claim to be the master mason" (PB); with Brian Sedgemore has been one of the two main battlers to save Barts from closure; has tried hard to avoid criticising the behaviour of Tory Westminster Councillors;

History: "My father went into the Commons when I was four, so I've had the backwash of Westminster at the breakfast table all my life"; was elected: Vice President, National Union of Students and General Agent, Oxford University Conservative Association '55; became a Camden Borough Councillor "the only year in which we took power in Camden" May '68; resigned from Camden Borough Council to work abroad '69; on returning, failed to find selection at Chester, Nantwich and Melton '73; contested Bedwellty against Neil Kinnock, receiving the lowest Tory percentage ever (11.8%), losing his deposit Oct '74; failed to be selected for Huntingdonshire, where John Major succeeded, because he and Chris Patten would not give up their gladiatorial battle for Bath Nov '76; was selected for London and Westminster South by-election, due to departure for Brussels of Christopher Tugendhat; was elected Feb '77; worried about resurgence of Mayfair prostitution Feb '78; opposed banning Arabs from buying central London houses May '78; attacked the payroll tax July '78; backed a Bill to ban indecent displays Jan '79; was appointed Assistant Whip May '79; called for curbs on pornography Feb '81; was promoted full Whip (Lord Commissioner) Sep '81; said men behind pornography terrorized Soho Mar '82; was named Under Secretary for Education with responsibility for further and higher education June '83; announced an extra £20m for polys to curb cuts in student places Oct '83; announced halving of minimum student awards Nov '83; announced flat rate for student travel, reduction of funds for Open University Feb '84; urged Open University to "reconsider its direction" June '84; when Mrs Thatcher was denied an honorary Oxford degree, commented: "no cause can be considered lost until the University of Oxford has espoused it" Feb '85; urged Open University to save needed £1m by reconsidering its partnership with BBC Apr '85; Chris Patten was promoted over him to become Sir Keith Joseph's deputy at Education Sep '85; was promoted Minister of State at the Treasury, succeeding Ian Gow (resigned over Anglo-Irish Agreement) Nov '85; announced 300 extra drug-detection customs officers Nov '85; "in the 1980s, I served longer on the [European] Community's Budget Council than any British Minister has done, continuously, since 1972" (PB); his defence of the Government's decision to hand over a top-up contribution to what it considered to be an illegal 1986 EEC Budget brought hoots of derision from Tory anti-Marketeers and Labour MPs (although the case was later won) Feb '86; denies having attended a meeting which discussed Westminster Council's plans for "designated sales" to Conservative voters of flats in marginal council constituencies Dec '86; favoured profit-related pay and employee shares Mar '87; voted against death penalty Apr '87; during the election campaign, refused to be critical of VAT collectors, though asked to by Mrs Thatcher May '87; was promoted Paymaster General (retaining his Treasury responsibilities) June '87; with political resistance to Lord Young's becoming party chairman because of clash of responsibilities with remaining Trade and Industry Secretary, he was unexpectedly named Chairman of Conservative Party in succession to Norman Tebbit ("a relief to party apparatchiks" - OBSERVER) Nov '87; was made a Privy Councillor Jan '88; attended a meeting in John Wheeler's office on the looming '90 council elections, in which there was passing reference toWestminster Council's 'designated sales' of flats in marginal council seats to Tory voters Mar '88; was sharply critical of Dr Jenkins, the anti-Tory Bishop of Durham Apr '88; admitted that Mrs Thatcher and Nigel Lawson did not share "exactly the same view" on exchange rate May '88; voted against restoring capital punishment June '88; when Lady Porter's lobbyists, GJW, approached him in their effort to curb Westminster's poll tax, they reported confidentially: "overall his Treasury loyalties seem to be stronger than his loyalties to Westminster" Tory Councillors May '89; accused Labour of having turned pro-European out of "a cynical thirst for power" May '89; in Euro-elections admitted Tories were trailing in the polls June '89; was "unceremoniously removed from the Tory chairmanship...after the aborted Euro-election campaign - not his fault" (Michael White, GUARDIAN) July '89; in reshuffle was unexpectedly named Northern Ireland Secretary by Mrs Thatcher, which was seen initially as a sideways shift into exile July '89; hinted at a possible alternative to the British-Irish Agreement July '89; excited comment when he said that it was difficult to envisage the purely military defeat of the IRA; but if the IRA renounced violence, a future British government might have to talk to them Nov '89; launched "talks about talks", appealing for an end to Unionists' "self-imposed exile", moving toward tripartite negotiations with a devolved parliament as the ultimate goal Jan '90; voted for embryo research Apr '90; expected to announce talks between Northern Ireland parties and Dublin, but Dublin backed off from reportedly agreed statement July '90; after failing to persuade Mrs Thatcher to stay on, backed Douglas Hurd for Leader/Prime Minister Nov '90; was awarded prize of the Tipperary Peace Convention for bringing "fresh hope" to people of Northern Ireland Jan '91; introduced new provision against financing terrorism from racketeering Feb '91; was mentioned as a possible new Speaker Mar '91; after 14 months of painstaking negotiations, launched a text for all-party negotiations with Dublin, which were welcomed by Irish Government; "exploited the absence of an alternative to cajole the North's political parties into their first direct talks with each other for 16 years" (David Hearst, GUARDIAN) Mar '91; announced Government's decision to privatize Northern Ireland electricity Mar '91; was unable to force the pace of negotiations when deliberations were bogged down for eleven weeks seeking a neutral venue and chairman July '91; his initiative ran into difficulties when Unionist leaders demanded a suspension of the British-Irish Inter-Government conference for the duration of the negotiations - expecting a strengthened position if there were a hung Parliament after impending general elections July '91; half-admitted talks had broken down July '91; saw constituent Asil Nadir in his surgery Sep '91; after suggesting the devolution of primary legislation from Westminster, received a 44-second ovation at party conference Oct '91; gave an unprecedented reception at Hillsborough Castle for the Catholics' new Cardinal Cahal Daly Oct '91; was mentioned as a possible future Speaker or Governor of Hongkong Oct '91; after 4 weeks of wrangling, reconvened talks at Stormont Nov '91; confirmed the Government would "continue fully to support and operate the Anglo-Irish Agreement" Dec '91; informed Dublin that talks had ground to a halt Jan '92; John Major rejected his offer to resign after provoking Unionist resentment when he sang "Oh My Darling Clementine" on Gay Byrne's TV show on Dublin's RTE in wake of IRA murders Jan '92; tried - but failed - to revive talks Jan '92; voted against Bill banning hunting with hounds Feb '92 retained seat with majority up from 12,042 to 13,369, a swing of 0.6% to Conservatives Apr '92; PM John Major asked him to make way in the Cabinet for younger men and encouraged him to stand for Speaker; he was replaced as Northern Ireland Secretary by Sir Patrick Mayhew; was defeated by Betty Boothroyd in contest for a new Speaker, by 372-238, a majority of 134, with 74 Tory MPs voting for Miss Boothroyd; she abstained from voting, he voted for himself Apr '92; received £8,049 in compensation for losing his Northern Ireland post Apr '92; on resignation of David Mellor over sex scandal and freebie holidays, was unexpectedly named Secretary of State for the National Heritage as "a safe and loyal pair of hands" (David Hughes, SUNDAY TIMES) Sep '92; accepted the BBC should continue to be supported by a license fee as a "national asset", "admired and respected all over the world" Nov '92; was criticized for announcing instantly that the fire damage at Windsor Castle would be made good by Government, and that it would be restored without change Nov '92; reduced by a third the number of cultural organizations devolved to regional support Dec '92; promised Britain's first state-sponsored lottery for 166 years would create millionaires, museums and harmless fun; came under fire for damage lottery would do to pools firms Dec '92; published Calcutt Report on press regulation and privacy, accepting the need for better guarantees of privacy but resisting recommended statutory control of the press (preferring a strengthened Press Complaints Commission) Jan '93; moved 2nd Reading of National Lottery Bill, refusing to promise help to endangered pools companies Jan '93; suggested a stronger Press Complaints Commission might be empowered to impose fines, if the press did not produce more suitable impediments; legal sanctions to stop intrusion into people's privacy were still on the Cabinet's agenda Feb '93; admitted the Queen had not been asked to contribute to the £30-40m required to restore Windsor Castle Mar '93; press executives offered him support for a ban on trespass, intrusive photography and illegal bugging Mar '93; outlawed sale of decoders for pornographic service from Red Hot TV Mar '93; was said to be thinking of anti-bugging and privacy legislation in '94-95 session Apr '93; backed John Patten on testing students Apr '93; backed Jocelyn Stevens in transferring responsibility for thousands of listed buildings in London from English Heritage to local boroughs Apr '93; was thought likely to be dropped in impending Cabinet reshuffle Apr-May '93; admitted he had written to Attorney General in 1991 on behalf of constituent Asil Nadir June '93; his office denied his losses as a Lloyd's 'name' would "cause any embarrassment" June '93; published survey of public opinion on BBC, showing most wanted BBC to continue a wide range of programmes, funded by license fee July '93; published consultation papers on protecting 500,000 listed buildings July '93; in Christchurch by-election was criticised for warning Tories planning to vote for Liberal Democrats that a Tory defeat there might speed a general election resulting in a Labour victory July '93; in review of Arts Council, reaffirmed his commitment to arms-length principle of funding, while proposing a reduction of its members from 20 to 12, and cuts in its powers of decision and in state financing July '93; failed to win Cabinet approval for publication of White Paper on disciplining the press Sep '93; announced relaxation of "present regulations on the ownership of ITV companies" (which resulted in soaring share values, allegation of "insider trading" and amalgamations) Nov '93; in the wake of the District Auditor's criticism of Westminster's "disgraceful and unlawful gerrymandering", admitted that he had heard "passing references" while party Chairman to Dame Shirley Porter's plans to sell homes in marginal council constituencies to Tory voters Jan '94; "as a man whose blood is half-Welsh, appearances to the contrary notwithstanding," congratulated film "Hedd Wyn" on its prize-winning and confirmed that he had set up a review on how to help the British film industry Mar '94; held a hastily-arranged meeting to mollify veterans' organisations protesting the light entertainment proposed by PR firm Lowe Bell to celebrate the 50th anniversary of the Normandy landings Apr '94; as anticipated, was dropped from National Heritage in favour of young Stephen Dorrell July '94; in his first speech from the backbench, he backed the Government and its NHS policy, even the Tomlinson Report on the over-provision of hospitals for London EXCEPT for the closure of Barts Oct '94; was host of a press conference of Westminster councillors protesting the risks they might face from having taken "decisions they had been advised were legal" (PB) Feb '95; savaged Health Secretary Virginia Bottomley for her "insensitivity" and lack of "moral courage" in trying to sneak out London hospital closures in a written answer; his attempt at a Private Notice Question was disallowed by Speaker Boothroyd because it was too narrowly drawn Apr '95; he voted against the Government on the submergence of Barts in the Royal Hospital despite the adverse findings of the York Health Economics Consortium May '95; pressed the need for universities to attract top quality scientific and technological brains to survive Oct '95; in the debate on Michael Howard's Asylum and Immigration Bill, whose principles he supported, said 70% of his surgery cases were asylum-seekers, who cost Westminster Council £10.5m a year Dec '95; was the most senior Tory MP to abstain, refusing to back the Government's proposal to strip benefits from 13,000 asylum-seekers Jan '96; said "I have not been critical of the [Westminster] District Auditor" Magill May '96; decided to stand again to protect the City of London; voted to curb MPs' mileage allowance but for basing pensions on £43,000 July '96; was "agnostic" on Michael Howard's Crime (Sentencing) Bill Nov '96; backed PM John Major's wait-and-see policy on joining a single European currency Dec '96; complained that accelerated bed closures at Barts had "exacerbated the distress of local people" Feb '97; retained his altered seat by a two-thirds reduced majority of 4,881, a notional pro-Labour swing of 11.5% May '97; said that in 120 hours of canvassing, no elector had urged a strategic authority for London May '97; urged better funding for London Underground June '97; backed Kenneth Clarke for Tory Leader June '97; in debate on London insisted it was made up of villages that did not need a strategic overview June '97; was initially named to the Health Select Committee but dropped because it made it impossible to make him Chairman of the Northern Ireland Grand Committee, as the Labour Government wished July '97; applauded Frank Dobson's decision to keep Barts open Feb '98; expressed the hope that Culture Secretary Chris Smith could help the D'Oyly Carte company, his grandfather having illustrated published editions of Gilbert and Sullivan Apr '98; was one of 18 Tory MPs voting for 16 as the age of homosexual consent

June '98;

Born: 3 March 1934, Hampstead, London

Family: Under James I's plantations policy, Basil Brooke from Cheshire captured Donegal Castle and laid out Donegal town; in 1669, his direct ancestors, also from Cheshire, took out their first land deeds in Cavan; he is thus related to the Brookeboroughs and Brookes of Fermanagh, Ulster; his great-grandfather, Donegal-born Stopford Brooke, a Victorian preacher, bought Wordsworth's Dove Cottage in the Lake District, five years before the National Trust was founded; "my great-grandfather was chaplain to 'Dear Vicky', Queen Victoria's daughter"; his grandfather, Leslie Brooke, was a children's book illustrator ('Johnny Crowe'), who illustrated Gilbert and Sullivan's published editions, and also a landscape and portrait painter; son, late Baron (Henry) Brooke of Cumnor, PC CH, former Hampstead MP and Home Secretary, and Baroness (Barbara) Brooke of Ystradfellte, for 10 years Conservative Party Vice Chairman; his brother, Sir Henry, is a Lord Justice of Appeal; m 1st '64 South American Joan Margaret (Smith), whose subsequent fatal cardiac arrest after a hysterectomy in '85 long dismayed him; 4s Jonathan '65, Daniel '67, Sebastian '68 - all fine cricketers - 1s dcd; m 2nd '91 divorcee Mrs Lindsay (Allinson), blonde, jazz-loving Conservative ex-deputy area agent;

Education: Marlborough; Balliol, Oxford University (President of the Union, MA); Harvard Business School (MBA);

Occupation: Shareholder (Director '64-79) in Ecole St Georges SA (Swiss girls' school) '64-; ex: Lloyd's Underwriter (74 syndicates listed in '94; suffered retrospective losses from '90 in '93) '77-97; Chairman of Spencer Stuart (originally US management consultants for whom he pioneered head-hunting in UK ("I was the first headhunter in the UK" (PB)); Director of its parent company '65-79) '74-79; Research Assistant at Imede (Swiss business school, Lausanne) '60-61; Swiss Correspondent of FINANCIAL TIMES '60-61; Shareholder: Patent Industrial Group Ltd (engineering) '75-80, Rantavan Resources Ltd (family company) '67-87;

Traits: Tall; beetle-browed; wooden walk; "he looks more like an extra from a grainy English film from the '50s" (Phil Murphy, YORKSHIRE POST); "has come to resemble Lord Wavell as played by C Aubrey Smith" (OBSERVER); old-fashioned dresser; "sports heavy three-piece suits of the kind that appear to have been handed down from father to son" (OBSERVER); wears braces (sometimes in black, yellow and red); "diffident", "bumbling manner" (David McKittrick, INDEPENDENT); "genially Woosterish" (Andrew Rawnsley, GUARDIAN); "unfailingly courteous...style is sober, verging on the ponderous...solidly reliable" (Robin Oakley, TIMES); "the air of an upper-class gent...slightly buffoonish in public manner, affable, but sharp and decisive...unthreatening, utterly loyal...assiduously discreet" (Colin Brown, Colin Hughes, INDEPENDENT); "treats everyone who comes to see him - including journalists - as grown-ups" (Donald Macintyre, SUNDAY CORRESPONDENT); serious: "always seemed odd to his contemporaries" (Phillip Whitehead ex-MP); "underneath all that affability there's something reserved about him" (Ministerial colleague); can ponder his next move endlessly, as in Northern Ireland; a wooden speaker whose speeches reveal a richly-furnished mind; conformist; knowledgeable and passionate cricketer (MCC member; has a near-perfect memory for Wisden statistics; in '89 co-set [with Sir Michael Quinlan] a full page cricket quiz for SPECTATOR; two days before the grim anniversary of internment and the beginning of one of the tensest fortnights in Northern Ireland's recent history, he relaxed by going off to a county cricket match in Weston-super-Mare; "has a penchant for eating his way through entire restaurant menus" (EVENING STANDARD); once narrowly lost a bet he could eat his way through each of the four courses on the five menus of a liner returning from New York; buys wood-block prints with a ceiling of £50; has had a dog named 'Benji'; classicist (used to quote Latin and Greek in Camden Borough Council); churchy (Chairman,

National Conference of Student Christian Movement '56; Lay Adviser to St Paul's Cathedral '80-); "a continuation of Selwyn Gummer by other means" (colleague); "a first-rate fourth-class mind" (Tom Braun, quoting Balliol song to tune of "Halls of Montezuma"); his ambition to become an Army officer was frustrated by a knee injury in National Service;
Address: House of Commons, Westminster, London SW1A 0AA; his seven-bedroomed Wiltshire country home, near Warminster, was put up for sale at £300,000 in June '93, after Lloyd's losses were disclosed;
Telephone: 071 219 5481/0254 (Fax) (H of C);

Rt Hon Dr (James) Gordon BROWN   **Labour**   **DUNFERMLINE EAST '83-**

Majority: 18,751 (51.3%) over SNP 5-way;
Description: Has vanishing mines, declining engineering, some electronics and computers but much unemployment; Labour is strongest in centre and north of constituency; its southeast coast is prosperous; has Rosyth dockyard plus its threatened naval base; also has the "newest petro-chemical plant in Europe";
Position: Chancellor of the Exchequer '97-; ex: Shadow Chancellor of the Exchequer '92-97; on Shadow Cabinet '87-97; on Labour's NEC '92-98; Shadow Trade and Industry Secretary '89-92; Shadow Chief Secretary of the Treasury '87-89; Spokesman, on Regional Affairs and Shipping '85-87;
on Select Committee on Employment '83-85; Vice Chairman of PLP Health and Social Security Committee '83-84; Chairman of Scottish Council of Labour Party '83-84, on its Executive Committee '77-83; Student Rector, Edinburgh University '72-75;
Outlook: The dynamic "tough but fair" (GB) 'Iron Chancellor' who was, in '98, the most popular Chancellor for two decades, but whose empire-building was reined in by Blair's '98 reshuffle; until curbed, he had placed supporters in every department, sometimes at its head, as with Harriet Harman; a monetarist curbed by his Maastricht restraints and Europhile ambitions; "he is ardently pro-European" (Will Hutton, OBSERVER); his real intentions are obscured by his talent for linked soundbites oft signifying little; "his arguments may be revisionist but they are rooted in recognisably Labour traditions in ways that Blair's are often not" (Michael White and Ewen MacAskill, GUARDIAN); "he is economically cautious and tough on spending pledges; but the real Brown is more complex than his reputation; he is also genuinely a man of the Left, driven by a desire to lower inequality and social exclusion and a believer in the scope of intelligent public action to raise growth and investment rates" (Will Hutton, OBSERVER); "I'm never sure when I turn up at the Treasury whether I'm going to see 'Red Gordon' or 'Iron Gordon'" (trade union leader); was the top election strategist who delivered the goods, but for the other Young Pretender; according to his biographer, Paul Routledge, he still resents having sacrificed his dream by stepping aside to give his formerly-close friend, Tony Blair, a clear run for the Leadership; the heir to the late John Smith's belief that the 1997 election could only be won by avoiding any spending commitments whatsoever; by controlling his colleagues' commitments, has largely persuaded the public to change their vision of Labour as necessarily a high-taxing and wastefully-spending party; rivetted this home by accepting the Tories' spending ceilings, and some of their techniques for

achieving it, like testing the disabled for fraud; still hopes to be a radical Chancellor, narrowing the gap between rich and poor; has been less successful in persuading the public that his vision is different from the Tories', despite his distinctive belief that boom-and-bust have been caused by too little capacity for growth in the economy; therefore tends to over-emphasise skill shortages and bottlenecks; "the most misunderstood of Labour's leaders" (Peter Riddell, TIMES); a convert both to Gavyn Davies's Chicago-style monetarism and to Robert Reich's belief that the longterm prosperity of a country depends on the value of its labour skills; an enthusiastic European who has never adequately sketched out the EC's economic benefits and liabilities; lost credibility as a realistic economic analyst when he refused to urge realignment before September 1992's 'Black Wednesday', even when Neil Kinnock and John Smith were willing; "accomplished at delivering lacerating speeches" (Andrew Rawnsley, GUARDIAN); very bright, skilful, punchy, prolific, inexorable, indefatigable, Scots gloom-monger; has a partisan's talent for hitting his opponents in the solar plexus while amusing his own side with his wit (in '91 claimed Conservatives were dependent on "a Greek billionaire moving his money out of Colonels and into Majors"); has "evangelical sincerity" (Terry Coleman, GUARDIAN); "the John Knox of the economic crisis, the son of the Manse who can find a ray of Presbyterian gloom for Labour in a cloudless sky" (Godfrey Barker, DAILY TELEGRAPH); "something of a Scottish Puritan in his zeal for the truth" (GUARDIAN); initially made his name exploiting leaks; "came of age in the Commons in 1988, when John Smith suffered his [first] heart attack; Brown, as his deputy, stood in for him against the then Chancellor, Nigel Lawson, and did a demolition job on the old thug that is still vividly remembered" (Charles Reiss, EVENING STANDARD); "as a whistle-blower he ranks with Tam Dalyell and Brian Sedgemore"; "a specialist in personal abuse" (John Major MP); "a rare example of effective Labour invective" (Peter Riddell, TIMES); "the Brown style, which certainly exudes gravitas and reflects an "capable of constructing an entire speech composed of nothing but sound bites" (Andrew Rawnsley, GUARDIAN);   "for a man who is both cautious and conservative in many ways, he is exceptionally open to new ideas and thrives on intellectual discussion"; has an "awsome single-minded loyalty to Labour" (Martin Kettle, GUARDIAN); has "the vigour of youth married to a statesmanlike gravitas, operating with a well-crafted text" (Ruth Wishart, SCOTSMAN); a "statistical wizard who does his homework and knows few interviewers will be numerate enough to challenge his figures" (John Williams, EVENING STANDARD); "from his formative years as the brilliant student rector, his overweening ambition was well known, but quite acceptable because he could 'nice' people to death" (Hugh Macpherson, TRIBUNE); initially a leading crusader for devolution; said to "hate the London Labour Party in particular with an envenomed, implacable loathing" (Bruce Anderson, SUNDAY TELEGRAPH); is thin-skinned about criticism, especially from political friends; formerly TGWU-sponsored;

History: "Learned his Christian socialism and...that strange oratorical mixture of Presbyterian doom and faintly self-satisfied righteousness, at the knee of his father, a Church of Scotland minister" (Godfrey Barker, DAILY TELEGRAPH); his Labour-voting father took him to see the misery when the sea wall broke and Kirkcaldy was flooded in the '50s; at 12 offered to canvas against Alec Douglas-Home at Kinross and West Perthshire by-election '63; wrote an article in Kirkcaldy High Scool magazine welcoming Harold Wilson's succession '63; joined Labour Party at 18, '69; was Chairman of Labour Club at Edinburgh University; presided over coup to oust the Principal, Lord Swan, from the Chair of Edinburgh University's Student Court '71; was second student to win election as Rector to Edinburgh University Student Court '72; edited Labour's 'Red Paper on Scotland' '75; was elected to Executive of Scottish Labour Party '77; was a key member of Labour's 'Scottish Vote Yes' in devolution campaign '78-79; contested Edinburgh South, challenging Tory social services cuts May '79; was on

Scottish Executive during the devolution explosion Mar '79; becoming its Chairman, "he united a squabbling party" (Tom Brown, DAILY RECORD) '83; adopted for Dunfermline East, was elected May '83; said only a big injection of funds could help the constituency's problems, with the closing of the mines and the decline in shipbuilding: "only a caring and expanding social services sector makes sense, because it is the quickest way of getting people back to work" June '83; accused the Government of a Watergate style cover-up, alleging that the Prime Minister had ordered the shredding of documents detailing plans for the abolition of wages councils, mortgage tax relief, the current system of child benefit and the introduction of private medical insurance with possible payments for hospital and GP visits June '83; said unemployment was the disease, not the cure July '83; urged inquiry into system-built housing July '83; voted for Kinnock for Leader and Deputy Leader Sep '83; attacked DHSS "super-snoopers" as a "callous assault on the civil liberties of the poor" Jan-Feb '84; challenged Chairman Norman Tebbit to make a statement about party donations from foreign firms Apr '84; urged investigations into conflicts of interest with "scandalous" increase in Tory MPs' consultancies and directorships Mar '85; with Merlyn Rees urged a Royal Commission into local and national police accountability May '85; fiercely cross-examined Ian MacGregor on dismissed miners May '85; was re-selected from shortlist of one July '85; asked Mrs Thatcher why job losses in north were over 10 times those in south Jan '86; claimed 31 Tory MPs had links with firms with South African connections (leaving out Labour MPs like John Cunningham) June '86; leaked a Government report to European Regional Development Fund projecting over 3m UK unemployed in 1990, Sep '86; leaked government plans to penalize unemployed who refused training Apr '87; added 8,000 to his majority June '87; opposed the Livingstoneite strategy of "sending out search parties for ever more discontented minorities", preferring to "mobilize the support of the majority of working people" June '87; opposed a Tribune Group poll agreement with the hard-Left Campaign Group July '87; was elected to Shadow Cabinet on the Tribune Group slate as joint eleventh with 88 votes July '87; was named shadow Chief Secretary of the Treasury, at 36 the youngest member of Labour's top team for many years July '87; co-authored Tribune Group pamphlet urging a cut-rate Labour Party membership for trade unionists Sep '87; claimed that "tax avoidance has become such a big industry that it is costing the country at least £1,000m a year - money that could be better spent on the NHS or reducing taxes for the ordinary citizens stuck with PAYE" Mar '88; claimed Nigel Lawson was the first Chancellor to make "inequality and social division the main weapon in his social and economic policy" Apr '88; trounced Chancellor Lawson with the quip about "not worrying about the Moonies next door"; "he is not paranoid; they really ARE out to get him" Oct '88; on Tribune slate, came top in the ballot for th Shadow Cabinet, with 155 votes, up from 88, Nov '88; accused Chancellor Lawson of "astonishing complacency" about increased burdens on mortgage payers Jan '89; was chosen to lead Labour's campaign to widen its membership Mar '89; claimed the £40m pensioners' concession on private medical insurance was "the ultimate in redistribution; it is not the rich supporting the poor; it is the poor compelled to support the rich" Mar '89; asked Mrs Thatcher to choose between her former adviser, Sir Alan Walters and her Chancellor, Nigel Lawson Oct '89; toured Europe with John Smith Oct '89; voted 4th on Tribune slate, again came 1st for Shadow Cabinet, with 162 votes Oct '89; was promoted Shadow Trade and Industry Secretary Nov '89; asked why a further £38m in Rover subsidies for British Aerospace had been concealed Nov '89; accused Government of "fecklessness, gullibility and incompetence" for not warning investors in Barlow Clowes before its collapse Dec '89; backed random breath testing Jan '90; urged a revitalization of Department of Trade and Industry Feb '90; complained UK firms were not investing in Eastern Europe Feb '90; with John Smith, sought to sell Labour policies to bankers, stockbrokers and industrialists Feb-Mar '90; indicated Labour would only buy back

2% of BT Apr '90; attacked Nicholas Ridley for his department's negligence on export of war materials to Iraq Apr '90; backed joint financing by Government and private sources for major projects like Channel Tunnel link; promised he would have a Labour Government "working at industries' side, but not on their backs"; outlined a plan to save film industry May '90; urged a ban on retired Ministers joining privatized company boards June '90; attacked Nicholas Ridley for refusing to do anything against Harrods-owning Fayed brothers June '90; at conference attacked "the mistaken policies of the discredited Ministers in a failed Government pursuing a bankrupt ideology" Oct '90; in Shadow Cabinet election received 138 votes Nov '90; with Tony Blair, did not take take part in vote on Gulf War, although he identified with families in Rosyth (minesweepers) and Leuchars (Tornados) Jan '91; attacked threatened closure of Ravenscraig Jan '91; from leaked documents, predicted closure of Rosyth naval base in his constituency Feb '91; led attack on privatization of British Technology Group Feb '91; produced policy document, 'Modern Manufacturing Strength - Building a World Class Economy' Feb '91; accused John Major of "evasiveness" over UK exports of war materials to Iraq Apr '91; blamed John Major for a "wholly inadequate, evasive and ultimately contemptible response" over Rover privatization "sweeteners" May '91; complained the Citizens' Charter was being diluted "from the already weak to the virtually worthless" June '91; opposed Lord Hanson's attempt at a 'hostile' takeover of ICI June '91; urged a reduction in bank charges to small businesses June '91; the Labour Party crisis, when John Underwood resigned because he wanted Mandelson protege Colin Byrne sacked, was attributed to his trying to prevent Byrne from over-favouring Gordon Brown and Tony Blair on radio and TV June '91; on the sidelines of the attack on the ERM by Peter Shore, Brown disclaimed still being a member of the Common Market Safeguards Committee June '91; complained Government had been "slow to act and even slower to come to the aid of small [BCCI] investors" July '91; informed John Major that UK had supplied Iraq with aircraft spares, armoured vehicles and mortar-locating radar sets for three years before the Kuwait invasion July '91; pushed for stronger utility regulators July '91; condemned Michael Howard's trade union law reforms as "cynically conceived, contrived in its arguments, consistent only in its hypocrisy, subversive and one-sided in its effects" July '91; urged an independent inquiry into exports to Iraq July '91; was urged as Kinnock's successor by MAIL ON SUNDAY Sep '91; came first in Shadow Cabinet election with 150 votes (up from 138) Oct '91; urged better consumer representation on public utlities Nov '91; was accused by the SUNDAY MAIL of having the 7th worst voting record of any Scottish MP Dec '91; accused Michael Heseltine of having deprived British regions of £100m in EC regional grants Dec '91; "far from the promised strong end-of-year economic recovery, Britain goes into 1992 with falling investment and manufacturing and construction output, rising unemployment and the fastest rising business failure rate in western Europe" Dec '91; urged protection of shoppers against misleading 'bargains' Dec '91; promised a Scots Parliament would be able to rebuild its economy Feb '92; toured Continental capitals withh John Smith Feb '92; claimed unemployment had doubled in London in two years Mar '92; was willing to "raise [the] tax level for only the very rich"; told Charter 88 that constitutional change was "integral to our future as a country" Mar'92; retained seat with majority down from 19,589 to 17,444, a swing to Conservatives of 2% Apr '92; declining to contest the leadership, backed John Smith for Labour Leader and Margaret Beckett for Deputy Leader; could not contest Deputy Leadership because both jobs could not be held by Scots; Smith recruited him and Tony Blair to add a radical edge to his bid Apr '92; came top in Shadow Cabinet election with 165 votes; was named Shadow Chancellor of the Exchequer July '92; while he was in charge, in John Smith's absence, resisted all efforts by Labour colleagues to urge the realignment of sterling in the ERM Aug-Sep '92; after 'black Wednesday' urged an international conference to stabilise turbulent currency markets Sep '92;

was elected to Labour's NEC Oct '92; criticised payments to libel lawyers Carter-Ruck to protect Chancellor Nigel Lawson against publicity for renting his flat to a sex therapist, which Treasury had tried to keep secret Nov '92; urged an "arms for Iraq" inquiry Nov '92; urged a windfall tax on excess public utility profits Jan '93; visited Washington with Tony Blair to meet Clinton's lieutenants Jan '93; launched a "budget for jobs", including "full and fulfilling employment" which Hugo Young found "not merely otiose but silly" Feb '93; claimed "we [plan to] tax and spend for a purpose justifiable if it increases the opportunities of individual people in our community and so augments national wealth"; this "redefining" of Labour's economic philosophy was described by Ian Aitken of the GUARDIAN as "a comprehensive junking of [Labour's] ethos ever since its foundation" Feb '93; demanded full compensation for people on income support and pensioners for increased cost of VAT on domestic fuel Mar '93; outlined Labour's new economic thinking: with little reference to incomes redistribution, planning or macro-economic guidlines, it concentrated on developing human skills, improving infrastructure and compelling the finance system to foster longterm investment Apr '93; in a Tribune Group pamphlet, he was accused by MPs Peter Hain and Dr Roger Berry of "unilaterally disarming on the questiuon of macro-economic policy" and "disregarding the necessity for a substantial stimulus to aggregate demand" to cut joblessness; he was also accused of having supported an "overvalued exchange rate within the ERM" Apr '93; was accused by Alan Watkins of having been "for some months now to have been on a kind of automatic pilot, which enables him to repeat meaningless phrases in a monotone" May '93; uncritically supported Social Chapter of Maastricht treaty May '93; accused high street banks of usurious rates on overdrafts June '93; Bryan Gould accused him of failing to seize the intiative on the economy when the Conservative Government was at its most vulnerable June '93; in a PLP debate, helped defeat Hain-Berry demand for Labour to propose a Keynesian expenditure of £10-15b to get the economy moving and mop up unemployment July '93; was threatened with a "Glasgow kiss" by colleague Dr John Reid for "boring the backside" off Labour MPs with a dissertation on economic policies July '93; was regarded as having become "an unfashionable figure" with "little fresh to say" (Peter Riddell, TIMES) July '93; complained local Rosyth dockyard had been unfairly treated in competition with Devonport for nuclear refits July '93; revealing Labour had abandoned all its election spending pledges, said he hoped Labour could cut taxes Aug '93; in contest for Labour's NEC, received 414,000 votes (seventh and last of those elected), down from 523,000 (3rd) previous year Sep '93; in contest for Shadow Cabinet came fourth with 160 votes (down from 165) Oct '93; with the help of his Deputy, Harriet Harman, proved that Tories had become the high-tax party Jan '94; demanded Norman Lamont close the tax loophole whereby banks sold repossessed houses to BES firms owned by top-rate taxpayers and then bought them back Mar '94; was baited in PRIVATE EYE for continuing with his £15,000-a-year column in the DAILY RECORD after it had sacked 64 journalists May '94; with the death of John Smith, which shook him, found that Labour opinion -including opinion-formers like Peter Mandelson - were tipping toward Tony Blair, partly because of his effort to convert Labour from Keynesianism to monetarism May-June '94; agreed to give his friend, Tony Blair, a free run for the Leadership of Labour, with the understanding that he would remain Shadow Chancellor and become Chancellor in Labour's next Government June '94; came 3rd, after Robin Cook and David Blunkett, in vote for constituency section of NEC, with 76,753 votes Oct '94; came 3rd, after Robin Cook and Margaret Beckett, in vote for Shadow Cabinet, with 167 votes Oct '94; Blair's strong victory and soaring popularity raised the question of whether he could retain Brown as Shadow Chancellor if his popularity continued to sag in the vote for Labour's NEC and for the Shadow Cabinet in Oct '94; was clobbered by a rampaging Chancellor Kenneth Clarke after he questioned his mini-Budget statement Dec '94; misleadingly told a MAIL ON SUNDAY interviewer that "my mother was a company director all her life", which she corrected to having been a "nominal" director of her family's small building business Apr '95; insisted that the welfare state would have to be modernised July '95; was coolly received when he warned annual conference that an incoming Labour would "not build a New Jerusalem on a mountain of debt"; he pledged a cut in VAT on fuel Oct '95; in Shadow Cabinet election again came 3rd, after Margaret Beckett and Robin Cook with 159 votes; although Beckett scored higher, her Leftwing wings were effectively clipped by bringing her Trade and Industry portfolio under his Treasury portfolio Oct '95; initially declined to reveal his £15,000 earnings from the DAILY RECORD in the Register of Interests Nov '95; warned that Tory plans to abolish capital gains tax would be the biggest transfer of wealth to the rich this century Nov '95; committed Labour to a possible starting income tax rate of 10p, "when affordable" and to penalise workshy youngsters on benefit Nov '95; protests from John Prescott and Robin Cook that he was over-reaching himself as chairman of the Shadow Cabinet's strategy committee by launching initiatives without proper consultation were met with a Blair statement that he had been doing a "quite brilliant job" Nov '95; expressed surprise at Bank of England Governor Eddie George's criticism of Chancellor Kenneth Clarke for cutting interest rates Dec '95; was defeated in Scottish Labour conference when he proposed claimants who refused jobs or training would be docked 40% of their benefit Mar '96; voted to keep the 3% cap on MPs' salary increase July '96; antagonised colleagues by announcing diversion of benefits from better-off 16-18-year-olds into an educational maintenance grant for the most needy 16-18-year-olds with minimum consultation with colleagues June? '96; again attacked the Conservatives for running a campaign against his windfall tax on the utilities in concert with the utilities; insisted: "Labour intends to use the windfall tax to get 250,000 people under 25 off benefit and into work" July '96; in the last pre-election contest for the Shadow Cabinet, he dropped from 3rd place to 14th (159, down from 188) July '96; in the final pre-election reshuffle, he was confirmed as shadow Chancellor and jointly responsible, with Peter Mandelson, for election strategy Aug '96; warned annual conference on the need for economic caution: "no quick fixes, no easy options, no voodoo economics" Sep '96; having wished to make the election manifesto pro-EMU enough to make a referendum on entry unnecessary, he reluctantly accepted the need to include a pledge for a referendum on entering EMU Sep '96; Lord (Denis) Healey apologised for deriding him as "too rigid" and having "no government experience whatsoever" after he was misled that Brown had criticised him as too anti-EMU; announced Labour's pledge of a referendum before EMU entry Nov '96; was dissuaded by Tony Blair, backed by John Prescott and Robin Cook from going for a 50% income tax on income levels over £100,000 annually, as a target for a Tory election campaign Nov '96; Brown returned to the argument, insisting a 50% top rate would add credibility to Labour's pledge not to tax the poor; Blair's preference for a 40% ceiling was finally confirmed in the Leader's Islington home Dec '96; opened the campaign for Wirral West, the last but crucial by-election Dec '96; was alleged to be horning in on Margaret Beckett's turf Dec '96; baited Tories on their Eurosceptic party within their party Dec '96; pledging Labour to "save and invest", confirmed 40p as Labour's top rate of income tax for five years Jan '97; informed the Queen that Labour would not honour Michael Portillo's pledge to pay for a new £60m yacht Jan '97; accepted Tory spending caps for first two years of a Labour Government, allegedly seeking to stay within Maastricht parameters Jan '97; agreed with the churches that special measures were needed to get long-term unemployed back to work Apr '97; after Tony Blair's speech was taken to mean possible privatisation of air safety control, explained that Labour could not rule it out Apr '97; exploited the report of the Institute for Fiscal Studies, which showed taxes had risen by £7 a week for the average family since 1992, Apr '97; insisted "the Tories are now in chaos on the single currency" Apr '97; retained his unaltered seat with a majority increased to 18,751, a 1.6% swing from the SNP May '97; was named Chancellor of the Exchequer May '97; transferred control over interest rates to the Bank of England but deprived the Bank of its supervisory role over other banks, transferring to the Security and Investment Board May '97; he raised £5b from the privatised utilities to finance "welfare to work"; his interim Budget took another £5b a year off the pension funds' tax credits July '97; "judge me on the long term," he told TIMES interviewers, emphasising his intent to end "boom and bust" and "short-termism" July '97; in his coolly-received party conference speech promised to adopt "Labour's enduring values" of "high and sustainable levels of growth and employment" to the global economy of the 21st century by creating "employment opportunities for all"; "just as you cannot spend your way out of recession, you cannot in a global economy spend your way through a recovery either" Sep '97; he all but ruled out joining the EMU until after the next election by insisting that Britain would have to observe how it worked for several years first; Britain was at a different stage of the economic cycle and there was a risk that the EMU might fail Oct '97; published his Register of National Assets, some saleable Nov '97; his Budget statement had the initial impact of stunning the Conservatives into near-silence, until City friends unscrambled an alleged £5b in concealed taxes Nov '97; published his plan for Individual Savings Accounts (ISAs) allegedly appealing to the half of voters who did not save Nov '97; the publication of Paul Routledge's semi-authorised biography indicated he still resented having agreed to make way for Tony Blair almost four years before Jan '98; on the third of Labour's welfare reform roadshows, he urged trust and confidence in the Government's plans to put the impoverished back to work Feb '98; he extended the term of Bank of England Governor Eddie George for a further five years Feb '98; launched his slightly redistributionist Budget which stayed within the Maastricht limits Mar '98; in a MORI Poll he earned the highest approval rating of any Chancellor for 20 years Mar '98; in a hilarious Parliamentary Press Gallery speech, twitted Tony Blair, Alastair Campbell, Peter Mandelson and Lord Irvine Mar '98; invited to Downing Street Ken Follette and his MP-wife Barbara Follette, Blair-discarded former leaders of 'Luvvies for Labour' Mar '98;

Born: 20 February 1951, Govan, Glasgow

Family: His family were initially mostly Dunfermline farm labourers; son, of Dr John Brown, Labour-voting Church of Scotland Minister and the first university graduate in the family, and Elizabeth (Souter); unmarried but long "one for the girls"; had a five-year affair with Princess Margarita, eldest daughter of ex-King Michael of Romania, who said: "it was a very solid and romantic story; I never stopped loving him but one day it didn't seem right any more; it was politics, politics, politics, and I needed nurturing"; she later had affairs with Ceaucescu's son, Valentin, a Prime Minister, her lesbian helper; she also acquired two illegitimate children; he had flutters with Sheena MacDonald, a long relationship with Marion Caldwell; after three years he unveiled his comely latest girlfriend, PR lady Sarah Macaulay in 1997;

Education: Kirkcaldy West Primary; Kirkcaldy High School ("did his O-levels at 14, his Highers at 15"); Edinburgh University ("a first in History before he was 20"); MA; PhD;

Occupation: Author: Values, Visions and Voices (with T Wright; 1995), John Smith: Life and Soul of the Party (with James Naughtie; 1994), Where There Is Greed (1989), Maxton (1986), Scotland - the Real Divide (editor; 1983), How the Tories Sold Out Invergordon (1982), The Politics of Devolution and Nationalism (with H Drucker) (1980), The Case for a Scottish Assembly (1979), The Red Paper on Scotland (editor; 1975); ex: Journalist: columnist on DAILY RECORD (£15,000 p a) '89-97; formerly Sponsored by TGWU (£600 p a to constituency party, 80% of election expenses) '83-95; Director (unpaid), 7:84 Theatre Company (Scotland); Editor, of Current Affairs, Scottish TV '80-83; Lecturer in Politics, at Glasgow College of Technology, Edinburgh University '75-76;

Traits: Dark, longish, stylish hair; "sometimes his lower jaw seems jammed in 'jut' mode"; he places "one hand on his rump, elbow out, in the 'I'm a little teapot' pose he has an unwitting habit of adopting" (Mattew Parris, TIMES); "smiles too little" (TIMES); seems to chew his cud when he speaks; "charming, plausible manner"; "a soft personal charm and good looks, slightly flawed by a 'lazy' squint - he is blind in the left eye following a Rugby accident at school - which apparently had the same aphrodisiac effect on young ladies as Byron's club foot" (Hugh Macpherson, SUNDAY TELEGRAPH); had three major operations on his remaining part-effective eye while at university; "his pulpit tone, deployed against the [former] fatuous optimism of the Treasury during the recession, can be severe, scornful and contemptuous"; "he seems to be two people, a man whose private persona is bafflingly at odds with his public; behind the ferocious piety and air of zeal which Brown [displays] for the Commons and the conference, there lurks a mind as relaxed, deft and witty as, say, Michael Heseltine" (Godfrey Barker, DAILY TELEGRAPH); "Gordon plays the dour Scot, who ends every sketch with the hilarious line, 'when it is prudent to do so!'" (Simon Hoggart, GUARDIAN); can "positively radiate gloom", "can brighten a room just by leaving it" (Peter Lilley MP); 'he moves from Lugubrious to Grumpy to Churlish and has come to rest at Despondent" (Michael Portillo MP); "an elusive personality"; "he is sociable, but also shy and private"; "monumentally self-disciplined"; "he is a person in whom mighty determination and instinctive caution exist side by side"; "has bit his nails to quick"; "notorious for being a bookworm"; "his offices and flats are a shambles; filing was never a strong point, but he always knows were to find things amid the sea of paper, books, government reports, destroyed typewriters and batterd word processors with which he surrounds himself"; "that contradiction in terms, a non-whisky drinking Scottish Labour MP" (Martin Kettle, GUARDIAN); still sports-obsessed after having been sports-crazy as a child ("I was particularly prone to the typical schoolboy fantasy of becoming a professional footballer"); exceptionally workaholic ("he keeps trying to learn to play effective golf and almost succeeds, and then gets sucked back into his books"); was friendly with Princess Marguerite of Romania; has been friendly since with barrister Marion Caldwell and his recent girlfriend, Sara Macaulay; "I play tennis and a bit of golf and obviously loved rugby before my eye injury"; put an ice axe through his thigh while hill-climbing with John Smith and Dr Lewis Moonie; still prays;
Address: House of Commons, Westminster, London SW1A 0AA; 11/10 Downing Street SW1; 48 Marchmont Road, Edinburgh EH9 1HX; bought a new house beside the Forth bridges;
Telephone: 0171 219 3429/6916/3025 (H of C); 0131 447 7726;

WADING IN FILES:
Apart from the boiled-down versions which appear in these books and on our computers, we have shelves and shelves full of information built up over our over forty years of existence. Since we are not run by accountants, we are not compelled to purge the best bits by having junior assistant librarians culling our files. If you want to write the biography of ex-MP Sir John Stokes, it will only cost you £30 to see his file. There you will find that he was so pro-Franco during the Spanish civil war, that Balliol put up its own anti-Franco candidate against him for President of the Oxford University Conservative Association. This win was the springboard for Ted Heath's political career. Postwar, having held this position helped him overcome the deep prejudice among Conservative selectors who resisted choosing as the candidate for a winnable seat the son of a carpenter and a housemaid.

Rt Hon Nicholas (Hugh) BROWN   Labour   **NEWCASTLE-upon-TYNE EAST and WALLSEND '83-**

Majority: 23,811 (57.3%) over Conservative 6-way;

Description: Diverse city seat, ranging from richest to poorest, often housed in big council estates; power plant manufacture (Siemens, formerly NEI Parsons) has overtaken shipbuilding since Swan Hunter was forced into bankruptcy by the loss of a helicopter carrier contract; in '95 17,000 voters were brought in from old Wallsend while 8,500 left it for Newcastle Central;

Position: Agriculture Minister '98-; ex: Chief Whip '97-98; Deputy Chief Whip '96-97; on Labour's National Policy Forum '93-97; Senior Whip (Organisation) '95-96; Deputy Spokesman on Health '94-95; Deputy to Leader of the Commons and Labour Campaign Co-ordinator '92-94; Deputy to Margaret Beckett, successively Shadow Chief Secretary and Deputy Leader '89-92; on Selection Committee '96-97; on Select Committee on Broadcasting '94-95; Chairman, PLP's Northern Group '93-94; Assistant Spokesman: on Treasury and Economic Affairs '87-94, on Legal Affairs '85-87; on Select Committee on Consolidation of Bills '84-87; Newcastle City Councillor '80-84;

Outlook: Gordon Brown's friend, formerly the "Great Thumbscrewer" (Quentin Letts, DAILY TELEGRAPH) 'promoted' to Agriculture Minister to remove him from the centre of personnel power, allegedly because he helped publicise the continuing Brown-Blair tension by helping with Paul Routledge's biography of Brown; sensible, moderate, witty, well-informed, locally-based trade unionist (GMB) who has risen rapidly since he first joined John Smith's team; was initially "the backroom fixer who helped organise the Brown and Blair campaigns for membership of Neil Kinnock's Shadow Cabinet in the late '80s; he would have organised Gordon Brown's Leadership campaign in 1994, had not the deal been struck which pushed Blair forward into John Smith's shoes" (Michael White and Peter Hetherington, GUARDIAN); "if you get on the wrong side of Nick, he can be pretty nasty to you; he's a good hater" (fellow Newcastle Labour MP, quoted in the GUARDIAN); "has always been a staunch believer that the role of individuals should be subservient to the good of the party" (TIMES); no headline-grabber, but widely respected in the PLP; was earlier a solid frontbench wind-up performer and economically-literate Finance Bill committeeman; has "a good deal of Newcastle...muscle" and regularly comes up "with chirpy common sense" (Tory MP Ian Taylor); an "astute" (DAILY TELEGRAPH) former City Councillor who "weeded out the extremists" (NEWCASTLE JOURNAL); one of Labour's best campaigners, who won the seat following the defection to the SDP of Mike Thomas; anti-foxhunting; was initially an active free-tripper; with Tory MP Michael Jack, has a background of as a soft-soap advertising salesman for Procter and Gamble;

History: At Manchester University he "reacted against the extremism of the 1968 generation" (Malcolm Rutherford, FINANCIAL TIMES), joining the Labour Party '68; was elected to Newcastle City Council May '80; there he became a leading member of a group dealing with housing issues in the east end of Newcastle; he clashed with the council leader, west-end-based Sir Jeremy Beecham, who objected to his razing a housing estate built by T Dan Smith and thereafter froze him out; selected for Newcastle East, Brown campaigned on

Copyright (C)Parliamentary Profile Services Ltd

unemployment and pushed Mike Thomas and the SDP into third place - one of Labour's best results June '83; attacked the Rates Bill as "intellectually contemptible" and based on CBI's desire to reduce unavoidable rates; urged reform of rates rather than put even higher burdens on city slum-dwellers Jan '84; complained that working class defendants were receiving rough justice from middle-class magistrates Jan '84; urged DTI to match Japanese and Korean subsidies for local shipbuilding yards Jan '84; introduced Bill to insist on maintained standards where local authorities put services out to tender Mar '84; urged investment in shipbuilding of money wasted on local food mountains July '84; defended the strike of Newcastle computer operators against their wage cut Oct '84; was on delegation to speed ordering of frigates for local Swan Hunter yard Nov '84; favoured stronger educational campaign against glue-sniffing Nov '84; demonstrated that Tyne-Tees TV interviewed twice as many Tories as Labour MPs Apr '85; as Assistant Spokesman on Legal Affairs, welcomed the end of the solicitors' monopoly in conveyancing May '85; was re-selected from shortlist of one Aug '85; insisted that northeastern Labour MPs, apart from Don Dixon, were not hostile to devolution Mar '86; attacked "podgy Tory lawyers" appointed to administer health authorities May '86; was criticised by CSEU union chief for suggesting Swan Hunter might go into receivership Aug '86; urged orders for two coal-fired power stations to avoid job losses Oct '86; opposed Kenneth Hind's Unborn Children (Protection) Bill Oct '86; prayed against Government changes in prosecution services Dec '86; opposed T Dan Smith's attempt to rejoin Labour Party Dec '86; complained about 800 more redundancies at NEI Parsons because of failure to order power plant Jan '87; on Labour's behalf, opposed Sir Edward Gardner's Human Rights Bill as giving Tory-leaning courts too much power Feb '87; inquired about export of local placenta to make blood products Mar '87; asked Mrs Thatcher why she was seeking to cover up MI5's effort to destabilise the Wilson Government Apr '87; increased his majority by 5,000 June '87; as Assistant Spokesman, was switched to John Smith's Treasury team July '87; visited China Shipbuilders as Swan Hunters' guest Aug '87; visited Washington and New York with British-American Parliamentary Group Nov '87; complained about Government's write-off of £63m in Rolls-Royce debts prior to privatization Jan '88; opposed moving Dr Marietta Higgs, the pediatrician specialising in child sex abuse, back to Newcastle from Cleveland before the inquiry had reported Jan '88; blocked the Newcastle Town Moor Bill because it was "a ramp for property speculators" seeking access to its 1,200 acres and because of the "arrogant" attitude of the city council sponsoring it without consulting local MPs Apr '88; claimed Government was handing out £290m in capital gains reliefs to wealthiest individuals; derided the Budget's changed taxes for married women, allowing husband to pass on part of his relief only if he wanted to, as "an insult to women" and "discriminatory" May '88; expressed fear that electricity privatization would threaten local mines July '88; among other Tory MPs, accused Bowen Wells of submitting amendments to Finance Bill which might help International Distillers and Vintners, which he served as a consultant July '88; accused Chancellor Lawson of having imposed the highest interest ratessince the war Aug '88; after reassurances, withdrew opposition to Town Moor Bill Nov '88; was re-selected unopposed Apr '89; in debate on Nigel Lawson's last Finance Bill, claimed he was "a fan of the Chancellor's increasingly frequent forays into self-parody"; derided tax relief for over-60 BUPA subscribers as making the Government into a highwayman demanding "your money or your life" May '89; accepted tax allowances where people's jobs required security expenditure, but criticized its use by Cabinet Ministers like John Gummer and others "converting chauffeurs into bodyguards for tax purposes and re-landscaping their gardens for 'security reasons'" May '89; backed Government's £60,000 ceiling on earnings qualifying for occupational pension schemes June '89; was named Deputy Spokesman to Shadow Chief Secretary, Margaret Beckett Nov '89; claimed Chancellor John Major lost the Government £500m through under-priced sales of Rover and Royal Ordnance to British Aerospace Nov '89; complained that 11 Conservative MPs had put down worrying amendments in committee: "it was our concern that it was companies and not constituencies that were being represented at this stage of the Finance Bill" Nov '89; demanded Trade Secretary Nicholas Ridley apologise for having "deceived and duped" Parliament "on a grand scale" in pretending big guns for Iraq were "steel tubes" Apr '90; worked with Chris Smith on Labour plans to extend workers' share ownership Apr '90; confirmed Labour's promise to increase pensions and child benefit would cost £3.3b in first year May '90; proposed methods of tightening up on tax avoidance and evasion June '90; challenged the wisdom and equity of ending the trust status of port authorities because of their many other functions July '90; having arranged a check-off system for Labour Party members in Swan Hunter, said: "I would like to see more encouragement given to ward membership canvasses and payroll check-off projects" July '90; when the Chief Executive of Tyne and Wear Development Corporation accused him of "seeming to work assiduously to chase jobs away" for criticising Newcastle's quayside scheme, challenged him to stand against him in the next election and let the voters decide July '90; visited the USA as guest of US Information Agency July-Aug '90; with others, failed to persuade Trade and Industry Secretary Peter Lilley to bail out local NEI Parsons over its £75m turbine contract with embargoed Iraq Sep '90; deplored cruel murder of Ian Gow, "an able Parliamentary opponent" and "a very kind and a very nice man" Oct '90; visited Taiwan with PLP delegation, as guest of Republic of China Oct '90; said Labour would probably apply the 50% top rate on income tax to salaries over £40,000 Nov '90; attacking below-value privatisation of electricity, asked John Major whether he would sell his home for 60% of its market value Dec '90; visited Japan to seek more investment in the northeast Mar '91; as an enthusiast for mobile telephones, was very cool about Chancellor Lamont's decision to impose on them a new £200 tax because he had been irritated by their use in his favourite Kensington restaurant June '91; re-stated Labour's intention of restoring water to the public sector and taking control of electricity's national grid June '91; said Lloyd's 'names' "ought to be able to benefit from the same tax reliefs in the way that companies can" June '91; asked why Newcastle Quayside Developments was allowed to trade while insolvent June '91; asked why Treasury did not act sooner on IMRO doubts about BCCI July '91; secured an adjournment debate on East Newcastle quayside development to complain about the behaviour and concealment of financial arrangements by the Tyne and Wear Development Corporation: "I cannot understand why the [Tyne and Wear] Development Corporation decided to choose a developer first and then set out to try to acquire all the land from others who were told that they were being kept out of the development consortia; in those circumstances, why on earth should those who are not part of the development consortia voluntarily agree to being kicked off their land?"; the Under Secretary, Robert Key, accused him of "seeking to justify his Luddite tendencies, representing, as he does, prehistoric socialism"; Mr Key warned him he "had better start packing his bags" because "people are exasperated" July '91; claimed Government had accepted a number of Labour's proposals in its Finance Bill July '91; again urged more investment in manufacturing industry Oct '91; was rebuffed by John Major when he asked for Government support for Roll-Royce's bid for Malaysian power projects Nov '91; was rated as being the northeast's third most active poser of written Parliamentary questions Nov '91; complained that Newcastle City Council was having to consider disposing of all its old people's homes under pressure from Whitehall Jan '92; urged Home Secretary Kenneth Baker to back a creative alternative to jail for local unemployed youngsters involved in crime Jan '92; visited Australia as guest of its government Jan-Feb '92; denied it was Labour's intention to increase income tax on the better-off Feb '92; retained seat with majority up from 12,500 to 13,887, a swing to Labour of 2.26% Apr '92; was re-named Deputy to the Deputy Leader,

Leader of the Commons and Campaign Coordinator, Margaret Beckett July '92; joked that 'Fort Victoria', the RN's first armed oil tanker, should be called 'HMS Delorean' because it cost much more to produce in Northern Ireland's Harland and Wolff shipyard than in his local Swan Hunter yard July '92; was tied for third place with Maria Fyfe for a place in MPs' ballot for Labour's new National Policy Forum Feb '93; visited New Zealand as guest of its government Apr '93; claimed that Chancellor Lamont employed the methods of Arthur Daley and used Alan B'stard as his role model in sneaking increases into the Budget by the "back door" May '93; warned that Swan Hunter would close without the £160m helicopter carrier order on which it was being undercut; claimed VSEL had undercut Swan Hunter because it had "massive financial resources which have been built up on the profits of the Trident submarine contract" May '93; with Stephen Byers of Wallsend, complained that the shares of VSEL had risen by 50% before it was announced it had won the contract for the helicopter carrier from Swan Hunter, whose 6,000 jobs were threatened June '93; asked for a Rosyth-style programme of guaranteed refits to keep Swan Hunter alive June '93; voted against restoring capital punishment, even for killers of policemen Feb '94; voted to reduce age of homosexual consent to 18 or 16, Feb '94; blamed the Government for having blocked Swan Hunter's bid to build Malaysian frigates Feb '94; on the death of John Smith, began canvassing for Gordon Brown as his successor, lining up 50 names before being called off May '94; flew to France to assess CMN, which was hoping to take over Swan Hunter May '94; protested hostile reference to CMN by Tory MP Keith Hampson June '94; moved motion urging submission to Committee of Privileges of the SUNDAY TIMES report that two Conservative MPs, Graham Riddick and David Tredinnick, had accepted £1,000 each for submitting questions July '94; voted for Beckett for Leader and Deputy Leader July '94; his decision to stand in Shadow Cabinet election weakened the GMB-based 'Jock and Geordie' coalition in the PLP he had previously helped organise Sep '94; he received 85 votes in the Shadow Cabinet contest on his first attempt but 12 short; was named Deputy Spokesman on Health under Margaret Beckett, a sidelining he apparently blamed on Peter Mandelson's advice Oct '94; left Select Committee on Broadcasting Jan '95; pointed out that until the closure of Swan Hunter, it had poured £1m a week into the local economy May '95; complained about the erosion of the "public service ethos" in the NHS because "the Conservatives believe in fragmented private markets" July '95; pointed out that if private companies built and owned hospitals, the nine-year contracts of some would end NHS use rather soon Oct '95; sharply criticised the National Blood Authority for closing five of 15 regional centres on the advice of inadequate management consultants, without ministerial approval Oct '95; received 84 votes in Shadow Cabinet election<0F>Oct '95; was promoted Deputy Chief Whip under Donald Dewar Oct '95; was placed on Committee of Selection Apr '96; was the target of a hostile Tory Parliamentary motion because he had blocked the award of British passports to 29 Chinese widows of servicemen who had died in defence of wartime Hongkong; this was attributed to Brown's not having been told about Donald Dewar's promise to support John Major's promise to the widows May '96; voted for 3% cap on MPs' pay rise and to curb MPs mileage allowances but backed pensions based on £43,000 July '96; in last pre-election reshuffle was retained as Deputy Chief Whip Aug '96; said he had "never been so angry over an NAO report" on why local Swan Hunter lost its bid to build a helicopter carrier to VSEL, forcing it into bankrupcy and the sacking of 2,500 workers Aug '96; in an interview with the INDEPENDENT warned that a Labour Government would imply much tighter discipline: he said that if he could prove someone had taped a recent confidential backbench briefing with Tony Blair and then leaked verbatim quotes to a malign Tory tabloid he would do all in his power to have the culprit expelled from the PLP and from the party itself, ensuring the losss of his or her Commons seat; "they would risk expulsion from whatever I co uld get them expelled from" Aug '96; was said to have phoned colleagues at annual conference: "Tony doesn't want to see photographs of MPs leaving the wrong bedrooms at the Blackpool conference" Sep '96; in the FABIAN REVIEW backed tighter Labour discipline as part of "co-operative working, not thought-policing": "sniping in the press, the leaking of sensitive party documents and the practice of unattributed briefing should have no part in a cohesive political party serious about governing the country" Nov '96; negotiated a deal whereby the Conservatives, for the first time in 18 years, were forced to concede its majority on the key Finance Bill Committee Jan '97; he was among a 'hit-list' of 80 pro-abortion MPs targeted by the Prolife Alliance Party Feb '97; retained his expanded seat with an addditional 10,000 majority on an 11.3% swing from the Tories May '97; was named Chief Whip and elevated to the Privy Council; he turned pink when the Queen stopped him when he sought to affirm his allegiance, having been called forward at the wrong point in the ceremony May '97; with a Labour majority of 179, instituted system of pagers to instruct the new arrivals in particular and a rota of 50 Labour MPs successively having a week to cultivate their constituencies June '97; investigated the charge that Welsh Secretary Ron Davies was threatening anti-devolution Welsh Labour MP Llew Smith June '97; suspended West Derby MP Bob Wareing while investigating his undeclared Bosnian Serb financial connections June '97; persuaded PLP to suspend new Govan Labour MP Mohammed Sarwar to avoid prejudging court action against him June '97; although an opponent of foxhunting, insisted there was no Government time for Michael Foster's Bill to ban it June '97; when Sir Gordon Downey confirmed Brown's complaint and found Bob Wareing guilty of having concealed his private company being paid to help a Bosnian Serb company, Wareing accused Brown of "having taken leave of his senses" in accusing him and having ignored a letter in which he confessed to feeling "suicidal" July '97; after the suicide of Gordon McMaster, Brown was asked to investigate; he started by suspending Tommy Graham, accused in McMaster's suicide letter July-Aug '97; he sent each of Labour's 417 MPs a photocopy of the newish rule: "no Member shall engage in a sustained course of conduct prejudicial, or detrimental, to the party" Aug '97; he acquitted Tommy Graham of having caused Gordon McMaster's illness or death but kept him suspended from the PLP pending the outcome of Labour's NEC inquiry in Tommy Graham's relationship with his local party Oct '97; the SUNDAY TIMES alleged he was "embroiled in a bitter political row over his close involvement" with Bruce and Freddie Shepherd, Labour-supporting local entrepreneurs attempting to build a £14m Morrison's superstore at Walkergate in Newcastle's depressed east end Oct '97; after 47 Labour MPs rebelled against cutbacks in lone parent benefits, he said leading rebels would be given a telling off and be "shown the yellow card" Dec '97; was promoted from Chief Whip to the Cabinet job of Agriculture Minister, replacing Jack Cunningham July '98; reversed the protested curb on the vitamin B6 July '98;

Born: 13 June 1950, Hawkhurst, Kent

Family: Son, late Reginald Claude Brown, clerk with South Eastern Electricity Board, and Gwenda Kathleen (Tester); unwed;

Education: Swatenden Secondary Modern; Tunbridge Wells Technical High School; Manchester University (BA '71);

Occupation: Formerly Sponsored, by GMB (£600 a year to constituency, 80% of election expenses) '83-95; its ex Legal Adviser '80-83, Researcher '78-80, to GMB (Northern Region); Executive: in Slade (dry-cleaners) '75-78, in Procter and Gamble's advertising division (initially extolled the virtues of Ariel; "I later moved on from that to Lenor, providing housewives with a softness and a freshness they have never known before") '74-75;

Traits: A Kent-born 'Geordie'; dark; stocky; full-faced; pointed nose; flat, parted brown hair; "a thick-set fellow who, at first sight, resembles the stud-collared bulldog called 'Spike' in the 'Tom and Jerry' cartoons; his mouth, when relaxed, sets to a Les Dawson grimace; you expect

him to speak gruffly, so when his first words came out, it was a surprise to hear them emerge in a soft, quite high-pitched voice" (Quentin Letts, DAILY TELEGRAPH); articulate; persuasive; hard-working; good-humoured, self-mocking wit; a "political junkie with no wife and kids to distract him" (Michael White and Peter Hetherington, GUARDIAN); "is irritated to have been described as 'grey' - but compared to many politicians he is a veritable rainbow" (NEWCASTLE JOURNAL); swimmer; fast traveller (85 minutes from Newcastle to Commons by plane and taxi); used to work two doors from Tory MP, Michael Jack, in a Newcastle office block, when both were in advertising for Procter and Gamble; agnostic (affirms instead of swearing on the Bible); 'Newcastle Brown';
Address: House of Commons, Westminster, London SW1A 0AA; 12 Downing Street, Westminster, London SW1A 0AA;
Telephone: 0171 219 4400/6814 (H of C); 0191 285 2227/9669 (Fax) (home);

Russell BROWN   **Labour**   **DUMFRIES '97-**

Majority: 9,643 over Conservative 6-way;
Description: Previously one of the two safest Conservative seats in Scotland, which Sir Hector Monro retained by 6,415 in '92; apart from Dumfries itself it embraces mostly small towns - including Lockerbie - and rural areas, spreading over nearly 2,500 square miles; it contains plants of ICI, BNFL, and the boiler-making subsidiary of Rolls-Royce; Robert Burns is buried there; its former mining areas were moved into Galloway in '83;
Position: Dumfries and Galloway Unitary Councillor (Labour Group Leader '95-) '95-; ex: Dumfries & Galloway Regional Councillor '86-96; Chairman, Public Protection Committee '90-94; Annandale & Eskdale District Councillor '88-96; "I served as a member of the Dumfries and Galloway Police Authority for 11 years, four of which were as its Chairman";
Outlook: A long-established locally-born local government stalwart who, on his first Parliamentary attempt, rode the anti-Conservative tide into a hitherto unbreachable fortress; he had pioneered local improvements like free travel for senior citizens on public transport, in partnership with private companies; one of Labour's few working-class members in the 'Class of '97';
History: He joined the Labour party '78; he was elected to Dumfries and Galloway Regional Council May '86; was elected to Dumfries and Galloway Unitary Council, becoming its Labour Group Leader May '95; was selected for Dumfries, made more vulnerable by the retirement of the sitting Tory MP Sir Hector Monro, after three decades Oct '96; claimed the Dumfries area had the second lowest average wage levels in Scotland Apr '97; became the first Labour MP for Dumfries, winning by 9,643 over the veteran Tory candidate Struan Stevenson on a near-record swing of 16.49%; "even in our wildest dreams, we had never contemplated the size of the eventual majority" May '97; asked International Development Secretary Clare Short how many refugees had returned to Rwanda, Burundi and Zaire May '97; asked the Scottish Secretary about his plans to improve Scottish food standards June '97; urged the amalgamation of the NHS trusts in sparsely-populated areas like his July '97; urged a further detailed survey of offshore Beaufort's Dyke and a public inquiry into the dumping there July

'97; his Maiden, in loyal support of Chancellor Brown's Budget, was largely a recital of all the advances which had first taken place in Dumfries July '97; was given a brief walk-on part in Tam Dalyell's enormously lengthy new adjournment debate on Lockerbie because he had "served on the Dumfries and Galloway Police Authority for 11 years, four of which were as its Chairman"; he was sure the two Libyan accused could receive a "fair trial" in Scotland and was opposed to the trial being handed over to a "third party" as desired by Dalyell July '97; backed ban on import of asbestos July '97; welcomed the Minimum Wage Bill as ending the need for some constituents to hold down two or three jobs to survive without relying on benefits Dec '97; co-sponsored motion urging the continuation of party political broadcasts Jan '98; pointed out risks for Scottish sheep exporters to France of the new EU requirement to split carcases to remove specified risk materials Feb '98; again supported the Government against Tam Dalyell, pointing out that even if the UK agreed to trying the Libyan accused in a neutral country, there was no "clear guarantee" from the Libyans that they "would hand over the two suspects" Mar '98;

Born: 17 September 1951, Annan, Dumfriesshire

Family: Son, of late Howard Russell Brown and Muriel (Anderson); married Christine Margaret (Calvert); 3d;

Education: Annan Academy;

Occupation: Former Plant Operative, in ICI Films, Dumfries '92-97; previously Production Supervisor, in ICI Explosives, Dumfries '74-92 (TGWU);

Traits: Slim face; short dark brown greying hair and beard; enjoys sport, particularly foootball (runs a local primary school football team);

Address: House of Commons, Westminster, London SW1A 0AA; 56 Wood Avenue, Annan, Dumfriesshire DG1 6DE;

Telephone: 0171 219 3000 (H of C); 01461 205365 (home);

Des(mond) BROWNE QC　　　　**Labour**　　　　**KILMARNOCK & LOUDOUN '97-**

Majority: 7,256 over SNP 6-way;

Description: The unaltered seat embracing the proud and independent town of Kilmarnock and smaller towns and communities; it contains the major bottling plant of Johnnie Walker whisky; in '92 the SNP became the leading challenger to Labour supremacy;

Position: On: Scottish Catholic Bishops' Conference Working Party on Child Sexual Abuse '95-, Scottish Council for Civil Liberties '76-, Scottish Office Consultative Committee on Child Law '92-94; Chairman, Children's Rights Group '81-86;

Outlook: Able, well-connected, socially-sensitive party loyalist and top Scots Catholic advocate, specialising in family law; was parachuted in as the last-minute replacement candidate for this SNP-threatened seat; formerly a local solicitor, he more than held the SNP at bay; is linked with Scottish Secretary Donald Dewar through the Glasgow law firm of Ross Harper and Murphy; also was "Gordon Brown's preferred candidate for the seat" (NEW STATESMAN);

History: Following an upbringing on a council estate at Steventon, as the son of an ICI process worker, joined the Labour Party at 23, '75; contested LibDem-held Argyll & Bute, running in Labour's traditional fourth place Apr '92; represented Labour in court, preventing a 'Panorama' interview with PM John Major being shown in Scotland on the eve of local elections May '95; was selected over eight others within 20 days of the election by Labour's NEC when the Labour MP-candidate, Leftwinger Willie McKelvey, had to stand down due to a slight stroke Apr '97; derided the policies of his main challenger, the SNP, as "dangerous pie in the sky"; rejected the claims of his SNP opponent, Alex Neil, saying "no one in the party believed a Blairite had been deliberately imposed on them", noting that "Willie McKelvey hasn't disappeared; he is here to help me"; claimed the main issue was job creation to ease the unemployment "epidemic" in certain housing estates and the extension of the M77 to Fenwick Apr '97; retained the seat with a majority over the SNP of 7,256, a slight (0.62%) swing from SNP to Labour May '97; led a motion congratulating Knockentiber Amateur Football Club for their victory in the Scottish Amateur Club Final May '97; expressed solidarity with jailed Indonesian union leader June '97; pressed PM Tony Blair to take measures against "the threat of organised crime emanating from Russia and eastern Europe" June '97; asked for encouragement for a local heritage facility training the young in old lacemaking skills June '97; his Maiden, understandably for an advocate specialising in child law, was on the Child Support Agency; he urged a £15 disregard and warned about the CSA's possible challenge to the European Convention on European Rights June '97; asked when Britain would incorporate into British law the European Convention on Human Rights July '97; urged a level playing field for Scotch whisky exports, particularly in India July '97; made one of the best contributions to the debate on the Social Security Bill, emphasising the need for the system's complete overhaul July '97; strongly supported the Scotland Bill, emphasising that popular support for Scottish home rule had been produced by the Conservative exploitation of its majority in England to impose unwanted legislation on Scotland Jan '98; pointed out that its state pensions put the UK second from the bottom of the '95 EU league table, blaming it on the Tories' breaking the link with average earnings Mar '98; opposed devolution to Scotland of minimum wage controls because low wages afflicted all regions equally, with a tenth earning under £3.20 an hour throughout the UK Mar '98; pointed out that the disproportionate use of custody sentences by the Kilmarnock Sheriff Court had been curbed by East Ayrshire's Social Work Department in persuading it toward more non-custodial sentences Apr '98;

Born: 22 March 1952, Steventon, Ayrshire

Family: Son of an ICI process worker; married; 2s: Daniel '85, Samuel '88;

Education: St Michael's Academy (RC), Kilwinning '64-70; Glasgow University (LLB) '70-74;

Occupation: Advocate, called to the Bar '93, specialising in child law; on Deans' Council, Faculty of Advocates '94-; Clerk to the Human Rights Committee, Faculty of Advocates '94-; formerly a Solicitor '76-92: Senior Partner, in McCluskey, Browne, Kilmarnock '85-92, Partner, in Ross Harper & Murphy, Glasgow '80-85; on Council of Law Society of Scotland '88-91;

Traits: Stocky; small, bird-like features; square face; speckled greying dark swept-back full head of hair; moderate in tone; Roman Catholic of working class origins;

Address: House of Commons, Westminster, London SW1A 0AA; 20 Glenlockhart Road, Edinburgh EH14 1BN;

Telephone: 0171 219 3000 (H of C); 0131 443 5439;

Our WESTMINSTER CONFIDENTIAL broke the 'Profumo Scandal'

Angela BROWNING   Conservative   **TIVERTON & HONITON '97-**

Majority: 1,653 (2.8%) over Liberal Democrat 7-way;
Description: A new small-town and rural constituency in inland Devon made up of the bulk of her former Tiverton and a small part of abolished Honiton, including 8,500 voters in and around the town itself; the Conservatives' main challengers are the Liberal Democrats;
Former Seat: Tiverton '92-97
Position: President, Women Into Business '92-; ex: Deputy Spokesman, on Education and Disability '97-98; Parliamentary Secretary, Agriculture, Fisheries and Food ('Minister for Food') '94-97; Government Co-Chairman of Women' National Commission '95-97; PPS, to Michael Forsyth '93-94; on Agriculture Select Committee '92-93; Secretary, Conservative MPs' Employment Committee '92-93; Chairman, Rights of Way Review Committee '93; on Department of Employment's Advisory Committee '89-92; Chairman, Western Area Conservative Political Centre; Vice Chairman, Tiverton Constituency; on National Advisory Committees: of Conservative Political Centre, of Small Business Bureau (Director);
Outlook: The "quick-witted and pugnacious" (INDEPENDENT) but self-retired former junior Minister who loyally and capably manned the BSE ramparts; was rated one of the three best women in John Major's Government; a Eurosceptic who was Redwood's '97 campaign manager; "I have always taken a very strong stand on issues like defence and a sound economy; on the other hand I also have a particular interest in...the mentally handicapped and mental illness" (AB); previously a caring new spokesperson for small business people, particularly the selfmade; was initially a very assiduous backbencher, more interested in solving real problems in a "One Nation" spirit than partisan posturing; in office could occasionally descend to low-level partisanship about alleged Labour councils' preference for lesbians; a well-trained, experienced executive in sales, management and training who specialised in collecting debts and credit control; one of the three women selected for safe Tory seats, after eight years on candidates' list, who became Robin Maxwell-Hyslop's successor; very conscious of barriers to women politicians, especially middle-aged ones: "there seems to be an age barrier imposed on women in politics" which Teresa Gorman had to hurdle with a lie; a strong advocate of "opening doors" and providing ladders for those born with limited opportunities; works for people with autistism and others with permanent disabilities, only partly because her son is autistic; she stood down from the front bench to help her son;
History: She came from a non-political family but "I have always been a Conservative and became actively involved with the party at about the age of 18" '64; she joined the Conservative Party '80; in the '80s she debated actively for 'Peace Through NATO' against CNDers, including Bruce Kent; spoke in defence debate at annual conference as a Tiverton representative Oct '84; was selected for Crewe and Nantwich, against Gwyneth Dunwoody Apr '86; as a small business spokesman at party conference, urged Government action to keep wages down and business rates low, with VAT threshold increased to £50,000 Oct '86; at Conservative Central Council, again urged the VAT threshold be raised Mar '87; at her formal adoption meeting insisted it was despicable of socialists like Mrs Dunwoody who lived in large houses and owned large cars to pour scorn on Conservative policies to give power and

independence to all ordinary people, pretending that Conservatives were not a "caring" party; she declaimed that "as someone who grew up as one of those people for whom doors have been opened, I am determined that we should continue the wider distribution of wealth and properties; that is the way forward for 'one nation'"; "Conservatives believe that true caring is endorsed by the ability to provide for the most needy - and not just to talk about it" May '87; was narrowly defeated by Gwyneth Dunwoody, with a fractional .7% swing from Tories to Labour June '87; served on Employment Department's Advisory Committee, specialising in women's employment from '89; was selected for Tiverton, as successor to retiring Robin Maxwell-Hyslop Nov '89; retained Tiverton, with majority increased to 11,089, a 1% swing from Liberal Democrats Apr '92; signed motion urging "a fresh start" on Maastricht after its rejection by the Danes June '92; made her Maiden on agriculture, welcoming improvements in CAP and help for sheepfarmers, but urged more; expressed her determination to work for those with permanent disabilities June '92; asked John Major to endorse her view that Shakespeare had to have "a central place in the teaching of English in our schools" July '92; was named to Select Committee on Agriculture, which was interpreted as a way of weaning her from Euroscepticism July '92; was elected Secretary of Conservative MPs' Employment Committee July '92; with 40 other Tory MPs, voted for an £11,000 extra office allowance for MPs, against Government's wishes July '92; flew to Dubai as guest of its Emirates Airline Sep '92; secured an adjournment debate to criticise "the antiquated and deeply unjust system of commercial leasehold", freezing the "huge escalation that took place in rents for shops and offices in the late 1980s", with rents soaring at over four times the increase in RPI from '85 to '90; also attacked long leases and their upwards-only rent revisions and original-tenant liability Nov '92; was uncertain about whether to support the Government's pit closure programme Dec '92; insisted there was a need for legislation to provide the disabled with rights Feb '93; raised the problems of small businesses which had to make training payments but had no hope of grants Feb '93; made pre-Budget representations on behalf of Federation of Small Businesses to Chancellor Lamont Mar '93; urged Chancellor to continue his previous year's first-year capital allowance for a further year, allowing small businesses a ceiling of at least £50,000 Apr '93; welcomed Finance Bill's change to cash accounting system because of slow payments and bad debts: "an egg producer in my constituency was told by a large supermarket that the payment terms that had previously been 30 days was to be changed to 60 without any question of renegotiation" May '93; became Chairman of Rights of Way Review Committee May '93; urged "proper compensation" for impending VAT on domestic fuel for "pensioners, the disabled, the frail, the elderly and people of whatever age who very much rely on heating" May '93; was named PPS to hard-Right Michael Forsyth, Minister of State for Employment, necessitating her coming off the Agriculture Select Committee June '93; as "a spokesman for the Small Business Bureau and Women into Business" she understood the problems of small suppliers dependent on threatened Devonport and Rosyth June '93; was concerned that rural schizophrenics were sometimes housed in urban conurbations July '93; while admitting that some exploited the Social Security net, insisted that "when a teenage girl has had a baby, there is a statutory obligation...to ensure that mother and child are cared for and that they have a warm, safe and clean environment" July '93; complained that fishermen allocated only 80 days at sea could not service their bank loans July '93; complained that in neighbouring Exeter people were afraid to go into the city centre at night but its Labour-led council would not install closed-circuit cameras Oct '93; on behalf of the Small Business Bureau applauded the Chancellor's abolition of statutory audits for unincorporated businesses with turnovers under £90,000 Dec '93; showed concern about "huge, unexpected and regular increases" imposed on local elderly in sheltered accommodation Jan '94; voted to restore capital punishment for killers of policemen Feb '94; voted to reduce age of homosexual consent to 18, not 16, Feb

'94; in 2nd Reading of Dr Berry's Bill on civil rights for the disabled - for which she voted - asked for attention to the needs of the autistic, as Special Counsellor to the National Autistic Society, and the mother of an autistic son Mar '94; agreed with Home Secretary Michael Howard in partly blaming parents for soaring crime: "many children come from backgrounds where parents have no respect for authority" Apr '94; again urged more extensive and sensitive handling of children with special needs May '94; critifised Lady Olga Maitland for being "in the wrong battle" in helping to torpedo Dr Roger Berry's disability Bill at the behest of the Tory Whips May '94; opposed limits on Sunday trading hours for garden centres like Otter Nursery in East Devon June '94; in the reshuffle, was named Parliamentary Secretary for Agriculture, Fisheries and Food, replacing Nicholas Soames: "I like my food, but I won't be having a brace of grouse and a pitcher of claret for breakfast every day" July '94; was thrown into the "tuna war" in the Bay of Biscay Aug '94; deplored the EU's failure to follow UK's lead in abolishing tethers in sow stalls Dec '94; deplored "extremist" demonstration at farm of William Waldegrave because of possible sale of calves into veal crates Jan '95; succeeded Baroness Denton as Government Co-Chairman of Women's National Commission Feb? '95; disparaged as "whingeing" Labour complaints about unequal treatment for women, wrongly claiming that Avon Council had cut funds for Boy Scouts to provide gym mats for lesbians Mar '95; after a partly successful tour of EU capitals, again urged Europe-wide adoption of Britain's ban on the veal crate "in the animals' best interest" Mar '95; invited Labour MP Dennis Skinner to come up and see her some time about dioxine levels on Bolsover's dairy farms Mar '95; opposed warning labels on food as an encroachment by the "nanny state" May '95; attacked "European nonsenses that arise from time to time and are batted away as quickly as possible" like the directive on nitrates in lettuces that threatened the UK lettuce industry June '95; defended the Conservative Government's "balanced view" on BSE and its avoidance of "responding to unfounded fears by banning material that is perfectly safe"; "even though there is no evidence that BSE can be transmitted to humans" "we have...taken proportionate action to ensure that the risk is removed" by destroying suspect cattle Jan '96; turned down an invitation from Michael Fabricant to tour Europe a deux dispensing superior British farm produce Feb '96; at an NFU meeting at Exeter University told worried farmers that scientists thought there "may be a link" between BSE and new CJD Mar '96; admitted 1m sheep and 1800 calves had been exported illegally with the complicity of her Ministry Mar '96; she banned Britain's top-selling pesticide for roses June '96; she admitted there were 20,000 tons of contaminated cattle feed still in store June '96; voted for a 3% cap on MPs' pay increases, against basing pensions on £43,000 July '96; in the reshuffle was left in place, despite widespread expectations of a promotion, not least because she had done so much better than her cackhanded boss, Douglas Hogg July '96; tried to assuage Tory MPs by saying the Government would not support "needless" slaughter of cattle, despite disturbing new research Aug '96; complained about townies who moved into country villages and complained about cowpats and farming smells Oct '96; voted against a total ban on foxhunting Nov '96; admitted the BSE crisis had cost the Government £855.1m in the last nine months of 1996, Feb '97; promised to publish soon a hygeine league table of slaughterhouses Mar '97; although she originally backed John Major on "wait and see" she suddenly opposed any further transfer of sovereignty to Europe, such as a single currency, insisting the transfer of gold reserves to a European central bank was a "step too far" Apr '97; after writing the Conservative Manifesto for Farming, narrowly retained her altered seat by a five-sixths reduced majority of 1,653, on a notional swing to the LibDems of 8.4%; she was "shell-shocked" about what happened elsewhere May '97; served as campaign manager for John Redwood as Leader May-June '97; switched to Ken Clarke for Leader June '97; was said to abstain against Redwood-Clarke deal to bar Hague June '97; complained of misdiagnoses of breast cancers in Devon hospitals June

'97; was named Deputy Spokesman on Education June '97; supported much of Labour's White Paper on Education, although she felt it was too strong on equality, too weak on opportunity and rising standards July '97; a flashflood hit her Myrtle Cottage home in East Devon, washing away her copy of the Dearing Report on Higher Education Aug '97; announced imminent withdrawal from her frontbench post as Deputy Spokesman on Education to spend more time with her autistic son, Robin May '98; retired June '98;

Born: 4 December 1946, Reading

Family: "My grandfather and brother were submariners"; daughter of Thomas Pearson, Chief Technician in Department of Physiological Chemistry, and Linda Frances (Cross); m '68 David Browning, accountant and rowing umpire; 2s Philip Grenville '70, Robin James '71, a sufferer from Asperger's Syndrome, a type of autism;

Education: The Hill School, Emmer Green; Westwood Girls (Grammar) School; Reading College of Technology; Bournemouth College of Technology;

Occupation: Management Consultant (Fellow of the Institute of Sales and Marketing Management); ex: Adviser, to Institute of Sales and Marketing Management '92-95; Area Sales Manager of domestic appliance firm, Training Manager, Marketing Consultant;

Traits: Blonde; hook nose; "trim, poised, well-groomed" (Matthew Parris, TIMES); caring; realistic ("the idea that there are women who run perfect homes and have delightful children who never get chickenpox without giving a month's notice is unrealistic"); her family are keen oarsmen; she enjoys the theatre and opera;

Address: House of Commons, Westminster, London SW1A 0AA;

Telephone: 0171 219 3565/5067/4038 (H of C); 01404 822103 (home); 01392 72652 (constituency);

Ian (Cameron) BRUCE   **Conservative**   **DORSET SOUTH '87-**

Majority: 77 (.2%) over Labour 6-way;

Description: Weymouth, the former Portland naval base and the marbled Isle of Purbeck; "some of the finest beaches, coves and cliffs in the whole of the country...Lulworth cove and the naked beauty of Studland", "the Purbeck Hills and the white horse that people know so well" (IB); formerly the political base of the Cecils;

Position: On the Information Select Committee '97-; Vice Chairman, Conservative MPs' Education and Employment Committee '92-; Joint Chairman, all-party Street Children Group '97-; Vice Chairman, PITCOM '97-; Vice Chairman, all-party Groups on Romania, Nepal and European Informatics Market Group '97-; Secretary, all-party Groups on Finland, Cable and Satellite '97-; Secretary, Parliamentary and Scientific Group '97-; ex: PPS, to Alastair Burt, Lord Astor and William Hague '92-94; on Select Committees: on Science and Technology '95-97, Employment '90-92; Vice Chairman '92-93, Secretary '90-92, Conservative MPs' Social Security Committee; Chairman: Conservative Candidates Association '86-87, Danbury Young Conservatives '66-69, Chelmsford Young Conservatives '67-69; Founder-Chairman of Trialogue (Yorkshire Conservative candidates' forum) '85-86;

Outlook: Outspoken, loyal, Rightwing manufacturing and employment consultant; assiduous defender of Defence jobs in his constituency; made a profession of taking delegations to Tory Ministers; "pursues the hallowed principle of asking a question at every opportunity, irrespective of his knowledge of the subject" (Simon Heffer, DAILY TELEGRAPH); "empty-headed" (Frank Dobson MP); his "brain works like a jigsaw puzzle with half the pieces missing" (ex-MP Alex Carlile); "with a tendency to see everything in black and white", regularly moans about "appalling traffic jams in Dorset" (Andrew Rawnsley, GUARDIAN); "the nerdiest internet nerd in the House, is normally in favour of people communicating electronically" (Simon Hoggart, GUARDIAN); can be a witty speaker, displaying a well-furnished mind; often barracks from his seat; Welsh-born of Scottish and Irish origins, he tries to speak on Scottish affairs; a selfmade man of working class origins who replaced the latest scion of the Cecils; anti: tobacco, dog registration, toll roads. unfettered unions, registered dock labour scheme; pro: better Dorset roads, caning, national identity cards;

History: He comes from a family that voted Labour "until converted by H Wilson"; "I have always believed, even when I thought I was a socialist, in a high-wage, high-productivity economy; when I thought I was a socialist, I was very young...a lad of 12 or 13 years working in the sweatshops" '60; his first affiliation was to the Conservatives '63; was elected Chairman, Danbury Young Conservatives '66; was elected Chairman, Chelmsford Young Conservatives '67; at Tory conference urged privatisation of Jobcentres Oct '82; contested Burnley, coming second with 38.2%, only 770 votes (1.5%) behind Peter Pike June '83; at Conservative conference complained EEC was not moving fast enough to remove trade barriers Oct '83; contested Yorkshire West in the European Parliament elections June '84; at Tory conference urged the reunification of Conservatives and Unionists, proposing a Unionist as Northern Ireland Secretary Oct '84; was not called to speak at Tory conference, when he wanted to urge the replacing of the whole tax and benefits system Oct '85; was selected as candidate for South Dorset, replacing retiring Viscount Cranborne Sep '86; at Tory conference rejected income tax cuts proposal, preferring cuts in industrial rates, and employers' National Insurance and Corporation Tax Oct '86; as its Chairman, organised and chaired the Conservative candidates' conference Apr '87; was elected with a majority unaltered from that of Viscount Cranborne June '87; in his Maiden denied the existence of a North-South divide, insisting there were more unemployed in South Dorset than in the Colne Valley; it was difficult to get married men with several children to take a (low-paid) job, and difficult to persuade employers to take even retrained men over 50 July '87; urged ban on all tobacco advertising and sponsorship and smoking in public places Nov '87; unsuccessfully introduced a clause in Employment Bill to abolish National Dock Labour Scheme Jan '88; voted to televise Commons Feb '88; urged reintroduction of corporal punishment Mar '88; led motion calling for Japanese reparations for their former POWs May '88; objected to secondary picketing of P&O at Dover May '88; asked about Bradwell Power Station, disclosing his "interest": "my brother works there" July '88; again urged national identity cards July '88; with other MPs, asked of DTI's role in collapse of Barlow Clowes companies Oct '88; again urged compensation for POWs of the Japanese Nov '88; claimed deregulation had improved safety on buses in his constituency Dec '88; to allay the plight of local egg producers after Edwina Currie's salmonella scare, ate two feasts of raw and cooked eggs before local TV cameras Jan '89; urged introduction of national identity cards Feb '89; supported upgrading pre-'73 war widows to level of post-'73 war widows Mar '89; complained that Government plans for electricity privatisation would "spell disaster" for Dounreay and research work at "Winfrith in my constituency" Nov '89; defended secret trade union ballots as enabling employers to make 11th-hour settlements Jan '90; applauded Employment Bill as part of "the sensible step-by-step approach of the Government in bringing industrial relations into the 1990s"; complained that when he had run an employment agency in Yorkshire, he had to sign up with the TGWU every driver he supplied Jan '90;

backed the Computer Misuse Bill against hackers Feb '90; there was a constituency fuss over his registering in Westminster where his poll tax was £195 on a flat, rather than £335 for his big suburban house in Weymouth; he promised to give the difference to charity, but not "because I feel guilty about it"; faced a poll tax protest of almost 1,000 in the middle of a gale Feb '90; insisted that, in his experience, lawyers were not as efficient as they claimed Apr '90; opposed dog registration Apr '90; promised support for resistance to shutdown of 22-year-old Winfrith heavy water reactor, with loss of 750 local jobs; June '90; dismissed dog registration as "simply bureaucratic nonsense" Oct '90; urged an insurance scheme or a simplification of statutory sick pay, recalling that when it had been transferred from DHSS to employers when he was a managing director, he had always been called on to puzzle out the rules' application Nov '90; complained that EC regulations were against part-timers; employers preferred full-timers but had to hire temporary staff on occasion, at a premium in London, but not elsewhere; "in the real world, people earn money on the basis of the demand for their particular skills," he said as the owner of a technical employment agency Dec '90; visited Argos headquarters at Milton Keynes, with all-party Group for the Retail Trade Dec '90; was named to Select Committee on Employment Dec '90; visited Israel as guest of Israeli Government Jan '91; came unstuck with a "typically sycophantic question" (Quentin Letts, DAILY TELEGRAPH), asking Chancellor Lamont "to encourage further spending" - he meant 'saving' - to beat inflation Jan '91; suggested Scottish independence might be liked by the English who would acquire financial and representative equality Feb '91; asked by the Whips to fill in during a Scottish debate, invited Scottish Secretary to visit a Dorset forest Mar '91; urged more and better roads, financed by taxation, not tolls Mar '91; visited Nepal as an election observer May '91; shouted that 'Majorism' could be defined as "winning the next election" June '91; criticised Norman Lamont's attempted £200 mobile phone tax as "a tax too far", "a tax on enterprise which we should not be imposing" July '91; visited Guernsey with his family as guest of Commodore Shipping Ltd July '91; retained seat with majority down from 15,067 to 13,508, a swing to Liberal Democrats of 2.1% Apr '92; in a witty speech on losing 20,000 voters under the new Boundary Commissions Bill, urged the same rules for seats apply throughout the UK, instead of Scotland being over-represented June '92; was re-named to Employment Select Committee July '92; against Government wishes, with 40 other Tory MPs voted for an increase of £11,000 in MPs' office allowances July '92; was elected Vice Chairman of the Conservative MPs' Employment Committee July '92; claimed no constituent had ever complained about working too-long hours July '92; visited ASTRA Satellite Control St ation in Luxembourg as guest of Societe Europeene des Satellites Sep '92; complained that Defence was spending £300m to move its Procurement Executive north of Bristol, "with the loss of thousands of jobs in my constituency and others " Oct '92; claimed Labour should "rush to its feet to welcome some of many developments" in the Trade Union Reform and Employment Rights Bill, since "we are engaged in a sensible operation to tidy up the law to ensure that trade union members who are paying for a service can keep control of their unions"; claimed that wages councils "have never worked" and many removed from their "so-called protection" found their wages rising faster Nov '92; was replaced on Employment Select Committee by Harry Greenway Nov '92; talked to Prime Minister and spoke on adjournment about RN cutbacks of almost 3,000 at local Portland naval base Dec '92; was attacked by Gordon Brown MP for taking "profiteering" Southern Electricity Plc as clients of Ian Bruce Associates; he replied that his only benefit from Southern Electricity had been two fax machines linking Westminster with his constituency office Jan '93; urged Defence to extend operational sea training instead of spending £600m on office blocks for civil servants Feb '93; as an Adviser to the Telephone Manufacturers' Association, urged the Minister to confer with them about thefts of mobile phones and their fraudulent alteration May '93; asked for EC KONVER money for Dorset as an assisted area May '93; insisted the Government "have bent over backwards to look after Rosyth and the Scottish defence industry", belying the claims of "the whingeing Jocks who have been sent here"; complained that "in order to keep to its long-term costings, the Royal Navy had to do a half-closure of Portland, leaving the helicopters where they were, and save money at Portland; my constituents have paid the price of trying to look after the best interests of people in Rosyth" June '93; visited Petroleum Research Centre in Pau as guest of ELF June '93; in debate on Defence Estimates 1992, admitted he had been pursuing the Ministry of Defence to cut its activities in his constituency June '93; backed Government's pit closure programme by pointing out that if domestic coal were priced higher, it would increase the cost of electricity Mar '93; observed Nigerian elections May-June '93; was described as Sir Wyn Roberts' "stoolpigeon" by Ted Rowlands?/Allan Rogers? MP July '93; visited Japan with Britain-Japan Parliamentary Group as guest of its government Nov '93; voted to restore capital punishment, especiall for killing policemen Feb '94; voted against lowering the age of homosexual consent below 21, Feb '94; said it was impossible to legislate effectively to attain equality between men and women because the markets determined their pay; Alex Carlile MP accused him of "playing the part of [an] ignoramus" May '94; again complained to Defence Secretary Malcolm Rifkind about transferring jobs out of Portland July '94; blamed GUARDIAN editor for working with a "blackmailer", Mohammed al-Fayed, to bring down the Conservative Government Nov '94; after being falsely promised that the 3rd Armoured Reconnaissance Regiment would be locally based, only to find it would go to the Chief Whip's constituency, threatened to rebel over transfer of further Defence jobs out of his constituency Apr '95; said that he found it impossible to persuade clients not to include age discrimination in their advrtisements Feb '96; urged data-matching as an excellent way of detecting fraud; the DSS had belatedly found that 30% of those employed by him in Yorkshire were also claiming benefit Mar '96; came 9th in the Private Members' ballot Oct '96; introduced Telecommunications (Fraud) Bill Nov '96; voted to retain caning Jan '97; voted to dis-assemble target guns rather than ban them Feb '97; welcomed the new prison ship from New York, urging locals to stop "whingeing" about it Mar '97; survived the election with the minute majority of 77 (.2%) over Labour, a pro-Labour swing of 15% May '97; supported William Hague for Leader May-June '97; raised the question of old germ warfare tests secretly carried out in the Westcountry 30 years before Nov '97; a "paid adviser" of the Telecommunications Managers Association asked how the new Radiocommunications Agency would charge for making parts of the radio spectrum available Nov '97; deriding him for his "empty-headed comments" Frank Dobson added, "they do show why, in as Tory an area as South Dorset, we got within 77 votes of winning the seat" Mar '98;

Born: 14 March 1947, Llantwit Fadre, Glamorganshire

Family: S late Henry Bruce, Scottish dry cleaning manager, and (Ellen) Flora (Bingham), Irish building society chief clerk; m '69 Hazel Roberts, recently his secretary, formerly an accounts executive and company director, previously clerical officer in Jobcentre and laboratory assistant; 1s James '74, 3d Kathleen '75, Maxine '77, Tasmin '78; ("my wife and I volunteered to be short-term foster parents when my wife was pregnant with out first child" '74);

Education: Kings Road Junior and Infant Schools, Chelmsford; Chelmsford Technical High School; Bradford University; Mid-Essex Technical College, Chelmsford;

Occupation: Chairman and Director of Ian Bruce Associates (ex Glidemark) Ltd (an employment agency; clients: Southern Electricity Plc, Saudi Arabian Bank, Ingres Ltd) '75- and of Bruce Associates (manufacturing consultancy) '75-; Parliamentary Adviser: to Telecommunications Managers Association (at £5-10,000) '89-, Trevor Gilbert and Associates (at £5-10,000) '97-, Priority 2000 '97-; Vice Chairman, (unpaid), of EURIM ("a company formed to monitor and collate information on the European Informatics Market as it affects EC and British legislation and to lobby the EC and British Ministers and Parliamentarians") '93-; Owner: of freehold reversion of properties in Huddersfield '85-; ex: Parliamentary Adviser, Federation of Recruitment and Employment Services '96-97, Chairman and Founder of BOS Group of companies, Huddersfield (employment agency; "in my first year of self employment, I paid myself nothing and my company lost £9,000"; "the sort of wages that I was able to offer when I started my business, attracted only women"; after increasingly good years, "sold out at an extremely good price" '75-85; Factory Manager, with Sinclair, ESI and BEPI ("I was made redundant"); Work Study Manager with BEPI ("I advised management when they were faced with the possibility of industrial action in the '60s and '70s"); Work Study Engineer with Sainsbury, Pye and Marconi; Student Apprentice, in electronics with Marconi;

Traits: Tall; slim; front-combed red hair; specs; outspoken; "yet another of the thin men wearing spectacles, aged somewhere between 25 and 45, who lurk on the Conservative back benches; they seem harmless, but vaguely troubling, like a shoal of sand-eels, forever diligent in search of an opening" (Andrew Brown, INDEPENDENT); "tall and thin, with a tendency to see everything in black and white, and topped off with a ball of red hair, Mr Bruce resembles nothing so much as a Belisha beacon" (Andrew Rawsley, GUARDIAN); Scouts enthusiast (Assistant District Commissioner for Venture Scouts, formerly in Huddersfield South West Scout Association); badminton player (member of Linthwaite and Golcar Badminton Club); Camping and Caravaning Club; enjoys sailing;

Address: House of Commons, Westminster, London SW1A 0AA;

Telephone: 0171 219 5086/5705 (H of C); 01305 833320 (home); 0305 786142 (constituency);

Malcolm (Gray) BRUCE   **Liberal Democrat**   **GORDON '83-**

Majority: 6,997 (16.6%) over Conservative 5-way;
Description: Formerly West Aberdeenshire, won in '66 by Liberal James Davidson; another former MP was the Tory, Colin ('Mad Mitch') Mitchell of Aden fame; in '95 it lost over a quarter of its inflated electorate in the Aberdeen suburbs to Aberdeen North, in exchange for 14,000 voters from the rural constituencies of Banff & Buchan and Moray; this made it a more rural seat and its political balance uncertain; one faulty estimate, by Robert Waller, gave the seat to the Tories by 8,500;
Position: Chief Spokesman, on Treasury Affairs '94-; on Select Committee on Treasury and Civil Service '94-; Vice President, National Deaf Children's Society '90-; ex: Spokesman: on Trade, Industry and Employment '92-94, Scotland '90-92, Environment and Energy '89-90, Natural Resources '88-89, Trade and Industry '87-88, Employment (for Alliance) '87, Energy '85-87, Scotland '83-85; on Select Committees: on Science and Technology '92, Trade and Industry '92-94, '87-90, Scottish Affairs '83-87; Leader, Scottish Liberal Democrats '88-92; Deputy Chairman, Scottish Liberal Party, '75-84, its Spokesman on Energy '75-83;

Outlook: The '94-new LibDem Treasury Spokesman who launched their new tax-increase programme earmarked for education, the NHS and public transport; the shrewd, fair-minded, even-tempered, regionally-based vote-winner who surprised the political world by retaining handsomely his seat, thought basically altered in the Tories' favour; has recently become the leading opponent of Ashdown's dream of a LibDem-Labour alliance, fuelling antipathy to Labour by sharp attacks on Gordon Brown's statistics and tactics; it was initially seen as "pedestrian" and presenting "a mish-mash of muddle, error and banalities" (Peter Riddell, TIMES); it was later made more distinctive and creditble -according to Chancellor Kenneth Clarke - and was reinforced by the '97 infusion of economically-literate new LibDem MPs; was previously particularly well-informed on North Sea oil questions; an analyst rather than an agitator; gave up as Leader of Scottish Liberal Democrats after '92's electoral setbacks; an assiduous local job-defender; a home-ruler and opponent of London-based centralised monopolies and a friend of decentralised "people-sized economies", with BT, CEGB and British Gas all regionalised; a moderate exponent of "good radical solutions to mainstream problems", not way-out fringe issues; "a lot of my attacks on the Government are, if you like, from the Right; [but] the market in many areas of this country doesn't work, it is not free, it is dominated by monopoliies, both private and public" (MB); opposes the nuclear deterrent, favours the phasing out of nuclear power; "a muscular speaker who can occasionally make a speech take off, he is liked and respected for his judgement" (Robin Oakley, TIMES); "able, ambitious, touchy" (ex-MP Clement Freud); "Bruce is not as lovable as [his predecessor as Scottish Liberal Leader Russell] Johnston, but is rather more energetic; he is a seriously committed politician, not easily given to admitting mistakes, but who does confess to a lot of frustration at the point where his energies crash into a wall of indifference" (Peter Jones, SCOTSMAN); anti-smoking; anti-racist ("I can tolerate almost anything except intolerance"); **History:** After an initial pro-Conservative period "probably because of tribalism" at Wrekin College, he had "a political reaction against the public school ethos of an elite, privileged middle class" (MB), joining the Liberals at 17, '62; joined the Liberal Club on his first day at Dundee University - when it was stil part of St Andrews - becoming its President '64; fought North Angus and Mearns against Alick Buchanan-Smith, with a "catastrophic" result Oct '74; was selected '75, contested West Aberdeenshire (later called Gordon) May '79; favoured: aid for rural areas '79, energy planning '80, cheap fuel for selected areas and industries '82; at Gordon was one of the surprise victors with a majority of 850 June '83; urged higher standards of helicopter safety in North Sea July '83; as the Liberals' Scottish Spokesman, urged all-party agreement on an early Scottish Parliament Dec '83; attacked increased fees for foreign students Jan '84; opposed building of any further nuclear power stations Mar '84; joined with Labour to support keeping Scott Lithgow in public ownership Mar '84; worked out a compromise between David Steel's desire to retain Cruise missiles and those wanting them removed Sep '84; opposed the closing of the Don Barracks in Gordon Nov '84; again spoke up for two engineer-constituents detained in Nigeria Feb '85; urged that break-up of National Bus should provide equal competition with already-operating small transport companies May '85; backed Rural Development Fund July '85; as the Liberals new Energy Spokesman, proposed a slowdown of North Sea oil extraction to safeguard reserves Sep '85; said: "I have always been opposed to an independent nuclear deterrent but I wanted to help break the nuclear impasse" Sep '85; said Liberals favoured full membership of European Monetary System Sep '85; urged a fuller exploration of alternative energy Oct '85; proposed a gradual switchover to non-nuclear energy, beginning with decommissioning of Magnox stations May '86; urged use of standing charges as fuel credits, to favour the pensioner against holiday home owners May '86; introduced Bill to conserve energy July '86; rebutted Peter Walker's argument that nuclear power was safe, cheap or necessary July '86; reaffirmed Liberal opposition to reprocessing nuclear fuel at Sellafield Aug '86; at Liberal Assembly backed David Steel and nuclear weapons but insisted that phasing out of nuclear power would depend on developing alternatives Sep '86; in the 1986 North Sea oil decline "processions of people came to my constituency surgery who had not only lost their jobs but found that, because of the downturn in activity, the fall in price of their houses had dropped them into sharp negative equity"; was criticised by standing committee chairman Ted Leadbitter for tabling an amendment to the Petroleum Bill - to introduce tax changes to stimulate North Sea oil - and leaving without voting Jan '87; complained that Government tried to stimulate new businesses without helping them survive difficult early days Feb '87; accused the Government of abusing the civil service for its own political ends Feb '87; broke the news of the job-losing Leyland-Daf deal Feb '87; welcomed Tory plans for trade union reforms which Labour described as a "blacklegs' charter" Feb '87; increased his majority by almost 9,000 in electorate enlarged by 10,000 June '87; urged a deft merger without unnecessarily ruffling the sensitivities of Social Democrats June '87; attacked the Government's allowing Murdoch to take over the previously pro-Alliance TODAY newspaper as a "disgraceful negation of duty", claiming it had given into blackmail in its own political interest July '87; threw doubt on Government statistics claiming 32,400 jobs were being created monthly July '87; attacked the over-simplification of the North-South divide, emphasising "a massive imbalance between London and the regions" Sep '87; at Harrogate Assembly backed electricity privatisation and urged a new federal constitution for Liberal Party Sep '87; was named Trade and Industry Spokesman Oct '87; in the wake of the Guinness betrayal of its promise to locate in Edinburgh, urged a new legally enforceable Code of Practice for takeovers Oct '87; opposed water privatisation Oct '87; insisted that the market could only be made to operate effectively by controlling monopoly and promoting effective competition Nov '87; welcomed the Monopolies and Mergers Commission's review of British Airways' attempted takeover of British Caledonian, which he had attacked as "one super mega-airline and a very fragmented group of small airlines competing for the crumbs" Nov '87; voted against fellow Liberal MP David Alton's abortion-curbing Bill Jan '88; was asked by Maggie Clay of the ALC to stand for the Leadership of the Social and Liberal Democrats when he secured a standing ovation for a powerful pro-merger speech Jan '88; urged a separate Scottish steel company when BSC was privatised Feb '88; attacked the Government for allowing the Nestle takeover of Rowntrees, as allowing the Swiss to "sit behind the barricade of the Alps and pick off our ripe cherries" May '88; a Thames TV poll placed him third for the Leadership with 6%, behind Ashdown (57%) and Beith (7%) May '88; became Paddy Ashdown's campaign chairman May '88; announced he would contest the Liberal Democrats' Scottish leadership as a tough devolutionist June '88; in the wake of Russell Johnston, was elected Leader of Scottish Liberal Democrats by 2,690 votes to Archy Kirkwood's 1,396 Aug '88; attacked poll tax as "wicked and evil" but not to be fought by law-breaking Sep '88; was named to Treasury team, as Spokesman on Natural Resources (Energy and Conservation) Sep '88; his Scottish Liberal Democrats were squeezed down to 7% in latest GLASGOW HERALD poll, 12 points below the Alliance at previous election Apr '89; in speech to Scottish TUC, urged a federal structure for Britain Apr '89; congratulated Mrs Thatcher on her ten years in office, but urged she "went around with her eyes and ears open but her mouth shut" May '89; was named Spokesman on Environment and Natural Resources Nov '89; opposed war crimes trials for elderly Baltic refugees in UK Dec '89; backed Greenpeace's protest against illegal dumping of flyash in North Sea Jan '90; backed Environmental Protection Bill, but urged something more radical Jan '90; launched Bill to control CFCs Jan '90; urged tougher targets for reduced acid rain and carbon dioxide emissions Feb '90; worried about the danger from releasing genetically modified mice Feb '90; came off Trade and Industry Select Committee Feb '90; voted for John Browne to resign for concealing his outside interests Mar '90; became fulltime Spokesman on Scotland, as part of his effort to knit the 9 Liberal Democratic MPs into a team Mar '90; voted with minority to ban smoking in public places May '90; supported split of Nature Conservancy Council into its Scottish, Welsh and English components May '90; accused Scottish Secretary Malcolm Rifkind of failing Scotland by failing to establish an independent Scottish steel industry May '90; warned of massive increases in Scottish water charges June '90; introduced Bill to help deaf with support for further and higher education Dec '90; representing "perhaps the biggest pig-producing area" in Britain", backed Sir Richard Body's Pig Husbandry Bill against sow cruelty Jan '91; said electricity privatisation plans were "not only ideologically motivated, they were ill-thought-out and shambolic" Jan '91; because a third of Grampian's workers were employed in North Sea oil, said all were shocked by unexpected Piper Alpha tragedy Mar '91; rejected Labour's Alternative Vote PR system for Scottish Parliament Mar '91; opposed council tax as a combination of "two most unpopular taxes - the rates and the poll tax combined" Mar '91; offered Labour a mixture of the Single Transferable Vote and the Additional Member system for a Scottish Parliament Mar '91; introduced Deaf People (Access to Further and Higher Education and Training) Bill, modeled on US legislation; cited how few educational institutions made provisions for the deaf Mar '91; claimed Sir Bob Scholey, Chairman of British Steel, had reacted with "sheer venom" against the Scottish steel industry July '91; urged a Scottish and Welsh Parliament as moves toward a federal Europe Sep '91; visited Spain's Catalan and Basque regions, sponsored by the Acton Trust Sep '91; accused Scottish Secretary Ian Lang of being "out of step" with Welsh Secretary David Hunt, who preferred the creation of "Europe of the regions" Oct '91; after Scottish Liberal Democrats won Kincardine, giving them 10 MPs to Tories' nine, cheekily wrote to John Major asking to discuss Scotland's constitutional position Nov '91; criticised Scottish Secretary Ian Lang for overlooking "overwhelming opposition" to opt-out of Foresterhill hospital Dec '91; in leaked party document, proposed a post-election aliance between the Scottish Constituional Convention and SNP in the event of another Tory election win Dec '91; backed miners' consortium seeking to reopen Monktonhall Colliery as a miners' co-operative Dec '91; blamed Government for closure of Ravenscraig Jan '92; objected to Labour's preference for Additional Member System for Scottish Parliament, which favoured them, rather than Liberal Democrats' preferred Single Transferrable Vote Jan '92; urged a stronger, more autonomous Scottish business sector to back self-governmet Jan '92; in four-cornered debate in Scottish Convention, claimed "the Conservative Party cannot resist the tide" toward Scottish self-government Jan '92; reporting on his trip to Spain, said the Basque and Catalan parties there wanted nothing to do with the SNP Feb '92; blamed Government and British Airways for having "sold down the river" the employees of bankrupted British International Helicopter, who were encouraged to transfer their pensions from BA to Maxwell Mar '92; an ICM-SCOTSMAN poll showed him as having improved his approval rating from 27% to 34% in two months Mar '92; retained seat with his majority down from 9,519 to 274, a swing of 8.56% to Conservatives, reflecting the upsurge of their support in the Aberdeen area Apr '92; after the party's poor showing in the election in Scotland - which he blamed on its identification with Labour in the Scottish Convention - stood down as Leader of Scottish Liberal Democrats, being replaced by Jim Wallace Apr '92; although BR and British Coal needed restructuring and access to new capital, said "the amount of money that has been spent in paving the way for privatisations in the past has been unnecessarily profligate" May '92; was named Spokesman on Trade, Industry and Employment May '92; urged stronger regulatory body for BR and British Coal June '92; defended Wages Councils against abolition July '92; was named to Select Committee on Science and Technology July '92; complained that Government was starving Grampian of needed infrastructure resources because of its buoyant oil economy July '92; warned: BR privatisation might make the Edinburgh-Aberdeen service a branch line July '92; called for legal changes to close a loophole on the ownership of former Scottish school buildings Sep '92; at annual conference again warned Liberal Democrats to keep their distance from Labour, recalling that the Tories had exploited their slogan, "a Liberal vote is a Labour vote" Sep '92; although he criticised Government for having "privatised in the dark", was criticised at party conference for having accepted too many Tory ideas in 'After Privatisation' Sep '92; identified the "dash for gas" which had closed some coal mines as being caused by the desire of regional electricity companies to "give themselves more bargaining power" against the "monopolistic position of the two generators" of electricity Oct '92; went on to Trade and Industry Select Commitee Oct '92; warned that agreement between EC and US on GATT would put a further squeeze on EC farm incomes Nov '92; blamed "botched electricity privatisation" and "mistakenly propping up an ailing nuclear industry" for unnecessary mines closures Nov '92; urged better treatment of small businesses by banks and suppliers, rather than abolishing needed safety and pollution controls Nov '92; although Liberal Democrats had favoured abolition of closed shop, opposed "further substantial and detailed interference in the working of trade unions" in Employment Rights Bill Nov '92; came off Science and Technology Select Committee Nov '92; complained about surcharges on package travel and Government incompetence in allowing bankrupt travel companies to trade Dec '92; attacked Labour for abandoning its alliance with local Liberal Democrats on Grampian Regional Council, in favour of Scottish Nationalists Jan '93; again criticised rapid way in which British Coal was being squeezed out of energy competition Jan '93; opposed the ousting of workers from tied cottages with sale of local Castle Fraser estate Feb '93; attacked the Government as "political cheats" for having "got into power by sheer dishonesty" as "a tax-cutting party" and then introduced "a tax-raising Budget" Mar '93; opposed the "vindictive" abolition of Wages Councils Mar '93; opposed Post Office privatisation Mar '93; voted against National Lottery Bill Apr '93; urged transitional arrangements out of fear that Government's changes in tax on North Sea oil might be "damaging", "introducing a depression in exploration and appraisal activity when the activity is already in a downturn" May '93; predicted either "non-viability for THORP or in a blank cheque that will cost us dear" June '93; said that "the programme of privatising gas and electricity has meant that, whether wilfully or through lack of foresight, coal is being squeezed out of the marketplace"; unless the Government reversed that, it would be "accused of total irresponsibility and vandalism in respect of a major energy resource" July '93; warned the Maxwell pension scandal might block EC acceptance of the British "way of managing pension funds"; "if the Germans had their way, our system would not be admitted in the EC" July '93; opposed pollution taxes on petrol as hurting rural constituents Sep '93; insisted a Labour connection would be "simply damning" with floating voters Sep '93; voted against restoring capital punishment, even for killers of policemen Feb '94; voted to reduce age of homosexual consent to 18 or 16, Feb '94; opposed Deregulation Bill to avoid weakening of consumer protection Feb '94; backed Trade Marks Bill, saying he had worked as a buyer of proprietary products for Boots, who had wasted a lot of money initially by marketing their own poor-quality toothpaste, and then did well with a better proprietary product later Apr '94; attacked Tories for levelling more taxes on lower incomes Apr '94; in major LibDem reshuffle, was promoted Chief Spokesman on Treasury Affairs replacing Alan Beith, allegedly because his pro-EU ideas were closer to the Leader's July '94; complained of slack supervision of high electricity prices Aug '94; said he was not afraid to target middle-incomes for higher taxes earmarked for education, health and public transport Aug '94; in his stumbling debut at the Brighton conference called for a new top rate of 50p income tax on those earning over £100,000 - reduced from 60% in Beith's previous proposals - and cuts in defence and road spending to finance £1.8m more on education Sep

'94; was taken off Trade and Industry Select Committee and put on Treasury and Civil Service Select Committee Nov '94; delighted in helping defeat the Tories on increased VAT on household fuel and heat Dec '94; his allegation that Labour's spending plans would mean a 5p increase in income tax was rejected by Labour Spokesman Andrew Smith as "a fantasy exercise" designed to prevent Paddy Ashdown cosying up with Tony Blair Jan '95; voted for Ashdown's Bill for a Referendum on major changes in relations with EU Feb '95; voted to ban foxhunting Mar '95; he started studying for the Bar even before the Boundary Commission changes which gave his voters in the Aberdeen suburbs to Aberdeen North and imported 14,000 rural voters from Banff and Buchan and Moray thus making altered Gordon seem a likely Tory win ("very Conservative" - Robert Waller, GUARDIAN) May '95; urged caution in approaching the single European currency, which might not start until 2003, Aug '95; at annual conference jibed that "for many years we have been saying we wanted to get rid of the Labour Party; now Tony Blair is doing it" Sep '95; voted against Iain Duncan-Smith's Bill to curb the European Court Apr '96; complained of the sharp impact of the beef ban on the best beef exporter in his constituency Apr '96; was concerned that the Private Finance Initiative would result in clinical services being operated by a private firm in at least one Scottish NHS hospital June '96; voted against 3% cap on MPs' pay rise, in favour of curb on MPs' mileage allowance July '96; urged an independent but accountable UK central reserve bank to "lock in" inflation Aug '96; opposed a closer LibDem-Labour relationship: "we're not going to be seduced by a simple offer of some kind of share in office as a result of an accidental freak of an out-turn at a general election" Sep '96; warning against "a confusing image of convergence", insisted Paddy Ashdown discuss relations with Labour with other LibDem MPs Nov '96; voted to dis-assemble target pistols rather than ban them Feb '97; on the day the Labour-LibDem agreement on constitutional reform was published, he told The TIMES there was no pro-Labour or anti-Tory favouritism in his economic approach Mar '97; insisted that the LibDem plan to increase by 1p the standard income tax and to 50% on earnings over £100,000 to put an extra £2b a year into education would provide a big boost Mar '97; as an opponent of foxhunting, he was on the 'hit-list' of The FIELD Apr '97; against the odds, he retained considerably altered Gordon by a majority of 6,997 over his Conservative opponent on a notional swing of 18.7% May '97; was re-named to the Treasury Select Committee July '97; alleged that Treasury took less than expected from BT in Windfall Tax, possibly because of BT's deal with Blair July '97; claimed Gordon Brown had cut expenditure by £5.25b by not compensating for larger-than-expected inflation July '97; at the LibDems' Eastbourne conference, claimed Gordon Brown's "something-for-nothing economics" did not add up Sep '97; campaigned with his fiancee Rosemary Vetterlein in Beckenham, thus helping to frustrate a Blair-Ashdown deal for the LibDems to give Labour a virtual free run there against the Tory, Jacqui Lait, who narrowly won Nov '97; Tony Blair made a waspish attack on him, suggesting that the Teletubby Tinky Winky could do a better job as the LibDems' Treasury Spokesman Dec '97;

Born: 17 November 1944, Birkenhead

Family: S David Stewart Bruce, hotelier and agricultural merchant who argued provocatively with his children, and Kathleen Emslie (Delf); m '69 Jane (Wilson), whom he met on a blind date in Liverpool; 1s Alexander '74, 1d Caroline '76, profoundly deaf; separated Nov '89 "on a wholly amicable basis" with "no other party...involved"; divorced '92; m 2nd '98 Rosemary Vetterlein, LibDem's '97 candidate for Beckenham;

Education: Kingsmead, Meols, Cheshire; Wrekin College, Shropshire (public school); Dundee University, when part of St Andrews (MA '66); Strathclyde University (MSc '70);

Occupation: Barrister, qualified 1995; Author: A New Life for the Country (1978), Putting Energy to Work (with others 1981), A New Deal for Rural Scotland (1983), Growth from the

Grassroots (with Paddy Ashdown, 1985); Journalist: Regular Contributor to ACCOUNTANCY AGE (£1-5,000) '97- Joint Editor/Publisher: Aberdeen Petroleum Publishing (Aberdeen-based specialists in oil and gas industry) '81-84; Marketing Director, Noroil Publishing House (UK) '75-81; Trainee Journalist, (with Robin Oakley, John Sergeant and Tony Bevins) on LIVERPOOL DAILY POST '66-67; ex: Researcher for North East Scotland Development Authority '71-75; Section Buyer: Boots '67-68, A Goldberg and Sons '68-69;

Traits: Small; lean; dark/greying; mild-mannered; persuasive; "solid and worthy" (LIBERATOR); "meticulous and dauntingly well-informed" (SCOTSMAN); a witty writer; not "easy to know or like" (Peter Jones, SCOTSMAN); "I probably suffer fools too gladly; but when I come across hectoring, arrogant, domineering, intolerant behaviour, I find my hackles rising" (MB); has learned sign language ("when I started, my daughter, who is deaf, fell about laughing because I'd learned English signs, not Scottish"); enjoys theatre, music, travel, "fresh Scottish air";

Address: House of Commons, Westminster, London SW1A 0AA; Grove Cottage, Grove Lane, Torphins, Aberdeenshire AB31 4HJ;

Telephone: 0171 219 4580/6233 (H of C); 01339 82386; 013982 386;

Karen BUCK   **Labour**   **REGENT'S PARK & KENSINGTON NORTH '97-**

Majority: 14,657 over Conservative 6-way;

Description: A new seat, a gift to Labour from the Boundary Commission: a combination of safe-Tory St John's Wood, with mixed Little Venice and Maida Vale and strongly-Labour Queen's Park, Harrow Road, Westbourne and Notting Hill; "we have the liveliest markets and hippest bars in town, we host the Notting Hill carnival", "the largest and most successful street festival in Europe" (KB); it also has "one of the highest proportions of private sector tenants in the UK" (KB);

Position: On the Select Committee on Social Security '97-; Westminster City Councillor (Chairwoman, Labour Group '95-, previously Chairwoman of Social Services, Housing, Social Services) '90-; on Queens Park Single Regeneration Budget Board '95-; ex: Chairwoman, of Westminster North CLP '88-90; on Paddington and North Kensington Health Authority '87-88;

Outlook: One of Labour's brightest Centre-Left feminist insiders, from Walworth Road and the Conservatives' sleaze-ridden Westminster Council; a potential minister with a very good ability to grasp detailed briefs; tends to work closely with her former colleagues from Westminster Council, Peter Bradley and Andrew Dismore; as Chairwoman of the Westminster Objectors Trust was "disgusted" by the 'homes for votes' scandal; an "inner-party hackette, though friendly to everyone" (RED PEPPER); a key advocate and final beneficiary of all-women short-lists; believes that "the House of Commons is terribly out of touch on so many issues because it is run by an oligarchy of middle-aged men", adding, "when we get more women in, the Tories will suddenly look terribly old-fashioned"; is in Greenpeace and Amnesty International, formerly in CND;

History: Joined the Labour Party at 20, '78; was elected to Wesminster City Council May

'90; she wrote to Peter Brooke MP to urge him to vote for full disclosure of MPs' interests in the Nolan debate Nov '95; was selected from an all-woman short-list for the new safe-Labour seat of Regent's Park and Kensington North Nov '95; this precipitated a legal challenge from thwarted aspirant Peter Jepson, a part-time law lecturer who secured a legal decision declaring such short-lists illegal Jan '96; the Labour Party decided to suspend further all-women short-lists but to retain the 38 already decided Jan '96; won the new seat with a majority of 14,657, a notional swing to Labour of 11.84% May '97; co-sponsored motion urging a public inquiry into the functioning of Westminster City Council June '97; in her Maiden contrasted the surface luxury of the affluent part of her seat with deprivation and squalor in its worst back streets June '97; campaigned in Uxbridge for Labour July '97; was named to the Select Committee on Social Security July '97; co-criticised Lord Rees-Mogg for his "black propaganda" in favour of Dame Shirley Porter before her court hearing Sep '97; backed the Greater London Authority Bill as "a balanced package" needed to solve the problems of a capital city but not requiring the re-creation of the GLC or two or more questions in the referendum Nov '97; welcomed the High Court's guilty verdict on Dame Shirley Porter Dec '97; co-sponsored motion criticising ex-PM John Major for failing to condemn Dame Shirley Porter on her being found "guilty of wilful misconduct" costing Westminster City Council £27m, which Ms Buck then spelled out in a speech Jan '98; deplored the situation of her many private sector tenants whose agreements "have turned out to be effectively worthless, with soaring rents" Jan '98; backed 'Operation Black Vote' "on its work to encourage black Londoners to participate" in the imminent referendum May '98; urged availability of low-cost housing in all parts of London to avoid "ghettoising" poor families on the worst estates May '98; spoke up strongly for London Lighthouse, charitable trust for HIV and AIDS June '98;

Born: 30 August 1958, Castlederg, County Tyrone;

Family: Daughter of Pat Buck; her Partner is Barrie Taylor; 1s;

Education: Chelmsford County High School for Girls; LSE (BSc in Economics, History and Politics; MSc Econ, plus MSc in Social Policy and Administration);

Occupation: Ex: the Labour Party's Acting Head of Campaigns and Elections '94-95, Campaign Strategy Co-ordinator '92-97, Health Policy Officer '87-92 (TGWU); Public Health Officer, Hackney '86-87 (NALGO); Specialist Officer in Disabled Employment, Hackney '83-86, Research and Development worker at Outset '79-83 (ASTMS);

Traits: Longish blonde hair with dark roots; fringe; sharp nose; specs; a rapid, strong speaker; displays a school-teacherish insistent logic; "steely-tongued" EVENING STANDARD); a good sense of humour; has great mastery of '60s trivia, including the names of obscure groups; enjoys music, cinema and squash; has suffered six burglaries, four in the same flat;

Address: House of Commons, Westminster, London SW1A 0AA; 254 Ashmore Road, London W9 3DD;

Telephone: 0171 219 3000 (H of C); 0181 960 1119 (home/Fax); 0171 286 9692 (constituency office);

WE'RE GETTING FATTER

MPs profiles tend to get fatter, like the papier mache masks we made in our youth by adding to a clay portrait model soggy strips of newsprint soaked in flour and water. Just as you can build up a strong papier mache mask, so too we hope we have transformed a dimly lit outline form into sharp features plus a few warts.

Richard (Haines) BURDEN   **Labour**   **NORTHFIELD, Birmingham '92-**

Majority: 11,443 (29.5%) over Conservative 5-way;

Description: Formerly marginal working-class seat in Birmingham's outer suburbs, all of whose wards were considered marginal, except Tory-leaning Bartley Green, which it lost to Edgbaston in '95; the site of Longbridge car plant, now BMW-owned. but is largely a residential area of varying qualities; it has a mix of council and private estates housing half its 13,000 workers;

Position: PPS, to Jeff Rooker '97-; Secretary, Birmingham Group of Labour MPs '97-; Chairman, all-party Motor Group '97-; Joint Chairman, all-party Advisory Council for Transport Safety '94-; Vice Chairman '98-, Chairman '96-98 Labour Campaign for Electoral Reform; Chairman, all-party Group on Electoral Reform '97-; Vice Chairman, Labour Middle East Council '94-; ex: Chairman '97-98, Secretary '94-97 Commons Motor Club; Secretary '96-97, Vice Chairman '95-96 PLP Trade and Industry Committee; Joint Secretary, all-party Parliamentary Water Group '94-97; Secretary, of JAWS (Joint Action for Water Services) '85-90; President, York University Students Union '76-77;

Outlook: The '92 captor of a marginal, since '97 possessor of a safe seat; in 'New Left for New Labour' - the former 'Supper Club' - but effectively sidelined in 1995 by becoming the first outside the hard-Left to protest publicly against Blair's attempt to convert ideology-based Labour into "a US-style party - a ruthlessly effective electoral machine"; his media-exaggerated critique was sparked by his dislike of Mandelson's "dirty tricks" campaign against the successful Liberal Democrat in the Littleborough and Saddleworth by-election; on opponent of dangerous fireworks; a youngish, hyperactive, publicity-seeking former NALGO official in the Midlands water industry; anti-privatisation (especially water); his local publicity has come from spotlighting Birmingham's NHS financial scandals; a pro-Arab he has also called for intervention in Bosnia to protect its Moslems; claims Antonio Gramsci and Rosa Luxembourg as his political heroes; a former Young Liberal, is still strongly pro-PR; a multi-cause groupie (Fabians, Labour Campaign for Electoral Reform, Co-operative Party, Labour Middle East Council, Trade Union Friends of Palestine, Greenpeace, SERA, CND and, formerly, Anti-Apartheid); formerly TGWU-sponsored;

History: He was initially a Young Liberal for four years from '72; became President of York University Students Union '76; joined the Labour Party '80; led the campaign in the Midlands against water privatisation, helping to found JAWS (Joint Action for Water Services) '85; was selected at 31 for Meriden Apr '86; with qualifications, supported decision to proceed with a superpit development at Hawkhurst Moor, Berkswell, if British Coal provided assurances that it was not possible to develop the field from existing pits and the environment was protected; was somewhat sympathetic because the Chernobyl disaster "has been a tragic but timely reminder about the dangers of relying on nuclear power" June '86; protested Government's effort to establish a local City Technical College with Hanson Trust backing, instead of better financing for existing schools Mar '87; came 2nd in Meriden with 26% of vote, marginally better than 1983, June '87; warned against water privatisation in pamplet, 'Tap Dancing - Water, the Environment and Privatisation' '88; was selected for Northfield over GMBman Phil Davis because Northfield CLP had swung Left Nov '89; warned against dumping on streets of elderly mentally-ill patients Dec '90; urged cut in interest rates Mar '91; again backed PR May '91; attacked planned opt-out by five Birmingham hospitals May '91; claimed he detected a "sea change" in political opinion Mar '92; narrowly retook Northfield by 630 votes, a 3.5% swing to Labour Apr '92; made his Maiden speech on poverty in outer city areas May '92; attacked the way the Conservatives had prepared water privatisation, especially Severn-Trent June '92; raised doubts about the "financial wisdom" of NHS reforms imposed on south and central Birmingham July '92; asked Health Secretary Virginia Bottomley why she was "colluding in the suppression of a report" on the "multi-million pound cash crisis in South Birmingham Health Authority which is threatening to close two hospitals" Oct '92; accused Government of planning to privatise the Careers Service; as a "trade unionist in the public services", "I endured a range of privatisation experiments - I have yet to come across one which has not cost the Exchequer far more than it has saved" Nov '92; with the Longbridge car plant in his constituency, fulsomely enthused about the abolition of motor car tax Nov '92; co-sponsored motion deploring as "deeply offensive" an Israeli Tourist Board advertisment showing a picture of East Jerusalem, captioned "It could only be Israel" Dec '92; complained that, under its Employment Rights Bill, the Government was trying "to make unions spend more money unnecessarily" Feb '93; warned that abolition of wages councils would produce "a cut in pay for some of the lowest-paid employees in the country" Feb '93; again raised the financial scandals in the West Midlands Regional Health Authority, including its pay-off to prematurely retired Sir John Ackers Feb '93; co-sponsored Helen Jackson's motion on water disconnections Mar '93; again raised its financial scandals, complaining that Birmingham's NHS was being run like a "glorified supermarket" but badly Apr '93; welcomed 40th anniversary of David Steel's Abortion Act 1967 as having abolished back-street abortions Apr '93; co-wrote to US President Clinton urging military intervention in Bosnia against Serb aggressors May '93; visited Jordan and occupied territories of Gaza and West Bank, as guest of pro-Arab Labour Middle East Council May-June '93; challenged Employment Minister Eric Forsyth as to whether British Government would accept EC directive to provide part-time women employees with 14 weeks maternity leave on full pay June '93; urged EC pressure on Israel to improve its behaviour toward Palestinian Arabs July '93; refused to accept Minister's mild reproach to Sir James Ackers, controversial, early-sacked former Chairman of West Midlands Regional Health Authority Jan '94; led motion opposing sale of Rover to BMW because its Longbridge workers were not consulted Feb '94; warned about safety dangers in excessive deregulation Feb '94; voted to reduce the age of homosexual consent to 16, Feb '94; complained that Severn-Trent's 700 prepayment water meters had led to about 400 disconnections May '94; again attacked Government proposals to weaken Health and Safety regulations May '94; complained about fleecing of local pensioner contributors by Teampace Holdings June '94; voted for Blair for Leader, Prescott for Deputy Leader July '94; deplored the decline of the water industry through privatisation and the growing denial of water to the impoverished through metering July '94; collaborated with Clare Short and editors of TRIBUNE and NEW STATESMAN to draft an alternative Left revision of Clause IV Nov '94; described lengthily how the "bureaucratic nightmare" of the NHS internal market was failing to provide a primary health care centre on a long-promised Birmingham site July '95; was "ashamed" of the "amorality" of the Mandelson-led dirty-tricks campaign against the successful LibDem candidate in the Littleborough and Saddleworth by-election July '95; he wrote to Leader Tony Blair to give him advance notice of a carefully-written critical article he had written for The NEW STATESMAN; he failed to have the article withdrawn after learning The TIMES would reprint his warning against turning Labour into a "US-style party - a ruthlessly effective electoral machine" centralised in a tight "inner sanctum" clique without any ideological base; "when any party starts to believe its own interests are, by definition, synonymous with those of the electorate as a whole then political arrogance is on the march" Aug '95; voted with hard-Left against Defence Estimates Oct '95; urged tightening of fireworks regulations Nov '95; introduced his Water (Conservation and Consumer Choice) Bill to set mandatory water leakage control targets Dec '95; deplored the deterioration of policing in Birmingham Jan '96; opposed penalising all Palestinian Arabs for the havoc wreaked by Hamas bombs Mar '96; introduced his Vaccine Damage Payments (Amendments) Bill to improve compensation drastically Apr '96; voted against rushing through the revised Prevention of Terrorism Act Apr '96; wrote to The GUARDIAN with 7 other pro-PR Labour MPs to urge the abandonment of the current "Tories' preferred system" May '96; opposed water metering, especially pre-payment meters, as encouraging "self-disconnection" May '96; said "I didn't see the need to remove Clause IV" June '96; deplored the additional delays imposed on NHS building projects in Birmingham through the Private Finance Initiative Jan '97; was listed among 30 mainstream semi-hard-Left MPs led by Robin Cook and John Prescott - tagged 'New Left for New Labour' (formerly the 'Supper Club') -half of whom subsequently secured office Apr '97; as an opponent of foxhunting, was on the 'hit-list' of The FIELD Apr '97; retained his altered, previously-marginal seat by a majority of 11,443, a notional pro-Labour swing of 13% May '97; became PPS to Jeff Rooker, Minister of State for Agriculture May '97; voted to ban fox-hunting June '97; pushed the Additional Member System as a form of proportional representation that did not cut the constituency link Nov '97; welcomed the European Parliamentary Elections Bill for introducing PR; he would have preferred an open-list system Nov '97; in an adjournment debate on Birmingham health services, urged more resources, more concentration on primary care and high-quality cancer care Mar '98; had an adjournment debate on international law in Israeli-occupied territories June '98;

Born: 1 September 1954, Liverpool

Family: Son, Kenneth Rodney Burden, engineer, and late Pauline (Ronnan) secretary; his partner is Jane;

Education: St Aidans Primary, Wallasey '59-65; Wallasey Technical Grammar '65-70; Bramall Grammar/Comprehensive '70-72; St Johns College of Further Education, Manchester '72-73; York University (BA Hons in Politics) '73-78; Warwick University (MA in Industrial Relations) '78-79;

Occupation: Author: 'Tap Dancing - Water, the Environment and Privatisation' (1988); formerly Sponsored, by TGWU (£600 p a to constituency, 80% of election expenses) '92-95; ex: Fulltime Official, of NALGO (initially a Branch Organiser in North Yorkshire '79-81; then a District Officer in Midlands, dealing largely with water industry '81-92) '79-92; Factory Worker '78; Students Union President '76-77; Hospital Porter '74;

Traits: Dark hair; no more soupstrainer moustache; mild-mannered; monotonous tone; discursive; enjoys motor-racing (won the Lords-Commons Brands Hatch race '94, team captain in '98); owns a '78 Lola Sports racing car;

Address: House of Commons, Westminster, London SW1A 0AA;

Telephone: 0171 219 5002/2318 (H of C); 0121 475 9295 (constituency); 0121 553 6051 (West Midlands);

LORDS PROFILES
We also do profiles of Lords, based on forty years of observation and the best files in the country, bar none. Price: £40 each.

Colin BURGON   Labour   ELMET '97-

Majority: 8,779 over Conservative 4-way;
Description: The unaltered marginal seat named after the last Celtic kingdom in England; it actually embraces the furthest eastern wards of Leeds; although it has some Labour wards, these are normally outweighed by the heavily-Conservative market town of Wetherby; this provided the previous Conservative MP with a majority of over 3,000 in '92;
Position: On Joint Committee on Statutory Instruments '97-; ex: Chairman and Secretary of Elmet CLP; on Labour's Yorkshire Regional Executive for six years; Chairman, Leeds Euro-CLP;
Outlook: A late-starting, steady-as-she-goes newcomer; knows that starting at 49 is not the easiest way to reach the Cabinet; only asked five written questions in his first year; a locally-based union-backed teacher-turned-local-government-officer who was third time lucky in the same seat, on what he thought was his last chance at 49; has campaigned against opencast mining in Elmet; is in Amnesty International and Friends of the Earth;
History: He joined the Labour Party '79; as Labour's election agent in Elmet later described the campaign as a "shambles", "we never even had a map of the constituency" May '83; was selected as Labour's candidate for Elmet by 40 votes to 7, Dec '85; expressed admiration for "the way Neil Kinnock has transformed the Labour Party since the last election, and his hold on the party is absolute" June '87; despite a 2.9% pro-Labour swing failed to unseat Tory MP Spencer Batiste by 5,356 votes June '87; was the Labour Agent in the Leeds Euro-election June '89; was re-selected for Elmet June '90; found it "extremely strange" that thieves broke into the regional HQ of his then union, NUPE, taking sensitive political documents but leaving valuables behind Apr '91; achieved only a 2.1% swing, failing to unseat Tory MP Spencer Batiste by 3,261 votes Apr '92; was again selected for Elmet, by then seen as a key marginal '95; Labour scored a clean sweep in Elmet district elections, May '95 and May '96; his election campaign was 55% financed by five unions, including a contribution of £2,100 from the GMB Apr-May '97; ousted Spencer Batiste with a majority of 8,779 on a swing of 10.91% May '97; led a motion calling for electoral registration officers to allow voters to cast ballots after "a genuine administrative mistake" May '97; in his humorous Maiden thanked Elmet's voters for "finally recognising my worth before it was too late", "given my advancing years"; he also criticised the social security system as "complex, inefficient and unfair"; "I especially welcome new criminal penalties for serious cases of deliberate evasion and fraud" July '97; was rated near the bottom of the 'Bottom 100' of written questioners among MPs, with only five posed in his first year May '98; urged Home Secretary Jack Straw to reduce the mixing of young offenders with juveniles at local Wetherby Young Offenders Institution May '98; urged PM Tony Blair to bid to hold the 2006 World Cup in England in "the great city of Leeds" May '98;
Born: 22 April 1948, Leeds
Family: Son of Thomas Burgon, tailoring worker, and Winifred (Feeley); m Kathy, health visitor; 1d Maria '91; now separated;
Education: St Charles RC Junior School; St Michael's College, Leeds; Becketts Park Carnegie College, Leeds (B Ed Hons) '70-74; Huddersfield Polytechnic (part-time study for MA in History):

Occupation: Ex: Local Government Policy and Research Officer for Wakefield Metropolitan Borough Council (GMB); previously a secondary school teacher at Foxwood School, Leeds, for 16 years; before that was a Clerical Officer in the CEGB, a Driver, and a Warehouseman;
Traits: Back-brushed light-brown hair; strong chin; good sense of humour; RC by education; interested in most sports, especially football (a Leeds United supporter); football coach (Leeds City Boys under-19s); youth club leader; enjoys music, the countryside, reading history, especially the American civil war;
Address: House of Commons, Westminster, London SW1A 0AA; 16 St John's Court, Thorner, Leeds LS14 3AX
Telephone: 0171 219 6487 (H of C); 0113 2875198;

John (Patrick) BURNETT   Liberal Democrat   DEVON WEST & TORRIDGE '97-

Majority: 1,957 over Conservative 6-way;
Description: Devon's largest seat, a sprawling, rural, largely inland seat, despite its shipbuilding port of Appledore; it embraces much of Dartmoor, including bleak Princetown with its fearsome prison; it has had a strong Liberal tradition, including the '58 victory of Mark Bonham-Carter in its previous incarnation as Torrington;
Position: Spokesman on Legal Affairs '97-; on the Council of the Devon Cattle Breeders Association, the Law Society's Revenue (Tax) Committee '84-96;
Outlook: Slightly unpredictable maverick and colourful eccentric; on one level a widely-based conservative LibDem victor interested in reforming the legal system and in helping local small local businesses and beef farmers; on another level can ham up his exploits as a former Royal Marine in Borneo or launch Commons speeches with which his colleagues may not agree; conservative on gun control and fox-hunting; a rooted local solicitor and farmer popular with fellow-farmers for his Euroscepticism; was able to capitalise on the rising tide of LibDem support in the Westcountry and the turmoil in Tory ranks after Emma Nicholson's defection in this seat;
History: Joined the Liberal Party; defended the decision of the Liberal-SDP Alliance group on the Devon County Council to raise rates by 19.8% against the criticisms of local Tory MP Sir Peter Mills, pointing out that almost all the increase was caused by the net cut in the Rate Support Grant by the Thatcher Government, the rest by increased spending on education Mar '86; was selected to contest Devon West and Torridge against the new Tory candidate Emma Nicholson May '86; at annual Liberal Assembly spoke of the "insolvency and misery" of many small farmers, urged an agricultural bank, an independent version of the Agricultural Mortgage Corporation, saying it would help farmers who were on the "interest rate treadmill" and enable new entrants to get into farming Sep '86; halved the Tory majority June '87; did not contest the seat in '92; was re-selected to fight it in Feb '96, following the withdrawal of the LibDem candidate, Matthew Owen, and the sensational defection to the LibDems of the sitting Tory MP Emma Nicholson in Dec '95; won the seat on a notional swing of 4.4% by a majority of 1,957 against a weak outside Tory candidate Ian Liddell-Grainger May '97; urged extra NHS funds for sparsely-populated areas like his June '97; urged the extension of the 30-month cull of beef cattle to 36 months for cattle farmers "using traditional extensive grass-based systems"

June '97; having come sixth in the ballot for Private Members Bills, introduced his Energy Efficiency Bill with all-party support June '97; voted against Labour's total handgun ban June '97; asked for statistics on imprisoned young offenders and on mandatory drug-testing July '97; in his Maiden gave qualified support to the Budget's attempt to end the boom-and-bust cycle, from which the southwest suffered particularly: "the brakes get put on the economy by dramatic increases in interest rates when overheating in the southeast demands it, which is usually just before the recovery reaches us" July '97; made a strong appeal to keep open Winsford, a local rural hospital July '97; as a former Marine, deplored the rumoured merger between the Royal Marines and the Parachute Regiment; pressed for two new replacement landing ships Oct '97; urged celebration of 333rd anniversary of the Royal Marines "in which I am proud to have served" Oct '97; welcomed the Strategic Defence Review, hoping it would back "a strong Navy with a flexible, experienced and expert amphibious force as an integral part of it" Oct '97; dismissed Lord Chancellor's legal aid changes as a "blunt knife" which would be "bad news for anyone with a borderline case" Oct '97; expressed severe doubts about the Lord Chancellor's legal aid reforms, denying local legal aid solicitors were "fat cats" Nov '97; voted against Mike Foster's Bill against fox-hunting Nov '97; asked "if the Paymaster General [Geoffrey Robinson] himself is the beneficiary of what is considered to be an extremely lucrative tax avoidance measure, how can he take part in...discussions and examinations without being the subject of glaring conflict of interest?" Jan '98; introduced 2nd Reading of his Energy Efficiency Bill to provide energy ratings for homes at the point of sale, an idea suggested by Peter Walker 14 years before Feb '98; complained that "many barristers return briefs to the CPS at the last minute at the outset of the trial, causing chaos to the criminal justice system" Feb '98; urged "that juries should set and decide on standards for honesty in fraud as well as other trials" Mar '98; urged an independent Secretary of State for Justice responsible to the Commons Mar '98; backed the retention of Territorial reserves for all three Services Apr '98;

Born: 19 September 1945, Oswestry, Shropshire

Family: Son of Aubone Burnett, solicitor, and Joan (Bolt); m '71 'Billie'/Elizabeth (Sherwood de la Mare); 2s Robert '78, George '79; 2d Alice '72, Laura '76;

Education: Ampleforth College, York; Royal Marines Commando Training Centre, Britannia Royal Naval College, Dartmouth; College of Law, London;

Occupation: Solicitor, specialising in taxation '72-: Senior Partner, in Burd Pearse (offices in Okehampton, Tavistock, Torrington and Hatherleigh); Cattle Farmer at Petrockstowe, near Oakhampton; "I am a shareholder in a renewable energy company, but as a trustee only"; ex: Royal Marines Officer '64-70

Traits: Tall; parted longish dark blond hair; broken nose; slightly deaf and inclined to shout; Roman Catholic (active in Torrington RC Church); personable, charming, effusive, confident;

Address: House of Commons, Westminster, London SW1A 0AA; Berry Farm, Petrockstowe, Okehampton, Devon EX20 3EY;

Telephone: 0171 219 3000 (H of C);

With all the destabilizing constituency changes, we think it necessary to try to have accurate seat descriptions. Some newspapers (like the SCOTSMAN and GLASGOW HERALD), some MPs, and especially The Almanac of British Politics by Robert Waller and Byron Criddle (Routledge), have been particularly helpful.

Simon (Hugh McGuigan) BURNS   **Conservative**   **CHELMSFORD WEST '97-**

Majority: 6,691 (11.4%) 18,260 (25.86%) over LibDem 6-way;
Description: A seat re-created in 1995, four-fifths from the previous Chelmsford seat, one fifth from Braintree; it contains the whole of the core of Essex's expanding, prosperous county town, with its outlying Tory-leaning villages; Chelmsford is the base for four GEC-Marconi companies, recently employing 3,500 as against 11,000 20 years before; Tories were formerly closely threatened by the Liberals;
Former Seat: Chelmsford '87-97
Position: Deputy Spokesman on Social Security '97-; ex: Under Secretary for Health '96-97; Whip '95-96; Assistant Whip '94-95; PPS: to Gillian Shephard '93-94, previously to Tim Eggar '89-93; Political Researcher for Sally Oppenheim '75-81;
Outlook: A new, reborn version of the old partisan loyalist: first a barracking backbencher, then a Whip and a junion minister; a wind-sensitive political weathervane, is one of the few Hague spokesman who recognises the Tories lost in May 1997 and that his town's Marconi employment base has shrunk to a third; is not ashamed to ask for help from the new Labour Government; "I am not of the Neanderthal school of politics, believing that anyone who is unemployed is a scrounger" (SB); was one of the Tories' best majority-builders, who made safe the marginal seat left him by Norman St John-Stevas; he held on to his seat with a lower swing than most of his Tory neighbours; because "he makes such powerful representations" is "loved in his constituency" (Robert Key MP); has attacked the "sanctimonious and dishonest campaign" by non-Tory media and Opposition MPs over the award of overseas 'trade and aid' contracts to British companies that had contributed to the Conservative Party -including locally-dominant GEC-Marconi; is an up-market version of David Amess as an Essex-booster ("that wonderful county which produces Essex man and Essex woman"); although formerly a "cerebral Thatcherite zealot" (Simon Heffer, DAILY TELEGRAPH) and Eurosceptic, has been a Major loyalist, even on Maastricht; became more partisan as Tory public opinion poll support sagged; an assiduous attender and speaker; initially a youthful 'wet', later "a one hundred percent supporter of Thatcher"; has been sensitive to the needs of local younger married; anti: abortion, litter; pro: NHS, lottery, Commons creche;
History: His family was Conservative; he himself was a Conservative from school days; "we lived abroad while I was growing up and I had never seen television or a newspaper until about 1962 and I really got interested in politics as a result of John Kennedy; the first events of a political nature I can really remember were the Cuban missile crisis and Kennedy's assassination; I saw him as a young man, an idealist who was seeking to change the world for the better, struck down early on in his career when his full potential had not been totally realised; it make me think it was a viable ambition to seek a political career"; helped found Rutland Young Conservatives '70; at 20 he helped the Presidential campaign of the Leftwing Democrat, Senator George McGovern - "we were all wets then" '72; he joined Sally Oppenheim's office as a Researcher when she was in Mrs Thatcher's Shadow Cabinet two months after he left university '75; was selected for marginal new Alyn and Deeside Apr '83; while canvassing in this seat he kept exchanging greetings with what turned out to be a mynah bird; he came within 3% of overtaking Barry Jones June '83; "he plotted against 'wets' at the

Institute of Directors" (Simon Heffer, DAILY TELEGRAPH) '83-87; was selected as a young married willing to live in marginal Chelmsford in succession to the 'bachelor' MP Norman St John-Stevas, who had held the seat for 22 years, the last time very narrowly - by 378 votes - against the challenge of Liberal Stuart Mole July '86; at annual conference urged Tory critics to "stop the whingeing" and "shout from the rooftops" "the record of this Government" Oct '86; announced in a press release that his wife was pregnant May '87; his substantial win was against the local bookies' odds June '87; supported a call for statutory protection against experimentation on the human embryo July '87; backed anti-abortion motion Oct '87; in his Maiden supported blocking the road of youngsters moving from school to "state subsidized indolence" on the dole, without training or further education Nov '87; deplored a possible Christmas postal strike Dec '87; supported David Alton's abortion-curbing Bill Jan '88; urged on the spot fines for litter louts Jan '88; his 10-minute Bill for a national lottery to provide extra "billions" for the NHS was defeated Feb '88; complained about rate increase by Liberal-controlled Chelmsford Council Apr '88; as a loyal Thatcherite, joined in baiting Tory MP Michael Mates during his speech backing a banded poll tax, calling Mates "disingenious" instead of disingenuous Apr '88; signed more anti-abortion motions Apr-May '88; warned Lords against changing poll tax legislation May '88; launched motion for a creche in Palace of Westminster, the first MP to do so May '88; visited the USA, sponsored by G Tech Corporation to study lotteries there May '88; again proposed a lottery to help finance the NHS July '88; visited Lake Como as guest of Konrad Adenauer Foundation Sep '88; urged more powers for magistrates to punish irresponsible license holders Nov '88; was 'minder' of Steve Norris during Epping by-election Dec '88; deplored Screaming Lord Sutch's behaviour to secure increased sponsors: "they are trying to turn the whole procedure into farce, just for self-publicity" Jan '89; visited Japan as guest of its government Mar '89; introduced Bill urging stiffer penalties against 'litter louts' Mar '89; defended freeze of child benefit, saying: "it is nonsense for my wife to receive a tax-free sum of money each week towards the upkeep of our child; I much prefer that money, or the money that my wife would have received as an increae in child benefit, to be taregeted on genuinely less well-off families" Apr '89; complained that Frank Cook had killed off his Litter (Fines) Bill May '89; congratulated John Moore on improved social benefits when fellow Tory MP Sir Anthony Meyer deplored growing gap between poor and rich May '89; criticised BR service into Liverpool Street May '89; was named PPS to Tim Eggar May '89; co-sponsored John Redwood's Euro-sceptic motion backing an EC based on "willing and active co-operation between independent sovereign states" May '89; staged debate on litter June '89; insisted there was no justification for able-bodied people claiming benefit if they had no intention of seeking work July '89; because he was the only member to turn up, a crucial meeting of the committee on BR's Kings Cross Bill had to be abandoned Dec '89; urged litter fines go to local councils to encourage them rigorously to enforce their powers Jan '90; introduced Bill to limit right of newly-qualified to drive powerful cars in their first year Jan '90; enthusiastically supported Environmental Protection Bill Jan '90; visited New York as guest of C L Global Partners Securities Corporation Apr '90; opposed excusing elderly people living with their families from poll tax as unfair to others May '90; visited Israel as guest of its government May-June '90; urged better protection of railway architecture June '90; visited East and West Germany as guest of Konrad Adenauer Foundation Sep '90; insisted "I do not believe that you can get a greener environment on the cheap" Oct '90; visited Denmark as guest of Danish Association of Teachers of English Nov '90; felt ousted Mrs Thatcher had been "very shoddily treated; it is a disgrace that her premiership should end in such sad circumstances; a little more gratitude should have been shown for her achievements" Nov '90; demanded suspension from Commons of all its poll-tax dodgers Jan '91; deplored Saddam Hussein's "despicable ecological devastion" Jan '91; urged full-day nursery schools instead of half-day sessions which were "no good for a lone parent who wants to work full-time instead of part-time" Feb '91; in debate on Family Policy admitted that he had felt guilty that his wife had gone back to work and his small daughter had been left in a creche charging £500 a month, more than it cost to send a child to a public school and beyond the reach of most; urged tax relief on such expenditures, to encourage more to go out to work Feb '91; complained about BR's service to Chelmsford Feb '91; backed Maintenance Enforcement Bill and Child Support Bill Feb '91; laughter drowned his question when he asked party Chairman Chris Patten, "had he had time to ruminate...?" Mar '91; opposed a place for David Owen in a Conservative Cabinet: "he damaged the Labour Party, he destroyed the Alliance, and it would be rather nerve-wracking if he came over to us" Apr '91; claimed there was little the Government could do to force banks to bring down their rates to small businesses June '91; urged tougher police action against squatters who inflicted serious damage July '91; cancelled his summer holiday to be an hand for an autumn general election July '91; visited Stuttgart and Prague as a guest of Konrad Adenauer Foundation Sep '91; deplored John Prescott behaving "like a yobbo on a building site" in referring to him and colleagues as "f*****g Tories" Nov '91; supported National Lottery Bill Jan '92; complained about civil servants who wore ear-rings and pony-tails Jan '92; retained seat with majority up from 7,761 to 18,260, a swing to Conservatives of 7.21%; he won election bets of £5 each from Mo Mowlam, Adam Ingram and Rhodri Morgan Apr '92; defended unemployed constituents against adjudication officer's refusal to support mortgage payments for a big house with a small mortgage May '92; demanded Douglas Hurd's confirmation of rumours that UK was supporting Jacques Delors' reappointment as President of European Commission June '92; defended Chelmsford against charge of an "abysmal cultural level" Sep '92; rejected CBI's call for MPs to reject salary increases, asking "if members of the CBI and the Institute of Directors, and especially the heads of privatised companies, would follow suit" Nov '92; again introduced Bill to limit initial right of new drivers to powerful cars; it was later dropped on 2nd Reading Jan '93; congratulated PM on securing Tornado order and "safeguarding thousands of jobs", including the HE high-tech company in his constituency Feb '93; enthused about increasing local grant-maintained schools Mar '93; raised problem of unemployment in Chelmsford's defence industries May '93; protested the US Congressional ban on image-intensifiers made in Chelmsford July '93; deplored the "demoralising" loss of jobs in defence industries in Chelmsford, particularly the various Marconi companies; emphasised need to re-skill them July '93; in an argument on the threatened coal industry, was sharply criticised by William Cash for "language that must be completely and utterly out of order" while PPS to Tim Eggar July '93; switched as PPS from Tim Eggar to Gillian Shephard July '93; visited Cyprus as guest of its House of Representatives and Greek Cypriot Brotherhood Sep-Oct '93; made a long and loyal speech defending the Government's closure of the coal mines Oct '93; was congratulated on "his magnificent effort in...securing £300,000 in KONVER [funds] from the European Community" (David Amess MP) Dec '93; while Adviser to Scope Communications, who had the McDonald account, hosted a reception for all MPs with McDonald burger restaurants in their constituencies Dec '93; urged Defence Minister Jonathan Aitken to award the contract for Type 911 tracker radar to local Marconi Radar Jan '94; accused Liberal Democrats of racism Jan '94; voted to restore capital punishment, especially for killers of policemen Feb '94; voted to reduce age of homosexual consent to 18, not 16, Feb '94; complained about the functioning of the Child Support Agency Feb '94; accused Sir David Steel of threatening Chelmsford jobs by pointing out that GEC had been favoured for 'trade and aid' contracts in Malaysia because of the company's contributions to the Conservative Party Mar '94; asked about orders for local Marconi Radar and Control Systems Mar '94; urged abandonment of the "hated M12 from the M25 to Chelmsford, which no one in south and mid-Essex wants" Mar '94; welcomed the road's death Mar '94; he won the 'Greasy Spoon of the Week' award from The GUARDIAN's Simon Hoggart for his "lickspittle question" about "steady and sustainable recovery" May '94; was named an Assistant Whip in the reshuffle July '94; during the "cash for questions" furore, it was pointed out that he was one of 7 MPs who worked for Parliamentary lobbyists, in his case Scope Communications (until promoted a Whip) Sep '94; when John Maples' letter advising the use of backbench 'yobbos' to put Labour's new Leader, Tony Blair, off his stride, it was pointed out that Burns was one of those "whose barracking has secured him promotion" to the Whips' Office (Stephen Bates, GUARDIAN) Nov '94; atttacked as "wicked, spiteful, politically-motivated vindictiveness" a move to remove bus passes from Essex children atttending grammar schools over three miles from their homes; he claimed this was an effort by Essex County Council, controlled by Labour and the LibDems, to pressure students into comprehensives Apr '95; sought to have Paddy Ashdown intervene against local LibDems on school bus passes May-June '95; attended the much-coveted Commonwealth Parliamentary Association meeting in Sri Lanka Oct '95; deplored the loss of another 230 jobs from two Marconi plants in Chelmsford, bringing the total to 2,000 jobs lost in two years from defence cuts Jan '96; was promoted from Whip to Under Secretary for Health, replacing John Bowis July '96; backed a 3% cap on MPs' pay increase, reduced mileage allowance; voted against a pension based on £43,000 July '96; backed better co-operation to improve child health Sep '96; rejected as too expensive and bureaucratic a Rowntree Foundation proposal for compulsory insurance to pay for residential accommodation in old age Sep '96; it was announced that Terry Smith, a stockbroking analyst, would stand against Burns for the Referendum Party Sep '96; warned that Ecstasy could be "very damaging" Feb '97; fought the campaign on "Britain is indeed booming - now is not the time to let Labour blow it" Apr '97; retained the altered and renamed seat with a majority halved to 6,691 on a notional anti-Tory swing of 7.2% May '97; became the campaign manager of Stephen Dorrell for Leader May '97; he switched his support to Michael Howard June '97; was named Deputy Spokesman on Social Security, under Iain Duncan-Smith, by the new Leader, William Hague June '97; staged an adjournment debate on the closedown of Marconi College and the loss of another 535 job losses at Marconi Comunications, ending the town's manufacturing base; he urged help from the new Labour Government June '97;

Born: 6 September 1952, Nottingham

Family: Son late Brian Burns, retired Army officer, and Shelagh (Nash); m '82 Emma (Clifford), interior decorator and Director of Colefax and Fowler; 1d Amelia Mary Louisa McGuigan '87; 1s 'Bobby'/Robert '91; separated '98;

Education: Christ the King School, Accra, Ghana; Stamford School; Worcester College, Oxford University;

Occupation: Adviser, to Scope Communications Management (Clients: McDonalds, Toyota, Tyne and Wear Development, W H Smith, Rank Xerox, Halfords, Allied Lyons) '93-94; on Political Opinion Panel, of Market Access International Ltd (money to Chelmsford charities) '88-94; Policy Executive, Institute of Directors '83-87; Director, 'What to Buy for Business' magazine (with Phillip Oppenheim) '81-83; Political Researcher, for Sally Oppenheim while in Shadow Cabinet and Minister for Consumer Affairs '75-81;

Traits: Six-footer; reddish-blond, centrally parted, front-combed hair; "long legs" (Quentin Letts, DAILY TELEGRAPH); "young, almost dashing" (DAILY TELEGRAPH); "believed to model himself on the late John F Kennedy" ('Peterborough', DAILY TELEGRAPH); "impish" (EVENING STANDARD); "a red-eyed new Tory whose hair may conceal brains" (Godfrey Barker, DAILY TELEGRAPH); "dim" (Edward Pearce, GUARDIAN); "the expression of a pious young Sunday school prize-winner" (Matthew Parris, TIMES); "obviously believes that

shouting at people is good for his soul" (Sir Russell Johnston MP); self-publicist ("knows a photo opportunity when he sees one" [DAILY TELEGRAPH), such as his day as a dustman '91; also tried a stunt when visiting the local fire brigade: "I went up a 70-foot ladder there, which wasn't my idea of heaven; one of my legs was shaking vigorously, but I was terrified of being thought a wimp, so I hooked it to one of the rungs to stop it shaking"); accident-prone (caught finger on security grill '91, misaligned bin when pretending to be a dustman, with result the cart's vicious teeth started to chew up the bin instead of the rubbish '91, tripped over 18-inch-high link-chain fence '92); excellent swimmer (recorded speediest time on Parliamentary team in Speedo Charity Swim '91); readily mouse-frightened ("I stood on my chair" when a mouse appeared in the Commons); tried to stop smoking ("I have stubbed out my last one") in preparation for swimming contest in '91, but was caught at the event with a surreptitious fag; is Clare Short's 'pair'; likes swimming and travelling;
Address: House of Commons, Westminster, London SW1A 0AA; 31 Hamlet Road, Chelmsford, Essex;
Telephone: 0171 219 3000 (H of C);

Paul BURSTOW   **Liberal Democrat**   **SUTTON & CHEAM '97-**

Majority: 2,097 over Conservative 6-way;
Description: The unaltered seat on the edge of the North Downs which has reverted to what was seen as the "false dawn" of a Liberal victory when Graham (now Lord) Tope won the '72 by-election there; over the next quarter century, it seemed to underline the observation that no matter how firmly local people trusted Liberal or LibDem councillors, they did not want them as MPs; this has been reversed dramatically, in a band of five seats in London's southwestern suburbs, not merely because of the local "Olga Maitland experience";
Position: Spokesman on Disability Rights and Social Services and LibDems' Team Leader on Local Government '97-; Sutton Borough Councillor (Deputy Leader '94-97, Chairman, of Environmental Services '93-96, '88-91) '86-; Political Secretary '96-97, Campaigns Officer '87-96, of Association of Liberal Democrat Councillors; on Liberal Democrats' London Regional Executives; ex: on LibDem Federal Policy Committee '88-90;
Outlook: Diligent, sensible and obviously ambitious new boy, the first of them to be made a LibDem team leader, serving in Paddy Ashdown's inner shadow-Shadow Cabinet; a leading young LibDem local government apparatchik who joined their '97 phalanx of five MPs from London's southwestern suburbs; in his case he had extra multi-party thanks for ending the shrill career of the Rightwing Serbo-Scottish aristocrat, Lady Olga Maitland; has been very assiduous as a written questioner, achieving 8th place among the 'Top 100' by posing 401 in his first year; very active on behalf of the blind and the disabled; a hyper-active member of the social-democratic wing of his party inclined to sympathetic but firm pressure on Labour; "constructive and sensible" (Nick Raynsford MP); a member of Charter 88; "I believe passionately in the need for decentralisation, which is vital for renewing our democratic life and for rebuilding a sense of community";
History: Joined the SDP '82; was elected to Sutton Borough Council May '86; joined the

Liberal Democrats from the SDP '88; on Sutton Council was responsible for local Agenda 21 and for sustainability and disability issues; he also led the council's development of award-winning environmental programmes; he only dented the majority of Lady Olga with a swing of 5.4% which shaved 30% off her 16,000 majority Apr '92; finished the job with a massive 13% swing, giving him a majority of 2,097 over Lady Olga May '97; in his Maiden, emphasised the need for more opportunities for the disabled; also said, "I look forward to the creation of a new strategic authority for London" May '97; launching a debate on 'Youth Crime', urged "a sophisticated, well-researched and successfully-implemented strategy to tackle crime" such as carried out in Sutton and Cheam's "Youth Awareness Programme" June '97; backed ban on fox-hunting June '97; welcomed the £5b in phased release of housing receipts, but insisted it no more than scratched the surface of housing need, including a £20b housing repair backlog June '97; urged "a national strategy on dementia care" June '97; warned against the centralising tendency of new Labour Government June '97; was active on the Local Government (Contracts) Bill, trying to secure more power and discretion for local authorities June-July '97; was critical of the Budget because of the Government's "self-imposed straitjacket" which would bring "another winter of crisis and chaos" in the NHS and elsewhere July '97; repeatedly urged improved facilities for blind and near-blind voters July '97; led motion urging retention of rail travellers' network cards July '97; introduced his Elections (Visually Impaired Voters) Bill July '97; co-sponsored motion complaining of polls' inaccessibility for the disabled July '97; opposed the Tory attempt to enable borough leaders to hold to account a directly-elected London Mayor Nov '97; urged "a more accountable system which raises [local government] tax on the basis of ability to pay and guarantees greater freedom of action for local councils" Dec '97; insisted that if cuts had to be made they should be made in benefits paid to middle-class families Dec '97; agreed that "the systematic abuse of power - and its financial consequences -by Dame Shirley Porter and David Weeks, as Leader and Deputy Leader of the Conserative majority on Westminster Council, is in a league of its own in the annals of local government misconduct and surcharge" Jan '98; co-sponsored motion attacking age discrimination Jan '98; complained for LibDems that Government allocations to councils were £1b short of what was needed Feb '98; urged better access to the polls for the blind and partially sighted Feb '98; complained about stoppage of disabled benefits after disabled benefits interviews Feb '98; pointing out that 1.75m children were working illegally, asked what resources would be committed to correct this Feb '98; complained that the Government were using "fantasy figures" in local government financing Feb '98; urged better publicity for carers discounts on council tax Mar '98; again urged PR for local government Mar '98; moved an amendment to the School Standards and Framework Bill to allow money to follow pupils squeezed out of school places by selection or the Greenwich judgment Mar '98; urged stronger legal protection against 'whisky scam' frauds Apr '98; warned that Labour's refusal of a two-question referendum would reduce turnout May '98;
Born: 13 May 1962, Carshalton
Family: Son of Brian Burstow, tailor, and Sheila (Edmond); married to Mary (Kemm);
Education: Glastonbury High School, Carshalton; Carshalton College of Further Education; South Bank Polytechnic;
Occupation: Director: Business Ecologic, Business Link London South (local government organisation) '96-97; previously ALDC Campaigns Officer, '87-96;
Traits: Front-combed dark brown flat hair; specs; small-featured; hyper-assiduous; "constructive and positive" (Alun Michael MP); a happy-clappy Christian whose strong-willed wife Mary save him from disorganised untidyness;
Address: House of Commons, Westminster, London SW1A 0AA;
Telephone: 0171 219 3000 (H of C); 0181 643 9904;

Christine BUTLER   **Labour**   **CASTLE POINT '97-**

Majority: 1,116 over Conservative 5-way;
Description: The unaltered, '83-created Essex seat consisting of Benfleet and refinery-dominated Canvey Island, along the north side of the Thames estuary, within the Port of London but just outside the Thames corridor; it is primarily a commuter area with nine out of ten electors owner-occupiers; until '97 this was the 77th safest Tory seat, providing its former Tory MP, Dr Robert Spink, with a majority of almost 17,000 in '92;
Position: On Select Committee on Environment, Transport and Regional Affairs '97-; ex: Essex County Councillor '93-97; Chairman, of the Essex Co-operative Development Agency;

Outlook: The local county councillor who delivered Labour's fourth most unexpected gain on a near-record swing of 16.94%, ousting the sitting Tory MP, Dr Robert Spink; "in this new optimistic era, I'd like to make sure all of Labour's policies are implemented, tackling unemployment first" (CB); was slow at first in mastering Parliamentary skills, concentrating on local issues; a pro-European, in the Co-operative Society, Fabian Society, Greenpeace;
History: She joined the Labour Party '73; was elected to Essex County Council for Castle Point May '93; Labour representation on the Castle Point Borough Council, which has the same boundaries as the Parliamentary seat, moved from a minority of four to full control May '95; ousted the sitting Tory MP, Dr Robert Spink, with a majority of 1,116, on a massive pro-Labour swing of 16.94% May '97; co-sponsored motion attacking the BBC for showing "a self-confessed paedophile" on the 'Kilroy' programme June '97; expressed solidarity with jailed Indonesian union leader June '97; asked about prospecting for sand and gravel in the Thames estuary July '97; co-sponsored motion warning of dangers of reduced use of pilots in the Thames July '97; was named to the Select Committee on Environment, Transport and Regional Affairs July '97; signed the European Movement's advertisement: "Europe: A Force for Fairness, Equality and Opportunity for Women" Nov '97; in her Maiden spoke of her constituency's need for "regeneration" Dec '97; urged promotion of telemedicine in the NHS Feb '98; supported Chris Pond's Employment of Children Bill: "I should like all employers and putative employers of children to be licensed or registered"; "employers should be certified as fit and proper people to employ children, and should be able to convince authorities that conditions in the workplace are suitable for children" Feb '98; urged a short, sharp Bill to end the voting rights of 750 hereditary peers Feb '98; urged equality of opportunity in scientific careers for women Mar '98; was rated one of the lowest of 'Bottom 100' written questioners with only four posed in her first year May '98;
Born: 14 December 1943, Lancashire
Family: Married to a teacher; has three sons and four small grandchildren;
Education: State primary and grammar schools; Middlesex Polytechnic (BA Hons);
Occupation: Former Research Assistant: in the pharmaceutical industry and in the NHS (MSF);
Traits: Short brown hair; gap-toothed; lived-in face;
Address: House of Commons, Westminster, London SW1A 0AA;
Telephone: 0171 219 5668 (H of C); 01268 684722 (constituency)

John (Valentine) BUTTERFILL   **Conservative**   **BOURNEMOUTH WEST '83-**

Majority: 5,710 (13.9%) over Liberal Democrat 7-way;
Description: The western bit of the traditional seaside resort, with a heavy proportion of retired middle class voters, plus the town's largest council estate; it has recently been infiltrated by unemployed Liverpuddlians lured there by unscrupulous hoteliers, partly converting it into a "Costa del Dole"; the '95 return of wards to Poole and acquisition of town-centre wards from Bournemouth East was politically neutral;
Position: On Chairmen's Panel '96-; on Trade and Industry Select Committee '92-; on Select Committee on Unopposed Bills '95-; on Court of Referees '96-;
Chairman of Trustees, Parliamentary Members Fund '97-; Trustee, Parliamentary Pension Fund '97-; Chairman, Conservative Party Rules Committee '98-; Vice Chairman '97-, Secretary '96-97, 1922 Committee; Chairman 95-, Vice Chairman '92-95 Conservatives' European Affairs Committee; Vice Chairman, Conservatives' Finance Committee '92-; Chairman, all-party Group on Occupational Pensions '92-; Secretary '96-, Vice Chairman '97- all-party Group on Building Societies; on the Board of Parliamentary Office of Science and Technology (POST) '95-97-; Vice Chairman, Parliamentary Group, of Conservative Friends of Israel '95-; on General Council of Management of the People's Dispensary for Sick Animals '89-; ex: PPS, to Dr Brian Mawhinney '91-92, to Cecil Parkinson '88-90; Vice President, Conservative Group for Europe '92-95; Vice Chairman '85-88, Secretary '84-85, Conservative MPs' Tourism Committee; Secretary, their Trade and Industry Committee '87-88; Chairman, Conservative Group for Europe '89-92; on National Council of European Movement '82-90;
Outlook: The conscientious, strongly pro-EU Rightwing voice of the investment community; Adviser to British Venture Capital Association at £10-15,000 ("I can see now why the hon Gentleman is retained at such generous rates; he clearly does his best for the industry" - Chief Secretary Alistair Darling); the sponsor of the failed British Time (Extra Daylight) Bill to put Britain on Central European Time; a party loyalist, offering Whip-planted questions to the PM, or Whip-inspired baiting of Tory rebels like Michael Mates; a well-informed, socially-responsible chartered surveyor and company director who feels it necessary to preface with anti-Labour sallies almost every show of social concern; has served Bournemouth after failing his political 11-plus in South London; 'wet' on social services, consumer protection and health; 'dry' on the economy, education and playing Rugby with South Africa; anti: hanging, dog registration, fluoride, Liverpuddlian 'scroungers' in Bournemouth, "whining egalitarian fanatics"; pro: caning, Zionism, tourism, EU (especially if expanded);
History: "I...came into British politics because of an enthusiasm for the European Community"; he joined the Conservative Party '57; failed as Tory Euro-candidate for London South Inner June '79; selected for the Croydon NW by-election, he regretted Shirley Williams was not fighting it: "she would have been a very beatable candidate"; he lost this Tory-held seat to the less-well-known Liberal, Bill Pitt Oct '81; was adopted for Bournemouth West in succession to retiring Sir John Eden (later Lord Eden of Winton) Mar '82; voted against restoring the death penalty July '83; warned against political indoctrination of school children Jan '84; urged rapid implementation of Lovelock Review of Citizens' Advice Bureaux Feb '84; backed Rugby tour of South Africa Feb '84; backed postal ballots for trade union elections

July '84; backed a blindness allowance Nov '84; urged retention of the zero rating of VAT on children's shoes Nov '84; deplored "unscrupulous hoteliers and boarding house operators in my constituency" who had lured unemployed from Liverpool to live off their benefits locally, converting Bournemouth into a "Costa del Dole" with resulting "increase in drug abuse and drug trafficking", "muggings, burglaries and prostitution" Dec '84; voted against fluoride in water Jan '85; expressed doubts about BBC going in for Breakfast Television Mar '85; put down a motion trying to ensure "that existing workers in the retail trade cannot be forced to work on Sundays" May '85; co-sponsored Roger Gale's liberalizing Licensing Acts (Amendment) Bill May '85; introduced an amending to the conveyancing Bill to ban anyone from offering conveyancing services where they already had a financial interest June '85; urged that better-off should revert to child tax allowances rather than receive child benefit June '85; co-sponsored motion urging Spain to recognize Israel before joining the EEC July '85; backed a free vote on Sunday trading Nov '85; urged a test for glaucoma be included in normal NHS eye test Jan '86; backed the scrapping of the Rent Acts Feb '86; fought for disclosure of salesmen's commissions and all other costs in insurance or investments Mar '86; opposed anti-Market MPs Teddy Taylor and Enoch Powell over the European Communities Bill June '86; urged curb on banks' advertising and "cold calling" in the Banking Bill, but worried about accounts disclosure, even in criminal cases Nov '86; claimed county councillors could save money by using management consultants Nov '86; sought a consensus to enable growth without profiteering in private rented sector Feb '87; strongly opposed banks and building societies being able to sell their own products, like life assurance Mar '87; felt the Financial Services Act should ensure a fair market in which investors were properly protected by the Securities and Investment Board: "I am particularly interested in the development of a unitized property market" May '87; criticized Bernie Grant for his "unhelpful and regrettable" Maiden speech warning of "powder keg" in inner cities July '87; denied there were any monopolistic trends in the press Nov '87; urged new radical reforms in social security Nov '87; urged British companies "invest in social projects in South Africa" Jan '88; urged lower rating on holiday caravans Feb '88; tried to limit rate increases for small businesses to 10% a year Mar '88; supported reintroduction of corporal punishment Mar '88; enthused about Chancellor Lawson's Budget, except for wanting a higher threshold for stamp duty on house sales Mar '88; at instigation of Whips, baited Michael Mates for his banded poll tax efforts Apr '88; defended imprisonment as last sanction for nonpayers of poll tax because it was aimed at the man who wasted his benefit "on beer and the betting shop" Apr '88; visited Amsterdam as guest of British Tourist Authority and British Midland Airways Apr '88; was defeated by Treasury when he submitted new clauses for Finance Bill on Home Annuity Loans, allowing interest on loans to be rolled up, net of tax relief and repaid along with the capital on the death of the annuitant; this plan, backed by 110 other Tory MPs, could have doubled the income of elderly home owners May-June '88; voted against restoring capital punishment June '88; visited North Cyprus as guest of Turkish Republic of North Cyprus Sep-Oct '88; resisted CBI move to get EC money to improve local roads Feb '89; agreed with Tony Benn MP in wanting "an outgoing Europe"; also said the EMS "as presently constituted" could not have coped with such violent changes of parity as between the pound Sterling and the dollar Feb '89; enthused about Chancellor Lawson's reduced taxes, repayment of debts and expanded economy Feb '89; loyally defended Government's uprating of pensions Apr '89; felt it extraordinary for the European Commission to seek to extend its activities into language training and transport infrastructure funds; urged more democratic accountability in EC, with European Parliament enhanced May '89; baited Neil Kinnock for abandoning unilateralism because it was unpopular May '89; urged easing of barriers to takeover bids in the EC May '89; as Chairman of Conservative Group for Europe, said the criticisms of its President, Edward Heath, of Mrs

Thatcher's attitudes toward the EC, made "quite a few people" "feel his behaviour is incompatible with membership of a Conservative organization"; he himself felt Heath's "behaviour has been most regrettable and very sad" June '89; overcame efforts of Thatcherites to oust Ted Heath as its President, a position held since three years after it was formed in 1974, but facilitated his departure July '89; voted against CofE ordaining divorced men July '89; urged cash help for Poland because it was already over-burdened with debt Nov '89; asked searching questions about pension funds Feb '90; again voted against C of E ordination of divorced men Feb '90; warned against allowing too much access by individuals to files held on them for fear of hindering combat of international fraudsters Feb '90; urged dismissal of Hackney finance officer Andy Murphy, leader of punk anarchist group 'Class War', for justifying attacks on police Apr '90; toured Bonn and Cologne as guest of Roads Campaign Council June '90; toured East Germany as guest of Konrad Adenauer Foundation Oct '90; opposed dog registration as impractical, suggesting widespread neutering instead Oct'90; introduced Registered Homes (Amendment) Act to prevent disqualified proprietors of care homes from remaining in that business by running smaller homes Jan '91; complained of policing burden on Bournemouth during party conferences there Jan '91; was made PPS to Dr Brian Mawhinney, then Northern Ireland Minister Mar '91; asked hostile questions about funding of British Fluoridation Society Apr '91; claimed "nearly twice as many babies at risk died when "the [Labour] party opposite was in power" June '91; again complained of a "bad lot" from Liverpool who contributed to Bournemouth's crime, prostitution and drug problems July '91; insisted that the CBI, "the Institute of Directors, the City and all our major companies" "are telling us that we must proceed further with economic and monetary union" because 53.3% of UK exports were going to the EC Nov '91; opposed European Parliament's resisting expansion of EC to embrace Nordic countries, Austria and Switzerland in European Economic Area of 19, Feb '92; retained seat, with majority over Liberal Democrats almost unchanged Apr '92; was defeated by Sir Peter Hordern for the Chairmanship of the Conservative MPs' European Afffairs Group by only two votes, but won its Vice Chairmanship with backing of '92 Group', with Eurosceptic MPs boycotting the election June '92; was named to Select Committee on Trade and Industry July '92; urged exclusion of land-owning charities and foreign investors from leasehold enfranchisement under Housing and Urban Development Bill Nov '92; joined the Positive Europe Group Jan '93; enthusiastically supported Maastricht treaty and subsidiarity in the name of "every industrialist throughout the country", despite sharp attacks by anti-Maastricht Tory MPs Mar '93; again urged corporal punishment for young thugs, like the one who beat up a 100-year-old constituent Apr '93; in an otherwise loyal defence of the Budget and even VAT on energy -despite his excess of elderly constituents - criticised absence of transitional arrangement for movement away from PRT (petroleum tax) Apr '93; the Whips removed him from the Finance Bill committee but the Treasury made minor concessions to his viewpoint June '93; PM John Major ordered a crackdown on housing benefit excesses after receiving a Butterfill dossier on local landlords who advertised on the Merseyside to fill their hotels with housing benefit clients: "it is a scandal people can build business empires on the back of th benefit system", said Butterfill Aug '93; as Rob Hayward's "minder-in-chief" at the disastrous Christchurch by-election, claimed that Conservative support was "firming up" in the last week before the deluge washing out the Tories' 23,000 majority; he alleged that "people had no idea what they were voting for" July '93; won 16th place in ballot for Private Members' Bills Nov '93; introduced his Insolvency (Amendment) Act "to give protection to purchasers of property which had been previously transferred at an undervalue" Dec '93; backed the "balanced approach" of the Budget's tax increases, including increases in the blindness allowance he had pioneered; urged abolition of "iniquitous" capital gains tax Dec '93; asked about statutory compensation for commercial properties affected by the Crossrail Bill Jan '94; opposed restoration of capital punishment, even for killing policemen Feb '94; backed reduction of age of homosexual consent to 18, but not 16, Feb '94; blamed the problems with pensions on inadequate regulation by the Securities and Investments Board Mar '94; blamed the Euro-poll disaster on media hostility May '94; applauded the variety of schools available in Bournemouth and condemned "the Liberal Democratic and Labour parties for trying to close down that choice" July '94; deplored the bailing of a local man charged with indecent assault who then committed 13 more offences including two rapes in his year on bail Aug '94; said: "I do not think that there is the remotest chance of anything but a handful of nations meeting the convergence criteria in the Community by 1999, let alone 1997" Feb '95; attacked the Liberal Democrats' "incompetent and insensitive" administration of Dorset, into which departing Bournemouth had been temporarily absorbed when it had lost its borough status July '95; in the boundary changes, he lost wards returned to Poole and gained some in the heart of the town from Bournemouth East July '95; regretting the adoption of the new Nolan rules tightening declaration of interests and the appointment of Sir Gordon Downey - against which he had voted - disclosed he was receiving between £10,000 and £15,000 each from the British Venture Capital Association and also the British Insurance and Investment Brokers Association Nov '95; already on the 1922 Committee's Executive, unsuccessfully contested the post of its Joint Secretary Nov '95; coming first in the Private Members' Ballot, he opted for a British Time (Extra Daylight) Bill to provide an extra usable hour of daylight, backed initially by 200 other MPs from all parties Nov '95; was attacked by SNP Leader Alex Salmond as "a would-be time bandit, threatening Scotland with daylight robbery" in advance of his Bill to adjust Britain to Central European Time Nov '95; attacked by Scottish Secretary Michael Forsyth, on a free vote his Bill turned out to have inadequate support; he won the vote by 93 to 85, but he was 7 short or the 100 votes needed Jan '96; on the Select Committee on Trade and Industry, led the campaign to water down its report on nuclear privatisation by eliminating one key recommendation: that Sizewell B be held back from the sale of nuclear power stations and kept in state hands Feb '96; emphasised the need to renegotiate the finances of the EU -especially the CAP - in enlarging it Mar '96; opposed 3% cap on MPs' pay rise and for pensions to be based on £43,000 July '96; came 18th in Private Members' Ballot Oct '96; introduced Policyholders Protection Bill Nov '96; voted to retain caning Jan '97; welcomed Chancellor Clarke's last Budget proposals, except for his increase in insurance premium tax and the still-high level of capital taxes (as Adviser to the British Insurance and Investment Brokers Association) Jan '97; deplored the "very irresponsible" campaign of the Children's Society which advertised "Why travel 6,000 miles to have sex with children when you can do the same thing in Bournemouth?"; this was explained by the society as "shock tactics" to publicise its local refuge in Bournemouth Feb '97; retained his half-changed seat with a halved majority of 5,710, a very low notional swing of 5.6% May '97; unsuccessfully contested the Chairmanship of the 1922 Committee, but was elected its Vice Chairman May '97; backed Kenneth Clarke for the Tory Leadership June '97; in an argument with Chief Secretary Alistair Darling, pointed out that, in 1986, he had insisted on the disclosure of all costs in direct selling of pensions, not merely salesmen's commissions July '97; as Chairman of the all-party Group on Occupational Pensions, pointed out that the "old-age pension has fallen relative to average gross male earnings from 20% in 1950 to 15% today; if nothing is done it will fall to about 9% by 2030"; the new Labour Government had damaged personal pernsions by changing ACT legislation and should reverse that July '97; was re-appointed to Select Committee on Trade and Industry July '97;

Born: 14 February 1941, Kingston-upon-Thames

Family: S George Thomas Butterfill, Lloyd's insurance broking executive, and Elsie Amelia

(Watts), Bank of England executive; m '65 Pamela (Ross-Symons) ex-Assistant Personnel Manager of Aquascutum; 1s James '75, 3d Natasha '69, Samara '74, Jemima '76;
Education: St Paul's School, Addlestone, Surrey; Caterham School; College of Estate Management;
Occupation: Chartered Surveyor, FRICS '74-: Consultant '92-, Senior Partner '77-92, of Curchod and Co (chartered surveyors; "my firm acts for 32 banks and building societies"); President, European Property Associates '78-; Director: Conservation Investments Ltd (real estate development; also a shareholder and director of subsidiaries) '85-, Conservation Properties Ltd (a subsidiary) '93-, Delphi Group Plc (IT Services) '9?-, Maples Group Ltd '92-98; Partner, in Butterfill Associates (financial, corporate and real estate consultants) '92-; Parliamentary Adviser: to British Venture Capital Association (at £10-15,000; Panellist: for Harris Parliamentary Panel (up to £1,000), Market Access Ltd (PR, lobbying, at up to £1,000) '92-; Political Opinion Panel of Business Planning and Research International (up to£1,000); ex: Managing Director, St Paul's Securities Group '71-76; Director: Islef (Building and Construction) Ltd '85-91, John Lelliott Development Ltd '84-88, Audley Properties Ltd (Bovis Group) '69-71; St Georges Property Company '84-88; Adviser, to British Insurance and Investment Brokers Association (at £10-15,000) '92-97, Independent Financial Advisers Association (at £10-15,000) '94-97 to Arrowcroft Group Plc '90-91; Pavilion Services Group Ltd (proprietors of motorway service areas and filling stations; also a shareholder) '92-96, Foxwell Securities Ltd (investment and development of real property) '93-96; Senior Executive, with Hammerson Group '64-69; Valuer, with Jones Lang Wootton '62-64;
Traits: Plump; parted brown hair; pudgy lined face; agreeable; worthy; no great presser of the flesh; shows old-fashioned politeness and felicity of phrase; "smooth, cautious and reticent" (Dennis Barker, GUARDIAN); has a deadly grasp of detail; very prosperous (may not be able to afford to become a junior Minister); caring (on PDSA council);
Address: House of Commons, Westminster, London SW1A 0AA;
Telephone: 0171 219 6383/6375 (H of C);

Rt Hon Stephen (John) BYERS   Labour   **TYNESIDE NORTH '97-**

Majority: 26,643 (59%) over Conservative 4-way;
Description: An altered solidly-Labour seat of windswept council estates and former pit villages, created in '95 from his former Wallsend seat, shorn of Wallsend itself, with 7,000 voters added from Tynemouth; its declining shipbuilding (Swan Hunter) has been transferred to the Newcastle East and Wallsend seat;
Former Seat: Wallsend '92-97
Position: Chief Secretary to the Treasury '98-; ex: Minister of State for Education '97-98; Deputy Spokesman '96-97, Assistant Spokesman '95-96, on Education and Employment; Whip '94-95; on Home Affairs Select Committee '93-94; Chairman: PLP Home Affairs Committee '92-94; Joint Chairman, all-party Police Committee '93-9?; Chairman, of Education Committee, Association of Metropolitan Authorities '90-92; Leader, Council of Local Education Authorities '90-92; North Tyneside Metropolitan Borough Councillor (Deputy Leader '85-92, ex Chairman of Education) '80-92; on Northern Region

TUC '90-92; Chairman, National Employers Organisation for Teachers '90-92; on Education Subcommittee of Labour's NEC; on Management Panel, of National Joint Council for Further Education;

Outlook: The Blair-approved rising politician who beat his Brown-approved rival, Alan Milburn, into Cabinet; initially intended as a union-curber before the election, was used in '97-98 as a school-improver; "able, ambitious, well-dressed, rational in debate and, perhaps more importantly, close to Peter Mandelson" (TIMES); "one of the new generation of bright, ambitious modernisers who form part of Tony Blair's northeast 'Mafia' of Labour high-flyers"; "despite representing the former mining and shipbuilding stronghold of Wallsend he is viewed with suspicion by old-style trade union leaders who know he is a passionate believer in putting distance between them and New Labour" (Joy Copley, DAILY TELEGRAPH); was an impressive, extremely well-informed moderate newcomer who could clobber opponents when challenged; was also an "expert user of Parliamentary questions to ferret out information damaging to the Tories" (GUARDIAN), including Mrs Thatcher's involvement in arms sales to Malaysia and Jonathan Aitken's in arms for Iraq; was said to deserve a "gold star" (MAIL ON SUNDAY) for his work against the Education Bill enacting opting out; with Geoffrey Hoon, outmaneuvred Government on Maastricht; a former leader of local education authorities and member of the Burnham Committee; a sleaze-probing former local law lecturer who graduated from local government; after a number of near-misses he was belatedly selected for a safe seat locally, having finally overcome the disadvantage of not being union-sponsored; acquired UNISON backing '92-95 after he reached the Commons;

History: Joined the Labour Party '74; opposed IMF intervention in Labour Government's financial policies Nov '76; was elected to North Tyneside Metropolitan Borough Council May '80; backed Leftish campaign for activist democracy in Labour Party '80-82; was selected for hopeless Hexham, endorsed by NEC Apr '82; contested Hexham against Geoffrey Rippon, losing by 8,308 votes June '83; switched his union membership from NATFHE to NUPE '84; became Deputy Leader of North Tyneside Council '85; failed to secure selection for Blyth against NUM-backed Ronnie Campbell Aug '85; failed by one vote to secure selection for Newcastle North against GMB-backed Doug Henderson (which was the occasion of a later protest to the NEC against the GMB's "stranglehold") Feb '86; was selected for safe Wallsend, after Ted Garrett announced he would not stand again after 25 years Oct '89; complained that Government was planning to privatise auditing of opted-out schools June '91; as Education Chairman of the AMA, said the news that three times as many schools were opting out in low-spending Conservative-controlled areas showed that "opting out is a policy which has backfired; it is a massive vote of no confidence in the policies of Tory education authorities" July '91; retained Wallsend with almost identical massive majority of 19,470 Apr '92; stepped down from North Tyneside Council May '92; in his Maiden deplored his constituency's loss of jobs in shipbuilding and platform-building and warned against a return to selective education May '92; complained about movement of regional aid from northeast to south June '92; urged opening up of judiciary to women and ethnic minorities through a Judicial Appointments Commission June '92; succeeded in having withdrawn the Lord Chancellor's rule that defendants had to produce 13 wage slips to qualify for legal aid June '92; urged acceptance of its Social Chapter to diminish resistance to Maastricht July '92; after extracting information in remorseless questioning, disclosed that, of the £2b pumped into 10 English urban development corporations, 6 of them had lost £67m on land purchases largely for commercial, rather than industrial, development July '92; complained that schools' league-tables would be distorted by excluding worst students July '92; insisted that schools were five times more likely to opt out of low-spending Conservative-run local education authorities in England; complained that Assisted Places Scheme, on which £500m had been spent since '81, had helped mostly middle class parents who had fallen on hard times, rather than working-class parents July '92; asked a string of probing questions on the finances of City Technology Trusts July '92; asked for inquiry by Audit Commission into poor schools being partly financed by Assisted Places Scheme Nov '92; deplored continuing delay on planned local sewage sludge plant Oct '92; produced statistics showing 77% of recently appointed top judges were from Oxford or Cambride and 84% had attended private schools Oct '92; on Education Bill, complained about Mao-style "period of permanent revolution"; deplored fact that new money was "not for education but to fund bureaucrats" Nov '92; deplored "the fiasco surrounding the publication of the school examination results league tables" Nov '92; insisted there was "a crisis of confidence in our legal system"; emphasized the judges were largely a self-perpetuating elite of male middle-class barristers; he urged automatic retirement at 65; to make up for shortages, urged the Continental system of taking young graduates into early judicial training instead of waiting until they make their names and piles in their forties Dec '92; provided statistics demonstrating that, even in predominantly Labour areas, magistrates appointed were mostly Tory supporters Dec '92; played a major role in committee on Education Bill Jan '93; after the Tyneside-built 'Ark Royal' sailed for the Adriatic, urged the upgrading of amphibious capability by the building of a landing-platform helicopter vessel, preferably at Swan Hunter Feb '93; complained about defective rates indices: "that index shows Cheltenham as poorer than Rotherham, Gloucester as poorer than North Tyneside" Feb '93; said, "our education system has been seen as a failure" because "academic education [is] reserved for the most able pupils while vocational education is for the less able" Mar '93; complained about continuing concentration of power in the hands of Education Secretary John Patten, against whom he quoted John Ruskin: "conceit may puff a man up but it can never prop him up" Mar '93; again urged maintenance of UK's "amphibious capacity", with a helicopter carrier built on the Tyneside Mar '93; when he complained to PM about unemployment, Mr Major said he had "neglected to mention" the 20% fall in Wallsend's unemployment Mar '93; welcomed 25 years of Abortion Act 1967 and its role in killing off "back-street" abortionists Apr '93; with Geoffrey Hoon MP, devised the new clause 75, enabling the Social Chapter to be added to Maastricht; warned that unless Social Chapter was endorsed with Maastricht treaty, there would be legal difficulties Apr '93; deplored blow to Tyneside's Swan Hunter shipyard, attacking Industry Minister Tim Sainsbury for "saying he was prepared to allow shipbuilding to die on Tyneside because that is what the market determined" May '93; complained that "a million pounds has been lost" on Brighton's City Technology College May '93; asked for inquiry into claim that Vickers undercut Swan Hunter because of a £40m sweetener for taking over Cammell Laird on Merseyside; also asked Stock Exchange's Surveillance Department and the National Audit Office to investigate a "startling" 50% rise in Vickers share price before it received helicopter carrier order June '93; urged Swan Hunter be allowed to complete work on 3 frigates June '93; complained that Government money were being diverted to fund propaganda urging schools to opt out July '93; complained that nursery and primary schools were "poor relations" compared with secondary schools Oct '93; urged the "need to restore bargaining rights to the 400,000 teachers in England and Wales" Oct '93; was named to Home Affairs Select Committee Dec '93; backed EC intervention funding to save Swan Hunter Dec '93; urged contribution from publishers HarperCollins toward estimate £300,000 cost of protecting Baroness Thatcher during promotional tour for her book, 'The Downing Street Years' Jan '94; voted against restoring capital punishment, even for killing policemen Feb '94; voted to reduce age of homosexual consent to 18 or 16, Feb '94; claimed that Government might have given prejudiced advice against his local Swan Hunter shipyard being suitable to build Malaysian frigates for which it had expensively bid Feb '94; complained about naming of a Conservative candidate to head a supposedly nonpartisan organisation advising schools on opting out Apr '94; on the death of John Smith, supported Tony Blair for Leader June '94; elicited from John Major the fact that Margaret Thatcher had, in June 1988, stopped off in Malaysia to arrange arms sales May '94; voted for Blair for Leader, Margaret Beckett for Deputy Leader July '94; expressing "anger and betrayal", predicted that 3,000 jobs would be lost as a result of Tyneside's loss of the 'Sir Bedivere' refit contract, including 900 at local Swan Hunter July '94; complained that millions in legal aid was being diverted to wealthy litigants but denied ordinary taxpayers needing "an hour's basic legal advice from a solicitor" July '94; exposed £5m in subsidies for lifestyle of top military brass Aug '94; was one of five 'modernisers' promoted to the Whips' Office Oct '94; described the spending of £500,000 on grace-and-favour homes for three Cabinet Ministers as "a waste of taxpayers' money" Nov '94; complained that £20,000 had been spent on sending abroad DTI Ministers' wives, Anne Heseltine and Christine Hamilton Nov '94; came off the Home Affairs Select Committee Dec '94; exposed huge costs of officers' personal cooks and housing allowances Jan '95; secured a printout showing that companies which had recruited former civil servants received the lion's share of massive consultancy contracts Feb '95; complained that the Maxwell brothers would benefit by £10m in legal aid Feb '95; urged an inquiry into the corrupted student loan system Feb '95; formally protested Michael Heseltine's and Richard Needham's refusals to reply to his questions on export guarantees Mar '95; lengthily challenged the suitability of R J Budge to take over the remnants of British Coal May '95; his motion criticised Chief Secretary Jonathan Aitken for having signed a gagging order covering documents needed by the defence in the Matrix Churchill case; the documents referred to the supply of arms to Iraq by BMARC, "a company of which he was a director at the relevant time"; "at the same" Aitken was "Deputy Chairman of Aitken Hume" which was "acting as financial advisers to Walter Somers, who produced part of the Supergun" June '95; investigated embargo-violating shipments of explosives to Iran by Royal Ordnance Oct '95; "after mightily impressing Tony Blair in the Whips' Office" (GUARDIAN), was named an Assistant Spokesman on Education and Employment on David Blunkett's team Oct '95; criticised the Education (Student Loans) Bill as short-changing both students and taxpayers Nov '95; alleged widespread misuse of Training and Education funds Nov '95; was put in charge of redrafting Labour's trade union employment rights, instead of Employment Spokesman Michael Meacher Nov '95; "in an unusual move by Mr Blair, Mr Byers was also given the job of looking after trade union rights; this led to a series of clashes with Michael Meacher, the Leftwing Shadow Cabinet member who was the official Employment Spokesman but was effectively sidelined" (Joy Copley, DAILY TELEGRAPH); in his TRIBUNE column deplored the action of 10 Labour MPs who, instead of abstaining as asked, voted with the LibDems to oppose a 1p cut in income tax Dec '95; asked Health Secretary Stephen Dorrell why there were 80,000 more administrators and 50,000 fewer nurses in the NHS Jan '96; his document on training was welcomed by the CBI but attacked by the GMB as abandoning Labour's commitment to a compulsory training levy Feb '96; in debate on educating 16-to-19 year-olds, insisted that the "knowledge-based revolution of the 21st century will require investment in human capital" May '96; complained that the Government's top training programme was producing ten times as many hairdressers, childminders and shop assistants as information technologists June '96; in Labour's election package on employment rights, drafted by him after consulting Tony Blair, unfair dismissal was protected from day one (instead of after two years), and an end to abuses of zero-hour contracts and phoney self-employment was pledged June '96; urged that a Labour Government should publish a league table of what the 100 biggest companies spent on training their employees July '96; in the last pre-election reshuffle he was confirmed as Deputy Spokesman on Education and Employment, under David Blunkett July '96; said: "we will immediately opt into the Social Chapter in principle" and then consult widely on implementation Aug '96;

welcomed suspension of threat of strike on London's Underground Aug '96; told four journalists attending the TUC's Blackpool conference at an off-the-record luncheon that Labour was about to "break the links with the unions altogether" and that, if there were a "summer of discontent" after Blair took power, there would be a ballot of Labour Party members on whether they wanted the unions to retain voting rights at the party conference and their seats on Labour's NEC; this was denied by Labour and he accused the journalists of "ludicrous misinterpretation" and being "prime candidates for the Booker Prize for fiction"; this denial enabled him to survive a two-hour cross-examination by his constituency officers Sep '96; John Edmonds, the GMB General Secretary, described his radio performance as "unimpressive" Sep '96; Labour's conference chairman, Diana Jeuda, described his remarks as "divisive and bad for morale" Sep '96; as "an insider, reputed to be a member of the small 'Labour into Government' group which has been doing some hard thinking about how a Blair administration might conduct itself during the first turbulent months in office...Mr Byers may have blurted out something he was supposed to keep secret" (Andy McSmith, OBSERVER); he was given a dressing-down by David Blunkett but his offer to resign was refused as only making matters worse Sep '96; attacked the Conservative Government's "disarray" for failing to produce its promised Green Paper on curbing walkouts and industrial disruption Oct '96; with Tony Blair, David Blunkett and Kim Howells was the target of a Leftwing petition for having advocated weakening Labour's links with the unions Nov '96; claimed that Tory claims about inward investment were misleading, since "the majority of inward investment comes from foreign investors making rich pickings from what's left of British industry"; "our nation's assets are being sold abroad, with profits being siphoned off overseas" Dec '96; rejected proposals by GMB leader John Edmonds for a tripartite forum involving the unions, employers and Government as "turning the clock back" Dec '96; exposed Conservatives for finding jobs for only 2,312 long-term unemployed, despite spending £50m Feb '97; wrote to DAILY TELEGRAPH that a Labour Government would "retain the essential elements of the '80s Tory trade union legislation...people should be free to join or not to join a trade union; there will be no return to the closed shop, no flying pickets and no secondary action" Apr '97; retained his renamed and altered seat by an enhanced majority of 26,643 May '97; was named Minister of State for Education, with responsibility for standards May '97; published a list of 18 schools not improving quickly enough, closing the first one a few days later May '97; instigated an emergency inspection of Hackney's schools June '97; introduced the White Paper, 'Excellence in Schools' July '97; introduced 2nd Reading of Education (Student Loans) Bill July '97; urged primary school parents to read with their children for twenty minutes a day July '97; admitted school repairs were a lottery July '97; urged speedier sacking of "grossly incompetent" teachers July '97; in leaked Cabinet document co-signed by Harriet Harman, urged penalising of the workshy young July '97; proposed closer links between private and state schools Oct '97; said incompetent teachers should be sackable within six months, not three years Nov '97; announced ambitious new literacy targets for every English education authority Jan '98; as long predicted, was promoted to Cabinet as Chief Secretary to the Treasury, in Alastair Darling's place July '98;

Born: 13 April 1953, Wolverhampton

Family: Son, Robert Byers, RAF radar technician, and Tryphena Mair (Jones); his partner, Jan, helped persuade him to shave his moustache in '95;

Education: Buxton County Primary; Chester City Grammar; Chester College of Further Education; Liverpool Poly (LLB);

Occupation: Formerly Sponsored, by UNISON (ex-NUPE; £600 p a to constituency, £2,200 toward '92 election expenses) '92-95; Author: 'Rates and Unemployment' (1982); ex: Chairman: National Employment Organisation for Teachers '90-92, Education Committee of

AMA '90-92; Senior Lecturer, in Law, Newcastle Poly '75-92 (NUPE '84-92, NATFHE '75-84);
Traits: Dark, parted shock of hair; specs; no more soupstrainer moustache, shed with that of Mandelson in '95; nice smile; assiduous; persistent; "slender and earnest policy wonk with shy smile" (GUARDIAN); "brilliant but grim" (David Aaronovitch, INDEPENDENT);
Address: House of Commons, Westminster, London SW1A 0AA; 11 Burn Avenue, Wallsend, Tyne and Wear, NE28 8SG;
Telephone: 0171 219 4085 (H of C); 0191 234 4426 (home); 0191 295 5917 (constituency office);

Dr Vincent CABLE   **Liberal Democrat**   **TWICKENHAM '97-**

Majority: 4,281 over Conservative 6-way;
Description: The long-Conservative affluent middle-class suburban seat across the Thames from the main local Liberal Democrat power-base in Richmond; in the end, Tories were ousted on both sides, here ditching the quirky veteran Toby Jessel; the seat contains Hampton Court Palace and is the home of Rugby Union; was only slightly changed in '95, with the return of East Twickenham; contains four Twickenham town wards plus Teddington, Whitton and the various Hamptons;
Position: Finance Spokesman on LibDems' Economics team '97-; London Spokesman on Metropolitan Police, Fire Services and Community Relations '97-; Chairman, LibDems Economics and Environment Panel '93-; Glasgow City Councillor '71-74 (when Labour);
Outlook: The new MP with a record number of adjournment debates; a rather academic intellectual economist who has won party plaudits despite his tendency to discursive economics lectures rather than sharp political points; his lectures are listened to in respectful silence by political opponents, except on the EMU, on which he is a fanatic; was initially a leading LibDem advocate of collaboration with Labour to keep the Tories in the wilderness for a decade at least; this was modified at the '97 Eastbourne conference when LibDems seemed to take fright at losing their identity in a Blairite takeover; but he insists "I would still be regarded as one of the Liberal Democrat Members arguing for good, constructive links with the current [Labour] Government"; a strong opponent of inflation, partly because its main victims are the poor; a specialist in international trade who became Shell's Chief Economist; a pro-European enthusiast for the Euro and opponent of import controls; a racial egalitarian with an wife of Indian origins; a political and geographic nomad: a former Labour Councillor in Glasgow, and former Special Adviser to John Smith who - via the SDP - has wound up as a Liberal Democrat MP for Twickenham;
History: His father was an active Tory; at school he was Liberal-inclined; at Cambridge he was Chairman of the Liberal Club while President of the Union; joined the Labour Party to work for a "more egalitarian, fairer society" '64; wrote a Fabian pamphlet on Kenya Asians '68; at 27 contested Glasgow Hillhead for Labour, gaining half as many votes as Tory MP Thomas Galbraith June '70; while a lecturer at Glasgow University won a seat on Glasgow City Council May '71; wrote Fabian pamphlet 'The Case Against Import Controls' '78; became

Special Adviser to John Smith, Labour's Trade Secretary '79; joined the SDP, having become concerned about Labour's drift to Left extremism '82; contested York for the SDP, coming 3rd with 23%, enough to unseat its Labour MP, Alex Lyon, and give the seat to Tory Conal Gregory June '83; was re-selected for York '86; polled a reduced vote of 16%, just enough to allow the sitting Tory MP to retain his seat June '87; selected for Twickenham, initially managed to reduce Toby Jessel's Conservative majority from 7,000 to 5,700, against the trend Apr '92; at annual conference attacked the accuracy of the Government's economic statistics, which included in GDP the costs of divorces and stolen goods Sep '96; in the NEW STATESMAN urged the need for practical co-operation between LibDems and Labour even before an election to inflict a lengthy defeat on the Tories Dec '96; worried by evidence of a rise in the Labour vote in a local by-election, concentrated his campaign on the need for tactical voting Apr '97; ousted Twickenham's Tory MP Toby Jessel, who had served 27 years, by a majority of 4,281, on a notional swing of 8.8%, May '97; endorsed Gordon Brown's giving the Bank of England US-style control over inflation to avoid political delays June '97; said it was "outrageous that world airlines should land at [Heathrow] one of the busiest and most congested airports [and] pay nothing to the taxpayer for the right to land and pay landing charges that are way below the economic and environmental cost that they cause" July '97; urged chess be encouraged by the Sports Council June '97; after trying to amend the Finance Bill, opposed curbing the Budget debate because its full impact was not understood: "local authority budgets are still capped despite the need to top up pension funds following the loss of tax credits on A[dvance] C[orporation] T[ax]" July '97; co-sponsored motion opposing a 12-lane super-highway to Heathrow July '97; tried to modify Labour's PFI Bill to ensure more adequate consultation with the public and the NHS professionals, but backed an early PFI-financed local hospital July '97; at LibDems' annual conference was scathing about Labour's Budget, attacking its new imposts along Tory lines; also insisted on a short timetable to join the Euro Sep '97; in debate on the Bank of England Bill emphasised that the Bank of England had responsibility "solely for short-term interest rates" and that long-term investment decisions were dependent on the markets Nov '97; complained that the Metropolitan Police were becoming "frayed at the edges" because of inadequate funding Nov '97; claimed that joining the Euro soon would cut Sterling's premium rate Jan '98; co-sponsord LibDem motion backing further leasehold enfranchisement Jan '98; urged Government to allow local authorities to raise taxes, "free of central Government capping and other centralised controls Mar '98; warned against UK's exclusion from areas of economic policy by failing to join the Euro early Apr '98; insisted that considerable convergence had already taken place in the EU: "there is virtually no divergence between the longterm bond markets in Italy and Germany"; "the rate of the bond yield in Italy is now lower than in the UK or the US"; "the market is telling us clearly - in a transparent, non-political way - that there is a greater prospect of longterm stability in Italy than in the UK or the US" Apr '98; complained of unfair advantages of BAA in pushing its Terminal 5 target at Heathrow May '98; urged the Treasury to resume its statistical series to test whether Labour's two budgets had made the tax system more regressive May '98; urged giving Richmond the right to discriminate against pupils migrating from low-tax areas like Wandsworth, with poorer schools May '98; was rated among the 'Top 100' written questioners, with 113 posed in his first year May '98; opposed import controls despite the threat posed by collapsing Asian currencies June '98; challenged PM Tony Blair to speed EMU referendum June '98;

Born: 9 May 1943, York

Family: Son, of late John Leonard Cable, a Tory joiner and fitter who became a technical lecturer, and Edith Pinkney; m '68 Maria Olympia (Rebelo), musician, teacher and historian with a PhD from Glasgow University; 2s: Paul '69, Hugo '79; 1d: Aida '72; his wife, of Indian

origin, is allegedly prone to sack his staff;
Education: Poppleton Road Primary School, York; Nunthorpe Grammar School, York; Fitzwilliam College, Cambridge University; Glasgow University (PhD);
Occupation: Author: The World's New Fissures (1994), The New Giants, China and India (1994), Foreign Investment and Development (with B Persaud; 1985), Protectionism and Industrial Decline (1983); ex: Chief Economist, Shell International '95-97; Special Professor of Economics, Nottingham University '96-97; Head of Economics, Royal Institute of International Affairs '93-95; in Group Planning Department, Shell '90-93; Director of Economic Division, Commonwealth Secretariat (ASTMS) '83-90; Deputy Director, Overseas Deelopment Institute '76-83; in the Diplomatic Service '74-76; Lecturer, in Economics at Glasgow University '68-74; Treasury Finance Officer, Government of Kenya '66-68;
Traits: Bald; grey fringe and sideburns; oval face; "comes over one-to-one as a frightenly intelligent though kindly professor" (LibDem colleague); enjoys ballroom and Latin dancing, classical music;
Address: House of Commons, Westminster, London SW1A 0AA; 102 Whitton Road, Twickenham TW1 1BS;
Telephone: 0171 219 1166 (H of C); 0181 892 0215 (constituency office);

Richard (George) CABORN   **Labour**   **SHEFFIELD CENTRAL '83-**

Majority: 16,906 (46.4%) over Liberal Democrat 8-way;
Description: The central area of the traditional steel and engineering city; over two-fifths in council houses; had 23% unemployment in '91; a Labour bastion reinforced by the addition of Nether Edge ward from Sheffield-Hallam;
Position: Minister of State for Regions, Regeneration and Planning '97-; ex: Spokesman on Competition '95-97; Chairman, of Select Committee on Trade and Industry '92-95; on Liaison Select Committee '92-95; Secretary: all-party Parliamentary Group on Southern Africa '87-92; National Treasurer '92-97, on NEC of Anti-Apartheid Movement '86-97;
Assistant Spokesman, on Trade and Industry '87-90; Chairman '87-88, Vice Chairman '86-87 of Tribune Group; Chairman, Sheffield District Labour Party; Vice Chairman: PLP Trade Union Group '87-92, Vice Chairman, PLP Anti-Apartheid Group ; on Select Committee on European Legislation '84-88; MEP for Sheffield '79-84; Chairman, UK Labour Party Group of MEPs '80-83; Vice President: Sheffield Trades Council '68-79, Sheffield District Labour Party; on BBC Advisory Council '75-78;
Outlook: Prescott's man, charged with saving the coal industry and setting up Regional Development Agencies as halfway houses to regional assemblies; an unexpected Minister in the inclusive Blair Government, recruited at the urging of his immediate boss, Deputy Prime Minister John Prescott; "one of Mr Prescott's closest allies" (Patrick Wintour, GUARDIAN); part of the little-noticed group of 30 'New Left for New Labour' group which, before the election, agreed with Prescott to influence the Blair leadership from within rather than oppose it from outside; "left the womb a fully-fledged socialist; no one has ever been truer to his principles" (PRIVATE EYE); "has won respect as an efficient, if indiscreet, convenor of the

Parliamentary Left" (Jonathan Foster, INDEPENDENT); was an "armchair guerilla" against Apartheid (ex-MI6man and Tory MP Cranley (now Lord) Onslow); backed the 1984-85 miners' strike, but has recently loathed his childhood friend, Arthur Scargill, as much as Michael Heseltine; a longtime pillar of the Sheffield trade union Left, became a Chairman of the soft-Left Tribune Group, a member of Bryan Gould's team and a Prescott campaign manager; his Parliamentary influence comes from his expert Chairmanship of the Select Committee on Trade and Industry '92-95; a strong regionalist; "Old Labour with a sense of humour" (INDEPENDENT ON SUNDAY); previously AEU-sponsored;

History: His father was a leading Sheffield Communist trade union official; his brother David was friendly with both Jimmy Reid and Arthur Scargill, who, when Young Communists, sometimes stayed over in the Caborn home, sleeping head to toe; joined the AUEW '59, the Labour Party '66; his politics were expressed as the AUEW's Convenor of Shop Stewards at steelmakers Firth Brown for the dozen years from '67; was elected MEP for Sheffield June '79; urged more orders for UK shipbuilding Feb '80; as Chairman of European Parliament's Economic Committee urged tighter control of multinationals Apr '81; backed continued steel quotas May '81; took wife to China Sep '81; supported Tony Benn for Deputy Leader Sep '81; opposed pro-EEC propaganda Oct '81; "he established himself as a man of principle, guaranteeing himself a seat in Parliament when he masterminded a series of brilliant campaigns as Chairman of the Sheffield District Labour Party; foremost amongst these was his campaign to stop the sale of council houses" (PRIVATE EYE); despite pressure from his Rightwing union President, Terry Duffy, was selected instead of former Defence Secretary, Fred (later Lord) Mulley, for Sheffield Park; David Blunkett, then Leader of Sheffield City Council, wrote that "it was the Militant Tendency that worked hardest to reject" "Richard Caborn on the grounds that he was mostly likely to be a strong defender of the 'firm Left' rather than susceptible to pressure or attack from factional groups" Feb '82; when Denis Healey attacked Caborn as having "lived high on the hog" as an MEP, David Blunkett pointed out that "Caborn had donated most of his income and in every other possible way placed his resources at the disposal of the Labour Party in Sheffield"; was endorsed by the NEC Mar '82; opposed force-feeding of geese Mar '82; urged inquiry into MEPs' economic links Nov '82; was elected for new Sheffield Central June '83; sponsored motion for referendum on Cruise missiles June '83; modified his demand for Britain's withdrawal from EEC in favour of working for radical changes in Brussels until Labour Party won power July '83; was concerned about glue-sniffing July '83; spoke at El Salvador Solidarity meeting on fringe of Labour Conference Oct '83; became a Trustee of the Miners Solidarity Fund, set up to ease hardships but later suspected of being a device to hide union funds; some £6m was contributed, but not fully monitored May '84; put down motion urging people to contribute taxes to peace fund rather than for military defence Mar '84; accused South Yorkshire police of unprovoked attacks on miners and himself Apr '84; with Scargillites Dennis Skinner and Martin Redmond, criticised Neil Kinnock for not appearing at mineworkers' support rallies Nov '84; congratulated Church of England for withdrawing £4.4m in investments from South Africa Dec '84; complained of impact on Sheffield of ratecapping Apr '85; introduced Bill to impose sanctions on South Africa July '85; was re-selected from a shortlist of one Dec '85; launched a campaign to save Sheffield MORNING TELEGRAPH Jan '86; proposed new Appeals Committee for Labour Party, to lower temperatures and diminish recourse to the courts Apr '86; his new sanctions Bill lost by 47, July '86; attacked Mrs Thatcher's plans further to privatise BSC Nov '86; claimed South Yorkshire's bus system had been devastated by the Transport Act Nov '86; helped to talk out the Parliamentary day, 11 December, in revenge for Government's peremptory processing of teachers' pay and conditions Bill Dec '86; pressed Defence Secretary George Younger on modernisation of short-range nuclear weapons after having been misled on it by Michael

Heseltine Mar '87; increased his majority by 2,500 June '87; urged revival of prosecution of those who had burned Anti-Apartheid and African National Congress offices and tried to kidnap ANC members Oct '87; was elected Chairman of the Tribune Group Nov '87; co-authored Tribune Group pamphlet urging trade union members be admitted to full membership of the Labour Party on payment of a small supplement to the political levy they already paid on their union dues Nov '87; pressed TRIBUNE to stop publishing ads offering Filipino women for marriage, but staff vote blocked him Nov '87; led a motion attacking Mrs Thatcher for impugning African National Congress Nov '87; became Secretary of the new South African Group, an all-party group of pro-sanctions MPs Nov '87; described scrapping of regional aid as "a major blow to regeneration of the regions and the urban areas" Jan '88; gathered 110 MPs' signatures urging Mrs Thatcher to intervene to ask for clemency for 'Sharpville Six' Feb '88; spearheaded all-party campaign which garnered over 100 MPs' signatures for release of Nelson Mandela Mar '88; led John Prescott's campaign team for the Deputy Leadership Mar-Sep '88; voted for Prescott and Kinnock when his constituency's General Management Committee wanted him to back Tony Benn and Eric Heffer Sep '88; drew up plan for Yorkshire and Humberside to have its own regional assembly and civil service, as part of Labour rethink on regionalism Sep '88; urged emergency plans to take advantage of looming Single Market Sep '88; backed plans for airport at Tinsley Park, with a speedy rail link to link to the Channel Tunnel Oct '88; derided Cecil Parkinson's plan to privatise British Coal as "an absolute disaster" and likely to "lead to further pit closures on a large scale" Oct '88; organised lobby to 'free Namibia now' Dec '88; complained about tightening of benefit to 16- and 17-year-olds since his constituency had the highest youth unemployment in the country Dec '88; criticised fellow Labour MPs Martin Redmond and Mick Welsh for killing off legislation for Sheffield's 'supertram' by their guerilla tactics to block the expansion of ports importing foreign coal Jan '89; with Hallam's Tory MP, Irvine Patnick, asked why local murderer John Taylor was twice freed from prison to kill again Jan '89; complained about Government's "negative attitude" towards Sheffield's World Student Games, although three times bigger than the Commonwealth Games Mar '89; claimed PM Thatcher had misled the Commons three times on SWAPO's role in Namibian ceasefire Apr '89; discussed with Sheffield's Traffic Commissioner the possibility of his being called in to act against High Street overcrowding through bus deregulation Apr '89; complained that Sheffield women led the list of women dying from breast and cervical cancer Sep '89; complained about threat from DTI Under Secretary Eric Forth to Citizens Advice Bureaux that they would be denied development funding if they did not accept monies from companies with South African links Nov '89; was re-appointed Assistant Spokesman on Trade and Industry Nov '89; insisted the main problem with industrial development in the West Midlands was "the tendency to pump ever more resources into the southeast" Dec '89; helped organise Newcastle conference on regional assemblies which was viewed with coolness by Neil Kinnock and David Blunkett Feb '90; was one of 35 Labour MPs urging Tory MP John Browne to resign for failing to declare his interests accurately Mar '90; told Mrs Thatcher that Sheffield Forgemasters, informed the DTI in July 1988 about Iraqi supergun specifications, had been told no export license would be required Apr '90; complained the Government's 50% cut in regional aid and lack of redistribution had helped overheat the south and under-utilise the north July '90; endorsed the recovery of £44.4m of illegal "sweeteners" from British Aerospace, as demanded by the European Commission Sep '90; supported Peter Snape's unsuccessful challenge to Chief Whip Derek Foster Sep-Oct '90; visited Hongkong as guest of its government Oct '90; visited Essen as guest of South Yorkshire Transport Oct '90; left Labour's front bench to concentrate on its regional policy, including regional assemblies Nov '90; asked why the case against Sheffield Forgemasters for exporting superguns to Iraq was being dropped Nov '90;

complained that all of Sheffield's planned reconstruction was "at risk because the standard spending asssessment under the poll tax has devastated the city"; he had the tenth poorest constituency in the country, but when the best parts of Sheffield were averaged in, the figures "do not look too bad, but the inner city problems in Sheffield are as acute as in any other major city"; "how can Sheffield be granted £400 less per secondary pupil than that calculated for Manchester when they are similar cities?" Dec '90; co-accused British Government of using Scotland Yard "as pawns in a conspiracy to obstruct justice" in the murder of six Jesuits in San Salvador Nov '90; signed motion opposing military action in the Gulf against Iraq Jan '91; was critical of Government policy on child benefit Jan '91; said "I don't think many regional MPs will stand for anything less than a commitment to elected regional assemblies" as a counterpoint to backing a Scottish Assembly Feb '91; welcomed President de Klerk's announcement of the repeal of anti-Apartheid laws as a good beginning Feb '91; chased the photographer who caught the semi-hard Left 'Supper Club' meeting in 'Westminster Arms' Feb '91; after he protested to the PM the absence of any Ministers at Sheffield's World Student Games, Sports Minister Robert Atkins suddenly appeared July '91; in view of Tory MP Hal Miller's 1988 warning, asked whether it was incompetence or conspiracy which allowed the export to Iraq of superguns from the Forgemasters plant in his constituency in the middle of the Iran-Iraq war Aug '91; after DAILY MIRROR contributed £100,000 to his Wembley Stadium musical tribute to Nelson Mandela, but not the full £150,000 promised, said: "we can't be critical of Maxwell; he provided a lot of help at short notice and lent Nelson Mandela his helicopter" Oct '91; complained that the regeneration of Sheffield was being stifled by the over-centralisation of power in London Nov '91; as Secretary of the Parliamentary Southern Africa Committee, urged an interim government for South Africa Nov '91; complained that not enough Maastricht discussion related to the proposed new role for European regions Dec '91; as a "product of a further education college", warned against isolating them or thinking them the same as polys Feb '92; retained his seat with majority down from 19,342 to 17,294, despite swing to Labour of 0.77% Apr '92; backed Bryan Gould for Leader, and led John Prescott's campaign for Deputy Leader Apr '92; was critical of Lloyds' bid for Midland Bank, because 1,750 of Midlands' local staff were in its head office in Sheffield May '92; was named a scrutineer for Labour's Chief Whip election June '92; was elected Chairman of the Select Committee on Trade and Industry, seeing off Stan Orme, former Cabinet Minister and Chairman of the PLP July '92; asked Michael Heseltine for a "longterm energy policy" Oct '92; was named to Liaison Select Committee Nov '92; after threatening resignation if there were no unanimity, his committee said many of the 31 pits earmarked for closure could be viable within a few years with £500m in subsidies; this could save £1.2m in redundancy payments Jan '93; said British Coal's response to his committee's report were "self-indulgent and over-pessimistic" Feb '93; complained that his Select Committee had sought additional markets for coal, while Michael Heseltine had endorsed mines closure programme Mar '93; complained to PM that his committee's inquiry into the Iraq supergun was being hamstrung by failure of the intelligence services to give evidence May '93; his Select Committee urged £100m in launch aid to help aerospace industry July '93; strongly defended his Select Committee's report on the mines against attack by Arthur Scargill at Labour's conference Oct '93; disclosed that the Government had refused to allow a vote on the 39 recommendations on coal made by his Select Committee, but instead had rejected its nine main recommendations, although "we have proved beyond any reasonable doubt that the cheapest way to produce electricity in the United Kingdom is coal-fired generation" Oct '93; again urged Government assistance to the aerospace industry, which had to compete with foreign Government-backed competitors Dec '93; protested when British Aerospace, following Rolls-Royce, had to be rescued financially by BMW because of "the lack of finance going into British manufacturing"

Jan '94; voted against restoration of capital punishment, even for killers of policemen Feb '94; voted to reduce age of homosexual consent to 18 or 16, Feb '94; urged Michael Heseltine to give Post Office more commercial freedom rather than privatise it May '94; urged a training levy, rejected by Michael Heseltine May '94; led John Prescott's successful campaign for the Deputy Leadership June-July '94; contested the post of Chief Whip, coming 3rd with 50 votes, after Peter Kilfyle with 73 and Derek Foster with 143 Oct '94; commenting on the revision of Clause IV, said: "I didn't see any real need to go down that course, but Tony [Blair] wanted to make a statement of his new leadership [and] in that context it's acceptable" Nov '94; complained to Michael Heseltine about the leniency of the control over pricing by the privatised electric utilities Feb '95; co-signed letter calling for Labour to include commitment to full employment in its constitution Mar '95; was among those, including John Prescott, who had let their Tribune Group membership lapse (INDEPENDENT) May '95; smelled a rat when Michael Heseltine, previously uncooperative, tried to get his Select Committee to investigate Jonathan Aitken and his involvement with gun exporters BMARC; he only proceeded when he secured "reasonably satisfactory" promises of access to information June '95; criticised OFGAS regulator Claire Spottiswoode's request for a 65% pay increase on a salary of £75,000 June '95; received 65 votes - with 107 needed - for the Shadow Cabinet Oct '95; at the suggestion of John Prescott, was named Spokesman on Competition, teamed with Peter Mandelson, under Derek Foster as the Shadow Chancellor of the Duchy of Lancaster Oct '95; came off the Select Committee on Trade and Industy Nov '95; was criticised by Michael Heseltine for "whipping up anxiety over short-termism as a justification for extensive interference in the market economy" Jan '96; when he called on the Government to investigate the "serious threat to the development of the UK broadcast industry" posed by Mr Murdoch's pay-TV monopoly, John Prescott said he was not reflecting (Blair) party policy Feb '96; in the debate on the Scott Report cited the frustrations of the Trade and Industry Select Committee in its efforts to investigate the supergun at his instigation, which had made it necessary to call in Sir Richard Scott Feb '96; insisted, in TRIBUNE, that Britain could only compete internationally if its most industrially-damaged regions were brought up to scratch June '96; complained to Sir Gordon Downey, Parliamentary Commissioner for Standards, that a leaked letter from Tory MP Sir Graham Bright showed that companies were being offered influence on Government policy in exchange for contributions to Conservative Party funds June '96; clashed with two Scargillites in public meeting near Sheffield, breaking one of their banners July '96; in Tony Blair's 'final' pre-election reshuffle, he was retained in post, nominally under Derek Foster July '96; told a TUC fringe meeting that Labour planned tighter profit caps for utilities through a tougher regulatory system Sep '96; in the run-up to the election was part of the Prescott-inspired 'New Left for New Labour' grouping of 30 Leftish MPs - mainly from the former 'Supper Club' - who would hope to have influence on the modernising Blairites Apr '97; was listed as one of over 80 MPs targeted by the anti-abortion Prolife Alliance Party Apr '97; retained his altered seat with a slightly increased majority of 16,906 over a Liberal Democrat, on a swing of only 2.8% May '97; a surprise in Tony Blair's inclusive government was his appointment to John Prescott's team at Environment and Transport as Minister of State for the Regions, Regeneration and Planning May '97; ruled out a northern regional assembly before 2002 because of legislative logjam despite pressure from northeastern Labour MPs during Scottish and Welsh devolution debates June '97; his approval of a proposed out-of-town shopping centre in Richmond, London, was taken as evidence of Labour relaxing restrictions designed to preserve traditional high street shopping July '97; following reported clashes over decentralisation between his boss John Prescott and Margaret Beckett and David Blunkett, insisted discussions were over a concordat on regional decision-making Sep '97; was put in charge of saving surviving coal industry Nov '97; said a range of incentives was being considered to encourage building on 'brownfield' sites Jan '98; introduced 2nd Reading of Regional Development Agencies Bill Jan '98; pledged there would be a rural representative on every RDA; insisted he would stick to inherited greenbelt policies Feb '98; was considering how to limit fast-growing leylandii conifer hedges Mar '98; the passage through the Commons of his Regional Development Agencies Bill presaged the '99 setting up of 9 RDAs in England, each with a £1b budget and substantial powers May '98;

Born: 6 October 1943, Sheffield

Family: Son, late George Caborn, engineer and AUEW District Secretary ("a pragmatic Communist of imposing presence who ran the engineering union in Sheffield in virtual autonomy" -INDEPENDENT), and Mary (Russell); m '66 Margaret (Hayes); 1s Steven '73, 1d Catherine '71;

Education: Hurlfield Comprehensive (left at 15); Granville College of Further Education; Sheffield Polytechnic;

Occupation: Formerly Sponsored, by AUEW (£600 for constituency, 80% of election expenses) '83-95; Chairman, Sheffield City Trust (held assets of £200m; no emoluments) '90-95; Director: Sheffield United Football Club (with £7,500 to a charitable trust) '95-97, Freedom Productions Ltd (organiser of ANC's fundraising events; no emoluments) '88-97, Sheffield Festival (no emoluments) '91-97; Engineer, then Convenor of Shop Stewards, Firth Brown '67-79; Engineering Apprentice '59-64;

Traits: Short; trim; dark blond; beard; receding hair; specs; 'Dick'; amateur footballer (scored own goal in MPs' football match against Press Gallery Dec '84); supports Sheffield United; has "a blunt self-confidence"; "wears lack of sophistication like a club tie" (Jonathan Foster, INDEPENDENT); "puritanical and ascetic in the extreme" (PRIVATE EYE); "Harry Perkins" ("could have been a model for [Chris] Mullin's Northern Leftwinger unwilling to abandon tenets but instinctively able to find expedients; indeed Mullin is known to have drawn on him" for the hero of A Very British Coup" - INDEPENDENT);

Address: House of Commons, Westminster, London SW1A 0AA; 29 Quarry Vale Road, Sheffield S12 3EB; 54 Pinstone Street, Sheffield S1 2HN (office); flat in Barbican;

Telephone: 0171 219 4211/6259 (H of C); 01742 393802 (Sheffield home); 01742 737947 (constituency office);

Alan CAMPBELL   **Labour**   **TYNEMOUTH '97-**

Majority: 11,273 over Conservative 5-way;

Description: The northeast's former last-remaining Tory seat, previously held by Labour only in '45-50; its alleged Tory leanings were not dented by the removal of rock-solid Labour Riverside ward in '95; a mainly coastal seat containing middle-class Tynemouth itself, North Shields, Cullercoats, Monkseaton and Whitley Bay;

Position: On Public Accounts Committee '97-; ex: Secretary and Campaigns Co-ordinator of Tynemouth Constituency Labour Party;

Outlook: Another pro-European Labour recruit from the chalk-face; "every inch the New Labour man" (Neil Sears, NEWCASTLE EVENING NEWS); won the seat with a huge swing (14%) on his first attempt, making him the seat's first

Labour MP in half a century; the size of his majority astonished even his faithful supporters; rather unusually for a Labour teacher, was in the NAS-UWT; interested in education and constitutional reform;

History: Joined the Labour Party at 30, '87; was selected for Tynemouth, where its long-sitting Tory MP, Neville ('Globe') Trotter, was retiring '95; gave the Conservative Government credit for attracting Siemens to the Tyneside; while local Tories were claiming they were "neck and neck" with Labour, he was helped by a NEWCASTLE JOURNAL poll which accurately predicted Labour would have a 21% lead; he pledged he would be "a local MP for local people and not a paid mouthpiece for a few wealthy interests", like the outgoing Tory Apr '97; won the seat by an unexpectedly large 11,273 majority, a notional swing of 14.19%, May '97; in his Maiden emphasised that Siemens' investment of £1b in a microchip plant in his constituency was a tribute both to local people and "an acknowledgement of Britain's key role in Europe; we meddle with that at our peril" June '97; backed ban on fox-hunting June '97; as a former teacher in one, co-sponsored motion backing comprehensives as "the foremost and most efficient way to provide secondary education" June '97; was named to the Public Accounts Committee Oct? '97; as "a new member" of the PAC, deplored the behaviour of Camelot, as outlined in its 20th Report, and urged "a significant overhaul of the system" Nov '97; co-sponsored the motion of Fraser Kemp to back the 22 Ryhope Street allotment holders and pigeon fanciers against its developer Jan '98; co-sponsored Fraser Kemp's motion paying tribute to fund raised by the Alzheimer-afflicted ex-MP Roland Boyes and his wife to raise money for an Alzheimer's Research Trust Jan '98; urged making available microfilmed copies of historic registration Apr '98; enthused about the establishment of the Jenkins Commission on electoral reform, although he was "not yet convinced that the present system does not meet the criteria as well as any"; he was somewhat sympathetic to the Supplementary Vote which would "enable the winner to claim at least 50% of the vote" June '98; was hit hard by the announced closure of the £1b Siemens plant in his constituency Aug '98;

Born: 8 July 1957, Consett, County Durham

Family: Son, Albert Campbell and Marian (Hewitt); m Jayne, a former student; 1s 1d;

Education: Blackfyne Secondary School, Consett, Co Durham; Lancaster University (BA Hons); Leeds University (PGCE); Newcastle University (MA);

Occupation: Ex: Teacher '80-96: former Head of 6th Form at a Whitley Bay High School where, in '96, two-thirds of its sixth formers went to university ("among the highest recorded levels" (AC) (NAS-UWT);

Traits: Dark brown parted hair; square face; good-looking; well-paced speaker; uptight on personal details;

Address: House of Commons, Westminster, London SW1A 0AA; 19 Sandringham Avenue, North Shields NE29 9AX;

Telephone: 0171 219 3000 (H of C); 0191 296 1318 (home); 01426 2033757 (pager);

UNEXPECTED REACTIONS
One can never predict the reaction of MPs to recording what they disclose about themselves to a lightly-attended House, forgetting about HANSARD reporters and TV cameras. We wrote sympathetically about two former Conservative MPs, one of whom overcame congenital deafness and the other born spastic. To our double astonishment, the first cursed us out to local TV reporters, the other enthused about the sympathy expressed.

Anne CAMPBELL   **Labour**   **CAMBRIDGE '92-**

Majority: 14,137 (27.5%) over Conservative 8-way;
Description: The university and city, with its 10,000 registered students; includes all but the very poshest bits within the city boundary around Grantchester in the southwest; in '83 it lost 10,000 voters to South West Cambridgeshire; unaltered in '95;
Position: PPS, to John Battle '97-; ex: on Science and Technology Select Committee '92-97; Chairman, PLP Science, Technology and Civil Service Committee '93-97; Vice Chairman: Parliamentary Office of Science and Technology '93-97, PLP Women's Group '93-97; Cambridgeshire County Councillor '85-89; Vice Chairman, Cambridge

Constituency Labour Party '89;
Outlook: Widely-respected, cerebrally-cool, superloyal, pro-EU Blairite statistician who, apart from Blair-worship, avoids over-stating a well-documented case of which she has direct knowledge; "I use my maths in that I am reasonably numerate, which many politicians are not; I have a great interest in science, technology and IT" (AC); "I feel very much part of the New Labour party and a supporter of Tony Blair's reforms; I think he has done exactly the right thing and my job when I go back to the constituency is to persuade the waverers of that" (AC); tends to consult widely in her constituency and elsewhere on emerging problems; is an information technology buff who once held a monthly hour-long E-mail surgery; "likeable and ambitious" (Matthew Norman, GUARDIAN); has "the charm, intelligence and moderation regarded as necessary for success in this supposedly sophisticated, liberal-minded constituency" (Alexander Chancellor, INDEPENDENT); can be seen by Tory opponents as "unnecessarily and unjustifiably sour" (Nigel Forman MP); pro: "some form of PR" (AC), a single European currency, military intervention in ex-Yugoslavia; anti-smoking; moved into politics to block Tory educational cuts; multi-cause groupie (Greenpeace, Socialist Education Association, Cambridge Progressive Co-operators); was MSF-sponsored;
History: She was born into a family "with a lot of political argument"; her father was "an old-fashioned Liberal", her mother "quite a staunch Conservative who used to canvas in Barnsley"; at Cambridge she was a contemporary of the 'Tory Mafia' - Clarke, Howard, Gummer, Brittan, Lamont - but did not know any of them "because I wasn't that political"; she joined the Labour Party at 23, '63; on her academic husband's sabbatical in Switzerland, she was struck by "just how awful the conditions were for Swiss women" who did not then have the vote '80; she "became interested in political activity in the early '80s when Tory-controlled Cambridgeshire County Council initiated a series of damaging cuts in the education service; I became Chair of an organisation which was a federation of parent groups called 'the Cambridgeshire Inter-PTA'; following that I became an elected member of Cambridgeshire County Council '85-89, where I helped put right some of the damage done by previous Tory cuts"; was selected for Cambridge by 51% to 49% over Mark Todd, who was later selected to fight Edwina Currie Nov '89; became confident that local academics were "looking for somebody competent who's anti-Tory and is prepared to fight for what is good for Cambridge" Nov '91; narrowly succeeded in winning Cambridge by 580 votes over new Conservative candidate Apr '92; in her Maiden, dwelt on the harsh realities of non-academic life in Cambridge, with "rising unemployment, chronic housing shortages and poverty just

Copyright (C)Parliamentary Profile Services Ltd

below the surface" May '92; boasted of Cambridge's record of tenant participation in its housing schemes, helping to minimise unsuitable accommodation June '92; deplored overlapping and inadequate planning and funding of scientific research June '92; initiated debate on special educational needs, insisting there had been a consensus around identifying children with special needs and providing for them in mainstream schools, but that specialist support had been progressively reduced July '92; was named to Science and Technology Select Committee July '92; sponsored motion deploring disposal by public authorities of land used for playing fields July '92; said she wanted "all schools to be able to accommodate their teaching methods and their specialities to the children within them" Nov '92; urged the Heritage Secretary to prevent the Royal Holloway's sale of Gainsboroughs, Constables and Turners to fund building work Nov '92; complained that Government had misled schools thinking of opting out that they would still be able to call on specialist local education authority support Mar '93; after visiting Germany with the Select Committee on Science and Technology, urged German-style measures to support "high-powered technical innovation" Mar '93; complained that DTI was not flexibly providing support for local firms hit by decline in defence orders Apr '93; the local elections showed Labour had strengthened its Cambridge position by 4%, the Liberal Democrats by 14%, with the Conservatives declining by 18% May '93; deplored "the Government's lack of an industrial strategy in the past 14 years" May '93; co-signed letter to President Clinton advocating military intervention in ex-Yugoslavia May '93; co-signed pro-OMOV GUARDIAN letter with woman Labour MPs June '93; chaired meeting on under-representation of women in science and technology, reporting: "it is far from easy to return to a career in research after taking time out to have children; it is at this stage that many women are lost to the profession; very few women are in positions of seniority in science and engineering" June '93; deplored stifling of creative research in Britain June '93; was elected Vice Chairman of the Parliamentary Office of Science and Technology July '93; attended workshop in Vienna on Parliamentary Technology Assessment as guest of Austrian Government Oct '93; criticised Education Secretary John Patten's attacks on student unions' activities as ranging "from the malign to the ridiculous" Nov '93; opposed restoration of capital punishment, even for killers of policemen Feb '94; backed reduction of age of homosexual consent to 18 or 16, Feb '94; although an opponent of the use of eggs from foetuses, resisted Dame Jill Knight's rushed, late-night amendment to ban their use while the Human Fertilisation and Embryology Authority was still carrying out consultations on a process which would take ten years to develop Apr '94; urged French-style subsidised child care to enable single mothers to work profitably Apr '94; co-wrote letter to GUARDIAN saying "first-past-the-post electoral system has brought 17 years of anti-consensus government with the Tories" May '94; was named as one of the "new intake modernisers" behind Margaret Beckett's Deputy Leadership bid June '94; voted for Blair for Leader, Beckett for Deputy Leader July '94; pointed out to Tory Minister Peter Lloyd that his party would have had 23 MEPs under PR, instead of an "abysmal" 18, July '94; complained that economic recovery was derived from consumer spending, not from more-needed increased investment in industry; urged tax changes to avoid research-crippling tax penalties on high-tech firms' incomes July '94; claimed to have more - perhaps 20,000 - Internet-connected constituents than any other MP Oct '94; attacked cuts in housing benefits, allegedly "to finance the Government's election bribe" Dec '94; with other modernising 'New Agenda Group' Labour MPs, published a new Clause IV Feb '95; repeated Blairite mantra, 'tough on crime, tough on the causes of crime' in support of Sir John Hannan's Proceeds of Crime Bill Feb '95; called for women to be gtiven to be given tax relief for child care expenses Mar '95; introduced Bill to stop discrimination against people who have had genetic tests or have a genetic predisposition to disease Apr'95; introduced Environmental Investment (Accelerated Depreciation) Bill to encourage investment in innovative environmental technologies June '95; urged Commons Leader to introduce 20p per mile allowance for cyclist-MPs and to reduce the car mileage allowance to the same level Aug '95; raised with the FCO the problem of a constituent arrested in Thailand for heroin smuggling Sep '95; urged HANSARD be put on the Internet Oct '95; complained about declining investment in research Oct '95; urged "a real restructuring of the social security system which will alleviate the poverty trap and allow parents to return to work without being worse off" Nov '95; on behalf of a constituent, prompted Labour's NEC to query whether Exeter's John Lloyd was "an appropriate candidate" (AC) Dec '95; wanted to limit Commons smoking to a few airtight rooms Dec '95; opposed privatisation of research laboratories, urging support for long-term core research June '96; pressed claim of Valkyrie aircraft, made by local Marshalls of Cambridge, as a replacement for Nimrod maritime patrol plane June '96; expressed concerns about the complex impact of genetic advances; regretted relatively low spend by UK pharmaceutical companies on R&D July '96; backed 3% cap on MPs' pay rise and a cut in their mileage allowance July '96; rejected Austin Mitchell's criticism of Tony Blair whom she described as "an extremely good Leader and is doing exactly what needs to be done: the...necessary...changes which were started by Neil Kinnock" Aug '96; came 13th in annual ballot for Private Members Bills Oct '96; called for amendment to the 1990 Human Fertilisation and Embryology Act to allow for consent to the use of embryos to be made exceptionally other than in writing Nov '96; proposed the provision of at least one computer terminal in every library to provide acccess to the Internet Nov '96; opposed Tory MP David Amess's attempt to restrict access to abortion Dec '96; opposed Tories' Social Security Administration Bill because data-matching was a violation of civil liberties and privatisation of functions would lead to unquantifiable leaks Feb '97; was one of the 72 anti-hunting MPs targeted by The FIELD Apr '97; retained her unaltered seat with her majority increased by over 13,500, a pro-Labour swing of 13.2%; this made her the first Labour MP to hold Cambridge in two successive elections May '97; was named PPS to Science Minister John Battle May '97; voted to ban fox-hunting June '97; co-urged joining a single European currency "as soon as it is practically possible" Oct '97; opposed Government's threat to end support for Oxbridge's collegiate system as a threat to a system which had produced 69 Nobel Prizes but supported widening social composition of incoming students to increase greatly the number from state schools Nov '97; pressed for allowance for cycling MPs Dec '97; backed Cynog Dafis's Road Traffic Reduction Bill Jan '98; secured 6.25p per mile for cycling MPs Mar '98; cheered Labour's Cambridge City Council for keeping rates lower than Tory-controlled Cambridgeshire County Council May '98;

Born: 6 April 1940, Dewsbury, Yorkshire

Family: Daughter, Frank Lucas, NHS statistician, and Susan (Chadwick); m '63 Archibald Campbell, Director of Interdisciplinary Research Centre in Superconductivity; 1s Diarmid '74; 2d Frances '65, Emily '67; 3 grandchildren;

Education: Birdsedge County Primary School, nr Huddersfield; Penistone Grammar School, nr Sheffield; Newnham College, Cambridge, (Parts I & II in Mathematics); Institute of Statisticians Qualifying Exam '78; Fellow of Institute of Statisticians '85-; Fellow of Royal Statistical Society '85-; Fellow of Royal Society of Arts '92-;

Occupation: Author: Calculation for Commercial Students (1972); Director, the Welding Institute (technology transfer; £5-10,000) '95-; Chairman, Opportunity Links (information service aiding parents into work; unpaid) '94-; ex: had Research Assistant provided by Consultants Recruitment and Training (£25-29,000) '95-97; Owner: holiday cottage in Britanny; Sponsored, by MFS (donated £2,000 to Cambridge CLP election fund) '92; Head of Statistics and Data Processing Department, National Institute of Agricultural Botany (MSF '83-, ex NATFHE) '83-92; Senior Lecturer, in Statistics at Cambridgeshire College of Arts and

Technology '70-83;
Traits: Blonde; high cheekbones; dimpled cheeks; sharp chin; "like a wise owl" (Nicholas Soames MP); "looks far younger than her years" (John Young, TIMES); presents human problems persuasively; tends to read her speeches; "resembles her boss, Tony Blair, in that she asks rude quesions in a sweet ingenuous fashion" (Simon Hoggart, GUARDIAN); enjoys tennis, skiing and gardening;
Address: House of Commons, Westminster, London SW1A 0AA; Alex Wood Hall, Norfolk Street, Cambridge CB1 2LD; 20 St Barnabas Road, Cambridge CB1 2BY;
Telephone: 0171 219 5089 (H of C); 01223 65777 (home); 01223 355511 (Cambridge Labour Party offices);

(Walter) Menzies CAMPBELL CBE, QC   **Liberal Democrat**   **NORTH EAST FIFE '87-**

Majority: 10,356 (24.8%) over Conservative 5-way;
Description: The prosperous rural bulk of the ancient kingdom of Fife, between the Tay and the Forth, sprinkled with fishing villages, resorts and solidly Conservative towns such as Auchtermuchty, Cupar and the ancient university town of St Andrews, birthplace of golf and the "monetarist Mafia"; it once returned Asquith; service industries outnumber the one-tenth of those employed in farming or fishing; it was only slightly altered from pre-'83 East Fife; it gained a mere 48 voters from Fife Central in '95;
Position: Chief Spokesman, on Defence and Foreign Affairs '94-; on Defence Select Committee '92-; on Labour's Cabinet Committee on constitutional reform '97-; Vice Chairman, on Executive of Scottish Sports Group '87-; Delegate to North Atlantic Assembly '89-; ex: Spokesman, on Defence, Sport and Scottish Legal Affairs '88-94; Spokesman on Arts, Broadcasting and Sport '87-88; on Trade and Industry Select Committee '90-92, Members' Interests Select Committee '87-90; Legal and Home Affairs spokesman of Scottish Liberal Party '79-83; Delegate to the Parliamentary Assembly of OSCE '92-97; Chairman: Scottish Liberal Party '75-77, its Policy Committee '77-79; on Departmental Committee on Scottish Licensing Laws (Clayson Committee) '71;
Outlook: The LibDem spokesman who is "a polished performer on television" with "the highest profile in the party apart from Mr Ashdown" but "may be considered too old" to succeed him (George Jones and Rachel Sylvester, DAILY TELEGRAPH); is one of Ashdown's inner circle favourable to a conditional Labour link; a highly-intelligent spokesman with the embarrassment of a more mature and cautious judgement than his chief, in fields in which Ashdown has a claim to competence; "few other LibDem spokesmen sound as authoritative" (Peter Riddell, TIMES); is said to impress Tony Blair (Steve Richards, NEW STATESMAN); the active, mainstream Scots QC who recaptured Asquith's old seat for the Liberals on his third try; has shown strong advocacy of home rule for Scotland; long close to David Steel and a friend from university days of Donald Dewar and late John Smith; a former athletic star, admits to being "obsessed" by anabolic steroids;
History: His parents were ILP and Labour: "there was a lot of political discussion at home

but it was more Workers Educational Association than formal Labour-trade union politics"; attracted to the Liberals by Jo Grimond, he joined the Liberal Club at Glasgow University '59, becoming its President in '62; while at Stanford University "the campus was in total ferment" because of the Vietnam war '66; his political interest was revived when the South African Rugby tour went to Scotland, when David Steel asked him to speak against it in Galashiels '70; was asked to contest Greenock but declined because he was planning to marry the month of the election June '70; contested Greenock and Port Glasgow Feb and Oct '74 and was "well beaten"; became Chairman of the Scottish Liberal Party '75; was adopted for East Fife Jan '76; urged a statutory pay policy Mar '79; at Scottish Liberal conference warned Liberal Parliamentary Party against voting against devolution, adding that only PR could allay "the legitimate fears" of people in rural areas that the Scottish Assembly would be dominated by Labour representatives from Strathclyde Mar '79; fought East Fife, coming second with 23% - twice the previous vote May '79; opposed individual UK athletes competing in Moscow Olympics May '80; warned against "intemperate" Liberal attacks on SDP as "political madness", acclaiming the Alliance as a heaven-sent opportunity: "I am fed up with the party forever being second; we have the opportunity to convert a lot of dreary footslogging into genuine and sustained political influence" Sep '81; warned of strength of commitment to 'home rule' for Scotland, rather than devolution and warned it could not be delayed until England was federated Mar '82; warned SDP that Alliance were committed to create a Scottish Parliament without a referendum and without necessarily waiting for regional assemblies to be established in England and Wales Feb '83; contested East Fife, coming second with 40.2%, under 6% behind Tory Barry Henderson June '83; wrote that pushing the phasing out of US bases from Scotland would detract from the campaign against Trident Apr '85; received the CBE for political and public services as former Chairman of the Scottish Liberal Party and member of the Clayson Committee Jan '87; attacked the Scottish Nationalists' "doomsday scenario" for UDI after the next general election as "an attempt...to open the back door to separatism" Mar '87; made much of the Alliance commitment to a Scottish Assembly with revenue-raising powers May '87; his was one of nine candidacies endorsed by the Campaign for a Tory-free Scotland, mostly successful May '87; increasing his share of the vote by 4.7%, he won the seat, unseating Barry Henderson in one of the Scottish Liberals' two gains June '87; in his Maiden speech he deplored the "regressive" poll tax - preferring a local income tax - and cuts in grants for St Andrews and local government July '87; at the Liberal Assembly he urged a small negotiating team to deal with the pro-merger SDPers, warning: "Bob Maclennan will be no pushover"; attacking the poll tax, he warned that the Government might introduce identity cards; "the prospect of Big Brother peering through the bathroom window to see how many toothbrushes there are there would be funny if it were not so pathetic" Sep '87; as the new Arts Spokesman he gave "a cautious welcome" to Richard Luce's proposals for increased Arts Council funding Nov '87; in the debate on the Firearms (Amendment) Bill he claimed there had been inadequate consultation with the shooting organisations and urged "sensible" modifications Jan '88; launched Private Member's Bill to control use of anabolic steroids in sport Feb '88; joined Conservatives on Members' Interest Committee in opposing Labour effort to formalise rules under which Ministers divest themselves of company holdings and directorships on taking office Mar '88; warned that poll tax on overseas students might harm his local St Andrews University May '88; backed Paddy Ashdown's Leadership campaign May '88; tabled an amendment trying to outlaw ticket touts June '88; was named Defence and Sports Spokesman on Paddy Ashdown's team Sep '88; since the Trident system would be mostly completed and paid for by the next election, "the option of cancelling Trident and starting again will not be available" Feb '89; visited Bulgaria as guest of its government Sep '89; was named Defence and Disarmament Spokesman, while retaining Sports Nov '89; again introduced Bill to ban use of steroids in sport Dec '89; voted against war crimes trials of elderly Baltic immigrants Dec '89; was added to Select Committee on Trade and Industry Feb '90; left the Select Committee on Members Interests June '90; again introduced Bill to ban ticket touts June '90; received gift of briefcase from Saudi Arabian government after a visit there Nov '90; with his wife, Elspeth, attended a seminar at Gleneagles Hotel as guest of Conoco (UK) Ltd May '91; again introduced Bill to ban ticket touts June '91; as one with "a moral objection to capital punishment" he could not see why it should be retained only in the armed forces June '91; won a place on Private Members' Bill ballot Nov '91; introduced Bill to establish and entrench a Scottish Parliament based on PR Dec '91; visited Saudi Arabia, Bahrein and Abu Dhabi, with travel paid by Liberal Democratic Middle East Council, with accommodation provided by governments of countries visited; the Emir of Bahrein gave him a wristwatch Feb '92; introduced 2nd Reading of his Home Rule (Scotland) Bill retained seat with a doubled majority, up from 1,477 to 3,308, a swing to Liberal Democrats of 2.14% Apr '92; was named to Defence Select Committee July '92; opposed Euthanasia Bill July '92; visited Democratic Party Convention in New York, with travel provided by Virgin Atlantic and accommodation paid for himself July '92; asked Government to back his Bill to ban anabolic steroids July '92; urged an independent review of university pay Aug '92; urged a review of Scotland's "creaking" legal system Sep '92; derided possibility of a centralised Lib-Lab pact Sep '92; attended commemoration of El Alamein. where his father-in-law had fought with 51st Highland Division Oct '92; complained MPs could be forced to spend £1,000 a year on fundraising party stalls Nov '92; urged a full-scale judicial inquiry into Matrix-Churchill affair; feared the Scott Inquiry would be "toothless" and unlikely to get to the truth about selling arms-making equipment to Iraq Nov '92; deplored inadequacy of EC reaction to crisis in former Yugoslavia Nov '92; co-signed INDEPENDENT letter urging rapid imposition of safe havens in Bosnia-Herzegovina Dec '92; supported previous action against Iraq but warned against any more "extravagant" reaction to further Iraqi provocation Jan '93; visited Zagreb with Defence Select Committee Feb '93; urged exclusion of tactical air-to-surface missiles because they were devised when "NATO's nuclear doctrine was one of flexible response" and Trident missile could now do the job Feb '93; despite doubts, supported renewal of Prevention of Terrorism Act Mar '93; voted against National Lottery Bill Apr '93; again insisted it was not necessary to have more warheads on Trident than on Polaris May '93; complained that Government, in awarding the £5b nuclear submarine refits solely to Devonport, had broken the promise to Rosyth dockyard made by Lord [George] Younger June '93; opposed sending 17-year-olds into action; also opposed use of death penalty under Army regulations; opposed discrimination against homosexuals; asked how long it would take for a Jamaican like US General Colin Powell to reach a senior rank in the UK June '93; welcomed UK's willingness to commit a brigade to Bosnia Aug '93; urged legally-binding contracts for Rosyth dockyard Aug '93; voted against restoring capital punishment, even for killing policemen Feb '94; voted to reduce age of homosexual consent to 18, but not 16, Feb '94; after Attorney General Sir Nicholas Lyell conceded he had had "overall responsibility" for the catalogue of errors leading to a failure to pass crucial information to the court in the Matrix-Churchill arms-for-Iraq trial, Menzies Campbell said: "Sir Nichoas Lyell's latest confession...has effectively sealed his fate" Mar '94; was promoted Chief Spokesman on Defence and Foreign Affairs, on the retirement of Sir David Steel from the latter job July '94; in the wake of the "cash for questions" inquiries, he gave up his £5,000-a-year Directorship of Westminster Communications Group, lobbyists Sep '94; criticised free-ranging agenda of LibDem conferences, allowing for contradictory policy statements without regard for public spending implications Sep '94; backed Ashdown's moves towards Labour, saying he would find it difficult to support a Tory Government in a hung Parliament Sep '94; backed Bill of

Labour MP David Jamieson to regulate activity centres, following pupils' deaths near Lyme Regis, but argued for retaining some risks and worried about cost implications Jan '95; again presented Bill to set up a Scottish Parliament elected by PR, reducing the number of Scottish MPs at Westminster Jan '95; sent terse memo to Paddy Ashdown complaining there had been a misunderstanding which explained his failure to recruit more than 19 Labour MPs to back the LibDem motion calling for a referendum on Europe; he complained that a copy of this memo had been stolen from the desk of his assistant Feb '95; was reported as moving toward a tougher line on protecting Bosnian Muslim enclaves May '95; accused Labour of descending to "tabloid character assassination" of LibDem candidate in Littleborough and Saddleworth by-election June '95; despite LibDem proposals to crack down on large-engine cars, was revealed by EVENING STANDARD as driving a 5.3-litre Jaguar Aug '95; it was suggested in the EVENING STANDARD his wife would never allow him to give up his lucrative practice at the Bar to become LibDems' Leader Sep '95; criticised as "clearly excessive" the "huge sums some people have won" on the National Lottery Sep '95; privately opposed LibDem conference vote to boycott French goods to protest renewal of nuclear testing in the Pacific, which he opposed as "scientifically unnecessary and politically inept" Sep '95; reaffirmed LibDem commitment to Europe, attacking John Major's concessions to Tory "Euro-nihilists" Sep '95; defended the nuclear deterrent but opposed overspending at Faslane and the French nuclear test Oct '95; attacked the Defence Secretary for his criticism of Special Air Services Oct '95; co-signed GUARDIAN letter calling for retention of open access for Nigerian asylum-seekers Oct '95; was named, with Tory MP Seb Coe and Labour MP Tom Pendry, to investigate drug-taking by British athletes Nov '95; urged sanctions against Nigeria for its "cruel and inhuman behaviour" Nov '95; his wife Elspeth said changes in Parliamentary sittings made little difference to Scottish MPs because, during the week "he still has no one to cook dinner for him in his horrible little flat" in London Nov '95; called for resignation of the Ministers responsible and a public apology to the businessmen involved in the Matrix Churchill case Nov '95; initiated debate on erosion of Ministerial responsibility, citing Douglas Hurd and the Pergau Dam Feb '96; after the Scott revelations, with Robin Cook tried to force resignation of Sir Nicholas Lyell and William Waldegrave, saying "the only reason they hang on in government is because the Government is so weak that it dare not get rid of them" Feb '96; complained of the "infection of anti-Europeanism" after William Waldegrave claimed Britain could exist outside the EU May '96; backed end of ban on homosexuals in the Forces May '96; opposed threat of non-cooperation with the EU, following its demands for a cattle cull to cut BSE June '96; urged UK passports for 3,000 non-Chinese Hongkong minority June '96; voted against a 3% cap on MPs' pay rise for a cut in their mileage allowance and for a pension based on £43,000 July '96; urged a total ban on land mines July '96; said "some of our thousands of councillors regard control of the local authority as a greater prize" than Westminster Sep '96; warned of cost and time-overrun on provision of 232 Eurofighters for the RAF Sep '96; warned that "Britain will never influence Europe so long as it sulks in its tent" after John Major attacked Brussels "dictatorship" after an adverse decision on the 48-hour directive Nov '96; named by SPECTATOR as the "Member to Watch", recalled he had once raced 60 yards indoors and beaten an obscure American athlete called O J Simpson Nov '96; attacked the Japanese-led consortium which had acquired the MOD's privatised married quarters for failing to disclose the company's structure Nov '96; dubbed it a "disgrace" that the Government was still pretending Gulf troops had not been exposed to organophosphates Dec '96; when formerly Europhile Health Secretary Stephen Dorrell urged renegotiation of the UK's Euro-link. quipped, "the Cabinet has given up on the general election and are now fighting the Leadership election" Jan '97; proposed MPs be compelled to lodge their income tax returns with the Commons Registrar of Members' Interests Mar '97;

backed European Movement Mar '97; retained his seat with a trebled majority of 10,356 on a pro-LibDem swing of 8.4% May '97; was retained as Chief Spokesman on Foreign Affairs and Defence May '97; urged revocation of arms export licenses for Indonesia May '97; again urged curb on Trident warheads to Polaris level May '97; was re-named to the Defence Select Committee July '97; was named a Substitute Delegate to the Parliamentary Assembly of the OSCE July '97; urged Defence Secretary George Robertson to set out the Government's strategic objectives in its defence review July '97; backed ban on visits of senior Indonesians to Farnborough defence show July '97; joined Labour's Cabinet committee on constitutional reform as one of its five Liberal Democrat members July '97; urged Clare Short to help Montserrat Aug '97; attacked Portillo's prior sale of MOD's married quarters as "driven by dogma and a poor memorial to his stewardship" Sep '97; was one of 14 LibDem MPs who opposed Mike Foster's anti-foxhunting Bill Nov '97; urged an inquiry into the transfer to Northern Ireland, at the request of the Protestant Unionists, of a murderer of a Celtic suporter Oct '97; backed Labour Government on use of force, if necessary, against Saddam Hussein Feb '98; backed Labour Government in seeking an EU code on arms exports Apr '98;

Born: 22 May 1941, Glasgow

Family: Son, late George Campbell, builder and ILPer, and late Elizabeth (Phillips), civil servant; m '70 bright, beautiful and witty Open University graduate Lady Grant Suttie (Elspeth Mary Urquhart), d of Major General R E Urquhart (who commanded the British 1st Airborne Division at Arnhem), who serves as his secretary; she and David Steel won a public apology and a "very substantial" sum from the STAR in May '87 for a libellous story linking them; 1 steps, James Grant Suttie;

Education: Hillhead Primary, Glasgow; Hillhead High, Glasgow; Glasgow University (a contemporary of John Smith); Stanford University;

Occupation: Advocate: QC '82- (once earned £20,000 a year); Panellist, for Harris Opinion Poll (at £1,000 a year) '95-; ex: Advocate Depute '77-80; Standing Junior Counsel to Army in Scotland '80-82; Chairman: Medical Appeal Tribunals, VAT Appeal Tribunal '84-87; Director, Westminster Communications Group (PR, lobbying; earned £5,000 a year for "less than one hour a week" serving clients: British Gas, British Railways Board) '93-94;

Traits: Tall; balding; "Ming"; "well-dressed, elegant" (his wife); "noticeably stylish" (Julie Kirkbride MP); when he left a suitcase behind en route to Torquay in '93, he 'phoned Austin Reed to order a suit to be dispatched to him); self-assured; clear-minded; "for many months I thought the honourable and learned Member for Fife North East, with his cutaway collars and striped shirts, was a member of the Conservative Party, and I bought him a number of drinks on that basis" (jokey John Patten MP); "has become incredibly grand and smartened up his accent" since student days (Alan Cochrane, SUNDAY TIMES); ex-runner (on Olympic team, Tokyo '64 and Commonwealth Games '66, Captain UK Athletic teams '65, '66, AAA 220 yards champion '64, '67; held UK 100-metre record '67-74); ex-Chairman, Royal Lyceum Theatre Company, Edinburgh; owner of a shotgun certificate;

Address: House of Commons, Westminster, London SW1A 0AA; 6 Lynedoch Place, Edinburgh EH3 6JN; Ellenbank, Gateside, Strathmiglo, Fife; a "horrible little flat" (his wife) in London;

Telephone: 0171 219 4446 (H of C); 0131 220 6066 (home); 0131 226 5071 (chambers);

Michael Grylls' payments from Ian Greer first emerged in PARLIAMENTARY PROFILES

'Ronnie' (Ronald) CAMPBELL   Labour   BLYTH VALLEY '87-

Majority: 17,736 (41.7%) over Liberal Democrat 3-way;

Description: A bleak industrial valley formerly dominated by coalmines, a power station and dockyards; it lost Bedlington and changed its name in '83; its pits have all closed; unemployment went to 18%, and Cramlington has become part of Newcastle's commuter belt;

Position: On Select Committee on the Parliamentary Commissioner for Administration (Ombudsman) '87-97; ex: Blyth Valley Councillor '74-88, Blyth Borough Councillor '69-74;

Outlook: One of "Blair's Bastards" (Professor Philip Norton) as one of the most frequent hard-Left Campaign Group rebels against the Labour Whip; was congratulated by Home Secretary Jack Straw for "the work that he is doing in his area and more widely in respect of young drug addicts"; otherwise, a rebellious, rumbustious, crudely class-conscious, hard-Left ex-miner; "archetypal Old Labour" (Tom Baldwin, SUNDAY TELEGRAPH); the most frequent target for Speaker Boothroyd's disapproval; "he always speaks with particular eloquence on any matter concerning his constituency...and of course he speaks with passion and knowledge about the coal industry" (Tory MP Quentin Davies): "I am a radical and a fighter" (RC); "I've never wanted to be a Minister and I don't think Tony Blair would want me to be [one]; I would nationalise everthing again and spend all his money" (RC); a warm-hearted, excitable, unsophisticated, Left-fundamentalist, local former miner-councillor; opposed the Gulf War; has recently opposed the EU and a single European currency; a very active constituency MP, based on a local office he finances from part of his salary; a loud supporter of the Campaign Group and, formerly, of Arthur Scargill, rather than of Militant; pro-Arab (including Libya); an enthusiast for conventional defence, including "two frigates a year built on Tyneside for the next ten years"; was NUM-sponsored;

History: He was elected to his NUM branch committee at 21 '65, to Blyth Valley Council from Croft ward May '69; was elected to Blyth Valley Council May '74; his predecessor, John Ryman, wrote thanking him for "all the support and loyalty in the past few difficult months" - a reference to Ryman's having been committed for trial on election corruption charges, of which only his agent was found guilty Oct '76; Campbell was fined £75 with £25 costs for breach of the peace when, as NUM branch chairman at Bates Colliery, he grabbed a policeman who had seized a picket - he later explained: "all working miners had been in the pit for some time when this happened and were not under any threat at the time of the incident" Dec '84; strongly supported Arthur Scargill's posture during the miners' strike, later saying: "his standpoint was absolutely right" '84-85; unsuccessfully challenged John Ryman in reselection contest for Blyth Valley May '85; invited Peter Heathfield and Derek Hatton to speak locally - Hatton did not make it but Heathfield announced the impending closure of Bates Colliery, where Campbell was employed Oct '85; sought selection for Liberal-held Berwick July '86; John Ryman announced he would not be standing again for Blyth Valley Sep '86; Campbell stopped fighting against demands for repayment of hardship loans extended during strike by Northumberland County Council Sep '86; the NUM announced he was its nominee for the Blyth Valley seat Oct '86; Ryman wrote to Blyth Constituency Labour Party saying he would not stand again on their behalf, later threatening to stand as an Independent Dec '86; Campbell was selected by a one-vote majority on the fifth ballot to succeed John Ryman from among 11 nominations including Euro-MP Gordon Adam and university lecturer-writer Ben Pimlott; disclosed he was a Catholic opponent of abortion and thought he lost some votes that way Dec '86; accused by retiring MP John Ryman of being a friend of a Militant, he replied "I never would be a member of Militant but there is a lad who comes to my house every week to sell me a copy of the Militant paper; I listen to what he has to say - they are not totally bad and and have some good ideas - but he has never asked me to join"; admitted to having spoken at two Militant meetings, one in London and one in Newcastle to raise funds for the striking miners, and to having invited Derek Hatton to speak Dec '86; urged miners' families to repay the Northumberland County loans made during the strike, saying: "you can't win in a legal battle" and warning they would face legal costs on top Dec '86; NEC endorsed his candidacy in wake of inquiry by National Agent David Hughes, as demanded by Ryman Jan '87; Campbell urged YTS trainees be given the full trade union rate for their age groups - at least £36 a week with union-negotiated top-ups Apr '87; Ryman did not stand and Campbell, having increased the Labour vote by 3,000, narrowly won by 853 voters over the SDP, who increased their vote by 5,000, with the Tory trailing badly in third place June '87; joined the hard-Left Campaign Group July '87; voted against the 21.9% pay increase for MPs, taking a miner's weekly pay of £210, with the rest going to the Blyth party July '87; opposed the expulsion from the Labour Party of his friend, Bob Newall, for selling MILITANT, which was not against party rules at the time Aug '87; in his Maiden speech he omitted paying a tribute to his predecessor, John Ryman; urged subsidies for British-mined coal and a rejection of dependence on foreign coal Oct '87; urged a new coal-fired power station on the Northumberland coast Nov '87; backed the right of MPs to bring in any researcher, including those with former IRA sympathies Nov '87; when he said he would follow the Labour Party line and oppose Alton's abortion-curbing Bill, his Blyth Valley councillor-wife, Dierdre, an Irish Catholic, publicly threatened to denounce him if he went against his Catholic conscience Dec '87; when the Campaign Group urged a three-line Whip in favour of abortion, Campbell retorted: "I am single-minded on this issue; I am a practising Catholic, so therefore on those grounds I will most probably vote for Alton; I don't believe in abortion at all, not even 18 weeks"; in the event he voted for David Alton's Bill to curb abortions Jan '88; visited Afghanistan as guest of Friends of Afghanistan Jan '88; voted against the Speaker's suspension of Dave Nellist, pro-Militant MP Apr '88; opened a constituency office financed by part of his salary, which was to deal with 5,600 inquiries a year Apr '91; co-urged the complete rehabilitation of Leon Trotsky June '88; his support (later denied) was claimed for 'Troops Out Now' rally July '88; visited North Korea at invitation of its government '89; pledged support to Militant-run Anti-Poll Tax Union Sep '89; co-signed INDEPENDENT letter urging rail links from Channel Tunnel to the north Oct '89; his re-selection was endorsed Oct '89; backed motion supporting fundraising for Communist daily MORNING STAR to ensure "diverse editorial opinion" Feb '90; co-urged boycott of Israeli goods to force end of brutality to Palestinian Arabs and occupation of their lands June '90; with Dennis Canavan and Bob Parry visited Libya, Iraq and Jordan as guest of POPEM Sep '90; voted against Gulf War Sep '90; complained about poor conditions and high demands imposed on local teachers Nov '90; having asked the Defence Secretary whether "he has sent any body bags to the Gulf", again voted against Gulf War Dec '90; complained about brutal treatment in Durham Prison meted out to constituent Darren Brook, a first offender, who had been beaten and killed by a fellow inmate Dec '90; in Ports Bill debate said that Blyth's port commissioners feared compulsory privatisation Jan '91; again opposed Gulf War Jan '91; complained about poll tax dodger's imprisonment for two months Apr '91; asked about local child abuse Apr '91; complained about lack of repairs for local schools June '91; was alleged by Conservatives to be a Militant sympathiSer Aug '91; again visited Libya with six other Labour MPs, organised by Bernie Grant MP Nov '91; urged restoration of diplomatic relations with Libya, but only after trial of its accused Lockerbie bombers Nov '91; asked the Government whether they intended to close down domestic coalmining and increasing imports of foreign coal Nov '91; the NEWCASTLE JOURNAL rated him the 13th most active written questioner of 29 local MPs and the 24th most active oral questioner of 28, Nov '91; complained that Government was jailing poll tax dodgers while allowing traders to flout the law on Sunday trading Dec '91; complained of rapid increase of environmentally damaging opencast mining while deep mining was being squeezed out Jan '92; when the Prime Minister made the customary "send me the details" request in answer to Campbell's harangue about an arthritic constituent facing a 15-month wait for treatment, he crossed the floor and handed the relevant papers to the PM Feb '92; threatened libel action against Conservative charge that he was an IRA sympathizer: "I have never, never agreed with the 'Troops Out' campaign and have had arguments with some of my colleagues because of it"; one of his sons was a marine Feb '92; retained seat with majority up from 853 to 8,044, a swing to Labour of 7.25%, almost wholly from a drop in Liberal Democratic vote from previous SDP runner-up Apr '92; visited China, with local accomodation and hospitality provided by its government Aug-Sep '92; opposed Euthanasia Bill Sep '92; in fraught paving vote on Maastricht turned on Paddy Ashdown behind him and accused him of treachery Nov '92; co-sponsored motion against the taxpayer being burdened by bill for restoring fire-damaged Windsor Castle Nov '92; relayed fears for their livelihoods of local cobble-boat fishermen Dec '92; was rated the second strongest Labour rebel against the Whip, with eight recent defiances, mostly on Maastricht Feb '93; co-sponsored Dennis Skinner's motion supporting Grimethorpe as a profitable pit Mar '93; decried 81% increase in unemployment in northeast since 1979, Mar '93; voted against 3rd Reading for Maastricht treaty Bill May '93; on the announcement of the closure of Swan Hunter, the last Tyne shipyard, asked DTI Minister Tim Sainsbury when he was "going to get off his backside and get something done in the northeast" May '93; blamed recession on "fast buck economy" which rewarded richest with tax cuts and allowed decline of manufacturing June '93; expressed his fear that safety would suffer in privatised mines, as had happened before Jan '94; voted against restoring capital punishment, even for killers of policemen Feb '94; voted to reduce age of homosexual consent to 18 or 16, Feb '94; complained that Blyth Valley "has become one of the biggest drug centres in the northeast", that local drug dealers were persuading their addicts to steal for them and were feeding them lethal cocktails Mar '94; co-sponsored motion urging decriminalisation of cannabis Apr '94; was described by Tory MP James Pawsey as "a staunch member of the Select Committee on the Parliantary Commissioner...always in attendance at meetings of the Committee" Apr '94; complained "the media are trying to make Tony Blair Leader May '94; backed John Prescott for Leader June '94; demanded an inquiry into the Gulf War Syndrome, claiming the Government had been 'fifty-faced on this issue" July '94; voted against EC Finance Bill Nov '94; signed motion calling for normalisation of relations with North Korea Mar '95; attacked the "inner sanctum of the Labour Party" for trying to "con the people in the south into believing we are an electable party"; "we now have a National Policy Forum set up by people educated at Oxford and Cambridge and who sit round the table and decide what Tony Blair's next policy is going to be"; "under Blair we are taking up Thatcher's ideas" Aug '95; signed Benn motion urging scrapping of Trident and other defence cuts Oct '95; voted against Defence Estimates Oct '95; in drugs debate, highlighted way in which addicts could obtain methadone illegally from GPs, saying: "there is no way that I would say that any drugs should should be legalised" Nov '95; with nine other Leftwing Campaign Groupies, defied the Labour Whip to vote against the Government's 1p cut in income tax Dec '95; was upbraided by Speaker Boothroyd for disorderly behaviour Dec '95; said he would no longer be a royalist after the death of the Queen: "I support the Queen, but after the Queen I don't think there will be anyone worth supporting" Mar '96; showed his horny hands and sinewy arms in response to Alan Duncan's jibe that the only thing that Labour had recently run was a bath Apr '96; voted for Bill Cash's Referendum Bill on European federalism June '96; was named in TRIBUNE as one of nine Left Labour MPs who would oppose a single European currency in his manifesto June '96; voted against a 3% cap on MPs' pay rise, in favour of a pension based on £43,000 July '96; he was named as one of "Blair's Bastards" by Professor Philip Norton for voting 24 times against the Whips since '92, Sep '96; complained about often being put under pressure "by my party and from women's organisations for speaking out against abortion...colleagues whom I had always regarded as friends say I could be de-selectedf over this" Jan '97; claimed Leftwingers in the PLP had kept their heads down "because we want Labour to win" Apr '97; said biggest pressure for a "fairer redistribution of wealth" would come in two or three years; claimed 60 Labour MPs would want tax increases and 100 would rebel to preserve links with the unions Apr '97; the North East Area of the NUM announced it could not contribute to the election expenses of its four previously sponsored local MPs, including Campbell Apr '97; retained his unaltered seat, doubling his majority to 17,736 on a 12.7% swing to Labour May '97; attacked Labour leadership's plan to vet centrally all candidates prior to local decisions as a drive for "middle-class clones"; "if you are a goody-goody clone you are going to be in; if you are on the Left, you are on your bike"; "we will only have candidates who are well-educated and well-groomed and certainly don't come from working-class backgrounds like me" July '97; was called to order by Speaker Boothroyd for "disturbing the House" July '97; after a visit to his constituency by Home Secretary Jack Straw, was congratulated in the Commons for his work with young drug addicts Nov '97; tried to speed up work of Royal Commission on longterm care for the elderly Dec '97; was discovered to have provided a Commons pass for Roger Pope, head of PR for the Electricity Association Nov '97; was banned from the Commons for a day for insisting on calling Michael Jack a "hypocrite", an 'un-Parliamentary' term Feb '98; urged the import of Australian-type family courts to sort out the Child Support Agency Feb '98; when he shouted "Liberal fudge!" at David Chidgey, the Deputy Speaker asked him to "conform to the rules of order of this House" Mar '98; congratulated the Government on beefing up Customs to stop drug importation Apr '98; was one of 31 Labour rebels who voted against abolition of student maintenance grants June '98;

Born: 14 August 1943, Blyth Valley

Family: Son, Ronald Campbell, retired joiner, and Edna (Howes); m '67 Dierdre Philomena (McHale), strongly-RC Blyth Valley councillor born in Ballina, County Mayo; 5s: Edward '68, Barry '72, Shaun '74, Brendan '74, Aidan '78; 1d Sharon '70;

Education: State primary; Ridley High School (secondary modern);

Occupation: Formerly NUM-sponsored (£600 p a to constituency, plus 80% of election expenses) '87-95; ex: Miner, at Bates Colliery for 27 years, 14 years at the coalface '59-86; "I have worked in conditions where I could not see my hands in front of me because of the dust from the [coal-cutting] machines, even though they had dust-suppressors; I worked in the mines when the water was coming in and I was soaked for hours on end" (RC); after the mine closed in '86 he signed on for the dole until elected to Parliament a year later;

Traits: Greying; retreating hair; chubby face, reddened when he shouts, in a Northumberland accent; "his accent makes Gazza sound like Brian Sewell" (Simon Hoggart, GUARDIAN); RC; "roguishly likeable" (Matthew Parris, TIMES), "sure to sparkle like [one of the] rough diamonds - uncompromising and brash without any of the bad grace of some of [his] tough backbench colleagues" (Simon Beck, NEWCASTLE JOURNAL); perhaps the only MP with a tattoo; enjoys restoring old furniture, including French polishing; philatelist; has been known

to provide Tony Blair with his stottie, a type of Geordie bap;
Address: House of Commons, Westminster, London SW1A 0AA; 4 Balfour Street, Blyth, Northumberland, NE24 1JD; 68 Broadway, Blyth, Northumberland NE4 2 PR; has a flat in Kennington after having lived in a Catholic hostel for homeless teenagers on the Caledonia Road for two months;
Telephone: 0171 219 4216 (H of C); 01670 355242 (home);

Dale (Norman) CAMPBELL-SAVOURS   **Labour**   **WORKINGTON '79-**

Majority: 19,656   (39.8%)   over   Conservative 5-way;
Description: A Lake District seat, with its Labour majority coming from the Cumbrian coastal industrial belt: Workington's council estates housing workers from its steelworks and formerly from Maryport's defunct docks; includes part of Sellafield nuclear power plant and the shut former Volvo/Leyland bus plant; in '95 9,000 voters were drafted in from rural Aspatria and Silloth wards formerly in Penrith and the Border;
Position: On Select Committees: on Standards and Privileges '97-, Intelligence and Security '97-; ex: Assistant Spokesman, on Food and Agriculture '92-94; Deputy Spokesman, on Overseas Development '91-92; on Select Committees on Agriculture '94-96, Members' Interests '84-92, Public Accounts '80-92, Procedure '83-91; Vice Chairman: PLP Agriculture Committee '93-95, PLP Footwear and Leather Industries Group '87-96;
Outlook: West Cumbria's sleaze-busting maverick with an unbeaten track record including having exposed Westminster Council's cemetery-selling and political cleansing, the Malaysian trade of dam aid for arms purchases and the Tory Whips' conspiracy to protect Neil Hamilton; a solitary, craggy, assiduous, puritanical crusader; has proclaimed that "no one will ever drive me into a lobby in support of a measure with which I do not agree"; "the Workington Savonarola" (Colin Welch, DAILY MAIL); "Labour's super-sleuth" (David McKie, GUARDIAN), "he demonstrates that puritanical inquiring independence which marks an MP down among Whips on both sides as unsuitable for office"; "sometimes conspiratorial, always assiduous", "awkward to the core" (Michael White, GUARDIAN); "perpetually a-tremble with news of some ghastly conspiracy", "he stalks the corridors of Westminster in grim pursuit of new evidence of dark dealings by the Tories, the Establishment, the City, MI5...almost everyone, in fact, in this wicked and self-serving world" (Matthew Parris, TIMES); "never to be under-estimated" (Edward Pearce, DAILY TELEGRAPH); "a master of Parliamentary procedure", with "forensic skill, persistence and a thick-skinned willingness to bore the pants off everyone else"; "for scowling propensity to see conspiracy in every bus queue, Campbell-Savours is king", "at the tabloid end of rat-smelling" (TIMES); "a conspiracy theorist to rival any JFKologist" (Robert Hardman, DAILY TELEGRAPH); "manages to invest every subject with a marvellous frisson of cloak and dagger excitement" (Sir Peter Tapsell MP); "has an unattractive habit of assuming that any allegation is automatically true" (Peter Lilley MP); anti: abortion, embryo experimentation, aggressive Bosnian Serbs, nuclear weapons and leakage, lowflying aircraft, Falklands war, bishop-baiting, late Tiny Rowland;

pro: THORP and nuclear power at Sellafield, EU, CofE, industrial democracy, Kurds, Arabs (on Labour Middle East Council), military intervention against Serbs and Saddam; a nationaliser within mixed economy; Backbencher of the Year (GUARDIAN 1985); has been UNISON-sponsored;

History: The son of wealthy parents, he rejected his inheritance when very young; he was a Rightwinger at the Sorbonne; "since my earliest years, I have been a passionate supporter of the European Community; I campaigned for entry to it as a teenager"; joined the Labour Party '65; was elected to Ramsbottom UDC May '72; contested Bury Council May '73; contested hopeless Darwen Feb and Oct '74, Bury Council May '76; was chosen over local mayor to follow Fred (later Lord) Peart as pro-EEC candidate Oct '76; contested Workington in by-election, losing it to Richard Page Nov '76; investigated bribery at French and Italian borders Aug '77; retook Workingtom May '79; in Maiden opposed abortion as taking of life July '79; urged better bank credit for small businesses Dec '79; fruitlessly urged Mrs Thatcher to intervene in BSC strike Jan '80; backed Access to Commons and Open Country and seatbelt Bills Feb '80; complained that monetarist policies and high £-Sterling were killing manufactured exports Nov '80; claimed "doctored" statistics caused closure of BSC's Workington iron foundry Dec '80; accused BSC chief Ian MacGregor of threatening to pull steel out of constituency unless Campbell-Savours stopped criticising BSC management Dec '80; his complaint was submitted to Commons Privileges Committee Jan '81; urged moratorium against exporting second-hand textile machinery Jan '81; because of conflict of evidence, Privileges Committee was unable to find for him, against MacGregor Apr '81; rejected idea that Tribune membership demonstrated belief in socialism Nov '81; urged reflation Nov '81; protested Canada Bill, partly over abortion Mar '82; made Arab-sponsored trip to Middle East Apr '82; voted against Falklands operation May '82; opposed seductive advertising of London Dockland Corporation June '82; urged job creation through home insulation and improvement July '82; "it was precisely because he approached the issue of an enterprise zone in [a constructive] manner and with enthusiastic endorsement in the early 1980s that he helped persuade me that there should be an enterprise zone" there (Michael Heseltine); opposed the RAF's lowflying exercises over Lake District Dec '82; urged same treatment for families of those killed in Ulster as in Falklands Dec '82; attacked wife beating Dec '82; "I supported Greenpeace during the 1983 demonstration over the Sellafield pipeline and subscribed to its legal costs" '83; urged the burning of the Serpell Report on making BR profitable Jan '83; complained Labour leaders were not getting message across "in the language of our people" hence "disastrous" polls Feb '83; supported PLO Apr '83; complained that the rich were getting richer, the poor poorer Apr '83; claimed the Food Advisory Committee was over-influenced by Conservatives consultants to the food industry June '93; was anti-hanging teller when restoration was again defeated July '83; backed Gwyneth Dunwoody for Deputy Leader Sep '83; feuded with local landowner, Lady Egremont, over salmon poaching Oct '83; opposed allowing banks and building societies to convey properties Dec '83; as a PAC member he felt let down that De Lorean's use of interest-free loans had not been monitored Jan '84; demanded Mrs Thatcher declare her interest because her son had links with firm seeking Oman contracts Jan-Mar '84; asked whether anyone had been contaminated by Sellafield leak Feb '84; asked why secret radar project - whose existence had been revealed by documents left in telephone booth - did not appear in annual statement to PAC Mar '84; published a minority report on Mrs Thatcher's links with Oman contract Apr '84; urged a review of FCO staff's entitlement to free boarding school education Aug '84; urged John Selwyn Gummer to stop bullying the bishops, especially Durham Nov '84; said every woman planning to have an abortion should see 'Silent Scream' Jan '85; voted for Enoch Powell's Bill to ban embryo experimentation Feb '85; put down motion urging stricter pesticide controls Mar '85; sought to protect an Aish and Company director who had 'blown the whistle' on its over-charging Mar '85; complained that Liberal MPs had not declared themselves as BSM-sponsored although BSM's £188,000 gift had persuaded Liberals to resist tougher regulations on driving instructors May-June '85; published first-ever PAC minority report on BOC's overcharging of NHS June '85; warned against society giving way to scientists on foetus experimentation July '85; attacked David Alton's proposal to phase out nuclear power as a "hysterical over-response" to problems of nuclear waste Nov '85; again urged action after a further Sellafield leak Jan '86; insisted Mrs Thatcher was not telling the truth about Westland Jan '86; urged an international offshore dump for nuclear wastes Feb '86; failed to secure debate on takeover of Leyland bus plant in his constituency Feb '86; complained BNFL management failures were impeding his effort for a reasonable approach to nuclear waste Mar '86; backed motion to protect special character of Sunday Mar '86; tried to stop a Lloyd's syndicate from insuring against kidnapping Apr '86; claimed "belching filth" of coal-fired power stations was worse than nuclear radiation May '86; was warned by Speaker over his anti-Tory "they don't care!" litany July '86; claimed Falklanders would not be able to police their fishing zone Oct '86; ran a protracted campaign to demand an investigation of Peter Wright's accusations of a plot to destabilise the Wilson Government and to question why Wright was attacked while Chapman Pincher and Rupert Allason MP were let off Nov-Dec '86; complained of injunctions against the BBC and NEW STATESMAN over the 'Zircon' programme Feb '87; urged restrictions on foreign women coming for late abortions Mar '87; urged expulsion of Tory MP Keith Best for multiple applications for BT shares Apr '87; spoke for two hours to talk out Bill to liberalise drinking hours May '87; named the six MI5 men in the "Wilson affair" May '87; co-sponsored both David Alton's abortion-curbing Bill and Edward Leigh's Bill to report abortion-seeking foreign girls to their home doctors Oct '87; claimed he was banned from putting questions on GCHQ Oct '87; complained of loose supervision of fraudulent charities by Charity Commission Oct '87; called for resignation of Lord Weinstock over standard of Marconi supplies to Defence Ministry Nov '87; complained about "hypocrisy" in prosecution of Duncan Campbell when officials had allowed release of classified information in GCHQ book by Rupert Allason MP Dec '87; implied that Alton's Bill should have made exceptions for handicap-prone foetuses Jan '88; said supervision of nuclear waste should "not be influenced by the whims of the monopolist employer and dominator of the West Cumbrian economy -British Nuclear Fuels" Jan '88; disclosed that 23 firms had overcharged Defence, with £30m in refunds being demanded Jan '88; opposed televising Commons, unless as a dedicated feed Feb '88; again attacked John Gummer for his "malicious and squalid" attacks on the clergy Feb '88; alleged three top Ulster policemen were exempted from prosecution on 'shoot to kill' allegations Feb '88; voted against Licensing Bill to extend hours Feb '88; his proposal of a fuller, tougher Register was rejected on the casting vote of Chairman Sir Geoffrey Johnson-Smith Mar '88; attacked John Gummer for "bishop-bashing" Mar '88; tried for emergency debate on shutdown of local brewery Mar '88; complained of sizeable VAT fraudsters being let off Apr '88; complained about company selling reading spectacles without eye tests Apr '88; accused Christopher Chope of misleading Commons over cost of valuing Richmond Terrace for DHSS new headquarters, having it valued privately for £44,000, when it could have been done by PSA for £2,000 May '88; voted against 26-week ceiling for abortions May '88; tabled 83 formal objections to the report of the District Auditor into the sale of three Westminster cemeteries for £1, which were sold on for sums reaching £5.5m, May '88; opposed raising limit for tax-free inheritance to £110,000 because inherited wealth "borders on the morally wrong" as he had argued with his wealthy parents May '88; highly praised Chief of Defence Procurement Peter Levene for having "shaken up the organisationa and given a good kick in the pants to a number of contractors who have been having it too good over the years" May '88; began intoning at Mrs Thatcher, "she's losing her grip!" May '88; his Bill to force into the open policemen who were Freemasons won 117 vote for and 16 against June '88; helped launch an investigation into lobbying June '88; voted against EC money resolution July '88; was recorded as AWOL by Whips for attending COHSE's annual conference without being paired July '88; visited Washington to discuss Congressional scrutiny of US intelligence services July '88; secured British Airways disclosures of extent they free-tripped 50-70 MPs annually July '88; in a MORI poll was rated joint 10th most popular backbencher Sep '88; voted against Defence Estimates, instead of abstaining Oct '88; asked the Government to prosecute the other MI5 officer who allegedly worked with Peter Wright to destabilize the Wilson Government Oct '88; infuriated Tory MPs on the Members' Interests Select Committee by asking lobbyists whether they were uneasy because one of their number - Sir Marcus Fox, a Director of Westminister (Communications) Ltd - was Chairman of the Commons' Committee of Selection Oct '88; waxed indignant about terms of purchase of Conservative Central Office's freehold from Conservative-controlled Westminster Council, and its subsequent sale for £2m more Nov '88; criticised DPP for not prosecuting companies for defrauding Defence over contracts for fear of their loss of overseas contracts Nov '88; urged equality for all MPs in being called to speak in Commons, instead of precedence for Privy Counsellors like the "whingeing" Edward Heath "who has never done a blind bit of good for the Labour Party" Nov '88; demanded more savings in British Army of the Rhine, where Defence had ignored "huge efficiency savings", thus losing "hundreds of millions of pounds" Nov '88; was elected by 65 votes to 49 over Merlyn Rees by PLP as Trustee to supervise £839,000 in 'Short Money' Dec '88; urged Labour appoint "a shadow Secretary of State for Environmental Protection" Dec '88; urged sacking from Health of Edwina Currie "because she's frightened the people of this country" over salmonella in eggs Dec '88; declined to support the Security Service Bill because its "absence of Parliamentary accountability is a fatal flaw" Dec '88; devised a Supplementary Vote electoral system whereby voters would vote for first and second choices; MPs who secured 50% or more would be elected but second choices of those knocked out would be redistributed Dec '88; with Nicholas Winterton, demanded more protection for investors than offered by Government's new self-regulatiory organisations (SRO) Dec '88; although an opponent of abortion, was so indignant about "procedural abuse" by Ann Widdecombe, the sponsor of an abortion-curbing Bill he had co-sponsored, that he refused to acquiesce in sabotaging other Private Members' Bills to facilitate her Bill's passage Jan '89; opposed Protection of Privacy Bill because he feared it would harm investigative journalism Jan '89; claimed Westminster Council was trying to "buy off" the district auditor investigating their cemetary scandal by awarding a £78,000 contract to Touche Ross, the firm of which he was a partner Jan '89; criticised Defence for trying to dodge PAC investigation of 'Pindar', the Thatcher-ordered massive £130m Defence Communications Centre under Westminster by splitting up its costs Jan '89; urged increase in motorway speed limit to 80 mph Feb '89; was suspended for a day by Speaker Weatherill for repeatedly demanding an inquiry into MI5's alleged blackballing of six Tory MPs as security risks Feb '89; as a "passionate supporter of the European Community", hoped it would protect a tenant farmer constituent from having his outbuildings annexed by a "feudal" neighbouring hotel-owner Feb '89; insisted "with gloomy and unctuous relish" (Colin Welch, DAILY MAIL) that MPs' researchers' passes should not "be handed round the Commons like confetti" after he discovered Pamela Bordes, SUNDAY TIMES Editor Andrew Neil's girl friend, had secured a pass from Henry Bellingham and been passed on to David Shaw; he later asked about a division bell having been authorised for her flat Feb-Mar '89; sought emergency debate to attack Transport Secretary Paul Channon for failures contributing to Lockerbie bombing Mar

'89; alleged a family link between Tory Minister Michael Howard and a former Deputy Chairman of a Lonrho subsidiary Mar '89; repeated allegations of 'phone-tapping of Harrods owners by OBSERVER owner Tiny Rowland; Rowland called him a "coward" for not repeating these allegations outside the libel-free Commons Apr '89; with other CNDers opposed Neil Kinnock's switch from unilateralism to multilateralism May '89; criticised OBSERVER Editor, Donald Trelford, for fabricating stories on behalf of its proprietor, Tiny Rowland May '89; urged the re-establishment of industries -like quartz clock movements in which he had been involved - to curb need to import them June '89; his amendment to reject an experiment to televise Commons until a satellite channel was available dedicated to its unedited coverage was defeated by 274 to 98, June '89; urged Tiny Rowland to give up the OBSERVER since he was misusing it to defend his commercial interests June '89; claimed most Labour MPs favoured electoral reform Sep '89; was rated the sixth most active intervener in other MPs' speeches Nov '89; his friend, Ann Clwyd, unsuccessfully asked Neil Kinnock to appoint him as her Deputy on Overseas Development Nov '89; claimed Government had lied to Commons over Lord Young's "sweeteners" to British Aerospace to make Rover more palatable Nov '89; asked Mrs Thatcher about involvement of Iraqi businessmen in UK's chemical, defence and communications industries Nov '89; claimed that Metropolitan Fraud Squad had leaked a copy of DTI's report into House of Fraser takeover to Tiny Rowland Nov '89; welcomed setting up of new National Nuclear Corporation to keep nuclear power in public sector Nov '89; complained that Lord Young had misled Parliament over Rover "sweeteners" Dec '89; complained that consultants had "juggled their waiting lists to do work within the private sector which they are unwilling to do in the NHS" Jan '90; raised a furore -including his suspension from Standing Committee E - when he demanded Michael Forsyth pledge not to rejoin his formerly-owned PR-lobbying firm, Michael Forsyth Associates Jan '90; was rebuked by Speaker Weatherill for complaining that MPs like Michael Grylls were being paid for referring clients to Ian Greer's lobbying firm Jan '90; reported Michael Mates MP for not having declared his consultancy with makers of flight simulators when Chairman of Defence Select Committee Jan '90; asked whether the Calcutt Inquiry would be able to investigate forgeries, among the Ulster "dirty tricks" alleged Feb '90; voted against EC agricultural funds Feb '90; as a member of the Members' Interests Select Committee, told Tory MP Peter Fry: "I have to tell you that in one year, 1985, half your Parliamentary interventions can be related directly to clients of public relations companies with which you had a direct involvement" Mar '90; was listed as a backer of SPUC Apr '90; accused Michael Mates MP, Chairman of Defence Select Committee, of being a "paid hack" of SGL Defence Ltd May '90; visited Hongkong as guest of Hongkong Government May-June '90; urged higher pay for Commons catering staff Aug '90; urged Michael Mates to resign his Chairmanship of Defence Select Committee or his consultancy with Link Miles Aug '90; visited China with local hospitality by Chinese Government Sep '90; was rated by MORI as sixth most popular backbencher Sep '90; notified National Audit Office of UK overpayment for Malaysian dam to secure arms contracts Sep '90; claimed there must have been a leak on ERM entry because the FTSE had risen by £16b in the hour and a half prior to the announcement Oct '90; said of the Gulf: "in the event...of a war being needed and required, I want to make it clear that I shall support it" Nov '90; said he "would support military conflict" in Iraq "as a position of last resort" Dec '90; admitted that Iraq war had shown that Tornadoes' low-flying exercises over Cumbria had paid off Jan '91; accused City discount house Gerard and National of having profiteered on ERM entry Jan '91; complained about seeing "ill-clad people, shuffling in the street with nowhere to go, people sleeping rough in indescribable squalor, caked in snow, lying on pavements and in shop doorways" at Euston Station Feb '91; urged stronger intervention against Iraq Feb '91; criticised the STAR for again being "inaccurate" about

Sellafield Mar '91; Michael Mates reported him for not declaring his COHSE sponsorship Apr '91; attacked Institute of Economic Affairs as a Tory front masquerading as a charity May '91; criticised for not mentioning his COHSE sponsorship (which brought him no remuneration), he claimed he did that deliberately to enable him to complain that Tories never disclosed equivalent company contributions to their constituencies Apr '91; complained that John Major had doctored HANSARD to cover a mistake May '91; submitted petition to Commons to publicise his complaints about redevelopment of Keswick Railway site Apr '91; visited Washington to lobby for international guarantees for Kurds, with help from Joseph Rowntree Reform Trust May '91; again complained about maltreatment of Kurds June '91; Speaker Weatherill, annoyed by his "mouthing things from a sedentary position [which] looked suspiciously like threats aimed in my direction", added: "the best thing that the honourable Gentleman could do would be for him to go to his constituency now" July '91; complained of slackness in prosecution of insurance fraudsman Richard Bruce July '91; complained that Bank of England had endangered councils' funds by failing to vet adequately the fraudulent BCCI bank July '91; complained that Commons Leader John MacGregor had been "nobbled" by Conservative committee chairmen, to prevent a debate on proposal that they not be allowed to have commercial interests in areas their committees investigated Sep '91; was named Deputy Spokesman on Overseas Development under his friend, Ann Clwyd Oct '91; complained that cyclone-battered Bangladesh was not receiving UK aid, although it already spent a quarter of its outside help on servicing its debt Nov '91; was rated the northeast's top Parliamentary question Nov '91; deplored shutdown of local Volvo bus plant Dec '91; visited India with local hospitality provided by its Government Jan '92; complained about Volvo's "asset-stripping" in Workington Feb '92; introduced Criminal Activity (Proscribed Equipment) Bill to han sale, possession or use of scanning receivers or skeleton keys Mar '92; visited Russia as guest of Future of Europe Trust Mar '92; was charged by John Browne as having been "out for my blood" Mar '92; retained seat with majority up from 7,019 to 10,449, a swing to Labour of 3.48%; insisted Labour lost because of Tory tabloid propaganda about Labour's "£35b mythical expenditure" Apr '92; urged tighter rules for MPs' declaration of interests, including sums received by (Tory) constituencies from businessmen June '92; was named Assistant Spokesman on Food, Agriculture and Rural Affairs July '92; insisted on asking questions about BSE ("mad cows disease"), despite beefy Tory pressure to keep quiet July '92; with some other Labour MPs, "positively supported the use of military intervention, in the form of air strikes against Serbian positions, because we believe that it is impossible to negotiate with fascism" from Aug '92; as a former "£100 entrepreneur" urged stronger ECGD support and help with overseas market research to encourage exporters Nov '92; claimed the Government had were threatening the ESA programmes, despite environmental promises to national park farmers Nov '92; asked: "will the £4,300 contribution by the Treasury to enable the Chancellor, [Norman Lamont], to evict a stripper from his home contain a VAT element?" Dec '92; urged more effective transfer of skills to overseas countries Dec '92; told Michael Heseltine Cumbria TEC would bid for a one-stop shop Dec '92; insisted that every time there was an incident at Sellafield, local MPs like himself were informed almost immediately, unlike the 1957 Windscale accident Feb '93; accused Government of having made bad errors in estimating compensation for hill livestock; urged a massive increase in lamb export to EC Feb '93; secured protest from Members' Interests Select Committee against John Gummer's failure to register the £2,000 improvement in his pond by Hillsdown Holdings, Britain's biggest meat company Feb '93; protested £17,000 paid to build unused police room at home of John Gummer Feb '93; attacked Luxembourg steel company for closing its West Cumbria plant Feb '93; protested Baghdad action against Kurds Mar '93; submitted voting modification to Plant Committee with 2nd choices of failed candidates being redistributed Mar '93; again urged air strikes against Serbians because "this cancer growing at the very heart of Europe has got to be stopped now before it spreads even further" Apr '93; with other interventionist Labour MPs, wrote to US President Clinton urging air strikes against Serbs May '93; warned that, with collapse of world wool price, farmers would stop sheering their sheep unless some wool continued to be subsidised May '93; strongly opposed destruction of the Potato Marketing Board June '93; complained that he was expected to register his constituency party's receipt of £600 from COHSE, but a Scottish Tory MP, Lord James Douglas-Hamilton, whose constituency received £10,000 from Wallace Mercer, a building developer, did not have to report it June '93; warned that unless THORP started working soon, it "would be an unmitigated disaster for my constituency", "five times that of the imminent job losses at Rosyth, and the local economy would be devastated" June '93; urged strong regulatory regime for Milk Marque, the successor to the Milk Marketing Board, since it would control 80% of production June '93; said he did not object to lobbyists as long as their operations were transparent and registered June '93; gave up his post of Assistant Spokesman on Agriculture because of deteriorating health Jan '94; deplored the closure of the accident ward at Barts, where his life had been saved Jan '94; led motion urging military intervention in Bosnia against Serb aggression Feb '94; was named to Agriculture Select Committee Mar '94; again demanded Tory MP Alan Duncan repay the "ratepayers of Westminster the £50,000 that he ripped off them" by financing the purchase of his neighbour's council house Mar '94; again attacking Serb aggression, said: "if Margaret Thatcher had been Prime Minister today, she would have sorted out this bloody...nonsense one and a half years ago; at least she demanded that fascism should be stopped in its tracks in the heart of Europe, whereas this Conservative Government have ducked the issue" Apr '94; claimed Philip Morris and Ian Greer Associates had collaborated in formulating amendments to cripple Kevin Barron's Tobacco Advertising Bill May '94; lengthily demanded that consultants should be banned from being members of the Committee of Privileges considering the sale of Parliamentary questions for £1,000 by two Tory MPs, to avoid "a stitch-up" July '94; privately warned against banning MPs' outside interests, but urged a ban on MPs being allowed to lobby for such interests July '94; blocked the naming of 17 MPs to the Privileges Committee to bar Tory MPs "with 18 directorships and 9 consultancies between them" from conducting a quick inquiry into "cash for questions" issues July '94; voted for Blair for Leader, Beckett for Deputy Leader July '94; called for a fully independent inquiry into standards following the walk-out of Labour MPs on the Privileges Committee Oct '94; accused Public Accounts Committee of "deliberately misleading the public" in claiming no commission was paid to Mark Thatcher in the Saudis' Al Yamamah arms contract Oct '94; again alleged that Michael Howard might have been improperly influenced by his Lonrho-employed relative in dealing with Mohammed al-Fayed in '87, when a DTI Minister Oct '94; described as "an outrage" the Privileges Committee's decision to conduct its "cash for questions" inquiry in private Oct '94; complained that Conservative Central Office was in breach of privilege in pressing Teresa Gorman's constituency association to de-select her Nov '94; decried Privileges Committee as "riddled with commercial interests" Dec '94; opposed Tony Benn on opening the Privileges Committee to public gaze because he had found MPs changed their minds more readily in private Dec '94; urged EU harmonisation of tobacco duty, decrying one-nation increases as encouraging smuggling Dec '94; left the Chamber rather than withdraw his charge that Lord Archer's Anglia TV share-dealings were a "criminal activity" Jan '95; staged sit-in in Members' Interest Select Committee to protest unprecedented membership of a Tory Whip, Andrew Mitchell Feb '95; in Nolan Committee testimony, also urged an "ethics registrar" responsible for investigations Feb '95; urged a national ID card scheme Feb '95; was reported to Speaker by Sir Geoffrey Johnson-Smith for gate-crashing Members' Interest Select Committee to protest its soft-peddling charges against

MP Neil Hamilton Mar '95; put down motion protesting Julian Lewis's threat to sue distributors of SCALLYWAG Mar '95; put down 12 questions on collapse of Barings Bank Mar '95; by 135 votes to 35 the Commons banned him from disrupting the Members' Interests Select Committee Apr '95; his colleague Brian Sedgemore dropped his attempt to install him as the Chairman of the new Commons Standards Committee June '95; insisted, after 25 years' experience on select committees, that they functioned better in private June '95; in debate on Nolan proposal to compel disclosure of consultancy earnings, claimed Tory MPs required these to finance their children at private schools; also attacked Sir Edward Heath for failing to disclose his full interests July '95; following SUNDAY TIMES disclosures about late Tory MP Barry Porter, urged a ban on MPs being paid to arrange meetings with Ministers Nov '95; voted with "awkward squad" against proposed Commons procedure changes Nov '95; backed appointment of Sir Gordon Downey to replace Members' Interest Select Committee Nov '95; attacked deception in purchase and shutdown of local Homepride factory by Campbell Soups multinational Nov '95; urged debate on multinationals' activities Dec '95; queried adverse impact of end of potato marketing deregulaton Jan '96; he urged a boycott of Campbell Soups; his motion attacking the multinational attracted 331 signatories, including 48 Tory MPs, only the 24th time in 48 years that a Commons majority signed an Early Day Motion Jan '96; urged opening of EU market to South Africa Feb '96; attacked DTI Minister Richard Page, his former electoral opponent, for having for 10 years provided a Commons pass to lobbyist Barry Joseph Feb '96; attacked the withdrawal of public funding of a scientist investigating BSE Mar '96; alleged 500 BSE-afflicted animals were entering the food chain every week Mar '96; opposed guillotining of revised Prevention of Terrorism Act Mar '96; claimed Agriculture Select Committee, which he had just left, had been remiss in not investigating BSE, despite his urging over 30 months June '96; described as "a joke" Home Secretary Michael Howard's claim that car crime had decreased since most people did not bother to report such crimes June '96; a National Audit report confirmed his complaint about fraud in the £1.3b TEC programme June '96; attacked MPs wanting pay increase to £43,000 as "Dickensian money-grubbers"; instead backed a 3% cap on pay rise, a £43,000 base for pensions and a cut in mileage allowances July '96; led assault on Paymaster General David Willetts, a former Tory Whip, by disclosing his letter to Tory Chief Whip Richard Ryder from Andrew Mitchell, Tory Whip and disputed member of the Members' Interests Select Committee Nov '96; asked Andrew Mitchell if, when a Whip, he had told Tory MPs how to vote on investigating Neil Hamilton's acceptance of money and gifts from al-Fayed Jan '97; alleged a "major public scandal" following a rise in share price of the Go-Ahead Group after its bid for the Regional Railways North East franchise Jan '97; the Standards and Privileges Committee agreed that Andrew Mitchell's appointment to the Members' Interests Select Committee "was a mistake which damaged the work of the Committee" Feb '97; with 97 other MPs supported the European Movement Mar '97; retained his seat with an enhanced majority of 19,656 on a notional pro-Labour swing of 11% May '97; opposed paying £16m to maintain royal palaces, insisting the royal family should do it themselves May '97; called for a new link between MPs and his union UNISON to avoid being "out of line with Nolan" June '97; was named to the Standards and Privileges Committee June '97; in his campaign to freeze out lobbyists, tabled 65 questions to every Labour Minister on how many times they or their officials had met lobbyists July '97; was named to the Intelligence and Security Select Committee Aug '97; visited Turkey to lecture on a code of conduct for Turkish Parliamentarians, paid for by the National Democratic Institute of Washington June '97; said some sort of appeal system was needed for corruption-charged MPs like Neil Hamilton Nov '97; urged a national identity card Feb '98; urged the people of Iraq be offered an alternative to the reign of Saddam Hussein Feb '98; tried to amend the anti-foxhunting Bill to allow hunting of foxes in the Lake District to protect lambs Mar '98; opposed as unjust the judicial proceedings for rape against Owen Oyston Mar '98;

Born: 23 August 1943, Swansea

Family: Son, late John Lawrence Campbell-Savours, wealthy Lloyd's Chief Surveyor of Shipping and "an engineer who worked in the nuclear industry", and wealthy, Welsh Rightwinger Cynthia Lorraine (Campbell-Jones), a pillar of the Glamorgan Society, who organised the Society for Individual Freedom dinner to celebrate Tory MP Gerald Howarth's '86 victory in BBC libel case; she purchased the Lordship of the Manor of Llangyfelach; his Thatcher-admiring mother had homes in Chelsea, Guildford and Glamorgan; "when I was a young man, I had an argument with my parents", "about whether it was right for people to inherit"; "I stand to lose a considerable inheritance from my family, as I have chosen to disinherit"; m '70 Icelander Gudrun Kristin (Runolfsdottir), whose brothers have worked on a whaling station; 3s Dylan '73, Owen '76, Marcus '81;

Education: Keswick School (direct grant); Sorbonne, Paris;

Occupation: Formerly Sponsored, by UNISON (ex-COHSE; £600 p a to constituency; 90% of election costs; no personal remuneration) '84-95; recently "a proportion of the salary of the constituency organiser is met by UNISON" '95-; ex: Community Worker '77-79; Managing Director and Technical Director of manufacturing firm he founded "making glass and tubular furniture...in the backroom of a cinema in Ramsbottom, Lancashire" '67-78; "I was once a clock manufacturer"; "I was an entrepreneur from the age of 21";

Traits: Tall; dark; sallow-skinned; wrinkled forehead; specs; hunched; gangling; wiry; cadaverous; foreign-looking ("the Nepalese Tam Dalyell"); "with dark piercing eyes, a low insistent voice, and a shock of curly silver hair blazing in the lights, he looked and sounded like the recording angel who will tick off your sins on Judgement Day" (Simon Hoggart, GUARDIAN); "dresses as though he were on the way to someone's funeral" (Andrew Rawnsley, GUARDIAN); Machiavellian (persuaded Tory MPs on the Members' Interest Select Committee to investigate charges in PARLIAMENTARY PROFILES on the pretence that Michael Grylls could be cleared); intense; "indefatigable" (John Hunt, FINANCIAL TIMES); "forthright in a schoolmasterly way, he regularly drives the Speaker to distraction with interminable points of order" (GUARDIAN); plot-happy; used to regularly intone a litany of accusations against Mrs Thatcher ("she doesn't care!", "she's losing her grip!"); half-Welsh, half-Scots; frail (had emergency operations on ulcerative colitis, injured legs '83, '84, came close to death at Barts in Dec '93); "glaucoma appears to be genetically transmitted within my family"; "with his stooped gangle and general dishevelment, he looks himself as if some ogre had recently used him to pick a big, rusty lock in his castle" (Andrew Brown, INDEPENDENT); "apotheosis of mournfulness" (Godfrey Barker, DAILY TELEGRAPH); "his spindly finger is always pointing rudely at the [Tory] Government" "like a particularly unsuitable conjuror at a children's party" (Craig Brown, TIMES); "wild, joyous, incoherent" (Colin Welch, DAILY MAIL); "clenched his fists and jumped up and down like a spoilt child refused a ride on the dodgems" (Quentin Letts, DAILY TELEGRAPH); "sanctimonious and distasteful" (Tory ex-MP John Biffen); active Christian; angler; linguist (French, Italian); good investigator (trapped the window cleaner who stole his portable telephone by having all the calls checked by BT);

Address: House of Commons, Westminster, London SW1A 0AA; The Coach House, Vicarage Hill, Keswick, Cumbria CA12 5QB;

Telephone: 0171 219 3513 (H of C); 017687 74747 (private office)/71111 (home); 0171 834 1117 (London flat);

Dennis (Andrew) CANAVAN   **Labour**   **FALKIRK WEST '83-**

Majority: 13,783 (35.9%) over SNP 4-way;
Description: Solidly working-class areas of Falkirk District ("cradle of the (Scottish) Industrial Revolution"), including most of Falkirk town and former parts of West Stirlingshire such as Denny, Dunipace, Bonnybridge and Banknock; the '95 boundary changes brought in 5,000 voters from Falkirk East;
Former Seat: West Stirlingshire '74-83;
Position: On the Select Committee on International Development '97-; Vice Chairman, all-party Hospice Group '90-; Spokesman, for Scottish Committee on Mobility for Disabled '77-; ex: on the Select Committee on Foreign Affairs '82-97; Chairman '89-97, Vice Chairman '83-89, PLP Northern Ireland Committee; Chairman: all-party Scottish Sports Parliamentary Group '87-??; Chairman '80-81, Vice Chairman '79-80, Treasurer '76-79, of Scottish Labour Group; Vice Chairman: PLP Defence Committee '87-92, PLP Foreign Affairs Committee '85-92, PLP Education Committee '83-85; Convener, of Scottish Group of PLP's Education Sub-Committee '76-87;

Outlook: The leading victim of the Blairite attempt to 'purify' the new Scottish Parliament; although tagged one of "Blair's Bastards", his hard-Left outflanking of Labour's leaders long predated Tony's advent; "a formidable tartan bruiser of the old school", "a sabre-toothed growler on Labour's awkward bench" (Robert Hardman, DAILY TELEGRAPH); "he is a man well-known for going his own way" (Donald Dewar MP); "has never risen far in the party's ranks due to an unfortunate trait of speaking his mind" (Ken Smith, Glasgow HERALD); a radical Leftwing supporter of Scottish home rule who long challenged the Tories' right to rule largely-Labour Scotland to the point of disrupting Commons and committee business; formerly "a Leftwinger favouring guerilla tactics" as "the Labour MP most committed to devolution" (Ewen MacAskill, SCOTSMAN); although a Campaign Groupie, was self-isolating because his "guerilla tactics" were tagged over-the-top by colleagues, especially Whips; also a militant supporter of a peacefully reunited Ireland; "well-known for his republican sympathies" (Peter Hetherington, GUARDIAN); as a Roman Catholic, is anti abortion and embryo experimentation and a member of the Christian Socialist Movement; pro: a united Ireland, 'Scotland United'; anti: EU, poll tax; can be reasonable on a Select Committee; was UNISON-sponsored;

History: At 11, refused to join in Coronation pageant at school '53; joined Labour Party '65; was election agent for William Baxter, Labour MP for Falkirk West Feb '74; was elected to Stirling District Council (becoming Leader of Labour Group) May '74; succeeding Baxter as candidate, was elected Oct '74; backed more defence cuts '74; was active in 'Scottish Labour Against the Market' Mar '75; objected to Civil List increase '75; supported united Ireland May '75; complained about heavy fine on unemployed youngster for potato-stealing Oct '75; backed SCOTTISH DAILY NEWS' workers co-op Oct '75; opposed anti-terrorist Bill Nov '75; moved Bill to ban corporal punishment Jan '76; was accused of calling SNP MP a "racialist swine" for having deserted Scotland to make his living in South Africa Jan '76; after helping defeat the Wilson Government's White Paper on public expenditure, he was verbally abused by Chancellor Denis Healey for opposing spending curbs (an action which lost Healey respect in the impending Prime Ministerial contest) Mar '76; menacingly confronted Tory MP Geoffrey

Rippon in Mace incident May '76; attacked the "privileged housing situation" of Princess Anne and her £700,000 Queen-bought estate June '76; visited Israel '76; urged more defence cuts July '76; tried to establish Scottish Anglers Trust July '76; urged cot deaths inquiry Sep '76; said Teddy Taylor was "paid lackey" of Globtik Tankers Mar '77; warned good Scotch whisky was being adulterated with "foreign rubbish" May '77; on the day Callaghan's son-in-law, Peter Jay, was named Ambassador to Washington, introduced Bill to make such appointments democratically accountable to Parliament June '77; persuaded British Airways to end ban on wheelchairs June '77; urged end of "denial of basic human and civil rights" in Czechoslovakia July '77; became Chairman of Scottish Council of 'Liberation' Oct '77; urged Rhodesian Minister, Duke of Montrose, be found a traitor for supporting UDI Nov '77; opposed Royal expense increase for "parasite", Princess Margaret Mar '78; served as front-runner on Scots devolution Feb '78; was barred from Commons for 24 hours for accusing Lord Thorneycroft of "stealing" £9m July '78; urged Freedom of Information Act July '78; investigated human rights in El Salvador Dec '78; campaigned fiercely for 'yes' vote on Scottish Assembly Mar '79; claimed Labour opponents of devolution were "disloyal" May '79; urged freedom for prisoner Jimmy Boyle '79; asked a question without wearing a tie July '79; investigated Hongkong, urged more democracy Sep '79; asked Queen about Blunt Nov '79; was concerned about arms sales to Chile Dec '79; urged river fishing be available to all Dec '79; was halted by coup en route to Afghanistan Jan '80; urged another referendum on EEC membership May '80; urged abolition of surviving private schools, and for most help to be given to those children most in need Sep '80; supported legal rights for Gaelic speakers Jan '81; complained about "international slave trade" in oil workers Feb '81; asked about SAS immunity for killings in Iranian Embassy Feb '81; introduced Bill to ban retention of MPs who change their party Mar '81; introduced Bill to force ex-EEC employees to disclose EEC earnings before election to Commons July '81; reproached Neil Kinnock for urging 'sensible Left' abstention against Tony Benn's bid for Deputy Leadership against Denis Healey Sep '81; asked about Mr Thatcher's intervention in North Wales housing development Oct '81; tried unsuccessfully for debate on failures in security (Blunt, Long) Nov '81; attacked "elite" controlling University Grant Committee Apr '82; introduced Bill to set up Scottish Parliament July '82; attacked Schroder Wagg for transferring its Argentine loan business to Zurich just before Falklands invasion May '82; opposed "purely military solution" to Falklands crisis May '82; opposed assisted places scheme for schools Oct '82; unsuccessfully opposed Michael Cocks for Chief Whip by 43 to 124 Oct '82; introduced People's Right to Fuel Bill Jan '83; demanded a ban on trade with Taiwan to stop counterfeits Jan '83; was involved in incidents when he visited Falklands with the Foreign Affairs Select Committee - telling the local Monsignor that Argentina had as much right to islands as Britain Feb '83; opposed expulsion of Militants Feb '83; was ordered from Commons for accusing Trade Secretary Lord Cockfield of "lining his pockets" over Anderson Strathclyde takeover bid Feb '83; as STOPP sponsor demanded end to corporal punishment Mar '83; tabled a ten-minute-rule Bill to compel MPs who changed parties after an election to stand again if they wanted to retain their seats Mar '83; introduced Bill to nationalise Anderson Strathclyde without compensation Mar '83; supported "inalienable rights of the Palestinian people" and the PLO Apr '83; backed All-Ireland Forum for peaceful reunification Apr '83; slated Michael Foot for nominating too many rejected MPs as Labour peers July '83; with four other pro-Home Rule MPs, supported campaign of Parliamentary disruption over the lack of a Tory mandate for Scotland Sep '83; left the Tribune Group for the hard-Left Campaign Group Sep '83; supported a Kinnock-Meacher ticket Sep '83; contested the NEC with CLPD, Labour Left Liaison and Campaign Group support, winning 59,000 votes Sep '83; opposed the 'witch-hunt' against Militant Sep '83; commended Maurice Bishop's "socialism" in Grenada Oct '83; on Campaign Group slate for Shadow Cabinet he was defeated with 35 votes Nov

'83; urged the Elgin Marbles be sent back to Greece Nov '83; introduced People's Right to Fuel Bill Nov '83; on the Foreign Affairs Select Committee delegation to Grenada, he was refused permission to visit jailed "Marxist" leaders Jan '84; introduced Bill to protect trade unionists in GCHQ Feb '84; opposed South African Rugby tour of UK Feb '84; had an adjournment debate on the role of Commonwealth Development Corporation in Philippines Feb '84; urged investigation into charitable status of four Rightwing pressure groups Feb '84; failed to persuade the Select Committee to condemn US invasion of Grenada Apr '84; again tried to set up a trust to administer freshwater fishing rights in Scotland Apr '84; urged a directly-elected assembly for Hongkong July '84; contested the Labour Conference Arrangements Committee, winning 1,520,000 votes Oct '84; on the Campaign Group slate for Shadow Cabinet he came nineteenth with 32 votes Oct '84; claimed that former Defence Secretary John Nott had misled the Commons on the course of the 'Belgrano' Nov '84; visited Sudan and Ethiopia with Foreign Affairs Select Committee Dec '84; urged amnesty for sacked Scottish miners Jan '85; insisted World Bank and EEC should help starving Africans Feb '85; introduced a Bill to make the Chancellor more responsible to Parliament, immediately before Nigel Lawson's Budget speech, the last MP to have that slot Mar '85; complained against Government refusal to supply documents for 'Belgrano' inquiry June '85; was re-selected from a shortlist of one July '85; put down a barrage of 73 question on dioxin poisoning from local Re-Chem plant Sep '85; fought the closure of a local foundry Sep '85; on the Campaign Group ticket for Shadow Cabinet, came 23rd with 34 votes Oct '85; introduced Bill to prevent disconnection of fuel in hardship cases Feb '86; introduced a ten-minute-rule Bill to allow part of registered objectors' taxes to go to peace fund Mar '86; introduced Bill to ban rubber and plastic bullets, defeated 184 to 85 Apr '86; voted with the Government on the Salmon Bill, opposing Home Robertson's amendment to extend the closed season Apr '86; introduced Bill to make Scottish bank notes legal tender throughout the UK July '86; on the Campaign Group slate for the Shadow Cabinet, came 16th with 36 votes Oct '86; employed guerilla tactics to oppose Scottish poll tax, including speaking from public gallery of committee room Dec '86; at Scottish Labour conference urged an unofficial Scottish Assembly with "sporadic raids" on Westminster if Labour did not win a majority Apr '87; introduced Bill to disqualify moonlighting MPs May '87; increased his majority by over 4,500 June '87; interrupted installation of Speaker to insist Labour had won the election in Scotland June '87; angered Donald Dewar and other colleagues by forcing a procedural vote on "I spy strangers!" to protest drafting in of English Tories to intervene in Scottish question time July '87; was one of four Labour MPs in Trotskyist-led anti-Apartheid demonstration on South African Embassy steps July '87; on the Campaign Group slate for the Shadow Cabinet, came 20th with 37 votes July '87; co-sponsored the hard-Left-plus-Trotskyist Chesterfield Conference Oct '87; was elected Convener of the all-party Scottish Sports Group Nov '87; supported MPs' right to allow entry to Commons for any researcher, including a former IRA sympathiser Nov '87; at special Scottish Labour conference, argued for an interim Scottish Assembly with Robin Cook's support, opposed by Donald Dewar Nov '87; voted for David Alton's abortion-curbing Bill Jan '88; Labour frontbenchers reported him to Speaker for trying to disrupt committees of which he was not a member Jan '88; defying Labour's policy, he pledged neither to register for nor pay poll tax, attacking Labour's Scottish Leader Donald Dewar for his "impotence" Feb '88; co-sponsored cross-party Bill with SNPers for a referendum on Scottish constitutional change Mar '88; backed Dave Nellist against Speaker's suspension Apr '88; opposed 26-week ceiling for abortion, favouring 18 weeks May '88; challenged Northern Ireland Secretary Tom King about extension of Ulster's shoot-to-kill policy to Gibraltar May '88; successfully moved motion in Foreign Affairs Select Committee urging a large increase in aid to poorest countries Aug '88; was fined £50 for refusing to register for poll tax Sep '88; his proposal of a mass campaign of poll-tax non-payment was rejected by David Blunkett for the NEC at Conference Oct '88; visited Eastern Europe with Select Committee Oct-Nov '88; co-launched Scottish 'Committee of 100' to fight poll tax Nov '88; blamed Labour's loss of Govan by-election to SNP on its policy of "sitting on its hands" on Scottish home rule after having won most Scottish seats Nov '88; co-sponsored Eddie Loyden's Data Protection (Amendment) Bill to include access to personal information bureaux Dec '88; voted against Government's Bill to compel loyalty oaths from Northern Ireland councillors, instead of abstaining as whipped Dec '88; blamed salmonella scare on Government's cutting scientific research Jan '89; was threatened with warrant sale of his property over refusing to pay fine for failing to register for poll tax Jan '89; appealed to SNP to join Constitutional Convention to bring pressure for a referendum on a Scottish Parliament Feb '89; became a member of Scottish Labour Action of radical home-rulers Apr '89; was devastated by death from skin cancer of his 16-year-old youngest son, Paul Apr '89; complained that Falkland islanders had been given right of abode in UK whereas Hongkong Chinese were denied similar rights; tabled an amendment to Select Committee report urging right of abode July '89; was one of 15 Labour MPs supporting non-payment of poll tax Sep '89; urged a much more sympathetic attitude toward starving Ethiopians Dec '89; at Scottish Convention argued that Scottish Parliament should claim all political power and then decide its relationship with Westminster and Brussels Jan '90; complained that quiet resignation of allegedly homosexual Scottish judge was "yet another Establishment cover-up" Jan '90; opposed "barbaric" sheriff oficers' warrant sales, admitting he had been "threatened" with one Feb '90; backed survival of MORNING STAR as helping provide "diverse editorial opinion" Feb '90; listed as a backer of Militant-led Anti-Poll Tax Federation, repeated: "I have not paid the poll tax and will not pay poll tax" Mar '90; opposed embryo research Apr '90; backed boycott of Israeli produce until its forces withdrew from occupied territories Aug '90; was teller in vote against Gulf War Sep '90; visited Gulf to try to see Saddam Hussein, with Ronnie Campbell MP and Robert Parry MP as members of 'International Peace Mission to the Gulf', organised by the Malta-based 'Peace Organisation of the People of Europe and the Mediterranean' Sep '90; at Labour Party Conference, spoke against risking hostages' lives by warlike actions in Iraq Oct '90; received 28 votes in Shadow Cabinet elections Oct '90; visited South Africa with Foreign Affairs Select Committee Oct '90; claimed Richard Needham's over-heard criticisms of Mrs Thatcher showed his "degree of expertise on diagnosis of mad cow disease" Nov '90; when Labour MP David Winnick urged military action against Saddam Hussein, he shouted, "why don't you volunteer to go to the desert?" Nov '90; urged sanctions and diplomatic pressure against Saddam Hussein rather than military action; was a teller in vote against war in Gulf Dec '90; cast anti-EC vote on Jonathan Aitken's amendment Dec '90; co-sponsored motion urging transfer of Gulf force from US command to UN Military Staff Committee Jan '91; backed Tony Benn in demanding a cease-fire in Iraq, claiming "millions of people outside this House support us!" Jan '91; successfully introduced Bill to abolish warrant sales, used to sell the property of Scots refusing to pay their poll tax Jan '91; complained about cut in Scotch whisky measure as a result of metrication proposal Jan '91; backed motion opposing bombing of civilians in Gulf Feb '91; complained Gulf war strategy was dictated by US, not UN Feb '91; opposed lifting sanctions on South Africa as yet Mar '91; deplored over-use of "lethal force" by security forces in Northern Ireland; applauded peace movement's resistance to intimidation, such as knee-capping Mar '91; was listed as still "definitely not paying" his poll tax, until Government announced it abolished Mar '91; was fastest MP in London Marathon (3hrs 28min) Apr '91; criticised Mrs Chalker for distributing mere chocolates to starving Kurdish children Apr '91; savaged validity of business plan of applicants for trust status for local Royal Scottish National Hospital May '91; opposed admission of Chilean "butcher" General Pinochet on arms-buying mission, after arms supplied to Middle East "created monsters such as Saddam Hussein, who caused the Gulf War that killed more than 100,000 people" June '91; backed cancellation of 'Gulf War Victory Parade' June '91; urged a 32-county Irish referendum on choices for constitutional change, not merely between united Ireland and United Kingdom July '91; asked whether it was legal to charge NHS patients for fertility treatments Oct '91; received 35 votes in Shadow Cabinet elections Oct '91; claimed local health board was lying about waiting times Nov '91; complained about NHS consultants giving more rapid operations privately Jan '92; complained about threatened closure of Hilda Lewis House for psychological assessment for children Feb '92; opposed Labour Government imposing Trident nuclear weapons on an unwilling Scotland Jan '92; again introduced Bill to abolish warrant sales in Scotland Mar '92; said: "I am proud to be a member of CND" Apr '92; retained seat with majority down from 13,552 to 9,812, a swing to SNP of 5.57% Apr '92; visited UDR Four in prison and campaigned for their release Apr '92; co-started resistance to Maastricht treaty Bill by backing vote for 'strangers' to withdraw May '92; became one of four Scottish Labour MPs in Scotland United to persuade the Scottish group of Labour MPs and Labour's Scottish Executive to demand a referendum on the government of Scotland June '92; sarcastically proposed Mrs Thatcher for Governor of the Falklands June '92; at Falkirk meeting of Scottish Labour MPs, urged a Parliamentary delegation of all Scottish opposition parties to demand a multi-option referendum from the PM July '92; opposed draft Euthanasia Bill July '92; received 26 votes in Shadow Cabinet elections July '92; derided payout of £60,000 to Balmoral Estate for planting: "they are always very ready to take handouts of taxpayers' money" Nov '92; sponsored motion opposing Government's paying to repair Windsor Castle Nov '92; was ousted as Vice Chairman of PLP's Defence Committee Nov '92; complained about West's differing attitudes toward Muslims in Iraq and Bosnia Jan '93; urged Government to reverse its "potentially disastrous decision" to axe the search and rescue helicopter flight from RAF Leuchars Jan '93; was tagged a top hard-Left rebel, with seven rebellions out of a possible nine against Labour Whips Feb '93; complained about local layoffs in Rosebank Distillery Feb '93; complained to Chancellor Lamont that VAT on fuel meant "many faced a choice between eating and heating" Mar '93; introduced Bill for a multi-option referendum on a Scottish Parliament Mar '93; voted against 3rd Reading for Maastricht treaty Bill May '93; John Major told him he needed "more rehearsal" after a contrived question about "headless chickens" and being "too chicken" June '93; complained to Speaker that "gerrymandered" local government boundaries might contaminate Parliamentary boundaries July '93; co-sponsored Jeremy Corbyn's Bill to give both sexes retirement pensions at 60, July '93; warned John Major that internment in Ulster would again be a recruiting ground for paramilitaries Nov '93; after Government's Railways Bill defeats there, baited John Major on whether he planned to "abolish the House of Lords" Nov '93; backed the Downing Street declaration, urging Sinn Fein to give up violence Jan '94; said of the "entanglement" (Douglas Hurd) betweeen aid for the Pergau Dam and Malaysia's purchase of arms: "the whole thing stinks" Feb '94; voted against restoring capital punishment, even for killing policemen Feb '94; voted to reduce age of homosexual consent to 18 or 16, Feb '94; raised the problems posed by the changed catchment area for St Modan's, the RC secondary school whose Mathematics Department he had headed May '94; voted for Margaret Beckett for Leader and Deputy Leader July '94; with other Campaign Groupies co-signed GUARDIAN letter attacking Criminal Justice Bill for criminalising protest and removing historic right to silence Oct '94; voted against EU Finance Bill Nov '94; had to be restrained by Deputy Chief Whip Don Dixon from lurching across the Commons floor to attack Chancellor Kenneth Clarke during the debate on imposing VAT on domestic fuel Dec '94; called for Burns Night to be made a national holiday in Scotland Jan '95; signed motion urging diplomatic relations with North Korea Mar '95; turned up for Commons vote from its gym wearing blue lycra shorts, orange T-shirt and plimsolls Mar '95; claimed Tony Blair had a "hidden agenda" to ditch all nationalisation during debate on Clause IV at Scootish Labour conference Mar '95; after revelation that the Labour Party Director of Finance was a major investor in privatised utilities and a director of a private health company, said "this is a sad reflection on so-called 'New Labour' and the type of people running it" July '95; attacked Tony Blair, saying educational policies should be based on principles of equality rather than an "attempt to justify the Leader's choice of school for his own son" Aug '95; claimed Labour conferences would soon have "flag waving and prolonged standing ovations for the Leader", like Tory conferences Aug '95; said "no Leader is infallible, and it would be an abuse of leadership to treat the membership as mindless zombies" Aug '95 backed Tony Benn's amendment scrapping Trident and cutting Defence spending to European average Dec '95; was listed in NEW STATESMAN as one of 12 Scottish Labour MP likely to leave Westminster for the new Scottish Parliament Mar '96; complained about "the stifling of democratic debate" in the Labour Party "and the autocratic manner in which policy is being made, often on the hoof", which drew from Tony Blair the joking response, "the next person who says I'm autocratic will be fired" Mar '96; voted against guillotine on revised Prevention of Terrorism Act and voted against it, claiming 27,000 had been detained, "the vast majority of whom were innocent" Apr '96; opposed new elections before the start of all-party talks in Northern Ireland Apr '96; urged more spending on Scottish further education June '96; voted for Bill Cash's European Referendum Bill June '96; despite Blairite leadership opposition to contest, became a candidate for the Shadow Cabinet, securing 42 votes, July '96; voted for a 3% cap on MPs' pay rise, a cut in MPs' mileage allowance and against basing MPs' pensions on £43,000 July '96; urged the two sides in Northern Ireland to emulate South African reconciliation July '96; responding to Blairite Kim Howells' saying the word "socialism" should be "humanely phased out", said it was "provocative and fuelled suspicions of a hidden agenda" Sep '96; was termed one of "Blair's Bastards" by Hull University researchers for having voted against the leadership 42 times since '92, Sep '96; backed Senator Mitchell's call for "the decommissioning of mindsets" in Northern Ireland Oct '96; was one of a group of Labour MPs who met a Sinn Fein delegation in Westminster Nov '96; said, "I think Tony Blair is going to be Leader of the Labour Party for many years and that that he will be the next Prime Minister; it would certainly be a big improvement on the disastrous Tory Government" Dec '96; accused Blair leadership of being "set on some sort of witch-hunt to get rid of people whom they view as dissidents" Feb '97; claimed that between 20 and 30 Labour MPs would back a continual windfall tax and that "even within the constraints of maintaining income tax rates there is still...a possibility of taxing the rich" Apr '97; retained altered seat with an enhanced majority of 13,783 on a notional swing of 4% against the SNP May '97; at first PLP meeting in Church House, urged Blair not to delay plans for a Scottish Parliament May '97; in debate on the Queen's Speech, the first in 20 years to which he gave "a general welcome", he urged "an injection of additional resources for the NHS and education, opposed both handing control of interest rates to the Bank of England and having a referendum on a Scottish Parliament, since the election result had been "the greatest mandate any government ever received for constitutional change" May '97; in debate on Referendum (Scotland and Wales) Bill insisted no meaningful parliament lacked revenue-raising powers June '97; observed the Irish General Election as the guest of the Electoral Reform Society June '97; voted to outlaw fox-hunting June '97; after 8 years was defeated in contest for Chairman of PLP's Northern Ireland Committee by Dr Norman Godman by 17 to 12, with Godman allegedly supported by Blairites and 'closet Unionists' July '97; was named to the International Development Select Committee July '97; urged "even more power" be transferred to the Scottish Parliament July '97; opposed "reactionary proposals" to "kick away the ladder of opportunity" by depriving university students of grants and forcing them to pay tuition fees July '97; announced the end of his second marriage, wishing all the best to his departing wife Brigid Aug '97; was not recognised by Speaker Boothroyd without his beard Oct '97; urged leadership pay attention to protests against lone-parent benefit cuts Nov '97; voted with 22 other rebels agains cuts in lone-parent benefits Dec '97; proposed an amendment to the Scotland Bill removing the Queen's prerogative over the appointment of a Scottish Chief Minister Feb '98; urged quarantine for pets be replaced by vaccination Feb '98; voted against military action against Iraq; secured promise from Foreign Secretary Robin Cook that Iraq would not be nuked Feb '98; urged Standing Orders for Scottish Parliament require an oath of allegiance to the Scottish people, instead of the Queen May '98; with Ian Davidson, was barred from standing for Scottish Parliament by Blairite panel June '98; voted against abolition of student grants; was accused by PM Tony Blair of allying himself with the Tory Opposition for asking why English, Welsh and Northern Ireland students should have to pay £1,000 more in tuition than others from the EU for their fourth year June '98; was one of 24 Labour rebels voting against Murdoch-style predatory newspaper pricing July '98; objected to naming Gus Macdonald Scottish Industry Minister and new life peer Aug '98;

Born: 8 August 1942, Cowdenbeath, Fife

Family: Son, Thomas Canavan, electrician, and Agnes (McCusker); m 1st '64 Elnor (Stewart); 3s: Dennis, Mark and Paul (who died of skin cancer at 16 in '89); 1d Ruth '68; m 2nd 'Brigid; separated '97; has four grandchildren;

Education: St Bride's Primary, Cowdenbeath; St Columba's High, Cowdenbeath (at 15 left as Dux [top scholar] with university entrance qualifications); Edinburgh University (BSc Hons, Dip Ed);

Occupation: Panellist: on Harris Parliamentary Panel (£1,000) '95- and Business Planning and Research International (£1,000) '95-, both "donated to Strathcarron Hospice"; formerly UNISON-sponsored: £600 annually to his constituency, 80% of election expenses) '84-95; ex: Parliamentary Adviser, to Civil Service Union '83-84; Assistant Head, of Holy Rood High School, Edinburgh '74; Head of Mathematics Department, St Modan's High School, Stirling '70-74; Teacher of Mathematics '68-70;

Traits: Short; slim; super-fit; formerly ginger-bearded; gravelly Scots brogue; "as sinister and cadaverous as an innkeeper from a story by Robert Louis Stevenson" (Craig Brown, TIMES); brainy partisan, sometimes short on tactical judgment; self-igniting cracker; invective-spraying; truculent: "star shouter" (Frank Johnson, TIMES), "swashbuckling" (John Hunt, FINANCIAL TIMES), "practitioner of the quivering upper lip" (Edward Pearce, DAILY TELEGRAPH); "Fairly Furious of Falkirk" (David Lister, INDEPENDENT); "Dennis the Menace"; top marathon runner with his personal best in '85 being 2hrs 58min; came first of five completing MPs '86, '91, '93; long-distance swimmer (200 lengths of RAC pool '92); regular runner (often trespassing on local laird's estate); ex-footballer (Scottish Universities International); hillclimber; convivial (to the point of incidents); pioneer of informal dress (a green safari suit in '84, '88; "I dress comfortably so I can get on with my work more efficiently" [DC]]);

Address: House of Commons, Westminster, London SW1A 0AA; 37 Church Walk, Denny, Stirlingshire FK6 6DF;

Telephone: 0171 219 4127 (H of C); 01786 812581; 01324 825992;

Majority: 10,439 (21.6%) over Conservative 6-way;

Description: Marginal, fickle, contradictory Suffolk port and industrial town which has often swung against the tide; was Labour's fourth most attractive marginal until '97; lost 20,000 voters to Central Suffolk in '83; lost 260 voters to Suffolk Coastal in '95;

Position: On Select Committee on Defence '97-; Joint Secretary, all-party Northern Cyprus Group '96-; ex: on European Standing Committee A '95-97; Director, Ipswich Port Authority '85-??; Ipswich Borough Councillor (Leader of Labour Group '76-91, Leader of Council '79-91) '73-92;

Outlook: The Humberside migrant ex-teacher with two profiles: a low one in the Commons - except on the Defence Select Committee -and a high one in formerly ultra-marginal Ipswich; in the Commons shows refreshing modesty about his knowledge and argues his cases factually and with restraint and humour; even his moderately frequent rebellions against Labour Whips are quietly executed; a Eurosceptic; is interested in a new role for carrier task forces; a supporter of electoral reform, particularly the German list system; after several free trips, is pro-Turkish on Northern Cyprus; his political hero was Denis Healey; he was also "an admirer of what Neil Kinnock [did] for the party"; "I'm Left on some things, Right on others", "very anti-hard-Left" (JC); has become a supporter of Blair: "Tony Blair is the toughest Leader the Labour Party has had in my lifetime; that is precisely what the party needs; Members will not agree with every decision; nevertheless he is imposing a unity on the party that is awesome; you may call it 'Stalinism'; I call it 'leadership'" {JC}; Cann was Ipswich's energetic, well-publicised "Leader of one of the best Labour Councils in the country" (Jack Straw MP) for almost a dozen years until '91 and remained a member of its Port Authority; "under his leadership, in nearly 12 years of Labour control of Ipswich Borough Council, Ipswich [was] transformed; considerable sums [were] invested in housing, sports facilities, entertainment venues, parks, environmental improvements and the town centre, and services have been improved in quality, quantity and efficiency"; "there can be few others who have retired from the leadership of a local authority after 12 successful years, at the peak of their political power" (Alistair Nicholls);

History: Joined the Labour Party '70; was elected for Valley ward to Ipswich Borough Council May '73, for Chantry Ward May '76; was elected Leader of the Labour Group on Ipswich Borough Council May '76; became Leader of Ipswich Borough Council when Labour achieved a majority on it May '79; criticised the "very poor record" for asking Parliamentary questions of the sitting Tory MP Michael Irvine Mar '89; won selection for Ipswich, defeating Don Edwards, Mary Honeyball, Andrew Mackinlay (later MP for Thurrock) and David Bull Apr '89; accused Tories of using a fraudulent poll tax prediction of £215 for Ipswich when the real figure would be £270 or so Apr '89; complained that NIIS was suffering "a death of a thousand cuts" June '89; said that "on balance" he favoured random breath-testing Sep '89; welcomed attendance of CEGB at inquiry occasioned by asbestos-related deaths exposed by Ipswich EVENING STAR Sep '89; a nation-wide poll sampling 10,000 people disclosed a 7% swing to Labour in East Anglia, which would unseat Michael Irvine MP in favour of Jamie Cann Oct '89; decried poll tax as "unjust, unrealistic and unmanageable" in putting heavy burdens on those less able to pay and removing it from those more able to pay Feb '90; complained that Government were penalising Ipswich by £5,011,000 in redistribution of business rate, because it was the only Suffolk district not controlled by Tories Apr '90; claimed that Labour's gain of two more wards in Ipswich council elections was "the great poll tax referendum" May '90; confirmed that Ipswich was in grip of recession; for the ordinary person who took out a mortgage in '88, there had been a recession for some time with the "drip, drip, drip" of unemployment figures going up; a number of Ipswich companies had managed to get through previous years of difficulty; "I hope and pray they will come tbrough the next 18 months"; but people who had been "hanging on by their fingernails" had to see early interest rate cuts Sep '90; announced he would stand down as Council leader in new year to concentrate on Parliamentary candidacy; dismissed as "beneath contempt" suggestion by his political opponent, Michael Irvine MP, that he was doing this to "distance himself" from council's problems, including £440 poll tax burden Nov '90; backed a new airport for Ipswich "but where it is will be up to the Suffolk County Council" Dec '90; said Labour would be pleased to discuss the future of the poll tax with Mr Heseltine, but only if he agreed to its abolition Dec '90; resigned as Leader of Ipswich Borough Council to dedicate himself to his Parliamentary candidacy Jan '91; claimed the Budget suggested a June election Mar '91; blamed "the collapse of such widely respected firms as Sadlers" on Tory incompetence Mar '91; criticised the Governments "all-too-small state pension increases" May '91; criticised PM John Major for having "sneaked" into Ipswich: "he should have visited local factories and offices to hear the opinions of people who have seen their colleagues made redundant and who fear for their own jobs" June '91; at a conference for East Anglian candidates, "I said that in Ipswich there were large numbers of skilled workers being made redundant" July '91; claimed that the derisory vote for the Conservatives at Walton by-election showed they were no longer a national force July '91; said unemployed cost each working person £7 a week and it was more profitable to spend this money on skill training and industrial investment Sep '91; urged Anglian Water to improve Ipswich sewers Sep '91; urged improvements on BR's line to Liverpool Street, London Sep '91; announced his support for electoral reform at meeting featuring Jeff Rooker: "in this county at the last general election, four people out of seven voted for the Tories, two for Labour and one for the Liberals - but all the Parliamentary seats went to Tories" Sep '91; announced he would not contest Ipswich Council in May, Feb '92; found a widespread feeling of economic betrayal Mar '92; opposed conversion of Ipswich Hospital to trust status Mar '92; the town bookmaker, Krullind's, offered 10-to-1 against his getting a majority of 2,500 or more but closed the book within a day because so much money poured in Apr '92; narrowly won Ipswich, ousting Conservative MP Michael Irvine by merely 265 votes Apr '92; in contest for successor to Neil Kinnock, supported John Smith as the man found to be most popular with Labour voters on the doorstep Apr '92; deplored the resignation of David Mellor as Heritage Secretary as "one of the few ministers who seemed to have any competence" Sep '92; complained of inadequacies of the Social Fund as applied to specific constituents' pressing needs Nov '92; was rated as a leading rebel against the Labour Whips, with five rebellions out of a possible nine Feb '93; visited Northern Cyprus as guest of its Turkish regime Apr '93; complained that the powers of Ipswich to function as a successful local authority had been steadily crippled by central government at high cost to local people needing cheap council housing and services Apr '93; voted against 3rd Reading for Maastricht treaty Bill May '93; when it was suggested that the MPs' visit to Northern Cyprus had been paid for by the fugitive businessman Asil Nadir - whose company owned the hotel in which the visiting MPs had stayed - said he had written to President Denktash to seek assurances that their trips were not funded by Mr Nadir; "if I do not receive that assurance, I intend footing the complete cost of the trip myself" June '93; visited Israel as guest of Labour Friends of

Israel June '93; complained that defence commitments had remained unchanged while UK's capacity to fulfill them had been sliced back, salami-style Oct '93; complained about the "thoroughly bad" non-domestic rate as "fundamentally flawed" and dangerous to local democracy Jan '94; voted against restoring capital punishment, even for killers of policemen Feb '94; voted to reduce the age of homosexual consent to 18, but not 16, Feb '94; urged a new-style carrier task force that could "put at least a brigade force ashore almost anywhere in the world and cover it" Feb '94; urged change in law to prevent houseowners who sold their properties for more than their valuation being asked for payment of back taxes Apr '94; visited North Cyprus and Turkey as guest of the Turks May-June '94; voted for Blair for Leader and Prescott for Deputy Leader July '94; urged Lady Archer to quit as Director of local Anglia TV because Lord Archer's admission of "grave error" in share purchases had "made her position on the board untenable" Aug '94; urged removal of security gates "which disfigure Downing Street" Oct '94; asked by local TV interviewer whether Clause IV, printed on the back of his Labour membership card, was close to his heart, replied: "not at all; I keep my wallet in the back pocket of my trousers" Jan '95; complained of underfunding of Suffolk police Feb '95; complained of sale of former US airbase, Bentwater, to Maharishi Foundation and its Natural Law Party partly because the departure of the Americans would leave a "deep dent in the local economy, and all the Ministry of Defence can do is hand over the base to a bunch of nutters who will use it to bounce up and down on their backsides" Feb '95; was attacked as "naive and foolish" and showing "a degree of malevolence and ignorance almost unparalleled" by Defence Minister Nicholas Soames when he again called for a review of sale of Bentwater, complaining that the Maharishi Foundation was a cult and that the university it planned would expose youngsters to indoctrination Apr '95; went on another visit to Turkish North Cyprus with six other MPs who were described as behaving "like lager-louts", despite the presence of Lady Olga Maitland, an accusation largely directed at Tory MP James Pawsey Sep '95; pointing out that 11,000 of Ipswich's 17,000 tenancies received housing benefit, attacked reliance on benefit, caused by rent rises high above pay increases Nov '95; opposed EU's imposing of recruitment of homosexuals after spending a month with the Royal Navy Feb '96; proclaimed his admiration of Tony Blair's "awesome...leadership" in imposing much-needed unity on the Labour Party Apr '96; voted against any increase in MPs' pay, in favour of a reduced MPs' mileage allowance July '96; was tagged as one of "Blair's Bastards" after Hull University research showed him voting against the Labour leadership 22 times since '92, Sep '96; failed to block privatisation of Port of Ipswich Sep '96; defended himself against Defence Secretary Michael Portillo's charge that he had "a very low profile" Apr '97; was targeted by The FIELD with 71 others for his opposition to fox-hunting Apr '97; after the prediction of "a thumping majority" in the EAST ANGLIA DAILY TIMES, retained Ipswich with a forty-fold increased majority of 10,439, on a pro-Labour swing of 10.5% May '97; with five other Labour MPs, voted to dis-assemble rather than ban target guns in a free vote June '97; was named to the Select Committee on Defence July '97; insisted: "we have no need for the RAF in Germany, but we have increased needs for a projection of air power overseas", "I hope the strategic defence review [produces] the birth of British power projection as carrier battle groups, with the capacity to put a brigade ashore and keep it going for as long as necessary"; "I am not sure that, essentially, we need Eurofighter" Apr '98;

Born: 28 June 1946, Barton on Humber

Family: His father's father was a Rhondda miner; his mother's father was a canal worker, on the canals to Leeds and York; son, of Charles Cann, initially a Rhondda miner but later a steelworks manager who "worked on Lancasters, Wellingtons and Hampdens in the second World War" (JC), and Brenda Julia (Chapman), shopkeeper; m '70 Rosemary (Lovitt) telephonist; 2s Jamie Charles Lovitt '70, Andrew John '72;

Education: Barton on Humber Church School; Barton Grammar; Kesleven College of Education (DipEd);
Occupation: Panellist, on Harris Parliamentary Panel (£1,000) '95-; ex: Director, Ipswich Port Authority '85-??; Deputy Head, Handford Road Primary School '81-92; Teacher, Handford Road Primary School '67-81 (NUT);
Traits: Dark, front-combed hair; long nose; wide mouth; strong chin; slight northern (Lincolnshire) accent; genial; convivial; outspoken; has a nice line in sardonic humour; used to play badminton, squash, snooker; now watches soccer and reads history;
Address: House of Commons, Westminster, London SW1A 0AA; 79 Woodbridge Road East Ipswich, Suffolk IP4 5QL;
Telephone: 0171 219 4171 (H of C); 01473 726670 (home); 01473 725063 (Agent John Mowles);

Ivor CAPLIN   **Labour**   **HOVE '97-**

Majority: 3,959 over Conservative 7-way;
Description: Brighton's smaller but more staid Siamese twin, with elegant Regency homes at the seafront, but seedier streets behind; has a significant Jewish minority and council estates at Portslade; until '97 it was considered a traditionally safe Conservative seat;
Position: Ex: Brighton and Hove Unitary Councillor (Deputy Leader '96-98) '96-98; Hove Borough Councillor (Leader '95-97) '91-97; Chairman, Hove Constituency Labour Party '85-91;
Outlook: A completely loyal, on-message Blairite former local Deputy Council Leader, unexpectedly catapulted into Parliament as Hove's first-ever Labour MP; is one of the three - with David Lepper and Des Turner - providing Labour with a first-ever clean sweep of the Brighton-Hove conurbation, on the back of prior victories in local government; a supporter of electoral reform; a member of the Co-operative Party, the League Against Cruel Sports and the Labour Friends of Israel; in the Campaign for Ending Animal Exports; as a (non-practicing) Jew is opposed to the campaign against religious slaughter promoted by the locally-based animal welfare group, VIVA;
History: Joined the Labour Party '79; was elected to Hove Borough Council May '91; became Leader of Hove Borough Council when Labour won the local election in May '95, giving it "a two-year opportunity to prove that Labour could deliver what it promised"; "during those two years we put in place plans to rehouse the residents of a decaying block of flats called Portland Gate"; "we also cut the price of bus passes for Hove pensioners, as we pledged we would"(IC); after selection as a candidate, considered himself "clearly the only candidate local enough to deal with the very difficult issues affecting Hove and Portslade", particularly the fact that "Brighton Health Care Trust is at breaking point"; contesting Hove against Robert Guy, the Tory replacement for Sir Tim Sainsbury, retiring after 24 years, Caplin won by 3,959, securing an almost record-breaking 16% swing to Labour, with the LibDem vote cut in half May '97; decided to combine continued Deputy Leadership of Brighton and Hove Unitary Council with being Hove's new MP May '97; said his first priority would be to see the new Health Secretary, Frank Dobson, to seek help for Brighton Health

Care Trust, which was "at breaking point" May '97; in Maiden expressed his support for a ban on export of live animals, not merely from nearby Shoreham; praised the Chancellor's decision to transfer control of interest rates to the Bank of England as having "generated confidence" in the financial services sector in which he had worked for 20 years June '97; urged a ban on EU subsidies being used to grow fibre flax on land of environmental importance June '97; co-sponsored motion urging ban on fox-hunting June '97; baited Peter Lilley on why he had left uncompensated 500,000 who had been mis-sold pensions July '97; recounted to Labour's annual conference at Brighton the secret of his success at Hove in the general election: the public-private rebuilding of decaying Portland Gate to time and to budget Oct '97; asked John Redwood: "is he happy for his constituents to be paid £2 or £2.20 an hour?" Dec '97; signed a motion warning Deputy PM John Prescott to build on "brownfield" rather than "greenfield" sites Dec '97; co-sponsored motion criticising the Canadian Government for subsidising the slaughter of 285,000 seals Mar '98; supported Government's issue of ISAs, insisting that there is no advantage in PEPs for low-income groups", with the authority of a former employee of Legal and General Mar '98; resigned as Brighton and Hove Unitary Councillor and Deputy Leader because of heavy legislative workload in the Commmons Mar '98; welcomed the investment of £11m in the Brighton West Pier Trust which, he claimed, would "generate in the region of £30m investment in the area" Apr '98; in debate on Sport deplored the sale of the grounds of Brighton and Hove Albion Football Club in Hove without any replacement by the former LibDem MP for Eastbourne, David Bellotti, which "meant that we had to play in Gillingham this year, a 150-mile round-trip for supporters" June '98;
Born: 8 November 1958, Brighton
Family: Son of late Len Caplin, accountant and a member of the Management Board of Brighton's Middle Street Synagogue, and Alma, a market researcher living in Hove; married to Maureen (Whelan); 1s 1d;
Education: King Edward's School, Witley; Brighton College of Technology;
Occupation: Ex: Sales and Marketing Quality Manager, Legal and General Assurance Society (MSF) '78-97;
Traits: Dark, receding hair; full-lipped; able speaker; an accomplished club cricketer (batsman/wicket-keeper); good footballer (scored winning goal for England in the MPs' game against Scotland); "he gets what he wants" (sporting colleague); from childhood a supporter of troubled, locally-based Brighton and Hove Albion Football Club; an animal lover (Executive Treasurer of AP - animal welfare group); enjoys music; a non-practicing Jew, is keenly aware of his background;
Address: House of Commons, Westminster, London SW1A 0AA; 31 Elder Close, Portslade, Hove BN41 2ER;
Telephone: 0171 219 3414 (H of C); 01273 292933 (constituency);

AN EXTENSION OF MPS

MPs have developed an added dimension, called researchers. Until recently only more sophisticated MPs used them. Or were used by them. One former Northwest MP, suddenly seemed fascinated with by Trans-Pacific trade, according to questions in his name. These were planted by his research assistant, an American PhD-aspirant, writing his dissertation with the help of answers provided by UK civil servants. Recently the number of questions has increased by a third, as researchers vie with lobbyists and cause groupies. One now has to distinguish between MPs' questions and those planted on them. Our monitoring does so.

Roger (Mark) CASALE   Labour   WIMBLEDON '97-

Majority: 2,990 over Conservative 8-way;
Description: The affluent southwest London seat which is the home of lawn tennis and many desirable residences rented out to tennis buffs; until '97 it was considered ultra-safe Conservative territory -their 95th safest seat - with only patches of Labour support around Haydons Road and South Wimbledon station; has recently become the site of the national headquarters of the GMB;
Position: On the Select Committee on European Legislation '97-; Co-Chairman of all-party Future of Europe Trust '97-; Chairman of the Party of European Socialists (London Association); Co-ordinator of Wimbledon Labour Party Regeneration Project; President, of the Wimbledon Council of Christians and Jews; ex: Vice Chairman and Secretary of Wimbledon Labour Party;
Outlook: A locally-active Europhile and internationalist; over-idealist, over-eager and over-loyal: self-described as "a one-stop shop" for constituents, a "local resource"; "it is, after all, possible that he is wired up to a computer himself with a microchip receiver [receiving] instructions from Millbank direct to his brain" (Simon Hoggart, GUARDIAN); an enthusiast for open government; a former special adviser to Larry [later Lord] Whitty and policy adviser to Tony Blair and John Prescott; has recovered from his surprise at capturing, so handsomely, a seat which is a by-word for suburban affluence; a Founder-Co-ordinator of European Socialist Initiative (ESI); a member of the Fabian Society, Labour Movement in Europe, Labour Finance and Industry Group;
History: He joined the Labour Party '84; was selected for "hopeless" Wimbledon which he, almost alone, did not regard as unwinnable; what surprised him was the extent of his victory when he defeated its two-term Tory MP, Dr Charles Goodson-Wickes by 2,990 votes on an exceptional 17.94% swing to Labour - the country's fifth highest May '97; backed ban on fox-hunting June '97; with Derek Wyatt, tried to start an "Unlikely Lads and Lasses Club" for over 80 new Labour MPs who succeeded despite being outside Labour's target seats; he said it would be to help such new MPs who had found entry "like going to a new school, only to find that there aren't any classes or teachers and that you have to find your own way" July '97; speaking "as a British patriot and a European", enthused about being part of a burgeoning Europe Nov '97; suggested that he would nominate the Metropolitan Police for an award Nov '97; enthused about the Government's help for the young unemployed Dec '97; backed the licensing of minicabs on which many local people depended; "I understand from the local police that many unlicensed minicabs are used by burglars to get away with their loot from the scene of the crime"Jan '98; urged PM Blair to persuade "as many employers as possible to support our New Deal programme giving young people the chance they deserve" Feb '98; welcomed the refurbishment of local railway stations Mar '98; insisted that "as in many other areas of Eurpean regulation, it is not so much the [European] Commission's policy as the enforcement of policy by member states that is the real issue at stake" Apr '98; said proudly that "those [European] Heads of State will know that our Prime Minister is committed to making the Euro a success" Apr '98; complained that his local Merton, Sutton and Wandsworth Health Authority was having to seek a bridging loan June '98; aroused widespread mirth when he told PM Blair of Wimbledon Park School, where, thanks to the

Government's New Deal for Schools, "all the children are wired up to computers" June '98;
Born: 22 May 1960, London
Family: Son, of Edward Casale, teacher at a Wimbledon school for 30 years, and Jean (Robins) occupational therapist who used to work at Kingston Hospital; m '97 Fernanda (Miucci);
Education: Hurstpierpoint College; Brasenose College, Oxford University (BA); Ludwig Maximilians University, Munich; Johns Hopkins University, Bologna Centre(MA); LSE (PhD candidate);
Occupation: Lecturer, in European Studies, Greenwich University; ex: Policy Adviser, to Tony Blair and John Prescott (GMB); previously head of a training institute in Germany;
Traits: Dark, parted, front-falling hair; full cheeks; sharp nose; dimpled chin; bored-sounding voice; multilingual (German, Italian); over-eager; "robotic", "oleaginous" (Quentin Letts, DAILY TELEGRAPH); one of the "willing greasers...ready to use their long sticky tongues in the Prime Ministerial service" (Simon Hoggart, GUARDIAN); supports Wimbledon FC; enjoys playing tennis, happily, also cooking, art and the theatre;
Address: House of Commons, Westminster, London SW1A 0AA; 17 Lingfield Road, Wimbledon SW19 4QD;
Telephone: 0171 219 4565/0789 (Fax) (H of C); 0181 540 1012; 0181 946 2462 (Fax) (constituency office);

'Bill' (William Nigel Paul) CASH   Conservative   STONE '97-

Majority: 3,818 (7.2%) over Labour 5-way;
Description: A sprawling, star-shaped seat created in '95 out of three equal remnants of the former Stafford, Mid-Staffordshire and Staffordshire-Moorlands constituencies, providing Bill Cash with a safe Conservative bolt-hole from his adversely redrawn Stafford seat; it embraces the small, Tory-voting towns of Stone, Cheadle, Eccleshall and Gnossall, many villages and the popular Midlands playground of Alton Towers;
Former Seat: Stafford '84-97
Position: On Select Committee on European Legislation '85-; Chairman: Parliamentary Friends of Bruges Group '89-, Millbank Group '94-, British
Kenya Committee '87-, Britain-East Africa Parliamentary Group (Secretary '85-88) '88-; Joint Chairman: Complementary Medicine Committee, all-party Jazz Group '91-; Vice President '92-, Secretary '88-92, Commons Cricket Team; Chairman, European Foundation (Goldsmith-funded until '96) '93-; ex: on Select Committees: on Statutory Instruments '86-91, Employment '89-90, Consolidation Bills '87-89; Chairman: Conservative MPs' European Affairs Committee '89-91, Conservative Small Business Bureau '86-89, all-party Widows and Single Parent Family Group '85-91; Vice Chairman '85-87, Secretary '84-85, Conservative MPs' Constitutional Affairs Committee; Vice Chairman '88-91, Secretary '87-88, Conservative MPs' Smaller Businesses Committee; Executive Council, Royal Commonwealth Society '84-86;
Outlook: "The most fanatical Euro-wonk of all" (Michael White, GUARDIAN); "he is the one the Establishment would most like to destroy because he not only organises but also has

the great strength of being insensitive" (Lord (John) Biffen); "I have to thank him for his assistance - without his work, we would not have done so well in the general election" (Chancellor Gordon Brown); he became the unexpected leader of the anti-federalist rebellion, putting down 240 amendments to the Maastricht Bill and voting against it 47 times; from his dugouts in 17 College Street and then from the Goldsmith-financed 'European Foundation' emerged the briefs which kept his anti-federalist colleagues going when he was not speaking himself against Maastricht; being sensitive to the threats to himself, he often abstained instead of voting against detested moves toward Euro-federalism; the formerly obscure and assiduous defender of traditional old-fashioned ethics and morality whose super-loyalty was seriously dented by Euro-federalism, which gave him "a messianic mission" (David Wastell, SUNDAY TELEGRAPH) and made him the "scourge of the federasts" (GUARDIAN); without Maastricht and Goldsmith and with his shrunken party now in Opposition and made up mostly of his sympathisers he has subsided as a news figure; not a rebel by nature, nor a chauvinist anti-European like the original anti-EEC 'irreconcilables'; until Maastricht was an RC-churchy Rightwing lawyer who had done much drafting for the Tories and was preoccupied with small businesses, simpler legislation, financial ethics and unemployment; from the famous name-tape and John Bright family, with nonconformist Quaker roots and a Catholic education; a former "watchdog for small shareholders" (FINANCIAL WEEKLY); was belatedly transformed into the de facto rebel leader by his constitutional opposition to federalism; became an unrelentingly anti-federalist speaker of almost filibustering dimensions; "a constitutional nit-picker of rat-like tenacity" (Michael White, GUARDIAN); had "an unrelenting desire to educate the party on what he sees as the 'con trick' of Maastricht" (Toby Helm, SUNDAY TELEGRAPH), together with "mind-numbing procedural expertise and mastery of the issue" (Donald Macintyre, INDEPENDENT ON SUNDAY); "the Ultimate European Deterrent" (Alan Watkins, OBSERVER); his longest speeches made the Commons "the only spot in the country that has a surplus of Cash" (ex-MP Edwina Currie); pro: alternative medicine, the EC (until Maastricht), private medicine; a leading Pro-Lifer; anti: abortion, pornography, unscrupulous moneymen, tougher sanctions on Apartheid South Africa, "social engineering", mine closures;

History: He was brought up in Sheffield, over-shadowed by its declining steel mills; was impressed by the 'One Nation' theme of Disraeli's 'Sybil'; an enthusiastic cricketer, was not active in Oxford politics - partly because of rigging of elections to the Oxford University Conservative Association - although he learned there that his father's family had been active in radical, nonconformist, Quaker politics for 100 years; joined the Conservative Party, becoming a temporary agent in Harrow '64; on the Forum and Literature Committee of the Primrose League, told Julian Critchley that the League was necessary to buttress the constitution and religious morality in relation to the law Sep '69; "I was a founder-member of 'Westminster in Europe'", voted to stay in EEC June '75; was legal adviser to acupuncturists when a Bill tried to drive them out of business '75; was legal adviser to the Cardiff Ship Repairers fighting the Aircraft and Shipbuilding Industries Bill '76; became Secretary of the Bow Group Home Affairs Committee '77; was an adviser in drafting Tories' trade union, small business legislation and the Child Pornography Bill '78-80; at Conservative conference attacked proportional representation as a Trojan Horse for the Alliance which Tories had to fight fiercely Oct '83; after 15 previous selection failures, partly due to his Catholicism, was selected to contest Stafford by-election caused by death of Sir Hugh Fraser, also RC Apr '84; won his first contest, with a heavily depressed majority - over 10,000 down from 14,277 - because of dairy farmers' complaints May '84; in Maiden condemned the lack of a national NUM ballot and intimidation by the NUM June '84; maintained that PR was a prescription for confused policies, horse-trading and increased power for the marginal few July '84; walked on to

Stoke-on-Trent miners' rally platform to demand that Arthur Scargill repudiate violence and intimidation Sep '84; addressed the Pro-Life meeting in Leamington, proposing a 2m-name petition Sep '84; welcomed the sequestration of the miners' assets and urged these be used to pay for policing the intimidatory and unlawful mass picketing Oct '84; urged tax cuts, greater work force mobility and radical review of business legislation Nov '84; was critical of Warnock Report's toleration of experiments with human embryos Nov '84; drew attention to AIDS and attacked sexual promiscuity Dec '84; formed Davy Group to co-ordinate Tory backbench action on miners' strike '84; co-sponsored and drafted Small Business Bill Jan '85; opposed fluoridation Jan '85; sponsored motion condemning the proposed implantation of human embryos into animals Feb '85; supported and served on committee of Enoch Powell's Unborn Children (Protection) Bill Feb '85; urged greater help for small businesses by reducing the impact of VAT Feb '85; in an article in TABLET warned that the dangers of human genetic engineering were "as important as the bomb" Mar '85; obtained independent inquiry into Stafford's outbreak of Legionnaires' Disease May '85; co-urged a Select Committee to investigate human embryo research and genetic engineering, despite opposition from Pro-Life group to which he was sympathetic July '85; on the Anglo-Irish Agreement, urged all to avoid "the language of hate and mistrust and to remember that people and children mean more than pieces of paper or political power" Nov '85; co-operated with Richard Shepherd in his battle to end Crown Immunity for hospital and prison kitchens Feb '86; warned that BT might be liable to prosecution for transmitting soft porn in its phone-ins Feb '86; lengthily resisted Eddie Loyden's Bill to abolish the right to surcharge and disqualify councillors operating outside the law Feb '86; sought to strengthen Winston Churchill's Obscene Publications Bill by specifying that human sexual activity, genital organs, urination and excretion could not be shown on TV Feb '86; said the Leftwing councillors in Lambeth and Liverpool deserved what they were getting in surcharges and disqualification for their willful misconduct Mar '86; warned against the Government allowing Harland and Wolff to win a naval contract with hidden subsidies Mar '86; supporting the European Community (Amendment) Bill, claimed Britain would be able to make great use of the opportunities the EEC offered if it used the mechanisms effectively Apr '86; again urged a Public Order Bill to reinstate the power of dispersal originally in the Riot Act of 1714 repealed by Roy Jenkins in '76, May '86; proposed amendments to Banking Bill to prevent the foreign takeovers of British banks '86; co-urged pharmaceutical companies be allowed to use their patents without generic competition for a further four years June '86; warned that, unless modified, the European Community (Amendment) Bill - which became the Single European Act - would have a vital impact on British commercial and industrial practices; tabled an amendment saying that nothing in the Act should derogate from the sovereignty of Parliament June '86; with the backing of 150 MPs, defended alternative medicine against a hostile report by the BMA May '86; supported the right of parents to withdraw children from sex education Oct '86; tabled an amendment to the Education Bill requiring local authorities to give all children seven and over every opportunity to play competitive games Oct '86; voted for Kenneth Hind's anti-abortion Unborn Children (Protection) Bill Oct '86; co-deplored the spread of Labour's "bully-boy tactics" to Parliament Dec '86; urged that only qualified practitioners of complementary medicine be allowed to practice Feb '87; introduced Protection of Shareholders Bill to establish a shareholders' committee for all public companies Feb '87; stopped Tam Dalyell from attacking the Prime Minister by calling "I spy strangers!" Feb '87; attacked Tam Dalyell as "a bounder and a cad" for alleging Airey Neave tried to destabilise the Wilson Government May '87; defended Lord Young's decision to allow Rupert Murdoch to buy TODAY without reference to the MMC July '87; defended the right of a Minister to send British Blowpipe missiles to Afghanistan July '87; backed Mrs Thatcher's resistance to pressure for more comprehensive sanctions on South Africa Oct '87; secured 150 signatures to motion banning use of human genes in animals Nov '87; introduced Right of Privacy Bill to make infringements of privacy by journalists acceptable only if their revelations were of public benefit; it had backing of 307 MPs Jan '88; urged 10-year limit on embryo experimentation Feb '88; warned of pitfalls in Bill against poison-pen letters Feb '88; complained of death of young constituent while awaiting "hole in heart" operation Feb '88; loyally pretended that a Tory Health Minister in 1944 was the parent of the NHS, rather than Aneurin Bevan in 1947-48, July '88; warned that "if there are benefits to be derived" from genetic engineering "they must be weighed most seriously against the incredible dangers" Dec '88; co-sponsored John Browne's Protection of Privacy Bill - based on his own previous Right of Privacy Bill - "to ensure that people have direct personal rights that they can sustain" Jan '89; told Tony Benn the Tories were on the point of splitting over EC federalism, which would realign politics in a way comparable to the alliance of his ancestor John Bright and Disraeli at the time of the 1867 Reform Bill Mar '89; was added to Employment Select Committee in place of Andrew Rowe, dropping from Consolidation Committee May '89; was elected Chairman of Parliamentary Friends of Bruges Group as smaller clone of Bruges Group headed by Lord Harris of High Cross; John Redwood was a co-founder May '89; continued in office as a Vice Chairman of Conservative Small Business Bureau May '89; introduced European Community (Reaffirmation and Limits of Competence) Bill to set EC's limits June '89; acclaimed PM Thatcher's "so far and no further" posture at Madrid EC summit June '89; warned against school teaching of sex or use of computers if in violation of parents' "deeply-held religious conviction" July '89; complained there was "no limit to the number of people who can come in or to the benefits that they can seek" under the "open-ended" Single European Act July '89; took Parliamentary Cricket Team to Barbados Aug '89; urged a reduction in rates of new Uniform Business Rate Oct '89; visited Kenya as Chairman of the East Africa Committee and Joint Chairman of the British Kenya Committee, at the invitation of the Kenyan Government Oct '89; rejected the need "to bind Germany into a federal Europe" Nov '89; replaced Europhile Ian Taylor as Chairman of the Conservative MPs' European Affairs Committee Nov '89; urged harsher punishment for drunken hooligans who attack the police Dec '89; visited Uganda at the invitation of the Ugandan Government, as Chairman of the East African Committee Jan '90; backed principle of Unified Business Rate Jan '90; was offered post of PPS to Foreign Office Minister Lord Caithness but turned it down to retain his freedom Feb '90; voted against punishing Tory MP John Browne for concealing his interests Mar '90; left Employment Select Committee, being replaced by Emma Nicholson Mar '90; after a Cabinet battle, supported Chancellor Major's compromise proposal of an ecu-based alternative to a single currency June '90; published his Bow Group pamphlet, 'A Democratic Way to European Unity: Arguments Against Federalism' June '90; pointed out, "60% of our trade deficit in 1989 was with the European Community" June '90; as a former member of the Select Committee on Employment accepted Rolls-Royce sackings as the "inevitable consequence of defence requirements" July '90; after ERM entry said, "we must draw a firm red line beneath this decision, making it clear that it doesn't constitute any sort of move towards Delors-style economic or political union" Oct '90; urged Chancellor Major to repudiate the suggestion that UK monetary policy would be made in Berlin Oct '90; after Mrs Thatcher's farewell speech said he was tempted to say "in the name of God, stay" Nov '90; was re-elected Chairman of the Conservative MPs' Foreign Affairs Committee over pro-EC challenger, Raymond Whitney, with 63% backing Dec '90; visited Turkey as guest of its government Apr '91; lodged a motion backed by 130 MPs condemning a single European currency at any stage June '91; was criticised for being too hostile to John Major in attacking him for being too "frightened" to veto an EMU treaty June '91; criticised by Chief Whip Richard Ryder for Bruges Group's letter attacking PM Major, Cash pointed out he was not a member of the extreme Bruges Group but of its clone, the Parliamentary Friends of the Bruges Group June '91; the Government tried to isolate him as Chairman of the Tory MPs' European Affairs Committee by Chancellor Lamont's telling committee that UK might proceed with other aspects of Economic and Monetary Union apart from a single European currency June '91; insisted there was no reason for amalgamating the Staffordshire regiment with the Cheshires Oct '91; backed Jonathan Aitken's amendment urging a referendum on Maastricht Nov '91; was ousted as Chairman of Conservative MPs' Foreign Affairs Committee by Majorite loyalist, Sir Norman Fowler, despite being backed by the '92 Group' Nov '91; SPECTATOR named him its 'Campaigner of the Year' for his anti-Maastricht activities Nov '91; his book, Against A Federal Europe, warned against German-dominated centralisation Nov '91; with eight others (including Margaret Thatcher), abstained at end of two-day Maastricht debate, with seven others (including Norman Tebbit) voting against; the Government had an 86 majority Dec '91; voted against talking out Referendum Bill on Maastricht Feb '92; retained seat with majority down from 13,707 to 10,900, a swing to Labour of 6.28% Apr '92; spoke and voted against 2nd Reading of Maastricht Bill as dragging us "into a federal Europe" May '92; with 17 other Tory MPs, plotted anti-Maastricht scenario at Carlton Club May '92; visited Canada, as guest of Air Canada May '92; opposed re-naming of federalist Jacques Delors as President of European Commission June '92; backed "fresh start" motion urging Maastricht delay, after Danish Referendum June '92; was renamed to Select Committee on European Legislation June '92; lost his place as Secretary of Commons Cricket Team to Labour MP Graham Allen, being named Vice President instead June '92; Sir Peter Hordern became Chairman of Conservervative MPs' European Affairs Committee, Cash thinking it "incongruous" to stand June '92; welcoming UK's ejection from ERM, abstained with seven others from supporting Government motion Sep '92; opposed draft Euthanasia Bill Sep '92; his constituency chairman said he had the backing of his association and 80% of constituents Oct '92; deplored pits shutdown affecting miners in nearby Trentham colliery, "many of whom live in my constituency" as "a callous reminder of the way in which people can be thrown out of work when imports of coal are pouring in from elsewhere in the world" Oct '92; after voting against Government on Maastricht paving debate, said he might have backed Government, had he been told 3rd Reading would be delayed until second Danish referendum Nov '92; having put down 240 amendments to Maastricht in his own name, made a 142-minute speech against Maastricht Bill Dec '92; claimed the concesssion offered to Denmark at Edinburgh summit were disingenuous and legally flawed Dec '92; said he would either vote against Government on pit closures or abstain; he abstained Dec '92; backed Osteopaths Bill as a legal adviser to complementary and alternative medical groups for "nearly 20 years" Jan '93; said Government was "in bigger trouble than before" over pit closures Jan '93; attended pro-referendum rally with Sir Teddy Taylor and Tony Benn Jan '93; was one of four Tory MPs to vote with Opposition against mine closures; said coal industry faced "unmitigated disaster"; asked if Trentham pit would have access to all coal purchasers, if privatised Mar '93; went on cricket trip to Antigua Mar '93; helped defeat Government 314-292 on Labour's amendment to Maastricht on the composition of an EC committee of the regions Mar '93; backed Ann Winterton's anti-abortion motion Apr '93; voted against 3rd Reading of Maastricht treaty Bill May '93; in rebellion-scoring, was tied with Nicholas Winterton as the leading Maastricht rebel, with 47 rebellious votes, 13 abstentions and two votes for the Government May '93; said the Edinburgh concessions to Denmark were meaningless since Maastricht treaty could not be changed May '93; tabled new clause 22, thought to block Labour's Amendment Two May '93; set up the European Foundation, one-third financed by Sir James Goldsmith '93; threatened to go to court to stop UK signing Maastricht treaty, at cost of £250,000 May '93; expressed concern about the new European

Parliamentary constituencies June '93; with two threatened pits in next constituency, was one of six Tory MPs who voted against Government on pit closures July '93; voted against Government amendments on Maastricht July '93; voted with Opposition in favour of Social Protocol to Maastricht July '93; was backed by Lord Alistair McAlpine as the best alternative to John Major as Prime Minister July '93; Young Conservatives who had invited him to Conference-fringe meeting were warned by Central Ofice that normal help with expenses would be withdrawn Sep '93; an attempt was made to destabilise him by publicising his Personal Assistant, ex-model Louise Hobkinson; his wife: "just because she is beautiful and has got long legs, I don't think that she should be thought of as any different from anyone who has worked for him before" Sep-Oct '93; voted with Opposition against Government's pit closures Oct '93; voted to restore capital punishment, especially for killing policemen Feb '94; voted against reducing age of homosexual consent below 21, Feb '94; voted against 2nd Reading for Kevin Barron's Tobacco Advertising Bill Feb '94; disappointed his enemies by winning an appeal against Boundary Commission, which gave him a safer seat at Stafford and the choice of another safe seat at Stone Mar '94; opposed dilution of Britain's right of veto in EC because it would "reduce the House of Commons to a cipher" Mar '94; claimed that in 1977 the Labour Government had sabotaged the Protection of Children Bill "which I took part in preparing" by going "to considerable lengths to table sheets of amendments to destroy the Bill" May '94; urged John Major to "ensure that we do not have a federalist as President of the Commission" and that "we do not have the Germans and French running the European Community" June '94; opposed the European Union (Accessions) Bill because it would deepen the Union as well as widen it July '94; after the EU's Court of Auditors' report exposing massive EU waste and fraud, questioned "the extent to which the British taxpayer should continue to pour money into this bottomless, fraudulent pit" Nov '94; extracted concession from the Government that the Public Accounts Committee would, in future, monitor the spending of EU funds in Britain Nov '94; his constituency chairman, Desmond Twigg, warned him off rebelling over British contributions to the EU Budget, saying "an election would be suicide for us and might also be suicide for him; he is a fine constituency MP [but] he is playing with fire" Nov '94; Cash avoided being among the eight rebels who lost the Whip after voting against the Government on the EU Budget, allegedly to keep open his hopes of moving to a safer seat following the adverse redrawing of his Stafford constituency Nov '94; highlighted the threats to rural life in the decline of shops, police stations and police stations and the threat of criminal elements linked to car-boot sales Dec '94; signed Sir Teddy Taylor's amendment calling for withdrawal from the Common Fisheries Policy Jan '95; abstained in vote on Commmon Fisheries Policy Jan '95; voted for LibDems' motion for a Referendum on Europe Feb '95; after Charles Wardle's resignation as Immigration Minister, claimed British exemption from the EU's open frontiers legislation was "not worth the paper it was written on" Feb '95; signed motion congratulating John Major for ruling out the Euro in '97, Feb '95; dubbed Euro-federalist MPs "federasts" Feb '95; urged resignation of Chancellor Clarke over his support for EMU Feb '95; proposed Bill to keep sovereignty of UK Parliament within EU Feb '95; abstained in vote on Government's European policies Mar '95; signed motion opposing talks with Sinn Fein until "huge progress" was made on decommissioning IRA arms Mar '95; wrote to Chief Whip Richard Ryder requesting a vote to preserve EU border controls Mar '95; was reported to be having a "tough fight" (GUARDIAN) with his Tory neighbour, Michael Fabricant, about safe Tory seats after boundary changes Apr '95; was accused by PM John Major of having "always misrepresented what I achieved at Maastricht"; Major also accused him of "claptrap" and, in the Commons, of "talking through the back of his head" June '95; backed enthusiastically and voted openly for John Redwood to replace John Major as Tory Leader July '95; was called on to withdraw from race for new Tory-safe constituency of Stone to avoid a battle over Europe by Europhile Tory MP Sir David Knox, who then stood down Sep '95; opposed large wage increases for charity bosses Oct '95; won libel action against DAILY MIRROR over allegations his campaign for a Maastricht referendum was funded by a Kuwaiti businessman Oct '95; claimed the European Court's 15 judges had a "gargantuan appetite for more power" Oct '95; was selected for the new Tory-safe seat of Stone Nov '95; claimed EU fraud was 15 times that admitted by its Court of Auditors Nov '95; urged PM John Major to veto the Spanish Foreign Minister's nomination as NATO Secretary General because of previous opposition to NATO and nuclear deterrence Dec '95; voted against Government on Common Fisheries Policy, helping to defeat it Dec '95; his pamphlet, 'Are We Really Winning on Europe?' urged ban on Euro during next Parliament Dec '95; local activists threatened not to campaign for him because of his disloyalty to John Major Jan '96; claimed his two-year-old European Foundation was distributed to 6,000 subscribers, including 150 MPs Jan '96; in pamphlet co-authored with Iain Duncan-Smith warned of a return to fascism in Europe if Chancellor Kohl's quest for a federal superstate was not defeated Feb '96; answered the Government's White Paper on Europe by calling for Maastricht's renegotiation Mar '96; voted for Iain Duncan-Smith's Bill to curb the European Court's jurisdiction Apr '96; claimed EU ban on British beef was illegal May '96; his Referendum Bill, urging Maastricht renegotiation, was backed by 95 MPs, including 74 Tories June '96; Europhile Tory MP Quentin Davies asked how he "could reconcile being a loyal [Tory] MP with receiving political funding from the head of a rival political party", the Referendum Party; Sir Edward Heath attacked as "abominable" his acceptance of funding for his European Foundation from "a French MEP living in Mexico"; under pressure from Downing Street as well, announced he would no longer accept money from Sir James Goldsmith; Baroness Thatcher thereupon made a contribution to the European Foundation as "vital both to the Conservative Party and to the country" June '96; described David Heathcoat-Amory as having "immense integrity and terrific guts" after his resignation as Paymaster-General over the single European currency July '96; voted against a lower MPs' mileage allowance and in favour of MPs' pensions at £43,000 July '96; told a packed conference-fringe meeting of his European Foundation, "we are heading for one country - a German Europe" Oct '96; won libel action over bribe allegations in the SCOTSMAN Oct '96; attended Dublin conference as guest of the European Movement Oct '96; accused Agriculture Minister Douglas Hogg of "weasel words" over ending the EU's beef ban Nov '96; abstained on Government's European policy Nov '96; attacking monetary union as a "disaster area", welcomed Michael Howard's hostile stance in Cabinet Dec '96; attacked as "disgraceful" that EU funds would support Jacques Delors' new "propaganda machine" 'Fondation Notre Europe' Dec '96; cited Sheffield University research showing 60% of Tory MPs were anti-Maastricht Jan '97; attacked Europhile Sir Edward Heath as a "totally divisive force within the party and a source of damaging disunity" Feb '97; voted for dis-assembling target guns, rather than banning them Feb '97; was re-elected for drastically altered and renamed Stone seat with a shrunken majority of 3,818, on a notional anti-Tory swing of 10% May '97; in debate on Queen's Speech, claimed the new Labour Government could not deliver on health, education and welfare because they "have adopted exactly th same policies as are embedded in the Maastricht Treaty" May '97; fuelled speculation that he might stand as a candidate in the Tory Leadership election to push a more Eurosceptic policy May '97; backed Redwood, then Hague in the Leadership ballots June '97; claimed most Germans opposed a single European currency; urged the Labour Government to veto the Amsterdam Treaty in its entirety at the coming Intergovernmental Conference June '97; put down an undebated amendment to preclude Scotland's MPs from voting on matters pertaining only to England, accusing the Labour Government of a "Stalinist dictatorship" in guillotining the Bill June '97;

demanded more resources for Staffordshire July '97; was thanked by the Europhile Chancellor, Gordon Brown, for facilitating Labour's victory in the general election Apr '98; recalling his vote against pit closures, backed Labour's mines review and called attention to the £5b German subsidies for their mines June '98;

Born: 10 May 1940, London

Family: "My great-great-grandfather founded the London and Brighton Railway in 1830"; the National Provident Institution and "the Abbey National Building Society [were] founded by my great-grandfather, William Cash, and his cousin, John Bright"; son. of Paul Cash MC (killed in action near Caen '44), and Moyra Roberts (Morrison); m '65 blonde, attractive Bridget/"Biddy" (Lee), whom he met while at Oxford; 2s William, Los Angeles novelist '67, Sam '72, 1d Letitia, artist '74;

Education: St Mary's Hall (RC); Stonyhurst College (RC; "I was taught extremely well in a very disciplined atmosphere"); Lincoln College, Oxford University (History);

Occupation: Solicitor '67-, William Cash and Co (private practice and administrative law) '79-, Consultant, to Radcliffe Crossman Block (£5-10,000) '86-; Adviser: Council for Complementary and Alternative Medicine '85-, Society of Company and Commercial Accountants Ltd '85-, National Market Traders' Federation '91-; Founder: European Foundation (which provides research and organisational assistance) '93-, and Editor, EUROPEAN JOURNAL '93-; Owner, land and property at Upton Cressett, Shropshire; lives in "beautiful medieval-cum-Tudor house, Upton Cressett Hall, resurrected from dereliction by Bill Cash MP, and his wife" (SUNDAY TIMES); in '87 he bought a house in Stafford for £8,000; Author: Visions of Europe (1993), Euope, The Crunch (1993), Against a Federal Europe (1991); ex: Partner, Dyson Bell and Company '71-79; Director, Community Task Force '78-88; Adviser: to British Foundry Association '86-91, Institute of Legal Executives '75-93, Politics International '91-94, Public Policy Consultants '86-89, Ogilvy and Mather Ltd '86-89, Campaign for Independent Financial Advice '87-89, MacLean Hunter Cablevision Ltd '89-90, Staffordshire Cable Ltd '89-90, Library Association '76-86 ("for well over 10 years I have been legal adviser to the Library Association"); in his Sheffield school days "I used to deliver post in the slum area of Attercliffe during Christmas holidays";

Traits: "Immensely tall (6' 4") and equally earnest" (David McKie GUARDIAN); grey-haired; specs; "Woosterish traditional jazz-lover...wrapped in a quite extraordinary pin-striped suit of which Jeeves would not have approved...a Roman Catholic, in many respects a rather European type of intellectual...can be pompous" (John Torode, INDEPENDENT); "patrician" (INDEPENDENT); "the Prince of Bores on the subject of Europe and admits that at the mere rumour of his approach colleagues dive into the nearest cupboard" (Graham Turner, SUNDAY TELEGRAPH); a "village cricketer of wiry frame and seriously unexciting expression, worthy and earnest and nature's captain of the Lloyds Bank XI v the Diocese of Southwell" (Godfrey Barker, DAILY TELEGRAPH); musical; has "relentless charm"; "humourless" (ex-MP Emma Nicholson); although his deceased war-hero father came from a Quaker family, "I was brought up a Catholic by my mother"; "I was brought up with the understanding that we were definitely not part of the Establishment; at school I became aware of all the Catholic martyrs and I've always known that Quakers, Catholics and Jews must stick together" (WC); cricketer (ran Lords and Commons cricket team '88-92; fast-medium pacer for Commons, Oxford Authentics and Free Foresters and Staffordshire Cricket Club); tennis player (played for Parliament against US Senators '86); gardener; served as a shirt model for brochure of Charles Tyrwhitt, a mail-order shirt company in '93; his opponents tried to create mischief in '93 by playing up the youthful beauty of his Personal Assistant, leggy ex-model Louise Hobkinson;

Address: House of Commons, Westminster, London SW1A 0AA; 37 St George's Square,

London SW1; Upton Cressett Hall, Bridgnorth, Shropshire; 43 Castle Street, Stafford;
Telephone: 0171 219 3431 (H of C);

Martin CATON   **Labour**   **GOWER '97-**

Majority: 13,007 over Conservative 6-way;
Description: "It snuggles around the southwest and
north of Dylan Thomas's 'ugly, lovely town of
Swansea'" (MC); it is a mixture of the seaside holiday
resort and affluent homes for Swansea commuters on
the Gower peninsula and its industrial working class
hinterland of Gorseinon, Pontardulais and Clydach;
Position: On Select Committees: on Welsh Affairs
'97-, Swansea Unitary Authority Councillor '95-; on
Welsh Labour Party Executive '95-; ex: Swansea City
Councillor '88-95;
Outlook: A pleasant, articulate, original-minded
Swansea councillor from "away", into whose lap a
safe Welsh seat has fallen after a rapid rise within
Welsh Labour ranks; was one of the tiny minority of 14 new Labour MPs who rebelled against
cuts in lone-parent benefits in Dec '97; before his election, served loyally as a Labour Agent in
local and Parliamentary elections; another example of Welsh Labour's willingness to select
non-Welsh-born MPs, like Hain, Hanson, Ainger, Marek, Lawrence and Alan Howarth; a
member of the Socialist Environmental Resources Association (SERA), Socialist Health
Association;
History: Joined the Labour Party at 24, '75; became Political Assistant to David Morris,
MEP for South Wales West June '84; was elected to Swansea City Council May '88; was
elected to Swansea Unitary Council May '95; on the announced retirement of Gareth Wardell,
was selected for Gower '96; raised the scare of possible VAT on food if the Tories returned to
power Apr '97; claimed the Conservatives had "insulted" Gorseinon by putting up a "Britain is
Booming" poster only yards from nine empty shops and three charity shops in a run-down part
of town Apr '97 was elected with a majority of 13,007, a swing of 7.5% May '97; his Maiden
speech was widely appreciated because he managed to mention and pronounce correctly
almost every village; this was considered very clever for a non-Welshman June '97; complained
about Welsh Development Agency's favouring the southeast of Wales at the expense of the
southwest June '97; expressed solidarity with jailed Indonesian union leader June '97;
complained that the Development Board for Rural Wales had only served mid-Wales, not his
patch July '97; was named to the Select Committee on Welsh Affairs July '97; pointed out that
only 6 of the 34 Welsh Labour MPs were unenthusiastic about a Welsh Assembly July '97; told
PM Blair that the "evidence of already deprived and disadvantaged children being
accommodated in children's homes and then physically and sexually abused shames our whole
society" Nov '97; rejected the argument that the close vote for a Welsh National Assembly
undermined its validity since it was on "an old register in a poll held at the end of a summer
[and which] was far higher than is achieved in local government or European elections" Dec
'97; voted against benefit cuts for single parents, one of only 14 new MPs Dec '97; wittily
urged an end of the "all-consuming" "monogamous love affair with the motor car to help us
become a nation of happy transport polygamists" Jan '98; led motion congratulating CND on
its 40 years battle "to remove the deadly threat of nuclear weapons" Jan '98; supported the

'Barnett Formula' allocation of Wales' share of Government expenditure, while sympathising with Plaid Cymru's effort to update and increase the share Feb '98; backed "sustainable development" while admitting people were entitled to ask, "are there theories at the bottom of your jargon?" Feb '98; urged a rural remit for the Welsh Development Agency to carry on throughout Wales the excellent work of the former Development Board for Rural Wales Feb '98;

Born: 15 June 1951, Bishops Stortford

Family: Son, of John Caton, grocer, and 'Jim'/Pauline (Gardner); married to Bethan (Evans); 2 stepchildren;

Education: Newport Grammar School, Essex; Norfolk School of Agriculture; Aberystwyth College of Further Education (HNC in Applied Biology);

Occupation: Political Assistant, to David Morris MEP for South Wales West '84-97; previously Scientific Officer, at Welsh Plant Breeding Station, Aberystwyth '74-84;

Traits: Brown, parted hair and beard; specs; loud voice; witty (in his Maiden disclosed his constituents were tagged "Jerks" because they were halfway between Llanelli (called "Turks") and Swansea (nicknamed "Jacks");

Address: House of Commons, Westminster, London SW1A 0AA; 26 Pontardulais Road, Gorseinon, Swansea SA4 4FE;

Telephone: 0171 219 5111 (H of C); 01792 892100 (constituency);

Ian (Arthur) CAWSEY   **Labour**   **BRIGG & GOOLE '97-**

Majority: 6,389 over Conservative 4-way;

Description: The north Lincolnshire market town of Brigg now linked with the larger, more pro-Labour port town of Goole, set amidst pro-Tory flatlands; as the home of John and Charles Wesley, was the birth-place of Methodism; until May '97 it was seen as a Tory marginal;

Position: Chairman, PLP Home Affairs Committee '97-; North Lincolnshire Unitary Authority Councillor (its Leader '95-97) '95-; ex: Humberside County Councillor (Chairman, Humberside Police Authority '93-96) '89-96; Director, Humberside International Airport;

Outlook: One of the "cheeky chappie" (Tory MP Edward Garnier) new interjectors; a Blairite locally-rooted council leader who captured a new seat largely overlapping with his municipal domain; his rise has been helped by his prominence as chairman of the local police authority and his work for neighbouring Scunthorpe MP, Elliot Morley; a former long-time IT-man;

History: He joined the Labour Party '77; contested Grimsby council seats in May '83, May '84, May '85; moved to Scunthorpe, becoming Personal Assistant to its new Labour MP, Elliot Morley June '87; was elected for Ashby ward in Scunthorpe to Humberside County Council May '89; contested Conservative-held Brigg and Cleethorpe against Michael Brown, registering a 5.8% swing to Labour, recovering 2nd place from the LibDems Apr '92; was elected Chairman of Humberside Police Authority May '93; was elected Leader of the North Lincolnshire Shadow Unitary Authority May '95; was selected for new Brigg and Goole, overlapping his previously-fought seat Apr '95; protested against the closure of local Binns, a

House of Fraser department store Jan '97; defeated his Tory opponent, Donald Stewart, by a majority of 6,389, on a notional swing of 13.9% May '97; in his Maiden, backed Labour's attempt to further control handguns, as a former Chairman of the Humberside Police Authority June '97; welcomed impending new measures to arm councils with powers to curb anti-social behaviour July '97; co-sponsored motion urging Government to be "tough on road crime" July '97; lengthily supported the Government proposal for a regional list for Euro-elections, claiming people could not identify with their current remote Euro-MPs in over-large constituencies Nov '97; co-sponsored motion urging the retention of mutuality by building societies Nov '97; led motion attacking the Canadian Government for subsidising the killing of 285,000 seals Mar '98; interjected into debate on fox-hunting that "three-quarters of the people in this country" supported its abolition Mar '98;

Born: 14 April 1960, Grimsby

Family: Son, of Arthur Henry Cawsey, fitter, and Edith (Shaw), clerk; m '87 Linda Mary (Kirman), child minder; 1s Jacob '93; 2d Hannah '88, Lydia '97;

Education: Wintringham School;

Occupation: Ex: Political Assistant, to Elliot Morley MP for Glanford and Scunthorpe '87-97; IT Consultant '85-87; Computer Systems Analyst, with Imperial Foods, in Grimsby and Hull (Seven Seas Healthcare) '82-85; Computer Programmer '78-82; Computer Operator '77-78;

Traits: Spikey, greying, light-brown centre-parted hair; chubby heart-shaped face; strong chin; slightly skewed mouth; "cheeky chappie" (Edward Garnier MP) with a cheery, jokey style; a local musician who performed with the '60s group 'The Moggies'; an enthusiastic sportsman who has made appearances for the local Labour Club on cold, wet Sunday mornings; Methodist;

Address: House of Commons, Westminster, London, SW1A 0AA; 10 Glover Road, Scunthorpe DN17 1AS; 7 Market Place, Brigg DN20 8AA; The Courtyard, Boothferry Road, Goole DN14 6AE (constituency)

Telephone: 0171 219 5237 (H of C); 01724 872560/ 01724 872560 (Fax)(home); 01405 767744/767753 (constituency);

'Ben' (James Keith) CHAPMAN   **Labour**   **WIRRAL SOUTH '97 (Mar)-**

Majority: 7,004 (14.6%) over Conservative 6-way;

Description: An essentially middle-class residential seat (dubbed 'Surrey-sur-Mersey'); Conservative strength rises to the West at prosperous Heswall, on the Dee; there is some Labour support at Port Sunlight and Bromborough on the Mersey side of the peninsula; "a blue chip Tory seat; a traditional Conservative heartland" (Ben Chapman); unchanged in the '95 boundary revision;

Position: PPS, to Richard Caborn '97-; Chairman: all-party Groups for China. Hongkong, Turkey '97-;

Outlook: The self-effacing by-election phenomenon who momentarily illuminated the whole political sky, revealing middle-class disillusion with the Tories, only to fall to earth as a reticent and obscure Labour backbencher who began to speak up after his first year; the consultant and former civil servant cleverly chosen and fielded by 'New

Labour' as a symbol of its transformation into a business-friendly party, feeling him able to attract disillusioned Tories; "we've chosen a 'Tory' candidate because this is a Tory seat" (senior Labour figure); "I worked with Ben for five years [when a civil servant] and never heard him express a political opinion; he is a blank piece of paper on which a script can be written" (his Tory opponent, Les Byrom); "there's nothing he can't handle" (Ben's daughter, Bridget);

History: He joined the Labour Party at 55 after leaving the civil service to set up his own trade and investment consultancy Apr '96; following the withdrawal of the previously-selected Labour candidate, Ian Wingfield, after allegations about his private life, Chapman was hurriedly chosen from among 40 would-be candidates for the Wirral South by-election caused by the death of its popular Conservative MP, Barry Porter; his selection was protested by hard-Left NEC members Diane Abbott and Dennis Skinner on the technicality that his party membership was less than the statutory two years Nov '96; the by-election campaign, expected to be the last before the general election, produced a huge turnout of high-level canvassers, led on Labour's side by Leader Tony Blair; Ian McCartney was Chapmen's 'minder'; the campaign slogan was "Ben Chapman Means Business" but his minders hardly allowed him to open his mouth; Blair countered the Tories' claim that Labour would threaten the closure of Harold Wilson's alma mater, Wirral Grammar School, by insisting "Labour poses no threat to grammar schools; where schools are good and parents want to keep them, they are under no threat" Feb '97; after a MORI poll accurately predicting a Labour victory over the Tories by 52% to 36%, the actual poll produced a landslide swing of 17%, producing a Labour majority of 7,888 on a high, 73% turnout, overturning the previous Tory majority of 8,183 Feb '97; despite John Major's telling Chapman not to bother unpacking his bags, since this had occurred in a seat never before won by Labour, the by-election was widely interpreted as the deathknell of Tory hopes for the ensuing general election nine weeks later; fighting the general election without the huge resources of the by-election, Chapman denied he had "been cut adrift on my own" and was re-elected with a similar majority and swing - 7,004 votes on a 15.4% swing from '92, one of the biggest in the country May '97; asked about the need to revise methods of calculating unemploymnent statistics and on the role of the Bank of England in setting interest rates May '97; asked how many local young jobless would benefit from welfare-to-work proposals June '97; was named PPS to Richard Caborn June '97; was commended by Foreign Office Minister Derek Fatchett for his "real understanding of the situation in China" when he urged a vigorous pursuit of a new relationship July '97; claimed that Liverpool's "image problem", born out of the past influence of Militant and poor labour relations in the '80s, was being overcome July '97; welcomed the National Lottery Bill as tightening up regulation of the Lottery, complaining that his constituency had been inequitably treated, ranking 628th in sums received Apr '98; pushed David Clark on millennium computer compliance in the Government Apr '98; complained about "harassment and victimisation" of "vulnerable witnesses" June '98; welcomed proposed freedom of information legislation June '98; urged speedier establishment of out-of-school-hours clubs June '98; urged better management of further education, citing the Wirral Metropolitan College which had "managed to create considerable debt by over-grandiose ideas, by straight mismanagement and by creating over-dependence on European funding that did not continue", forcing campus closures July '98;

Born: 8 July 1940, Kirkby Stephen

Family: Son, late James Hartley Chapman, farm labourer, and late Elsie Vera (Bonsfield); m '70, Jane Deirdre (Roffe); 3d: Bridget '71, Charlotte '73, Clare '75; divorced '84;

Education: Appleby Grammar School, Westmorland;

Occupation: Founder-Director, Ben Chapman Associates (consultancy on Far Eastern trade and investment) '95-; Director, of China Gateway-Northwest '96-; on Advisory Board, China Technology Link '96-; Director, Wirral Chamber of Commerce '96-; Owner: of holiday flat and cottage in Appleby and a commercial rented leasehold property in Manchester; ex: Director for Trade and Industry, Government Office for the Northwest '94-95; Regional Director for the Northwest, DTI '93-94; Deputy Regional Director for the Northwest and Director for the Merseyside, DTI, '91-93; Commercial Counsellor, Beijing '87-90; Assistant Director, DTI '81-87; First Secretary (Economics), Accra '78-81; First Secretary (Commercial) Dar es Salaam '74-78; Board of Trade '70-74; Rochdale Inquiry into Shipping '67-70; Ministry of Aviation/BAA '62-67; MPNI '58-62; Pilot Officer, RAFVR '59-61;

Traits: "Dapper in a double-breasted navy blue pin-stripe suit and nippy black moccasins, speaks BBC RP" (Polly Toynbee, INDEPENDENT); chubby jowls; well-manicured appearance; "diffident air", a "master of self-effacement" (Jon Hibbs, DAILY TELEGRAPH); "sometimes appears too reticent to be a politician" (Russell Jenkins, TIMES); enjoys opera, theatre, music, sculpture, football;

Address: House of Commons, Westminster, London SW1A 0AA; Anvil Cottage, Village Road, Heswall, Wirral L60 0DZ;

Telephone: 0171 219 3000 (H of C); 0151 342 7293;

Sir Sydney (Brookes) CHAPMAN   Conservative   **CHIPPING BARNET '79-**

Majority: 1,035 (2.1%) over Labour 7-way;

Description: Previously Reginald Maudling's North London, semi-rural, suburban seat under its old name of Barnet; it includes Barnet, New and East Barnet; parts of Cockfosters, New Southgate and Whetstone; and villages of Totteridge, Arkley and Monken Hadley; in the '95 reduction of Barnet's seats from four to three, it gained 11,000 voters from Freirn Barnet in the former Finchley constituency;

Former Seat: Handsworth, Birmingham '70-74;

Position: Chairman '97-, Member '94- Commons' Accommodation and Works Committee; President: of Friends of Barnet Hospitals '81-, Barnet Society '88-, Tamarisk Trust '81-; ex: Whip '88-95: Vice Chamberlain of HM Household '92-95; Lord Commissioner '90-92, Assistant Whip '88-90; on Select Committees: on Public Service '95-97, on Environment '83-87, Commons Services '83-87, Unopposed Private Bills Committee '80-88, Race Relations and Immigration '73-74; on Commons' Administration Committee '92-95; PPS to: Norman Fowler '79-83, Michael Alison and Paul Dean '73-74; Chairman, Parliamentary Group for Consultancy '80-88; on all-party Animal Welfare Group '73-74; on Executive, Conservative National Union '61-70; National Chairman, Young Conservatives '64-66; President: Arboricultural Association '83-89, London Greenbelt Council '85-89; Vice Chairman, Wildlife Link '85-89;

Outlook: Pleasantly cheerful mainstream architect-planner who was the only local Tory to survive, narrowly, Labour's '97 tidal wave, despite having been obscured for seven years after '88 by his climb up the Whips' ladder ("since I've become a Whip, it has been hard to obtain any coverage"); was also the only local Tory not to seek public support by objecting to changes in local hospital dispositions; a longtime advocate of wholesale tree-planting who has shown "able leadership of the movement to protect the greenbelt in the capital" (former Tory

Minister Robert Jones); in his first stint for Handsworth a liberal-minded Heathman, returned for Barnet a Rightish building company director, still a civilised environmentalist (especially on old houses, trees and green belt); pro: EC, police, hanging; anti: juggernauts, acid rain, Stansted, Sunday trading, Soviet nukes;

History: He was elected to Executive of the Conservative National Union '61; was adopted for Stalybridge and Hyde Nov '62; was elected National Vice Chairman of Young Conservatives Feb '63; contested Stalybridge and Hyde Oct '64; wrote 'Blueprint for Britain' '65, 'Social Security in the '70s' '66, 'Local Freedom' '68; was selected for Handsworth, beating local Alderman, Anthony Beaumont-Dark, and David Knox Dec '69; was elected as Sir Edward Boyle's successor in Handsworth June '70; in Maiden warned against pollution of countryside by pylons and breweries Nov '70; his tree-lovers' Bill was talked out by John Farr Feb '71; voted against the Government on museum-entry charges Jan '72; opposed a deal with Ian Smith Mar '72; launched 'Plant a Tree in '73' Mar '72; urged ban on hare-coursing Mar '72; said juggernauts must be kept out of villages Sep '72; tried to introduce Bill to preserve interesting buildings Oct '72; backed construction of new Parliamentary building May '73; was defeated for Handsworth by John Lee Feb '74; became Director of National Tree Week Mar '75; was rejected for Chippenham, City of London, Dorking, Wycombe and others '75-78; was selected for Chipping Barnet in succession to Reginald Maudling from among 250 applicants Apr '79; voted to curb abortion, allow hanging again July '79; co-sponsored Bill to increase access to countryside Feb '80; urged ban on Russian-produced Christmas cards June '80; urged GLC to get rid of every ugly parking meter Feb '81; wanted marches curtailed to save police costs June '81; criticised Labour's verbal assaults on Metropolitan Police July '81; wanted rates replaced quickly Nov '81; urged increased access for British products to Japan Oct '82; complained that GLC's cheap fares policy would cost ratepayers £1,200m by end of 1985-86, Feb '82; raised problem of heavy lorries in urban areas May '82; backed Michael Heseltine plan for Vauxhall Cross development June '82; said USSR was spending 50% more than USA on arms Feb '83; spoke of Londoners' utter dismay at Ken Livingstone's pro-IRA Ulster trip Mar '83; urged quick abolition of GLC and rating system Mar '83; worried about Soviets' nuclear lead Mar '83; urged release of imprisoned Soviet Jew July '83; voted to restore hanging for all types of killing July '83; worried about Government's "vague if not contradictory" green belt circular, urging development instead of derelict land in conurbations Aug '83; recoiled 'Plant a Tree in '83' Nov '83; urged tighter rules on airguns Nov '83; welcomed the Town and Country Planning Bill Dec '83; applauded Government's withdrawal of two greenbelt circulars Feb '84; the Government resisted his amendment to Rates Bill giving further relief to business ratepayers Mar '84; worried that VAT on building industry would encourage demolition rather than conservation Apr '84; blamed the Government for reducing areas of special scientific interest Nov '84; headed a motion backing Mrs Thatcher's refusal to recognise or meet the PLO Nov '84; contested the 1922 Committee unsuccessfully Nov '84; signed an anti-Stansted motion Dec '84; signed a rebel motion urging local authorities be allowed to spend their money on house building Jan '85; urged the government to do more to cut UK's acid rain emission Jan '85; welcomed US space weapons Jan '85; co-sponsored David Clark's Wildlife and Countryside (Amendment) Bill Feb '85; urged priority on reducing tax burden on lower paid and increasing incentives for unemployed to find work Mar '85; urged replacement of government art funding by private contributions sparked by tax concessions Mar '85; in an adjournment debate he backed a vitrification process which made asbestos waste harmless Apr '85; was one of five most vociferous opponents of the Sunday Trading Bill, and was one of 26 Tories voting against it May '85; co-signed letter of 'Third Term Group' of Tories urging end of rent controls on future tenancies May '85; was one of 17 Tories to vote against expanding Stansted June '85; as 'Third Term Groupie' he co-signed letter to Chancellor urging raised thresholds rather than cut in basic rate of income tax Dec '85; welcomed the Latent Damage Bill's new demands on faulty architecture but urged a longstop of 15 years from construction, particularly for retired architects June '86; while the acting Chairman of the Environment Select Committee he allowed Labour MPs to ban a strikebreaking TIMES correspondent from a trip, to Mrs Thatcher's indignation July '86; backed Labour's effort to save common land Sep '86; complained about the shortage of police in London's suburbs Mar '87; co-sponsored Chris Smith's Environment and Safety Information Bill Oct '87; in wake of hurricane he asked whether Church Commissioners insured their property against acts of God, showing a lack of faith Nov '87; urged another national tree-planting year Nov '87; sponsored BR's British Railways (London) Bill to link North and South London, demolishing the Blackfriars-Holborn viaduct Jan '88; complained of the RAWP-produced shortage of nurses in Barnet Jan '88; as Chairman of the Committee on the Dartford-Thurrock Crossing Bill, complained of its lack of technical back-up Feb '88; saw through British Railways (London) Bill to enable BR's new Thameslink to cross Thames Mar '88; urged extra pay to attract staff to Northern Line, whose operations he was monitoring Mar '88; voted against Government's proposal to charge for testing eyes Apr '88; led a debate on need to defend green belts May '88; backed free optical and dental examinations July '88; asked if better safety precautions on oil rigs would have a bad effect on balance of payments July '88; in the 11-10 vote on Ecclesiatical Committee allowing ordination of divorcees, was in the minority opposed May '89; asked about safety of Channel Tunnel's concrete lining July 88; asked about state of Church of England property investments Oct '88; again voted against Government charge for eye tests Oct '88; urged a continued and well-researched Government programme against pollutants, especially sewage into North Sea Nov '88; in the mini-reshuffle following Edminia Currie's resignation, was named an Assistant Whip, requiring him to abandon a £10,000 outside job as Parliamentary consultant to a development company Dec '88; voted against ordaining divorced men July '89; again voted against ordaining divorced men Feb '90; was promoted full Whip or Lord Commissioner July '90; retained seat with majority down from 14,871 to 13,951, a swing to Labour of 3.91% Apr '92; was promoted to Vice Chamberlain, the fourth most senior Whip who informs the monarch daily about Parliamentary happenings Apr '92; was named a member of Commons' Administration Committee June '92; arrested for drunken driving, was found to be under the limit Sep '92; announced Government's 319-316 victory at end of Maastricht paving debate Nov '92; announced 317-317 tie vote on Maastricht, the Speaker ruling in the Government's favour July '93; as a Whip was the Commons sixth most devoted attender Dec '93; as his Whip warned Finchley Tory MP Hartley Booth against resigning over his affair with researcher Emily Barr and thus causing a by-election Jan '94; voted to restore capital punishment, especially for killing policemen Feb '94; voted to reduce age of homosexual consent to 18, but not 16, Feb '94; Tory MPs being ousted from offices in Dean's Yard to provide sleeping berths for security guards criticised him for not defending their interests: "some flunky only has to tell him some decision has been taken for security reasons and he buys it!" (DAILY TELEGRAPH) Apr '94; was named to Commmons Accommodation Committee Dec '94; as a Whip was the Commons third best attender Dec '94; unlike fellow local MPs, Sir John Gorst and Hugh Dykes, did not stoke up opposition to threatened closure of Accident and Emergency department of Edgware Hospital: "I appreciate it is difficult to persuade anyone living near a hospital that services will be improved by closing an A&E department but I sincerely believe this to be the case" June '95; ended eight years in the Whips' Office by standing down as Vice Chamberlain of the Household, receiving a knighthood for his services July '95; was released from the Commons Administration Committee July '95; was named to the Select Committee on Public Service Oct '95; on reaching 60, said he was becoming interested in 'ageism' Oct '95; in debate on Edgware Hospital, insisted: "whatever the opprobrium the Government now face, tomorrow the people will realise they took the right decision in the long term for the benefit of our constituents and for that of the NHS" Nov '95; claimed the Commons' terrace, which had been raised by four feet to avoid flooding, could now be lowered because of the impact of the Thames Barrier Feb '96; claimed bus deregulation had "led to buses reaching parts of Chipping Barnet undreamt of ten years ago" Mar '96; admitted "political damage has been done" by the revelations about Dame Shirley Porter and her Westminster Council misdeeds May '96; urged the "inefficient, uncompetitive and adversarial" construction industry "get its act together" to achieve effective lobbying May '96; introduced Party Wall (Etc) Bill July '96; voted for 3% cap on MPs' pay rise but a pension based on £43,000 July '96; urged more flexible tree-planting as part of National Tree Week Nov '96; was named a Substitute Delegate to the Assembly of the Western European Union Dec '96; was listed as a wait-and-see pragmatic on the single European currency Dec '96; asked for assurance that none of the planned 4.4m new homes would be built on greenbelt land Feb '97; narrowly held his altered seat by only 1,035 votes, on a notional anti-Tory swing of 14.1%, which cut his majority to one-fifteenth of what it had been; it still made him the only surviving Tory MP in formerly solidly-Tory Barnet May '97; in the second round of the Tory Leadership ballot, voted for William Hague on all three ballots June '97; in a debate on 'cowboy' wheel clampers, argued for private landowners being allowed to charge an official maximum limit for people trespassing on their property July '97; as Chairman of the Accommodation and Works Committee, announced the delayed £250m Portcullis House, with office space for 200 MPs over Westminster Station, would be ready for occupancy in 2001, Dec '97; on the 25th anniversary of his National Tree Year initiative, urged its revival for the Millennium Mar '98;

Born: 17 October 1935, Macclesfield, Cheshire

Family: Son, late W Dobson Chapman, architect/town planner, and late Edith Laura (Wadge); m '76 Claire Lesley McNab (Davies); 2s David '70, Michael '81, 1d Laura '77; separated '84, dvd '87;

Education: The Leas, Hoylake; Rugby; Manchester University (MA in Architecture '58);

Occupation: Chartered Architect and Surveyor/Town Planner; no longer practicing) Dip Arch '58, ARIBA '60, Dip TP '61, AMTPI '62, FRTPI '78, FRSA '80, Hon FFB '80; Hon FB Eng; Hon Assoc Landscape Institute; Hon Assoc British Veterinary Assoc;; Author: 'Town and Countryside' (1978); ex: Director, Capital and Counties Property Company Ltd '80-88; Parliamentary Consultant, Lovell Group (ex-Director Lovell Construction Ltd '82-85) '85-88; Columnist, ESTATE TIMES '78-81; Associate Partner in McDonald, Hamilton and Montefiore '71-76; Consultant on Private Planning to Eliot, Son and Boynton '71-79; Director of Information at British Property Federation '76-79; Lecturer in Architecture at Wigan Mining and Technical College '64-70;

Traits: Tall; specs; shambling; genial smiler; witty; self-mocking; persuasive; polite; adroit; he sold his personalised license plate (SC34) for £2,000 in '86;

Address: House of Commons, Westminster, SW1A 0AA;

Telephone: 0171 219 4542 (H of C);

We reach the uncovered parts of MPs the press no longer notice, because the correspondents leave the Press Gallery too early.

David CHAYTOR   Labour   BURY NORTH '97-

Majority: 7,866 over Conservative 4-way;
Description: Prosperous Lancashire textile town made more so as a Manchester commuter suburb via the M66; four-fifths of voters are owner-occupiers; is famous for its black puddings, its football club and as the birthplace of Sir Robert Peel; a long-standing marginal which, until '97, resisted the pro-Labour trend with the help of an attractive Tory MP, Alistair Burt, and its strongly pro-Tory town of Ramsbottom; **Position:** On the Deregulation Committee '97-; Calderdale Borough Councillor (Chairman of its Labour Group) '82-; **Outlook:** A major new contributor to the environment debate; the third-time-lucky aspirant who finally won in his home town; a "Left-leaning" (NEW STATESMAN) "Old Labour" (SUNDAY TIMES) lecturer-councillor forced to shift from Yorkshire back to Lancashire by the imposition of an all-women short-list on the Calder Valley, which he had fought twice before; a "smoothie who won't cause Blair any trouble, though not a true believer; aspires to office but unlikely to get there" (RED PEPPER); a member of the Full Employment Forum, Amnesty International, formerly of Anti-Apartheid; as a Calderdale councillor, he helped secure a multi-million pound flood protection scheme for Todmorden;
History: He joined the Labour Party at the time of the miners' strike and the three-day week "because of what Heath was doing to British industry" '73; was elected to Calderdale Borough Council May '82; was selected to fight Calder Valley, where Labour had been pushed into 3rd place in the previous election Jan '86; insisted that "Mrs Thatcher's criminal record is the real issue" May '87; failed to oust the sitting Tory MP, Donald Thompson, but restored Labour to 2nd place, 6,045 votes behind June '87; was re-selected to fight Calder Valley Sep '90; securing a swing of only 1%, left Donald Thompson still almost 5,000 votes ahead Apr '92; Calder Valley was designated an all-women's contest; his wife tried instead but failed to be selected Feb '95; he was selected instead for his home town, the key marginal of Bury North, occupied by the barnacle-like Tory Minister Alistair Burt '95; said, "we're good at educating the elite, hopeless in developing the potential of the majority...which doesn't come cheap"; said he backed Blair's "fair tax" strategy but he could "live with" an increase in the top rate of tax Mar '97; said he thought the monarchy was "slowly destroying itself" and would "wither away into one of those [Scandinavian-style] bicycle monarchies" Mar '97; ousted Burt by a majority of 7,866 on a swing of 11.19%, May '97; in his lengthy Maiden complained against discrimination in funding: "why is Bury allowed to spend only £79 per person on capital expenditure when Bolton is allowed to spend £118, Rochdale £120, Trafford £175 and Oldham £219?" June '97; backed ban on fox-hunting June '97; asked about strengthening democracy in Albania June '97; asked about costs of alcohol abuse June '97; urged encouragement of cycling June '97; protested under-financing of further education colleges June '97; pressed for help for smaller professional football clubs June '97; urged inspection of private nurseries June '97; urged the Government to undertake strategic planning in further education colleges, instead of the existing "shambles of the internal market", if it wished to avoid "a series of bankruptcies and closures" June '97; asked about the cost of expanding NATO June '97; expressed solidarity with jailed Indonesian union leader June '97; asked about control of air rifles July '97; probed abuse of ground rents July '97; was named to the

       Copyright (C)Parliamentary Profile Services Ltd

Deregulation Committee Aug '97; was one of the 14 new Labour MPs who voted against cutting benefits for lone parents Dec '97; opening his debate on Fuel Poverty and Energy Efficiency, pointed out that most winter deaths from hypothermia could be avoided Jan '98; co-sponsored motion congratulating CND for 40 years of "fighting to remove the threat of nuclear weapons" Jan '98; backed Cynog Dafis's Road Traffic Reduction Bill because"people understand now that the great car economy has taken us to the brink of economic disaster" Jan '98; urged a reform of inherited local government financing allocations, complaining his local "schools in Bury are in one of the small group of authorities with chronically low per capita funding; consequently, they struggle to obtain basic materials" Mar '98; welcomed Chancellor Brown's Budget but deplored "the unfortunate absence of any reference to pensioners"; he added: "I understand the Government's point about separating out the issue of need and the issue of family structure"; "I have tried hard to agree with that, but I simply cannot accept that the needs of a two-earner family paying the higher rate of income tax are equal to those of a lone-parent family; I cannot believe that the difficulties of bringing up and caring for children are the same for two parents as for one" Mar '98; led motion congratulating Chancellor Brown on "the progress made towards as a green taxation policy" Mar '98; complained about the over-preoccupation with the "graduate elite" instead of "the needs of unskilled 16 and 17-year-olds in low-grade, dead-end jobs" Mar '98; introduced a Bill to increase the amount of recycled paper in newsprint Mar '98; criticised import of Georgian plutonium because of the number of nuclear accidents, "some of which were made public and some of which were concealed" Apr '98; urged further reforms of CAP, including encouragement of organic farming Apr '98; urged further use of fiscal policy to encourage emissions cuts Apr '98; was rated as one of the 'Top 100' written questioners, with 138 posed in his first year May '98; initiated Plutonium debate, praising the nuclear industry for its "phenomenal record of technological innovation" but urged it to "solve for this countrty and others the legacy of 40 years of mistakes" May '98;
Born: 3 August 1949, Bury
Family: He is married, with one son and two daughters;
Education: Bury Grammar School; Huddersfield Polytechnic; London University (BA, M Phil); Leeds University (PGCE);
Occupation: Head of Continuing Education, Manchester College of Arts and Technology '93-97; Senior Lecturer, Continuing Education, MCAT, '90-93; Senior Staff Tutor, Manchester College of Adult Education '83-90; Lecturer in Adult Education (helping adults who failed the 11-plus to secure university entrance) '73-83; (NATFHE/TGWU)
Traits: Centre-parted hair; lantern-jawed; craggy; handsome; "a fluent pavement performer" (Andrew Rawnsley, GUARDIAN); cyclist and walker;
Address: House of Commons, Westminster, London SW1A 0AA; 7 Lumbutts, Todmorden, OL14 6JE;
Telephone: 0171 219 6625/0952 (Fax; H of C); 01706 812052 (home); 0161 764 2023/763 3410 (Fax; constituency office);

WE'RE GETTING FATTER
MPs profiles tend to get fatter, like the papier mache masks we made in our youth by adding to a clay portrait model soggy strips of newsprint soaked in flour and water. Just as you can build up a strong papier mache mask, so too we hope we have transformed a dimly lit outline form into sharp features plus a few warts.

David (William George) CHIDGEY **Liberal Democrat** **EASTLEIGH '94-**

Majority: 754 (1.4%) over Conservative 5-way;
Description: Formerly a marginal suburban area north and east of Southampton, including the railway centre of Eastleigh; in '83 it lost its outer, more rural areas to Romsey-Waterside while taking over Woolston from Southampton-Itchen; in '95, as the fourth largest constituency, it lost 13,000 voters in Chandlers Ford and Hiltingbury to Romsey, while 10,000 voters in Woolston returned to Southampton-Itchen
Position: Spokesman, on Trade and Industry '97-; ex: Spokesman, on Transport '94-97, on Training and Employment '94; Winchester City Councillor '87-90;
Outlook: The somewhat unexpected '97 survivor of '94's famous LibDems' by-election victory; Conservative Stephen Milligan's more sober successor, a commonsensical civil engineer with wide overseas experience; has shown a social democratic approach to transport; "a bright and affable addition to the Liberal Democrat benches" (George Jones and Philip Johnston, DAILY TELEGRAPH);
History: Joined the Liberal Party '85; was elected to Winchester City Council May '87; deplored the overcrowding of trains which contributed to the casualties in the Clapham train disaster Dec '88; contested Hampshire Central against successful Conservative, Edward Kellet-Bowman in Euro by-election (coming third after Labour) Dec '88 and in the Euro-election June '89; at annual conference criticised the Government, complaining that too many firms regarded training as a cost rather than an investment; "when you get a recession, this is one of the first things to be cut back; this is resulting in an appalling lack of training and the situation is getting worse" Sep '91; contested Eastleigh against Sir David Price's successor, Stephen Milligan, coming second with 28% of the poll Apr '92; on the death of Stephen Milligan, was chosen to contest the seat again; he claimed: "the Liberal Democrats are the clear challengers to the Conservatives in Eastleigh, as they are across the south of England; people in Eastleigh are worried about Britain's long-term economic future and about prospects for jobs in Eastleigh; they are worried about changes in the NHS which are diverting resources from hospital beds to perks for accountants and managers; they are worried about crime, and angry about Michael Howard's rejection of the Chief Constable's request for extra officers in Hampshire" Mar '94; according to his Labour opponents, his campaign was started a week early, while the political moratorium resulting from John Smith's death was still on; Liberal Democrats insisted Labour were already distributing leaflets in the constituency May '94; insisted that people would pay higher taxes if the reasons were explained to them May '94; won the seat with a majority of over 9,000; it was not the sort of landslide majority achieved at Newbury and Christchurch because the Labour vote held up to within 500 votes of the 15,768 achieved in 1992, with the Conservatives collapsing into 3rd place; he became the LibDems' 23rd MP June '94; in his Maiden, paid tribute to Stephen Milligan as a hardworking constituency man who argued on policies, not personalities; urged the reform of the Child Support Agency to allow an Australian-type appeals system to achieve corrections of its "draconian operations" July '94; opposed the Department of Employment's targeting of BIG ISSUE vendors as social security fraud suspects Sep '94; was named the LibDems' Transport Spokesman, on top of Training and Employment Nov '94; opposed EU's proposed limit on power of motorcycles as a threat to Triumph's product range Nov '94; urged training and

Copyright (C)Parliamentary Profile Services Ltd

investment in infrastructure to mop up longterm unemployment Dec '94; again urged major restructuring of CSA Dec '94; opposed Job-Seekers Allowance as forcing unemployed into deadend jobs; urged benefits be paid to employers as a training subsidy to improve the skills of the unemployed Feb '95; his questions disclosed that excess absenteeism in Government cost £350m a year Feb '95; said Hampshire, as the most "defence-dependent economy", had suffered badly from defence cuts Feb '95; backed Bill for referendum on Europe Feb '95; urged BT to extend CLI (Caller Line Identification) to the emergency services to cut response times Mar '95; urged more Government contracts for his local Vosper-Thorneycroft shipyard May '95; opposed the call of Tory MP Alan Duncan for Britain to withdraw from the ILO June '95; urged unions not to restrict their party links to Labour June '95; claimed his party was the first to fight ageism Sep '95; was named Transport Spokesman Nov '95; claimed Tory privatisation allowed "predatory companies...an opportunity to run down rail rolling stock, maximise their profits and at the end of the contracts hand back a derelict railway" Feb '96; voted for Labour MP John McFall's Bill to ban animal cruelty Mar '96; opposed time-limiting debate on Prevention of Terrorism Bill Mar '96; urged more resources to train and educate engineers and technicians Mar '96; voted against Iain Duncan-Smith's Bill to curb the European Court Apr '96; urged renegotiation of rail privatisation to maximise rail improvements instead of benefiting lawyers and accountants Apr '96; attacked award of Network South Central to a French company as taking "privatisation, already a black farce, to undreamed of depths with British taxpayers subsidising French shareholders" Apr '96; expressed fear that London and Continental Railways, contracted to build the Channel Tunnel rail link, might "walk out from the project and leave the public holding the purse strings and shelling out more cash to make it viable" Apr '96; claimed rail privatisation had been "driven by the sort of manic belief that competition and market forces are the ultimate goal in trying to provide an efficient railway system" Apr '96; claimed Labour's refusal to commit itself to reacquire Railtrack meant privatisation could not be halted Apr '96; attacked practice of discharging demented elderly patients from hospitals and trying to force them to pay for needed medical care June '96; initiated debate on Hampshire's NHS cuts June '96; voted against a 3% cap on pay rise for MPs but for cutting MPs' mileage allowance and for pensions based on £43,000 July '96; launched paper urging more use of motorcycles instead of cars to reduce pollution and congestion Sep '96; insisted Tory talk of Tube privatisation showed Tories were "sacrificing the safety of millions to fund short-term tax bribes" Jan '97; described as a "train ride from Hell" his journey from Euston to Runcorn to speak in the Wirral South by-election Feb '97; somewhat unexpectedly retained his altered seat by the narrow majority of 754, down from the by-election's 9,239, but a notional 11.3% anti-Tory swing from the '92 general election May '97; was re-appointed Transport Spokesman May '97; insisted the London Underground should remain and be managed as an integrated system June '97; welcomed decision to abandon the controversial Salisbury bypass but described as "unsustainable" the decision to go ahead with the Birmingham Northern Relief Road July '97; urged extra money for speed cameras by adding £10 to the fines of those caught speeding July '97; was named Spokesman on Trade and Industry Sep '97; initiated debate against anti-competitive practices in funeral industry Nov '97; urged regional variations in national minimum wage May '98; urged ban on predatory pricing in national broadsheets June '98;

Born: 9 July 1942, Basingstoke

Family: "I am the first male member of my family this century not to have folllowed a professional career in the Army" (DC); son, of Major Cyril Chidgey, retired Army officer, and Hilda Doris (Weston); m '65 April Carolyn (Idris-Jones), probation officer; 1s David '65, 2d Joanna '69, Caitlin '71;

Education: Brune Park County High School; Royal Naval College, Portsmouth; Royal Naval

College, Portsmouth; Portsmouth Polytechnic;
Occupation: Mechanical and Aeronautical Engineer, CEng, FICE, FIHT, MCIT: with Admiralty '58-64, Chartered Engineer and Project Director, Brian Colquhoun and Partners '73-94, as Associate Partner and Overseas Director '84-94; as a student apprentice, he worked in the Portsmouth Dockyard; Owner: of residential rented property in Southsea;
Traits: Heavily built; jowly; specs; calm; measured; has common sense; "one of Westminster's less charismatic politicians" (John Rentoul, INDEPENDENT); unconventional as an engineer; "Easy Rider" (because of his enthusiasm for motorcyles, which he has never ridden);
Address: House of Commons, Westminster, London SW1A 0AA;
Telephone: 0171 219 6914; 01703 620007;

Malcolm CHISHOLM   **Labour**   **EDINBURGH NORTH & LEITH '97-**

Majority: 10,978 (26.84%)) over SNP 7-way;
Description: A new name for for three-quarters of his former Edinburgh-Leith constituency with 9,000 voters added from Edinburgh Central and 4,500 from Edinburgh East; despite some Conservative strength in New Town and Stockbridge, it is still a traditionally Labour seat containing the 'Trainspotting' council estates of Granton, Royston and West Pilton; the depressed industrial areas around Leith docks have been partially gentrified with modish wine bars and warehouses converted into flats;
Former Seat: Edinburgh-Leith '92-97
Position: Ex: Under Secretary, Scottish Office, May-December '97; Assistant Spokesman, Scottish Affairs '96-97; Scottish Whip '96; Chairman, Lothian Regional Labour Party '88-89; Chairman, Leith Constituency Labour Party (Secretary '88-90) '90-92;
Outlook: The resigner turned super-enthusiast; the first ministerial casualty of the Blair Government, widely respected, by Blair among others, for giving up a job he loved in protest against one-parent benefit cuts ("I know [he] feels strongly about that issue" - Tony Blair); his brief recent fame overcame his low profile south of the Border, where he was derided as spurning the "cheap thrills of HANSARD appearances, the easy lure of a high profile and endless committee work" (DAILY TELEGRAPH Diary); the DAILY TELEGRAPH had clearly ignored his informed Commons speeches criticising Tory economics skewed to favour the rich, or his crusade for better breast cancer services; as a recent convert to moderate devolution was judged by former Tory MP and Minister Allan Stewart "a good sound chap with a good sound Unionist record" for having voted against devolution in '79; until his December 1997 resignation, was one of few Leftwingers given jobs by Blair in May '97; a thoughtful, intellectual Leftist, one of the Campaign Group's only four '92 new recruits, who left the Group, abandoning hard-Left politics in '94; uses his cool intelligence instead of the hot emotions of his predecessor, Ron Brown, to support "class politics"; believes the Labour Party is "a crusade or it is nothing"; his crusades have been for better breast cancer services, one-parent benefits and a fair shake for the poor;
History: He voted 'no' to devolution in the Scottish referendum '79; he joined the Labour Party '80; became Secretary of Leith Constituency Labour Party '88; the local Leith party's

Management Committee censured Ron Brown over the Apr '88 Mace incident, but narrowly avoided criticising him - by 27 votes to 25 with six abstentions - over his poor voting record June '88; Chisholm was one of three shortlisted for re-selection by Leith, including the MP, Ron Brown; in the three 600-word messages from each, Lord Provost Eleanor McLaughlin raised the question of whether "working class interests are being best served" by Ron Brown; in his statement, Chisholm stayed out of personal confrontation, setting out instead a lengthy list of Labour Party policy priorities on public ownership, phasing out of nuclear power and weapons and the need for a Scottish Assembly, more strength for trade unions, reversing the decline of council housing and increasing pensions; "if selected as a candidate, I shall be accountable to the members of Leith Labour Party at all times; I undertake to carry out my work with self-discipline and without discrediting the Left; if elected, I shall vote regularly in Parliament, and deal to the best of my ability with the many problems that our unjust social system inflicts on the people of Leith, problems that have intensified so much during the last ten Tory years" Sep '89; the local party re-selected Ron Brown in the first ballot, with 54% for Brown, 33% for Chisholm and 13% for Eleanor McLoughlin Oct '89; Brown was then tried, found innocent of stealing the knickers of his former secretary-lover, Nonna Longden, but fined £1,000 for malicious damage to her seaside flat; his champagne celebration of what he described as a "moral victory" irritated his Leith constituency party; when he refused to resign Jan '90, Leith CLP secured NEC approval for re-running the re-selection contest without Brown being included Feb '90; Chisholm was elected the new Chairman of the Leith CLP Feb '90; after a delay forced by Brown, the MP was de-selected Apr '90; Malcolm Chisholm was selected over Elizabeth Maginnis 91-39, with Ron Brown not allowed to stand Sep '90; confronting Ron Brown in the campaign, Chisholm insisted that Labour Party was still "a crusade or nothing" and he would go on fighting the regional council over teachers' pay Mar '92; retained Leith with a majority reduced to 4,985 from 11,327, due to Ron Brown's standing as candidate (4,142 votes) and doubling of SNP vote to 8,805 Apr '92; was one of four Campaign Group's new recruits after they had lost four in the election; backed Ken Livingstone for Leader May '92; joined in effort to disrupt Maastricht treaty endorsement by device of excluding strangers from the Visitors' Gallery May '92; in his Maiden complained that Leith was being de-industrialised, with 20% unemployed May '92; complained that the Government had forced the poor to use expensive credit to pay for the poll tax, social fund repayments and enforced rent increases June '92; urged more sympathy for women fearful of giving the Child Support Agency the name of their child's father for fear of violence June '92; backed Edinburgh campaign to bring local cemeteries into public ownership June '92; supported Jeremy Corbyn's Bill to give pensioners equal retirement at 60, July '92; co-sponsored Tony Benn's Bill for a referendum on Maastricht Sep '92; with fellow Edinburgh Labour MPs Gavin Strang and Alistair Darling, campaigned to save the European Fighter Aircraft to keep jobs at GEC Ferranti in Lothian and Fife Sep '92; urged abandonment of "unjust, arbitrary and morally indefensible" primary-purpose rule banning immmigration by foreign spouses where UK entry was the main reason for marriage; deplored it as forcing women to stay with husbands for four years although "treated intolerably by their husbands" under threat of deportation Oct '92; said the Left was lining up against the Maastricht treaty because "savage public expenditure cuts" would be needed under the treaty Oct '92; urged more public investment in unprivatised Scottish water and a ban on disconnections; "if it came to disconnections in Scotland, I would support and become involved in direct action to stop any of my constituents from having their water turned off" Dec '92; strongly deplored NHS "chaos" in Scotland, although milder than in England, warning that "an ideological obsession with the market will destroy the National Health Service unless action is taken to check it" Jan '93; criticised Labour front bench for accepting Maastricht treaty's establishing of control of inflation as the first priority of economic policy Jan '93; pressed Labour Defence Spokesman David Clark to take a harder line against the US attack on Baghdad Jan '93; warned John Major against changing the law "which makes the obscenity of water disconnection illegal in Scotland" Mar '93; deplored oil tax changes which were losing jobs in Scotland May '93; voted against 3rd Reading of Maastricht treaty Bill May '93; complained that "VAT on heating is the most regressive taxation imaginable"; "VAT on heating is almost a second poll tax and will do as little good for the Conservative Party as the poll tax" because it made the deprived even more deprived May '93; co-sponsored Ken Livingstone's motion attacking US bombing of Iraqi intelligence headquarters without UN authorisation June '93; urged John Major to send a Government Minister to join Anti-Racist Alliance in demonstration June '93; co-sponsored hard-Left Campaign Group amendment on Defence expenditure, urging its reduction to the European level and cancellation of Trident July '93; backed Edinburgh "zero tolerance" campaign against male brutality as a way of correcting the imbalance between power-abusing men and victimised women who thus became responsible for family homicides July '93; blamed Tories both for shrinkage of tax base and growth of unemployment which together caused increase in PSBR; instead of accepting responsibility, Tories were perpetuating myths about crime being the product of one-parent families July '93; described Boris Yeltsin as a Rightist addicted to "hard-line monetarism" and opponents like Alexander Rutskoi and Rusland Khasbulatov as Keynesians Oct '93; voted against Defence Estimates, instead of abstaining Oct '93; voted against European Economic Area Bill Oct '93; voted for a lesser increase in MPs' pay Nov '93; backed Peter Shore's anti-Maastricht amendment Dec '93; urged improved nursery care Dec '93; called for more Government money for local government to prevent the risk of rent increases to pay for repair to frost-damaged pipes in Edinburgh's council houses Jan '94; opposed imposition of a guilotimne on the Finance Bill, claiming the Government was trying to avoid a vote on the extension of VAT Feb '94; co-sponsored Tony Benn's motion attacking low taxes on the rich and calling for "a clear socialist commitment" to soaking the rich to provide "full employment, planned defence diversification, the rebuilding of our infrastructure, the extension of essential public services and the regeneration of British industry" Feb '94; voted against restoring capital punishment, even for killing policemen Feb '94; voted to reduce age of homosexual consent to 18 or 16, Feb '94; urged a substantial improvement in government-funded child care Apr '94; voted for Margaret Beckett for Leader and Deputy Leader July '94; co-signed Campaign Group's letter to the GUARDIAN opposing the alleged criminalising of protest and the removal of the right to silence in the Conservatives' Criminal Justice Bill Aug '94; left the Campaign Group "and hard-Left politics" '94; attacked the replacement of Unemployment Benefit by the Job-Seekers' Allowance as "not helping the unemployed to gain jobs, but helping the unemployed to lose benefit in order to fund next year's election bribes" Jan '95; attacked the Budget's new burden on ordinary people, claiming "the richest 1% have cumulatively gained £75b in tax cuts, while the poorest fifth have suffered a rise in their tax contributions from 31% of income in 1979 to 39% in 1992" and that "14m people live on incomes of less than £115 a week - 1 in 4 - a rise from 1 in 10 in 1979" Jan '95; asked PM John Major if Rothschild's Bank, who were managing the privatisation of Railtrack, would "keep a seat warm" for the Transport Secretary, John MacGregor Feb '95; introduced debate on breast cancer, highlighting UK's much lower survival rate, blamed on long waiting times, misdiagnoses, inadequate treatment and shortage of research funds Feb '95; complained about stereotyping of domestic violence as a working class problem, citing a poster showing two fists tattooed with "Love" and "Hate", asking "which one will she get tonight?" Mar '95; criticised Chancellor Clarke's "rhetoric that somehow single parents were advantaged" but expressed relief that "he did not abolish the lone-parent premium or single-parent benefit paid when single parents go into work" Nov '95;

backed Tony Benn's amendment scrapping Trident and cutting defence expenditure to the West European average Dec '95; was commended by SNP MP Margaret Ewing for his campaigning role in Scotland on breast cancer services Feb '96; opposed low housing expenditure, claiming there was "a massive housing crisis in Scotland" Mar '96; voiced doubts about financing Scottish hospitals by Private Finance Initiatives (PFI) and opposed "clinical services being put out to the private sector" May '96; following the resignation of Assistant Scottish Affairs Spokesman John McAllion over Tony Blair's decision to hold a pre-legislation referendum on devolution, he was promoted Assistant Spokesman in his place, covering constitutional affairs, health, housing and local government June '96; was reminded by Scottish Secretary Michael Forsyth that he had voted 'no' in the '79 Scottish devolution referendum June '96; was described by Tory MP and former Minister Allan Stewart as "a good sound chap with a good sound Unionist record" July '96; he attacked Michael Forsyth's claim that Scotland got more than its share of revenues under the Barnett Formula July '96; called on the Government to back Edinburgh-based GEC-Marconi Avionics' bid for the Sea King airborne early warning contract to protect "this country's employment and industrial base" June '96; voted for a 3% cap on MPs' pay rise but a pension based on £43,000 July '96; was confirmed in the last pre-election reshuffle as Assistant Spokesman on Scottish Affairs July '96; was listed as one of "Blair's Bastards" for having voted 24 times against the Labour leadership since '92, in Hull University research Sep '96; accused the SNP of "cruel and cynical deception" for pretending the Scottish economy could become the "tiger economy of Europe" Sep '96; dismissed the SNP's proposed "Scottish Budget" as "the economics of the tooth fairy" Nov '96; having failed to get Lord James Douglas Hamilton to rule out reliance on PFI, insisted that it was "totally unacceptable to the public that the medical profession should be run by private finance" Feb '97; dismissed SNP promises to monopolise North Sea oil taxes, saying "no one will ever take the Nationalists seriously" Feb '97; urged an "all-out war against E-coli in Scotland"; ruled out further commercialisation of NHS care of the elderly Feb '97; was targeted with 71 other MPs for anti-hunting views by The FIELD Apr '97; retained his altered, renamed seat with an increased majority of 10,978, with an anti-SNP notional swing of 6.1% May '97; was named Under Secretary for Scotland, responsible for Local Government and Transport May '97; was included in the Cabinet Committee on Women's Issues chaired by Harriet Harman July '97; launched "a New Deal for Lone Parents" in Scotland July '97; claiming it was possible to find the £60m to avoid lone-parent benefit cuts, resigned from the Government to join 46 other Labour MPs voting against the cuts; in his letter to PM Tony Blair, explained: "firstly, in-work benefits for lone parents are an obvious work incentive"; "secondly, the lone-parent income support benefit cut will make it more difficult for a lone parent to make the transition from welfare to work" Dec '97; in a GUARDIAN article attacked the cuts as a "massive betrayal of the principles we have set ourselves for modernisation...of the welfare state" Dec '97; was praised by his former boss, Scottish Secretary Donald Dewar for his "realism" in claiming the increase in Scottish water charges were due to under-investment during 18 years of Conservative Government Dec '97; in a Parliamentary question, asked Tony Blair to review the lone-parent benefit cuts in a comprehensive review of the social security budget Jan '98; in a TIMES letter claimed that "only by admitting we made a mistake (over lone-parent benefits) can we regain the trust of the British people for much-needed welfare reform" Jan '98; welcomed the "technically brilliant" Scotland Bill setting up a Scottish Parliament as a "tremendous opportunity" and its proportional representation system as leading to "less confrontational and more co-operative politics"; he insisted "it is far more in Scotland's interest to be part of a large voting bloc - the United Kingdom" in dealing with Europe Jan '98; claimed that lone-parent families would have even less to spend on heating their damp Scottish dwellings - a quarter of all Scottish homes -

if they lost their jobs after taking up employment Jan '98; promised to "go on challenging the Government unceasingly until, like errant teenagers, they see the error of their ways" Jan '98; urged many-faceted advances for women which he had observed evolving as "a member of the Cabinet Subcommittee on Women" Feb '98; welcomed Gordon Brown's Budget for its "remarkable redistributive heart", making up for lone-parents cuts by increasing child benefit payments; said Government was "back on course to deliver Old Labour objectives in New Labour ways" Mar '98; welcomed Government's proposals to clean up corruption in Scottish local government through a new National Standards Commission May '98; welcomed Scottish Parliament as part of "asymmetric devolution, which is practiced in many countries" May '98;

Born: 7 March 1949, Edinburgh

Family: Son, Malcolm Chisholm, primary school teacher, and Olive (Richardson); m '75 Janet (Broomfield) writer of historical novels (Bodley Head Prize in '90 for A Fallen Land); 2s, 1d;

Education: George Watson's College; Edinburgh University (MA, Dip Ed);

Occupation: Ex: Teacher, at Broughton High School (EIS representative '89-90) '87-90, Castlebrae High School (EIS representative) '76-87; between university and his first teaching job he worked in the NHS as a Porter and Nursing Auxiliary for two years;

Traits: Tall; slim; auburn hair; balding; moustache; "dignified-looking" (Edward Pearce, DAILY MAIL); previously restrained; has "tenacity, enthusiasm and infinite patience" (Patricia Wynn Davies, INDEPENDEMT); enjoys watching football;

Address: House of Commons, Westminster, London SW1A 0AA; 107 Bellevue Road, Edinburgh 7 EH7 4DG;

Telephone: 0171 219 4613 (H of C); 0131 556 4707 (home);

Christopher CHOPE OBE   **Conservative**   **CHRISTCHURCH '97-**

Majority: 2,165 over Liberal Democrat 5-way;

Description: A seat north and east of Bournemouth - with the UK's highest proportion of detached homes (55%) - recently famed for its dramatic swings: the Tories' 10th safest seat, which provided the late Robert Adley with a 23,000 majority in 1992, it registered the 3rd biggest swing in recent history (35%) when it returned Liberal Democrat Diana Maddock with a 16,000 majority in the July '93 by-election; although it reverted narrowly to the Tories in '97, even this represented a notional swing of 18.28% from the previous general election;

Former Seat: Southampton-Itchen '83-92

Position: Assistant Spokesman: on Trade and Industry '98-, on Local Government '97-98; ex: Chairman, Conservative Parliamentary Candidates Association '93-97; on DTI Deregulation Task Force on Transport and Communications '93-97; on Local Government Commission for England '94-95; on Health & Safety Commission '93-97; Under Secretary, for Transport '90-92, for Environment '86-90; Vice President, of Selsdon Group; PPS, to Peter Brooke '85-86; on Select Committee on Procedure '84-86; Secretary, Conservative MPs' Environment Committee '83-86, Shipping and Shipbuilding Subcommittee '85-86; on Executive Committee of Society of Conservative Lawyers '83-86; Leader of Wandsworth Council '79-83;

Outlook: The return of the ultimate ideologue of the hard-Right; a would-be hard-hitter whose muscles are bound to Rightwing ideology; formerly a Cromwellian company commander in the Tories' onslaught on Labour's town halls; a fervent advocate of the poll tax and compulsory tendering; a Rightwing scion of St Andrews and the Adam Smith Institute, later in the 'No Turning Back' group of Thatcherites; "specifically dry" with "hard economic liberal convictions" (Edward Pearce, SUNDAY TELEGRAPH); long part of "the St Andrews privatisation Mafia" (PRIVATE EYE); formerly London's leading privatiser of public services and proselytiser for standing up to the public service unions from his one-time Wandsworth base; "a man conscious that local government finance is the crucible, the cauldron, the cockpit" (Frank Johnson, TIMES); his threatened "venomous attack" had "all the serpentine terror of attack by [a] slow-worm" according to Labour's Glenda Jackson;

History: An acolyte of Dr Madsen Pirie at St Andrews, he was in the Federation of Conservative Students in the late '60s; with Harvey Proctor and Piers Merchant, was a member of the Universities Group of the Rightwing 'Monday Club' Dec '69; was elected to Wandsworth Borough Council May '74; became Leader of Wandsworth Borough Council May '79; steamrollering his opponents, cut Wandsworth's costs by selling its properties; boasted he had cut 2,000 employees (20%), had cut rates but increased expenditure June '82; was awarded an OBE for his services to local government June '82; was selected for Itchen, which 'Bob' Mitchell had narrowly won for Labour before defecting to the SDP Dec '82; campaigned against Labour's defence policy as likely to lose jobs at Vosper-Thorneycroft; won Itchen, with a majority of 5,290 over the sitting SDP MP 'Bob' Mitchell, with Labour's John Denham coming 3rd June '83; he made his Maiden speech against any MPs' pay rise beyond 4%, saying "we must set an example" July '83; voted for the restoration of death penalty for all categories July '83; took on controversial far-Right Harry Phibbs as his researcher Aug '83; attacked the "complacent cabal" of local government officers for "pulling the wool over the eyes of elected councillors" instead of "cutting out waste" Jan '84; visited South Africa, as a guest of its government Jan-Feb '84; backed playing Rugby with South Africa, and increased trade with it Feb '84; claimed ILEA was "systematiclly wrecking education in inner London" in preparation for a "Leftist takeover" Feb '84; criticised building societies for not giving mortgages on system-built homes Mar '84; was one of five Tories seeking to make it mandatory for employers to get employees' permission before deducting political levy Apr '84; headed a motion urging action against misuse of student funds for political purposes June '84; he asked Mrs Thatcher to appeal to the TGWU to end the "pointless" dock strike in Southampton July '84; visited the USA as a guest of the State Department Sep '84; called for advertising on BBC and the fading out of license fees Nov '84; criticised the Government for delaying orders for Type 22 frigates, causing unemployment in his constituency Nov '84; co-signed a letter, claiming pre-Thatcher full employment was really over-manning Dec '84; voted against fluoridation Jan '85; had an adjournment debate on the black economy and shoddy work in the building trade Jan '85; initiated a debate urging the abolition of "outdated" wages councils Feb '85; at his behest, the Government dropped a clause from the Transport Bill to allow representations on the unroadworthiness of applicants (later restored in the Lords) Apr '85; was one of two Tory members of the Procedure Committee who favoured time-tabling all Bills May '85; introduced a Bill to transfer sub post offices to an independent licensing body, instead of "bribing" some of them to close down by "spurious financial targets" June '85; in an adjournment debate attacked local authorities (like Southampton) which set up "fraudulent sham" companies with ratepayers' and taxpayers' money and without accountability June '85; was one of the 13 authors of the super-Thatcherite 'No Turning Back' pamphlet rejecting caution Nov '85; elicited from the Attorney General that Lord Kagan's firm had been given 7 years to pay its fine Feb '86; asked about police powers to deal with witchcraft Feb '86; again urged time-tabling of Bills, clashing with Leader of the Commons John Biffen Feb '86; complained that supplementary benefits failed to keep up with rising costs, compelling rest-home owners to waive charges for elderly residents Mar '86; sought reassurance that the local Vosper-Thorneycroft shipyard would not face unfair competition Mar '86; complained that some petrol stations were charging 10p more than necessary Apr '86; asked how many cleaning contracts had been kept in-house despite lower tenders from outside June '86; expressed fears that Vosper-Thorneycroft might lose experienced teams through loss of orders June '86; was promoted Under Secretary for the Environment Sep '86; announced he would stop "propaganda on the rates" Nov '86; caused consternation when he suggested an Ealing Labour councillor convicted of indecency should resign, just when the House was agog with similar rumours about a leading Tory MP Nov '86; announced his support for a Whitehall reorganisation which would end the £2.8b Property Services Agency Jan '87; announced ILEA members would be subject to disqualification in cases of surcharges Jan '87; defended retrospective clauses in the Local Government Finance Bill Jan '87; denounced a Labour council which advertised for a Director of Social Services in LABOUR WEEKLY Feb '87; made concesssions to Toby Jessel in latter's opposition to wildlife-destroying Government plans to clear Thames river banks up to Hampton Court Mar '87; voted to restore hanging for "evil" murders Apr '87; refused Tony Banks' request for an independent audit of the savings the Government claimed would come from abolishing the GLC Apr '87; he increased his majority by 1,500, with SDPer 'Bob' Mitchell being forced into 3rd place by Labour June '87; became responsible to Environment Secretary Nicholas Ridley for PSA affairs and to Minister of State Michael Howard for poll tax and compulsory competitive tendering June '87; despite three negative reports, asked for further investigation of the possiblity of private provision of MPs' new offices July '87; claimed the poll tax was the last chance to save local government finances from "an advanced state of senility and decay" July '87; despite Treasury caution because of falling Stock Market, urged quick privatisation of Crown Suppliers Nov '87; claimed local councils could save a further £600m through compulsory tendering Jan '88; admitted the poll tax would cost twice as much to collect but denied the need for a national identity number system Feb '88; denied misleading the Commons by refusing to admit that the PSA could have valued DHSS headquarters at Richmond Terrace for £1,500 instead of the £40,000 charged by Cluttons Apr '88; investigated transferring Crown Suppliers' civil servants to the private sector without their agreement or legislation May '88; curbed local government publicity considered propaganda by Government July '88; voted against ordination of divorced men July '89; denied security would be endangered by privatisation of Defence bases Sep '89; claimed Bill ending council house rent subsidies would establish a truthful rent pattern Nov '89; was jeered at AMA conference when he alleged bad management over escalating rent arrears Feb '90; sought to embarrass non-poll-tax-paying Militant MP David Nellist in disclosing he had registered for the poll tax in low-tax Wandsworth rather than high-tax Coventry Feb '90; saw no prospect of reversing poll tax, insisting he had experienced worse resistance when privatising the Wandsworth dustmen Mar '90; announced cash incentives to lure council tenants into private dwellings Mar '90; voted against embryo research Apr '90; after rumours held that Mrs Thatcher was unhappy about his privatisation of PSA and Crown Suppliers, was moved sideways into Transport as Under Secretary for Roads and Traffic July '90; announced compulsory seatbelts Nov '90; through his boss, Cecil Parkinson, urged Mrs Thatcher to contest the 2nd round of the Leadership contest Nov '90; announced 20 mph speed limits near schools Dec '90; announced introduction of speed limiters on all heavy goods vehicles Feb '91; with fellow Thatcherite Michael Forsyth, tried to persuade Michael Heseltine not to abolish the poll tax Mar '91; was named as one of the Selsdon Group favouring privatising the NHS

Oct '91; announced regulations curbing car alarms July '91; defended screen-washing gangs lurking at lights July '91; with Thatcherites Eric Forth and Edward Leigh was listed as considering resignations over the Maastricht summit Dec '91; was punched in the face while canvassing; lost his seat to Labour's John Denham by 551 votes Apr '92; admitted the market-testing of civil service departments was pointless in view of EU regulations on retaining the same pay and conditions May '93; unsuccessfully sought candidacy for Eastleigh, lost to LibDems at by-election June '94; was selected for Christchurch, which had been lost to LibDem Diana Maddock in the 3rd biggest by-election swing '94, Nov '95; said he would oppose a single European currency Apr '97; recaptured Christchurch from Diana Maddock with the reduced majority of 2,165, which represented an 18.28% notional swing from '92; it was the only Tory reversal of a by-election loss May '97; in the Tory Leadership contest, joined the campaign team backing Michael Howard May-June '97; led the attempt to deny a 2nd Reading to Labour's Firearms (Amendment) Bill to ban most handguns June '97; asked the Attorney General whether he was "aware that many persistent burglars on their seventh conviction are not even being sent to prison?" June '97; the new Tory Leader, William Hague, named him Local Government Spokesman July '97; was given additional responsibility for quarrying because his team leader, Norman Fowler, having become a £25,000 Director of Aggregates Ltd, could no longer speak on that subject Oct '97; in the Road Traffic Reduction Bill urged special treatment for vehicles for the disabled and children Mar '98; his opponent, London Transport Minister, rejected his support for more roadbuilding of the sort that was already costing £20b Apr '98; was named Assistant Spokesman on Trade and Industry June '98; deplored the Government's "complacency" on the problems of small business June '98;
Born: 19 May 1947, Eastbourne
Family: Son, of late His Honour Robert Charles Chope, retired Circuit Judge, and Pamela (Durell); m '87 'Christo'/Christine (Hutchinson), fine arts archivist who worked as his secretary; 1s 1d;
Education: St Andrew's School, Eastbourne; Marlborough College; Dundee University; St Andrews University (LLB Hons) where he was a contemporary of Michael Fallon and Michael Forsyth, and was influenced by Dr Madsen Pirie;
Occupation: Barrister, Inner Temple, '72-; in Lord (Peter) Rawlinson's chambers; ex: on DTI Deregulation Task Force on Transport and Communications '93-97; Special Adviser, Ernst & Young (accountants and management consultants) '92-97; on Local Government Commission for England '94-95; on Health & Safety Commission '93-97;
Traits: Tall; blond; specs; angular features; Boy Scout manner; exhibits a studied greyness and wooden manner; as a Minister was "an inveterate droner", "one of the most insufferably boring fellows in the House" (Stuart Wavell, GUARDIAN); in local government was considered brave to the point of foolhardiness by his Tory friends; by his opponents was known as "Chopper" Chope, "unscrupulous and crude", "rasping and aggressive, willing to break all the rules" (a Labour opponent, quoted in GUARDIAN; "pitiless" (Frank Johnson, TIMES): Rottweiler owner;
Address: House of Commons, Westminster, London SW1A 0AA; 63 Roupell Street, Waterloo SE1 8SS;
Telephone: 0171 219 3000 (H of C); 0171 633 9129;

Judith Ann CHURCH   Labour   DAGENHAM '94-

Majority: 17,054 (47.2%) over Conservative 6-way;

Description: The long, thin, Dagenham-dominated seat, stretching north from the river Thames, mainly of council house dwellers who have Ford's as their largest employer; pre-'97 only marginally safe for Labour; in '95 it acquired another 1,700 voters in a minor boundary change;

Position: On the Executive of IPPR '92-; ex: on the Deregulation Committee '95-97; on Labour's National Executive Committee '92-94; Co-Chairman (with Gordon Brown), of Labour's Economics Commission '92-94; on the Plant Commission '91-93; Chairman, Hornsey and Wood Green CLP '89-90;

Outlook: Enthusiastic, pro-European Blairite 'moderniser' who has had little response to her super-loyalty; has gone quiet, compared with '97-vintage 'Blair's Babes'; a former union full-timer as MSF's Health and Safety Officer, was the first woman to be elected to the trade union section of the NEC, was earlier seen as "one of Labour's rising stars", "a convinced supporter of electoral reform, on the board of the think-tank IPPR and co-founder of the economics magazine, NEW CENTURY" (Martin Linton, GUARDIAN); "a considering woman who argues her case with logic and humanity" (Kirsty Milne, OBSERVER); was sponsored by UCW;

History: She was politicised by her experience as a factory inspector: "I was interviewing people in hospital who had lost bits of their bodies in machinery, or suffered terrible electric burns; they were accidents that could have been prevented"; she was also shocked by the closedown of factories as a result of the Thatcher Government's '79-81 deflation: "I would go to inspect places which suddenly weren't there anymore"; within three months she joined the Slough Labour Party '80; transferred to the Hornsey and Wood Green CLP '87; she was elected Chairman of Hornsey and Wood Green Constituency Labour Party, where she strongly resisted entryism '89; she was selected for Stevenage by 57% over 32% for Brian Hall, for 20 years the Leader of Stevenage Borough Council, both of them MSF Nov '89; said: "the yuppies who have been voting for Margaret Thatcher are getting older, turning into family people; they are going to start minding about schools and hospitals and whether the equipment in the local playground is falling apart"; "we have to remind people that taxes are our collective purchasing power; we can't each go round paying for schools and refuse collection on our own" Feb '90; was named to the Plant Commission ??? '91; in Stevenage, she came second in the general election, increasing the Labour vote by 53% and its share by 12%, moving it from third to second place Apr '92; was elected to the Trade Union Section of Labour's National Executive Committee, coming seventh with 4,743,000 votes, the first woman so to succeed Sep '92; on the Plant Commission, although an enthusiast for electoral reform, voted for first-past-the-post rather than Supplementary Voting Mar '93; in an article in the FABIAN REVIEW called for the regeneration of old industrial "brown field" sites into high-tech areas for the next century Apr '94; with ten nominations, was shortlisted for Dagenham with three others by an NEC selection committee, after Bryan Gould announced he would be stepping down to return to New Zealand Apr '94; was selected by Dagenham; she was tied in the 4th round at 100-100 with Chris Pond of the Low Pay Unit, but won with more first preferences Apr '94; was elected with a 13,344 majority, double that secured by Bryan

Gould June '94; opposed the closure of Oldchurch Hospital's Accident and Emergency unit July '94; in her Maiden, as a UCW-sponsored MP, warned against the "pin-striped predators" tearing apart the Post Office at the behest of the Treasury and Michael Heseltine July '94; decided not to stand again for the Trade Union Section of Labour's NEC July '94; voted for Blair for Leader, Beckett for Deputy Leader July '94; urged Government to develop a UK Plc information superhighway Nov '94; with other Blairite modernisers - Anne Campbell, Tony Wright and others -published a new version of Clause IV Feb '95; introduced a Women and Information Technology Bill to "address the serious under-representation of women in IT at all levels" Mar '95; was named to Deregulation Committee Mar '95; backed decision to impose an all-women short-list in Slough, where she grew up May '95; claimed that the basic change in employer-employee relations at Dagenham had increased profits and wages July '95; backed Blair's decision to drop all-women's short-lists, claiming "we have broken through and changed the culture of the party" July '95; defended Blair against Leftwing critics Ken Livingstone and George Galloway, urging them not to communicate their grievances through the media Aug '95; at GUARDIAN conference-fringe meeting, told of BMW-drivers coming over to Labour out of fear of losing jobs and homes Oct '95; in an extension of the annual reshuffle, was assigned to Youth on the team of Mo Mowlam, Spokesman on Northern Ireland Oct '95; warned of danger from unqualified gas representatives when British Gas lost its monopoly Nov '95; attacked cuts in lone-parent benefits in Chancellor Clarke's Budget Dec '95; was the only Labour MP at PLP to defend Harriet Harman's sending her son to a selective school in Bromley, pointing out how inadequate many London schools were due to poor resources and the social mix Jan '96; introduced Childcare (Local Provision) Bill to make provision for local implementation of a national childcare strategy Apr '96; urged greater female representation in Northern Ireland political life, as part of the development of its proportional representation Apr '96; voted for MPs' pensions to be based on £43,000 July '96; retained her seat with a majority of 17,054 on a 16.2% swing from '92, May '97; welcomed first question time as "more like a modern dialogue and not a bear garden," adding: "I'm sure the women had an impact on it" May '97; was a signatory to the European Movement's advertisement: "Europe: A Force for Fairness, Equality and Opportunity for Women" Nov '97;
Born: 19 September 1953, London
Family: Daughter, the late Edmund Church, who worked in the City in the export credit business, and Helen (Anderson), a nurse now retired; her former partner, Peter Mitchell, was an employment law specialist for the TUC; 2s: Matthew '88, Edward'91; separated '95;
Education: St Bernard's Convent and Grammar School, Slough '57-72; Leeds University (BA Hons in Mathematics and Philosophy) '75; Huddersfield Polytechnic (Certificate in Technical Education) '78; Aston University (Diploma in Occupational Health and Safety) '81; Thames Valley College (Diploma in Management Studies) '84;
Occupation: Formerly UCW-sponsored '94-95; ex: National Health and Safety Officer, MSF '86-94; HM Inspector of Factories, for Health and Safety Executive '80-86; Process Researcher, for Mars UK and a chemical company '78-80; Mathematics Teacher, in West Africa, with Voluntary Services Overseas '75-77;
Traits: Dark, curly, short hair; pleasant smile showing good teeth; "comely" (Peter Oborne, EVENING STANDARD); "exemplifies the shoulder-padded socialists" (Lesley Thomas, SUNDAY TIMES); "telegenic and earnest " (TIMES); "I used to think you could be too glamorous or your colleagues would think you were a bimbo; but that's rubbish; if you look back at us 15 years ago, we were probably a bit drab" (JC); is said to hate her neighbour Margaret Hodge, calling her "a two-faced bitch"; can hide her status: after snubbing Tory MP Charles Hendry at the opera, later apologised: "Sorry, Charles but the chap I was with didn't know I was an MP"; "I think I'm the only MP with a poster of Keanu Reeves in my office"

(JC); articulate; likeable; witty; thoughtful; RC by education;
Address: House of Commons, WestminsterLondon SW1A 0AA;
Telephone: 0171 219 6000 (House of Commons);

Michael ('Mick') CLAPHAM   **Labour**   **BARNSLEY WEST & PENISTONE '92-**

Majority: 17,267 (40.9%) over Conservative 4-way;
Description: The unaltered remaining half of the old Penistone seat, north of the Peak District, from the sheep-raising Pennine farms down to the mining outskirts of Barnsley; it includes the towns of Penistone, Hoyland and Dodworth; it has over 20 closed collieries and over 20,000 lost pit jobs; unemployment rises from 18% in Barnsley to 40% in former mining villages;
Position: Chairman, all-party Group on Occupational Safety and Health '96-; ex: PPS, to Alan Milburn, May-Dec '97; on Trade and Industry Select Committee '92-97; Vice Chairman, PLP Trade and Industry Group '96-97; on Branch Committee of NUM '65-70;

Outlook: A union loyalist in the hard-Left Campaign Group, he has made a comeback after a difficult time in Scargill's backyard for his differing defence of a shrunken coalmining industry: "I had a bad time for a couple of years" (MC); a locally-popular former coalface miner turned lecturer and top NUM official; once friendly to Arthur Scargill, he mourns the "tragedy" of Scargill's self-segregation in his "stillborn Stalinist anachronism"; his political hero is another ex-miner, Aneurin Bevan; says, "I see socialism operating on two levels: one is ethical; the other is about how you organise the rsources of society to benefit people by a more equitable distribution"; he resigned as Alan Milburn's PPS in protest against the Blair Government's December 1997 lone-parent benefit cuts; has proved to be a restrained, factual and effective defender of a mining industry under terminal attack; until the '92 election was Head of NUM's Industrial Relations Department; his speeches concentrate on miners' and union problems; also wants a political rather than a military solution to Ulster's problems; is an enthusiastic supporter of defence cuts to release "£8b a year" to "increase social provision and better the nation's economic infrastructure"; anti-nuclear (Greenpeace); pro-Soviet (British-Soviet Friendship Society); was NUM-sponsored;
History: After having left the Labour Party in the '60s in protest against Harold Wilson's appeasement of the US over Vietnam, rejoined the Labour Party at 36, '79; was backed by NUM and Arthur Scargill initially for selection for Barnsley Central in succession to Roy Mason, but was pipped at the post by Eric Illsley, who finally secured NUM backing against his closest NUPE rival, helped by the story - repeated in PRIVATE EYE - that Clapham had signed nomination papers in '79 for a 'Troops Out' candidate, the father of a convicted IRA bomber, against ex-miner Roy Mason when Ulster Secretary Dec '86-Jan '87; "it was my intention to focus attention on the Irish question; to construe the fact that I signed his nomination papers as an act which supports terrorism is totally absurd"; announced he would seek selection for Barnsley West when Allen McKay said he would not stand again; he was in a quandry when Arthur Scargill, whom he had known since the '60s - when he was a coalface worker -refused to rule himself out and tried to persuade Allen McKay to stay on until the

mid-90s, Sep-Oct '89; was selected for Barnsley West and Penistone Jan '90; retained seat by a virtually identical majority of 14,504 votes Apr '92; in his Maiden pointed out that his constituency had lost 20,000 pit jobs in the previous decade, although miners had almost trebled their productivity May '92; co-sponsored motion opposing opencast coal mining May '92; emphasised that the four pension schemes in the mining industry held over £12b "which is a great attraction to an asset stripper"; British Coal had already taken £735m from it in pensions holidays, which would continue until 2001; urged copper-bottomed guarantees for all pensioners in the industry June '92; pointed out that the safety record of British Coal was much better than its foreign or domestic private competitors June '92; was named to Trade and Industry Select Committee as its only ex-miner Oct '92; led motion opposing "dash for gas" and guaranteeing 65m ton takeup of coal by generators Nov '92; insisted that he wanted all 31 surviving pits to be saved, not merely 25; this could be done by transferring to coal the nuclear levy and ending taking electricity from France Feb '93; was vilified by Arthur Scargill for accepting the Trade and Industry Select Committee's plan to close 31 pits Feb '93; defended the agreed pit-saving decisions of the Trade and Industry Select Committee against the pit-sacrificing Government White Paper Mar '93; co-sponsored amendment by ex-miner MPs to save all 31 threatened pits Mar '93; voted against 3rd Reading of Maastricht treaty Bill May '93; in debate on Employment Rights Bill insisted that part-time workers should have a statutory right to an itemised pay slip to enable them to make claims against folded small businesses June '93; in debate on Trade Union Reform Bill attacked clause enabling employer to "offer a bribe" of higher wages if employees gave up right to belong to a union of his choice June '93; complained that cut in Arts Council funding would affect mainly smaller theatrical companies July '93; complained that the Mines (Health and Safety) Bill's removal of the safety role of the pit deputy would undermine British Coal's outstanding safety record Oct '93; ridiculed the "Back to Basics" philosophy in the Queen's Speech as meaning "deregulation", "low wages, poor working conditions and a lack of representational rights" Nov '93; insisted that markets for coal were the crucial area but "the Governement have failed to deal with that point" Jan '94; supported anti-US motion on North Korea Feb '94; opposed Deregulation Bill because of its adverse impact on health and safety regulations Feb '94; voted against restoring capital punishment, even for killers of policemen Feb '94; voted to reduce age of homosexual consent to 18 or 16, Feb '94; warned that privatisation would end the support given to miners for industrial diseases Mar '94; introduced Bill to reduce to ten years the period of underground work required for miners to qualify for benefits for chronic bronchitis and emphysema Apr '94; secured a debate to pay fuller tributes to just-deceased Labour MPs Apr '94; voted for Prescott for Leader, Beckett for Deputy Leader July '94; in the Queen's Speech debate, deplored the "further reduction in the share of the national income going to the public sector" Nov '94; co-wrote TRIBUNE article defending Clause IV and claiming the "UK privatisation model has run its course", on behalf of the miners' group of MPs Jan '95; complained of impact of Tory Government's "standstill Budget" on education in Barnsley Feb '95; called for money to clean up water courses polluted by minewater from defunct pits June '95; claimed one-third of Barnsley households had at least one person suffering from a disabling disease June '95; voted for Tony Benn's defence amendment calling for scrapping of Trident and curbing of defence spending to the West European average Oct '95; urged a minimum wage to stimulate the economy, complaining that 18% of Barnsley's males were unemployed Nov '95; complained that Barnsley 2.8% increase in Standard Spending Assessment (SSA) for '96-97 was a freeze in real terms Jan '96; deplored the "tragedy" of Arthur Scargill's departure to form his own party: "the Labour Party is the dominant political force and it is the place where socialists should be"; Scargll's alternative was a "still-born Stalinist anachronism" Jan '96; claimed the EU's Social Chapter "could save European manufacturing industry" Feb '96; again opposed nuclear privatisation on safety grounds, insisting "profits and plutonium do not mix" Mar '96; asked about risk to workers from slaughtering BSE-infected cattle Mar '96; alleged Tory Government was abandoning its two-year training period for probation officers to bring in ex-servicemen to instill discipline Apr '96; was listed in INDEPENDENT as one of 26 Labour MPs in Parliamentary Humanist Group Apr '96; attacked cuts in accessibility to Reduced Earning Allowance by miners with pneumoconiosis June '96; attacked partial privatisation of nuclear industry as meaning the decommissioning costs of the older power stations would have to be met by the taxpayer June '96; attacked Tory Government for its inflexibility in recognising and compensating miners with emphysema and chronic bronchitis June '96; insisting public ownership of energy utilities would be "back on the agenda within 10 years", attacked slipping safety precautions in private mines and deplored opencast mining July '96; opposed 3% cap on MPs' pay rise July '96; urged more funds for Barnsley's depressed areas Feb '97; retained unaltered seat by enhanced majority of 17,267 on a pro-Labour swing of 5.3% May '97; was named PPS to Alan Milburn, Minister of State for Health May '97; voted to ban fox-hunting June '97; co-wrote to GUARDIAN protesting lack of access to material on Jonathan Aitken's involvement with BMARC in arms-for-Iran when his Select Committee on Trade and Industry was investigating June '97; in the wake of the RJ Budge warning of an impending disaster for remaining coal mines, formed a discreet lobby with colleagues Paddy Tipping and Kevin Barron to save remaining 11,000 mining jobs Nov '97; was told by PM Tony Blair about a six-month deal between coal producers and power generators; hours later he resigned as PPS to Alan Milburn as one of the Labour MP opposing cuts in lone-parent benefits Dec '97; voted against military action against Iraq Feb '98; urged more educational emphasis on the creative arts Feb '98; again urged a ban on white asbestos, asking PM Blair to backdate payment for asbestosis to the onset of the disease Mar '98; blamed fall in union membership almost wholly on unemployment May '98; urged that multinationals like Rio Tinto be pushed "to promote human rights and protect the environment in areas of the world where they practice" May '98; having broadened his 'save the coalmines' lobby into allied industries, was delighted by the Government's reprieve for the coalmining industry June '98; complained about Portugal's treatment of a constituent, Professor David Lowery June '98; derided John Redwood as "a classic case of Festinger's theory of cognitive dissonance because he did one thing and says another" July '98;

Born: 15 May 1943, Barnsley

Family: Son, late Thomas Clapham, miner, and Laura Alice (?maiden?); m '65 Yvonne (Hallsworth); 1s, 1d;

Education: Leeds Polytechnic (BSc Hons); Leeds University (PGCE); Bradford University (MPhil);

Occupation: Formerly Sponsored, by NUM (£600 p a for constituency and 80% of election expenses) '92-95; ex: Head, NUM Industrial Relations Department '83-92; Deputy Head, Yorkshire NUM Compensation Department '77-83; College Lecturer, '75-77; Miner '58-70 (left for further education);

Traits: Dark, pleasant-looking; front-combed, centre-parted hair; heavy, arched eyebrows; "looks like a character out of 'Sons and Lovers' (Anne Perkins, GUARDIAN); acts with "cutomary modesty" (Ann Clwyd MP); loyal (especially to miners and ex-miners); humanist; enjoys squash, walking, reading;

Address: House of Commons, Westminster, London SW1A 0AA; 19 Lawrence Close, Higham, South Yorkshire S75 1PE; 18 Regent Street, Barnsley Yorkshire S70 2HG;

Telephone: 0171 219 5015 (H of C); 01226 384714 (home); 01226 730692 (office); 01742 888239 (Agent, Trevor Cave); 01742 888239 (regional party);

Majority: 3,075 (6.1%) over Labour 6-way;
Description: The South Hertfordshire commuter towns of Potters Bar, Borehamwood-Elstree, Radlett and Bushey - all but the last were previously in South Hertfordshire; mostly middle-class, except for the vast Borehamwood GLC overspill estate; it contains Elstree film studios; in '95 it lost the 5,500 voters in London Colney ward to St Albans;
Position: Deputy Spokesman, on Home Affairs '97-; ex: Under Secretary, for the Environment '95-97; on Select Committees: on Members' Interests '94-95, Health '92-93; PPS, to Lady Blatch '93-95; Secretary, Conservative MPs' Education Committee '92-93; Treasurer, of Oxford University Conservative

Association;
Outlook: One of the few Tory front-benchers chastened by his near-defeat in the formerly-safe seat previous held by Cecil Parkinson; recently transformed into a moderate and sensible spokesman, replacing the former combative young superloyalist Rightwinger; was judged by the GUARDIAN's Simon Hoggart of having been given in '95 a "brown-nose promotion" as a reward for his naive, stoogey questions and over-egged Government-supporting speeches; at the Whips' behest, helped to block Dr Roger Berry's disabled rights Bill in '94; was somewhat more restrained about legal and constituency problems, like local unemployment and Elstree's threatened studios; pro-Zionist (Conservative Friends of Israel); a Leeds barrister, property company director and former Lloyd's 'name' with inherited wealth, was rewarded with Cecil Parkinson's safe seat after four times fighting doggedly in hopeless ones - Bootle (twice), Yorkshire South and Barnsley East with unquestioning loyalty to earlier Thatcherite dogmas;
History: His rich farmer father was a Conservative Councillor; he joined the Young Conservatives; became Treasurer of Oxford University Conservative Association; was selected to fight hopeless Barnsley East '86; was delighted by drop of 429 in local unemployment, bringing rate down from 20.5% to 20% Mar '87; lost Barnsley East to Terry Patchett by an even greater majority than his predecessor, achieving a 5% swing to Labour June '87; strongly supported motion backing the poll tax at annual Conservative conference Oct '87; as candidate for hopeless Yorkshire South in Euro-election, backed Mrs Thatcher's belief in Europe as "an association of independent and democratic nations linked by trade and co-operation in matters of common interest and not for the Community to become a federation of states governed by a central bureaucracy" Sep '88; lost Yorkshire South contest June '89; at Conservative annual conference urged the swift introduction of the poll tax; also repeated his opposition to a federal Europe: "we do not want full European Union in a federal state" Oct '89; was selected to fight Mike Carr on the death of Bootle's Allan Roberts Apr '90; insisted "the extreme Left is still very much in place in the Labour Party in Merseyside; the selection of the Labour Party candidate [Mike Carr] in this constituency...looks like nothing more than a cheap confidence trick to tell the people that Merseyside is free of Leftwing influence" Apr '90; during his hopeless effort to overturn the bequeathed Labour majority of almost 25,000, was supported by Kenneth Baker, Chris Patten, Michael Howard, Michael Heseltine, Michael Portillo and David Trippier; "we've had very little abuse," he said, "the people of Bootle admire Mrs Thatcher's guts" May '90; his Tory vote went down to 9% from a previous 20%; he finished

23,500 behind Labour and only 41 votes ahead of the Liberal Democrats; this represented a 9.8% swing from Tories to Labour May '90; loyally agreed to to fight Bootle again after the sudden death of Mike Carr MP Aug '90; welcomed the Thatcher Government's "positive record of achievement" on the Merseyside; claimed the Unified Business Rate would "benefit northwest business to the tune of over £300m when in full force" Oct '90; claimed Bootle Tories had offered a poll tax £104 lower per couple Oct '90; at annual Tory conference a month before Mrs Thatcher was deposed, claimed Tories were "united in support of the Government's policies" Oct '90; was again defeated at Bootle, this time by Joe Benton, achieving a fractionally higher percentage of the vote and finishing 371 ahead of the Liberal Democrat Nov '90; was short-listed for Nigel Lawson's safe Blaby seat Dec '90; at 34, was selected for Hertsmere over Sir Paul Beresford, after Cecil Parkinson announced his impending retirement Mar '91; retained seat by 18,735 votes, almost identical with Parkinson's last majority, but a 2% swing to Labour Apr '92; was elected Joint Secretary of Conservative MPs' Education Committee with David Faber, defeating Lady Olga Maitland June '92; urged setting of performance targets for courts "so that the public can know which courts are the most successful" June '92; was named to Health Select Committee July '92; visited Argentina and Uruguay as guest of Inter-Parliamentary Council Against Anti-Semitism July '92; enthused about choice of grant-maintained status by a constituency school as a "beacon of hope" Nov '92; said parents had every right to information about their children's examination performances and would "feel huge disappointment if some teacher unions boycotted their children's tests" Dec '92; complained about rundown of St Albans hospital on behalf of Peter Lilley and himself Feb '93; urged encouragement to Israelis over Golan heights, despite deportation to Lebanon of Palestinian Hammas extremists Feb '93; welcomed Home Secretary Michael Howard's promise of tougher action against juvenile offenders, including more secure training centres Mar '93; amidst usual super-loyal claims that "Conservative values" were "shared more widely than ever before among the electorate", admitted that Hertfordshire "went into recession earlier than some other parts of the country" and "there is no lack of concern about unemployment" there; agreed that only growth would solve the problem but admitted that most local people insisted that growth was still "fragile" June '93; backed Israel's "progress" on curbing Jewish settlements on the West Bank June '93; proposed to introduce Right to Silence (Amendment) Bill to permit court comment if accused refused to answer quesstions June '93; urged John Major to redress "the absence of a power for the courts to send persistent juvenile offenders into secure accommodation" July '93; asked PM John Major a stooge question about Britain's agenda on "cutting deficits, deregulation and improving the flexibility of the labour market" July '93; introduced Bill to double maximum sentence for young offenders July '93; insisted social security expenditure was too high and had to be reviewed July '93; urged "careful monitoring" of "innovative" workstart pilot project aimed at "getting the long-term unemployed back into work" Oct '93; with a score of other Tory Rightwingers, threatened to vote against the Government on further defence cuts Oct '93; asked stooge question about local NHS reforms which would "help managers and professionals to work together with purchasers to promote high-quality care and best clinical practice" in his constituency Oct '93; fed Environment Under Secretary Tony Baldry a stooge question about how much better off single people were in Tory areas Oct '93; with five other loyal Rightwingers, decided to try to rid 1922 Commitee of fervent anti-Maastricht Rightwingers Sir George Gardiner, John Townend, Sir Rhodes Boyson and James Pawsey Nov '93; welcomed Michael Howard's law and order proposals in Queen's Speech, pretending to expect Labour's Home Office spokesman Tony Blair to back them as well Nov '93; voted to restore capital punishment, especially for killers of policemen Feb '94; voted to reduce age of homosexual consent to 18, but not 16, Feb '94; with threatened Elstree studios in his constituency, backed film industry proposals to make Britain more attractive to US film-makers by fiscal incentives Mar-Apr '94; opposed Paddy Ashdown's proposal to abandon UK's "national veto" as handing Westminster's power over to Brussels Apr '94; with Lady Olga Maitland and others put down Government-sponsored crippling amendments to kill off Dr Berry's disabled rights Bill May '94; asked stooge question of PM John Major, attacking signalmen's strike and berating Labour for not taking a Tory line June '94; welcoming "the significant fall in serious crime", urged Tony Blair to give up his campaign for the Labour leadership in the country to return to the Commons to welcome the fall in serious crime June '94; declaring his interest as a Lloyd's 'name', insisted that protecting the environment should have priority when ships with dangerous cargoes were sinking July '94; claimed inward investment would be attracted most by "continuing the economic policies which have brought the UK such great and growing successes throughout the '80s and '90s" Oct '94; denies he was briefed by lobbyist Ian Greer, active in blocking efforts to ban tobacco advertising '94; was added to Select Committee on Members' Interests Dec '94; was promoted Under Secretary for the Environment, yielding his post on the Members' Interests committee July '95; welcomed Tory MP Andrew Hunter's Bill to impose on-the-spot fines of £10 on dog-owners refusing to clean up after their dogs Mar '96; rejected as unnecessary the proposal of Tory MP David Ashby to give the partner of a gay tenant the right to inherit the tenancy in the event of death, since same-sex couples could register as joint tenants Mar '96; voted to extend the waiting period for divorce and against no-fault divorces Apr '96; rejected Labour MP Richard Burden's effort to introduce compulsory controls of water leakage May '96; voted for 3% cap on MPs' pay rises, cuts in their mileage allowances and against pensions based on £43,000 July '96; endorsed Tory MP Harry Greenway's Bill to make punishable by on-the-spot fines of £100 night-time noises exceeding 35 decibels Dec '96; opposed EU-wide bans on noise pollutions, insisting cultural differences made it an issue of strictly national concern Dec '96; announced Tory Government's abandonment of plans to ban smoking in all public buildings, but said people "who have chosen not to be smokers should be able to expect an area in public places which is smoke-free" Dec '96; narrowly retained his formerly-safe seat with his majority slashed to one-sixth, 3,075, on a pro-Labour swing of 15.1% May '97; backed William Hague for Leader May-June '97; was named Deputy Spokesman on Home Affairs, under Dr Brian Mawhinney June '97; argued for the "deterrent value of prison" for young offenders against new Home Secretary's effort to emphasise education and training for them Aug '97; removed the Commons pass from his researcher, Stuart Pollock, revealed as a Consultant to the loan firm City Mortgage Corporation (CMC), linked to US fraudsters, whose managing director, David Steene, had donated £20,000 to William Hague's leadership campaign Aug '97; after a long period of restrained opposition tried to become aggressive on Labour's inadequate supply of secure accommodation for young delinquents, invoking Home Secretary Jack Straw's taunt of its being "remarkably poorly researched" since the Major Government had taken nearly seven years to provide 170 places, some unusable Feb '98;

Born: 14 September 1956, Beverley

Family: Son, late Leonard Clappison, wealthy farmer, and Dorothy (Blashill), farmer; m '84 Helen Margherita (Carter), solicitor and former university law tutor; 1s Henry '87; 2d Charlotte, '85, Christabel '89;

Education: Patrington School (state primary); St Peter's School, York; Queen's, Oxford University (Scholarship);

Occupation: Barrister, called to the Bar '81, with chambers in Leeds '82-; Director and Shareholder, L Clappison Ltd, his late father's firm from which he receives rental income; also receives rental income from "other properties", including "six rented houses" and a "small hairdresser's" in Patrington, North Humberside; is actively involved in his family's farm near

Patrington, run by his mother in the wake of his father's death; ex: Lloyd's Underwriter, in a score of syndicates, six of them open '82-94;
Traits: Chubby; rounded face; pug nose; front-combed, parted dark brown hair; initially displayed an almost infantile, stoogey super-loyalism; "Mr Oleaginous" (Simon Hoggart, GUARDIAN); "pugilistic" (Victor Smart, OBSERVER); had a "slightly sententious manner", "sounds like a pompous third-former, reading out his Nature Study project to apathetic and sadly unconcerned classmates" (David Aaronovitch, INDEPENDENT); a determined fighter, even in impossible circumstances like fighting rock-safe Labour seats like Bootle;
Address: House of Commons, Westminster, London SW1A 0AA; 7 Foxhill Avenue, Weetwood, Leeds LS16 5PB;
Telephone: 0171 219 5027/4152 (H of C); 01532 786038;

Rt Hon Alan (Kenneth McKenzie) CLARK　　　Conservative　　　**KENSINGTON & CHELSEA '97-**

Majority: 9,519 over Labour 9-way;
Description: The new seat whose concentration of wealth makes it the second safest in the country for a Tory candidate; the habitat of the mythical 'Sloane Ranger'; contains many of London's famous institutions, set in exclusive residential areas;
Former Seat: Sutton, Plymouth '74-92;
Position: Vice Chairman, of 1922 Committee '97-; ex: Minister of State, for Defence '89-92, for Trade '86-89; Under Secretary, for Employment '83-86; Secretary, Conservative MPs' Home Affairs Committee '82-83, '76-81; Vice Chairman '80-83, Secretary '79, their Defence Committtee; on Select Committee on Sound Broadcasting '76-83;

Outlook: The dashing, cynical, wealthy Renaissance Prince of the chauvinist hard-Right; "I'm a political junkie; I couldn't stay away from it"; believes "it is natural to be proud of your race and your country"; a maverick who is cynical about everything but his Thatcher-worship (until recently); exposed this and many other personal and political secrets in his fabulously popular diaries; a blurter of the needs of realpolitik, like the need for an overnight slaughter of 600 IRAmen; "Mr Clark is terrific at thinking the unthinkable; what he just can't do is think the thinkable" (Simon Hoggart, GUARDIAN); like many Rightwing nationalists, is anti-German and anti-American but pro-Russian; is deeply suspicious of the EU, thinks NATO has outlived its usefulness; is deeply suspicious of pro-European Tories like Michael Heseltine and Kenneth ("puffball") Clarke; a believer in 'Fortress Britain' who would have struck a peace deal with Hitler in 1940; self-described as "romantic and reactionary"; "I am a reactionary populist Tory, [a] hanger but not a flogger", "like Gengis Khan, only richer" -with £28m at last count; is against cruel sports except for Europhile-baiting; was an open opponent of Devonport dockyard privatisation; "the first Tory Minister to resign to spend more time with other people's families" (Labour MP John Reid);
History: He decided he wanted to be a politician at Eton; he joined the Conservative Party '58; joined the Rightwing, pro-Empire Monday Club; rejected as unwinnable the candidacy offered for the Swindon by-election '69; was banned from the Tories' candidates' list as too reactionary, on the orders of Ted Heath '69; was adopted as candidate for Sutton, Plymouth

Sep '72; said Uganda Asian immigrants should be told: "you cannot come into the country because you are not white" '72; won Sutton Feb '74; urged Ted Heath be dropped as Leader Mar '74; opposed Channel Tunnel, though it would benefit his Kent landholding, because "the English Channel has always protected us from invasion" Apr '74; supported a part-elected Tory Shadow Cabinet July '74; opposed sanctions against Ian Smith's Rhodesia Nov '74; opposed talk of coalition May '75; attacked Plymouth's Workers' Education Association as a "school for scroungers" Sep '75; was among 28 Tory MPs who voted against devolution after being asked by the Whips to abstain Jan '76; warned that the Tories were losing their working-class base Dec '76; opposed Hitachi being allowed to build TVs in the UK Apr '77; backed SPUC May '77; warned against banning National Front march in Manchester in response to the "insatiable" hunger of the "extreme Left" Sep '77; rebelled against sanctions against Rhodesia Nov '78; opposed sale of Harriers to China Dec '78; talked out Ethnic Groups Grant Bill Mar '79; opposed fluoridation of water Aug '79; opposed Cruise deterrent Nov '79; was named Chairman of committee to investigate Britain's civil defence May '80; opposed interfering with wage levels June '80; warned that UK civil defence was inadequate and run by those "ignorant of their task" July '80; warned against further cutbacks in British defence spending Dec '80; urged defence cuts be made in Rhine Army, not in the Navy May '81; urged a referendum on capital punishment Nov '81; backed Keith Speed in his resignation from office over Royal Navy cuts May '81; opposed judicial whipping Mar '82; suspected collusion over Argentine landings in the Falklands; warned against betrayal of the Falklands Apr '82; insisted UK had no nuclear independence since US permission was needed to launch US-provided missiles Jan '83; expressed sympathy for the police in shooting of innocent Stephen Waldorf, alleging his companions in the car were "tainted with criminality" Jan '83; said Government's subliminal approach in anti-CND advertising was demeaning Feb '83; was appointed Under Secretary for Employment June '83; although a non-drinker was accused of being "incapable" by Clare Short, when he mocked a statement on equal pay for women by reading it slowly July '83; launched the start-your-own-business Enterprise Scheme for the unemployed Aug '83; resigned as Patron of the Anti-Hunt Council because the Government announced it did not intend to legislate against hunting Aug '83; attacked Esperanto, saying, "if you want an international language, it should be English" Sep '83; urged the rejection of Jo Richardson's Sex Equality Bill, insisting it would inhibit the employment of women Dec '83; survived Michael Heseltine's demand he be sacked for "slightly treasonable" remark on the BBC, admitting Ministers had given in to admirals in placing Harpoon missiles in the USA, instead of the UK, giving Americans "a tremendous vested interest...against arms control" Apr '84; was accused of having made a remark about "Bongo-Bongo Land" Oct '84; nodded in agreement with Teddy Taylor's anti-EEC remarks while on the Front Bench Jan '85; admitted he was "totally ashamed" of the Government's decision to privatise the Devonport dockyard July '85; with Lord Young's backing, he opposed Home Office plans to introduce US-style contract compliance Oct '85; avoided voting for the Government's Dockyards Bill by arranging an out-of-town engagement Dec '85; revealed massive dole frauds in 25 towns Dec '85; was promoted Minister of State for Trade at DTI in Paul Channon's place as part of reshuffle after Leon Brittan's resignation over Westland Feb '86; defended Multi-Fibre Agreement because "free trade, like unilateral nuclear disarmament, is fine only as long as everyone is doing it" Feb '86; admitted it was unlikely International Tin Council could be rescued Mar '86; was again pointedly absent on the dockyard privatisation vote Mar '86; in a letter to Frank Field, he admitted job losses from South African sanctions could not be quantified June '86; warned GATT against a flood of protectionist measures which could cause a world trade collapse Sep '86; announced he favoured US consultants for Devonport dockyard rather than a management buy-out Oct '86; although not consulted, opposed Paul Channon's refusal to refer to the MMC the BTR bid for Pilkington Jan '87; voted for Geoffrey Dickens' Bill to hang child murderers Jan '87; voted for Sir Ian Percival's Bill to restore hanging for "evil" murderers Apr '87; threatened retaliatory action unless the Japanese stopped import discrimination Apr '87; again declared his opposition to the Channel Tunnel June '87; lost two-thirds of his majority, largely due to job losses from dockyard privatisation June '87; the Japanese congratulated him on his reappointment as Trade Minister June '87; backed David Alton's abortion-curbing Bill Nov '87, Jan '88; privately gave ambiguous advice to Matrix-Churchill executives about exports of arms-making equipment to Iraq Jan '88; opposed the "protectionist" EEC's effort to limit non-EEC TV programmes to 40% of transmissions Mar '88; urged "real teeth" for GATT Mar '88; opposed plans for a nuclear waste store in Devonport dockyard Apr '88; his effort to label some furs as caught by leghold traps was opposed by Canadian Indians May '88; was reshuffled sideways as Minister of State for Defence Procurement July '89; a leak of his defence cuts, reducing the Navy from 48 to 32 destroyers and infantry battalions from 55 to 32, put him at odds with Defence Secreraty Tom King and defence chiefs May '90; Tom King's 18% cuts were less swingeing July '90; was sent by Mrs Thatcher as her emissary to bolster Arab support for the multinational military force in the Gulf Aug '90; horrified by Mrs Thatcher's fall - for which he would never forgive Michael Heseltine - backed John Major as her successor Nov '90; the SUNDAY TIMES disclosed the ambiguous advice he had given to Matrix-Churchill Dec '90; announced NATO was obsolete Dec '90; became a Privy Councillor Jan '91; claimed Britain's European partners "ran for their cellars" on the Iraqi invasion of Kuwait Jan '91; was quoted as saying, "what we need now is the ability to create an alliance with Russia against the Japanese" Jan '91; claimed one of his last acts as Defence Minister was to try to persuade Mrs Thatcher to authorise the sale of Hawks to the Iraqis Mar '91; as a landowner in Scotland was described by Scots Labour MP Brian Wilson as "a parasite on the people of the Highlands and Islands" Apr '91; HM Customs investigators indicated their intention of interviewing him and Lord Trefgarne over the sale of munition-making tools to Iraq Apr '91; was attacked in a GUARDIAN letter for attending a party hosted by the far-Right historian, Hitler-apologist David Irvine Dec '91; fined for doing 99 mph in his Porsche on the M5 in Somerset, said he thought the police car pursuing him was his personal escort Jan '92; voted for the anti-hare-coursing Bill of Labour MP Kevin McNamara Feb '92; before the Commons Trade and Industry Select Committee claimed the first he knew about the Iraqi 'supergun' was when it was seized by Customs in Apr '90 at Teesport Feb '92; at the last minute, he decided not to contest his seat again Mar '92; at the Old Bailey trial of Matrix-Churchill executives, caused the collapse of the trial when he admitted he had been "economical with the actualite" in telling executives to emphasise the likely peaceful use of their machine tools when Whitehall knew they were destined for Iraq's arms factories Nov '92; the Crown Prosecution Service decided not to prosecute him over the export of arms-making equipment to Iraq Mar '93; admitting the drug of politics was too strong for him, put his name forward for the Newbury by-election Mar '93; revealed that Government ministers' phones were routinely tapped by MI5 May '93; claiming that no British interests were at stake, urged withdrawal from ex-Yugoslavia May '93; his frank 'Diaries' were hailed as unequalled since those of 'Chips' Channon June '93; was arrested in London for driving through a police bomb cordon Feb '94; was accused by South-Africa-based Judge Harkness of having had intercourse with his wife and daughters Oct '94; claimed favour of Prince the Cabinet was "top-heavy with federalists -Hurd, Clarke, Heseltine and Hunt - who were all turnoffs and Heathite groupies who should have been consigned to the knackers' yard years ago" Dec '94; attended the Coventry Cathedral funeral of the animal rights activist, Jill Phipps, who had been run over Feb '95; claimed that 'New Labour" were no more than "a bunch of people in suits who want to win an election" Mar '95; joined animal rights protesters at Dover docks to oppose the export of live sheep and calves, accusing police of "pushing up the profits of a load of thugs in the haulage industry" Apr '95; it was rumoured he was taking instruction in the Catholic faith May '95; a leak from the Scott Report named him and two other ministers who had deliberately failed to inform Parliament of the decision to relax the guidelines on defence sales to Iraq from Dec '88, Nov '95; having admitted his decision not to stand again was an error, sought selection for the new safe seat of Kensington and Chelsea, along with John Maples and Michael Fallon, but they lost out to Chelsea's sitting MP, Sir Nicholas Scott Nov '95; sought unsuccessfully to be selected for Sevenoaks, Dorset North and Tunbridge Wells '95-96; in a rerun of Kensington and Chelsea after Sir Nicholas Scott had been found drunk on a pavement, Clark was successful in being chosen from a short-list of four on the third ballot Jan '97; Elizabeth Peacock MP - about whom he had been rude in his 'Diaries' - wondered how Kensington and Chelsea could choose a "self-confessed philanderer, reprobate and adulterer who has been extremely rude about people in trade yet is no aristocrat himself, his family having made their money in the cotton trade" Feb '97; campaigned as an opponent of the single European currency Apr '97; won the seat by 9,519, despite a notional swing to Labour of 12.93%, at 69 the oldest member of the '97 intake May '97; was elected a Vice Chairman of the 1922 Committee May '97; in the Leadership contest, joined the campaign team of Michael Howard May-June '97; deplored as a "tragedy" the collapse of the libel trial against the GUARDIAN of his close friend Jonathan Aitken June '97; asked Scottish Secretary Donald Dewar if the cost of getting the Hyundai factory for Fife would cost the taxpayer £120,000 per job June '97; said, "I do not hunt and I do not permit hunts to cross land that I own" but urged opponents of fox-hunting to make some concessions to countrymen July '97; welcomed Labour's defence review because it would be policy-driven, not Treasury-driven, but was hostile to the Eurofighter project July '97; blamed journalists for suicide of Gordon McMaster, citing the remorseless hunting of his own wife and family Aug '97; in his BBC TV series suggested the Conservatives may have undermined the monarchy in 1936 by forcing the Abdication because they thought Edward VIII was an unsuitable monarch Sep '97; objected in a letter to The TIMES to balloting Tories to endorse William Hague and his reform principles as a single question; Hague just wanted Tories to sign a "blank cheque on a small coterie of management consultants" Sep '97; in his BBC TV 'History of the Conservative Party' blamed the Tory election defeat on Mrs Thatcher's "ruthless economic Darwinism" which damaged "the fabric of the British nation state" Oct '97; at a fringe meeting at the Blackpool annual Conservative conference suggested "the only solution for dealing with the IRA is to kill 600 in one night" Oct '97; describing the IRA as "the most resilient and formidable of all resistance movements in the west", favoured allowing Gerry Adams and Martin McGuinness to take their Parliamentary seats Nov '97; told pro-Europeans Michael Heseltine and Ken Clarke to resign from the party or stop criticising William Hague Nov '97; attacked foxhunting as "despicable" and staghunting as "utterly repellent" but Mike Foster's Wild Mammals Bill was "badly drafted" and gave the police "draconian powers" Nov '97; insisted the defence industries must be valued not primarily as employment engines but for their research and high technology Dec '97; won his law action against the EVENING STANDARD for its spoof diary which might seem written by him; the EVENING STANDARD had to pay £250,000 in legal costs Dec '97-Jan '98; said he was "seriously interested" in becoming Mayor of London Jan '98; warned that if sanctions were relaxed against Iraq "only a tiny group of children or the sick, assembled for a photocall for the world's press, would receive any aid; the rest of the oil revenue would go straight to the military machine that Saddam Hussein so menacingly continues to assemble" Jan '98; worried that the military commitment against Saddam Hussein was retributive and the Government had not thought through the political and other possible consequences, warning it could be "the precursor of a very long war" Feb '98; criticised the "ludicrous and megalomaniac", "environmentally damaging" Channel Tunnel Rail Link, which would probably end by costing £16b Mar '98; complained that the BBC was "dumbing down" by concentrating on special interest lobbies Mar '98; protested at having been "named and shamed" by English Heritage over needed improvements to his Grade I Saltwood Castle for which he had never asked for a grant for repairs May '98; defended Britain's football hooligans in Marseilles as defending themselves as targets of the French June '98;

Born: 13 April 1928, London

Family: Descendant of wealthy Paisley thread manufacturers; son of the late multi-millionaire Lord (Kenneth)) Clark, OM. CH, famous art expert, collector, lecturer ('Civilisation') and writer, and the late Elizabeth (Martin), "remarkable but alcoholic" (David Piper, GUARDIAN); m '58 Caroline Jane (Beuttler), whom he courted at 14 and married at 16, and who still says, "I know he is a S-H-one-T, but I love him"; 2s James '60, helicopter pilot, and Andrew '62, former Captain in the Life Guards;

Education: Eton College ("an early introduction to human cruelty, treachery and extreme physical hardship"); Christ Church, Oxford University ("a complete waste of time" until he became a star pupil of Hugh Trevor-Roper; MA); Inner Temple;

Occupation: Military Historian who worked under Sir Basil Liddell-Hart; Author: BBC TV series, "Alan Clark's History of the Tory Party" (1997), The Donkeys, A History of the BEF in 1915 (1961), The Fall of Crete (1963), Barbarossa, The Russo-German Conflict, 1941-45 (1965), Aces High (1973), A Good Innings, Viscount Lee of Fareham (1974), Diaries (1993); Columnist, with fortnightly column in NEWS OF THE WORLD (at £65,000 a year) '97-; Owner: of a fabulous collection of inherited paintings worth £12m, despite transfers in lieu of tax; of Saltwood Castle (50-roomed 14th Century castle acquired from father of Lord ('Bill') Deedes after the '29 crash); The Manor House, Seeend, Wiltshare (for sale for £1.25m in '97), Broomhayes Farm, Wiltshire; Town Farm, Bratton-Clovelly, Devon (for sale for over £150,000 in '98); Eriboli Estate (27,000 acres) and harbour in Sutherland, bought for £425,000 in '84 and kept undeveloped; Shareholder, with six $10,000 (nominal) shares in Woods Petroleum field in Brunei; Barrister (non-practicing); Marshall of the Southeast Assize '53-??; ex: Lecturer, Services Division, Department of Extra-Mural Studies, Oxford University;

Traits: Aquilinely handsome, despite age lines; rakish look; permanent sneer; a cynical realist; has "an aggressive contempt for hypocrisy" (George Hill, TIMES); couldn't-care-less cavalier style (claims to have urinated out of his ministerial window on passers-by); elitist ("I believe in privilege"); "I have no guilt about being rich"; "an old-fashioned combination of hauteur and noblesse oblige" (GUARDIAN); gamey; witty; a pithy dispatcher of his contemporaries (asked which great figure from the past he would like to lunch with, he replied "Sir Geoffrey Howe"); non-drinker; engagingly frank about his own faults (admitted "I deserve to be horse-whipped" for his philandering); a genuine animal lover (almost went to war with the BBC because of the threat to have Hannah, his pet rottweiler, put down in the wake of its biting a litigious BBC cameraman);

Address: House of Commons, Westminster, SW1A 0AA; Saltwood Castle, Hythe, Kent CT21 4QU;

Telephone: 0171 219 3000 (H of C); 01303 265 445 (home);

Our WESTMINSTER CONFIDENTIAL broke the 'Profumo Scandal'

Rt Hon Dr David (George) CLARK   **Labour**   **SOUTH SHIELDS '79-**

Majority: 22,153 (56.8%) over Conservative 5-way;
Description: The coalmining and shipbuilding city at the mouth of Tyne, with a sideline as a North Sea seaside resort; safe-Labour since 1935; was reinforced by 5,700 voters from Jarrow in '95;
Former Seat: Colne Valley '70-74;
Position: President: Northern Ramblers '79-, Open Space Society (Chairman '79-87) '87-; Chairman, Forestry Group '79-; ex: Chancellor of the Duchy of Lancaster '97-98; Defence and Disarmament Spokesman '92-97; Delegate, to North Atlantic Assembly (Vice Chairman of its Socialist Group '92-97) '92-97, '82-88; Spokesman: on Agriculture and Rural Affairs '87-92, on Environmental Protection '86-87; Deputy Spokesman: on Environment '81-86, Defence '80-81, Agriculture '73-74; Chairman, PLP Northern Group (Vice Chairman '85-86) '86-87; Vice Chairman: PLP Agriculture Committee '83-87, PLP Environment Group '72-74; Secretary, all-party Wool Textile Group '71-74; Treasurer, British-Swedish Parliamentary Group '88-92;
Outlook: The sacked Cabinet Minister who went bald awaiting his press-heralded execution; his widely-admired Freedom of Information White Paper was the subject of tussles with Lord Irvine and Jack Straw, but the year-long negative briefing was attributed to Peter Mandelson, who allegedly coveted his job; Clark previously was one of the victims of Blair's last-minute switches in Ministerial appointments in '97; the Defence Secretary post to which he seemed entitled by his long and patient search for a consensus among Labour MPs went to George Robertson as recompense for losing the post of Scottish Secretary to Donald Dewar; instead he was landed with producing a Freedom of Information Act which could pass Lord Irvine's scrutiny; when it did, to general acclaim, it was too late to cancel his execution; his pre-election achievement of a multilateralist consensus was also under-estimated: as his having "put [the] defence issue to sleep for Labour" (John Rentoul, INDEPENDENT); an able, assiduous, loyal, worthy, and widely-respected moderate; "the very model of informed reason" (Matthew Parris, TIMES); "talks sense enough, but too quietly" (Edward Pearce, GUARDIAN); has the disadvantage of a bland image: "Clark the Obscure" (Andy McSmith, OBSERVER), "wholly unobtrusive" (John Rentoul, INDEPENDENT); but can display a "dyspeptic undertaker's" manner in delivery"; his Defence effort was more complex than his five years as Labour's Gummer-baiting Agriculture Spokesman; an ex-Solidarity Centrist with a wider constituency among his colleagues; Eurosceptic (on Common Market Safeguards Committee); pro-NATO; in CSM (Christian Socialist Movement); basically an environmentalist crusader, badger-protector, footpath bulldozer and libertarian Rambler who made Green issues sexy; "the first career Green politician to have reached the front bench on either side of the House" (Charles Glover, DAILY TELEGRAPH); "tireless and genuine in his passion for the great outdoors" (INDEPENDENT); had "an uncompromising attitude towards farmers and developers who have scant regard for the need for conservation in the countryside" (Jon Craig, NEWCASTLE JOURNAL); was UNISON-sponsored;
History: Joined the Labour Party '59; contested Withington Mar '66; won Colne Valley from Liberal Richard Wainwright June '70; attacked environmental pollution July '70; visited South Sudan to clear its Government of killing Christians Nov '70; worried about overladen foreign

lorries Mar '71; opposing entry, said only one-third supported the EEC Oct '71; led Ramblers along disputed right of way Oct '72; criticized farmers for allowing bulls on footpaths May '73; defended brass bands July '73; opposed use of crossbow Nov '73; urged food subsidies for poorest Dec '73; lost Colne Valley back to Richard Wainwright Feb '74; contested it again Oct '74; was adopted for South Shields to succeed Arthur Blenkinsop Nov '75; protested increases in school meals Feb '78; was elected May '79; urged one-member one-vote to select Labour candidates Dec '79; tried, but failed, to introduce Access to Commons and Open Countryside Bill Feb '80; condemned as "aesthetic vandalism" plans to dump nuclear waste under Cheviot Hills Oct '80; as Deputy Defence Spokesman, visited Hongkong defences Jan '81; criticised shortage of 3,000 men in Services Feb '81; warned against "Draconian" cuts in Royal Navy May '81; attacked high-handed railway police May '81; was attacked by unilateralist Martin Flannery for "misrepresenting" Labour's defence policy Aug '81; rejected Bennite "witch hunt" claims Sep '81; wrote: "I am against the installation of Cruise missiles in the UK, the use of chemical weapons, the development of the neutron bomb, the decision to buy Trident, and Britain having an independent nuclear deterrent; I believe we are spending too much on defence and that this level must be reduced to that of the European NATO average" Sep '81; quietly resigned as Deputy Spokesman on Defence because his views on Defence were not in accord with those of the Labour Party nationally: "I resigned as the deputy Labour spokesman on defence in 1981 when the party went unilateralist because I was a multilateralist" Oct '81; said shipyards needed more cash Nov '81; claimed Britain was becoming world's nuclear "dustbin" Mar '82; collected 21 votes for Shadow Cabinet Nov '82; demanded share of Norwegian rig-supply trade Feb '83; insisted the Wildlife Act was no bar to farmers destroying countryside and wildlife Mar '83; promised greater countryside access under Labour, with less deference to the 5% who were farmers May '83; backed Roy Hattersley for Leader and Deputy Leader Sep '83; urged the withdrawal of the "inadequate" green belt circular Oct '83; with Don Dixon bid for more cash for South Tyneside Nov '83; on Solidarity's slate, won 24 votes in Shadow Cabinet contest Nov '83; attacked paying landowners for not doing environmental damage Mar '84; criticized "export of acidification" June '84; met Mrs Thatcher to try to stop Plessey's switch from South Shields to Plymouth June '84; found "deplorable" a South African tour by nine rebel hockey players Aug '84; in OBSERVER article again called for greater access to countryside Aug '84; urged more control over aeriel crop-spraying Aug '84; won 60 votes for the Shadow Cabinet Nov '84; having come fourth in the Private Member's ballot, introduced a Bill to amend the Wildlife and Countryside Act Dec '84; after his green allies helped fight off Government's watering down, his Bill to amend the Wildlife and Countryside Act to prevent badger-baiting and protect scientific sites received Royal Assent June '85; led an all-party delegation to Environment Secretary Patrick Jenkin to favour the Northern route for Okehampton bypass July '85; scored a remarkable double with a second Bill to amend the Wildlife and Countryside Act July '85; criticised tax concessions to plant Scottish forests Sep '85; tried to woo the Greens with a Jobs and Industry Charter for the Environment Sep '85; at Labour's conference claimed that environmental protection would create thousands of jobs Oct '85; urged better development of alternative energy Oct '85; on the Solidarity slate, won 80 votes for Shadow Cabinet Oct '85; claimed Nirex had been most insensitive in their nuclear waste siting Mar '86; accused MAFF of "obsessive secrecy" about radioactivity in lambs June '86; complained to Mrs Thatcher about UK Ministerial incompetence and confusion in dealing with aftermath of Chernobyl June '86; attacked National Trust for buying houses which the English Heritage should buy, instead of saving open spaces Aug '86; secured wide backing for Bill to save common land Sep '86; was elected to the Shadow Cabinet for the first time with 89 votes; was named Spokesman on Environment Protection, including responsibility for nuclear waste (after turning down

Transport) Nov '86; was shocked by alleged efforts of his friend John Cunningham to diminish his status in the Shadow Cabinet to No 2 to Cunningham at Environment Nov '86; was elected Chairman of PLP's Northern Group Nov '86; wrote a ten-year plan for Shadow Cabinet proposing spending £10b to create 200,000 environmental jobs Jan '87; attacked Nicholas Ridley's plans to allow developments on surplus farmland as the "rape of the UK countryside...for a quick buck" Feb '87; in the Sizewell debate attacked the Government's "obsession with nuclear power" Feb '87; attacked abandonment of nuclear dump sites as squalid election bribery May '87; more than doubled his majority June '87; despite a Leftward tilt among new Labour MPs, was re-elected to Shadow Cabinet with 87 votes; was named Spokesman for Agriculture and Rural Affairs July '87; called for an inquiry into marketing of radioactive Cumbrian lambs Nov '87; blamed CAP for costing an extra £11.50 a week for average UK family Dec '87; was the only Shadow Cabinet member to vote against televising Commons Feb '88; complained that Chernobyl-irradiated lamb had gone into food chain Apr '88; claimed Government policy was worsening plight of poor farmers May '88; asked about unexamined new Chernobyl radiation hotspots in Southwest England June '88; accused Government of "betrayal" of hill farmers July '88; urged opening up of countryside, providing hard-pressed farmers with additional income from tourism Aug '88; came fourth in Shadow Cabinet election with 128 votes, up from 87 votes and 14th place Oct '88; complained that Government was suppressing information on Chernobyl impact just as it had over 1957 nuclear accident at Windscale/Sellafield Jan '89; demanded details of 21 protein processing plants which supplied salmonella-contaminated feed to egg producers Jan '89; urged better control of CAP fraud Mar '89; opposed irradiation of food May '89; feared loss of access with sale of Forestry Commission land Aug '89; visited Brazil to study rain forests Sep '89; at Labour's conference called for the "greenest agriculture policy in Europe but also the safest and cleanest food policy" Oct '89; came 13th in ballot for Shadow Cabinet with 111 votes, down from 128; he was renamed Spokesman on 'Food, Agriculture and Rural Affairs' Nov '89; was rated the 7th most assiduous Commons questioner in the previous Parliamentary year Nov '89; backed Government ban on stubble-burning Nov '89; backed voluntary code for egg producers to combat salmonella Dec '89; protested closure of Institute of Food Research Jan '90; backed control of imported eggs Jan '90; protested dumping of industrial waste into North Sea Jan '90; welcoming Government's belated agreement to give full compensation for BSE-infected cattle, blamed problem on slow Government reactions Feb '90; urged more rapid testing of newer, safer pesticides Mar '90; backed labelling of genetically-altered foods Mar '90; urged aerial surveys of persisting Chernobyl-caused radioactivity Mar '90; complained that imported eggs did not have to conform to high standards of UK producers Mar '90; urged continued ban on hunting minke whales May '90; criticized John Gummer for religious bigotry in claiming vegetarianism was "wholly unnatural" May '90; claimed Government was concealing real extent of 'mad cow disease' (BSE) May '90; complained Agriculture was clashing with Health over seafood contamination May '90; said: "irradiation will become a charter for food cowboys" June '90; complained about "poor standard of food hygiene in this country" June '90; warned that uncertificated beef, unsuitable for export, could be sold in UK June '90; welcomed ban on bovine somatotropin July '90; complained that Government was hiding information about dioxins in dairy herds near incinerators Aug '90; urged improved abattoir hygiene Sep '90; urged tightening of his 1985 legislation to curb badger-baiting Sep '90; came 7th in Shadow Cabinet election with 118 votes, up from 111, Oct '90; backed a 30% cut in EC farm support Oct '90; urged tighter BSE controls, including ban on breeding from offspring of "mad" cows and random sampling of cattle heads in abattoirs Nov '90; supported Government on updating GATT Nov '90; resisted Government's plans to allow irradiation of school meals when it was banned in prison meals Jan '91; visited New Zealand at invitation of its government Feb '91; in Ribble Valley by-election was accused by Agriculture Minister Gummer of not eating beef sausages because of BSE threat Feb '91; with Nick Brown MP, visited Japan to seek further industrial investment for northeast Mar '91; accused Government of continuing its "cover-up" of impact on UK soil of Chernobyl disaster Apr '91; announced Labour's intention of establishing a consumer-orientated Department of Food and Farming Apr '91; accused Agriculture Minister Gummer of scuppering a research project to identify BSE because it might show the extent of "mad cow disease" Apr '91; criticized set-aside as "stupid" in asking that "consumers should pay rich landowners for doing nothing" May '91; remained a member of Common Market Safeguards Committee June '91; accused Agriculture Minister Gummer of "being sanctimonious about saving the dolphin in public, and then sabotaging them in private" June '91; began asking about pigs' "blue ear disease" June '91; complained about Government's "sloppy" drafting of 1988 Merchant Shipping Act, which had been overturned by European Court of Justice, allowing Spanish to establish UK fishing companies July '91; complained average family of four were paying an extra £16 a week for the "socially and economically indefensible" CAP July '91; promised Agriculture Minister Gummer support for resistance to unreasonable EC demands July '91; emphasized Labour would have a free vote on banning country sports like fox-hunting Aug '91; criticized as a "national scandal" the secret sale of Forestry Commission land, mostly to unlisted purchasers Aug '91; urged ban on drift nets above 2.5km to protect dolphins Sep '91; came 10th in Shadow Cabinet election, with 122 votes Oct '91; visited Japan at invitation of its government Nov '91; was rated the most active written questioner among northeastern MPs Nov '91; disclosed that 7 farmers were receiving over £70,000 for set aside, and 70 receiving over £30,000; "very rich people who don't need the money are being given obscenely big state handouts for doing nothing" Dec '91; complained that food and drink trade deficit had reached a quarter of the massive trade deficit Jan '92; demanded supply of surplus food to childen and old instead of accepting EC directive to plough it back into ground Feb '92; retained seat with majority slightly down from 13,851 to 13,477, despite a swing to Labour of .08% Apr '92; backed John Smith for Leader Apr '92; complained that CAP was "riddled with fraud and with money being siphoned off for the use of the IRA and the Mafia" May '92; said it was "outrageous that farmers and landowners are obtaining huge tax concessions on the understanding that public access is given" without the public being informed June '92; voted with Government in favour of King's Cross Railways (No 2) Bill June '92; claimed CAP changes would increase taxes June '92; demanded Royal Navy protect British fishermen against French trawlers June '92; complained that 90% of eggs in Birmingham had been found to be sub-standard June '92; insisted that UK was afflicted with BSE because Tories had eased regulations for renderers, allowing sheeps' scrapie to be passed on to cattle July '92; came 18th and last, with 104 votes, in election to John Smith's new Shadow Cabinet; was named Spokesman on Defence, Disarmament and Arms Control July '92; after Swan Hunter sackings, urged defence diversification Aug '92; complained about inadequacies in SA80 assault rifles, as revealed by Falklands Government's rejection Aug '92; in his first speech as Labour's Defence spokesman, accepted involvement of UK troops in Bosnia in peacekeeping role Sep '92; urged tighter rules on movement of former serving officers into private defence companies Sep '92; ranked as 8th most assiduous written questioner, with 211 questions in 1991-92; with 111 replies, was 18th most successful receiver of written answers in '92-93 session up to July '92, Oct '92; attacked close down of Wessex helicopter bases at RAF Manston, RAF Brawdy and RAF Leuchars as cost-cutting which would cost lives Oct '92; asked how Iraqis' use of gas against Kurds had affected UK exports of arms to Iraq Nov '92; failed to secure extension of Scott Inqiry to exports to Iran Nov '92; urged shooting down of Serb planes if they flouted the ban on military flights over Bosnia Dec '92; after collapse of Matrix Churchill case, urged independent inquiry into export to Iraq of defence technology Nov '92; urged coherent UN coalition strategy against Iraqi provocation Jan '93; urged Trident nuclear warheads be limited to 192 Jan '93; demanded statement from Government to explain Prime Minister's unequivocal support for President Clinton's attack on Baghdad without Security Council authorization Jan '93; said US raid on Baghdad should be referred back to UN, because responses to Saddam Hussein's provocations were "getting out of hand", but declined hard-Left invitation to become more critical Jan '93; co-urged stronger, better-financed UN peace-keeping operations Feb '93; welcomed Defence Secretary Rifkind's reprieve of four regiments as an admission the armed forces were over-stretched Feb '93; urged better training and housing for sacked soldiers: "how can we ask people to risk their lives one day and put them on the dole queue the next?" Feb '93; challenged uneven basis of competition between Swan Hunter and Vickers over helicopter landing ship Mar '93; in view of break-up of Communist world, strongly supported non-proliferation and ban on nuclear testing Mar '93; resisting increased Labour back-bench support for armed intervention in Bosnia, urged a quicker recall of Security Council to impose tougher sanctions on Serbia, while rejecting air strikes or lifting of arms embargo as akin to trying "to douse a fire with petrol" Apr '93; urged consideration of ethnic safe havens in Bosnia Apr '93; backed a fullscale defence review instead of "salami slicing" under Treasury pressure Apr '93; claimed it was "potentially dangerous" to withdraw British troops from Belize May '93; urged defence diversification to provide jobs for sacked Swan Hunter workers, since unemployment was already 29% in South Tyneside May '93; said Labour would support reinforcements for peace-keeping in Bosnia May '93; said Labour accepted need for defence cuts but insisted they should emerge from a defence review, accompanied by diversification of defence industries to avoid sacking of 100,000 defence workers May '93; complained about missing Defence documents on export of arms technology for Iraq May '93; quoted Alan Clark's diaries in ridiculing "Options for Change" as a poor substitute for a defence review June '93; urged Gurkha troops for UN and replacement of HMS Fearless and Intrepid June '93; met Bosnian Serb leader Radovan Karadzic, paid for by the Yugoslav-born lobbyist John Kennedy Aug '93; visited Bosnia as guest of Yugoslave Federal Government Aug-Sep '93; visted Azerbaijan as guest of British Petroleum Sep '93; came seventh with 133 votes for Shadow (up from 104) in Shadow Cabinet poll Oct '93; welcomed Government's cancellation of TASM missile "which we have been demanding" Oct '93; attacked Government for withholding from Scott Inquiry hand-written notes by Ministers Nov '93; complained that Royal Arsenal fraud by a senior Ministry of Defence official had "not only threatened Britain's military capacity but also the jobs of thousands of loyal defence workers" Nov '93; welcomed Government limiting of Trident's warheads to the 192 that "we have been calling for" Nov '93; voted against restoring capital punishment, even for killers of policemen Feb '94; voted to reduce age of homosexual consent to 18 or 16, Feb '94; was injured while visiting British troops in Bosnia Feb '94; urged consideration of new risks from land mines in Bosnia, with British troops taking over patrols of the battle zone Mar '94; voted for Tony Blair for Leader, Margaret Beckett for Deputy Leader July '94; MoD confirmed he had been briefed three times Aug '94; claimed Government Inspectors report criticising Aldermaston Atomic Weapons Establishment "proves what we have been saying for some time" Oct '94; received 109 votes (13th) for the Shadow Cabinet; was retained as Defence Spokesman Oct '94; attacked Government's "high complacency" following disclosure of British Intelligence telephone and modem numbers Nov '94; tabled a series of questions on Gulf War innoculations Dec '94; attacked proposal to use the expensively refitted 30-year-old HMS Sirius as a missile target Dec '94; questioned dismissal from a rape crisis centre of a former seaman alleged to be homosexual in RN dossier Jan '95; object to spending £1m a year on batmen when 18,000 servicemen had been sacked Jan '95; objected to Government's refusal to sign the Chemical Weapons Convention Jan '95; criticised the hiring of Lt Comdr Christopher Parke by computer company Informix months after he had awarded it an RN computer database contract Feb '95; opposed an enhanced defence role for an expanded EU including four neutrals Fwb '95; was forced to back down after he promised Labour would review, "within a month of being elected" the Services' ban on homosexuals, which Admiral Lord Hill-Norton dismissed as "the sort of bloody silly thing the Labour Party would do" Apr '95; attacking as "barbaric" the Bosnian Serbs' seizure of hostages, backed the dispatch of more British troops May '95; declared the MoD the "Ministry of Waste" after the NAO listed 25 orders running massively over-budget and an average of 3 years late May '95; dismissed Tories Defence White Paper as a "fraudulent prospectus", with spending set to "fall by £1.6b over the next three years" with 31,000 losing their jobs May '95; outlined a Defence Diversification Agency in TRIBUNE June '95; urged independent inquiry into Government's having spent £120m on Rosyth but still pretending it might site nuclear submarine base at Devonport Sep '95; claimed Britain was secretly collaborating and perhaps help finance French nuclear tests in the Pacific Sep '95; at Labour's annual conference staged a photocall in a space suit on Brighton beach to protest landmine proliferation Oct '95; questioned Defence Secretary Michael Portillo about his extreme Rightwing adviser and "Rasputin", David Hart Oct '95; was named in press reports attributed to Peter Mandelson as a "dud" likely to be reshuffled Oct '95; received 141 votes (9th) for the Shadow Cabinet; was retained as chief Defence Spokesman Oct '95; urged a strategic defence review Oct '95; criticised Government's Hart-inspired plan to buy US F15s off the shelf, claiming that Labour would defend defence employment in British industry Oct '95; attacked MoD's "financial waste and mismanagement" in its £248m Bristol Procurement Executive building Nov '95; attacked as "economic madness" the sell-off of its 60,000 servicemen's houses Jan '96; claimed racism had blighted MoD recruitment among minorities Mar '96; citing JANE'S, said "our amphibious shipping is barely fit to go to sea" May '96; on his return from Bosnia, pledged Labour to keep British troops there even if the US pulled out June '96; with Foreign Affairs Spokesman Robin Cook bracketed Leader Tony Blair, while Labour's foreign and defence policy was unveiled; a six-month defence review to match resources to commitments was promised, with Trident retained June '96; while thought to have done his Defence job well, was judged by Blairites to be neutral in the divide between Old Labour and New Labour; allegedly angered Blair by suggesting Labour would review the issue of homosexuals in the armed forces July '96; urged removal of Tory fund-raiser John Beckwith from bidding for MoD housing July '96; voted against a 3% cap on MPs' pay rise, for a pension based on £43,000 and a cut in MPs' mileage allowance July '96; was re-elected to Shadow Cabinet with a high vote of 205 (9th); was retained as shadow Defence Secretary in Blair's 'final' pre-election Shadow Cabinet reshuffle July '96; welcomed contract for 232 Eurofighters Sep '96; atttacked Government's retreat from ban on landmines Sep '96; attacked bid for MoD housing by Japanese-led consortium, including Tory-financing band of Tory Treasurer Lord Hambros Sep '96; attacked privatisation of Defence Intelligence Staff computer system Sep '96; welcomed defeat of anti-Trident motion at Labour conference Oct '96; disavowed his one-time CND membership, pointing out that, as a multilateralist, he had resigned as Deputy Spokesman on Defence when the party went unilateralist Nov '96; backed Tory MP Michael Colvin, Chairman of the Defence Select Committee in opposing MoD's plan to allow public to examine plans for new SAS headquarters Dec '96; urged declassification of all drugs used on Allied troops in Gulf War Dec '96; asked why Tory Government had not asked for private capital to be involved in BRITANNIA replacement Jan '97; was target by Prolife Alliance Party because of his support for abortion Feb '97; retained his South Shields seat with a majority of 22,153, a swing to Labour of 11.2% May '97; was named Chancellor of the Duchy of Lancaster in the Cabinet

Office, with responsibilities for open government, having lost his expected Defence Secretary's post to George Robertson, who lost out to Donald Dewar as Scottish Secretary May '97; announced the opening to public inspection of Labour's information retrieval system Excalibur June '97; admitted his "mistake in not registering his '93 meeting with Radovan Karadzic, thinking it a UN-paid trip June '97; announced a 5,000-strong "People's Panel" to test public reaction to Government policies July '97; complained of a "smear campaign" over the £60,000 spent on studying "people's panels in the USA, Canada and Australia Oct '97; announced active consideration of voluntary 'smart cards' for every citizen, to improve public services Feb '98; ordered an elite team of intelligence agents to try to break into Government files to see if they were hacker-proof Apr '98; his White Paper on Freedom of Information was extremely well-received July '98, as had been his report on Millenium Compliance June '98; was sacked from the Cabinet, blaming it on his insistence on living in the northeast and missing out on the London cocktail circuit July '98;

Born: 19 October 1939, Castle Douglas, Scotland

Family: Son, George Clark, gardener, and Janet (Smith); m '70 Christine (Kirkby); 1d Catherine '71;

Education: Bowness Elementary; Windermere Grammar; Manchester College of Commerce (evenings); Manchester University (BA Econ, MSc, President of the Union); Morecambe College of Further Education; UMIST; Sheffield University (PhD '78);

Occupation: Sponsored, by UNISON (ex-NUPE; £500 p a to constituency, 80% of election costs, £100 in expenses) '79-; Director '89-, Adviser '83-89, Homeowners Friendly Society; Author: We Do Not Want The Earth (1992), Victor Grayson, Labour's Lost Leader (1985), Colne Valley, Radicalism to Socialism (1981), The Industrial Manager (1966); ex: Lecturer: in Politics at Huddersfield Poly '74-79, in Administration and Government at Salford University '65-70; Trainee Manager, in US textile mill '64; Student Teacher '59-60; Textile Laboratory Assistant '57-59, Forester '56-57;

Traits: Blond, retreating hair; genial; earnest; dedicated; worthy; hardworking; "tireless and genuine" (INDEPENDENT); "quietly spoken", "fresh-air fanatic" (Jon Craig, NEWCASTLE JOURNAL); optimist (bet on Labour victory, '92); Scot; fell-walker; gardener; watches football (esp Carlisle United); was injured while visiting British troops in Bosnia;

Address: House of Commons, Westminster, London SW1A 0AA; Three Gables, Barmoor Lane, Ryton, Tyne and Wear NE40 3AB;

Telephone: 0171 219 4028/6201/6801 (H of C); 0191 413 7370; 0191 454 0364;

WELCOME WORDS

One of the MPs' bouquets most welcome among the occasional brickbats is the frequent refrain: "Thanks for recalling that speech! I had completely forgotten ever making it...."

PROSPECTIVES SATISFACTION

The 1 May 1997 general election increase in the number of Labour and Liberal Democrat MPs provided what might be called "archive satisfaction". In a fair number of cases we have been tracking such candidates as "possible" victors for as many as four or five contests, badgering them for information and writing up their profiles, just in case. In their cases - as in the case of the 17 'retreads' - there was the satisfaction of knowing that the previous efforts were not wasted.

Dr Lynda (Margaret) CLARK QC   **Labour**   **EDINBURGH-PENTLANDS '97-**

Majority: 4,862 over Conservative 7-way;
Description: The perennially-marginal southwestern Edinburgh suburbs, capped by the beautiful Pentland Hills; until '97 it remained stubbornly Tory with Conservative-leaning Colinton and Balerno outvoting the Labour-leaning estates of Wester Hailes and Sighthill;
Position: On Edinburgh University Court '95-; on Scottish Legal Aid Board '91-94;
Outlook: The most senior woman Advocate practicing at the Scottish Bar, who collected the most senior Tory scalp at the election, that of the former Foreign Secretary, Malcolm Rifkind; her scalping knife has been less evident at Westminster; a confirmed homeruler: "as a Scots lawyer with more than 20 years' experience, I know that Scots law and development have suffered badly from the present [pre-devolution] system"; a successful professional - one of only seven women QCs in Scotland - from a poor working-class Dundonian background, brought up in an inner city tenement and then in a council flat; she prospered in the conservative climate of the Scottish Bar, despite a reputation as a Leftwing feminist; "a true Blairite in the English mould; an example of Scottish sovereignty residing with Tony Blair as far as New Labour is concerned; she mouthes Blairite cliches with the passion of a senior QC" (RED PEPPER); has started slowly in Parliament, certainly so far as written questions are concerned, having posed only two in her first year; formerly on the Scotttish Council for Civil Liberties; UNISON (ex-NUPE);
History: She joined the Labour Party at 36, out of concern at the state of the party '83; was selected to fight the hopeless seat of North East Fife, held by Liberal Democrat Menzies Campbell '91; narrowly retained her deposit, as the Labour vote was squeezed from 6.6% to 5.5% by Menzies Campbell Apr '92; emphasised her sex in seeking selection for Pentlands, claiming she would attract media attention as a woman standing against a Cabinet Minister Oct '95; "I have benefited from years of free education, good NHS care, local authority housing and a Labour-inspired system which has encouraged equal opportunity; I am shocked and angry at the results of 16 years of Tory policies and legislation" Oct '95; criticised as inexperienced Scotland's first woman judge, Sheriff Hazel Aronson, and was accused -wrongly she felt - of sour grapes July '96; ; an ICM poll in the OBSERVER four days before polling put her ahead with 42%, Rifkind trailing on 34%, the SNP at 15% and LibDems at 7% Apr '97; she ousted Malcolm Rifkind with a majority of 4,862, with similar percentages: Labour (43%) Conservative (32%), SNP (13%), LibDems (10%), on notional swing of 9.8% May '97; made her witty Maiden speech in support of Scottish devolution May '97; co-sponsored motion deploring Air UK's "discriminatory and insulting" treatment of disabled passengers July '97; insisted that "the British Parliament has never been an exercise in academic logic"; "in our system, the Queen in Parliament is sovereign; any legislation approved by the Queen in Parliament is legal and constitutional"; implied that the 'West Lothian question' was one of many anomalies; "no other country that claims to be a democracy has hereditary peers voting on legislation; Conservative Members have lived with that anomaly for many years" July '97; asked how David Clark's White Paper proposals for open government would work; "is it intended that constituents should come to us before going to the Commissioner?" Dec '97; asked whether legal aid money could be targeted at the industrial tribunal system Mar '98; was

Copyright (C)Parliamentary Profile Services Ltd

rated as one of the poorest of written questioners in the 'Bottom 100', with only two posed in her first year May '98;
Born: 26 February 1949, Dundee
Family: Daughter of a van driver and worker at National Cash Registers, Dundee; her mother was a shop assistant for 40 years; she is married; does not disclose her parents' or husband's names;
Education: Lawside Academy, Dundee; St Andrews University (LLB Hons '70); Edinburgh University (PhD '75);
Occupation: Advocate at the Scottish Bar '77-, QC '89-; member of the English Bar '88-; ex: on the Scottish Legal Aid Board '91-94; Law Lecturer, Dundee University '73-76; has special expertise in medical law;
Traits: Dark shoulder-length hair; snub-nosed; toothy smile; "smart, confident" (Greg Neale, SUNDAY TELEGRAPH);
Address: House of Commons, Westminster, London SW1A 0AA; 7 Regent Terrace, Edinburgh EH7 5BN; Advocates' Library, Parliament Square, Edinburgh EH1 1RF;
Telephone: 0171 219 2915 (H of C); 0131 226 2881; 0131 558 9154 (home);

Dr Michael CLARK   Conservative   RAYLEIGH '97-

Majority: 10,684 (20.8%) over Labour4-way;
Description: A new name for what is essentially the pre-'97 Rochford seat, shorn of 10,000 voters in Rochford itself; it remains a solidly Conservative area, embracing suburban commuter towns newly expanded northwest of Southend in semi-rural Essex, including five villages from old Chelmsford, Maldon and South East Essex; "stretching from the outskirts of Chelmsford in the West to Foulness in the East"; adjacent to Bradwell nuclear power station;
Former Seat: Rochford '83-97
Position: On Chairmen's Panel '97-; Chairman, Select Committee on Science and Technology '97-; on 1922 Committee '97-; Vice President, Parliamentary and Scientific Committee '94-; Chairman: all-party Anglo-Russian Group '94-, Anglo-Venezuelan Group '95-; on Advisory Panel, Conservation Foundation '95-; ex: Chairman '94-97, Vice Chairman '90-94, Secretary '87-90 all-party Chemical Industry Group; Chairman, all-party Parliamentary Group for Energy Studies '92-97; Chairman '90-93, on Executive '87-94 British Group of Inter-Parliamentary Union; Chairman '93-98, Treasurer '89-93 Board of the Parliamentary Office of Science and Technology; Chairman '89-92, member '83-92 of Select Committee on Energy; on Select Committee on Trade and Industry '92-94; Vice Chairman '87-90, Secretary '86-87 Conservative MPs' Energy Committee; on Liaison Committee (of Select Committee chairmen) '89-92; Secretary, Parliamentary and Scientific Committee '85-88; Treasurer, British-Malawi Parliamentary Group '87-90; Secretary, British-Nepalese Parliamentary Group '85-90; Chairman '80-83, Vice Chairman '78-80, Treasurer '75-78 Cambridgeshire Conservative Association;
Outlook: Widely-respected, hard-working, thoughtful, independent-minded mainstreamer; the only serious energy intellectual in the Commons; the highly-regarded former Energy Select Committee Chairman whose coal analyses avoided all the errors of Lords Parkinson and

Wakeham, Tim Eggar and Michael Heseltine; "an acknowledged expert on the coal industry" (GUARDIAN) who angered the Government and its Whips by "getting it right all along" (Sheila Gunn, HOUSE MAGAZINE) on the coal crisis; "he should have been an Energy Minister" (PRIVATE EYE); can adapt rapidly to changed circumstances; a shrewd and experienced industrial chemist and management consultant, formerly a chemical plant manager with ICI; has "rare courage" in "putting his constituents before his promotion prospects" (GUARDIAN); can very occasionally play the 'wise fool'; a Eurosceptic; Rightish on law and order; "I speak as a friend of the nuclear industry";

History: "I was born, brought up and went to school in Nottinghamshire" "with many coalminers' sons; some of my own family worked in the pits in Manton and Bevercotes"; he joined Retford Young Conservatives '51, Cambridge University Conservative Association '57; was a founder-member of the Ratepayers Association in Marske, Yorkshire '62; contested hopeless Ilkeston against Ray Fletcher May '79; at Tory conference urged a great improvement in educational standards, but rejected vouchers Oct '79; was runner-up to Teddy Taylor in selection for Southend East in by-election Feb '80; was selected for Rochford over Norman St John Stevas, partly because he had a wife: "we find we can get an awful lot of work out of a good wife" Feb '83; was elected June '83; in Maiden supported privatisation of BT in expectation of better service but warned: "we must be careful we do not move from a public monopoly to a private monopoly" July '83; voted for restoration of death penalty for murders of police, prison officers, or caused by terrorism and shooting July '83; was one of 12 Tories abstaining in criticism of Government's GCHQ policy Feb '84; backed Rugby Union tour of South Africa Feb '84; was one of 40 Tory rebels on political levy, preferring opting in to opting out Apr '84; visited Israel as its government's guest May-June '84; led a motion insisting on better delivery of Russian mail (to dissidents) July 84; opposed Sir Keith Joseph's increased parental contribution to grants Nov '84; opposed further development of Stansted airport Dec '84; backed freedom for councils to spend more of their own money from house sales on housebuilding Jan '85; attacked cut in Rate Support Grant for Rochford Jan '85; co-signed letter urging higher VAT on non-standard goods to avoid taxing books and children's shoes Jan '85; voted against Enoch Powell's Unborn Children Protection Bill Feb '85; rebelled against 'top peoples' pay increase July '85; backed nuclear generation as "one of the safest forms of electricity generation" Oct '85; was one of 32 Tory rebels on shire rates Jan '86; was one of six Tories on Energy Select Committee demanding concessions on British Gas privatisation Mar '86; was cheered when he criticised Geoffrey Dickens for abusing Parliamentary privilege in accusing doctor in Clark's constituency of raping child (of which he was later found innocent) Mar '86; opposed Government on Sunday trading (although he had previously welcomed Auld Report and urged end of limits on shop hours) Apr '86; was disclosed to have been the eighth most assiduous attender of committees in 1984-85 session May '86; said Essex had nothing to fear from nuclear waste dump because Bradwell was so patently unsuitable May '86; opposed Kenneth Hind's Unborn Children (Protection) Bill Oct '86; called for guarantees for holiday makers Dec '86; urged the end of the Advanced Petroleum Revenue Tax because it had squeezed cash flow out of oil companies when they needed it, at the start of oil field development Dec '86; opposed Bradwell as a nuclear dump because it was wet, over-populated and earthquake-prone Feb '87; complained Government was penalising Tory shires and helping Labour councils with grants Mar '87; claimed nuclear power was needed and its threat was quantifiable May '87; his majority went up by over 6,000 June '87; previously its Secretary, was elected Vice Chairman of Conservative MPs' Energy Committee July '87; criticised the decision to close a "cost-effective" cancer unit at Southend Nov '87; in response to Energy Secretary Cecil Parkinson's proposal to force privatised electricity boards to buy 20% nuclear power at a premium price, said it would be to long-term advantage of nuclear industry if it was "exposed to the full rigours of competition" Feb '88; acclaimed the contributions of the chemical engineering industry, in which he had worked Mar '88; complained that use of wheel clamps had gone too far July '88; asked Social Services Minister Tony Newton to ensure that Dr Higgs and Wyatt, accused of over-reacting to child sexual abuse, would never exercise independent authority in this field July '88; complained of state of A13 and A127 Oct '88; introduced Bill to compel registration of professional chemists Oct '88; with Sir Trevor Skeet backed retention of a separate, publicly-owned nuclear company Dec '88; chairing the committee which sat on the Associated British Ports No 2 Bill, warned of "potentially horrendous" effect on domestic coal industry of large-scale coal imports; agreed to quarterly reports on coal imported Feb '89; complained of inadequate spending on southeastern roads Mar '89; became Treasurer of Parliamentary Office of Science and Technology Mar '89; pointed out that, whatever party was in power, for every ton of coal burned, three tons of carbon dioxide would be produced May '89; after listening for an hour to "outrageous" accusations by Labour MPs left the Chamber; seeing the sponsors of the Associated British Ports No 2 Bill, said: "since I am being accused of being in your pocket, I had better say 'hello' to you" May '89; flatly denied charges by Martin Redmond and Dennis Skinner that he had any interest to declare in connection with North Killingholme Cargo Terminal Bill or Associated British Ports (No 2) Bill: "had it not been for the coal issue, the Bill, promoted by Associated British Ports, would probably have gone thorugh the House largely unopposed; Assocated British Ports wanted facilities to import iron ore, other chemicals and raw materials necessary for industry in Lincolnshire and the north of England"; said the new port facilities were useful and cheap foreign coal imports could be monitored May '89; was again criticised in motion by Labour MPs for having broken the rules for private Bills by communicating with sponsors of Associated British Ports No 2 Bill July '89; was promoted Chairman of the Energy Select Committee in succession to Sir Ian Lloyd Nov '89; was consequently appointed to Liaison Committee Dec '89; urged progress for Associated British Ports (No 2) Bill because of usefulness of improved ports for non-coal industries Jan '90; visited Bulgaria with Roy Hughes in IPU "flying squad" Feb '90; claimed nuclear costs would remain stable Feb '90; visited Turkey as guest of its government Mar '90; voted against Bill to give 50,000 Hongkong Chinese families right of abode in UK Apr '90; chaired press conference of Energy Select Committee, saying cost of nuclear power was at least twice as high as the CEGB had claimed, which had not been taken into account by Cecil Parkinson in his "ill-prepared" privatizing of electricity June '90; visited South Africa as guest of South African Chamber of Mines Aug '90; visited Israel and Jordan with Baroness David on IPU delegation Nov '90; urged the horrors of war "be made abundantly plain to Saddam Husein" Dec '90; urged more plants to demonstrate clean coal-burn technology Feb '91; in discussion of Cullen Report on Piper Alpha disaster, spoke against background of his own experience as an ICI plant manager; said unions should be recognised but that safety should not be watered down by negotiation; said the Cullen recommendations should have been put into place five years before by operators, saving 167 lives Mar '91; said British Coal was unsuitable for privatisation, except for its opencast operation, since deep mines would have to be "drastically" reduced in number, provide limited proceeds for Government and have an adverse effect on balance of payments June '91; visited Sweden to inspect its nuclear waste storage facility as a guest of UK Nirex Sep '91; complained that people in southeast were being penalized by higher council tax on their more expensive homes Nov '91; claimed coal industry was coping well with changes Dec '91; complained about "outrageous behaviour" of Brussels in refusing at the last minute to participate in Energy Select Committee hearings Jan '92; co-signed motion urging Malcolm Edwards be confirmed in his job as Commercial Director of British Coal Jan '92; visited Moscow and Kiev as guest of Russian and Ukrainian governments Feb '92; in Moscow on IPU mission, urged careful and tactful aid for Russia Mar '92; retained his seat with majority up from 19,694 to 26,036, a swing to Conservative of 3.82% Apr '92; signed the "fresh start" motion urging a delay in Maastricht endorsement June '92; sought to retain an Energy Select Committee or at least a Subcommittee June '93; his Energy Committee's report, 'Clean Coal Technology and the Coal Market after 1993' urged the Government to develop a national energy strategy for the next decade July '92; was appointed to Trade and Industry Select Committee (Energy having been absorbed into DTI) July '92; signed motion urging Government to remain out of ERM Sep '92; with five other Tory MPs, voted against Government on its "precipitate and badly-handled" pit closures, demanding a review which attempted to save all 31 pits; attacked Lord Wakeham for having ignored the sensible warnings of his Energy Select Committee Oct '92; was infuriated by his Energy Select Committeed closed down Oct '92; voted against Government in paving debate on Maastricht, despite having been warned by Mark Lennox-Boyd that he would not be allowed to represent the Government at an energy conference in Canada Nov '92; again backed a "long-term energy strategy" including generators near mines using clean-coal technology and "run of the mine" coal Nov '92; criticised Government's withdrawal from fast-breeder reactor technology Nov '92; was recruited as a Consultant to British Gas, to take effect after Trade and Industry Select Committeed completed its investigation into the future of coal and the "dash for gas" Nov '92; said: "surely it is better that we subsidise the coal industry rather than unemployment"; was reported as having persuaded Conservatives on the Trade an Industry Select Committee to back its proposal to switch the subsidy from the nuclear to the coal industry Jan '93; somewhat unexpectedly, welcomed Michael Heseltine's White Paper on pit closures apart from "single reservation" that "it would be a breach of the Treaty of Rome for France to be prohibited from exporting [energy] to the United Kingdom"; "it is a shame that this is not a two-way street and a two-way interconnector"; urged a declaration that "a management buy-out of British Coal will not be permitted"; said he accepted the White Paper because "the deal that we have now is the only deal on the table"; when challenged as to whether he accepted the White Paper's acceptance of more gas generators because he had been offered a consultancy with British Gas, he replied: "I reported that to the Chairman and members of the Select Committee"; "I offered to step down from the Select Committee if the members wished me to do so; they wished me to remain on the Select Committee" Mar '93; was one of 4 Maastricht rebels who voted with Government Mar '93; said he was hoping 15 pits could be saved but would be content if only 12 could be kept going for at least two years May '93; was estimated to have been the 41st of 47 'Maastricht rebels', with two rebel votes, 51 abstentions and 9 supporting votes May '93; voted with Conservative majority on pit closures, not with handful of rebels July '93; was made Chairman of the Board of the Parliamentry Office of Science and Technology, Sir Gerard Vaughan complaining that he had been excluded by the Whips because he had abstained on the Maastricht paving vote the previous November, forgetting that Dr Clark had voted against it July '93; complained that "we have not sold any coal over and above what we would have sold if the [Heseltine] White Paper had not been produced", largely because over-stocked privatised generators were not willing to increase their stocks; again urged curb on gas generators; again rebutted Martin Redmond's "absolutely untrue" statement that he had had any declarable interest when Chairman of the committee considering the Associated British Ports (No 2) Bill July '93; paying his own fare, visited Indonesia as guest of the Speaker of the Indonesian Parliament Sep '93; paying his own fare, visited Mexico as guest of the Turkish Ambassador to Mexico Oct '93; said Government had provided British Coal with all the financial support it had requested Oct '93; voted to restore capital punishment, especially for killers of policemen Feb '94; voted against reducing age of homosexual consent below 21, Feb '94; admitted that a lot of Essex Tories would not be campaigning for the European Parliament because they saw it as "counter-productive, worse than useless and a waste of time and money" Mar '94; in wake of 'cash for questions' revelations, left no stone unturned in revealing all his interests in the Register of Members Interests Oct '94; introduced Road Traffic (New Drivers) Bill to require drivers qualified for less than two years to retake the test if they had accumulated five penalty points: "mile for mile, a young driver is seven times more likely to have an accident than a middle-aged man" Feb '95; signed Kenneth Baker's Eurosceptic motion insisting it was not in Britain's interest to join a single European currency in '97, Feb '95; backed privatisation of nuclear industry, claiming that the reasons he had had for not supporting privatisation previously - such as unpredictable decommissioning costs - were no longer relevant May '95; was among 25 Tory MPs abstaining to protest EU fishing policy Dec '95; voted for Iain Duncan-Smith's Bill curbing the European Court Apr '96; voted for Bill Cash's Bill for a referendum on Euro-federalism June '96; congratulated the Conservative Government on its multi-stage privatisation of the energy industries, which had cut energy costs and introduced new sources July '96; voted against a 3% cap on MPs' pay rise, voted for MPs' pensions based on £43,000 and for a cut in MPs' mileage allowances July '96; voted to retain caning Jan '97; retained his renamed, altered seat with a halved majority of 10,684, on a notional anti-Tory swing of 12.57% May '97; backed Hague for Leader June '97; was named Chairman of the Science and Technology Select Committee July '97; insisted that the Japanese had to compensate surviving POWs early, while there were still many alive, instead of waiting a decade, when most would be dead Apr '98;

Born: 8 August 1935, Worksop, Nottinghamshire

Family: Son, late Mervyn Clark, builder and contractor, and Sybilla Norma (Winscott); m '58 Valerie Ethel (Harbord), teacher; 1s Jonathan '63; 1d 'Kate'/Catherine '61, who has worked as his secretary;

Education: Babworth Road Primary, Retford; King Edward VI Grammar, Retford; King's College, London (BSc Hons Chemistry; Fellow '87-); Minnesota University (Fulbright Scholarship '56); St John's College, Cambridge (PhD Chemistry);

Occupation: Management Consultant, formerly with P A Management Consultants Ltd (ASTMS/MSF) '81-93; Director '93-, Adviser '91-93, MAT Group Ltd (international transport company); Adviser: British Gas (£1-5,000) '93-, Royal Society of Chemistry (£1-5,000) '87-, British Chemical Engineering Contractors Association (£1-5,000) '87-; ex: Director: Courtney Stewart International (management consultants) '78-81; Divisional Marketing Manager, St Regis Paper Company '73-78; Executive, PA International Management Consultants '69-73, Smiths Industries '66-69; Industrial Chemist: ICI '60-66 (becoming Factory Manager);

Traits: Greying, wavy hair, balding on top; fair-minded; "charming, gentle soul" (Tory colleague); can be "deliberately naive" (Donald Dewar); gardener; DIY fan; bridge player; golfer;

Address: House of Commons, Westminster, London SW1A 0AA; 150 Free Trade Wharf, the Highway, Wapping, London; Rochford Hall, Rochford, Essex SE4 1NN;

Telephone: 0171 219 4016 (H of C); 01702 542042;

Majority: 1,980 over Conservative 8-way;
Description: The north Kent seat which is the largest of the three Medway Towns, with the onetime role of housing those working in the now defunct Chatham Navy Dockyard; until '97 was rated the Tories' 107th safest seat; it is over 80% owner-occupied, with only 10% in council housing; it remained in the hands of Tory MP James Couchman from '83 to '97, partly because of the previous neck-and-neck position of his LibDem and Labour opponents;
Position: Gillingham Borough Councillor (Labour Group Leader '89-90, Deputy Group Leader '83-89) '82-90;
Outlook: A slow-starting newcomer who asked only two written questions in his first year; his button can best be touched by discussions of the Channel Tunnel Rail Link, the 'New Deal' and other keys to regenerating the Thames Corridor and the Medway Towns; "New Labour" (NEW STATESMAN); a locally-born and locally-resident TUC and AEU administrator and ex-councillor who was one of the most unexpected '97 victors, with "a magnificent result" (Alan Howarth MP);
History: He joined the Labour Party '75; was elected to Gillingham Borough Council May '82; became Deputy Leader of the Labour Group on Gillingham Borough Council May '83; became Leader of the Labour Group on Gillingham Borough Council May '89; contested Gillingham, narrowly moving Labour from 3rd to 2nd place; this neck-and-neck place of his opponents enlarged Jim Couchman's majority to 16,638, Apr '92; re-selected for the seat, won it by a majority of 1,980, on a near-record notional swing of 16.02%; he was helped by a squeeze on the LibDem vote and by a combined vote for the Referendum and UK Independence parties larger than his majority May '97; backed ban on fox-hunting June '97; opposed Eurotunnel's open lattice goods wagons as unsafe June '97; co-sponsored motion attacking Tory-controlled Kent County Council for its moratorium on capital expenditure on schools June '97; in a letter to the GUARDIAN praised Frank Dobson's efforts to open up the NHS to public involvement Jan '98; asked if young people with exceptional needs could enter the New Deal early if they chose to do so Jan '98; was at the local Priestfield Stadium where Matthew Fox was killed in an otherwise good-humoured and well-policed match Mar '98; in the Channel Tunnel Rail Link debate, urged its full development, not merely to Ebbsfleet but to Stratford and St Pancras and beyond, via the West Coast line to Edinburgh; this could lead to the regeneration of the whole Thames Corridor, bringing 50,000 new jobs, including those in the Medway towns Mar '98; was rated among the 'Bottom 100' of written questioners, with only two posed in his first year May '98;
Born: 29 April 1957, Gillingham
Family: Son, of Gordon Clark, rtd journalist, and Avo Sheila (Warner) Gillingham Councillor '84-, Mayor '94-95; m '80 Julie (Hendrick); 2c;
Education: Gillingham Grammar School; Keele University (BA in Economics and Politics); University of Derby (DMS '96)
Occupation: Manager: of the TUC'S National Education Centre, of the TUC (AEEU) '86-97; Resident Assistant to the President of the AEU '80-86;
Traits: Parted dark hair; retreating forehead; heart-shaped face; specs; estuarial cockney

speech; joined the Army for "a 36-hour survival course" in January '98;
Address: House of Commons, Westminster, London SW1A 0AA; 50 Maidstone Road, Bounds Green, London N11 2JR;
Telephone: 0171 219 5207/2545(Fax) (H of C); 0181 361 8382 (home);

'Tony' (Anthony) CLARKE   **Labour**   **NORTHAMPTON SOUTH '97-**

Majority: 744 over Conservative 6-way;
Description: A populous seat which, as the Tories' 131st safest, until '97 was thought the fief of the former Tory Deputy Speaker, Michael Morris, and possibly beyond Labour's grasp; it contains half of Northampton and affluent commuter suburbs to the south, some of which were removed in '95; it houses Church's shoes, Carlsberg, Barclaycard, Panasonic and MFI;
Position: Northampton Borough Councillor (Chairman of Environment Services '94-97) '91-
Outlook: A young, locally-born, locally-based councillor who unseated Deputy Speaker Michael Morris, ending his a 23-year stint; as local Chairman of Environment Services and a committed environmentalist, led many local green initiatives; a football enthusiast and social work trainer; a Leftwinger formerly in the the local Campaign Group;
History: He joined the Labour Party '89; was elected to Northampton Borough Council at 28, May '91; at 32, was selected to contest almost out-of-reach Northampton South '95; Northampton was visited during the election campaign by Tony Blair and John Prescott, mainly to support the capture of more-winnable Northampton North, where Tory rebel Tony Marlow was vulnerable to a 3.6% swing Apr '97; was backed by several local unions Apr-May '97; Tony Clarke was elected for Northampton South, on a 13.38% notional swing, securing a majority of 744; this was half of the 1,405 votes cast for the Referendum Party candidate; the UKIP candidate, also called Clark, won 1,159 votes, taking votes from Tony Clarke May '97; asked the Home Secretary what proportion of crimes he estimated to be linked to drug abuse May '97; co-sponsored motion urging the Nationwide to remain a mutual building society June '97; co-sponsored motion urging more care in extraction of coal and aggregates July '97; in his Maiden showed pride in being "the first member of the town for many years to serve the place of my birth"; he also celebrated the victory at Wembley of his team, Northampton Town, as showing "that anything is possible under a Labour Government" July '97; complained that the inherited debts of local hospital trusts made it difficult to take advantage of new opportunities Dec '97; backed the Road Traffic Reduction Bill, on the basis of his "frustrating" experience as former Chairman of Environment Services for Northampton, "one of the first towns to undertake "real-time air-quality monitoring" Jan '98; complained about stolen tapes in the Hillsborough disaster Feb '98; expressed his "despair and dismay at the inadequate [football] ticket allocations from the French" Mar '98; was rated in the 'Bottom 100' of written questioners, having asked only 3 in his first year, because he does not believe in them May '98; was shot at in Albania while observing elections there June '98;
Born: 6 September 1963, Northampton
Family: Son, of Walter Arthur Clarke, engineer rtd, and Joan Ada Iris Clarke; divorced; is

married with two children;
Education: Lings Upper School, Northampton; Institute of Training and Development (Certificate of the Institute of Safety and Health);
Occupation: Former Social Work Trainer (Disability), with the Northamptonshire County Council (GMB) '84-97;
Traits: Burly; bearded; straight-talking; local football enthusiast (Vice Chairman of the Northampton Town Football Club Supporters' Trust; Manager and Coach of the Northampton Labour Club football team);
Address: House of Commons, Westminster, London SW1A 0AA; 30 Ethel Street, Northampton NN1 5ES;
Telephone: 0171 219 4469 (H of C); 01604 150044/250055 (Fax);

Charles (Rodway) CLARKE   **Labour**   **NORWICH SOUTH '97-**

Majority: 14,239 over Conservative 7-way;
Description: The centre of historic Norwich, including the cathedral close and the University of East Anglia; it has been the classic Labour marginal, sometimes its only East Anglian seat; in '95 some Tory-leaning suburbs were added;
Position: Parliamentary Secretary, Education and Employment '98-; ex: on Select Committee on Treasury Affairs '97-98; a PLP Delegate to Labour's National Policy Forum '97-98; Chairman, all-party Cycling Group '97-98; Vice Chairman, all-party Estonia Group '97-98; Chief of Staff to Labour Leader Neil Kinnock '83-92; Hackney Borough Councillor (Chairman of Housing, Vice Chairman of Economic Development) '81-86; President, of the National Union of Students '75-77;
Outlook: One of the first two of the 'class of '97' - with Patricia Hewitt - to be promoted to office; the shrewd and able politician who has finally come out of the backroom; a forceful extempore speaker who initially took some time to find a new niche, because of his background; an "effective fixer, talented and ambitious, but his historic connections with Kinnock could hold him back" (NEW STATESMAN); a mandarin's son who was first a Marxist student radical ("further to the Left than Wedgwood Benn"), then a Kinnock intimate but who initially sounded mildly Blairite but then settled into his own place; this was after his embarrassing experience of voting for lone-parent cuts which he privately opposed; was the last-minute replacement for ailing ex-MP John Garrett, which made him one of the few high-flying metropolitan staffers to come through the localising grid of Labour's OMOV (one-member, one-vote);
History: He became the sabbatical President of the Cambridge Students Union '72; called for the nationalisation of Oxbridge; was elected to the National Executive of the National Union of Students '73; joined the Labour Party '74; was elected President of the NUS '75; was accused by Conservatives in the NUS of "peddling the Moscow line" during a fraternal visit to Bucharest; spent a year in Cuba organising for its World Youth Festival also attended by Peter Mandelson, Paul Boateng, Fiona Mactaggart and Nigel Evans; all worked to block pro-Communist motions '78; was elected to Hackney Borough Council May '81; joined Neil Kinnock's staff as a Researcher '81; followed Kinnock to the office of Leader of the

Opposition as his Chief of Staff after Kinnock replaced Michael Foot as Labour Leader June '83; with Patricia Hewitt, helped write Kinnock's conference speech attacking Derek Hatton and the Liverpool Militants Oct '85; "was swiftly marginalised after Kinnock's departure" from office; after the death of Ron Leighton MP, was short-listed for Newham North East but not selected; complained about irregularities, with two other candidates, Charlotte Atkins (later MP for Staffordshire-Moorlands) and Claude Moraes Apr '94; these irregularities were put right before the selection of Stephen Timms; beating TRIBUNE editor Mark Seddon among others, Clarke was selected for Norwich South, "without assistance from the leadership" (RED PEPPER) Oct '96; in an article for the NEW STATESMAN, warned against believing in poll predictions of a massive Labour majority because the fickle voting public, spurred on by a hostile press, might turn on Labour, as in '92, Jan '97; warned that "the millions of Labour Party [supporters] who believe the party's job is to offer hope to those who now have little are asking" "whether New Labour is committed to change at all" Apr '97; at an election hustings, admitted he had smoked cannabis a couple of times in his teens, but opposed its legalisation Apr '97; retained Norwich South with a majority of 14,239, a swing to Labour of 10.10% which more than doubled the majority May '97; in his Maiden, urged rapid passage of promised Bill to put Private Finance Initiative into action, to enable the construction of the delayed Norfolk and Norwich Hospital May '97; came reluctantly to the conclusion that the new PFI-built hospital would be erected at Colney, a few miles outside the city and inaccessible to those without cars: "it's fundamentally unsatisfactory, but our hands are tied; to try to cancel the PFI contract would cost tens or even hundreds of millions of pounds, which would have to come out of the Health Service budget" June '97; co-sponsored motion approving of environmental initiatives by Anglia Water and Cambridge Water Company July '97; was named to Select Committee on Treasury Affairs July '97; strongly backed the Bank of England Bill as shifting the basis of decisions from "the febrile concerns of the market place in the City" to the "real needs of the economy" with more public disclosure of the Chancellor' targets Nov '97; urged the Government to press the Japanese for a full apology and appropriate compensation Nov '97; urged the encouragement of cycling, to catch up with European levels Dec '97; was elected a PLP representative on Labour's National Policy Forum, with the highest vote of the male '97 intake Dec '97; on the day he supported the Government in voting for cuts in lone-parent benefits, sent Social Security Secretary Harriet Harman a private letter insisting that it was "fundamentally wrong to discriminate financially against those who make the choice to be a parent and so do not seek work"; he also insisted that there would not be in place "the range of work opportunities and child care provisions which would make work a realistic alternative for single parents"; he added that "almost everyone I know in the PLP is outraged by what the Government is doing" but he had decided to support the Government "because I believe that it is better to treat this decision as an error of judgment from which the Government will learn rather than a division in principle from which there can be no retreat" Dec '97; in the subsequent meeting of the Norwich Labour Party, his explanation of why he had backed the Government on lone-parent benefits was greated with silence while the new Labour MP for Norwich North, Dr Ian Gibson, was applauded for voting against penalties on lone parents Dec '97; in the NEW STATESMAN urged an early transformation of the Lords into an elected second Chamber Jan '98; in the debate on the Bank of England Bill, backed the right of the Treasury Select Committee to vet members of the Monetary Policy Committee Jan '98; in the Treasury Select Committee spoke against continuing the Barnett formula, with its excessive generosity for Scotland Jan '98; campaigned against transfer of MAFF's Central Science Laboratory from Norwich to York; said, "the clear consensus view in Europe is that before joining the Euro, Britain will be required to make some kind of statement fixing an exchange rate betweeen Sterling and the

Euro; that does not appear to be the view of the British Treasury; it is a misunderstanding that needs to be clarified" Mar '98; predicted that from the beginning of '99 "the Euro will circulate more widely in the UK than people, including those in the Treasury, currently expect" Apr '98; persuaded the PLP to change its regional organisation from that of the Labour Party to parallel the Government's regional offices May '98; his campaign to remove borrowing limits from local authority airports like Norwich was accepted by John Prescott June '98; on the Treasury Select Committee attacked as "unfair" the fact that the costs of mis-selling pensions by firms like Prudential were being borne primarily by policy-holders rather than share-holders July '98; was promoted Parliamentary Secretary for Education and Employment (School Standards) July '98;

Born: 21 September 1950, London
Family: Son, of Sir Richard Clarke KCB, ex Permanent Secretary at the Ministry of Technology, and Brenda (Skinner) psychologist; m '83 Carol Marima (Pearson) researcher whose mother came from Estonia; 2s Christopher '87, Matthew '90;
Education: Highgate School; King's College, Cambridge '69-73 (BA in Maths and Economics);
Occupation: Ex: Chief Executive, QPA (public affairs consultancy which advised the Association of District Councils, among others) '92-97; Chief of Staff, to Labour Leader Neil Kinnock '83-92; Researcher, to Neil Kinnock as Education Spokesman '81-83; Lecturer, in Maths (part-time), City Literary Institute '81-83; Organiser, Hackney People in Partnership '78-80; President, of the NUS '75-77;
Traits: Burly; shortish blond beard, once much longer ("I have no plans to shave it off"); matey beer drinker; elusive; chess-player; enjoys walking, to the discomfiture of his government driver, deprived of overtime;
Address: House of Commons, Westminster, London SW1A 0AA; has moved to Norwich;
Telephone: 0171 219 6496 (H of C);

Eric CLARKE   Labour   **MIDLOTHIAN '92-**

Majority: 9,870 (28%) over SNP 5-way;
Description: The old Midlothian seat south of Edinburgh minus the Calders and Livingston New Town; now based mainly on the largely-defunct Midlothian coalfield (including Bilston, once scene of bitter strike clashes) with its small working-class communities and growing sunrise industries; three-fifths of its workers travel to Edinburgh to work; in '95 it lost 13,000 voters in Penicuik to Tweeddale, Ettrick and Lauderdale;
Position: On Scottish Select Committee '97-, '92-94, Broadcasting Select Committee '97-; Joint Treasurer, all-party Parliamentary Beer Club '94-; ex: Scottish Whip '94-97; NUM's man on Labour's NEC '84-88;
Lothian Regional Councillor '74-78; Midlothian County Councillor '62-75, on Scottish Council for Development and Industry '75-78; on South and West of Scotland Forestry Advisory Commission '76-78; Joint Secretary, of Coal Industry Social Welfare Organisation Scotland '78-89;
Outlook: A widely-respected 'democratic Marxist' showing the loyalism typical of a lifelong

trade unionist: withdrew his public protest against the '97 Harman benefit cuts to protest privately to Chancellor Brown; an able, experienced, low-profiled, semi-hard Left veteran ex-miner who succeded Alex Eadie; was sacked by Arthur Scargill from his leadership of the Scots miners in '89; is active in Commons despite being a belated Westminster entry, after serving 16 years as a Councillor in Scotland; "a member of an endangered species: a Scottish Labour Member who knows what he is talking about" and expresses himself "in his customary robust way" (Tory ex-Minister Allan Stewart); "I am aware of the constructive approach [he] has taken and the dedication that he has shown in the interests of the [mining] industry" (Michael Heseltine MP); is involved, as Adviser, in Scottish Coal; was NUM-sponsored; **History:** Was a radical at school; joined the NUM at 16 as a young miner '49; was elected to Midlothian County Council '62; was named JP for Midlothian '63; joined the Labour Party '64; campaigned against cuts in children's milk from June '70; was selected as Labour candidate for Clackmannan and East Stirling '74; was elected to Lothian Regional Council May '74; opposed cuts in public services by Callaghan Government '76; resigned as Clackmannan's Labour candidate on being elected a full-time official, as General Secretary of Scottish NUM '77; in letter to LABOUR WEEKLY wrote: "the concept that Marxists are totally opposed to the Parliamentary system and are completely undemocratic is nonsense, and the conclusion that they have no part in the Labour Party is bordering on arrogance"; "I am a socialist and in my vocabulary of political terms, socialism means democracy at all levels within the Labour Party and in life; let us drop the term 'democratic socialist'" Aug '79; in Energy debate at party conference, spoke for NUM in backing a composite urging a "triple alliance" of coal, conservation and alternative energy, with only cautious support for nuclear energy Sep '82; narrowly failed to be elected to the trade union section of Labour's National Executive, with 3,159,000 votes; urged imposition of statutory code of conduct on media, who had "freedom and irresponsibility" because "they are responsible to big business"; they only treated the occasional erring Tory Minister badly; "all the personality assassinations are [aimed at] the leaders of this party and at the trade union officials" Oct '83; was elected to trade union section of National Executive Committee at annual conference with 3,310,000 votes; in Defence debate urged more trade unionists to join CND; deplored Labour's Defence spokesmen in Parliament as being "too close to the NATO and too close to the United States' policies"; he wanted US arms out of Scotland: "go back to where you belong and do not come back!" Oct '84; was again elected to trade union section of Labour's National Executive with 3,356,000 votes Oct '85; on behalf of Labour's NEC, supported a Scottish Assembly Sep '87; at Scargill's behest, was dropped as NUM's nominee to Labour's NEC Oct '88; as a continuing critic of Arthur Scargill, was made redundant as General Secretary of Scottish Area of NUM July '89; with 52% of the vote, was selected to succeed fellow ex-miner Alex Eadie at Midlothian, defeating Ted Matthews (37%) and Dan Lennie (11%) Aug '89; at party conference urged an "all-out campaign for the democratisation of South Africa, the scrapping of Apartheid, and the freeing of Nelson Mandela and his colleagues" Oct '89; urged as good safety precautions for offshore oil production as miners had achieved in their industry, after many disasters Aug '90; at party conference urged British Coal to reopen Monktonhall colliery itself instead of trying to privatise a slimmed down version Sep '90; retained seat with majority of 10,334, down from 12,253 because of doubling of SNP vote Apr '92; in Maiden charged PM John Major with wanting to "return to the dark ages of the coal owners" by privatising British Coal; expressed concern about Monktonhall colliery May '92; warned that privatisation of British Coal would mean drop in safety standards, pointing out that no private mines supplied 'self-rescuers' which enabled miners to go through smoke-filled atmosphere to safety; "I want the industry transferred from public ownership with safety absolutely guaranteed" June '92; urged a contingency plan in case Germans withdrew from European Fighter Aircraft consortium, with by-products for future technology June '92; was elected to Scottish Affairs Select Committee July '92; urged continuity of CIN, the effective organisation that had run the miners pension fund July '92; warned Energy Minister against prematurely selling Frances colliery in Fife Oct '92; warned that water privatisation would benefit the few and harm the many Dec '92; complained that mink were "ecological disasters" because they slaughtered ducklings and other birds and animals Dec '92; complained that cuts in local government expenditure were leading to deterioration of fabric of schools and education Feb '93; co-sponsored Skinner-led amendment urging saving of all threatened pits Mar '93; urged Government to reconsider its oil tax proposals in order to keep up exploration for new sources of oil May '93; his Bill on Maritime Safety was dropped after its 2nd Reading July '93; derided as "pure propaganda" "the Government's formula for the closure of economically viable collieries" because "there was a total lack of effort in encouraging generating companies to buy British and secure a market for coal" or to end "a subsidy of £1.3b a year" "built in for nuclear power" or any effort to close obsolescent Magnox stations July '93; visited Cyprus to attend a rally to commemorate the Turkish invasion, as a guest of the Morphou Association Oct '93; complained that Sainsbury's were using "a form of blackmail" against staff reluctant to work Sundays by saying their chance of promotion might be affected by unwillingness to work on Sundays Nov '93; made a scathing critique of the Government's "reform" of Scottish local government Jan '94; voted against restoring capital punishment, even for killing policemen Feb '94; voted to reduce age of homosexual consent to 18, but not 16, Feb '94; voted for John Prescott for Leader and Deputy Leader July '94; was named Scottish Whip Oct '94; came off the Scottish Select Committee Nov '94; reacting to the suggestion that Labour might reconsider its opposition to nuclear power, said "there should be a moratorium on any nuclear power" Jan '95; assigned Helen Liddell to sit on a committee considering the Scottish Children's Bill when, as she insisted as an economist, she wanted to sit on the Finance Bill committee Jan '95; initiated a debate on the "deplorable conditions" of the Forth Rail Bridge, threatening to "hold the Government solely responsible if any accident happens to anyone because of the lack of maintenance and care" Feb '95; was reported as joking at the large turnout of Labour women MPs for a debate on women's lives on a rainy International Women's Day, "of course, they would be in here; it's not much of a day for hanging out the washing" Mar '95; called for the lodging of the plans of old mine workings regionally, to reduce the travel costs of individuals or developers interested in subsidence June '95; raised the anomaly that parents and carers of severely handicapped children under five were ineligible for Disability Living Allowance July '95; co-sponsored the Bill of Labour MP Alan Meale to ban cruelty to animals Jan '96; expressed regret that the cash-strapped NUM could no longer support ex-miner MPs' constituency parties; "I make no apology for being a sponsored MP; it takes the miners' MPs to look after the mining communities" Feb '96; opposed proposed gas-fired Gartcosh Power Station as a threat to fully half of Scottish coal production Mar '96; voted against Iain Duncan-Smith's bill to curb the European Court Apr '96; voted against a 3% cap on MPs' pay rise, voted for a pension based on £43,000 and to retain MPs' high mileage allowances July '96; in Labour's last pre-election reshuffle, was retained as Labour's Scottish Whip July '96; introduced Witness Protection Bill on behalf of Irene Adams MP Nov '96; urged the retention of the proposed electricity interconnector linking Scotland and Northern Ireland which "will burn the equivalent of 600,000 tons of coal" Feb '97; retained his altered seat with a majority of 9,870 on a 1.5% notional swing from the SNP May '97; was dropped as Scottish Whip May '97; was restored to the Scottish Select Committee and named to the Select Committee on Broadcasting July '97; visited Cyprus as guest of the Greek Cypriot Federation Oct '97; strongly supported the Scotland Bill establishing a Scottish Parliament, saying "we want the same as people in former colonies who now have freedom" Oct '97;

opposed Harriet Harman's decision to implement the Tory benefit cuts to lone parents, saying: "our children and our children's children will not thank us if we don't deal with the matter now" Nov '87; urged an integrated fuel policy, with an investment in clean-coal technology to secure use of coal reserves instead of wasteful gas generation Nov '97; withdrew his name from a motion criticising Harman's benefit cuts after being told by Whips that it would be "more efficient" to write to Chancellor Gordon Brown Dec '97; acclaimed the emerging Scottish Parliament, warning that "anyone who dares to stand in its way will be walked over and forgotten forevermore..." Jan '98;

Born: 9 April 1933, Edinburgh

Family: Son, Ernest F Clarke, railway guard, and Annie (Reid), laundress; m '55 June (Hewat), shop assistant; 2s Paul Andrew '57, Stephen Richard '61; 1d Susan Margaret '59; 1 grandson, Ben Clarke;

Education: St Cuthberts School, Edinburgh; Holy Cross Academy, Leith; W M Ramsey Technical College; Esk Valley College;

Occupation: Parliamentary Adviser, to Scottish Coal (£5-10,000) '97?-; Panellist: for Harris Parliamentary Panel (£1,000) and British Planning and Research International (£1,000), both paid to Midlothian Constituency Labour Party '95?-; ex: Adviser, to Mining (Scotland) Ltd (cooperative aimed at taking mines closed by British Coal into co-operative ownership, mainly by Scottish miners) '92-97?; Sponsored, by NUM (£750 p a to constituency, 80% of election expenses) '92-95; Unemployed '89-92; General Secretary, Scottish NUM '77-89; Miner (Roslin Colliery '49-51, Lingerwood Colliery '51-69, Bilston Glen Colliery '69-77) '49-77;

Traits: Parted grey-white hair; burly build; Scottish accent; "I am half Irish and half Scots"; "I am proud to be of peasant stock, but I am not an inverted snob" (EC); "blunt-spoken" (Peter Jones, SCOTSMAN); self-mocking MCP; can seem over-serious or portentous (ridiculed HOUSE MAGAZINE's "stupid" request for his political hero by replying "Charlie Chaplin"); "I am a keen angler": enjoys trout fly-fishing, carpentry, gardening;

Address: House of Commons, Westminster, London SW1A 0AA; 32 Mortonhall Park Crescent, Edinburgh EH17 8SY;

Telephone: 0171 219 6373 (H of C); 0131 664 8214 (home); 0131 654 1585 (office); 0131 654 1586 (office Fax); 0141 332 8946 (regional party);

Rt Hon Kenneth (Harry) CLARKE QC   Conservative   RUSHCLIFFE '70-

Majority: 5,055 (8.1%) over Labour 6-way;

Description: Nottinghamshire's unaltered southernmost constituency; mostly rural and suburban, it is almost 80% owner-occupied; its biggest centre is West Bridgford (middle-class commuter town across the Trent from Nottingham) with its Nottingham Forest football ground and Nottinghamshire County Council headquarters;

Position: President '97-, Patron '80-97, Tory Reform Group; Vice President, European Movement '97-; ex: Chancellor of the Exchequer '93-97; Home Secretary '92-93; Education Secretary '90-92; Health Secretary '88-90; Chancellor of Duchy of Lancaster (Deputy Trade and Industry Secretary) '87-88; Paymaster General (Deputy Employment Secretary) '85-87; Minister of State, Health '82-85;

Parliamentary Secretary, Transport '79-82, Deputy Spokesman: on Industry '76-79, Social Security '74-76; Whip (Lord Commissioner) '74, Assistant Whip '72-74; Secretary, Conservative MPs' Health and Social Security Committee '74; PPS to Sir Geoffrey Howe '71-72; Vice Chairman, British-American Parliamentary Group '87-89; Delegate, to Council of Europe and Western European Union '73-74;

Outlook: The Europhile Leader most '97 Eurosceptic Tory MPs consigned to the well-cushioned boardrooms; he so established himself as much the punchiest Tory politician of the Major era that even some of his Eurosceptic critics voted for him to succeed Major as Leader; since Hague's victory has only appeared occasionally in his Brown-baiting role, spending most of his time with lucrative companies, where he earns over £200,000; "there is something very appealing about a politician who apparently doesn't give a damn about what his colleagues think of him and actually seems to enjoy flaunting the fact; watching him at the Despatch Box defending the...single [European] currency reminds me of Landseer's painting of 'The Stag at Bay'; he may be a rather portly stag and one with an unlikely taste for cheroots, Hush Puppies and Nottingham Forest, but he is still able to see off a pack of slavering Tory hounds" (Tony Banks MP); the very bright, able, combative, no-nonsense 'One Nation' reformer; unlike his prior roles in Education and Health, as Chancellor had a sure feeling for the British economy; "temperamentally a seat-of-the pants man" (Peter Riddell, TIMES); was "the first innumerate Chancellor Britain...had for 14 years; there is no evidence he knows much about economic policy or anything whatever about the refinements of exchange rate management and reading the monetary aggregates" but had "a proven capacity to shake up departments, combined with a saloon bar vocabulary and what looks like an uncalculated defiance of anything that smells of political correctness" (Hugo Young, GUARDIAN); the most thuggish top politician since Denis Healey; having outstripped Michael Heseltine, became the vocal leader of pro-European Tories, claiming it is possible to have economic and monetary union without a federal United States of Europe; his pro-European vision led him to have to be restrained from slugging it out with the anti-Maastricht Eurosceptics in '94; "my politics are the politics of the hard Centre"; "I have always regarded myself as a 'One Nation' Tory and still do" (KC); insists: "my hero was Iain Macleod", "an extremely enlightened, liberal man, but he was also an extremely partisan, aggressive and rather activist politician"; "he became one of the most hated men in the Conservative Party" (KC); "I hold all the classical liberal views, on hanging, race and all that sort of thing [including abortion]; my sense of social justice is quite strongly developed; I remain committed to the NHS and the state education system" (KC); a punchy satirist, who still enjoys using Gordon Brown as his punching bag (claims Brown is so dour that his local wine bar won't let him during 'Happy Hour'); "he is extremely clever, insouciant, fun and capable of clever footwork; if there were rabbits in the hat, he would [have been] the Chancellor to find them" (Labour MP Austin Mitchell); formerly "a Prime Minister in waiting" (Peter Riddell, TIMES) and "the heir-all-too-apparent" (GUARDIAN); announced his intention of becoming Major's successor when the latter called it a day; but the chance of that being successful was frustrated when on his initial confident belief that the two-thirds of Eurosceptic Tory MPs would be converted to the European single currency was overturned in '97 when the proportion of Europhobes was increased by the election; "courage is half of politics and he's certainly got courage; I trust his judgement less" (Lord Rees-Mogg); was "said to be the only member of the Cabinet admired by Margaret Thatcher" (Sarah Baxter, NEW STATESMAN)); "has two notable gifts essential to a good Prime Minister": "the first is apparently unlimited self-confidence; the second, which springs from the first, is a clear idea of what must be achieved and the ruthlessness and intellect to carry out the necessary action" (Simon Heffer, EVENING STANDARD); "Kenneth Clarke can afford to take risks; he can fly by the seat of his pants because he is extremely able, and has this most amazing speed of thought" (quoted by Valery Elliott, SUNDAY TELEGRAPH); "the kind of politician who will cross a road in order to get into a fight" (Lord (Douglas) Hurd); "everyone knows that Kenneth Clarke uses arguments like clubs to beat his opponents" (Lord Rees-Mogg, INDEPENDENT); has the "impulse to punch before he thinks" (OBSERVER); "believes that aggression can make up for ignorance" {Lord (Roy) Hattersley); "the thinking man's lager lout" (fellow Minister); "a spectacularly effective political ruffian" (Ian Aitken, GUARDIAN); "famously ignorant of economics" (ex-MP Bryan Gould); "the cuddly axeman" (Donald Macintyre, SUNDAY CORRESPONDENT); his "speciality is the Good Old Ken approach -the jokey-blokey knockabout style that disarms hostile questioning by implying that nothing should be taken too seriously" (John Williams, EVENING STANDARD); "the classic barrister - bright, ill-informed and opinionated"; "he travels light, relying more on instinct than substance; such talents serve him well, so long as he does not have to stand still too long in any one place, which so far he has not" (Martin Kettle GUARDIAN); can be seen alternately as socially-concerned and also as a hard-faced union-basher, grinder of do-gooders' faces and blaster of education's "outdated '60s nostrums"; "without losing radical push, he conveys the sense of being something better than an opportunistic ideologue" (Hugo Young, GUARDIAN); after 'wet' beginnings as co-founder of 'Nick's Diner', suffered a Rightward political 'change of life' which disclosed him as a sharp-tongued opponent of nurses, doctors, teachers and ambulancemen; as Health Secretary and Education Secretary he swallowed the Rightwing agenda while rejecting the loonier ideas of the Rightwing think tanks; "adapted rather than submitted" to Thatcherism (OBSERVER); described his policies as "Thatcherism with a human face"; even before that, had long been an advocate of trade union 'reforms' and pay ceilings; "one of the toughest exponents of controlling public expenditure in the Cabinet" (former Chief Secretary); "his unflappability and his affable approach" were belatedly "seen by Mrs Thatcher as essential skills for the task of selling the reforms of the NHS to a doubting public" (INDEPENDENT); in his adaptation to Thatcherism lost a lot of friends and made powerful enemies; at Health "was the 'bulldozer' riding roughshod over the doctors and the unions" (Victoria Macdonald and James Le Fanu, SUNDAY TELEGRAPH); was "the focus of probably the most expensive [£1.9b] personal campaign yet against a single politician", by the BMA (Donald Macintyre, SUNDAY CORRESPONDENT); "he is not a details man; in fact sometimes it's quite staggering what he doesn't know, but he has a very clear overview of what he wants to do"; formerly worked in tandem with his old university mate, Norman Fowler, and then Lord Young ("Lord Young's representative on earth" - Andrew Rawnsley, GUARDIAN); a rare Minister who can reply without a visible brief; a pragmatist willing to take the tough decisions; "he believes himself to be a man of the people"; "he maintains his proletarian habits and appears not to have forgotten his roots; hence his love of soccer and pints of beer" (OBSERVER); "no ideologue and certainly no monetarist, and the combination of earthy common sense with a traditionally Conservative approach to social policy has moved some colleagues to suggest that their party may have another Baldwin on its hands" (GUARDIAN); "I'm vehemently opposed to Proportional Representation" (KC);

History: His maternal grandfather, Harry Ernest Smith, a Raleigh toolroom engineer and Communist Party member, often argued politics with Ken's father in his presence; Ken's father had become an opponent of unions when a wartime pit electrician; Ken decided to become an MP when he was seven; "even in short trousers I was following the politics of the Attlee Government" '47; at Cambridge University initially joined both the Bow Group and the moderate-Labour 'Campaign for Social Democracy' '59; supported Harold Macmillan's failed bid to join the EEC '60; was elected Chairman of the Cambridge University Conservative Association '61; defended right of Conservative Association to invite fascist Oswald Mosley on free speech grounds Nov '61; was elected President of the Cambridge Union and Chairman of the Federation of Conservative Students Feb '63; at Cambridge Union pledged to keep women out: "I have always been against women in the Union; the fact that Oxford has admitted them does not impress me; they will soon realise what a mess they are in" Mar '63; was rated by VARSITY as the nicest, the most grown-up, the most academically considerable of the 'Cambridge Mafia' '63; contested hopeless Mansfield Oct '64, Feb '66; wrote pamphlets for Birmingham Bow Group: 'What's Wrong with General Practice?' '65, 'Immigration, Race and Politics' - which mixed racial harmonization (more ethnic police, making racial discrimination by employers a criminal offence) with curbs on swamping (immigrant population should not exceed 50% with mortgages refused when it reached that ceiling and schools limited to a third of pupils from immigrant families) - '66, and 'Regional Government - A West Midlands Study' '69; retook Rushcliffe from Labour's Tony Gardner June '70; in his Maiden, congratulated new Education Secretary, Margaret Thatcher, for allotting a purpose-built comprehensive to his constituency, with the support of the local Conservative authority July '70; was named PPS to Sir Geoffrey Howe, then Solicitor General; worked with him on Industrial Relations Bill and European Community enabling legislation '71-72; was named Assistant Whip Apr '72, full Whip (Lord Commissioner) Jan '74; attacked Labour proposal of referendum on staying in EEC May '74; as Deputy Spokesman on Social Services urged an invested pension fund instead of Barbara Castle's tax-based pensions Sep '74; opposed increased National Insurance contributions from the self-employed Nov '74; urged abolition of earnings rule for pensioners Jan '75; having voted for Sir Geoffrey Howe as an "intelligent abstention", showed overt displeasure over Mrs Thatcher's victory as Leader Feb '75; urged end of "political cat-and-dog fight" in pension field Mar '75; attacked "army of scroungers" exploiting welfare system Jan '76; his effort to provide pubs with flexible hours and 'family rooms' in his Licensing Amendment (No 2) Bill was killed by the anti-alcohol lobby Jan '76; was named Deputy Spokesman on Industry Nov '76; attacked huge subsidies for BL and others without requirement of improved management Apr '77; attacked Labour's blacklist of firms breaking pay ceilings '78; opposed import control on Japanese cars Nov '78; was named Parliamentary Secretary for Transport under Cambridge chum Norman Fowler May '79; guessing that Sealink would be first part of BR to go, insisted denationalization was pragmatic, not doctrinaire Jan '81; helped make it easier for BR to reopen closed lines May '81; reduced lead in petrol but resisted its complete elimination Oct '81; was promoted Minister of State for Health, after a fight with Mrs Thatcher on his behalf by his chum, Norman Fowler Mar '82; exaggerated that NHS payments by overseas visitors would yield £6m a year Mar '82; backed Pill for under-16s May '82; had rough handling from NHS strikers in Liverpool, resulting in a "pathological hatred" for the "health service unions" (Ian Aitken, GUARDIAN) Aug '82; announced £11m health research trust, restrictively funded by tobacco companies Oct '82; angered NHS unions by allegedly breaking unwritten agreement Nov '82; insisted on limited prescribing; tightened up medical deputizing service July '83; was promoted Privy Councillor Jan '84; expressed concern over continued prescribing of banned drugs Feb '84; introduced Water (Fluoridation) Bill Jan '85; was promoted to Cabinet as Paymaster General and No 2 to Lord Young as Employment Secretary Sep '85; claimed trade union reform was one of the Thatcher Government's "success stories" Oct '85; 7% of backbenchers supported him as a successor to Mrs Thatcher, with Kenneth Baker (35%), Norman Tebbit (16%), Peter Walker (9%) ahead of him Jan '86; voted against restoring hanging Apr '87; devised a plan to outlaw the closed shop and give members of unions the right to break strikes even if their union had voted for industrial action May '87; in the post-election reshuffle was transferred without enthusiasm to DTI as No 2 to Lord Young June '87; said that authorities who opposed urban renewal would be leapfrogged June '87; insisted the acceptance of the

Murdoch bid for TODAY, without a reference to the MMC, was required by the paper's uneconomic status July '87; pressed for use of local labour in developing inner cities but resisted making it a statutory requirement July '87; admitted Labour-governed Glasgow was the UK's best example of urban regeneration Oct '87; was rated at 12-to-1 to becoming Leader by SUNDAY TELEGRAPH Oct '87; dismissed as a "grandiose scheme of dubious scientific and commercial value" the EC's bid to launch a manned space flight by 1999 Oct '87; after months of infighting, was finally promoted to inner-city supremo by Mrs Thatcher Dec '87; toured the US for inner-city ideas Jan '88; announced a virtual standstill in Britain's funding for the European Space Agency Feb '88; voted to televise the Commons Feb '88; voted against restoring hanging Mar '88; when Mrs Thatcher announced there would be a hot-line for businessmen interested in the inner-city programme, he irritated her by saying he would not be answering the calls himself Mar '88; sold nationalized British Shipbuilder's Govan yard to Norwegian company, Kvaerner Industries, for £6m plus £12m in secret Euro-subsidies (which later prevented Sunderland yard from being sold by Tony Newton) Apr '88; voted for a 26-week ceiling on abortion May '88; mocked the "little Englander approach" of MPs opposing the Swiss Nestle takeover of Rowntree June '88; agreed to allow British Aerospace to sell on Rover within 5 years without penalty (as disclosed 18 months later) July '88; was appointed Secretary of State for Health July '88; refused to return from his Spanish holiday to cope with nurses' pay dispute; on holiday read Dr David Owen's Our NHS, extolling internal market Aug '88; looking at NHS reforms, rejected Rightwing proposals for a switch to private health insurance; initially opposed the eye and teeth test charges imposed on him by Mrs Thatcher, managing to defuse the Tory conference revolt against them Oct '88; after her salmonella-in-eggs blurt-out, urged Edwina Currie to keep quiet, protected her from a Commons mauling over her exaggerated statement, but did not try to stop her resigning; left it to Chief Medical Offer Sir Donald Acheson to try to rescue the situation Dec '88; declined to resign from Cabinet although he wholly opposed Mrs Thatcher's Bill to force football clubs to introduce a national identity scheme Jan '89; with Agriculture Minister John MacGregor agreed to an independent inquiry into mounting food poisoning Feb '89; published his NHS reform blueprint, 'Working for Patients'; its core was an 'internal market' for the NHS, with competition from hospital trusts for funds from budget-holding GPs; it retained Mrs Thatcher's proposals for tax incentives for the retired to help them retain private health insurance, against which he and Chancellor Nigel Lawson had argued Jan '89; announced it would "make sense" for all 2,000 hospitals eventually to become trusts Feb '89; his proposals secured the united opposition of all wings of the medical and nursing professions (including those in Nottingham); said: "I do wish the more suspicious of our GPs would stop feeling nervously for their wallets every time that I mention the word 'reform'" Mar '89; attacked BMA for "scurrilous nonsense" in leaflet denouncing his plans for performance-related doctors' contracts Apr '89; 280,000-strong Royal College of Nurses and 32,000 GPs voted to campaign against his NHS 'reforms' after he dismissed opposition as a waste of money Apr '89; 150 local GPs urged anti-Tory votes in Vale of Glamorgan by-election, lost by Tories Apr '89; Tory-dominated Social Services Select Committee criticized pace of his NHS 'reforms' May '89; appointed Sir Robert Scholey, British Steel Chairman, and Sir Graham Day, Rover Group Chairman, to NHS policy board May '89; was subjected to a "misleading and unscrupulous" (KC) £600,000 BMA advertising campaign against his NHS 'reforms' May '89; warned Cabinet that "over-generous" 8.8% BR settlement would be paid for with disputes in the NHS June '89; previously agreed GPs' contract was rejected by BMA, with deal put out for ballot June '89; 75% of those polled by Gallup thought his 'reforms' would lead to NHS cuts in services and eventual privatization July '89; accused BMA of spending millions on "irresponsible and misleading shroud-waving" July '89; after their 3-to-1 rejection by family doctors - blamed on his "bullying tone" - decided to impose GPs' contracts July '89; the BMA launched a further £750,0000 campaign against his 'reforms' July '89; Mrs Thatcher gave him another Minister, Lord Trafford, to help pilot his Health Bill through the Lords July '89; claimed: "about 80 to 90% of the White Paper has in fact been accepted"; "an unreformed Health Service would eventually have collapsed because the attempt to just meet lobby-led demand for more resources, having an uncosted base, with no sensible internal organization, would have produced a costing gap between people's satisfaction with the service delivered and the service's ability to get the money it constantly required" July '89; secured truce with BMA over indicative limits on prescribing, by dropping legally binding fixed-cash limits Sep '89; ambulancemen began overtime ban against 6.5% offer Sep '89; was rated by Ladbroke's at 16-to-1 - down from 12-to-1 - as a successor to Mrs Thatcher Oct '89; favoured 24-week ceiling for abortion Oct '89; introduced Bill to implement his NHS 'reforms' Nov '89; secured £2.6b extra for NHS from Chief Secretary Norman Lamont Nov '89; with Mrs Thatcher's support, strongly resisted pay claims of ambulance workers and other NHS unionists; put Army on standby Nov '89; 76% of GPs rejected contract he offered them Nov '89; announced £26m for medical audit Dec '89; 4.5m people signed a petition backing ambulancemen's dispute Dec '89; was recommended by Norman Tebbit as a "vigorous and combative" possible future Tory Leader who could be "getting on with things I want to see done" Jan '90; briefed Sunday lobby journalists that he was prepared to be "flexible" about minority of "paramedical" ambulancemen but not mere "professional drivers"; he dismissed as "pointless" TUC-organized demonstrations by 1m in support of ambulancemen's 16-week dispute, to whom he offered 9% increase over 9 months Jan '90; announced a new body to ensure standards of clinical care were maintained after introduction of internal market in NHS Feb '90; voted against ordaining divorced men as clergymen Feb '90; the ambulancemen's dispute ended in a draw, with some ambulancemen getting up to 23.4% more over 24 months, but Clarke refused fireman-type inflation-proofing Feb '90; introduced Human Fertilization and Embryology Bill, voting in favour of continued research Apr '90; succeeded in reversing Lords amendment to ring-fence community care funds June '90; rejected opticians' claim that eye tests had fallen by a third since charges were imposed June '90; announced phasing in of community care, delaying it by two years July '90; secured a £2.3b increase for NHS in 'Star Chamber' negotiations Oct '90; again refused to compensate haemophiliacs infected with AIDS by NHS blood Oct '90; in an ICM poll was Cabinet's low man with 18% approval and 60% disapproval Oct '90; while still in the last stages of applying the NHS 'reforms', was made Education Secretary, as the 'hard' man to replace John MacGregor, who had gone 'soft' on the educational Establishment Nov '90; despite Mrs Thatcher's renewed support for them, said: "I have never being in favour of vouchers"; indicated he would overturn MacGregor's rejection of teacher appraisal Nov '90; said he would vote for Mrs Thatcher in first round of Leadership battle; after Mrs Thatcher failed to win outright on the first round, "I advised her that she should not go on, and in my opinion, she ought to step down"; told her: "if you fight on, it will be like the Charge of the Light Brigade"; "I would have resigned had she gone on," but did not threaten her with this Nov '90; despite Alan Clark's claim to have heard rumours that "that pudgy puff-ball" might stand, Clarke supported 10-years-older Douglas Hurd to succeed as Prime Minister, dragging Hurd out of dinner to bully him into declaring his immediate candidacy Nov '90; urged end of poll tax Nov '90; opposed transfer of Education management to central Government Nov '90; announced compulsory teacher appraisal on classroom performance every two years Dec '90; endorsed Tory Reform Group's 'The Right Way Forward', urging European integration, a social market, improving quality of life and tackling social divisions Jan '91; offered incentives to schools to opt out of local authority control Jan '91; held back £35m from university budgets to ensure they reached pay settlements satisfactory to the Government Feb '91; was accused of crippling music teaching in schools Feb '91; before Select Committee, laid the blame for decline in reading standards on local authorities and teachers; backed phonic methods of teaching, deriding others as "cranky" Mar '91; said his "ideal" was "where all secondary schools are grant-maintained" Mar '91; having resisted Michael Heseltine's proposal to finance all education centrally, announced plans to take FE and 6th-form colleges out of local authority control Mar '91; threatened School Examinations and Assessment Council for sabotaging his requests Mar '91; postponed teachers' pay Bill for further consultations Mar '91; postponed his belated plan to penalize GCSE candidates for poor spelling Mar '91; visiting Japan, acclaimed its education system as the best in the developed world Mar '91; conceded an independent pay review body to teachers in exchange for an agreement not to strike over pay and conditions Apr '91; said he would no longer insist on 5-year moratorium on change of status for grant-maintained schools Apr '91; labelled DAILY MIRROR readers as "morons" after they voted him a "prat" for saying anyone who could afford it wouild prefer to put their children through fee-paying schools Apr '91; in interview in INDEPENDENT insisted that by schools becoming grant-maintained, unnecessary bureaucracy could be cut: "modern public services are best provided by delegated management, encouraging diversity in response to competition" May '91; ruled out further money for university pay May '91; a poll showed his Labour spokesman opponent, Jack Straw, had 10% more popular backing than he May '91; criticized School Examinations and Assessment Council for presenting unworkable tests for 7-year-olds June '91; Labour MP and ex-headmaster Gerry Steinberg said he would not trust his increased powers under School Teachers' Pay and Conditions Bill: "those in the Health service did not trust him, the teachers do not trust him, and I certainly do not" June '91; named BP manager David Pascall, formerly in Mrs Thatcher's Policy Unit, as Chairman of National Curriculum Council and Rightwing economist Lord (Brian) Griffiths, former head of the Policy Unit and Chairman of Centre for Policy Studies, as Chairman of the Schools Examination Assessment Council July '91; backed down on his threat to stop subsidizing adult classes Sep '91; promised to privatize schools inspection and provide parents with full information about schools Sep '91; at annual Tory conference was lukewarmly received for "a long, worthy trudge through the jargon of education policy" (John Williams, EVENING STANDARD) Oct '91; said head teachers' salaries should depend on examination results and truancy rates Oct '91; announced slimming down of Her Majesty Inspectorate, from 480 inspectors to 175, with their role reduced to accrediting and supervising privately-organized inspectois Oct '91; announced Bill to provide league tables of results and publication of results of privatized inspectors; derided HMI as out-of-date failed teachers Nov '91; announced 8.6% increase in Education spending Nov '91; claimed Labour-controlled Newcastle had more non-teachers than teachers on its education pay roll, when Newcastle insisted it had 47 teacher-advisers and 2,200 teachers Nov '91; urged a May or June election Jan '92; named Eric Bolton and Daphne Gould as Stratford School governors to strengthen its head against Muslim chauvinists Jan '92; radically shifted teacher training from theory in colleges to practical training in schools Jan '92; demanded fundamental changes in primary teaching, including restoration of streaming and a return to "chalk and talk", rejecting "highly questionable dogmas" from the '60s, like group work Jan '92; named BP executive David Pascall to extricate the National Curriculum Council from the antagonistic grip of the educational establishment; he replaced Duncan Graham who later accused him of subverting the history curriculum and trying to interfere with teaching methods Jan '92; was named 'Radical of the Year' by the Thatcherite 'Radical Society' in gratitude for "the screams of pain that Clarke has brought from the NUT" (his Cambridge chum Professor Norman Stone) Feb '92; said: "our education policy represents Thatcherism with a human face" Feb '92; his Bill to privatize school inspections suffered two defeats in the Lords Feb '92; accepted Lords' curbs on his power to control appointments, student admissions and duration of courses Feb '92; claimed only Tories could bring UK "smoothly and sensibly" out of recession, in contrast to union-dominated Labour with their "massive increases" in taxes Feb '92; claimed Assisted Places Scheme "breaks down social barriers and widens opportunities for children from less well-off families" Feb '92; accepted teachers' recommended pay rise of 7.5% Feb '92; voted against Bill to ban hunting with hounds Feb '92; his claim that Lords curbs on privatized school inspection was union-inspired was derided as "utter tripe" by Labour's Baroness Blackstone Mar '92; in a poll, three times as many said they would not buy a used car from him as those who would Apr '92; retained seat with majority down from 20,839 to 19,766, a swing to Labour of 5.51% Apr '92; was named Home Secretary Apr '92; decided to delay the re-introduction of the Asylum Bill while rethinking the Government's approach to refugees May '92; addressed Police Federation, announced the Sheehy inquiry, designed to destroy their privileged pay formula, remove a tier of police management and merge a number of forces May '92; in the wake of UK's devaluation and exit from ERM, forcefully argued in Cabinet for early re-entry Sep '92; with John Major and Norman Lamont lying low, made statements supporting Lamont on all media channels, saying he would resign if Lamont were forced out Sep '92; was rated second to Michael Heseltine by William Hill as John Major's successor, at 6-4 against Sep '92; after Europhobe Lord (Norman) Tebbit had told annual conference that a Cabinet Minister (Clarke) had not read the Maastricht treaty, he had to be separated from Tebbit by Chief Whip Richard Ryder in "incandescent" argument over Maastricht at Lord Archer's party; he had attacked Tebbit over his conference speech, saying: "you've declared war on the Government", "we have no choice but to take you on!" Oct '92; re-introduced modified Asylum Bill, softening the policy towards asylum seekers but clamping down on foreign visitors by requiring visas Oct '92; Euro-sceptic Tories warned against his becoming Chancellor or Prime Minister: "he is too Leftwing and too zealously pro-Maastricht to have the support of the Rightwing of the Conservative Party in Parliament" (Lord Rees-Mogg, INDEPENDENT); he replied that the forced ERM exit was "a disastrous setback"; we may be out of the ERM for now but we have to restore currency stability "at a reasonable level" Oct '92; a former adviser, Duncan Graham, accused him of having subverted the national curriculum for political purposes and of interfering over teaching methods when Education Secretary Oct '92; refused to grant any form of pardon to Derek Bentley, hanged 40 years before (he was later given a posthumous conditional pardon by Home Secretary Michael Howard after court had ruled Clarke had "erred in law") Oct '92; claimed he had no option but to sign certificate of immunity for Home Office documents in Matrix Churchill case Nov '92; having previously agreed to entry for 600 Bosnian refugees, expanded it to 4,000 Nov '92; announced that Parliament would vote on three options for Sunday trading: total deregulation, substantial deregulation or minimal deregulaton Nov '92; disclosed that Home Office press officer had searched confidential files to discover whether US Presidential candidate Bill Clinton had applied for British citizenship to avoid Vietnam draft, allegedly in response to a journalist's query Dec '92; announced that deliberate transmission of the HIV virus would not be made a criminal offence Dec '92; announced legislation to allow incompetent police officers to be sacked Dec '92; appointed as chief of prison service Derek Lewis, former head of satellite TV company, who had never been inside a prison Dec '92; was said to have clashed with Michael Howard over his plans to reduce local authority representation on police authorities Jan '93; said he did not think UK should rejoin the ERM in the immediate future Jan '93; ordered the extradition to the US of two British women accused of conspiring to murder late Bhagwan Shree Rajneesh; their lawyers later charged him with having "made an error in law and miscontrued the ambit of his discretionary powers" Apr '93; announced he would seek to allow courts to "take into account all the offences for which the offender is being dealt with" and to "restre to the courts their power to have full regard to the criminal record of an offender"; also abolished unit fines, for which he was widely praised May '93; in the wake of the Newbury by-election loss, John Major was persuaded by his Chief Whip, Richard Ryder, that he had to sack his unpopular former campaign manager, Norman Lamont, as Chancellor if he was not to face a challenge to himself in the autumn, perhaps from Kenneth Clarke; despite expected opposition from the Euro-sceptic Right, Major chose to sack Lamont and put Clarke in his place; some of Clarke's friends thought he had been handed a poisoned chalice May '93; the GUARDIAN's Hugo Young claimed he was "the first innumerate Chancellor Britain has had for 14 years" May '93; said: "our membership of the Exchange Rate Mechanism certainly helped us to achieve the low level of inflation which is one of the best bases for making industry competititve as we move into the recovery; the five-point reductions in interest rates before we left the ERM were as valuable as the four additional point reductions that we have made since we left the ERM June '93; a poll showed that the VAT on fuel he had inherited from Lamont had only 5% support in the electorate, a quarter of the support the poll tax had had Sep '93; was ready to give Bank of England more independence in setting timing of interest rate changes Sep '93; in an unusually boring speech, told the Conservative Party Conference: "any enemy of John Major is an enemy of mine" Oct '93; at SUNDAY TELEGRAPH debate summarized his politics as "free market economics combined with enlightened social reform" Oct '93; introduced a Budget with the biggest increase in taxation and the tightest curbs on public spending since the war, plus a compensation pack for VAT on fuel to the delight of Tory MPs, including the suspicious Right; there was no immediate appreciation that it presupposed a three-year freeze on public sector pay and would cut post-tax income by over 3.5%, Nov '93; attacked Delors' White Paper on reform on the basis of a FINANCIAL TIMES report which wrongly suggested the European Commission wanted to borrow £6b a year to fund infrastructure projects; this hostility made him seem so Euro-sceptic that PM John Major had to apologize for him Dec '93; severely damaged his reputation by dismissing as "piffle" in TV interview with David Frost the information on record taxes coming that his own Treasury officials had revealed to the SUNDAY TIMES Jan '94; voted against restoring capital punishment, even for killers of policemen Feb '94; voted to reduce age of homosexual consent to 18, but not 16, Feb '94; damaged his own efforts to present himself as a reborn Eurosceptic by saying in Bonn that he supported an eventual single currency if the terms were right {"I have always been a supporter of economicand monetary union") June '94; fought unsuccessfully to retain Stephen Dorrell as his Financial Secretary, in the hope of promoting hm Chief Secretary; this was overruled by PM John Major who, seeing this as too much of a pro-European cabal, promoted Dorrell to National Heritage Secretary June '94; he was pushed into an interest rate rise by Bank of England Governor Eddie George, despite his own hesitation Sep '94; urged Budget deficit cuts to qualify for Euro entry Oct '94; he raised the stakes before the crucial Euro-Budget vote by warning back-bench rebels that the Cabinet would resign en masse if they tried to call John Major's bluff over a threatened general election Nov '94; his Budget report was unexpectedly better than expected, with growth higher, inflation lower, exports bigger and unemployment down; he was unexpectedly defeated on the second tranche of VAT on home fuel tax and imposed higher taxes on motor fuel and drinks Nov '94; for a fortnight he seemed to overshadow PM John Major as he set the pace for the civil war against the Eurosceptic Right in the Conservative Parliamentary party Dec '94; aroused sharp comment from Eurosceptic Tory MPs for suggesting a single European currency was possible without any sacrifice of sovereignty by the "nation state" ("it is quite possible to have monetary union without political union; it is a mistake to believe that monetary union need to be a huge step on a path to a federal Europe") Feb '95; in Brussels said Britain would "work constructively" toward a single currency Feb '95; gave way to John

Major in replying to Gordon Brown, with the PM accepting that a single currency would raise "economical and political and constitutional issues" Feb '95; accused anti-Maastricht Eurosceptic Right of undermining the pound Sterling Mar '95; in gaffe praised Consett's steelworks and nappy factory, both closed years earlier Mar '95; accused of stealing the clothes of Labour's Gordon Brown, snapped: "you can't steal the clothes from a man who just walked naked into the debating chamber; every time I listen to Gordon Brown, it's quite clear he doesn't have an economic policy; nothing that's economic; nothing that's policy" Apr '95; resisted pressure from Bank of England Governor Eddie George to increase interest rates May '95; in MORI Poll Tory voters thought the party would be more likely to win under his leadership June '95; again resisted pressure from Bank of England Governor to raise interest rates June '95; he backed Major against challenge of John Redwood, whose Rightwing programme he dismissed as having no appeal to the ex-Tory voters deserted to Blair June '95; again resisted Bank of England pressure to raise interest rates July '95; predicted Britain would meet all the Euro requirements in the next year July '95; caved in to pressure from Tory backbenchers on plans to tax executive ("fat cat") share options, limiting tax only to those schemes agreed after his announcement July '95; in the wake of John Major's defeat of John Redwood, proclaimed himself a 'One Nation' Tory in a GUARDIAN interview, that even Tory voters expected a modern Welfare State: "it means strong health care and strong education and also making sure you maintain spending to produce the high-quality public services of the type that people demand" July '95; attacking 'Europhobic editors", warned against risks of UK being left out of a single European currency Oct '95; proposed a voucher scheme to let a million 16 to 19-year-olds choose their own form of advanced education Oct '95; having hinted to party conference of rolling programme of tax cuts, most of his economic advisers warned against large-scale tax reductions Oct '95; his cautious Budget cut of 1% on basic rate was welcomed more by Centrist moderates than Rightwingers demanding heavy cuts in state expenditure and income tax Nov '95; MORI Poll recorded lowest rating since '79 of public confidence in Tory economic policy, of minus 41%, Nov '95; under pressure from Education Secretary Gillian Shephard, agreed to ease councils' capping on schools spending Nov '95; was attacked by Gordon Brown for suggesting the lowest 10% were not genuinely poor but employed good tax accountants Dec '95; again said UK should keep its options open on joining Euro in '98, Dec '95; cut interest rates over objections of Bank of England Jan '96; resisted Cabinet pressure for referendum over joining the Euro Feb '96; derided the view that the UK, outside the EU, could become a "Switzerland with nuclear weapons, stranded on the sidelines of world politics" May '96; warned in OBSERVER interview that "the extremes of Euroscepticism and Reagonomics are two of the major dangers facing Right-of-Centre British politics" May '96; reluctantly agreed to non-cooperation with EU partners over beef ban June '96; voted against 3% cap on MPs' pay rise and MPs' pension based on £43,000, but for cut in mileage allowance July '96; for 4th year, announced freeze on public sector pay Sep '96; ridiculed idea that repeated currency devaluation guaranteed economic success Oct '96; in conference speech derided Gordon Brown's policy as based on "the Dolly Parton school of economics - an unbelievable figure, blown out of all proportion, with no visible means of support" Oct '96; retained his seat with his majority reduced by three-quarters to 5,055 (8.1%), on a pro-Labour swing of 11.5% May '97; was the first to enter the Leadership contest following John Major's resignation, warning that the Tories would make themselves "unelectable" if they swung too much to the Right; urged Tories to "combine a social conscience with economic competence" and avoid "mean-mindedness and narrow nationalism"; Gallup Poll gave him 27% to William Hague's 12% in public approval May '97; he was backed by pro-Europeans Heseltine, Hurd and Howe; on the first ballot he received 49, Hague 41, Redwood 27, Lilley 24, Howard 21; Howard was eliminated and Lilley dropped out to back Hague in a 'stop Clarke' move; hinted he would make Lilley his Chancellor of the Exchequer; on the second ballot he led by 64 votes to Hague's 62 and Redwood's 38; made a widely-derided 'stop Hague' pact with John Redwood, which DAILY TELEGRAPH's Boris Johnston compared to 1939's Ribbentrop-Molotov Pact; in the final vote Hague beat him by 92 votes to 70; he quit the front bench June '97; attacked Gordon Brown's "unnecessary" Budget, scorning his transfer of interest rate control to the Bank of England July '97; became Chairman of Unichem at £120,000, replacing deceased Lord Rippon Sep '97; became President of the Tory Reform Group Oct '97; derided Hague's refusal to consider joining the Euro for 10 years as meaningless by the next election; said he might challenge William Hague for the Leadership if the Conservatives lost the next election on their anti-Euro policy Oct '97; was booed by Tory MPs when he welcomed Chancellor Gordon Brown's longterm commitment to the Euro, only regretting his insistence that Britain could not be ready for some years Oct '97; in DAILY TELEGRAPH urged a cross-party coalition, including the City, CBI and TUC to win a referendum on the Euro before the next election Oct '97; in Commons attack on Gordon Brown deplored fact that, since the election, economic growth had already "fallen away very rapidly" Nov '97; with Lord (Roy) Jenkins and Neil Kinnock was named a Vice President of the pro-Euro European Movement Nov '97; with other pro-European grandees wrote to INDEPENDENT promising PM Tony Blair support for joining the Euro after a referendum Jan '98; claimed the Budget was "putting a considerable burden of extra taxation on the very businesses that must create jobs if more people are to move from welfare into work" Mar '98; sailed in during debate on Scottish Parliament Bill to make a powerful Dalyell-style anti-devolution speech as a "Unionist" May '98;

Born: 2 July 1940, Nottingham

Family: A grandfather sold the DAILY HERALD at trade union rallies but left the Labour Party when pacifist George Lansbury lost out as Labour's Leader; grandson of Harry Ernest Smith, a Raleigh toolroom engineer and Communist Party member; son, of late Kenneth Clarke, a workaholic who was successively a watch repairer, a film projectionist, a wartime colliery electrician and the owner of a jewellery business, and late Doris (Smith), a highly intelligent woman who died an alcoholic; m '64 - with John Selwyn Gummer as his best man - 'Gill'/Gillian Mary (Edwards), "a formidable blue-stocking Tory with a tinge of Laura Ashley liberalism" (INDEPENDENT), an Oxfam trustee who prefers Rugby to soccer; 1s Kenneth Bruce '65 who attended King Edward School, Birmingham, at £2,250 a year, later becoming a management trainee at local bank; 1d Esther 'Sue'/Susan '68, who attended Edgbaston High School at £1,971 a year, then became a student nurse, dressed like a punk (with tattoo) and nearly bit off an opponent's finger in a pub disco 'cat-fight' Jan '88; she qualified as a nurse '91; he claims to have had Fabian-type hesitations about sending his children to fee-paying schools;

Education: Langley Mill Primary; Bulwell Primary; Nottingham High School (scholarship boy at this fee-paying school which John Major in '96 mistakenly described as a grammar school; the alma mater of DH Lawrence; he lost his regional accent there; "the grammar school system suited me down to the ground"; "it gave me all the opportunities and a life I have very much enjoyed"); Gonville and Caius College, Cambridge (BA Hons, LLB; President of the Union '63);

Occupation: Chairman, Unichem (£120,000) '97-; Deputy Chairman, British-American Tobacco (£50,000?) '97-; Director: Foreign and Colonial Investment Trust (£18,000) '97-; Adviser, to Daiwa Europe Ltd (on economic and financial matters; £25,000?) '97-; ex: Sponsored, in his '97 Leadership campaign: by Nat Puri (£32,000), Sir Geoffrey Leigh (£5,000), Christopher Saunders (£1,000), John Stevens MEP (£1,500), Brendan Donnelly (£2,500); Barrister '63-, Gray's Inn; was on Midland Circuit '63-79; QC '80-; ceased practicing in '79;

Traits: Blond; forelock; potbellied; portly ("Piglet"), "packs a paunch"; "bits of his body flop out" (Harriet Harman MP); "I am always fighting an unsuccessful struggle with my weight, which, if I drank a little less beer, I would succeed in"; "that pudgy puff-ball" (Alan Clark MP); "in an age when most politicians come blow-waved and air-brushed, there is something rather refreshing about one who looks as though he has just rolled out of bed after being up until four in the morning indulging his passion for jazz at Ronnie Scott's" (Andrew Rawnsley, GUARDIAN); "when Kenneth Clarke was appointed to the Treasury...his appearance on the steps of that august institution startled the nation and brought despair to the TAILOR AND CUTTER; the new Chancellor of the Exchequer was flying his Garrick Club tie, wearing his younger brother's two-piece suit, and sporting a pair of suede Hush Puppy brogues that had scruffed for Nottingham and England" (Julian Critchley MP, YOU); he brought "a cheerily raffish style to the Cabinet, wearing his hair longer than the average and enjoying the occasional jazz club evening; those working close to him are well aware of his penchant for poisonous small cigars" (Robin Oakley, TIMES); gave up smoking for 48 hours in '93; "I am a very informal, relaxed sort of guy; I hate formal dress; I dislike pomp and don't naturally take to ceremonial; it rather goes with the working-class boy at Cambridge image" (KC); "I always wear Hush Puppies; people began to talk about it not long ago, which led me to notice that other people weren't wearing them any more; now I wear them out of a certain bloody-mindedness" (KC); "I have a very low boredom threshold - I have to do things all the time"; "during the week I seem to need about four or five hours a night"; "at the weekend I catch up with sleep"; "I am completely useless at DIY and deeply dislike it" (KC); "I am hedonistic; but if there was a clash between politics and beer, I would put politics first and beer second" (KC); "he was very much a loner as a child and is very detached emotionally, very much apart; he is an iceberg - 75% under water" (brother Michael Clarke); he displays "ruthlessness from being starved of love by his mother; [has] genetically-inherited high intelligence on his mother's side and a father who displaced his unfulfilled ambitions on to his son" (psychologist Oliver Jones); deploys "combative skills", "hard work, a perpetual smile and a hope for better things" (Jim Naughtie, GUARDIAN); "a voracious appetite for work" (Michael Hatfield, TIMES); "talks very fast indeed and faster still when under pressure" (David Selbourne, INDEPENDENT); "can talk the hind leg off the Recording Angel, but [his] jolly, obstreperous manner is thoroughly agreeable (Edward Pearce, SUNDAY TELEGRAPH); Nottingham Forest supporter; "no religious convictions" (KC); had early ambitions to become a works driver for Ferrari, to play the tenor saxophone, and become Chief Secretary to the Treasury; was an enthusiastic bridge-player at University (with Norman Stone); "a fully paid-up member of the human race" (Anthony Howard, SUNDAY TIMES); "he passes Julius Caesar's famous test: 'fat, sleek-headed, sleeps like a log'" (Michael White, GUARDIAN); has an "ordinary bloke approach" (Peter Riddell, TIMES); an "up-market lager-lout" with "robust intelligence" (Hugo Young, GUARDIAN); "has natural authority; he is not personally wounded by criticism" (Martin Ivens, TIMES); "we disagree entirely on Europe but, unlike some people, he doesn't take it personally if you disagree" (John Townend MP); "he is always infuriatingly calm and says, 'it's part of life's rich tapestry'" (his wife, Gillian); a modern-jazz enthusiast (at Ronnie Scott's, often with ex-MP Sir Jim Lester); "I started by buying New Orleans stuff and early black jazz; my taste now is more modern - Charlie Parker, Stan Getz, Art Blakey"; his jazz favourites include Louis Armstrong, Duke Ellington, Thelonious Monk and Billie Holliday; cannot resist opportunities to exploit the media, even when ill-prepared ("the idea of Ken Clarke in purdah is about as realistic as [former SUN editor] Kevin MacKenzie editing the CHURCH TIMES" (No 10 official); "gregarious, ebullient, portly and thuggish; the only Cabinet Minister who regularly drinks and gossips in Annie's Bar" (OBSERVER); "paunchy and rumpled, he is a dreadnaught in suede

shoes" (John Williams, EVENING STANDARD); bird-watcher; collects political memorabilia;
Address: House of Commons, Westminster, London SW1A 0AA; house in West Bridgford, across the Trent from Nottingham; formerly shared "a rather grotty flat" (Gill Clarke) in Lambeth with other MPs;
Telephone: 0171 219 4528/5189/4162 (H of C);

Rt Hon 'Tom' (Thomas) CLARKE CBE   Labour   **COATBRIDGE & CHRYSTON '97-**

Majority: 19,295 (51.3%) over SNP 5-way;
Description: The renamed Strathclyde seat, 90% of whose voters come from his former Monklands West, with 8,000 from former Monklands East; it is based on the heavy industry town of largely-Catholic Coatbridge, together with rural bits of North Lanarkshire and East Dunbartonshire; its Gartcosh steel plant and Cardowan mine have been closed, along with whisky-distilling Buchanan's; it was safe enough for Labour to have resisted '82's 'Falklands Fever'; it was later plagued by accusations of bias and nepotism on Monklands Council in favour of Coatbridge rather than neighbouring largely-Protestant Airdrie;
Former Seat: Monklands West '83-97, Coatbridge & Airdrie '82-83;
Position: Ex: Minister of State, for Culture, Media and Sports ('Minister for Film and Tourism') '97-98; Spokesman: on Disabled Peoples' Rights '94-97, Development and Co-operation '93-94, on Scotland '92-93; Assistant Spokesman, on Health (Personal Services) '87-90, on Scottish Education and Health '86-87; on Select Committees: on Health '91-92, on Scottish Affairs '83-87; Vice Chairman, Parliamentary Panel on Personal Social Services '87-90; Secretary, UN Parliamentary Group '85-??; Chairman, PLP Foreign Affairs Committee '83-86; Vice Chairman, PLP Parliamentary Affairs Committee '83-86; Vice Chairman, British-Netherlands Parliamentary Group, British-Papua New Guinea Parliamentary Group; Treasurer, Overseas Parliamentary Group; Governor, British Film Institute '87-??; President, Convention of Scottish Local Authorities '78-80, Vice President, Scottish Council (Development and Industry) '76-78; Provost of Monklands District Council '74-82;
Outlook: An "Old Labour member of the 'Scottish Mafia'" (SUNDAY TELEGRAPH), sacked in the first reshuffle; one of the Shadow Cabinet members not made a Cabinet Minister in '97, perhaps as retrospective punishment for undermining Labour's campaign in the '94 Monklands East by-election; a respected, persuasive, over-anxious, local-government-rooted, pro-devolution, former Provost-fixer; hypersensitive about Monklands Council; "boring but safe" (David Hencke and Michael White, GUARDIAN); in '92 was unexpectedly elevated to Scottish Spokesman, his highest role yet, by John Smith, his friendly neighbouring MP, before being replaced by George Robertson;; after his illness, settled for Development and Co-operation in '93, then Disabled Peoples' Rights in '94; "one of Westminster's 'Mr Nice Guys'" (GUARDIAN); "over the years he has demonstrated a sincere regard for the rights and circumstances of those who are mentally ill and mentally handicapped" (Tory MP Sir Peter Lloyd); secured passage of 1986 Disabled Persons Act, on which £27m was spend in '89-90,

although only half-implemented; a Centre-Right moderate at home, radical on self-determination and on 3rd World; sensitive to Scottish joblessness and Philippines' violations of civil rights; an enthusiast for overseas development and free-tripping; anti: EC, Apartheid, abortion (RC); dislikes working on committees; charmer of Tory ladies, especially Mrs Thatcher and Dame Jill Knight ("such a delightful man and uses that charming Scottish accent"); formerly GMB-sponsored;

History: He joined the Labour Party at 16, '57; became election agent for near-blind James Dempsey at 18 (youngest in the country) Oct '59; at 22 was elected to Coatbridge Council May '64; was elected Provost (Chairman) of Monklands District Council May '74; voted 'yes' in devolution referendum May '79; served on the Stodart Committee of Inquiry into Local Government in Scotland which reported in Jan '81; as long expected, was adopted as successor to deceased MP James Dempsey May '82; was elected for Airdrie and Coatbridge at by-election, with 10,000 majority June '82; called for expulsion of Militants June '82; in Maiden urged more investment in his area of Scotland to reduce smell of sewage and mop up unemployment July '82; introduced Young Persons' Rights Bill '82; in adjournment debate complained of violations of civil rights in Philippines Jan '83; criticized TIMES allegation that Ethiopian aid was being diverted into Soviet arms Apr '83; warned that growth of cable TV threatened British film industry July '83; accused ODA Minister Tim Raison of "appalling complacency" on Philippines rights violations Aug '83; pleaded to keep local Cardowan colliery open Aug '83; again raised Phillipines civil rights violations Aug '83; backed Roy Hattersley for Leader and Deputy Leader Sep '83; defeated David Winnick to become Chairman of PLP Foreign Affairs Committee Nov '83; co-urged BBC to show anti-nuclear 'War Game' Dec '83; co-protested US mining of Nicaraguan waters Apr '84; urged full diplomatic relations with Argentina instead of 'Fortress Falklands' June '84; went on an officially-sponsored visit to USA Sep '84; spoke against the Marcos regime at Labour conference fringe meeting Oct '84; urged Mrs Thatcher to back UNESCO instead of clinging to "US coat-tails" Nov '84; procured spending of £500,000 on Glasgow hospital housing Dec '84; after serving on its committee, voted for Enoch Powell's Bill to ban embryo experimentation Feb '85; criticized government for its aid cuts Mar '85; was re-selected from a shortlist of one June '85; headed an anti-SDI motion July '85; was a speaker at an SPUC launch meeting on embryo transplants July '85; visited Botswana and Swaziland, witnessing a South African cross-border attack Aug '85; coming first in ballot for Private Member's Bill, resisted SPUC pressure to do an anti-abortion Bill; opted to establish minimum care standards for mentally handicapped Nov '85; his Bill was extended to physically handicapped Dec '85; secured passage of his Disabled Persons Act unopposed, to cheers Apr '86; was on Whitelaw-Healey IPU delegation to Moscow May-June '86; supported sanctions to end Apartheid Aug '86; visited North Korea Oct '86; complained of Government's failure to implement his Disabled Persons Act Dec '86; when Harry Ewing fell ill, Leader Kinnock asked him to join Scottish team Dec? '86; paid sponsored visit to India Jan '87; urged wider recruitment for Scottish universities Mar '87; urged stronger action against warrant sales for debt Mar '87; was rated by Adam Smith Institute as being one of the five most interventionist MPs Apr '87; increased his majority by 6,000 June '87; was named Assistant Spokesman on Personal Social Services July '87; complained his Disabled Persons Act was not being applied to disabled school leavers Sep '87; voted for David Alton's abortion-curbing Bill Jan '88; admitting "the Prime Minister has not always been wrong", ignored her advice to back televising the Commons Feb '88; voted against a 26-week ceiling for abortion May '88; was on Archbishop's mission to Iran to try to free Beirut hostages June '88; complained of death of Bahadur Singh, after racist beatings in Barlinnie Prison July '88; complained that 3rd World countries would be "pressurized into accepting a programme of privatization" before receiving

UK aid Feb '89; pointed out Treasury was being saved millions by those devoting themselves to looking after the mentally ill Apr '89; led for Opposition on Children's Bill Apr-May '89; complained about cuts in aid to Africa May '89; complained that Government was spending enormous sums on inadequately inspected private residential homes Apr '89; said the case for family courts was overwhelming Oct '89; was again named Assistant Spokesman on Personal Social Services Nov '89; complained about ineffective triggering and inadequate sums for severe weather payments Dec '89; urged more food for Ethiopia Dec '89; urged strengthened economic sanctions to speed solution for South Africa Feb '90; like most Catholic MPs, opposed embryo research Apr '90; attacked as "pathetic and humiliating" Scottish Secretary Malcolm Rifkind's refusal to force British Steel to keep open their Ravenscraig plant May '90; was on standby to repeat journey to Iran to try to break diplomatic deadlock June '90; deplored Government's plan to delay introduction of community care July '90; was reappointed to Board of British Film Institute by Arts Minister David Mellor Oct '90; was replaced by Jeff Rooker as Assistant Spokesman on Personal Social Services - apparently at instigation of Robin Cook - with promise from Neil Kinnock of a post in a Labour Government Nov '90; complained of unhygienic delivery practices in Scottish meat industry Dec '90; joined the Health Select Committee Jan '91; strongly urged help for the impoverished and starving in Sub-Saharan Africa Jan '91; backed Rosie Barnes' Bill for no-fault compensation in NHS Feb '91; was mistakenly identified as attending a meeting of the semi-hard Left 'Supper Club' Feb '91; deplored failure to implement first three sections of his Disabled People Act May '91; visited Vancouver Island to inspect forest at invitation of Greenpeace and Women for the Environment, deploring "wanton destruction" of old forests May '91; deplored further British Steel closures in Scotland, with resulting unemployment and dereliction; "more than 85% of the derelict land in Lanarkshire is my district" July '91; as a member of Health Select Committee, described as "dirty tricks of the worst kind" the leak to Health Secretary William Waldegrave of committee's draft report July '91; was smeared as a "CP supporter" by Rightwing 'Economic League', to which he replied "And me a former altar boy! I thought I was known as a moderate" Sep '91; was involved in Labour's manifesto effort to give more help to independent film makers Oct '91; visited Latvia on IPU delegation Nov '91; pushed amendment to Further and Higher Education Bill to ensure rights of handicapped Feb '92; retained seat with majority down from 18,333 to 17,065, a swing to SNP of 3.37% Apr '92; again raised question of keeping out of prison the mentally ill and handicapped June '92; urged support of friends or advisers of individuals being assessed in community care July '92; unexpectedly succeeded in contest for Shadow Cabinet, coming 17th with 105 votes, including support of fellow devolutionist George Galloway; to wide surprise was named Scottish Spokesman, replacing the tired veteran of nine years in office, Donald Dewar July '92; opposed privatisation of Scottish prisons Nov '92; after a meeting of Scottish Labour MPs on forthcoming boundary changes broke up in disorder, took two months' sick leave to recover from "recurring viral infection"; "his illness may reawaken questions in a number of MPs' minds as to whether Mr Clarke is the right man for a demanding political post" (Peter Jones, SCOTSMAN) Nov '92; deplored the "American-style attempt to smear John Smith and myself" over accusations of pro-Catholic nepotistic favouritism in Monklands local government Jan '93; was welcomed back to Commons "fully restored, we all hope, to health" by Scottish Secretary Ian Lang Jan '93; aroused some concern when he pledged to restore Scottish water only to public control, if privatised Feb '93; again aroused irritation when he derided the worthlessness of the Scottish financial industry which employed over 200,000 Feb '93; despite such "gaffes", his position was temporarily safe because John Smith, a midd-class modernizer, required the support of Clarke as a "working class traditionalist" (Peter Jones, SCOTSMAN) Feb '93; dismissed as "ludicrous tokenism" Government offer of stronger

Scottish Grand Committee instead of Scottish Parliament Mar '93; after SNP MPs backed Tory Government on Maastricht, urged SNP members, "sickened at their party"s lack of integrity", to join Labour Mar '93; welcomed study of Germany, which showed economic decision-making was devolved to its lander Mar '93; demanded Scottish Secretary Ian Lang climb down on Scottish water privatization May '93; "welcomed Helen Jackson's Bill to outlaw water disconnections May '93; condemned British Coals intention to sell or lease Fife's Frances Colliery, for fear it would be shut if no buyer was found June '93; complained that "instead of a considered reform of local government, what we have is a shabby political exercise designed to manipulate local government on behalf of the minority [Conservative] party" July '93; joined with other non-Conserservative Scottish parties to oppose Tories' local government 'reforms' Aug '93; joined delegation to Brussels of Coalition for Scottish Democracy, including Sir Russell Johnston and Scottish Nationalist, to urge Scottish self-determination on European Parliament Sep '93; opposed the idea that all candidates for vacant Labour seats and key marginals be women until the party had as many women as men in Parliament Oct '93; came 13th with 120 votes, up from 105, in contest for Shadow Cabinet Oct '93; was made Spokesman on Development and Cooperation, a less-demanding post, being replaced as Scottish Spokesman by George Robertson Oct '93; voted against restoring capital punishment, even for killers of policemen Feb '94; voted to reduce age of homosexual consent to 18 or 16, Feb '94; reacted very negatively to Labour candidate Helen Liddell's acceptance of some of the criticism of nepotism on Monklands Council during by-election campaign for Monklands East June '94; asked PM John Major whether Royal Ordnance intended to make land mines June '94; undermined candidate Helen Liddell's chances in Monklands East by-election caused by John Smith's death by dismissing as "McCarthyite smears" allegations of malpractice on Monklands Council which he formerly led, despite the candidate's call for an inquiry to secure a narrow victory over the SNP; Clarke was accused of "an act of unforgivable stupidity" for contradicting Liddell; "if we had lost the by-election he would have been guilty of murder; as it is, he is only guilty of manslaughter" June-July '94; voted for Blair for Leader, Beckett for Deputy Leader July '94; attacked as "outrageous and inflammatory" the suggestion of Peter Riddell that he was elected to the Shadow Cabinet as its "token Catholic", insisting it was because of his former chairmanship of the Scottish local government organisation COSLA and his disabled rights legislation Oct '94; polled only 83 votes, with 97 needed, losing his seat on the Shadow Cabinet Oct '94; was named Spokesman on Disabled Peoples' Rights Oct '94; dismissed the Government's Disability Discrimnation Bill as "a public relations exercise" and backed Labour MP Harry Barnes' Civil Rights (Disabled Persons) Bill as superior Jan '95; claimed that Tory Britain was slipping down the European league table in social welfare Feb '95; urged properly-adapted vehicles for the disabled Mar '95; his call for a Disability Rights Commission to enforce anti-discrimination laws was defeated by 299 to 286, Mar '95; criticised the reduction in the role of Remploy workshops for the disabled June '95; unexpectedly polled 107 votes, winning the 19th and last place in the Shadow Cabinet; was retained as Disabled Rights Spokesman, despite an allegedly acrimonious demand for a better post from Tony Blair Oct '95; dismissed as "a small group of militants" disabled protesters who sat in at Labour headquarters in Walworth Road Mar '96; demanded an apology from Conservative Central Office for issuing a dossier falsely describing him as a member of the semi-hard Left Supper Club, which had opposed the '91 Gulf War Apr '96; voted against a 3% cap on MPs' pay rise, in favour of a pension based on £43,000 and for a cut in MPs' mileage allowance July '96; was re-elected to the Shadow Cabinet with 175 votes, just ahead of last-place Harriet Harman July '96; backed compensation case of constituent whose wife had died of CJD Dec '96; was the only Shadow Cabinet member not to be targeted by the anti-abortion Prolife Alliance Party Dec '96; retained his renamed and altered seat with a majority of 19,295, on a notional swing of 3.1% swing from the SNP May '97; instead of a Cabinet Post, was made a Minister of State, 'Minister for Film and Tourism' and promoted a Privy Counsellor May '97; visiting the Cannes Film Festival in his new role, urged the employment of more disabled actors and better disabled access to theatres May '97; press reports of "disasters" during his latest visit to the Cannes Film Festival undermined hopes he would survive in office May '98; was sacked on the same day he entertained Liz Hurley and Hugh Grant on the Commons terrace July '98;

Born: 10 January 1941, Coatbridge

Family: Son, James Clarke, miner, and Mary (Gordon); unwed;

Education: All Saints Primary, Airdrie; St Mary's Secondary (later called Columba High School), Coatbridge; Scottish College of Commerce;

Occupation: Formerly Sponsored, by GMB (£600 p a to constituency, and 80% of election expenses) '83-95; "a contribution of more than 25% of my election expenses at the 1997 general election was made by GMB Union to Coatbridge and Chryston Constituency Labour Party"; Governor (unpaid), of British Film Institute, '87-; ex: Director, 'Give Us a Goal' (film short) '72; Assistant Director, Scottish Film Council '66-82; held "various clerical jobs" until '66; started working life at 16 as an office boy with Glasgow accountants '56;

Traits: Blond, balding, egg-head; specs; "affable" (TRIBUNE); concerned; sensitive; "anxious" (David Hencke, GUARDIAN); trustworthy; practical; discursive; showman; his election speeches "are straight out of the Aneurin Bevan declamatory school" (Fred Bridgland, SCOTSMAN): soft Scots brogue; golfer; amateur film-maker (won prize with 'Give Us A Goal' '72; ex-President, Amateur Cinematographers' Central Council); on being benched by Kinnock in November '90 said: "the one thing I refuse to do is sulk or become involved in petty jealousies; I have seen too many people destroyed by that"; RC (former altar boy); "I really do love Chinese food";

Address: House of Commons, Westminster, London SW1A 0AA; 27 Wood Street, Coatbridge, Lanarkshire ML5 1LY;

Telephone: 0171 219 6997 (H of C); 01236 22550;

David (Gordon) CLELLAND   **Labour**   **TYNE BRIDGE '85-**

Majority: 22,906 (65.7%) over Conservative 5-way;

Description: A reinforced Labour stronghold: an ultra-deprived area on both sides of the Tyne, linking old, small Newcastle Central and old Gateshead West, with bits of Gateshead East, Blaydon, Newcastle North and Newcastle West; a quarter were unemployed in '91; over two fifths of its multiply-deprived voters live in council houses; has strong minorities of Jews and Indians and some Poles; in '95 13,000 voters were brought in from Gateshead East to make up for depopulation;

Position: Assistant Government Whip '97-; Chairman: PLP Trade Union Group '94-, Secretary and Treasurer, PLP Northern Group '90-; on all-party Greyhound Group '91-; ex: Assistant Opposition Whip '95-97; Chairman '90-97, Vice Chairman '88-90, PLP Environment Committee; Chairman, PLP Regional Government Group '92-93; on Select Committees: for

Energy '89, Home Affairs '86-89, Parliamentary Commissioner for Administration (Ombudsman) '86-87; Leader, Gateshead District Council '84-85; Chairman, Gateshead Recreation Committee '76-84; Vice Chairman, Gateshead Area Health Authority '82-84;

Outlook: Assiduous but low-profiled, regionally-minded, locally-born-and-raised mainstream Centre-Left Tynesider; recently a Whip, as suitable for an active trade union loyalist; a former skilled local government leader who has gained Parliamentary experience rapidly since his '85 by-election victory; "moderate, capable and popular" (DAILY MAIL); Eurosceptic; was formerly AEU-sponsored;

History: His family were Labour supporters; at 26 joined the Labour Party "on the same day as his father [rejoined] and his father's best friend, Harry Cowans" joined the party (Malcolm Boughen, NORTHERN ECHO) '69; was elected to Gateshead District Council May '72; voted for Tony Benn for Deputy Leader, because he was thus mandated Sep '81; after defection to SDP of John Horam MP, was selected to contest Gateshead West (which later disappeared) June '81; was elected Leader of Gateshead Council May '84; led Council delegations to demand aid for Tyne and Wear in '84 and '85; failed to reach shortlist for Gateshead East, won by Joyce Quin Feb '85; was beaten by Hilary Armstrong in selection for Northwest Durham by one vote, 34 to 33 Apr '85; was selected to contest Tyne Bridge on death of Harry Cowans, by 46 to 35 on the fourth ballot from a shortlist of five Nov '85; was elected with a slight increase in Labour's share of the votes (58%), with SDP coming second Dec '85; in Maiden speech complained of Government's continual attacks on rate support grants, capital spending and housing programmes, leaving his Tyneside area to face "the difficulties of escalating crime rates, plummeting housing starts, high unemployment and low incomes" Jan '86; opened debate on Labour's demand for Government funds for legal aid centres Mar '86; complained that the understandable uncertainties in nuclear plant construction had deepened the problem of employment in NEI in Gateshead May '86; contrasted low rate of prosecutions on tax swindles with the high rate of prosecutions on social security frauds June '86; initiated adjournment debate on providing expenses for people attending immigration appeal tribunals July '86; was accused by Home Minister David Waddington of "sneering at Thatcherism" July '86; on returning from visit to US prisons with Home Affairs Select Committee, said: "I don't think keeping a person incarcerated is something people should make a profit out of" Oct '86; was reproached by Speaker for suggesting Mrs Thatcher had told lies about the Westland affair Oct '86; tabled motion condemning Newcastle District Health Authority for treating as a dismissible offence of theft the use of tea, milk and sugar by nursing staff Nov '86; was on a delegation to the Environment Secretary to complain of the problems faced by Gateshead Council Nov '86; complained of deterioration of service with deregulation of buses Nov '86; visited Poland on IPU delegation Dec '86; attacked the Government's hypocrisy in local government finance, in practicing illegality while attacking others for doing so Jan '87; reproached Environment Secretary Nicholas Ridley for the chaos he was causing by his revised announcements on rate support grant Mar '87; called for John Stanley's resignation for misleading the Commons over a number of years on nuclear defence decisions Mar '87; doubled his majority June '87; complained of lack of compensation for local man wrongly jailed for 14 months Oct '87; warned that cutback of investment in coal mines was forcing closure of local engineering works Nov '87; attacked the Government's "myth" that trade unionists were sheep Feb '88; called for kosher food for Jewish prisoners Mar '88; urged the exclusion of the northeast from the Regional Development Grants (Termination) Bill with the area being allowed autonomy for distributing aid Mar '88; wrote to Mrs Thatcher in an effort to save local Marconi plant July '88; protested the loss of free school meals by 6,000 children in Newcastle and Gateshead Oct '88; was elected Vice Chairman of PLP's Environment Committee Nov '88; left the Home Affairs Select Committee, for the Energy

Select Committee Jan '89; again criticized Tyneside's City Technology College and the awarding of a contract to build it to a subsidiary of John Laing Plc, a sponsor of the CTC Jan '89; was one of three Labour MPs (the others Bruce Grocott and James Lamond) who spoke against reserved places for women on Labour's Shadow Cabinet July '89; backed pressure to link Channel Tunnel to north Oct '89; left the Energy Select Committee Nov '89; opposing the latest Employment Bill, recalled opposing the 1988 one as well: "we opposed the creation of a Commissioner for the Rights of Trade Union Members - or CROTUM for short; that would be a rather unfortunate acronym if we ever got a Senior Commissioner..." Jan '90; led motion opposing all-seated football stadia on grounds that "many fans prefer to stand on the terraces" Jan '90; supported MORNING STAR's fund raising to retain "diverse editorial opinion" Feb '90; complained that council house building had fallen from 111,000 per year in the '70s to 21,000 in the '80s Feb '90; urged nuclear cuts but backed orders for Challenger II tanks Feb '90; sharply attacked poll tax Dec '90; preferring continued sanctions, opposed Gulf War; then emphasized that "this war is against Saddam Hussein and his henchmen, not against ordinary families in Iraq" Jan '91; complained that Government policy was killing off manufacturing industry in the northeast June '91; urged the Prime Minister to make an early decision to select the Challenger II as the British Army's main battle tank, to avoid "killing off the British tank manufacturing industry" June '91; backed proposal to make bookmakers contribute a share of their takings to stop decline of greyhound racing July '91; was reluctant to support local bypasses for fear of greater exhaust fumes from increased traffic Sep '91; among the 30 northeastern MPs, he was shown to have asked the 9th most frequent oral questions, and the 19th most frequent written questions Nov '91; expressed concern about the "impartiality" of the planned local government commission "because the Secretary of State for the Environment has already pre-empted the commission's decisions by expressing the view that Cleveland and Humberside will be abolished"; ridiculed the idea of need for compulsory competitive tendering because "throughout the years local government, under the control of whichever political party, has been involved in competitive tendering" Feb '92; retained seat with majority down from 15,553 to 15,210, despite a swing to Labour of 1.65% Apr '92; convened a meeting of Regional Government Group Jan '93; complained that Tyneside seats, with heavier unemployment and social problems, were discriminated against in rate support grants; complained about Tory-led quangos: "I remember well the occasion of the Northumberland Plate at Gosforth Park racecourse a few years ago; I asked what the small groups of local gentry were gathered together to discuss, and was told that they were deciding who should be the Chairman of the Training and Enterprise Council; and so they did, in between the Brown Ale Handicap and the Federation Cup" Feb '93; complained in adjournment speech about damage to local properties from construction of A1 Newcastle Western Bypass Feb '93; complained that Government was closing down all the Tyneside's most modern industries: Swan Hunter, Plessey and Marconi May '93; with Gerry Steinberg, attacked two muggers during a trip to Jerusalem with Labour Friends of Israel as guest of Israeli Government May-June '93; won 13th place in ballot for Private Members' Bills Nov '93; introduced Sale and Supply Goods Bill to ensure that goods sold were as described, fit for their purpose and of merchantable quality; it received a 2nd Reading Feb '94; voted against restoring capital punishment, even for killers of policemen Feb '94; voted to reduce age of homosexual consent to 16, Feb '94; the Boundary Commissioners proposed to make his seat safer by awarding it pro-Labour Riverside ward from Tynemouth, refusing to abolish Tyne Bridge as earlier proposed Feb '94; complained that the northeast, with "a proud history of manufacturing excellence" had been hard-hit by the shrinkage of the nation's manufacturing base under the Tories Mar '94; again urged alternative to Government's devastating A1 Western Bypass Mar '94; urged Defence Secretary Malcolm Rifkind to order a further 200-plus Vickers Challenger

II tanks June '94; voted for Blair for Leader, Beckett for Deputy Leader July '94; voted against EC Finance Bill Nov '94; backed regional devolution for the northeast, claiming the Tory Government had "stamped uniformity across Britain despite the dissenting views of people in different parts of the country" Jan '95; the Boundary Commissioners finally decided to bring his diminished voting population up to scratch by adding two wards from Gateshead East '95; was named an Assistant Whip Oct '95; though anxious to preserve exports to Saudi Arabia, because of 1,000 tank-making jobs at local Vickers factory, supported the free-speech rights of Saudi dissident Mohammed al-Masari Jan '96; went on Parliamentary delegation to Saudi Arabia, paid for by Royal Saudi Embassy Mar '96; voted to cap MPs' pay rise at 3% July '96; in Labour's final pre-election reshuffle, was retained as an Assistant Whip July '96; was re-elected to his altered seat by a majority increased to 22,096 on a notional pro-Labour swing of 10.5% May '97; was named an Assistant Government Whip May '97;

Born: 27 June 1943, Gateshead

Family: Son, Archibald ('Clem') Clelland, BR technician and good friend of late MP Harry Cowans, and Eleanor Ellen (Butchart); m '65 Maureen (Potts), school meals assistant; 2d Jillian '65, Vicki '69;

Education: Kelvin Grove Boys School, Gateshead; Gateshead, Hebburn and Charles Trevelyn (Newcastle) technical colleges;

Occupation: Formerly Sponsored, by AEUW (as its former NEI Reyrolle shop steward '68-81; £600 p a to constituency and 80% of election expenses) '85-95; ex: National Secretary, National Association of Councillors and editor of its journal, COUNCILLOR '81-85; Apprentice '59-64, Electrical Tester '64-81 at NEI Reyrolle (where he was made redundant, with 800 others, after 22 years) '59-81;

Traits: Balding; egg-shaped face; "diminutive", "sporting the nattiest cloth cap that Parliament has seen for some time" (NEWCASTLE JOURNAL); energetic; "cheery, pipe-smoking" (DAILY MAIL); "worthy, earnest, perhaps a little dull" (SUNDAY EXPRESS); displays a dry Geordie sense of humour (he told Kenneth Clarke, on a visit to Gateshead: "Your CATS (City Action Teams) are all very well, but what we really need is MICE - More Inner City Expenditure"; also joked about tagging a Senior Commissioner for the Rights of Trade Union Members as SCROTUM); golfer;

Address: House of Commons, Westminster, London SW1A 0AA; 24 Fountains Close, Gateshead, NE11 9PX;

Telephone: 0171 219 3669 (H of C); 0191 477 2559 (constituency office);

UNINTENDED PAIN

One former MP, now in the Lords, but with a son now in the Commons, told of how he had tongue-lashed his wife for disclosing to us that the family owned an island off the coast of Scotland. To his credit, he was contrite when reminded that he himself had confided this over a convivial luncheon.

IMPATIENT CLIENTS

Clients who are aware that updating our four-volume PARLIAMENTARY PROFILES takes time, take advantage of our special offer. If they want to know about a particular politician urgently, they ask us to update them specially and Fax the profile. We charge £35 per updated profile in this special service.

Geoffrey (Robert) CLIFTON-BROWN   Conservative   COTSWOLD '97-

Majority: 11,965 (23.4%) over Liberal Democrat 6-way;
Description: A new constituency, created in '95, embracing half the electorate from his Cirencester and Tewkesbury seat, shorn of Tewkesbury, and with Tetbury added at the southen end to form a constituency running along the Cotswold Hills; it includes many pretty towns and villages - Cirencester, Bourton-on-the-Water, Stow-on-the-Wold and Chipping Campden - providing second homes for affluent Londoners and Midlands businessmen; this area has been a Tory redoubt since 1910;
Former Seat: Cirencester & Tewkesbury '92-97;
Position: On: Public Accounts Commission '97-, Public Accounts Committee '97-; Vice Chairman '97-, Secretary '92-95 Conservative MPs' Committee on European Affairs; Secretary, all-party Group on Population, Development and Reproductive Health '97-; Vice Chairman: Small Business Bureau '95-, Charities Property Association '97- ; ex: PPS, to Douglas Hogg '95-97; on Environment Select Committee '92-95; Vice Chairman '84-86, Chairman '86-91, North Norfolk Conservative Association; on Conservative Eastern Area Executive Committee '86-91;
Outlook: Assiduous, highly partisan, wealthy, class-conscious hereditary Norfolk farmer, businessman and chartered surveyor who was Nick Ridley's more mainstream successor; a traditionally Rightwing recent Old Etonian recruit from the hereditary political squirearchy, with five former MPs in his family, including his great-great uncle, ex-Speaker Clifton-Brown; well-informed on agricultural economics; one of the few hard-line supporters of Michael Howard's approach to law and order; an ultra-loyal partisan, so keen to bait Labour, whether in Opposition or in Government, that he has to be curbed by the Speaker; "I always thought he was a better horseman than a Parliamentarian" (Liberal Democrat MP Nigel Jones); he also deplored the Tory Government's "confiscatory" leasehold enfranchisement measures, which he found "abhorrent"; an advocate of world birth control; a farmer on family's 900-acre farm near Gresham; had a property grounding as a chartered surveyor; claims a "pragmatically positive" view of Europe as a daffodil-exporter to the Netherlands; was initially a supporter of a "fresh start" after the Danes rejected Maastricht, but was bought back into line by a post on the Environment Select Committee; supports a pollution tax to encourage more efficient use of fossil fuels;
History: He joined the Conservative Party at 15, '68; says the stimuli to his early political activity were the "repeal of the trade union laws and privatisation in the 1980s"; became Vice Chairman of North Norfolk Conservative Association '84; became Chairman of the North Norfolk Conservative Association and joined the Conservatives' Eastern Executive Committee '86; at party conference supported Mrs Thatcher's strong negotiating stance on arms reduction Oct '86; at party conference backed Sir Geoffrey Howe's stance on the Single European Act and the creation of the internal market by 1992, Oct '87; at party conference disagreed with the new concept of set-aside of farming land, to curb agricultural over-production Oct '88; wrote to his local newspaper that "the EC should only be involved in those areas of national policy where the 12 states acting in concert can achieve more than by acting as individuals"; the Social Chapter "is one of those grey areas which fall in between these two categories"; "Britain, with her world wide service industry has most to gain from the free and unrestricted

corporate structure" Oct '89; after Nicholas Ridley's anti-German explosion, resignation from the Cabinet and the announcement of his retirement from the Commons, won selection as his successor at a secret ballot of party members Dec '90; retained the seat by 16,058 votes, an increase over Nick Ridley's last majority, achieving a 1.42 swing to the Tories from the Liberal Democrats Apr '92; in his Maiden said 'set-aside' of agricultural land was "not the best way forward in the longer term"; predicted that "if the current Boundary Coommission's proposals are accepted , I shall be the last and the most short-lived" Tory MP to represent Circencester and Tewkesbury June '92; backed the motion calling for a delay on Maastricht and a "fresh start" on EC negotiations after the initial Danish rejection June '92; water had to be treated as "a precious resource" because its needed purification would make it increasingly expensive; public authorities should help privatised water companies - "an outstanding successs" - to reach new standards June '92; warned the world's population would double again in the next 50 years June '92; urged a higher sugar quota for UK farmers July '92; was named to Environment Select Committee July '92; was elected Secretary of the Conservative MPs' European Affairs Committee and Housing Improvement Subcommittee July '92; warned the world's population would double again "in the next 30 to 40 years" July '92; urged early legislation "to strengthen the law against the curse of new-age travellers" Oct '92; endorsed the Autumn Statement Nov '92; strongly supported the pilot 'workfare' scheme of his former MP, Ralph Howell, to help the demoralised unemployed and restore the work ethic Nov '92; made a super-loyal intervention in Prime Minister's questions to call attention to wonders achieved for the motor car industry by Government's abolition of car tax Dec '92; joined the pro-EC 'Positive Europe Group' Jan '93; complained that the local authorities had accumulated debts of £54.4b, a "fantastic figure" which had to be serviced; even Gloucestershire - "my authority" - was £124.4m in debt, yet it had "some 7,000 acres of valuable agricultural land" Feb '93; complained that stud farmers were treated more harshly in UK than their competitors in Ireland and France Feb '93; urged curb on coal use to cut carbon dioxide emission Feb '93; urged basing coal-burning energy policy on proper research, like that done by the Coal Research Establishment in his constituency Mar '93; as "a businessman" welcomed reduction of Customs and Excise's "quite unnecessarily draconian powers as regards penalties" in Norman Lamont's last "excellent" Budget; also urged use of simplified, US-style self-assessment for self-employed with "a £300 reduction to anyone who is prepared to change to the new system" Mar '93; welcomed CAP package John Gummer brought back from Brussels including a 30% increase for UK farmers; additionally, "the package has not discriminated against our large farmers" Mar '93; showered PM John Major with stooge questions such as "will he welcome today's unemployment figures?" Apr '93; complained about subsidised moves by companies and jobs out of his constituency into the northwest Apr '93; complained of slowness of council tax appeals "when they have not been paid any interest on the amount that they have [wrongly] paid" May '93; after serving on the Standing Committee on Peter Atkinson's Hedgerows Bill, Labour MP Peter Hardy, a bird-lover on the Council of the RSPB, accused Clifton-Brown of having "delayed us a great deal in Committee"; Clifton-Brown countered that "over the past 20 years, I have had a net gain on my farm of more than one mile of hedgerows"; he still wanted the Bill to punish farmers only when they deliberately damaged or destroyed hedgerows May '93; "as a potato grower" urged the Government to "go slowly on abolishing" the Potato Marketing Board because "it would be folly to lose the stability that the Board brings until we have a regime, however lightweight, across Europe to which we can oblige our Community partners to adhere under Maastricht"; complained that recent doubling of potato imports had cost "30,000 acres of potatoes that we could be growing in Britain; it amounts to a loss to our balance of trade of £125m" June '93; backed the Government on replacing the Milk Marketing Board with the Milk Marque dairy cooperative: "what on earth is wrong with farmers coming together in a strong co-operative to face a market of strong buyers?" June '93; was named to the Opposed Bill Committee on the British Waterways Bill June '93; criticised the Government's leasehold reform in its Housing and Urban Development Bill as "a reprehensible piece of legislation which amounts to confiscation"; insisted that "where a property owner's interest is acquired, as it were, compulsorily, he should be compensated for the full diminution in the value of his property"; he also described the Leasehold Reform Act 1967 as "abhorrent" June '93; complained about local errors in application of Mental Health Act July '93; urged sale of surplus housing stock held by Ministry of Defence in his constituency at RAF Rissington July '93; because the Hercules were the "frontline workhorses for all three services and the oldest aircraft are now more than 30 years old", urged early tender for its replacement Oct '93; helped his constituents oppose the building of a carbon processing plant in a local village Nov '93; although he was expecting a cheque for £60,000 for growing less on his 900-acre farm, said EC set-aside payouts should be limited to £50,000 Nov '93; enthused about Kenneth Clarke's first Budget, particulary its "granny bonds, for which I have called for some time"; his doubt was limited to scaled-down audits of companies with turnovers below £90,000, because of risks to creditors: "I hope that those business will be required to add a caveat on their invoices, letterheads and quotations, so that all their creditors and customers know precisely with what type of businesses they are dealing" Dec '93; having served on the Standing Committee on the British Waterways Bill, deplored the time and money wasted on a handful of objectors Jan '94; voted to restore capital punishment, especially for killers of policemen Feb '94; voted to reduce age of homosexual consent to 18, but not 16, Feb '94; co-sponsored amendment allow "reasonable corporal punishment of male pupils" in secure training centres Mar '94; suggested that Labour amendments were impeding the Criminal Justice and Public Order Bill which could have prevented a murder by "a suspect who was out on bail for a string of serious sexual offences" Mar '94; warned that, despite GATT agreement, CAP expenditure could still mount Mar '94; when repeatedlfy baiting the Opposition, Speaker Boothroyd reminded him: "we are here not to discuss Labour and Liberal Democrat policies, but to question the Executive"; when he proved incapable of rephrasing his question, she moved on to the next questioner Apr '94; helped talk out Roger Berry's Civil Rights (Disabled Persons) Bill Apr '94; opposed any challenge to John Major before the election May '94; urged better facilities for tourists, to take advantage of the Channel Tunnel June '94; asked a battery of questions on wildlife conservation as applied to those with sporting rights July '94; opposed payment of criminal injuries compensation to those on substantially higher than average earnings Jan '95; urged Gloucestershire County Council sell some of its 5,000 acres of agricultural land to reduce its debt Feb '95; backed the Agricultural Tenancies Bill as "one of the most important milestones in the postwar history of agriculture" because it made farm lets available to younger farmers by removing the security of tenant farmers' tenure Feb '95; in the wake of the early retirement of his constituent, Air Chief Marshal Sir Andrew ('Sandy') Wilson, he called for generous pay and conditions for senior Service pensonnel to ensure "maintenance of quality" Feb '95; called for limits on the use of restriction orders by licensing magistrates Feb '95; acted as Teller against Labour MP Harry Barnes' Civil Rights (Disabled Persons) Bill Feb '95; criticised the Church Commissioners' management of pension funds May '95; told PM John Major his constituents preferred a Europe of nation states to a European superstate May '95; opposed Lord Nolan's proposal for a Parliamentary Commissioner to vet MPs' outside interests, claiming that thereby "democracy is irredeemably damaged" May '95; praised Tory Government's proposed policy to involve children in sports Oct '95; initiated debate on explosion of world population, urging more overseas aid for family planning and criticising Vatican's negative attitude Nov '95; claimed Labour were "not only soft on crime but soft on the bogus asylum seekers" Nov '95; complained of poor reception quality of BBC's Radio Cotswold Dec '95; urged means testing of social security benefits Jan '96; claimed low council house rents impaired mobility Jan '96; complained that "under the present [social security] system a millionaire can claim unemployment benefit for a year without being means-tested" Jan '96; defended the threatened local National Fire Service College based in Moreton-in-Marsh May '96; said his postbag was "ten to one in favour of gun-using folk" resisting the costly handgun ban in the post-Dunblane Firearms Bill Nov '96; proposed abolishing the state pension in his pamphlet 'Privatising the State Pension', alleging pensioners could receive an average of £280 a week from privately-funded pensions Nov '96; accused LibDem-controlled Gloucestershire County Council of a debt of £150m, compared to £25m when the Tories last ran it in '85, Feb '97; admitted he had earlier blocked Tory MP Peter Ainsworth's Hedgerow Bill, conceding that "a small minority of farmers acted totally irresponsibly" but claimed "it is in hunting and shooting areas we find the best hedges" Mar '97; easily retained his truncated, renamed Cotswold seat with a majority of 11,965 on a notional swing of 1.2% from the LibDems, the only pro-Tory swing in the country May '97; was named to the Public Accounts Commission June '97; urged Foreign Secretary Robin Cook to urge the primacy of US involvement in NATO when meeting President Clinton June '97; was named to Public Accounts Committee July '97; acted as Teller against the 1st Reading of Labour MP Mike Foster's anti-foxhunting Bill Nov '97; complained that increased petrol duties would hit poor pensioners in rural areas Apr '98; complained about poor morale in RAF Apr '98;

Born: 23 March 1953, Cambridge

Family: Among his ancestors were five MPs, including his grandfather; his great-great uncle, Hexham MP Colonel Douglas Clifton-Brown, was Speaker of the Commons, '43-51; nephew of Edmund Vestey; son of R L Clifton-Brown, farmer; m '79 Alexandra (Peto-Shepherd), journalist; 1s Edward '85; 1d Jacqueline '83;

Education: Tormore School, Upper Deal, Kent; Eton; Royal Agricultural College, Cirencester;

Occupation: Director (formerly Managing Director), of GRCB Farming Company (family farming business based on Gresham Hall and 900 acres at Gresham, Norwich which received £60,000 in set-aside money in '93); Shareholder, in Alder Investment Ltd (investment management); Owner, of agricultural holdings in Gloucestershire as well as Norfolk, with "small amounts of forestry in Scotland"; Chartered Surveyor (Associate, Royal Institute of Chartered Surveyors), formerly an Investment Surveyor, with Jones, Lang Wootton in London '75-79; ex: Director, East Beckham Produce Partnership;

Traits: Short; rugged; square-faced; thin-lipped; curly, parted, dark brown hair; youthful-looking; squashed face; tends to shout or be over-emphatic when he speaks; "bumbling" (DAILY TELEGRAPH); "diminutive C-B, [his] face, one of the least expressive in the House, usually fails to betray emotions such as love, hatred or comprehension" (David Aaronovitch, INDEPENDENT); "I hold a firearms certificate and a shotgun certificate; I own firearms and shotguns and have shot all my life" (GC-B); suffered a black eye from being kicked by his horse's knee when thrown;

Address: House of Commons, Westminster, London SW1A 0AA; Gresham Hall, Gresham, Norwich, Norfolk; agent: Hayward Burt, Cotswold Conservative Association, 7 Rodney Road, Cheltenham, Gloucestershire, GL50 1HX;

Telephone: 0171 219 5147 (H of C); 01242 514551 (constituency);

Ann CLWYD (Roberts)   **Labour**   **CYNON VALLEY '84-**

Majority: 19,755 (59.1%) over Plaid Cymru 4-way;
Description: A South Wales Labour stronghold, centred on Aberdare (after which it was previously named) between Merthyr and the Rhondda, bordered by the Brecon Beacons national park; it retains one deep pit, the workers' cooperative Tower Colliery; "we have the worst housing, the highest male unemployment in Wales and some of the worst health problems" (AC);
Position: Chairman, Parliamentary Human Rights Group '97-; Chairman, Campaign Against Repression and for Democratic Rights in Iraq (CARDRI) '84-; ex: a Spokesman: on Foreign Affairs '94-95, on Employment '93-94, on National Heritage '92-93, on
Wales '92, Overseas Development '89-92, on Women's Affairs '87-88, Education (Primary and Pre-school) '87-88; on Select Committee on European Legislation '85-87; Chairman: PLP Health and Social Security Committee '85-87; Vice Chairman: PLP Defence Committee '85-88, British-Vietnam Parliamentary Group '87-88; MEP for Mid and West Wales '79-84; on Labour Party NEC '83-84; Chairman, Tribune Group '86-87; on Arts Council '75-80; Vice Chairman, Welsh Arts Council '75-79; on Royal Commission on National Health Service '76-79;
Outlook: Twice-sacked (by Kinnock and Blair) senior woman in the awkward squad; her high intelligence and foresight - as over the Pergau Dam - can be obscured by quarrels with colleagues; a hard-hitting, hard-working, semi-hard Leftwinger, who has fallen back from her high as Labour's Spokesman on 3rd World; with an unbridled tongue in the Over-The-Top Tendency, she seemingly can only oppose in terms of shrill indignation and occasional vituperation; part of her energies, devoted to challenging privilege, corruption or oppression, can be misrepresented as furthering her own position; "her credentials as a tough, yet feminine, campaigner were confirmed by her decision to become the first Western politician to travel into Iraq from Iran to meet Kurdish rebel leaders" in 1991 (Robin Oakley and Sheila Gunn, TIMES); "tediously righteous she may be, but this dogged campaigner for the world's oppressed has real courage and stamina"; "whether the subject is Colombia, Iraq, Indonesia, Nigeria or Turkey - torture, child labour or malnutritious - Ms Clwyd's pressure in the Chamber causes an irritated tightening in the Ministerial jaw; she won't give up and she won't shut up" (Matthew Parris, TIMES); "she absolutely sees herself as a victim of backstairs party machinations, definitely not as an accident-prone publicity-seeker" (Jan Moir, GUARDIAN); has a journalist's nose for scandal; can show more impulsiveness than judgement (as in her attack on Baroness Chalker and her conclusions about SAS activities in training the Khmer Rouge); "apart from Glenys Kinnock, she is the best-known woman in Welsh politics" (GUARDIAN); did not get on with her Welsh former Leader; until '97 was Wales' only woman MP, the first to represent a mining valley; "articulate and Welsh-speaking" (INDEPENDENT); a "honey-blonde rebel against the tough, sexist world of Welsh Labour politics" (PRIVATE EYE); "a tough Parliamentary performer who...managed to force herself to the forefront of public attention despite holding the relatively low-profile portfolio of Overseas Development" (DAILY TELEGRAPH); a semi-hard Leftwinger with soft edges: formerly on the harder, pro-Campaign-Group fringe of the Tribune Group; a staunch campaigner for women's equality, Kurds, East Timorese, the 3rd World and against nuclear

weapons and Indonesian and Turkish militarists; a former anti-Marketeer who came to see the EC less "as a straightjacket, but more as a stretchable, elastic girdle"; pro: PR, CND; formerly TGWU-sponsored;

History: As a student she supported a woman Plaid candidate against Labour's Megan Lloyd George in Carmarthen by-election '57; joined Labour Party '68; contested native Denbigh June '70; was short-listed for Aberdare Sep '72; was selected for Gloucester July '74, contested it Oct '74; tried for Caerphilly '77; became Chairman of Cardiff Anti-Racialism Committee '78; was in the running for Ogmore but missed out after a dubious count which picked Ray Powell Aug '78; was elected MEP for Mid and West Wales, insisting that Labour nationally had conducted a "feeble and mean-spirited campaign" for Euro-elections June '79; alleged £7.5m could be saved if all Community institutions were held in Brussels Nov '79; urged more help for Welsh flood victims Jan '80; during Anwar Sadat's visit to Luxembourg, she thumped a security man who had struck her, having refused her entry Feb '81; supported Welsh weight-lifters claim for independence from UK team Dec '81; suggested an EC register of lobbyists Jan '82; led campaign for aid for snow-crushed Welsh farmers Jan '82; urged Labour to think again on withdrawal from EC Apr '82; urged Welsh fishermen to take advantage of EC aid Jan '83; won recognition for minority languages including £56,000 for Welsh Feb '83; since Labour's previous policy of withdrawal was a "dead duck", urged the party "get its act together" to improve EC representation July '83; was surprised not to be short-listed for Rhondda May '83; campaigned to sever EC links with Turkey Sep '83; was elected to Women's Section of National Executive with 4.74m votes Oct '83; accused Defence Ministry of intimidation at Greenham Common Jan '84; said there were more cases at the European Court against the UK for breaches of equal rights legislation than against any other country Jan '84; was considered a possible successor to Dr Roger Thomas at Carmarthen Feb '84; was selected for Cynon Valley by-election over four ex-MPs after Ioan Evans' death; in the campaign completely supported the miners' strike; attacked VAT on fish and chips: it "discriminates against working people" Apr '84; was elected for Cynon Valley - the fourth woman elected for a Welsh seat and the only one sitting - putting up Labour's share of votes May '84; in Maiden deplored discrimination against South Wales mines June '84; stood down from European Parliament June '84; voted to retain GMC selection for MPs July '84; was on Rightwing trade unionists' 'hit list' designed to knock her off the NEC as too Left Aug '84; on NEC voted with Kinnock and soft-Left to widen participation in re-selection Sep '84; signed 'Socialist Charter' with other semi-hard and hard Leftwing MPs Oct '84; was knocked off NEC with vote reduced to 1.77m; replying for the NEC at conference, described housing cuts as the Tories' "top crime"; urged more public control of construction industry and strengthened tenants' rights Oct '84; maintained that NATO's offensive concepts contradicted its claim to be a defensive alliance Oct '84; attacked "catastrophic" rate-capping Nov '84; opposed further developments at Stansted and Heathrow, urging more flights for Cardiff Nov '84; was angered by Hitachi's suggestion that its local TV plant workers should retire at 35, Dec '84; at CND press conference with Bruce Kent, accused the Ministry of Defence of misleading Parliament on NATO strategy Dec '84; briefly joined Campaign Group's disruptive pro-miners' demonstration in Commons Jan '85; pressed for pregnant women not to have to pay for dental treatments begun before pregnancy Mar '85; urged an independent inquiry into victimisation of local strike-breaker Mar '85; headed a campaign for a women's hairdresser in the Commons Apr '85; joined a women's protest at the Home Office against a twelve-month sentence for a Greenham Common woman Apr '85; urged reinstatement for five miners sacked for spitting at strikebreaker Apr '85; headed a motion complaining of flooding of her Commons office May '85; was only Labour MP who abstained instead of voting against increase in VAT contribution to EEC, in protest against anti-EC sentiments July '85; complained against wounding statements by Michael Heseltine and US Chief of Staff of SHAPE in interview with PLP Defence Committee July '85; led a Labour motion against 'Star Wars' July '85; led a demand for an emergency PLP debate on absence of 38 Labour Mps from vote on top people's pay, which was lost by 17 votes July '85; was again defeated for NEC with 1.41m votes Oct '85; headed a motion attacking use of Commons facilities to host Mecca's 'Miss World' beauty contest Nov '85; introduced Bill to bring men's retirement age down to 60 Dec '85; opposed further development of nuclear power until waste could be safely disposed of Dec '85; complained about continued imprisonment of Turkish peace campaigners Dec '85; was reported by the promoters as absent from compulsory attendance at Felixtowe Docks Bill committee after walking out in protest against being accused of bribery by the TGWU and against outdated procedure, which later led to changes in Private Bill procedure Jan '86; with Roland Boyes founded PAW (Peace and Animal Welfare) to protest warfare experiments on animals Feb '86; introduced Bill to ban identifiable tobacco products from TV Feb '86; urged more powers for European Parliament which, she claimed, was already more effective than Commons Apr '86; won "substantial damages" from PRIVATE EYE for its claim she had "used her promiscuity as a means of attaining her political ambitions" May '86; pressed for an end of Crown Immunity for hospitals whose unhygienic catering she had investigated when on Welsh Hospital Board June '86; defeated the re-selection challenge of hard-Leftist ex-MP Reg Race by 54 to 27, July '86; with 600,000 votes, was again defeated for NEC Sep '86; was elected Chairman of Tribune Group -the first woman - over Ron Davies and Stan Thorne Nov '86; was accused of "sexism" by two women Tories when she demanded a register of MPs' close relatives after allegations that Edwina Currie's husband's accountancy firm was given a DHSS contract Dec '86; as Chairman, failed to stop a Tribune Group debate and vote against the sacking of Norman Buchan as Arts Spokesman Jan '87; asked why 'Zircon' project expenditures had not been reported to Public Accounts Committee Feb '87; denied Soviet-American agreements rendered Labour's unilateralism anachronistic Mar '87; expressed Tribune Group's annoyance with Neil Kinnock's acceptance of delay in removal of US Cruise missiles from UK pending Geneva agreements Mar '87; after Keith Best disclosures, claimed people were outraged about "MPs lining their pockets at their expense" Apr '87; increased her majority by over 8,000 June '87; disclosed Tribune Group had rejected by 37 to 27 her scheme for a joint Shadow Cabinet slate of eight Tribune and four Campaign groupies June '87; was made Deputy Spokesman on Women and on Primary and Pre-School Education July '87; secured 2.7m votes, but was not elected to NEC, despite TGWU and LCC backing Sep '87; introduced her Unfair Reporting and Right of Reply Bill to establish a Media Complaints Commission Oct '87; was re-elected Vice Chairman of PLP Defence Committee Nov '87; Chief Whip Derek Foster sought to have her disciplined for her absence on an Oxfam-sponsored trip to Kampuchea, but Neil Kinnock dissuaded him; in adjournment debate on Kampuchea after her visit, she accused Prince Sihanouk of being a puppet of Khmer ('Killing Fields') Rouge, while Vietnam-supported government was refused recognition and aid Jan '88; her right-of-reply Bill was sunk by anonymous Tory MP shouting "object!" Feb '88; claimed her constituency had "worst housing, the highest male unemployment in Wales and some of the worst health problems" Mar '88; supported random breath tests Mar '88; urged wider nursery education Mar '88; again urged better Westminster facilities, especially for women MPs, including a swimming pool May '88; declined to support withdrawal of Whip from Ron Brown MP for Mace incident May '88; urged an appeal body if women were denied an abortion May '88; complained of inadequate sums offered to improve housing in valleys constituencies like hers June '88; as the only front-bencher to vote against Defence Estimates instead of abstaining, was dropped as Assistant Spokesman on Education and Women's Affairs, despite her reminding Kinnock he had often rebelled himself Oct '88; deplored phurnacite pollution in her constituency Nov '88; voted against Prevention of Terrorism Bill instead of abstaining Dec '88; urged PR be considered in Labour's policy review Dec '88; attacked Welsh Water for increased disconnections Dec '88; co-sponsored Tony Worthington's Right of Reply Bill, like hers in previous session Dec '88; sought emergency debate on listeria poisoning Jan '89; dismissed "neurotic" fears of the Press that a legal right of reply would swamp newspapers with space-consuming complaints Feb '89; visited East Timor with Tory MP Richard Alexander Mar '89; criticised Government for allowing attendance at Baghdad arms fair Apr '89; was among 50 Labour MPs who criticized Neil Kinock for dropping unilateralism May '89; visited Vietnam and Kampuchea, sponsored by aid agencies Sep '89; again sharply attacked Labour's jettisoning of unilateralism July '89; unexpectedly, received 111 votes (joint 13th) in contest for Shadow Cabinet, despite avoiding Tribune slate; after promising to abide by collective Shadow Cabinet responsibility, was named Spokesman on Overseas Development and Co-operation Nov '89; asked Neil Kinnock for Dale Campbell-Savours as a deputy, but was offered instead Dr Lewis Moonie and then George Foulkes, part-time Nov '89; sought emergency debate on famine in Eritrea Nov '89; presented petition opposing support of Khmer Rouge Jan '90; visited Ethiopia for HTV Mar '90; urged help to liberalise and modernise Vietnam's economy Mar '90; urged relief for "crippling burden of 3rd World debt" Mar '90; backed embryo research Apr '90; with Joan Lestor wrote Shadow Cabinet document urging linking of UK aid programme to country's human rights record Apr '90; voted for voluntary euthanasia May '90; visited Hongkong as guest of its administration May '90; warned of danger to 3rd World trade of Single European Market May '90; after being re-selected said: "Labour's re-selection process for MPs is a torture drawn up by masochists suffering from dyspepsia" June '90; accused Nicholas Ridley of being an "aristocratic football hooligan" and "indolent and insolent Little Englander" for insisting that Nigeria's £60m credit could only be spent on equipment and supplies from UK-based companies July '90; after being refused access to Kurdish villages by Baghdad, claimed Saddam had displaced at least 100,000 Kurds July '90; urged careful targeting of generous aid to Eastern Europe July '90; urged end of arms and other support for Khmer Rouge July '90; after visit to West Bank, complained about Israeli abuses of Palestinian human rights Aug '90; on Pilger TV programme told of meeting two military Britons in Cambodia; asked Prime Minister to investigate whether they were SAS; claimed there was evidence UK gave Khmer Rouge training Oct '90; asked about pollution standards of UK's overseas power projects Oct '90; received 102 votes (11th), in contest for Shadow Cabinet Oct '90; having been tipped off by a Malaysian journalist, asked about corruption in UK bid for Malaysian hydro-electric Pergau project Oct '90; criticised John Major for not offering Lynda Chalker a Cabinet post Nov '90; urged write-off of 3rd World debt Dec '90; visited Malaysia and Thailand to study population problems for International Planned Parenthood Federation; was given confidential information suggesting that up to £35m in bribes had been paid to Malaysian agents for British companies to secure contracts for Pergau dam Jan '91; was said to have reservations about Gulf War Jan '91; sharply criticised Lynda Chalker for delays in funds to feed starving Africans Jan, Feb '91; complained that Gulf War was diverting attention from starving Africa Mar '91; with a TV camera crew, travelled to Iraqi border to visit trapped Kurdish refugees, smuggling in a key communications component for Kurds Apr '91; made a harrowing and widely-admired speech - lauded on the front page of DAILY TELEGRAPH - describing the horrors of her five days on Iraq's border with Iran Apr '91; urged a UN-supervised referendum in East Timor May '91; complained that Government's response to crises in Iraq, Bangladesh and Sub-Saharan Africa had been "slow and shamefully inadequate" May '91; secured admission that Britain had trained non-Communist anti-Vietnamese insurgents for Cambodia June '91; again urged help for Iraqi refugees July '91; was forced to apologise for libelling two Britons in jumping to the conclusion they were SAS men training Khmer Rouge to lay mines against Cambodian civilians, on which John Pilger embroidered his TV 'disclosures' July '91; secured release of Welsh hostage held by Kurdish guerillas in Turkey Sep '91; in Shadow Cabinet election received 137 votes (4th, top woman) Oct '91; co-urged peace between PLO and Israel Oct '91; backed Geraint Howell's motion for a Welsh Parliament Nov '91; Overseas Development Minister Lynda Chalker congratulated Dale Campbell-Savours on finally having become Ms Clwyd's official deputy, twitting him for the "unofficial work he has done for so long for the hon Member for Cynon Valley, for which perhaps he has not been thanked as much as he should have been" Nov '91; after another trip to Iraq, urged more aid to harassed and oppressed Kurds Nov '91; citing a recent political murder, urged Government to curb its aid to Kenya Nov '91; visited India with hospitality provided by its Government Jan '92; visited Moscow with her Deputy, Dale Campbell-Savours, and others to investigate British food aid, funded by Future of Europe Trust; found UK beef stacked in a warehouse because not colour-coded Feb '92; visited Turkey as guest of Turkish women's organisations Mar '92; retained seat with majority down from 21,571 to 21,364, a swing to Conservatives of .24% Apr '92; blamed Labour's defeat on macho style and playing down of 3rd World problems Apr '92; after withdrawal of her favoured candidate, Gordon Brown, initially decided to contest Deputy Leadership, with strong support from Brian Sedgemore; her manifesto backed electoral reform, urged a Bill of Rights and a pro-EC stance; complained about unions' role in leadership switch: "it would be tragic if a rift were to occur because some trade union leaders acted undemocratically during the current contests for the Leader and Deputy Leader"; she was blocked by need for nomination by 55 Labour MPs Apr '92; accused Baroness Chalker of having failed to stop aid cuts of 17% and "hot-footing it down the corridor [to the Lords], days after being rejected by the voters of Wallasey, to wrap herself in ermine while pontificating on the poverty of two-thirds of humanity"; her "personal attack" was criticised as jealousy by Foreign Secretary Douglas Hurd and others May '92; after spending four days in Rio de Janeiro for the Earth Summit, claimed John Major's departure after a day or two was an "absolute disgrace" (but accepted a lift back to London on the PM's plane) June '92; attended first Iraqi Opposition conference, "paid for by Iraqi Opposition groups" who were financed by the CIA June '92; contested Shadow Cabinet; received 133 votes (10th); was unhapppy about being named Welsh Spokesman, in succession to Barry Jones; criticised Leader John Smith for not giving "very high profile jobs" to Shadow Cabinet women July '92; was overheard loudly but unsuccessfully asking John Smith to be allowed to reply to emergency debate on mines closures, instead of scheduled Energy Spokesman Martin O'Neill Oct '92; John Smith named Ron Davies as Labour's Welsh Spokesman, shifting her to National Heritage Spokesman, replacing resigned Bryan Gould; the TIMES, anticipating this, said: "there are few better qualified than Clwyd" Nov '92; urged curb on English Heritage chief Jocelyn Stevens as an "asset stripper and an axeman" Nov '92; urged Queen to contribute to repair of Windsor Castle after fire Nov '92; opposed privatisation of BBC, even at its fringes Nov '92; after an acrimonious exchange of letters, Speaker Betty Boothroyd threatened publicly to clamp Mrs Clwyd's car because parking "in Speaker's Court is by permission of the Speaker", claiming it was accorded to the Speaker and Government Ministers - while dissenting Mrs Clwyd "continues to leave her car in the Court, thereby taking someone else's parking space and, by her conduct, causing embarrassment to the servants of the House whose duty it is to enforce the regulation"; Mrs Clwyd insisted she and other MPs should have the same rights as Ministers Jan '93; under pressure from pro-pools Labour MPs, urged protection of pools employees when National Lottery came in Jan '93; complained to Chairman of Independent Television Commission that Granada TV was not living up to its franchise commitments Feb '93; urged an 'Old People at Risk Register' after releasing letter from constituent who was later murdered Mar '93; supported Sir Malcolm Thornton's amendment to Lottery Bill to allow pools companies to compete "freely and fairly" Apr '93; criticised "politicisation" of BBC, calling for more impartial regulators Apr '93; complained to ITV Chairman that Tyne Tees TV was failing to carry out its statutory duties Apr '93; complained that most of the money left to the British Library by George Bernard Shaw had been diverted to the British Museum May '93; speaking for Labour on Privacy and Media Intrusion, backed a Freedom of Information Act, a code of conduct for journalists, a statutory right of reply to correct factual inaccuracies, a curb on media monopolies, the abolition of bugging and telephoto intrusion and the right of privacy for ordinary people, but no inhibition of investigation into the "lives of the rich and powerful" June '93; complained that Murdoch was using satellite profits to cut price of TIMES, endangering the INDEPENDENT Sep '93; opposed takeover of small ITV companies by their bigger brothers Sep '93; published Bill to protect ITV from hostile takeovers until the end of '96, Oct '93; alleging a "cynical chauvinist plot" by older MCP Labour MPs, was knocked off Shadow Cabinet, receiving 104 votes, down from 133; Oct '93; was replaced as National Heritage Spokesman by Mo Mowlam, becoming John Prescott's Deputy Spokesman on Employment instead Oct '93; despite offers of a Millbank office from her old feuding partner from Ogmore selection days, Ray Powell -suspected to be an organiser of the anti-feminist plot - delayed relinquishing the office, off Speaker's Court, that went with her former job; Powell threatened in the press: "if she doesn't move out soon, I'll simply pile all her stuff in the corridor and change the locks" Dec '93; voted against restoring capital punishment, even for killers of policemen Feb '94; vote to reduce age of homosexual consent to 16, Feb '94; staged a 27-hour underground protest, helping to win a reprieve from closure of local Tower Colliery, but miners then accepted redundancy deal Apr '94; in adjournment debate on Tower Colliery, claimed "Neil Clarke, the Chairman of British Coal, has debased, demeaned and diminished public life"; "in the conversation that I had with him, he lied, lied and lied again" Apr '94; introduced Regulation of Cosmetic Surgery Billl to "establish registration procedures for cosmetic surgeons in order to set mininum standards of training and practice" June '94; voted for Blair for Leader and Prescott for Deputy Leader July '94; urged industrial tribunals try to reinstate employees rather than compensate them for dismissal July '94; the SUNDAY TIMES revived her '90 revelation about the Pergau Dam and arms contracts corrupton Feb '94; urged inquiry into East Timor atrocities July '94; attacked Social Security Secretary Michael Portillo for blaming EU for the axing of help for the disabled when he himself had negotiated the directive Aug '94; backed rail signalmen's strike despite Tony Blair's coolness Sep '94; aided by the "assisted places scheme" for women Labour MPs, polled 94 votes for the Shadow Cabinet, making her runner-up in 19th place, 3 votes behind successful Ann Taylor Oct '94; she was made an Assistant Spokesman on Foreign Affairs under Robin Cook; was also made a Deputy to John Prescott Oct '94; in GUARDIAN letter rebutted claim of Tory MP Patrick Nicholls that figure of 200,000 East Timor casualties was "wholly unsubstantiated" Nov '94; condemned British aid to Indonesian Government as part of 45-minute speech on East Timor atrocities Dec '94; tabled motion on East Timor atrocities Jan '95; helped celebrate re-opening of Tower pit in Hirwaun as a "model" workers' co-operative Jan '95; fiercely rejected male resistance to all-women short-lists, warning women would not wait "another hundred years" Feb '95; queried £1.35m spent on housing of UK Ambassador to the Yemen Feb '95; urged continued sanctions against Iraq, citing its human rights violations Mar '95; was sacked with her fellow Foreign Affairs Assistant Spokesman Jim Cousins for investigating, without the Whips' permission, Turkish attacks against the Kurds, after which she and Cousins fell out; she and Cousins left Robin Cook without lieutenants during Foreign Office questions; she insisted she would not have secured permission because the Pairing Whip, Ray Powell, was her 17-year-long enemy Apr

'95; after being sacked by Blair, said, "he had to do it to prove he is a toughie" Apr '95; complained to John Major and Lord Nolan about appointment to board of GEC of Tory MP and former Minister, Richard Needham, who had visited Indonesia when GEC and British Aerospace were negotiating £500m in contracts Sep '95; referred to National Audit Office the spending of British aid funds in East Timor whose occupation by Indonesia was of dubious legality internationally Oct '95; asked about pension funds of privatised mining industry Oct '95; in Shadow Cabinet, polled 72 votes (down from 94), making her 8th runner-up Oct '95; acclaimed £2m profit from local Towr miners' co-operative as "sociaslism in action" Dec '95; backed Tony Benn's defence amendment urging the scrapping of Trident and cutting spending to West European average Dec '95; attacked British role in training Indonesian police Jan '96; said she was "sickened" by the revelations in the Scott Report as one who "witnessed at first hand the victims of Halabja and realised that the shells that were delivered on Halabja were made by the lathes of Matrix Churchill" Feb '96; was told she had not "lost her talent for being offensive" when she asked Welsh Minister Rod Richards whether he was telling "the whole truth, part of the truth or his version of the truth" about the higher death rate and incidence of breast cancer in Wales Feb '96; urged inquiry into childhood illnesses from local derelict phurnacite plant Feb '96; voted both against the Prevention of Terrorism Act and guillotining of its debate Apr '96; although silent on the subject, was considered to be one of the half-dozen Welsh MPs opposing devolution May '96; took up with Speaker Boothroyd the blocking of her motions on Welsh child abuse; shouted "object" to Government's tribunal proposals because it would make the matter sub judice June '96; despite Tony Blair's opposition, contested Shadow Cabinet election, receiving 94 votes; complained that whole leadership pressure had been to ensure election of Harriet Harman, who won last place with 149 votes July '96; voted against a 3% cap on MPs' pay rise, for pension based on £43,000 and a cut in mileage allowance July '96; on behalf of their disfigured victims, again called for controls on cosmetic surgeons Sep '96; urged Saddam Hussein be tried by international tribunal Sep '96; urged more Government aid for sufferers from bronchitis and emphysema, often miners Nov '96; opposed Bill of anti-abortion Tory MP Elizabeth Peacock to outlaw skull-crushing "partial-birth abortion", because this was rarely used in UK and clinicians should retain their freedom Dec '96; backed additional compensation for former prisoners of the Japanese, disclosing: "my uncle died in a Japanese war camp" Dec '96; after Australian holiday, complained that Airtours treated travellers like cattle Jan '97; was one of 72 MPs targeted by anti-abortion Prolife Alliance Party Feb '97; asked Home Secretary Michael Howard about tapping of mobile phones Mar '97; was listed as pro-EU in European Movement advertisement Mar '97; spoke to US Congress, with airfare paid for by Iraqi expatriates Apr '97; retained her unaltered seat with a slightly smaller majority of 19,755, this time over the Plaid May '97; complained about absence of Freedom of Information Act in Queen's Speech May '97; was elected to one of six places on PLP committee to liaise with new Labour Government June '97; spoke at Washington seminar, with her airfare paid for by Americans for Democratic Action June '97; in PLP meeting attacked new Defence Secretary, George Robertson, for allowing senior Indonesian military men to attend a British arms fair June '97; was listed as a member of the Christian Socialist Movement June '97; asked about impact on sheeps' eyes in Porton Down experiments with water cannon (exported to Indonesia) June '97; urged International Development Secretary to curb misdirected increased aid to Indonesia, no longer a poor country July '97; asked Speaker about slowness of Foreign Office in answering 38 of her questions on arms for Indonesia July '97; launched anti-Saddam campaign in Strasbourg, with expenses paid by Iraqi expatriates July '97; asked Welsh Secretary about maximising number of women in Welsh National Assembly July '97; asked Tony Blair whether it was responsible to ask Hungary, Poland and the Czech Republic to increase their defence spending to qualify for NATO, in view of other demands July '97; resisted conformist pressures on Labour Mps, insisting: "we are not androids, we are not going to be manipulated, and we'll speak out about things we disagree with" Aug '97; criticised Foreign Secretary Robin Cook's visit to Indonesia, unless he also visited East Timor Aug '97; revealed that the late Princess Diana had invited her to Kensington Palace to discuss landmines Sep '97; was "genuinely sad" to learn of 11 new arms contracts with Indonesia Oct '97; was cleared of having driven through a red light in Cardiff after conducting her own defence Dec '97; rebelled with 46 other Labour MPs against cuts in lone-parent benefits, after receiving evasive reply Dec '97; claimed the extent of the £3.2m of inherited cuts in lone-parent benefits would "stiffen the resolve among the 47 Labour MPs who hae already refused to support the lone-parent benefit cuts" Jan '98; fiercely attacked Foreign Minister Derek Fatchett for Labour's failure to cancel arms export licenses to Indonesia May '98; spoke movingly on anti-personnel-mines legislation, recalling her conversation with Diana, Princess of Wales July '98; was one of 24 Labour rebels voting against Murdoch-style predatory newspaper pricing July '98;

Born: 21 March 1937, Denbigh

Family: Daughter, of Welsh-speaking Gwilym Henri Lewis and Elizabeth Ann (Jones); her pen-name, Clwyd, derives from her second name; m '63 broadcaster Owen Roberts, recently a free-lance producer, previously Assistant to Head of Programmes, BBC Wales;

Education: Halkyn Primary; Holywell Grammar; The Queen's School, Chester; University College, Bangor (no degree: too much fun and student politics);

Occupation: Parliamentary and Political Adviser, to IPMS (including CME and STE; £1-5000) '95-; Journalist and Broadcaster (NUJ): Welsh Correspondent: GUARDIAN and OBSERVER '64-79; formerly Sponsored: by TGWU (£600 p a to constituency, 80% of election expenses) '85-95, Society of Telecom Executives (Adviser '86-93) '93-95; ex: BBC Studio Manager '59-64; Reporter and Producer (free-lance) '64-79; Student-Teacher, Hope School, Flintshire '55-56;

Traits: Small; attractive; blonde; "lissom"; "shapely"; "glamorous" (Colin Welch, DAILY MAIL); articulate; vivacious; determined; headstrong; manipulative; Welsh-speaking; "I can look calm on the outside and not be very calm on the inside" (AC); "indefatigable"; "wry sense of humour" (Patrick Wintour, GUARDIAN); "feline" (Godfrey Barker, DAILY TELEGRAPH); "curmudgeonly" (Jim Lester MP); "agreeably erratic, mildly larky" (Edward Pearce, GUARDIAN); interacted bitchily with Lynda Chalker; "she smiles sweetly as she dishes the dirt"; "the smile never wavers even when she's asked a question she doesn't like; it stays in place, but stiffens like a curl of stale icing" (Jan Moir, GUARDIAN);

Address: House of Commons, Westminster, London SW1A 0AA; 70 St Michael's Road, Llandaff, Cardiff; Flat 6, Dean Court, 6 Dean Street, Aberdare, Mid-Glamorgan CF44 7BN;

Telephone: O171 219 3437/6609 (H of C); 01222 562245; 01685 871 394;

REWRITING HISTORY

Some MPs have an amazing capacity for trying to rewrite their own histories. The late Robert Adley tried to excise the fact that he had supported Enoch Powell's tirade against coloured immigration in 1968, protesting: "But that was before I was an MP!" A Labour MP repeatedly denied a line in her profile that she had refused to applaud an acclaimed Kinnock speech at conference, until the message was passed via her husband that this was observed first-hand at a distance of twenty feet.

Majority: 3,802 over Conservative 4-way;
Description: A compact seat on Nottingham's northeastern fringe, favoured by its middle-class commuters; in its pre-'83 version as Carlton, it was able even to resist Labour's '66 high tide; 80% of its homes are owner-occupied; only 11% are council house tenants;
Position: Rushcliffe Borough Councillor (Labour Group Leader '87-) '83-; on Labour's Central Region Executive; on Labour's National Policy Forum '93-;
Outlook: The loyal intervener who was the archetypal teacher-councillor, involved in trying to raise the horizons of local working-class children; the first-ever Labour MP for this seat, who beat an able young Minister, Andrew Mitchell; was third-time lucky, having fought the same seat twice before; was a Leftwinger in the '60s, '70s and '80s as a unilateralist, opponent of the Vietnam War and an opponent of EEC entry; his causes reflect his preoccupations: Socialist Educational Association, League Against Cruel Sports;
History: At school he opposed the US war in Vietnam '68; opposed UK's entry into the EEC '72; joined the Labour Party at 25, '78; was elected to Rushcliffe Borough Council May '83; contested Rushcliffe against Kenneth Clarke, coming 3rd, June '83; was selected for Gedling Nov '85; first fought Gedling, restoring Labour to 2nd place above the SDP June '87; contested the seat again, raising the Labour vote from 24% to 34% and reducing Tory MP Andrew Mitchell's majority from 16,539 to 10,637 Apr '92; raised with Minister Andrew Mitchell the MRC report on the Institute of Hearing, alleging that new government guidelines would effectively deprive veterans with war-damaged hearing of their war pensions Dec '96; although 108th on Labour's target list, he decided "we can win Gedling" Apr '97; on a swing of 13%, ousted Andrew Mitchell by a majority of 3,802 May '97; asked about raising the basic state pension May '97; made a generous tribute to Andrew Mitchell in his Maiden, which concentrated on securing smaller classes, a higher status for teachers and ending pupil alienation June '97; pressed for action "to stop the illegal trade in wild animals and plants" June '97; co-enthused about comprehensive education "as the foremost and most efficient way to provide secondary education" June '87; backed expansion of school sports June '97; co-urged ban on fox-hunting June '97; urged the need for education about international development July '97; helped press the Government to be "tough on road crime" July '97; backed curbs on detention of asylum seekers July '97; backed focus groups as "the way forward for the Government that will be welcomed by most people" July '97; loyally supported the Finance Bill against Tory scoffers July '97; insisted that people did not claim benefits to which they were entitled because "the Conservative Pary created a culture in which people believe that anyone who claims benfit is a scrounger" July '97; enthused about the chance of England hosting the soccer World Cup in 2006, July '97; urged debate on the "dramatic increase in the number of permanent exclusion from our schools" Oct '97; applauded the establishment of the Pension Provision Group to "deal with the mess that we are in" Nov '97; loyally supported all the Government's decisions on public services Nov '97; co-sponsored motion attacking hunting of wild mammals with dogs Dec '97; introduced Labelling of Products Bill to provide consumers with key facts Jan '98; led a motion attacking fur farming of mink and fox Jan '98; with 68 other mainly-new MPs backed more building on "brownfield" sites Jan '98; urged a

fairer share for social housing to mop up the homeless Feb '98; pushed an early debate on Lord Justice Stuart-Smith's report on the Hillsborough disaster in view of "continuing disquiet, upset, anxiety, worry and concern" Feb '98; "welcomed the General Teaching Council as helping to re-establish teachers' morale, and showing that "this Government are one of the best-performing Governments on education" Mar '98; urged the quick application of the Crime and Disorder Blill to curb anti-social behaviour on his local estates Mar '98; urged more time to discuss animal welfare Apr '98; loyally welcomed the National Child-Care Strategy May '98; congratulated Government on helping pensioners with their fuel bills May '98; urged extension of Education Action Zones to "tackle the incredible levels of under-achievement" May '98; loyally backed the Government's Teaching and Higher Education Bill, insisting "I do not believe that it is the lack of grants that will deter students from going on to higher education"; he insisted that the maintenance grant system had failed poorer students; as a Deputy Head Teacher he had found "we could not raise their expectations and we could not create a culture of educational achievement" June '98;

Born: 17 June 1953, London

Family: Son, of Edwin Coaker, policeman, and (he doesn't know his mother's maiden name); m '78 Jacqueline (Heaton), teacher; 1s Matthew William '86, 1d Laura Clare '84;

Education: Oaklands Primary School; Drayton Manor Grammar School, Hanwell, London; Warwick University; Trent Polytechnic (BA Hons);

Occupation: Deputy Head Teacher, of Nottingham's Big Wood Comprehensive '95-97; Teacher, ("the best teacher I ever had" (local voter) (NUT) '76-95;

Traits: Tall; burly; flat hair with deep widows peaks; long, oval face; formerly had a small moustache; London accent; was the manager of Nottingham Academicals Football Club;

Address: House of Commons, Westminster, London SW1A 0AA; 6 Ingleby Close, Cotgrave, Nottinghamshire;

Telephone: 0171 219 3000 (H of C); 0115 989 2721 (home);

Ann (Margaret) COFFEY   **Labour**   **STOCKPORT '92-**

Majority: 18,912 (40.5%) over Conservative 7-way;

Description: The more Tory-leaning western half of Stockport, with middle-class Heatons to the north and Davenport to the south; it has engineering and foodstuffs; in '83 it lost Brinnington with its council housing and gained Davenport and part of Offerton and Cale Green; Brinnington's return in '95 helped Labour;

Position: PPS, to Tony Blair '97-; ex: Assistant Spokesman, on Health '96-97; Assistant Whip '95-96; on Select Committee on Trade & Industry '93-95; on Parliamentary Panel of USDAW '92-95?; Vice Chairman, PLP Trade and Industry Committee '93-??;

Secretary, PLP North West Group '93-??; Stockport Borough Councillor (Leader of Labour Group '88-92, Spokesman on Education '88-89, Spokesman on Social Services '86-88) '84-; ex: on Stockport Area Health Authority '86-90;

Outlook: A low-profiled, locally-focussed loyalist and Blair's second PPS; the former social worker and councillor who finds "the Commons offers the tantalising prospect of endless opportunities to debate - but very rarely to change - things"; "she appears impeccably Blairite and cautious, if anything to a fault"; "with her strong grounding in town hall politics, looks a reliable choice to play a straight bat" (David Brindle, GUARDIAN); "I don't see myself in Leftwing or Rightwing terms" (AC); Inverness-born social worker who acquired special northwestern expertise from having been leader of Oldham's fostering and adoption team; as expected, has taken a keen interest in reforming the Children Act and adoption law; has a practical approach to trying to solve well-anticipated problems with realism ("there is nothing worse than promising what you cannot achieve" [AC]); in politics she spent eight years on Stockport Council, half as its Leader; in her Parliamentary candidacies, worked up from a hopeless contest in Cheadle to take a hopeful marginal in Stockport; "very committed to electoral reform" (AC);

History: She feels the most important political influences on her were "my student experiences in the '60s and the feminist movement of the '70s"; joined the Labour Party '76; was elected to Stockport Borough Council May '84; was selected for hopeless Cheadle, endorsed by the NEC Jan '86; became Spokesman on Social Services on Stockport Borough Council '86; came 3rd in Cheadle, with 9% of the vote, 2% better than in 1983, June '87; became Spokesman on Education on Stockport Borough Council '88; became Leader of Labour Group on Stockport Borough Council '88; was selected for marginal Stockport, defeating two other candidates overwhelmingly Feb '90; won seat by 1,422 votes, ousting Tony Favell, the personally popular former Tory MP Apr '92; in Maiden, said local parents like herself faced a "nightmare scenario" and "chaos" in their children's education, with imposition of headlong reforms including opt-outs on top of Stockports just-completed reform of its secondary schools May '92; urged higher standards of support in residential homes for the elderly, which could be achieved at lower cost in local authority homes if councils were allowed to borrow the money needed to re-equip them June '92; warned that "because of the prescriptive nature of the legislation" setting up the Child Support Agency, DSS officers would "recover a few million pounds by taking the clothes off children's backs and the food out of their mouths" but would do "nothing to dispel poverty or to improve the welfare of children and it humiliates hundreds of our citizens" June '92; said: "I strongly suggest that the registration for small [residential] homes should be the same as for larger homes" July '92; warned about inadequacy of support for British Aerospace, which had a plant locally Sep '92; as a former specialist in adoption, warned Government to close the loopholes left in the Children Act 1989; also sharply criticized the "illogicality" of sections of the Adoption Law Review Nov '92; complained that her constituency had 7,000 on its waiting list, "the hidden homeless", who were having to live "in intolerable circumstances for a long time" Nov '92; asked for help for 54 traumatised Bosnian Muslim refugees in Stockport Nov '92; urged better street lighting to deter crimes and vandalism and make people feel safer Dec '92; urged more funds to aid urban regeneration Feb '93; visited Japan as guest of Japanese Government Mar '93; asked PM John Major what more he was doing to ensure that the Saudi Arabian Government gave an anticipated contract to endangered Ferranti in her constituency Apr '93; co-sponsored motion celebrating 25th anniversary of Abortion Act Apr '93; voted against National Lottery Bill Apr '93; with other women Labour MPs co-signed GUARDIAN letter backing one-member one-vote June '93; insisted that "if it is right to send itemised pay slips to employees, it is right to send them to all employees" June '93; complained to PM John Major about doubling of rent to over £50 a week to an elderly constituent in housing association flat June '93; complained that £4m Europa House in her constituency had been rejected in favour of a £20m Glasgow office building for a new integrated Army personnel centre June '93; the Tory agent for her constituency was made redundant July '93; urged pensions for foster carers, who saved Government huge amounts Dec '93; expressed concern about local authorities being able to pay for secure training places at £2,000 a week without committed Government resources Jan '94; co-sponsored motion calling attention to the chance that the use of nuclear weapons might be declared illegal Feb '94; voted against restoring capital punishment, even for killers of policemen Feb '94; voted to reduce age of homosexual consent to 18 or 16, Feb '94; urged Government to show generosity to Stockport Council for making available secure accommodation for which no provision was made in standard spending assessment Mar '94; urged victims be given advance notice before their attackers were released from prison, to prepare themselves psychologically Mar '94; welcomed application of European directive giving part-time women workers maternity benefits Apr '94; voted for Blair as Leader and Prescott as Deputy Leader July '94; proposed community treatment rather than custodial treatment for young offenders in debate on Criminal Justice and Public Order Bill Oct '94; urged more openness in the operation of hospital trusts, especially in discharging old people on grounds of "increased efficiency" Nov '94; was named as part of the 'New Clause IV Campaign' to mobilise party members to support change Dec '94; again urged more consultation, citing unwelcome cuts in speech therapy services Feb '95; criticised loss of jobs and Treasury revenue in privatisation of regional electricity companies Feb '95; urged better after-care in mental illness June '95; introduced Bill to register all fostering agencies Oct '95; appointed an Assistant Whip, was dropped from the Trade & Industry Select Committee Nov '95; after the death of a local child, urged an inquiry into adequacy of local ambulance service Dec '95; complained about inflexible and stressful working practices in Commons Feb '96; because of gas fire risks, protested cuts in Health and Safety Executive Mar '96; speaking for the first time from the Dispatch Box during International Women's Week, urged a Cabinet Minister for Women and more women Tory Parliamentary candidates Mar '96; with Tessa Jowell and Irene Adams began a 'Talking to Women' tour Apr '96; voted against a 3% cap on MPs' pay rise, in favour of a pension based on £43,000 and for a cut in MPs' mileage allowance July '96; was named as an Assistant Spokesman on Health, specialising in community care July '96; defended Blackpool North's Labour candidate, Joan Humble, against attacks by threatened local Tory MPs Nov '96; backed tougher discipline for Labour MPs, warning "the electorate do not like parties that are divided by internal warfare" Dec '96; urged a legal framework for treating the elderly to prevent local authorities charging them for services Dec '96; criticised the Asylum and Immigration Act 1996 for cruelly withdrawing benefits from asylum-seekers Mar '97; with 71 others, was targeted by The FIELD for her opposition to fox-hunting Apr '97; was re-elected for previously marginal Stockport with a quadrupled majority of 18,912 on a notional pro-Labour swing of 15.2% May '97; was named as Tony Blair's second PPS May '97;

Born: 31 August 1946, Inverness

Family: D late John Brown MBE, "one of seven from a poor urban background" who was in the RAF, and Marie (Mackay), "a nurse from a poor rural background" (AC)); m '73 Thomas Coffey; divorced '89; 1d Kate '77, "with whom I get on in spite of everything"; Kate went to Sussex University;

Education: Because her father was in the RAF, her early education was diverse: in Kinloss, Nairn and Cornwall; Polytechnic of the South Bank (BSc in Sociology); Manchester University (MSc; PG Certificate in Education; Certificate of Qualification in Social Work);

Occupation: On Parliamentary Panel of USDAW ("no personal financial benefit") '92-95; ex: Social Worker: Team Leader in Fostering and Adoption for Oldham '88-92; Social Worker: in Cheshire, '82-88, Stockport '77-82, Wolverhampton '75-76, Gwynedd 73-74, Birmingham '72-73; Trainee Social Worker, Walsall (NALGO) '71-72;

Traits: Tall; slim; pleasant-looking; dark hair; wears centre-parted bangs; because she was moved around so much as a child, because of her father's RAF postings "I think it made me a

very good survivor"; "I suppose my ambition is to be competent in everything I do"' "I am one of those people who, from time to time, feels guilty about not going to the gym"; "I like chess but am not very good at it"; "I would like to do more water-colour painting" (AC); hopes that politics will not dominate every aspect of her life; she admires women who can juggle family and political obligations;
Address: House of Commons, Westminster, SW1A 0AA;
Telephone: 0171 219 4546 (H of C); 0161 491 0615 (constituency office);

Harry (Michael) COHEN   **Labour**   **LEYTON & WANSTEAD '97-**

Majority: 15,186 (38.6%) over Conservative 5-way;
Description: This seat, reshaped and renamed in '95, is three-quarters old Leyton, topped up by 15,000 mostly Tory-leaning voters from abolished Wanstead and Woodford; basically an East End seat with some good and some poor terraced houses; Asians and blacks, including Somalis, make up a third of its voters; it also has a second-division football club, Leyton Orient;
Former Seat: Leyton '83-97
Position: On Defence Select Committee '97-; Vice Chairman '92-, '86-87, Chairman '87-92, PLP Defence Committee; Alternate Delegate, to OSCE Assembly (Vice Chairman, its Co-operation and Convergence with Eastern Europe Subcommittee) '92-; ex: Vice Chairman, PLP Treasury and Civil Service Committee '87-88; Waltham Forest Borough Councillor '72-83;
Outlook: A shaven and mellowed, increasingly-effective operator, deflected recently to the Defence Select Committee; has also shifted his focus to the OSCE Assembly, where he resists US Rightwingers placing too heavy a burden on new NATO members; the widely-popular, hyper-assiduous hard-Left pacifist prober of nuclear and government computer secrets; a strong defender of women, gays' and ethnic minority rights; "a Leftie of the 'cheeky monkey' school" (Matthew Parris, TIMES), "he provides the East Ender's answer to what the West End calls 'bottom' in politics; Cohen has no 'bottom' at all, but has a lively mind, a sharp eye for emperors without clothes and a gift for one-liners; although beholden to the predictable Left causes, Cohen is no machine-politician; perhaps it is his humour, perhaps his taste for minority campaigns, but Cohen sounds like his own man; he lacks the sourness of his comrades, and is liked by those who notice" (TIMES); "a small, irascible, [formerly] bearded presence but capable of largeness of mind"; he "sometimes speaks raucously for himself, sometimes raucously for a few fellow Leftwingers," occasionally speaks "raucously for the whole House, or at least for an awful lot of it" (Colin Welch, DAILY MAIL); "a good solid performer who has been a good mate on difficult issues" (Dennis Skinner MP); a receptive funnel for Leftwing lobbyists and researchers; a Leftwing accountant and Jewish pro-Arab; a prolific spawner of Private Member's and 10-minute-rule Bills; initially Labour's Livingstoneite replacement for SDP defector Bryan Magee; a loyal Campaign Group activist, at first as an acolyte of Tony Banks and Jeremy Corbyn; originally thought endangered by boundary changes; anti-nuclear (and pro-Clinton); animal-lover; unexpectedly popular with Tories, partly because of his assiduity, East End wit and verbal felicity ("following my vote against

war in the Gulf, one of the tabloid papers described me as a treacherous swine, because I voted to save our soldiers' bacon"); "very popular" (ex Tory Minister David Trippier); "one of the aficionados" of data protection who "always speaks with great seriousness and expertise" (Tory ex-Minister Tim Renton); "always argues passionately on behalf of whatever case he raises" (Tory Minister Charles Wardle); "always extremely succinct, logical and clear in his argument" (Tory ex-Minister Roger Freeman); "a strong supporter of the rights and privileges of back benchers seeking to introduce legislation" (Tory MP Michael Colvin); "a tireless campaigner for human rights in all sorts of areas" (Tory ex-MP Jerry Hayes);

History: He joined the Labour Party at 16, '65; was elected to Waltham Forest Borough Council at 23, May '72; was selected for Leyton, in wake of Bryan Magee's defection to SDP and NEC-endorsed July '82; signed statement of pro-Arab Labour Middle East Council urging recognition of PLO as "the legitimate representative of the Palestinian people" and supporting their "inalienable rights...to self-determination" Apr '83; was elected for Leyton, pushing Bryan Magee into third place June '83; in Maiden supported Greenham Common women and Nuclear Free Zones July '83; joined Campaign Group July '83; favoured a heavy-lorry ban for London July '83; voted against Defence Estimates July '83; was one of five hard Left Labour MPs to provide an audience in the Commons room for Sinn Fein MP Gerry Adams July '83; urged government to protest US involvement in Central America July '83; co-signed a letter to TIMES protesting the "obvious war intentions of President Reagan" in Nicaragua Aug '83; worried about British military personnel in Kenya Jan '84; instead of abstaining, voted against union ban at GCHQ Feb '84; introduced Bill to avoid immigrants losing their entry clearance because the spouse has died - as in the Afia Begum case - or there has been a divorce Mar '84; signed all-party plea for Shcharansky Mar '84; was rebuked by Speaker for "reprehensible" smear of Leon Brittan by quoting disgruntled MI5 officers in PRIVATE EYE about his behaviour on the Libyan Embassy siege June '84; with Banks, Corbyn and Chris Smith shouted "object!" to introduction of Prevention of Intimidatory Picketing Bill July '84; in debate on Warnock Report, complained about those who hijacked embryo experimentation for their anti-abortion obsession Nov '84; attacked Government for refusing to act on acid rain Jan '85; criticised the Interception of Communications Bill as "puny" and "ineffective" in proposing "a toothless poodle" rather than an effective watchdog Mar '85; in Budget debate described unemployment as the "Government's central weapon of fear" to keep wage settlements low Apr '85; was accused of selfishness by the Speaker for repeatedly asking questions on security matters at the time of the Bettany affair May '85; Speaker refused as "unbecoming" his motion criticising BUPA for telling Princess Michael its doctor's prize-winning work was on peptic ulcers when it was on testicles May '85; wrote to Lord Chancellor urging the removal of a local magistrate who called the rape of a prostitute "a contradiction in terms" May '85; LABOUR HERALD criticised "vacillating" Labour Party for allowing a free vote on the Powell Bill on embryo experimentation May '85; his questions showed a tenth of the population were on police computers, including spent convictions June '85; in LABOUR HERALD disclosed that 4,000 miners' cars were on police computers June '85; introduced his ten-minute-rule Racial Harassment Bill, the first on this subject July '85; was re-selected from short-list of one July '85; again called on Government to introduce a Bill to ban racial harassment Aug '85; went on US tour sponsored by US-UK Parliamentary Group Sep '85; his article in Corbyn-edited LONDON LABOUR BRIEFING urged Racial Harassment Bill Oct '85; in debate on Armed Forces Bill said homosexuality should be no basis for discrimination -also urged allowing trade unions in armed forces Nov '85; with most of the Campaign Group, voted against the Anglo-Irish Agreement Nov '85; opposed the Animal Experiments Bill as inadequate; said he preferred stunning before ritual slaughter, brought in by consultation, not legislation Feb '86; after having been "the first Western Parliamentarian to meet

[Afghanistan's] new leader, Doctor Najeeb", wrote a sympathetic article about the regime in the Trotskyist LABOUR HERALD, repeating uncritically Dr Najeeb's claim that the Soviets were there "to protect our country from outside interference" June '86; co-attacked US bombing of Libya from UK bases Apr '86; urged tougher penalties for dog-fighting June '86; in adjournment debate urged the Birmingham pub bombing case be sent to the Court of Appeal July '86; queried Masonic links in the police Dec '86; asked for a statement on French kissing and AIDS Dec '86; introduced Bill to give either parent of small children statutory right to paid leave Feb '87; in adjournment debate urged weeding out of police computer records Feb '87; introduced Bill to amend Data Protection Act May '87; participated in demonstration on steps of South African Embassy but police refused to arrest him July '87; with Corbyn and Diane Abbott visited hunger-striking Tamils Aug '87; sponsored Unemployed Workers' Charter at TUC Sep '87; in debate on Data Protection he urged fewer exemptions and wider and simpler access Oct '87; with Joan Ruddock was dropped by Labour as a candidate for Defence Select Committee because of MoD doubts about making documents available to them, as CNDers Nov '87; backed the right of Commons access for Corbyn's ex-IRA-sympathising research assistant Nov '87; again introduced Bill to amend Data Protection Act Nov '87; welcomed Arms Control and Disarmament Bill giving powers for USSR inspectors to visit UK INF missile sites Dec '87; headed a motion urging Israel to stop brutality on West Bank and withdraw Jan '88; was suspended from sitting after criticising Speaker for refusing to call him on ratecapping of his local council Feb '88; was accused of filibustering against David Alton's abortion-curbing Bill Feb '88; accused John Gummer of bishop-bashing Mar '88; visited Cyprus as guest of Friends of Cyprus Apr '88; backed Dave Nellist against Speaker's suspension Apr '88; co-sponsored Tony Benn's Bill against foreign nuclear bases Apr '88; criticised Israeli murder of Abu Jihad Apr '88; backed John Browne's Bill against dog-fighting by amending it to ban advertising such fights Apr '88; complained about cuts in Waltham Forest health services May '88; focussed on racism in Special Branch June '88; was found to have asked the most questions in the previous year July '88; tried to limit Government's data available to poll tax registrars July '88; backed Benn's effort to revolutionise the constitution July '88; co-urged UK to condemn Iraqi gassing of Kurds Sep '88; voted against money resolution for EC Oct '88; voted against Defence Estimates, instead of abstaining Oct '88; co-sponsored motion opposing China's suppression of Tibet Oct '88; re-introduced Parental Leave Bill for working parents of young children, to allow them three months' paid leave during the first two years of their child's life Nov '88; voted against loyalty oaths in Northern Ireland, instead of abstaining Dec '88; voted against Prevention of Terrorism Bill, instead of abstaining Dec '88; welcomed Security Service Bill as putting MI5 on a statutory footing but deplored the permission it gave to break into the homes of suspects without a warrant Dec '88; on Valentine's Day, introduced his Poll Tax (Restoration of Individual Privacy) Bill to bar "an orgasm of privacy abuse" by poll tax collectors pursuing partners and ex-partners Feb '89; paid tribute to Palestinian Intifada and deplored "well over 300 murders inflicted by the Israeli occupying forces" Feb '89; 'Black Sections' announced his was one of the seats they would target Feb '89; opposed new automatic exit barriers on London Transport Feb '89; in reply to his specific question, Mrs Thatcher denied a change in UK policy or guidelines on supplying equipment to Iraqi arms factories (answers which figured in the '94 Scott Inquiry) Apr '89; suggested Hillsborough disaster might have been caused by a computer failure which made it impossible to realise there was plenty of space on the terraces Apr '89; co-protested Neil Kinnock's abandonment of unilateralism May '89; complained bitterly that City of London Bill "steals Leyton's forest land and gives it no proper replacement" May '89; complained "the Government are riding roughshod over" "the Data Protection Act 1984" May '89; backed dog registration June '89; introduced Bill banning useless animal experimentation June '89; urged monitoring of servicemen who might contract AIDS in African bordellos June '89; urged "a strategic planning authority for London" to deal with its roads and markets June '89; complained about huge pay rises for the boss of P&O June '89; was rated as having asked the 4th most questions (551) in '88-89, Jan '90; again voted against EC measure Jan '90; opposed sale of information from electoral registers Jan '90; proposed Poll Tax (Restoration of Privacy) Bill Jan '90; urged redeployment of Royal Navy vessels on anti-drugs work with US Coastguard Feb '90; criticised Michael Colvin's anti-hacking Computer Misuse Bill as "ill-defined and lopsided"; urged charge be laid also against owners of computers left open to interference Feb '90; had adjournment debate to protest UK Government's approval of reopening of Hongkong ivory market which threatened declining African elephants Feb '90; introduced his Rape in Marriage (Offence) Bill to make it a criminal offence Feb '90; worried that sailors on nuclear submarines were exposed to radiation Feb '90; backed fund-raising by MORNING STAR as providing "diverse editorial opinion" Feb '90; said "people are fed up with being bled white and blue" by poll tax Mar '90; insisted he remained committed to not paying his poll tax: "it may be gesture politics, but I will have my five minutes in court" Apr '90; having served on committee for Computer Misuse Bill, urged search warrants be issued by circuit judges rather than more compliant justices of the peace; also worried about MI5 being authorised to hack into computers May '90; put down blocking motion and filibustered to stymie London Regional Transport Bill May '90; signed advertisement of Joint Committee for Palestine urging boycott of Israeli produce until violations of Palestinian Arabs' human rights ceased June '90; introduced Computers (Compensation for Damage) Bill July '90; introduced Declaration of War and Commitment of Troops Abroad (Constitutional Arrangements) Bill to ensure that war could not be declared or troops committed overseas without Commons approval July '90; introduced Mortgage Assistance Bill to allow for shared ownership where mortgagor was unable to meet repayments July '90; led motion condemning "Iraq's invasion of Kuwait as a clear act of aggression" but opposing the Government's "efforts to make war in the interests of cheap oil for the United States" Sep '90; claimed Mrs Thatcher was "using war in the Gulf as a political tool" to bolster her challenged leadership Nov '90; just back from Bangladesh, urged more aid for it and rest of 3rd World, financed by cuts in arms trade Dec '90; repeatedly opposed Gulf War Dec '90, Jan '91; decided not to move his Declaration of War (Requirement of Parliamentary Approval) Bill Jan '91; alleged Government was planning to reintroduce conscription Jan '91; backed Sir Richard Body's Pig Husbandry Bill to abolish cruelty to pregnant sows Jan '91; warned against new war aims, including assassination of Saddam Hussein and invasion of Iraq Feb '91; co-complained that Kuwait had been liberated but not Palestinian Arabs Feb '91; co-complained about "barbaric slaughter of innocent men, women and children in Baghdad" caused by US bombing Feb '91; sought to have "consenting homosexual behaviour removed from the list of serious sex crims" in Criminal Justice Bill which "increased penalties for consensual gay relationships" Feb '91; introduced Bill to ban hare-coursing Feb '91; complained London was being over-charged for council tax because its expensive property did not have separate regional banding Apr '91; deplored excessive force used against Iraq, including 50% more bomb tonnage than used in Vietnam war May '91; led motion deploring Government incompetence on AIDS and HIV May '91; introduced Sexual Offences (Amendment) Bill to protect women at risk June '91; lengthily and sharply criticised the "inept" "shysters" of London Regional Transport for depriving his constituents of bus services July '91; in the run-up to the general election, the Conservative Party alleged he was a Militant-sympathiser Aug '91; urged Home Secretary to reform the Metropolitan Police, which had split over reforms Oct '91; claimed that, as with the poll tax, the Government was not allowing local councils enough time to secure the computer software to collect council tax

Nov '91; co-sponsored Tony Benn's pro-referendum amendment to Bill endorsing Maastricht Nov '91; went on good-will trip to Libya organized by Bernie Grant MP Nov '91; introduced debate deploring "increasing use of knives in crimes of violence" Dec '91; with Tony Benn, Ken Livingstone and others co-urged "a commitment from the next [Labour] Government to withdraw from Ireland" Jan '92; introduced Hare Coursing Bill to ban the 'sport' Mar '92; introduced Newsprint Recycling Bill requiring a minimum content of recycled paper Mar '92; described Norman Lamont's Budget as "bent as a £28b note"; retained seat with majority up from 4,641 to 11,484, a swing to Labour of 8.84% Apr '92; was elected by PLP to North Atlantic Assembly May '92; was rebuked by new Speaker Boothroyd for attacking "the monarch's private greed" for retaining a claim on the property of anyone in the Duchy of Lancaster who died without leaving a will June '92; urged admission of RSPCA inspectors to factory farms June '92; introduced Homicide (Defence of Provocation) Bill, to change the definition of provocation, allowing plea of manslaughter for sustained domestic violence "which drives some women out of desperation to act" July '92; introduced new Sexual Offences (Amendment) Etc Bill, which redefined rape and also made rape of a male a specific criminal offence Oct '92; was rated the 13th most assiduous poser of written questions in '91-92, with 180 posed Oct '92; was rated the 8th most active poser of written questions in first half of '92, with 160 posed Oct '92; was ousted as Chairman of PLP's Defence Committee by pro-Trident John Hutton, being demoted to Vice Chairman Nov '92; asked PM John Major to be "a little less economical with the actuality" about Matrix Churchill trial Nov '92; urged better relations with Libya which was probably not "solely responsible" for Lockerbie bombing, and "progressive easing of sanctions" against Iraq, because of child malnutrition there Nov '92; was refused information about use of primates in laboratories to test medical counter-measures against chemical and biological weapons Nov '92; accused Home Under Secretary Charles Wardle of being "rude and racist" about deportation of Ugandan Dr Munuku Mulopwe, which he had tried to stop Jan '93; on St Valentine's Day, introduced Weddings Bill to provide for flexible marriage sites Feb '93; introduced debate on Animals (Scientific Procedures) Act 1986 to try to reduce use of animals in unnecessary laboratory tests Feb '93; again introduced Hare Coursing Bill Feb '93; asked about fatal accidents at Aldermaston Feb '93; secured debate on operational guidelines for Child Support Agency Apr '93; backed school supply of contraceptives for teenagers Apr '93; again enthused about Nuclear Non-proliferation Treaty Apr '93; introduced amendment to Sexual Offences Bill - to abolish assumption that a boy under 14 was incapable of sexual intercourse - and to remove words describing gay sex as "unnatural" Apr '93; introduced his Abortion Clinic (Access) Bill to ban harassment or intimidation May '93; co-urged new hearing of case which kept Winston Silcott in prison after being released as one of the 'Tottenham Three' May '93; challenged UK Government's claim to buy Trident missiles from US at £24m per missile when it cost the US £49m per missile May '93; co-sponsored Jeremy Corbyn's Bill to give pensioners equal retirement at 60, July '93; the Boundary Commission's intention of reducing the number of local seats, threw a cloud over his political future July '93; was greeted with questions, "is it Harry?" when he appeared beardless in Commons Oct '93; accused Government of contriving to have "London Underground going down the tube" by killing its management's 10-year modernisation plan Oct '93; complained the Government was creating tensions with Washington by undermining US efforts towards non-proliferation Oct '93; voted against Defence Estimates, instead of abstaining Oct '93; was rated the 12 most active quesioner in the 1992-93 session, with 571 questions Jan '94; was found to be the 10th most active questioner in the previous year, with 403 questions costing £39,000 to answer Feb '94; voted against restoring capital punishment, even for killers of policemen Feb '94; voted to reduce age of homosexual consent to 18 or 16, Feb '94; again urged a new law to deal with racial attacks

Mar '94; again criticised M11 Link Road scheme Mar '94; organised visit of Soviet Ambassador to PLP Defence Committee Apr '94; accused Tory Minister David McLean of "a lamentable error of judgement" in having failed to take seriously Cohen's 1990 query about "mad cat disease", dismissing it as "a crazy panic over pet food", although McLean's successor had admitted to 47 cases of feline spongiform encephalopathy May '94; again introduced Bill to make it easier for women to plead provocation as a homocide defence after years of violent abuse May '94; again urged tougher UK persuasion of EC partners on animal welfare, to prevent curbs on "freedom from hunger and thirst and from distress" June '94; posed series of questions on Porton Down tests on animals June '94; led motion attacking partnership of Holiday Inn with Chinese Government to build a hotel in Tibet July '94; introduced Bill to allow payments for unfair dismissal to come from Redundancy Fund if employers became insolvent July '94; voted for Margaret Beckett for Leader and Deputy Leader July '94; backed Tory MP Giles Brandreth's Marriage Bill to extend sites for marriages July '94; introduced ten-minute-rule Bill to allow a plea of provocation for battered wives who kill their violent partners July '94; co-signed Campaign Group letter protesting Criminal Justice Bill's alleged criminalising of protest and removal of right to silence in court Aug '94; challenged alleged over-provision of hospital beds in London in debate he launched Oct '94; introduced Bill to provide equitable division of pensions in divorces Nov '94; voted with other Eurosceptic rebels against the EU Finance Bill Nov '94; was credited with voting in 59% of all divisions in the '93-94 session Dec '94; voted against extension of Sunday pub licensing hours Feb '95; complained of discrimination against women Mar '95; co-wrote GUARDIAN letter opposing "draconian police powers to stop and search, which will send shivers of alarm through black communities across Britain" Apr '95; attacked as "an abuse of state power" raid of MoD police on Greenpeace headquarters May '95; claimed that in World War II Britain was "very happy to have many men of homosexual orientation lay down their lives for this country" May '95; backed 'Women Against Rape' and 'Legal Action for Women' in campaign against CPS for prosecuting only 20% of rape cases May '95; claimed a majority of London Labour MPs wanted to lift the Services' ban on homosexuals June '95; spoke for 150 minutes against Westminster closing down gay bars June '95; called for ban on export of landmines in TRIBUNE Oct '95; voted against Defence Estimates with 23 other, mostly hard-Left, Labour rebels Oct '95; blamed the spread of the deadly MRSA staphylococcus in hospitals on privatising cleaning services Dec '95; opposed expansion of MI5's role as a threat to civil liberties Jan '96; attacked disproportionate deaths in custody of members of ethnic minorities Feb '96; again urging nuclear disarmament, deplored waste of £155m on nuclear submarine 'Renown' Feb '96; urged removal of poverty traps in welfare-to-work, which had caught his foster son, Mark Feb '96; with 24 other Labour rebels, mainly hard-Left, voted against guillotining and renewal of Prevention of Terrorism Act Apr '96; with other Campaign Groupies, co-signed letter to GUARDIAN urging scrapping of Trident July '96; was listed as one of "Blair's Bastards" in Hull University research for voting against the leadership 36 times since '92, Sep '96; dismissed the Royal Yacht as a "silly status symbol" Jan '97; was targeted by the Prolife Alliance Party for his pro-abortion role Feb '97; urged lifting of "cruel sanctions" harming Iraqi children Feb '97; voted against creating a national police service Feb '97; urged getting 600,000 young off the dole instead of the 250,000 planned by Labour Apr '97; retained extended, renamed seat with an enhanced majority of 15,186 on a notional swing of 11.8% May '97; complained his local Whipps Cross Hospital was £4m in the red May '97; complained of potential traffic complications from local impact of Channel Tunnel Link and its Stratford station June '97; was named to Defence Select Committee July '97; was named an Alternate Delegate to the Parliamentary Asssembly of OSCE July '97; presented Bill to bar school absenteeism July '97; helped calculate the cost of NATO expansion Nov '97; was one of 47

Labour rebels against cutting lone-parent benefits Dec '97; urged Home Secretary Jack Straw to set Reggie Kray free in the new year Dec '97; again complained about Iraqi sanctions harming almost 1m children Jan '98; voted against military action in Iraq Feb '98; said, "we must resist pressure from militarists and US Rightwingers to insist on high defence spending across Europe and especially in the new countries" July '98; was one of 24 Labour rebels voting against Murdoch-style predatory newspaper pricing July '98;

Born: 10 December 1949, Hackney

Family: S Emanuel Cohen, ex taxi-driver, and Annie (Cohen); m '78 divorcee Ellen Hussain (nee Laffy), FE college lecturer; a stepson Mark '34, petshop owner, a stepdaughter, Leila Hussain '33 who was his secretary, recently a mental health social worker; one foster-son, Mark '75;

Education: George Gascoigne Secondary Modern; East Ham Technical College (day release); Chartered Institute of Public Finance and Accountancy; Birkbeck College (MSc in Politics and Administration '92-94);

Occupation: Beneficiary, of donation from UNISON (£500 p a "paid into my office costs allowance") '92-95; Accountant (ACTSS): ex: Auditor, in Local Government and NALGO;

Traits: Short; slight; dark; formerly bearded; Jewish; "ever-affable" (Charles Kennedy MP); "cuddly" "straightforward" (Michael White, GUARDIAN); "a Cockney sparrow of an MP, short and cheeky" (TIMES); his "awkward stance when he rises from his place suggests that he has left the coat-hanger in his trousers" (Simon Heffer, DAILY TELEGRAPH); "rocks as he debates, right thumb tucked into the top of his trouser" (Quentin Letts, DAILY TELEGRAPH); "swarthy, [ex-]bearded and bespectacled" with an "awkward, shambling walk", "he reminded me of the amiable Russian revolutionary who turns up in the Railway Children" (Colin Welch, DAILY MAIL); "he sounds a kindly if rather vulnerable little chap, and seems to invite concern as to whether he has any sheltered hostel to go to at night" (Matthew Parris, TIMES); his musical tastes were considered the "funkiest" (Martin Linton, GUARDIAN) among Labour MPs in '96 because of his preference for Sid Vicious, Sex Pistols, Stranglers, Leonard Cohen, and Iggy Pop and Debby Harry; initially showed tasteless humour, later improved; has a talent for vivid phrases, contrasts and sharply pointed questions like that which skewered Mrs Thatcher on sales of arms to Iraq;

Address: House of Commons, Westminster, London SW1A 0AA; 1 Lytton Road, Leytonstone, E11 1JQ;

Telephone: 0171 219 4137/6376 (H of C);

TAPPING INTO OUR COMPUTERS
The factual way in which we compress MPs' involvement in issues, big and small, has turned out to be a goldmine for those using our computers for searches. A client asked for a search on the Falkland Islands. To our surprise, the printer churned out over 30 pages of information which, cleaned up, yielded 10,000 words of information on all the positions taken by all the politicians involved, including the furious reactions to late Nicholas Ridley's 1980 proposal to hand the islands over to Argentina and then lease it back. We only charge £250 for such a computer search. Call us at 0171 222 5884 or Fax us at 0171 222 5889.

Majority: 3,842 over Conservative 9-way;

Description: The home of both Fulham FC and Chelsea FC; a '95 amalgam of the evenly-balanced five most southerly parts of Hammersmith merged with partly-yuppified Fulham; despite such infiltration, it is the UK's 16th poorest borough; 35% of the constituency's households are on benefit, with 53% of its schoolchildren entitled to free school meals; nevertheless until May '97 this seat was expected to be held by the Conservatives;

Position: On the Deregulation Committee '97-; Hammersmith and Fulham Councillor (its Leader '91-) '91-; ex: Hammersmith Borough Councillor (Chief Whip til '86) til 91;

Outlook: The Leftish Leader of Hammersmith & Fulham Council who unexpectedly captured its new Parliamentary seat; a "principled and hard-working 'Hain-ite', sympathetic to the Left" (RED PEPPER); was a supporter of old Clause IV; a slow starter in the Commons, rating as one of the 'Bottom 100' for having posed only two written questions in his first year;

History: He came from a Labour family, his psychologist mother becoming Mayor of Barnet and his brother, Neale, becoming a leading objector to the Conservatives' 'homes for votes' ramp on Westminster Council; Iain joined the Labour Party '78; elected to Hammersmith Borough Council, became its Chief Whip; resigned as Chief Whip on Hammersmith Council, in protest against service cuts '86; became Leader of Hammersmith and Fulham Borough Council May '91; when Westminster City Council's misdeeds were under attack in Parliament, the then Tory MP for Dover, the widely-criticised David Shaw, made libel-proof attacks in the Commons against the whole Coleman family, against Iain's brother Neale, as well as his mother and father; his father was erroneously accused of having run "the Ann Summers chain of sex shops"; his brother was misleadingly accused of causing the suicide of the Tory councillor Dr Michael Dutt by raising the 'homes for votes' scandal in which Dr Dutt was involved; Shaw refused to repeat the charges outside Parliament, where he could have been sued for libel May '96; was criticised by the sitting Tory MP, Matthew Carrington for becoming Mayor during the election campaign; unexpectedly, Iain won the Hammersmith and Fulham seat, defeating Fulham's former Tory MP, Matthew Carrington by 3,842 votes, on a notional swing of 10.06%, May '97; in his Maiden welcomed the Bill offering a phased release of council housing funds; in his constituency, 6,000 families were on the housing register, 2,724 were on the housing transfer list; social housing was desperately needed "with a three-bedroom flat in South Fulham costing an average of £200,000" June '97; launched motion to provide surviving gay partners with same protection against eviction as heterosexual partners July '97; was named to the Deregulation Committee Aug '97; co-sponsored motion criticising ex-PM John Major for not condemning Dame Shirley Porter after the High Court had found her "guilty of wilful misconduct" costing Westminster Council £27m Jan '98; backed Hillingdon Hospital strikers May '98; was rated among the 'Bottom 100' for having posed only two written questions in his first year May '98; urged Board of Trade President Margaret Beckett to investigate banks' and building societies' sharp practices in mortgage lending June '98;

Born: 18 January 1958, London

Family: His father worked in the '70s for the same company that owned the Ann Summers

shops; his mother, Pamela, Mayor of Barnet '95-96, was an NHS psychologist for 30 years; his brother, Neale, was a Westminster Labour Councillor for 8 years; m '96 Sally (Powell) 1 s;
Education: Tonbridge School;
Occupation: Leader, of Hammersmith and Fulham Borough Council (UNISON, ex-MSF) '91-; previously a local government administrator in Ealing and Islington;
Traits: Full-faced; parted thinning hair; retreating hairline; specs; worried expression; has been an Arsenal FC season ticket-holder for over 20 years and very rarely misses a match, home or away;
Address: House of Commons, Westminster, London SW1A 0AA;
Telephone: 0171 219 4486/2820 (Fax; H of C); 0171 381 5074/386 5415(Fax; constituency);

Tim(othy William George) COLLINS CBE   Conservative   **WESTMORLAND & LONSDALE '97-**

Majority: 4,521 over Liberal Democrat 4-way;
Description: The slightly altered sprawling eastern Cumbria seat; largely agricultural and Tory but also a tourist haven, taking in the southern Lake District; it has some light industry in Kendal; a "curious mixture of farmers in tweeds and sprightly geriatrics in spotless Barbours" (INDEPENDENT);
Position: Whip '98-; on Select Committee on Agriculture '97-98; ex: Media Consultant, to Conservative Party Chairman Dr Brian Mawhinney '96-97; in Prime Minister John Major's Policy Unit '95;
Outlook: The new Tories' classiest, wittiest Labour-baiter; the ultimate former back-room "whizz-kid" who made a delayed start as an able counter-propagandist - due to his father's accidental death - but began by backing his old boss Michael Howard for the Tory Leadership; the highly-regarded former party press apparatchik who won this safe seat in the wake of his services to former PM John Major; "razor-sharp" (James Blitz, FINANCIAL TIMES); "the finest communications chief since Michael Dobbs 10 years ago" (Peter Oborne, EVENING STANDARD); thought likely to be "his generation's Norman Tebbit, but with gentler manners" ('Quidnunc', SUNDAY TIMES); has become an active constituency MP; has a "good feeling for politics and a passionate loathing of Labour"; "he has developed a formidable political brain which can come up wih a counter-offensive at speed; after a political controversy has died down, it is often his sulphurous words, whispered anonymously by Mr Collins, that stick in the mind" (Russell Jenkins, TIMES); the former "Conservative Central Office media guru who claimed the credit for John Major's victory at the [1992] general election" (Paul Routledge, INDEPENDENT ON SUNDAY); spent his whole previous career in Westminster, whether Smith Square or Downing Street; a cautious Eurosceptic who has remained apart from the near-religious war over Europe which has raged in the columns of the DAILY TELEGRAPH;
History: His family were Essex Conservatives, active mainly as councillors; his mother was Chairman of the Epping Forest Conservative Association; he joined Conservative Central Office after university '86; festooned his Pimlico flat with photographs of Margaret Thatcher;

worked as a ministerial aide to Cabinet Ministers David Hunt and Michael Howard, and as speech-writer to Prime Ministers Margaret Thatcher and John Major; protested against the dropping of his heroine, Margaret Thatcher Nov '90; reappeared as a Major loyalist Dec '90; was with John Major "throughout the historic [and victorious] day and night of 9th April 1992" (TC); in briefing the press, claimed that Major's "Back to Basics" speech was aimed at "rolling back the permissive society" Oct '93; was there to brief the press when John Major defeated John Redwood, describing it as a "crushing, clear-cut victory" although 109 Tory MPs failed to support Major; described some of Redwood's suporters as a "swivel-eyed barmy army from Ward 8 at Broadmoor" July '95; he denies that he was recommended by John Major or Central Office for selection to follow Michael Jopling at Westmorland and Lonsdale; he was able to reassure local selectors about his Rightwing roots; his selection made him one of only two bachelors picked for safe Tory seats July '95; on his selection, retired from Central Office but was re-appointed as a Media Adviser by Dr Mawhinney Nov '95; was rewarded with a CBE June '96; with five other loyal Tory candidates for safe seats, wrote to the DAILY TELEGRAPH stating that "the Prime Minister must be prepared to put Britain's interest first in negotiations with Europe even if this means standing alone" but that "Britain is right to make a full and constructive contribution to the debate within Europe before any decisions are taken on a single currency" Dec '96; was drafted in by Dr Brian Mawhinney to be the party's media guru at the Wirral South by-election; "Mr Collins' job is to harry and harass Labour at every turn to ensure that it does not inflict such a humiliating defeat that voters go to the polls in the general election with a stirring victory for Labour still fresh in their minds" (Russell Jenkins, TIMES) Feb '97; he blamed the disastrous result at Wirral South on the media not getting the Government's message Feb '97; retained Westmorland with a shrunken majority of 4,521 over the Liberal Democrat challenger, after a swing from the Conservatives of 10.26% May '97; backed his former boss, Michael Howard, for the Tory leadership May-June '97; in his Maiden admitted that since his constituency stretched from Yorkshire into Lancashire, it was unwise to comment on the War of the Roses or test cricketers Mike Atherton and Geoff Boycott June '97; accused some Labour local authorities of "blackmail" over early education June '97; objected to curbing the Budget debate July '97; urged US-style repositioning of lorry exhausts July '97; urged extra subsidies for sheep farmers since "much of the beauty of areas such as the Lake District depends on the hard work of hill farmers" July '97; was named to the Select Committee on Agriculture July '97; made a powerful speech at the Tories' annual conference at Blackpool Oct '97; complained the Blair Government was selling the pass on European federalism Nov '97; again attacked European federalism Jan '98; made a wholly hostile attack on the Regional Development Agencies Bill Jan '98; on the Agriculture Select Committee, helped bait Agriculture Minister Jack Cunningham on the understated costs of moving his office Mar '98; asked the Speaker whether PM Blair would clear up his relations with Rupert Murdoch about which his press office had "scandalously abused and insulted journalists" Mar '98; spoke movingly of a constituent's pains from Adhesive Arachnoiditis Mar '98; baited MP Tony Blair on his conversation with Italian PM Prodi about BSkyB's access to Italian TV Mar '98; had only limited hesitations about the Government's Crime and Disorder Bill Apr '98; opposed penalising farmers who had admitted honest errors on complex EU forms Apr '98; in his well-informed contribution to the RAF debate, described Ernest Bevin as "the outstanding British Foreign Secretary of this century" Apr '98; asked whether 28-year-old Tim Allan was to be paid £100,000 by BSkyB "because of his mastery of the motor scooter or because of his access to the heart of Government?" Apr '98; opposed giving bail to anyone previously convicted of murder, rape or manslaughter Apr '98; suggested both Tony Lloyd and Robin Cook should resign over the 'arms for Sierre Leone' shambles May '98; was put in charge of liaison with Labour over Proportional Representation May '98; was named a Whip

in the reshuffle, leaving the Agriculture Select Committee June '98;
Born: 7 May 1964, Epping, Essex
Family: Son, of late William Collins, Conservative dairy farmer who died from the electrification of his farm pond in May '97, and Di(ana) (May), Chairman of Epping Conservative Association; m July '97 Clare (Benson) teacher;
Education: Chigwell School; LSE (BSc in International Relations); King's College, London University (MA in War Studies);
Occupation: Ex: Senior Strategy Consultant to WCT Live Communication '95-97; Media Adviser, to Conservative Party Chairman '95-97; in Prime Minister's Policy Unit, 10 Downing Street, '95; Director of Communications, Conservative Central Office '92-95; Founding Chairman, of CCO Conferences Ltd, a company which contracted for services for Central Office, with a turnover of £1m) '94-95; Press Secretary to PM John Major during election campaign Mar-Apr '92; Special Adviser, to Michael Howard at Employment (where he helped campaign against the minimum wage, '90-92; Special Adviser, to Michael Howard and David Hunt, at Environment '89-90; Staffer at Conservative Research Department '86-89;
Traits: Boyish-looking; fresh-faced; front-combed hair; "amiable, mild-mannered" (Chris Moncrieff, HOUSE MAGAZINE): "self-esteeming" (Paul Routledge, INDEPENDENT ON SUNDAY); "looks like Harry Enfield playing a computer nerd"; "he does not drink" (Russell Jenkins, TIMES); "a dead ringer for those chilling Hitler clones, The Boys from Brazil" (MAIL ON SUNDAY); "Trekkie" (a fan of Star Trek, Dr Who and Thunderbird); a Fanta-quaffing junk-food addict; dislikes exercise; "something of a split personality - quiet to the point of gaucheness, but also capable of being uproariously funny"; his Commons speaking style can be boring in tone;
Address: House of Commons, Westminster, London SW1A 0AA;
Telephone: 0171 219 5151 (H of C);

'Tony' (Anthony John) COLMAN   Labour   PUTNEY '97-

Majority: 2,976 over Conservative 10-way;
Description: The leafy, affluent, middle-class seat on the south bank of the Thames which seemed to have become safely Conservative, partly due to the 'Wandsworth effect' of low rates set by its efficient Tory local government; these assumptions were upset by the adverse reactions evoked by its high-profile former Tory MP, David Mellor; despite his many talents, he attracted criticism for his sexual activities, his many partly-declared business interests, and his pro-Europeanism, which made him a target for his Referendum Party opponent, Sir James Goldsmith, since deceased;
Position: PPS to Adam Ingram '98-; Chairman, PLP Trade and Industry Committee '97-; Chairman: Public-Private Partnership Scheme '96-, Labour London Research Centre '94-; ex: on the Select Committee on Treasury Affairs '97-98; Merton Borough Councillor (Leader '91-97) '90-98; Chairman: Low Pay Unit '90-98, UK Standing Committee on Local Government Superannuation '94-98, Local Authorities Mutual Investment Trust '94-98; Vice Chairman, ALA '91-95; on Executive, Labour Finance and Industry Group '70-92; on the Price Commission '77-79;

Outlook: A major new figure at the interface between the Blair leadership and local government; an extremely rare example of a wealthy former captain of industry transformed into a Labour borough chieftain; sensitive to children's special educational needs, as he showed in Merton; "everyone's favourite to be the first of the new intake for promotion" (TIMES); has an "obsession with local government finance" (Robert Hardman, DAILY TELEGRAPH); "the archetypal Christian Socialist Blairite" (Simon Sebag Montefiore, SUNDAY TIMES); "a moderniser" who "favours PR" (NEW STATESMAN); has quoted Thomas Rainborowe, leader of the Levellers, in support of a London mayor and strategic authority elected by PR; a leading member of London Agenda 21 and also a member of the Fabians, the Christian Socialist Movement, Labour Finance and Industry Group;

History: He joined the Labour Party at 29, '72; was named to the Price Commission by the Labour Government '77; contested hopeless South West Hertfordshire against Geoffrey Dodsworth, coming 2nd with 28%, a 5% drop from the previous contest May '79; was elected to Merton Borough Council May '90; became Leader of Merton Borough Council May '91; was selected to contest Putney against David Mellor July '95; like David Mellor and the Referendum Party leader and Putney candidate, Sir James Goldsmith, suffered a break-in, concluding: "someone is clearly trying to undermine the democratic process" Nov '96; after his police constable brother had to face, unarmed, a criminal with a .22, "as a local government leader, I led the movement within London borough councils to pass resolutions proposing a total handgun ban, which were adopted by the UK Local Government Association"; avoided attacking David Mellor for his steamy personal life: "I'm on my third marriage, so I can't talk" Apr '97; admitted that, unlike himself, most local Labour authority leaders preferred London's mayor to be selected from the majority group on any strategic London authority Apr '97; the former Liberal Democrat candidate said, "given the electoral arithmetic in Putney, the only candidate who can beat David Mellor is Tony Colman" Apr '97; won the seat by a majority of 2,976, by London standards a moderate 11.18% swing to Labour; the count was disfigured by extreme taunting between Goldsmith and Mellor May '97; in his Maiden promised to fight his constituency's NHS hospital cuts, air and noise pollution and unemployment; concentrated on economic regeneration, as Chairman of the widely-supported consortium London Agenda 21 Initiative; he also pledged his support for a mayor and London strategic authority, elected by proportional representation June '97; strongly supported the Government's Bill virtually banning handguns, citing his police constable brother's experience with a criminal armed with a .22 and the derisory demonstration (by 78) and vote (90) for the Sportsmen's Alliance candidate in the Putney contest June '97; strongly supported the Government Bill for phased release of housing receipts to increase social housing; he contrasted the behaviour of Merton, the council he had led, in building 3,000 social housing units, and that of Conservative-led Wandsworth which had emphasised selling off its housing stock, often unsuitably; he cited a constituent who, at 78, had had to buy her council flat with a 25-year-long mortgage; "now at the age of 86, she faces huge bills, large service charges and large capital charges amounting to more than £10,000" June '97; urged reversal of severe pre-election cuts imposed on local Queen Mary's University Hospital in Roehampton June '97; as head of the local authorities' pension group, wrote privately to Chancellor Gordon Brown warning that the planned Budget abolition of Advance Corporation Tax "would add at least 3% - or £300m to [local authority] employers' pension costs and compensation would be needed, otherwise there would be further cuts in local services unless there was an increase in the revenue support grant" June '97; when this letter was quoted by a Tory MP, he was compelled to disclose in the Commons that he had received a letter from the Minister for Local Government, Hilary Armstrong, "which plainly states that when the actuarial figures are given following revaluation or the fresh look in 1998 and if it is found that there is a problem, the Government will take such factors into account in determining local authority provision for 1999-2000 and subsequent years" July '97; congratulated Government on closing two meat plants violating anti-BSE rules July '97; was named to the Select Committee on Treasury Affairs July '97; he asked, successfully, for a "pathfinder project for the use of PFI in social housing" July '97; as "a humble back-bencher" took pride in the Local Government (Contracts) Bill, quickly worked out between the new Government and his Public-Private Partnership July '97; strongly criticised the Multilateral Agreement on Investment reached at Earth Summit 2 for its restrictions on hiring local personnel and on use of local materials in manufacturing, pointing out he was the former manager of a multinational (the United Africa Company) July '97; in a letter to the GUARDIAN on vitamin B6 wrote: "I hope the Government will take the initiative if it emerges a mistake has been made in deciding to change the regulation of this vitamin" Aug '97; deplored the "noise pollution" of 1,200 daily flights into Heathrow, largely over Putney Oct '97; backed further consultation on the Wireless Telegraphy Bill, emphasising the importance of proper management of the radio spectrum for radio-controlled taxis and fishermen at sea Oct '97; in the name of the 23 out of 32 Labour-controlled London boroughs, backed an elected mayor and an elected assembly Nov '97; after visiting Ireland with an all-party group, backed the Public Procession Bill Dec '97; in his lengthy speech on Special Educational Needs, emphasised the need to identify autism and treat it sensitively, preferably within mainstream schools, as had been done in Merton Dec '97; congratulated by Minister Frank Field for his local authority's work against housing benefit fraud, he urged Mr Field to persuade banks and building societies to share information with the all-London team against fraud, instead of hiding behind the Data Protection Act 1988, Feb '98; in a debate on Thames Riverside Development favoured "coherent" development backed by local amenity groups over the inappropriate efforts of developers, preferably endorsed by a reconstituted Thames Working Party Feb '98; complained that his Tory-controlled Wandsworth Council was "sitting on more than £30m of balances and refusing to pass a Labour Group proposal for a lower council tax of £295" Mar '98; left the Treasury Select Committee - where he was replaced by David Kidney - to become PPS to Adam Ingram, the Northern Ireland Minister specialising in economic development Mar '98; backed the Late Payments Bill on the basis of his previous experience as a Director of the Burton Group, whose prompt payments enabled designers and manufacturers to pay their cloth manufacturers May '98; led motion backing the Government's unconditional support of emission cuts at Kyoto May '98;

Born: 24 July 1943, Upper Sheringham, Norfolk

Family: Son, of William Benjamin Colman and Beatrice (Hudson); his police constable brother Ronald won the British Empire Medal for disarming a criminal; "a cousin of mine fishes for crab and lobster in the North Sea"; m 3rd Juliet, personnel executive; 5s, 1d, 2 stepc;

Education: Paston Grammar School, North Walsham; Magdalene College, Cambridge; University of East Africa; LSE;

Occupation: Chairman: GLE Development Capital Ltd ("on a pro bono basis; it has a factoring and invoice-discounting subsidiary" [AC]) '90-; Aztec '90-; Leader, Merton Borough Council '91-97; ex: Director, Burton Plc '81-90, Chief Executive, for Development and Concessions for Burton: Top Shop (which he helped Ralph Halpern set up), Top Man, Dorothy Perkins and Evans '69-90; he denies having received a £750,000 payoff from the Burton Group; United Africa Company/Unilever Plc '64-69;

Traits: Long, narrow face; pinched nose; large spectacles; neat blond coiffure; over-serious, hard corporate-man mien; "mellifluous" (Piers Merchant MP); "a prissy, keen man of good works and public service"; his "dapperness is high game-show camp; his hair has tinges of a red-blonde colour" (Simon Sebag Montefiore, SUNDAY TIMES); long-winded; "can lapse into worthy boffinry" (Robert Hardman, DAILY TELEGRAPH); a Norwich City FC fan;

enjoys swimming and the theatre;
Address: House of Commons, Westminster, London SW1A 0AA; 'Phoebus', 14 Lambourne
Avenue, London, SW19 7DW;
Telephone: 0171 219 2843 (H of C); 0181 879 0045 (home);

Michael (Keith Beale) COLVIN   **Conservative**   **ROMSEY '97-**

Majority: 8,585 (16.5%) over Liberal Democrat
5-way;
Description: A new seat, created in '97, nearly half
from his previous Romsey and Waterside seat and the
rest in nearly equal proportions from Eastleigh,
Southampton-Test and Hampshire NW; a
safe-for-Tories area stretching from the Southampton
suburbs to The Wallops in north Hampshire;
removing Tory-leaning areas from Southampton-Test
and Eastleigh made those seats more vulnerable;
Former Seat: Romsey & Waterside '83-97; Bristol
NW '79-83;
Position: On Defence Select Committee (Chairman
'95-97) '92-; Delegate, to Council of Europe and
Western European Union '97-; on Executive of 1922 Committee '97-; on Executive of UK
Branch of Commonwealth Parliamentary Association '93-; on British-Irish Parliamentary Body
'92-; Captain, House of Commons Shooting VIII '83-; Vice Chairman '97-, Chairman '87-97
British-Gibralt Parliamentary Group, British-Lithuanian Parliamentary Group '92-; Vice
Chairman: British-Bophuthatswana Parliamentary Group '87-, British-Sudan Parliamentary
Group '92-, Parliamentary Beer Club '94-; Secretary, all-party British-Taiwan Parliamentary
Group '97-; Chairman, Council for Country Sports '88-; Secretary, Licensed Trade
Parliamentary Group '87-; ex: PPS: to Richard Luce '83-87, to Baroness Young '83-85; on
Select Committees: on Energy '90-92, Employment '79-83; on Liaison Committee '95-97;
Chairman '92-97, Secretary '87-92 Conservative MPs' Foreign Affairs Committee; Chairman,
Conservative MPs' Aviation Committee (Vice Chairman, '80-82, Secretary '79-80) '87-92,
'82-83; Chairman '82-83, Secretary '81-82, West Country Conservative MPs; Vice Chairman
'81-83, Secretary '80-81, Conservative MPs' Smaller Businesses Committee; Secretary,
Conservative MPs' Shipping and Shipbuilding Sub-Committee '82-83; Vice Chairman, British
Field Sports Society '86-98;
Outlook: Thoughtful if wobbly Thatcherite-Eurosceptic big farmer-landowner and defence
and aviation specialist; a leader of the post-Hungerford and post-Dunblane "gun lobby" (David
Mellor); a spokesman for the field sports who was a fervent rebel against attempts to curb
handguns; a somewhat secretive former lobbyist for pre-Mandela South Africa; a friend of the
Prince of Wales, but not of the late Princess; also a friend of ex-MP John Browne and lobbyist
Ian Greer; a party loyalist who hired a private ambulance to race through red lights to help him
vote for the fishermen after a double hip operation; "cannot be trusted" on badger protection
(Tony Banks MP); was spokesman for National Licensed Victuallers' Association until it
secured flexible open hours for pubs like his in Licensing Act 1988; champion free-tripper as
Vice Chairman and Chairman of Tory MPs' Foreign Affairs committee (and formerly of their
Aviation Committee); pro: British Airways, liberal licensing hours, reformist South African
whites, wider share ownership, privatisation of CAA, better treatment for the elderly in

nursing homes, a bigger merchant fleet (as a Cayzer son-in-law);
History: Was elected to Tangley Parish Council for twelve years from May '64, to Andover Rural District Council for seven years from May '65, to Hampshire County Council for five years from May '70, to Test Valley Borough Council for two years from May '72; was elected Vice Chairman of Winchester Conservative Association '73; worked as a part-timer on Trade and Industry, in Conservative Research Department for three years from '75; was adopted for Bristol North West July '75; claimed comprehensive education meant going at the pace of the slowest Nov '75; alleged British Aerospace nationalisation would cost 20,000-30,000 jobs July '76; backed a coalition government Oct '76; said police should be paid more than others Feb '77; welcomed Bristol tax rebels Mar '77; claimed business could not flourish under Labour Oct '78; backed Bristol firemen July '78; captured Bristol NW from Labour June '79; urged a new Centre Party Jan '80; urged ballots in unions Apr '80; urged more backing for Inmos computer chip company July '80; launched 'An Open Tech' pamphlet Nov '80; urged curbs on finance for British Airways Jan '81; backed Namibian anti-SWAPO regime Nov '81; urged break-up of BAA July '82; urged government to recognize importance of children's play Oct '82; urged privatization of NHS services Oct '82; was selected for Romsey and Waterside Mar '83; was critical of the handling of unemployment during election campaign and urged rethinking June '83; opposed the phasing out of tax allowance on new shipbuilding May '84; opposed the slicing off of BA's routes just when it was becoming successful June '84; expressed doubt about the Trident decision, since it put "all our nuclear eggs in one basket" June '84; complained about the multiplication of clubs at the expense of pubs July '84; again urged flexible hours for pubs like his Aug '84; warned the Government to rethink its Civil Aviation Bill, particularly its limit of 275,000 movements at Heathrow Nov '84; urged help for a larger, modernized merchant shipping fleet Dec '84; said universal Sunday trading might produce many more part-time jobs but work-sharing, job creation and the abolition of Wages Councils were needed Mar '85; backed the Sporting Events (Control of Alcohol) Bill July '85; after the Select Committee on Foreign Affairs decided to interview Oliver Tambo, he asked the Government not to hold talks with "terrorist organizations" Oct '85; backed the preliminaries to the Anglo-Irish Agreement Nov '85; supported Mrs Thatcher over Westland Jan '86; visited South Africa as a guest of its government Feb '86; his pamphlet, 'Time Gentlemen Please', again urged a liberalization of pub opening hours, allowing any 12 opening hours between 10am and midnight May '86; cited BBC as reporting that 450,000 blacks in the homelands might die if South Africa's already faltering economy did not recover July '86; visited Bophuthatswana as a guest of its government Oct '86; led Parliamentary action for official recognition of Bophuthatswana Nov '86; was sceptical of Boeing's promised offset work if Nimrod were abandoned for its AWACs system Dec '86; fought CEGB plans for a coal-fired power plant at Fawley Mar '87; urged support for Play Board to encourage children's play opportunities Apr '87; actively supported reformist Dennis Worral's South African election campaign May '87; urged an automatic sentence of a year at least for any person convicted of acts of violance against licensees and their staff July '87; backing the BA/BCal merger, he wrote to the TIMES that a referral to the MMC was unnecessary because the Transport Secretary and BAA had enough supervisory powers Aug '87; in an adjournment debate he urged better-financed training of doctors for general practice Oct '87; again visited Bophuthatswana as a guest of its government, successfully invoking rainfall after six months' drought Dec '87; voted against David Alton's abortion-curbing Bill Jan '88; urged support for the European Fighter Aircraft project Feb '88; urged proper written testing after the educational reforms, not variable airy-fairy oral assessments Mar '88; urged guaranteed research and development after electricity privatization, including the Marchwood establishment in his constituency Mar '88; voted for 26-week ceiling on abortion May '88; was

dissatisfied with Firearms (Amendment) Bill, which showed Government's lack of comprehension May '88; was elected Chairman of Council for Country Sports, aimed at countering advances of the League Against Cruel Sports May '88; criticised BBC's Mandela concert June '88; co-sponsored motion backing free dental and optical tests July '88; attended Republican Convention in New Orleans as part of Conservative Central Office team Aug '88; helped dissuade Energy Secretary Cecil Parkinson from allowing the construction of a massive coal-fired power station and coal port at Fawley, in his constituency, near the Esso plant, the largest oil refinery in Europe Oct '88; as Chairman of the Council for Country Sports opposed the National Trust resolution to ban hunting on its land, insisting "those who take part in field sports have a vested interest in conservation of the countryside" Oct '88; urged "identity card schemes and fewer off-licenses" - but not fewer pubs like his - to curb "lager louts" Oct '88; visited Munich as guest of Hans Seidel Foundation Nov '88; spoke against and voted against dental and optical charges Nov '88; was credited with having helped persuade Mrs Thatcher to get rid of Edwina Currie and help the poultry farmers hurt by Mrs Currie's exaggerations about salmonella in eggs Dec '88; visited Michigan as guest of Conference of Committees for Democracy Dec '88; visited Angola as guest of Unita Feb-Mar '89; visited Bophuthatswana as guest of its President Mar-Apr 89; backed setting up of Hearing Aid Council Apr '89; urged more runway-building - including a fifth terminal at Heathrow - to counter air traffic jams in southeast May '89; visited Washington and Chicago, as guest of United Airlines, British Aerospace, British Airways and Rolls-Royce May '89; welcomed abolition of Apartheid in South African coalmines June '89; as guest of Rolls-Royce attended Paris Air Show June '89; as guest of IATA atended their annual conference in Marakesh June '89; welcomed F W de Klerk's visit to UK June '89; visited Rome as guest of Air Europe, meeting the Pope June '89; visited Seattle as guest of British Airways and Boeing July '89; during railway strike demanded a ban on strikes in public sector July '89; urged liberalization rather than US-style deregulation in European civil aviation July '89; welcomed Lord Young's compromise on curbing brewers' rights to own licensed premises as a "simple tenant of a major brewer" July '89; visited Canada and USA as guest of Bombardier, Air Canada, Textron Lycoming, Rolls-Royce and British Aerospace Sep '89; as an Adviser to Licensed Victuallers, claimed "the public house is an extremely responsible place in which to drink" Oct '89; visited Berlin air conference as guest of British Aerospace Oct '89; visited South Africa as guest of South African Coal Industry Oct '89; visited Munich as guest of Hanns Seidel Stiftung Nov '89; came 3rd in ballot for Private Member's Bills Nov '89; after being shown the Law Commission's report, successfully introduced a Government-backed Bill against computer hacking Dec '89; deplored "the continued condemnation of South Africa on the basis of largely obsolete disinformation sedulously propagated by the Anti-Apartheid Movement" Jan '90; co-sponsored attack on Peter Hain for his anti-Apartheid 'World in Action' telecast Jan '90; urged more generous support for private residential homes forced to pay their nurses more Jan '90; sought to allow local markets to trade on Sundaya, if councils wished it Feb '90; joined the Energy Select Committee Feb '90; was one of 23 Tory rebels who favoured better compensation for ex-servicemen who were victims of Pacific nuclear testing Feb '90; said, in support of his Computer Misuse Bill, allowing hackers to be sentenced to five years for unauthorized access: "there is a very real risk that, if nothing is done, the UK could well become a sort of international hackers' haven" Feb '90; claimed reintroduction of rates would be even more unpopular than poll tax Mar '90; was one of 32 Tories who voted against Government to provide extra cash to ease the plight of elderly people in difficulty over fees for private residential homes Mar '90; animal welfare activists called for his expulsion from the RSPCA after he praised angling and parents who introduced their children to field sports Mar '90; tried to prevent punishment of adjacent Tory MP, John Browne, who had "suffered enough" after he had been found guilty of having concealed his interests: "he has been pilloried unmercifully and unjustifiably in the national press"; "his particularly acrimonious divorce and the determination of his ex-wife to destroy him were largely responsible" Mar '90; his anti-hacking Bill competed its Commons passage May '90; denied receiving money from lobbyist Ian Greer while admitting he saw his firm once a month on average and had recommended his PR firm to companies May '90; urged promotion to Cabinet of the Minister for the Arts June '90; after death threats had been received from a "twisted minority" of Badger Bill supporters, asked whether it was right for MPs who objected to a Bill to be named by its supporters July '90; opposed public access to farm tracks: "if the public are allowed to wander willy-nilly on every bit of common land, they will end up spoiling it for everyone" Sep '90; toured USA as guest of British Airways, Roll-Royce, General Dynamics, United Technologies and British Airways Sep '90; was flown to Brussels by GEC Avionics Sep '90; visited Kenya as guest of its government Oct '90; visited Munich as guest of Hans Seidel Foundation Nov '90; was first MP to lead a Parliamentary Group to visit Forces in the Gulf Oct '90; was rated the "most-travelled MP" with 18 freebies in the previous two years Jan '91; in succession to Neil Hamilton, became an undisclosed and unregistered Consultant to SNI (Strategy Network International), organised by South African intelligence and serving South African clients, receiving £10,000 '91; welcomed meeting between Nelson Mandela and Chief Buthelezi Jan '91; backed the Badgers Bill with reservations Feb '91; questioned the CAA's allowing Air Europe to carry on flying under a massive and mounting burden of debt Mar '91; offered to introduce MPs to a pretty 3-year-old pit bull bitch named Holly, who "wouldn't hurt a flea", when Home Secretary Kenneth Baker promised to ban killer dogs May '91; tried to amend Badgers Bill to allow the use of terriers in badger setts for fox control May '91; with Sir Nicholas Bonsor and Nicholas Soames helped to kill Hare Coursing Bill May '91; expressed concern about the "disappearing rivers" of Hampshire May '91; visited Gibraltar as guest of its government and Chamber of Commerce June '91; urged the British-Spanish agreement on Gibraltar's airport be spelled out more comprehensively, like the international airport at Basle July '91; complained that Lord King did not seem to like competition from British Caledonian, which was the real reason he was cutting BA's contriibution to the party July '91; visited Japanese aerospace industry thanks to British Aerospace, Cathay Pacific, Rolls-Royce, Virgin Atlantic Airways and Westland Sep'91; visited Toulouse as guest of Airbus Industrie Oct '91; helped lead campaign to kill Kevin McNamara's Wild Animals (Protection) Bill as being aimed mainly "to end hunting with hounds"; claimed RSPCA had been the victim of "entryism" by people anxious to ban fox hunting, which would risk 16,500 jobs and £148m in trade Feb '92; complained of inadequate supervision by LAUTRO and FIMBRA of home equity schemes, devised by reliable companies like Royal Life but deployed by "high pressure salesmen on a naive and financially unsophisticated public"; "we now know that many of the advisers and salesmen were dishonest and have been sent to prison"; "how could those people have been allowed by the companies concerned to compound their fraud under a regulated system?" urged merger of LAUTRO and FIMBRA Mar '92; retained seat with majority almost unchanged, a swing to Liberal Democrat of 1.07% Apr '92; was said to have suffered heavy losses at Lloyd's May '92; was named to Defence Select Committee July '92; rebelled in favour of an additional £11,000 in office expenses for MPs July '92; opposed draft Euthanasia Bill July '92; urged a nuclear weapons system as well as Trident Aug '92; as a friend of the Prince of Wales, spoke of "profound disquiet among colleagues on both sides of the House at the thought that the Princess of Wales might one day become Queen" Dec '92; urged a redrawing of the map of Bosnia, to be underpinned by the UN Apr '93; in wake of Tories' Newbury by-election defeat declared Chancellor Norman Lamont "is now a political liability; I think he should be sacked; his time is up" May '93; stormed at Tory Euro-rebels that they would be "turkeys voting for Christmas" if they let the Prime Minister down over the Maastricht treaty July '93; again urged purchase of more EH101 support helicopters July '93; urged improvement in John Major's image: "somebody should buy him a few jazzy ties" Aug '93; complained of "absence of an overall defence strategy" in Defence White Paper Oct '93; opposed the idea of fellow Tory MP-farmer, Geoffrey Clifton-Brown, that set-aside subsidies for big farmers should have a ceiling of £50,000 - which he had received for his 1,000 Hampshire acres: "it flies in the face of natural justice; why should a guy be penalized because he has more acres?" Nov '93; welcomed the idea "that we should widen rather than deepen the European Community"; urged an increase in the Territorial Army to compensate for cuts in the Regular Army, a bargain since Territorials cost a sixth as much to maintain Nov '93; was lobbied by Ian Greer to opposed Kevin Barron's Bill to ban tobacco advertising Jan-Feb '94; in a press release, praised PM John Major for being "most sympathetic" about wartime Channel Island deportees in a cancelled meeting which never took place Feb '94; opposed restoration of capital punishment, except for killers of policemen Feb '94; voted to lower age of homosexual consent to 18, but not 16, Feb '94; urged better self-regulation of private pensions Mar '94; welcomed privatisation of coal in motion June '94; was named with ten other Conservative MPs as having failed to register their Lloyd's syndicate numbers -although he had submitted the numbers but banned their publication June '94; as Captain of the Commons Shooting Club, resisted plans to convert its rifle range into a creche July '94; was exposed as having having been recruited in '91 for £10,000 annually by black Rightwing lobbyist Derek Laud - of whose lobbying firm he was a Director - to serve, as as a successor to Neil Hamilton MP, as an unregistered Consultant to SNI (Strategy Network International), organised by South African intelligence and serving South African clients; he had asked questions without disclosing his interest; he described his non-registration as an "oversight" Oct '94; described financial advisers Knight Williams as "a sore on the reputation of the financial services industry"; it had a stand at the Conservative Conference, despite having been fined for previous serious financial infringements Oct '94; claimed his pig farmers were under threat from unfair competition from the Netherlands, France and Denmark Dec '94; complained that Spain was unfairly "laying seige to Gibraltar", urging its full entry to the EU, by which it should be protected; urged implementation of the '87 airport agreement, without disclosing his son-in-law, James Gaggero was Deputy Chairman of its only scheduled airline, GB Airways Dec '94; opposing fellow Tory MP Peter Viggers, urged New Forest become a unitary district Jan '95; defended the Government's Agricultural Tenancies Bill providing shorter tenancies Feb '95; signed Kenneth Baker's motion opposing a European single currency Feb '95; urged Government to buy 25 more Westland helicopters Feb '95; did not disclose his directorship of lobbyist Ludgate Laud Feb '95; in debate on John McFall's anti-fox-hunting Bill, asked whether it was a coincidence that on the day of the poll tax riots, no fox-hunts were sabotaged Mar '95; urged more troops for Bosnia July '95; was exposed by the SUNDAY TIMES as having failed to register his directorship of Ludgate Laud or its client National Transcommunications Ltd when he asked questions about or criticised the subsidies of its rival the BBC transmission services Nov '95; urged expansion of NATO Nov '95; was attacked in local press for driving dangerously in a private ambulance to vote in a lost fishing vote, while recovering from a hip operation Dec '95; suggested that young offenders sent to boot camp might volunteer for the army Jan '96; backed sale of MoD property, including Admiralty Arch, if other departments could not use them Jan '96; as Chairman of the Defence Select Committee reluctantly agreed to ask Defence Minister James Arbuthnot for identity of foreign buyers of 58,000 MoD married quarters Mar '96; after Dunblane, opposed "knee-jerk" ban on handguns, preferring they were kept in gun clubs Mar '96; warned Tony Blair there were 2m involved in shooting and opposed to losing target pistols May '96; voted for Bill Cash's European

Referendum Bill June '96; revealed he had written to 300 English-language newspapers urging expatriates to register to vote, as Chairman of 'Conservatives Abroad' June '96; defended Government sell-off of MoD married quarters July '96; warned Chancellor Clarke against any further defence cuts July '96; opposed Tory Government's ban on handguns Nov '96; urged better compensation for handgun owners, to avoid "legalised robbery" Dec '96; judged a single European currency unlikely and unworkable but worth negotiating Dec '96; voted to restore corporal punishment Jan '97; claimed sabotage of feed for game birds on his Tangley estate Jan '97; voted for dis-assembling of handguns held at home Feb '97; claimed that a rabbit had a 50% chance of getting away from the falcons used on his estate Feb '97; he retained his 60%-altered and renamed seat by the halved majority of 8,585, on a notional pro-LibDem swing of 11.8% May '97; backed Peter Lilley in first round of Tory Leadership contest, Hague in the second and third May-June '97; opposed Labour Government's tougher anti-handgun legislation June '97; was retained on the Select Committee on Defence, but not as its Chairman July '97; was elected Secretary of the all-party British-Taiwan Parliamentary Group July '97; backed Hague's democratisation of Conservative Party, but envisaged a 30% members' share in electoral college to elect the Leader Oct '97; was fined £1,000 and ordered to pay £11,000 costs for contiminating his neighbours' water with his farm slurry Mar '98;
Born: 27 September 1932, London
Family: S late Captain Ivan Beale Colvin RN and Joy (Arbuthnot) OBE; "his great great-uncle...successfully introduced a Bill to ban bear-baiting" (Ralph Atkins, FINANCIAL TIMES); m '56 Nicola (Cayzer) daughter of Baron Cayzer, Life President of British and Commonwealth Holdings; 1s James '65, 2d Amanda (former 10 Downing Street secretary) '57, Arabella, married to Gibraltar airline's Deputy Chairman, '60;
Education: West Downs, Winchester; Eton; RMA Sandhurst; Royal Agricultural College, Cirencester;
Occupation: Partner, in Colvin Farms Partnership (Tangley Estates: 1,000 acres - for which he received £50,000 for set-aside in '93 - with Tangley House, near Andover, Hampshire, and Colvin Farms, Essex; Forester: Langley Woodlands, Cramond and Harthill Estates in Scotland; Lloyd's Underwriter ("we went in open-minded; we knew that we could well be signing a blank cheque"; lost money from Lloyd's after '89) '87-; Consultant: Caledonian Investments (£10-15,000, including cost of an assistant) '??-, Meridian Broadcasting Ltd (local TV; £1-5,000) '95?-, Federation of Retail Licensed Trade (Northern Ireland; £1-5,000) '9?-; Panellist: Harris Parliamentary Panel (£1,000) '95?-, Business Planning and Research Intenational (£1,000) '95-; Director: Accrep Ltd (property investment) '62-76; Royal British Legion Training Company Plc (unpaid) '83-; ex: Director: Broad Abandonment and Research Technology Plc (unpaid) '93-95, Laud Ludgate (imitation-Greer Rightwing lobbyists led by black Tory Derek Laud) '95-96; Consultant: SNI (Strategic Network International; organised by pre-Mandela South African intelligence, with South African clients; succeeded Neil Hamilton; £10,000 annually) '91-92, Thames Heliport '93-94, CUK (aerospace) '93-94?, National Licensed Victuallers Association '84-88, British Field Sports Society (Vice Chairman) '87-??; Beneficiary, of half the value of £10,000 worth of pre-Christian era Celtic coins found on his Tangley estate '94; Publican: Tenant of 'The Cricketer's Arms', Tangley, Hampshire whose freehold he bought in '93 and sold in '94 ("for the record, Mr Colvin [leased] the pub to save it for the village and he makes little money from it" (SUNDAY TIMES); Account Executive, J Walter Thompson '57-61; Regular, in Grenadier Guards (Captain in '56) '50-57: served in Berlin, Suez, Cyprus '50-57;
Traits: Silver-haired; slim; good-looking; intelligent; "lucid and thoughtful" (Edwina Currie MP); qualified pilot and parachutist; "accomplished artist of professional standard" (DAILY TELEGRAPH); designer; "a three-quarters Scot" (MC); "I am both marksman and

sportsman" (MC); has had Tibetan spaniels called 'Coco' and 'Punch'; has complained that drag-hunting lacks the excitement of fox-hunting because it is like "kissing your sister"; **Address:** House of Commons, Westminster, London SW1A 0AA; Tangley House, nr Andover, Hants SP11 0SH;
Telephone: 0171 219 5208/4208 (H of C); 0171 828 6664 (London flat); 01264 730215 (home); 01794 512132 (constituency office);

Michael CONNARTY   Labour   FALKIRK EAST '92-

Majority: 13,385 (32.2%) over SNP 5-way;
Description: An industrial seat based on the oil refining community of Grangemouth and Bo'ness at the inner end of the Firth of Forth, which refines 40% of North Sea oil; nearly half its voters live in council houses; in '95 the last part of Falkirk town was transferred to Falkirk West, while 7,500 voter were brought in from the former Clackmannan seat;
Position: On Information Select Committee '97-; Chairman '97-, Vice Chairman '96-97, Tribune Group; Chairman '97-, Treasurer '94-97 all-party Parliamentary Group on the Chemical Industries; Vice Chairman, PLP Scottish Group '96-; ex: PPS to Tom Clarke '97-98; on European Standing Committee A '93-97?; Secretary, PLP Science, Technology and Civil Service Committee '92-97; Co-ordinator, PLP's Scottish Task Force on Youth Skills and Training '94-97; on Scottish Executive of Labour Party '83-92, '81-82,; Stirling District Councillor (Leader '80-90) '77-90; Chairman, Scottish Local Government Committee '88-90; represented Scotland on NEC's Local Government Committee '88-91; Founding Secretary, Labour Co-ordinating Committee (Scotland) '78-81; Vice Chairman, Central Regional Labour Party '79-82; on Salmon Fisheries Board for Forth River;
Outlook: "Now regarded by colleagues as 'sensible Left' after a turbulent career in local government" (Michael White, GUARDIAN); the former hyperactively Leftwing Stirling Council Leader and pamphleteer; formerly a Gramsci-influenced semi-hard Leftwinger, "a kilted version of Ken Livingstone" (Ian Bradley, TIMES); "a real Leftwing Bogeyman" (his 1987 opponent, Tory ex-MP Michael Forsyth); in Commons debates still looks back to his earlier incarnation; "as lively and ideas-productive as ever" (Hugh Cochrane, GLASGOW HERALD); a military interventionist in ex-Yugoslavia: "the only one I have heard who is in favour of sending a military expedition into Bosnia to impose a solution" (Foreign Secretary Douglas Hurd); economically literate; a Scots home-ruler who hoped to contest the Scottish Parliament but withdrew from the selection process; cause groupie: CND, Socialist Education Society, Fabian Society, Labour Campaign for Electoral Reform; was CWU-sponsored;
History: He joined the Coatbridge and Airdrie Labour Party at 15, '63; joined the Stirling Labour Party '73; displacing a sitting SNP Councillor, began a local government career in which he placed CND stickers on Stirling Council vehicles, refused a civic reception for the RAF but granted one for a visiting East German delegation, was taking to court by the Tories for allowing trade unionists to participate in Council meetings and increased rates by 122% May '77; at annual conference, attacked ex-PM James Callaghan for the power of his patronage, arguing that the party should be able to elect Cabinet Ministers Oct '77; as Leader

of Stirling Council, challenged the Government's financial constraints on local government, by exploiting their draconian "excessive and unreasonable" clause to curb expenditure May '80; supported Tony Benn for Deputy Leader Sep '81; was adopted for Stirling Feb '83; fought Stirling (which, after boundary changes incorporated 23% of Kinross and West Perthshire), branding his Tory opponent, Michael Forsyth, as a "hardline" "careerist" but lost after polling 27.9% June '83; was surcharged for refusing to raise rents to Government-specified levels '84; tried for East Kilbride selection, but lost to Adam Ingram, who got 40 votes to his 20, 10 ahead of Militant-backed Rob McKenzie Mar '85; was re-selected for Stirling from a shortlist of four with 38 votes to 11 to 6 to 5 and re-endorsed by the NEC Dec '85; chaired the working group which convinced the Labour Party in Scotland that the sale of council houses and their repurchase could be accomodated within the party's housing policy '86; moved successful resolution on Labour's Scottish Council, calling on Labour local authorities to boycott the Youth Training Scheme until three conditions were met Feb '87; at Stirling was narrowly defeated - by 548 votes (not 948 as reported by the press) - by Michael Forsyth, after increasing Labour's share by over 8% June '87; said: "the hard-Left label that in the past was attached to us, possibly because of what the Conservative Government was doing and the way we over-reacted, no longer applies," adding: "I don't think it is a softer image, I think we are different people" June '87; after Harry Ewing announced he would not stand again for Falkirk East, won its selection contest by 56% to 26% for Esther Quinn June '89; twinned Stirling with Nicaragua's Pearl Lagoon Oct '89; gave up his Leadership and Council seat in Stirling to move to Falkirk '90; retained Falkirk East with majority of 7,969, down from 14,023, mainly because of 4,000 increase in SNP vote Apr '92; in Maiden said that there had been 1,000 job losses in Grangemouth, despite hundreds of millions invested by BP and ICI May '92; with hard-Left and nationalists, divided Commons on "I spy strangers" ploy to delay 2nd Reading of Maastricht treaty May '92; urged more sensitivity to people heavily in debt to avoid bankrupcy June '92; criticised "cheap and patchwork" Bankrupcy (Scotland) Bill which forced people in debt to spend great sums on accountants and lawyers Oct '92; preferred COSLA's way of running water authorities to that proposed by Scottish Secretary Ian Lang Nov '92; backed idea that Queen should pay for repairs to Windsor Castle Nov '92; urged more technology transfer from university research in fields like fibre optics Dec '92; disclosed he had taken part "in the vigil when the rolling mill at Gartcosh was closed...I lived within a mile of that plant" Jan '93; deplored shutdown of Scottish operations of Lilley Group Jan '93; complained that Government were again offloading responsibilities on local government without providing the resources to fund them Feb '93; urged national database for missing persons Feb '93; co-celebrated 25th anniversary of Abortion Act; expressed concern about "the massive increase in the use of caesarian sections" in childbirth Apr '93; co-urged "military force" against "racially-motivated fascism which the Serbian aggressors embody" Apr '93; asked: "is it not time to end the delay, to stop buck-passing to the Americans and to commit ourselves to military intervention to deal with ethnic cleansing and create a safe haven now for those Bosnians who are left in their own country" May '93; co-wrote to President Clinton urging military intervention in ex-Yugoslavia May '93; voted against 3rd Reading of Maastricht treaty Bill May '93; insisted "we should be talking about putting together a peace-making force to guarantee Macedonia's borders" June '93; backed retention of Trident refitting at nearby Rosyth, which employed some of his constituents June '93; urged better ring-fencing of residential drug and alcohol projects June '93; insisted a Conservative Government could not fully impose its will on Scottish local government because they would be resisted by local officials as well as dominant non-Conservative councillors; the Scottish Labour Party's Local Government Committee had produced better criteria for reforming local government than the Government had; Tory changes had caused a deterioration, as in Stirling, where the grass was now a foot high July '93; was named to European Standing Committee A Nov '93; complained of EC's impact on Scottish Agriculture; farmers were going out of business in the Forth Valley because of inadequate milk quotas; urged a road bypassing the Avon gorge between Lothian and Central regions Dec '93; welcomed the Anglo-Irish Downing Street Statement, recalling: "I lost a relative in 1973 in a pub-bombing in Belfast" Dec '93; complained of the Government's renewed "asset-stripping" drives Jan '94; voted against restoring capital punishment, even for killers of policemen Feb '94; voted to reduce age of homosexual consent to 18 or 16, Feb '94; again attacking the Government's Local Government (Scotland) Bill, said "if I wanted to be partisan, I would encourage them to go ahead with the proposals, which would be disastrous for them" May '94; recalled that even Mrs Thatcher had considered that selling the Post Office was "a privatisation too far" July '94; urged the inclusion of the amount received by MPs for their consultancies in the Register of MPs' Interests July '94; voted for Blair for Leader and Prescott for Deputy Leader July '94; compared the Tories' Queen's Speech to 'The Secret Life of Walter Mitty' and 'Billy Liar'; alleged a £40-50b deficit in the PSBR Nov '94; claimed that vast majority of youths on youth training schemes did not get jobs Dec '94; complained Grangemouth masters did not allow pilots aboard Jan '95; urged "a decent Christian burial" for the "disappeared" victims of Ulster paramilitaries June '95; urged a properly co-ordinated science policy Oct '95; signed motion honouring Greek war sacrifices Oct '95; backed Tony Benn's defence amendment urging Trident-scrapping and cutting spending to West European average Oct '95; spotlit Scottish failures in Private Finance Initiative Oct '95; following rumours of top Labour tensions, praised Blair's leadership and warned that "back-benchers would not forgive those who put their egos and personal ambition before the disciplined advance to a Labour victory" Nov '95; predicted Britain would become a tax haven laundering other countries' currencies instead of selling them manufactures Dec '95; accused Tory government of a "smash and grab" raid on Post Office profits because public would not permit its privatisation Dec '95; emphasised community care needs of disabled Mar '96; said he would contest the Scottish Parliament May '96; was listed as one of 26 Labour MPs in Parliamentary Humanist Group Apr '96; after a spat in which he called Tony Banks a "hypocrite" for not voting for a pay rise, voted against a 3% cap on MPs' pay rise, in favour of pensions based on £43,000 July '96; was described as one of "Blair's Bastards" by Hull University researchers for have voted against Labour's leadership 21 times since '92, Sep '96; speaking as an MP sponsored by the UCW, urged proper compensation for injured postmen Nov '96; spotlit drug problems and suicides in Cornton Vale, Scotland's only women's prison Jan '97; urged a "cold climate allowance" to cut cold-related deaths Jan '97; retained his altered seat by 13,385 votes on a pro-Labour swing of 8.2%, securing the seat's highest-ever vote for a Labour candidate May '97; was named PPS to Tom Clarke, also Coatbridge-born, Minister for Film and Tourism May '97; urged PM Tony Blair to sequester criminal assets to finance better witness-protection schemes June '97; in debate on the Scotland Bill, said "my great worry is that the Scottish Parliament should ever become like this place", "it is a big idea that should not be nibbled at" Jan '98; urged an investigation of water privatisation "to see just how badly the Tories swindled the public" Mar '98; called for abolition of feudal tenure in Scotland June '98; spoke strongly in favour of local councillors' public service June '98;

Born: 3 September 1947, Coatbridge

Family: S Patrick Connarty, electrician's mate, and Elizabeth (Plunkett), Labour Party member; m '69 Margaret Mary Doran Depute Director of Education and ex-headteacher; 1s Brian Boyd '73, 1d Laura Ann '78; separated '93; reunited '95;

Education: St Bartholomew's, Coatbridge; St Patrick's High, Coatbridge; Stirling University (President, Students' Association, BA Econ); Glasgow University (Dip Ed; not completed);

Jordanhill College (DCE);
Occupation: Panelist, for Harris Opinion Panel (£1,000) '95-and Business Planning and Research International (£1,000) '95-; Writer: contributor to TRIBUNE, and formerly to LABOUR WEEKLY; Co-Author: 'Building Real Unity: Making Councils Accountable' (1982), 'Socialist Policies for District Councils' (1984), 'Socialist Housing Policies' (l984), 'Socialist Education Policies' (l985), 'Socialist Policies for Regional Councils' (1986); formerly Sponsored, by Union of Communication Workers (£800 p a to his constituency, plus Development Fund Grant; in the final year of sponsorship, his constituency received £8,000) '92-95; ex: Teacher, of children with learning difficulties in Falkirk (EIS - President of its Central Region '82-83) '76-92; Treasurer, Scottish Carpet Workers Union, in Stirling '74-75; Toymaker, making 'Cindy' dolls (TGWU shop steward at Triang, Canterbury) '72-73; Worker, in steel industry '62, '64;
Traits: Greying brown hair worn long on top; deepset eyes; sharp chin; "smart suit and plentiful hair", obsessively active; "an impenetrable rush of earnest phrases" (Sandra Barwick, INDEPENDENT); wordy; discursive; "I am...known to my Scottish colleagues for my spiky style" (MC); "I am by nature a person who is suspicious of any authority; I have naturally suspicious nature" (MC); unpompous (posed as a pregnant man, folded a Napoleonic hat to intervene in a Commons vote); enjoys his family, hillwalking and watching Falkirk Football Club; Scots-Irish; Catholic-educated humanist;
Address: House of Commons, Westminster, London SW1A 0AA; Ashgrove, California Road, East Stirlingshire FK2 0NH;
Telephone: 0171 219 5071 (H of C); 01324 714807 (home); 01324 474832 (agent);

'Frank' (Francis) COOK   Labour   **STOCKTON NORTH '83-**

Majority: 21,357 (48%) over Conservative 4-way;
Description: It has the massive ICI chemical plant in Billingham; strongly pro-Labour council estates merge to the northwest with large tracts of farmland; in '95 3,500 largely non-Labour voters were moved into Stockton South;
Position: On Select Committee on Defence '92-; on Chairmen's Panel '94-; Delegate: to North Atlantic Assembly '88-, to CSCE Parliamentary Body '91-; Chairman, all-party Landmines Eradication Parliamentary Group '96-; Chairman '92-, Vice Chairman '87-92, all-party Parliamentary Group on Alternative Energy; on Board of Visitors of Royal Navy Detention Quarters and Colchester Military Corrective Training Centre '88-; Captain of Pistols in MPs' Shooting Range; ex: Whip (Northern and Energy) '87-89; on Select Committees: on Procedure '88-92, on Employment '83-87, Transport, Employment, Agriculture, Foreign Affairs; Chairman '89-90, Vice Chairman '92-93, '88-89 PLP Northern Group; Chairman, Stockton Labour Party '81-83;
Outlook: Veteran hard Leftwing Catholic maverick mellowed by his exposures to the Defence Select Committee and NATO meetings; an ex-Regular recently a fellow-traveller more of the gun lobby than the Campaign Group; initially was an assiduous sponsor and signer of the latter's hard-Left motions and amendments; a 'happy warrior' of the Left and, post-Dunblane, of the gun lobby; occasionally serves as the spokesman of ICI, whose plant

dominates his constituency at Billingham; a former Regular, whose son is also a Regular; has an unusual interest in guns although he claims he has "never owned or wanted to own a firearm"; is a defence-minded and security-minded unilateralist: "I am 'pro' safe-nuclear and very 'anti' unsafe-nuclear"; now a hardline opponent of drinking and driving; he achieved his first Parliamentary task by dumping his seat's ex-MP, Bill (recently Lord) Rodgers, of whom he was a long-time critic, even when Rodgers was in the Labour Party; formerly MSF-sponsored;

History: He joined the Labour Party '50; campaigned against staying in the EEC May '75; was persuaded to stand against sitting MP and SDP defector, Bill Rodgers, by latter's FINANCIAL TIMES article alleging that Cook posed a threat to him; beat Tony Blair and others for selection as candidate for Stockton; was NEC-endorsed Nov '81; his selection was opposed by Sir John Boyd, Rightwing AEU General Secretary Dec '81; opposed expulsion of Militants '82-83; complained that old Stockton voters would never be able to show their disapproval of Bill Rodgers because of boundary change Jan '83; was narrowly elected to changed seat, pushing Rodgers into third place, June '83; urged anti-glue-sniffing campaign in schools July '83; opposed nuclear waste dumping July '83; expressed concern about US forces' threat to Nicaragua July '83; was initially listed as a member of Campaign Group as well as Tribune Group Sep '83; co-sponsored Eric Heffer for Leader, Michael Meacher for Deputy Leader Sep '83; tried for emergency discussion of local dumping of intermediate-level radioactive waste in a mine under his home in Billingham Oct '83; flew to Moscow with other MPs in Labour Action for Peace Dec '83; tipped off by a former workmate, began inquiring into safety at the Hartlepool AGR, where control rods were getting stuck in the reactor Feb '84; in an adjournment debate, again opposed the deposit of nuclear waste in Billingham May '84; quietly resigned from both Tribune Group and Campaign Group Oct '84; was reselected by a large majority Mar '85; when, after another leak, he and others called for Sellafield to be closed until safe, John Cunningham accused them of "calling for 11,000 people to be put out of work" Feb '86; introduced a Bill to establish an independent commission to promote "clean renewable alternative sources of energy" Feb '86; called for an inquiry into Sunday trading May '86; urged the shutting of the Hartlepool nuclear reactor until it could be made safe May '86; attacked the incompetence, dishonesty and treachery of NIREX May '86; urged further Norwegian-style wave-power research Dec '86; insisted nuclear waste be kept only in isolated engineered storage remote from inhabited communities Feb '87; opposed Sizewell because of its PWR system Feb '87; proposed the registration and licensing of accommodation agencies Mar '87; urged a Royal Commission into child abuse May '87; in the absence of Bill Rodgers, increased his majority by 8,000 June '87; in an amendment, urged MPs "to declare their intention to forsake their [driving] license or their liquor" - having been banned in '85 for three years himself after his second drink-drive conviction in 10 years July '87; with Mo Mowlam and Ted Leadbitter urged a judicial inquiry into sex abuse, without any public statements (by Stuart Bell) July '87; complained about nuclear-contaminated railway wagon at Hartlepool power station Aug '87; insisted in the GUARDIAN that the phasing out of nuclear power would not mean a job loss Sep '87; said he would support the reduction of the legal limit for abortion to 24 weeks but thought Alton's ceiling of 18 weeks was "unrealistic" Oct '87; applied to buy his council home, in which he had resided for 24 years Oct '87; urged Tory MP Andrew MacKay to step outside to see if he was "gutless" during a debate on concessionary TV license for pensioners Nov '87; complained of cuts in the North Tees District Health Authority Nov '87; urged an investigation of the possible cancerous effects of overhead power lines Jan '88; voted for David Alton's abortion-curbing Bill's 2nd Reading Jan '88; in an adjournment debate, raised the inadequate reward paid Jim Cormack who blew the whistle on a "fraud of gigantic proportions" in stealing diesel fuel at Faslane nuclear base Feb '88; backed

Tory Catholic MP Sir Hugh Rossi's effort to make religion a core subject in the school curriculum because "we need the opportunity to explain regularly the code of ethics which we hold dear, the way in which we interpret it and the scripture on which it is based" Mar '88; asked for assurances that new and tighter controls of nuclear effluents would be applied Mar '88; again demanded an inquiry into overhead transmission lines Mar '88; co-deplored Baghdad's gas attack on Kurds Apr '88; urged a Select Committee on abortion May '88; introduced a Bill to set up a Renewable Energy Development Agency June '88; the Butler-Sloss Report on child sex abuse in Cleveland, referred to his prior call for a royal commission on the subject, partly to clarify the number of cases in which adults later disclose they had been sexually abused as children; in the Commons he told of a "58-year-old woman who is visited three times a week by her 82-year-old father; that may be funny in a music hall, but is not funny in real life" July '88; introduced Bill to enable cabbies to ban smoking in their cabs July '88; deplored job losses from Swan Hunter's failure to win RN orders July '88; Environment Secretary Nicholas Ridley misleadingly wrote to him that his PPS, Nicholas Soames, had not attended a meeting of CET, a nuclear waste disposal company July '88; Nicholas Ridley later admitted Soames had attended a CET meeting Aug '88; again urged a Renewable Energy Development Agency Aug '88; as Vice Chairman of all-party Alternative Energy Group, urged an independent review on wave power, after doctoring of consultant's report on Salter's "nodding duck" system Aug '88; voted for John Prescott for Deputy Leadership Oct '88; co-urged a full-scale military review, since current commitment to a five-day war could not be sustained if munitions ran out after two days; disclosed he had joined Parliamentary Armed Services Trust; described the "degree of real, vile hostility" extended to British servicemen in parts of Northern Ireland Oct '88; attended a seminar at NATO Defence College in Rome Oct '88; co-urged decent rail links to North for Channel Tunnel Oct '88; had his head shaved on TV to raise £4,300 for Children in Need Appeal Nov '88; introduced Bill to establish a National Cervical Cancer Foundation Nov '88; helped elicit the figure that disposing of nuclear waste disposal might cost Government £4.35b Nov '88; demanded to know the local Labour Party "coward" who had anonymously exposed him to criticism for having bought his council house in Billingham at a 54% discount, bringing it down from £15,550 to £7,153 Dec '88; co-sponsored Tory MP John Browne's Protection of Privacy Bill Dec '88; co-sponsored Joan Ruddock's Control of Pollution (Amendment) Bill to register carriers of controlled wastes Dec '88; complained that pensioners were losing transitional protection Dec '88; asked about costs to CEGB because they had to close down poorly-designed AGR nuclear reactors before refuelling Dec '88; complained about constituency activists seeking to discredit him in the run-up to re-selection Jan '89; led attack on Freedom Association for seeking to support 'rebel' cricketers willing to play in South Africa Jan '89; with others, backed Dr Marietta Higgs as having been 90% accurate in her claims of sex abuse of Cleveland children Feb '89; when 30 MPs put down a motion urging the abolition of hare coursing, he typically put down his amendment: "forthwith" Mar '89; with other unilateralists, rejected Neil Kinnock's conversion to multilateralism May '89; was accused of resisting Simon Burns' Control of Litter (Fines) Bill May '89; led a motion expressing concern that food irradiation could cause illness, partly because it could not prevent botulism June '89; put through Bill for Cleveland County Council making it unnecessary to raise Newport Bridge June '89; with anti-abortion Tory MP Nicholas Winterton, urged a Select Committee on Abortion Oct '89; after the Deal bombing, pointed out that wives of serving personnel at three British Army units in West Germany were canvassed for jobs as security guards Oct '89; urged shifting of BBC's local Cleveland presenter, Graham Robb, who aspired to become a Tory candidate Oct '89; claimed security was too casual at the Guards' Wellington Barracks off Birdcage Walk, where Mrs Thatcher's helicopter landed Nov '89; asked Mrs Thatcher why her nuclear energy adviser, Lord Marshall, had to resign while Cecil Parkinson continued in office Nov '89; voted against War Crimes Bill Dec '89; emerged as the most assiduous of motion signers in '88-89, Dec '89; as Vice Chairman of the all-party Alternative Energy Group, backed Tory MP Tony Spellar's demand for more serious backing for "alternative cheaper, safer and more efficient forms of renewable energy" Apr '90; admitted he was uncertain about how to vote on embryo experimentation, being repelled by the emotional nature of the arguments of the Pro-Lifers with whom he should sympathise as a Catholic Apr '90; collapsed, suffering from low blood pressure and exhaustion Apr '90; introduced a 10-minute-rule Control of Toxic Waste Residues Bill; he knew the chances of getting it on to the statute book were "about as rare as rocking-horse droppings" May '90; complained that, the previous July, there had been "an unscheduled, uncontrolled and hitherto undisclosed release into the atmosphere of substantial quantities of irradiated material from the nuclear establishment at Harwell" July '90; after being driven to vote from Westminster Hospital, had prolonged absence after serious colonic cancer operations Oct '90; in a letter to him, Nuclear Electric admitted that they had been unable to correct a design fault on their most-recently-completed AGRs, which would cost £500m a year in lost electricity revenue and another £50m a year in extra research and modifications, blowing wide open the long pretence that nuclear energy was cheaper than coal Nov '90; while recuperating, helped constituency wives fly to see their husbands in Iraq Dec '90; did not vote with party majority backinh Gulf War Jan '91; expressed concern about level of radiation at Trawsfynydd Lake adjoining nuclear power station June '91; led a delegation to Strasbourg to protest attempted takeover of ICI by Lord Hanson July '91; complained that UK Government was not supporting Davy bid for refurbishment of Indian steel plant on same basis as German government was supporting their companies' bids Oct '91; complained about unflattering portrait of Queen foisted on Commons extension by Patrick Cormack MP Nov '91; complained that Michael Heseltine had blocked a cartel agreement between ICI and Finnish state fertilizer company Kimera which included their running ICI's Billingham plant Dec '91; complained that he had been unable to meet an Environment Minister despite six months of trying to lead an all-party delegation from Stockton to complain that councillors' allowance resulted in reduced benefits Mar '92; retained seat with majority up from 8,801 to 10,474, a swing to Labour of 1.51% Apr '92; demanded a royal commission to investigate the issue of Barclays' Bank, Philips and Shell expropriating the intellectual property of an advertising agency and pushing it into bankrupcy May '92; was named to Defence Select Committee July '92; complained about "surreptitious" local Defence job losses, disclosed in response to planted questions Dec '92; co-signed TIMES letter complaining that UN lacked "a structure and the staff to make contingency plans and meet the Security Council's calls for emergency actions; its financial resources are depleted; too many nations are in arrears with their payments and its communications cannot cope with the increasingly complex tasks it has to discharge" Feb '93; challenged Education Secretary John Patten for having devalued tests by over-applying them; he disclosed that "in a previous capacity, I was responsible for the formulation, standardization and application of various forms of educational testing" May '93; complained that service families in Tidworth and Cyprus had to live in "hovels" July '93; in Maastricht debate admitted he was a convert to the EC; insisted the Social Chapter would not be a threat to ICI in his constituency; when Tory MPs told him ICI's chief was against Social Chapter he telephoned Sir Denys Henderson to try to argue him out of it July '93; represented Commons in Washington at Scientific and Technical Committee of North Atlantic Assembly, where he received frightening information about nuclear waste in the US Nov '93; again raised the problem of Barclays Bank and Philips and Shell appropriating the logo devised by Hook Advertising Agency, with the bank putting the squeeze on the ad agency Nov '93; again slammed Barclays Bank for exploiting a customer, and Bank of England for failing to supervise the bank adequately Jan '94; voted against restoring capital punishment, even for killers of policemen Feb '94; backed reduction of age of homosexual consent to 18 or 16, Feb '94; urged an inquiry into why a businessman jailed for fraud and deception ws given £2.5m of public money to start a new £8m Teesside factory Apr '94; voted for John Prescott for Leader and Deputy Leader July '94; because the world situation was much more unstable with the end of the 'cold war' and British forces were over-stretched, opposed any further defence cuts, particularly the closure of local Eaglescliffe military depot Oct '94; backed cancelling of Trident to make up for revenue from cutting VAT on fuel Dec '94; urged referenda on single European currency and Northern Ireland Dec '94; opposed abolition of Cleveland County Council as a "Tory vendetta" and "fragmentation of the Teesside conurbation" Jan '95; criticised the £227m remote-controlled 'Phoenix' spy aircraft, eight years behind schedule and known to its GEC-Marconi makers as the 'Bugger-Off' because of its habit of not returning after its launch Mar '95; urged a full hearing at home for rogue trader Nick Leeson who caused collapse of Barings Apr '95; condemned French for resuming nuclear testing in the Pacific July '95; after his third trip to Bosnia with the Defence Select Committee, described the situation as "fraught with mendacity" July '95; opposed easing of sanctions against Serbia July '95; backed Clare Short's call for an inquiry into cannabis, criticising Mandelson's LibDem-bashers for having gone "overboard in quite a disgraceful manner" in the Littleborough and Saddleworth by-election July '95; urged a new agency to concentrate on family problems, involving sophisticated policemen inured to sexual abuse cases Dec '95; urged sale of unwanted MoD properties to local authorities for council housing June '96; voted against a 3% cap on MPs' pay rise, for a pension based on £43,000 and a cut in mileage allowances July '96; complained the locally-built sunken MV Derbyshire had had substandard construction imposed by the management July '96; voted against Tory Government's post-Dunblane gun-curb legislation, claiming it was unenforceable Nov '96; criticising police diligence, claimed the Dunblane killer had been allowed to build up an arsenal because he was a Freemason Dec '96; addressing 1,000 gun-owners in newly-formerd Sportsman's Association, opposed "ignoring real criminals and penalising the law-abiding" by banning target guns Dec '96; voted for dismantling of target weapons rather than outlawing them; urged right to possess weapons temporarily, citing recently-deceased Tory MP who had a German machine-gun and 1,000 rounds Feb '97; visited Laos to introduce British solar developers Mar '97; retained his slightly-altered seat with a doubled majority of 21,357 on a pro-Labour notional swing of 13.5% May '97; voted to ban fox-hunting June '97; asked new Home Secretary Jack Straw how he expected to train new police marksmen and whether he wanted to do away with target-shooting altogether June '97; claimed nobody would choose a .22 calibre pistol as a murder weapon because it was so difficult to conceal; with four other Labour MPs, rebelled against new Labour Government's Firearms (Amendment) Bill, claiming "unforgiveable negligence" by the Dunblane police June '97; as Chairman of the all-party Landmines Eradication Parliamentary Group, criticised Tory MPs for pressurising Princess Diana to cancel a Commons meeting June '97; estimated the cost of compensating handgun owners at £300m -twice the official estimate - because of the need to pay off dealers Aug '97; was a rebel against "primitive, unjustified and totaly unwarranted" lone-parent benefit cuts which rendered his surgeries "pretty bloody heart-breaking; I don't want to add to that" Dec '97;

Born: 3 November 1935, West Hartlepool

Family: Son late James Cook, gardener, and Elizabeth (Collier); m '59 Patricia (Lundrigan); 1s Andrew '65, 3d Christine '60, Maxine '62, Nicola '63; his son Andrew, a Regular, had responsibility for mainenance of armoured personnel carriers in Gorazde; divorced;

Education: Corby School, Sunderland; De La Salle College, Manchester ("I was a product

of...Catholic schools and Jesuit Catholic schools"); Institute of Education, Leeds;
Occupation: Formerly Sponsored by MSF (ex-AEU-TASS; £600 p a to constituency and up
to 80?% of election expenses) '83-95; MSF contributed more than 25% to his election
expenses Apr-May '97; Consultant (unremunerated), to United Expatriates (advice to workers
abroad) '87-; Chairman (unremunerated), Eurosolar (UK) '94-; Vice President, Eurosolar '94-;
Trustee and Director (unremunerated), of Faithfull Foundation '92-; Director, of SAFE
(Struggle Against Financial Exploitation; unremunerated) '93?-; ex: Project Manager and
Senior Construction Planning and Field Engineer for Capper-Neill International
(AUEW-TASS) '66-83; previously schoolmaster "for six years in a voluntary Church school
before entering state education" '57-66; gravedigger, Butlins Redcoat; steel works transport
manager; was in Parachute Regiment (secured early discharge when they wanted to demote
him from parachutist to pay clerk because he had a short tendon from meningitis) '53;
Traits: Short; close-cropped hair; pink complexion; "clever; fluent; amusing" (Michael White,
GUARDIAN); "one of Labour's more macho Members" (John Hunt, FINANCIAL TIMES);
health-troubled (collapsed from exhaustion '90, had bowel cancer operation '90, more surgery
'94, early meningitis); belated battler against Demon Rum; climber; fellwalker; music-lover
(including New Orleans jazz); RC ("I'm an MP who is a Catholic and not a Roman Catholic
who is an MP and I have to represent all my constituents to the best of my ability"); has a
voice-activated mobile phone (when he said "drop dead, you bastard" to a motorist carving
him up, the mobile phone replied "OK");
Address: House of Commons, Westminster, London SW1A 0AA; 84 Southwark Park Road,
London SE16 3RE;
Telephone: 0171 219 4527/4006 (H of C); 01642 563041 (home);

Rt Hon 'Robin' (Robert Finlayson) COOK   Labour   LIVINGSTON '83-

Majority: 11,747 (27.4%) over SNP 6-way;
Description: New overspill town halfway between
Glasgow and Edinburgh, with lots of social problems
and political volatility; it has former mining area
around the Calders and Broxburn; in '95 it lost 5,000
SNP-inclined voters in Kirkliston to Edinburgh West;
has among the highest concentrations of Catholics in
Scotland;
Former Seat: Edinburgh Central '74-83;
Position: Secretary of State for Foreign and
Commonwealth Affairs '97-; President, Socialist
Environment and Resources Association '90-;
Chairman, Labour's National Policy Forum '94-; ex:
Foreign Affairs Spokesman '94-97; Trade and
Industry Spokesman '92-94; Health Spokesman '89-92; Social Services Spokesman '87-89;
Deputy Spokesman, Trade and Industry '86-87; Campaigns Co-ordinator '85-86; Spokesman,
European and Community Affairs '83-85; Deputy Spokesman, Treasury and Economic Affairs
'80-83; on Select Committee on Transport '79-83; Vice Chairman, PLP Defence Committee
'75-79; Chairman: PLP Scottish Housing Sub-Committee, all-party Group on Penal Reform;
on Council of Europe '77-80; Edinburgh Town Councillor '71-74;
Outlook: The most brilliant debater, tactician and strategist on Labour's front bench,
transformed into one of its best Ministers; a "hugely intelligent, sharp-tongued perfectionist"

(TIMES); has "a sense of mission that has meant keeping faith with basic principles" (INDEPENDENT); is held back mainly by his appearance, arrogance and exposures of his private life ("Robin Cook's handling of his elopement with Gaynor Regan has set British records for sheer cackhanded incompetence" [Paul Routledge, INDEPENDENT ON SUNDAY]); with the best, most detached and realistic analytical ability, his pragmatic Euroscepticism is capable of accepting, with cautious realism, a single European currency, as one of his few calculated risks in foreign affairs; the acceptable face of old Labour, and "by instinct...an unreconstructed Keynesian" (Donald Macintyre, INDEPENDENT), "he is fast moving...towards a fusion of the ideas of the old and new Left" (Ewen MacAskill, GUARDIAN); "Cook's poor relationship with [Gordon] Brown remains one of the Foreign Secretary's consuming passions, something of which his loyal staff are only too aware; Mr Cook is known to go into a depression when the Chancellor is doing well, a mood his officals have nicknamed 'Brown Dog'" (Con Loughlin and David Wastell, SUNDAY TELEGRAPH); he retains a penetrating ability to discomfit opponents with caustic, under-the-skin insinuations as well as well-researched damaging facts; domestically is a highly competitive and ambitious loner rather than a team man because of his independent judgements; bed apart, has almost always managed to be in the right place at the right time, then exploiting his opportunities to the full by productive hard work; "has political nerve, doggedness and sharp debating intelligence" (Geraldine Bedell, INDEPENDENT ON SUNDAY); decided not to contest the Leadership in '94 because he expected to win only a quarter of the votes; became John Smith's campaign manager in '92 after having cooled on Neil Kinnock, for whom he did the same job in '83; the picador who was the sarcastic shriveller of Health Secretaries William Waldegrave and John Moore; "Cook's fire penetration on Health [was] 500% more effective than that of the late Mr Michael Meacher and his blunderbuss" and had the "virtues of the fact-ingesting Scotch dominie" while capable of "deploying statistics with model elegance and cruelty" but his "frostbitten arrogance... has spoiled Mr Cook for some of his colleagues" (Godfrey Barker, DAILY TELEGRAPH); "if he ever offers you a bouquet, have it sniffed for explosives before raising it to your nose; and if the flowers are not wrapped in Semtex, you may be sure there will be hornets inside, nursing hangovers" (Andrew Brown, INDEPENDENT); "his best speeches are "well researched, sweetly written, incisively read...with the sort of jokes which...leave a sting behind" (David McKie, GUARDIAN); "the most witheringly destructive, resourcefully scornful Dispatch Box talent in...Parliament" (Mark Lawson, TIMES); earlier, was the most clear-minded of quiet unilateralists; is still hostile to nuclear power; a soft-Left radical intellectual and libertarian; no longer cool on devolution; has long favoured the Alternative Vote for electoral reform; was RMT-sponsored;

History: "I started reading the NEW STATESMAN when I was 14" '60; he came to Labour through unilateralism '63, joining the party in '65; ran the Labour Club at Edinburgh University '65; was elected Chairman of Scottish Association of Labour Students '65; decided he was against EEC entry '66; contested Edinburgh North against the Duke of Buccleuch June '70 and took over the local party with Martin O'Neill; was elected to Edinburgh City Council May '71, becoming its Chairman of Housing; he served with John McWilliams, George Foulkes, Malcolm Rifkind and Lord James Douglas-Hamilton; was selected for Edinburgh Central Sep '72, won it by 961 votes on 28th birthday Feb '74; "I joined the [Tribune} Group when I came [to the Commons] in 1974", it was "not then part of the PLP establishment"; introduced Bill to bring Scottish divorce law into line with English Jan '75, but failed Mar '75; urged better and cheaper alternatives to prison for those like shoplifters Apr '75; accused employers of pressing 'yes' vote on EEC employees June '75; urged referendum on devolution Jan '76; urged Select Committee on South African arms Apr '76; complained about expensive signals intelligence May '76; sharply attacked John Mackintosh's pro-devolution proposals July '76; denied widespread 'scrounging' July '76; tried to set up agencies to give jobs to young July '76; urged liberalisation of Scottish homosexuality law Oct '76; complained about nuclear waste disposal plans Dec '76; led Scottish Labour revolt against cut in Rate Support Grant Dec '76; warned against over-investment in nuclear reprocessing Feb '77; urged decriminalising of drunkenness Nov '77; claiming no enthusiasm for devolution in his constituency, announced he would campaign against it in referendum Nov '77; introduced pro-homosexual Sexual Offences (Scotland) Bill Dec '77; led Labour anti-devolution vote campaign in Scotland Jan '78; argued that the 40% minimum was unrealistic Feb '78; queried airlift of plutonium oxide to Scotland Mar '78; initiated debate on accountability of Special Branch May '78; questioned wisdom of belonging to NATO July '78; urged dropping of secrets case against Duncan Campbell Sep '78; deplored Queen's visit to Iran as supporting its Shah Nov '78; staged adjournment debate against AGR nuclear power station at Torness Nov '78; was elected to Tribune Group's Steering Committee July '79; claimed nuclear power was expensive and unnecessary in Scotland July '79; introduced Bill to make security services accountable Dec '79; won equality with England for Scots gays July '80; challenged suitability of Lord Diplock to control phone tapping July '80; attacked Cruise and Trident in Glasgow demonstration Oct '80; demanded indexing of tax allowances Mar '81; voted against Defence Estimates instead of abstaining May '81; criticised Tony Benn for contesting Deputy Leadership without consultating others June '81; admitted nuclear power was not uneconomic July '81; attacked use of Diego Garcia as nuclear defence base Aug '81; accused Government of hiding likely nuclear casualties Sep '81; Home Secretary admitted to him that Special Branch were trailing political suspects Feb '82; attacked Militant Tendency Apr '82; warned Falklands expedition "might prove to be a military failure and a diplomatic failure" Apr '82; said £1b spent on Falklands war should have gone elsewhere June '82; voted against Northern Ireland Emergency Powers Bill June '82; with 73 votes was a runner-up for Shadow Cabinet Nov '82; attacked Robin Leigh-Pemberton's appointment as Governor of Bank of England Jan '83; expected to have Tony Benn as opponent in selection for Livingston Mar '83; supported self-determination for Palestinians and recognition of PLO Apr '83; was adopted for Livingston May '83; recanted on opposition to devolution and called for a federal constitutional settlement June '83; with Jack Straw and Jeremy Bray proposed a revamped party July '83; was Neil Kinnock's campaign manager in Leadership bid, declining to do the same job for Roy Hattersley July-Oct '83; was elected to Shadow Cabinet, with 78 votes (10th) Oct '83; was named European Spokesman Nov '83; with 71 votes was elected fifteenth and last man on the Shadow Cabinet Oct '84; was retained as European Spokesman (although he wrote he was "still unconvinced that it was a good idea to join the Common Market") Nov '84; having spelled out his outspoken criticism of Walworth Road's structures, he was switched from European Spokesman to Campaign Co-ordinator Jan '85; was considered a possible Chief Whip June '85; urged Labour to concentrate its fire against the Alliance Sep '85; with LCC backing, received 200,000 votes for NEC's constituency section Oct '85; after being re-elected to the Shadow Cabinet in fifth place with 105 votes on a joint Tribune-Campaign slate, was retained as Campaigns Co-ordinator (after refusing Agriculture and being refused Defence) Oct-Nov '85; introduced a Private Member's Bill to open up the board meetings of the five Scottish development corporations to the public and press Dec '85; opposed Denis Healey's proposal that Labour hang on to Polaris and use it as a bargaining counter with the Russians Jan '86; complained Scotland was providing twice as much expensive nuclear power as required May '86; in the wake of Chernobyl, helped agree a Labour policy compromise - a phase-out of UK's nuclear power May '86; urged Liberals to stop their "dirty tricks" July '86; received 207,000 votes for the constituency section of Labour's NEC Sep '86; in negotiations over a joint slate, Campaign Group initially refused to support him and Stan Orme July '86; was criticised by Tam Dalyell's constituency party for backing the building of a competing RC school in Livingston Sep '86; after 18 months off the Front Bench he lost his place on the Shadow Cabinet (with 78 votes, two votes behind just-successful Michael Meacher) Oct '86; was appointed a Deputy Trade and Industry spokesman (specialising in the City) under John Smith Oct '86; ran George Howarth's successful by-election Oct-Nov '86; disclosed irregularities in the way Cazenove had bid for Guinness shares the previous May, Jan '87; attacked as "utterly pointless" the security service's search of the NEW STATESMAN Jan '87; failed initially in his effort to show the 'Zircon' film Jan-Feb '87; supported the Alternative Vote as a fair reform of the electoral system but resisted tactical voting for the Alliance, which might make a deal with the Tories May '87; was re-elected with his majority up over 6,000 June '87; secured 95 votes (8th) for the Shadow Cabinet, charging the hard Left with being "fixated with stopping the Right from carrying out an imaginary plot" June '87; was named Social Services Spokesman July '87; urged Scottish Labour Party to set up an interim Scottish Assembly of 50 Scottish Labour MPs, inviting other Scots MPs to join them in an interim Assembly of Opposition MPs Aug '87; at conference warned John Moore he was "not going to launch his campaign for the party leadership on the bodies of claimants" Sept '87; received 172,000 votes for constituency section of NEC Sep '87; predicted 700,000 welfare claimants would be excluded by new Social Security Bill Nov '87; asked Tony Newton how putting up dental charges encouraged people to look after their teeth Nov '87; urged indexation of child benefit Nov '87; published details of the halving of funds allocated to DHSS areas for social fund payments Dec '87; warned nurses to "think long and hard" before going on strike Jan '88; criticised the Kinnock-Hattersley statement of Labour aims as insufficiently interventionist Feb '88; condemned Chancellor Lawson's proposals as "a Budget for the greedy, paid for by the needy" Mar '88; made widely-acclaimed Moore-shrivelling speech attacking social security changes as doing three times the damage the Government admitted Apr '88; accused the NHS of wasting money on agency-supplied outside manpower June '88; criticised the National Communications Union for its "most grotesque and offensive intrusion into civil liberty" in sacking John Golding over an alleged sexual lapse June '88; said it was "nonsense on stilts" for Britain to pretend to be a nuclear power July '88; welcomed the Butler-Sloss report into child sex abuse in Cleveland July '88; was told to shut up after he had publicly advocated non-payment of poll tax July '88; was credited with having defeated Tony Benn's challenge to Neil Kinnock Oct '88; at Labour fringe meeting confirmed his support for proportional representation Oct '88; in contest for Shadow Cabinet won 119 votes (5th) Nov '88; was co-rated (with Gordon Brown) as 'Front-Bencher of the Year' for their "elegant destruction" of the Tory Front Bench Dec '88; his proposal for Labour to support decommissioning of Sizewell B was rejected by Kinnock and NEC May '89; condemned Government's naming of British Steel chairman Sir Robert Scholey and Rover Group chairman Sir Graham Day to new NHS Policy Board May '89; came 2nd in ballot for constituency section of Labour's NEC (404,000 votes), with Ken Livingstone being pushed off; attributed it to activists' preference for those wanting to win the next general election Oct '89; on Tribune slate came 5th in ballot for Shadow Cabinet, with 141 votes (3rd); was named Health Spokesman Nov '89; launched LCC's pro-PR pamphlet 'Getting It In Proportion' May '90; was again elected to constituency section of NEC with increased vote of 440,000 (2nd); voted against Kinnock's departure from unilateralism at party conference Oct '90; won 125 votes (4th) in Shadow Cabinet elections Oct '90; was said to be sceptical about Gulf War, but would not discuss it, because of Shadow Cabinet collective responsibility Jan '91; challenged the use of UN resolutions to justify "bombing runs deep into Iraq" Feb '91; asked whether the new NHS would be "safe in the hands of estate agents" because of enormous potential sales of its properties Mar '91; deplored closure of 9,000 NHS beds in previous year Mar '91; said Basildon's cutback in vasectomies was reducing choice Apr '91; Gallup Poll showed public preferred him to his opponent, Ken Clarke May '91; welcomed pro-PR shift by Labour candidates in marginals May '91; said Monmouth voters were making his 'Dont Trust the Trusts' slogan an issue in by-election May '91; denied that his claim that trust hospitals were "opting out" was a "big lie", as claimed by John Major in wake of Tories' loss of Monmouth by-election May '91; presented a 30-point health plan, including ban on tobacco advertising June '91; after having voted for the Dog Registration Bill was bitten by a rottweiler at a New Forest barbeque July '91; trade union leaders polled by NEW STATESMAN placed him as the fourth most effective front-bencher Aug '91; countered William Waldegrave's claim that waiting lists had gone down by pointing out the statistics were six months out of date Sep '91; came 2nd in constituency section of NEC with 469,000 votes Sep '91; polled 149 votes (2nd) in Shadow Cabinet election Oct '91; voted with Kinnock on Shadow Cabinet to urge conference to remit a motion to cut Defence expenditure Sep '91; a TODAY poll rated him 21% ahead of his adversary, William Waldegrave, with Labour moving into a poll lead as a result of his assaults on NHS 'reforms' Oct '91; backed a separate Health Tax, but was opposed on this by John Smith Oct '91; was named 'Parliamentarian of the Year' by SPECTATOR Nov '91; after initially coming out flatly against two-tiered fund-holding, said Labour would phase out GPs' budget-holding Jan '92; acclaimed Scottish Labour's adopting Additional Member form of PR for Scottish Assembly Jan '92; said that Scottish MPs should not serve as ministers for England and Wales in any portfolio devolved to a Scottish parliament; this was half-repudiated by Neil Kinnock Feb '92; said £50m saved on abolition of tax relief for private health insurance should be spent on improving cancer services Feb '92; his election launch of Labour's health blueprint was overshadowed by controversy over Labour's TV film charging 'Jennifer' had waited 11 months for an ear operation Mar '92; claimed Labour would reverse increases in prescription charges Apr '92; accused Tories of accepting 2,000 advertising sites from Hanson's Imperial Tobacco in exchange for killing off a White Paper opposing smoking Apr '92; retained seat with majority down from 11,105 to 8,105, a swing to SNP of 5.58% Apr '92; again said, "Labour must commit itself to PR", because PR would have produced a Lib-Lab government Apr '92; although he coveted the top post himself, was named campaign manager to John Smith, who became Labour's Leader Apr '92; produced a compromise with unions over block vote, allowing them to keep their voting power in leadership election if they swallowed one-member one-vote for candidates June '93; demanded explanation of £15m in untraced contributions to Tories June '93; blamed Labour's defeat partly on having drafted its proposals in 1989 and "then we froze them in aspic" July '92; received 149 votes (3rd) for new Shadow Cabinet; was named Trade and Industry Spokesman (although he coveted the Treasury post, which only partly explained his subsequent hostility to Gordon Brown) July '92; said of Heseltine's success in securing a majority of 22 for his White Paper on coalmine closures - with only 4 rebels: "he is not mining a seam for his back benches, he is digging a pit for them to fall into because, in a year's time, none of those pits will still exist" Mar '93; in Gallup Survey of public trust of politicians, he was trusted by 36%, mistrusted by 64% Apr '93; attacked Michael Heseltine for not rescuing collapsed DAF lorry company Apr '93; launched 'Making Britain's Future' which urged pension funds to invest in long-term industrial projects Apr '93; urged more commercial freedom for Post Office May '93; was said to oppose an early showdown with unions over block votes May '93; accused Ministers of cover-up on super-gun for Iraq May '93; pressed Conservatives to return the money they had had from fugitive tycooon Asil Nadir June '93; attacked Government for fraudulent promise to save coal mines July '93; with disclosure that another fugitive businessman, Octav Botnar, had contributed £90,000 to Tories, again insisted on "disclosure of party donors" July '93; after 3rd tranche of BT shares was sold, urge BT be allowed to compete with cable TV July '93; claimed Royal Bank of Scotland was giving

preferential treatment to Tories, allowing them a "phenomenal overdraft" of £14m Sep '93;
came fourth with 517,000 votes (up from 426,000) for constituency section of NEC Oct '93;
came top of poll for Shadow Cabinet with 177 votes (up from 149), which he took as a tribute
to his fight against mines closures Oct '93; made another explosive attack on the fraudulence
of Government's promise to save coalmines from closure Oct '93; pointed out to Chancellor
that "the Government's financial deficit is bigger as a proportion of GDP than ours was in
1975" Dec '93; voted against restoring capital punishment, even for killing policemen Feb '94;
voted to reduce age of homosexual consent to 18 or 16, Feb '94; as "an enthusiastic racegoer"
welcomed Sunday racing May '94; after John Smith's death, refused to stand for Leader or
Deputy Leader of the Labour Party, despite considerable urging; he estimated he could not
secure more than a quarter of Labour MPs' votes June '94; voted for Blair for Leader, Prescott
for Deputy Leader July '94; derided as doctrinaire the proposed sale of the Royal Mail July
'94; attacked the predatory pricing of Murdoch papers July '94; laid down a barrage on Lord
Archer's alleged "insider trading" in Anglia TV shares, on whose board Lady Archer sat
Aug-Sep '94; topped poll for constituency section of Labour's NEC with 83,923 votes Oct '94;
expressed reservations about Blair's plans to rewrite Clause IV Oct '94; topped poll for
Shadow Cabinet with 187 votes; was switched to Foreign Affairs Spokesman, instead of the
Treasury he coveted, but which Gordon Brown had snared in his deal with Blair; in
compensation he was made Chairman of Labour's National Policy Forum Oct '94; in
TRIBUNE claimed "there can be a socialist foreign policy" Feb '95; again topped poll in
constituency section of NEC with 85,670 votes Oct '95; came second to Beckett in Shadow
Cabinet ballot with 181 votes Oct '95; clashed with Gordon Brown over latter's proposal to
cut benefits for unemployed youngsters who refused work or training Nov '95; criticised Tory
Government over its arms sales to tarnished Nigerian regime Nov '95; demanded resignations
of Tory Ministers in Scott Report debate, claiming William Waldegrave had misled the
Commons over 30 times Feb '96; alarmed Europhobes like Peter Shore when he said the
advent of a Labour Government would increase the likelihood of Britain joining a single
European currency Mar '96; announced Labour would grant full nationality rights to 5,000
non-Chinese in Hongkong on the colony's reversion to China May '96; claimed William
Waldegrave was "living in cloud cuckoo land" when he claimed "we could be outside the EU"
May '96; in Birthday Honours was promoted to the Privy Council June '96; was re-elected to
Shadow Cabinet with 214 votes, dropping to fifth place July '96; at the STUC conference said
Labour must "speak for the poor" as the "party of social solidarity" ??? '96; expressed doubts
about UK's early membership of the single European currency; insisted the Social Chapter was
a "necessary antidote to open markets" Sep '96; described as "wholly dishonest" the SUNDAY
TIMES' claim he had attacked Blair on poverty or opposed the strategy of wooing the middle
classes Sep '96; initiated discussion with LibDems on electoral and Lords reform, devolution
and Freedom of Information Oct '96; said it would not be in UK's interest to stay out of Euro
in medium or long term because of inward investment and strength of Sterling Oct '96; said a
referendum on the Euro was more likely in the first five years of a Labour Government than its
first five months Nov '96; was named the SPECTATOR's 'Parliamentary Debater of the Year'
because of his Scott Report speech Nov '96; predicted a Labour landslide Apr '97; retained
altered seat with an enhanced majority of 11,747 on a notional 3.8% swing from the SNP May
'97; was named Foreign and Commonwealth Secretary; secured the most Leftwing group of
junior ministers the FCO had ever seen; proclaimed an "ethical foreign policy", signing up to
the Social Chapter, "constructive enlargement" of the EU and his intention of making the UK
"one of the three major players in Europe and to draw the line under sterile negative
confrontation"; backed previous government's opposition to majority voting on defence and a
fully-fledged EU defence policy May '97; reportedly opposed Blair's proposal to ban Cabinet

Ministers from standing for Labour's NEC May '97; backed US decision to renew China's trade benefits, denying this clashed with defence of human rights May '97; at first meeting with other EU foreign ministers, reiterated insistence on British control of borders, immigration and asylum May '97; said the Euro must be "credible" and accepted by the British people in a referendum June '97; opposed lifting Nigeria's suspension from the Commonwealth until it showed "very serious progress" in human rights June '97; his reluctant decision to allow £160m of contracted "soft" arms exports to Indonesia caused 140 Labour MPs to sign a protest motion July '97; told Croatian President Tudjman UK had vetoed IMF loan over its war crimes and human rights record July '97; after his attack on Burma's military fascists for their "deeply oppressive regime" Malaysian PM Mahathir Mohamad threatened to boycott ASEAN summit Aug '97; announced the end of his marriage to Dr Margaret Cook as he was about to depart with her on holiday, having been tipped off that the NEWS OF THE WORLD was going to splash his affair with his secretary, Mrs Gaynor Regan Aug '97; after flaws showed in the handling of volcanic Montserrat, he ordered a review of UK's 13 remaining such dependencies Aug '97; topped the constituency section of Labour's NEC with 118,726 votes Sep '97; described as "wholly unacceptable in the modern world" the sentencing for murder of two British nurses by a secret Saudi Arabian court Sep '97; he blocked two Indonesian arms contracts Sep '97; during Queen's tour of India, his remark that Britain had a historic duty to mediate between India and Pakistan over Kashmir was countered by PM Gujral's retort that Britain was a "third-rate Power poking its nose in" Oct '97; the DAILY MAIL claimed he had flown back from India to spend two days with his mistress Oct '97; Buckingham Palace, in an unprecedented statement, said it was happy with the FCO's handling of the Queen's Indian tour Oct '97; he announced no Nigerian would attend the Edinburgh Commonwealth summit Oct '97; he announced he had invited the UN, the Arab League, the Commonwealth and the Organisation of African States to confirm that alleged Libyan Lockerbie bombers would be accorded a fair trial in Scotland Oct '97; said "we will use our [EU] presidency to give EMU the best start we possibly can" because it was in Britain's interest that the Euro succeeded, "even though we will not be taking part in the first wave" Nov '97; on a visit there, warned Czech Republic to treat better its 300,000 gypsies, warning that false asylum seekers could not find UK homes Nov '97; in Poland pledged to remember its victims of Nazi persecution Nov '97; rejected Spain's suggestion of shared sovereignty in the absence of agreement by Gibraltar's inhabitants Dec '97; welcomed the "constructive approach" of senior Tory Europhiles - Clarke, Heseltine, Heath and Howe - in offering support to Blair on the Euro Jan '98; denying he would quit the Cabinet to become Scotland's 'First Minister', he cleared the way for Donald Dewar Jan '98; urged Saddam Hussein to comply with Security Council demands, warning Tony Benn it weakened pressure on Saddam to exaggerate divisions among the major Powers Jan '98; overcame initial resistance of Algerian regime to EU initiative to discuss massacres Jan '98; warned US against imposing sanctions on firms dealing with Iran as threatening US-EU relations Jan '98; his attempt to replace his hostile Tory-minded secretary, Anne ("impossible to work with") Bullen, inherited from Douglas Hurd, with his mistress-secretary, Gaynor Regan, was blocked by the FCO; instead he accepted a civil service replacement Jan-Feb '98; under pressure, he abandoned his outside job as tipster-columnist for the GLASGOW HERALD, being replaced by SNP Leader Alex Salmond Feb '98; needing all the Cabinet support he could get in his media-enlarged domestic troubles, he "buried the hatchet" with his old rival Gordon Brown, who told him to "hang in there" Feb '98; visited Kuwait and Saudi Arabia to secure more support against Iraq, but the Saudis announced their opposition to military action against Saddam Feb '98; 23 Labour MPs opposed his military threat against Iraq Feb '98; rejecting Lord Chancellor Irvine's call for press curbs, insisted the public had a right to know about his marriage break-up Feb '98; angered the Rightwing Israeli

Government by his symbolic meeting with a Palestinian Arab at Har Homa, the disputed Israeli building site in East Jerusalem; British Zionists snubbed him by cancelling a dinner in his honour Mar '98; his Jewish predecessor, Sir Malcolm Rifkind, doubted his "diplomatic skills" Mar '98; Speaker Boothroyd disputed his claim that a statement on his Middle East visit was not advisable because there was no policy change Apr '98; the Commission for Racial Equality found "very disappointing" that he had only appointed one person of Asian origin, to the Marshall Aid Commemoration Commission, since assuming office Apr '98; by staging his wedding a week early, when news would be dominated by the Ulster talks, he largely avoided publicity for his marriage to Gaynor Regan Apr '98; an EVENING STANDARD poll of businessmen showed a sharp drop in his approval rating July '98;

Born: 28 February 1946, Bellshill, Lanarkshire

Family: Only child of Peter Cook, a headmaster from a Lanarkshire mining family, and Christina (Lynch); m 1st '69 Dr Margaret (Whitmore) consultant haematologist at Livigston's St John's Hospital; 2s Christopher '73, solicitor, Peter '74; divorced '98; m 2nd '98 Gaynor Regan, ex-secretary;

Education: Aberdeen Grammar School; Royal High School, Edinburgh; Edinburgh University (MA Hons, 2.1 in English Literature; failed to finish his PhD on Dickens and the Victorian novel);

Occupation: Journalist: recently a jump-racing correspondent for GLASGOW HERALD '91-98, formerly TIMES columnist '84-85, Defence Correspondent for the NEW STATESMAN '81-83; formerly Sponsored, by RMT (ex-NUR; £600 p a to constituency, 80% of election expenses) '79-95; also received in '93 contributions towards research costs from UNISON, National Communications Union and Union of Communication Workers and equipment from AEEU and ISTC; office support from World Affairs Research Trust continued until May '97; ex: Consultant (without fee), to Library Association '79; Tutor-Organiser, for WEA in Southeast Scotland District, '70-74; Teacher, of English in Bo'ness Academy (comprehensive school) '69-70;

Traits: Small; red-haired; bearded; somewhat portly; "looks like a squirrel with a bad shave" (Jan Moir, SCOTSMAN); "his habit of raising his right eyebrow makes him look indignant, demented or both (Peter Hillgrove, OBSERVER); "looks like Lenin and talks like Miss Jean Brodie" (Alan Watkins, OBSERVER); "Mr Cook tends to gabble; he swallows whole strings of syllables so that words slither down his throat like tapeworms" (Simon Hoggart, GUARDIAN); "leprechaun-like, chuckling into his red beard" (Edwina Currrie MP); "he's a good talker, and he seems a good listener too; he's interesting, witty, amusing; he could probably laugh a woman into bed" (an Edinburgh family friend, DAILY TELEGRAPH); "Little Red Rooster" - "he stands with his chest thrown out and one leg forward like a scruffy bantam cock, so confidently aggressive that you expect the forward foot to have a spur on the heel with which to rake the carpet" (Andrew Brown, INDEPENDENT); "he struts around like such a fine turkeycock that one cannot help noticing he is even more impressed with his own oratory than those around him; he behaves more like a lawyer in an American courtroom drama; his apparent belief that the brief is everything, the reality of secondary importance seems uppermost" (Steve Crawshaw, INDEPENDENT); "may be sparkling company, witty and sharp, but he has few friends, even fewer die-hard allies and, unlike his arch-rival Gordon Brown, makes little effort to woo backbenchers; as a consequence, he has enemies by the barrelful, including those who resent what they see as his arrogance: his belief that he is one of the brightest, if not THE brightest in the Cabinet" (Con Coughlin and David Wastell, SUNDAY TELEGRAPH); "once revered as a razor-sharp Parliamentary performer Robin Cook emerges [from disclosures about his domestic life] as a spoiled, selfish spendthrift" (Margarette Driscoll, SUNDAY TIMES); "he cannot cope with...the give-and-take of a

modern marriage between two intellectual equals, equal in the workplace, equal in the support mechanisms they put in place for each other"; [his former wife believes that] "what he wants and needs is the support of younger women who adore him and look up to him" (Linda McDougall, Westminster Wives); "of course Robin wants to be Leader - but I don't think plastic surgery has advanced that far" (Shadow Cabinet colleague); "my looks and personality are very much of a school swot; I'm not good-looking enough to be party Leader" (RC); highly intelligent ("one of the best intellects in his party" -Ewen MacAskill, SCOTSMAN); workaholic; soft-spoken; self-spoofing; "lithe and guileful" (Mark Lawson, TIMES); "alleged excess of bumptiousness" (David McKie, GUARDIAN); "frosty arrogance" (Godfrey Barker, DAILY TELEGRAPH); uses "barbed tones" (Ivor Owen, FINANCIAL TIMES) and "devastating sarcasm" (Ewen MacAskill); "can strut while standing still" (Andrew Brown, INDEPENDENT); admits he has the classic characteristics of an only child: reserved, defensive and private; "I have always had the character of the school swot; I was not massively popular at school; but as an only child I was not particularly fussed to be popular or gregarious" (RC); wanted to be a Presbyterian minister but, partly under the influence of George Bernard Shaw's rationalism, lost his faith at 19; "has many admirers but almost no friends" (Labour Front-bencher) except Frank Dobson and John Prescott; unclubbable; was a VE-baby; instead of the London flat he shared with John Prescott and Frank Dobson, had a room in a Victoria hotel for four nights, then a Pimlico flat; enjoys French cuisine, Alsatian wines and, above all, Italian ice cream; has a passion for horses and jump-racing; fancies himself as a tipster; "has a genuine, almost child-like enthusiasm for jump-racing" (John McCririck); horses "are my hobby, what keeps me sane; I try to ride every weekend, very much rough riding; I have no pretensions to be a great horseman" (RC); "the most exciting sights and noises I know are, first the colour and noise of a large field coming into a steeplechase fence, which is a tremendous spectacle; the other is the clang of tin ballot boxes as they hit the gymnasium floor coming of the back of a truck on election night" (RC);
Address: House of Commons, Westminster, London SW1A 0AA; Chevening, Kent; 1 Carlton House Terrace, London SW1; his Pimlico flat is now rented out;
Telephone: 0171 219 5120/4431/6136 (H of C); 0131 339 8329;

Yvette **COOPER**   Labour   **PONTEFRACT & CASTLEFORD '97-;**

Majority: 25,725 over Conservative 4-way;
Description: A West Yorkshire Labour stronghold, previously largely based on coalmines, all but one shut; it still retains factories in Pontefract, potteries in Castleford, a power station at Ferrybridge, glassworks and chemical works at Knottingley and Castleford, plus liquorice fields;
Position: On Select Committees: on Education and Employment '97-, Intelligence and Security '97-;
Outlook: A vestal 'golden girl' of 'New Labour'; "one to watch" (NEW STATESMAN): the "dazzling star of the Blairite nomenklatura" (Simon Sebag Montefiore, SUNDAY TIMES); a young journalist, formerly on the INDEPENDENT, shoehorned into a super-safe West Yorkshire seat after Sir Geoffrey Lofthouse had been squeezed out; "no doubt talented, she has nonetheless benefited from leadership patronage because of close links

to senior Blairites" (TRIBUNE); a former Adviser to late John Smith and Gordon Brown, she is now the wife of Brown's adviser, Ed Balls; is also the grand-daughter of a miner and the daughter of a union leader; whatever the origins of her talents, she soon showed them by seeming to reply ably for the Government in economic debates soon after her Maiden;

History: She joined the Labour Party '87; advised Labour Leader John Smith '91-92; she worked on Bill Clinton's staff in Arkansas '92; she advised the team of Labour's 'Shadow Chancellor' Gordon Brown '93-94; in her article for the INDEPENDENT ON SUNDAY predicted that Chancellor Clarke's latest Budget would not win the Tories the election July '96; she was short-listed for the safe seats of Wentworth Dec '96 and the all-woman contest at Warrington North, where she competed with Valerie Vaz, Valerie Shawcross and winner Helen Jones Mar '97; having failed on these occasions, Sir Geoffrey Lofthouse was squeezed out of Pontrefract and Castleford by the carrot of a life peerage and the stick of not being allowed to continue as Deputy Speaker; she was fielded with four other NEC nominees: Tony Benn's son Hilary, Blair adviser and ex-SDPer Derek Scott, Kirklees Council Leader, John Harman, AEEU convenor Cath Ashton, none from the constituency; she won, after a "virtuoso performance", winning the selection conference over with "a combination of research and pep" (Martin Wainwright, GUARDIAN) Apr '97; retained the seat with a majority of 25,725, on a 6.6% swing May '97; in her Maiden enthused about Gordon Brown's "wise and radical" "people's Budget" because of its help in curbing youth unemployment July '97; backed motion urging curb on detention of asylum-seekers July '97; made impressive, economically-literate speeches defending the Government in its pensions policy July '97; was named to the Select Committees on Education and Employment, and on Intelligence and Security July '97; opposed prematurely killing off the coal industry by ending its exclusion from fair competition in the energy market Nov '97; welcomed the 'Welfare to Work' programme particularly because a survey of her constituency had shown 48% of the young unemployed "had no educational or vocational qualifications at all", twice the national average Dec '97; at her Eastbourne wedding to Ed Balls, which attracted all the Blair-Brown glitterati, her sleek and chic midnight blue gown was outshone by the gold lame trouser suit of Marie Elena Robinson, the over-dressed operatic wife of the Paymaster General Jan '98; applauded the Budget her new husband had helped on for giving an extra £500 to "some of the poorest families in the country" Mar '98; attacked as "a kamikaze thing to do" John Redwood's proposal to derail the Euro Mar '98; in a pro-coal article in TRIBUNE emphasised the uncertainty about nuclear and gas-fired energy Mar '98; backed the Government's Teaching and Higher Education Bill as a better way to secure both further education and higher education for working class kids who, in her constituency, left education in droves at 16; she herself had doubled her income by taking a Master's at LSE for which she had taken out a "career development loan"; "I have only just finished paying it back" June '98;

Born: 20 March 1969, Inverness

Family: Her grandfather "began his working life in pits as a teen-ager"; daughter, of Tony Cooper, General Secretary, Engineers and Managers Association, and June (Iley); married '98 Ed Balls, Adviser to Chancellor Gordon Brown;

Education: Eggars Comprehensive School, Alton, Hants; Alton Sixth Form College; Balliol College, Oxford University (1st in PPE); Harvard University (Kennedy Scholar '91-92); LSE (MSc Econ);

Occupation: Journalist, on the INDEPENDENT (leader-writer and economics columnist) '95-97; Research Associate, Centre for Economic Performance, LSE '94-95; Adviser, on Youth Unemployment, to Labour's Treasury team, led by Gordon Brown '93-94; Staffer, in Bill Clinton's 'War Room' in Arkansas '92; Economic Researcher, for Shadow Chancellor John Smith '91-92;

Traits: Short; elfin look; short brown hair; heart-shaped face; brainy; articulate; has a sense of humour: as "a Finance Bill virgin, friends and family asked, 'how was it for you?'; I have to say that 'it was a strange experience'"; tended to wake her new husband at 4am when calling from the USA on a select committee visit, not discounting the time difference; confesses to having two washing machines and two kitchen sinks as "the only way to avoid bow legs from lugging huge bags between London and the constituency";
Address: House of Commons, Westminster, London SW1A 0AA;
Telephone: 0171 219 5080 (H of C); 01459 106 221 (pager);

Robin **CORBETT**   Labour   **BIRMINGHAM-ERDINGTON '83-**

Majority: 12,657 (31.3%) 4,735 (12.88%) over Conservative 4-way;
Description: A slice of North Birmingham from the fumes of Spaghetti Junction to the blossoms of middle-class Sutton Coldfield; it has Fort Dunlop, Jaguar's Castle Bromwich complex and a host of motor component producers; in '95 the large Kingstanding council house ward was added from Perry Barr, reinforcing Labour's hold;
Former Seat: Hemel Hempstead '74-79;
Position: On Home Affairs Select Committee '97-, '84-86; Chairman '97-.Secretary '85-97 Australia and New Zealand Group; Chairman, all-party MS Group '97-; Vice Chairman: Friends of Cyprus '87-, Indo-British Group '97-, Motor Industry Group '87-; Sponsor, Terrence Higgins Trust '87-; ex: Deputy Spokesman: Disabled People's Rights '94-95, National Heritage (Media and Broadcasting) '92-94; Deputy Spokesman '87-88, Assistant Spokesman '85-87, '89-92 on Home Affairs; Whip (West Midlands) '84-85; on Select Committees: on Agriculture '96-97, '83-84, Expenditure '76-79; Chairman: PLP Home Affairs Committee '83-86, Labour Agriculture Group '77-78; Secretary, Labour Civil Liberties Group '74-79; Vice Chairman, all-party Animal Welfare Group '76-79; co-opted to Food, Agriculture Sub-Committee of NEC '74-79; Chairman of Farm Animal Welfare Co-ordinating Executive (13 animal-caring organizations); on Council: of Royal College of Veterinary Surgeons '85-92, Save the Children Fund '87-90; on Committees of Campaign for Victims of Crime, Reform of Animal Experiments;
Outlook: Sidelined veteran trendy, commonsensical Left-Centre radical; able former middle-ranking front-bencher downgraded to a select committee for age and being 'Old Labour'; previously a punchy frontbencher who skilfully led for Labour on Broadcasting Bill; a doughty crusader against tabloid intrusion and smear, who used their own vivid, straight-from-the-shoulder style against "the sewer SUN"; an Australian-born happy warrior; an able campaigner, environmentalist, animal defender, consumerist and civil libertarian; from the family which inspired the BBC series "Living With The Enemy"; a Euro-sceptic (ex Labour Common Market Safeguards Committee); pro-Greek on Cyprus (Friends of Cyprus); also pro: single parents, rape victims, alternative energy, UN; critic; anti: gutless Press Council, nuclear weapons, 'bugs', computers, drugs, fox-hunting, press monopolists; detests Murdoch, but not enough to refuse the loan of Sky TV satellite equipment in '90; "obliging and conscientious" (JOURNALIST); was USDAW-sponsored;

History: His family was deported back from Australia when Robin was one; according to the Economic League, he began writing for the Communist CHALLENGE from Mar '54; joined the Labour Party '63; contested Hemel Hempstead Mar '66, West Derbyshire in the by-election (caused by resignation of Aidan Crawley); complained that George Brown refused to speak for him Nov '67; again contested Hemel Feb '74; won it Oct '74; initiated debate on civil liberties Nov '74; opposed naming rape victims Dec '75; opposed cover-up of Metropolitan Police corruption Feb '75; urged ban on sale or installation of 'bugs' May '75; urged rent be collected from squatters Aug '75; voted against Prevention of Terrorism Bill Nov '75; tried to end need for waiter service of drinks at pubs Nov '75; was rebuked by Roy Jenkins for saying IRA had a spy inside Special Branch of Scotland Yard Mar '76; was co-sponsor of Kenneth Clarke's Bill to ease licensing laws Jan '76; opposed training Chilean airmen in UK Jan '76; his rape reform Bill - guaranteeing anonymity for the complainant woman and male defendant until conviction - became law Dec '76; won 17,000 votes in constituency section of NEC Oct '76; introduced Bill to ban export of live animals Apr '77; opposed expansion of Luton Airport Apr '77; stressed danger of using crossbows May '77; urged ban on National Front meeting July '77; expressed concern about video surveillance Aug '77; worried about security vetting at Cheltenham Nov '77; attacked high railway fares Jan '78; urged curbs on youthful alcoholism June '78; complained about horses bought at sales for meat processing abroad Mar '79; talked PM James Callaghan into agreeing to set up a Standing Royal Commission on Animal Welfare Mar '79; accused Mrs Thatcher of "playing to the gutter" over immigration Apr '79; was defeated at Hemel May '79; "it was terribly hurtful when I lost in 1979; you feel hurt, dirty, shabby, it's all your fault"; objected to supporters of Tony Benn for Deputy Leader announcing their organisations without consulting them July '81; after being replaced as the candidate by the then hard-Left half-black candidate, Paul Boateng, an appeal was launched to NEC July '82; urged Militant Tendency to split off and found its own party Aug '82; was adopted for Tory-held marginal Erdington, Birmingham (against Charles Morris, Anne Davis and Lord Mayor) May '83; narrowly won seat (with help of canvassers from Hemel, where Boateng ran third) June '83; supported a plan to save Dunlop tyre factory in constituency Aug '83; nominated Neil Kinnock and Denzil Davies for Leader and Deputy Leader Sep '83; alleged a cover-up over safety of system-built council flats Oct '83; co-alleged that John Biffen misled Commons over Murdoch purchase of SUNDAY TIMES Oct '83; was elected Secretary of Birmingham Labour MPs Dec '83; was Tony Benn's 'minder' in Chesterfield by-election Dec '83; introduced Bill to allow leaseholders the right to choose their own insurers Jan '84; urged a review of Bail Act Feb '84; backed Northfield Report recommendation that more publicly-owned farms be made available for letting Mar '84; attacked proposal to make incest legal for over-21 brother and sisters as "an offence to every married couple" Apr '84; led a motion complaining of Spanish tax advantage in car exports July '84; attacked the "offensive and humiliating" defence questioning of the named victim in the Hutchinson wedding day rape-murder case Sep '84; deplored leniency of 5-year sentence for rapist of 6-year-old girl Oct '84; opposed too-wide powers for intimate body search for too many drugs Oct '84; was on Labour delegation which clashed with Kenneth Clarke over appointments to West Midlands Health Authority Dec '84; backed right of under-16 girls to confidential contraception Jan '85; arranged a Commons showing of banned '20:20 Vision' programme on security surveillance (Massiter) Feb '85; was re-selected Mar '85; urged better safeguards in Interception of Communications Bill Mar '85; after tour of US he urged a 'Fortress Britain' approach to halting a tidal wave of killer drugs May '85; on Labour working party he voted against setting up 'black sections' May '85; attacked BBC ban on 'Real Lives' programme on Northern Ireland Aug '85; urged 500 more customs officers to fight drugs Aug '85; was named an Assistant Spokesman on Home Affairs in place of resigning Robert Kilroy-Silk Nov '85;

demanded a debate on alleged abuse by MPs of temporary admissions system Dec '85; urged more work on non-animal tests for major diseases Jan '86; urged prosecution of SUN for breach of anonymity of rape victims in Ealing vicarage case Mar '86; alleged cuts in customs men had given green light to drug barons Oct '86; expressed concern about Birmingham pub bombings verdicts Oct '86; was one of five Birmingham Labour MPs who wrote to Bernie Grant and Linda Bellos warning them against attending an "illegal" launch of Birmingham 'black sections' Apr '87; a poll showed 60% of constituents knew his name - twice as many as the national average May '87; despite a SUNDAY EXPRESS prediction he would lose, he multiplied his majority ten-fold, while spending the least of any successful candidate June '87; was promoted Deputy Spokesman on Home Affairs June '87; attacked the Government's refusal to refer Rupert Murdoch's purchase of TODAY to the MMC July '87; urged a ban on imports of furs from countries still using steel-jaw leg-traps Nov '87; after being banned from driving for a second time wrote BIRMINGHAM POST article favouring random breath tests Dec '87; opposed needlessly restricting rights of law-abiding shooters because of one madman Jan '88; said the "smutty" racing industry were the main sponsors of the rejected Sunday Sports Bill Jan '88; demanded more cash for temporarily-closed Birmingham Children's Hospital Feb '88; supported Bill to ban dog-fighting Apr '88; in debate on "sloppily drafted" Firearms (Amendment) Bill, urged power for Chief Constables to investigate mental health of gun-certificate holders May '88; congratulated Government on tightening up his 1976 Sexual Offences (Amendment) Act on anonymity for rape victims, if not for defendants June '88; visited Cyprus as guest of pro-Greek 'Friends of Cyprus' July '88; visited Soviet Union to view the Lada plant as guest of all-party Motor Industry Group Nov '88; co-criticised attacks on anti-SAS "Death on the Rock" Nov '88; attacked Tories' "bully-boy tactics" in pushing through post-Hungerford Firearms (Amendment) Bill Nov '88; urged resignation of judge who excused ex-constable for abusing his daughter because his wife was pregnant Nov '88; worried about threats to regional TV in new Government broadcasting plans Dec '88; attacked "outrageous" choice of Lord Chalfont as Deputy Chairman of Independent Broadcasting Authority: "he was put in there to do the Prime Minister's bidding" Jan '89; backed John Browne's Protection of Privacy Bill because "the excesses of the sewer SUN and other tabloids have reached such proportions in the quest for sensation and sleaze that action must now be taken"; "punitive damages would persuade the sleaze sheets to start cleaning up their act"; cited his experience at the hands of a fellow journalist when "my wife and I lost a baby in a cot accident"; "every citizen should have a right to privacy"; ridiculed newspapers having an in-house "ombudsmen" on their payrolls; the SUN's "ombudsman" had said: "I'm the man who's got to deal with all these whingeing pinko pooftahs" Jan '89; named Colin McColl as "the new head of MI5" Jan '89; again complained about the "day-in day-out abuses of gutter journalism on papers like the sewer SUN, who are not just careless about people's privacy, but who see the misuse of people's privacy as a short-cut to circulation and profit" Apr '89; complained the Official Secrets Bill would lead to "an extension of secrecy" May '89; urged a ban on tail-docking, ear-cropping, de-barking and de-clawing of dogs in accordance with Convention of Europe for Pet Animals May '89; backed public funding of BBC May '89; put the block on the jumbo-sized development envisaged by developer Peter de Savary in his private Hayle Harbour Bill June '89; was helicoptered to Hayle to see the extent of the dereliction there July '89; he removed his block, provided there were regular town polls of the development monitored by the Electoral Reform Society July '89; was named an Assistant Spokesman on Home Affairs (Shadow 'Minister for Broadcasting') Nov '89; led for Labour on the Broadcasting Bill, urging a higher quality threshold; claimed the Government put cash ahead of quality in TV, treating viewers as no more than parcels to be sold off to advertisers Dec '89; promised a Labour Government would force Rupert Murdoch to choose between

Sky TV and News International Jan '90; backed all-party pressure to have TV3 carry religious broadcasts as a public service obligation Feb '90; opposed giving police more power to seize tapes and transcripts before transmission, unless authorised by a judge Mar '90; supported distinctive Channel 5 for TV May '90; complained that under-anaesthetised animals may have been used in experiments May '90; urged a measured response to IRA terrorism, within the law, while seeking a political solution Sep '90; visited Australia as guest of Australian Parliament Oct '90; repeated Labour's call for "quality before cash" on TV Oct '90; welcomed Sir Geoffrey Howe's resignation, "I think he has had enough of her tantrums; she is now friendless in Cabinet and I would not be surprised to see her go before the next general election" Nov '90; opposed Murdoch's satellite monopoly through merger with BSB Nov '90; co-sponsored Roy Hughes' Badgers' Bill Dec '90; backed motion opposing military force to retake Kuwait from Iraqis Jan '91; said a Labour Government might fund the BBC from direct taxation Feb '91; urged resignation of Lord Chalfont as Chairman of Radio Authority, since he was a Director of Shandwick's, which promoted four London radio stations May '91; as a Trustee of Terrence Higgins Trust, defended its use of explicit photographs re AIDS June '91; was still in anti-EC Common Market Safeguards Committee June '91; backed a register for all dogs, not merely dangerous ones under Dangerous Dogs Bill; deplored limited action on rottweilers, alsatians and dobermans June '91; on Labour's behalf, promised a Freedom of Information Act Jan '92; described as a "disgraceful slur" the Government's ban on security guards being represented by a union affiliated to the Labour Party Jan '92; listing the "unfettered mayhem and distress, annoyance and damage" caused by hunts, promised Labour would bring in a Bill to ban hunting with hounds early in the life of a Labour administration Feb '92; backed a paperback version of Salman Rushdie's Satanic Verses Mar '92; retained seat with majority up from 2,467 to 4,735, a swing to Labour of 3.12% Apr '92; in first-round ballot for Chairman of the PLP, came fifth with 21 votes May '92; was named Deputy Spokesman on the National Heritage July '92; attacked appointment of Jocelyn Stevens (an "unsuitable, ideological ignoramus") as Chairman of National Heritage, fearing it would lead to to many monuments being "doomed to neglect" Oct '92; urged more practical design of cars to deter theft Oct '92; backed Clive Soley's Freedom and Responsibility of the Press Bill as an effort to balance the freedom of the press with its responsibility in an era when editors had lost their independence to monopoly owners and watchdogs had lost their teeth Jan '93; agreed the BBC's allowing John Birt to be employed as a self-employed contractor was "astonishing" Mar '93; derided the "friendless" Press Complaints Commission Apr '93; urged trials for West Midlands police disciplined for having stolen from dead people Apr '93; sought to protect local charitable lotteries from rules for National Lottery Apr '93; urged better British financial support for British films Apr '93; in the wake of Denktash's "sheltering of Mr Nadir", urged British action against the militarily-imposed Turkish regime in Northern Cyrus July '93; warned that Government cuts threatened pensioners' free bus passes Aug '93; again visited Cyprus as guest of 'Friends of Cyprus' Sep '93; visited Hongkong with his wife, as guest of its government Oct '93; after Mo Mowlam became his new boss in the wake of an ambush by Labour's MCPs, commented: "the obvious answer is to reserve four places for women, not to put them into competition with men" Oct '93; visited France as guest of West Midlands PTA Nov '93; opposing Granada TV's takeover of LWT, said, "television for London needs to be made by people who live and breathe the concerns of its own people" Jan '94; urged tightening of food laws after discovery that Latero Flora for AIDS sufferers was contaminated by bacteria Feb '94; voted against restoring capital punishment, even for killers of policemen Feb '94; voted to reduce age of homosexual consent to 16, abstaining from voting for 18, Feb '94; voted for Blair for Leader, Prescott for Deputy Leader July '94; backed SUNDAY TIMES' subterfuge in securing expose of 'cash-for-questions' Tory MPs Graham Riddick and David

Treddinick July '94; criticised axeing of 100 jobs at Central TV in Birmingham following Carlton takeover Sep '94; was switched from Broadcasting Spokesman to Disabled People's Rights Deputy Spokesman under Tom Clarke Oct '94; criticised Tory Government's Disability Discrimination Bill for failing to tackle access to education of those with learning difficulties Jan '95; voted against extending Sunday licensing hours Feb '95; urged better compensation for crime victims than offered in Criminal Injuries Compensation Bill May '95; was dropped, with other veterans, from Labour's Front Bench Oct '95; was named to Agriculture Select Committee Jan '96; urged review of convictions in Carl Bridgwater murder case Dec '95; urged more money for Birmingham hospitals Dec '95; with 29 other Labour MPs, voted against guillotining of revised Prevention of Terrorism Bill/Act Apr '96; voted against 3% cap on MPs' pay rise, in favour of pension based on £43,000 July '96; found "extremely distasteful" press coverage of Mandy (pregnant with 8 foetuses) Allwood Aug '96; described as "crackpot" the advice of Severn-Trent Water during drought: that people pave over lawns Aug '96; tabled raft of questions on animal cruelty Feb '97; was targeted by The FIELD for his anti-hunting views Apr '97; retained his favourably altered seat by a trebled majority of 12,657, a notional pro-Labour swing of 7.3% May '97; as Vice Chairman of Friends of Cyprus, urged Turkish Cypriot leader Denktash to join negotiations for EU entry June '97; backed bar on fox-hunting June '97; opposed BBC's downgrading of 'Yesterday in Parliament' June '97; was named to the Home Affairs Select Committee July '97; urged "a more independent Police Complaints Authority" because "the police are still seen to be investigating complaints themselves" Mar '98; urged improved cancer treatment for under-65s be "focused on offering deprived communities extra health care and advice" Mar '98;
Born: 22 December 1933, Fremantle, Western Australia
Family: A claimed forefather was Miles Corbet who signed the death warrant of Charles I; son, Thomas Corbett, English foundry worker of Irish descent who was deported from Australia with Robin in '35, and Marguerite Adele (Mainwaring); has a twin; m 1st Patricia (Essex) '54, dvd '64; 1s Adam '62, 1d Susannah '61; m 2nd '70 Val (Jonas) Hudson, South African-born journalist-scriptwriter-novelist (co-author of Splash); 1d Polly '75 (on whom the BBC series "Living with the Enemy" was based);
Education: Holly Lodge Grammar School, Smethwick, Staffs;
Occupation: Consultant, on Public Affairs and Communications; was USDAW-sponsored (£600 p a to constituency, 20% of election expenses) '85-95; received more than 25% of his election expenses from USDAW Apr-May '97; Author: Can I Count on Your Support (1986) (canvassing stories for Save the Children), Tales from the Campaign Trail (1987); ex: PRman: Director: Robin Corbett Associates '83-85, Link Organization (Holdings) Ltd '83-85, Binary Public Relations '79-83; Senior Labour Adviser, IPC Magazines '72-74; Editorial Staff Development Executive, IPC Magazines '69-72; ex-Journalist: FARMERS' WEEKLY (Assistant Editor) '60-70, BIRMINGHAM MAIL '59-61 (on NEC of NUJ '64-69); ex-Owner of one-third share in a greyhound syndicate;
Traits: Tall; rugged; "fuzzy hair and aquiline nose...striking figure" (SUNDAY EXPRESS); "Colonel Gadaffi look-alike" (Commons policeman); humorous; brash, bright; trendy; persistent;"direct and confident" (Paul Johnson, GUARDIAN); "I'm not ambitious - not in the sense that I'd kill to become this, that or the other"; cat lover; collects bric-a-brac; formerly convivial (twice banned from driving for a year, most recently in '87); had a diesel Rover fastback in '91; ex pipe-smoker; loves creamed potatoes but denies he misspells "potato" like Dan Quayle;
Address: House of Commons, Westminster, London SW1A 0AA; Flat 7, Spiral Court, 12 Wheelwright Road, Erdington, Birmingham B24 8NU; 96 Piccotts End, Hemel Hempstead, Herts HP1 3AT;

Telephone: 0171 219 3420 (H of C); 01442 252866; 0121 373 1147/8662;

Jeremy (Bernard) CORBYN   **Labour**   **ISLINGTON NORTH '83-**

Majority: 19,955 (55.6%) over Conservative 4-way;
Description: The less gentrified end: a rundown inner city area with low wages, high unemployment and high drug dependency; multi-ethnic, including many Irish-born and Turkish Cypriots;
Position: On Social Security Select Committee '90-; Vice Chairman: London Labour Party '88?-, PLP Health and Social Security Committee '84-; PLP Foreign Affairs Committee '93-, Northern Ireland Committee '93-; Chairman: Campaign for Non-Alignment '90-, Joint Committee on Kurdistan '88?-, Committee for Human Rights in Grenada '83-, Stop Child Labour Campaign '97?-; Secretary, PLP Central and Latin America Committee '??-; on CPLD Executive '83-; Vice Chairman, Labour Action for Peace '??-; on National Council of CND '??-; ex: Chairman '93-96, Vice Chairman '85-93, London Group of Labour MPs; Secretary, Campaign Group '87-95?; Hackney Borough Councillor (Chairman: Community Development '75-78, Public Works '78-79, Planning '80-81) '74-83; Haringey Councillor '81-83;
Outlook: Hyper-active quasi-Trotskyist (LONDON LABOUR BRIEFING) hard-Leftist attempting visually to mellow; has moved out of Oxfam-reject clothes into a smart burgundy jacket; "a sort of Parliamentary Sandanista" (Tory ex-MP Tristan Garel-Jones); "too close to the IRA" (Tory ex-MP Terry Dicks); "a rare and increasingly sought-after example of the unreconstructed Left" (Matthew Parris, TIMES); since he has escaped the fate of his more primitive and obstreporous Militant fellow-entryists is "as much an endangered species as the badgers, deer and other wild life he tries so hard to protect from hunters" (Michael White, GUARDIAN); has "energy and dedication", "naivety and preoccupation with never being outflanked on the Left" (Robert Low, OBSERVER); so deviant that only the deliberately politically-illiterate Tory MP Nigel Evans could score by describing him as "perhaps not New Labour but certainly Real Labour"; an excellent, hyper-assiduous constituency MP, he was overwhemingly re-selected by his increasingly safe constituency just before it voted 2-to-1 for a Blairite watering-down of Clause IV in '95; a unilateralist; a keen defender of the wronged 'Guildford Four' and 'Birmingham Six'; as a troops-out backer of a united Ireland has been the most frequent host to leading Sinn Feiners, including Gerry Adams; "each time he has been reprimanded by the Labour leadership but never had the whip withdrawn" (James Landale, TIMES); a defender of asylum-seekers; a former poll-tax resister; an opponent of blood sports; an environmentalist, including Antarctica; a prolific spawner of small, short-lived hard-Left groups, some of which he has headed; also fertile in producing ten-minute-rule Bills; can make "a confounded nuisance of himself from a sedentary position which is only mildly preferable to the nuisance that he makes of himself when he stands up" (Tory ex-MP Sir Nicholas Bonsor); "he speaks with great conviction, and I have no doubt that, over the years, he has totally convinced himself" (Tory MP Sir Geoffrey Johnson-Smith); "has the almost unique capacity to make a significant, important and worthwhile case" - access to Westminster by the disabled - "sound almost positively unattractive" (Tory ex-MP Sir Geoffrey Howe);

"what he possesses in verbosity, he clearly lacks in a sense of humour" (Tory ex-MP Hugh Dykes); obsessed with picketing and other "extra-parliamentary" activities and foreign tripping to show "revolutionary solidarity"; a leading Campaign Groupie and contributor to quasi-Trotskyist LONDON LABOUR BRIEFING and SOCIALIST ORGANISER; formerly sponsored by UNISON (ex-NUPE);

History: He joined the Labour Party and CND at school '66; was sympathetic to the Socialist Organiser Alliance of Trotskyist entryists; joined LONDON LABOUR BRIEFING editorial board - led by Ken Livingstone and Ted Knight and designed to push the London party Leftward - as General Secretary '79; became a Labour Agent for Trotskyist Ted Knight in Haringey, with subsequent questions about undeclared expenses May '79; was elected to Executive of Greater London Labour Party Mar '81; at Brighton he threatened a purge of soft-Left Labour MPs - led by Neil Kinnock - who had abstained from voting for Tony Benn for Deputy Leader Sep '81; succeeded SDP defector Michael O'Halloran as candidate for Islington North, with its large Irish community, beating off the challenge of then semi-Trotskyist Paul Boateng by 39 to 35, Feb '82; as Chairman of Hornsey Labour Party proposed issuing party card to Trotskyist Tariq Ali against NEC wishes April '82; wrote: "the Party leaders are hellbent on an unremitting war on the socialists in the party - they have no intention of unilaterally disarming or taking power from the City...there must be a total defence of ANY socialist threatened with expulsion from the party" Sep '82; condemned the division of Haringey into two seats Sep '82; was elected to Executive of Campaign for Labour Party Democracy, although he opposed registration, as required by Labour Party Feb '83; was elected for Islington North, defeating ex-Labour SDPer John Grant June '83; organised Sinn Fein leader Gerry Adams' visit to Commons July '83; called for a "London-wide lorry ban" July '83; worried about the US threat to the sovereignty of Nicaragua and the South African threat to Lesotho July '83; voted against Defence Estimates July '83; attended Turkish political trial Sep '83; proclaimed himself a member of the hard-Left Campaign Group Sep '83; attacking Kinnock as a "preaching careerist", supported Eric Heffer for Leader, Michael Meacher for Deputy Leader June-Oct '83; visited Turkey for Turkey Solidarity Campaign from where he wrote deploring its military rulers Sep '83; spoke against 'witch hunt' (expulsion of Militant leaders) Oct '83; spoke for "No Socialism Without Gay Liberation" Oct '83; urged annual Labour conference to proclaim to Central Americans, "we stand with you against American imperialism" to avoid "another Vietnam" there Oct '83; failed to secure entry of Gerry Adams to a Brighton Labour conference fringe meeting organised by the Labour Committee on Ireland Oct '83; again opposed continuing exclusion from Labour Party of Trotskyist Tariq Ali Oct '83; after visiting Grenada, he urged debate on arrests of members of its New Jewel Movement Dec '83; refused initially to criticise Archway road-widening protesters who harassed inquiry inspector into resignation Feb '84; urged better care for the elderly Feb '84; demanded stronger Labour and TUC support for striking miners Apr '84; was allegedly involved in Livingstoneite plot - "Target '87" - to deselect moderate London Labour MPs Mar-May '84; attacked bitterly the "shabbby and squalid" Bill to replace the GLC with a Tory dominated quango May '84; defended the ILEA as a "unique education authority" May '84; attacked cuts in the London NHS May '84; introduced a Bill to abolish standing charges for gas, electricity, water and telephone services for pensioners and the poor July '84; helped stop the Intimidatory Picketing Bill by shouting "object!" July '84; was arrested in Trotskyist-led anti-Apartheid demonstration outside South Africa House July '84; urged a blitz against drug addiction from which 15% of constituency's young men suffered Aug '84; marched in favour of 'Troops Out of Northern Ireland' Aug '84; was unsuccessful candidate of City Trotskyists for National Committee of Anti-Apartheid Movement Oct '84; invited IRA spokesmen to speak at House of Commons a fortnight after the Brighton bombing Oct '84;

belatedly admitted two convicted Sinn Feiners had visited the Commons to discuss strip searches Nov '84; unrepentant, was reprimanded by Chief Whip Michael Cocks for "thoughtlessness" of the highest order" for IRA invitations Dec '84; invited into Commons striking miners who were expelled after chanting "Coal Not Dole" from gallery Jan '85; helped stage a demonstration on the miners' strike which forced the suspension of the Commons, without consulting the Labour Party leadership Jan '85; introduced a Bill to abolish standing charges for pensioners Jan '85; again attacked ratecapping Apr '85; criticised the Government's refusal to negotiate with nine Leftwing local authorities refusing to set a rate Apr '85; after a private meeting in May, criticised Home Secretary Leon Brittan for not giving asylum to Tamils June '85; introduced a Bill to guarantee heat and light for pensioners June '85; said it was "absolutely disgraceful" for Roy Hattersley to have visited Madeira on behalf of a merchant bank (for Roy's friend Lord Williams) June '85; in an adjournment debate, attacked UK supply of arms to Chile July '85; urged an amnesty for sacked miners July '85; visited Cyprus as guest of EDEK Oct '85; was a speaker with Tony Benn, Diane Abbott and Peter Heathfield at a Socialist Action meeting Oct '85; in a TV debate on Militant efforts to oust Robert Kilroy-Silk, described local plots as "healthy debate" Oct '85; urged greater Labour activity against Israeli attacks on the PLO Oct '85; attacked as "a disgrace" Neil Kinnock's refusal to stand by hard-Left councils Oct '85; clocked up a low attendance at official standing committee meetings '84-85; voted against Anglo-Irish Agreement Nov '85; went to Paris as guest of Western Sahara Solidarity Campaign Nov '85; urged more generous NHS pay Mar '86; urged solidarity with the people of El Salvador Apr '86; spoke in Florence for European Solidarity with Chile June '86; attacked the "unaccountable" policing of London July '86; visited Cuba and Nicaragua, where he found US policies were dictated by the need "to maintain a financial structure which enslaves most of Latin America" Aug '86; on Campaign Group slate, received 31 votes for Labour's Shadow Cabinet in his first effort Oct '86; served on the Social Security Bill Committee in which John Major ended single payments and the death grant and introduced the Social Fund '86; was alleged to have given £45 to a "clever confidence trickster" who passed himself off as an IRA bomber seeking to flee London Jan '87; introduced a Bill to provide for a better life for old age pensioners Mar '87; at a troops-out meeting he stood in silence for a minute to honour the eight IRAmen shot dead in an SAS ambush May '87; complained the British Government had helped keep the Pinochet regime in power in Chile July '87; nominated on the Campaign Group slate, he received 39 votes for the Shadow Cabinet July '87; urged support for a campaign against Labour Party economies Aug '87; intervened on behalf of Tamil asylum-seekers Aug '87; was summoned by Chief Whip Derek Foster for appointing as his research assistant, Ronan Bennett, a former anarchist and IRA sympathiser who, in 1975, was sentenced for the murder of an RUC inspector, which sentence was quashed a year later Sep '87; appealed for funds for CAMPAIGN GROUP NEWS Oct '87; was a sponsor of the Chesterfield 'Socialist Conference' open to Trotskyists outside the Labour Party Oct '87; fought the Commons security ban on his researcher, Ronan Bennett Oct-Nov '87; was on hit-list of moderate Labour leaders to curb Leftwing control of London Labour Party Dec '87; was a guest at the prison wedding of Paul Hill of the Guildford Four Feb '88; co-sponsored Tony Benn's Bill to end British jurisdiction in Northern Ireland Mar '88; was one of 15 hard-Left Labour MPs in the Campaign Group who backed the Benn-Heffer challenge to the Kinnock-Hattersley leadership Mar '88; was beaten by Glenys Thornton in contest for Chairman of London Labour Party Mar '88; was first MP to protest Saddam Hussein's gas bombardment of Kurds in Halabja Mar '88; tried for an emergency debate to discuss the London parents' poll against the abolition of the ILEA Apr '88; backed Militant MP Dave Nellist against his suspension by the Speaker Apr '88; co-sponsored Tony Benn's Bill to ban the siting of foreign nuclear, chemical and biological weapons in Britain;

deplored US control over 157 installations by over 30,000 privileged servicemen Apr '88; defied party policy in sharing a platform with Sinn Fein speaker Richard MacCauley May '88; deplored insidious influence on police of Freemasons June '88; protested increase to 20% of Labour MPs needed to nominate someone to contest the leadership June '88; voted against EC money resolution July '88; deplored celebration of enthronement of William and Mary - instead of the triumph of the Parliamentary armies over the King during the civil war - because William and Mary were imported to "forever guarantee the powers of the landowning classes as well as bringing with them the Protestant religion and the discrimination against Catholics that followed" in Ulster July '88; complained that Paul Hill of the Guildford Four had been moved 47 times as a prisoner July '88; urged release of Israeli-arrested Palestinian trade unionist Machmoud Masawri Sep '88; accused Labour leadership of retreating into appeasing Thatcherism Oct '88; urged support for Palestinian 'Intifadah' (Uprising) Oct '88; on the Campaign Group slate, received 31 votes for Labour Shadow Cabinet Nov '88; was elected Vice Chairman of the PLP's Northern Ireland Committee Nov '88; protested the West's involvement in the just-ended Iran-Iraq war, which had caused 500,000 fatalities Nov '88; was elected Vice Chairman of PLP's London Labour MPs Nov '88; voted against Prevention of Terrorism Bill, and Ulster loyalty oaths, instead of abstaining Dec '88; became Chairman of Campaign for Non-Alignment, with aim of withdrawing UK from NATO in wake of changes in eastern Europe Dec '88; deplored deportation of Sri Lankan Trotskyist Viraj Mendis Jan '89; defended himself against criticisms of having allowed Ronan Bennett the run of the Palace of Westminster by saying he had never been informed about the charges against him Jan '89; introduced Elimination of Poverty in Retirement Bill Jan '89; voted against Speaker's exclusion of Jim Sillars Mar '89; made a plea to retain hedgerows Mar '89; raised the problems of Kurdish refugees May '89; co-deplored Neil Kinnock's abandonment of unilateralism May '89; presided over Sheffield meeting of Bennite-Trotskyist 'Socialist Conference' June '89; favoured turning Antarctic into a world environment park, without allowing mineral exploitation July '89; said: "we live in a dirty, polluted and dangerous city and I get more and more angry as I cycle round London having my lungs blasted full of exhaust from cars" July '89; co-deplored imprisonment of Mrs Khalil by Israelis July '89; shared platform with Sinn Fein leader Gerry Adams at meeting on fringe of Labour's annual conference Sep '89; visited Paris as guest of the Kurdish Institute of France Oct '89; urged "full compensation" for Guildford Four and reopening of case of Birmingham Six Oct '89; visited Brussels as guest of European Institute on Relations with Latin America Oct '89; stood surety for the Guildford Four when they were released on bail Oct '89; was found to have been the 11th most active intervener in the speeches of other MPs in previous two years Nov '89; addressed annual conference of the [Stalinist] Communist Party of Britain Nov '89; demanded a fresh investigation into the Birmingham Six, who had confessed after beatings and abominable treatment Nov '89; claimed Government was hellbent on trying to destroy the ambulance drivers Dec '89; won the 'Worst Dressed MP' contest, according to the GUARDIAN's Andrew Rawnsley, "for his exquisite examples of the traditional dress of north London: jackets from last year's jumble and trousers which are the most eloquent case for mercy killing" Dec '89; as a friend of asylum-seekers, was unhappy about Labour frontbenchers' hostility to right of abode for 50,000 Hongkong Chinese families Jan '90; again introduced Elimination of Poverty in Retirement Bill, to require monitoring of retired people and eliminate standing charges on gas, electricity and water and telephone rental Jan '90; supported fund-raising by Stalinist MORNING STAR to retain "diverse editorial opinion" Feb '90; admitted he had never been successful with a Bill under the ballot procedure, although he had introduced seven ten-minute-rule Bills Feb '90; urged John Browne to resign for concealing his outside interests Mar '90; supported the Militant-run Anti-Poll Tax Federation Mar '90; helped launch hard-Left 'Labour Party Socialists' with Tony

Benn and ex-MP Reg Race Apr '90; opposed designation of Finsbury Park as a redlight district May '90; introduced Bill to prohibit "barbarism" of hunting and killing of deer with dogs June '90; attacked as a smear Geoffrey Dickens' claim he had deliberately missed a statement on local IRA bombing June '90; urged better facilities for disabled June '90; urged better access to Westminster for disabled July '90; complained of under-funding of Islington Health Authority and its merger July '90; attacked poll tax July '90; urged recall of British forces from Gulf: "the armed presence out there makes things worse; it heightens the chances of war"; voted against the Gulf War Sep '90; was taken to court by Labour-controlled Islington Council for non-payment of poll tax Sep '90; received 26 votes for Shadow Cabinet, overwhelmingly from Campaign Groupies Oct '90; deplored accidents to cyclists Oct '90; urged a peaceful solution of Gulf crisis Nov '90; urging a warmer welcome in adjournment debate, said: "since I have become a Member, I have spent a lot of time dealing with the problems of asylum-seekers from many countries, including Iran, Iraq, Chile, Colombia and a number of Asian countries, particularly Sri Lanka and China" Nov '90; was retained as Secretary of Campaign Group Nov '90; again introduced Elimination of Poverty in Retirement Bill Dec '90; was named to Social Security Select Committee Dec '90; co-sponsored amendment urging peaceful freeing of Kuwait, based on economic sanctions and UN police forces Jan '91; voted against Gulf War Jan '91; co-deplored bombing of civilians in Iraq Feb '91; appeared in court for refusing to pay his £481 poll tax set by Islington Council Feb '91; helped set up 'Labour Against the [Gulf] War'; warned of secret war aims, including ouster of Saddam Hussein Feb '91; deplored impact of Gulf War on region's ecology Mar '91; supported Chris Mullin's view that Judith Ward could not have commited M-62 bus bombing Mar '91; attacked US for killing "at least 100,000 poeple in the Gulf War" but was unable to stop killing of Kurds Apr '91; introduced Asylum Seekers and Refugees Bill to facilitate their entry by a Refugee Protection Agency, a review board to hear appeals and charter of rights May '91; the Campaign Group put him and Dave Nellist on its slate in place of Jo Richardson and Audrey Wise May '91; introduced Abolition of Deer Hunting Bill June '91; attacked exploitation of Latin America July '91; was labelled a "Militant sympathiser" by Conservative Central Office Aug '91; spoke against expulsion from the Labour Party of Militant supporters Dave Nellist and Terry Fields Sep '91; supported Gulf War deserter Sep '91; led amendment pressing for defence industry diversification Oct '91; defended rights of Sahrawi people of Western Sahara Dec '91; with other hard-Leftwingers, urged British withdrawal from Ulster Jan '92; led competing hard-Left amendment urging end of "abhorrent" nuclear weapons Jan '92; opposed "awful" King's Cross Railways Bill, preferring the main terminal to be at Stratford Jan '92; urged solution of Central America's social and economic problems Feb '92; again urged his Elimination of Poverty in Retirement Bill Feb '92; urged an international trial for Lockerbie accused Feb '92; deplored spread of racism in Europe Mar '92; was supported in his re-election campaign by members of the Birmingham Six and Guildford Four, whose cases he had fought Mar '92; intervened on behalf of death-fasting Tamil convicted of murder Apr '92; retained seat with majority up from 9,657 to 12,784, a swing to Labour of 4.57% Apr '92; blamed Labour's defeat on its failure "to offer people an alternative vision of society and a coherent programme for implementing it" Apr '92; was named to Social Security Select Committee July '92; co-sponsored Tony Benn's Bill for a referendum on Maastricht Sep '92; in ballot for constituency section of Labour's NEC, received 22,000?/17,000? votes Oct '92; again introduced Elimination of Poverty in Retirement Bill Nov '92; was rated as one of the most assiduous anti-Maastricht rebels, with seven rebellions against the Labour Whips out of a possible nine Feb '93; again spoke up for self-determination of people of Western Sahara Feb '93; opposed Maastricht because it strengthened the European Commission without any increase in strength of European Parliament Mar '93; voted against 3rd Reading of Maastricht Bill May '93; opposed

PR because it would lose Labour seats May '93; led Campaign Group amendment to Defence Motion, urging cuts to West European average June '93; again urged special handling of unaccompanied children seeking asylum June '93; introduced his Pensioners' Equality Bill to harmonise retirement at 60 July '93; in ballot for constituency section of Labour's NEC, received 16,000 votes Oct '93; unusually, spoke up for a local company, the Simkin Partnership Oct '93; again urged cuts in defence expenditure and diversification of defence industries Oct '93; urged limitation of wage increases to those MPs who did not earn more than £2,000 outside Nov '93; urged Government to keep its contacts in Northern Ireland "with all political parties, including Sinn Fein Jan '94; voting against restoring capital punishment Feb '94; voted to reduce age of homosexual consent to 18 or 16, Feb '94; voted for Margaret Beckett for Leader and Deputy Leader July '94; polled 16,418 votes in constituency section of Labour's NEC Oct '94; polled 31 votes in Shadow Cabinet election Oct '94; voted against EU Finance Bill Nov '94; voted for a LibDem amendment urging a referendum before further EU federalisation Feb '95; deplored the fact his constituency had voted 64.6% for Blair's watered-down Clause IV Apr '95; condemned London's hospital closures May '95; opposed NEC's vetoing of candidacy of Liz Davies, a contributor to his favourite LONDON LABOUR BRIEFING, as "totally unacceptable" Sep '95; polled 22,457 votes for NEC Sep '95; again introduced his Elimination of Poverty Bill Oct '95; paid tribute to Greece's record in World War II Oct '95; attacked US victimisation of Cuba and its desire to make Mexico "a cheap-labour pool" Oct '95; voted against Defence Estimates Oct '95; with hard-Left and "awkward squad" voted against Commons procedure reforms Nov '95; attacked "dreadful" Asylum and Immigration Bill as motivated by "xenophobia" and "backward populism" Dec '95; backed Tony Benn's defence amendment scrapping Trident and cutting spending to west Europe's average Dec '95; again opposed renewal of Prevention of Terrorism Act which had never "stopped a single IRA bomber" Feb '96; opposed Labour support for a new law making mandatory a life sentence for re-offending rapists Feb '96; urged assessment of the monarchy Apr '96; was Teller for the Noes opposing renewal of the Prevention of Terrorism Act Apr '96; initiated an adjournment debate on threat to flora and fauna of Antartica Apr '96; voted for Bill Cash's referendum on Europe June '96; voted for a 3% cap on MPs' pay rise, against a pension based on £43,000 July '96; co-signed GUARDIAN letter urging scrapping of Trident July '96; raised issue of child labour in Britain July '96; ignoring Tony Blair's wish for an uncontested Shadow Cabinet, entered the ballot, receiving 37 votes July '96; backed Clare Short's attack on spin-doctors but preferred blaming "the direction in which Tony Blair is trying to take the party" Aug '96; the Shadow Cabinet voted unanimously to condemn his hiring a Commons room to launch Gerry Adams autobiography, the hiring being cancelled Sep '96; was rated the third topmost of "Blair's Bastards" by Hull University researchers, having voted 64 times since '92 against the leadership Sep '96; again contested the NEC, receiving 25,529 votes Sep '96; opposed the giant Millennium Wheel as "an eyesore" Oct '96; was carpeted by Chief Whip Donald Dewar for meeting a Sinn Fein delegation in the Commons Nov '96; escaped punishment under Labour's new rules after signing Socialist Workers Party petition pledging to fight any Labour weakening of union links or retention of "Tory policies" on the welfare state, by claiming he did not know it was an SWP document Dec '96; urged a "substantial rise" for the "worse-off" public sector employees Jan '97; was targeted by anti-abortion Prolife Alliance Party Feb '97; retained his seat by an enhanced majority of 19,955, on a 6.7% swing from the LibDems May '97; urged new Home Secretary Jack Straw to give asylum to Nigerian dissident Abdul Onibiyo, previously deported by Michael Howard June '97; voted with four other Leftwingers in first rebellion against capping Somerset and Oxfordshire councils June '97; was under pressure for tabling motions without showing them first to Labour Whips July '97; opposed Blair leadership's move toward centrally-approved register of potential candidates as a "pretty appalling vista" July '97; attacked pressure on impoverished East Europeans to buy expensive NATO weapons July '97; urged a better sharing of the world's wealth to prevent the poorest dying at birth and the wealthiest living to 90, July '97; objected to student tuition fees Aug '97; becoming fifth runner-up, polled 39,565 in NEC election Sep '97; voted with 46 other Labour MPs against cuts in lone-parent benefits in Social Security Bill, with four others to oppose its 3rd Reading Dec '97; backed Chris Pond's Employment of Children Bill Feb '98; voted against military action against Iraq Feb '98; was one of 24 Labour rebels voting against Murdoch-style predatory newspaper pricing July '98;

Born: 26 May 1949, Chippenham

Family: Son, David Benjamin Corbyn, electrical engineer, and ????? (?Maiden?), teacher, both Labour Party members; his equally hard-Left brother, Andrew, was an oil expert in Mozambique; his brother Piers was a well-known London squatters' leader in the '60s; m 2nd Claudia; 3 children '88, '92, '93 (one born while he was lecturing to NUPE members elsewhere in the same hospital);

Education: Adams Grammar School, Newport, Shropshire; North London Polytechnic (did not complete degree);

Occupation: Formerly Sponsored by UNISON (ex-NUPE; £600 p a to constituency, 60% of election expenses and £100 for his office expenses) '83-95; Director, of Campaign Group News Ltd (publisher of SOCIALIST CAMPAIGN GROUP NEWS '93?-, Red Rose Labour and Socialist Club (unremunerated) '93?-, Blackstock-Highbury Vale Trust (unremunerated) '93?-; Shareholder, in Hornsey Labour Party Premises Society Ltd (no dividend received); Joint Owner, of freehold of property in London N19; ex: NUPE Area Officer 75-83; Researcher: for AEU (APEX) '73-75, Tailors Union '71-73;

Traits: Slight; bearded; "his bearded and flint-like features appear to have been carved from rock, after the brutalist manner of early Socialist Realism; he never smiles" (Matthew Parris, TIMES); "solemn, bearded and intense", "gaunt and stricken", "like...some Renaissance Crucifixion" (David McKie, GUARDIAN); bitter-tongued; manipulative; "he can be so nice, but when he thinks he's right about something important, he becomes a different person" (Labour MP-colleague); a "spray-on proletarian" (Edward Pearce, DAILY TELEGRAPH); formerly "the nearest thing Parliament has to a Greenham Common man"; used to come "to the House in a jacket refused by Oxfam and corduroy trousers crying out to be put down" (Andrew Rawnsley, GUARDIAN); his new "red jacket...burns like a beacon" (Max Davidson, DAILY TELEGRRAPH); "I dress in a comfortable and casual style in which I feel best able to serve my constituents"; had a black dog called 'Mango'; cyclist ("I have had the same bike since I was 12"); vegetarian; formerly very close to Diane Abbott;

Address: House of Commons, Westminster, London SW1A 0AA; 16 Turle Road, London N4 3LZ (home); 129 Seven Sisters Road (office);

Telephone: 0171 219 3545 (H of C); 0171 263 7538 (home); 0171 263 9450 (office);

CHECKING DRAFTS
We submit drafts of our profiles to MPs to minimise errors and reduce the threat of libel actions. It sometimes produces amusing insights. One MP, whose daughter was reported as having been arrested for prostitution, set us straight. She had gone to Bristol to procure drugs. When arrested, she claimed she was offering sexual favours, knowing it would incur a much lighter sentence.

Sir Patrick (Thomas) CORMACK   Conservative   STAFFORDSHIRE SOUTH '83-

Majority: 7,821 over Labour 4-way;
Description: A safe Tory suburbanised seat on the western edge of the West Midlands; formerly rural, it is now overwhelmingly populated by young, white middle-class owner-occupiers in postwar housing; this development helped defeat Jennie Lee in '70, when it formed a third of her Cannock seat; in '74 it was was renamed Staffordshire SW, then Staffordshire South in '83; by '92 it was the biggest seat in the county; in '95 the Boundary Commission reduced its numbers by 16,000, over 10,000 going to Stafford and the rest to new Cannock Chase;
Former Seat: Staffordshire SW '74-83, Cannock '70-74;
Position: Deputy Shadow Leader of the House '97-; on Select Committee on Modernisation of the Commons '97-, Joint Committee on Privileges '97-, on House Services Committee (Accommodation and Works '91-)'79-; on Ecclesiastical Committee '71-; on Royal Commission on Historical Manuscripts '83- Chairman: all-party Arts and Heritage Committee '79-, all-party Anti-Slavery Society '87-, all-party Finnish Group '92-; Vice Chairman: all-party Group for Release of Soviet Jews '74- (its Chairman '71-74); Chairman '92-, Treasurer '87-92, British-Finnish Parliamentary Group; on General Synod of Church of England '95-; ex: on Chairmen's Panel '83-97, PPS, to Michael Alison and Paul Dean '70-73; on Select Committees on National Heritage '92, Education '79-83; Chairman: all-party Bosnia and Croatia Groups '92-97, all-party Forestry Group '87-92, all-party Committee for Widows and One-Parent Families '74-77 (its Vice Chairman '77-83); Chairman '79-83, Vice Chairman '83-84, Conservative MPs' Forestry Subcommittee;
Outlook: The belated appearance on the front bench, after 27 years, of a shrewd, rebellious Centrist; "one of the finest Parliamentarians" (Michael White, GUARDIAN); was among the first Conservatives to realise how completely they had lost Middle England over their greed, incompetence, incessant quarrels over Europe and by moving too far to the Right; a mainstream traditionalist, a monarchist loyal to the Prince of Wales ("most royally loyal" - Andrew Rawnsley, GUARDIAN); recently, because he has seen it as another Holocaust, has been a belligerent defender of more aggressive peacekeeping in Bosnia ("persistent...in advocating a more interventionist policy in former Yugoslavia" - Douglas Hurd); can also be a bustling Bishop-like figure out of Trollope, orotund of figure and speech; "I have to own up to being an unashamedly nostalgic romantic" (PC); "he brings to our...ecclesiastic heritage not just immense expertise but...passionate commitment" (Tory ex-MP Iain Sproat); a churchy leader of the "sanctimony school" (late Lord Bruce-Gardyne) of Church of England Anglo-Catholics; anti: the ex-Bishop of Durham and women ordained as priests; "know the type: Queen's own Bombastineers - Clerical Section" (Edward Pearce, NEW STATESMAN); a culture-vulture, philistine-baiter and aesthetic heritage defender; a canny fighter for old churches, historic buildings, the genteel of modest means - and Soviet Jews; Euro-enthusiast (in Positive Europe Group '93-); was a cushioned thorn in Mrs Thatcher's flesh, particularly over the poll tax; also against excessive privatisation; "he is not always certain that he is wholly with his own party, and for that reason we like him even more" (Labour MP Tony Banks); "pompous twit" (Tory ex-MP Terry Dicks);
History: His mother was an active Conservative Party worker; "I got a taste for election

meetings as a schoolboy in the '50s in Grimsby"; joined Young Conservatives at 16, '55; became Vice Chairman, East Midlands YCs '61; at 25 contested hopeless Bolsover ("at what they had reckoned to be potentially the most riotous assembly, I read my press release to the school caretaker and the police sergeant who had come to keep order") Oct '64, Grimsby (against Tony Crosland) Mar '66; was selected for Cannock '67; taught part-time locally, guaranteed against earnings loss by local landowner Major Monckton '69-70; overturned Jennie Lee's 11,000 majority to win Cannock June '70; a month later contested 1922 Committee Executive July '70; attacked those "pushing extortionate wage claims" Dec '70; attacked "captains of industry" for lacking "guts" and "slavishly giving in to the bullying tactics of the more irresponsible union leaders" Apr '71; filibustered against Nabarro Bill May '71; introduced Historic Churches Preservation Bill June '71; said he had changed his mind and would support EEC entry July '71; introduced Unit Pricing Bill to ensure marking of price per unit Apr '72; defeated Fergus Montgomery in fierce battle to fight Staffordshire SW May '72; local Tory Executive passed vote of no confidence in him, reversed by Association Aug '72; introduced Container and Packaging Control Bill Apr '73: attacked £73m for MPs' new building May '73; urged metrication July '73; resigned as PPS Nov '73; urged formation of a coalition government May '74; introduced Cinematograph and Indecent Displays Bill June '74; introduced Bill to reform the rates Dec '74; attacked "brutal aggression [in Cambodia] of the North-Vietnamese-sponsored forces" Apr '75; attacked Wealth Tax Sep '75; defended corporal punishment in schools Jan '76; attacked sponsoring of pornographic play Mar '77; his Bill attacked transformation of London skyline into "mini-Manhattan" Mar '77; helped secure Mentmore pictures for nation May '77; escorted expelled John Cordle to door of Commons July '77; urged Mrs Thatcher to name Edward Heath party Chairman Dec '77; introduced Rating Reform Bill Mar '78; precipitated emergency debate on suspension of TIMES Nov '78; co-sponsored Bill to bar indecent displays Nov '78; urged better support for national heritage to stimulate tourism Dec '79; opposed sharp increase in fees for overseas students Dec '79; urged cancellation of Moscow Olympics Jan '80; rebelled on school transport charges Feb '80; urged debate to protest EEC butter for Russia Feb '80; introduced Soviet Union (Temporary Powers) Bill to impose sanctions on USSR June'80; urged tax incentives to encourage returnable bottles Dec '80; attacked cuts in Arts Council grants Feb '81; opposed Forestry Bill to privatize Forestry Commission land Feb '81; abstained against RN cuts July '81; strongly urged reflation Oct '81; rebelled on referenda on rates rises Nov '81; criticised policies of Chancellor Sir Geoffrey Howe Dec '81; urged ban on word 'Chairperson' Mar '82; urged Lord Carrington and John Nott to resign over Falklands Apr '82; rebelled on cuts in unemployment pay July '82; rebelled over benefit cut Nov '82; attacked Ken Livingstone's invitation to Sinn Fein Dec '82; urged lifting of ban on Sunday shopping only in smaller shops Feb '83; co-sponsored Allaun's Right-of-Reply Bill Mar '83; criticised appointment of Ian MacGregor to NCB Mar '83; on 150th anniversary of Wilberforce's death, urged final end of slavery everywhere and elementary rights in the USSR July '83; co-complained of delay in Theatre Museum July '83; opposed contraceptives for under-16 girls without parental consent Dec '83; voted against Rates Bill Jan '84; abstained from supporting GCHQ union ban Feb '84; backed freedom for Shcharansky Mar '84; backed strike-breaking Staffordshire miners Mar '84; was one of four Tory MPs to vote against poll tax [Local Government (Interim Provisions)] Bill on 3rd Reading May '84; urged a wide rebellion against the Rates Bill Mar '84; was among 19 Tory rebels against suspending GLC elections Apr '84; introduced elimination-style electoral reform Bill to ensure MPs represented over half their constituents May '84; attacked the "total contempt" with which the Arts Minister was treating MPs June '84; complained that unemployed thrifty in their fifties were being penalised for previous savings June '84; obliquely criticising the Bishop of Durham, he asked for Durham's orphans to be "brought up to believe in the virgin birth" and the other "essential tenets of the Christian faith" June '84; urged Arts Minister to hold "tutorials for the Philistines" June '84; again unsuccessfully contested Executive of 1922 Committee Nov '84; rebelled against Keith Joseph's increase in parents' contributions to undergraduates Nov '84; was among two dozen Tory rebels against abolishing GLC Dec '84; complained about failure to apply anomalous Sunday trading legislation Dec '84; complained about too much power being placed in hands of Environment Secretary Dec '84; led the demand for a mini-GLC Dec '84; threatened to rebel against an extension of VAT Dec '84; was among 40-odd 'wets' who urged government to allow local authorities to spend a proportion of their house sales money on house-building and infrastructure Jan '85; opposed Norman Tebbit becoming Chairman of the Conservative Party Aug '85; urged Mrs Thatcher to broaden her administration Aug '85; said MP-PRmen should not speak on behalf of a client in the Commons Nov '85; introduced Bill to allow local authorities access to criminal records of potential child abusers Dec '85; voted against the Channel Tunnel, one of 6 Tory MPs Dec '85; urged a mandatory two-year imprisonment for drunken drivers who cause death Dec '85; criticised Mrs Thatcher's style over Westland and urged Leon Brittan to resign Jan '86; urged tax deductibility as the real answer to the financial problems of the arts Jan '86; provocatively urged a Heseltine-style 'European solution' to BL's problems, rather than General Motors Feb '86; helped defeat Government on Shops Bill to allow Sunday trading Apr '86; as its Editor, had issue of HOUSE MAGAZINE pulped for publishing "politically contentious" material against Mrs Thatcher Jan '87; complained that Arts budget was minute Mar '87; rebelled against charging farmers for hygeine inspection Mar '87; was re-elected June '87; successfully co-campaigned for funds for haemophiliacs infected by the AIDS virus Nov '87; backed Sir George Young's initial effort to make poll tax made "more fair by banding the rate of charge in proportion to ability to pay" Dec '87; urged Chancellor Lawson to devote to the NHS a further 1p or 2p from income tax cuts Jan '88; voted against Government's failure to uprate child benefit Jan '88; backed televising the Commons Feb '88; asked how Stalker memoirs could be both a tissue of lies and a breach of confidence Feb '88; rebelled on full poll tax for student nurses Apr '88; rebelled on poll tax for aged Apr '88; rebelled with Michael Mates' on banding proposals for poll tax Apr '88; opposed charges for eye and dental checks Apr '88; in Ecclesiastical Committee said ordination of divorced and remarried men was incompatible with the Christian doctrine of the indissolubility of marriage May '88; visited Moscow with East-West Human Rights Group Feb '89; said Israel's friends were running out of patience over its ignoring of PLO's conciliatory gestures Feb '89; toured USA with British-American Parliamentary Group Mar '89; led the cheers for Sir Geoffrey Howe after he had been downgraded by Mrs Thatcher from Foreign Secretary to Leader of the Commons July '89; urged more aid for AIDS-afflicted haemophiliacs Nov '89; objected to Parliament Square being dug up for new Westminster tube station Nov '89; voted against War Crimes Bill Dec '89; urged state aid for cathedrals Dec '89; urged Arts Minister Richard Luce to ratify the 1970 UNESCO Convention Dec '89; visited Paris as guest of House of Fraser Dec '89; thought ambulance strike would be worth settling at 6.8% if the unions agreed to a no-strike deal Jan '90; refused to vote for Student Loans Bill because the Vice Chancellors had not been consulted Feb '90; told Commons of his participation in East-West talks Feb '90; urged help for Royal Shakespeare Company Feb '90; pointed out 70 fellow Tory MPs supported transfer of education expenditure to central Government (to cut poll tax) Mar '90; was a teller against punishing John Browne MP for concealing his interests Mar '90; said, "I think Mrs Thatcher should be giving increasing thought to whether there might be some merit in having a new captain on the bridge for the next election" Mar '90; refused to vote further for NHS and Community Care Bill when Kenneth Clarke introduced a guillotine too early ("one guillotine too far") Mar '90; voted with Opposition to provide more help for elderly in homes Mar '90;

visited Bucharest as guest of Emenescu Trust Mar '90; said poll tax was "fundamentally unfair" Apr '90; opposed giving too much power to Education Secretary Apr '90; in abortion debate, said, "first, the interests of the mother are and must be paramount"; women who were victims of rape or incest must have the chance to have the pregnancy terminated; or if there was evidence of severe abnormality Apr '90; said, "the British people like pomp and circumstance" after Mrs Thatcher cut back on Royal Household finances July '90; urged a Ministry of the Arts, Heritage, Tourism, Films and Broadcasting July '90; suggested Iraqis be bombed by leaflets disclosing unpleasant things about Saddam Hussein Sep '90; urged help for haemophiliacs Oct '90; deplored Sir Geoffrey Howe's resignation Nov '90; when he heard Mrs Thatcher was threatening to fight again in the second round for the Leadership, he raised his eyebrows and said, "if I were her, I would sleep on it" Nov '90; again attacked poll tax Dec '90; again opposed War Crimes Bill, insisting a fair trial was no longer possible Mar '91; waved his order paper in celebration of abolition of poll tax, saying: "I have been implacably opposed to this tax from the word go, as Opposition Members know; I did not support it at any stage"; urged abolition of 20% contribution in council tax Mar '91; urged reform in the shape of two-round elections, with a repeat for those who hadn't attained 50% in the first round May '91; was rated as one of the most rebellious Tory MPs, with six dissents in '89-90 session Aug '91; abstained against Defence cuts Oct '91; waxed indignant about big stores flouting Sunday trading laws: "the people violating the law are quite deliberately holding Parliament in contempt in this quite intolerable way" Nov '91; as an old opponent of the poll tax, backed the new council tax Nov '91; angered fellow members of his Works of Art Committee by hanging the controversial painting of the Queen by Henry Mee, without full consultation Nov '91; sought emergency debate on rushed aid for Kurds Nov '91; backed law change to prevent courtroom libels (such as launched against Labour MP Greville Janner by a child molester) Dec '91; urged "tough deterrent action" against those attacking Dubrovnik, "a world heritage site" Dec '91; said "I have never in my 22 years in this House heard a more silly proposition" when Teresa Gorman tried to force the Commons to have as many women as male MPs Jan '92; retained seat with majority down from 25,268 to 22,633, a swing to Labour of 4.14% Apr '92; attacked "the pack of greedy voyeurs" in the Sunday press June '92; co-stressed "the moral need for an immediate end to the present horror in Bosnia" by curbing the aggressive Serbian Government which "has actively instigated the infliction of terror and massacre upon the peoples of Croatia and Bosnia in turn"; urged the use of an aircraft carrier force in the Adriatic, with regular air patrols June '92; was again named to Accommodation and Works Committee June '92; was named to National Heritage Select Committee July '92; when Tory Whips opposed Nicholas Winterton's re-appointment to Health Select Committee, on grounds he had been around too long, it was pointed out that Cormack had served 12 years on select committee July '92 opposed draft Euthanasia Bill July '92; angered like his constituents about threat to close 31 coalmines, thought he had won a "real review" of pit closures from Michael Heseltine and Tim Eggar Oct '92; left the National Heritage Select Committee Nov '92; promised to give ordination of women a hard time Nov '92; again said, "Serbia has persistently been the aggressor" in former Yugoslavia Nov '92; insisted the taxpayer must foot the bill for the Windsor fire Dec '92; said, "it is inconceivable that we could have a crowned King and a crowned Queen not speaking to each other" Dec '92; co-launched 'Action for Bosnia' Dec '92 ; was uncertain about pit closures review Dec '92; urged an "internationally guaranteed" peace for Bosnia, with all heavy weapons taken from all sides, particularly the Serbs, who had killed 200,000 in what "amounts to genocide" Jan '93; was attacked as a "squit" by Sir Nicholas Fairbairn for having chosen Michael Hopkins as architect for the "hideous, hippopotomic carbuncle" of a new Parliamentary building in Bridge Street Jan '93; co-sponsored the restrictive Shops (Amendment) Bill of Labour Whip Ray Powell ("whom I am delighted to call my honourable Friend on this occasion") Jan '93; was one of three Tory MPs who abstained on mines closures Mar '93; spoke strongly against threat to Staffordshire school music service Mar '93; mixed his support for Maastricht with repeated demands for a common policy on Bosnia Mar '93; celebrated reprieve of Staffordshire Regiment, whose amalgamation with Cheshire he had fought Apr '93; said, "I am thoroughly frustrated and ashamed; I have always wanted an ultimatum, backed up by action, which the Serbs know they can't get away with; we have got to use air strikes, and there will be a need for certain ground involvement as a peacekeeping force" Apr '93; supported Ray Powell's Shops (Amendment) Bill to keep Sundays special May '93; was considered by late Robert Adley to be one who was "anxious about the effects of [railway] privatisation, but could not be relied on to rebel" May '93; congratulated Transport Secretary John McGregor for listening to complaints and amending Railways Bill May '93; said war in ex-Yugoslavia could have been stopped in Dubrovnik June '93; urged John Major to save Sarajevo July '93; on Ecclesiastical Committee demanded Archbishop of Canterbury safeguard promotions of opponents of women's ordination July '93; before voting against it, admitted to being "distressed" by proposal to ordain women as priests; "I do not believe that a woman can be a priest any more than she can be a father"; warned he might follow Ann Widdecombe and John Gummer into the Roman Catholic Church Oct '93; sharply criticised British Coal Chairman Neil Clarke as "a half-hearted pessimistic salesman [who] does no good to the industry" Oct '93; said he would vote for Government on Defence Estimats only "with great reluctance": "we won our battle over the Staffordshire Regiment, but it was a small victory; we have cut too deep already" Oct '93; as a signatory to a letter to John Major warning of a possible revolt over defence cuts, said he was prepared to vote against the Budget if front-line capability was jeopardised Nov '93; was overruled by Speaker in his design for Commons Christmas card Nov '93; warned in Sunday trading debate "if we abolish Sunday as a special day, we cannot get it back, it is gone for ever" Dec '93; insisted "the whole credibility" of the UN as a peacemaker was at stake in Bosnia Dec '93; deplored those who "rob, pillage and sell cultural objects and view them merely as money"; "commercialism has done great damage in many walks of life"; suggested reconsidering the return of the Elgin Marbles Feb '94; told pro-privatisation Michael Heseltine: "I view Royal Mail Plc as favourably as your old regiment being replaced by Group 4 at Buckingham Palace" May '94; in the Commons successfully sponsored Lord Renton's Bill to outlaw the "market overt" legalising stolen goods sold in Bermondsey Market between dawn and dusk July '94; following speculation about the divorce of Prince of Wales and Princess Diana, said "the marriage has irretrievably broken down and the sooner it's over, the better" Oct 94; insisted on an "MPs Only" section in Bellamy's Canteen in the new Parliament Street office building, excluding researchers and secretaries Oct '94; urged end of VAT on church repairs Dec '94; urged a summit of world leaders on Bosnia on Foreign Secretary Douglas Hurd Dec '94; insisted the Tories' loss of the Dudley by-election showed "people in Middle England are fed up with what they see as doctrinaire championing of privatisation" Dec '94; was knighted in New Years Honours Jan '95; predicted the Tories would suffer "the most catastrophic defeat in its history at the next election unless some of my colleagues can learn to practice a self-denying ordinance and realise that bickering today spells doom tomorrow" Mar '95; said, "division over Europe was at the root of the party's troubles and the biggest impediment to recovery" Apr '95; after the Bosnian Serbs had taken UN peacekeepers hostage, said they were now "trying to hold the international community to ransom" after committing the "most appalling atrocities" May '95; claimed another change in Tory Leadership would be "the final nail in the party's coffin" May '95; called for lift of arms embargo to let Bosnia resist Serb aggression July '95; attacked as "deplorable taste" the Playboy TV advertisement mentioning "morgasms" Oct '95; as the representative of Lichfield diocese, attended his first General Synod Nov '95; said it was not "necessarily in the best public interest" to privatise HMSO, preferring to have it taken over by Parliament Dec '95; criticised "headstrong" Princess Diana as "badly advised or doesn't take advice", after she threw doubts on her husband's kingly attributes on 'Panorama' Dec '95; preferred BBC to be wholly financed from the public purse, rather than partly privately-financed Jan '96; attacked with revulsion the offer for sale of the Royal Naval College, Greenwich, as the "son of a master mariner" Feb '96; voted against the extension of Sunday pub licensing hours Feb '96; derided Home Secretary Michael Howard's claim that some asylum seekers had self-inflicted wounds, insisting he "would rather the system was abused by one perverse individual who had mutilitated himslf...than that someone who has been tortured was sent back to further torture and torment" Feb '96; after Prince of Wales' private call had been intercepted, introduced Protection of Privacy Bill to make it an offence to buy or sell transcripts of private conversations without consent of both parties Mar '96; described the reaction to BSE as "urban panic" and an effort to create a "steak-rejecting society" Mar '96; opposed panic over the Tories' loss of their Staffordshire SE seat - a defeat he had predicted Apr '96; deplored the behaviour in TV sitcom 'Men Behaving Badly' July '96; said of TV: "there is no worse crime against humanity than the destruction of childish innocence" July '96; spoke and abstained against Government Bill restricting asylum-seekers from three-days grace in seeking asylum July '96; voted against 3% cap on MPs' pay rise, for pensions based on £43,000 and cuts in mileage allowances July '96; opposing radical change, insisted "I believe the stability of our democratic system depends on the survival of the monarchy" Aug '96; led CPA delegation to Hongkong Oct '96; opposed siting a giant Ferris-wheel opposite the Commons Oct '96; urged the Church of England to remain "neutral, at the very least" on fox-hunting since "there are many fine examples of hunters in the Bible" Dec '96; urged English Heritage to provide more core funding for church buildings Dec '96; attacked colleagues as "Europhobes masquerading as Eurosceptics" Dec '96; voted to restore caning Jan '97; on the Firearms (Amendment) Bill, claimed no legislation could deal with maniacs and police should have sussed out the Dunblane killer Feb '97; led campaign to give UK citizenship to 5,000 non-Chinese in Hongkong, saying "they should be given the security their loyalty to the Crown merits" Feb '97; voted to dis-assemble target guns rather than ban them Feb '97;criticised Bishop of Worcester for his pro-Labour comments Mar '97; with 96 other MPs, backed European Movement's pro-EU campaign Mar '97; retained his altered seat by a majority reduced by two-thirds, to 7,821, on a pro-Labour swing of 9% May '97; seconded Peter Lilley for the Tory Leadership May '97; after Lilley lost, failed to persuade him to back Kenneth Clarke June '97; was named to the new Select Committee on Modernisation June '97; was named Deputy Shadow Leader of the Commons, under Gillian Shephard June '97; as part of Opposition tactics, opposed guillotining of the Finance Bill and the Referendum (Scotland and Wales) Bill June '97; opposed proposals of new Commons Leader Ann Taylor to clear out to many old Commons customs, possibly allowing clapping Aug '97; urged "a period of silence" on Princess Diana after her "very partisan political comments" describing the previous Tory Government as "hopeless" and backing the new Labour Government on landmines Aug '97; urged a cautious approach to changing Commons procedures Nov '97;

Born: 18 May 1939, Lincolnshire

Family: Son, Thomas Charles Cormack, local government officer and master mariner, and Kathleen Mary (Harris), active Tory; m '67 Kathleen Mary (McDonald); 2s Charles James Stuart '69, who contested West Renfrewshire for the Tories in '97, Richard '71;

Education: St James' Choir School, Grimsby; Havelock School, Grimsby; Hull University;

Occupation: Consultant, to Patrick Cormack and Partners (PR firm - clients: Federation of Personnel Services '72-93, Federation of Engineering Design Companies '74-91,

Linford-Bridgeman Ltd [conservation and restoration company] '84-, Machinery Users' Association [£5-10,000] '79-, SAC Designs Ltd '82-91, Parliamentary Communications Ltd [publishers of HOUSE MAGAZINE] '81-, Colebrand Ltd [private company in high technology] '85-, NNEB (National Nursery Examinations Board) '83-, Watercolour Facsimiles Ltd '86-90); Programme Adviser, Catholic University of America [£1-5,000] '89-; Journalist (Institute of Journalists): Editor, the HOUSE MAGAZINE [£5-10,000] '83-, President, of FIRST MAGAZINE [£1,000]; Visiting Fellow, St Antony's College, Oxford '94; Author: English Cathedrals (1984), biography of William Wilberforce (1983), Castles of Britain (1981), Westminster: Palace and Parliament, (1981), Right Turn (1978), Heritage in Danger (1976); Trustee, Historic Churches Preservation Trust; on Historic Buildings Council; ex: Chairman, Aitken Dott Ltd '84-88; Director, Aitken Dott Ltd (The Scottish Gallery) '88-91, Aitken Dott Ltd (Art in Business) '84-90, Landywood Cabinet Company '86-87, Historic Houses Hotels Ltd '80-88; Watercolour Facsimiles Ltd '86-90, Watercolour Foundation '88-90; Shareholder, in Collectors' Commemoratives Ltd (commemorative pottery) '75-79; Associate Editor, of TIME AND TIDE '77-79; Consultant, to Thomas Tudor Organisation '72-74; Company Training Officer of Ross Group '66-67; Schoolmaster: Brewood Grammar School, Staffordshire '69-70, Wrekin College '67-69, St James' School, Grimsby '61-66;
Traits: Rounded; owlish; fruity-voiced; "a large man with a biggish head, large spectacles, a wide mouth that is often set in a shallow downwards curve...Sir Patrick...who looks as though he has never rejected a steak in his life - or any other foodstuff for that matter -... reminds me of the large Toad, Mr Jackson, who sat in Mrs Tittlemouses's kitchen saying 'tiddly, widdly, widdly'; he is the only MP who is paired - satisfactorily for all concerned - with himself" (David Aaronovitch, INDEPENDENT); bright; shrewd; assiduous; "Bunteresque" (MAIL ON SUNDAY); "seems to be cultivating a kind of jowly sagacity nowadays which suggests he may be in training for the Woolsack" (David McKie, GUARDIAN); can display a "perma-sulk" or "saturnine smugness" but "his face usually glares with apparent disdain in the presence of the uncouth - such as most of his colleagues - that makes him look as if he has mumps" (Simon Heffer, DAILY TELEGRAPH); "the air of those people who say 'ssshh' to you in public galleries"; "a man of such majesty that even colleagues do not always appreciate how majestic he is" (Matthew Parris, TIMES); churchy (General Synod, Rector Warden of St Margaret's, Westminster; "there are those of us who feel very deeply and passionately about the Church of England as by law established"); "a capacity for sanctimonious pomposity" (Gerald Kaufman MP); his "frock-coated presence has lent tone to many a St Margaret's memorial service" (ex-MP Sir Julian Critchley); collects political pottery; "a Fellow of the Society of Antiquaries, he seldom fails to place FSA after his name" (DAILY TELEGRAPH); in '94 he became its Vice President;
Address: House of Commons, Westminster, London SW1A 0AA; Dolphin Square, SW1; a house in Enville, Staffordshire;
Telephone: 0171 219 3420/5096 (H of C);

TAKING US SERIOUSLY
We noticed that politicians began to take us seriously after it became apparent to them that most press profiles and biographies relied on the facts in our four-volume PARLIAMENTARY PROFILES. Our profiles even follow politicians to their graves. We noted one obituarist who relied on us completely, causing us to break out into the famous comic song enjoining American academics to plagiarise.

Majority: 16,159 (33.5%) over Conservative 6-way;
Description: A formerly marginal seat of skilled working-class owner-occupiers; a long strip of the eastern fringe of Bristol, containing major parts of the old pre-'83 Cripps-Benn safe-for-Labour Bristol Southeast, and some of the old Northeast; in '95 it lost 10,000 voters in Hengrove to Bristol South and picked up 17,000 in St George East and West from Kingswood; overall this helped Labour;
Position: PPS, to David Blunkett '97-; Deputy Chairman, Parliamentary Labour Party '97-; on PLP's Liaison Group '97-; ex: on Select Committees: on Home Affairs '95-97, on Agriculture '92-95; Co-Chairman, PLP Women's Group '92-97; Head of Elections and Training Department of Labour Party '85-86; Bristol Area Regional Organiser '81-85; South West Region's Women's Organiser '76-81; Organiser, Taunton '74-76; TGWU-sponsored;

Outlook: An attractive lady who packs a mean semi-hard Left punch; has low-profiled significance as a trusted link between David Blunkett (his PPS), the PLP (its Deputy Chairman) and the interface between the Leadership and backbenchers (elected to its Liaison Group); as Co-Chairman of the PLP's Women's Group, became a key figure in "the sisterhood" of feminist Parliamentarians as soon as she recovered from surgery soon after she captured the seat in '92; she and Dawn Primarolo were until '97 the only Labour women MPs in the West Country; "symbolises drive and ability coupled with a hectic family life" (Michael White and Alan Travis, GUARDIAN); as Tory Ministers soon learned, she has the formidable backing of her husband, Professor Peter Townsend, the Labour movement's most effective academic statistician and redistributionist; Labour's former Southwest Regional Organiser turned candidate, then MP, having been "head-hunted especially for the job" (Michael Lord, BRISTOL EVENING POST); she proved her competence and appeal as a campaigner by taking the seat in '92 with a then near-record 6.78% swing to Labour; in '97 she played a leading role in ousting William Waldegrave from Bristol West by exposing his role, in the Treasury, of underfunding Bristol; a multi-cause groupie (Haldane Society of Socialist Lawyers, Co-operative Party, One World); was TGWU-sponsored;
History: Her most important early political influence was "watching my grandmother's face at Christmas 1948 when my father explained to her that NHS treatment was free"; joined the Labour Party '58; was named full-time Organiser for Taunton '74, Women's Organiser for South West '76, South West Area Regional Organiser, (only the second woman to achieve this) '81; was named Head of Elections and Training Department in Walworth Road, Labour headquarters '85; after her marriage to Professor Peter Townsend, retired from Walworth Road to study for the Bar '86; on qualifying, had a "convincing victory" (BRISTOL EVENING POST) when she was selected for Bristol East, defeating Councillor Pam Tatlow and the previous candidate, ex-MP Ron Thomas by 52% on the first ballot Jan '90; her Bristol East Constituency Labour Party called on the Labour Party to back a mass "wont pay" campaign on the poll tax; she said she would not pay her own poll tax "voluntarily" but would not encourage others to break the law Feb '90; was attacked by her opponent, Jonathan Sayeed MP, for refusing to pay her poll tax Mar '90; she did eventually pay it; urged wholesale reform: "the House of Lords should go, and be replaced by an elected second Chamber"; "I'd

also support the abolition of the Lord Chancellor's office"; also family courts to improve divorce and less discrimination against women at the Bar Oct '90; she was allegedly seen locally as "the reasonable face of Labour; her hobbies include such safe, middle-aged pursuits as knitting and gardening; she is a skilfully-chosen antidote to the extemists of the Labour-dominated [Bristol] City Council" (Frances Hardy, DAILY MAIL) Mar '92; recaptured Bristol East by 2,692 votes, a swing to Labour of 6.78% Apr '92; in her Maiden pointed out that Bristol now had equal representation, two women and two men; deplored the deterioration of Bristol's economy and the failure of Bristol Development Corporation, which "has managed to arouse the hostility of residents, business people and virtually every community group", partly by proposing "without holding a public inquiry, to build a dual carriageway on stilts through my constituency which will carry 42,000 vehicles a day"; she wanted to know why British women were "at the bottom of the European league in maternity pay and maternity rights" May '92; urged tougher pressure on water companies to avoid their breaching the 1976 drinking water directive in her constituency, where analysis had shown banned pesticides and faecal coliform; the Department of Environment had put off Bristol Water's need to conform until the late '90s; "my constituents are being asked to pay by a Marie Antoinette Government who say, 'Let them drink Perrier'" June '92; was named to Select Committee on Agriculture Oct '92; warned that expected cuts in invalidity benefit would come without any basis of information: "in reply to a series of Parliamentary answers addressed to me on 30 October, Nicholas Scott, the Minister for Disabled People, was unable to give any information about distribution of income of invalidity benefit recipients and their families; furthermore, he was unable to give trends in the income of these people for the late '80s and early '90s; what a way to go about creating a nation at ease with itself!" Nov '92; led motion attacking curbs on legal aid Jan '93; in NHS debate warned that the Avon dental service was breaking down Jan '93; complained of impact of cuts on urban programme on her constituency, with male unemployment at 43% in Barton Hill Feb '93; urged a debate on the Jopling Report to reform Parliamentary hours, to allow MPs to have "a decent home and family life", thus enabling more women to consider becoming MPs Feb '93; introduced Justice Bill to help investigate alleged miscarriages of justice Feb '93; with 1,400 of 5,000 Rolls-Royce job losses hitting Bristol, urged Assisted Area status for Avon, recognised by the EC as "the most defence-dependent urban area in Europe" Mar '93; celebrated 25th anniversary of Abortion Act Apr '93; voted against 3rd Reading of Maastricht Bill May '93; complained that allowing employers to bribe employees with higher pay if they gave up their unions would "have the effect of negating trade union membership", "an attempt to turn the industrial relations clock back to 1906"; she cited the Bristol printing company, Arrowsmith, which had locked out workers and de-recognised unions because this behaviour was condoned by the Government June '93; in debate on domestic violence said legislation "completely fails women who are brave enough to go to court; the law is a mess - I say that as someone who, before becoming a Member of Parliament, was a barrister specialising in domestic violence law"; urged "a proper network of refuges...so that women can seek refuge quickly and safely for themselves and their children" July '93; secured the statistics demonstrating that under Mrs Thatcher the living standards of the top 10% improved by 62%, while the poorest 10% had a cut in real income of 14% Oct '93; as a result of the CofE's ordination of women "I felt that the Church to which I was supposed to belong, but with which I have had little to do in my adult life, included me for the first time" Oct '93; led a widely-supported motion to reverse the "precipitate recommendations of the Committee on Toxicity of Food" which resulted in banning comfrey tablets Nov '93; Social Security Under Secretary Alistair Burt complained that she had been wrong in claiming that statistics on poverty had been "wrongly withheld"; "as I have repeatedly said in correspondence with [Mrs Corston], this Department makes available to bona fide researchers the base data set from which the households below-average income statistics are obtained, to enable them to undertake what further analysis they choose under the conventions they prefer"; "she was...reminded that the base data set could be made available to her research advisers" - clearly her husband, Professor Peter Townsend - "in the computer-readable form of their choice; this repeated an offer first made some months ago, which I understand her researchers have now taken up" Jan '94; sharply criticised the Government's new Criminal Justice and Public Order Bill as missing "a unique opportunity to restore confidence in our criminal justice system"; "there is a need for an independent body to review miscarriages of justice, as recommended by the Runciman Commission"; "the right to remain silent in the face of questioning, accusations and interrogation is a fundamental principle that has been in existence for 350 years"; she objected to "child jails" for young offenders because existing secure places were under-funded; "offending behaviour is frequently associated with family breakdown and sentencing to closed institutions a long way from home will serve only to exacerbate that problem" Jan '94; voted against restoring capital punishment, even for killing policemen Feb '94; voted to reduce the age of homosexual consent to 16 or 18 Feb '94; led a motion urging Government to abide by a judgement of the International Court of Justice if it declared nuclear weapons illegal Feb '94; in Prime Minister's questions asked whether PM knew the richest fifth had increased their income by £6,000 a year since 1979 while the poorest fifth had had their incomes cut by £3,000 a year, which he tried to deny Feb '94; in Sex Discrimination debate pointed out that Labour had more women MPs than the other parties together, and in 20 years the Tories had not even had "a single half-day committed to debating sex discrimination"; British women's percentage of men's pay, at 67%, was the lowest in the EC Mar '94; introduced her ten-minute-rule Bill to enable local authorities to use a microchip to identify permanently stray dogs, to avoid the costly business of repeatedly rounding them up and kenneling them Mar '94; caught out the PM in a comprehensive rebuttal to his false statement in February that the disposable income of people "at all ranges of income has increased" since 1979, pointing out that, according to Government statistics, the "poorest 10% of families with children had an average household income which was £438 per year lower in 1992 than in 1979"; "the incomes of the second poorest 10% are also smaller - by an average of £281 per year - than in 1979" May '94; urged more Government funding for cheaper rented housing in Bristol's deprived areas June '94; voted for Margaret Beckett for Leader and Deputy Leader July '94; asked Agriculture Minister about diet and nutrition July '94; denied the job of running the loathed Child Support Agency was unsuitable for a woman, insisting "to be in public life at all, women have to be very tough" Sep '94; opposed too much flexibility in placating Labour Party opponents of all-women short-lists for fear of "giving the green light" to male monopolists Sep '94; said that, because some local Labour parties were having difficulty with the new rule about alternating men and women delegates, was no reason for dropping it Sep '94; urged a debate on childhood asthma and the polluting environment Oct '94; denied misrepresentation in COSMOPOLITAN that she had favoured decriminalising hard drugs Dec '94; co-signed Campaign Group letter alleging Criminal Justice Bill criminalised protest and removed right of silence in court Dec '94; claimed there was "a national child care gap of 400,000 places" for the 45% of women who were at work Jan '95; found it "extraordinary that it was acceptable for the House [of Commons] to have a rifle range but not a creche" Jan '95; voted against extending Sunday pub licensing hours Feb '95; complained that the poorest 20% had a lower disposable income than in '79, but BT's Sir Iain Vallance could call his £770,000 pay "modest" Feb '95; introduced Bill to provide more information to curb domestic violence Mar '95; co-signed GUARDIAN letter urging Labour's commitment to full employment Mar '95; introduced Bill to eliminate sexism in language of Acts of Parliament May '95; tabled motion and held debate defending Bristol

Cancer Help Centre against criticisms of higher death rates from Imperial Cancer Research June '95; argued for lifting of quarantine, citing only two rabid dogs in living memory July '95; condemned "vicious racist attacks" on young blacks by 20 fairground workers in Bristol July '95; in letter to INDEPENDENT criticised Frank Field's welfare reforms as "Victorian" - which Field denied -insisting "the challenge for the Labour Government is the reformulation of the strengths of the public sector" Aug '95; was appointed to head a team of MPs under John Prescott to co-ordinate PLP efforts to win the general election Oct '95; co-sponsored Tony Benn's amendment to Defence Estimates, urging Trident-scrapping and spending cuts to West European average Dec '95; regretted Labour decision not to appeal tribunal veto on all-women short-lists Feb '96; claimed three-quarters of those earning under £3.50 an hour were women, with 800,000 earning less than £2.50; urged "zero tolerance" of violence against women Mar '96; expressed concern that press reporting on Bristol's black drug dealers would fuel race hatred Apr '96; in paper co-written with Peter Hain and Derek Fatchett, published in the NEW STATESMAN, urged a future Labour Government consult with backbenchers to avoid being "run from Whitehall and Downing Street" Apr '96; backed parental leave to enable fathers to share child upbringing July '96; complained that Bristol had received less tax assistance than any comparable city, blaming William Waldegrave from his days in the Treasury; he lost his seat three months later Feb '97; had adjournment debate on harmful effects of anti-malarial drug Lariam Mar '97; was listed in GUARDIAN as one of 30 in 'New Left for New Labour' - largely the former 'Supper Club' - backing Prescott and Cook against Blairites Apr '97; was targeted by The FIELD as an opponent of hunting Apr '97; retained beneficially-altered seat by an enhanced majority of 16,159, on a notional pro-Labour swing of 11.9% May '97; was one of five women to take all but one of the seats in PLP Liaison Group with new Govenment June '97; was elected Deputy Chairman of the PLP June '97; with Derek Fatchett and Peter Hain sent memo to Labour's General Secretary Tom Sawyer urging a strong role for the unions and annual conference July '97; was named PPS to David Blunkett Aug '97; was named by Ann Clwyd as one of the Labour women MPs the late Princess Diana expressed an interest in meeting Sep '97; urged PM Blair that the NHS be made more open to staff concerns like the excessive deaths among cardiac child patients in Bristol Royal Infirmary June '98;

Born: 5 May 1942, Hull

Family: D Laurie Parkin, former glove-maker then trade union official, and late Eileen (Russell); m 1st '61 Christopher Corston; 1d Sarah '63 doctor; 1s David '65 primary school teacher; m 2nd '85 Peter Townsend, Professor of Social Policy at Bristol University; five stepchildren: Matthew '52. Adam '53, Christian '57, Benjamin '62, Lucy '76;

Education: Huish and Westfield Primaries, Yeovil; Yeovil Girls High School; Somerset College of Art and Technology; Open University; London School of Economics (LLB '89); Inns of Court School of Law;

Occupation: Barrister (in Bristol, specialising in domestic violence law) '91-92; Director, Tribune Publications Ltd (unpaid) '93-; was Sponsored, by TGWU (£600 p a to constituency, 80% of election expenses) '93-95; ex: Head of Department for Elections and Training, Labour Party '85-86 (TGWU); Bristol Regional Organizer, Labour Party (APEX & NULO) '81-85; South West Region Women's Organizer, (APEX & NULO) '76-81; Taunton Organizer '74-76 (APEX & NULO);

Traits: Dark hair; pert; pretty; intelligent face; friendly smile; "softly-spoken", "attractive, articulate and oozes reasonableness"; "vegetarian" (LEGAL BUSINESS); "as a child I was required to go to church three times on a Sunday; by the time I had become a young woman, I felt that the Church had nothing to say to me; I felt excluded"; "I concluded that the Church would rather I arranged the flowers and sang nicely, because there seemed to be no other way

of my influencing it"; her political hero is Mary Wollstonecraft because she was aware in 1794 that education was the key to the liberation of women; her political hate-figure is Kenneth Baker "who represents the unctuous Brylcreem style that I find repellent"; had a hysterectomy in '92; enjoys reading, walking, gardening and knitting;
Address: House of Commons, Westminster, London SW1A 0AA;
Telephone: 071 219 4575 (H of C); 0454 231686 (home); 0272 259279 (constituency office);

Brian COTTER   **Liberal Democrat**   **WESTON-SUPER-MARE '97-**

Majority: 1,274 over Conservative 4-way;
Description: The large, mostly traditional Bristol Channel resort town in the North Somerset estuary whose Tory majorities were slipping even before the '97 election;
Position: Small Business Spokesman '97-; on the Deregulation Committee '97-; on the National Executive of Liberal Democrat Parliamentary Candidates Association; ex: Woking District Councillor '86-90;
Outlook: Sensible, efficient and capable if not spectacular Spokesman; a not very partisan newcomer ("I hate all this point-scoring" [BC]); a small plastics manfacturer and company doctor on the LibDem's conservative wing; an internet anorak interested in small business's role in job creation; won on his second try by exploiting the tactical vote; in Charter 88, Amnesty International, Green Liberal Democrats;
History: He joined the Liberals '83; was elected to Woking District Council May '86; selected to contest Weston-super-Mare, he cut Tory MP Jerry Wiggin's majority from 7,998 to 5,342 Apr '92; was re-selected; Jerry Wiggin stepped down, as did the local Green candidate, who moved to adjoining Woodspring; at annual LibDem conference, backed 5% VAT on tourism; complained that for every £1 spent in the Westcountry on tourism, £40 was spent in Scotland Sep '96; in the election campaign concentrated wholly on tactical voting, with a former Chairman of the local Labour Party helping with "we must not let wasted votes for Labour let the Tory scrape in"; Cotter's election literature emphasised a bar chart illustrating how this had happened previously Apr '97; managed to defeat by 1,274 votes the able new pro-European Tory candidate and former MEP for the area, Margaret Daly, helped by a Referendum Party vote of 2,280 May '97; urged better monitoring and regulation of shipping in the Bristol Channel June '97; asked Minister to "reduce the regulatory burden on small businesses" June '97; pressed for cuts in business rates June '97; urged a review of credit reference agencies June '97; in his Maiden emphasised his role as the LibDems' Small Business Spokesman, saying, "if just one job were to be created in every small business, it would solve the employment problem in this country"; he endorsed the planned late-payment Bill and regional development agencies; he also called for a "fairer rating system" and warned that the windfall tax "will inevitably hit consumers and pension fund holders" July '97; he urged a reassessment of the "deregulation initiative" July '97; was named to the Deregulation Committee Aug '97; urged more support for innovative small businesses, especially from financiers Nov '97; exploded: "I hate all this point-scoring" Dec '97; asked about advice for head lice in schools

Dec '97; welcomed proposed Regional Development Agencies Jan '98; led motion urging protection of dwindling tiger population from illegal poaching Jan '98; urged more intense concentration on the millennium bug and policing of the internet Mar '98; urged faster payment by Government of its bills Mar '98; urged more generous funding for schools Apr '98; challenged the "startling arrogance" of Conservatives in warning about a threatened industrial recession despite the damage they had done to industry in their 18 years in office Apr '98; congratulated Government on proposing interest on late payments May '98; co-sponsored motion deploring supermarket profiting on low beef prices for farmers May '98; urged more Government emphasis on small business start-up guidance and support June '98;

Born: 24 August 1938, Ealing

Family: Son, of Dr Michael Cotter, GP, and Mary (Nugent); m '63 Eyleen Patricia (Wade); 2s, 1d;

Education: St Benedict's School, Ealing; Downside School, Bath;

Occupation: Managing Director, of Plasticable Plc (plastics manufacturing company employing 27 people), earlier its Sales Director; was previously unemployed for a year;

Traits: A de Gaulle look-alike; long face; beaky nose; crooked smile; receding grey-blond, straggling, parted hair; discursive, chatty style; charming but accident-prone; doughty and formidable; reminds one of Larry Grayson, camp but not gay; educated in Benedictine public schools; enjoys reading, films, gardening, walking; has "an e-mail address and was one of the first MPs on the website" (BC);

Address: House of Commons, Westminster, London SW1A 0AA; Belmont House, Brinsea Road, Congresbury, Bristol BS19 5JF;

Telephone: 0171 219 4357 (H of C); 01934 832755 (home); 01934 876919 (Fax);

'Jim' (James Mackay) COUSINS   Labour   NEWCASTLE-upon-TYNE
                                                                 CENTRAL '87-

Majority: 16,480 (35.8%) over Conservative 4-way;

Description: A formerly marginal seat, created in '83, with no overlap with old safe-Labour Newcastle Central (now in Tyne Bridge); it now surrounds Town Moor, just North of the city centre; it has considerable owner-occupied middle-class housing as well as multi-occupied rundown mansions; many lecturers, teachers, students, doctors, nurses and some non-whites in Wingrove and Jesmond; home of Andrews Liver Salts and Lucozade (closed down); in '95 it acquired the safe Labour ward of Sandyford from Newcastle East;

Position: On Treasury Select Committee '97-; Chairman '97-, Vice Chairman '95-97, PLP's Northern Group; Treasurer, Office of Science and Technology '91-; ex: Assistant Spokesman: on Foreign Affairs '94-95, on Trade and Industry '92-94; on Select Committees: on Public Service '95-97, on Trade and Industry '89-92; Chairman '91-92, Vice Chairman '88-90, of the Tribune Group; Tyne and Wear County Councillor (Deputy Leader '81-86) '73-86; Wallsend Borough Councillor '69-73; on Northern Regional Health Authority '78-80;

Outlook: Highly-intelligent, low-profiled, rooted local fixer who lost his footing on the promotional ladder through an unauthorised trip with Ann Clwyd to Kurdish areas; his previous interest in foreign affairs was on the Iraqi supergun, when on the Trade and Industry Select Committee, where he was an effective questioner; semi-hard Leftwinger (in the 'Supper Club', a former Tribune Group Chairman); is a firm regionalist, an advocate of a North East Regional Assembly; persuasive but not overly partisan; was rated the seventh most assiduous questioner in '93-94; a former local lecturer-councillor who captured a key target seat from Piers Merchant and then strengthened his hold; has "intelligence and clear thinking" but was "something of a wheeler-dealer" (Phil Murphy, NEWCASTLE JOURNAL); "a fixer who likes to lead from behind" (Newcastle official); was partly responsible for bringing Komatsu and Nissan to the area; looks back "with pride" on his record as a Tyne and Wear Councillor: "we defended free fares for pensioners over 12 difficult years, AND introduced Britain's one and only integrated public transport system"; was MSF-sponsored;

History: He was initially a member of the Liberal Party; joined the Labour Party '66; was elected to Wallsend Borough Council May '69; was elected to Tyne and Wear County Council Apr '73; was appointed to the Northern Regional Health Authority as a Tyne and Wear Councillor '78; was dropped when he was "just beginning to understand how it worked" because he belonged to the wrong, i e Labour, party '80; was elected Deputy Leader of Tyne and Wear County Council '81; as Chairman of the Tyne and Wear Planning and Transportation Committee, was partly responsible for the creation of the Tyne and Wear Metro - Britain's first integrated transport system '81-83; as expected, was selected from a shortlist of four men and one woman by 42 to 17 on second ballot for marginal Newcastle Central, previously narrowly won by Tory Piers Merchant Nov '85; attacked closure of Fleming Memorial Hospital Nov '86; criticised withdrawal of public funds from St Camillus Hospital at Hexham Nov '86; attacked local "bus chaos" Dec '86; promised to fight sacking of 140 academics at Newcastle University Jan '87; complained of the "ultra-Right anti-democratic clique inside the spy Establishment" exposed by Peter Wright May '87; said it was a "vicious trick" to deprive the old and poor of community alarms May '87; was convinced he would capture the seat because many local interest groups had been alienated by the Conservative Government May '87; was elected, ousting Piers Merchant June '87; handed over his first week's pay to local SOGAT strikers June '87; in his belated Maiden he said that social security claimants were "reluctant to claim" partly because of "the Government's distrust of those on benefit"; he complained that the social security benefits system was a disincentive to work Nov '87; voted with hard Left to allow Jeremy Corbyn's ex-IRA-sympathising researcher access to Commons Nov '87; like Ken Livingstone, he was initially without a desk or telephone; insisted this had no political significance, joking: "hardline Leftwingers like me have very little in common with Rightwingers like Ken" Jan '88; filibustered in committee against poll tax Bill, speaking for one hour and 40 minutes on one amendment Feb '88; complained about continued inadequate financing for scientific research Feb '88; said that if Regional Health Authorities were abolished, "I would fear that the medical aristocracy might be replaced by more ruthless managers"; they should be replaced with a group independent of government, with moral authority, representing the interests of the patients of the region and able to put them to the Government Apr '88; complained that local poor were being offered loans rather than grants July '88; claimed hard-up families were being driven into the clutches of loan sharks after being cut by £15 a week Aug '88; as Chairman of Labour's Parliamentary Science and Technology subcommittee, urged better Government funding for scientific research Sep '88; was elected Vice Chairman of Tribune Group Nov '88; joined protest against persecution of political prisoners in Iran Jan '89; expressed anger that the rebuilding of a 101-year-old local school was again being deferred Jan '89; was named to Select Committee on Trade and Industry, replacing Joe Ashton Jan '89; while serving on the Companies Bill he was alerted to the weak position of ordinary investors, who were helpless to influence the decision-makers; "for the first time I could see all sorts of deficiencies in the way companies and financial services operated, not to mention the secrecy" Mar '89; co-urged Labour to emphasise 'green' environmental issues June '89; complained the Government was subsidising the tarting up of Gray Street in the commercial centre of Newcastle, while neglecting people on outlying estates Sep '89; warned that student loans would introduce a "two-tier education system" Oct '89; urged the building in of "proper regulation of accountancy and accounting standards" into the Companies Bill Oct '89; said it was "very disturbing" that only two of the 21 investigations launched by the Investigations Division of Trade and Industry into insider dealing had been completed Nov '89; dismissed as unworkable the "confetti of controls and cash limits" the Government was working into its NHS and Community Care Bill Dec '89; forced a change in over-reliance on food vouchers in his local social security office Jan '90; despite his questioning, Trade Secretary Nicholas Ridley refused to explain why he had not disqualified the Fayed brothers as company directors of the House of Fraser Mar '90; warned a Newcastle conference of an impending crisis for the elderly and mentally handicapped if community care were to be under-funded Mar '90; asked a brace of questions about the Accounting Standards Board Apr '90; voted against war in the Gulf Dec '90; after 500 questions, was attacked by John Redwood, then Minister for Corporate Affairs, for his "campaign of vilification" against the accountancy profession, because he urged higher standards in protecting pension funds or insurance investments Feb '91; was photographed in the Westminster Arms meeting of the semi-hard Leftwing 'Supper Club' Feb '91; asked Securities and Investment Board Chairman Sir David Walker to take preventive steps to clamp down on misleading advertisements promoting high-risk, high-return investments Feb '91; claimed "a Government who could subsidise chemical plant construction in Iraq to the tune of several hundred million pounds during the 1980s have no need to cheat children of £2.30 per week by freezing child benefit as they have since 1987" Feb '91; complained about the destruction of DTI records on British arms sales to Iraq Mar '91; was hostile to Lord Hanson's bid for ICI: "he is shaking the tree and waiting to see if any apples fall; someone who has £7b in his back pocket can clearly shake any tree he wishes; that is one of the perils of the free market system" June '91; blamed the Government for "the ridiculous machinery" of NHS reforms "which is now crumbling around the Government" Oct '91; was rated as asking the second largest number of written questions among 29 Northeastern MPs, and the twelfth most frequent oral questions Nov '91; said "the Attorney General should enforce the existing law [on Sunday trading] after all the hoo-hah about collecting and enforcing the poll tax" Dec '91; voted to defer Far Eastern trip of Trade and Industry Select Committee in order to complete its report on the Iraq 'super-gun'; succeeded in getting Alan Clark to call Nicholas Ridley a liar on the subject ("an exaggeration") Feb '92; claimed NHS waiting lists were lengthening Feb '92; during election campaign his claim to have secured a local liver transplant unit was challenged by the Tories; retained seat with majority up from 2,483 to 5,288, a swing to Labour of 3.49% Apr '92; was retained on Select Committee on Trade and Industry May '92; accused the Government of "going for a cover-up" on £20b sales of Tornado aircraft to Saudi Arabia after "totally unsatisfactory" answers to his string of questons about who had profited from "the biggest arms deal in history" (Adam Raphael, OBSERVER) May '92; as its outgoing Chairman, supported a move to revitalise the Tribune Group and make it more independent of the leadership, after the election of Centre-Right John Smith as Leader aroused fears the Left would be marginalised May '92; was named Assistant Spokesman on Trade and Industry under Robin Cook July '92; having become a spokesman, was dropped from Select Committee on Trade and Industry Oct '92; in his Maiden speech as a Spokesman, complained the DTI was not helping hard-hit small businesses by, for example, exempting small shops from the uniform business rate Nov '92; warned that the Government's announced plan to privatise Parcel Force would weaken the Post Office Apr '93; at the press conference on the Iraqi super-gun report by the Trade and Industry Select Committee, said that "at least two Whitehall departments have been lying and lying for a number of years" May '93; claimed that Government had applied volatile swings to industry in the '80s, "the same as electro-convulsive therapy" and were later taking credit for those who survived June '93; visited France with all-party Parliamentary Space Group as guest of British Aerospace and Matra Marconi June '93; was ranked 12th among the most frequent receivers of written answers in the '92-93 session, Jan '94; complained that Trade and Industry had slowed down growth of jobs by its slow processing of telecommunications applications Jan '94; deplored the privatisation of the Commercial Division of AEA Technology as "a disaster for British technology exports and the British taxpayer" Feb '94; voted against restoring capital punishment, even for killing policemen Feb '94; voted to cut age of homosexual consent to 16, not voting on 18, Feb '94; was rated the seventh most assiduous questioner among MPs in the year to February 1994, asking 419 questions, costing £41,000 Apr '94; after the death of Labour Leader John Smith, tried to organise support for Robin Cook as his successor May '94; Cook having refused to stand, voted for Margaret Beckett for Leader and Deputy Leader July '94; urged Michael Heseltine to safeguard the livelihood of sub post offices by protecting their payment of benefits - 40% of their income - against being poached by banks and supermarkets July '94; was named Assistant Spokesman on Foreign Affairs under Robin Cook by the new Leader, Tony Blair Oct '94; asked a lot of questions about the veiled Anglo-American Mutual Defence Agreement Dec '94; voted against extending Sunday pub licensing hours Feb '95; complained that self-regulation of professions was no more than an "institutionalised conspiracy" in debate on Medical (Professional Performance) Bill; called for clearer definition of "serious" in doctors' "serious misconduct" Apr '95; was sacked by Tony Blair as Assistant Spokesman on Foreign Affairs for being absent without Whips' permission in Kurdish areas with Ann Clwyd, who also was sacked for missing crucial votes; he went along with her to observe Turkish Army attacks on Kurdish villages; he wanted to leave the war zone before she did; she accused him of "bleating and whimpering", "I had to hold his hand"; he insisted his were "sensible decisions" and he tried to "protect her from herself" Apr '95; complaining to Environment Secretary John Gummer about the capping of Newcastle's spending, was told it was the Tory Government's "purpose to make sure the people of Newcastle do not pay the full penalty for having voted Labour" June '95; after Michael Heseltine's surprise disclosure about BMARC's shipping forbidden artillery to Iran asked about the Chief Secretary, "how is Mr Aitken ever to clear his name in the face of this disgrace, this dishonour and these deceits?" June '95; was named to the Public Services Select Committee ??? '95; accused the Government of lying and the intelligence services of "demonstrable incompetence" in the Scott Report debate, demanding further, deeper investigations Feb '96; complained of four suspicious deaths in his local Royal Victoria Infirmary Apr '96; voted against a 3% cap on MPs' pay rise and for a cut in their mileage allowance July '96; when he asked about civil service leaks, Deputy PM Michael Heseltine alleged a network of pro-Labour leakers Dec '96; complained that the two-in-five Newcastle children on benefit were being short-changed by the Government Feb '97; he became a target of the Prolife Alliance Party Feb '97; claimed the Government's North East Office was inaccessible to local people Mar '97; said, "Labour wants a better deal for the North and we need our own regional voice to do this" Apr '97; retained his favourably-altered seat with an enhanced majority of 16,480 on a notional pro-Labour swing of 9.9% May '97; after Regional Affairs Minister Caborn warned there was no chance of a North East Regional Assembly before 2002, said it was "very important a clear direction was taken towards democratic government in the North[east]" June '97; vote to ban fox-hunting June '97; was

named to the Treasury Select Committee July '97; again urged a "regional development strategy" for the Northeast, "one of the most disadvantaged regions in Europe" which "bumps along at the bottom of the table of every social and economic indicator" Jan '98;
Born: 23 February 1944, Shepherds Bush, London;
Family: Son, Charles 'Jack' Cousins, printing compositor, and Grace (Rich), shop assistant; m '?? Anne (Morison) "influential Tyne and Wear Councillor"; 2s Charles, Jonathon, 1 steps Nicholas, 2 stepd Alison, Katherine; sixth-former Katherine died at 18 in '90 from a pulmonary embolism (blood clot) as a rare side-effect of having started the pill a month earlier;
Education: City of London School; New College, Oxford University; London School of Economics;
Occupation: Panellist: on Harris Parliamentary Panel (£1,000) '95?-, Business Planning and Research International (£1,000) '95?-; formerly Sponsored, by MSF (£600 p a to constituency party, a third of election expenses) '89-95; MSF provided more than 25% of his election expenses Apr-May '97; ex: Lecturer at Bradford University, Sunderland Polytechnic (ASTMS) '68-87); Contract Researcher and Lecturer on steel, shipbuilding and inner city job markets for trade unions, Commission on Industrial Relations and Departments of Employment and Environment; Research Officer, Durham University;
Traits: Tall; burly; greying beard; specs; a John Osborne look-alike ("any resemblance is purely facial!" [JC]); "has never entirely trusted the press, and, on occasions colleagues - he has too often given the impression of being a secretive politician", "hardly a man of the people" (Phil Murphy, NEWCASTLE JOURNAL); enjoys composting;
Address: House of Commons, Westminster, London SW1A 0AA; 37 Sanderson Road, Newcastle-upon-Tyne, NE2 2D4; 21 Portland Terrace, Jesmopnd, Newcastle NE2 1QQ;
Telephone: 0171 219 4204 (H of C); 0191 281 2235 (home); 0191 281 9666 (office);

'Tom' (Thomas Michael) COX　　　　**Labour**　　　　**TOOTING '74-**

Majority: 15,011 (32.6%) 4,107 (8.03%) over Conservative 9-way;
Description: Unaltered cosmopolitan seat in South London between Brixton and Wimbledon with many Greek Cypriots, a quarter of non-whites; it was expanded in 1983 to take in Tory-inclined areas from Battersea South; is afflicted with kerb crawlers in Bedford Hill;
Former Seat: Wandsworth Central '70-74;
Position: Delegate, to Council of Europe and WEU (Rapporteur: on Children '95-96, Asbestos '96-97) '80-; on Executive of Commonwealth Parliamentary Association '92-; Chairman '95?-, Vice Chairman '83-95?, Secretary '??-83 British-Cyprus Parliamentary Group; Chairman, British-Taiwan Parliamentary Group '97-; Vice Chairman: British-Cameroon Parliamentary Group '87-, British-Ivory Coast Parliamentary Group '87-; Treasurer, British-East African Parliamentary Group; Secretary: Franco-British, British-Somali, British-Liberian Parliamentary Groups; ex: Whip (Lord Commissioner) for Greater London '77-79, Assistant Whip '74-77;
Outlook: Left-leaning partisan battler for social and international causes who has repeatedly frustrated Wandsworth Tories anxious to oust him from their 'flagship borough'; refused a

peerage to make his seat free for a young "Blair Babe"; a hard worker in the constituency, especially in fighting Wandsworth Tory councillors and the local scourges of kerb crawlers and loud music; a leading Commons spokesman for the Greek Cypriots; socially concerned (on Wormwood Scrubs board); a crusader against National Front; pro: prison reform, CND, Greeks in Cyprus, Kashmiri freedom fighters, Taiwanese, democratic Argentinians; anti: Turks, tobacco for children, loud music, Tory-led Wandsworth Council; a wide-ranging free-tripper as an IPU and WEU activist and for a plethora of foreign-linked Parliamentary groups; obsessively secret about his modest background; as a former power station worker was EETPU-sponsored; "one of Labour's natural journeymen" (Walter Ellis, DAILY MAIL); **History:** He joined the Labour Party at 14, '44; was elected to Fulham Borough Council '5?; became Fulham Borough Council Alderman '60; was elected to Hammersmith Council May '64; contested Stroud Mar '66; contested GLC elections May '67; won Wandsworth Central June '70; deplored youthful drug-taking, unnecessarily frequent industrial accidents July '70; deplored assaults on bus drivers and conductors Dec '70; was stopped from speaking by National Front Sep '71; opposed EEC entry Oct '71; urged arms amnesty Mar '73; complained that electricity boards were unwittingly helping landlords oust unwanted tenants May '73; urged Register of MPs' Interests June '73; introduced Bill to prevent giving of fraudulent degrees July '73; became an Assistant Whip '74; was promoted full Whip (Lord Commissioner) in place of Tom Pendry Jan '77; despite Callaghan appeal, voted against PR for European Assembly Dec '77; opposed prison haircuts for Rastafarians Apr '81; warned about possibility of new Brixton riots unless "this Government tackles the really root cause of the problem" Apr '81; voted for Healey against Benn Sep '81; wanted kerb crawlers prosecuted under Vagrancy Act Nov '81; opposed National Front march through black areas Dec '81; asked why Thatcher Government was not as much against Turkish military fascists as those of Argentina Apr '82; again attacked kerb crawlers Apr '82; urged an "immediate truce" in the Falklands May '82; had adjournment debate on maltreatment of Greek Cypriots by Turks July '82; accused Mrs Thatcher of a "hysterical outburst" in "smearing the leaders of the CND" and converting Britain into "Reagan's European fortress" Apr '83; attacked Government's "destruction of job opportunities" May '83; unexpectedly retained Tooting May '83; co-sponsored motion welcoming Greek Cypriot President Kyprianou July '83; backed Bill to abolish standing charges for utilities Jan '84; secured promise of action against kerb crawlers Feb '84; wanted stricter control of poultry slaughter Mar '84; urged better prison conditions June '84; expressed concern about asbestosis among power station workers -his old job - and demolition crews July '84; opposed changes in housing benefit Oct '84; co-sponsored Janet Fookes' Bill against kerb crawlers Jan '85; lined up with Tories in Committee, against Clive Soley and Alf Dubs, to keep kerb crawlers in Fookes Bill, despite possible risk to innocent drivers Feb '85; opposed increases in charges for overseas students Mar '85; deplored Tony Marlow's "grave disservice" and Matthew Parris's filibuster which killed off Fookes' Bill to punish kerb crawlers May '85; was re-selected by 27 to 24 on second ballot, beating off challenge of Keith Vaz June '85; criticised police for kicking in doors of blacks and Asians Oct '85; urged UK to stop dragging its feet over South African sanctions June '86; urged reinforcement of Metropolitan Fraud Squad to cope with City fraud Feb '87; urged more help for areas of urban deprivation, instead of rate-capping Mar '87; voted against televising Commons Feb '88; again complained about night flights Feb '88; warned of need for precision in Bill to ban dog-fighting because of risk of judicial misinterpretation Apr '88; urged allowing prisoners to telephone distant relatives July '88; asked Mrs Thatcher what a £48 a month rise in mortgage repayments would do to young people struggling for home ownership July '88; opposed the entry to Britain of CIA-backed anti-Communist UNITA leader, Dr Jonas Savimbi July '88; deplored the continued use of police cells to hold remand prisoners Dec '88; the Black Sections movement said it wanted to take over his seat Feb '89; was renamed a Delegate to Council of Europe Apr '89; visited China as on WEU mission, serving as Rapporteur May '89; urged a more active British role in reuniting Cyprus Oct '89; visited East and West Germany on IPU mission Dec '89; accused the new Minister for Housing, Michael Spicer, of wanting to preside over a nation of people sleeping in cardboard boxes Jan '90; asked a brace of questions on prison conditions Jan '90; visited Romania on IPU mission Feb '90; complained that for hours on end and day after day, his constituents suffered from fighting between prostitutes and their pimps; many ordinary women in Bedford Hill would not go out in the evenings because they would be accosted by kerb crawlers Feb '90; urged resignation of Tory MP John Browne for concealing his outside interests Mar '90; opposed Ken Livingstone's amendment to Sexual Offences Bill, designed to avoid entrapping the wrong people for kerb crawling: "I give greater support to the rights of women who live in my constituency and who need to be able to walk home without continual harassment and abuse" May '90; visited Argentina on IPU mission Oct '90; asked another brace of questions on prison conditions Oct '90; complained about "noise pollution" - loud music - in his constituency Oct '90; co-sponsored Andrew Faulds' Children and Young Persons (Protection from Tobacco) Bill Dec '90; visited Syria and Turkey on IPU mission Dec '90; visited Wembley with all-party Football Committee Feb '91; called attention to Cypriot help for Gulf War Mar '91; reported on his visit to Nepal to observe its elections June '91; in debate on anti-social behaviour, concentrated on loud music and Wandworth Council's cuts in social services June '91; was renamed a Delegate to Council of Europe June '91; deplored the number of small businesses which had gone to the wall in London Nov '91; complained about deterioration of London Transport Feb '92; visited Washington to urge renewed Anglo-American initiatives in Cyprus, as part of pro-Greek 'Friends of Cyprus' delegation Feb '92; was expected to lose his grip on Tooting because its Tory 'flagship borough', Wandsworth, had twice avoided demanding poll taxes; but Wandsworth managed to stir its yuppies into hostility by over-spending on education and then sharply cutting on educational expenditure Mar '92; retained his seat with his majority up from 1,441 to 4,102, a swing to Labour of 2.53% 'Apr 92; was renamed to Council of Europe May '92; again raised the 1974 Turkish invasion of Cyprus May '92; complained about grossly over-crowded prisons June '92; deplored fraudulent organisation of commercial boxing Oct '92; was rated as the 25th most assiduous questioner Oct '92; staged debate on sufferings of Kashmiri freedom fighters Dec '92; was on delegation to see Foreign Secretary Douglas Hurd about misbehavour of Indian security forces in Kashmir Jan '93; urged improved civil rights for the disabled Feb '93; again raised human rights of Kashmiris Apr '93; complained about drop in manufacturing jobs in London June '93; opposed draft Euthanasia Bill Sep '92; staged an adjournment debate on Cyprus, blaming Turkish Cypriot leader, Rauf Denktas for torpedoing peace talks July '93; voted to keep Sunday special in Sunday trading debate Dec '93; launched another debate on Cyprus, deploring the '74 "brutal invasion by the Turkish army"; attacked the obduracy of Turkish Cypriots and Ankara in refusing "a settlement that ensures the rights of both the Greek and Turkish Cypriot communities" Dec '93; was again named Delegate to Council of Europe Dec '93; voted against restoring capital punishment, even for killing policemen Feb '94; voted to reduce homosexual age of consent to 16, but did not vote for 18, Feb '94; his free trip to the Falklands was frustrated by Labour Whips operating "guerilla tactics" Mar '94; voted for Blair for Leader, Beckett for Deputy Leader July '94; on 20th anniversary of Cyprus invasion, again attacked Turks, especially the threat to united North Cyprus with Turkey, if Cyprus joined the EU July '94; warned about misuse of imported pen that turned into penknife Nov '94; secured debate on Tory-led Wandsworth Council and its obsession with low council taxes, contrasting the needs of "the [middle-class] people who had moved into the borough and who need very few council services and those who do need the services"; urged more

low-cost rented property Dec '94; his Researcher, Frederick Morgan, was named in the OBSERVER as a lobbyist for Westminster Advisers Ltd Jan '95; supported the Proceeds of Crimes Bill of Tory MP Sir John Hannan to curb international money laundering; emphasised need to strengthen extradition, to secure return of Turkish Cypriot Asil Nadir, for example Feb '95; backed improvement of pension rights for MPs like himself, elected before '83, enabling them "at long last to get a reasonable pension to look after them in old age" July '95; backed motion attacking DAILY MAIL for leaving Greece off list of Britain's wartime allies Oct '95; atttacked Turkish Cypriots for failing to allow agreed settling of ghost town of Famagusta Nov '95; opposed reforms of Commons procedures, in company of hard-Left and 'awkward sqyad' Nov '95; attacked impact of Wandsworth health budget cuts on local St George's Hospital Dec '95; backed Tory MP John Marshall's Sexual Offences Bill aimed at Britons abusing children abroad Apr '96; attacked Wandsorth Council for its stinginess on day centres for the elderly Apr '96; as Chairman of the Britain-Cyprus Parliamentary Group urged Cyprus's admission to EU, not allowing a Turkish veto June '96; voted against 3% cap on MPs' pay rise July '96; urged return of all occupied areeas of Cyprus to their rightful owners (mainly Greeks) Dec '96; raised the crisis in London hospital services, especially St George's accident and emergency department Dec '96; welcomed Foreign Secretary Rifkind's Cyprus visit Dec '96; visited Greece on invitation of Greek Parliament Jan '97; was a target of Prolife Alliance Party Feb '97; as an opponent of fox-hunting, was a target of The FIELD Apr '97; refused the offer of a peerage if he stood aside for a Blairite candidate, Sally Morgan Apr '97; retained his once-threatened seat with a majority almost quadrupled to 15,011 on a swing of 12.3% May '97; as a Council of Europe Rapporteur in its Report on Asbestos, complained of the enormous lmovement of this dangerous substance among it 40 member-states June '97; visited US to attend conferences, paid for by International Co-ordinating Committee for Justice in Cyprus June '97; voted to ban fox-hunting June '97; became Chairman of the British-Taiwan Parliamentary Group July '97; co-signed INDEPENDENT letter attacking Turkish behaviour towards Kurds Aug '97; urged a complete ban on use of asbestos Dec '97; enthusiastically urged improved relations with democratic Argentine leadership July '98;
Born: i9 January 1930, London
Family: Refuses to disclose family background;
Education: London council school (undisclosed); LSE (course);
Occupation: Parliamentary Adviser, to Ancient Order of Foresters Friendly Society (unpaid) '97?-; formerly Sponsored, by EEPTU (£2,012 toward election costs in '79) '70-95; ex: Labourer in Battersea Power Station '49-70; Miner in South Wales '45-48;
Traits: Dark; thinning hair; specs; prewar-style moustache; a punchy debater on a few subjects; "eloquent and passionate" (Nick Raynsford MP); has a loud voice ("the Tooting Stentor" - David McKie, GUARDIAN); "his manner, as ever, that of a permanently enraged greengrocer" (Matthew Parris, TIMES); RC; tight-lipped about personal and educational background; "nice chap" (Tory opponent); "lacklustre" (SDP opponent); likes gardening; "an interest in greyhound racing" (ex-MP Hugo Summerson);
Address: House of Commons, Westminster, London SW1A 0AA; 171A Tranmere Road, London SW18 3QX;
Telephone: 0171 219 5034 (H of C); 0181 946 2641 (home);

James (Douglas) CRAN   Conservative   **BEVERLEY & HOLDERNESS '97-**

Majority: 1,211 (2.3%) over Labour 5-way;
Description: A new rural and suburban seat, created in '95, to the north and east of Hull; half its voters come from former Bridlington, two-fifths from old Beverley and the rest from abolished Boothferry; it stretches from the minster town of Beverley via the Hull suburbs to the ornithologists' redoubt at Spurn Head;
Former Seat: Beverley '87-97
Position: Whip '97-; ex: on the Administration Committee '97-98; PPS, to Sir Patrick Mayhew '95-96; on: Northern Ireland Grand Committee '96-97, Select Committee on Northern Ireland '94-95, Trade and Industry Select Committee '87-92; Vice Chairman: Conservative MPs' Northern Ireland Committee '92-94, Conservative MPs' Horticulture and Markets Subcommittee '87-88; Secretary: Conservative MPs' European Affairs Committee '89-91, Constitutional Affairs '89-91; Vice Chairman, all-party Anglo-Mongolian Parliamentary Group '93-94, all-party Order of St John Parliamentary Group '94-95; Secretary, all-party Anglo-Malta Parliamentary Group '92-94; Sutton Borough Councillor (Chairman of Housing '75-79) '74-79;
Outlook: A flinty Aberdonian Eurosceptic and Ulster unionist whose "quirkiness makes him difficult to predict" (DAILY TELEGRAPH); "I am a pretty Rightwing character...but I am not particularly daft" (JC); in '97, voted for Michael Howard, then John Redwood, finally for William Hague; a leading Rightwinger who voted against Maastricht from its 2nd Reading becoming the 'chief whip' of the rebels and their "most thoughtful strategist" (TIMES); "the chief puppet-master of the Conservative Euro-rebels...who came within a few minutes of bringing down the Prime Minister" (Nicholas Wood, TIMES), but later decided that dumping Major would bring in Heseltine; one of the former Tory businessmen "who object to the way they say EC growth hampers trade" (Michael Prescott, SUNDAY TIMES); was also one of the "constitutionalists...who argue that British law and sovereignty are being eroded at every turn by Brussels" (Philip Webster, TIMES); "I am not a natural rebel; I find it quite difficult; I live in the hope that behind the scenes when you talk somebody, somewhere, will listen; the longer I have been here, the more I have realised that nobody at all is listening"; "as long as most MPs want to be Ministers, they will never have much influence, because to do that they have got to keep in with the system and the system rewards conformity" (JC); was initially an opponent of MPs' accepting lobbying consultancies: "as soon as...one accepts money for lobbying in Parliament, one ceases to use one's own independent mind" (JC); "he itches to bring in management consultants to get the place efficiently organised" (Madeleine Bunting, GUARDIAN); initially an assiduous, independent-minded, constituency MP; normally a party loyalist; was "probably the closest Lord Young had to a supporter on the [Select] Committee" which reported adversely on Young's 'sweetened' sale of Rover to British Aerospace (Ralph Atkins, FINANCIAL TIMES); is tough on crime and punishment, anxious to bring back capital punishment and caning and put juveniles in secure accomodation and expel travellers and other trespassers; was one of the most zealous of the '87 newcomers - "a reputation for being a very hardworking constituency Member" (Colin [recently Lord] Moynihan); initially a full-timer enthusiastic about Urban Development Corporations and concerned about possible causes of child cancer clusters; a former CBI Regional Director with long-standing political

Copyright (C)Parliamentary Profile Services Ltd

ambitions who succeeded Sir Patrick Wall at Beverley; an economic Rightwinger with social and environmental awareness;

History: He won the National Youth Speaking Contest and DAILY MIRROR Trophy '68; joined Conservative Research Department '70; was elected to Sutton Borough Council May '74; contested Shettleston, Glasgow Oct '74; was selected for Gordon (ex West Aberdeenshire) instead of sitting MP David Myles Mar '83; contested Gordon, losing by 1.8% to Liberal Malcolm Bruce June '83; was selected for Beverley to replace retiring Sir Patrick Wall Sep '86; retained seat June '87; in his Maiden he insisted "sloganizing does not help to solve the intractable problem of inner city deprivation", "it is the lack of economic regeneration that exacerbates social problems"; he had "helped to lobby for the Black Country Urban Development Corporation" July '87; worried that the BA/BCal merger might exclude small independents from Gatwick July '87; with others, complained about plans to cut child benefit Sep '87; voted against David Alton's abortion-curbing Bill Jan '88; backed a Bill to compel rear seatbelts in cars Feb '88; enthused about the DTI's enterprise initiative Mar '88; again complained about child cancer clusters in his constituency and persuaded the Government to investigate the emissions of Rio Tinto-Zinc's Capper Pass tin-smelting plant Mar '88; backed the reintroduction of corporal punishment Mar '88; complained about five efforts to amalgamate the East Yorkshire Health Authority with the Hull Health Authority Mar '8; urged better information technology to make British business more competitive Apr '88; objected to argument that UK should emulate Korean subsidies for shipping June '88; asked about childhood cancer clusters Oct '88; asked about dirty, overcrowded trains Oct '88; joined Friends of Bruges to support Mrs Thatcher in her fight against "creeping" EC federalism Mar '89; launched debate to curb bugging Mar '89; when Labour MP Harry Barnes proposed civil disobedience against poll tax, countered: "the result of your actions would lead to anarchy in this country, and destruction of democracy" Mar '89; called on Government to relocate more civil servants out of London May '88; urged safer motor coaches, with safety belts and shatterproof glass May '88; visited East and West Germany as guest of Konrad Adenauer Foundation Sep '88; introduced Control of Electronic Surveillance Devices Bill, to curb bugging May '89; was a co-sponsor of Bill Cash's European Community (Reaffirmation and Limits of Competence) Bill which rejected the ERM, EMU, the Social Chapter June '89; complained of the "extravagant campaign" being conducted by the Brewers' Society and some of the major brewers against Lord Young's effort to break their monopoly, under which "six large brewers...control 75% of beer production, 74% of brewers' tied houses and 86% of loan ties" June '89; complained that management's "own snouts are...too deeply in the pay trough" June '89; urged more Government action to assess and research child cancer clusters July '89; said 2.5% attendance at Church of England services was "a national disgrace" Oct '89; was elected Secretry of the Conservative MPs' European Affairs Committee, with Bill Cash being elected Chairman Nov '89; as a former Chief Executive of the National Association of Pension Funds, accused Michael Meacher of trying to "dupe" employees that they could get something for nothing Jan '90; disclosed he had come under pressure from brewers after backing Lord Young on cutting back on their tied houses: "one representative of a brewer made it clear to me in oblique terms that if I didn't back the breweres in what they were saying, then, of course, perhaps some money might be withdrawn from the Conservative Party" (WORLD IN ACTION) Jan '90; said employers might feel their pension schemes were becoming too complex and costly Jan '90; claimed that in 25 years up to 1987 about 51% of those killed in England and Wales were killed by those previously convicted of homicide Feb '90; voted with Opposition to compensate servicemen damaged in nuclear tests Mar '90; opposing the admission of 50,000 Hongkong Chinese families, voted against British Nationality (Hongkong) Bill giving them the right of abode Apr '90; urged artificial lighting of all motorways Apr '90; on Trade and Industry Select Committee tried to eliminate criticisms of Lord Young for his role in paying "sweeteners" to sell Rover to British Aerospace May-July '90; raised the problem of constituency leukaemia clusters, possibly due to unsuitable radiation limits on radioactive raw materials used in local smelters, RTZ's Capper Pass plant, as exposed in Baxter Report July '90; urged "gradual" cut in defence costs because of the uncertainty of Soviet politics July '90; visited Mexico as part of IPU team to support anti-drug campaign Oct '90; again visited Germany as a guest of the Konrad Adenauer Foundation Oct '90; claimed the Statutory Sick Pay Bill was "relatively innocuous" Nov '90; insisted industrialists wanted price stability above all Jan '91; abstained in debate on Economic and Monetary Union, insisting that the end of sterling as an independent currency would be disastrous Jan '91; was absent from the Select Committee's final vote on its report on Lord Young's sale of Rover to British Aerospace: "I was unaware that the Rover report in its entirety had been adopted" Feb '91; refused the latest of six offers to become a PPS, saying "if it doesn't pay then it isn't worth it" Feb '91; urged Britain to go more aggressively for Kuwaiti contracts Feb '91; was not enthusiastic about the Budget: "the VAT increase is going to bear down very heavily on the car industry; I wish he had done something about the special car tax to compensate" Mar '91; supported more bypasses, since "my village of Tickton in east Yorkshire, is lucky enough to have a bypass" separating "me and my neighbours from all the heavy traffic which previously went through the centre of my village" July '91; with other anti-Marketeers, demanded a referendum before Maastricht was brought before Parliament Nov '91; was voted out as Secretary of Conservative MPs' European Affairs Committee, along with its equally anti-Brussels Chairman, Bill Cash Nov '91; was one of a dozen who abstained against the Maastricht summit, with seven voting against Dec '91; visited Norway as guest of Parliamentary Armed Forces Scheme Feb '92; backed Richard Shepherd's Referendum Bill Feb '92; Mrs Thatcher spoke for him in the election campaign Mar '92; he retained the seat with his majority up from 12,595 to 16,517, a swing of 2.3% to Conservative Apr '92; with other Eurosceptics, convened at Carlton Club May '92; co-authored and co-sponsored the Euro-sceptic motion urging "a fresh start" on Maastricht, after the Danes turned it down in their referendum June '92; voted for £11,000 in higher office allowances for MPs, against wishes of Whips July '92; visited Malta as guest of its government Sep '92; voted against returning Britain to ERM Sep '92; visited Hongkong and Taiwan as guest of their governments Sep-Oct '92; was one of 18 Tory MPs to gather in the Carlton Club to plot their opposition to the Maastricht Bill Oct '92; backed the Government's mines closures Oct '92; was elected Vice Chairman of the backbench Conservatives' Northern Ireland Committee Nov '92; as one of the 26 rebels who stood out against the Government in the paving vote on Maastricht, described his "very intimidating experience": "there are some very physically big Whips who come up - particularly to a new Member; and so you have maybe five Whips come up to you, and they start bullying you; they'll cajole you, they'll even shove you around" Nov '92; claimed that the NHS was doing rather well in his constituency, except in orthopaedic surgery and dentistry Jan '93; threatened to try to stop Maastricht by voting with Labour to include the Social Chapter, explaining: "we have not come all this way to stumble at the last fence; we are looking to amend the Bill; I am a pragmatist...if we can win a vote, we should go for it" Feb '93; resisted Douglas Hurd's threat to delay the Maastricht Treaty if the rebels forced the Commons to back its Social Chapter: "this sort of exhortation is not going to help us defeat this particular scheme because frankly it has got the effect of making everybody look into the nooks and crannies of Parliament" Feb '93; voted with Opposition to defeat Government - Major's first defeat - over composition of an EC Committee of the Regions Mar '93; "was button-holed by three angry senior Tory MPs after rebels forced a division but then pulled out to keep the Government guessing about their strength for later votes" Mar '93;

voted with Labour against the motion to continue the Maastricht "until any hour" Mar '93;
ignored Michael Heseltine's appeal for a truce on Maastricht; also clashed with 1922
Committee Chairman Sir Marcus Fox over whether the Maastricht rebels had damaged the
party Mar '93; objected to Government's tactics on Social Chapter: "the Government is quite
determined to go to any lengths to avoid a vote on the Social Chapter" Apr '93; rejected John
Major's criticism of rebels: "this sort of language will not make it easier to get over the
bruising we have had over the past six to twelve months; it alienates rather than binds
together" Apr '93; was rated one of the top Maastricht rebels, with 30 votes against the
Government, 30 abstentions and only one vote for the treaty May '93; voted against 3rd
Reading of Maastricht Bill May '93; after Norman Lamont was sacked, Cran said: "the Right
has lost a Chancellor and gained a Welsh Secretary" May '93; after Michael Mates was forced
out of office, Cran said of Major: "the poor man can't win!" June '93; voted against
Government on Maastricht, then with Government on the Social Chapter July '93; urged
Chancellor Clarke to scrap the second stage of the planned increase of VAT on fuel in '95,
Aug '93; was not satisfied with John Major's ECONOMIST promise not to rush back into the
ERM: "I would very much have preferred the Prime Minister to say a single currency was not
on the agenda, not now, not ever"; had his invitation to speak to Sutton YCs cancelled at
instigation of Central Office Sep '93; claimed Ken Clarke and Michael Heseltine were "rocking
the boat" by reaffirming their belief in an eventual single currency for Europe Nov '93; backed
the Queen's Speech's concentration on law and order, particularly the need for juveniles' secure
training centres and expulsion of travellers Nov '93; signed anti-EC amendment Dec '93;
visited Israel with Conservative Friends of Israel as guest of its government Jan '94; after the
TIMES demonstrated that voters would soon be paying more tax under the Tories than they
had under Labour, he warned: "the Tory Party has to demonstrate that it is a low-tax party,
and if it cannot", "then we shall bear the consequences" Jan '94; voted to restore capital
punishment, specially for killing policemen Feb '94; voted against reducing age of homosexual
consent, either to 16 or 18, Feb '94; was named to Select Committee on Northern Ireland Mar
'94; following doubling of Britain's EU Budget contribution from £1.7b to £3.5b, claimed "the
British people will increasingly realise that our membership of the EC is very costly indeed"
June '94; was falsely rumoured to have been promised a job in the summer reshuffle as a
symbolic Maastricht rebel July '94; was named with other Tory Eurosceptics as part of an
international Rightwing front against European federalism Sep '94; to keep his powder dry for
later battles against Euro-federalism, pledged his backing for the Government in the key vote
on the EU Budget on which 8 Tory Eurosceptics lost the Whip Nov '94; signed Sir Teddy
Taylor's amendment urging withdrawal from the Common Fisheries Policy Jan '95; with 100
other Tory MPs backed Ken Baker's Eurosceptic motion praising Major for opposing joining a
single European currency in '97, Feb '95; with the abolition of Humberside County, opposed
the inclusion of Goole in the restored East Riding Feb '95; attacked untimeliness of
Archbishop of Canterbury's remark that "the English need to ask forgiveness for a brutal
domination and crass insensitivity in the 800 years of our relationship with Ireland" Feb '95;
attacked as "a stab in the back" President Clinton's allowing Gerry Adams to visit the US; also
opposed US involvement in decommissioning of IRA arms Mar '95; became PPS to Northern
Ireland Secretary Sir Patrick Mayhew in place of tabloid-smeared Richard Spring, who
replaced him on the Northern Ireland Select Committee May '95; described as "absurd" the
Law Officers' advice that British Ministers could be held liable personally for refusal to
implement an EU directive on the 48-hour week June '95; was one of a group of Rightwingers
who concluded that John Major's departure would probably result in pro-EU Michael
Heseltine's succession June '95; was "set up for a fall" (DAILY TELEGRAPH) by
neighbouring Tory Eurosceptic MPs in the boundary changes by being steered away from

safer Haltemprice - largely based on his Beverley seat - which went to David Davis, while he was left with more-marginal Beverley and Holderness June-Oct '95; praised the Budget, but not its VAT increase, threatening he would no longer buy new cars or, possibly no more new suits Nov '95; opposed new rule requiring MPs to disclose outside earnings as "intrusive and damaging" (having acquired a consultancy) Dec '95; voted against Government's Family Law Bill with eight other anti-divorce MPs June '96; voted for a 3% cap on MPs' pay rise, for a cut in their mileage allowances and against a pension based on £43,000 July '96; resigned as PPS to Sir Patrick Mayhew, allegedly to concentrate on nursing his extensively-redrawn and "vulnerable" constituency; he claimed 18 months in the job was enough Sep '96; voted to restore caning in schools Jan '97; had to contribute £1,000 to Amnesty for having, along with the DAILY MAIL, libeled comedian Jeremy Hardy as supporting the IRA for having called for a retrial of Danny McNamee for blowing up four Household Cavalry soldiers, which Hardy claimed was a miscarriage of justice Jan '97; received a contribution of more than 25% of his election expenses from Eurosceptic businessman Paul Sykes Apr '97; narrowly retained his altered Beverley and Holderness with a majority of only 1,211 on a near-record notional pro-Labour swing of 16% May '97; in the ballot for the new Conservative Leader, first backed Michael Howard, then John Redwood and, after hesitation - "I'm not sure he's a heavy hitter in the House" -William Hague rather than Ken Clarke "a heavy hitter who hasn't got the right agenda, particularly on Europe" May-June '97; was named an Opposition Whip by Hague June '97; was named to the Administration Committee July '97; urged pump-priming for the multiply-deprived East Yorkshire Victorian seaside town of Withernsea, which he had inherited with the boundary changes; "I probably did not get many votes from the town and the area, but that does not matter"; "I am a pretty Rightwing character...but I am not particularly daft"; "I know pefectly well that there is no alternative to the pump-priming that only Government can provide" Dec '97; deplored the killing of David Keyes in Maze Prison and urged "a fully independent inquiry" Mar '98; left the Administrative Committee June '98;

Born: 28 January 1944, Kintore, Aberdeenshire

Family: Son, James Cran, farm grieve turned greenkeeper, and Jane (McDonald); m '73 Penelope Barbara (Wilson); 1d Alexandra Penelope '81;

Education: St Paul's School, Aberdeen; Ruthrieston School, Aberdeen (Dux Medallion winner '59); Aberdeen College of Commerce; Aberdeen University; Heriot Watt University, Edinburgh;

Occupation: Parliamentary Consultant, to the Board of Lincoln National (UK) Plc (life asurance, pensions and unit trusts; £5-10,000) '94-; on Pension Trustees Forum Advisory Council '92-; ex: West Midlands Director CBI '84-87, its Northern Director '79-84; Chief Executive '73-79, Secretary '71-73, National Association of Pension Funds; Researcher in Conservative Research Department '70-71;

Traits: Dark, parted hair; specs; sharp nose; self-satisfied expression; neat; "with his steel-rimmed spectacles, reassuring Scottish burr and sober dark suits, he looks more like a country doctor than a political assassin" (Nicholas Wood, TIMES); shy; puritanical; assiduous; perfectionist; "the sort of well-groomed, compact Scot you expect to inhabit an executive-size corporate office rather than be pondering the British system of government in the Commons tearoom" (Madeleine Bunting, GUARDIAN); praises saving "not only as a Scotsman but an Aberdonian, and we are famous for our capacity to save money": claims to be Highland Scots Presbyterian, although he did say, "I am a cross between a Scotsman and a Yorkshireman, a devastating combination as far as the saving ethic is concerned; I have been saving since I was so high because it was inculcated in me; my parents insisted that I save threepenny Post Office savings stamps"; "my savings ratio is such that if it were repeated by everybody else we would have very high levels of unemployment" (JC) ; "very decent"; "impatient" (his wife); suffered

from mild meningitis after being injected for a myelogram;
Address: House of Commons, Westminster, London SW1A 0AA;
Telephone: 0171 219 4445/5069 (H of C);

Dr Ross CRANSTON   **Labour**   **DUDLEY NORTH '97-**

Majority: 9,457 over Conservative 7-way;
Description: The historic iron-working Black Country town newly divided on a different axis, with both halves being considered marginal -until '97;
Position: Solicitor General '98-; ex: on Select Committee on Home Affairs '97-98; Chairman, Board of Trustees, Public Concern at Work (the whistleblowers' charity) '96-97; on Legal Advisory Panel National Consumer Council til '97;
Outlook: The newly-promoted highly-intelligent, academic Blairite; worthy and assiduous, was always eager to provide informed background and loyal support in any debate, initially in the numbing style of a lecturer reading to a captive audience; assisted Richard Shepherd secure protection for 'whistleblowers' in the Public Interest Disclosure Act; has been active in setting up the all-party Group for Vaccine-Damaged Children; he was implanted into the seat from which Labour veteran Dr John (later Lord) Gilbert was squeezed out; a respected, well-read Australian-born Barrister-Recorder, formerly Professor of Commercial Law at LSE, and an authoritative and prolific legal author; a former Labour candidate against William Hague for hopeless Richmond, Yorkshire; a member of the Society of Labour Lawyers and the Labour Finance and Industry Group;
History: He arrived in Britain in '73, joining the Labour Party '74; contested hopeless Richmond, Yorkshire against William Hague, retaining Labour's traditional 3rd place, with an almost identical percentage of votes Apr '92; three weeks before the '97 election, after 70-year-old Dr Gilbert had been squeezed out by the offer of a peerage and a ministerial post in Defence, he was selected by an NEC committee from its list of seven candidates, without the involvement of the Dudley constituency; this procedure was apparently devised to select, instead, Tony Blair's friend and former flatmate, Charles Falconer QC, due to become Solicitor General, who was allegedly ruled out because his children attended private schools; Falconer was therefore made a peer to become Solicitor General; when Cranston was selected, it only required endorsement by his constituency association; he was "unanimously endorsed by all members present" according to the CLP Chairman, Alan Harvey; a former MP and continual aspirant, Geoff Edge, complained: "the issue is not whether Ross Cranston is an able candidate; it is that we know nothing about him and have had no say in his selection" Apr '97; Cranston was elected by a majority of 9,457, a notional swing of 9%, whereas the swing to Labour in Dudley South was 11%; Mark Atherton, a Scargillite 'Socialist Labour' candidate who was top of the ballot paper, attracted 2,155 votes (4%) May '97; urged more use of local museum to encourage culture and economic regeneration May '97; expressed solidarity with jailed Indonesian union leader June '97; blamed the windfall tax on the Conservatives' lax price controls in the early '90s July '97; was named to Select Committee on Home Affairs July '97; ridiculed the Tories' continued commitment to tax relief on pensioners' BUPA payments July '97; loyally backed Gordon Brown's removal of tax relief on dividend payments to pension

funds, despite former Labour Treasury Minister Denzil Davies' pointing out that, under the previous Labour regime, "pension funds used not to pay tax on dividends, rent from property developments and gilts" July '97; at Law Society fringe meeting in Brighton claimed Labour policy on youth crime was based on empirical evidence while Tory policy had been based on populism Oct '97; backed the Bank of England Bill "without deviation and without hesitation" Nov '97; predicted 200 changes in legislation on offshore trusts Jan '98; spoke of securing a 'New Deal' posting at the Dudley Zoo for a young constituent unemployed for seven years Jan '98; opposed Teresa Gorman's referendum on an English Parliament as unsuitable and "not necessarily a progressive instrument" Jan '98; backed Home Secretary Jack Straw's attack on unscrupulous and even criminal immigration advisers, urging compensation for wronged immigrants Feb '98; warned against allowing misbehaving policemen to retire prematurely on phoney health grounds Feb '98; urged more sensitive handling of child witnesses Feb '98; backed Employment of Children Bill, emphasising the need to avoid exploitation and health dangers Feb '98; asked how soon bribery of MPs would be made an offence Mar '98; in the debate on new ISAs, pointed out that Nigel Lawson had introduced PEPs to spread share ownership, not encourage saving Mar '98; backed publication of rail surveys Mar '98; urged closer collaboration between the Prison and Probation services Mar '98; enthused about local tree-planting in the Dibdale area of his constituency Mar '98; welcomed the Budget as "one more piece of the jigsaw" of ensuring "a fairer society" Apr '98; pointed out to complaining Peter Lilley that "the quarterly system of Corporation Tax payment operates in the US, Germany, France, Australia, Canada, Japan and a host of other countries and that we are simply coming into line" Apr '98; complained of inaccessible-for-the-handicapped old museums Apr '98; urged Paymaster General Geoffrey Robinson to take "the news of this brilliant ['New Deal'] programme to other parts of Europe" Apr '98; complained of the excessive bureaucracy in the Crown Prosecution Service June '98; wrote that by "protecting the public interest whistleblower the new [Public Interest Disclosure] law will protect the safety and well-being of children in care and the public" June '98; urged an overdue review of the law applying to small businesses June '98; the Public Interest Disclosure Act, on which he collaborated with Richard Shepherd, became law July '98; he was promoted Solicitor General July '98;

Born: 23 July 1948, Brisbane, Australia

Family: Son, of Frederick Hugh Cranston, clerk/paint salesman, and Edna Elizabeth (Davis); m '88; 1d; separated '94; divorced;

Education: University of Queensland, Australia; Harvard University; Wolfson College, Oxford University (DPhil, DCL);

Occupation: Barrister '76-; Recorder '97-; Bencher, Gray's Inn '98-; Author: Consumers and the Law (1984), Principles of Banking Law (1997), Legal Ethics and Professional Responsibility (1995), Law, Government, and Public Policy (1987), Legal Foundations of the Welfare State (1985), Regulating Business (1979); ex: Cassel Professor of Commercial Law, LSE '93-97; Assistant Recorder '91 Consultant '88-96: to the Commonwealth Secretariat, World Bank, IMF, UN; Lecturer, at Warwick University '75; he "worked [with] the West Midlands County Council's Trading Standards Department for 3 months in the 1970s" (BIRMINGHAM POST):

Traits: Neat, close-cropped dark receding hair with bald pate; "a friendly expression" (Matthew Parris, TIMES); can be mistaken for Malcolm Savidge by Matthew Parris; intelligent; careful; articulate; soft-spoken; residual Australian accent; initially read his speeches like a law lecturer with captive students;

Address: House of Commons, Westminster, London SW1A 0AA; lives in Lewishaam;

Telephone: 0171 219 2647/4195 (H of C);

David CRAUSBY   Labour   BOLTON NORTH EAST '97-

Majority: 12,669 over Conservative 5-way;
Description: Part of the former pioneering cotton-spinning town - the birth-place of Samuel Crompton - that turned to initially-prosperous engineering; a former knife-edge marginal embracing depressed inner-city and middle-class suburbs; it was tipped toward Labour by the '95 addition of inner-city Halliwell;
Position: On Select Committee on Administration '97-; ex: Bury Metropolitan District Councillor (Chairman of Housing '85-92) '79-92; Chairman, Bury North Constituency Labour Party '87;
Outlook: A well-rooted, low-profiled but sharp local politician and trade unionist (AEEU); was second-time lucky in this seat, where he has long worked as an engineer and AEEU trade unionist; this came after an earlier failure in Bury North, his home town; one of the few skilled engineers in Labour's '97 entry; he backs proportional representation;
History: He joined the Labour Party '74; was elected in his home town to Bury Metropolitan District Council May '79; was selected 43-24-7-1 to contest marginal, Tory-held Bury North Oct '85; protested to local MEP Barbara Castle against the impact of bus deregulation on Ramsbottom, in particular Jan '86; despite a national swing to Labour, he suffered a 3.5% swing to the Conservatives, with Bury North's sitting Tory MP, Alistair Burt, increasing his majority from under 3,000 to almost 7,000 June '87; after Ann Taylor had failed to win the seat in '84 and Frank White had failed to take it in '87, was selected for Bolton North East Mar '90; warned that the seat was "not typically northern" and that in a region of marginal seats "we're not going to get much help from other constituencies"; pointed out that the sitting Tory MP, Peter Thurnham, "plays to people's prejudices quite well and [even if] he's not a sparkling character, he has won twice"; he failed to take the seat, despite cutting Thurnham's majority from 813 to 185, Apr '92; stayed on to fight the seat again, helped by the boundary revision which made it a Labour marginal and caused Thurnham to announce he would not fight it again '95; Thurnham later left the Conservatives for the Liberal Democrats Feb '96; Crausby claimed, "Conservatives are coming over to us in droves"; "I've never met that throughout my political career" Apr '97; he won the seat with a majority of 12,669 after a pro-Labour swing of 10.17% May '97; co-sponsored motion urging better funding for further education colleges June '97; backed ban on fox-hunting June '97; urged trying to persuade the USA that "our common policy on Bosnia should be 'in together, out together'" June '97; in his Maiden urged the rebuilding of Bolton's engineering base and the conversion to a university of the Bolton Institute of Higher Education July '97; co-sponsored motion congratulating Bolton Wanderers on their promotion to the Premier League July '97; told PM Blair how he welcomed having, "for the first time in our history, a national minimum wage that will protect our people from the low wages that create poverty" Mar '98; co-sponsored motion opposing the buying out of Great Western Holdings without adequate consultation Mar '98; welcomed the Crime and Disorder Bill as "enabling law-abiding citizens to live peacefully and harmoniously without unnecessary interference from others", especially when reinforced by the 'New Deal' for the young unemployed and initiatives like Bolton Safer Cities which had alread curbed crime locally Apr '98; complained that local councils were not passing on fully their education funds May '98;

525

Born: 17 June 1946, Bury
Family: Son of Thomas Crausby, industrial labourer/club steward, and Kathleen (Lavin); m '65 Enid (Noon), who was also active in the AEEU; 2s both of whom attended university;
Education: Bury primary; Derby Grammar School, Bury;
Occupation: Engineering Turner: former full-time Shop Steward and Works Convenor at Beloit Walmsley (Bolton engineering works) for 18 years; previously an Engineering Turner (AEEU);
Traits: Dark, receding hair; broad forehead; medium build; Mediterranean appearance; persistent; quiet-spoken; earnest; a football enthusiast (Bury FC and Bolton Wanderers);
Address: House of Commons, Westminster, London SW1A 0AA; 139 Red Lane, Bolton;
Telephone: 0171 219 4092 (H of C);

(Constance) Ann CRYER   **Labour**   **KEIGHLEY '97-**

'62-65;

Majority: 7,132 over Conservative 4-way;
Description: The loveliest and most northerly part of Bradford metropolitan district, including the Bronte country and Haworth as well as the textile town of Keighley, with its possibly 10,000 Asians and heavy unemployment; unaltered in '95, but in '83 Ilkley Moor, predominantly-Tory Ilkley and Addingham's 10,000 electors were added from Ripon and Skipton;
Position: Vice President, Keighley and Worth Valley Railway Preservation Society '94-; JP Bradford; Delegate, to Council of Europe '97-; Treasurer, Parliamentary CND '97-; ex: on Social Security Appeals Tribunal '87-96; Darwen Borough Councillor

Outlook: A more restrained version of her widely-popular hard-Left late husband, Bob; is in the Campaign Group; opposed poll tax payment and the wars in Vietnam, the Falklands and the Gulf; backed the '84-85 miners' strike and opposed subsequent pit closures; strongly anti-EU (in Common Market Safeguards); CND; "as an MP, I'll inevitably think to myself, what would Bob have done in my position? But at the end of the day, I'll make my own decisions; I'm not a continuation of him, not Bob Cryer Mark Two"; "she's seen as a decent, honest person who brought up her family in Yorkshire; she's trustworthy" (local party member);

History: Joined the Labour Party at 18, '58, CND '58, the Co-operative Party '65; was elected to Darwen Borough Council May '62; was on Aldermaston marches '62, '63; after her husband's death, refused to enter the selection contest as his successor at Bradford South ("it was too soon, I wasn't up to it") June '94; urged on by her daughter Jane ("you've virtually done the job for years"), agreed to enter the all-women's short-list to contest Keighley - once held by her late husband - against its Tory incumbent, Gary Waller, rather than see the seat go to a 'Blairite moderniser'; she won selection July '95; campaigned against rail privatisation from '95; campaigned against green belt erosion and in favour of retaining the Settle-Carlisle rail link and for a tougher line against crime ("Keighley people are frightened in their homes") Apr '97; Lord Attenborough campaigned for her Apr '97; won the seat, ousting Gary Waller, with a majority of 7,132 on a pro-Labour swing of 10.21% - with her son John winning

Hornchurch May '97; in her Maiden speech, in which she was very cautious about referring to her late husband, she backed the Labour Government's priority for "human rights, world-wide; I trust that that commitment will extend not only to the Muslims in Kashmir but to the long-suffering women in Afghanistan" May '97; she joined the Campaign Group, but not necessarily the same wing as her son John May '97; backed ban on fox-hunting June '97; led motion urging elimination of all nuclear weapons, with strict and effective international control July '97; led motion attacking 40% bonuses self-awarded by Yorkshire Water directors July '97; co-sponsored motion deploring BA's selling off of its catering division July '97; co-sponsored motion deploring police attacks on peaceful demonstrators in Kenya July '97; co-sponsored motion to print out a consolidated version of the principal treaties of the European Union July '97; co-sponsored motion opposing any cut in lone parent child benefit July '97; had an adjournment debate on Bronte-sanctified Top Withens in her constituency July '97; was one of the Leftwing MPs who urged the Government to "negotiate away" its nuclear weapons, ditch NATO expansion and scrap the Eurofighter project Aug '97; voted against cuts in lone-parent benefits Dec '97; in debate on women, paid tribute to Annie Besant, the Irishwoman who supported Indian independence, and her own suffragette grandmother Dinah Place Feb '98; spoke against the local threat by Bradford to build 1,500 houses in the "beautiful area of the Aire Valley around Sisden", which she had been fighting for three years Mar '98; in 2nd Reading of Human Rights Bill emphasised privacy rights of families of MPs and Ministers Apr '98; criticised the Indian and Pakistani nuclear tests May '98; opposed backdoor privatisation of the BBC May '98; voted against the Government on student maintenance grants June '98;

Born: 14 December 1939, St Annes-on-Sea, Lancashire

Family: Her grandmother, Dinah Place ('Dainty Dinah') was a leading suffragette and an ILP activist; daughter of Allen Place, shoemaker, then labourer and ILP and Labour activist, and Margaret Ann (Ratcliffe), "a very skilled producer of soft furnishings" (AC); m '63 Robert Cryer, teacher and lecturer, MP for Keighley '74-83, MEP for Sheffield & North Derbyshire '84-89, and MP for Bradford South '87-94 (when he was killed in a motor accident which she survived); 1s John '64, Labour MP for Hornchurch '97-; 1d Jane '65, solicitor; 5 grandchildren;

Education: Highfield Infants, St John's Junior, Darwen; Spring Bank Secondary Modern, Darwen; Bolton Technical College (secretarial diploma); Keighley Technical College (O-lvels);

Occupation: Writer, Boldness Be My Friend (a memoir to her late husband); Personal Assistant, part-time to her husband, as MP and MEP '74-94; Researcher, part-time for Essex University '69-70; Clerk, at ICI and GPO '55-64;

Traits: Handsome; aquiline features; white hair; suffered from post-traumatic stress disorder for a long time after she and her husband were involved in their '94 car crash;

Address: House of Commons, Westminster, London SW1A 0AA; 32 Kendall Avenue, Shipley, West Yorks BD18 4DY; Bob Cryer House, 35 Devonshire Street, Keighley, West Yorks BD21 (constituency office);

Telephone: 0171 219 3000/4838/6649 (H of C); 01274 584701 (home & Fax); 01535 210083/210085 (Fax);

LORDS PROFILES

We also do profiles of Lords, based on forty years of observation and the best files in the country, bar none. Price: £40 each.

Majority: 5,680 over Conservative 6-way;
Description: An unchanged suburban seat on London's Essex fringe, three-quarters owner-occupied, often by skilled workers; 15% of them work at Ford's Dagenham plant; until '97 this was considered safe for Conservatives;
Position: On Deregulation Committee '97-;
Outlook: "A rising star of the Left" (TIMES) and one of the worries of Whips and Blairites: a hard-Left journalist who claims to share "the ideals and beliefs" of his late father, the widely-admired Bob Cryer; but there was, at first, a much harder edge to his political position, illustrated by his refusal to pay the normal tribute in his Maiden to his predecessor, Robin Squire, generally regarded as a decent Centre-Left Tory; "I don't want to be pally with the Tories, I want to grind them into the dirt" (JC); "like his late father, may be more Leftwing than is good for his career, but he has spoken well and sparingly in the House" (DAILY TELEGRAPH); this 'class war' approach is more in line with the Trotskyist LABOUR BRIEFING and Communist MORNING STAR for which he worked than with his late father's good-humoured application of his Leftwing views; strongly anti-European ("when I was canvassing in Hornchurch, I hardly met anybody who was in favour of a single currency"); favours renationalisation of all the public utilities; proclaims his links with Tony Benn and Jeremy Corbyn, as well as his father's friend and collaborator, Dennis Skinner; with his mother, Ann, is the first Commons mother-and-son pair since the Oppenheims in '83-87; in the Campaign Group, the Labour Euro-Safeguards Committee and the First-Past-the-Post Group;
History: He was raised in a very Leftwing family, his father becoming the MP for Keighley when he was 9, Feb '74; joined the Labour Party at 15, '79; after his father's death in a car crash, sought to follow him at Bradford South, but the choice fell to Gerry Sutcliffe, Leader of Bradford City Council May '94; claimed that Labour was trying to fudge its commitment to renationalise Britain's railway system Jan '95; in TRIBUNE hailed the achievements of Jeremy Corbyn Jan '95; in TRIBUNE claimed Labour's NEC was being sidelined or used as a rubber stamp by the Blair leadership July '95; was selected for Hornchurch, thought "hopeless" by the Labour leadership, since it required a 9.5% swing to capture it Sep '95; in TRIBUNE cited criticisms of the redrafting of Clause Four because of the "absence of specifics and a general acceptance of the economic status quo" Nov '95; was attacked in TRIBUNE by Stephen Twigg, Islington Councillor and candidate for Southgate, for his inaccurate criticisms of Islington's poor education record Feb '96; in TRIBUNE predicted that Labour was in for a "summer of discontent" over the Blair leadership's plans to provide only minimal rights at work and social security protection, while retaining much of the Conservative's trade union legislation June '96; somewhat unexpectedly captured Hornchurch from its incumbent Tory MP Robin Squire by a majority of 5,680, on a pro-Labour swing of 15.95%, one of London's highest; this made him Labour's 41st least-expected victor May '97; in his Maiden he paid homage to Tony Benn, Jeremy Corbyn and Dennis Skinner, but said of his predecessor only "the constituency elected a Conservative Member of Parliament for 18 years"; emphasised, "I was elected to this Chamber to defend universal benefits, free and universal health care, jobs and living standards" May '97; raised the threat of closure for Romford's Oldchurch Hospital May '97; asked for a review of the Child Support Agency May '97; called for the scrapping of

the CSA June '97; complained that further education colleges were "marked by gross underfunding, anarchic organisation and an almost complete lack of strategic planning" June '97; backed Labour Government's halt in sales of Forestry Commission land June '97; urged the creation of Grand Committee for London June '97; co-sponsored his mother's motion to abolish nuclear weapons under strict and effective international controls July '97; criticised the Labour leadership for dropping plans to renationalise railways July '97; urged a debate to show the dangers of PR July '97; attacked the Tories for their mis-selling of pensions, with "25,000 miners being conned out of their occupational schemes" July '97; co-sponsored Campaign Group motion protesting refusal of entry clearance for Nigerian Abdul Onibuyo July '97; called for the restoration of the earnings link with state pensions and the rebuilding of SERPS July '97; was named to Deregulation Committee Aug '97; was one of the Leftwing MPs who urged the Government to "negotiate away" its nuclear weapons, ditch NATO expansion and scrap the Eurofighter project Aug '97; urged a delay in consideration of the Labour leadership's 'Partnership in Power' "because there hasn't been enough time to debate it" Sep '97; complained that the planned cut in single parents' benefit failed "to deliver hope and sustenance to the socially excluded but could make their lives even worse" Oct '97; complained of "thuggish" and anti-union behaviour by Principals of further education colleges Nov '97; urged the abolition of special Privy Councillors' speaking priorities, to cut the time others had to wait to speak - "the longest that I have waited was seven hours and I did not get called at the end of it"; welcomed the retention of personal voting by MPs: "as a new Member, I have found that it is possible to buttonhole Ministers in the Lobby, but nowhere else" Nov '97; was one of the rebel Labour MPs who voted against cutting lone-parent benefits Dec '97; complained about underfunding of London Underground Jan '98; co-sponsored motion backing Government's use of liquid petroleum gas in its car fleet "to improve national air quality" Jan '98; co-sponsored motion backing alternative fuels Jan '98; congratulated Government on help for pensioners' fuel bills Jan '98; complained of the "nightmare that the Child Support Agency has wreaked across the country" Feb '98; congratulated Health Secretary Dobson on keeping open Oldchurch Hospital Feb '98; urged a debate on the shortage of speech therapists Feb '98; complained that US electricity giants had bought up 60% of UK's supply and distribution companies Feb '98; urged a debate on sport Apr '98; backed an early referendum on the Euro: "if that happened, unlike 20 years ago, the 'nos' would win" Apr '98; urged PM Tony Blair to ban import of white asbestos, an "especially deadly substance" May '98; was one of 33 Labour MPs who rebelled against scrapping maintenance grants and introducing tuition fees for undergraduates June '98;

Born: 11 April 1964, Darwen, Lancashire

Family: Son, of late Robert ('Bob') Cryer, teacher and lecturer, MP for Keighley '74-83, MEP for Sheffield & Derbyshire North '84-89, MP for Bradford South '87-94 and Ann Cryer, MP for Keighley '97-; m Narindar (Batas); 1s, 1d ;

Education: Oakbank School, Keighley; Hatfield Polytechnic (BA in Literature and History); London College of Printing;

Occupation: Journalist '88-: on LLOYD'S LIST '96-97, TRIBUNE '93-96, LABOUR BRIEFING (where he "personally penned several of the more fascinating profiles in the popular series, 'Class Traitor of the Month' - PRIVATE EYE) '96-97, MORNING STAR ("he is fondly remembered as a colleague; he was a sub-editor working in news and features; he wasn't penning 3000-word pieces on Kim Il Sung and he didn't come to work in a tank", Deputy Editor Paul Corry); Insurance Underwriter ("it may surprise Hon Members to learn that a raving firebrand like me was a yuppie for a few years; I worked as an underwriter - but I could not get out fast enough") '86-88;

Traits: Young; reddish hair; specs; "I have supported Leeds all my life, so my life has been an

aching void in many ways" (JC); likes railways, architecture, old sport cars; a "voracious reader" (JC);
Address: House of Commons, Westminster, London SW1A 0AA; 65 Haverhill Road, Balham, London SW11;
Telephone: 0171 219 3000 (H of C); 0181 673 2124 (home);

John (Scott) CUMMINGS   Labour   EASINGTON '87-

Majority: 30,012 ((71.6%) over Conservative 5-way;
Description: Dominated by Durham's East coast mining communities of Easington, Hordern and Murton, now without any working mines; once contained "four of the remaining six collieries in the old Durham area" (JSC); because of the domination of mining, "there is a lack of an enterprise culture" (JSC), making it the country's third poorest district; it includes the new town of Peterlee; since '83 it again contains Seaham, scene of Ramsay Macdonald's '29 and '31 victories and his '35 defeat by 'Manny' Shinwell; "we have fine Saxon and Norman churches, beautiful denes and woodlands and, of course, a delightful coast...the people who populate the area came from Cornwall, following the closure of the tin mines in the 1860s; there are also people who emigrated from Ireland, following the potato famine in the 1840s" (JSC);
Position: On Select Committee on Environment, Transport and Regional Affairs, '97-; Delegate to Council of Europe and WEU '93-; Treasurer, all-party British-Czech and Slovak Parliamentary Group; ex: Whip, (Northern Region '94-95, Overseas Development '95-97) '94-97; on Environment Select Committee '87-92; Vice Chairman, Coalfield Community Campaign '85-87-; Easington District Councillor (its Leader '79-87) '70-87; on Northumbrian Water Authority '77-84; on Aycliffe and Peterlee Development Corporation '80-87;
Outlook: An 'Old Labour' Whip who did not make it into the 'New Labour' Government; "I've always been in the NUM since I started work and still regard myself as a mining MP" (JSC); a locally-born, locally-rooted, formerly NUM-sponsored former pit electrician and Council Leader; on the fringe between the semi-hard Left in the 'Supper Club' and the hard Left in the Campaign Group, whose motions he often backs; as extreme a miners' defender as Dennis Skinner or Arab defender as George Galloway, but less heterosexual than either; despite, or because of this, a fervent RC opponent of abortion; he inherited from Jack Dormand the rock-safe seat once held by Shinwell, Macdonald and Sidney Webb - and made it even safer; a sixth-generation child of the pits who feels disinherited; "all my life I have lived within 400 yards of a working pit"; anti: coal privatisation, gas power, abortion, embryo experimentation, Zionists; pro-Arab; an assiduous questioner on all subjects related to his area (especially the A19); "sure to sparkle" with Ronnie Campbell "like rough diamonds - uncompromising and brash - without any of the bad grace of some of their tough backbench colleagues" (Simon Beck, NEWCASTLE JOURNAL);
History: He joined the Labour Party at 16, '59; was elected to Easington District Council May '70; became its Leader May '79; was selected to replace retiring Jack Dormand as Easington's Labour MP Dec '85; attacked David Steel and David Owen for describing him as

one of 101 "hard Left" Labour candidates: "the performance of the Alliance in the local elections earlier this month, when Labour won nine more seats, mainly at their expense, shows that the Labour Party principle of fighting elections on policies and not personal smear campaigns strikes a chord with the electorate" May '87; retained the seat, increasing the Labour majority by 10,000 June '87; backed motions opposing abortion and embryo experimentation July '87; supported the Early Day Motions of Frank Cook throwing doubts on the safety of Heysham 2 (nuclear) Power Station July '87; in his Maiden speech he complained about the loss of local coal pits, the Government's parsimony in funds for council housing and the loss of control over Peterlee new town "the only success story in the area" July '87; welcomed the several Private Members' Bills curbing the 1967 Abortion Act Nov '87; backed David Alton's abortion-curbing Bill Jan '88; co-sponsored a motion attacking the use of aborted freeze-dried unborn children as earrings Jan '88; asked about toxic wastes being offloaded at the local port of Seaham Feb '88; identified with the serving staff at the Commons: "conditions in the kitchens are very poor and if this was not a royal palace, the Health and Safety Executive could be called in" Feb '88; visited Iraq, Kuwait and Bahrein as guest of Gulf Centre for Strategic Studies in group of eleven MPs led by Tony Marlow, but did not register this through "an oversight"; thought Saddam Hussein "an absolutely horrifying figure; he just oozed wickedness - cobra eyes, a really fearful figure" Feb '88; urged an effort to publicise public rights of way Mar '88; welcomed Mother Teresa's anti-abortion statement Apr 88; backed Gwyneth Dunwoody's effort to avoid discrimination against furs caught by Canadian Indians May '88; voted against a 26-week ceiling for abortions May '88; sided with Tony Marlow in urging "the regime in Tel Aviv" to "cease at once its terrorist activities" May '88; supported the rehabilitation of Leon Trotsky June '88; welcomed as "a victory to celebrate" the dumping of Durham coal waste at sea, instead of by coastal tipping at Easington June '88; backed the Kinnock-Hattersley team, while his flatmate Ronnie Campbell backed Benn and Heffer June '88; accused Government stinginess of being responsible for putting further and higher education out of the reach of working-class families June '88; urged a "once and for all" solution to pollution caused by dumping of mine waste June '88; urged better protection for badgers and badger setts Sep '88; urged help for pre-'73 war widows Mar '89; claimed 8,000 locals on income support had lost out in upgrading of benefits Apr '89; attacked "appalling" policy of being generous in grants for new City Technical Colleges while penny-pinching with normal secondary education May '89; urged more generous treatment for local ex-prisoners Aug '89; attacked decimation of deep-mined coal mines to benefit opencast and imported coal produced by child and slave labour June '89; expressed fears that parents of mentally handicapped children would have to travel further because of community health service changes Jan '89; urged recognition of PLO Dec '89; criticised Israel's Rightwing Premier, Yitzhak Shamir, for establishing new settlements for influx of Russian Jews Jan '90; backed boycott of Israeli goods until their withdrawal from West Bank and Gaza Strip June '90; opposed Gulf War against Iraq Sep '90; complained Northern Electric had spent £4.9m on privatisation including £1.8m on advertising Oct '90; again opposed Gulf war Dec '90; co-sponsored motion urging real ale be made available in Commons bars Dec '90; again opposed Gulf War Jan '91; backed a new sewage treatment plant at Hendon to prevent beach contamination May '91; urged higher minimum wages for security men Sep '91; was rated the 28th and last northeastern MP in terms of oral questions and the 11th in terms of written questions Nov '91; backed George Galloway's motion recalling 11 years of US intervention in Vietnam, leaving 2m dead and countless others maimed Dec '91; led motion deploring closure of Murton colliery, in which he had worked for 29 years Dec '91; backed George Galloway's motion attacking US involvement in El Salvador and East Timor Dec '91; backed an enterprise zone for East Durham to provide a "kick start" for an area deprived of mining jobs Jan '92;

asked about human rights in Israel and Kuwait (but not Iraq) Jan '92; retained seat with majority up from 24,639 to 26,390, a swing to Labour of 2.10% Apr 92; visited China, with local travel and accomodation paid by Chinese Association for Friendship and Understanding Aug-Sep '92; co-sponsored Dennis Skinner's motion demanding scrapping of pit closure programme in wake of devaluation Sep '92; sharply attacked Michael Heseltine's "disgraceful" and "insulting" statement on mines closures, criticising the "incestuous relationship between [electricity] supply companies in the northeast and gas-fired power stations"; asked "who will get their grubby hands" on the "tremendous amount of money - £15b -in the mineworkers' pension scheme"? Oct '92; urged easing of tobacco taxes to help hard-pressed corner shops Feb '93; when moderate pro-miner Labour MPs welcomed report that Grimethorpe Collier was viable, co-sponsored Dennis Skinner's amendment demanding all pits be saved Mar '93; backed motion opposing US "unilateral action...in authorising a missile attack upon Iraq" July '93; opposed easing of mining safety regulations: as "an electrician underground...many was the occasion when I had recourse to the miners' regulations in the top pocket of my waistcoat against the under-manager, the manager and the group manager" Oct '93; raised alarm about the stopping of pumping operations at Easington Colliery: "that will destroy the colliery, which was up for bids" Oct '93; indicated he would accept privatisation of Easington Colliery, since "we are talking about 600 jobs" Oct '93; was named an alternate Delegate to the Council of Europe and Western European Union Dec '93; said, "it is perhaps the first time - at least in the past 150 years - that a Member for Easington has spoken in the Chamber without having a working colliery in his constituency"; "at the flick of a switch more than £20m worth of expensive coalmining equipment and machinery has been left to flood at Easington Colliery; he blamed it on the Tory desire to "slim the industry down for privatisation"; warned that "the people of Durham and Sunderland are sitting on an ecological time bomb" from unpumped mine waters Jan '94; in a Campaign Group motion co-warned of threat of war in Korea as a result of US intervention there Feb '94; voted against restoring capital punishment, but in favour of reducing age of homosexual consent to 18 or 16, Feb '94; voted for Blair for Leader, Prescott for Deputy Leader July '94; was named a Whip Oct '94; said 15,000 jobs had been lost locally in 10 pits closed since '79, forcing ex-miners to work for £1 an hour as packers; urged the delayed plan for 235 acres of enterprise zone be implemented Nov '94; backed Campaign Group motion urging diplomatic recognition of North Korea Mar '95; voted for Tony Benn's amendment to Defence Estimates, urging scrapping of Trident and cutting spending to West European average Dec '95; claimed Easington had become the country's 3rd poorest area with the closing of Easington colliery; urged the Government to "give a little back to Easington, which has paid in blood, sweat and tears" Jan '96; attacked the exclusion of Commons catering staff from improved catering facilities to be at variance with John Major's "classless society" June '96; voted to cap MPs' pay rise at 3%, to cut their mileage allowance but to base their pension on £43,000 July '96; had to appeal to local party members to fund his re-election campaign when the NUM revealed there was no money to fund its formerly sponsored MPs Apr '97; in campaign called for concessionary TV licenses for pensioners, wages for ex-Servicemen; also claimed thatafter two years in government some Labour LMPs would press for more than the parrty's five election pledges: "Gordon Brown will never say there is no money for it; he could say we realise that inequalities exist and as soon as the public purse permits we will react to it" Apr '97; retained selt with an enhanced majority of 30,012 on a swing of 7.8% May '97; formerly a Whip, was sidelined to Select Committee on the Environment July '97; visited Slovakia on the all-party Czech and Slovak Group Oct '97;
Born: 6 July 1943, Murton, Easington
Family: "I am a sixth generation child of the coal industry; we have had six generations at Murton Colliery who have been born and bred for the pit"; s, George Scott Cummings, who

was 51 years a miner, and Mary (Cain); unmarried;
Education: Murton Council Infants', Juniors' and Seniors' schools; Easington Technical College;
Occupation: Parliamentary Adviser: to National Association of Licensed House Managers (unpaid) '97?-, National Associatoin of Coouncillors (unpaid) '97?-; ex: NUM-sponsored (£400 p a for his constituency, 80% of election expenses) '87-95; Pit Electrician at Murton Colliery (NUM) '58-87;
Traits: Full-faced; stubbly light grey hair; high widow's peak; an emotional style, especially when discussing the "betrayed" mining industry; well-read; RC; adores Jack Russell terriers: his deceased 'Grit Gritsky' had stood on picket lines at Murton colliery chewing on its favourite Maggie Thatcher doll; deplores the way orang-utangs are kept in London Zoo, telling the keeper: "you are the one who should be in a cage"; "has caused a stir in the past for proudly declaring his bi-sexuality" (EVENING STANDARD); his Kennington flatmate was fellow ex-miner Ronnie Campbell, with six children;
Address: House of Commons, Westminster, London, SW1A 0AA; 18 Grasmere Terrace, Murton, Seaham, Durham SR7 9NW;
Telephone: 0171 219 5122/5663 (H of C); 0191 526 1142 (home); 0191 5818249 (agent); 0191 5273773 (constituency office)

Lawrence (Francis) CUNLIFFE   **Labour**   **LEIGH '79-**

Majority: 24,496 (53.3%) over Conservative 4-way;
Description: Lancashire coalfield with light industry replacing mines in Leigh, Atherton and Hindley; a safe Labour seat since '22; in '95 Hindsford ward (comprising part of Atherton) was lost to Eccles, in exchange for Lightshaw ward from Makerfield; this switch was expected to shave few votes off an impregnable Labour majority;
Position: Alternate Delegate to Council of Europe and Western European Union '93-; Chairman: all-party Minerals Group, all-party Association of Non-Profitmaking Clubs '87-; Vice Chairman: all-party Racing and Bloodstock Industry Group, all-party Leisure and Recreation Industry Group; Treasurer: all-party Rugby League Group, all-party Cricket Group; ex: Whip (for North West and Energy) '85-87; on UK Executive, Commonwealth Parliamentary Association '89-94; Chairman, NUM Parliamentary Group; on NUM Area Executive '57-??, NUM Parliamentary Panel; on Services Committee (Catering Sub-Committee) '81-83; Bolton District Councillor '74-79; Farnworth Borough Councillor '60-74;
Outlook: Shrewd, moderate, occasionally rebellious Lancastrian former mining engineer; an opponent of pornography and a longstanding enthusiast for a North West Regional Assembly; formerly an NUM-sponsored ex-Gormley man; has a half-joking style but has been deadly serious about his dismay about the destruction of the mining industry; an opponent of select committees ("a waste of time and money"); sponsored the Scarman-encouraged Citizens' Compensation Bill; pro-Zionist; favours voluntary-aided and grant-maintained Christian schools; an RC pro-Lifer; anti: abortion and embryo research; a low-profile operator except

when mines are threatened or woman trouble pushes him into headlines; "has a ,reputation among fellow Mps of being a hardworking constituency man" (DAILY MAIL);
History: Was elected to NUM Area Executive '57, to Farnworth Council '60; became Mayor of Farnworth; after fighting an anti-immigrant candidate, was beaten by Cyril Smith at Rochdale by-election Oct '72 and general election Feb '74; was elected to Bolton Metropolitan Council May '74; was selected to follow long-inactive Labour MP Harold Boardman '78, elected May '79; favoured 100% grants to encourage replacement of motor buses by trolley buses, to save oil June '79; favoured limiting Abortion Act July '79; supported RC Bishop of Hexham in backing free school transport Nov '79; complained about slowness of Manchester-London mail Feb '80; visited Israel '80; opposed televising Parliament Jan '80; opposed reduction in local bus services Feb '81; his constituency suffered infiltration from Militants June '81; again visited Israel Oct '81; supported effort of retarded patient to free herself from mental hospital Dec '81; urged long-term international guarantees of Falklands security May '82; introduced Bill to compel full disclosure before sale of public assets July '82; urged positive discrimination in favour of north west July '82; was Doug Hoyle's 'minder' in Warrington by-election July '82; visited US to observe elections Sep '82; opposed using live animals for research Nov '82; warned against arms reaching PLO Dec '82; backed Eritrea against Ethiopia Dec '82; asked about cash limits on Family Practitioners Committee expenditure Jan '83; again defended Israel's position Apr '83; was re-adopted for Leigh Apr '83; backed Royal Commission on Pornography June '83; supported freedom of Jews to leave USSR July '83; was embarrassed by allegations about woman friend Jan '84; predicted collapse of bus and train services Aug '84; again was thought to be under threat from Militant and hard Left Oct '84; co-sponsored motion urging a Royal Commission to investigate use of live animals in research Nov '84; co-led a motion opposing generic prescribing Jan '85; backed more flexible pub hours Mar '85; was re-selected from short-list of one June '85; took adjournment debate (for ill Terry Lewis) opposing opencast mining Jan '86; attacked the financial provisions of the Coal Industry Bill Nov '86; added 4,000 to his majority June '87; voted for 2nd Reading of David Alton's abortion-curbing Bill Jan '88; again voted against televising the Commons Feb '88; demanded equality for clubs with pubs under Licensing Bill Apr '88; opposed 26-week abortion ceiling May '88; co-sponsored Bill to establish a North West Regional Assembly Oct '88; voted for Neil Kinnock as Leader Oct '88; like other NUM-sponsored ex-miners, strongly opposed the Associated British Ports (No 2) Bill, fearing that development of Immingham port would increase cheap coal imports Nov '88; came 6th in draw for Private Members' Bills; opponents of abortion were disappointed when he declined to introduce an Alton-style abortion-curbing Bill, although a Catholic Dec '88; urged an full inquiry into funeral costs which, he found, included profit margins of 500-1,500% Feb '89; successfully introduced 2nd Reading of his Citizens' Compensation Bill, as recommended by Lord Scarman; its intention was to deal "with the enormous difficulties that injured people face" - because of high legal costs - "in seeking compensation" for things like medical negligence; Solicitor General Sir Nicholas Lyell urged him to abandon his proposed Compensation Advisory Board, which judges would ignore Mar '89; complained that Citizens' Compensation Bill had been "hijacked" and "decimated" because he had been forced to drop the first four clauses in Committee to get it through quickly while Tory MP James Arbuthnot added a narrowing alteration the Speaker considered a "wrecking amendment" July '89; on Coal Industry Bill said free competition had been abandoned for price intervention; nuclear power continued to be subsidized, particularlyh the Magnox "white elephants"; despite cheaper coal, 30,000 more miners would be sacked, to "fatten the goose prior to privatization of the coal industry" Dec '89; said miners would have to work harder and longer to produce cheap coal for privatized electricity Dec '89; "as an officer of the all-party Rugby League

[Parliamentary] Group" opposed imposition of all-seater stadia on Rugby League grounds which had average attendances of 3,500-4,000 a week Jan '90; as an RC opposed embryo research, voted for 18-week limit on abortion Apr '90; asked Mrs Thatcher why building society chiefs should award themselves 50% pay increases while their luckless customers felt the pinch June '90; urged easing of cold weather payment claims for elderly Jan '91; backed motion encouraging "new independent Christian schools and schools of other faiths to apply for voluntary-aided status and extend eligibility for grant-maintained status" Feb '91; complained about funeral directors "ripping off the public, urging standards and a registration council to maintain them Apr '91; complained that despite Wigan's being a model local authority, judged by the SUNDAY TIMES to be the third most efficient in the country, it had been capped three times, the last time costing 400 teachers' jobs Feb '92; retained seat with majority up from 16,606 to 18,827, a swing to Labour of 1.71% Apr '92; did not vote in election for Leader or Deputy Leader July '92; co-sponsored NUM MPs' motion urging use of devaluation to halt closures so that more coal could be exported Sep '92; complained about three mines closures in "last seven and a half months", reporting "the feelings and the depression of miners, with an average age of 27 years, who have moved from pit to pit with the guarantee that there will be no compulsory redundancies and who have been totally isolated and neglected and are now near, not to hope, but to despair"; asked President Michael Heseltine "how can he reconcile the fact that he proposes to close profitable pits with the fact that uneconomic, dangerous nuclear power stations are being highly subsidised - to the tune of £1,260m a year levy - and still command 20% of our total energy market?" "could not the production from profitable pits replace at least 50% of that and save 10,000 miners' jobs?" Oct '92; backed motion urging the bill for restoring Windsor Castle should be paid by the Windsors, "one of the world's richest families, whose head does not pay income tax" Nov '92; urged the transfer of "about half the nuclear levy for Magnox stations" to "help most of the collieries to survive" Feb '93; said, "I am the self-assigned chairman of the organization that seeks the abolition of all select committees; they are a waste of time and money" Mar '93; voted against National Lottery Bill Apr '93; asked Energy Minister Tim Eggar why he over-emphasised the Modified Colliery Review Procedure, since so "many pits that have gone through that procedure, regardless of their productivity, economic value and viability, have been closed; if there is no market for coal, what is the point of re-introducing this red herring for miners - as if it were something that would ultimately save them and their industry? would it not be far better to act instantly by cutting coal imports further, by ceasing opencast mining and by controlling our oil imports and gas reactor services more closely?" Oct '93; was named an Alternate Delegate to the Council of Europe and Western European Union Dec '93; was accused by DAILY MAIL's Nigel Dempster of being friendly with an eighteen-year-old researcher, who worked for John Watts, his co-Chairman of the all-party Nonprofitmaking Parliamentary Group Feb '94; co-sponsored Dale Campbell-Savours' motion urging military intervention in Bosnia against "Serbian aggression" Feb '94; voted against restoring capital punishment or reducing the age of homosexual consent from 21, Feb '94; backed Sunday racing, since racing had become part of the leisure industry May '94; voted for Blair for Leader, Prescott for Deputy July '94; voted against extension of Sunday pub licensing hours, complaining there had been no consultation with the drinking clubs Feb '95; in debate on John McFall's anti-hunting Bill, recalled being forced to hunt and set snares as a child with his grandfather; his memories of being forced to bludgeon baby weasels to death had haunted him for 50 years: "I can still hear the echoes of those penetrative shrills as those animals died" Mar '95; voted against a 3% cap on MPs' pay rise, in favour of lower mileage allowances, for a pension based on £43,000 July '96; voiced public's "grave and growing concern about televised pornography", citing DAILY MAIL's claim there were 27 hard-core porn films available on satellite TV every night; urged Government to make it an offence to make, sell or possess pirated decoder cards to access banned satellite channels; he also attacked accessibility to children of pornography on the internet Nov '96; his place as an Alternate Delegate to WEU was renewed Dec '96; retained his seat with a majority of 24,496 after a notional pro-Labour swing of 10.7% May '97; urged voluntary or compulsory identity cards to deter under-age drinking, "one of the principal reasons for the rise in youth crime" June '97; voted to bar fox-hunting June '97; as a "long-standing member of the Arospace and Technology Committee of the WEU" pressed for a commitment to the Eurofighter, to retain "the viability of British Aerospace productive capacity" to protect 10,000 local jobs in Lostock factories in Bolton and on aircraft wings in Chadderton July '97; urged Regional Minister Dick Caborn to "place on a fast track regional government for the northwest region" where "limited self-rule is imperative" and there was "unanimity among the CBI, all employers federations, local government, trade unions and MPs about the need to get it off the ground as quickly as possible; is it really necessary to hold a local referendum before we do that?" Nov '97; was one of 14 Labour MPs who abstained against the Social Security Bill cutting single parents' benefits Dec '97; cited the "astounding success of the American drug courts, which have a specialised judge and a specialised team of workers" Mar '98; rebelled against abolition of student maintenance grants June '98; demanded of PM Blair an early ban on fox-hunting July '98;

Born: 23 March 1929, Worsley, Manchester
Family: S Francis Cunliffe, ex-miner; m '50 Winifred (Haslem); 3s, 2d; divorced '85 on grounds of his friendship for Elizabeth Payne;
Education: St Edmund's Roman Catholic School, Manchester; Ruskin College, Oxford (union course);
Occupation: Formerly Sponsored by NUM (£600 p a for constituency, plus 80% of election expenses) '79-95; Adviser, Club Institute Union '92-97; Engineer in NCB's Walkden Area Engineering Services, Worsley, Manchester '49-79;
Traits: Unexpectedly black hair, replacing a previously retreating hairline; long-faced; hooded eyes; crooked smile; "bears a striking resemblance to Mr Tom Jones without the shaky hips" (Colin Brown, HOUSE MAGAZINE); shrewd; genial; joking manner (said, "I am in the springtime of my senility"); RC ("I go to mass every Saturday evening")
Address: House of Commons, Westminster, London SW1A 0AA; 396 Manchester Road, Worsley, Manchester M28 5WH;
Telephone: 0171 219 4185 (H of C); 01204 75136;

KEEPING PARLIAMENTARY SECRETS
A rueful MP claimed, with some truth, that the best way to keep something secret is to make a speech about it in the Palace of Westminster. He was commenting on the emptiness of the Press Gallery (except for HANSARD writers and the Press Association). Long gone are the days when serious newspapers carried a full or half-page summarising Parliamentary debate. Of late, Westminster has been used as a source of news stories. In our old-fashioned way, we read HANSARD daily and watch the Commons and Lords on the Parliamentary Channel. Parliamentary debaters are very self-revealing in debate. And we don't mean only Kerry Pollard MP, in whose Maiden he disclosed that until 12 he had to drop his trousers regularly to prove that Kerry was not a girl's name.

'Jim' (James) CUNNINGHAM   **Labour**   **COVENTRY SOUTH '97-**

Majority: 10,953 (21.9%) over Conservative 8-way;

Description: A new seat, created in '95, out of three-quarters of his former Coventry SE seat and half of formerly Tory-held Coventry SW; some analysts rated it a Tory marginal until '97; it stretches from the blitzed and rebuilt city centre to peripheral council estates, leafy suburbs and Warwick University's campus;

Former Seat: Coventry SE '92-97

Position: On Trade and Industry Select Committee '97-; ex; on Home Affairs Select Committee '94-97; Chairman, Tribune Group '96-97; Coventry City Councillor (Leader '88-92) '72-92; Chairman, Labour's West Midlands Joint Committee;

Outlook: Low-profiled trade union loyalist addicted to reading his speeches; an opponent of young drunks from the city which was the first to ban public drinking; the local former council leader chosen to mobilise the loyal Labour vote to resist the blandishments of its popular, expelled pro-Militant former Labour MP, Dave Nellist, who refused to accept his rejection; a Scots engineer and former Rolls-Royce shop steward;

History: He arrived in Coventry from Scotland '62; joined the Labour Party '67; was elected to Coventry City Council May '72; became Chief Whip '85, Deputy Leader '87, Leader of Coventry City Council '88; was selected by a postal ballot of over 200 party members - defeating ex-MPs Oonagh McDonald and Geoff Edge - to stand as Labour's official candidate replacing expelled Militant sympathiser Dave Nellist, who then described him as "the imposed candidate" Feb '92; just before the election a BIRMINGHAM POST poll of the constituency gave him 32% against 30% for Dave Nellist and 28% for the Conservative, Mrs Martine Hyams Mar '92; narrowly held this normally safe Labour seat with his 11,902 votes securing a majority of only 1,311 - down from 6,653 - with Dave Nellist coming in 3rd, with 10,311 votes Apr '92; in his Maiden speech, he emphasized unemployment in Coventry and its lack of resources from the Government: "Coventry South East, like the rest of the country, suffers from a lack of resources to develop its education system"; "Coventry South East has a major council housing problem because of the lack of Government resources to carry out the necessary repairs and to deal with homelessness"; he urged the Government not to "mislead the country into thinking that they are involved in hard negotiations over Britain's rights when in fact they are putting on a charade - a half-hearted attempt to kid the Europeans that we want to play a major part as members of the European Community" May '92; voted for fellow-Scot John Smith for Leader, Bryan Gould for Deputy Leader July '92; urged Chancellor Lamont to extend income tax to the Queen, to which Lamont replied "I have no plans to do so" Nov '92; complained that Government's propaganda had misled people into giving up their state pensions Nov '92; voted against both full and partial deregulation of Sunday trading, preferring to "Keep Sunday Special" Dec '93; was added to Home Affairs Select Committee, replacing Donald Anderson Feb '94; asked a brace of questions about the role of Health Management Trust Ltd, established by the West Midlands Regional Health Authority Feb '94; voted against restoring capital punishment, not even for killing policemen Feb '94; voted to reduce age of homosexual consent to 18, after voting for 16, Feb '94; complained of the "scandal" that the skilled engineers of Matrix Churchill had lost their jobs without receiving full redundancy or pensions and without being allowed to testify to the Scott Inquiry Apr '94; voted for Blair for Leader, Prescott for Deputy Leader July '94; after asking Downing Street for financial help for a group of sacked workers, received a leaflet, "How to Claim Legal Aid" Aug '94; to expose the use of family credit to subsidise low wages, he cited a constituent, a lone mother earning £1 an hour Aug '94; urged Government aid for R&D for Coventry's aircraft industry Nov '94; highlit Coventry Airport's problems of noise, crashes and airworthiness Jan '95; raised question of fatal crash of freight aircraft used to export live animals from Coventry Airport Feb '95; urged licensing and registration of private security agencies Nov '95; said, "I am not one of those who would like a British Federal Bureau of Investigation" Jan '96; in Scott Report debate concentrated on collapse of Matrix-Churchill, losing 600 skilled engineering jobs Feb '96; opposed Tory MP Iain Duncan-Smith's Bill to curb jurisdiction of European Court Apr '96; was uncertain about use of security services to combat organised crime June '96; proposed a Pensions Trustees Bill June '96; was elected Chairman of the Tribune Group July '96; proposed Witness Protection Bill to protect witnesses and victims of anti-social behaviour July '96; his Researcher, David John Collins ('Deejay') was described in GUARDIAN as a "New Labour weenie" who was "bombarding the press with near-identical letters savaging those who dare to dispute with the leadership" Sep '96; asked a brace of questions on alcohol-related questions Oct '96; in adjournment debate featured youthful drinking and consequent crime Feb '97; introduced 10-minute-rule Bill to control airport noise Feb '97; asked questions on tax on private pension contributions, seen by the SUNDAY TELEGRAPH as a precursor to Gordon Brown's tax hikes Mar '97; as an opponent of hunting, was a target of The FIELD Apr '97; retained his redrawn and renamed seat with an enhanced majority of 10,953 on a notional swing of 13.5% in what was thought to be a marginal seat; he was helped by the decline of the vote of the pro-Militant ex-Labour MP, David Nellist, to 3,262, May '97; was named to Trade and Industry Select Committee July '97; read his loyal speech wholly supportive of Gordon Brown's Budget, alleging that "under the Conservatives' so-called tax cuts were nothing more than an underhand shift from direct to indirect tax, from progressive to regressive tax, from taxing the rich to taxing the poor" Mar '98;

Born: 4 February 1941, Coatbridge, Lanarkshire

Family: Son, Adam Cunningham, a former miner and then a steel worker, and Elizabeth (Farell); m '85 Marion Douglas (Podmore); 1s, 1d, 1steps, 1stepd;

Education: Columba High School, Coatbridge; Tillycoultry College; Ruskin College (courses on Labour Movement and Industrial Law);

Occupation: Ex: Engineer, formerly at Rolls Royce Aerospace '72-92; MSF Senior Shop Steward '72-92;

Traits: Slim; white, parted hair; tends to read whole speeches in a pedestrian manner; enjoys football, music, visiting historical buildings;

Address: House of Commons, Westminster, London SW1A 0AA; 457 London Road, Coventry, West Midlands;

Telephone: 0171 219 6362 (H of C); 01203 304340 (home); 01203 553159 (constituency);

We reach the uncovered parts of MPs the press no longer notice, because the correspondents leave the Press Gallery too early.

Rt Hon Dr 'Jack' (John Anderson) CUNNINGHAM   **Labour**   **COPELAND '83-**

Majority: 11,944 (28.9%) over Conservative 5-way;

Description: Whitehaven renamed, with the port, nearby Haig colliery (closed in '86) and controversial, leaky Sellafield (ex Windscale) nuclear power and reprocessing plant; in a region with high unemployment Sellafield provides jobs directly and indirectly supports half the working population; the seat includes some of the spectacular scenery of the Lake District National Park;

Former Seat: Whitehaven '70-83;

Position: Minister for the Cabinet Officer and Chancellor of the Duchy of Lancaster '98-; Deputy Lieutenant, Cumbria '91-; ex: Minister of Agriculture, Fisheries and Food '97-98; National Heritage Spokesman '95-97; Trade and Industry Spokesman '94-95; Foreign Affairs Spokesman '92-94; Shadow Commons Leader '89-92; Spokesman, on Environment and Sport '83-89; Deputy Spokesman, on Industry '79-83; Under Secretary, Energy '76-79; PPS, to James Callaghan '72-76; on Committees of Privileges, Services (Chairman its Computer Subcommittee), Televising the Commons '89-92; on Select Committee on Science and Technology 70-76; Chairman '82-83, Vice Chairman '79-82 PLP Northern Group; on Executive Committee of Labour Solidarity '81-86;

Outlook: The PM's new "enforcer" set the task of knocking together the heads of rival Cabinet Ministers; the tough-minded veteran formerly set the task of cutting back the subsidies for Britain's most handout-dependent but crisis-ridden industry; an unexpected job for Tony Blair's close adviser, rejected in '95 for the Shadow Cabinet as too laid-back and too boring a speaker by fellow Labour MPs; "that rare bird, a Labour MP with Ministerial experience' (TIMES); "no one could be older Labour" (Alan Watkins, INDEPENDENT ON SUNDAY); a very bright, highly-educated, regionally-rooted, radical Right-of-Centre moderate; formerly in the Solidarity group; "one of the brightest lights of his political generation" (Andrew Rawnsley, GUARDIAN) in other fields; "as an operator, he is very professional, very skilled and very managerial" (senior Labour colleague); has the "ability to conjure up sharp, tabloid-style quotes" (Charles Hymas, YORKSHIRE POST); "one of the most effective dealers in political venom in the business", because "he does it with a smile which makes it all the more deadly"; "when Jack Cunningham does a hatchet job on you, you remain politically scarred for life" (NEWCASTLE EVENING NEWS); suffers from the failure of his colleagues to rally round when in trouble ("in terms of his chums, he is a bit of a loner; in fact you have difficulties just thinking who they are" [senior Labour colleague]); a long-time opponent of the hard Left, partly over nuclear power; also developed prickly relationships with fellow Right-of-Centre colleagues Roy Hattersley and Gerald Kaufman; was mocked by media journalists for his lack of serious interest in culture when National Heritage Spokesman; but showed his politician's skills by wrong-footing Michael Heseltine over Labour's being landed with the overdraft for the Millennium Exhibition at Greenwich; was also late John Smith's "closest Shadow Cabinet friend" (Donald Macintyre, INDEPENDENT ON SUNDAY) after running his tight election campaign in '92; has been backed by Mandelson for his "abundance of presentational skills", his "mastery of the soundbite, good looks, [and] authoritative TV presence" (INDEPENDENT); others see a self-indulgent man who prefers fishing in Norway in July to his frontbench duties; "Dr Cunningham's ability to misread the House of Commons is

unparalleled" (Simon Hoggart, GUARDIAN); in the foreign affairs post he successfully sought, was a cliche-rusted, blunter blade than his sharp predecessor, Gerald Kaufman and had difficulty in coping with his skilled professional opponent, Douglas Hurd; left most of the running on Maastricht to his deputy, George Robertson, and on Bosnia to Paddy Ashdown; this did not change the general Labour judgement that he is self-indulgent, which was reflected in his low votes for the Shadow Cabinet until corraled by Blair's Whips; a talented scion of the northeast's influential Cunningham family; a highly-skilled sharp-tongued controversialist, was formerly particularly adept at baiting Patrick (now Lord) Jenkin and late Nicholas (then Lord) Ridley; until '97 was one of Commons' two PhDs in chemistry; until '97 was a well-paid adviser to big chemical companies; with Sellafield as his constituency's dominant employer, was embarrassed by nuclear leaks into seeming ambivalence as Labour's long-standing Environment Spokesman '83-89; unequivocally favours safe nuclear power but is sharply critical of unsafe nuclear power; favours electoral reform but opposes deals with Liberal Democrats; was GMB-sponsored (his father was its Northern Secretary);
History: After delivering its leaflets from childhood, joined the Labour Party at 16, '55; was elected to Chester-le-Street District Council May '69; was selected for Whitehaven over Gerald Kaufman; was considering emigrating to US for an academic post when he was elected MP for Whitehaven (later renamed Copeland) June '70; urged a Regional Development Minister July '70; warned that the northeast was deteriorating because of Tory opposition to regional policies Feb '71; became unofficial PPS to James Callaghan '72; his father was arrested in Poulson scandal July '73; was appointed to Subcommittees on national policy on sea-bed engineering and on computer industry of Select Committee on Science and Technology Nov '73; urged full-scale investigation of cancer threats at Windscale (later Sellafield) Jan '74; partly out of personal loyalty to his father, who had pleaded guilty to corruption, James Callaghan named him his official PPS Mar '74; renewed his Windscale inquiry demand Nov '74; called for wholesale reform of Parliamentary procedures Mar '75; thanked Tony Benn for not storing spent fuel at nuclear power stations Mar '76; led James Callaghan's successful team in post-Wilson Leadership contest March-April '76; was named Energy Under Secretary (under Tony Benn) Sep '76; urged siting of Government analytical chemists in Cumbria Nov '76; screened Tony Benn from answering questions on IMF-imposed gas price increases Mar '77; urged special Minister for northeast Jan '81; with Giles Radice became Co-ordinator for northeast of moderates' 'Labour Solidarity' organisation June '81; successfully reversed redrawing of constituency, which would have made it a Tory seat June '81; on slate of Manifesto moderates, failed to be elected to Shadow Cabinet Nov '81; attacked CEGB financing of Korean cable-laying ship Feb '82; warned Royal Navy cuts would mean "thousands of redundancies" in northeastern shipyards Mar '82; warned privatisation would mean "asset stripping" of shipyards Nov '82; won 67 votes for Shadow Cabinet, failing to get on Nov '82; demanded controls on dangerous pesticides Dec '82; led opposition to Telecommunications Bill Nov '82; demanded more information on 1957 fall-out from Windscale (renamed Sellafield) Feb '83; led Labour's successful team at Darlington by-election Mar '83; wanted Michael Foot to step down as Leader Apr '83; attacked involvement of Communists in trade union voting for Labour's new Leader June '83; backed Roy Hattersley against Kinnock for Leader Sep '83; with Manifesto backing, won 89 votes (5th) in Shadow Cabinet election, the highest-placed newcomer Oct '83; was named Environment and Sports Spokesman Nov '83; spoke of "real anger" of constituents about radioactive Sellafield discharges and asked whether individual managers might be charged Dec '83; was re-elected to the Shadow Cabinet with 106 votes (joint 3rd) Oct '84; was named a Shadow Cabinet representative on Campaigns Strategy Committee Oct '84; after the Government's majority dropped to a record low of 23 on the Local Government Bill (poll tax), asked how it would

react to its "moral and humiliating defeat" Dec '84; in Shadow Cabinet elections he received 95 votes Oct '85; was re-adopted from a shortlist of one Nov '85; received 93 votes in Shadow Cabinet election Oct '86; remained overall Environment spokesman but just-elected Dr David Clark was given Environmental Protection and Development and Green issues, somewhat to Cunningham's discomfiture Nov '86; Kinnock ignored his urging that Labour should fight the election on the poll tax; after a rearguard fight, hailed Labour's commitment to a slow phasing out of nuclear power as meaning local jobs were safe ("a safe future for Sellafield") May '87; despite sharp attacks on Labour as anti-nuclear and on his own pro-safe-nuclear position from pro-nuclear Tories and an anti-nuclear Green candidate, retained his slimmish majority June '87; was re-elected to Shadow Cabinet on the Solidarity slate, with 88 votes (joint 11th) July '87; insisted water should remain in public ownership and control Oct '87; came under gays' attack when he criticised but did not force a vote against a Tory proposal to ban local councils and schools from promoting homsexuality, since it had never been their duty or practice to promote homosexuality Dec '87; resisted hard-Left efforts to "put a spanner in the works" of the poll tax, saying: "any idea of illegality is not consistent with the position of a democratic socialist party" Feb '88; urged a Labour commitment to science and technology in the 1990s Feb '88; accused the Government of "seeking political gain from aiding and abetting bigotry" in promoting the anti-gay Clause 28 Mar '88; claimed that nine out of ten in his constituency would have to pay more in poll tax than in rates Mar '88; urged tighter controls to block genetic engineering for military or mischievous purposes May '88; disclosed that Environment's incompetent drafting still allowed local authorities to hinder companies insisting on discrimination against women or the disabled June '88; demanded an inquiry into discovery of high-level plutonium pellets at Drigg dump for low-level nuclear waste July '88; received 88 votes (14th) in Shadow Cabinet contest Nov '88; visited USA "partly funded by myself, the American Overseas Programme and private sector companies based in the USA" May '89; received 125 votes (8th) in Shadow Cabinet contest; was named Campaign Strategy Co-ordinator and shadow Leader of the House Nov '89; was consequently named to Committee of Privileges and Services and Television Committees Nov '89; all his computer discs, including internal party strategy papers, were stolen Dec '89; Tory MPs hostile to a Labour motion demanding disclosure of fees for MP-consultants, asked how much he was receiving from Albright and Wilson (UK) Ltd Feb '90; with his wife, visited Hongkong as guest of its Government and Japan as guest of Japanese Atomic Industrial Forum Apr '90; voted against War Crimes Bill Apr '90; visited USA as guest of National Democratic Institute June '90; received 99 votes (13th) for Shadow Cabinet Oct '90; more confidential papers were stolen Nov '90; again offered Labour backing for UN action in Gulf Jan '91; backed recommendations of Ibbs Committee on Commons services Jan '91; derided 'looney-Left' Lambeth Council for "patently ridiculous" motion urging withdrawal of troops from Gulf Feb '91; falsely claimed Labour candidate was set to win Ribble Valley Mar '91; attacked as a "disgrace" the unprecedented use of the guillotine to get through the Commons in one day the Bill to reduce the poll tax Mar '91; backed use of Parliament Act to override Lords on War Crimes Bill Mar '91; again voted against War Crimes Bill May '91; badgered John Major over changed HANSARD record to correct misnamed medical magazine, claiming nothing was "as cheap as fiddling the record" May '91; sipped champagne over Labour's advances in council elections May '91; told Paddy Ashhdown: "don't call us; we won't call you; there will be no pacts or deals" May '91; baited Government over guillotine to contrive rebellion-threatened vote on dog registration in small hours June '91; claimed £10m spent on publicising Citizen's Charter was thinly-disguised Tory election propaganda July '91; was criticised for taking his normal summer break, fishing in Norway, during London's G-7 conference, when Government was under siege over BCCI, largely by Labour MPs fearing an autumn election; to "dismay" of

Neil Kinnock, he did not address last pre-recess session of Shadow Cabinet July '91; travelled to France to address Unisys seminar Aug '91; declined to end his connection as its Adviser when Albright and Wilson were found to be discharging high levels of heavy metals into the Irish Sea from Whitehaven plan, saying: "if any company breaks the law on discharges in the environment, it must face the consequences" Sep '91; accused John Major of fearing to face the electorate Sep '91; a Greenpeace poll suggested his seat was under threat because of his support for an underground and undersea nuclear waste repository at Sellafield Oct '91; received 121 votes (12th) in Shadow Cabinet contest Oct '91; was rated the northeast MP who had asked the 9th most oral questions and the 17th most written questions Nov '91; accused Tories of having squeezed Dr Kumar's Labour victory at Langbaurgh by exploiting racism Nov '91; claimed Labour was running neck-and-neck in London Nov '91; urged electronic voting in the Commons and shorter sitting hours Nov '91; backed expulsion from Labour Party of David Nellist MP as a Militant member Dec '91; "as someone whose motor car has just been stolen and used in a ram raid" he backed the Government's Aggravated Vehicle-Taking Bill Dec '91; claimed guillotining of Bill to privatise school inspectors was to enable Tories to hold April election Jan '92; as leader of Labour's campaign committee was criticised for under-using the talents of Mandelson's favourites: Gordon Brown and Tony Blair Feb '92; was a tough chairman of Labour's early election press conferences, ruthlessly protecting Neil Kinnock from Tory tabloids trying to rattle him Mar '92; on BBC's 'Today' programme, "reaffirmed his claim to the title of 'Britain's touchiest breakfast politician'" (GUARDIAN) in loudly protesting questions which had not been agreed on Mar '92; retained seat with majority up from 1,894 to 2,439, a marginal swing to Labour of .53% Apr '92; was "discreetly blamed for pushing his Leader into the damaging two-step with Paddy Ashdown on electoral reform" (John Williams, EVENING STANDARD); co-nominated his friend John Smith Apr '92; was charged of election expense irregularities because of interview with him in BNFL newsletter; no chzrges were ever brought Apr '92; denied there was any "conspiracy" to manoeuvre John Smith into Labour's leadership Apr '92; angered unions by calling for a severe reduction of their presence on Labour's NEC May '92; resisted criticisms of his work as election Campaigns Co-ordinator, especially from John Prescott June '92; British Nuclear Fuels was cleared of breaching electoral law by promoting his re-election by publicising his support for an underground nuclear waste dump at Sellafield June '92; received 124 votes (12th) in Shadow Cabinet contest; as he hoped, was named Foreign Affairs Spokesman (despite Gerald Kaufman's warning to John Smith against his appointment) July '92; backed Government on air-exclusion zone for southern Iraq Aug '92; refused to be bounced by media into criticising Government on its caution in Yugoslav crisis Aug '92; was criticised by interventionist, Leftwing TRIBUNE for his "shabby performance"; "unless Mr Cunningham bucks his ideas up in the next month, he will deserve to lose his job" Aug '92; after 'Black Wednesday' said: "these claims that the ERM caused the recession, caused high interest rates, fly in the face of the facts" Sep '92; welcomed British troop deployment in ex-Yugoslavia and sanctions against Serbia Sep '92; welcomed Labour conference's overwhelming vote for closer union with EC Oct '92; said it was wrong to go ahead with Maastricht Bill until Danes had reversed their 'no' vote Oct '92; led opposition to backing paving vote on Maastricht as a vote of confidence in Major: "we say quite clearly we do not have any confidence in him or his government" Oct '92; backed extension of democracy in Hongkong Nov '92; welcomed deployment of US Marines in Somalia to protect aid-providers Dec '92; criticised absence of "any coherent strategy" by Government toward Iraq and Arab world Jan '93; deplored Israeli Government's deportation to no-man's land of Arab extremists Jan '93; disclosed Labour would insist on separate vote against opt-out from Maastricht's Social Chapter Jan '93; was elevated to the Privy Council Feb '93; insisted the protocol on the Social Chapter could simply be folded into the main body of the Maastricht treaty without the inclusion of the British opt-out Feb '93; attended conference in South Africa as guest of European Socialists, with hospitality from HM Ambassador there Feb '93; lobbied the Prime Minister to give the go-ahead for the THORP reprocessing plant in his constituency June '93; visited Egypt and Israel as guest of those governments June '93; was accused of having "left most of the Maastricht maneuvering to his skilful deputy, George Robertson, and...most of the running on Bosnia to Paddy Ashdown" (SUNDAY TELEGRAPH) Sep '93; received 107 votes - down from 124 - in Shadow Cabinet elections, tying for last place with David Blunkett; despite this implicit criticism of his performance as Foreign Affairs Spokesman - "not so much a Shadow Foreign Secretary as a phantom one" (Andrew Rawnsley, GUARDIAN) - was kept in place by Leader John Smith, an opponent of reshuffles Oct '93; criticised PM John Major for refusing to lift the ban on union rights at GCHQ Dec '93; after lunching with PLO's Yasser Arafat, asked Foreign Secretary Hurd about an international presence on the West Bank Dec '93; visited Hongkong and China as guest of their governments Jan '94; complained about Douglas Hurd's "vacillation" over Bosnia Jan '94; asked for rigorous inquiry into UK loans for Malaysia's Pergau Dam and consequent arms deals Jan '94; criticised hard-Left Labour MP George Galloway for honouring Saddam Hussein on TV Jan '94; favoured enlarged European Union Feb '94; voted against restoring capital punishment, even for killing policemen Feb '94; voted to reduce age of homosexual consent to 18 and 16, Feb '94; claimed colleagues were urging him to stand in the Labour leadership election, but they never surfaced; the OBSERVER said he could "almost certainly find the 34 MPs he would need to sign his nomination papers, but after that he would probably come bottom of the poll" May-June '94; was judged to have made "a lazy botch of foreign affairs...compounded by his loud truculence in debate" (Edward Pearce, GUARDIAN) June '94; voted for Blair for Leader, Beckett for Deputy Leader July '94; with support from the leadership, received 120 votes (10th) for Shadow Cabinet; was named Trade and Industry Spokesman by Tony Blair Oct '94; derided the £475,000 salary of British Gas chief executive Cedric Brown as an "abuse of monopoly power" Nov '94; endorsed Labour plans to tax speculative short-term share dealings Jan '95; called for an investigation of Chief Secretary Jonathan Aitken's BMARC links with arms for Iran Mar '95; was snubbed by Blair in assigning Robin Cook to lead in Scott Report debate June '95; despite support from the leadership, was voted off the Shadow Cabinet after 12 years, receiving only 100 votes, seven less than Tom Clarke, the lowest man elected; despite this, was named National Heritage Spokesman Oct '95; made moderate attack on the National Lottery, urging it be run by a non-profit organisation rather than Camelot which allegedly made £1m a week Oct '95; supported alternative to Government's proposal to limit to newspaper companies with less than 20% of national circulation if they sought to own TV companies up to 15% of total TV audience Nov '95; introduced himself as the shadow Secretary for the Environment, a post he had held in '83-89, Dec '95; backed continued dumping of waste at Sellafield (opposed by neighbouring MP Dale Campbell-Savours) Dec '95; backed a cross-party alliance to block exclusive TV rights for Murdoch to eight major sporting events Jan '96; was reportedly angered by junior Art Spokesman Mark Fisher's statement that Labour would reopen talks with Greece about the Elgin Marbles Apr '96; in the first post-Nolan Register, was shown to be earning up to £30,000 from three consultancies, more than any other Labour frontbencher May '96; Tony Blair urged his MPs to vote Cunningham into Joan Lestor's vacated place; with this backing regained his place in the Shadow Cabinet with 190 votes (12th) July '96; claimed that tapping "one of the world's greatest wells of talent in the creative industries" could yield 500,000 new jobs Oct '96; although invited by Virginia Bottomley, refused to underwrite the escalating costs of the Millenium Dome Nov '96; was roasted in an interview by Marianne Macdonald in the

INDEPENDENT ON SUNDAY over the paucity of cultural events attended after a year in the job Dec '96; succeeded in forcing Michael Heseltine to capitulate to Labour's terms for supporting the Millennium Exhibition in Greenwich, if it ousted the Conservatives from power Jan '97; again headed the list of Shadow Cabinet members with up to £30,000 in outside earnings Feb '97; retained his previously marginal seat by a majority inflated to 11,944 on a pro-Labour swing of 11.8% May '97; was unexpectedly named Minister of Agriculture to "take on" the farmers' subsidies May '97; announced an end to "the aggressions and intransigence of the past" with a new approach to the EU beef ban and the quota-hopping fishing dispute May '97; conceded quota-hoppers' licenses could not be removed May '97; was allegedly part of the Cabinet's 'English Lobby', with Jack Straw and Frank Dobson, hostile to aspects of Scottish devolution May '97; threatened a unilateral ban on EU beef imports into Britain unless EU adopted UK measures to protect people from BSE June '97; welcomed decision of fast-food chain McDonald's to end its 15-month ban on British beef June '97; saying "many farmers recognise the days of high subsidies and protection from market forces are over", urged an end to farm subsidies and their replacement with EU aid to rejuvenate rural areas June '97; allegedly angered his civil servants by moving them to Lambeth, taking over their Whitehall offices for himself and his ministers July '97; apologised for illegal beef exports to the Continent July '97; withdrew his threat of a beef import ban against EU states following EU agreeement on new sanitary standards for Continental abbatoirs July '97; announced a review of quarantine regulations Oct '97; in reply to Margaret Beckett's letter on the minimum wage, urged the exclusion of share fishermen and inclusion of "benefits in kind" for farmworkers Oct '97; did not take part in vote on Foster's anti-hunting Bill Nov '97; hired firm to rename and restyle his Ministry to make it more "people-friendly" Nov '97; opposed plan to build windmills on edge of Drigg, the UK's biggest radioactive dump Dec '97; ordered butchers to separate meat from the bone in T-bone steaks; was attacked for "insufferable arrogance" by William Hague, whom he accused of "breathtaking hypocrisy" Dec '97; announced a £85m plan to aid beef farmers, together with a year-long inquiry into BSE and proposals to slim down the industry drastically; urged "a rationalisation of the beef sector", citing his local hill farmers who had to be subsidised by £24,000 a year to produce an income of £10,000 Dec '97; attacking the CAP fiercely, told NFU its subsidies would be phased out within a decade Jan '98; announced plans for the Food Standards Agency Jan '98; his Ministry's house-moving, estimated to cost £930,000, came to more Feb '98; his T-bone regulations were dented by a Scottish court Apr '98; was named PM Blair's "enforcer" as Minister for the Cabinet Office and Chancellor of the Duchy of Lancaster July '98;
Born: 4 August 1939, Newcastle
Family: Grandson of a Durham miner; son, of Freda (Anderson) and 'Andy' (Andrew) Cunningham, former GMWU northeastern regional boss and jailed associate of T Dan Smith and John Poulson; m '64 Maureen (Appleby), recently an Open University graduate; 1s Jonathan '73, 2d Catherine '69; Alexandra '71;
Education: Jarrow Grammar School; Bede College, Durham University (Union President, Chemistry Hons '62, PhD in Chemistry - until '97 one of two in Commons - '66);
Occupation: President: of the Industry Forum (unremunerated) '95-, the £1,000 Club (unremunerated) '95-; ex: Adviser: on Industrial Policy to Albright and Wilson (chemical giant; £5-10,000) '80-97, Hays Chemicals (£5-10,000)'93-97, Centurion Press (£5-10,000) '92-97; Sponsored: by GMB (65% of agent's salary, plus some of '92 election costs, £2,033.73 of '79 election costs "including direct benefit to me") '70-95; Adviser: to Leather Chemicals '84-92?, Dow Ltd (US chemical giant) '85-92; Regional Officer of GMWU (now GMB) with responsibilities in the chemical industry, education and research fields '69-70; Teacher '68-69; Fellow in Chemistry, Durham University '66-68;

Traits: Tall; long-headed; dark short hair; pale skin, normally permanently tanned (allegedly from frequent trips abroad, hence "Mr Permatan"); "the slightly austere look of a modern-day Dracula" (Charles Hymas, YORKSHIRE POST); "languid, quick-minded, poised, articulate and cool, he is one of this Cabinet's surprise stars"; "has the saturnine good looks of a swarthy praying mantis, and the adenoidal menace of a slightly sadistic junior geography master; he speaks as though twisting a small boy's ear as he hammers home the admonition, 'our COUNTRYSIDE (twist) cannot AFFORD (twist) to TAKE (twist) that SORT of RISK!' Ouch!" (Matthew Parris, TIMES); "both arrogant and defensive", now scowling, now smiling superciliously", "a sort of John Prescott without the charm" (SUNDAY TELEGRAPH); sonorous; shrewd; articulate; practical Geordie intellectual; "the accents of cultivated Wearside" (Edward Pearce, DAILY TELEGRAPH); his posh Geordie speech resulted in his being misunderstood as describing Monmouth Tory Roger Evans as "Turd of Turd Hall" when he really said "Toad of Toad Hall"; "unclubbable" (Labour friend); "an able and likeable man but with a vicious temper when aroused - and a certain relish for arm-twisting and knuckle-dusting" (Bruce Anderson, SUNDAY TELEGRAPH); "Mafia-efficient"; "to say he is tough is an understatement"; has "robust self-sufficiency; he clearly possesses a strong belief in himself but it means he is often seen as arrogant and solitary" (Phil Murphy, YORKSHIRE POST); "an arrogant bastard" who "doesn't suffer fools gladly" (Labour friend); "is well ahead of the pack as the politician most likely to lose his temper" (David Lister, INDEPENDENT); "there's an element to his approach that is to do with being a scientist: the feeling that scientists know best; people don't like it" (Labour friend); squash-player; fell-walker; fast driver (fined £150 for doing 103 mph '89); "I like fell-walking; I'm a soccer-nut; I've supported Newcastle United all my life, which is part of the culture of the area I grew up in; I like angling;" loves his annual late-July fishing holiday in Norway;
Address: House of Commons, Westminster, London SW1A 0AA; Dolphin Square, London SW1; 18 Caragh Road, Chester-le-Street, County Durham DH2 3EA; 3 Carter Lane, Whitehaven, Cumbria;
Telephone: 0171 219 5222/6234/3738 (H of C); 0191 388 3492 (home); 01946 2813 (constituency); 01905 776696 (Secretary);

Roseanna CUNNINGHAM　　　　**Scottish National**　　　　**PERTH '97-**

Majority: 3,141 (7.1%) over Conservative 6-way;
Description: The former Perth and Kinross seat shorn in '95 of 7,500 voters in Kinross (moved into the Ochil constituency); apart from Perth and smaller Auchterader and Crieff, it consists of vast tracts of rolling farmland and hills; as Kinross and West Perthshire it once provided the blue chip base for Sir Alec Douglas-Home '63-74, then, as a Tory-SNP marginal, a precarious seat for the exotic Sir Nicholas Fairbairn '74-95; on his death, it fell to the SNP in May '95;
Former Seat: Perth & Kinross '95-97
Position: Spokesman: on Arts and Broadcasting, Employment, Home Affairs, Environment, Land Reform, Leisure and Sports '97-; Joint Vice Chairman, all-party Renewable and Sustainable Energy Group '97-; on SNP National Executive; ex: SNP party spokesman on the

Environment '91-95;
Outlook: Glasgow-based Leftwing feminist nationalist; deplores the Commons' "Boys' Own atmosphere", preferring "Australian directness and a healthy disrespect for authority figures"; anti: blood sports, nuclear weapons, monarchism ("Republican Rose"); became the '95 by-election winner despite attempts to block her candidacy; Glasgow-born but Australian-raised; former council solicitor-turned-barrister; was NALGO convenor of Dunbarton District Council;

History: She left Glasgow with her parents for Perth in Western Australia when she was 8, '60, remaining there until 23; it was during this exile, she says, that she started believing in an independent Scotland and resolved to return home to work for it; by the age of 16 she was corresponding with the SNP from Australia '69, joining the party on a visit to Scotland '71; returned home at 23, '76; was named SNP Research Officer '77; after legal education became a local government solicitor with Dumbarton, then Glasgow district councils, leaving the last after legislation barring certain senior grade local government officers from political activity Mar '89; was selected as SNP candidate for Perth and Kinross, defeating SNP Deputy Leader Alasdair Morgan Feb '91; campaigned against incumbent Tory, Sir Nicholas Fairbairn as "out of touch"; Sir Nicholas helped by attacking coloured immigrants, forcing Viscount Whitelaw to cancel a supporting speech; she halved Fairbairn's majority to 2,094, Apr '92; as SNP's Environment Spokesman, campaigned against Government's water privatisation proposals "trampling over the wishes of the Scottish people" Jan '93; after the death of Sir Nicholas Fairbairn, withdrew her name from the SNP's candidate list after the leak of MEP Winnie Ewing's allegation that she had had an affair with Donald Bain, previous husband of SNP Parliamentary Leader Margaret Ewing, currently Winnie's daughter-in-law Feb '95; a week later, with the backing of Maggie Ewing, who dismissed "foolish prurient stories" as "of no present relevance", re-entered the race with the backing also of party leader Alex Salmond; she admitted to a seven-month affair, but only after the Bain's marriage had broken down; was re-selected as candidate Mar '95; she denied the seat was "a tweedy Conservative constituency' but one with many "second and third generation Nationalists" Mar '95; her Tory opponent, John Godfrey, a London-based investment banker, had been dismissed by Sir Nicholas Fairbairn as an "unelectable clone"; he attacked her as "Republican Rose" because she had said the Queen "is at the apex of the class system"; Labour's young candidate, Douglas Alexander, was strongly supported by visits from Tony Blair and seven Shadow Cabinet members; she won the seat with a majority of 7,311 May '95; in her Maiden, said the Scots were enthusiastic about the EU; she supported the Social Chapter and a £4 minimum wage June '95; as the SNP's Environment Spokesman, insisted "the days when Scotland gets every dangerous substance dumped on its doorstep, while it's fleeced of its natural resources, are coming to an end"; she emphasised decrepit Dounreay, munitions dumping in Beaufort Dyke and the decommissioning of the Brent Spar oil platform Oct '95; urged restoration of benefits for 16- and 17-year-olds to avoid increase in homelessness Nov '95; attacked as "objectionable" the Asylum and Immigration Bill's restrictions of asylum-seekers' rights Dec '95; urged more funds for Scottish Film Production Funds, to make it comparable with funding of Irish film industry Jan '96; urged decentralisation of "deeply centralist" BBC, which made only 3% of its programmes in Scotland, Wales and Northern Ireland, with 17% of UK's population Feb '96; urged more council housing for her constituency, despite the Tories' "ideological bias" Mar '96; backed the Bill of Labour MP Angela Eagle to give part-time workers equal sick leave rights Apr '96; opposed guillotining of anti-terrorist Bill Apr '96; insisted that "a policy of full employment should not be discarded as unobtainable" June '96; with Alex Salmond and Margaret Ewing crashed the First Scottish Standing Committee to protest the presence of English MPs June '96; voted for 3% cap on MPs' pay July '96; criticised dominance of sporting

estates interests on Deer Commision for Scotland, citing enormous damage done by deer July '96; launched motion attacking absentee ownership of Eigg Oct '96; attacked as "beyond belief" the post-Dunblane fielding of a pro-gun candidate against anti-gun Scottish Secretary Forsysth Oct '96; supported the "Scottish consensus" favouring ban on all handguns Oct '96; co-signed all-party TIMES letter urging a computer in every library Nov '96; attacked dereliction of absentee landlords on local Blackford estate Nov '96; attacked the Tories as the party of "law and order legislation" rather than "law and order", having put through 33 Acts in 18 years while crime rates soared Nov '96; attacked Tories' "narrow Unionist dogma" which prevented Scotland from escaping the ban on British beef Nov '96; attacked the "obscenity" of fuel poverty among its elderly in energy-rich Scotland in debate secured on Scottish cold weather payments Jan '97; became the first SNPer to retain a seat won in a by-election, with a 3,141 majority on a notional pro-SNP swing of 6.6% in her altered seat May '97; voted to ban fox-hunting June '97; urged more powers for Scottish Environment Protection Agency June '97; at SNP conference clashed with her colleague Alasdair Morgan in urging an elected head of state in an independent Scotland, insisting "most people believe the SNP is already a republican party" Sep '97; described Scottish Protestant James Campbell, who killed a Celtic supporter and was transferred to the Maze, as "no political prisoner; he is a thug" Oct '97; "as a nationalist, I regard the devolution scheme as half a loaf"; derided the Tories' claim that devolution would marginalise Scotland, insisting it would reverse that situation; called for broadcasting to be accountable to the Scottish Parliament, out of the reach of "the London-centric broadcasting base that has trouble seeing beyond the M25" Jan '98; attacked cuts in local authority funding which caused closure of rape crisis centres Feb '98;
Born: 21 July 1951, Glasgow
Family: Daughter, of Catherine and late Hugh Cunningham, who thought educating girls was a waste of time; he died of Alzheimer's in '94; unmarried;
Education: Attended school in Perth, Western Australia; University of Western Australia (BA Hons in Politics '75); Edinburgh University (LLB '82); Aberdeen University (Diploma in Legal Practice '83);
Occupation: Scottish Advocate '90- (no longer practicing); ex: Solicitor: in Glasgow firm of Ross, Harper & Murphy '89-90; with Glasgow District Council '86-89, Dunbarton District Council '83-86; SNP Researcher '77-79;
Traits: Reddish blonde; straight-haired; pleasant-looking; serious of mien; no Aussie accent despite 16 formative years down under; "bright, attractive and straightforward" (Geraldine Bowditch, TIMES); determined; interested in 'Star Trek' and other science fiction and martial art 'Akaido';
Address: House of Commons, Westminster, London SW1A 0AA; 14/367 Argyll Street, Glasgow G2 8LT
Telephone: 0171 219 6424 (H of C); 0141 221 5641;

DOORSTEPPING JOURNALISTS

We accept that one of the weaknesses in this volume is paucity of information about the parents of politicians. We find it valuable to know whether the father of an MP is a multi-millionaire property developer or a plumber. But some MPs claim that their parents fear press intrusion. Any pressman with experience of doorstepping journalists or aggressive photographers can understand some trepidation. But our jury is still out on whether this is the main reason for withholding such information.

Rt Hon David (Maurice) CURRY   Conservative   **SKIPTON & RIPON '87-**

Majority: 11,620 (21.4%) over Liberal Democrat 4-way;

Description: A huge, sheep-rich, rural '83-created Pennine-straddling seat in North Yorkshire in the heart of the Dales; combines two stripped old seats: Skipton deprived of small mill towns of Barnoldswick and Earby (now in Lancashire) and Sedbergh and Dentdale (now in Cumbria); Ripon lost Ilkley and Otley to West Yorkshire; in '95 Boroughbridge's 5,600 voters were moved into the new Vale of York constituency; 250,000 of its sheep are sold in Skipton Market annually;

Position: Ex: Shadow Minister of Agriculture June-Nov '97; Minister for Local Government '93-97, and Housing '94-97, and Southwest '96-97; Minister of State '92-93, Parliamentary Secretary '89-92, for Agriculture and Fisheries; on Select Committee on Agriculture '87-89; Secretary, Conservative MPs' Agriculture Committee '87-89; MEP for North East Essex '79-89; Budgetary Spokesman, for European Democrats in European Parliament '85-87, Vice Chairman, its Budget Committee '84-85, Chairman, its Agriculture Committee '82-84;

Outlook: A Europhile defector from William Hague's Shadow Cabinet after only four months because he could not live with its decision to stay out of the Euro for a decade; previously one of the outstanding middle-rank Ministers, who was seen by Labour opponents as a decent type trying to mitigate the actions of his more populist-reactionary superiors in Environment; "if they want to portray me as a nice guy, that's fine"(DC); comes from a family of socially-minded teachers; formerly "one of the best intellects in John Major's junior ranks", with a "good brain and palpable decency" (Matthew Parris, TIMES); was rewarded with promotion initially for coolly surviving the anger of British and French fishermen when Fisheries Minister; despite his ten-year immersion as an MEP in Brussels and Strasbourg, a strong pro-European ("for me...the creation of Europe seems to be the most important task that my generation can undertake"); a very bright, realistic, well-informed and witty former FINANCIAL TIMES journalist; a former EC farm surplus reformer returned to his native north from the "exile" of the European Parliament only to find the Commons rather frustrating after some Ministerial achievement because he found himself in the minority in a quasi-religious war which offended his rationality and idealism;

History: His first political affiliation was to the Newcastle West Conservative Association in '67; contested hopeless Morpeth, taking 23% of vote Feb and Oct '74; founded the Paris Conservative Association '77; managed to win selection for the safe North East Essex Euro-seat against Paul Channon (Mrs Thatcher's nominee for the Tories' leadership in the European Parliament) Jan '79; won North East Essex by 65,641 votes May '79; at Tory conference urged expansion of UK agricultural production, insisting "the farmer needs reassurance" Oct '79; attacked the EEC's Budget as one "of hopelessness, of paralysis" Dec '79; voted for freeze on payments for dairy products in surplus after describing Commission proposals as "sheer bloody financial irresponsibility" Mar '80; complained of chronic surpluses of Community dairy products May '80; complained of EEC threat to Stilton and Sherry June '80; urged changes in EEC regulation of apple industry to allow fairer competition for British apples Sep '80; insisted the import of New Zealand butter into the EEC was "plain common sense" Nov '80; urged an end to "guaranteed prices for unlimited production" by EEC Feb '81;

called for a "breathing space" for UK apples against threat from France Mar '81; again insisted that unlimited financial responsibility for agricultural production must end Mar '81; described as a "total catastrophe" the overthrow of his report calling for moderate food price rises in favour of one urging a 14% hike Mar '82; succeeded Sir Henry Plumb as Chairman of the EEC Agriculture Committee May '82; warned of threat of US-EEC "war" over agricultural exports Oct '82; tabled resolution approving proposal for EEC to bear the whole cost of supplying school children with processed milk products - his scheme provided milk at same price as sticky drinks May '83; expressed concern about behaviour of English football hooligans in Luxembourg Nov '83; warned of threat of intensified violence in French farm politics to keep out British lamb Jan '84; retained his seat with 54,302 vote majority June '84; complained that failure of EEC to control its own surpluses was a cause of shortages in Third World by depressing agricultural prices in starvation-threatened areas Mar '85; backed setting aside of farm land to reduce excess production while protecting farmers May '86; emphasized that reforms in agricultural policy were likely to cause short term increases in expenditure and that it was unrealistic to expect that economies in agriculture could finance significant expansions in non-agricultural programmes Sep '86; was selected for Skipton and Ripon on the impending resignation of John Watson Sep '86; became General Rapporteur for the EEC's Budget '87; elected June '87; urged an investigation of the overlooked Chernobyl 'hot spot' in North Yorkshire which found its way through sheep into the food chain Nov '87; in his Maiden, he urged unity to "enable us to stand on our own feet" in defence, to guarantee against a US departure Nov '87; backed stabilizers as the best restraint on the CAP Nov '87; called for the reviving of constituencies like his as "a working countryside", unhindered by Sunday trading limits and clashes between Government departments Feb '88; voted to televise the Commons Feb '88; spent fortnight in New Zealand as guest of its government Mar '88; aroused ire when he said North Yorkshire's nuclear 'hot spot' was peripheral and not worth seriously investigating: "I can't see anybody growing any funny bits from the back of their heads" Apr '88; said that control of EEC farm surplus spending was gradually being established May '88; backed the privatization of the Settle-Carlisle line May '88; voted against restoring capital punishment June '88; was the "minder" to William Hague in the by-election in neighbouring Richmond Jan-Feb '89; insisted that "the choice for the UK [in Europe] is quite clear: it is engagement or withdrawal; I do not believe that there is a halfway house; I do not believe in a second-class citizenship in Europe"; urged a more pragmatic approach, and a distinction between economic and monetary union; " I feel that the case is, on balance, in favour of joining the ERM before long" May '89; was promoted Parliamentary Secretary for Agriculture and Fisheries, replacing Donald Thompson July '89; pointed out that 700,000 salmonella-infected chickens had been slaughtered Oct '89; after European Commission ruled there was no evidence British beef imports carried BSE, said he hoped France would "climb back off this rather silly political limb they are on" in banning British beef May '90; he said, "if it's on, I'm off", after fishermen's organization offered him crab at a dinner, after having been warned it was unhealthful June '90; resisted giving in to French "terrorism" by curbing live animal exports Sep '90; visited Kenya and Uganda Sep-Oct '90; refused to compensate plum growers for frost damage Oct '90; urged farmers to diversify Nov '90; in "a marvellous coup" (David Maclean MP), saved the whole knacker industry for five years Dec '90; insisted "we are not seeking to drive agriculture back to the 1930s"; but ruled out direct income support for farmers, preferring a quantitative control on crops based on voluntary set-aside Jan '91; admitted that EC farm subsidies were higher than America's, but both were outstripped by Japan Jan '91; insisted the eight-day tie-up proposal for UK fishing boats "reflects scientific advice" Mar '91; claimed only another 17 Spanish fishing boats had won back the right to fish British waters under the court ruling overturning the 1988 Merchant Shipping Act July '91;

told farmer they had "reached the end of the road in producing basic commodities in return for a guaranteed price" July '91; claimed EC Farm Commissioner Ray MacSharry's proposals to switch support from larger to smaller food producers were "perverse and discriminatory" Sep '91; urged a "genuine reform" of CAP Oct '91; told MPs' delegation the Government had ruled out a decommissioning grants scheme for fishing boats Dec '91; retained seat with majority up from 17,174 to 19,330, a swing to Conservative of 0.42% Apr '92; was promoted Minister of State Apr '92; coped effectively with an upsurge of anger from Tory backbenchers over aggressive French fishermen attacking a British fishing boat; told French radio (in French): "there is in France this feeling that there are rules for everbody except for the French" June '92; introduced 2nd Reading of Sea Fish (Conservation) Bill June '92; defending Government's "vigorous and comprehensive action", predicted BSE would be "on the downward path" July '92; criticized "damned silly" blockade of Russian fish by British fishermen Mar '93; his talks with fishermen ended in deadlock when he insisted their blockade against Russian imports would not force Government to act for them Mar '93; told French to desist after their fishermen burned the White Ensign and hijacked three Royal Navy sailors Mar '93; deplored both French destruction of British fish and British destruction of Russian fish Apr '93; was pelted with paper missiles by 500 fishermen and their wives in Derby protesting the Sea Fish (Conservation) Bill May '93; was promoted Minister for Local Government and Planning, in Environment, on the recommendation of Environment Secretary John Gummer, his former boss at Agriculture May '93; admitted that John Gummer had met rich Hongkong Chinese "fellow Conservatives in the margins of public duties" June '93; said economic regeneration from Channel Tunnel Rail Link should take place in East Thames Corridor, not in lovely Mid-Kent July '93; insisted England's big cities did not need a second tier of regional government (thus excluding regional government for London, Birmingham and Manchester) Sep '93; came under fire from Tory backbenchers for Local Government Commission's uneven movement toward unitary authorities Dec '93; made minor simplifications of planning procedures Dec '93; appointed two more to Local Government Commission to speed its work, former Tory MP Christopher Chope and Margaret Hodge, then still an aspirant Labour MP Dec '93; praised Planning Inspectorate Jan '94; voted against restoring capital punishment, even for killing policemen Feb '94; voted to reduce age of homosexual consent, to 16 as well as 18, Feb '94; told Bob Wareing that if he did not like the three quangos spending £641m in the Merseyside, "we can arrange to cancel the funding" May '94; against a background of 10 years in the European Parliament, insisted "it is a mistake to believe that power and responsibility exist in defined chunks"; "I have never believed in the thesis that giving more power to the European Parliament necessarily means that an equivalent amount of responsibility is removed from this or another national Parliaments" July '94; had Housing added to his portfolio, inherited from Sir George Young July '94; at party conference sought to calm Tory fears that new unitary authorities would put an end to some historic councils, claiming "there is no covert agenda to impose a uniform structure" Oct '94; in harshest council spending cuts for years, announced councils outside London would be capped if they exceeded spending limits by more than .5%, Dec '94; provided 150 refuge places for London homeless in winter shelter programme Dec '94; defended splitting of Cleveland County into four unitary authorities Jan '95; denied political bias in setting Standard Spending Assessments, citing £1,030 per head for Tory boroughs and £1,189 for Labour boroughs; "if that's fiddling, I've not done a very good job" Feb '95; said he was flexible on Rowntree-financed report that rented housing was too low, insisting the '80s right-to-buy for council tenants had "changed the sociology of Britain than anything else since the war" Feb '95; derided as "an annual ritual" North Shropshire's complaints about spending cuts, as voiced by John Biffen Feb '95; confirmed low uptake of Government's 1993 "rents-to-mortgages" scheme Feb '95; introduced powers of eviction against noisy council tenants Apr '95; after disastrous Tory council election results, asked civil servants to investigate feasibility of ending capping so taxpayers would blame profiligate Labour councils and not the Tory Government June '95; was evicted by a LibDem Mayor from Ripon Town Hall premises, where he had held his surgeries July '95; told party conference police would be more active in dealing with rough sleepers; promised there would be no French-style "sluice them down and go-away" approach to beggars Oct '95; sustained only platform defeat for his Treasury-demanded resistance to suspending council capping Oct '95; announced measures against anti-social council neighbours, including use of professional witnesses Oct '95; dropped his plans for rounding up rough sleepers following police objections Dec '95; proposed a liberal policy on public housing allocations in consultation paper, giving preference for pregnant women or people at risk from abuse Jan '96; in Scott Report was cited as one of 13 MPs who received "designedly misleading" answers on arms-for-Iraq, in his case from William Waldegrave Feb '96; extended help for rough sleepers to Bristol Mar '96; introduced mitigations to Housing Bill, extending temporary accommodation for homeless to two years, instead of one Mar '96; extended right-to-buy to housing associations Apr '96; extended rights to inherit council tenancy to homosexual partners Apr '96; voted for a longer, 18-month cooling-off period before divorce Apr '96; was given added responsibility as 'Minister for the Southwest' Apr '96; said, "I do not seek to impugn the [District] Auditor" in his adverse findings on Tory-led Westminster Council, which were still under appeal May '96; announced fund to renew run-down inner-city council estates, provided tenants agreed to privatisation June '96; suggestions he might replace BSE-damaged Agriculture Minister Douglas Hogg were not realised; instead he was promoted to the Privy Council June '96; voted for 3% cap on MPs' pay rise and cuts in mileage allowances and against a pension based on £43,000 July '96; rejected as "unnecessary and possibly dangerous" call of Shadow Home Secretary Jack Straw to jail noisy or intimidating council neighbours Sep '96; extended rough-sleeper funds to more provincial towns Oct '96; as 'Minister for the Southwest' extended dualling of A30 Nov '96; also backed separation of Cornwall from Devon in EU fund applications Dec '96; was considered to be one of the 20 Ministers Chancellor Clarke claimed would resign if PM John Major gave in to the Eurosceptics on a single currency Dec '96; claimed Labour's minimum wage would devastate West Country's economy Apr '97; all five Tory seats in the southwest were lost; he retained his altered seat with a reduced majority of 11,620, on a notional pro-LibDem swing of 4.6% May '97; with Michael Jack acted as Ken Clarke's campaign managers in Tory Leadership contest May-June '97; was named Shadow Minister for Agriculture by successful William Hague June '97; urged higher payments for culled cattle for hill farmers July '97; with fellow Europhiles Sir George Young and Stephen Dorrell, urged William Hague to retain "not for the foreseeable future" as the Tory attitude to the Euro, instead of "not for a decade" Oct '97; following Shadow Cabinet decision to adopt "not for a decade", resigned as Shadow Minister for Agriculture, three days after Ian Taylor Nov '97; partook in day-long conference of 'Mainstream', the organisation of the Tory Centre-Left Nov '97; warned that "not for a decade" "risks leaving us marooned by events, marginalised in debate, and alienated from sections of the electorate who would normally look to us as their instinctive home" Nov '97; caused Labour laughter when he announced he was voting with the Tories against ratification of the Amsterdam Treaty, when Heath, Clarke and Heseltine absented themselves Nov '97; was named in the SUNDAY TIMES as having given a Commons pass to a lobbyist Nov '97; criticised system of PR for European Parliament which involved large multi-member constituencies as "a negation of representative democracy" Nov '97; urged the integration of Labour's education action zones in wider regeneration programmes Dec '97; claimed Labour's local government awards were much as he would have delivered them but, unlike his, were above the "pain threshold" Feb

'98; insisted the only way to reform CAP was to go for "direct aid divorced from production" May '98; was one of 18 Tory MPs voting for 16 as the age of homosexual consent June '98;
Born: 13 June 1944, Burton-on-Trent, Staffordshire
Family: His grandfather was a second-class stoker in Dorman Long, Middlesbrough; son, of Thomas Harold Curry, "headmaster of a primary school within sight of Armley jail in Leeds" (DC) who had started as a butcher's boy and then worked for a tailor before training as a teacher, and Florence Joan (Tyerman), who teacher-trained as a mature student and also taught in a rough area of Leeds; his aunt was a rural headteacher, his uncle a schools inspector specialising in truancy and delinquency; m '71 Anne Helene (Roullet), a native of Bordeaux with an Oxford DPhil in Egyptology; a sculptress, she was commissioned by the House of Commons Arts Committee to do Lord Jenkins of Hillhead; 1s Alexander, twin daughterss Isobel and Nathalie '74;
Education: Grange Street Junior School, Burton; Ripon Grammar School; Corpus Christi, Oxford University (BA MA Hons in Modern History); Kennedy School of Government, Harvard University, where he studied under Dr Henry Kissinger (Kennedy Scholar);
Occupation: Author: The Food War (1982); Owner: "a farm in Saffron Walden, Essex, where he used to be an MEP, a cottage in Masham, Yorkshire, as a constituency base, a desirable London flat and a villa in Provence" (MAIL ON SUNDAY '94); ex: Journalist: Columnist for FARMING NEWS '83-89, previously on FINANCIAL TIMES (Exports Editor, International Companies Editor, Brussels Correspondent, Paris Correspondent and European News Editor) '70-79; NEWCASTLE JOURNAL '67-70; Adviser: to Warburg Group {on EC legislation) '88-89, to Thackrays of Leeds '88-89, to Building Employers Confederation (on EEC and taxes) '87-89; to Christopher Morgan Marketing and Public Relations ("I have never met Asil Nadir and I didn't make any representations on his behalf") '84-88, to Morgan Grenfell (on EC) '79-80;
Traits: Flat, parted hair; specs; "with his sensible specs, neatly-parted hair and pleasant Despatch Box manner...gives every impression of being an intelligent, reasonable, rational man" (Andrew Rawnsley, GUARDIAN); "kindly and clever": "a keen intellect, a coldly logical approach, and a bloodcurdling way of speaking; there is a resemblance to Spock in 'Star Trek'; I think Curry is a Vulcan; his ears appear to be pointed at the top and, unlike humans, he cannot pronounce his r's"; "speaks as though attempting a funny voice for a duck in a children's cartoon"; "talks as might a fridge-freezer granted the gift of speech" (Matthew Parris, TIMES); "self-deprecating" (John Meikle, GUARDIAN); "quick on his feet" (George Jones, DAILY TELEGRAPH); persuasive; realistic; very sharp wit (described the European Council spokesman as sounding like "a brothel keeper promoting the virtues of chastity"); "a light wit made even lighter by a funny French accent" (Claudia Fitzherbert, DAILY TELEGRAPH); a master of ironical contrasts; "I was once a train-spotter...at Ripon station; that was almost a definition of optiminism because nothing went through Ripon station - even when there was a railway line there"; "congeniality is second nature to me"; athletic (windsurfer, formerly top MEP squash player, ex schoolboy sprint record holder); kept in shape in Environment by running up the 284 steps to his 15th-floor office; speaks fluent French (has a French wife);
Address: House of Commons, Westminster, London SW1A 0AA; Newland End, Arkesden, Essex CB11 4HF; Park View, Fearby Cross, Masham, nr Ripon, North Yorkshire;
Telephone: 0171 219 5164/6202 (H of C); 0179985 550 (home); 01765 89137 (constituency);

Majority: 7,182 over Conservative 6-way;
Description: The largely middle-class north-of-Merseyside commuter seat which now also embraces the heart of Liverpool's docklands; it was made famous by Shirley Williams' '81 capture of it for the SDP, interrupting its semi-permanent stay in Conservative hands; its '97 fall to Labour was due partly to the removal of Maghull from the communities of Crosby and Formby and the addition of two Labour-leaning wards from Bootle;
Position: On Select Committee on Science and Technology '97-; Crewe and Nantwich Borough Councillor '95-;
Outlook: A Left-of-Centre Welsh chartered engineer, feminist and animal-lover who took this altered seat from a highly-respected Tory on a swing of over 18%; an extremely able speaker and engineer who commands high fees for lecturing to fellow-engineers, which she contributes to her constituency party; denies being looney Left as suggested by Derek Draper; insists: "I am not [Leftwing]; I am in the Centre, extremely rational and reasonable" (CC-T); a newcomer rarely-seen in the winter of '97-98, having taken six months off "to bond with my [new] baby" (INDEPENDENT ON SUNDAY); has confused many by winning as 'Mrs Curtis-Tansley', then changing to 'Curtis-Thomas' while WHO'S WHO insists she is married to Michael Lewis; a rare woman chartered mechanical engineer who held top jobs in industry (including Shell); the first Labour MP for Crosby and the first female chartered engineer to enter the Commons; says, "I want to promote manufacturing science and technology to girls in school and women returners" (CC-T) she used both 'Emily's List' and the Labour Women's Network to ensure her candidacy; an active animal rights defender, in the League Against Cruel Sports and the Whale and Dolphin Society; also in the Fabian Society and Co-operative Society;
History: She joined the Labour Party; was elected to Crewe and Nantwich Borough Council May '95; sought selection in the all-women contest for Chester Jan '96; was selected for Crosby Mar '96; complained about the sex discrimination she had suffered as a woman as a fitter and mechanical engineer, in a BBC phone-in May '96; was criticised by anti-abortion Tory MPs Ann Winterton and Elizabeth Peacock as a beneficiary of 'Emily's List' which helped Labour women candidates financially in return for a commitment to a 'woman's right to choose' if elected; this was calculated to damage her, since a quarter of her electors were Catholics Mar '97; was supported during the campaign by John Moore Jr, a deviant Littlewoods Pools heir Apr '97; although her seat was 120th on Labour's target list, on the eve of poll a LIVERPOOL DAILY POST head-count predicted it would fall to her Apr '97; captured the seat from its widely-respected incumbent Tory MP, Sir Malcolm Thornton, by a majority of 7,182, on a near-record pro-Labour notional swing of 18.15%; this made her the 33rd least-expected Labour victor May '97; in a document on potential trouble-makers, compiled at the instigation of Peter Mandelson and carried out by Derek Draper, she was allegedly described as "clinically insane", according to Derek Draper May '97; expressed solidarity with jailed Indonesian union leader June '97; urged primary school teachers be qualified to teach science to 5-to-8-year-olds July '97; asked whether industrialists would be consulted over the proposal for a European patent system based on a single patent application July '97; in her Maiden, complained that, as a chartered engineer, her profession was very

under-represented in the Commons, although engineering "is probably the most innovative and exciting profession" July '97; was named to the Select Committee on Science and Technology July '97; Derek Draper, a former Mandelson aide, disclosed that the Minister Without Portfolio had asked regional organisers on 2 May for information on unexpected victors who were potential Leftwing troublemakers, in which she was tagged as "clinically insane"; she replied: "I can fully understand when organisations have new members why they would be concerned to know more about them; I am not [Leftwing]; I am in the Centre, extremely rational and reasonable" Nov '97; took some months off to "bond with my baby"; made a powerful statement on behalf of the eight families in her constituency who had lost loved ones in the Hillsborough disaster: "at least one family comes to see me at every surgery that I hold" May '98; asked how many teachers and care staff were currently under investigation after retrospective allegations of sexual abuse by former pupils May '98; spoke up for a constituent, former police inspector Raymong Herring, forced to resign after complaining of noise at the tennis club near his home June '98; agreed with her Whip that she would become fulltime in the Commons from October, July '98;

Born: 30 April 1958, Neath, Glamorgan

Family: Daughter of Joyce Curtis; m 1st Mr Tansley; 2d; m 2nd Michael Thomas, former railway engineer; 1c;

Education: Mynyddbach Comprehensive School for Girls, Swansea; University College, Cardiff, University of Wales (BSc in Mechanical Engineering); Aston University (MBA); "I am researching the ethical framework of the private and public sector for a PhD" (CC-T):

Occupation: Chartered Mechanical Engineer; ex: Dean, Faculty of Business and Engineering, University College of Wales, Newport; Partner, in Business Services for Industry (TGWU); previously Head of Strategic Planning, for Birmingham City Council, Head of Environmental Affairs, Shell Chemicals, Head of UK Distribution, Shell Chemicals; initially a Fitter;

Traits: Tall; has short, bobbed, reddish hair; brilliant speaker; since only 3% of engineers are women, initially felt "very lonely"; early on in the Commons, she was said to be a "candidate for the 'Don't You Know Who I Am?' Trophy", mythically awarded by Commons staff (Paul Routledge, INDEPENDENT ON SUNDAY); repaired a Commons lift, explaining, "I carry a miniature toolbox with me because you never know when it will be useful, and because I drive a Fiat" (CC-T); has installed a video link between her Commons office and her home so she can inspect her children's cleaned teeth each evening;

Address: House of Commons, Westminster, London SW1A 0AA; 30 Elmstead Crescent, Leighton, Crewe CW1 3PX

Telephone: 0171 219 3000 (H of C);

ANOREXIA OR OBESITY

Profiles, like politicians, can be very slim or very full-bodied. This can depend on how varied and colourful is the past of the MP concerned, or the quality of the newspapers reporting them. Some politicians are paranoid about disclosing anything beyond the bare minimum and then complain if second-hand information beyond the bare essentials turns out to be less than accurate. Others turn to their libel lawyers as an expensive threat. We adhere to the quaint idea that if people have decided to plunge into the glass fishbowl of politics they are not entitled to wear wetsuits. After all, most wrongdoing has been exposed by the media's investigative journalists, very little by politicians themselves.

Majority: 6,961 (17.3%) over Labour 5-way;
Description: A farming area mainly of Welsh-speakers, largely on hill farms, or in small towns; it has two colleges of the University of Wales: in Lampeter and Aberystwyth, the latter an important centre of learning and research; includes some 'in-comers': pot-throwing '60s refugees, hippy settlements and retirement colonies; has the holiday coast of Cardigan Bay (including Cardigan itself); but has few job opportunities for the educated young; in '95 it relinquished North Pembroke as far as Fishguard, acquired in '83, thus reverting to its original county identity;
Former Seat: Ceredigion and Pembroke North

'92-97

Position: Spokesman on Agriculture and Environment '92-; on Education and Employment Select Committee '97-; Vice Chairman, Renewable and Sustainable Energy Parliamentary Group '9?-, Secretary, all-party UK Eurosolar Parliamentary Group '9?-; on National Executive of Plaid Cymru; ex: on Welsh Select Committee '95-97; Plaid Cymru Vice Chairman, for Publications and Publicity; was NUT-sponsored;

Outlook: Intense Leftwing Welsh nationalist, conservationist and former teacher trade unionist who believes Wales has to reinvent itself; the first MP officially to half-represent the Greens; father of the Energy Conservation Bill later adopted by Alan Beith and of '98's successful Road Traffic Reduction Bill; "the best MP in terms of environmental issues" (BBC's WILDLIFE MAGAZINE); has "served with distinction" (Tory ex-Minister Eric Forth) on Education Bill committee; pro: EU; anti: nuclear weapons or energy, Turkish mistreatment of Kurds; initially surprised the local political world by doubling the Nationalist-Green vote to oust the popular, rooted, veteran former MP, LibDem Geraint Howells, later Lord Geraint; despite an idealism which appeals more to Islington do-gooders than to West Wales hill-farmers, in '97 he more than doubled his majority without official Green backing; hard-working and productive locally and in Westminster (259 questions in his frenetic first year);

History: The first major political influence on him was his father, the radically-Left and ideologially-liberal Minister in the Welsh Calvinistic Methodist Presbyterian Church of Wales; Cynog wrote the Manifesto of the Welsh Language Society (Cymdeithas yr Iaith Gymraeg) '71; as a Plaid candidate, contested Ceredigion, coming 4th with 13% of vote June '83; at Plaid's National Executive meeting pointed out that a new generation of young people were already engaged in setting up businesses and providing jobs; this meant the Plaid's planned support for Welsh small businessmen would win their favour Sep '85; contested this seat, coming 4th with 16% of vote June '87; a Plaid-Green whispering campaign concentrated on 'time for a change', with a thrusting, 54-year-old Cynog Dafis being contrasted with the ageing, ailing sitting MP, 67-year-old Geraint Howells; it was suggested that Howells would only stay on for two more years, when he would be elevated to the Lords; an appeal was also made, on 'green' grounds, to the 5,000 new young 'incomers' on the electoral roll '91-92; unexpectedly, Dafis won the seat by 3,193 votes, doubling support to 31% of the vote, a swing of over 13%, ousting Geraint Howells; Dafis made the point he was "the first MP to represent the Green Movement"; "the remarkable result was an expression of a number of factors including an upsurge in Welsh national consciousness and support for the idea of a Welsh Parliament, but what really made the difference and caused such a dramatic result was the fact that I was standing on an explicitly green programme, had the word 'Green' on my ballot paper" Apr '92; in Maiden complained about plans to semi-privatise BR, with the risk to railway connections to Fishguard and Aberystwyth in his constituency; linked public transport with limiting CO2 emissions May '92; voted with Scottish Nationalists and Scottish Labour nationalists to bar strangers from Commons to disrupt beginning of Maastricht debate May '92; in debate on Earth Summit insisted that "our pattern of production and consumption" were "unsustainable" June '92; urged John Major to stay longer in Rio and to sign the Biodiversity Treaty, and to miss out his scheduled visit to Germany over the European Fighter June '92; complained about soaring price and low quality of water in Wales June '92; sponsored motion criticising EC plans to hinder organic producers July '92; helped forge a compromise between Sealink Stena ferry company and local Fishguard fishermen, locked out of old moorings for security reasons July '92; complained about EC directive penalising retailers of organic food imports July '92; opposed legalisation of euthanasia Sep '92; the Green Party acclaimed as a major achievement the appointment of a Green Party activist as his Parliamententary researcher Sep '92; complained that Government were reneging on even its limited Rio commitments on the environment Oct '92; was rated the 3rd most active Parliamentary questioner Oct '92; complained that local farmers' moneys from animals sold at auction had gone into accounts of insolvent auctioneers Oct '92; complained that the Government were trying to eliminate local government powers over education behind a screen of the "illusion of parental consent", which was particularly transparent in Wales, where only three schools had opted out Nov '92; deplored UK's continued testing underground of nuclear weapons Nov '92; opposed compulsory competitive tendering for council house management Nov '92; complained of late payment of debts by big business to small businessmen Jan '93; introduced his Energy Conservation Bill as a 10-minute-rule Bill to require councils to draw up plans to achieve energy savings of 10-30%, cutting fuel bills and limiting CO2 emissions Feb '93; complained about "crippling" costs of upgrading small and medium-sized abattoirs to "the current interpretation of the European hygeine regulations" Mar '93; in a barrage of written questions, sought to enhance the rights of pupils requiring assessments for special education, despite Government's effort to dismantle local education authorities Mar '93; a "half-Welsh" Tory, Michael Fabricant, complained about the number of Parliamentary questions he had asked, as "an exorbitant waste of taxpayers' money" Mar '93; drafted amendment to Education Bill to enable Welsh grant-maintained schools to buy in services like music instruction from local education authorities Mar '93; urged retention of Aberystwyth's rail connectiions Mar '93; as a former head of English, complained that the Government's "constant chopping and changing" had inflicted damage and sapped the energy and undermined the morale of teachers Apr '93; moved an amendment to Railways Bill to "protect the interests of rail users living in rural areas" May '93; with David Alton, complained about Chinese maltreatment of Tibetans in forced labour camps May '93; urged more regional development for Wales June '93; claimed his Energy Conservation Bill had received support from 110 councils July '93; demanded resources for the Welsh Language Bill, to make it more than a totem of linguistic equality July '93; won 'Best Newcomer' award from GREEN MAGAZINE July '93; with others, opposed continued US embargo against Cuba July '93; attacked unilateral US missile attack on Iraq July '93; voted against Defence Estimates Oct '93; urged more research into hypertrophic cardiomyopathy Nov '93; his Energy Conservative Bill had acquired the backing of 330 MPs by Nov '93; deplored the go-ahead for THORP since the material it produced "could be used for making nuclear weapons should it fall into the wrong hands" Dec '93; complained "the substantial hike in fuel costs over the next three years will have considerable impact on scattered rural areas of Wales" Dec '93; with other Welsh MPs urged restoration of Welsh as a core subject for 12-14-year-olds Jan '94; deplored Welsh Secretary's "astonishing" failure to set up a special body to develop sustainable development policies for Wales in parallel with Scotland Jan '94; congratulated Alan Beith on his taking over his own Energy Conservation Bill Feb '94; asked whether the Government's new Deregulation Bill would lead to a boom in out-of-town supermarkets Feb '94; voted to reduce age of homosexual consent to 18 or 16, Feb '94; welcomed the EC's new Committee of the Regions as "a vitally important mechanism for the representation of the interests of the small nations and regions of Europe" and insisted it "should become the second chamber of the European Parliament" Mar '94; complained about the heavy work being loaded on to teachers by frequent curriculum changes: "being a rather hard-boiled old nut who spent some years in the teaching profession, I find it astonishing that teachers are willing to participate in all that; if somebody had asked me four years ago to undertake that work in addition to my existing responsibilities as a head of English, I would have shown them the door"; also complained: "it is clear to me that the hidden agenda is to water down the intellectual, theoretical and educational content of teacher-training" May '94; attended Commission for Sustainable Development at the UN May '94; urged Education Secretary Gillian Shephard to "spare Wales this madness...this divisiveness and deliberate sabotaging of the comprehensive ideal" by proposing schools opt out of the state system June '94; proposed Bill to require Government and local authorities to draw targets for traffic reduction July '94; urged more cheap rented accommodation and renovation of older Welsh housing July '94; after the Green Party's suspension of Jonathon Porritt for urging tactical voting for the Plaid in Euro-elections, the Welsh Greens demanded Dafis drop the Green half of his label Aug '94; co-signed GUARDIAN letter criticising Turkish maltreatment of Kurds Oct '94; he insisted he still had Green Party support, after various ballots Nov '94; urged radical policy to conserve transport and heating energy to cut CO2 emissions sharply Nov '94; asked Foreign Office about Nigerian dissident Ken Saro Wiwa Jan '95; asked about rail through-ticketing in Wales Jan '95; backed Home Energy Conservation Bill of LibDem MP Diana Maddocks Jan '95; co-signed GUARDIAN letter against Sizewell B Feb '95; opposing criminalising natural forms of hunting with animals, he abstained against John McFall's Bill against hunting with dogs Feb '95; because of his defence of 'natural' hunting, the Welsh RSPCA objected to the BBC WILDLIFE MAGAZINE having tagged him "the best MP in terms of environmental issues"; he said he would support a ban on hunting with hounds and horses, if alternative methods of hunting, including falconry, ferreting and rabbiting were maintained Mar '95; introduced Road Traffic Reduction Bill as a 10-minute-rule Bill Apr '95; launched motions on waste incineration and registration of contaminated land Apr '95; in GUARDIAN letter urged absorption of Welsh quangos into a Welsh Parliament May '95; urged a Cornish regional assembly June '95; with the fielding of local candidates by the Ceredigion Green Party, the pact linking them with the Plaid was declared "untenable" by him, ending his designation as jointly Plaid-Green July '95; replaced his Plaid colleague Elfyn Llwyd on the Welsh Select Committee Oct '95; with two Plaid colleagues, joined hard-Left Campaign Group in opposing Defence Estimates Oct '95; deplored impact on working-class students of student loans Nov '95; deplored excessive Welsh home-ownership Jan '96; rejected Tory nursery voucher scheme Jan '96; urged ban on aerial advertising Jan '96; attacked the "insulting inadequacy of Labour's proposals" for a Welsh Parliament in comparison with those for a Scottish Parliament Feb '96; urged sharp cut in dependence on fossil fuels after 'Sea Empress' tanker disaster Feb '96; the £9,000 sponsorship of his researcher by the Network for Social Change and the Marmote Trust was disclosed in the Register of Members' Interests Feb '96; introduced another Road Traffic Reduction Bill Mar '96; attacked the uniform business rate for closing local high street stores Apr '96; opposed the Bill of Iain Duncan-Smith to exclude the UK from the jurisdiction of the European Court Apr '96; on the Broadcasting Bill voted to retain the 20% limit on cross-media ownership of TV stations May '96; urged "co-operation [with the EU] in a firm constructive spirit" to end the beef ban instead of following "some Tory Eurosceptics [who] actually want the ban to continue in order to bolster their anti-European case" May '96; voted against 3% cap on pay rise for MPs, in favour of cuts in their mileage allowances July '96; deplored TV advertising's encouragement of consumerism and squandering of world's resources July '96; urged inquiry into employment aspects of sale of Trecwn RNAD depot Aug '96; again criticised Turkish mistreatment of Kurds Sep '96; focussed on underfunding of local hospital Nov '96; left the Chamber, thinking he had been ordered out after Gallery demonstrators had applauded his attacks on arms sales to Indonesia Dec '96; focussed on underfunding of local health authority Jan '97; criticised North Pembrokeshire ambulance service Feb '97; urged higher targets than posed by recent Earth Summit Mar '97; again raised jobs issue on new sale of Trecwn RNAD depot Mar '97; attracted CND support in election campaign because of his opposition to nuclear weapons; he had no Green opponent Apr '97; was re-elected with more than doubled majority of 6,961 over Labour for his altered seat, on an unusual 2.5% notional swing from Labour; his Labour opponent conceded Dafis had "a very strong personal vote" May '97; was named to the Education and Employment Select Committee July '97; voted against Mike Foster's Bill against hunting with dogs Nov '97; voted against military action in Iraq Feb '98; insisted that both Welsh and English should be equally used in the Welsh National Assembly with simultaneous translation equipment provided Feb '98; after friendly negotiations with Transport Minister Glenda Jackson, achieved 3rd Reading for his new scaled-down Road Traffic Reduction Bill, with Conservatives' tolerant approval Apr '98; co-urged ending reprocessing at Dounreay and Sellafield May '98; warned of threat of collapse of Welsh family farming May '98;

Born: 1 April 1938, Swansea

Family: Son, Welsh-speaking George Davies, Welsh Calvinistic Methodist Presbyterian Minister, and English-speaking Margaret Annie Joanna (Morgan); three of his brothers were miners, the fourth a tenant farmer who "graduated to Port Talbot's Abbey steelworks"; m '64 Llinos Iorwerth (Jones), Tutor-Organiser of Welsh for Adults, who persuaded him to change their surname from Davies to Dafis; 2s Arthur Iorwerth, Rolant Morgan; 1d Luned Gwellian; one son is married to a Basque, giving him a Spanish-speaking granddaughter;

Education: Aberaeron County Primary; Aberaeron County Secondary '49-54; Neath Boys' Grammar School '54-56; University College of Wales, Aberystwyth (BA in English '60, MEd '78);

Occupation: Supported, by Network for Social Change, who provided £13,700 for the employment of a Research Assistant '97-98; Owner, 32 acres of agricultural land '92-; ex: Parliamentary Adviser: National Union of Teachers and National Union of Teachers of Wales '93-95; Research Officer, Department of Continuing Education, University College, Swansea '91-92; Editor, of MDULDdraig Goch, monthly newspaper; Head of English, in Ysgol Dyffryn Teifi (comprehensive school), Llandysul '84-91, English teacher: Aberaeron Comprehensive '80-84, Newcastle Emlyn Secondary Modern '62-80, College of Further Education, Pontardawe '60-62;

Traits: Dark; greying; lean; high cheekbones; lined face; very intense; "looks like he's been to a non-stop, year-long party; he's got deep grey rings around his eyes and he seems almost exhausted" (Patrick Fletcher, WALES ON SUNDAY); Unitarian; Welsh-speaking ("I spoke Welsh to my father, English to my mother, English to my siblings" (CD); enjoys jogging, music; not a Rugby enthusiast: "when the missionary zeal of a group of young Valleys teachers foisted the oval ball on my West coast bilateral school in 1950, I quickly learned to get put on

the wing and hop over the touchline whenever trouble approached" (CD);
Address: House of Commons, Westminster, London SW1A 0AA; Crug yr Eryr Uchaf,
Talgarreg, Llandysul, Dyfed;
Telephone: 0171 219 4002 (H of C); 0154 555 632 (home); 01559 363 419 (constituency
office);

Tam DALYELL   **Labour**   **LINLITHGOW '83-**

Majority: 10,838 (27.13%) over SNP 5-way;
Description: An '83 seat, largely West Lothian,
without the previous Labour strongholds of Bo'ness
and Livingston; "Bathgate is where the voters are."
"scrappy, mine-scarred country, hit hard by the
demise of Scottish coal and steel" (Matthew Parris,
TIMES), but bolstered recently as the recipient of
52% of Scotland's foreign investment; in '95 the seat
lost 7,000 voters in SNP-inclined Queensferry to
Edinburgh West, reducing the longstanding
Nationalist threat;
Former Seat: West Lothian '62-83;
Position: Ex: on Labour Party NEC '86-87;
Spokesman on Science '80-82 (sacked over Falklands
vote); PPS, to R H S Crossman '67-70, '64-66; on Select Committees: on European
Legislation '79-83, '74, Science and Technology '67-68, Public Accounts Committee '62-66;
Delegate to European Parliament '74-79; Chairman: PLP Foreign Affairs Committee '79-80,
'74-75, Scots Labour MPs '74-75, PLP Sports Group '64-74, PLP Education Group '64-65;
Vice Chairman: PLP Liaison Committee '74-76, Defence Group '72-74;
Outlook: Scotland's threatened most veteran political pillar; the newish rebel from the old
Establishment; "I'm Ancient Labour; I want nothing from the party leadership, so they cannot
control me" (TD) the obsessional Etonian Unionist Cassandra who "never wearies of his
well-doing" ('Cross-Bencher', SUNDAY EXPRESS); the closet 10th Baronet who persists in
his Quixotic crusades when others have long wearied, insisting "the first quality is not to mind
being a bore" (TD); "a campaigner of the drone-till-they-drop school" (David Aaronovitch,
INDEPENDENT) has the required "forensic skill, persistence and thick-skinned willingness to
bore the pants off everone else" (TIMES); "Tam is unembarrassable; although Members
sometimes groan when he gets up to speak, they understand perfectly what he is trying to do
and most of them respect him" (OBSERVER); "the Great Backbencher: he rumbles Ministers
and forces explanations which would otherwise never be put before the public...the Unlikely
Laird of the Binns...he is in one way The Cat Who Walks Alone, ever-sceptical of the
accepted view and ready to challenge authority, but he is no outsider" (Jim Naughtie,
SCOTSMAN); his campaigns have stretched through his nearly four decades in the Commons,
like trying to sink Scottish devolution in the late '70s and '90s, or raising the 'Belgrano' issue
'82-84, or depicting Mrs Thatcher as a liar over Westland, or predicting ecological disasters in
the Gulf War in '90-91, or endless appeals for an end to sanctions against Iraq and Libya since
'93; still unanswered is his "West Lothian question" about why Scots MPs should be able to
vote on English matters while English MPs lose their right to vote on devolved Scottish
matters; has recently acquired strong strains of disguised pacifism and undisguised gullibility;
has had fifteen adjournments exculpating Gaddafi for Lockerbie and wept copious tears for the

Iraqi children starved by Saddam; he "does not realise that swallowing the poisoned propaganda of Saddam Hussein leads to a total destruction of the intellect" (Emma (now Baroness) Nicholson); was "the Cassandra of the [Gulf] conflict" (Donald Anderson MP), "an instrument of Saddam Hussein's policy" (Douglas Hogg MP); "an earnest, amiable, political eccentric" who "has the engaging habit of treating his political opponents as people who have been led astray" (Matthew Moulton, SCOTSMAN); "I am a Euro-fanatic"; "I would...bring the troops out of Ulster tomorrow"; "I ferociously support nuclear power" (TD); "a person of real qualities, although he is sometimes funny, ingenuous, a blurter-outer" (R H S Crossman MP); "obsessive" (Robin Oakley, TIMES); "he will spot sinister connections between the most unlikely events" (Chris Moncrieff, PRESS ASSOCIATION); "he has the unique ability...to get under the skin of Ministers" (Peter Riddell, FINANCIAL TIMES); "Dalyell's fragmentation bombs - 50 or 100 [Parliamentary] questions at a time - are designed to blow holes in the screen" surrounding officials; his crusades almost always have a serious point, but he does not notice the long toes he tramples as he hurls yet another point of order; "his inherent respect for the hierarchies of public life are at war with an internal targeting system which puts him in the ranks of outsiders" (GUARDIAN); "if Tam has suffered from a self-destructive bluntness, it is largely the straight talk of the gentleman who refuses to dissemble or to trim" (Colin Bell, SCOTSMAN); formerly a Fabian, was later applauded by the hard Left for whom he became a cult figure for his opposition to the Falklands War, becoming "the only Campaign Group member to own peacocks" (Andrew Marr, INDEPENDENT); he is pro-Arab partly because of his family's links there, despite his long association with pro-Zionist Dick Crossman; a science enthusiast, who strongly favours: nuclear power generation, animal vivisection (for science), organ transplants, small islands (Aldabra, Diego Garcia) and constituents - "I'm a very, very assiduous constituency MP"; was RMT-sponsored;

History: He was sponsored for membership in the Cambridge University Conservative Association by fellow undergraduate John Biffen '53; became its President '54; was beaten by Richard Moore when he tried to become a Tory President of the Cambridge Union '54; "I joined the [Labour] Party at the time of Suez" Nov '56; was adopted for hopeless Roxburgh, Selkirk and Peebles ("I liked the Borders because the Dalyells are Border reivers -cattle thieves") '57; contested it, coming third with highest Labour vote ever Oct '59; was selected for West Lothian '61; was elected at the West Lothian by-election which precipitated Harold Macmillan's "Night of the Long Knives" because the Tory vote was reduced by 70% June '62; urged PM Harold Macmillan to "look beyond your own nose" by exploring the deep Nov '62; launched two-year-long Standing Conference on the Sciences in major cities '62; supported election of Harold Wilson '63; urged widespread nationalisation of aircraft industry Mar '63; urged curbs on "robber bands" of cowboy hire-purchase firms May '63; complained of "irregularities" in new town of Livingston Sep '63; urged improved scientific education Oct '63; met President Nasser during his honeymoon trip to Cairo Jan '64; deplored brain drain of scientists to USA Feb '64; urged control of Palace of Westminster be transferred from Queen to Speaker and Commons Commission July '64; was named PPS to RHS Crossman Oct '64; was elected Chairman of PLP's Education Committee Dec '64; urged Labour annual conference become a "grassroots" affair, with a "two-way traffic" Dec '64; after a Parliamentary delegation to southeast Asia, concluded the British war in Borneo was "a totally unnecessary conflict" and told PM Harold Wilson he had been "taken for a ride" by Singapore's Lee Kuan Yew; he then felt constrained briefly to resign as PPS to R H S Crossman Sep-Oct '65; as PPS to R H S Crossman signed a letter warning Harold Wilson against selling out to Ian Smith Nov '65; fought Harold Wilson's attempted secret transfer of Diego Garcia to US Navy '66; revisited Indonesia June '66; urged a withdrawal of British "colonial" military power from southeast Asia July '66; received 48,000 votes (23rd) for constituency section of Labour's National Executive Oct '66; opposed later-abandoned Anglo-French 'swing-wing' aircraft advocated by Denis Healey Jan '67; resumed his post as PPS to R H S Crossman Sep '67; successfully urged an alternative to Aldabra as an Indian Ocean staging post, harassing officials in Whitehall and Washington Oct '67; as an advocate of withdrawal, was attacked by Singapore Premier Lee Kuan Yew on BBC-TV and at Parliamentary Press Gallery luncheon Jan '68; when George Brown resigned, urged R H S Crossman to make a bid to become Foreign Secretary Mar '68; complained that Britain was supporting an authoritarian regime in Singapore Mar '68; Scottish Labour conference backed his allegation that devolution "can only lead to separatism" Mar '68; opposed use of CS gas pistols by police Apr '68; was censured by the Committee of Privileges for a breach of privilege and a gross contempt of the House for giving an embargoed document on the Porton Down chemical warfare establishment to the OBSERVER July '68; urged debate on anti-Arab activities of Lt Col "Mad Mitch" Mitchell in Aden July '68; urged a ban on germ warfare Aug '68; again warned of danger of germ and gas warfare Oct '68; was dropped from Science and Technology Select Committee for leaking its document to the OBSERVER Nov '68; visited Indonesia, Japan and Australia May-June '69; investigated organ transplants for his boss, R H S Crossman, Social Services Secretary Sep '69; helped his friend Jim Sillars win the South Ayrshire by-election Mar '70; urged testing of school children for drugs Nov '70; introduced Bill to facilitate organ transplants May '71; voted with Labour's dissident pro-Brussels minority to enter the EEC Oct '71; visited Beijing with Scottish Trade Delegation Nov '71; registered his baronetcy to enable his son to inherit it: "I don't believe in using inherited titles myself" '72; urging him to quit, described Harold Wilson as "an albatross round the neck of the Labour Party" Dec '73; urged withdrawal of British troops from Northern Ireland "within days rather than weeks" to prevent "getting deeper and deeper into the Irish bog" May '74; said, "neither of us wants a phoney, sham, talking-shop kind of [Scottish] Assembly" Aug '74; challenged delay in publication of diaries of his friend, the late R H S Crossman Nov '74; led Parliamentary delegation to Brazil '75; urged beekeepers be allowed to sell honey without bowing to EEC dictates June '74; again urged Labour Government to end internment and bring troops out of Ulster Dec '74; became the leader of resistance to a Scottish Assembly Feb '75; urged a referendum on Scottish devolution Oct '75; urged an Anglo-French Channel Tunnel rail link Dec '75; warned Michael Foot he and 70 other Labour MPs would fight devolution June '76; began second phase of his campaign to kill off devolution Bill, ridiculing conversion of Royal High School into Assembly building July '76; insisted devolution was no way to "dish the Nationalists" Sep '76; criticised Lord Home for backing a referendum on Scottish independence Sep '76; helped block development of oil terminal at Nigg Oct '76; served on European Parliament's Committee on Budgets Dec '76; was again elected a delegate to European Parliament Jan '77; was one of four Labour MPs voting against their Government on devolution Jan '77; claimed devolution meant "dismemberment" of UK; voted against Labour Government's attempt to curb devolution debate; claimed Scottish Assembly would become an anti-English launching pad for a separate state Feb '77; claimed the Americans had been wrong in opting for the fast breeder reactor Apr '77; insisted he was not meeting with any hostility in Scotland, although "I had inflicted my strident anti-Assembly view on the House of Commons, day after day, and voted against both the Scotland and Wales Bill on 2nd Reading, and against the guillotine motion" May '77; opposed cuts in BBC external services Aug '77; voting against it, said the devolutionary Scotland Bill provided not the "remotest chance of a settlement of a lasting nature between Scotland and England" Nov '77; was frequently the only opponent to speak against John Smith, sponsoring the Labour Government's Devolution Bill, repeating chunks from his new book Devolution: the End of Britain? Dec '77; was one of 34 Labour rebels who defeated Government on George Cunningham's amendment imposing a minimum of 40% of affirmative votes to achieve Scottish devolution Jan '78; voted against 3rd Reading of Scotland Bill Feb '78; made seventh effort to allow doctors to take transplant kidneys from all except opt-outs Mar '78; opposed direct elections to European Parliament May '78; voted with Tories to sustain a Lords amendment to prevent the 71 post-devolution Scottish MPs from voting in Westminster on English and Welsh matters July '78; opposed proportional representation for Scottish Assembly July '78; challenged Devolution Minister John Smith to dissociate himself from 'Yes' leader, Lord Kilbrandon, who had said the break-up of the UK "would be no bad thing" Oct '78; was expelled from a closed session of European Commission of Human Rights for protesting analogy drawn between Scottish schools' use of tawse (strap) with life in Nazi Germany Oct '78; defeated effort to finance Scottish "Yes" (to devolution) campaign with national money Nov '78; his six-time opponent in West Lothian, SNP Chairman William Wolfe, decided to stand down Nov '78; insisting "devolution does equal separation," urged a two-day referendum on devolution to maximise turnout Nov '78; campaigned with fellow anti-devolutionists George Cunningham and Jim Sillars for 'no' vote in referendum, to embarrassment of pro-devolution Labour Party Feb '79; complained that BBC coverage of the referendum had been pro-devolution Mar '79; the indecisive vote in favour of devolution gave a further blow to the already staggering Labour Government - neutralised by the 40% hurdle of the "Midlothian requirement" Mar '79; introduced motion to allow organ transplants unless there was an opt-out May '79; Scottish devolution was finally buried by the incoming Tories, after his help in fighting it June '79; introduced another Bill for organ transplants Oct '79; was elected Vice Chairman of PLP Liaison Committee Nov '79; attacked threatened boycott of Moscow Olympics Feb '80; attacked "delusion" of thinking devolved Scottish Assembly could solve economic crises Feb '80; strongly opposed Peter Fry's efforts to bar animal experiments Mar '80; as Scottish Labour Party moved to advocating home rule, said: "they know not what they do" Mar '80; attacked sanctions against Iran May '80; warned computer malfunctions could bring mankind to "the brink of nuclear extinction" June '80; was named Science Spokesman by new Leader Michael Foot Dec '80; warned Soviet Ambassador against invading Poland Dec '80; spoke lengthily against Countryside Bill to extract concessions on marine nature reserves June '81; voted for Tony Benn for Deputy Leader, against Denis Healey Sep '81; offered to resign as Science Spokesman because he did not support even Michael Foot's lukewarm backing for Falklands expedition Apr '82; saw Mrs Thatcher privately -who said "always glad to see the awkward squad" - over the Falklands Apr '92; was dropped as Spokesman by Foot for voting against the Falklands War instead of abstaining May '82; he began his campaign to expose Thatcher Government's misdirection and misinformation in the Falklands conflict, allegedly to prevent a peaceful settlement; heard about alleged war crimes in 3rd Battalion of Parachute Regiment but decided not to do anything "because it was not part of my case against the Falklands War to denigrate British servicemen" Oct '82; received 48 votes (82 qualified) in Shadow Cabinet election Nov '82; alleged Thatcher Cabinet contemplated "nuking" Argentine military base of Cordoba if Falklands task force had been sunk May '83; supported Jeremy Corbyn's letter attacking US on Nicaragua Aug '83; received 113,000 votes for NEC Oct '83; stood for Shadow Cabinet, receiving 46 votes (with 72 qualifying) Oct '83; in the South Atlantic debate he described the Falklands War as "a chronicle of deception which has besmirched the name of our country" June '84; received 57 votes for the Shadow Cabinet (with 71 qualifying) Oct '84; was reselected on a shortlist of one July '85; received an increased but inadequate 268,000 votes for the constituency section of the NEC Sep '85; was elected to Executive of hard-Left Campaign Group Oct '85; disclosed that Colette Bowe had leaked the Westland letter on behalf of Leon Brittan Jan '86; asked Mrs Thatcher if the US had told her they would use anti-personnel cluster bombs in their UK-based Libyan air raid Apr '86; claimed that Mrs

Thatcher had looked the other way after inspiring the Solicitor General's letter against Heseltine in the Westland affair July '86; was elected to the NEC with 376,000 votes, displacing Eric Heffer with 251,000 Sep '86; in Shadow Cabinet elections he secured 42 votes (down from 70) Oct '86; was expelled by Speaker for refusing to withdraw remarks about Mrs Thatcher's deception over Westland Oct '86; lost hard Left favour when he led the argument on imposing a candidate on Militant-controlled Knowsley North Nov '86; alleged his phone was being tapped Dec '86; tried to get the Security Commission to investigate the forging by MI5 of Swiss bank statements implicating Lord Glenamara, then Ted Short Jan '87; raised the propriety of EDS, a computer firm which had lied to the Immigration Service and employed Mark Thatcher, being considered for an £800m government contract Jan '87; complained about the 'Zircon' raid on the Glasgow BBC Feb '87; deplored the £25m Sizewell inquiry as an expensive lawyers' ramp leading to the wrong conclusion; he would have preferred an AGR to the PWR urged by Layfield Feb '87; he ceased being a member of the Campaign Group Mar '87; again accused Mrs Thatcher of "deception of Parliament" over the Westland affair in the wake of the 'World in Action' report Apr '87; he was the only Scottish Labour MP not to sign a call for a Scottish Assembly Apr '87; withdrew rather than withdraw his charge that Mrs Thatcher had deceived the Commons over Westland Apr '87; Malcolm Rifkind severed relations with him for refusing to withdraw or substantiate allegations that he had known about the raid on the Glasgow BBC Apr '87; attacked the role of Norman Tebbit and Airey Neave in having helped MI5 destabilise the Wilson Government May '87; was attacked by the Alliance as one of 101 'hard Left' candidates May '87; his majority dropped slightly because of appeal of ex-Labour SNPer Jim Sillars June '87; received 36 votes for the Shadow Cabinet (84 qualifying) July '87; the hard-Left Campaign Group having dropped its support - because he only backed them a quarter of the time in NEC votes - he lost his seat on the NEC with 149,000 votes Sep '87; supported Jeremy Corbyn's right to introduce any researcher he wanted into the Commons, including a previously jailed ex IRA supporter Nov '87; was expelled from the Commons for five sitting days for again saying Mrs Thatcher had "told a necessary and indispensible lie" about Westland Nov '87; again raised the question of Mrs Thatcher's refusal to be candid over Westland Dec '87; appeared on the Wogan show after being excluded from the Commons Dec '87; launched an adjournment debate on the Prime Minister's Private Office, pointing out "the accelerating arrogance of power of No 10 Downing Street" Apr '88; in NEW SCIENTIST he suggested nuclear waste could be reprocessed on the Northern coast of Scotland Apr '88; urged an inquiry into SAS operations against IRA gunmen in Gibraltar May '88; voted with hard-Left and anti-Marketeers against providing money for European Communities (Finance) Bill July '88; was suspended again for accusing Mrs Thatcher of having lied to the Commons July '88; was again suspended from the Commons Dec '88; supported the demand that the Official Secrets Bill include the right for 'whistle-blowers' to disclose secrets in the public interest, as Clive Ponting had to him over the Belgrano Feb '89; backed chess for schools as a great challenge for clever pupils May '89; was again suspended for claiming that Mrs Thatcher had lied in January 1986 about the Westland affair July '89; voted against the Gulf War Sep '90; received 42 votes for Shadow Cabinet Oct '90; said "I have never been more uptight about any issue than I am about a Gulf war - in particular the ecological consequences of the military option"; warned that Kuwait would not be "liberated" but "obliterated" because Saddam Hussein had "deep-mined at least 300 of the Kuwaiti oil wells", whose igniting would result in significant global warming, according to King Hussein of Jordan, Saddam's collaborator; urged Denis Healey be sent to Baghdad as a mediator; was accused of "making himself an instrument of Saddam Hussein's policy" by Douglas Hogg Dec '90; predicted the Gulf War "would probably involve the use of nuclear weapons" Jan '91; voted against bombing of Iraqi civilians Feb '91; said, "I am an unashamed friend of the nuclear industry", praising Sellafield in particular Apr '91; introduced Bill to preserve ancient forests July '91; at a Labour conference fringe meeting, spoke up for nuclear power Oct '91; received 26 votes for Shadow Cabinet Oct '91; visited Libya with six other MPs as guest of Mathaba, with approval of Foreign Office, to see "Libyan officials" Nov '91; urged Government supervision of sales of historic buildings Nov '91; warned that Libya could be swept by a fundamentalist revolution if it released the British-requested Lockerbie suspects Mar '92; retained seat with majority down from 10,373 to 7,026, a swing to SNP of 3.92% Apr '92; received 26 votes for Shadow Cabinet July '92; said he would vote for Maastricht May '92; complained of secret dumping of live ammunition at sea Sep '92; at annual conference said "there is a very strong case for saying that the nuclear energy industry may be the greenest form of energy of all" Sep '92; received 17,000 votes for constituency section of National Executive Oct '92; was rated the 14th most assiduous Commons questioner Oct '92; in debate on the Arab world, in which he disclosed that both his parents had been fluent Arab-speakers, he urged conciliation with Colonel Gaddafi and deplored as "a crime" "the destruction of Gaddafi's home in Tripoli, the killing of his three-year-old daughter and the bombing of working-class homes in Benghazi in 1986 by [US] bombers based in Britain"; also tackled the falsification of British relations with Saddam Hussein, including disclosures of discussions with fellow Old Etonian Alan Clark Nov '92; urged caution about military involvement in Bosnia, since Yugoslavia's guerillas had held down 37 German divisions in wartime Dec '92; again spoke up for nuclear energy and for an early start-up for THORP Dec '92; was one of 17 MPs who voted against Clive Soley's Freedom and Responsibility of the Press Bill Jan '93; feared that some of the liberated ex-Communist countries were losing their church objects through organised theft Feb '93; opposed continued nuclear testing Feb '93; listed a dozen diseases escalating in Iraq because of sanctions Feb '93; introduced motion on Transplantation of Human Organs allowing "hospitals to take the organs of anyone, other than people who have contracted out" (later dropped) Mar '93; voted against National Lottery Bill Apr '93; said "I am a Euro-fanatic" Apr '93; saw Foreign Secretary Douglas Hurd on returning from Baghdad; said "thousands of babies are literally dying weekly in Iraq as a result of sanctions" May '93; complained of beach pollution May '93; visited Iraq with George Galloway May '93; urged easing of sanctions against Iraq and Libya, complaining of Iraqi children's malnutrition through sanctions June '93; asked whether there were contingency plans for "withdrawal or evacuation" from Bosnia June '93; repeated "I am a passionate and unreconstructed pro-European", insisting on having the Social Chapter July '93; expressed doubts that Saddam Hussein had ever tried to kill President Bush July '93; at annual conference received 16,000 votes for constituency section of National Executive Oct '93; said he was no longer in favour of punishing British soldiers for possible Falklands misdeeds 11-12 years after the event Nov '93; after another visit to Iraq with George Galloway, claimed sanctions were consolidating Iraqis behind Saddam Hussein Nov '93; John Smith said, "I'm glad you went; thank God you didn't tell me"; came 9th in poll of most impressive Parliamentarian Nov '93; again urged a review of Iraqi sanctions policy Dec '93; claimed local government reforms threatened Roman Catholic education Dec '93; said, "in my 31 years as a Member of the House I have never known a more ill-thought-out piece of legislation from both Governments than the reforms in the Local Government (Scotland) Bill" Jan '94; voted against restoring capital punishment Feb '94; voted to reduce homosexual age of consent to 18 or 16, Feb '94; saw PM John Major to urge easing of sanctions on Iraq to help ill and starving children there Mar '94; again urged easing of sanctions against Iraq and Libya Apr '94; was described as "Lord Haw-Haw" by Tory MP Emma Nicholson for demanding the facts about Saddam Hussein's actions against her marsh Arabs June '94; voted for John Prescott for Leader and Deputy Leader July '94; urged a trial of suspected Libyan Lockerbie bombers at

The Hague, under Scottish law July '94; defended use of foetal ovarian tissue in fertility treatment July '94; attacked predatory pricing of Murdoch's TIMES July '94; failed to be . elected to NEC with 28,433 votes Oct '94; alleged "massive corruption at the heart of the British state" over Mark Thatcher's involvement in arms sales Oct '94; helped show 'The Maltese Double Cross' to challenge the Anglo-American view that Libya alone was responsible for the Lockerbie bombing Nov '94; was accused of behaving "in a rather dotty manner" by Foreign Minister Douglas Hogg Dec '94; began campaign to repair the Forth Rail Bridge Dec '94; warned by his constituency party not to obstruct plans for a Scottish Parliament, he attacked devolution as "election-losing nonsense" Jan '95; had another long adjournment on Lockerbie, implicating Syria or Iran rather than Libya, but was factually punctured by Foreign Secretary Douglas Hurd Feb '95; opposed deeper military involvement in Serbia, warning Blair against backing Major as Foot had supported Thatcher over the Falklands May '95; again raised the "wicked" and "counter-productive" sanctions against Iraq June '95; sought emergency debate on French nuclear testing in the Pacific July '95; with Tony Benn sought Commons recall to debate escalation of war in ex-Yugoslavia Aug '95; co-signed GUARDIAN letter of Committee for Peace in the Balkans Sep '95; complained of lack of career prospects for academic research scientists Oct '95; made representations on behalf of former 'Desert Rats' wishing to visit war graves in Libya Nov '95; with other members of the 'Awkward Squad' voted against procedural reforms Nov '95; opposed 10-minute limit on backbench speeches, claiming that if Michael Foot and Jack Mendelson had been so limited in the '60s, British troops would have been sent to Vietnam Nov '95; opposed continued sanctions on Iraq and Libya as producing "a generation...growing up to hate the West" Nov '95; opposed sale of CCTV extracts of people having sex in doorways as opening them up to blackmail Nov '95; opposed expulsion of Libyan diplomat from UK as posing a threat to 5,000 British citizens working in Libya Dec '95; urged a referendum before setting up a Scottish Parliament Feb '96; opposed age discrimination in job advertisements Feb '96; claimed 560,000 Iraqi children had died since the Gulf War Feb '96; backed Don Touhig's Public Interest Disclosure Bill to protect "deep throats" like Belgrano-leaker Clive Ponting Mar '96; opposed nuclear privatisation Mar '96; claimed PC Yvonne Fletcher had been shot by UK-US intelligence officers from buildings other than the Libyan Embassy May '96; blamed BSE on cuts in UK's scientific infrastructure June '96; attacked Blair's two-question referendum on Scottish Parliament as "vacuous" and "absurd nonsense" June '96; voted against a 3% cap on MPs' pay, to cut MPs' mileage allowances and to base pensions on £43,000 July '96; urged a referendum after devolution legislation July '96; backed allegation that Royal Highland Fusiliers had tortured Iraqi prisoners in the Gulf War Aug '96; with 12 other Europhile Labour MPs, wrote pro-Euro pamphlet 'Jobs, Growth and Security' Sep '96; was fourth runner-up in NEC elections, with 35,790 votes Oct '96; was one of 9 Labour MPs to vote for dis-assembling target guns rather than confining them to gun clubs Feb '97; indicated he would seek a 12th adjournment to attack faulty FBI evidence against two Libyan accused Mar '97; with 96 other Europhile MPs, backed European Movement campaign Mar '97; was re-elected with an enhanced majority of 10,838 in his altered constituency on a swing from the SNP of 4.1% May '97; opposed Tony Blair's altering of PM's question-time to one half-hour as "short-circuiting the House of Commons" May '97; said he would vote 'No' to a Scottish Parliament but 'Yes' to its tax-varying powers May '97; initiated a 100-minute Lockerbie adjournment July '97; despite promises to his constituency party he would not be part of a 'No' campaign, derided devolution as "the de-wiring of Britain" and "a motorway to a separate state, without an exit", insisting "I am not going to be silenced" despite constituency threats of de-selection Aug '97; in an eve-of-referendum article in the anti-devoluton DAILY TELEGRAPH warned poorest would be hardest hit by taxation of a Scottish Parliament Sep

'97; the referendum produced a 74% 'Yes', with West Lothian (including Linlithgow) voting 80% in favour Sep '97; was one of 25 who voted against military action against Iraq, warning about bombing biological agents or an "anthrax installation" Feb '98; praised the Welsh Labour MPs dissenting on devolution Mar '98; welcomed Georgian nuclear waste Apr '98; had his 14th adjournment on Lockerbie Apr '98; voted against Government's abolition of student maintenance grants June '98; voted against reducing age of homosexual consent to 16, June '98; recalled his '80 warning of a Pakistani nuclear bomb June '98; had his 15th Lockerbie adjournment debate July '98; objected to naming Gus Macdonald as Scottish Industry Minister and new life peer Aug '98;

Born: 9 August 1932, Edinburgh

Family: Descendant of General Tam {'Bluidy Tam') Dalyell, a 17th century soldier of fortune and one-time commander of the Russian Army, who pursued Scottish Covenanters, one of the very few to escape from the Tower; his grandfather and great-grandfather were Residents of the East India Company and Nepal; only child of late Lt Col Gordon Dalyell, Indian Civil Service and Resident in Bahrein, who was in the tent when the line was drawn in the sand between Kuwait and Iraq, and Eleanor Isabel (Loch), "an even better Arabic speaker than my father" (TD); m '63 - with Very Rev Dr David Steel officiating - to RC Kathleen (Wheatley), daughter of late Baron Wheatley, ex Labour MP; 1s Gordon Wheatley '65, 1d Moira '68;

Education: Harecroft Hall (Prep) School, where "most of the other boys were children of the 'atomics' who worked at Drigg/Calder Hall; one term in 1944 four of them left mysteriously; two months later we got postcards from them post-marked New Mexico; they had gone to Los Alamos (for the A-bomb tests)" (TD); Edinburgh Academy; Eton ("Birley's Eton was a very civilised place"); King's College, Cambridge University; Moray House Teachers' Training College;

Occupation: Journalist: columnist on NEW SCIENTIST '68-, INDEPENDENT obituarist, columnist on SCOTTISH DAILY RECORD '66-70; Author: Misrule (1987), A Science Policy for Britain (1983), Thatcher's Torpedo (1983), One Man's Falklands (1982), Devolution: The End of Britain (1977), School-Ship 'Dunera' (1962), The Case for School-Ships (1960); Tenant of 'The Binns' (seventeenth Century mansion at Linlithgow, handed over to the National Trust for Scotland by his mother in '44); formerly Sponsored, by RMT (ex-NUR; £750 p a for constituency, plus 80% of election costs) '79-95; Schoolmaster at Bo'ness High School '56-60, Deputy Director of Studies aboard School-Ship 'Dunera' '61-62;

Traits: "A physique apparently constructed in a vivisection laboratory" (GUARDIAN); requires a pillow in the wake of hip operation; had a clumsy walk, with shuffling gait, even before his hip operation ("I'm afraid my mama, whom I love dearly, had a design fault in her"); ankle-length trousers; a joint "Worst Dressed MP...who in winter sports a range of pullovers which have seen better days, some of them possibly over a century ago" (David McKie, GUARDIAN); "a rather tortured look...as if permanently infuriated and baffled by the inscrutable nature of the world" (Frank Johnson); probing; outspoken; persistent; pertinacious; the tenacity of a limpet; "the Linlithgow bloodhound" (Andrew Marr, INDEPENDENT); "hippopotamus-skinned" (TD); suspicious; "burns with righteous anger, but burns slow" (Godfrey Barker, DAILY TELEGRAPH); "often injects a note of solemn fantasy" (Colin Welch, DAILY MAIL); "I am the second best-mannered man in the House of Commons; the man with the most beautiful manners is Tony Benn" (TD); Church of Scotland (wife is RC); "the worst driver in Bathgate" (his assistant, Harry); had a passion for squash; frugal eater; eats apple cores; still well-connected (the Earl of Rosebery's family are constituents and friends);

Address: House of Commons, Westminster, London SW1A 0AA; 'The Binns', Philpstoun,

                                Copyright (C)Parliamentary Profile Services Ltd

Linlithgow, West Lothian EH49 7NA;
Telephone: 0171 219 3427 (H of C); 01506 83 4255;

Rt Hon Alistair (Maclean) DARLING   **Labour**   **EDINBURGH CENTRAL '87-**

Majority: 11,070 (25.9%) over Conservative 7-way;
Description: The historic heart of Scotland's capital, with pro-Labour high-density tenements and the Royal Mile, from the Castle down to Holyrood House and the proposed site of the new Scottish Parliament; middle-class, suburban Murrayfield made it marginal normally; in '95 Labour's position was strengthened by the loss of Tory-leaning New Town ward to Edinburgh North and Leith and by the addition of Stenhouse council estate from Edinburgh West;
Position: Secretary of State for Social Security '98-; ex: Chief Secretary to the Treasury '97-98; Deputy Spokesman, on Treasury Affairs '95-97; Assistant Spokesman, on Treasury Affairs '92-95; Assistant Spokesman, on Home Affairs '89-92; on Plant Commission on Electoral Systems '90-93; Vice Chairman, PLP Transport Committee '87-88; Lothian Regional Councillor (Chairman of its Transport Committee '86-87) '82-87;
Outlook: Fast-rising, highly-competent product of the 'Sensible Left' who made his mark as Gordon Brown's very able lieutenant as Chief Secretary; "one of the ablest members of a generally able Cabinet and...willing to talk openly about his transition from municipal Leftwinger to impeccable moderniser" (Lord (Roy) Hattersley, GUARDIAN); "a reputation as the safest pair of hands in the Government" (Rachel Sylvester and Alice Thomson, DAILY TELEGRAPH); "quietly impressive; looks good and sounds good; enjoys excellent relations with Gordon Brown; highly respected by Treasury officials because of his ability to master even the most complex brief"; "the driving force behind the reforms of [financial] regulation and [was] seen as the steadying influence in the Treasury line-up"; "chillingly numerate", "the least partisan [of the Brown team] with at least one foot firmly in the Blair camp"; "one of the few true Blairites in the Scottish Labour Party" (TIMES); was "seen as a Blair agent in the...Treasury team" (MAIL ON SUNDAY); "fluent and combative enough to run a department" (DAILY TELEGRAPH); a talented, articulate, assiduous, ambitious, shrewd, moderate Scots advocate, better at reasoned argument than Gordon Brown's linked sound-bites; remains loyal to Brown while outshining him in advocacy to the extent that often he was offered to the media in Brown's place in the run-up to the election; self-described as "a reformer, not a radical"; a realist who admitted he would not push his opposition to predatory newspaper pricing in view of PM Blair's cultivation of Murdoch's support; earlier showed his ability on Labour Review Group and "his work behind the scenes on stitching up the proportional representation issue" for a Scottish Parliament (Chris McLaughlin, SCOTSMAN); was early considered "one of Labour's brightest new MPs"; "Scottish Tories will admit privately that he has been one of the most impressive performers among the Scottish Labour MPs" (Ewen MacAskill, SCOTSMAN); "feels Scottish", although he was born in London and lived in both England and Scotland until his family settled in Scotland when he was 12; a belated, unfanatical convert to devolution; the former regional councillor

who, in his first Parliamentary contest, ousted Sir Alex Fletcher, No 3 on Scottish Labour's 'hit-list';

History: His paternal grandfather was a Liberal candidate in '45; a great-uncle was a Tory MP; his late father voted Conservative; his mother voted Labour first in '97; after university, he joined the Labour Party in Edinburgh '77; initially he believed that Scottish devolution was "rubbish"; "I was a doubter in 1979"; "I was not convinced"; "the idea that a Scottish Assembly dependent for more than half its income from Westminster, could build in isolation a different type of society from the rest of the UK seemed implausible"; "at the end of that day, I actually voted 'Yes' - George Cunningham's 40% requirement was too much"; moving a composite motion against the Government's civil defence plans at annual conference, described it as "a con trick" and a "sham" that was "designed to protect the elite in this country; it has nothing to do with protection; it has nothing to do with survival", "the top officials and the Ministers who start the war in the first place will be down their boltholes while the rest of us fry on top"; urged "nuclear-free zones" instead Oct '81; was elected for the Haymarket-Tollcross area of Edinburgh to the Lothian Regional Council May '82; was selected for newly-created Edinburgh Central from a shortlist of two by 48 to 2, Oct '85; in a letter to the Scottish Office, complained that the Scottish Development Department had refused to give Edinburgh District Council legal powers to supervise private landlords, to avoid their exploiting and dispossessing young single homeless Nov '85; at conference of the Scottish Labour Party, predicted that the Auditor of Local Authority Accounts who had deemed Edinburgh District Council to be illegal in its expenditures would be proved wrong; criticised the Conservatives for implementing policies which led to the courts being substituted for politics, insisting that Labour should sweep away such laws Mar '86; in the local government elections covering the seat, the Labour vote exceeded the Tories' by 11,012 to 8,642 May '86; charged that the poll tax shifted "the burden of paying for local services from people living in more affluent areas and the commercial sector to those living in the less well-off neighbourhoods" Apr '87; succeeded in capturing Edinburgh Central from Sir Alex Fletcher June '87; urging better funding of the NHS, predicted that the junior doctors' dispute at the Royal Infirmary was just a symptom of what was to come June '87; in his Maiden he complained about the Government's interference in local government July '87; complained about the failure of Guinness to set up its headquarters in Edinburgh, as promised in the takeover battle for Distillers July '87; read pages of the banned Peter Wright book, Spycatcher, on the steps of the Scottish Academy Aug '87; complained that Edinburgh was being penalised for the extra £1m it had to spend to collect the poll tax Dec '87; in a battery of questions, asked about the tax losses from company loans for house purchase Feb '88; warned that the Budget would produce a "major balance of payments crisis" Mar '88; introduced a Bill to amend the law on Scottish solicitors May '88; was drafted into Labour's Policy Review Group on the individual and democracy July '87; told Mrs Thatcher that her policy of tranferring wealth from the poor to the rich and getting the rich to give it back by charity was nonsense, as shown in St Lukes May '88; demanded to know whether the Government, to make Scottish electricity boards saleable, would write off their debts at public expense July '88; after a year in Parliament he came to the conclusion that the balance of power had shifted so far to the southeast that Scotland could only survive and prosper with a federated regional government with taxation powers July '88; received damages from NEWS OF THE WORLD for its false allegation that he had been absent from a debate on the NHS because he was drinking July '88; said, "I do not want to make a final commitment on whether I pay [my poll tax] until after the Govan conference; I won't criticise people who refuse to pay" Sep '88; complained that the introduction of means testing to improvement grants would stop improvement work on Scottish tenements Sep '88; was named Assistant Spokesman on Home Affairs, under Roy

Hattersley Nov '88, whom he then persuaded to withdraw his opposition to a Bill of Rights; complained that deregulation of buses had enabled bus companies "to get rid of unprofitable services" as he had discovered as Chairman of the Lothian Region's Transport Committee Dec '88; in a SCOTSMAN interview, promised a Labour Government would give a Scottish Assembly top priority Jan '89; accepted the attractions of identity cards but warned against their possible abuse by Government Feb '89; said Labour might offer four or five bills enthrenching positive rights Feb '89; with Lord Young's help, won a year-long battle to prevent Australia's Elders' bid for the Scottish and Newcastle Breweries in his constituency Mar '89; complained that EC integration meant that "if anybody going to any European port of entry - for example, Athens, Amsterdam or wherever - is refused entry, they are refused not just for that country but for the whole of the European Community" May '89; co-authored Labour's Review Group proposals to democratise the legal system, without promising a Bill of Rights (which he himself favoured) May '89; opposed enfranchising the overseas "teaplanter who has been sitting on his verandah for two decades" June '89; accused immigration officers of having precipitated the crisis at Heathrow in 1986 that gave Ministers their justification for Commonwealth visas July '89; urged more TV broadcasts in Gaelic July '89; at Fabian Society conference proposed replacing the Lords with an elected second chamber of 200, plus devolution; insisted PR was "peripheral" to such structural changes Jan '90; at Scottish Convention said, "there is no reason why the Scottish Assembly should not introduce a Bill of Rights if it so wished" Jan '90; tried to save regional broadcasting within ITV Jan '90; opposed reliance on "David Mellor's expressions of good will" to guarantee independence of small regional ITV companies or priority for quality broadcasting Feb '90; pointed out that, under EC rules, a Frenchman married to a Pakistani would be able to come to Britain with their children via France and Germany without complying with rules applying to a British national Feb '90; complained that the Government, using a statutory instrument, was allowing advertising companies unrestricted access to electoral registers Feb '90; opposed sale of of IBA's £300m transmission system Mar '90; said he favoured the passing of the War Crimes Bill but saw great difficulties in establishing identities in court after almost 50 years Mar '90; opposed Government plans to give British passports to 50,000 Hongkong Chinese families, since the Chinese Communists would not recognise the passports' validity Apr '90; opposed Conservatives' plan to target 300,000 expatriate British voters in South Africa as bolstering a flagging party with affluent white "extremists" Apr '90; supported voluntary euthanasia May '90; promised stateless Hongkong Indians a Labour Government would treat their problems with "particular sympathy" June '90; said rowdy late-night pubs in Edinburgh should have their licenses suspended if residents objected June '90; asked, if Mrs Thatcher cared so much about the family, why she had blocked EC proposals for three months' parental leave at the birth of a child? July '90; urged a "continuous register" to improve voters' registration July '90; visited Hongkong at invitation of its government Aug '90; attended Anglo-Spanish conference on Developments in Europe, in Toledo, at invitation of Spanish Government Oct '90; was named to Professor Plant's 'Working Party on Electoral Systems', partly because of "his work behind the scenes on stitching up the proportion representation issue" for the Scottish Assembly (Chris McLaughlin, SCOTSMAN) Oct '90; said the £1m spent on advertising student loans could have helped cash-starved Edinburgh University Oct '90; opposed the use of public funds to finance private building in Scotland Nov '90; signed motion opposing military conflict in the Gulf, preferring prolonged economic sanctions against Saddam Hussein Jan '91; predicted Scottish hospital waiting lists would stretch out if Gulf War cases flooded the hospitals Jan '91; accused the Government of indifference to the financial plight of Scottish universities Jan '91; said, "there is no question of going back to first-past-the-post" for a Scottish Assembly Mar '91; admitted he doubted the War Crimes Bill "would work in practice" Mar '91; accused

Government of using delay to reduce immigration Mar '91; insisted Britain's 19th century constitutional settlement had to be updated by devolution May '91; warned against lumping homes in the same area into the same valuation band for council tax June '91; said he was no longer a member of the anti-EU 'Common Market Safeguards Committee' June '91; deplored Home Secretary Kenneth Baker forcing asylum seekers and immigrants to rely on strife-ridden UKIAS July '91; wrote: "there will have to be harmonisation of EC immigration policies if the Single Market is to work" July '91; deplored Arab diplomats "driving a coach and horse through the immigration rules" by falsely claiming imported domestic workers would be working in their embassies Sep '91; at conference said a Bill for a Scottish Assembly would be published within days of Labour forming a government Oct '91; urged a speeding up of immigration cases Nov '91; said Labour would use the German system of PR - the Additional Member System - for elections to the Scottish Assembly; then visited Germany for further study of its federal structure and the industrial benefits of wider higher education Jan '92; persuaded Immigration Minister Peter Lloyd to modify asylum rules Jan '92; claimed immigration control within EC would stiffen through greater co-operation; "if we abandon frontier controls, the logic of the introduction of identity cards will become overwhelming; identiy cards are unnecesssary and will create more difficulties than they will solve"; said Labour would allow the Asylum Bill to pass if Government abandoned blanket finger-printing for asylum-seekers and the need for visas for all transit passengers Mar '92; despite a drop of nearly 2,700 in its electoral register, largely of poll-tax dodgers, retained his seat with his majority down from 2,262 to 2,126, a swing to Conservative of 0.04% Apr '92; backed John Smith for Leader, Margaret Beckett for Deputy Leader Apr '92; accepted the Boundary Commission Bill, while demanding better registration June '92; as Immigration spokesman approved of new Home Secretary Ken Clarke's shelving of the Asylum Bill, but deplored Government's withdrawal of funds from UKIAS, urging an alternative structure to advise immigrants July '92; submitted a report on the future of Scottish devolution to the one-day Scottish Labour conference July '92; asked about financial crisis of Lothian Health Board July '92; was switched as Assistant Spokesman to Treasury and Economic Affairs, under Gordon Brown July '92; with other Edinburgh Labour MPs Gavin Strang and Malcolm Chisholm, stepped up campaign to save locally-produced European Fighter Aircraft Sep '92; objected to police use of logs of telephone calls without warrants Oct '92; complained the Bank of England had failed to use its powers to supervise BCCI, perhaps because it was used by British and American intelligence agencies Nov '92; urged action to prevent banks from disclosing personal financial data to third parties without permission Feb '93; again deplored failure of Bank of England to take responsibility for failing to supervise BCCI, where "tens of thousands of people lost their entire savings" Feb '93; demanded to know which banks had been aided by the Bank of England in the banking crisis of mid-1991 Mar '93; voted for Supplementary Voting, a form of PR, on Labour' Plant Commission on electoral reform Mar '93; claimed Government's proposals on insider dealing were "totally inadequate" Apr '93; complained the Government had altered its tax regime on North Sea gas and oil without warning May '93; again urged more clear and precise rules against insider trading May '93; asked why Michael Mates intervened on behalf of Asil Nadir when he was not a constituent May '93; objected to Tory MPs being allowed to vote on tax breaks in reserve funds for themselves as Lloyd's names June '93; urged tighter control of NatWest for keeping details of political and religious affiliation of its customers July '93; accused Chief Secretary Michael Portillo of cynically preparing "to raid public services and increase taxes now to pay for pre-election tax cuts later" Aug '93; criticised precipitate plan for a second road bridge across the Forth before a rail bridge was considered Sep '93; won 60 votes in his first contest for the Shadow Cabinet Oct '93; visited Frankfurt Stock Exchange at invitation of German

Government Dec '93; backed an urgent review of the Serious Fraud Office, preferring "a new centralised body" Dec '93; demanded a full investigation of pensions scandal involved bad advice for those leaving SERPs for PEPs Dec '93; urged a reformed Bank of England Dec '93; warned that Government's new legislation on insider dealing would be ineffective, badly applied, undermine London as a financial centre and provide riches only for lawyers Jan '94; opposed Nicholas Budgen's proposal to make the Bank of England independent of the Government Jan '94; opposed Government's insurance tax and the ability of the private health care industry to provide tax break on private health care premiums Jan '94; welcomed Government's decision to put a new statutory duty on auditors, but insisted more was required "against fraud and other crimes of dishonesty" Feb '94; urged a scrapping of the self-regulatory system, making the Securities and Investments Board responsible for the regulation of financial services Feb '94; criticised the Government's decision to leave trade union representatives off the Bank of England's Court of Directors for the first time since 1947, Mar '94; in a motion said "predatory pricing, with the intention of forcing rivals out of the market, will reduce choice and undermine competition" July '94; in the Leadership elections after John Smith's death, voted for Blair as Leader, Margaret Beckett as Deputy Leader July '94; in the ballot for the Shadow Cabinet, received 61 votes, with 97 required Oct '94; was promoted to third man in Labour's Treasury team, serving as Spokesman on banks Oct '94; denied rumour that Labour would also impose a windfall tax on high street banks, insisting they could not be compared with public utilities; he said Labour would bring in a new banking regulator who would be "a cross between the Office of Fair Trading and a consumer watchdog" Jan '95; said Labour would punish inside dealers and concentrate investigative and disciplinary powers in the Security and Investments Board Feb '95; received 67 votes for the Shadow Cabinet, with 107 needed Oct '95; with Gordon Brown's backing, was promoted to Deputy Spokesman on Treasury Affairs, or shadow Chief Secretary Oct '95; voted against Iain Duncan-Smith's Bill to remove the UK from the jurisdiction of the European Court Apr '96; lectured the Fabians on 'Stakeholding'; promised Labour would encourage longterm saving May '96; said MIRAS would "be left for the time being" May '96; voted for the 3% cap on MPs' pay rise July '96; was one of the dozen rising loyalists whom Mr Blair would have liked to see in the Shadow Cabinet who agreed not to stand in the last pre-election contest, to ease the leadership's effort to keep Harriet Harman July '96; his position as Gordon Brown's deputy was confirmed in Tony Blair's last pre-election reshuffle July '96; denied the 'feel-good factor' was returning, helping Tory prospects Aug '96; promised not to be a City-basher: "the City employs 2.8m people and contributes 18% to our GDP; we want not only to protect those jobs but to encourage even more to be created" Oct '96; explained Labour's plans to replace the Tories "Ken and Eddie Show" with a Monetary Policy Committee to advise the Governor Nov '96; denounced Tory plans to organise groups of privatised utilities against Labour's plans for a windfall tax Nov '96; after a very successul fortnight on TV discussing the Budget, was said to have come under pressure from Charles Whelan in Gordon Brown's office to shave his allegedly voter-irritating beard Dec '96; warned all Labour frontbenchers to clear all spending commitments with the Treasury team Dec '96; concentrated his fire on securing a pledge from Chancellor Clarke that he would not put VAT on food, after claiming to have incriminating film of the Chancellor and PM John Major discussing it Jan '97; said a new Royal Yacht would be an asset, but Labour, not having committed any funds to it, would expect it to be privately funded and more extensively used Jan '97; asked the Financial Secretary Michael Jack about the alleged Tory plan to privatise the tax-raising system Jan '97; became a target of the Prolife Alliance Party Feb '97; his participation in the Labour team which toured City boardrooms was said to have helped neutralise the City Apr '97; was re-elected for his altered seat by a much enhanced majority of 11,070 on a notional swing of 8.4% swing from the Conservatives May

'97; was promoted to the Cabinet as Chief Secretary of the Treasury and made a Privy Councillor May '97; the new Treasury moved rapidly to impose his wholesale reforms in banking and financial services regulation because uncertainty was causing poaching of senior staff of City watchdogs; he denied trying to punish the Bank of England but emphasised its BCCI and Barings failures May '97; insisted public spending would be more sharply focussed on "people's priorities" June '97; helped to tone down the "Braveheartish" language of the early drafts of the White Paper on a Scottish Parliament June '97; dismissed the claim of Bank of Scotland Governor Sir Bruce Pattulo that the average Scots wage earner would be £300 a year poorer, insisting "we have made sure there is a level playing field, because the corporation tax regime will be the same the the length and breadth of the kingdom" Aug '97; as the first Labour Cabinet Minister to appear at a LibDem conference fringe meeting, warned that "there are no easy solutions, no quick fixes" and "co-operation and responsibility is a two-way process" Sep '97; announced a £250m switch to the NHS from the Defence and DTI budgets to stem rising winter waiting lists Sep '97; continued for a further year the freeze on public sector pay Sep '97; the loss of his increasingly stubbly beard, favoured by his wife but opposed by Labour's spin-doctors, caused comment Sep '97; with Gordon Brown, was the butt of Cabinet colleagues' criticism for following Tony Blair's lead in not taking his salary increase Sep '97; launched the Paisley South by-election with praise for Labour's windfall tax, NHS spending and welfare-to-work scheme Oct '97; introducing the 2nd Reading of the Bank of England Bill, argued that its new Monetary Policy Committee would improve price stability and free interest rates from "narrow party political manipulation" as practiced by Ken Clarke Nov '97; opposed a Treasury Select Committee veto on Bank of England appointments Nov '97; promised any eventual proposals for the disabled would be "entirely consistent with our principles of fairness and opportunity" Nov '97; while considering tax concessions, replaced Harriet Harman on BBC's 'On The Record' as Labour MPs' opposition mounted over single-parent benefit cuts Nov '97; defended Geoffrey Robinson's overseas trust as having been set up by a Belgian woman living in Switzerland, and therefore not a way of avoiding tax in Britain Nov '97; promised to close tax loopholes Jan '98; again helped Paymaster General Geoffrey Robinson dodge questions about his offshore trust by fielding his questions Jan '98; asked about his previous opposition, in July '94, to predatory newspaper pricing, admitted he would no longer be pushing it, in view of the PM's position Feb '98; asked the Foreign Office to curb open-ended expenditure on keeping diplomats' children at private boarding schools Feb '98; raised expectations, soon realised, that the Government would lift the £50,000 limit on tax-free PEPS Mar '98; replying to the Budget debate, hailed it as "the biggest modernisation of the tax and benefits system for 20 years"; "we are supporting families by increasing child benefit by the largest amount since its introduction almost 20 years ago" Mar '98; was promoted Social Security Secretary, replacing Harriet Harman; promised to deliver on welfare reform July '98; denied reports he had insisted on Frank Field's removal Aug '98;
Born: 28 November 1953, London
Family: Son, late Thomas Young Darling, engineer, and Anna (Maclean); m '86 Margaret/'Maggie' McQueen (Vaughan) journalist on the GLASGOW HERALD; 1s Calum '88; 1d Anna '90; "when you have two young children you can't have any hobbies; your hobby is looking after them, although [when] pacing up and down at two in the morning I sometimes wish I was going up a mountain the next day";
Education: "I went to seven different primary schools, which left its mark; it made me adaptable and not afraid of change"; Loretto School ("I didn't enjoy boarding school" but denies having said, "I would not inflict on my own son what was inflicted on me"); Aberdeen University (LLB);
Occupation: Advocate '84-; no longer practicing; formerly Sponsored: "my constituency

party receive[d] £300 p a from the General Municipal, Boilermakers and Allied Trades Union" '90-95; Solicitor, '78-82; Director, Edinburgh Old Town Trust (charitable) '87-89;
Traits: Handsome; grey hair. black eyebrows and, formerly, a grey beard; he claims he could only shave his beard after the election because his election photos showed him with one; compact; dour; "smartly dressed" (SCOTSMAN); "his grey hair and [former] close-cropped beard are accompanied by saturnine jet black eyebrows and penetrating eyes that seem better suited to an Italian art-house movie than an Edinburgh courtroom" (Ivo Dawnay, FINANCTIAL TIMES); "beautiful, soft, white, nylon-like hair and a classless accent with just the faintest hint (very New Labour) of Educated Scot"; "grows smoother at every session" (Matthew Parris, TIMES); "a gent", "blessed with a fine small-screen countenance"; "not many members of the Opposition front bench could have sat for Van Dyck" (Edward Pearce, GUARDIAN); "courteous and articulate" (Christopher Monckton, EVENING STANDARD); displays "dry wit" (SCOTSMAN); "cynical humour" (Ivo Dawnay, FINANCIAL TIMES); "smooth, quiet, well-mannered and thoughtful" (Tory ex-Minister Michael Jack MP); can be "scarily insulting" (GUARDIAN), telling an obstreperous Tory MP, "if I knew your name, I'd reply to you"; parsimonious (has been seen eating home-made sandwiches with his tea in Strangers Cafeteria; "I am not one of those people who gets up at four in the morning and has muesli before climbing a mountain and dashing off a novel in the afternoon"; "I think I am always going to have a restlessness about me"; "I'm not clubbable or laddy" (AD);
Address: House of Commons, Westminster, London SW1A 0AA;
Telephone: 0171 219 4584 (H of C); 0131 662 0123 (constituency);

Keith DARVILL   **Labour**   **UPMINSTER '97-**

Majority: 2,770 over Conservative 4-way;
Description: The long, thin constituency on London's eastern fringe, on the Essex border at the end of the District Line; in its northern part is the giant Harold Hill council estate, in its southern part are the middle class suburbs of Cranham and Emerson Park; in '95 it lost Conservative-leaning Ardleigh Green ward; "most of the residents of this seat [like me] have come from the inner part of east London or are members of families born there", "part of the well-known eastward drift that has taken place since the 1920s" (KD);
Position: Chairman, Upminster Constituency Labour Party '94-97;
Outlook: The "charismatic" (Patrick Hennessy, EVENING STANDARD) local self-made solicitor who ousted the former Foreign Office Minister, Sir Nicholas Bonsor Bt, like all but one of the Tories in the near-Essex suburbs; the first-ever Labour MP for this seat; has been a model of loyal but not-quite-sickening support for the Government; as a school governor for over 15 years has an involved, nonpartisan approach to improving education; is no devotee of written questions, having asked only three in his first year; is in the Fabian Society, Co-operative Party, the Society of Labour Lawyers;
History: He joined the Labour Party '71; was selected to contest Upminster '95; helped by almost half of the LibDem vote, unexpectedly ousted Sir Nicholas Bonsor Bt by a majority of 2,770 votes, with a pro-Labour swing of 15.38%, May '97; backed outlawing of fox-hunting

June '97; expressed solidarity with jailed Indonesian union leader June '97; in his Maiden attributed his victory to the fact that Upminster voters, mostly immigrants from east London, had "returned to Labour"; he loyally supported the Budget proposals July '97; in the Schools debate, speaking as a school governor for over 15 years, warned against overloading governors, or undervaluing local education authorities' expertise or undermining teachers' morale; he also supported early testing to detect dyslexia July '97; backed curbs on detention of asylum-seekers July '97; spoke up for local partnerships in policing Nov '97; urged better funding and integration for London Underground Jan '98; hailed the "cross-agency co-operation" of Barking and Havering Health Authority, the local hospital trusts, local authorities and local Labour MPs Feb '98; strongly supported the Government's proposal for a one-question referendum on an elected mayor and assembly for London, which had been "well-aired" and widely supported Feb '98; urged Government to back small and medium-sized businesses in expanding exports Apr '98; was rated among the 'Bottom 100' for written questions, having asked only three in his first year May '98; urged partnerships between the police, local communities and local organisations as the best way to fight youth crime in areas like Harold Hill June '98;

Born: 28 May 1948, Forest Gate, London
Family: Son, of Ernest Arthur Darvill, docker, and Ellen May (Carke); m Julia (de Saren); 2s, 1d;
Education: Norlington Secondary Modern, Leyton E10; East Ham Technical College; Thurrock College of Further Education; Polytechnic of Central London; College of Law, Chester;
Occupation: Solicitor '82-; deals largely with property (TGWU)
Traits: Blond, parted hair; heart-shaped face; youthful looking; "charismatic" (Patrick Hennessy, EVENING STANDARD); enjoys tennis, badminton, sports generally and gardening;
Address: House of Commons, Westminster, London SW1A 0AA;
Telephone: 0171 219 5106 (H of C); 01708 222687 (constituency);

Edward DAVEY	**Liberal Democrat**	**KINGSTON & SURBITON '97-**

Majority: 56 over Conservative 7-way;
Description: A merger of two formerly Conservative seats in London's southwestern suburbs: former Surbiton linked to that part of Kingston-upon-Thames south of the main railway into London; what remained unsure until the '97 general election was the extent to which Liberal Democrat victories on Kingston council would be translated into a Parliamentary seat;
Position: Public Spending and Taxation Spokesman on LibDems' Treasury team '97-; ex: on Liberal Democrat Federal Policy Committee '94-95; Chairman, of the Costing Group on the LibDem Manifesto '94-97; on LibDem Policy Groups on Economics, Tax and Benefits, Transport;
Outlook: The first MP for this new seat which he so little expected to win that he was delivering leaflets in Richmond on the next to the last weekend of the campaign; fitted into the

Parliamentary team quickly because of his previous experience as the LibDems' economic adviser; was one of the clever young backroom boys transmuted into a rising star on the LibDems' front bench; was one of those insiders instrumental in forming the policy for a penny on income tax to pay for education; is respected by Labour Ministers for his economic expertise, if not his patronising whiplashing ("I always enjoy his speeches" -Helen Liddell MP); slightly blotted his copybook early on by being clumsily against a LibDem-Lab dialogue, at the instigation of his radical-activist local party; wanted a strategic authority for London, elected by PR, but is opposed to a separate directly-elected mayor; a former Senior Economics Adviser to LibDem MPs; one of the young LibDem apparatchiks who secured their five-seat sweep in the southwestern London suburbs; "conservation is his big issue" (INDEPENDENT ON SUNDAY);

History: He was active at Oxford "discussing the minutiae of energy conservation and green economics" (ED) '86; he joined the Liberal Democrats '89; was selected for the new Kingston and Surbiton seat following the abolition of the old Kingston seat Mar '95; at annual conference argued against demands from Scottish LibDems for a cut in VAT on hotel services as "incredibly inefficient and costly" at a time when the party was calling for a tax increase to fund education Sep '96; captured Kingston and Surbiton from Tory MP Dick Tracey by 56 - the third smallest majority - on the basis of a 13.6% swing May '97; in his Maiden complained about the punishing cuts imposed on education in Kingston June '97; tried to save Thames Ditton Lawn Tennis Club from demolition June '97; backed motion favouring abolition of hunting with hounds June '97; in the debate on exchange rate, insisted that Austin Mitchell always argued for devaluation, "a recipe for inflation"; an independent central bank was better July '97; criticised the rapid passage of the Finance Bill, because it contained "a dramatic change in fiscal policy" not foreshadowed in Labour's manifesto; the Budget was "designed for political considerations, not economic ones, and aimed at fulfilling a political project and bulding a war chest for the next election", "that is why Liberal Democrat Members will vote against the Second Reading"; he described Chancellor Brown's willingness to accept Kenneth Clarke's ceilings as "Clownism" July '97; urged help for non-taxpaying pensioners with the lowest incomes July '97; claimed Kingston would need more police if all the club license applications were accepted Nov '97; urged a two-question referendum on London's new government structure Nov '97; backed access to their family files by Barnardo's children Dec '97; supported the Bank of England Bill Jan '98; backed deregulation of emergency contraception Jan '98; backed licensing of London minicabs Jan '98; urged generous settlement for Kingston Jan '98; opposed closure of paediatric unit at Atkinson Morley Hospital, Wimbledon Jan '98; claimed people were "disillusioned" by Labour's restructuring of London's government Feb '98; opposed 3% cap on Kingston Council Feb '98; urged improvements for the A3 Kingston bypass, "the busiest stretch of non-motorway road in Europe" Feb '98; expressed puzzlement over why Chancellor Brown was not spending more on public services in view of the surpluses exposed by the Red Book Mar '98; co-sponsored LibDem motion attacking Cricket Board for its treatment of female employees Mar '98;

Born: 25 December 1965, Annesley-Woodhouse, Nottinghamshire

Family: Son of late John George Davey, solicitor, and late Joan (Stanbrook) teacher;

Education: Nottingham High School (head boy); Jesus College, Oxford University (BA in PPE, First Class Hons); Birkbeck College, London University (MSc Econ);

Occupation: Management Consultant, with Omega Partners '93-97; Director, of Omega Partners Postal (specialising in new markets for post offices) '96-97; Senior Economic Adviser to the LibDems in Parliament '89-93;

Traits: Parted light-brown hair; long jaw; cleancut; personable, good-looking and presentable; very bright; can seem self-satisfied and patronising; enthusiastic and waggy-tailed;

received a Chief Constable's Certificate and an award from the Royal Humane Society for
rescuing a woman who had fallen onto the track at Clapham Junction station;
Address: House of Commons, Westminster, London SW1A 0AA;
Telephone: 0171 219 3152 (H of C); 0181 399 3774;

Mrs Valerie DAVEY   **Labour**   **BRISTOL WEST '97-**

Majority: 1,493 over Conservative 7-way;
Description: The city's formerly-Conservative
heartland, including the University and the more
fashionable residential slopes of Clifton and Redland,
as well as inner-city, multiracial St Paul's; the addition
of Tory-leaning Westbury-on-Trym was thought
likely to save the seat for embattled William
Waldegrave;
Position: On the Select Committee on Education
and Employment '97-; ex: Avon County Councillor
(Leader of its majority Labour Group '92-96) '81-96;
Outlook: The education-preoccupied former Avon
Council Leader and ex-teacher who ended William
Waldegrave's Commons career and the Tories'
long-standing hold on the seat by exploiting tactical voting; favours electoral reform; a
Methodist who taught in Tanzania; in Amnesty and Action for South Africa;
History: She formed her convictions when she worked among the poor in Tanzania in the
'60s; she joined the Labour Party '70; was elected to Avon County Council May '81; became
Leader of the Labour Group on Avon County Council May '92; was selected for Bristol West,
in the knowledge that Labour had come 3rd with 24.8% in '92, with her LibDem opponent
having come 2nd with 30.7%, '95; expressed her concern about homelessness and sleeping
rough in Bristol on BBC TV's 'Midnight Hour' Jan '97; she concentrated her campaign on
getting back from the LibDems the tactical votes which had gone to them in '92, when they
were best-placed to oust William Waldegrave; she argued bitterly with their "dishonest" bar
graphs which portrayed Bristol West as a two-horse (LibDem v Tory) contest, ignoring
pro-Labour local and Euro elections after '92; her case was helped considerably by the
publication, four days before polling, of an ICM poll - confirmed by canvassing returns - which
showed her ahead of Waldegrave by 39% to 31% with the Liberal Democrat, Charles Boney,
trailing badly with 24%; she sent an eve of poll leaflet on this to every household Apr '97; won
the seat, ousting William Waldegrave by a majority of 1,493, a notional swing to Labour of
12.08%, May '97; in her Maiden complained about the past under-funding of Bristol, including
an allocation of only £17,500 for repairing its schools; she also complained of inadequate
funds for curbing growing homelessness June '97; urged a review of "the role and function of
the Equal Opportunities Commission" June '97; supported the outlawing of fox-hunting June
'97; expressed solidarity with jailed Indonesian union leader June '97; urged increased
concentration on children with special educational needs July '97; was named to Select
Committee on Education and Employment July '97; co-expressed concern about injured
employees whose companies had gone into liquidation July '97; co-sponsored motion urging
use of capital receipts to build 400,000 homes a year "to a minimum standard that guarantees
easy acces for people with disabilities, the elderly and able-bodied alike" Nov '97; urged seeing
cycling "as an important part of an integrated transport system" Dec '97; backed education

action zones Dec '97; backed the Independent Commission on Voting Systems, hoping it would lean toward PR Dec '97; urged a more imaginative approach to teacher recruitment, making it easier both to enter the profession and leave it Feb '98; expressed concern about a Bristol cemetery, housing 40,000 graves - including Indian philosopher Raja Rammohun Roy - threatened by a profiteer May '98; was rated among the 'Bottom 100' having posed only 7 written questions in her first year May '98;

Born: 16 April 1940, Sutton, Surrey

Family: Daughter, of Mr Corbett, much-transferred branch manager for W H Smith; married '66 Graham Davey; 1s, twin d;

Education: Attended three different state primary schools; attended three different state secondary schools; Birmingham University (MA); London University (PGCE);

Occupation: Full-time Councillor '82-; ex-teacher (in Tanzania in the '60s and Wolverhampton in the '70s) (NUT);

Traits: Tall; light brown straight hair; metal-framed specs; snub nose; blue-stocking school-teacher look; "sartorially the model 'New Labour Woman'" (David Hill, OBSERVER); Methodist; a forceful and accomplished speaker, not needing notes; enjoys homely pursuits (gardening, making marmalade); expressed interest in videophones;

Address: House of Commons, Westminster, London SW1A 0AA; 29 Norton Road, Knowle, Bristol BS4 2 EZ;

Telephone: 0171 219 3000 (H of C); 0117 909 3491 (home);

Ian (Graham) DAVIDSON   Labour-Co-op   **GLASGOW-POLLOK '97-**

Majority: 13,791 (42%) over SNP 7-way;

Description: A southwest Glasgow seat, south of the Clyde and its shrunken shipyards; redrawn in '95, it is made up of roughly equal numbers of voters from former Pollok and former Govan, mostly housed in vast council estates blighted by unemployment and crime; it is rated the country's 5th most unhealthy constituency; Militant activity by Councillor Tommy Sheridan is strong in Pollokshields;

Former Seat: Glasgow-Govan '92-97

Position: On Committee of Selection '97-; Chairman: MSF Group '97-; Vice Chairman: PLP Aerospace Committee '93-, PLP Defence Committee '97-, Co-op Group '97-, all-party Warm Homes Group '97-; Secretary: PLP Trade Union Group '97-, Tribune Group '97-; ex: on Parliamentary Panel on Private Legislation '93-97; Strathclyde Regional Councillor (Chairman, Education Committee '86-92) '78-92; Convenor of COSLA Education Committee '90-92; Convener, of Scottish Joint National Committee on Teachers' Salaries '90-92; Glasgow Chairman of Labour Co-Ordinating Committee '78-89; President, Jordanhill Students Association '75-76; Chairman, National Organisation of Labour Students '73-74;

Outlook: Sharp-tongued Leftwinger, "quick and cutting in debate" (SCOTSMAN); an emerging Scots critic of Blairism who sought unsuccessfully to contest the Scottish Parliament; the SCOTSMAN once thought "his prominent role as Strathclyde's Education Chairman, embroiled in school closures, disagreements with the Catholic Church, and concern about crumbling classrooms" was "of dubious value to his ['92] campaign" although it established local credibility; he can simultaneously back more Royal Navy spending in local Clydeside shipyards and Bennite proposals to cut Defence spending; reflects the strong feelings of decent working-class people terrorised by teenage criminals in his council estates; a Euro-sceptic who worked for MEP Janey Buchan;

History: He was first politicised by Liberal teacher Isabel Hilton at Galashiels Academy; he joined the Labour Party '68; was elected Chairman of National Organisation of Labour Students '73; led student teachers in a protest against Strathclyde over job cuts '76; was elected to Strathclyde Regional Council May '78; with Mike Watson was considered a possible candidate to take on Militant in Provan and Pollok Dec '84; became Chairman of Strathclyde's Education Committtee, thus heading the largest education authority in western Europe '86; was considered a possible candidate for Govan by-election caused by Bruce Millan's departure for Brussels but was pipped by Bob Gillespie, who was then destroyed by Jim Sillars Sep '88; was selected for Govan, with the task of ousting Jim Sillars, the SNP's top street-fighter Apr '90; an EIS (Scottish teachers' union) official predicted that he could face industrial trouble "unless he learns to bite his bloody tongue" May '90; said the debate on Scottish self-government had a low priority among all but the young, who increasingly took home rule for granted Dec '91; as Chairman of Strathclyde's Education Committee, made a deal with nearby Health Care International to keep open half-empty Dalmuir School with HCI paying for space to provide staff childcare there Feb '92; despite having many Catholic voters in the constituency, said he still supported David Steel's 1967 Abortion Act and deplored "those who seek to use religious affiliation as a means of gathering support; they are divisive"; he was in favour of integrated schools, with the consent of the Catholic community, while his SNP opponent, Jim Sillars, backed the survival of Catholic schools; the local Catholic paper FLOURISH, urged Catholic voters to oppose Labour Mar '92; recaptured Govan by a majority of 4,125, ousting Jim Sillars (as Labour had also done in old Govan to Sillars' wife Margo Macdonald, also a by-election winner) Apr '92; his deal with Health Care International was reversed at an Education Committee meeting he could not attend Apr '92; was accused of having used, on behalf of Strathclyde, the "tactics of bullying non-negotiation" in his previous relations with Educational Institute of Scotland by its General Secretary James Martin June '92; voted for John Smith for Leader, Bryan Gould for Deputy Leader July '92; wrote that the Labour-separatist organisation 'Scotland United' was leading up a "dead end" and contained the seeds of a breakaway party like 'Scottish Labour' set up by the then Labour MP Jim Sillars in the '70s Sep '92; in witty Maiden urged the expansion of Govan to include Pollok and Eastwood; spoke highly of Jim Sillars Oct '92; on returning from Belize, asked about Government's commitment to keeping Belize independent of Guatemala; also complained about misfiring SA80s with which the 45 Commando there was armed Oct '92; said Labour wanted "efficiency, effectiveness and economy" in public services Nov '92; complained that delegation of power to trusts and agencies gave their chief executives the right to site their offices and decide on staff rewards, which might work against dispersal and pay policies Nov '92; complained that the Government had not published the Quayle Munro report into Scottish water and sewerage, warning that Scots were being alienated from the political process over centralisation of power in the Scottish Office and Conservative-dominated quangos Dec '92; complained that he had received a letter from the Scottish Secretary congratulating him on higher payments for non-existent hill farmers in his urban constituency Feb '93; voted against 3rd Reading of Maastricht Bill Mar '93; voted for referendum on Maastricht Apr '93; said, "I was brought up in an area in which many Rugby Union players went on to play Rugby League; it always struck me as extremely unfair that those players, when they reached the end of their League playing days, were not allowed to return to Rugby Union to put something back in the game as coaches" Apr '93; expressed fears that National Lottery "will be raised from those who can afford it least to be spent on those who can afford it most"; its money might be spent instead of state funds instead of as additional to state funds; feared Lottery would result in job losses among those employed by the pools in his constituency; urged guarantees that new lottery jobs would go to them; voted against National Lottery Bill Apr '93; urged a thorough defence review to see what defence objectives the British economy could afford; suggested that the fourth Trident submarine did not have to be fully commissioned May '93; congratulated Prime Minister for sacking Chancellor Lamont and invited him to Govan to "tell the people there that he will sack any Minister who proposes a drastic reduction in the already inadequate level of invalidity benefit" June '93; urged a debate on the qualifications of those manning outdoor pursuit centres, such as that in Lyme Regis where lives were lost July '93; was named a member of the Parliamentary Panel to act as Commissioners to act under the Private Legislation Procedure (Scotland) Act 1936, Nov '93; voted for Keep Sunday Special Option Dec '93; in Boundary Commission recommendations for Glasgow, his seat would lose Hillington, Cardonald and Mosspark to Pollok, while gaining Pollokshields and Langside from Pollok; this would provide an increased Tory vote, while leaving Govan safe for Labour; since Mike Watson's Glasgow Central would disappear, he was expected to contest the new Govan and Davidson (and Jimmy Dunnachie) the new Pollok Nov '93; voted against restoring capital punishment, even for killing policemen Feb '94; voted to reduce age of homosexual consent to 18 or 16, Feb '94; asked about GPs' ability to discriminate against elderly patients Apr '94; protested that the new local government boundaries for Scotland would cut up educational catchment areas; the new small areas would be unable to maintain many services and have to waste money on three layers of bureaucracy May '94; urged payment for new elected councillors May '94; voted for John Prescott for Leader and Deputy Leader July '94; complained: that legal system could not cope with "marauding" local youth gangs, also about reoffending by teenage criminals while awaiting trial; for them he urged conditional bail or curfew, also eviction of drug dealer from council estates Feb '95; complained of unfair competition from heavily-subsidised Korean and German shipbuilders May '95; visited South Africa on Parliamentary Rugby Tour, funded partly by Turnbull Associates and British Aerospace May '95; after constituency boundary changes, opted to contest new Pollok, made up half of his old Govan, agreeing to let old Pollok's MP, Mike Watson, to have a free run in new Govan; accused Labour MP George Galloway of stirring up racial tension against his friend Mike Watson in support of Mohammad Sarwar Aug '95; again urged Government to ensure flow of Royal Navy orders to Clydeside shipbuilders Oct '95, but backed Tony Benn amendment to Defence Estimates urging Trident-scrapping and reduction of spending to West European average Dec '95; visited Cayman Islands at invitation of its government Feb '96; voted against Tory Eurosceptic Iain Duncan-Smith's Bill to remove UK from jurisdiction of European Court Apr '96; said he would be willing to contest the Scottish Parliament May '96; was Mike Watson's campaign manager in failed selection contest for new Govan May-June '96; voted against 3% cap on MPs' pay rise, in favour of a cut in mileage allowances and a pension based on £43,000, a £9,000 increase July '96; was named one of "Blair's Bastards" by Hull University researchers for having voted 20 times against the party leadership since '92, Sep '96; again complained of delays in trying violent local criminals and drug-pushers; backed tagging of under-16 offenders Nov '96; tried to stiffen the Tory Government's Crime and Punishment (Scotland) Bill which, he alleged, could lead to releasing housebreakers back into the community Jan '97; complained about threats to his canvassers from Sheridan's Militant supporters Apr '97; was re-elected for very much altered and renamed seat by an enhanced majority of 13,791 on a notional swing of 8.9% from the SNP; the Militant vote also declined May '97; was named to the Committee on Selection June '97; voted to ban fox-hunting June '97; visited South Africa on Rugby tour, funded by Virgin Airways, Travel Unlimited, Sealink

(South Africa) and Power Construction June '97; as Secretary of the soft-Left Tribune Group, wrote to new Mps: "I have checked with the Chief Whip's office and membership will not blight your career" Nov '97; welcomed the Scotland Bill as "excellent" but felt the Scottish Parliament should be built in Glasgow and deplored the varying size of constituencies and tagged the second-class regional list as "freeloaders"; repeated his intention of contesting the Scottish Parliament for the Co-operative Party Jan '98; as Secretary of the PLP's Trade Union Group, seemed reassured by Margaret Beckett about Government's alleged backtracking on its election pledge to restore trade union recognition, saying "there is going to be a dialogue" Feb '98; warned Government against exploiting the "gut loyalty" of local Labour authorities by delaying housing improvement money Feb '98; accused the Conservatives of trying to "stir up religious feeling for party advantage" by urging the transfer of control of abortion to the Scottish Parliament (where Catholics would be strongly represented among West of Scotland Labour people) Mar '98; won enough nominations to contest new-look NEC June '98; with Dennis Canavan protested their being barred from contesting Scottish Parliament by Blairite panel June '98;

Born: 8 September 1950, Jedburgh

Family: Son, Graham Davidson, dental mechanic, and Elizabeth (Crowe); m '78 Morag (Mackinnon); 1s Colin '83, 1d Christine '79;

Education: Jedburgh Grammar School; Galashiels Academy; Edinburgh University (MA Hons); Jordanhill College (Teacher's Qualification);

Occupation: Parliamentary Adviser, to Association of University Teachers (unpaid) '97-; has had occasional staff support from MSF; ex: Sponsored, by Scottish Co-operative Party (who paid more than 25% of his '92 election expenses)'90-95; ex: Consultant in Voluntary Services (MSF) '85-92; Chairman, of Govan Initiative (economic regeneration) '88-92; PA/Researcher, MEP Janey Buchan '78-85; NOLS Organiser '77-78;

Traits: Tall; dark; shiny dome; moustache; outspoken (especially in Glasgow); witty (congratulated Ken Maginnis as "a front row forward who can actually write in sentences"); enjoys Rugby ("a leading light of the Parliamentary men's XV" - DAILY TELEGRAPH), running and swimming (took first prize in '96 contest with Tory MPs);

Address: House of Commons, Westminster, London SW1A 0AA;

Telephone: 0171 219 3610 (H of C); 0141 946 3887 (home);

Rt Hon (David John) Denzil DAVIES   **Labour**   **LLANELLI '70-**

Majority: 16,039 (38.9%) over Plaid Cymru 5-way;

Description: Farming, tinplate, formerly anthracite and the golden sands of Pembrey; in '95 it lost 5,500 voters to Carmarthen East and Dinefwr;

Position: Ex: on Public Accounts Committee '91-97, '74; on Shadow Cabinet '84-88; Spokesman on Defence '84-88, Deputy Spokesman '82-83, '83-84; Spokesman on Wales '83; Deputy Spokesman: on Foreign and Commonwealth Affairs '81-82, Treasury '79-81; Minister of State, Treasury '75-79; PPS to John Morris '74-75; on Select Committees on: Public Accounts '74; European Secondary Legislation '74-75; Wealth Tax '74-75, Delegated Legislation '72; Chairman, Welsh Labour MPs '82-83;

Outlook: The brilliant, witty, Welsh Keynesian politician-barrister who represents the mating of Bill Cash and Tam Dalyell; has recently manned the rampart against Euro-centralism, even making a kamikaze effort to enter the Labour leadership campaign to highlight this danger; as the 'Welsh Tam Dalyell' led opposition to devolution to a Welsh Assembly for economic reasons rather than linguistic; he is Welsh-speaking and the WESTERN MAIL initially said that "of the younger South Wales Labour MPs, Mr Davies is probably the most sympathetic to Welsh aspirations"; he insists that Wales' 15% deficit makes devolution unreal; "one of the cleverest backbenchers" but "a loner with a self-destructive streak" (Michael White, GUARDIAN); in fact, he operates in tandem with his personal-political friend, Merthyr Tydfil's MP Ted Rowlands, also a former Minister; as Treasury's former Minister of State, Denzil has opposed entrenching the deflation implicit in the Maastricht treaty: "sometimes it is necessary to trade inflation against unemployment; sometimes it is necessary to realign the currency either upwards or downwards to protect industrial capacity" (DD); "his intellectual distinction is recognised" ('Smallweed', GUARDIAN); "when he was Tony Blair's age, Mr Davies had everything going for him" as "among the brilliant politicians of his generation"; "even now his grasp of detail is infinitely superior to the average MP's, as he demonstrated during his dogged opposition to the Maastricht Treaty" (Andy McSmith, OBSERVER); his Ministerial experience will remain behind him so long as Labour is led by pro-Europeans; one of the last of Labour's able ex-Ministers; a realistic, undoctrinaire, sensible Left, high-flying 'kamikaze' who threw in his job as Defence Spokesman in '88 when Neil Kinnock again neglected to consult him; a talent for understanding economic complexities and presenting them effortlessly; until his sudden resignation in '88 could "claim to have achieved a remarkable amount inside the party to help it unite around an agreed [multilateralist] policy" (Peter Kellner, NEW STATESMAN); was a pragmatic opponent of nuclear weapons and proponent of conventional defence without having been a unilateralist; had much more Parliamentary support than in the party at large;

History: His blacksmith father "was a strong trade unionist, a lifetime member of the TGWU" which tried to secure compensation for his blindness; Denzil joined Labour Party at 18, '56; "I tried to play a little part" in Megan Lloyd George's Carmarthen by-election "mainly by tearing down Liberal posters" Feb '57; he was involved in Labour politics at Oxford; was selected for Llanelli as Jim Griffiths' successor '69, elected June '70; resisted transfer of gunnery range from Shoeburyness to Pembrey Aug '70; published anti-EEC pamphlet with John Morris, Neil Kinnock, Brynmor John, Elystan Morgan Sep '71; opposed Llanelli Rugby Club's tour of South Africa May '72; urged EEC regional aid for Wales Apr '73; refused to attend constituency dinner for British Lions, just back from South African tour Aug '74; argued against staying in EEC May '75; was only backbencher to be promoted, to Minister of State at Treasury June '75; urged more investment in industry, curbing of less-productive Government expenditure Feb '76; expressed reservations about Labour's plan for import controls or surcharges Feb '76; opposed nationalisation of building societies Mar '77; at 39 was promoted youngest Privy Councillor Jan '78; attacked EEC's disproportionate spending on farm surpluses Apr '78; opposed Tories' forced direction of pension funds Dec '78; opposed increase of VAT to 15% July '79; derided enterprise zones as "pathetic" while industry was declining June '80; insisted next Labour Government should regulate pension funds May '80; insisted local councils should buy British July '80; named by Michael Foot to deal specifically with the EEC, said Treaty of Rome was unsuitable for UK Dec '80; attempted to save local Dupont steelworks Mar '81; defended BBC Overseas Service against cuts Oct '81; as Deputy Defence Spokesman warned that Trident purchase would cripple conventional defences Feb '82; claimed that if Argentina had waited a few months UK would not have had an RN task force for the Falklands, with 'HMS Hermes' in the knackers yard and 'HMS Invincible' on its way to Australia Apr '82; was granted Freedom of Gibraltar for his efforts to secure British citizenship for its inhabitants Oct '82; was promoted Shadow Welsh Secretary by Michael Foot Apr '83; after Callaghan's attack on Labour's unilateralist election plank, he described former PM as "confused" and Polaris as "clapped out" May '83; contested Shadow Cabinet, though on neither Tribune Group nor Campaign Group ticket July '83; entered campaign for Deputy Leadership as a Silkin-backed non-factional "anti-ticket" candidate July '83, securing a derisory 3.525% of vote Oct '83; was restored as Deputy Spokesman on Defence Nov '83; after asking about discrepancies in the sightings of the 'Belgrano', received concocted answers, falsified with the help of Clive Ponting; elicited the admission that 'Belgrano' was sighted a day earlier than previously claimed Mar-Apr '84; insisted it was "criminally irresponsible" to put Cruise missiles on land in densely populated parts of the country May '84; received 40,000 votes for Labour's NEC Sep '84; elected to the Shadow Cabinet in twelfth position with 81 votes, was named chief Defence Spokesman Oct '84; suggested that the logbook of 'HMS Conqueror', the sub that sank the 'Belgrano', had been "lost" because it was "embarrassing" Nov '84; described as "scandalous" the appointment of Peter Levene (head of United Scientific Holdings, a big defence contractor) as Chief of Defence Procurement Dec '84; scored heavily, with a "clever forensic performance" (John Hunt, FINANCIAL TIMES) when he charged the Government with concealing and distorting information about the 'Belgrano' in arguments over disclosures by Clive Ponting (whom he refused to see because he did not "condone breaches of trust by civil servants or by Ministers") Feb '85; when Michael Heseltine announced the privatising of Devonport and Rosyth naval dockyards, he asked whether the nation's defence would be handed over to Securicor Apr '85; demanded a debate on sweeping secret emergency powers, including the handing over of military and civil resources to the US in time of crisis Sep '85; received 75,000 votes for Labour's NEC Sep '85; in the debate in which withdrawal from NATO was defeated, he committed Labour to a stronger conventional defence within NATO and said Labour would send back all Cruise missiles Oct '85; although not backed by either the Tribune Group or Campaign Group, he was re-elected to the Shadow Cabinet in thirteenth position with 90 votes Oct '85; after the collapse of the Cyprus secrets trial, he asked about the methods use to try to extract confessions "from those young and inexperienced airmen" Oct '85; claimed US Defence Secretary Caspar Weinberger had duped Defence Secretary Michael Heseltine to secure endorsement of 'Star Wars' Dec '85; attacked the Bill to commercialise the management of the naval dockyards as one of the most ill-prepared and irresponsible ever, providing an agency system more suitable for a fast-food establishment Dec '85; attacked US efforts to produce a new generation of nerve gases Apr '86; angered the hard Left by confirming "that the money saved by cancelling Trident should be used for non-nuclear defence" July '86; received 78,000 votes for Labour's National Executive Sep '86; warned Labour Conference the party would have to unite behind its moderate non-nuclear defence policy or risk failing Oct '86; said that the Reykjavik Summit should never have broken down over 'Star Wars' Oct '86; after an excellent interview on 'Weekend World' he was re-elected to Shadow Cabinet in third position with 102 votes Oct '86; said that, under a Labour Government, Britain would remain in NATO even if NATO retained its nuclear umbrella strategy Oct '86; opposed the scrapping of Nimrod for its Boeing competitor Dec '86; claimed the NATO doctrine of "flexible response" was "completely incredible and completely out of date" Jan '87; said Labour would not discourage British firms from contracting for 'Star Wars', even if Labour did not approve of the project Mar '87; agreed with Kinnock that a Labour Government would delay the removal of US Cruise missiles from Britain pending the outcome of East-West talks Mar '87; complained about the "appalling state" of RAF air defences resulting from spending on the "nuclear obsession" Apr '87; enthused about the 'zero option' as a more constructive choice for NATO May '87; increased his general election majority by 7,000 votes June '87; was re-elected to Shadow Cabinet in sixth place with 111 votes July '87; wanted to be Foreign Affairs Spokesman; turned down three jobs (Wales, shadow Commons Leader, shadow Chief Secretary) before Kinnock renamed him Defence Spokesman July '87; as a former Treasury Minister he was named to Labour's committee to revise its economic policies July '87; CND vetoed his two preferred non-unilateralist Deputy Spokesmen: John McWilliam and Allan Rogers July '87; received 65,000 votes for Labour's National Executive Sep '87; in the Defence debate, ridiculed the idea of Trident being "an independent deterrent": "what we are buying is access to a common pool of missiles, all owned by the United States" Oct '87; resigned in the middle of the night in a telephone call to Chris Moncrieff of Press Association, saying he was "fed up with being humiliated", because Kinnock had again made changes "on the hoof" in Labour's defence policy without consultation, "and he is supposed to be a future Prime Minister"; Kinnock, attributed this reaction to "deep personal stress" - the break-up of Denzil's marriage June '88; abstained from supporting Kinnock in Leadership election Oct '88; had the second worst Parliamentary vote record, after blind and ailing David Blunkett, ranking 609th in the previous 17 months Oct '88; deplored the catastrophic deterioration of Britain's balance of trade, particularly with the EC Nov '88; in the wake of the SNP's Govan victory, again urged a Welsh Assembly, partly as a counterweight to the over-centralization of Mrs Thatcher Nov '88; was nominated for "Kamikaze of the Year" for his resignation when Kinnock was moving closer to his own non-unilateralist position Dec '88; sought to speed trial in Germany of son of a constituent accused of kidnapping the Lufthansa representative in Bolivia Feb '89; dismissed Labour's front bench criticism of the Government policy: "the Labour Party idea that you should have credit controls is rubbish; there is no way you can control credit except by controlling the price of credit and the price of credit is Bank Rate"; "Mr Lawson was right when he wanted to take Britain fully into the European Monetary System and he is right again to put up interest rates; Mrs Thatcher has got it all wrong; she should support the Chancellor and not try to undermine him; she should just shut up"; blamed the Prime Minister's monetarism for "the highest inflation rate in western Europe", "the worst balance of payments deficit of all the industrialized nations" and "the highest interest rates among all our main industrial competitors" June '89; predicted the reunification of Europe, but warned the radical Right against trying to "push change too fast and propel the countries of eastern Europe towards a kind of Hayekian Rightwing capitalist society"; predicted "German economic domination of the countries to the east of Germany, which we now call eastern Europe" July '89; said: "my constituency and Carmarthen contain at least 50m tons of mineable anthracite reserves; apart from the dwindling pocket of anthracite in the West German coalfield", "there is no anthracite between Llanelli and Poland"; "despite that, and despite the potential markets, British Coal has walked away from anthracite" Dec '89; derided Chancellor Major's first Budget as "timid" Mar 90; was appointed to the Select Committee on the Armed Forces Bill Dec '90; opposed the Cardiff Barrage Feb '91; complained that a third of the industrial jobs in his constituency had gone since 1979, Feb '91; backed the end of capital punishment in the Forces June '91; backed David Shaw's amendment to the Finance Bill to permit allowances for plant and machinery; said he would like higher Corporation Tax with a greater range of allowance for plant and machinery, expecially for manufacturing July '91; opposed entrenching deflation in the Maastricht treaty, because of the need for flexibility to defend employment or industrial capacity; urged Wales to create the technical skills "without which we cannot develop the Welsh economy" Nov '91; decried the "arrogance" of Chancellor Kohl, President Mitterand and Jacques Delors for transferring "forever, economic and monetary power from democratically elected countries to a non-elected [European] Commission and a non-elected [European] Central Bank" Dec '91; was added to the Public Accounts Commitee Dec '91;

there were baseless (EVENING STANARD) reports that a victorious Neil Kinnock would send him to Brussels as a Commissioner Jan '92; insisted Britain's net contribution to the EC would never go down; welcomed the EFTA countries entry Feb '92; retained seat with majority down from 20,935 to 19,270, a swing to Conservative of 1.95% Apr '92; warned Baroness Blackstone that the distinctive British Labour policy she sought would be curbed by Maastricht's pressure for convergence May '92; warned that "once we have completed stage 2" under Maastricht, "the reality will be that we shall have very little option but to sign up for stage 3" - Economic and Monetary Union - which would "entail a massive substantial shift of power over money and our fiscal and economic policy"; attacked Labour's reasoned amendment as providing "no escape and no hiding place" from the longterm impact of Maastricht May '92; was confirmed on the PAC June '92; warned that "Maastricht demands a central bank as the sole controller and arbiter of monetary policy; that has never been the Labour Party"s policy"; "Maastricht demands the pursuit of price stability which in the end can only mean nil inflation at the expense of all other economic goals, including a reduction in unemployment; again, I submit that that has never been my party's policy" July '92; after Britain was expelled from the ERM, said it was "intended, all along, to take the first step along the path to Economic and Monetary Union and, finally, to a federal Europe"; said ERM had failed to "create a zone of monetary stability"; between 1979 and 1990 "the French franc was devalued against the mark by 45%" Sep '92; sought to defend his local anthracite pit, Betws, from being closed despite demand being bigger than supply Oct '92; claimed "the Maastricht treaty is the wrong treaty at the wrong time for Europe, as Europe has developed in the past few years"; "the pursuit of Economic and Monetary Union will intensify the recession throughout western Europe", risking "social cohesion and the social fabric"; "price stability is really the new gold standard"; warned that the Single European Market would be dominated by fewer big companies: "factories will close, jobs will be lost and unemployment will increase" Nov '92; said that Maastricht was another major step toward European union since it would "transfer a substantial amount of democracy from the Parliaments and elected Governments of all 12 countries to non-democratic institutions" Jan '93; was chalked up as having rebelled five times against the Maastricht treaty Bill Feb '93; insisted that the last anthracite mine in his constituency could only be re-opened by private owners, because of the stupidities of electricity privatization Mar '93; criticized the Government for making a deal with the Welsh and Scottish nationalists to get through the Maastricht treaty: "are we now to conclude that for a majority in the modern Conservative Party the European Union takes pride of place over the British Union?" Mar '93; also pointed out that Government borrowing was £50b (or 8%), when the Maastricht treaty would only allow 3%; pointed out that Britain had a £13b deficit in manufacturing and £8-9b deficit in food: "we can no longer pay for our food imports by exporting manufactured goods" Apr '93; insisted "the European political class wants European integration without democracy"; voted against 3rd Reading of Maastricht treaty Bill May '93; Ann Clwyd attacked his new wife, Ann Carlton, for denouncing the "harridans" who backed quotas for women in the party's higher echelons Oct '93; urged the creation of more unitary authorities in reforming Welsh local government Nov '93; co-sponsored motion warning against the deflationary character of the convergence provisions in Maastricht Dec '93; in an angry attack on the Child Support Agency, warned that its unfairness "will probably bring down the Government and the Tory Party" Feb '94; voted against restoring capital punishment Feb '94; voted to reduce age of homosexual consent to 18, but not 16, Feb '94; claimed the new Welsh local government reorganization would prove as expensive and unpopular as that of 1972, whose committee stage he had attended; if the Secretary of State wanted to do something for democracy in Wales, he could allow trusts and quangos to be elected Mar '94; claimed that European Union was "a type of superior welfare state for [Europe's] political class" but would add to the 20m already unemployed May '94; unexpectedly threw his hat in the Labour leadership ring, but was only able to raise seven of the 34 sponsors needed; accused Tony Blair of having economic priorities similar to those of John Major June '94; voted for Prescott for Leader, Beckett for Deputy July '94; in adjournment urged licensing of local cockle industry Oct '94; in PAC debate criticised sums spent on installing computers and paying off managers Oct '94; voted against increased payments to EU Nov '94; claimed EU Budget payments would reach £35b by '99, Dec '94; backed referendum on Euro-federalism Feb '95; voted against extending Sunday pub licensing hours Feb '95; claimed the single European currency could lead to break up of UK since Welsh would like Irish-style independent rights June '95; with 9 Leftwing rebels voted against 1p cut in Budget Dec '95; criticised the 408-page length of the Finance Bill Jan '96; helped set up an anti-Euro "People's Europe", claiming 50 MPs' support and predicting 20m unemployed Feb '96; attacked the "authoritarian" European Court of Justice as "a state court which serves an increasingly centralised European state" Mar '96; said his election manifesto would show his opposition to the Euro and the need to reduce spending by £12b to meet Maastricht requirements May '96; urged Blair to "play hard" on the beef ban to persuade the EU to "give in" May '96; voted for Bill Cash's Referendum Bill June '96; voted against 3% cap on MPs' pay rise, for pension based on £43,000 July '96; quoted Ernst & Young prediction of 500,000 more UK job losses under Euro July '96; his pamphlet, 'The Single Currency: Axeing Labour's Programme' claimed cost of Euro would equal closing half the hospital trusts or two-thirds of secondary schools July '96; opposed leadership's plans for loyalty test for centrally-approved list of candidates July '96; was listed as one of "Blair's Bastards" by Hull University researchers for having voted against the leadership 22 times since '92, Sep '96; claimed Euro would represent the surrender of powers to EU's "bankers, bureaucrats and lawyers" Oct '96; attacked the support for the Euro of the "chattering classes who write for pseudo-radical newspapers such as the GUARDIAN and the OBSERVER and who live at the bottom of think tanks" Dec '96; claimed Welsh independence, as advocated by Plaid Cymru, was "economically impossible" because of the £9b or 15% deficit of the Welsh economy Feb '97; was one of the few Labour MPs to oppose joining the Euro in his election address Apr '97; was re-elected for his slightly altered seat with a majority of 16,039, a notional 0.1% swing from Plaid Cymru May '97; attacked the Franco-German "European elite" for wanting to "take democratic power out of the people's hands" June '97; opposed Gordon Brown's handover of interest-rate power to the Bank of England as saying: "I, the Chancellor, am not a man you can trust" June '97; urged the debt of Dyfed-Powis Health Authority be wiped out July '97; attacked the proposed Welsh Assembly for its PR element, and as diminishing the power of the Commons, leading to the "unbundling of the British unitary state" on which Wales was dependent economically July '97; in the Welsh referendum campaign claimed the Welsh Office only pretended the Assembly would dismantle quangos, which required primary legislation Sep '97; attacked Bank of England Bill as warning voters: "do not trust us with your money, we are just politicians" Nov '97; enjoyed himself ridiculing the varying national contributions to the European Union budget Dec '97; complained that part of the Welsh Assembly would be elected by "the worst kind of PR system" Jan '98; warned Plaid MPs that "unbundling the unitary state" too far would make the UK Cabinet into an English Cabinet Feb '98; warned about the changes in the Government of Wales Bill and that its "assymetrical form of decentralisation may create instability" Mar '98; attacked the Euro's launch as marking "a substantial transfer of power from democratic governments and Parliaments to undemocratic, bureaucratic and largely unaccountable institutions", "another step in the march towards a centralised European state" Apr '98; opposed Government's abolition of student maintenance grants and introduction of tuition fees June '98;

Born: 9 October 1938, Conwil Elfed, Carmarthen

Family: S Gareth Davies, "a blacksmith until he was involved in an industrial accident and lost his eyesight" (DD); m 1st '65 Mary Ann (Finlay) of Illinois; dvd Jan '88 - "a particularly stressful divorce" (Nicholas Comfort, DAILY TELEGRAPH); 1s Steven '70, 1d Jane '67; m 2d '89 Ann Carlton, the writer-politico who opposed all-women short-lists as "'wimminest' pottiness" and was savaged by Ann Clwyd for writing against "harridans" who supported quotas for women in the party's higher echelons;

Education: Conwil Elfed Primary; Queen Elizabeth's Grammar School, Carmarthen; Pembroke, Oxford University (first class Hons); Gray's Inn (Bacon Scholar, first class Law degree);

Occupation: Barrister, in London '88-. '66-75 (after a gap of 13 years); Head of Chambers in Goldsworth, Gray's Inn (he denied violence against a woman barrister in an altercation June '98) '97- ex: Lecturer in Law at: University of Chicago '63-64, Leeds University '65-66, East London College of Commerce '6?-6?;

Traits: Dark; greying; forelock; lippy; gangling; "almost languid", "Welsh lilt" (John Hunt, FINANCIAL TIMES); witty; fun-loving; can also be gloomy; self-described as legally "pedantic" and "old-fashioned"; occasionally volatile temperament" (Colin Hughes, INDEPENDENT); "a reputation for waywardness and an inclination to melancholy" (Donald Macintyre, SUNDAY TELEGRAPH); "brooding and impulsive" "a mischievous wit" "saturnine and emotionally Celtic"; "he has a deeply humane side which he prefers not to talk about: when the hysteria over the Thorpe case was at its height", "he took the former Liberal Leader's son into his home to live a normal life away from the glare of publicity" (Nicholas Comfort, DAILY TELEGRAPH); convivial (he won "substantial" damages from Jasper Carrott and the BBC for allegations that he missed a Commons debate because he was drunk); "personable, persuasive" (Terry Campbell, WESTERN MAIL); Welsh-speaking; Calvinistic Methodist; an enthusiastic supporter of Llanelli Rugby Club;

Address: House of Commons, Westminster, London SW1A 0AA; 11 Belsize Square, London NW3;

Telephone: 0171 219 5197 (H of C); 0171 794 3479 (London home); 015542 56374 (constituency);

Geraint (Richard) DAVIES   Labour   **CROYDON CENTRAL '97-**

Majority: 3,897 over Conservative 6-way;

Description: Croydon's skyscraper-dominated commercial and shopping centre, embracing New Addington council estate; Croydon is "the largest London borough" and it "commands one-fifth of the capital's economy" (GD)

Position: On the Public Accounts Committee '97-; Chairman, of PLP's Environment, Transport and the Regions Committee '97-; Croydon Borough Councillor (Leader '96-, previously its Housing Chairman '94-96) '86-;

Outlook: A clever, quick-witted, new loyal Blairite intervener who enjoys being pulled up sharply by the Speaker or Deputy Speaker for calling John Redwood "Mr Deadwood" or referring to Eric Forth as a "rogue Parliamentarian"; "I am a committed supporter of New Labour" (GD); "he will be a real asset to the Labour Whips" (Tory MP Michael Jack); the third-time-lucky Croydon Council Leader who ousted his former council sparring partner, Tory ex-MP David Congdon; one of Labour's few new recruits from the private sector ("my background is in multinational marketing and in running my own small business"); Chairman, of Labour Finance and Industry Group; in Croydon Co-operative Party, SERA;

History: He joined the Labour Party '82; became Assistant Secretary of the Croydon North East CLP '83; was elected to the Executive of the Croydon Central CLP Feb '84; was elected to Croydon Council for New Addington May '86; contested the very safe Tory seat of Croydon South against Sir William Clark, coming 3rd with 10%, having increased the Labour vote by a third June '87; fought Croydon Central against Sir Paul Beresford, increasing Labour's vote from 9,516 to 12,518, largely at the expense of the Alliance Apr '92; became Chairman of Housing of Croydon Council when Labour secured a majority May '94; was re-selected to contest Croydon Central, expected to provide a Conservative majority of 15,500 on '92 projections '95; denied TIMES report that his emergence as Leader of Croydon Council represented a "Leftwing takeover" May '96; won Croydon Central by 3,897 over former Tory MP David Congdon, on a notional swing of 15.48% to Labour May '97; in his Maiden, apart from enthusing about Gordon Brown's masterly Budget, boasted about the regeneration of Croydon as "an emerging European city" with its new cultural centres and tram system in whose creation he had participated as Council Leader June '97; defended Labour's plan for London's restructuring Nov '97; referred to John Redwood as "Mr Deadwood" until corrected by the Deputy Speaker Dec '97; defended better funding for London Underground after Tory years of underfunding Jan '98; backed Government's use of liquid petroleum gas in its car fleet Jan '98; punctured pieties about Northern Ireland by asking about new trams in Croydon Apr '98; said money markets saw Sterling at 2.7 to the Deutschmark/Euro in five years time May '98;

Born: 3 May 1960, Dorking, Surrey

Family: Son of David Thomas Morgan Davies, senior civil servant, and Betty (Ferrer); m '93 Dr Vanessa (Fry); 2d Angharad Mair '94, Meirian Sian '97;

Education: Birchgrove Junior School (where Ted Rowlands MP gave him an Investiture Mug in '69); Llanishen Comprehensive, Cardiff; Jesus College, Oxford University (MA PPE);

Occupation: Tour Operator: Managing Partner, Pure Crete (specialist green travel company) and Managing Director, Pure Aviation Ltd (GMB) '90-; previously Marketing Manager, Colgate Palmolive Ltd and Unilever (MSF) til '82;

Traits: Balding; broad face; broad retreating forehead; thin face; small mouth; intelligent; quick-witted; articulate; Cardiff-educated; refers to small prompt cards; overuses "holistic" and "really"; enjoys partisan politics, hill-walking, particularly in Wales, and community singing; a former Boy Scout, used his remembered skills to save a life by mouth-to-mouth rescuscitation and heart massage in Mumbles July '98;

Address: House of Commons, Westminster, London SW1A 0AA;

Telephone: 0171 219 4599/5962 (Fax) (H of C); 0181 680 5877 (home); 0181 680 5833/688 9951 (Fax) (constituency);

These profiles show our monitoring is top-notch; check with us on 0171 222 5884.

Majority: 2,692 (5.1%) over Labour 7-way;

Description: A new seat, created in '95 in southwest Lincolnshire, with just over half its voters from his former Stamford and Spalding and the rest from former Spalding; prosperous, industrialised, ancient Stamford is "the loveliest stone town in England" (JQD);

Former Seat: Stamford & Spalding '87-97

Position: Deputy Spokesman, on Social Security '98-; Vice Chairman, of European Movement '95-; ex: on Select Committees: on Standards and Privileges '95-98, Treasury '97-98; Treasury and Civil Service Select Committee '92-97; Secretary: Conservative MPs' Finance Committee '92-93, Trade and Industry Committee '92-93; PPS, to Angela Rumbold '88-91; Vice Chairman, Positive Europe Group '93-98; Secretary to the Macleod Group '92-97; Chairman, 'City in Europe' Committee '75, Treasurer, Cambridge University Conservative Association '65;

Outlook: Sophisticated, well-informed, rich, normally loyal, ambitious Rightwing financial adviser and former merchant banker and diplomat; formerly a "dedicated workhorse...worth every last penny of his [former] £34,085 pay" (Anthony Bevins, INDEPENDENT); "a cat that walks alone" (Edward Pearce, EXPRESS); was 'Backbencher of the Year' (SPECTATOR) until he belatedly reached the front bench in '98; his resumption of undiluted Labour-bashing in Opposition won him entry to the the Hague front bench in '98, while other pro-Europeans decamped; a highly-knowledgeable economist with a remarkable ability to speak lengthily without notes, albeit tinged with arrogant superiority; "enjoys a repertory of technical tax knowledge which he deploys in a fashion as unamiable as his social contempt, which is of the accentuated or minor public school kind" (Edward Pearce, HOUSE MAGAZINE); a pro-European (in Positive Europe Group, Vice Chairman of European Movement); "I was a great admirer of Margaret Thatcher, but I was very disappointed by her Bruges speech which was a terrible shock to me"; "it always seemed to me the European Union is the natural framework for the completion of the Thatcherite revolution" (JQD); "I am very much a 'One Nation' Conservative; our task is not just to defend the interests of the successful" (JQD); backed the Leadership bids of pro-Europeans Heseltine in '90 and Clarke in '97; was "regarded by contemporaries as being [one of the two] most openly ambitious of their ['87] intake" (Peter Riddell, FINANCIAL TIMES); was little noticed outside until his herdsman allowed a flock of sheep to starve in '91; until '96 "he... pandered to the Whips' every whim...always toed the party line" (Alice Thomson, TIMES); he surprised his colleagues in '96 when he "seized on the Scott Inquiry to carve himself a niche as the official conscience of the Conservative Party" (Jon Hibbs, DAILY TELEGRAPH); he turned savagely on promoted colleague David Willetts, rejecting his casuistry in nobbling the Chairman of the Members' Interests Select Committee; colleagues blamed it on frustrated ambition; opponents were more charitable: "like a ferret down a rat hole", "once he is convinced of a case intellectually, nothing will sway him from it" (Labour MP Diane Abbott, former colleague on the Treasury Select Committee); his "ability to speak without notes on any subject for any length of time the Whips care to allot him is unparallleled" (Labour Minister Alistair Darling); "intellectually overwound" (Godfrey Barker, DAILY TELEGRAPH); "I have always been in favour of capital punishment for premeditated and unprovoked murder" (JQD); ardent free-tripper, the favourite on the

German circuit;

History: "My father used to vote Labour and my mother has always voted Conservative; my father's political roots were in the 1930s when he had gone to Oxford and was very much influenced by the climate of opinion there; he was a strong suporter of Attlee and Bevin and he always thought the welfare state was a wonderful thing" (JQD); Quentin himself was elected Treasurer of Cambridge University Conservative Association '65; became Chairman of 'City in Europe' Committee (in 1975 Referendum campaign) May-June '75; fought the Ladywood, Birmingham, by-election after Brian Walden opted for TV; said the area had been "disgracefully neglected" by Labour because it was considered a safe seat; "socialism has knocked on the head the small businesses of 100 to 200 men in which Birmingham abounds, while it protects the ICIs of this world and it has made many people feel fools for going to work when they could make as much at home on social security; it has insulted people's intelligence over inflation, undermanned the police by refusing them proper pay and made Ladywood a place where many people are unable to go out at night"; he said he was "quietly confident" of winning but lost by 3,825 votes, 28.4% of the vote; blamed his defeat partly on violence three nights before the by-election Aug '77; was selected to fight Stamford and Spalding, where Sir Kenneth Lewis was retiring, Mar '86; won with a 2,000 larger majority June '87; in his Maiden he insisted: "it is not macro-economic demand deficiency, but supply-side deficiencies from which we suffer"; also "restrictive practices and artificial obstacles to the growth of productivity" July '87; welcomed the pension provisions of the Finance Bill because "it is pernicious to discriminate against early leavers" - of which he had been one July '87; insisted that the Government deserved "the wholehearted appreciation both of the House and of the general public" in the exercise of their judgment to launch the sale of BP shares and that "the main problem with the underwriters is that the foreign underwriters have not underwritten their commitment to BP with investing institutions" Oct '87; urged Western collaboration to aid the Afghan rebels, unless the Russians withdrew Dec '87; voted against the Alton Bill to curb abortions Jan '88; blamed regional disparities of employment and prosperity on national pay bargaining Feb '88; was greeted by a storm of Opposition jeers when he criticised the reluctance of TV news organisations to make their Northern Ireland films automatically available to the police, for fear of their crews' safety; he said: "there is no more fundamental duty for any citizen than to contribute to the maintenance of law and order and to do everything possible to prevent crime, particularly violent crime and murder" Mar '88; became PPS to Angela Rumbold, then Minister of State for Education Oct '88; introduced Bill to allow contingent fees for lawyers Oct '88; told Chancellor Lawson he was "superb" Nov '88; the Adam Smith Institute rated him as tied with Eric Forth for the most freedom-loving MP, having voted for the most free-market measures in 1987-88, Apr '89; voted against personal identity numbers Apr '89; visited Italy as guest of Konrad Adenauer Foundation Sep '89; expressed pro-ERM views Oct '89; visited South Africa as a guest of its government Nov '89; after unpleasantly interrupting Merlyn Rees, and calling for all war crimes to be punished, voted against War Crimes Bill aimed at aged Baltic immigrants Dec '89; condemned Iran for its anti-Rushdie fatwa Feb '90; voted against punishing Tory MP John Browne for concealing his interests Mar '90; urged a "tough budget" Mar '90; complained about low-flying RAF planes in his constituency May '90; visited USA as guest of US Information Agency Sep '90; backed Michael Heseltine in the Leadership contest Nov '90; urged the Government not to be left out if the EC opted for a single currency Jan '91; with Margaret Ewing and Paul Flynn, visited Lithuania, Latvia and Esthonia, with fare paid from public funds, but local hospitality provided by the three countries; encouraged them to "expand the area of their de facto independence"; according to Flynn he challenged a Soviet soldier to "go home" (in Russian) Mar '91; claimed Labour's demand for a training tax was wasteful, as he had discovered in running a Morgan Grenfell subsidiary in France; under compulsion he had spent money on training people in Spanish and knitting Apr '91; opposed a statutory minimum wage as leading to "higher inflation, higher unemployment or a mixture of the two" July '91; participated in conference in Germany and Czechoslovakia as guest of the Konrad Adenauer Foundation Sep '91; was fined £1,500 after half the lambs on his estate died from underfeeding by a herdsman Oct '91; Labour MP John Home Robertson said he "seems to want to treat the workforce of the United Kingdom in the same way as he treats his sheep" Dec '91; claimed the Social Chapter would cost BR and NHS £500m a year each Jan '92; participated in a Moscow conference as guest of Konrad Adenauer Foundation Jan '92; an OBSERVER study rated him the 10th least "green" MP Mar '92; retained seat with majority up from 13,991 to 22,869, despite a swing to Labour of 3.23%, because of a LibDem collapse Apr '92; described Mrs Thatcher's opposition to Maastricht as "more than a little perverse" after having pushed through the Single European Act June '92; was named to Treasury and Civil Service Select Committee July '92; rebelled by voting to increase MPs' office allowance by £11,000 July '92; participated in conference in Italy as guest of Konrad Adenauer Foundation Sep '92; opposed draft Euthanasia Bill Sep '92; Labour jeers greeted his admiration of Chancellor Lamont on the Treasury Select Committee Oct '92; participated in conference in Italy organised by Konrad Adenauer Foundation Oct '92; expressed doubt that there was "a genuinely competitive market in banking" Nov '92; participated in conference in Bonn organized by Konrad Adenauer Foundation Nov '92; participated in conference in Spain organized by Spanish-British Tertulia Nov '92; participated in conference in Versailles organised by Franco-British Colloque Dec '92; joined the Positive Europe Group Jan '93; denounced the press's bugging, long-range photography and theft of letters as comparable to the "operations of secret police in totalitarian societies" Jan '93; opposed Treasury help for BCCI victims because it would damage financial market integrity Feb '93; claimed social costs had reached "at least 50% of the cost of labour" in the EC Apr '93; congratulated Chancellor Lamont for his "courageous" Budget and having survived "a sustained and often malicious campaign of abuse" (a month before Lamont was sacked) Apr '93; insisted the ERM crisis was not terminal because "governments, in practice never have allowed free floating" and a fixed or single currency would only come after a "high degree of convergence" Apr '93; participated in conference in Belgium as guest of Hans Seidl Foundation May '93; when he described the US-dominated International Monetary Fund as "the ultimate independent, depoliticised monetary institution" in interrogating Lord (Denis) Healey, Lord Healey dismissively retorted: "anyone who thinks the the IMF is an independent body needs his head examining" July '93; urged effective air-to-surface missiles for Eurofighter 2000 July '93; participated in conference in Estonia as guest of Ko nrad Adenauer Foundation Sep '93; participated in conference in Italy as guest of Konrad Adenauer Foundation Oct '93; was named to European Standing Committee B and First Standing Committee on Statutory Instrumens Nov '93; urged caution in future rate cuts Jan '94; co-sponsored Nicholas Budgen's Bill to give Bank of England more independence Jan '94; served as election observer in Russia Jan '94; voted to restore capital punishment Feb '94; voted to reduce the age of homosexual consent to 18, but not 16, Feb '94; visited Copenhagen as guest of Unibank May '94; urged "greater transparency" in Europe May '94; protested the withdrawal plans for a new Stamford bypass July '94; urged interest rates be raied "sooner rather than later" July '94; praised Jopling procedural reforms but opposed plans to curtail late-night sittings and time-limiting of speeches and increasing reliance on statutory instruments Dec '94; dubbed Serbian taking of British UN troops an "act of war" Dec '94; opposed talks with criminal-supporting Sinn Fein or amnesties for those charged or convicted of serious crimes Dec '94; was dubbed by OBSERVER "Westminster's most widely-travelled backbencher" with a free trip every other month since '92, seven of them for the CDU-linked

Konrad Adenauer Foundation Jan '95; hailing UK's economic recovery, denied it stemmed from devaluation on leaving the ERM Jan '95; voted against extension of Sunday pub licensing hours Feb '95; queried Cabinet Secretary Sir Robin Butler's admission to only limited enquiries into Neil Hamilton's links with Mohammed al-Fayed whereas PM Major had claimed Hamilton was cleared by an investigation Mar '95; urged Chancellor Clarke to cut taxes "at the end of this year and for a number of years to come" Apr '95; said he had "some hesitation about publishing the financial earnings of MPs derived from activities relating in some way to advice on politics or on Parliament" and that "the amount of remuneration is not especially material" May '95; was named to the Select Committee on Standards and Privileges June '95; praised PM Major for securing release of Bosnian hostage troops June '95; expressed his fear of a Eurosceptic takeover of the Conservative Party July '95; criticised the Bank of England report on collapse of Barings for not having any input from rogue trader Nick Leeson Aug '95; was thrice a guest of Konrad Adenauer Foundation in Italy and Brussels Sep, Oct '95; after the redrawing of Lincolnshire seats, he was selected for new Grantham and Stamford Sep '95; attended Barcelona conference half-paid for by Centre for Economic Policy Research Nov '95; warned that ban on free-tripping would "ensure that the only people who speak...are ignorant" Dec '95; within a few days of the announcement of a campaign against the Tory ultra-Right by the 'Macleod Group' of Centre-Left MPs, including a Euro-federalist pamphlet by him, it was shelved at the instigation of party Chairman Brian Mawhinney's aide, Michael Mates; Mates complained that Davies' pamphlet would play the same game as Portillo's supporters Jan '96; complained that Baroness Thatcher had not done "her homework" in calling for more spending cuts Jan '96; introduced Journalistic Corrupt Practices Bill to ban chequebook journalism Feb '96; in the SUNDAY EXPRESS said he would probably vote against the Government on the Scott Report Feb '96; on 'Breakfast with Frost' alleged the Government had misled MPs over arms-for-Iraq Feb '96; having urged William Waldegrave to resign, his own rebellion, supported by Richard Shepherd, reduced Government's majority to one at end of Scott Report debate Feb '96; his Euro-federalist pamphlet urging economic, foreign and defence union was published, on his insistence Mar '96; did German lecture tour financed by British Chamber of Commerce in Germany and the Deutsch-Englische Gesellschaft Mar '96; went to Saudi Arabia on Parliamentary delegation, invited by Majlis-al-Shura Mar '96; attended Koenigswinter conference at Cambridge Mar '96; was named by the OBSERVER as the hardest-working MP on committees, having attended 111 meetings Mar '96; co-wrote TIMES letter with other Tory Europhiles deploring PM Major's European position as "a precarious straddle between opposing positions" Apr '96; the new, more explicit REGISTER of MEMBERS' INTERESTS showed him as having earned up to £41,000 (up to £25,000 from NatWest Securities, up to £15,000 from the Chartered Institute of Taxation) May '96; introduced 2nd Reading of his Journalistic Corrupt Practices Bill citing Rupert Allason's Soviet-style mistreatment by DAILY MIRROR May '96; attacked the accuracy of the Black, Murdoch and Rothermere press on BSE May '96; in TV debate claimed "Bill Cash taking money from [Sir James Goldsmith] the head of another party is like me taking money from Tony Blair" June '96; was accused by Tory Eurosceptics of having put up Chris Mullins to ask PM Major about Cash's taking money from Sir James Goldsmith June '96; urged "de-escalation" of BSE clash with EU June '96; voted against a 3% cap on MPs' pay rise; voted for a pension based on £43,000 and a curb on MPs' mileage allowances July '96; urged a single European currency in the DAILY TELEGRAPH July '96; defending Ken Clarke in the SUNDAY TIMES insisted that "only the mindless or the deliberately self-defeating could want to precipitate the departure of the Chancellor who has presided over so much success" Oct '96; with other Europhile Tories co-wrote letter to TIMES defending EMU Oct '96; savaged Paymaster General David Willetts in cross-examination in Standards and Privileges committee over his "profoundly misleading" "weasel words" describing his 1994 meeting with Sir Geoffrey Johnson-Smith, Chairman of the Members' Interests Select Committee Nov '96; his shocked loyal partisan Tory colleagues nastily attributed his sharpness to his inability to share Willett's promotions Nov '96; denied EMU would threaten "national sovereignty" in OBSERVER article Dec '96; was cited in SUNDAY TIMES as one of Ken Clarke's "suicide squad", likely to resign the Whip if Clarke was forced to quit Dec '96; was listed in DAILY TELEGRAPH as one of 104 Tory candidates backing "wait and see" on the Euro Dec '96; criticised Coopers and Lybrand for not having detected the serious lack of control in Barings Dec '96; was voted 'Personality of the Year' by GUARDIAN readers Jan '97; voted to restore corporal punishment Jan '97; visited Versailles as guest of Franco-British Colloque Jan '97; won Freedom of Information campaign award for his questioning of David Willetts Feb '97; was one of 97 MP-supporters of European Movement's pro-EU campaign Mar '97; introduced Bill against age discrimination Mar '97; was re-elected for redrawn and renamed seat by the reduced majority of 2,692 on a notional swing of 13.3% swing to Labour May '97; attended Amsterdam conference, half-paid by Centre for Economic Policy Research May '97; backed Ken Clarke in Leadership contest May-June '97; was renamed to the Standards and Privileges Select Committee and the renamed Treasury Select Committee June '97; urged the publication of the DTI report on al-Fayed's bid for House of Fraser and the 1987 Guinness bid for Distillers June '97; attended Trilateral Conference in Berlin as local guest of German Foreign Office June '97; was warned over "irrelevance and needless repetition" for his hour-long filibuster on a clause in the Finance Bill July '97; as guest of the Konrad Adenauer Foundation attended Cadenabbia conference Sep '97; attended University of Siena conference at Pontignano Sep '97; said elections were "won and lost on the middle ground of politics" in the Tory conference-fringe GUARDIAN debate Oct '97; at invitation of Konrad Adenauer Foundation, attended Berlin conference on NATO enlargement Oct '97; attacked as a "disgrace" the Standards and Privileges Committee handling of the Neil Hamilton case Nov '97; was named SPECTATOR's 'Backbencher of the Year' Nov '97; urged Home Secretary Jack Straw to "stop bringing forth an endless raft of unnnecessary, bossy, nannying, tyrannical rules and regulations progressively criminalising perfectly honest and honourable activitites from pistol shooting to eating beef on the bone" Jan '98; claimed the Chancellor's appointments to the new Monetary Policy Committee, unless confirmed by the Treasury Select Committee, were a "wonderful additional power of patronage, and might be a way of rewarding Mr Bernie Ecclesone or conciliaitng Mr Rupert Murdoch" Jan '98; fiercely attacked the tax-free limit of £50,000 in PEPs and TESSAs as perverse socialist egalitarianism Mar '98; on the Treasury Select Committee, challenged Chancellor Brown for not having taken enough out of consumption Apr '98; in his debut as Deputy Social Security Spokesman, accused the Government of "systematic evasion" and "shameless financial chicanery" May '98;

Born: 29 May 1944, Oxford

Family: S Dr Michael Ivor Davies, GP, and Thelma (Butler); "if my parents were to predecease me...I would not stand to inherit any substantial wealth"; m '83 Chantal (Tamplin), ex merchant banker, recently his secretary, daughter of Lt Col R Tamplin, Military Knight of Windsor; 2s: Alexander Sebastian Quentin '87; ????? '??; their nanny, allegedly "the best nanny in England" (EVENING STANDARD), was approached by the Duchess of York;

Education: Dragon School, Oxford; Leighton Park; Gonville and Caius College, Cambridge University (BA History, 1st Class Hons); Harvard University (Frank Knox Fellow);

Occupation: Adviser: to NatWest Securities (the investment banking arm of the NatWest Group; £20-25,000) '93-, Chartered Institute of Taxation (at £10-15,000) '93-; Panellist: on Market Access Parliamentary Panel (£1,000) '93-, Harris Parliamentary Panel (£1,000) '94?-; Owner: of some acres in Lincolnshire and survivors of herd of sheep; ex: Director, Dewe

Rogerson International Ltd '87-94?; Director '81-87, Consultant '87-95?, Morgan Grenfell and Company Ltd '81-87; Director-General and President: Morgan Grenfell France SA '78-81, Banque Morgan Grenfell en Suisse '81-87; Manager, later Assistant Director, Morgan Grenfell and Company '74-78; Diplomat '67-74: Third Secretary, FCO '67-69, Second Secretary, Moscow '69-72, First Secretary FCO, '73-74 (having left the Foreign Service with a tiny deferred pension, "I am one of the many casualties of the present pension system");

Traits: Dark; square-visaged; "plumping, balding"; "keen, eager, Brylcreemed" (Godfrey Barker, DAILY TELEGRAPH); self-satisfied; "loud confident voice, loud confident pin-striped shirts" (Michael White, GUARDIAN); can show "scorn...of the lip-curling and nose-getting-up sort"; "a rather old young man"; "an ambitious, able, unpopular, City type in seizure-inducing chalk-stripes"; "he combines high ability with a putting-off manner" (Edward Pearce: NEW STATESMAN, HOUSE MAGAZINE, EXPRESS); "he is all public school and la-di-da accents" (Tory backbencher, to Christian Wolmar, INDEPENDENT); "one of the most intelligent and succinct of Tories" (Quentin Letts, DAILY TELEGRAPH); can show "considerable tenacity and courage" (GUARDIAN); "colleagues say he is neither clubbable nor a thinker, although he gained a first at Cambridge" (Alice Thomson, TIMES); "a humourless intelligence...a complete pain in the arse....it could be understood why such an intelligent man never made it to being a Minister...his failure to understand that people in error do not always need to have their errors explained to them" (Philip Hensher, former Commons Clerk) "even when he tries to ingratiate himself with someone, he's offensive" (a Tory colleague, according to PRIVATE EYE); has a weakness for using economic gobbledygook; skier; plays "bad tennis" (JQD); multilingual (French, Russian, some Italian); has sensitive nostrils (sent back a £55 bottle of Pouilly Fumee because "the bouquet is not quite right" - according to Labour MP Brian Sedgemore);

Address: House of Commons, Westminster, London SW1A 0AA; 23 Great Winchester Street, London EC2P 2AX; has a "vast Lincolnshire mansion" (EVENING STANDARD);

Telephone: 0171 219 5200 (H of C); 0171 588 4545 (office);

Rt Hon Ron(ald) DAVIES   **Labour**   **CAERPHILLY '83-**

Majority: 25,839 (57.1%) over Conservative 6-way;

Description: The town of Caerphilly (cheese and castle) plus parts of the Rhymney Valley (declining coal, steel, transport);

Position: Secretary of State for Wales '97-; ex: Spokesman, on Wales '92-97, Agriculture '92; Deputy Spokesman, on Agriculture '87-92; Vice Chairman, PLP Employment Committee '84-86; Welsh Whip 85-87; Rhymney Valley District Councillor '69-84;

Outlook: The "archetypal [South] Welsh politician" with an "instinctive atavism" who "has forced New Labour into an uneasy test of its tolerance, not because of what he has done but what he is"(Roy Hattersley); a "bright but abrasive operator who likes his own way; often tetchy, outspoken and spars with officials to test ideas....a strong Commons fixer who can help win over the Left" (TIMES); "a more skilful operator than he is given credit for" (Anthony Bevins, INDEPENDENT); "a seasoned professional, he has been one of the unexpected successes of the Cabinet" (Stephen Castle, INDEPENDENT ON SUNDAY); "I see myself as radical Labour" but "I have always been a moderniser in the sense that I think the Labour Party must recognise and face new challenges and send new messages" (RD); an evolving moderniser, although rooted in the 'Old Labour' habits of South Wales political boyos; "the antithesis of Mandelson Man, he was nonetheless a cautious moderniser before Tony Blair became Leader, warning [South Wales'] Labour council bosses of their 'culture of arrogance'" (Andrew Adonis, OBSERVER); the hard-hitting, soft-Left convert to the Welsh language and devolution who managed to improve the Welsh devolution Bill while it went through the Commons, converting South Wales bosses to his vision of a Welsh Cabinet, over which he expects to preside; has transformed himself into the accepted leader of Wales's home-rulers, partly by insisting on using partial PR to avoid domination of the Welsh Assembly by the "Valleys Taffia"; "he has been through hell and back again to get a Welsh Assembly" (Dafydd Wigley, Plaid Leader); a republican; gaffe-prone, as shown by his becoming "spectacularly offensive about the Prince of Wales, mainly because of the Prince's passion for blood sports which he loathes" (Roy Hattersley); heavily partisan since he learned you earn more votes by bombast than courtesy; "an effective organiser" (Nicholas Timmins, INDEPENDENT); has been accused of male chauvinism by pro-quota feminists; environment-sensitive ("as someone with a lifelong interest in the natural world and the natural history of these islands" [RD]); has "obvious prejudice" (Sir Nicholas Bonsor MP) against Tory fox-hunters; peace-minded (Labour Action for Peace), especially in Central America and the Arab world; opposed the Gulf War; pro: badgers, hedgehogs, adders, Welsh Parliament, PLO; anti: pesticides, nuclear dumping, Derek Foster, Ray Powell, Cardiff Bay Barrage; was NUPE/UNISON-sponsored;

History: "It wasn't until I went to college that I became more politically conscious and got a harder edge to my politics"; he joined the Labour Party '65; was elected to his local council, Rhymney Valley District Council May '69; "I did try for a seat in Kidderminster, just to see if I could do it"; narrowly missed selection for Caerphilly Sep '77; also missed selection at Ogmore Aug '78; at the time of the initial devolution vote leaned toward devolution but kept silent out of loyalty to Neil Kinnock, leader of the 'Wales Says No' campaign; on the way to the polling booth, was accosted by a local Welsh Nationalist who urged him to vote 'Yes', making him change his mind; "when my opponents want me to do one thing, i feel inclined to do the other" Mar '79; after Kinnock led the soft-Left abstainers who enabled Deputy Leader Denis Healey to survive Tony Benn's challenge in Sep '81, he supported Kinnock's de-selection for talking like a Bennite in Wales and behaving like a Healey supporter in London; "Kinnock believes Davies was central to - and possibly leader of - the campaign to de-select him" (Roy Hattersley) '81-82; was selected for Caerphilly after Ednyfed Hudson Davies defected to the SDP; backed the PLO as "the legitimate representative of the Palestinian people" and supported "the inalienable rights of the Palestinian people to self-determination" Apr '83; Neil Kinnock "spoke at my eve of poll rally, so we were good friends even though there were tensions"; retook the seat June '83; favoured the abolition of private health care, and opposed Chief Constables' memoir writing June '83; sponsored motions calling for a referendum on Cruise missiles June '83, against nuclear waste dumping July '83; was alarmed at the US threat to peace in Central America July '83; introduced a motion opposing nuclear dumping in the Atlantic July '83; voted against Defence Estimates July '83; attacked as "the most brutal treatment of workers I have ever seen" the moonlight flit of a local grant-aided textile company Aug '83; co-nominated Kinnock as Leader Sep '83; urged Mrs Thatcher to condemn the US presence in Grenada and to call for their withdrawal Oct '83; unsuccessfully urged Mrs Thatcher to incorporate into UK law article 6 of European Convention on Human Rights, guaranteeing a fair and public hearing by an independent and impartial tribunal Nov '83;

strongly backed a local crime prevention scheme launched experimentally in the Machen area Dec '83; sponsored amendment to motion supporting Local Government Access to Information Bill calling for its early passage into law June '84; complained that David Mitchell, the Parliamentary Secretary for Transport, was promising Tory MPs priority information to favour bus deregulation Dec '84; in the debate on the Wildlife and Countryside (Amendment) Bill insisted that loopholes in environment protection had to be closed to leave Wales with anything worthy of conservation Feb '85; asked a series of searching questions on the impact of pesticides Jan-Mar '85; was reselected unopposed Mar '85; attacked as "deliberately precipitate and provocative" the closure of the Bedwas pit near Caerphilly Apr '85; in the debate on the Queen's Speech complained that the breakdown in law and order were made inevitable by the tensions caused by the Government's economic policies, especially in depressed industrial communities Nov '85; suggested to Mrs Thatcher that it would be better to use the polygraph (lie detector) in Downing Street than in GCHQ Jan '86; attacked as a "glaring and dangerous" loophole in the gun laws the ability of foreigners to buy unlimited shotguns and ammunition June '86; introduced a motion to protect hedgehogs June '86; contesting the chairmanship of the Tribune Group, was defeated by Ann Clwyd Nov '86; increased his general election majority by 7,500 June '87; warned "there is abundant evidence to show the effect of lead in water supplies on the developing brains of young children" Aug 87; "I got frustrated because I felt the PLP wasn't as organised as it should have been and I felt there were a lot of missed opportunities; I guess it was for that reson that I fell out with the then regime in the Whips' Ofice"; "because I was agitating for change, I got sacked by Derek Foster" as Welsh Whip in an argument over whether the (paid) Pairing Whip should be elected by Labour MPs; "the following day Neil [Kinnock] put me on the front bench in the Agriculture team" as Deputy Spokesman July '87; objected to the irrelevant powers taken in the Firearms (Amendment) Bill intended to prevent another Hungerford Jan '88; bemoaned the irrelevance of the Farm Land and Rural Development Bill, intended to reduce surpluses Feb '88; introduced Bill to allow public access to the Forestry Commission's regional advisory committee meetings Feb '88; voted against Licensing Bill (to ease hours) Feb '88; complained of over-planting of conifers in Welsh uplands Mar '88; co-deplored murder of PLO deputy leader Abu Jihad Apr '88; co-congratulated PLO leader Yasser Arafat on his "statesmanlike" handling of the Kuwaiti airplane hijacking Apr '88; replying for the Opposition on the Spitalfields Bill, deplored the failure to seek the approval of most local inhabitants May '88; complained that increased spending on agriculture had resulted in cuts in farm incomes and destroyed environment May '88; urged better protection for adders June '88; announced to the Tribune Group he would seek to replace as Chief Whip Derek Foster who had been over-tolerant of Campaign Group delinquencies June '88; called for a ban on continued experiments on dairy cows with Monsanto's super-hormone BST July '88; received 64 votes in Chief Whip's contest against 107 for Derek Foster, with Jeff Rooker receiving 41 Oct '88; complained that inadequate port of entry examination allowed in much contaminated meat Jan '89; promised Labour would bring in a Food Protection Agency Mar '89; voted, mainly with Tories, against Right of Reply Bill Apr '89; served as John P Smith's "minder" in capture of Vale of Glamorgan by-election Apr '89; attacked Government's "indecision and evasiveness" over BSE May '89; opposed irradiation of food because consumer would remain ignorant July '89; accusing Nicholas Ridley of being an "environmental Genghis Khan", urged better protection of environmentally-threatened sites July '89; received 83 votes in his renewed challenge to Chief Whip Derek Foster who had 124, Nov '89; was named Deputy Spokesman on Food and Agriculture, under David Clark Nov '89; was rated as most active questioner in '88-89 session, with 689 questions Nov '89; co-sponsored Hedgerows Bill Nov '89; opposed use of BST Nov '89; opposed £90m Cardiff Bay Barrage Bill Nov '89; backed fund-raising for

MORNING STAR to provide "diverse editorial opinion" Feb '90; led motion against Cardiff Bay Barrage Feb '90; received 58 votes for Shadow Cabinet (85 required) Oct '90; complained the Cardiff Bay Barage would cause "considerable destruction of wildlife" Oct '90; urged a ban on fur-farming and export of live horses Oct '90; backed Welsh Parliament Nov '90; co-sponsored Roy Hughes' Badgers Bill Dec '90; backed Campaign Group motion warning against "the very dangerous consequences of a Gulf War" Jan '91; backed Sir Richard Body's Pig Husbandry Bill to end tethering Jan '91; backed Badgers Bill, attacking Tory filibustering Feb '91; introduced Wildlife and Countryside (Amendment) Bill as a tribute to its just-deceased originator, Donald Coleman Mar '91; complained the Government was whipping the Cardiff Bay Barrage Bill, theoretically a Private Bill Apr '91; lashed out against Tory MPs trying to sabotage Pig Husbandry Bill Apr '91; attacked "arrogant and selfish" fox-hunting Tory MPs for trying to weaken Badgers Bill to protect fox-hunting; pointed out foxes were a menace on Welsh sheep farms, but could be curbed by shooting May '91; backed an amnesty for holders of illegal pesticides used to keep down predators against gamebirds July '91; announced intention of introducing a Protection of Wild Mammals Bill to extend to wild animals the protection afforded domestic species; Parliament would be asked, on a free vote, to ban the hunting of foxes and deer with hounds Aug '91; received 83 votes for Shadow Cabinet (up from 58) Oct '91; sponsored motion against fox-hunting Nov '91; objected to the undemocratic and lavish way in which the Cardiff Bay Barrage was being pushed at the expense of other infrastructure needs Nov '91; claimed the Government's farm policies had failed both the farmer and the consumers but helped the supermarkets Dec '91; backed tighter control of bailiffs: "bailiffs have the power to take almost anything they want" Jan '92; strongly backed Kevin McNamara's Wild Animals (Protection) Bill against Tory MPs defending fox-hunting Feb '92; was given police protection after fox-hunters tried to force him off the road for his having sponsored a failed Bill to bar fox-hunting Mar '92; retained seat with majority up from 19,167 to 22,672, a swing to Labour of 3.24% Apr '92; co-nominated Bryan Gould for Labour's Leadership May '92; opposed Cardiff Bay Barrage Bill June '92; managed John Evans' unsuccessful campaign to oust Chief Whip Derek Foster June '92; agreed with Jeff Rooker that blank ballot papers had been handed to Whips by Labour MPs "who think there may be some advantage to themselves in doing so" June '92; received 89 votes for Shadow Cabinet (104 required); was named Agriculture Spokesman July '92; insisted on the need to discuss more openly 'mad cow disease' or BSE July '92; was rated 20th most active questioner and the 30th most copious receiver of written answers for 1991-92, Oct '92; was elected to the Shadow Cabinet over George Robertson by 125 votes to 88 in the place vacated by Bryan Gould; was named Welsh Spokesman by John Smith; his place as Agriculture Spokesman was taken by Gavin Strang Nov '92; reassured Council of Welsh Districts that a Labour Government would recognise there would be a "plurality of representation" on EC's Committee of the Regions Jan '93; accused Welsh Secretary David Hunt of "ruling by quangos": "over 1200 people appointed by one man oversee one and a half billion pounds of expenditure and the influence of community, of common good of any democratically expressed intent it pushed to one side by Tory supporters" Feb '93; insisted that the unitary authorities being proposed by the Government were only feasible in the context of a Welsh Assembly, instead of a proliferation of quangos Mar '93; in winding up for Labour on the mining crisis, hectored Mrs Peacock but refused to make way for her, giving him "the distinction of making the crassest winding-up speech of the year" (Donald Macintyre, INDEPENDENT ON SUNDAY) Mar '93; announced he had joined a local company known as Quality Training Services, which had taken over collapsed Commercial and Industrial Training Services Ltd in his constituency July '93; voted against requirement to vote for four women in Shadow Cabinet elections, holding it would not guarantee more women on Labour's frontbench; instead proposed guarantee of places to four women coming highest in poll July '93; co-urged lifting of US blockade on Cuba July '93; received 121 votes for Shadow Cabinet, up from 89, Oct 93; in letter to PLP Chairman Doug Hoyle demanded a "thorough investigation" of claims that he had helped rig Shadow Cabinet elections against leading women politicians; claimed he had been the victim "of a deliberate dirty trick designed to undermine my position as an elected member of the Shadow Cabinet" Oct '93; sharply attacked John Redwood's proposed local government changes Nov '93; urged John Redwood to resign as Welsh Secretary after he had denied knowing the Conservative affiliations of new Welsh Development Agency Chairman, David Rowe-Beddoe Jan '94; attacked Welsh Secretary John Redwood for his attack on Dennis Skinner's sex life Mar '94; attacked John Redwood for allegedly intending to abolish the Development Board for Rural Wales July '94; after John Smith's death, nominated John Prescott for Leader ("to ensure there was a three-way contest"); voted for Blair for Leader, Prescott for Deputy Leader July '94; was re-elected to Shadow Cabinet with 113 votes Oct '94; criticised Welsh Tory Minister Rod Richard's attack on Welsh Labour councillors as "short, fat, slimy and fundamentally corrupt" as "crass, unjustified and unwarranted" Dec '94; unveiled Labour's Welsh Assembly plans "as a focus for a new Welsh sense of identity", blaming the absence of tax-raising powers on Wales' poverty May '95; predicted Wales would be "a Tory-free zone after the next election" when the Conservatives lost Monmouth, their last local authority May '95; dismissed as "a contemptuous insult to the people of Wales" the appointment of Yorkshirman William Hague as Welsh Secretary July '95; organised a boycott of Hague's first question time, allegedly to Blair's displeasure July '95; attacked Hague as "weak and inefficient", challenging the cost of his fact-finding tour of Wales Aug '95; despite a summer-long hostile whispering campaign against him by Blairites, polled unexpectedly well in Shadow Cabinet election, coming 4th with 157 votes (up from 113) Oct '95; ridiculed experiment of holding Welsh Grand Committee in various venues in Wales, insisting "the greatest need...is for the representatives of the Welsh people to control our own devolved affairs in Wales, in our own directly-elected assembly" Nov '95; in BBC Wales TV interview claimed Prince of Wales was not worthy of respect: "he spends time talking to trees, flowers and vegetables, and yet he encourages his young sons to go into the countryside to kill wild animals and birds for fun, for sport; is this person a fit sort of person to continue the tradition of monarchy?"; on the edited-out section of the interview, admitted he was a republican and said the Prince could not ascend the throne while "living in sin" with Camilla Parker-Bowles; he was forced by Tony Blair to apologise Mar '96; urged experiment with simultaneous translation from Welsh in Welsh Grand Committee Mar '96; was listed as one of 26 humanists among Labour MPs Apr '96; told the HOUSE MAGAZINE he favoured a "consensual" approach to Welsh devolution, involving "Liberals, the Nationalists and even Conservatives who share our views" Apr '96; welcomed the belated inquiry into child-abuse in north Wales childrens' homes June '96; publicly backed Labour's new devolution policy - for a pre-legislation referendum -although only informed two days before, not consulted and, according to Paul Flynn MP, having the choice of accepting or resigning June '96; voted against a 3% cap on MPs' pay rise and for a pension based on £43,000, £9,000 higher July '96; initially supported Blair's desire to avoid a Shadow Cabinet election to avoid losing Harriet Harman; when it was held, was re-elected in 11th place with 201 votes, despite press reports that Blair "detested" him and "would like to see him go" (GUARDIAN) July '96; described as "brutal, unnecessary and inhumane" the shackling to a hospital bed of an imprisoned constituent until two hours before he died of cancer Jan '97; was a target of the anti-abortion Prolife Alliance Party Feb '97; having been present, he insisted Tory defector Alan Howarth's selection for Newport East was "perfectly fair and democratic" Mar '97; denied allegation of Sir Ray Powell, the discarded Pairing Whip, that he had offered

him a peerage if he stood down to make way for a Blairite candidate Apr '97; was re-elected with an enhanced majority of 25,839 on a 5.8% swing from the Conservatives May '97; despite press predictions, was appointed Secretary of State for Wales and a Privy Counsellor May '97; threatened to discipline Welsh Labour MPs campaigning against the Referendum on a Welsh Assembly promised in the party's manifesto May '97; welcomed support for a Welsh Assembly of retired veteran Tory MP Sir Wyn Roberts, emphasising "the extent of our commitment to consensual politics [as] reflected in the alternative member [electoral] system by which people will be elected to the Assembly"; this form of PR was introduced by him to avoid domination of the Assembly by more populous south Wales and its "Valleys Taffia" of Labour bosses May '97; rejected as "fantasy" the claims of anti-devolution MP Llew Smith that he had threatened him with expulsion if he campaigned against devolution; also that one of Davies' office staff had warned Smith that relations between his constituency party and the Welsh Office might suffer; Blair defended Davies against this charge when repeated by William Hague June '97; presented the devolution White Paper, 'A Voice for Wales', creating a 60-seat Welsh National Assembly, 40 elected by constituencies, 20 by a form of PR from a party list, with no tax-raising powers and sovereignty remaining in Westminster July '97; his proposals were criticised by Welsh Labour MPs Alan Williams, Denzil Davies, Ted Rowlands, and Allan Rogers July '97; claimed "a clear majority, not as large as I would have liked" when the referendum in Wales ended with a narrow .6% 'Yes' majority Sep '96; in a rare tribute Plaid Cymru leader Dafydd Wigley said Davies "has been through hell and back to get a Welsh Assembly" Sep '97; moved 2nd Reading of Government of Wales Bill Dec '97; despite bids from Swansea, decided that Cardiff would be the site of the Welsh National Assembly Mar '98; secured amendments "to establish a Cabinet-style of decision-making" to Government of Wales Bill, which received 3rd Reading Mar '98; announced he would seek to become Wales' first First Secretary in '99, yielding his post as Secretary of State for Wales Mar '98;
Born: 6 August 1946, Machen, Gwent
Family: Son, late Francis Ronald Davies, ex-fitter, "an active trade unionist who worked in the railway industry, the steel industry and the chemical industry until he was made redundant from all three", and Beryl (Richards), a primary school teacher; m 1st '71; divorced '80; m 2nd '81 Christina Elisabeth (Rees), local government officer and "an impressive squash player - Welsh international 57 times, a judo black belt, a marathon runner [who] has played tennis and hockey for British and Welsh universities" (DAILY TELEGRAPH); 1d Angharad;
Education: Machen Primary; Bassaleg Grammar ("I didn't particularly like the old-style values and morals" [RD]); Portsmouth Poly; University College of Wales, Cardiff; London University;
Occupation: Director, Quality Training Services (local firm which took over training abandoned by collapsed Commercial and Industrial Training Services; unpaid) '93-97; formerly Sponsored, by NUPE/UNISON (66% of election expenses) '83-95 ; Adviser, to NATFHE '85-89; Further Education Officer, Mid-Glamorgan Local Education Authority '74-83; Tutor-Organiser with Workers' Educational Association '70-74; Teacher '68-70;
Traits: Egg-shaped face; trim; articulate; "a more sensitive and less secure man than his public image suggests" with "a remarkable capacity for becoming involved in mildly absurd controversy" (Roy Hattersley); "often assaults Conservative Members" in a "bombastic way"; "he makes many aspersions against our characters, our habits and our motives" (James Paice MP); formerly courteous; "a classic Labour male chauvinist pig" (Emma (recently Baroness) Nicholson ex-MP), rugby and squash player; runner; he and his wife are not Welsh-speaking, but he has been learning; his daughter attends a Welsh-medium school; humanist;
Address: House of Commons, Westminster, London SW1A 0AA; The Old Mill House, Draethen, Lower Machen, Newport, Gwent;

Telephone: 0171 219 3552/5990/4727/2747 (H of C); 01633 440555 (home); 01443 8323390 (agent);

Rt Hon David (Michael) DAVIS   Conservative   **HALTEMPRICE & HOWDEN '97-**

Majority: 7,514 (15.2%) over Liberal Democrat 6-way;

Description: A new seat, created in'95, mostly from old Beverley but with nearly a third of its voters from his abolished Boothferry seat; a mixture of Hull suburbs like Haltemprice, small towns like Howden and villages; it was wisely chosen by Davis in preference to nearby Brigg and Goole which absorbed nearly half his former voters but fell to Labour;

Former Seat: Boothferry '87-97

Position: Chairman, Public Accounts Committee '97-; ex: Minister of State, Foreign and Commonwealth Office '94-97; Under Secretary, for Public Service '93-94; Whip '90-93; PPS to Francis Maude '89-90; Chairman, Conservative Collegiate Forum '89-93?; on the Executive of Industrial Society '85-87; on CBI's Financial Policy Committee '77-79; Chairman, Federation of Conservative Students '73-74;

Outlook: A shrewd-tough dynamic operator, once tipped as "the next-Tory-Leader-but-two" (Matthew Parris, TIMES), who cannily sidelined himself as the skilful chairman of the PAC - "the best job in Opposition" (DD) - away from the vicious civil war among would-be Tory leaders; as 'Minister for Europe' had been John Major's "one-man awkward squad" trying to scale down Euro-federalism, while serving as "emissary to the [Eurosceptic] barbarians in the Tory Party" (Matthew Parris, TIMES); was described variously as "a charming bastard" and "a master of constructive obstructionism"; he had previously made a dubious reputation among fellow Eurosceptics as "the government's bovver-boy", the party's unflinching bone-crusher" (Donald Macintyre, INDEPENDENT) and self-described the "Eurosceptic for Maastricht" Whip '90-93 when he browbeat colleagues into voting for Maastricht, displaying "tough tactics and single-mindedness" (Andrew Grice, Michael Prescott SUNDAY TIMES); this earned him the reputation among some Maastricht rebels as "a thug, a bully and a careerist who sacrificed his Eurosceptic principles for ambition" (Nicholas Wood, TIMES); as 'Minister for Europe' had "a natural and amply-reciprocated dislike for the endlessly seductive lore and culture of the Foreign Office" (Donald Macintyre, INDEPENDENT); in the Office of Public Service, where he replaced Robert Jackson (a Fellow of All Souls like William Waldegrave), it was said: "we used to have two Fellows of All Souls; now we have one Fellow of All Souls and one fellow who is all balls"; a locally-born, highly-regarded, high-flying industrial intellectual (a former Director of Tate and Lyle); "a new-model Tory, a supporter of the meritocracy" (Colin Brown, INDEPENDENT); "one of the sharpest products of the 1987 election intake" (Nicholas Wood, TIMES); a Rightwinger who made his reputation initially as the scourge of the Dock Labour Scheme and then as a tough Whip - Richard Ryder's "enforcer" - during the Maastricht debates, a post for which he was recommended by Europhile Tristan Garel-Jones, although a Eurosceptic; on Alan Clark's approved list ("good strong chap, very much our sense of humour"); "a [former] Whip with the profile of a Rugby forward and the aggression of Schwarzenegger" who made "David Lightbown look like a pussycat" (DAILY TELEGRAPH); "he's a fine man; he's got brains; he can do joined-up writing and he can do joined-up thinking; and he's tough" (Tory Minister); anti-abortion; normally superloyal (except over eye tests): "I am a loyalist, essentially, at the end of the day" (DD); "I am a fan of the late, great Iain Macleod" (DD);

History: He first became active in Conservative politics in '69; became Chairman of the Federation of Conservative students '73; at annual conference urged laws to facilitate worker participation Oct '73; as a corporate strategist for Tate and Lyle from '84, he developed a plan to make a better-financed and more efficient NHS more effective for the patient; was selected for safe Boothferry to replace retiring Sir Paul Bryan Nov '86; retained the seat with a slightly increased majority because of the sag in Liberal votes June '87; in his belated Maiden he welcomed the Government's success in making UK industry more competitive but warned that the Wall Street crash and the cheaper dollar would make British exports there more difficult; markets elsewhere would show the effects of Japanese competition; discreetly urged the Government to "inject more demand into the economy - that is a commonsense approach, not a Keynesian one" to keep up Britain's "creditworthiness" Nov '87; asked the Northern Ireland Secretary to make more resources available "to enable schools from different religious backgrounds to undertake joint educational projects" Nov '87; voted for David Alton's Bill to curb abortions Jan '88; in the GUARDIAN he proposed a reorganized NHS based on District Health Authorities armed with standardized information on real costs and paid by results, with a patient's right of transfer in a limited internal market Jan '88; opposed the televising of Parliament because, during over two years in Canada, he had seen featured on TV mainly the short bits of bitter confrontation Feb '88; made a superloyal but thoughtful defence of Nigel Lawson's Budget and economic strategy Mar '88; voted against charges for eye tests despite pressure from the Whips, including interviews with Tony Newton, Edwina Currie and John Moore Apr '88; introduced Ten-Minute-Rule Bill to limit registered Dock Labour Scheme to lifetime of those in current employment under it May '88; again backed David Alton's abortion-curbing Bill May '88; served as Teller for those favouring privatization of BR Nov '88; co-sponsored Bill to exempt sports from Sunday limitations Dec '88; published CPS pamphlet, 'Clear the Decks', urging early end of Dock Labour Scheme, which had turned into a "legislative monster" blighting large sections of the northeast Dec '88; talked to Downing Street Policy Unit about abolishing Dock Labour Scheme '88-89; was named PPS to Francis Maude Jan '89; in letter to FINANCIAL TIMES, insisted abolition of Dock Labour Scheme could not wait Feb '89; Cabinet Committee accepted his scheme to abolish Dock Labour Scheme Feb '89; again claimed the Dock Work Scheme encouraged bad labour practices ("bobbing", "welting", "ghosting") and its abolition would create 50,000 jobs May '89; insisted a strike in de-registered docks would be "temporary and fragmentary" May '89; was named Chairman of the Conservative Collegiate Forum Nov '89; insisted that "loans will not curtail higher education for our youngsters but will have the opposite effect" Dec '89; in report for Centre for Policy Studies, 'The Power of the Pendulum', urged imposition of pendulum arbitration as a substitute for right to strike in statutory monopolies Nov '89; voted against a War Crimes Bill Dec '89; voted for Teresa Gorman's Bill to abolish Rent Acts Jan '90; in article for TIMES, urged more backing for more productive applied science, instead of pure science in which Britain had led Jan '90; deposited petitions against Humberside County Council Bill Feb '90; opposed punishment of Tory MP John Browne for concealing his interests Mar '90; in Budget debate, claimed the City and Labour Opposition had both misread the financial statistics Mar '90; backed 18-week ceiling on abortions Apr '90; in a period of near-drought, his new neighbours in Howden accused him of filling his lake with tapwater May '90; urged simultaneous squeeze on all sources of IRA income, which he estimated at £5.3m a year Nov '90; was excluded from Tristan Garel-Jones inner circle despite being recommended by Alan Clark; supported John Major during the Leadership election Nov '90; was promoted an Assistant Whip by John Major Nov '90; voted to restore capital punishment for killing policemen Dec '90; Mrs Thatcher spoke for him during the election campaign Mar '92; retained seat with majority down from 18,970 to 17,535, a swing to Labour of 3.25% Apr '92; as Foreign Office Whip, attended meeting of 'No Turning Back' Euro-sceptics, including Peter Lilley, Michael Portillo, John Redwood, Steve Norris, Edward Leigh; reported back to Richard Ryder, Douglas Hurd and John Major that Euro-sceptics wanted Maastricht abandoned in wake of its rejection in Danish referendum June '92; as Chief Whip Richard Ryder's chief "enforcer" on Maastricht, attracted the enmity of new MPs who had signed the Euro-sceptic "fresh start" motion June-July '92; attended the Conservatives' Blue Ball equipped with portable telephone to recall Tory MPs for two tight votes on Maastricht July '92; attended Third European Round Table Discussion at Cadenabbia, Lake Como, as guest of Konrad Adenauer Foundation Oct '92; was promoted Under Secretary for Public Service, under William Waldegrave, replacing Robert Jackson May '93; made his ministerial debut introducing amendments to the House of Commons Disqualification Act 1975 June '93; attended Fourth European Round Table Discussion at Cadenabbia, Lake Como, as guest of the Konrad Adenauer Foundation Oct '93; in a written answer disclosed that under a revised Civil Service Code, civil servants had to disclose if they were Freemasons Oct '93; voted for total deregulation of Sunday trading Dec '93; welcomed the increased number of British graduates who had applied for jobs with the European Commission in Brussels Feb '94; voted to restore capital punishment, especially for cop-killers Feb '94; voted against reducing age of homosexual consent to 18 or 16, Feb '94; after outside bets in the press on promotion to the Cabinet, was promoted Minister of State ('Minister for Europe') at the Foreign Office - replacing pro-European Tristan Garel-Jones -despite alleged doubts of Foreign Secretary Douglas Hurd; "although Mr Davis is rightly regarded as a Major loyalist, he is also as [Euro]sceptical a Minister as the Foreign Office could tolerate" (Robert Shrimsley, DAILY TELEGRAPH) July '94; in Cyprus debate refused to recognise the 'Turkish Republic of Northern Cyprus, recommending Turkish-opposed admission of Cyprus to EU Dec '94; defending the Anglo-American Mutual Defence Agreement said UK's nuclear explosive capacity had been reduced by a quarter recently Dec '94; was named - as a one-man 'awkward squad' - to represent UK in preparations for the EU intergovernmental conference to review the Maastricht treaty, with a brief to oppose greater EU integration and to press for a decentralised EU, flexible enough to allow enlargement Jan '95; put up a disastrous performance in debate on LibDem proposal for a referendum on Euro-federalism Feb '95; promised Tory MPs better consultation before the '96 IGC than they had enjoyed before the Maastricht Treaty Feb '95; said "a world free of landmines is a laudable objective" but an international agreement was impossible to reach Mar '95; outlined Major Government's stand-pat objectives for '96 EU IGC Mar '95; considered direct rule for Gibraltar to deal with drug-running and clean up its banking and legal systems May '95; was completely isolated among the 14 Euro-federalists in the IGC 'Reflection Group', the others pressing for more majority decisions June '95; strongly supported John Major against John Redwood in the Tory Leadership contest June '95; was named as a possible successor to ailing Chief Whip Richard Ryder, while he hoped for a Cabinet post June '95; claimed enough EU states opposed radical extension of majority voting Sep '95; announced UK climbdown on its campaign for a radical reduction in the powers of the European Court of Justice Oct '95; denied Sir Edward Heath's claim that being anti-European was a vote-loser Dec '95; was contradicted by pro-EU Chancellor Clarke when he opposed an EU-sponsored pro-Euro publicity drive in the UK Jan '96; backed an extended 18-month cooling-off period in divorce reform Apr '96; asked Ministers for their EU-related agenda to prepare disruption in retaliation for EU beef ban, adding: "those who know my [multi-ethnic] origins will realise just how much distaste I have for the extremes of xenophobia about which one learns from time to time" June '96; emphasised Britain's basic defence commitment to NATO, not EU June '96; he denied he had threatened to resign on the eve of the EU Florence 'summit' over not being promoted a Privy Counsellor or put in charge of the "botched" beef ban negotiations, replacing Agriculture MInister Douglas Hogg June '96; "I am here and will be here in November," he told anxious Americans anxious for a deal on the Test Ban Treaty before the US elections in November; he refused to do a deal until India and Pakistan were on board ???-??? '96; confirmed the Government would refuse export licenses for British-made landmines Oct '96; welcomed proposed worldwide ban on chemical weapons Nov '96; co-signed letter of support for Sir Nicholas Scott on eve of his de-selection for Kensington and Chelsea Nov '96; warned of Greco-Turkish arms race on Cyprus Dec '96; claimed that under Labour there would be "six surrenders to the EU in six weeks" Dec '96; was named to the Privy Council Jan '97; insisted UK was still committed to nuclear defence, despite 20% reduction in capacity Mar '97; retained his altered and renamed seat by 7,514, on a 9.5% notional swing to the LibDem May '97; backed Michael Howard in the first round of the Tory Leadership contest May '97; attacked Labour's abandonment of the national veto in numerous areas June '97; wound up for the Conservative front bench June '97; assumed the Chairmanship of the Public Accounts Committee July '97; introduced the latest 25 PAC reports, promising to be even tougher than his predecessor, Robert Sheldon Nov '97; had adjournment debate to express his fear the Labour Government was abandoning anti-missile defence research, despite 38, often rogue, states having ballistic missile systems Dec '97; in debate on an English Parliament, insisted "I am British" and "every part of the Union has gained from and contributed to the hybrid vigour that is produced from the many strains of talent in a single United Kingdom"; "the Government's devolution policy is little more than an unstable gerrymandered mess" Jan '98; secured NAO access to Royal Household accounts Jan '98; defended PAC's exposure of the "theft of taxpayers' money by a British Embassy employee" in Amman, acclaiming the PAC's exposure record, including the Pergau Dam, defending its questioning as "tough but polite" Feb '98; warned that the Budget's attempt to end the poverty trap and unemployment trap would cost about £2.8b in the first year and grow Mar '98; as Chairman of PAC he secured NAO access to Camelot accounts May '98; warned that taxpayers could spend billions on cleaning up after nuclear industry May '98; urged doubling of select committee financing with half going to pool of researchers, lawyers and accountants June '98; urged Metropolitan Police to use sanctions against policemen abusing sick leave July '98; criticised as "intolerable and totally unacceptable" the wrong decisions of the Child Support Agency as proved by the National Audit Office July '98;

Born: 23 December 1948, York

Family: "I have lines in my family that go back to the west of Scotland, to mid and south Wales, and to south Armagh in the north of Ireland"; one grandfather "was the son of a wealthy trawlerman but he was also a Catholic and a Communist who took part in the Jarrow march"; "his father took him aside and told him he had to choose: he could either succeed in the business as a good Catholic or he could remain a Communist; he walked, losing his entire inheritance"; son, of Elizabeth (Brown) and a Welshman; adopted son of Ronald Davis, Polish Jewish printworker; his half-sister has been a clerical officer in an east Midlands employment office; m '73 Doreen Margery (Cook); 1s Alexander '87, 2d Rebecca '74, Sarah '77;

Education: The Bec Grammar School; Warwick University (BSc); London Business School (MSc); Harvard University (Advanced Management Programme);

Occupation: Author: The BBC Guide to Parliament (1989), Company Rescue (1988); ex: Director: Tate and Lyle '87-90, Globe Investments (Britain's largest investment trust, which

British Coal's Pension Fund tried to take over in '90) '89-90, Buckingham Plc '90; Tate and Lyle's Strategic Planning Director '84-87; President, of Zymaize (a Canadian sweetener manufacturer which he turned around from a loss-maker to a profit maker as "what the Americans call a corporate trouble shooter" - YORKSHIRE POST) '82; Managing Director, Tate and Lyle Transport '80-82; Financial Director, Manbre and Garton (taken over by Tate and Lyle) '77-80; Tate and Lyle Executive '74-77;

Traits: Good-looking; parted, wavy, tonsured hair; "boyish" with a "knowing grin" (EVENING STANDARD); a determined expression; "thoughtful, technocratic but politically ruthless" (Nicholas Wood, TIMES); a complex but rational mind; a behind-the-scenes operator; "straight and courteous" (Sir Russell Johnston ex-MP); in 1990 he tried his hands at a novel set in the Middle East, The Sword of Allah, but the Gulf War events overtook his fiction; "my family has a touch of madness"; as a young man he climbed mountains, flew light aircraft and parachuted out of them doing cartwheels; recently he has concentrated on long-distance walking, starting with 100 miles along the Wolds;

Address: House of Commons, Westminster, London SW1A 0AA; Spaldington Court, Spaldington, nr Howden;

Telephone: 0171 219 4183/5873 (H of C); 01430 430 365;

'Terry' (Terence Anthony Gordon) DAVIS   Labour   HODGE
                                                    HILL, Birmingham '83-

Majority: 14,200 (41.6%) over Conservative 4-way;

Description: East Birmingham seat remade in '83 mostly of old Stechford (once decorated by Roy Jenkins) with 3,000 voters from Small Heath, with 7,000 gone to Yardley, and 4,000 others returned; half owner-occupiers, half council tenants; curiously, Labour does better in Washwood Heath, mostly owner-occupied with a quarter of its population black (many non-voting), than in the Shard End and Hodge Hill council estates, full of skilled white workers; many residents work in the motor industry;

Former Seat: Stechford '79-83; Bromsgrove '71-74;

Position: Delegate to WEU (Leader: UK delegation '97-, Socialist Group '96-, Labour delegation '95-; Chairman its Rules Committee '95-96) '92-; Delegate to Council of Europe (Leader: UK delegation '97-, Labour delegation '95-, Chairman: Development and Rules Committees '95-98) '92-; Delegate to Assembly of OSCE '97-; ex: Deputy Spokesman on Industry '87, Treasury and Economic Affairs '83-86, on Health and Social Services '80-83; Whip (West Midlands) '79-80; on Public Accounts Committee '87-94, '79-80; on Expenditure Select Committee '73-74; Chairman: of PLP Industry Group (previously Vice Chairman) '80-81; Vice President '82-95, Secretary '95-97 Socialist Health Association; Secretary, Parliamentary Group on Industrial Common Ownership '85-87; MSF Parliamentary Committee '88-89, West Midlands Labour MPs '73-74, ASTMS Parliamentary Committee '87, '73-74; Secretary, Parliamentary Group on Population and Development '87-90; Treasurer, Parliamentary Group on Population '85-90;

Outlook: A former low-profiled, disciplined 'Old Labour' workhorse, on its front bench '80-87; has recently grazed mainly in the WEU and Council of Europe and in finding housing for Brummy constituents; this is mainly because he is out of sync with the Blairite leadership; an informed and pragmatic Eurosceptic who believes in "co-operation and partnership" not integration; was initially wrongly lumped with Centre-Right 'Solidarity' because he had long supported one-member one-vote; recently has been lumped with the hard-Left because he has long opposed Defence Estimates, Prevention of Terrorism powers and opposed the Gulf War; a colleague observed "the trouble with you, Terry, is that you insist on thinking for yourself!"; an able, canny, independent-minded West Midlands former motor car manager; for seven years was an extremely effective PAC inquisitor (initially teamed with Ian Gow, latterly with Alan Williams); an active constituency man, especially on housing; progressive on women's questions; assiduous cultivator of ethnic minorities; formerly tireless in marching through division lobbies; scourge of lying civil servants; formerly MSF-sponsored;

History: His family were Conservatives; joined the Labour Party '65; was elected to Yeovil Rural District Council May '67; contested Bromsgrove unsuccessfully June '70; unexpectedly won the Bromsgrove by-election, overturning its 10,879 Tory majority in Heath Government's first by-election loss May '71; attacked the Ian Smith regime July '71; voted against EEC entry Oct '71; opposed cyanide dumping Jan '72; opposed unification of Herefordshire and Worcestershire May '72; lost new seat of Bromsgrove and Redditch to Hal Miller Feb '74; contested Bromsgrove Oct '74; lost Stechford to Tory Andrew Mackay at the by-election caused by Roy Jenkins' departure for Brussels Apr '77; was appointed Adviser to Albert Booth at Employment Feb '79; narrowly retook Stechford from Mackay May '79; said low pay was the problem at BL, where he had worked June '79; was appointed West Midlands Whip Nov '79; voted for Silkin, then Healey in Deputy Leadership contest Nov '80; was promoted Deputy Health Spokesman Dec '80; warned against loss of Midlands jobs if gas showrooms were privatised and appliances imported June '81; opposed charging foreign visitors for medical treatment, saying abuse was minimal Mar '82; successfully tabled amendment to enable close friends of mentally ill to agree treatments May '82; promised next Labour Government would ban cigarette advertising Dec '82; increased his majority to a comfortable 5,000-plus May '83; supported Roy Hattersley for Leader, Neil Kinnock for Deputy Leader Sep '83; contested Chief Whip's post, winning 25 votes Oct '83; was named Deputy to Roy Hattersley as Treasury Spokesman Nov '83; on the Solidarity slate, received 48 votes for Labour's Shadow Cabinet Oct '84; was re-selected over a single opponent Feb '85; sought to amend the Finance Bill to give tax relief for working mothers with children in nurseries May '85; hesitated to contest the Chief Whip's post while Michael Cocks was being opposed by the Left for reselection June '85; on the Solidarity slate in Shadow Cabinet contest, received 52 votes Oct '85; attacked plans to hand over control of the British car industry to Ford and General Motors, insisting that Americans did not like "door mats" Feb '86; argued against Mrs Thatcher's claim that the Americans were justified in bombing Libya because of Libya's alleged complicity in the Munich nightclub bombing Apr '86; argued for the exclusion of South African investments from the Personal Equity Plan July '86; in contest for Shadow Cabinet received 48 votes Oct '86; was dropped from Treasury team by Roy Hattersley Oct '86; voted against Kenneth Hind's Unborn Children (Protection) Bill Oct '86; was reinstated on the Front Bench as Industry Spokesman, replacing Geoffrey Robinson Jan '87; attacked the slimming down of the Austin Rover Group Jan '87; in a joint letter with Roy Hattersley and Denis Howell, rejected the "invasion" of Bernie Grant and Linda Bellos to give Brummies advice on 'black sections' Apr '87; supported Airbus on Labour's behalf May '87; was not reappointed a Deputy Spokesman July '87; warned that West Midlands was having the worst NHS crisis Nov '87; was again added to Public Accounts Commission Nov '87; voted against televising the Commons Feb '88; at the PAC he demonstrated that information had been withheld deliberately by officials of the Ministry of Agriculture and Intervention Board for Agricultural

Produce Feb '88; two civil servants apologised to PAC for having lied in response to his questions about documents he had seen them read on a train Mar '88; insisted Government had injected an extra £63m into Rolls Royce before privatisation in response to threat of resignation by its Chairman, Sir Francis Tombs Mar '88; claimed civil servants had "fiddled the figures" because they had not met Mrs Thatcher's demand they save 5% in their expenditure Apr '88; warned that British Aerospace would close down some of the smaller Rover companies it was being given May '88; voted against Prevention of Terrorism Bill, instead of abstaining Dec '88; introduced Junior Hospital Doctors (Regulation of Hours) Bill to cut hours Feb '89; said he had pressed for a PAC inquiry into the Rover's under-priced sale as "a former employee of British Leyland' Nov '89; disclosed that Cabinet Office was instructing civil servants to create new files marked "Not for National Audit Office Eyes' to frustrate audit checks Jan '90; claimed West Midlands allowed consultants more time for private work than any other regional health authority Jan '90; complained of inadequate control by Universities Funding Council Mar '90; supported Michael Colvin's Computer Misuse Bill May '90; urged councillors allowances be brought in line with those of MPs and civil servants May '90; opposed Midlands Metro Bill Oct '90; voted with Campaign Groupies against rushing into the Gulf War Dec '90; urged noise limits on night flying from Birmingham International Airport Dec '90; backed Campaign Group motion emphasizing the "very dangerous consequences of a Gulf War" Jan '91; backed a Campaign Group motion demanding cancellation of Birmingham arms exhibition, abolition of the Government's Defence Export Services Organizaiton and guarantees for armaments workers put out of work Feb '91; backed a Campaign Group motion condemning "the barbaric slaughter of innocent men, women and children in Baghdad, which was caused by bombing" Feb '91; with Bill Michie, proposed a negotiated settlement with Iraq, including the withdrawal of all Iraqi forces from Kuwait Feb '91; served as Teller against Midland Metro Bill which adversely affected his constituents Feb '91; backed a Campaign Group motion deploring poor aftermath of Gulf War Apr '91; co-sponsored Campaign Group motion demanding open planning by NATO in new international situation Dec '91; retained seat with majority up from 4,789 to 7,068, a swing to Labour of 2.79% Apr '92; was selected as an Alternate Delegate to the Council of Europe June '92; predicted an "almighty row" when it was disclosed that Auditor General Sir John Bourn would not be allowed to examine Royal Family accounts July '92; urged resignation of scandal-tainted Sir James Ackers, Chairman of West Midlands Regional Health Authority Oct '92; in PAC debate claimed that Rover Group had been "given away" not "sold" to British Aerospace Oct '92; described the 14-year-long £450m British Library saga as resembling "an appalling soap opera" Nov '92; demanded Attorney General Sir Nicholas Lyell "simply say sorry" to the Matrix-Churchill executives put at risk Nov '92; introduced National School Health Service Bill, to provide regular health reviews; it was later dropped after its 2nd Reading Nov '92; on PAC sharply challenged Treasury's payment of Chancellor Lamont's libel lawyer's charges over the ousting of the "sex therapist" to whom he had rented his flat Jan '93; urged Prime Minister to save the 2,000 jobs at Leyland DAF, then in the hands of a receiver Feb '93; joined in sharp attacks on the expensive scandals of the secretive West Midlands Regional Health Authority, shouting "disgraceful" at Health Under Secretary Tom Sackville for his lame explanations Feb '93; on PAC pointed out that costs and delays of Tornado GR1 bombers had soared because Defence Ministry work definitions had been insufficiently "taut" Feb '93; was rated among the top Maastricht rebels, with eight votes against the Bill by Feb '93; on PAC, demonstrated that health service for the physically disabled was "grossly inadequate" Mar '93; on PAC, helped uncover "ghosts" who helped workers in civil service canteens to be paid twice Mar '93; helped spotlight failure of Lord Chancellor's Parliamentary Secretary to inform PAC of judges' protests against cuts in legal aid Mar '93; helped force Trade and Industry's Permanent

Secretary disclose that Girobank was sold for £73m when its asset value was £170m Mar '93; voted against National Lottery Apr '93; voted against 3rd Reading of Maastricht Bill May '93; obtained confidential memorandum which disclosed that private firm, Mailforce of Northampton, had mishandled 150,000 Inland Revenue tax packs and codes, sending some to rival firms, with information being leaked about persons working for 440,000 companies June '93; complained that "a taxpayer would wonder why we think the Treasury could manage the British economy when they cannot run a teashop" July '93; in PAC debate urged "quicker and more rough and ready reports" to stop spending scandals sooner Oct '93; voted against Defence Estimates, instead of abstaining Oct '93; it was revealed that over £10m had been squandered by the West Midlands Regional Health Authority after investigations started when he passed documents to Sir John Bourn, the Comptroller and Auditor General; the RHA's Chairman, Sir James Ackers had been forced to resign Nov '93; further PAC disclosures indicated Government waste of £2.5b a year, whiich he described as "the tip of an iceberg" Dec '93; backed Peter Shore's anti-Maastricht convergence motion Dec '93; was re-selected as an Alternate Delegate to the Council of Europe Dec '93; voted against restoring capital punishment, even for cop-killers Feb '94; voted to reduce homosexual age of consent to 18 or 16, Feb '94; after seven years' service, left the Public Accounts Committee on being eleced a delegate to the Council of Europe Assembly May '94; voted for John Prescott for Leader and Deputy Leader July '94; was a rebel, voting against EU Finance Bill NOv '94; at Prague Council of Europe meeting criticised "academics from ivory towers" prescribing what was best for workers they had never met; then the academic who had spoken, Czech Professor Igor Tomes, disclosed he had spent 20 years in a steel mill after being purged in '68, Nov '94; voted for LibDem motion for referendum on further Euro-federalism Feb '95; voted against extension of Sunday pub hours Feb '95; with 29 hard-Left Labour rebels voted against guillotining Prevention of Terrorism Bill Apr '96; in rare Commons speech urged Government funds be used, not to cut taxes but to increase employment "to undertake the work in front of our eyes - housing shortage, the terrible provision of care in the community, social services" July '95; co-deplored omission by DAILY MAIL of Greece as World War II ally Oct '95; in Scott Report debate, deplored loss of local Matrix Churchill and BSA Tool jobs after their directors' arrest; attacked William Waldegrave's 38 misleading letters, "using his incompetence as a shield" Feb '96; urged a referendum on further integration into the EU, hoping to see "co-operation partnership and working together" as an alternative to "integration" Mar '96; with 25 hard-Left and LibDem rebels voted against renewal of the Prevention of Terrorism of Act Apr '96; complained that EU was not seen as relevant to UK's social problem and, instead of trying to solve them, preferred to "spend money on propaganda" Mar '96; voted for Bill Cash's European Referendum Bill June '96; was named as one of "Blair's Bastards" in Hull University research for having voted 36 times against the Labour leadership since '92, Sep '96; was re-named delegate to Parliamentary Assembly of Council of Europel and Assembly of WEU Dec '96; reaffirmed his opposition to a single European currency, claiming the EU was "dominated by people aged well over 60 whose minds were set in concrete by the Second World War" Dec '96; was re-elected with a majority of 14,200 on a 12.1% swing from the Conservatives May '97; backed Blair in resisting EU takeover of WEU June '97; was named a UK delegate to Assembly of OSCE June '97; voted to outlaw fox-hunting June '97; endorsed Defence Secretary Robertson's policies but urged him to read PAC and NAO reports to secure cost-effectiveness and avoid the costly scandals of the previous decade, also to take more cognisance of "the fact that this country's defence is now based on collective defence", particuluarly "the WEU as the hard core of NATO" Oct '97; suggested that "both Saddam Hussein and President Clinton, for different reasons, need a war" Feb '98;
Born: 5 January 1938, Stourbridge

Family: Son Gordon Davis, retired insurance man, and Gladys (Avery); m '63 Anne (Cooper), ex-teacher, Bromsgrove candidate in '79 and Hereford and Worcester County Councillor '73-85, on NEC '87-89, '84-85, '82-83; 1s John Gordon, 1d Katherine Margaret; **Education:** King Edward VI Grammar School, Stourbridge; University College, London (LLB, Union President); School of Business Administration, Michigan University (MBA); **Occupation:** Parliamentary Adviser, of Public Service, Tax and Commercial Union (PTC), who contribute £1-5,000 to his secretarial and office expenses '97?-; ex: Adviser, to Inland Revenue Staff Federation ("who contribute [£1-5,000] to my secretarial and office expenses" '84-95?; Sponsored, by MSF (£350 for election and £350 p a for constituency expenses in '79; "no payments are received by me") '79-95; MSF paid more than 25% of his '97 election expenses; Manager: with British Leyland '74-79, Rootes-Chrysler '68-74, Clarks Shoes, '65-68; Internal Auditor with Esso Petroleum '62-64;
Traits: Tall; dark; beetle-browed; crumpled Teddy Bear face; dark-suited; genial; sensible; personable; salesmanlike; dependable; conscientious;
Address: House of Commons, Westminster, London SW1A 0AA; 48 Hodge Hill Common, Birmingham B36 8AG;
Telephone: 0171 219 4509 (H of C); 0121 730 2246 (home); 0121 747 9500 (constituency office);

(Thomas) Hilton DAWSON   Labour   **LANCASTER & WYRE '97-**

Majority: 1,295 over Conservative 6-way;
Description: The marginal but Tory-leaning seat based on historic Lancaster, combined in '95 with the Tory-leaning small town of Poulton le Fylde and its rural hinterland; until the '97 election, it was expected - on '92 projections - to produce an 11,000-plus Conservative majority;
Position: On the Select Committee on Administration '97-; Lancaster City Councillor (its Deputy Leader '91-95) '87-97;
Outlook: The former child-care social worker and foster care manager and Deputy Leader who became the seat's first Labour MP in 27 years; feels "we need to make this country child-centred" (THD); with a small majority and a rural hinterland is one of Labour's five most vulnerable MPs to attacks from the Tory-backed Countryside Alliance; a supporter of Charter 88 and backer of PR; a rebel on gun law; "he usually leads with his chin" (Tory neighbour Michael Jack MP);
History: He joined the Labour Party '78; was the Labour Agent for Morecambe and Lonsdale in the general election June '83, and for Lancaster June '87; became Deputy Leader of Lancaster City Council May '91; was selected to contest the new Lancaster and Wyre seat '95; won the seat by 1,295, defeating the former Tory MP for Wyre, Keith Mans, on a notional swing of 10.6%; his majority was exceeded by the Referendum Party vote of 1,516, May '97; in his Maiden enthused about his beautiful and historic constituency but deplored its rendering plant which "blights the future and must go"; he also warned against being stampeded by the Dunblane tragedy into violating the rights of "law-abiding individuals" to do target-shooting June '97; voted with five other Labour MPs against a ban on all handguns June '97; expressed solidarity with jailed Indonesian union leader June '97; asked about BSE and landfill June '97;

asked about protection for children threatened by domestic violence June '97; asked about hundreds of thousands of tons of life-threatening waste products from BSE rendering June '97; asked about end of beef ban June '97; urged cancellation of the debts of poor countries July '97; led motion urging a Children's Rights Commissioner July '97; urged reconsideration of legislation on mobile homes July '97; voted against Government on cuts in lone-parent benefits Dec '97; welcomed Cynog Dafis's Road Traffic Reduction Bill as a step toward more "envrionmentally friendly and efficient vehicles" Jan '98; co-sponsored motion urging the establishment of a Ministry for Rural Affairs Feb '98; urged more influence for parish and town councils on estimates for housing needs Feb '98; complained that Tories were not "really serious about getting the beef ban lifted" Feb '98; backed the final leg of the Heysham M6 link road to boost the regeneration of run-down industrial areas Feb '98; urged more concentration on social services Feb '98; in debate on Adoption and Fostering, warned that "adoption is not a panacea; it is an over-simplification to say that it can be a solution for all children who have ben abused and then come into care; nor is fostering as an alternative to adoption invariably better than residential care" Mar '98; enlisted PM Tony Blair's sympathy for HANSARD reporters who had to sit up all night to record the "excruciating banality" of Tory MPs resisting the Minimum Wage Bill Mar '98; urged parents be allowed to retain their "crucial and seminal" place in supervising their children, rather than their teachers Mar '98; supported merger of local health trusts Mar '98; opposed motion of his colleagues attacking payment to Mary Bell by amending it to point out that "Mary Bell was herself a child of 11 years when she committed the grave crimes for which she was convicted of manslaughter some 30 years ago, believes that the concept of rehabilitation should form a vital part of humane criminal justice" May '98; warned about the impending worldwide shortage of chocolate May '98; complained that those leaving care were "grossly under-represented" among the "young people who go on to higher education"; "these people have explicit financial needs, and at least they should be supported through the long vacations" June '98;

Born: 30 September 1953, Stannington, Northumberland

Family: Son of Harry Dawson, teacher, and Sally (Renner) teacher; m '73 Sue (Williams); 2d: Charlotte '77, Helen '81;

Education: Ashington Grammar School, Northumberland; Warwick University (BA in Philosophy and Politics); Lancaster University (Social Work Diploma);

Occupation: Social Services Manager (UNISON, ex NALGO/NUPE) '89-97; in Lancashire Social Services '82-; Social Worker '79-; Community Worker '77-79; Kibbutz volunteen '76; Clerk '76; Brickworks Labourer '75;

Traits: Parted dark hair; good-looking;

Address: House of Commons, Westminster, London SW1A 0AA; 1 Malham Close, Lancaster LA1 2SU;

Telephone: 0171 219 4207 (H of C); 01253 899847 (constituency);

EXPLOSIONS

Sometimes an explosion unveils those who rely on our volumes. After the 1994 explosion damaged the Israeli Embassy in London, an eagle-eyed Welsh fan of ours scanned one of the pictures of its damaged interior and spotted a set of these volumes. A similar photograph of the interiors of other embassies would often show the same - foreign diplomats have been among the most enthusiastic about our interest in the positions of MPs on crises abroad, such as the deep split in the Commons over former Yugoslavia.

Stephen (Richard) DAY Conservative CHEADLE '87-

Majority: 3,189 (6.1%) over Liberal Democrat 4-way;

Description: The south of Manchester suburban seat with the greatest portion of 'top people' in the northwest; the eighth healthiest constituency in the country; a stronghold of Liberal voting in the '60s, when Dr Michael Winstanley held somewhat different boundaries '66-70; its strongest pro-Liberal wards were removed to form Hazel Grove in '74; in '83 it lost Wilmslow and acquired Bramhall; in '95 1,500 voters were added from Wythenshawe;

Position: Whip '97-; Co-Chairman, all-party West Coast Main Line Group '93-; Vice Chairman: all-party Non-Profit-Making Parliamentary Group '95-, Association of Conservative Clubs '95-; Joint Secretary, Friends of Northern Cyprus '92-; ex: on Environment, Transport and Regional Affairs Select Committee '97, Social Security Select Committee '90-97, Catering Committee '97-98; Co-Chairman: Parliamentary Advisory Council for Transport Safety '89-97; Vice Chairman, CPA (UK) '96-97; Secretary, Conservative MPs' Health Committee '92-??; Chairman, Yorkshire Area Conservative Political Centre '84-86; Otley Town Councillor '79-83, '75-76, Leeds City Councillor '75-80;

Outlook: Rooted, caring, low-profiled constituency MP with an unusual quota of common sense; unexpectedly promoted a Whip by Hague; preoccupied with social services and transport, especially transport safety; would have preferred railways to be "regionalised" before privatisation; father of the law for rear seatbelts for children in cars; normally loyal, but not on charges for tests for eyes and teeth or mishandling of coal mines or BR or Post Office privatisation; likes to rebel in stealth, without attracting media attention; pro: animal welfare (including foxes), Israel and Turks in Cyprus; a former Yorkshire salesman who inherited a safe Cheshire seat after his previous effort in Bradford West;

History: He joined the Conservative Party '67; won a seat on Leeds City Council May '75; won a seat on Otley Town Council May '79; was selected for Bradford West Dec '82; contested Bradford West against Max Madden taking 33% of the vote and losing by 3,337 votes June '83; at annual conference he urged Tories to learn from the Liberals, preaching their own message to the people and fighting more locally Oct '84; was selected to succeed Tom Normanton at Cheadle, elected with the same 55% of the vote June '87; won fifth place in the ballot for a Private Member's Bill July '87; in his Maiden he supported the Government's Employment Bill, especially its insistence that even non-voting members of union executives should be elected regularly Nov '87; voted for David Alton's Bill to curb abortions Jan '88; backed protest against International Cricket Conference for preventing "those cricketers who play and coach in South Africa gaining international representation" Jan '88; for his own legislation he opted for the oft-attempted Motor Vehicles (Wearing of Rear Seat Belts by Children) Bill which had its Government-backed, unopposed 2nd Reading Feb '88; welcomed the new prosperity which had come to the northwest Mar '88; opposed Government's new proposals to charge for eye and teeth tests Apr '88; supported Mates amendment for banding of poll tax Apr '88; backed further time for David Alton's abortion-curbing Bill May '88; his seatbelt Bill, slowed down in the Lords by the resistance of 'libertarians' like late Lord (Jock) Bruce-Gardyne, became law June '88; urged rapid inquiry into crash of Barlow Clowes investment house and compensation for investors June '88; backed free optical and dental examinations July '88; again moved to help Barlow Clowes investors Oct '88; voted against dental charges Nov '88; backed random breath testing Dec '88; visited Northern Cyprus with Parliamentary Friends of Northern Cyprus, as guest of its regime Mar '89; complained that Government had mishandled the issue of older war widows Nov '89; accused Labour and the BMA of circulating false charges against NHS reforms Nov '89; co-sponsored motion backing Turk Cypriots for having "declared their own state iin northern Cyprus" Nov '89; refused to take seriously the challenge to Mrs Thatcher by Sir Anthony Meyer, but admitted he would support Michael Heseltine if Mrs Thatcher stepped down Nov '89; attacked Government rejection of random breath-testing as "astonishing and cynical" Jan '90; urged life sentences should mean just that because a man who murdered a constituent had been released after twelve years for a previous murder Feb '90; rebelled to force government to provide extra cash to help elderly people and their relatives struggling to meet fees of private residential homes Mar '90; backed campaign for compulsory rear seatbelt wearing Apr '90; backed smoke hoods after Boeing 737 fire at Manchester in which 55 died May '90; visited Israel as guest of Conservative Friends of Israel; "I met the cost of the flight for my wife" June '90; was one of 11 Tory MPs who voted with Opposition to provide ring-fenced finance for enhanced local authority community care June '90; was named to Social Security Select Commitee Dec '90; backed use of cameras to deter speeding Dec '90; opposed linkage of Iraqi aggression with Israel's occupation: "Iraq's invasion of Kuwait was an act of naked aggression, but Israel's occupation of the West Bank and Gaza was brought about by decades of Arab intolerance of the state of Israel" Jan '91; as Co-Chairman of the Parliamentary Advisory Council for Transport Safety, backed random breath-testing Feb '91; having served on the committee on the National Health Service and Community Care Bill, was sure that the reforms were "the one way in which to save the NHS for the year 2000" Apr '91; was a Teller (with Teresa Gorman) for Bill to exempt video shops from being banned from Sunday trading May '91; urged Government to reconsider smoke hoods for aircraft Oct '91; congratulated PM Major on more NHS spending Nov '91; urged reminders of need for rear passengers to belt up Feb '92; said that although Cheadle was "a prosperous constituency", its businessmen were facing "serious difficulties" Feb '92; with Hugh Dykes moved an amendment to Railways Bill - later adopted in Lords - to allow BR to bid for its privatised chunks Mar '92; retained seat with majority up from 10,631 to 15,778, a swing to Conservative of 4.53%, largely from decline of Liberal Democrats Apr '92; was confirmed on Social Security Select Committee July '92; was one of 41 Tories who voted for £11,000 additional office allowance for MPs, against Whips' wishes July '92; opposed voluntary euthanasia Sep '92; urged Government action against Arab boycott of Israel, to herald Israeli PM Rabin's "welcome visit" Nov '92; said that "for the public to believe that they can rely on the state to provide a basic pension that will meet all their needs is, in the modern age, living in cloud cuckoo land"; "those who rely totally on existing state benefits definitely struggle" Nov '92; hesitated on how to express his unhappiness about pits closures Dec '92; warned against curbs on press for fear it might limit investigations of scandals like Barlow Clowes or Maxwell Jan '93; admitting "there are no easy answers" to causes of crime; insisted persistent offenders had to be "removed from circulation" Mar '93; was one of three Tory MPs who abstained against the Government on its handling of the coalmines, with four voting against Mar '93; co-deplored 3.7m abortions in 25 years of Abortion Act Apr '93; urged BR be allowed to bid for chunks of its operations, since "we shall rely on it if the franchise system breaks down" May '93; protested increased air flights over Stockport July '93; urged continued production of 146 at Woodford plant of British Aerospace in his constituency Dec '93; as Parliamentary Consultant to NALGO, complained that attacks on the NHS "may be construed by members of that union to be an attack on them"; "the NHS is a great institution; I am proud to say that I rely totally on the NHS for my health provision" Jan '94; warned against agreeing to Sinn Fein requests that British Government became a "persuader of the the people of Northern Ireland to join an united Ireland" Feb '94; voted to restore capital punishment, especially for cop-killers Feb '94; voted against reducing age of homosexual consent, either to 18 or 16, Feb '94; "as one who has been at the receiving end of an IRA bomb and has been hospitalised as a result, as was my wife, I perceive the greatest threat to civil liberties to be terrorism itself" Mar '94; urged early completion of the Manchester Airport Eastern Link Road and the upgrading of West Coast Main Line Apr '94; was among 7 Tory MPs backing motion opposing Post Office privatisation July '94; co-signed letter to EVENING STANDARD defending Turkish Cypriots July '94; welcomed MORI Poll showing most Tory constituency chairmen opposed Post Office privatisation Oct '94; signed Kenneth Baker's motion congratulating PM John Major for asserting it was not in UK's interest to join a single European currency in '97, Feb '95; voted against extending Sunday pub hours Feb '95; co-signed motion urging "huge progress in decommissioning" before Sinn Fein were admitted to Northern Ireland talks Mar '95; voted for John McFall's Bill against fox-hunting and animal cruelty Mar '95; opposed "Labour's ridiculous proposals for regional assemblies" as "getting in the way of private industry" June '95; with 22 other Tory MPs voted in favour of full disclosure of outside earnings, as recommended by the Nolan Report Nov '95; despite expressing concern over rail privatisation, did not vote against the Major Government on this issue Feb '96; in rail safety debate, expressed his reservations about the method of rail privatisation, but claimed "privatisation in general has been a great success for the people of this country" Apr '96; voted for Bill Cash's European Referendum Bill June '96; voted to restore caning Jan '97; urged proper local environmental safeguards in expansion of Manchester Airports Jan '97; urged big developers be forced to pay costs of appeals, win or lose, because costly appeals made councils afraid of refusing planning bids Apr '97; was re-elected by a majority down to 3,189 on a notional 11% swing to the LibDems, leaving him as one of only two remaining Conservative MPs in the Manchester-Liverpool conurbations May '97; was an early backer of Hague for Leader June '97; was only Tory of 119 MPs signing anti-foxhunting motion June '97; voted to outlaw fox-hunting June '97; was named to the Environment, Transport and Regional Affairs Select Committee July '97; was one of eight Tory MPs to vote for Mike Foster's anti-hunting Bill on 2nd Reading Nov '97; was named a Whip Nov '97; was named to Catering Committee Mar '98;

Born: 30 October 1948, Leeds

Family: Son, late Francis Day, engineer and shop assistant, and Anne (Webb); m 1st '71; 1s Alexander '72; m 2nd '82 Frances (Booth); separated amicably after 15 years, blaming the "pressures of Parliamentary life" Nov '97;

Education: Otley Secondary School; Park Lane College of Further Education, Leeds; Leeds Polytechnic (MIEx);

Occupation: Parliamentary Consultant, to NALGO section of UNISON (at £1-5,000)'91-; ex: Consultant, Chromagene Photographic Laboratories Ltd (previously the Sales Executive and Representative of this Leeds firm producing photographs, printing and exhibition displays '86-87) '87; Sales Executive, PPL Chromacopy (Leeds and Manchester) '84-86, AH Leach and Company Ltd (Brighouse firm in Hunting Group) '80-84, Larkfield Printing Company (Hunting Group) '77-80; Assistant Sales Manager, William Sinclair and Sons (stationary manufacturers in Otley) '70-77; Sales Clerk, William Sinclair '65-70;

Traits: Blond; slim-faced; specs; young-looking; genial; engaging; side-less; "a jolly fellow whose sanity belies his daft interest in [northern] Cyprus" (Paul Routledge, INDEPENDENT ON SUNDAY); sports-minded (former member of Otley Sports Council); enjoys movies, history (esp Roman) and music; "I am not a religious fanatic; indeed, I am not a regular

churchgoer";
Address: House of Common, Westminster, London SW1A 0AA; Cheadle Conservative Association, Mellor Road, Cheadle Hulme, Cheadle, Cheshire, SK8 5AT;
Telephone: 0171 219 3616/6200 (H of C); 0161 6875 (constituency);

Mrs Janet (Elizabeth Ann) DEAN   Labour   BURTON '97-

Majority: 6,330 over Conservative 4-way;
Description: The brewing town which was Conservative 1950-97 because pro-Labour Burton and Uttoxeter were outvoted by their pro-Tory rural hinterlands; even before the election, this balance was tilted in '95 when it lost two strong Tory wards; despite three breweries and JCB factories, it has high unemployment;
Position: On Catering Select Committee '97-; ex: Staffordshire County Councillor '81-97; East Staffordshire Borough Councillor (Mayor '96-97) '91-97; Uttoxeter Town Councillor (Vice Chairman: Social Services '93-96, Highways '85-93)'95-; Founder-Member of Uttoxeter Crime Prevential
Panel, President, Uttoxeter Citizens' Advice Bureau; on Arthritis Research Campaign;
Outlook: The motherly, ultra-busy three-level local government activist who ousted barrister-MP Sir Ivan Lawrence QC, the one-man fan club of Michael Howard; she was previously active on local issues like fighting, successfully, for the Uttoxeter bypass and against the closure of the local magistrates' court; "known to favour traditional Labour values, [she] did not receive a visit from Mr Blair"; local journalists described Mrs Dean, a former Mayor of East Staffordshire, as a John Prescott fan who "could not really be described as New Labour" (Job Rabkin, INDEPENDENT);
History: She joined the Labour Party '71; was elected to Staffordshire County Council May '81; was elected to East Staffordshire Borough Council May '91; was elected to Uttoxeter Town Council May '95; was selected from an all-women short-list to fight Burton July '95; her constituency's JCB plant was visited by Tony Blair Oct '96; campaigned that the Tories had "betrayed" homeowners; they "lied about mortgage tax relief, cutting it two years running" Apr '97; won the seat, ousting Sir Ivan Lawrence by a majority of 6,330 on a swing of 9.30%, becoming the second-ever Labour MP for Burton May '97; asked Chancellor Gordon Brown about his discussions with business about his welfare-to-work proposals since, having "six of the poorest wards in the West Midlands", they could help her constituency July '97; led motion deploring absence of local abbatoirs July '97; urged the Child Support Agency institute a simple percentage formula on "non-resident parents" to restore respect and provide needed child support Feb '98; urged more help from the National Lottery, because "my constituency has some of the most depried wards in the West Midlands" Apr '98; was tagged one of the 'Bottom 100' for having asked only 8 written questions in her first year May '98; asked PM Tony Blair to congratulate her local out-of-school club May '98;
Born: 28 January 1949, Crewe
Family: Daughter, of late Harry Gibson, farmer, and late Mary Elizabeth (Walley); m '68 late Alan Dean, railway clerk and town and borough councillor who died in '94; 2d: Carol Ann '70, Sandra Marie '72;

Education: Elworth Primary School, Cheshire; Winsford Verdin County Grammar School, Cheshire;
Occupation: Bank Clerk, at Barclays Bank '65-69; Clerical Worker, at Bass Charrington, Burton '69-70 ("before raising a family")
Traits: Blonde; broad face; chubby; seamstress (made wedding dresses for both daughters and nine bridesmaids in the same year);
Address: House of Commons, Westminster, London SW1A 0AA; Suite 13, Cross Street Business Centre, Cross Street, Burton Upon Trent, DE14 1EF
Telephone: 0171 219 6320 (H of C); 01283 509166 (constituency);

John (Yorke) DENHAM   **Labour**   **SOUTHAMPTON-ITCHEN '92-**

Majority: 14,209 (26.4%) 551 (0.99%) over Conservative 3-way;
Description: The largely working class area of the south coast's port city; has a "reputation for volatile voting behaviour" (DAILY TELEGRAPH); the removal of St Luke's ward to Southampton-Test and the acquisition of Woolston from Eastleigh in '95 was expected to help Labour;
Position: Minister of State '98-, Under Secretary '97-98, for Social Security ('Pensions Minister'); ex: Assistant Spokesman on Social Security '95-97; on Environment Select Committee '93-95; Vice Chairman, PLP's South East and South West Group '93-97?; Vice Chairman, Tribune Group '94?-95?;
Secretary, PLP Environment Committee '93-97; Southampton City Councillor '89-; Hampshire County Councillor '81-89; President, Southampton Labour Party '84-86;
Outlook: Energetic, young, idealistic internationalist who has outgrown his early flirtation with "extra-Parliamentary action"; "I am happy with the moderniser label; what has dominated people like me for the last few years was getting the Labour Party to understand the world in which we now live: a world in which 10 times as many people sell life insurance as dig coal" (JD); he believes in empowering organisations to enable people to run things for themselves, like tenants' control in Southampton; a housing expert who was the Housing Chairman of Southampton; helped expose the Wessex computer scandal; an architect of Labour's recovery in the south who has successfully worked to end his isolation as a south coast Labour MP by developing a campaigning strategy for building wider support locally; has favoured military intervention in ex-Yugoslavia; sees Britain's problems only soluble with allies in Europe and internationally; is a critic of the World Bank;
History: His paternal grandfather was a traindriver and union and ILP activist; his father was a Labour supporter, his mother a Conservative; he joined the Labour Party at 22, '75; was accused by Itchen's then-Labour MP, Bob Mitchell, of "trying to turn student union politics into the real thing" '76; as a leading member of the Clause 4 Group was an organiser of the democratic opposition to the Militant Tendency in the Labour Party Young Socialists and National Organisation of Labour Students for the six years from '76; as Itchen's delegate to annual Labour conference, moved the composite motion demanding a ban on the export of live animals, abolishing all blood sports and cruel intensive farming while studying alternative forms of medical experimentation not involving live animals Oct '79; was selected for Itchen

over Bryan Gould by one vote, on the announced intention of retirement by Bob Mitchell; was NEC-endorsed Nov '80; was elected to Hampshire County Council May '81; supported Tony Benn against Denis Healey in contest for Labour's Deputy Leadership Sep '81; organised 29 candidates to issue a statement insisting that "extra-Parliamentary action must play a major role in the efforts of the Labour Movement to establish a democratic socialist society in Britain" Feb '82; explained: "we can quite legitimately look for the kind of campaigning which means that the government effectively has to go to the country" Feb '82; warned that if Cruise missiles were to come they should be blockaded at Southampton docks Feb '82; was accused of belonging to a "Trotskyist organisation" by Douglas Eden in the DAILY TELEGRAPH May '83; campaigned against Trident, claiming its abolition would release funds for a bigger conventional Navy, likely to benefit Southampton shipyards June '83; came third, receiving 27.1% of the vote at Itchen, with Chris Chope winning by 5,290, and Bob Mitchell, by then in the SDP, coming second with 31.5% June '83; was selected again for Itchen by a vote of 32-11-8 from a shortlist of three Aug '85; made impassioned speech to annual Labour conference as the National Organiser of War on Want in favour of practical solidarity with 3rd world against "multinational companies" and "international banks" Sep '85; on Channel 4 said he was campaigning on jobs, health and a non-nuclear defence Oct '86; received 32% of the vote, 6,716 votes behind Christopher Chope, with SDPer Bob Mitchell coming 3rd June '87; at annual conference complained that Southampton was vying with Brighton as "the bed-and-breakfast capital of the South", exploited by "the bed-and-breakfast entrepreneurs, Mrs Thatcher's new risk-takers" Oct '87; at same conference warned against "the platitudinous repetition of economic policies that may have been relevant in 1976" but were "no help for the 1990s; nor are vague calls for public ownership, however desirable in themselves, which do not face up to the limited impact of buying subsidiaries of a global company"; "there is no purely British socialist economic policiy that we can now implement on our own; international action is essential; and just a few hours away from here is a place called Europe, and it is about time we stopped thinking of it as a strange amalgam of an evil Common Market and the playground for the worst elements of our football supporters; because there are people over there, and socialists, and trade unionists very much like us; and it is hard to believe, I know, comrades, but many of them have given far more thought to these issues - the issues of control, regulation, planning and regional policy in tackling the transnational companies - than our chauvinistic party has even begun to do; we do not have long, comrades; we do not have long to forge those links, but we had better do it quickly" Oct '87; was re-selected for Itchen; he retook Itchen by the slim majority of 551 votes, a swing to Labour of 6.59% Apr '92; presented a petition calling for a ban on stag-hunting in the New Forest June '92; asked about fire safety in large low-rise buildings June '92; complained that Government was driving a six-lane highway through Twyford Down, dumping the excavated chalk across the River Itchen Valley, "a site of special scientific interest" June '92; introduced Bill to bring civil airports within the scope of planning legislation, to enable Southampton Council to control the expanding airport at Eastleigh July '92; as a cricket lover, congratulated Hampshire Country Cricket Club on their victory in the Benson and Hedges Final July '92; voted for Bryan Gould for Leader and Deputy Leader July '92; said NHS money was being misspent, as illustrated by the Wessex RHA computer scandal Oct '92; asked about National Audit Office's computer specialists, in view of "£43m recently wasted by the Wessex Regional Health Authority" Nov '92; complained there was now too much student housing in inner-city Southampton which created behaviour problems and the deterioration of housing Nov '92; said: "I have believed passionately for many years, and have a great deal of practical involvement, in advancing tenant participation"; he complained that "the impact of [competitive tendering] is destroying the progress that has been made towards tenant participation" Nov '92; complained that, because of the absence of an effective licensing system for travel companies, 40,000 had lost their holidays with Bath-based Land Travel Dec '92; urged more environmental information Dec '92; deplored Labour's "unhelpful polarisation" between "modernisers" or "Clintonisers" and "traditionalists"; preferred Dawn Primarolo's idea of "taking inspiration from reality" in solving the practical problems of deeply-frustrated constituents dealing with redundancy and repossession; "we have to motivate our core vote but we can also reach out to voters in the private sector in ways which are radical and do not automatically accommodate Rightwing ideas; we have to show that there are massive things wrong with the way the system works, how the banks treat small businesses, how the endowment mortgages people took out might not pay up, how their personal pension money may be disappearing" Jan '93; urged the removal of the low-rent test from the Housing and Urban Development Bill, on the ground that it was inserted "as a result of lobbying by big [landlord] interests against the interest of ordinary people who happen to be leaseholders", who had a "right to ensure that those restrictions are fair, just and understandable"; tenants should have a right to veto any changes in management Feb '93; complained that EC trade policies were not co-ordinated with those of GATT and the Group of Seven; "if the European Community moves steadily, as I believe it should, towards monetary convergence and monetary union, the question of who represents economic interests and institutions such as the IMF and the World Bank must be faced"; "the World Bank is experiencing increasing failure; the proportion of policies and projects that work has halved, with failures rising from 15% to 40% over ten years" Feb '93; again raised "the waste of millions of pounds" by Wessex Regional Health Authority on computer installations Feb '93; in adjournment speech, welcomed the PAC's intention of examining the Wessex computer scandal which "it might not have done had it not been for inquiries by COMPUTER WEEKLY, the INDEPENDENT and myself"; claimed the Department of Health had long known what was going wrong but had concealed the truth Mar '93; welcomed Abortion Act on its 25th anniversary Apr '93; insisted that Labour councils were involved in many partnerships with the private sector, in contrast to the Tory "myth" Apr '93; co-demanded intervention in ex-Yugoslavia: "we believe the Left has a particular duty to stand up against the kind of pure, racially-motivated fascism which the Serbian aggressors embody" Apr '93; gave up as Chairman of Housing on Southampton Council but remained a Councillor May '93; after serving on the committee on the BR-privatising Railways Bill, again described it as based on "ideological dogma" May '93; co-wrote to US President Clinton urging military intervention in ex-Yugoslavia May '93; complained that union members in ABP Southampton were not being paid as well as non-union employees with contracts June '93; claimed that the North-South divide was outdated in unemployment: "there are more unemployed in the south; the rise in unemployment has been sharpest in the south since the second quarter of 1990; there are as many employment blackspots in the south as the north" mainly because of defence cuts July '93; in the wake of Labour's poor showing in Christchurch, where Labour's candidate - for whom he had been "minder" - came third, co-wrote a document, "Winning in the South", urging Labour to emulate Liberal Democrats in concentrating on street-campaigning Aug '93; at a conference fringe meeting, insisted Labour had to make itself relevant to southern voters Oct '93; voiced the fears of BR pensioners in the Southampton area about Treasury threats to their funds Nov '93; voted to "keep Sunday special" Dec '93; was named to Environment Select Committee Dec '93; blamed pension firms for mis-selling pensions because their salespeople were often poorly trained and working on commission only, "putting enormous pressure on them to break the rules" Jan '94; complained about Michael Portillo's "outrageous" foreigner-bashing Feb '94; opposed restoration of capital punishment, even for cop-killers Feb '94; backed reduction of homosexual age of consent to 18, Feb '94; complained that the 70,000 who had bought council flats leases with the council remaining the freeholder could not sell them because would-be purchasers could not get mortgages Feb '94; urged "value for money in tendering for new minehunters" Mar '94; complained that "since the beginning of the 1980s, at least 13,000 manufacturing jobs have been lost in the Southampton and Eastleigh travel-to-work area"; some of these were due to Government cutbacks in aerospace industry Mar '94; complained that New Forest had not yet received national park status, despite Conservative manifesto promise Apr '94; was "minder" in Eastleigh, where Labour pushed Tories into 3rd place June '94; urged industrial nations to create "an enabling environment" to stimulate economic growth in developing world June '94; attacked poor value of double-glazing and home improvement guarantees July '94; voted for Blair for Leader, Beckett for Deputy Leader July '94; deplored inadequacy of private pensions, most not being seen through to full term July '94; attacked acts of Brays private detective agency against Twyford Down protesters Dec '94; tabled motions on inadequacy of private pensions, urging their holders back into SERPS Jan '95; urged a unitary council for Southampton Jan '95; pressed for regulation of endowment mortgages Feb '95; insisted "people understand and do not resent justified inequalities in our society, but they resent rampant unfairness and greed that sit side by side with deep poverty" Feb '95; tabled motion calling for end to deer-hunting by the New Forest Buckhounds Mar '95; secured a debate on pension mis-selling based on his own experience May '95; claimed Southampton General Hospital was fiddling waiting list statistics June '95; welcomed return of Southampton's powers as a unitary authority July '95; was promoted Assistant Spokesman on Social Security, specialising in pensions, under Chris Smith Oct '95; criticised over-reliance on personal pensions in letter to INDEPENDENT Oct '95; retired from Environment Select Committee Nov '95; urged OFT to investigate Stagecoach's monopoly of Hampshire public transport Dec '95; pressed for Vosper-Thorneycroft to be allowed to bid to build minehunters Dec '95; charged Government promotion of private personal pensions was at expense of working people Apr '96; criticised management of Southampton NHS trust May '96; pressed for early pension-splitting between divorced couples June '96; with Chris Smith launched Labour plan for 'Stakeholder' second pensions June '96; backed 3% cap on MPs' pay rise, pension based on £43,000, a rise of £9,000, plus cuts in MPs' mileage allowances July '96; was re-named Assistant Spokesman on Social Security, now under Harriet Harman July '96; later denied informing Institute of London Underwriters that it was no part of his proposals that Labour would touch pension funds Oct '96; claimed "Tory pensions policy is like a pensions Titanic -millions are sailing unknowingly towards a retirement disaster" Dec '96; claimed changes to criteria for deafness pensions would hit war pensioners Dec '96; when Government back-tracked on war pensions, he claimed it had been "caught red-handed with its fingers in the pockets of war pensioners" Jan '97; claimed Conservatives' Basic Pension Plus scheme would cost £150b Mar '97; was listed in The FIELD as one of its 72 anti-hunting targets Apr '97; retained his marginally improved seat with an enormously improved majority of 14,209, on a notional swing of 12.3% May '97; his appointment as Under Secretary for Social Security was hailed in the City by big investment institutions May '97; insisted that "the Chilean national pension scheme has serious drawbacks as a model for pension provision in the UK" June '97; annouced far-reaching pensions review under his leadership to create a 'Stakeholder' pension for millions without ocupational pensions July '97; said "this country takes fraud against our social security system very seriously" after workers were encouraged to inform on employees who did not pay National Insurance Aug '97; reassured disabled workers that the "benefit integrity project is simply about ensuring that disabled people receive the right amount of disability living allowance - the amount to which they are entitled" Mar '98; insisted "we are committed to honouring our manifesto promise to try to find ways of getting more automatic help to the poorest pensioners" through pilot schemes Mar '98; urged ethical investment of pension funds

July '98; was promoted Minister of State replacing sacked Frank Field July '98;
Born: 15 July 1953, Seaton, Devon
Family: His paternal grandfather was a train driver active in the union and ILP in the '20s and 30s; his maternal grandfather was the prewar head of the Southampton Post Office; son, Albert Denham, Labour-supporting East Devon teacher, and Beryl Frances (Spence), secretary and former Conservative supporter; m '79 Ruth (Dixon) social worker and Convenor of Campaign Committee of Southampton Labour Party; 1s Edward '90; 1d Rosie '87; separated '96;
Education: Uplyme Primary school, Devon; Woodroffe Comprehensive, Lyme Regis; Southampton University (BSc Chemistry);
Occupation: Author: 'Winning in the South' (jointly 1993), 'A Democratic Voice' (National Youth Bureau, 1979), 'Reconstruction' (Labour Co-ordination Committee 1983), 'Profits Out Of Poverty?' (War on Want 1986); Chairman, Eastpoint Centre (community charity) '86-92; ex: Adviser, to National Union of Insurance Workers, from which he received "a modest contribution to my office research costs" '94-96; Consultant, to voluntary organisations on lobbying '88-92; Campaigns Organiser, War on Want '84-88; Head of Youth Affairs, British Youth Council '79-82; Transport Campaigner, Friends of the Earth '77-79; Adviser, Energy Advice Centre, Durham '77;
Traits: Dark; parted hair; good-humoured; intense; "a personable young man with the beginning of a Jimmy Carter smile" (Augustus Tilley, DAILY TELERAPH); "charming" (SUNDAY TIMES); "energetic" (Donald Macintyre, INDEPENDENT ON SUNDAY); "sartorially, Denham straddles the gap between the extra-Parliamentary and the Parliamentary; he unpegs his Michael Foot duffle coat to reveal a sharp brown-striped shirt and tie; charming and intent, he would never be mistaken for the humourless automata who typify Militant activists" (David Lipsey, SUNDAY TIMES); enjoys: sport (Hampshire County Cricket Club) and cooking;
Address: House of Commons, Westminster, London SW1A 0AA; 3 Tides Reach, Southampton SO18 1GE;
Telephone: 0171 219 4515 (H of C); 01703 235157 (home); 01703 702080 (Agent: Mike Creighton);

Rt Hon Donald (Campbell) DEWAR   Labour   GLASGOW-ANNIESLAND '97-

Majority: 15,154 (44.7%) over SNP 9-way;
Description: A seat renamed and altered in '95 but based three-quarters on his former Garscadden constituency in northwest Glasgow with the rest from Glasgow-Hillhead; its voters mostly come from the vast council estates of Knightswood, Yoker and Drumchapel, the last a byword for social deprivation; in health terms, it is the UK's 8th least healthy seat; former Hillhead voters from Glasgow's West End are more middle-class but not numerous enough to break Labour's invincible grip;
Former Seat: Garscadden '78-97; Aberdeen South '66-70;
Position: Secretary of State for Scotland '97-; ex: Chief Whip '95-97; Social Security Spokesman '92-95; Scottish Spokesman '83-92; Deputy

Spokesman: on Scotland '80-83, Local Government '82-83, Housing '80-82; PPS to Anthony Crosland '67-69; on Select Committees: on Scottish Affairs (Chairman '79-81, member '69-70), Expenditure '78-79, Public Accounts '66-68, Education and Science '69-70; on Liaison Committee '80-81; in Labour's Shadow Cabinet '84-97; on Scottish Council of Labour Party; Patron, of European Movement '90-92;

Outlook: The architect of Scotland's Parliament who triumphed over the Cabinet's devolution-sceptics only to be threatened by the SNP; compares himself to Kerensky as "a middle-class man who read books and did not make it" (DD) ; "he combines grip with vision, philosophy with bite; he is a master of detail who never gets lost in detail"; "in the range of his vocabulary, agility of his logic, the floweriness of his rhetoric, Mr Dewar is the Commons all-comers champ" (Matthew Parris, TIMES); "a strange amalgam of both old and new Labour, deeply rooted in the party's Scottish tradition, yet devoted to the Blairite revolution"; a "first-rate debater, assiduous master of any brief; cool head and sensitive political antennae" (Peter Hetherington, GUARDIAN); "one of those rare politicians who possess compassion and intelligence in equal measure" (Max Davidson, DAILY TELEGRAPH); his "'stick insect' appearance belies a politician with bottom" (Austin Mitchell MP); "a scion of Glasgow's professional classes", "a typical Scottish Labour laird and a prime example of the party's academically-inclined, legally-trained oligarchy"; "widely respected on both sides" "for all-round integrity and scrupulous reasonableness"; his "networking has proved crucial in keeping the potentially faction-ridden Scottish party united", as has "his extreme caution, which has led crueller critics to accuse him of being more calculating civil servant than vision-driven politician" (Ivo Dawnay, FINANCIAL TIMES); "very intelligent and convincing" (Frank Johnson, TIMES); "an endearing attachment to rectitude" (Edward Pearce, DAILY TELEGRAPH); "a man of such uprightness that when he gets to heaven, God will ask him to hear HIS confession" (Andrew Rawnsley, OBSERVER); an excellent constituency MP; "I don't see politics in terms of absolutes; I don't believe there is a monopoly of compassion in any one party" (DD); "he is sometimes too reasonable and tends to see the other side of arguments; that can be dangerous" (George Foulkes MP); was a fiery opponent of the poll tax who wanted to stop short of organised illegality; formerly a loyal Manifesto-Solidarity groupie; capable of putting a moderate case in rapid-fire immoderate language; long a pro-devolution would-be SNP-beater with a cautious approach to overly provocative devolutionary hotheads; is inclined to under-statement in his private life and views; was RMT-sponsored;

History: At Glasgow Academy he pinned Labour's election posters inside his coat and flashed them as he walked past May '55; he joined the Labour Party '56; met his hero, Hugh Gaitskell, at Glasgow University's Labour Club; became its Gaitskellite Chairman in succession to John Smith '60; campaigned for John Smith at East Fife by-election '61; at 25 was selected for Aberdeen South by its moderate selection committee after being recommended by his close friend John Smith as "another good Gaitskellite" '62; contested it Oct '64; won it at 29, unseating Lady Tweedsmuir Mar '66; said firm opposition to Ian Smith was needed in Rhodesia Nov '66; became PPS to Tony Crosland ("I never established a rapport with him") '67; backed David Steel's Abortion Bill '67; loyally defended Regional Employment Premium June '67; urged reform of Scottish divorce law Jan '68; tried to abolish 'not proven' verdict Feb '69; attacked as "crazy" efforts to restore hanging to Scotland Dec '69; asked for time for Scottish divorce Bill Dec '69; sponsored Divorce (Scotland) Bill Apr '70; attacked South African cricket tour as "a desperate and dangerous mistake" May '70; lost Aberdeen South to Iain Sproat, spending eight years out of Parliament from June '70; was in running for safe Stirling and Falkirk June '71; gave up Aberdeen South Nov '71; was one of five on Labour's Scottish Executive who voted for devolution but were out-voted by six anti-devolutionaries Dec '75; was selected as by-election candidate for Garscadden Mar '78; campaigned as a Centre-Left moderate, strong on Europe, pro-NATO, cool on state control; told SPUC he would vote to modify the Abortion Act for which he had voted; after having "almost despaired of going back to Westminster", was unexpectedly elected comfortably over SNP for Garscadden at by-election Apr '78; opposed extra police powers added by Tories in Scottish Criminal Justice Bill Jan '79; said loss of devolution referendum was serious blow for Labour Mar '79; said Tory attempt to create offence of "vandalism" was "totally fraudulent" Mar '79; attacked threat to sell homes of elderly Nov '80; on becoming deputy Scottish Spokesman resigned as Chairman of Select Committee on Scottish Affairs Jan '81; urged under-spenders be punished like over-spenders Feb '81; his constituency was threatened with Militant infiltration Feb '81; helped launch moderates' Labour Solidarity, going on its Steering Committee Feb '81; expressed doubts about use of tape recorders in confessions Apr '81; became Scottish Co-ordinator of Labour Solidarity June '81; asked why horrific rape charges were dropped against three Glasgow youths Jan '82; attacked as "primitive blackmail" attempts to force up Glasgow's rents by 25% Dec '82; attacked "mean" and "Philistine" attitude of Lothian Tories toward arts funding Dec '82; alleged Scottish police were undermining detention safeguards Apr '83; wrote a eulogy of Hugh Gaitskell for the SCOTSMAN Sep '83; supported Roy Hattersley for Leader and Deputy Leader Sep '83; on the Solidarity slate with 60 votes was tied third runner-up in Shadow Cabinet election Oct '83; opposed extension of council house tenants' 'right to buy' Nov '83; was promoted full Spokesman on Scotland Nov '83; opposed proposals for a high-profile disruptive campaign for devolution on the grounds that English MPs would not tolerate it Dec '83; attacked Government for not doing more to save Scott Lithgow shipyard Jan '84; urged a cautious approach to the inter-party Campaign for a Scottish Assembly Feb '84; attacked Alex Fletcher for "mismanagement" in selling off an education college for £5m less than it was worth Feb '84; pressed the NUM not to endanger Labour's position in the local elections by blocking coal supplies to Ravenscraig May '84; was elected to Shadow Cabinet with 75 votes Oct '84; carefully avoided giving direct backing to the NUM strike when speaking at a miners' rally in Edinburgh Nov '84; in a review of Castle diaries was anti-Castle and anti-Wilson Nov '84; voted for Enoch Powell's Bill against embryo experimentation Feb '85; demanded an independent review of the cases of 200 miners sacked for alleged strike misbehaviour Mar '85; won a partial victory over Scottish Secretary George Younger on aid for ratepayers hit by revaluation May-June '85; supported Caborn's Bill advocating sanctions against South Africa July '85; was reselected from a shortlist of two by 40 to 22 against semi-Trotskyist Oct '85; was elected to Shadow Cabinet with 88 votes, after the joint Tribune-Campaign slate was thought to threaten him Oct '85; attacked Robert Maxwell for use of barbed wire around his Glasgow news plants April '86; was tipped by the GUARDIAN as a possible moderate replacement for Denzil Davies as Defence Spokesman Aug '86; predicted Labour gains in the next general election, including Gordon Wilson's seat in Dundee Sep '86; was again elected to Shadow Cabinet, with 88 votes Oct '86; announced Labour's plans for a Scottish Assembly with tax-raising and economic planning powers Nov '86; again attacked the poll tax, this time as an "anti-social fraud" Jan '87; again predicted 50 seats for Labour in Scotland in the looming general election Apr '87; increased his vote from 56.2% to 67.7% and his majority by over 5,000 June '87; on the Solidarity slate, was again elected to Shadow Cabinet, with 93 votes July '87; was angered by Dennis Canavan's gesture politics in crying "I spy strangers" (English Tories) during a Scottish debate July '87; questioned the Government's commitment to future funding of housing associations Oct '87; resisted calls for a 'Constitutional Convention' to challenge the Government's legitimacy in Scotland, warning that it would end up driving Labour into the Nationalist camp Nov '87; unveiled Labour's Scotland Bill for a

Scottish Assembly with the power to vary the rate of income tax in Scotland Nov '87; said he was prepared to accept a Scottish Select Committee with Scots Tories on it representing English seats as preferable to no committee at all Jan '88; led Labour's debate on the Government of Scotland Jan '88; abstained on David Alton's abortion-curbing Bill Jan '88; alleged a "squalid conspiracy" by the Government in using backbench Tory Allan Stewart to amend the School Boards (Scotland) Bill to allow opting out Mar '88; against his wishes, Labour's Scottish Executive voted to support a strategy including a non-payment campaign against the poll tax as a last resort Apr '88; voted against a 26-week ceiling for abortion May '88; received 119 votes (joint 5th) for Shadow Cabinet Nov '88; was startled and damaged by SNPer Jim Sillars' victory over Labour's tattooed candidate at Govan by-election Nov '88; led the walkout of Scottish Labour, Liberal Democratic and SNP MPs in protest against Government's failure to set up the Scottish Select Committee Dec '88; after previously scoffing about Convention, sat down with SNP and Liberal Democrats for talks about getting a Scottish Convention under way Jan '89; sharply opposed opt-out of Scottish schools Mar '89; at Labour's annual Scottish conference urged a "Scotland independent within the UK" and "emerged as a driving force uniting Left and Right, quasi-nationalists and moderate devolvers in the battle to establish a Scottish Parliament" (Peter Hetherington, GUARDIAN) Mar '89; was attacked as a "Scottish 'Uncle Tom'" by SNP's Jim Sillars MP Apr '89; on a rare trip abroad, visited Bavaria to study German devolution May '89; succeeded in helping to hold Glasgow Central in by-election June '89; helped win the Tories' last two Euro-seats, North East Scotland and South of Scotland June '89; defended Scottish universities' four-year courses Aug '89; at Labour's Brighton conference, warned against poll tax protests becoming a poll tax rebellion; Labour councils would have to do their legal duty in collecting poll tax Oct '89; received 109 votes (15th) for Shadow Cabinet Nov '89; voted against War Crimes Bill Dec '89; said he would not propose a fully-sovereign Scottish Parliament which would make the UK unworkable and be rejected by Westminster Jan '90; claimed the Scottish Development Agency was being abolished because "it is an unacceptable reminder of the considerable success of the public sector" Jan '90; presented Labour's property-based alternative to poll tax, saying: "the vast majority of people live in a house that reflects their income" Feb '90; severely embarrassed Scottish Secretary Malcolm Rifkind by spotting that elderly English poll taxpayers were being given rebates despite their savings which had not been offered to their Scots equivalents when poll tax was introduced the previous year; he forced Rifkind to threaten resignation to secure the same concession for Scots retrospectively Mar '90; was criticised by Scots Labour MPs for his presentation of a property-based "roof tax" May '90; attacked Scottish Secretary Rifkind for having failed to intervene strongly enough to stop British Steel from closing its Ravenscraig strip mill May '90; criticised Scottish Secretary Rifkind for dropping large sections of law reform Bill under pressure from his own lawyer-backbenchers July '90; attacked Mrs Thatcher for forcing promotion of her "ideological toy-boy" Michael Forsyth on Rifkind Sep '90; rejected SNP's proposal of a multi-option referendum on Scotland's future as a cheap political stunt Sep '90; urged Rifkind to enter into a dialogue on devolution; promised: "Labour will deliver a Scottish Parliament" Sep '90; received 115 votes (joint 8th, up from 109) for Shadow Cabinet Oct '90; blamed SNP campaign of non-payment for poll tax surcharge Nov '90; became Patron of European Movement Nov '90; said "I would give a lot to be there" at the setting up of an eventual Scottish Parliament Jan '91; expressed concern that "very nearly one in four of children under 16 in Scotland live in households dependent for their living on income support" Jan '91; indicated to Liberal Democrats that he would prefer a modified Additional Member system of PR for a Scottish Parliament, which he saw as injecting a much-needed new political dynamic into Scotland Mar '91; attended European Development conference in Sweden as guest of

Swedish Social Democratic Party Oct '91; received 122 votes (joint 10th) for Shadow Cabinet Oct '91; urged separate Scottish Bills on reforming local government finance and higher education Oct '91; complained about the Local Government Finance Bill on council tax being rammed through its Committee stage in three weeks Nov '91; complained of payments to big Scottish landowners for not planting trees Dec '91; accused SNP of linking up with Militant against poll tax payments, ignoring warning by their ex-Leader, Gordon Wilson, against a rash and selfish adventure Dec '91; criticised British Steel and Tories for breaking promises to keep Ravenscraig open Jan '92; made a lack-lustre contribution to televised debate on 'Scotland - A Time To Choose' Jan '92; was attacked by George Galloway for having been caught "half asleep" on home rule, insisting on a new team to launch a counter-offensive Feb '92; criticising his own contribution, Dewar proposed Labour should sell its devolution policy as 'home rule' Feb '92; retained seat with majority down from 18,977 to 13,340 over Dick Douglas, ex-Labour MP who had defected to SNP, a swing to SNP of 4.99% Apr '92; after election urged a multi-option referendum for Scotland Apr '92; worked hard to overcome post-election apathy to get Labour supporters to polls for council elections May '92; before Shadow Cabinet election was discussing whom he would appoint as junior Scottish spokesmen; received 121 votes (14th) for John Smith's new Shadow Cabinet; with Tom Clarke's unexpected election to Shadow Cabinet, John Smith had opportunity to shift Dewar to Social Security, relieving anti-Dewar pressure built up by George Galloway and 'Scotland United'; Dewar had had enough of running the hard-to-handle Scottish Labour establishment July '92; said there was "major room for improvement and a shift in the balance of power towards Scots running their own affairs within this country" July '92; announced that Labour had abandoned its election pledge to increase the basic pension by £5 for single pensioners to provide a minimum guaranteed income for poorer pensioners July '92?; was again elected to Shadow Cabinet with 121 votes Oct '93; attacked Social Security Secretary for "scapegoat politics" aimed at the unemployed, single parents and the ill Oct '93; complained that the Government was imposing an "unfair increase" of another £2.2b in National Insurance, mainly on lower and middle incomes Nov '93; complained Labour had been "gagged" by the Government's decision to rush through debate on raising National Insurance contributions and shifting the burden of sick pay on to employers Dec '93; pressed hard for a review of the widely-attacked Child Support Agency Feb '94; opposed restoration of capital punishment, even for cop-killers Feb '94; backed reduction of age of homosexual consent to 18 or 16, Feb '94; agreed that Britain should not be a "soft touch" for scroungers but insisted Government should "concentrate on reducing waste and inefficiency in Social Secuirty and dealing with the chaos of the Child Support Agency, pensioner poverty and cuts in incapacity benefit" Feb '94; welcomed Gordon brown's decision not to contest Labour Leadership as "a disappointment to many of his friends, but taken in the best interests of the party" (DD) June '94; voted for Blair for Leader, Beckett for Deputy Leader July '94; polled 142 votes (4th) in Shadow Cabinet elections; retained his place as Social Security Spokesman Oct '94; did not rule out taxing child benefit Oct '94; deplored Government scheme to deny benefits to unemployed refusing low-paid jobs Nov '94; described as a "bitter anti-climax" the report of the Tory-dominated Social Security Select Committee urging easing pressure on absent fathers Nov '94; described as "a financial sentence of death" Social Security Secretary Peter Lilley's plans to cut income support for mortgage interest payments Dec '94; urged a common retirement age at 63, not 65, as proposed by Government Feb '95; backed Blair on revising Clause IV, despite opposition of his own constituency party Apr '95; said Frank Field's proposal of means-tested state benefits were "not on the agenda at present" May '95; defended minimum wage, attacking Lord Young of Graffham for taking a huge wage from Cable and Wireless while criticising the "greed" of teachers July '95; with Nick Raynsford, published a survey showing building societies feared more repossessions if Government required people to take out mortgage insurance July '95; described as "keeping it in the family" the appointment of Lt Gen Sir Thomas Boyd-Carpenter - son of a Tory peer and brother of a future Tory peer - as Chairman of the Social Security Advisory Committee Aug '95; dismissed Richard Burden's criticism of a Blairite "Stalinist" inner sanctum, insisting Blair had empowered "ordinary members of the party" Aug '95; was named -with Robin Cook and David Miliband to committee to spot "policy vacuums" and identify campaigning themes Sep '95; polled 156 votes (5th) for Shadow Cabinet; was named Chief Whip, replacing Derek Foster Oct '95; summoned Keith Vaz after 'Dispatches' programme alleging vote-rigging, intimidation and racism in Leicester Nov '95; was named 'Member to Watch' in SPECTATOR awards Nov '95; defended late John Smith against Hugo Young's charge of Anglophobia Dec '95; declared himself satisfied after a less-than-expected rebellion by 10 Leftwing MPs against Tories 1p cut in income tax Dec '95; prewarned Harriet Harman about hostility at PLP over her sending her son to a selective grammar school Jan '96; after Clare Short's breaking ranks over taxation policy, emphasised need to behave like "a government-in-waiting" in GUARDIAN letter Apr '96; urged "Tories with a conscience to leave the Government benches" after Labour's resounding victory in SE Staffs by-election Apr '96; with four other Shadow Cabinet members, voted for a one-year, rather than 18-month, divorce cooling-off period Apr '96; initially opposed as unworkable Jack Straw's proposal of curfews to combat juvenile crime June '96; defended Labour's front bench research trust, insisting most came from businessmen, not unions June '96; defended pre-legislation devolution referendum which caused resignation of extreme home-ruler John McAllion June '96; voted for 3% cap on MPs' pay rise and cuts in their mileage allowances July '96; polled 212 votes (6th) in Shadow Cabinet election, demanding Ann Clwyd and Diane Abbott withdraw charges the election had been rigged July '96; promised Labour would ban privately-owned handguns Aug '96; defended possible Lib-Lab co-operation in a "common cause" Sep '96; in joint press conference with LibDem Chief Whip Archie Kirkwood, urged stronger machinery for policing MPs' conduct Oct '96; with Robin Cook, George Robertson and Jack Straw, formed team to negotiate common programme of constitutional reform with LibDems Oct '96; defended free votes on abortion against Scots RC Cardinal Winning's attack on Tony Blair Oct '96; carpeted Ken Livingstone, Jeremy Corbyn and Alan Simpson for meeting Sinn Feiners in the Commons Nov '96; assured Left that new code to discipline MPs "for bringing the party into disrepute" would not stifle debate Dec '96; after talks with LibDems, gave assurance of priority for Scottish and Welsh devolution Bills in Labour's first year in office Jan '97; his claimed one-vote victory over the Government on grant-maintained schools was declared a tie Jan '97; after the Tories lost their majority with the Wirral South by-election, said he might put down a no-confidence vote if he had the Ulster Unionists on side Feb '97; retained his altered and renamed seat with a 15,154 majority, on a notional swing of 4.3% from the SNP May '97; was promoted Secretary of State for Scotland and a Privy Counsellor; warned hereditary peers they would lose their voting rights if they blocked the devolutionary legislation he would be steering through May '97; after Tory MPs tabled 250 amendments to his devolutionary legislation, imposed the guillotine June '97; the GUARDIAN claimed he "stands alone as a full-blooded advocate of devolution" against Jack Straw, leader of the curbing "English Lobby" in the Cabinet's ministerial team on devolution; he lost out on retaining the existing number of Scottish MPs in Westminster and giving Scotland separate rights to legislate on abortion June '97; angered SNP by rejecting Royal High School site for Scottish Parliament July '97; his 'Scotland's Parliament' White Paper was attacked by Tory spokesman Michael Ancram as breaking up the Union and welcomed by SNP Leader Alex Salmond as having "no glass ceiling" to prevent moves to full independence July '97; the all-party launch of the 'Scotland Forward' referendum campaign was marred by his refusal of questions about Gordon McMaster's suicide Aug '97; the campaign was crowned by a three-quarters 'yes' vote for a Scottish Parliament and a two-thirds vote favouring its tax-raising powers Sep '97; he was allegedly embarrassed by Peter Mandelson's claim a Scottish Parliament could not order a referendum on independence, after Dewar had secured that right in a Cabinet battle Sep '97; Downing Street distanced itself from his remarks to Edinburgh journalists that a Lockerbie trial of the two Libyan accused was unlikely and "the time has come to move on" Sep '97; his first choice of press chief for the Scottish Office, Gordon Brown's brother John, was vetoed by No 10 in case it seemed like nepotism Oct '97; he unified Scottish water in the public sector, responsible to the new Scottish Parliament, but replaced manifesto-promised mutualisation by a public-private partnership in investment Dec '97; in the published version of the Scotland Bill, his battle was won to retain the Barnett Formula giving Scotland a higher proportion of spending per head on education and health Dec '97; his ex-wife's second husband, Lord Irvine, discussing the Scotland Bill with friends, said "I wrote it; all of it" (TIMES) Dec '97; Dewar announced he was a candidate for Scotland's First Minister after Robin Cook dropped out, allegedly at Blair's instigation Jan '98; with the almost complete support of Scottish Labour MPs, apart from Tam Dalyell, secured passage of the Scotland Bill setting up Scotland's Parliament, skating over the "West Lothian question" Jan '98; apologised to Sean Connery for "speculation" that Ministers had blocked his knighthood because of his support for the SNP Jan '98; chose the site of a former brewery near Holyrood Palace for the new Parliamentary building and launched its design competition Jan '98; was accused of panicking - after a poll showed the SNP 41%-to-36% ahead of Labour - by promising the new Scottish Parliament would assume its full powers soon after the May '99 election, instead of waiting until Jan 2000, May '98; on scientific and economic advice, agreed to ending Dounreay reprocessing after eight years June '98; named friend Gus Macdonald as new Scottish Industry Minister and life peer Aug '98;

Born: 21 August 1937, Glasgow

Family: S Dr Alasdair Dewar, consultant dermatologist, an "intellectual doctor with gently nationalistic views" who was long confined to a sanitorium with tuberculosis, and Mary (Bennett), who suffered a serious brain operation when he was small; he was "an only child, a very lonely child; a fish out of water in my school with no social experience at all"; m '64 Alison (McNair); 1s Iain '68 (went to art school), 1d Marian '65 (has worked for trade union); separated '70, divorced '73; she then remarried in '74 Alexander/'Derry' (later Lord) Irvine; "I have not remarried because I have not remarried" (DD);

Education: Prep school in Hawick while his parents were both ill; Moss Park Primary ("I stood out like a sore thumb": "a quiet child with spectacles and not much confidence"); Glasgow Academy (fee-paying day school where he was a "total misfit", incapable of spelling or sports); Glasgow University (President of Union '61-62, MA, LLB);

Occupation: Solicitor: qualified '64, Consultant '92-97, Partner '75-92 in Ross Harper and Murphy, Glasgow '75-97; formerly Sponsored, by RMT (ex NUR; £750 for constituency, 80% of election expenses) '82-95; ex: Broadcaster, on Radio Clyde '76?-79; Social Work Reporter for Lanarkshire '70-75;

Traits: "He may have the skull-face of the Giles cartoon schoolmaster Chalky, the warmth of an Aberdeen breeze, and the charisma of a senior chemistry don, but by golly he carries authority"; "vinegary, rude, unbridled in mockery; [has] grisly elegance;" "pervading wry pessimism"; "looks and sounds like a cadaverous Dickensian magistrate"; "he exudes a sort of bleak, gale-lashed Calvinism"; with "that whiff of the archaic, evoking an ascetic probity" (Matthew Parris, TIMES); tall; dark; angular; lean; specs; forelock; hunched; beaky ("his nose stabbing at the Tories as if they were whelks to be picked" Colin Welch, DAILY MAIL); "the man for whom image consultants coined the phrase 'style-challenged': look along the green

rows of tidy suits and polished faces, and you are sure to see him, slumped, arms folded, sublimely indifferent to the shirt straying from his waistband and a lock of hair straying over his forehead" (Margaret Vaughan, GLASGOW HERALD); Dennis Skinner "once confided to me that, apart from him, I was the worst-dressed Member" (DD); has a troubling back, with an extra vertebra, which makes him exercise his right leg after inactivity, giving him "the air of a bespectacled stork warming up for a run"; "a considerate man with little sense of self-importance"; dyslexic ("I once spelled Garibaldi five different ways, all wrong, in one essay" (Colette Douglas-Home, SCOTSMAN); untidy (police thought his office had been burgled, but he had to admit it always looked that way); rapid speaker; acerbic; "witty and engaging" (David McKie, GUARDIAN); "selectively gregarious" (Roy Hattersley); "another Dewar virtue turned vice is his strong personal loyalty," "which is widely deemed to betray a lack of ruthlessness bordering on the unprofessional" (Ivo Dawnay, FINANCIAL TIMES); "wanders the corridors of Westminster as a figure of Gothic gloom, a constant worrier, a pessimist - though in private he can be jovial company"; "the lang streak of misery" (Ewen MacAskill, SCOTSMAN); "the only time he is truly happy is when he is totally depressed" (Shadow Cabinet colleague); "has the capability to exhaust time and encroach upon eternity" (Lord Douglas-Hamilton MP); "humorous, receptive and amiably conspiratorial" (SCOTSMAN); a workaholic who rarely takes holidays, almost never goes abroad (long without a passport, almost like Dennis Skinner): "I'd rather just be around Glasgow" (DD); "his passions outside politics are varied - from 18th and 19th century Scottish history to the post-impressionist school of Scottish 'colourists' - McTaggart, Peploe, Cadell - and even American football, he has an affection for the chatter of constituents" (Peter Hetherington, GUARDIAN);
Address: House of Commons, Westminster, London SW1A 0AA; "while in London, he shares a flat with colleagues in South London; at weekends and holidays, lives in the Glasgow house that he inherited from his father" (DAILY TELEGRAPH): 23 Cleveden Road, Glasgow G12 0PQ;
Telephone: 0171 219 4031/5153 (H of C); 0141 334 2374 (home); 0141 552 2416 (constituency);

Andrew DISMORE   Labour   **HENDON '97-**

Majority: 6,155 over Conservative 6-way;
Description: The '95 merger of old Hendon North with two wards of old Hendon South in northwest London; a multi-class seat with upper-middle-class Mill Hill (including the public school), middle-class Edgware, and the vast council estate of Burnt Oak; it is also multi-ethnic with a fifth of non-white residents and a sizeable Jewish minority;
Position: On Select Committee on Accommodation and Works '97-; ex: Westminster City Councillor (Leader of its Labour Group '90-, their Whip '82-90) '82-97;
Outlook: The former Leader of the minority Labour Group on embattled Westminster City Council who won an unexpected victory in Hendon, ousting the veteran Tory MP and PRman, Sir John Gorst; the first Labour MP there since 1950; an assiduous written questioner who posed 106

in his first year; a very hardworking, dogged campaigner with a bright legal mind; resourceful and hard-hitting but not overly charming or charismatic; on Westminster Council was thought better as Labour's Whip than as the Leader of the minority Labour Group; a Left-of-Centre solicitor interested in the rights of accident victims; in CND, the Fabian Society, Co-operative Party, Action for Southern Africa, and the Society of Labour Lawyers;

History: He joined the Labour Party '74; was elected to Westminster City Council May '82; became Whip of its minority Labour Group Dec '82; became Leader of its minority Labour Group May '90; he agreed with the thesis that Westminster Council Tories under Shirley Porter had deliberately waived millions of pounds of repair bills to encourage Tory supporters to buy flats to increase the Tory vote in marginal wards; said "I would be extremely surprised, given the importance of the home-for-votes sales drive, if the associated problem of the high leaseholders' bills were not brought to the attention of the leading members running the council at that time" Jan '95; was selected to contest Hendon against Sir John Gorst, who had been active in defending Edgware Hospital '95; unexpectedly won Hendon from Sir John Gorst, by a majority of 6,155 on a high pro-Labour notional swing of 16.21% May '97; in a meeting with new Minister Alan Milburn, learned that it was considered a waste of money and would raise false expectations to promise to save the Accident and Emergency department of Edgware Hospital May '97; continued to campaign for Edgware Hospital, securing a commitment to building of new Edgware Community Hospital June '97; asked about an enhanced Rough Sleepers' Initiative June '97; asked about statutory bereavement payment under the Fatal Accidents Acts June '97; in his Maiden, backed a London-wide authority and emphasised that in Hendon "5,000 families - almost one in four households of working age - have no breadwinner" June '97; backed outlawing of fox-hunting June '97; expressed solidarity with jailed Indonesian union leader June '97; "as a personal injury lawyer" complained that a the life of a child killed in an accident - perhaps mown down by a drunken driver - was "worth practically nothing" June '97; asked a brace of questions on the Criminal Injuries Compensation Scheme June '97; complained about "the previous Government's education policy, which turned out illiterate and semi-literate pupils from primary school" June '97; led motion calling for a public inquiry into the running of Westmister City Council; this was signed by over 100 MPs, but was brought to a halt by the lawyers for Dame Shirley Porter who pointed out there was a court action pending June-July '97; asked about regulation of immigration advisers July '97; led a motion in praise of Boosey and Hawkes July '97; co-wrote a letter to TIMES deploring Lord Rees-Mogg's "black propaganda" defence of Dame Shirley Porter Sep '97; urged pressure on PM Netanyahu to secure mutually advantageous settlement with Palestinian Arabs Nov '97; backed efforts to speed personal injury compensation Nov '97; urged efforts to overcome prejudice against those suffering from mental illness Dec '97; introduced debate on scandals in Westminster City Council Jan '98; urged increased taxation of casinos Jan '98; backed Road Traffic Reduction Bill Jan '98; complained of 600 racist sites on internet Mar '98; suggested "it would be in the best interestof all Cypriots if Cyprus were to accede to the European Union" Mar '98; claimed conditional fees had become increasingly popular with solicitors' clients Mar '98; claimed that pensioner poverty was a serious problem in Colindale and Burnt Oak Mar '98; complained about inadequate flood precautions in Edgware area Mar '98; "as a fellow member of the GMB" complained about non-recognition of its women workers in the casino industry: "is not that another example of bad employers trying to defeat the will of the work force because there is no law to protect them?" Apr '98; urged reform of court procedures to avoid delays Apr '98; pointed out that it was possible, even in London, to secure low-cost housing, citing how Barnet had "negotiated for 17 of the 60 homes being built locally by John Laing" to be rented through the Paddington Churches Housing Association; the same had been done with ex-MoD housing May '98; complained that the Greenwich Judgment had complicated school placement in Hendon, with Hertfordshire pupils coming in: "specifically, a grant-maintained school in my constituency -the Mill Hill County High School - has selected 45% of its pupils by aptitude and admitted another 110 pupils who are siblings of existing pupils; the net result has been that there are absolutely no places for children who live even in the same street as the school" May '98; was rated one of the 'Top 100' for written questions, having posed 106 in his first year May '98; complained about the slowness and inadequacies of investigative procedures in local government, despite the Westminster disclosures June '98; urged a Palestinian-Israeli settlement, required for the "economic stablity" of both June '98; complained that the "rather restrictive interpretation by the Metropolitan Police of data protection rules, they refused information to his local Victim Support June '98; called attention to Lord Neill's retention by Dame Shirley Porter while he held a Parliamentary post reporting on "probity in national and local government"; Lord Neill then dropped his Porter brief June '98; endorsed hiring a Chief Executive for the CPS, freeing up lawyers' time for lawyering rather than managing June '98; bridled at estate agent advertising for a "public-school-educated" negotiator July '98;

Born: 2 September 1954, Bridlington, Yorkshire

Family: Son, of Brenda and Ian Dismore, hotelier;

Education: Bridlington Grammar School; Warwick University (LLB); LSE (LLM);

Occupation: Solicitor: Partner, in Russell Jones, Walker, working largely "as a personal injury lawyer" (AD) '95-; ex: Partner in another firm '78-95; previously was an Employee of GMBU;

Traits: Parted dark hair; thick specs; dimpled chin; sharp nose; dogged; tenacious; dependable; resourceful; short on humour or charisma; is interested in modern Greek language and history;

Address: House of Commons, Westminster, London SW1A 0AA; 6 Leamington Road Villas, London W11 7HS;

Telephone: 0171 219 3000 (H of C); 0171 221 4720 (home);

'Jim' (James) DOBBIN   **Labour & Co-op**   **HEYWOOD & MIDDLETON '97-**

Majority: 17,542 over Conservative 5-way;

Description: These two Labour-leaning towns from Rochdale borough in Greater Manchester had a further 17,000 LibDem/Tory-leaning voters added from Rochdale itself in '95; it was expected to show a Labour majority of 8,000 on '92 projections;

Position: On Select Committee on European Legislation '98-; ex: Rochdale Metropolitan Borough Councillor (Leader '96-97, Deputy Leader '90-92) '94-97, '83-92; Chairman, Rochdale District Labour Party; Chairman, Rochdale Credit Union; Alternate Director, of Manchester Airport '96-97; on Community Health Council; on Rochdale Health Authority;

Outlook: Scottish-born local political fixer; one of '97's oldest entrants; "has established a reputation for campaigning hard" on traffic pollution (John Prescott MP); rebelled on cuts in sole parent benefits; self-effacing, but "doesn't miss a trick" (Rochdale colleague): a former NHS microbiologist and manager; is an enthusiast for decentralisation; RC anti-abortionist (in

Labour Life); in Amnesty International; ex-Fabian;

History: He was born into a Fife mining family; has been a Labour supporter from school days; joined the Labour Party '75; was elected to Rochdale Borough Council May '83; was elected Deputy Leader of the Labour Group on Rochdale Council May '90; was selected to contest Bury North May '90; was congratulated by Labour MPs "for his forethought and concern in taking up the plight of the employees of Stormseal UPVC" which went into receivership, after failing to pay wages and refusing its employees the protection of a union Feb '91; lost Bury North to Alistair Burt by 4,764 votes on a 2.1% pro-Labour swing Apr '92; disputed Paddy Ashdown's statement that he would not prop up the Tories, since "that is what they are doing in Rochdale" where the LibDems were in alliance with the Conservatives to control the council June '95; was selected to contest Heywood and Middleton in successon to retiring Jim Callaghan, with the backing of the local "T&G Mafia" Feb '96; remained on the Rochdale Council "to maintain continuity", after 10 local Labour gains ousted the Tory-LibDem alliance, with him becoming the new council Leader May '96; retained Heywood and Middleton with a majority doubled to 17,542 on a notional swing of 9.9% May '97; expressed solidarity with jailed Indonesian union leader June '97; in his Maiden, urged a redefinition of relations between central and weakened local government July '97; voted against cuts in benefits for lone parents Dec '97; was named to Select Committee on European Legislation Feb '98; complained about ill health caused by traffic pollution Mar '98; co-sponsored Graham Stringer's motion opposing acquisition of Great Western Holdings by First Group Plc Mar '98; complained about local "cowboy" housing developer, the Kiely brothers, who offered their own solicitors for conveyancing and also provided mortgages from linked firms; asked: "how can that be allowed in 1998?" Apr '98; was rated among the 'Bottom 100' for only posing 4 written questions in his first year May '98; co-sponsored motion attacking "abortion virtually on demand" May '98; urged provision of better health information for men over 40, June '98;

Born: 26 May 1941, Kincardine, Fife

Family: Son, of late William Dobbin, ex-miner, and Catherine (McCabe); m '64 Patricia Mary Duffy (Russell) teacher; 2s Barry Liam '71, Patrick '75; 2d Mary Louise '65 clinical and educational psychologist, Kerry Jane '69;

Education: Holy Name Primary, Oakley, Fife; St Columba's High School, Fife; St Andrew's High, Kirkcaldy, Fife; Napier College, Edinburgh; Fellow of Institute of Medical Laboratory in Microbiology;

Occupation: NHS Medical Scientist at Royal Oldham Hospital (MSF) '73-94; Alternate Director, of Manchester Airport '96-97; ex: NHS Microbiologist '61-94: worked for two Scottish Regional Health Authorities and one in Oldham;

Traits: Balding; grey beard; steel-rimmed spectacles; shaggy; self-effacing; behind-the-scenes manipulator/fixer; RC; Celtic football fan;

Address: House of Commons, Westminster, London SW1A 0AA; 43 Stonehill Drive, Rochdale OL12 7JN;

Telephone: 0171 219 4530 (H of C); 01706 342632 (home); 0589 519215 (pager); 01706 361135/361137 (Fax; constituency);

WEEKLY UPDATES

The weekly shifts in Parliamentary conflicts are analyzed by us in WESTMINSTER CONFIDENTIAL (£50 for 40 issues). A sample issue is available to you on request.

Rt Hon Frank (Gordon) DOBSON **Labour** **HOLBORN & ST PANCRAS '83-**

Majority: 17,903 (47.1%) over Conservative 10-way;

Description: Camden's southern half: Bloomsbury, Holborn, King's Cross, St Pancras, Somers Town, Camden Town, Regent's Park, Kentish Town, Primrose Hill; nearly half its voters are local authority tenants; a fifth are non-white, mostly Bangladeshi; in '95 Gospel Oak ward was transferred to Hampstead and Highgate;

Former Seat: Holborn and St Pancras South '79-83;

Position: Secretary of State for Health '97-; ex: Spokesman: on Environment '94-97, on London '93-97, on Transport '93-94, on Employment '92-93, Energy '89-92, Health '85-87; Shadow Leader of Commons and Campaigns Co-ordinator '87-89; Deputy Spokesman: on Health '83-85, Education '81-83; on Select Committees: of Privileges '89, Televising Commons '88-89, Environment '79-83; Chairman, PLP Greater London Group (Secretary '80-83) '83-87; Camden Councillor (its Leader '73-75) '71-75;

Outlook: One of Labour's unexpected 'tops of the pops', who has won popular approval despite problems with turning around his NHS "supertanker", including resistant waiting-lists; a rumbustious, aggressively partisan, witty, soft Leftist with bluff common sense, a knockabout style and an eagle eye for private "rip-offs"; a beneficiary of Blair's inclusiveness, but not of Blairite spin-doctoring; is unexpectedly back in the Health slot after long preparation for Environment; a traditional 'Old Labour' Left-pragmatist rather than a 'New Labour' Blairite; "not one of Labour's 'beautiful people' but a seasoned backroom operator" (SUNDAY TELEGRAPH); "brilliant" (Brian Sedgemore MP); "one of the canniest survivors in Westminster", "he deliberately hides his cultured intelligence under a bluff manner" (Rachel Sylvester and Alice Thomson, DAILY TELEGRAPH); "a highly professional politician who knows how to put the boot in" (Donald Macintyre, SUNDAY TELEGRAPH) - including accusing Tories of having put in NHS reforms "on the advice of a heroin addict and prescription fraudster"; "that magnificent old pugilist" (Ian Aitken, GUARDIAN); not originally an enthusiast for Blair's plan for an elected London mayor; a favoured by-election 'minder' despite his Bermondsey and Greenwich debacles (blame the candidates!); a radical internationalist (was on Executive of Chile Solidarity Campaign, and National Committee of Anti-Apartheid '80-85); anti-EC, pro-Greek; anti-nuclear; formerly RMT-sponsored (his grandfather and father were NUR members);

History: Joined Labour Party '58; was elected to Camden Council May '71; was elected Leader of Camden Council '73; instigated Compulsory Purchase Order on 36 Centrepoint flats; resigned on becoming Assistant Secretary to Local Government Ombudsman '75; was adopted as Lena Jeger's successor for Holborn and St Pancras South July '78, defeating Tory Robert Key there May '79; was on Chile Solidarity Committee deputation in protest at Foreign Office Sep '79; warned against dangers of sharp cuts in London Transport staff Oct '79; said all AGR nuclear power stations had been flops Nov '79; urged prosecution of Rhodesian sanctions-busters Dec '79; introduced Bill to strengthen Habeas Corpus Apr '80; opposed major nuclear power programme May '80; opposed break-up of ILEA June '80; urged UK leaders be compelled to remain above ground if they released nuclear deterrent Aug '80; urged Labour's boroughs to slap Compulsory Purchase Orders on land due to be sold by

Copyright (C)Parliamentary Profile Services Ltd

Tory-controlled GLC Sep '80; urged Michael Foot contest Labour Leadership as caretaker (because of his age) Oct '80; helped organise uproarious ban on Black Rod to give "short, sharp, shock" to Michael Heseltine's rent-raising plans Oct '80; attacked amnesty on "traitorous and illegal" Rhodesian "sanctions busters" Feb '81; opposed President Reagan's proposed joint address to Parliament March '81; voted for John Silkin, then Tony Benn for Deputy Leader Oct '81; disclosed only 17 Cabinet Ministers would be protected in nuclear bomb shelters Oct '81; was promoted Deputy Spokesman on Education, under Neil Kinnock Nov '81; staged debate to demand more jobs and training for youth Mar '82; attacked delay in solving gas explosion June '82; set up NHS Unlimited, to curb expansion of private medicine July '82; urged Namibia be rid of South African troops July '82; wanted curbs on local pimps and kerb-crawlers Dec '82; was minder at Bermondsey's disastrous Peter Tatchell by-election Feb '83; urged protection for tenants of short-life Crown-owned houses Feb '83; was chosen for reshaped constituency in preference to Jock (later Lord) Stallard Apr '83; won seat June '83; was elected Chairman of PLP's London Group June '83; backed Greeks in Cyprus July '83; complained about deportation to Turkey of Somers Town family July '83; backed Kinnock for Leadership and Deputy Leadership and served on his think tank Sep '83; contested Shadow Cabinet, winning 24 votes Oct '83; was named Deputy Health Spokesman, under Michael Meacher Nov '83; supported the campaign to keep the women-only South London Hospital Jan '84; backed better organ donations, his father having died of kidney failure Feb '84; charged Mrs Thatcher with "personal hypocrisy" when he disclosed that the private hospital to which she had gone for an eye operation had borrowed its equipment for her operation from a nearby NHS hospital Mar '84; conducted the first national survey to demonstrate the government was not providing the extra money or staff for adequate cervical smear testing Apr '84; told Mrs Currie: "when you go to the dentist, HE needs an anaesthetic" Apr '84; complained that the performance of the Metropolitan Police was "appallingly bad" May '84; accused the Government of "fiddling" the hospital waiting list figures Sep '84; won 26 votes for Shadow Cabinet Oct '84; led Labour's attempt to block Enoch Powell's Unborn Children (Protection) Bill to ban embryo experiments Nov '84; led a motion attacking anti-abortion campaigner Mrs Gillick Jan '85; led the opposition to limited list prescribing Jan '85; welcomed Michael McNair-Wilson's Bill to improve hospital complaints procedure Feb '85; described Nicholas Ridley as "the most arrogant, inept and stupid member of the present Cabinet - which means he has to work very hard for the title" Feb '85; his survey showed the health authorities were inadequate in collecting private fees and monitoring consultants' private work quotas Apr '85; warned US companies contemplating management takeovers of NHS hospitals that the next Labour government would "send them packing" May '85; said it would be impossible to outlaw "surrogacy for love" June '85; accused the Government of disgraceful cuts in aid to Bangladesh June '85; described Mrs Thatcher's new Cabinet as "the same collection of halfwits and ne'er-do-wells as before" Sep '85; won 87 votes for Shadow Cabinet on joint Campaign-Tribune ticket, but lost the runoff against close friend Bob Hughes for last place Oct '85; was re-selected from a shortlist of one Oct '85; said a future Labour government would use compulsion to take over private hospitals, remove all their subsidies and charitable status and decrease tax relief for private medical insurance Oct '85; told the BMA Labour would ban tobacco sports sponsorship and advertising except at point of sale Jan '86; welcomed Richard Shepherd's Bill to remove Crown Immunity from hospital kitchens Feb '86; ran Nick Raynsford's by-election campaign which took Fulham Apr '86; produced the first national survey of provision of treatment for infertility July '86; nominated Neil Kinnock for re-election but not Roy Hattersley Sep '86; promised total abolition of prescription charges in lifetime of next Labour Government Sep '86; won 69 votes for Shadow Cabinet on Tribune slate Oct '86; urged more explicit language to fight AIDS Nov '86; asked what companies had advised Wessex RHA on its computers; Health Minister Tony Newton listed four but omitted Arthur Andersen and Company which, with IBM, had won the first of the large computer contracts three months before Dec '86; his clause to end Crown Immunity in all hospitals, defeated in the Commons, was reinserted in the Lords Jan '87; complained that the Tube was becoming a haven of violence Apr '87; was re-elected with a 3% increase in his vote June '87; won 91 votes for Shadow Cabinet on the Tribune slate July '87; asked to be Energy Spokesman but agreed for two years to be Shadow Leader of the Commons and Campaigns Co-ordinator July '87; in the debate on Jeremy Corbyn's ex-IRA research assistant, said MPs had to secure the safety of the House of Commons, while preserving its liberties Nov '87; conducted a one-man inquiry into the King's Cross fire, exploiting revelations from union insiders Nov-Dec '87; criticised Government for failing to set up the Scottish Select Committee Jan '88; urged televising of Commons, admitting: "in respect of our behaviour, I doubt whether we have a reputation to damage" Feb '88; warned that ordinary people would be thrown out of Camden after the Housing Bill became law because rents would be driven up still further June '88; "in the European elections, when Labour did so spectacularly well, he should have been the man taking the plaudits; instead the credit went to that interloper from New Zealand, Mr Bryan Gould" (SUNDAY EXPRESS) June '88; claimed John Wakeham was acting like a "vile blackmailer" in saying it would be more difficult to persuade Mrs Thatcher to support Short Money for the Opposition if it resisted the Housing Bill June '88; received 116 votes (7th) for Shadow Cabinet (up from 91) Nov '88; complained that the Prevention of Terrorism Bill gave a victory to terrorism by according the IRA the "loathsome privilege of being acknowledged as a very dangerous threat" capable of diminishing "the openness of society" Jan '89; urged General Medical Council to investigate "dubious [kidney] transplant activities in private hospitals" Feb '89; tried to block King's Cross Bill to build £250m terminal locally for Channel Tunnel rail link Mar '89; spoke movingly of heroism in King's Cross fire Apr '89; deplored the soaring cost of the Government's publicity machine May '89; strongly backed televising Commons June '89; collected petitions to defend NHS against Government reforms July '89; complained of scale-down of mega-hospital at Euston July '89; deplored secrecy surrounding £15b Tory funding Sep '89; was described as unhappy in his post as Shadow Leader of the Commons Sep '89; deplored cut in school meals for 3m children: "children who study with an empty stomach do not do well in class" Sep '89; deplored £10,000 spent on US "jolly" for managers of Hampstead Health Authority Sep '89; in the '88-89 session was the 13th most assiduous questioner, with 316 questions Oct '89; was 6th on the Tribune Group slate for Shadow Cabinet Oct '89; received 118 votes (10th); was named Energy Spokesman Nov '89; claimed: "Chancellor [Nigel Lawson]'s resignation clearly resulted from the Prime Minister's high-handed, intolerable and disloyal treatment of Cabinet colleagues" Nov '89; predicted Mrs Thatcher would remain because "the rest of the Cabinet is spineless" Nov '89; was named Energy Spokesman, replacing Tony Blair Nov '89; derided withdrawal of nuclear stations from privatisation: "the most blatant rip-off, with the public picking up the nuclear liabilities and the private sector getting the non-nuclear assets" Nov '89; warned that UK would enter the '90s again as a net importer of fuel Dec '89; complained of cuts in dental care Dec '89; welcomed writing off of British Coal's debts, but not its threatened privatisation; opposed enlargement of private pits Jan '90; urged studies of nuclear power plants to establish the level of the leukaemia hazard Feb '90; accused Energy Secretary John Wakeham of secret subsidies to nuclear electricity industry in the form of sites Mar '90; attacked John Wakeham's promise of £2.5b to Nuclear Electric Mar '90; pledged Labour government would take whatever necessary powers "to control and regulate the [privatised electricity] industry in the interests of consumers, the environment and the longterm interests of the whole country", possibly repurchasing the National Grid Apr '90; said Labour would establish an Energy

Efficiency Agency and a Renewable Energy Agency June '90; urged dismissal from Thatcher Cabinet of Cecil Parkinson for his bungling of nuclear energy disposal June '90; forced into the open John Wakeham's private negotiations with Lord Hanson on trade sale of PowerGen July '90; described electricity privatisation as "one unending series of write-offs, rip-offs and pay-offs" July '90; promised NUM "a secure future for the coal industry" July '90; pledged Labour would not build any more nuclear power stations, adding that Sellafield would have to be retained for decommissioning purposes Oct '90; described the joining of the ERM as "the last throw of a gambler" Oct '90; secured 96 votes (16th) for Shadow Cabinet Oct '90; led Labour's attack on privatisation of electricity supply Jan '91; urged tougher electricity watchdog Feb '91; compained Energy Secretary Wakeham had under-priced Natonal Power and PowerGen by £250m in sale of their shares Mar '91; described electricity privatisation as "a system of outdooor relief for the City" Apr '91; blamed Piper Alpha disaster on inadequate Government safety standards Mar '91; blamed management of London Zoo for its financial crisis Apr '91; visited coal gasification plants at Montebello and Cooolwater as guest of Texaco Apr '91; complained of threatened use of orimulsion, "front-runner for the title of the filthiest fuel in the world" Apr '91; was rated the "top complainer" to Camden's Housing Department May '91; said he was no longer a member of Common Market Safeguards Committee June '91; deplored Government's failure to restrain profits of gas and electricity companies July '91; was involved in Liverpool's Walton by-election July '91; accused Tories of using £150m in taxpayers' money to publicise their charters July '91; asked John Major if he knew, when he accepted £100,000 contribution from Li Ka-shing, that latter was involved in King's Cross property development Sep '91; complained that threatened privatisation of British Coal "would mean nearly every pit in Britain would close" Oct '91; complained that Government had failed to improve its energy efficiency Oct '91; received 134 votes for Shadow Cabinet (up from 96), coming joint sixth after having "led a forceful onslaught on big pay rises for the heads of privatised industries and on business contributions to Tory party funds" (Philip Webster, TIMES) Oct '91; defended having published leaked Rothschild report urging privatisation of a drastically slimmed British Coal Nov '91; refuted John Major's speech on opening a private pathology laboratory in Camden, pointing out that hospital waiting lists had gone up by 194% since Major was an unsuccessful local candidate in 1974, Dec '91; complained of £150m spent by Government to publicise their Citizen's Charter Jan '92; derided Trade Secretary Peter Lilley for the "humiliating climbdown" in accepting EC conditions for paying £121m to mining towns facing pit closures, which Dobson had provoked Feb '92; promised Labour would curb coal imports Feb '92; asked John Major how many other Cabinet Ministers had visited Hongkong to touch wealthy Chinese for contributions to Tories Feb '92; retained seat with majority up from 8,853 to 10,824, a swing to Labour of 3.57%, despite spending most of his time helping Glenda Jackson win Hampstead Apr '92; backed John Smith for Leader, Margaret Beckett for Deputy Leader Apr '92; debating British Coal privatisation, said: "whatever else happens, the cost of coal privatisation must not be borne by the body and blood of the British miner" May '92; asked about chance for a referendum on Maastricht June '92; received 140 votes (4th) in contest for John Smith's new Shadow Cabinet, up two places; was made Employment Spokesman, at his request July '92; asked for a meeting with Metropolitan Police Commissioner to fight vice and drugs in King's Cross area; said magistrates were encouraging prostitutes by imposing low fines Aug '92; accused Tories of having cut industrial work force by a third since taking power in 1979, Sep '92; said: "we need to put full employment back at the heart of economic policy" Nov '92; insisted there were really 4m out of work Dec '92; demanded John Major lift the threat to over a quarter of a million jobs, including miners Jan '93; opposed any compulsory training courses Jan '93; urged Jobcentres to vet new job offers for vulnerable young women Feb '93; welcomed official figures of reduced unemployment but wondered whether this was another "fiddle" in the statistics, which had already been "fiddled" 27 times Mar '93; deplored inadequacy of Chancellor Lamont's help to only one in 30 of unemployed Mar '93; after another murder there by a drug addict, claimed "virtually all the drug users and pushers, most of the prostitutes and all of their clients, come from outside King's Cross; they come to the area because it has been allowed to become a seedy supermarket for drugs" Apr '93; claimed 4.5m people had lost their jobs since polling day with all but 320,000 had found other ones Apr '93; said "Tory Ministers should stop talking Britain down; every time they go to Brussels they whinge that Britain can only compete if British workers have lower pay, longer hours and worse working conditions" May '93; complained to Home Affairs Select Committee that John Major and other Ministers had sought donations from foreign businessmen while abroad on Government business June '93; demanded resignation of Tory MP Michael Mates for borrowing a car from Asil Nadir's PRman: "he shouldn't get a car from an organisation promoting the interests of a fugitive from justice" June '93; opposed clause allowing employers to bribe employees not to join unions June '93; agreed to transfer Labour-voting Gospel Oak ward to Glenda Jackson's more marginal constituency July '93; claimed a "scandal" in subsidising of Tory-led Westminster at the expense of Labour-led Camden July '93; demanded to know why Tory Deputy Chairman, Gerald Malone MP, had concealed his meeting with the fugitive businessman Asil Nadir Aug '93; urged Government to stop "playing politics with our schools" Aug '93; complained Government was trying to close Barts and University College Hospital to flog their sites to property developers Aug '93; complained that "compared with this time last year, there are 155,000 more people out of work and 750,000 fewer people in work" Aug '93; claimed Employment Secretary Michael Howard had secretly spent £4.8m to bail out the 60 skillcentres of Astra Training Services to prevent its collapse just before the '92 elections Aug '93; insisted, "everything must be geared to economic growth and rising employment" Sep '93; demanded to know why convicted forger Patrick Doyle had been allowed to acquire 13 Astra Training Services centres Oct '93; complained Government was weakening safety in mines Oct '93; in Shadow Cabinet election was tied for second place with John Prescott with 163 votes each Oct '93 ; recommitted Labour to "full employment" Nov '93; was displaced as Employment Spokesman by John Prescott, exploiting his new 'in' with Labour Leader John Smith; after loudly protesting - and being rewarded with new post of Spokesman for London as well -Dobson agreed to become Transport Spokesman Nov '93; complained Jubiilee Line extension should not be "left to the whim of property developers"; demanded to know why Government was blocking proposed EC legislation on higher safety standards for drivers of minibuses Nov '93; demanded to know whether it was true London's bus deregulation had been put off; welcomed delay, when announced, as saving London from being "gridlocked" Nov '93; after London Transport Minister Steve Norris first proposed privatising London Underground and then denied it the same day, said he was "unfit to be in charge of a whelk stall, let alone London Transport" Dec '93; backed 'Keep Sunday Special' as urged by shopworkers union, USDAW Dec '93; deplored the "shoddy" investigation of the Marchioness disaster, which he blamed on "the slack, idle and incompetent Department of Transport" Dec '93; claimed Government's deregulation would end transport safety regulations Jan '94; said the abandoned £135m plan for an international terminal at King's Cross was "a perfect example of public money thrown down the drain" Feb '94; voted against restoring capital punishment, even for cop-killers Feb '94; voted to reduce age of homosexual consent to 18, or 16, Feb '94; complained that ABB was not being allowed to lease much-needed new trains to seedy Northern Line Mar '94; after BR-privatisation was delayed for a further year, insisted "the Government must now drop the whole crackpot scheme" Mar '94; ridiculed Government's long period of indecision over Channel Tunnel rail link Apr '94; led an attack on the decline in the NHS in London Apr '94; as 'minder' in the Newham North East by-election, appealed to voters to protest against "London's shambolic transport system, homelessness and Mrs Bottomley's 'search-and-destroy' mission in hospitals" June '94; voted for Blair as Leader, Margaret Beckett as Deputy Leader July '94; attacked Railtrack for its "cavalier attitude" toward safety in the signalmen's strike July '94; attacked £1m share option for retiring privatised ManWeb electricity company chiefs as "just another round in the privatisation rip-off" Aug '94; urged Government to pay up and settle the signalmen's strike Aug '94; joked that he would found Labour Agnostics and Atheists Against All Religion to curb the spread of Christian Socialism Oct '94; his promise that Labour would reverse break-up and privatisation of the railways was qualified by a leadership statement that this might not be achieved in Labour's first term Oct '94; received 137 votes (6th) for Shadow Cabinet; was promoted Spokesman on Envrironment, retaining London Oct '94; promised Labour would return power to elected councillors from "rent-a-creep quangos" Nov '94; urged extraordinary audit by NAO of Westminster City Council after disclosure it had spent nearly £100m since '87, £72m on homes-for-votes scam Jan '95; in Nolan Committee submission, proposed ban on foreign and large secret party contributions and cap on general election spending Jan '95; proposed tougher audits of councils, including loony- Left ones Jan '95; dubbed the Government's rate support grant "a party political racket designed to help Tory areas and keep Tories in power" especially in Westminster Feb '95; welcomed Environment Secretary John Gummer's sacking of Local Government Chairman Sir John Banham Mar '95; welcomed record-breaking local Labour gains as "proof-positive that Labour is a national party again" May '95; commenting on adverse report on Islington Council having encouraged paedophiles, insisted "what happeneed in Islington was indefensible but I don't think there is a wider problem for Labour in equal opportunities because a load of child-molesters happened to dump themselves on Islington Council" May '95; insisted the grants to Westminster City Council were "rotten to the core" and if Norwich received the same grant per head it need not collect council tax and could give every taxpayer an £816 rebate June '95; condemned his local Camden Council for "waste and incompetence" in uncollected rents and allowing housing-benefit frauds July '95; spent the summer attacking the private water companies for their their inadequate services and their directors' 'fat cat' salaries July-Aug '95; opposed abolition of mortgage tax relief because of "desperate" situation facing mortgage-payers Aug '95; was applauded at annual conference in Brighton, promising to abolish compulsory competitive tendering in local government, back elected mayors and impose penalties on poor-performing councils Sep '95; after Brian Mawhinney attacked Camden for its grant to the Hopscotch Asian Women's Group, which turned out to be Home-Office-backed and linked to Princess Anne's 'Save the Children' fund in aiding Bangladeshi women, he accused him of being "guilty of the most slapdash preparation of his first major speech as Tory party chairman" Oct '95; received 142 votes (8th) for the Shadow Cabinet; retained post as Spokesman on the Environment and London Oct '95; complained that Government was forcing up council taxes Nov '95; welcomed Government's Bill to make compulsory audits of local government, urging it be extended to Health Dec '95; reported Westminster Council to DPP for housing homeless in asbestos-riddled housing Dec '95; opposed sale of Property Services Agency as a "bonanza for the usual band of accountants, advisers and consultants" Jan '96; attacked "deplorable" record of privatised water companies Jan '96; admitted ambivalence on an elected mayor for London, "but it is worth having a go" Mar '96; threatened poor-performing councils with "hit squads" Mar '96; accused the Government of being "a collection of swindlers looking after their friends" in rating Westminster as UK's fourth most impoverished place Apr '96; launched Labour's 'A Voice for London' proposals of a slimmed-down Greater London Authority, with only two paragraphs on an elected mayor Apr '96; was harangued with neighbouring Labour MP

Glenda Jackson for not voting against the renewal of the Prevention of Terrorism Act Apr '96; hailed the Magill report demanding Dame Shirley Porter and five others repay £32m for gerrymandering Westminster to save Tory control, claiming the Conservative Government including ex-Minister and local MP, Peter Brooke, was "up to its neck in the scandal" May '96; voted against a 3% cap on MPs' pay, to reduce MPs' mileage allowance, increase their pay and pensions to £43,000 July '96; after several speeches attacking Tory-controlled Westminster Council for "votes for houses" ramp, received 211 votes (7th), up from 142, in ballot for Shadow Cabinet July '96; was retained as Spokesman on Environment and London in Blair's 'final' pre-election Shadow Cabinet July '96; attacked award of 'charter marks' to privatised water companies, including two fined 42 times for pollution Dec '96; having lunched at the same restaurant, was able to confirm that Europhile Kenneth Clarke was the source of the BBC story that he had warned Eurosceptic party chairman Brian Mawhinney to "tell your kids to get their scooters off my lawn", threatening to lead a Cabinet walk-out Dec '96; denied Labour's spin doctors had tried to have him remove his beard: "if it was good enough for Abe Lincoln, it is good enough for anyone" Dec '96; warned Labour councils incoming Government would not change Tory-planned spending limits for next financial year Jan '97; released correspondence between DTI and Shell showing Government planned to dump 75 deep-water oil rigs in the Atlantic trough Jan '97; announced Labour plans to curb gazumping Feb '97; was accused with neighbour Glenda Jackson of shunning local Irish community Apr '97; was allegedly "banished to the outer reaches of Labour's election campaign" (Andrew Pierce, TIMES) Apr '97; was re-elected with increased majority of 17,903 on a pro-Labour notional swing of 10.5% May '97; his promotion to Secretary of State for Health and Privy Counsellor was "the biggest surprise of the Blair Cabinet" (Andy McSmith, OBSERVER) May '97; accepting it would take long to turn around the NHS "supertanker", he refused to reverse closure plans for Edgware Hospital's A & E department; announced more money for breast screening May '97; insisted cuts in still-free prescriptions would be "over my dead body" June '97; after considering the problems, announced a ban on sports sponsorship by tobacco companies June '97; promised a "no holds barred" NHS spending review; announced a review of London health care, with hold on hospital closures; began purge of Tory chairmen from hospital trusts June '97; as part of the Cabinet's so-called 'English Lobby' resisted Donald Dewar's effort to shift responsibility for Scottish abortions to Scottish Parliament July '97; announced forthcoming end of GP-fundholders' advantages on waiting-lists July '97; announced his plans to end the Tories "inefficient" internal market, cut waste, bureaucracy and paperwork and spend an extra £1.2b the next year July '97; described as "disgusting" models who smoked on catwalks Aug '97; admitted waiting lists would go on rising for some time Aug '97; was compelled to tone down his "off message" party conference speech, including reference to sacking health board members with private insurance Sep '97; announced he was considering making cannabis available for treatment of multiple sclerosis Oct '97; obtained another £250m to stave off winter crisis in hospitals Oct '97; obtained £269m for home care for elderly to free hospital beds Oct '97; announced overhaul of breast-screening Nov '97; announced plans to limit number of prescription issued by GPs Nov '97; PM Blair asked him to abandon the ban on tobacco sponsorship of Formula One racing (without disclosing Bernie Ecclestone's £1m contribution to party funds); was untypically evasive in BBC interview, but accepted Blair's Formula One policy Nov '97; was appalled by need of Warwickshire Health Authority to recheck 18,000 cervical cancer smears Nov '97; admitted that waiting lists, rising at 1,000 a week, would take long to turn around Nov '97; made a statement on Utting Report on child abuse in residential homes Nov '97; announced a commission to reform the system of paying for longterm care Dec '97; announced 'The New NHS' White Paper, phasing in abolition of internal market and replacing GP fundholding by larger primary care groups Dec

'97; was reported "seething" over Education Secretary David Blunkett's alleged claim that their departments would only get more money if £26m was cut from disability benefits Dec '97; announced appointment of 'waiting-list buster' Dec '97; ordered NHS managers to prosecute anyone assaulting NHS staff Dec '97; denied political bias in new appointments when Tories pointed to his naming the wife of Labour's Lord McIntosh as Chairman of Great Ormond Street Hospital Trust Dec '97; was alleged to back David Blunkett against Tony Blair in Cabinet argument over welfare reform Jan '98; announced scrapping of "care in the community" arrangements for mentally-ill patients as causing the deaths of innocent people Jan '98; suggested easing abortion rules to achieve easier, earlier terminations Jan '98; accepted Turnberg Report on improving London health care, especially for its most deprived; Barts was saved, eventually as a cardiac and cancer centre Feb '98; reaffirmed intention to ban tobacco advertising Feb '98; claimed £500m would shorten waiting lists within 12 months Mar '98; was mooted as a 'stop Livingstone' candidate for London's mayor; made it clear he preferred being Health Secretary - "the one job I wanted" Mar '98; was jeered by nurses when he apologised for paying their increases in stages Apr '98; set new targets to ensure that, within a year, waiting lists were brought down to those inherited May '98; in the DAILY TELEGRAPH's Gallup Poll, he was rated by 50% as having done a good job, a bad job by 36% May '98; announced half of the 1,000 board members he had appointed had been women and the proportion of non-whites had doubled June '98; said he would earmark much of the £21b secured for the next three years to ensure results; there was some scepticism about his promise to recruit up to 7,000 additional doctors and 15,000 more nurses July '98; ruled against compensating haemophiliacs suffering hepatitis C from contaminated NHS blood products July '98;

Born: 15 March 1940, Dunnington, York

Family: Son, late James William, railwayman whose kidneys packed up, and Irene (Shortland); m '67 Janet Mary (Alker) PhD, social researcher who was embroiled in a row in '96 on Hackney Council's reorganisation after becoming Assistant Director for Education at £48,310 '96-98; 2s: Tom '69 (who was unemployed after leaving Sheffield University), Joe '75, 1d Sally '68 (worked for Glenda Jackson MP); his children attended Sir William Collins School;

Education: Dunnington County Primary; Archbishop's Holgate's Grammar School, York; LSE (BSc Econ);

Occupation: Formerly Sponsored: by RMT (ex-NUR; his father and grandfather were NUR members; it paid 25% of agent's salary, 80% of election costs) '79-95; Owner, of house in Dunnington (although occupied, "no significant income is derived"); ex: Co-Presenter (with Robin Squires and Simon Hughes) of Capital Radio's 'Party Pieces' '83-87; Assistant Secretary, of Local Government Ombudsman (at £12,000) '76-79; Senior Administrative Officer: Electricity Council '70-75, CEGB '62-70;

Traits: Stocky; full white beard; pot belly; Father Christmas look-alike; "Dobbo"; "Lucullan grin" (Godfrey Barker, DAILY TELEGRAPH); "a rather delightful chuckle" (late Sir Anthony Berry MP); "designer gruffness" (Paul Routledge, INDEPENDENT ON SUNDAY); "hirsute and well-upholstered Marxist (Groucho Tendency) with the most fearsome laugh"; "an engaging mixture of joviality and bullying", "genuinely nice as well as a bruiser" (GUARDIAN); a "superficially cuddly character but with a tendency to produce excessively venomous speeches; the overall effect is rather like being bitten by a teddy bear"; "half Old Testament prophet, half David Bellamy" (Andrew Rawnsley, GUARDIAN); "a jolly Yorkshireman with large empathies, a galumphing manner and the subtlety of iron ore" (Edward Pearce, HOUSE MAGAZINE); "a verbal bruiser...one of the few genuinely funny people in politics...looking like a cross between George V and Mr Punch" (INDEPENDENT);

he gets on with anyone who makes him laugh, including Nicholas Soames and Alan Clark; "his jokes are unusuable, even at a Rugby club dinner" (Alan Clark MP); Cromwell is a hero, but not puritanism; admits he "eats too much"; bright; assiduous; ebullient; cocky; had jaundice as a child;

Address: House of Commons, Westminster, London SW1A 0AA; 22 Great Russell Mansions, 60 Great Russell St, London WC1 3LP;

Telephone: 0171 219 5040/4452/5840 (H of C); 0171 242 5760 (home); 0171 267 1676 (constituency);

Jeffrey (Mark) DONALDSON   **Ulster Unionist**   **LAGAN VALLEY '97-**

Majority: 16,925 over Alliance 8-way;

Description: A largely rural area with the thriving market town of Lisburn -the Army's headquarters in Northern Ireland - at its core; it contains the Maze prison; in '96 it lost the nationalist heartlands of Twinbrook and Poleglass to West Belfast and urban Carryduff to Strangford but gained mainly Protestant Dromore;

Position: Vice Chairman, Standing Committeee on Public Order, Northern Ireland Forum '96-; Secretary, Ulster Unionist Council '88-; ex: Assistant Grand Master of the Orange Order '94-97; Chairman, Ulster Young Unionist Council '85-86; Northern Ireland Assemblyman '85-86;

Outlook: The Ulster Unionists' young No-man who broke ranks over the Good Friday Agreement, possibly hoping to replace his Leader, David Trimble earlier than expected by distancing himself from the Agreement; "seen as a weather-vane of Unionism" (GUARDIAN); the "one man [who] kept two Prime Ministers, the American President and the world's media on a knife-edge" because "just as the peace agreement for Northern Ireland appeared to have been clinched" he "cried 'foul'" (TIMES); has refused to compromise with Sinn Fein-IRA unless it dismantles its fighting organisation and decommissions its weapons; formerly "the rising star of the Ulster Unionist Party" (Mark Simpson, BELFAST TELEGRAPH), "a strong public defender of the Orange Order" (NEW STATESMAN); an articulate media-aware young Lisburn businessman, Ulster Unionist apparatchik and former No 2 in the Orange Order who inherited the seat but not the caution of retired James (now Lord) Molyneaux; "the cherubic visage, masking the same old principles with more user-friendly presentational skills" (John Mullin, GUARDIAN);

History: The baby of the Ulster Unonists, he was seven when his cousin was the first policeman to be killed by a bomb in the Troubles '70; he joined the Young Unionists at 18, '81; became Election Agent to Enoch Powell in South Down Apr '83; was elected Chairman of the Ulster Young Unionist Council '85; was elected at 22 as the youngest member ever to the Northern Ireland Assembly May '85; was elected Secretary of the Ulster Unionist Council '88; was part of the Ulster Unionist negotiating team in the Northern Ireland constitutional talks '91; was elected Assistant Grand Master of the Orange Order '94; was elected to the Northern Ireland Forum at the top of the poll May '96; was selected as the Ulster Unionist candidate to succeed retiring James Molyneaux by over two-thirds of the vote Jan '97; pledged his constituents to remedy the "democratic deficit", help local business development and secure enough resources for health and education Mar '97; after the DUP decided to contest Lagan Valley for the first time since '83, said "I'm disappointed at the decision of the DUP to oppose me; I've long been a supporter of Unionist unity; I was brought up to believe that unity is strength, division is weakness" Apr '97; retained Lagan Valley by a majority of 16,925, despite a notional 8.5% swing to the Alliance Party May '97; in his Maiden speech urged more inward investment, particularly in the Lagan Valley - rather than West Belfast - and "a real peace that recognises the rights of the people of Northern Ireland to determine their own political future, free from the threat of terrorist violence and political interference" May '97; led motion urging PM Tony Blair to urge President Yeltsin to veto Duma's "draconian law" curbing religions July '97; after seeing PM Tony Blair complained the Government had "caved in" to the IRA, "giving them virtually everything they had asked for" July '97; insisted the Ulster Unionists would still "confront the Sinn Fein as appropriate" Sep '97; urged further Government support for Belfast's Bombardier Shorts company Dec '97; led debate on lapses in Maze prison Jan '98; ostentatiously tore up the Framework Document at Lancaster House Feb '98; asked for Government funding for small locally-owned hotels Feb '98; urged Sinn Fein's permanent exclusion from the talks Mar '98; said that Martin McGuinness, Sinn Fein's chief negotiator, might have been elected for Mid-Ulster because of organised voting fraud Mar '98; previously "seen as Trimble's ultimate heir, was turning against his Leader" (SUNDAY TIMES) Apr '98; a senior member of the UUP's negotiating team, he told his Leader, David Trimble, just as the peace agreement seemed clinched, that he could not sit on an Executive Commmitttee with Sinn Fein members without guaranteed IRA decommissioning; he walked out of Stormont Castle Buildings as Trimble led his delegation into the conference room to deliver his agreement; Blair's and Ahern's verbal guarantees were insufficient; after President Clinton's intervention and PM Blair's written guarantee, he was misquoted as saying he was back "on board" Apr '98; PM Tony Blair made a special effort to separate him from the other five UUP No-men May '98; promised to support the UUP campaign for the Assembly, but was denied a candidacy May '98; a majority of Unionists voted 'yes' in the Referendum, but he was one of six UUP MPs (out of ten) who voted 'no' May '98; said, "I'm a democrat; I accept the people of Northern Ireland have voted [yes]; but I don't think people who voted 'no' have anything to be ashamed about" May '98; warned of "renewed violence" by "organisations [which] are not really committed to peaceful and democratic means but are engaged in a tactical ceasefire" June '98; opposed Northern Ireland (Sentences) Bill because "prisoners and murderers will be released" and many of those not yet charged for terrorist crimes would only serve two years if charged and convicted of murder June '98; again demanded Sinn Fein be denied office because of new alleged IRA atrocities July '98; with 9 other hard-liners, voted against 3rd Reading of Northern Ireland Bill July '98;

Born: 7 December 1962, Kilkeel, Co Down

Family: Son, of James Donaldson, civil servant, and Sarah Anne (Charleton); m '87 Eleanor; 2d Claire '90, Laura '92;

Education: Kilkeel High School, Co Down; Castlereagh College, Belfast (Diploma in Electrical Engineering);

Occupation: Partner, in a financial services and estate agents' business in Lisburn and Dromore;

Traits: Youthful-looking; centre-parted short dark hair; full face; Celtic good looks; impassive expression; bright;

Address: House of Commons, Westminster, London SW1A 0AA;

Telephone: 0171 219 3000 (H of C);

Brian (Harold) DONOHOE   **Labour**   **CUNNINGHAME SOUTH '92-**

Majority: 14,869 (42%) over SNP 6-way;
Description: A slightly shrunken version of old Central Ayrshire, centred around Stevenston, Kilwinning and the growing seaside new town of Irvine with its chronic unemployment, despite its Finnish-owned paper mill;
Position: On Select Committee on Environment, Transport and Regional Affairs '97-; Chairman '96-,Vice Chairman '95-96, PLP Scottish Group; Secretary-Treasurer: all-party Gardening Group '97-, Whisky Group '97-; ex: on Transport Select Committee '92-97; on Executive, PLP Scottish Group '93-94; Treasurer, Cunninghame South Constituency Labour Party '85-92; Secretary, Irvine and District Trades Council '73-81; Chairman, North Ayrshire and Arran Local Health Council '77; Convenor, Scottish Political and Education Committee of TASS '73-79;

Outlook: Quiet, low-profile Scots loyalist, whose mobile rang mistakenly on May '97; wants the Scottish Parliament to be able to control an integrated Scottish rail network; is somewhat outshone by his voluble neighbour, Brian Wilson; an admirer of Gordon Brown but not of "manipulator" Mandelson; insists he "passionately believes in the ethos of Scottish local government" (BD); a politically-ambitious former trade union full-timer (NALGO/UNISON) and ex-draughtsman who was a union activist well before he joined the Labour Party;

History: As a draughtsman, joined TASS '68; was named Secretary of the Irvine and District Trades Council '73; became Chairman of Cunninghame District Industrial Development Committee '76; was named Chairman of the North Ayrshire and Arran Local Health Council '77; joined the Labour Party '80; joined TGWU-ACTSS '81; was elected Treasurer of the Cunninghame South CLP '85; was in the running for selection for marginal Ayr against Rosina McCrae, Keith Macdonald and David Foley, with Macdonald later winning it Oct '85; the sitting MP for Cunninghame South, David Lambie, announced he would not stand again Dec '89; Donohoe won selection for Cunninghame South although Tom Dewar and Anna Donn were rated as having better chances Mar '90; retained seat by 10,680 votes, down from 16,633, because of the doubling of the SNP vote Apr '92; joined the Tribune Group Apr '92; in his Maiden, opposed the Government's "intention to wind up the [new town] development corporations and dispose of their assets"; "to suggest stripping the development corporations of their assets at this time, with...the rundown of ICI in Stevenston, is irresponsible"; "we need an injection of resources"; warned too against single-tier local authorities as the "automatic choice"; also called for the upgrading of Ayrshire's connecting roads May '92; expressed concern about the discovery of clusters of brain tumours among 5-to-7-year-olds in the Ayrshire and Arran Health Board area May '92; visited Indonesia as guest of British Airways June '92; voted for John Smith for Leader, John Prescott for Deputy Leader July '92; was named to Transport Select Committee July '92; joined with three other Ayrshire Labour MPs to urge Ayr's Tory MP, Phil Gallie, to oppose mines closures because of its impact on 200 local workers making mine switchgear Oct '92; urged Secretary of State Ian Lang to refuse to privatise Scottish water and sewerage if the "vast majority of people say 'no'" Nov '92; visited Singapore as guest of Singapore Airlines Dec '92; complained that the Conservative Government had immediately picked up the tab for the Windsor Castle fire but insisted on voluntary organisations financing other disasters Jan '93; opposed replacement of the free-fall

    Copyright (C)Parliamentary Profile Services Ltd

nuclear bomb at a cost of £3b Feb '93; voted against 3rd Reading for Maastricht treaty Bill May '93; said the Government's projected local government changes could not be justified because of its "cost and disruption" and the increase in unaccountable bodies July '93; visited Norway as a guest of its Government Sep '93; visited USA as a guest of British Airways Oct '93; complained about winding up of Irvine Development Corporation just as job losses were being announced at Jetstream in Prestwick Oct '93; voted to "keep Sunday special" Dec '93; after seeing Secretary of State Lang together with Brian Wilson, said he was "appalled" by Government's "gerrymandering" proposals to "reform" Scottish local government Jan '94; voted against restoration of death penalty, even for cop-killers Feb '94; backed reduction of homosexual age of consent to 18 or 16, Feb '94; deplored 30,000 murders in Colombia, especially of street children Mar '94; asked PM John Major to "condemn the lies and deceptions contained in last week's Tory Party broadcast" on Birmingham Apr '94; complained that the Irvine Development Corporation's staff were "unhappy" because "the Government have welshed on the redundancy package which was on offer" Apr '94; asked PM John Major who he thought his "Brutus" would be May '94; urged Gordon Brown to contest the Labour Leadership and not stand aside for Tony Blair May '94; described as "at the very best tasteless and at worst disgusting" the SUN's publication of topless pictures of a murdered constituent, Sandra Parkinson July '94; he nominated Margaret Beckett but voted for John Prescott as Leader and Deputy Leader July '94; having elicited the spending of £11,000 on foreign travel and hospitality for Ministers' wives, said, "one would have thought they could stay at the British embassy" Oct '94; was reproached by Speaker Boothroyd for "a totally ludicrous waste of the House's time" when, during an exchange about informing other MPs when visiting their constituencies, he asked whether the MP for Westminster North had to be informed when MPs came to the Commons Feb '95; as one who had been defrauded of £200 by "phone cloning", demanded action against such fraudsters Apr '95; criticised presence of Peter Mandelson at dinner given by President Chirac instead of Shadow Cabinet members like John Prescott May '95; opposed sale of Scottish Homes and Irvine Development housing stock in the wind-up of Irvine New Town June '95; explained "there are times you need to take books from the Library" when it was disclosed he drove once a month to his constituency, at a roundtrip cost of £576 on MP's allowance June '95; said he had not travelled on a ro-ro ferry since working in a maritime design office in the early '70s June '95; after Clare Short urged an inquiry, he was named in INDEPENDENT as an MP willing to discuss legalisation of cannabis July '95; voted against Iain Duncan-Smith's Bill to curb the European Court Apr '96; when he asked DTI Minister John Taylor how many questions were rejected because disproportionately costly, that formula was repeated May '96; voted against a 3% cap on MPs' pay rise, in favour of a pension based on £43,000, up £9,000 July '96; attacked "utter shambles of the Crown Office and the judicial system" after constituent Gavin McGuire, a released murderer, reoffended June '96; PRIVATE EYE claimed lobbyists Lowe Bell used him and Alan Meale MP to reassure Stagecoach, who were taking over Sweden's nationalised bus company, that Labour was not as hostile to the company's growing monopoly as it had been while Brian Wilson was Transport Spokesman Sep '96; attacked Budget as bad for the unemployed and businessmen requiring longterm policies Dec '96; was attacked as "down in the gutter" by Tory MP Phil Gallie after revealing probable election dates from senior Tory MPs' diaries, the preferred one being 17 April, the second 1 May, Dec '96; was re-elected with an increased majority of 14,869 on a swing of 6.6% from the SNP May '97; took a call from 10 Downing Street concerning a junior Agriculture minister's job when he was mistaken for Lord Donoughue until he was put through to Tony Blair; "I was a Minister of State for eight seconds" May '97; as Secretary of the Commons Gardening Group planted red roses named 'Madame Speaker' on the Speaker's Terrace in honour of Speaker Boothroyd May '97; was

named to Select Committee on Environment, Transport and Regional Affairs July '97; claimed restrictions on powers proposed for Scottish Parliament made difficult the creation of an integrated transport system in Scotland Jan '98; again urged Scottish control of its own rail network since 95% was internal to Scotland Mar '98;
Born: 10 September 1948, Kilmarnock, Ayrshire
Family: Son, George Donohoe, teacher, and Catherine Sillars (Ashworth), secretary; m '73 Christine (Pawson) teacher; 2s: Graeme '77, Craig '79;
Education: Patna Primary; Waterside Primary; Loudoun Montgomery, Irvine; Irvine Royal Academy; Kilmarnock Technical College (ONC Engineering, Electrical and Mechanical);
Occupation: Beneficiary, of "small contribution towards constituency expenses made in 1994 by UNISON"; ex: Union Official, in NALGO '81-92 (TGWU-ACTSS '81-92); Contract Draughtsman at ICI '77-81; also worked at Ailsa Shipbuilding at Troon as an apprentice fitter-turner '65-70 (TASS '68-82);
Traits: Front-combed dark parted hair; beefy Irish good looks; worries about his name not being spelled correctly; enjoys cycling, foreign "fact-finding tours" (BD) and gardening; has a quarter of an acre garden on the almost frost-free west coast of Scotland; had a fellowship with Unilever under the Parliamentary and Industry Trust '93-94;
Address: House of Commons, Westminster, London SW1A 0AA; 5 Greenfield Drive, Irvine, Ayrshire KA12 0ED;
Telephone: 0171 219 6230 (H of C); 012942 274419 (home); 01294 276844 (constituency office); 0374 646 600 (mobile);

Frank DORAN   **Labour**   **ABERDEEN CENTRAL '97-**

Majority: 10,801 over Conservative 5-way;
Description: A '95-new seat embracing the city centre, made up of equal bits of Aberdeen North and South, with pro-Labour council estates from the north and some Tory-leaning areas from the south; on a '92 projection, was expected to go Labour by over 5,000 votes;
Former Seat: Aberdeen South '87-92;
Position: Ex: Assistant Spokesman, on Energy (under Tony Blair) '88-92;
Outlook: Cautious, Rightward-moving former semi-hard Leftwinger who was in the 'Supper Club' and opposed the Gulf War; has recently been described as part of the pro-Blair 'Network' in the Scottish Labour Party; has kept a very low profile since returning as a 'retread'; is not universally popular locally; in '87 won former Aberdeen South from Gerald Malone, but was the only Labour MP to lose his seat in '92 - after personal and professional problems; was formerly sponsored by GMB;
History: He joined the Labour Party '76; fought district and regional council elections in '80 and '82; contested the Euro-constituency of North East Scotland, calling for reform of the CAP June '84; was selected for Tory-held Aberdeen South from a short-list of six on the fourth ballot by 25 to 24, Sep '85; won the seat from Gerald Malone June '87; in his Maiden complained that while the Scottish Development Agency was trying to create jobs in Aberdeen, Government policies were creating unemployment in its university and shipyards

Oct '87; with five other new Labour MPs, sponsored a Bill urging a Peace-Building Fund to "encourage and initiate non-military peace-building initiatives" Oct '87; he and three other Labour MPs involved (George Galloway, William McKelvey, Ernie Ross) submitted a lengthy complaint to the IBA about the Channel 4 and Scottish TV programmes on the Dundee Labour Club Nov '87; claimed that the Government had been unable to put down the necessary secondary legislation for the "regressive" poll tax because "they cannot work out what to put into them, so hastily prepared and ill-thought-out is the measure" Dec '87; put down a motion condemning the SNP "calling for a campaign of non-registration for and non-payment of the poll tax" without warnings about the penalties Jan '88; co-sponsored a motion attacking the arrest in East Germany of nuclear disarmers Feb '88; supported much more generous funding for Aberdeen University, which was losing 500 jobs Mar '88; co-urged selective economic sanctions against Israel for the death of Abu Jihad, Deputy Leader of the PLO Apr '88; rushed back from a "magnificent victory" in Aberdeen's local elections to speak against David Alton's Abortion (Amendment) Bill, urging an appeal system for a woman who had been denied an abortion May '88; backed improved procedures in child sexual abuse, which had long been under-reported May '88; opposed privatising St Andrews' golf course, long run successfully by the local authority July '88; after the local Piper Alpha disaster, killing 167, urged a wider inquiry than allowed under Scots fatal accident law July '88; protested against an exodus of workers because of low wages and dangerous oil rig practices Aug '88; the press reported a legal action by his brother-in-law, Graham Lamont, demanding repayment of a £15,000 loan and a Law Society investigation of Doran's law firm's financial transactions Sep '88; claimed the Government had failed to carry out its statutory responsibilities on oil rig safety before the Piper Alpha disaster Oct '88; was named an Assistant Spokesman on Energy (Oil and Gas), under Energy Spokesman Tony Blair Nov '88; urged faster compensation for Piper Alpha victims Dec '88; reported sacking of oil worker for reporting safety violations Jan '89; backed confidentiality of social work records Jan '89; praised Scotttish Secretary Malcolm Rifkind for saving 400 jobs by subsidising the building of a ferry at local Hall Russell shipyard Feb '89; failed to secure debate on delayed report into the '87 Chinook helicopter disaster Apr '89; claimed loss of 40% of North Sea oil production through accumulated shutdowns Apr '89; introduced Employers' Liability Bill to require provision of death-in-service insurance benefits Apr '89; tried to mediate with Thomson Newspapers in strike at Aberdeen Journals over NUJ recognition Aug '89; urged Government to support local Raeden Centre for severely handicapped children rather than Budapest's Peto Institute Oct '89; protested Government's failure to release report on previous year's Ocean Odyssey explosion Oct '89; was criticised by Law Society of Scotland's disciplinary tribunal Jan '90; urged expansion of compulsory no-fault compensaton to cover all oil-rig workers Mar '90; sought unsuccessfully to exempt Scotland from lowered limit for abortions, claiming existing Scottish practice was more flexible Apr '90; claimed macho management threats had provoked offshore strikes Sep '90; welcomed support of Cullen Report into Piper Alpha tragedy for union safety representation Nov '90; opposed opt-out of Aberdeen Royal Infirmary from health board control Dec '90; co-opposed military action against Iraq until sanctions had operated longer Jan '91; Dundee Procurator Fiscal submitted a report on his business dealings in Dundee and Edinburgh Jan '91; underlined risk of Aberdeen port privatisation under the Ports Bill Jan '91; urged a no-fault liability scheme to avoid long delays in hospital negligence cases Feb '91; was named as a member of the semi-hard Left 'Supper Club', along with John Prescott, Margaret Beckett and Michael Meacher Feb '91; urged a tougher Health and Safety regime, with its headquarters moved to Aberdeen Mar '91; press reports claimed he had moved in with Joan Ruddock, who had left her husband Mar '91; he sought to keep secret the £2,500 fine of the Scottish Law Society for his professional misconduct over money borrowed from his brother-in-law June

'91; complained about cancelled operations caused by underfunding of Aberdeen Royal Infirmary Oct '91; asked why a helicopter flew in a snowstorm, killing 11 oil-rig workers in resultant crash Mar '92; was the only Labour MP to lose his seat - to Raymond Robertson - on a pro-Tory swing of 3.3% Apr '92; worked for Trade Union Co-ordinating Committee on campaign for political fund ballots which enabled unions to fund Labour Party; also worked as Researcher for Joan Ruddock; seeking selection for the new Aberdeen Central seat, stressed his local campaigning record; defeated veteran Aberdeen North MP, Bob Hughes, by one vote, forcing latter's retirement Oct '95; with five other Labour candidates, was identified by the SCOTSMAN as part of a pro-Blair "Network" in the Scottish Labour Party Jan '97; after a low-key campaign, won Aberdeen Central by a majority of 10,801, a pro-Labour swing of 8.02% May '97; complained about Aberdeen's 1,500 unemployed under-25s June '97; urged more expenditure on drug abuse in Scotland June '97; asked about 'black' fish July '97; complained about insufficient action on fishing problems July '97; complained that the equalisation of business rating had cost Aberdeen £30m Mar '98;

Born: 13 April 1949, Edinburgh

Family: Son, Francis Anthony Doran, painter and decorator, and Betty (Hedges); m '67 Patricia Ann (Govan), former community worker, later Tayside Regional Councillor; 2s Francis Richard '69, Adrian '71; separated '91; has been close to Joan Ruddock, according to press reports;

Education: Ainslie Park Secondary; Leith Academy; Dundee University (LLB Hons)

Occupation: Researcher, for Joan Ruddock '92-97; Scottish Organiser, for Trade Union Co-ordinating Commitee on Political Fund Ballots (GMB) '92-96; Solicitor, in Dundee and Edinburgh, (specialising in family law and mental health '77-87; no longer practising) Assistant Editor, Scottish Legal Action Group Bulletin '75-78;

Traits: Slightly-built; dark, receding hair; snub nose; canny-looking; guarded;

Address: House of Commons, Westminster, London SW1A 0AA;

Telephone: 0171 219 3000 (H of C);

Rt Hon Stephen (James) DORRELL   Conservative   **CHARNWOOD '97-**

Majority: 5,900 (10.5%) over Labour 5-way;

Description: A new seat created in '97 out of four others, lumping together the white, middle-class, owner-occupied, Tory-leaning outer suburbs of Leicester: 20,000 came from his former Loughborough constituency, 22,000 from Rutland and Melton, 15,000 from Blaby, 14,000 from Bosworth; it was expected to be among the safest Tory seats;

Former Seat: Loughborough '79-97

Position: Ex: Spokesman, on Education and Employment '97-98; Secretary of State for Health '95-97, National Heritage Secretary '94-95; Financial Secretary to the Treasury '92-94; on the Public Accounts Committee '92-94; Under Secretary, for Health '90-92; Whip (Lord Commissioner) '88-90; Assistant Whip '87-88; PPS, to patron Peter Walker '83-87; on Transport Select Committee '79-83; Secretary: of Conservative MPs' Trade Committee '79-80, their Finance Committee '80-82, their Northern Ireland Committee '82-83; Secretary, Parliamentary Group

on Population and Development '80-87; on the Board of Christian Aid '85-87;
Outlook: The new backbench one-man think-tank; the rejected Europhile 'middle way' politico-businessman, squeezed off the front bench by the increasing weight of Rightwing Eurosceptics, and by disappointment with his year's performance as Opposition Education Spokesman: was "left floundering by the supremely confident David Blunkett" (Andrew Pierce, TIMES); his reputation sank further after the publication of his reaction to the scientists March '96 warning about transmission of BSE to humans; once allegedly viewed by John Major as his "natural successor" and "seen as the best Leftwing leadership contender of his generation" (Stephen Castle, INDEPENDENT ON SUNDAY); but he failed to adapt successfully to the changed balance of Tory power; he so often 're-positioned' himself - "moving crablike to the Right" (Joanna Pitman, TIMES) - that he alienated Centre-Left Tory Europhiles without convincing Rightwing Eurosceptics; he could have made it easier for himself by explaining his opposition to the impact of Continental-style labour laws on his family's Dutch plant; he had plenty of time to adjust; he would have been promoted to Cabinet in '93 had it not been for the PM's need to preserve Europhile-Eurosceptic balance; he sees himself as "a Midlands businessman with strong views about how society should develop" (SD); "one of the few ministers with personal experience of manufacturing industry" in "his family's industrial clothing firm" (David Wastell, SUNDAY TELEGRAPH); is a sharp-honed partisan with a well-endowed analytical mind but dubious judgment; "exuding sweet reasonableness and being recognisably a member of the human race" (Stephen Bates, GUARDIAN); a Tory mirror-image of Tony Blair, equally a boyish, socially-concerned honest intellectual; formerly a rebellious, 'One Nation' Leftwing youngster from Peter Walker's Tory Reform Group stable; "he likes following the logic of ideas as an academic game and he can really clobber you if your arguments don't stack up; but, like a good academic, he is delighted if you can trip him up; most ministers hate that" (a senior civil servant); initially contemptuous of Mrs Thatcher's "simplistic, mechanistic monetarism"; favourable to industrial exports; pro-EMS; anti-racialist, anti-hanging; "his original promotion was long delayed by Mrs Thatcher, probably because he was PPS to Peter Walker" (John Cole, NEW STATESMAN); was initially harnessed as a Whip; then, as Health Under Secretary, where he outshone the No 2, Virginia Bottomley, and enjoyed a close relationship with Health Secretary William Waldegrave; was put into Treasury in '92 as Number Three to become "Mr Privatisation"; he then became head man at National Heritage before rescuing the NHS from Virginia Bottomley;
History: "I was certainly following politics as an 11 or 12-year-old, and then, when I went to Uppingham, I became more seriously and actively involved"; at Oxford he was an officer of the University Conservative Association and Chairman of PEST (Progress for Economic and Social Toryism) '72; served as Personal Assistant to Peter Walker in election in his native city of Worcester Feb '74; contested Worcester Council May '74; contested hopeless Kingston-upon-Hull East against John Prescott Oct '74; was selected for Loughborough, then a Labour marginal Mar '76; resigned from its Conservative Club after it blackballed an Asian Sep '78; after rejecting manifesto commitment to shrink immigration, he won Loughborough from Dr John Cronin (its Labour MP for 24 years) to become youngest MP May '79; voted against restoring hanging July '79; supported abolition of Prices Commission July '79; was one of 19 Tories who voted against Government's proposals to ban foreign fiances, for immigrants alone Dec '79; said he regarded the fight against anti-Semitism exactly the same as the fight against racialism Dec '79; said Tories had to be rescued from hands of Rightwing monetarist "radicals" Mar '80; was one of five Tory MPs who voted against Government's tightening of immigration rules on Asian fiances Mar '80; described Conservative Party as "the lesser of two evils" Apr '80; was only Tory to vote with Labour against abolishing Clegg Commission on

public sector pay comparability May '80; said too few Tories represented industry and too few showed interest in unemployment July '80; ousted Rightwinger Nicholas Budgen to become Secretary of Tory MPs' Finance Committee Dec '80; abstained against increasing petrol duty by 20p per gallon Mar '81; complained gas appliance industry did not export because of "cosy" relationship with British Gas June '81; abstained on Heseltine's referendum on rates proposal Nov '81; backed inquiry into anti-Asian racialist attacks Nov '81; complained that Government's economic package was "economically divisive" Dec '81; urged more birth control in 3rd World May, July '82; fought immigrant repatriation May '82; opposed Government finance for Channel Tunnel June '82; voted for an amendment to restore the 5% cut in unemployment benefit July '82; abstained against Government cut of 5% in unemployment benefit Nov '82; backed Chancellor's cuts in personal taxation Mar '83; was named PPS to Peter Walker, to Mrs Thatcher's distress June '83; introduced Bill to afford registration of service marks by amending 1938 Trade Marks Act July '83; voted against restoring hanging July '83; moved 2nd Reading of his Service Marks Bill, talked out by Robert Wareing Nov '83; was the architect of the playful ploy of holding up score-cards on Kinnock's performance Feb '84; asked for increased funding for assisted places May '84; urged joining the EMS to avoid currency fluctuations July '84; although a PPS, he signed motion opposing Sir Keith Joseph's increase in parental contributions to grant, resisting Whips' entreaties Nov '84; urged reform of insolvency law to prevent re-emergence of wound-up companies Apr '85; defended his boss, Peter Walker, against CROSSBOW accusations that he had had secret discussions on proportional representation with David Owen Aug '85; attacked Jeffrey Archer's attack on "workshy" young unemployed Oct '85; his renewed call to join the EMS was rejected by the PM Margaret Thatcher Mar '86; urged all University departments be allowed to combine teaching and research May '86; asked the Chief Secretary to the Treasury, John McGregor, to confirm that since the bulk of people got their health and education from the state, improvements must come from public expenditure June '86; opposed Kenneth Hind's Unborn Children (Protection) Bill banning embryo experimentation Oct '86; tried to infiltrate 'wet' young Tories into the increasingly Rightwing Greater London YCs Dec '86; insisted the concept of "democratic supervision" of the police was not consistent with their operational freedom Feb '87; supported the privatisation of Rolls-Royce Apr '87; his appointment as an Assistant Whip was received with astonishment; it was allegedly part of the price Peter Walker exacted for remaining as Welsh Secretary for a few more months June '87; voted to televise the Commons Feb '88; voted against restoring capital punishment June '88; voted against a 26-week ceiling on abortions June '88; was promoted a full Whip or Lord Commissioner in the reshuffle Dec '88; was promoted Under Secretary for Health in the reshuffle, replacing Roger Freeman, probably on the urging of departing Peter Walker May '90; unveiled plans to get homeless mentally-ill people off the streets of central London July '90; urged speedier closure of Victorian mental hospitals Nov '90; supported Michael Heseltine in Leadership election Nov '90; said the British pharmaceutical industry was a "world-beater" with eight of the 20 best-selling drugs; the industry's patent rights had already been reinforced and more was being considered Nov '90; disclosed the Government rejected the EC's desire to ban tobacco advertising Nov '90; rejected proposal to allow organ transplants unless the deceased had specifically refused permission: "nobody has a right to my organs other than me" Mar '91; said, "Mr Cook's use of statistics during this week's [NHS] debate gave a whole new meaning to the phrase 'cooking the figures'" May '91; claimed Labour Party put its union paymasters in hospitals before their patients Sep '91; was named Health's Minister in charge of 'green' issues Sep '91; accused Labour Spokesman Robin Cook of rewriting the dictionary when he spoke of "privatisation" of the NHS Oct '91; supported Tory candidate at hopeless Hemsworth by-election Oct '91; said NHS "support functions will be opened up to competition from the commercial sector" Nov '91; told Camden voluntary agencies dealing with the mentally ill and homeless, "we're none of us too proud to learn and it's a fact that in this area there hasn't been a record of conspicuous success" Nov '91; allowed GPs to use alternative and complementary therapists within their practices Dec '91; deplored unnecessary secrecy about records of children fostered, including HIV and tendency to abuse other children sexually: "it defied common sense that foster parents should be expected to take on these difficult cases without being aware of what they are taking on" Dec '91; urged satellite hostels - near hospitals - for the severely mentally ill Jan '92; defended the intial refusal of North Devon Health Authority to sanction an operation on former Liberal Leader Jeremy Thorpe to implant foetal cell to cure his Parkinson's Disease, on the ground that the success rate for over-'50s was 30% Jan '92; was involved in U-turn in deciding to set aside £12m to compensate those infected with HIV by NHS transfusions prior to the treatment of blood Feb '92; said he would tackle the "grotesque" gap between the mentally ill in hospitals (£26,250 a year) and those living in the community (£107 a year) Feb '92; resisted the pressure of GPs to be paid for out-of-hours visits Mar '92; retained seat with majority down from 17,648 to 10,883, a swing to Labour of 5.93% Apr '92; was named Financial Secretary to the Treasury by John Major with the task of privatising as much of the civil service as possible Apr '92; insisted there was no "final state of knowledge" on the right balance between public spending and taxation May '92; won colleagues' support for his "rent-a-room" tax concessions to small private landlords May '92; backed tax concessions to family firms like his own: "we do not believe in a one-generation enterprise society" June '92; resisted Labour proposals for tax breaks for industrial investment June '92; with Chancellor Lamont in Tuscany, it was left to him to defend the ERM outside the Treasury Sep '92; backed more employee participation Oct '92; refused bloodstock industry a lower rate of VAT Oct '92; warned that anti-Maastricht vote would be an "unwarranted act of national self-humiliation" Nov '92; was given responsibility for giving substance to the pledge of greater private sector involvement in big infrastructure projects Dec '92; named Giles Brandreth MP as his PPS Feb '93; was alleged to have clashed with Energy Minister Tim Eggar over the type of contracts that were eligible for transitional relief under the Petroleum Revenue Tax changes; he was reluctant to allow oil companies tax relief on binding contracts previously made Apr '93; claimed "we are now starting to emerge from a long recession" Apr '93; in the reshuffle following the dismissal of Chancellor Lamont, was considered by John Major as a replacement as Welsh Secretary for fellow Walker disciple David Hunt; but the PM felt he had to replace a departing Rightwing Eurosceptic (Lamont) with another (John Redwood) May '93; Dorrell refused to say whether Government was reconsidering its manifesto pledge to maintain the value of Child Benefit May '93; told the GUARDIAN "I am aware as the Minister responsible for tax that we [ministers] do not pay any tax on car journeys from home to work and from work to home; the reason is simply our large red boxes" May '93; opposed Rightwingers' "ideological purity, which the true Tory regards as neither feasible nor attractive" May '93; bowing to backbench pressure, put an upper limit of £80,000 on the new price-based method of calculating tax on company cars June '93; submitted a plan to merge tax and national insurance to the new Chancellor, Kenneth Clarke June '93; had to sack his agent to try to reduce a projected £20,000 deficit in his association July '93; was said to be anxious to transfer to new seat of Charnwood as boundary changes made Loughborough very marginal Aug '93; inflation moved up marginally hours after he proclaimed Britain was living in "an inflation-free world" Sep '93; admitted increased taxes would slow recovery but this would help prevent consumer recovery getting out of control Dec '93; in a "headline-grabbing speech" vetted by John Major to the 'wet' Tory Reform Group, he "rubbished the Rightwing views of his immediate boss, Michael Portillo" (INDEPENDENT); attacked "the exaggerated histrionics of flag-waving nationalists" with their "narrow, inward-looking view of patriotism" Jan '94; admitted private agencies could not yet compete equally with Government departments whose basic costs were not wholly registered Jan '94; agreed that "price stability is what creates the circumstances for maximised economic growth" Jan '94; opposed restoration of capital punishment, even for cop-killers Feb '94; backed reducing age of homosexual consent to 18, but not to 16, Feb '94; agreed "we have introduced Budgets that have put up taxes" but insisted net pay had also gone up Feb '94; said only state action could secure a just and free society Feb '94; admitted taxes might not be cut before next election Mar '94; was said to have retreated on Clause 241 of the Finance Bill, which would have given the Inland Revenue powers to raid accountants' offices after accountant-MP Michael Stern spearheaded a counter-attack Mar '94; in the first speech by a Tory Minister to a TUC conference since the early '70s, warned that public sector pay increases could only come from increased efficiency Mar '94; told civil service unionists that 91 agencies, employing 350,000 staff or 60% of civil service, should be privatised Mar '94; retreated on a clause in the Finance Bll which eliminated the right of heirs to take inflation into account when calculating Capital Gains Tax Apr '94; admitted he had not known that his PPS, Giles Brandreth had headed a company which went bust owing the taxpayer £200,000 Apr '94; in a speech to Manchester Business School, emphasised the primacy of the market in delivering growth and the limitations of politicians in giving strategic direction to the economy; the role of government was to underwrite social stability through law enforcement, to provide health care and a welfare safety net, and to deliver good education Apr '94; said the '80s boom had been "built on sand" because of monetary indiscipline May '94; was accused by Lord Hanson of "sounding like a socialist" for equating high dividends with low investment July '94; was promoted to Cabinet as Secretary of State for the National Heritage, replacing Peter Brooke, to the accompaniment of laughter from his father, because "it was an area so far from my expertise" (SD) July '94; refused to intervene to prevent threat of test match coverage being lost to Sky TV by the BBC Aug '94; extended export license time to allow for British bidders for Canova's 'Three Graces', instead of the Getty Museum Aug '94; insisted extra public spending should go to education or health rather than the arts Aug '94; spoke to Centre-Left Tory workshop seeking a less Thatcherite contingent after next election Sep '94; was discharged from PAC Oct '94; warned Heritage was not "a money fountain" for minority activities Oct '94; launched the National Lottery Nov '94; accused Jack Straw of trying to impose a "straight-jacket" of "political correctness" around the monarchy when he urged it be slimmed down Dec '94; probed Cabinet support for ban on invasions of privacy by bugging and long-range lenses Jan '95; rejected cap on National Lottery jackpots Jan '95; was attacked for owning homes near Loughborough, in Worcester and London and saying "homes are for living in, not for investment" by Eurosceptic Lord McAlpine Feb '95; was accused of being "a gamekeeper from the Treasury" who refused to turn "poacher" by National Heritage Select Committee Chairman Gerald Kaufman Feb '95; repeated Government pledge to keep the BBC's charter and license fee for a decade Feb '95; ignored Labour objections to appointing Sir Bernard Ingham, Baroness Thatcher's former Press Secretary, to the Press Complaints Commission Feb '95; rejected calls for tougher privacy laws after exposures of MPs Jonathan Aitken and Richard ('Three-in-a-Bed') Spring Apr '95; defended use of £12.5m in Lottery money to purchase Churchill papers from Tory MP Winston Churchill Apr '95; rejected call from Michael Grade to ban Rupert Murdoch from bidding for Channel 5, Apr 95; Rupert Murdoch asked "Stephen Dorrell, who is he?" when told that Dorrell might curb his expansion in the UK Apr '95; was mooted as a possible replacement for Jeremy Hanley as party Chairman May '95; rejected accusations of his philistinism May '95; referred to French actress Jeanne Moreau at Cannes Film Festival as a "distinguished French actor" May '95; was promoted Health Secretary in straight swap for least-believed Cabinet Minister, Virginia

Bottomley, with a mandate to reverse her unpopular excesses July '95; announced end of programme of NHS reforms July '95; warned Tories against too dramatic an assault on the £80b Social Security budget, urging a "middle way" between rampant welfarism and unrestrained capitalism Aug '95; his call for doctors to report on slipshod colleague cause a stir in the profession Aug '95; urged the views of the public be heeded more on hospital closures Aug '95; announced plan to sack thousands of NHS managers and employ more staff involved in patient care Aug '95; was selected for new, safe Charnwood seat, carved out of his redrawn, imperilled Loughborough seat Aug '95; urged doctors to curb "less effective" treatments to focus on the best Sep '95; indicated reprieve for cottage hospitals Sep '95; reaffirmed his belief in 'care in the community' despite murders by paranoid schizophrenics Sep '95; rejected call for partial NHS privatisation from Sir Duncan Nichol, ex-NHS Chief Executive, as a threat to the poor Sep '95; authorised building of four privately-financed NHS hospitals Oct '95; reportedly sought £300m more for Health in Budget Oct '95; tried to calm middle-class fears about sacrifice of pensioners' homes to pay for care by confirming consideration of a plan for state to pay for nursing, but not accommodation Oct '95; announced cut of 10,000 NHS managers Dec '95; after Government advised schools to ban beef, said: "I am absolutely certain that British beef is wholly safe, we do not believe BSE is transmissable to humans, but against the possibility we might be wrong about that, we have also put in place various controls within slaughterhouses" Dec '95; he was accused of issuing a "boozers' charter" in increasing approved alcohol limits on the run-up to Christmas Dec '95; announced more rigorous guidelines in discharging mentally-ill patients from hospitals, admitting care in the community was not yet working Dec '95; launched review of Social Security spending Jan '96; backed code of practice to curb growth of under-age alco-pops drinking Jan '96; urged the public be persuaded to avoid useless NHS spending like "excessive" Caesarian sections and "ineffective" ear grommets Jan '96; a report commissioned by him in '92 showed 39 mentally-ill patients had killed others and 240 killed themselves because of inadequate supervision Jan '96; outlined plans for GPs to take over minor hospital care and nurses to take on GPs' routine tasks Jan '96; predicted half of GPs would be fundholders in four months Jan '96; admitted disquiet about legal hospital discharges of mentally-ill patients Feb '96; announced plans for 400 "group homes" to provide 5,000 mentally-ill with 24-hour care Feb '96; his new guidelines to restrict emergency and intensive care services to critically ill patients with a chance of survival came under attack after a 10-year-old died after being ferried between four hospitals Mar '96; his reputation was severely dented by Harriet Harman despite his shouting introduction of the National Health Service (Residual Liabilities) Bill to try to rescue the Private Finance Initiative to build hospitals which had been frustrated by the absence of Government guarantees to private builders if trusts went bust Mar '96; supported PM John Major and Foreign Secretary Malcolm Rifkind in call for collective Cabinet responsibility in any referendum on the Euro when six Eurosceptic Cabinet Ministers backed a free vote Mar '96; after scientists' warning that 10 had already died, insisted there was "no scientific proof" that BSE could be transmitted to humans; he also resisted compensating human victims of BSE Mar '96; repeated "the product (beef) is to all intents and purposes, safe to eat", opposing huge expenditure on unnecessary slaughter; described the EU beef ban as "outrageous and totally unjustified" and accused Harriet Harman of "ferreting around in the sewer of party political advantage" on BSE Mar '96; agreed with the SUN on BSE that "it isn't the cows that are mad, it's the people" Mar '96; voted with three other Cabinet Ministers for an 18-month, rather than 12-month, divorce cooling-off period Apr '96; dismissed as "interesting gossip" the report that he had taken over from Ken Clarke as the favoured leadership candidate of Europhile Tories Apr '96; called for the European economy to be deregulated Apr '96; insisted the state should only provide a "safety net" for elderly care, with insurance providing the rest May '96; announced cut of £40m in unnecessary NHS red tape May '96; ordered 20% increase in paediatric care May '96; in speech to Tory Reform Group praised Margaret Thatcher as a One Nation Tory - despite her own denials - urged a Europe "a la carte" and insisted welfare state benefits should be confined to health and education May '96; on a free vote, opposed Government-backed amendment to limit the waiting period for divorce to 18 months June '96; yielded to threatening rebel local Tory MPs Hugh Dykes and Sir John Gorst by agreeing to retain a casualty unit instead of closing Edgware Hospital's A & E department June '96; backed a 3% cap on MPs' pay rise and curbs on MPs' mileage allowances and voted against a pension based on £43,000, a £9,000 increase July '96; with Social Security Secretary Peter Lilley challenged European Commission on unauthorised spending July '96; claimed Labour's devolution plans threatened civil war in Britain July '96; his appointment by party Chairman Brian Mawhinney as constitutional supremo annoyed Welsh and Scottish Secretaries William Hague and Michael Forsyth Aug '96; rejected calls for further curbs on fertility treatment after wide publicity for Mandy ('eight foetuses') Allwood Aug '96; following rape publicity, promised legislation to curb NHS lay managers releasing mentally-ill patients against medical advice Sep '96; a Gallup survey showed he was the second least-known of 13 Cabinet Ministers, with only 12% recognising his photograph Oct '96; at party conference-fringe meeting opposed widening of political powers of EU institutions Oct '96; his NHS White Paper proposed GPs' surgeries in supermarkets but dropped his much-trailed defence of cottage hospitals Oct '96; attacked the Lib-Lab pact on constitutional reform by Robin Cook-Robert Maclennan as showing "these two Leftwing parties intend to carve up Britain and split the UK" Oct '96; allegedly "went to the wire" to secure an extra £1b for the NHS in Budget Nov '96; unexpectedly sided with Cabinet's Eurosceptics against Major's 'wait and see' policy on EMU Dec '96; urged a recasting of Britain's relationship with the EU, preventing its drifting into a superstate Jan '97; the Government survived a vote on health policy after he reassured Sir John Gorst about Edgware Hospital Jan '97; said hospitals' mixed-sex wards would be phased out Jan '97; was chosen by PM John Major to go down to the local pub to brief the press after the Cabinet's Chequers meeting to finalise the Tory manifesto Jan '97; proposed amendment to his own NHS Primary Care Bill to drop plans for GPs' surgeries in supermarkets Feb '97; set up inquiry into Ashworth top-security mental hospital Feb '97; was ditched by John Major as constitutional supremo, without warning, at the behest of Scottish Secretary Michael Forsyth, after he had said a Scottish Parliament could be abolished Feb '97; said Britain would not join the Euro on its January 1999 launch, with PM John Major saying he had made a mistake, after which he said his "thought processes were blurred" Mar '97; launched "planned partnership schemes" insuring elderly against the cost of longterm care, with Government providing £1.50 for every £1 of insurance Mar '97; proposed sell-off of state residential care homes and provision of vouchers for residential care Mar '97; was re-elected for new seat of Charnwood by the much-reduced majority of 5,900 on a major notional pro-Labour swing of 14.2% May '97; said, "it was not the voters who got it wrong last week, it was the Conservatives", especially on devolution May '97; made a short-lived bid for the Tory Leadership with the public backing of only two MPs, David Faber and Simon Burns, no outside contributions and low public support (2% in a MORI Poll); he withdrew and backed Ken Clarke; but of his eight suporters he was only able to deliver himself to Clarke May-June '97; was named Spokesman on Education and Employment by William Hague June '97; attacked Labour's imposition of student tuition fees as "a shabby, opportunistic smash-and-grab raid on the budgets of low-income families" July '97; did not attend the crucial conference-eve meeting of the Shadow Cabinet at which it was decided not to consider joining the Euro for a decade Oct '97; stayed in Shadow Cabinet after Ian Taylor resigned after Hague's commitment not to discuss entering the Euro for a decade Nov '97; he dropped John Major's pledge of "a grammar school in every town" Nov '97; ridiculed lower charge for Scottish students on four-year courses Nov '97; SUNDAY TIMES disclosed that LibDem spokesman had asked 20 written questions without his asking a single written queston on education Dec '97; was embarrassed by the disclosure that he had approved in '90 and expanded in '95 a deal by which an NHS staffman made £8.6m from a £20m failed developement of a nationwide computer code to standardise NHS patient care Jan '98; was criticised by Labour for speaking against the minimum wage without disclosing that his family firm, Faithful Group Ltd, of which he was a Director, did not recognise unions Apr? '98; he was reproached for not having declared this, but cleared of any serious impropriety May '98; he retired from the front bench, being replaced by David Willetts June '98; warned his Tory colleagues they could not make a comeback while Europhobic June '98; documents published about the March '98 BSE crisis cast a shadow on his judgment July '98;

Born: 25 March 1952, Worcester

Family: Son, late Philip Dorrell, ex-Director of Faithful (the Worcester-based family overall firm), and Christine (Wilkes), a Director of Faithful; m '80 Penelope Annette Wears (Taylor), of half-Franco-Belgian parentage, a classics graduate of Cardiff University, recently also a Director of Faithful running 'The Cheshire Cat' a children's wear shop in Worcester; 2s Philip '93?, William '97; 1d Alexandra '88?;

Education: Local prep school; Uppingham; Brasenose, Oxford (BA '73; he was taught international law by Bryan Gould);

Occupation: Director '97-, '75-87, Chairman '84-87 of Faithful Group Ltd (family industrial clothing firm; Shareholder, with 22%; unions are not recognised; turnover reached £17m, profits £1m in '95; "profits have grown steadily over the past few years from less than £300,000 in 1986 to more than £1m in 1991; it has recently opened a [new] factory in Worcester and expanded into Europe" - Peter Oborne, EVENING STANDARD; "it has four factories in this country and two in the Netherlands" - INDEPENDENT) '75-; ex: Owner of a quarter share in a Tiger Moth;

Traits: Thin, long-faced; dark, parted hair; gangly; hunched; boyish; "he would be handsome in a handknit" (Chrissy Iley, SUNDAY TIMES); "fresh-faced" (Peter Oborne, EVENING STANDARD); ambitious; courageous; personable; "gaunt...known by his mischievous civil servants as 'the Grim Reaper'" (Matthew Parris, TIMES); "the voice would probably be marked down as Estuary Oxbridge; the face would go straight into the English Sensitive category"; "the world of the luvvy is so far from his world - the world of the provincial professional bourgeoisie"; "he appears to lack the typical politician's vanity and he cultivates a cool, rational and passionless style" (Joanna Pitman, TIMES}; "my roots are very much in the Midlands; I don't want my children to be engaged in a kind of fashionable metropolitan set" (SD); "hard to dislike'; shows "soft-spoken attentiveness"; "often coming over as a civil servant or a problem-solving manager rather than a politician" (Jonathan Steele, GUARDIAN); "he often gives the impression of barely considering what impression he is making" (Sandra Barwick, SUNDAY TELEGRAPH); playful (led the romp of holding up scorecards on Kinnock's performance); flier (RAFVR '71-73); "well-informed", "sincere" (Sir Teddy Taylor MP); "rather smug" ('Black Dog', MAIL ON SUNDAY); was a member of the Pudding Club, a supper club founded by Tim Smith, and the Blue Chip Club; "modestly rich" (Peter Oborne, EVENING STANDARD); old chum of Peter Luff;

Address: House of Commons, Westminster, London SW1A 0AA; 65 Marsham Court, Marsham Street, London SW1; has a Georgian home in Worcester "cannily bought in 1982 as a shambles for only £40,000" (Sandra Barwick, SUNDAY TELEGRAPH);

Telephone: 0171 219 6624/4472/4849 (H of C);

'Jim' (James Patrick) DOWD   Labour   LEWISHAM WEST '92-

Majority: 14,317 (38.2) over Conservative 6-way;
Description: South London's former supermarginal; "an inner-London seat, but mainly suburban in character" (John Maples); it has nothing of Lewisham but is made up of residential Forest Hill, Sydenham, and Catford;
Position: Whip (Lord Commissioner) '97-; ex: Assistant Spokesman on Northern Ireland '95-97; Opposition Whip '93-95; Chairman, West Lewisham Constituency Labour Party '77-; ex: Lewisham Borough Councillor (its Mayor '91-92, Chairman of Finance '90-91, Chairman of Central Services '87-90, Deputy Mayor '87, '90-91, Deputy Leader '85-87, Chief Whip til 85) '74-94; on Lewisham and North Southwark District Health Authority '84-90;

Outlook: A relaxed but skilful Whip who has shown, as a stand-in, he can be as successful and quick-witted a junior Minister as he displayed as an Opposition Spokesman; an opponent of first-past-the-post, despite the near-record swing it gave him in '97; Southeast London's witty former telephone engineer who has become an expert on the area's hospital and transport inadequacies; a locally-active mainstream councillor for 20 years who finally made it in his third Parliamentary bid, against able, persuasive John Maples; pro-CND but did not share the attitudes of some hard-Left fellow councillors; as a Police Committee Chairman "managed to steer a delicate line between the demands for increased accountability and the practical realities of day-to day co-operation with the police" (CATFORD NEWS); in Greenpeace and International Fund for Animal Welfare;

History: He joined the Labour Party '70; was elected to Lewisham Borough Council May '74; was appointed to the Lambeth, Lewisham and Southwark Area Health Authority May '76; was author of council resolution threatening to withhold payment of police precept as expression of total dissatisfaction with performance of the local police force Apr '80; selected for hopeless neighbouring Beckenham, was NEC-endorsed Jan '82; became first-ever Chairman of Lewisham's Police Committee May '82; contested Beckenham, coming 3rd with 15.5% June '83; was named to Lewisham and North Southwark District Health Authority Mar '84; after ex-MP Chris Price withdrew, was selected for Lewisham West by 38 to 32 on third ballot from a short-list of 3 men, two women Nov '85; became Deputy Mayor of Lewisham temporarily on the death of Tom Bradley Jan '87; promised to badger the Transport Minister to accept London Regional Transport's plan to extend the Bakerloo line to Lewisham Feb '87; led anti-nuclear march through Lewisham May '87; after John Maples campaigned against the "extravagant, inefficient loony-Left excesses" of Lewisham Council, lost to him by 3,772 votes (8%) June '87; was re-selected for Lewisham West over five other candidates, including a former Labour Government Minister, Albert Booth Mar '90; insisted that "unemployment in this constituency has risen more sharply than anywhere in south London" Aug '91; fought the effort of Guys and Lewisham Hospital Trust to bill Lewisham Council for £25,000 for burning its own medical waste Oct '91; retook Lewisham West with a majority of 1,809, ousting talented and persuasive Treasury Minister John Maples with a swing of 6.23% Apr '92; in his Maiden, urged the rebuilding of London's manufacturing industry June '92; disclosed he was nowhere as enthusiastic about the former Greater London Council as Ken Livingstone and Tony Banks; expressed doubts about the gerrymandering opportunities under the new

650   *Copyright (C)Parliamentary Profile Services Ltd*

Boundary Commission June '92; complained of the traumas suffered by Londoners from the deterioration of their ambulance service Oct '92; defended small businesses against the pressures of the banks and big businesses, who were slow payers Nov '92; complained that neighbouring Tory Bromley was refusing funds to help AIDS sufferers and their carers Dec '92; voted against Ray Powell's restrictive Shops (Amendment) Bill Jan '93; complained that Britain's withdrawal from UNESCO at the behest of Washington "has done immeasurable harm to this country and to the organisation" Feb '93; claimed the Budget showed the Conservatives "really are economic idiots of quite supreme proportions" because they used "the proceeds of capital sales to fund revenue"; complained: "some 17.5% of all the economically active adults in my constituency are unemployed" Mar '93; welcomed the 25th anniversary of the Abortion Act Apr '93; was one of 44 Labour MPs who wrote to President Clinton to urge military intervention in ex-Yugoslavia May '93 ; co-sponsored a motion attacking the US for its bombing attack on Iraqi intelligence headquarters in Baghdad without UN authorization June '93; complained about Government's having forced the closure of a Lewisham hostel for the homeless, only to reprieve it for the months before the elections July '93; voted for a lesser increase in MPs' pay Nov '93; was appointed Opposition Whip Nov '93; visited NATO/SHAPE in Brussels as a guest of the North Atlantic Council Nov '93; again complained that southeast London had virtually no Underground Dec '93; again demanded "the establishment of a strategic authority responsible for co-ordinating many of the services provided to the people who visit or live and work in London" Mar '94; said the Tomlinson Report - which "brought in its train serious threats to some of the finest centres of medical excellence in the world" - had been instituted because there was no London-wide NHS authority; pointed out that "the chairman of the Lewisham (Hospital) Trust [Sir Philip Harris] resigned after I placed questions on the order paper [in June '93], asking what the hell he was doing launching a £100m carpet company as the same time he was running a hospital" Jan '94; claimed the Deregulation Bill represented "a total surrender to the interests of big brewers, who are such generous backers of the Conservative Party" Feb '94; voted against restoring capital punishment, even for cop-killers Feb '94; backed reduction of age of homosexual consent to 18 or 16, Feb '94; ridiculed the idea that London had a surfeit of hospital beds because so many people had moved into the suburbs Apr '94; pointed out that NHS hospitals had long been changing before the latest "reforms" -southeast London's 12 hospitals had already come down to four; claimed that the hospitals were being run like "the Mad Hatter's tea party" Apr '94; voted with Tories on the Deregulation Bill, to secure a free vote on Sunday racing May '94; repeated need to extend Underground into south London July '94; nominated Tony Blair for Leader, Margaret Beckett for Deputy Leader but voted for Blair for Leader, Prescott for Deputy Leader July '94; deplored Government's failure to get long-term unemployed back to work, only 43,000 of 840,000 interviewed Nov '94; dubbed the Government's Single Regeneration Budget a "cut-price gameshow approach" Jan '95; urged retention of Guy's Hospital Feb '95; again defended Guy's because of the pressure the closure of its A & E department would put on King's College and Lewisham hospitals May '95; wittily baited PM John Major, congratulating him for having acquired a Deputy, Michael Heseltine, after five years in office July '95; again urged an end to first-past-the-post elections; Mrs Thatcher knew "that PR threatens to be the nemesis of the Tories" July '95; was promoted an Assistant Spokesman on Northern Ireland under Mo Mowlam Oct '95; moved an amendment on police and Army powers in Northern Ireland, recounting how he had heard the explosion on a bus in Aldwych six miles away in Lewisham Feb '96; in debate on renewal of Prevention of Terrorism Act recalled how his shamed Irish-born father had been unable to go to work on the day after the 1974 Birmingham pub bombing which had prompted the introduction of the Act Mar '96; voted against Bill of Iain Duncan-Smith to curb European Court Apr '96; voted against an Ulster Unionist amendment designed to thwart nationalist demands on the Northern Ireland Forum Apr '96; voted against a 3% cap on MPs' pay rise and for a pension based on £43,000, a £9,000 rise July '96; urged an extension of the East London Tube line from New Cross to Croydon July '96; was retained as Assistant Spokesman on Northern Ireland in Labour's last pre-election lineup July '96; complained of decline in NHS facilities in Northern Ireland Dec '96; secured withdrawal of comic advertisement suggesting Mona Lisa would look even more miserable if she lived in Lewisham Feb '97; he was one of 72 anti-hunting MPs targeted by The FIELD Apr '97; retained his formerly marginal seat with his majority enormously increased to 14,317 on a near-record anti-Tory swing of 17% May '97; was promoted Government Whip (Lord Commissioner of the Treasury May '97; was complimented by usually-abrasive Conservative MP Nigel Evans for his first Despatch Box performance standing in for Employment Minister Ian McCartney Mar '98;

Born: 5 March 1951, Bad Eilsen, West Germany

Family: "Family mythology has it that, via my paternal [Irish] grandmother (maiden name Reagan), a link to a moderately successful 'B' movie actor can be established; personally I feel this owes more to Irish romanticism than verifiable fact"; son, late James Patrick Dowd, Irish-born RAF and Post Office veteran, and late Elfriede Anna (Janocha), German-born former local government housing officer;

Education: Dalmain Road Infants and Junior Schools, London; Sedgehill Comprehensive; London Nautical School;

Occupation: Telecommunications Systems Engineer; ex: Engineering Consultant, and former Service Manager, Plessey Company, later GEC-Plessey Telecoms (MSF ex-ASTMS) '73-92; Station Manager, Heron Service Station '72-73; Telephone Engineer, with GPO (was one of 2,500 apprentices taken on in '67) '67-72;

Traits: Dark hair; half-Celtic good looks; chirpy, genial chatterer; keeps his Whip's desk obsessively tidy; this led five of his colleagues to litter it with ashtrays, used cups and newspapers; he threatened a Parliamentary motion naming them and demanding their "hanging, drawing and quartering"; had cat called 'Trotsky'; enjoys visiting Cornwall and the theatre;

Address: House of Commons, Westminster, London SW1A 0AA; 7 Surrey Mount, Forest Hill, London SE 23 3PF;

Telephone: 0171 219 4617/4130 (H of C); 0181 699 5870 (home); 0181 699 2001 (constituency);

WADING IN FILES:

Apart from the boiled-down versions which appear in these books and on our computers, we have shelves and shelves full of information built up over our over forty years of existence. Since we are not run by accountants, we are not compelled to purge the best bits by having junior assistant librarians culling our files. If you want to write the biography of ex-MP Sir John Stokes, it will only cost you £30 to see his file. There you will find that he was so pro-Franco during the Spanish civil war, that Balliol put up its own anti-Franco candidate against him for President of the Oxford University Conservative Association. This win was the springboard for Ted Heath's political career. Postwar, having held this position helped him overcome the deep prejudice among Conservative selectors who resisted choosing as the candidate for a winnable seat the son of a carpenter and a housemaid.

David (Elliot) DREW   Labour & Co-op   STROUD '97-

Majority: 2,910 over Conservative 4-way;
Description: This sprawling, mainly rural, slightly-altered seat stretches from Gloucester in the north to Bristol in the south, and is bordered by the Severn to the west; Stroud is its main town; "some 40% of the work force are still involved in manufacturing" (DD); in '95 it lost Tetbury to the new seat of Cotswold and picked up two wards from Gloucester; until the '97 election it was considered safely Conservative, with Tory MP Roger Knapman twice having registered majorities of about 13,000;
Position: On Select Committees: on Procedure '97-, on Modernisation of the Commons '98-; Chairman, PLP Committee on Agriculture '98-, Vice Chairman, PLP Committee on Rural Affairs '97-; Stonehouse Town Councillor '87-; ex: Gloucestershire County Councillor '93-97; Stroud District Councillor '87-95; Stevenage Borough Councillor '81-82;
Outlook: A well-informed, open-minded, idealistic and objective Christian Socialist lecturer who narrowly won a seat only once before gained by Labour, in '45; his sensible contributions are somewhat undermined by a portentous manner; because of the largely rural nature of his seat, he is vulnerable to any threat from the Tory-backed Countryside Alliance; a reformer flexibly loyal to Blairism; another of Labour's incoming teacher-councillors; a multiple cause groupie: Christian Socialist Movement, Labour Campaign for Electoral Reform ("supported electoral reform over many years" [DD]), Charter 88, Socialist Educational Association, Labour Party Rural Revival. formerly Anti-Apartheid; National Officer of the Economics Association;
History: He joined the Labour Party at 17, '69; was elected to Stevenage Borough Council May '81; was elected to Stroud District Council May '87; campaigned for public housing and to keep open Standish Hospital '91; contested the Stroud Parliamentary seat against incumbent MP Roger Knapman, picking up 4,500 votes to recover second place from the Liberal Democrat but still 13,405 votes behind Knapman Apr '92; was elected to Gloucestershire County Council May '93; was re-selected for Stroud Mar '95; captured the seat for Labour for the first time since 1945, by a majority of 2,910 on a notional swing of 11%, May '97; when he won, Peter Mandelson was said to say, "I never thought he'd win, so I didn't bother to get his name off the [candidates] list" May '97; asked Home Secretary what plans he had to incorporate the European Convention on Human Rights into domestic law May '97; co-congratulated Government on restoring trade union rights to GCHQ May '97; in his Maiden backed the phased release of housing receipts but attacked developers seeking to exploit greenfield sites June '97; asked the Chancellor of the Exchequer if he would review the proposal to end tax relief on profit-related pay, particularly for the first £1,000 of income June '97; urged further compensation for former prisoners of war in Japanese prison camps June '97; co-sponsored motion urging compulsory sprinkler syatems for single-storey supermarkets and superstores July '97; co-sponsored motion deploring difficulties for injured employees of liquidated companies July '97; urged bus re-regulation in view of Stagecoach's super-profits and deterioration of its services July '97; said on TV that he was "very unhappy" about new tuition burdens on university students and its special impact on those from poorer families Sep '97; urged a debate on how to improve relations between the NHS and local community

services Oct '97; although a supporter of the single transferrable vote, accepted the Government's proposal of a regional list because it would enable Labour voters in the southwest to elect Labour MEPs for once Nov '97; having led a survey of Gloucestershire's tenanted small holdings as a county councillor, urged their universal retention Nov '97; disputed the basis of assumptions on expected migration into Gloucestershire on which the planning need for 6,000 new houses was based Nov '97; deplored the inherited agricultural crisis -"never in recent years have so many agricultural products been in so much difficulty"; urged the supermarkets to replace foreign imports of beef with improved UK beef Dec '97; welcomed Cynog Dafis's Road Traffic Reduction Bill Jan '98; joined in an all-party meeting to resist too much building on greenfield sites Jan '98; in the Protection of the Countryside debate said: "I welcome a return to a plan-led, bottom-up, localised system"; "we must revitalise the cities if we are to protect the countryside" Jan '98; was named to Select Committtee on Modernisation of the Commons Feb '98; backed a Ministry for Rural Affairs Feb '98; strongly supported the retention of Stroud's maternity unit while recognising the need for a review Feb '98; supported an open list system for European elections, with an investigation of the closed list system if adopted Feb '98; urged better collaboration between local health and social services to avoid bed-blocking, as happened in Gloucestershire Feb '98; urged Deputy PM John Prescott to stick to a ceiling of 25 new houses in a village if that was all that local plans envisaged Feb '98; had a meeting with Chancellor Brown as Chairman of Labour's new Committee on Rural Affairs to warn against hitting country-dwellers in new taxation Feb '98; enthused about Chancellor Brown's Budget Mar '98; invited Education Secretary David Blunkett to christen Stroud's first new indoor school loo installed with promised new funds Mar '98; urged cautious spending on social housing on top of the capital receipts released by the Government Mar '98; asked for a debate on bovine tuberculosis, a threat only second to BSE Mar '98; urged a better localised supply of organic produce Apr '98; claimed only "rogue employers" rejected the national minimum wage Apr '98; urged a role for voluntary home improvement agencies like his Care and Repair England in improving fuel efficiency, especially if properly financed on a longterm basis June '98; urged better support and guidance for the parents of young offenders June '98; was one of only 14 Labour MPs (and of only two from the '97 intake) who opposed the reduction of the homosexual age of consent to 16, June '98;

Born: 13 April 1952, South Gloucestershire

Family: Son, of Ronald Montague Drew, company accountant, and Maisie Jean (Elliott), health worker; m 1st Olga (Samson); divorced '89; m 2nd '91 Anne Hilary (Baker) teacher; 2s: Laurence '84, Christopher '91; 2d Amy '82, Esther '92;

Education: Downend C of E Primary; Kingsfield School, Kingswood, Bristol; Nottingham University (BA in Economics); Birmingham University (PGCE); Bristol Polytechnic (MA in Business History, M Ed);

Occupation: Director, Care and Repair Stroud (voluntary home improvement agency; unremunerated) '88-; Author, The Electronic Office (1989); ex: Senior Lecturer, in Education, University of the West of England (formerly Bristol Polytechnic) '86-97 (NATFHE); previously a school teacher in Dene Magna, Forest of Dean '86-87, Maidenhill Comprehensive, Stonehouse '83-86, Stevenage '76-82;

Traits: Parted dark hair; droopy, chubby face; hooded eyes; soupstrainer moustache; is unusually conciliatory but has a portentous style suggesting self-importance and self-righteousness; deeply involved in church affairs; sporty: enjoys cycling, Rugby and cricket;

Address: House of Commons, Westminster, London SW1A 0AA; 17 Quietways, Stonehouse, Gloucestershire GL10 2NW;

Telephone: 0171 219 6479 (H of C); 01453 825603 (home);

Julia DROWN **Labour**

Majority: 5,645 over Conservative 6-way;
Description: The more Tory-leaning half of Wiltshire's premier industrial town just off the M4; initially based on the GWR's massive locomotive works, that works' decline has been compensated for by new industries, with a burgeoning population; the '95 split put Swindon's town centre and middle-class housing in this new seat, along with villages from former Devizes; the ex-Tory MP for unified Swindon, Simon Coombs, chose this as more likely to enable him to survive;
Position: On Select Committee on Health '97-; Vice Chairman, all-party Further Education Group '98-; ex: Oxfordshire County Councillor (Vice Chairman, its Labour Group and Spokesman on Social Services) '89-96; Chairman, Oxfordshire Co-operative Development Association;
Outlook: "A National Health Service high-flyer before leaving [her job as Finance Director of Radcliffe Infirmary] NHS Trust" (Clare Longrigg, GUARDIAN) in protest against the Tories' internal market; her aims remain unchanged: "I want to see the restoration of the Health Service and patients seen according to need" (JD); was a founder-member of the Campaign to Close Campsfield Detention Centre in Kidlington (her ward as a county councillor); multiple cause groupie: was on Executive of World Development Movement, in Labour Women's Network; Amnesty International, Greenpeace, Friends of the Earth, CND; with Swindon North's Labour MP, Michael Wills, supports a University for Industry, located in Swindon;
History: She joined the Labour Party '86; was elected for North Kidlington to Oxfordshire County Council May '89; was selected for the new seat of Swindon South Sep '95; resigned as Finance Director of Radcliffe Infirmary over internal market Apr '96; won Swindon South, ousting Tory MP Simon Coombs by a majority of 5,645, a pro-Labour notional swing of 14.57% May '97; in her Maiden, urged the redevelopment of Princess Margaret Hospital May '97; led a Parliamentary motion calling for the retention of the mutual building society status of Nationwide, based in Swindon June '97; urged drastic overhaul of the "Tories' CSA", to "make the agency foster co-operation between the agency and parents and between parents and children, that it should provide support to families rather than pulling them further apart and be fair to both partners and that it should give proper incentives for people to go to work and to co-operate with the agency" June '97; co-sponsored motion opposing exports of arms to Indonesia July '97; backed human rights for Yemen July '97; co-sponsored motion to compel installation of sprinkler systems in single-story supermarkets and superstores July '97; was named to the Select Committee on Health July '97; again urged ring-fencing of mutual building societies Aug '97; led motion welcoming the Government's release of capital receipts for housing, urging new housing be built to a "minimum standard that guarantees easy access for people with disabilities, the elderly and able-bodied people alike" Nov '97; urged the end of VAT on converting houses into flats, to ease the need for new building of 4.4m houses Nov '97; urged redirection of NHS funds into dentistry since no one was being allowed on to NHS dental lists in her constituency Nov '97; led a debate opposing local storage of possibly BSE-infected meat and bones Dec '97; introduced Energy Efficiency (Information) Bill to enable homebuyers to learn how energy-efficient their homes are Dec '97; surveyed insurance companies to make sure their small print did not discriminate against transsexuals Jan '98;

again criticised the inefficiency, inflexibility and unreasonableness of the Child Support Agency, including the inability of a constituent to reach the CSA, despite making 40 calls Feb '98; urged ending of rate-capping and the return of more control of business rates to local councils Feb '98; urged giving local councils greater control over density of housing construction Feb '98; attacked the idea that Labour was giving women only the choice of going out to work: "nothing is more valuable and often more satisfying than bringing up children" Feb '98; again backed constituents' protests against storing rejected, possibly BSE-infected meat and bones in Wroughton in her constituency Mar '98; contrasted the need for an ethical arms policy with the demand of most MPs that arms production continued in their constituencies; urged the costs of arms research be included into the cost of arms Apr '98; asked how much debt relief had been achieved for the poorest countries Apr '98;

Born: 23 August 1962, London

Family: Daughter, of David Drown, picture restorer, and Audrey (Harris) nurse; Partner, Bill Child, lecturer; their first daughter, Ruby, died within 7 hours Aug '98;

Education: Hampstead Comprehensive '73-80; University College, Oxford University (BA in PPE, after starting in Physics); CIPFA;

Occupation: Public Service Accountant (CIPFA): worked for NHS '85-96: as Director of Contracts, Finance and Information at Radcliffe Infirmary '90-96;

Traits: Parted long straight brown hair; long neck; long thin nose; a thin, almost two-dimensional head; pleasant but serious; enjoys cinema, music;

Address: House of Commons, Westminster, London SW1A 0AA; 39 Victoria Road, Swindon SN1 3AT

Telephone: 0171 219 2392 (H of C); 01793 615444 (constituency);

Alan (James Carter) DUNCAN   Conservative   **RUTLAND & MELTON '92-**

Majority: 8,836 (16.8%) over Labour 5-way;

Description: East rural Leicestershire including the Duke of Rutland's Belvoir seat; prime fox-hunting country, with beauty spots like Rutland Water and the Vale of Belvoir; Rutland was the smallest former county but was linked to Melton Mowbray in '83; includes Pedigree Petfoods at Melton, Castle Cement at Ketton, and RAF Cottesmore; it was made classier and more rural in '95 by moving 22,000 voters from the Leicester suburbs into the new Charnwood seat and adding 9,000 from Harborough villages;

Position: Deputy Spokesman, on Health '98-; ex: Vice Chairman, Conservative Party '97-98; Parliamentary Political Secretary to Leader William Hague '97-98; PPS, to Brian Mawhinney '95-97, '93-94; on Social Security Select Committee '92-95; Chairman, Conservative MPs' Constitutional Affairs Committee '94-95, Secretary, Conservative MPs' Environment Committee '92-93?;

Outlook: William Hague's miniaturised Mandelson replica teamed with Ann Widdecombe: "not since Kenneth Williams and Hattie Jacques camped it up in 'Carry on Doctor' have we had such an odd couple in the health profession" (Rachel Sylvester and Alice Thomson, DAILY TELEGRAPH); "the Rasputin of the Right" (Michael Gove, TIMES); "that clever, pinch-faced ideologue" (David Aaronovitch, INDEPENDENT); "clever and energetic, but he is also hyperactive, impetuous and a libertarian of the hard-Right"; he has "nerve" and "staying power" and "is unshakeable in his view that Blair will crumble"; "like other small men with big ambitions, Duncan likes a good scrap" (Paul Routledge, INDEPENDENT ON SUNDAY); the economic libertarian who rushes in where more prudent Tories fear to tread; was blamed for unwisely advising William Hague to accuse Tony Blair of making political capital from the funeral of Princess Diana; his 1995 book, 'Saturn's Children', called for a minimalist state reversing "a century of creeping collectivism", with Inland Revenue officials as "the moral equivalent of the Gestapo"; he is an enemy equally of "Christian Socialism, High Toryism, One Nation Toryism, Civic Conservatism and Liberal Democracy"; it also included four "most intelligent" pages (Labour MP Paul Flynn) on drug liberalisation, since excised; William Hague's former Westminster landlord who emerged as his spin doctor, obsessed with Tony Blair and Peter Mandelson; from his first days as an assiduous new boy he spoke as though an old parliamentarian loaded with political honours, having "invested 20 years of my life in getting into Parliament" (AD); a nakedly ambitious, wealthy young Rightwing oil trader who jumped nimbly from Mrs Thatcher's to John Major's bandwagon and then to that of his friend, William Hague; his copybook was slightly blotted for the Major Government by his initial opposition to Maastricht, for Labour by his allegedly using his neighbour's £50,000 discount to acquire his Gayfere Street council house at less than full price; is against a United States of Europe and, above all, a single European currency; worries about the welfare state having created a "thuggish under-class";

History: His grandfather was a friend of the Liberal leader, Sir Archibald Sinclar; he became a Liberal when eleven, '68; was defeated as a Liberal candidate in school mock election '70; says he has been a Conservative "ever since my balls dropped"; joined the Young Conservatives in southwest Hertfordshire at 15, '72; joined the Oxford University Conservative Association, aligning himself with its anti-TRG Rightwing '76; became President of the Oxford Union '79; with William Hague, was active in Devonshire ward of the Battersea Conservative constituency association from '82; was selected for hopeless Barnsley West and Penistone '86; said: "I want to see as many rich miners as possible and the best way to achieve it is to have a profitable mining industry"; claimed that many local Tory supporters were "frightened to admit in such a traditionally staunch Labour area that Mrs Thatcher's values are the ones they also support, for they fear they might be ostracised" Sep '86; lost Barnsley West and Penistone to Allen McKay by 14,191 votes, a swing from Tories to Labour of 3.7% June '87; was shortlisted for Richmond, after the announced retirement of Leon Brittan, but was just pipped at the post by his friend and former lodger, William Hague Nov '88; made an enthusiastic speech at conference, ending with a question, "Do we support the Thatcher economic policy?" to which he replied, "We do, we do, we do!"; was complimented by Chancellor Nigel Lawson for "so ably catching the mood of the conference"; next day ex-Tory-MP Matthew Parris wrote: "Mr Duncan, Duncan, Duncan is clearly looking for a safer seat, seat, seat" Oct '89; was selected for the Tories' third-safest seat, Rutland and Melton, in the wake of Michael Latham's announced retirement; he defeated 300 other aspirants, including ex-MP Michael Ancram (later adopted for Devizes) May '90; signed the letter of John Bercow, Rightist former Chairman of the disbanded Federation of Conservative Students, pledging fulsome support to Mrs Thatcher Nov '90; two hours after Mrs Thatcher resigned, made his Gayfere Street house available for John Major's campaign headquarters, at the request of William Hague, his friend and Norman Lamont's PPS, installing extra telephones, a computer and a fax machine; he became a member of the Major campaign team Nov '90; co-authored 'Bearing the Standard', a pamphlet in which ten young prospective Tory candidates urged more "social cohesion' and a "wider Europe" Sep '91; was credited with the view that the welfare state was creating a "thuggish underclass" Mar '92; John Major stopped his battle-bus in Melton, despite its huge majority Mar '92; retained seat by an enlarged majority of 25,535, with Labour now taking second place Apr '92; in his Maiden welcomed the inheritance tax proposals in the Finance Bill; urged a recovery "without massive house price inflation" June '92; signed the Euro-sceptic motion urging a "fresh start" after the Danish referendum rejection of Maastricht, to the sorrow of John Major June '92; backed Government spending cuts to offset demand-led spending on unemployment benefit June '92; in debate on Sittings of the House, opposed morning sittings July '92; visited Germany and Hungary as guest of the Konrad Adenauer Foundation Sep '92; was loudly cheered at a meeting of the Rightwing '92 Group' when he said the Conservative Party's problems stemmed from an imbalance between the Rightwing Parliamentary party and the Centre-Left Cabinet, which needed redressing by promoting more Rightwingers; he was supported by John Biffen Oct '92; described John Major as "impressive and persuasive" after being called in to have his backing for Maastricht reinforced Nov '92; voted with the Government on the Maastricht Bill, helping to give them their three-vote majority Nov '92; asked Edward Heath to confess that "much of his European passion - his passion for the European ideal - is based on a severe distrust of the United States" Nov '92; was named to the Social Security Select Committee Nov '92; was invited by biographer-minister Jonathan Aitken to meet ex-President Richard Nixon Dec '92; his and Lord Cochrane's Gas (Exempt Supplies) Bill received royal assent Jan '93; co-sponsored Simon Burns' Bill on Newly-Qualified Drivers Jan '93; was Teller for the opponents of the Right to Know Bill Feb '93; asked PM John Major whether he agreed "that criminals, even teen-age criminals and other young offenders, are responsible for their own actions and deserve to be punished accordingly" Feb '93; asked PM John Major not to tax the Queen because she might be "inexorably drawn into the forum of party-political conflict" if she had to "choose between two leaders, one with a high-tax policy and the other with a low-tax policy" Feb '93; in Budget debate complained that "we have lacked long-term finance in industry"; blamed the recession partly on Mrs Thatcher's refusal to tackle, in time, Chancellor Nigel Lawson's "surreptitious" inflationary decision to shadow the Deutschmark, partly on the ERM's conversion from an adjustable system to a non-adjustable system, preventing the lowering of interest rates; "I am against a single currency"; "I judge the PSBR to be dangerously high" Mar '93; amended Railways Bill to ensure that BR's successors would offer artefacts and document to the York Railway Museum Mar '93; when he did not fully agree with Baroness Thatcher over mortgage tax relief, she said, "if that's what you really think, there's the door" May '93; complained that the Gas (Exempt Supplies) Act which he had piloted through the Commons for Lord Cochrane was being held up by the Health and Safety Executive May '93; visited Italy as a guest of the Konrad Adenauer Foundation May '93; in a pamphlet published by Demos, urged abolition of mortgage tax relief because tax breaks for property had harmed finance for industry June '93; backed the Government's plans to close and privatise coalmines because that was the judgement of those dominating the energy market July '93; in debate on Finance Bill warned "it is necessary to build economic confidence", but not to worry about attacking a "fragile recovery" July '93; as a member of a 'No Turning Back' research group, proposed the scrapping of child benefit and the end of separate but overlapping benefits for different groups July '93; insisted farmers were "perfectly reasonable" in allowing access to their land but had few powers to remove disruptive people July '93; returned with six heads of antlers from a stalking holiday in Scotland to address 1,000 hunt supporters opposed to a move to ban hunting with hounds on land owned by the county council Oct '93; preferred to help the elderly with small savings rather than young unmarried mothers Nov '93; said, "we will have nothing to do with anyone who describes themselves as a 'chairperson', 'chairholder' or 'chair'" Nov '93; was named PPS to Dr Brian Mawhinney Dec '93; defended the Government's guillotining of two short social security Bills, which resulted in

Labour breaking off "usual channel" relations Dec '93; was rated as the third most assiduous back-bencher after Dennis Skinner and Bob Cryer, with a 95.52% participation rate Dec '93; it was disclosed that he had acquired a neighbouring council house valued at £190,000 by advancing £140,000 to his neighbour, who was entitled to a £50,000 discount; he acquired his neighbour's house after three years, the neighbour used the £50,000 to renovate the house, after which the neighbour continued to live rent-free; when this became known, LibDem constituents urged his de-selection, one Liberal Democrat saying "most people here think Duncan is a fly boy who is just out to feather his nest"; while insisting his transaction was "totally above-board, totally legal and something I have never tried to hide," he felt it necessary to resign as Dr Mawhinney's PPS after only 17 days Jan '94; warned the press it had been an "unwarranted invasion of privacy" to pursue his father's suicide four years before; his father, who suffered from terminal cancer, had shot himself with his own gun Jan '94; it was alleged by the MAIL ON SUNDAY that Innovisions Ltd, a company of which he had been Chairman and part-owner until its bankruptcy in '93, had used £14,000 of its employees' income tax and national insurance contributions to stave off the receivers Jan '94; said the Coal Industry Bill was "long overdue": "if oil and gas can survive and thrive in the private sector, so can coal" Jan '94; backed the restoration of capital punishment for killers of policemen Feb '94; backed reduction of age of homosexual consent to 16; asked his homophobic Tory colleague, Dr Robert Spink, "why does my honourable Friend think that the solution to two 18-year-olds consenting to have sex together is to send them to prison?" Feb '94; urged registration of acupuncturists Feb '94; Labour MP Dale Campbell-Savours again demanded he repay to Westminster Council the £50,000 discount given the neighbour whose house purchase he financed Mar '94; over 200 Opposition MPs signed a motion criticising his behaviour in buying his neighbour's council house, with 15 Tory colleagues defending it as "a perfectly legal transaction" Mar '94; was nominated for the Procedure Select Committee (but blocked by Dale Campbell-Savours' objection) Mar '94; thanked the Prime Minister for restoring the "valiant little county of Rutland" June '94; agreeing with the Duke of Edinburgh's claim that absolute poverty had been abolished, said, "you don't see children in the streeet any more with bare feet and rickets" June '94; personally confronted Gerry Adams in Westminster, demanding an apology for the murder of Airey Neave Nov '94; resisted efforts of women MPs to establish a creche at Westminster as "the collectivisation of child care around the place or work", saying "no! no! no!" in imitation of Mrs Thatcher, "someone who brought up twins with no help from the state" (but the backing of a rich husband) Jan '95; defended Army's involvement in fox-hunting, saying "mob rule and class war should not be allowed to stop the Army doing something that is perfectly legal; hunting is good exercise for horses; there is something inherently noble and nothing cruel in the great and glorious death of the fox in the field" Feb '95; backed Ken Baker's motion congratulating PM John Major for ruling out Britain joining a single currency in '97, Feb '95; led resistance to Harry Barnes' Civil Rights (Disabled Persons) Bill on grounds of cost Feb '95; denied "the poor had got poorer" but proposed "a citizens' income" of £53 a week Feb '95; was active in Tory moves to oust Labour MP Greville Janner as Chairman of the Employment Select Committee, saying "he has turned the select committee system into a vulgar stunt on prime-time TV" Mar '95; tabled an amendment to disability Bill to ensure the benefit went only to those genuinely incapable of work Mar '95; his amendment to the Gas Bill forced British Gas to hive off its £17b pipelines business to a subsidiary Apr '95; his book, 'Saturn's Children', co-written with Dominic Hobson, was a cry for a minimalist state with minimum taxes supporting only defence and health; urged all benefits be replaced by £53 a week payment May '95; sympathised with constituents' complaints about slogan of locally-brewed Ruddles Beer - "Rutland, home of Ruddles Best, and very little else" May '95; clashed with Peter Hain over 'Dispatches' TV programme exposing his taking up amendments to Gas Bill in the interest of the British Holiday and Home Parks Association, moved by its paid lobbyist Sir Jerry Wiggin misusing the name of committee member Sebastian Coe May '95; as part of the Conservative counter-attack on Lord Nolan's proposal to compel MPs to disclose earnings from consultancies, he harangued Lord Nolan on the street, warning him that he was playing "a very, very dangerous political game" which could "end up obliterating the professional classes' representation in the House of Commons" May '95; urged the UK withdrawal from the ILO, an "international quango that allows trade unionists to go on freebies at taxpayers' expense" June '95; his Harborough neighbour, Edward Garnier, was accused of "hostile action" in applying for selection for redrawn Rutland and Melton June '95; praised Michael Portillo for backing PM John Major, instead of challenger John Redwood June '95; praised Manchester Liberalism as having "released all the strengths and energies" of 19th century Britain, describing minimum wage proposals as "cretinous" July '95; with Charles Hendry, David Willetts and Michael Mates was named an ad hoc spin doctor to guide the press at the Conservative Party Conference Oct '95; was again appointed PPS to Brian Mawhinney, now Conservative Party Chairman, consequently leaving the Social Security Select Committee Oct-Dec '95; alleged Labour's aim in demanding disclosure of MPs' outside earnings was "a sinister and cynical exercise" to drive high-calibre Tories out of politics Nov '95; made a citizen's arrest of demonstrators who sprayed paint over his boss, Brian Mawhinney, in protest against the Government's asylum and immigration policy; he claimed £1,000 damage to his suit, Dr Mawhinney claimed £200 Nov '95; Conservative Central Office denied he was keeping a count of Speaker Boothroyd's displays of anti-Tory bias after she slapped down Welsh Office Minister Rod Richard's attack on Tony Blair's child going to a selective school Dec '95; defended Prince Charles against attack by Labour's Shadow Welsh Secretary Ron Davies, whom he described as "a shallow politician who demeans the Labour front bench" Mar '96; as 'minder' to Tory candidate Jimmy James at the crucial by-election for Tory-held SE Staffs sent young Tories to disrupt Labour photo-opportunities; he predicted a 5,000 Tory majority; the result was a Labour majority of 14,000 on a record 22% swing Apr '96; at magistrates court hearing of case against the paint-throwers, he claimed to have kept his hands behind his back to avoid being accused of assault by "tutored demonstrators" Apr '96; opposed Labour MP Angela Eagle's Part-Time Employees Bill as costing firms an estimated £1.5b and certain to destroy jobs Apr '96; was alleged in TIMES to being considered as a tough Rightwing Minister to undermine Education Secretary Gillian Shephard's resistance to increased selectivity in schools June '96; attended lecture by Sir James Goldsmith at house of neighbour-friend Jonathan Aitken June '96; in Budget debate urged abolition of inheritance tax Dec '96; was named as intending to oppose a single European currency in his election address Mar '97; with other of Neil Hamilton's friends, allegedly helped block Downing Street's effort to drop him as Tatton's candidate Apr '97; retained his seat with a majority slashed by two-thirds to 8,836 on a 14.5% notional swing to Labour May '97; became chief aide to former lodger William Hague in Leadership contest May-June '97; in final round, urged Baroness Thatcher to back Hague June '97; was named Hague's Parliamentary Political Secretary and Vice Chairman of the Conservative Party June '97; was named a member of 'Le Cercle', a discreet, exclusive Rightwing think tank chaired by his disgraced friend, Jonathan Aitken June '97; as the Labour leadership cooled over Mike Foster's anti-hunting Bill, he kept insisting "Blair wants the Bill" July '97; his influence over Hague was said to be responsible for abrupt resignation of Francis Halewood, Tories' acting Director of Communications Sep '97; he was held responsible for Hague's accusation that Blair was making capital of Princess Diana's death; this allegedly occasioned the Shadow Cabinet remark, "Margaret Thatcher said, 'Every Tory Leader should have a Willie, our Leader has a prick'"; he was shifted from his hands-on public relations role to a more ambiguous strategic advisory role in the party's high command Sep '97; at the instigation of William Hague, excised the drugs chapter from paperback edition of his book, 'Saturn's Children' in which he ridiculed prohibition and urged legalisation of drugs distribution June '98; he was promoted Deputy Spokesman on Health, under Ann Widdecombe June '98; he ridiculed "the people's waiting lists" June '98; he was one of 18 Tory MPs to vote to reduce age of homosexual consent to 16, June '98;

Born: 31 March 1957, Rickmansworth, Hertfordshire

Family: Son, late Wing Commander James Grant Duncan OBE, onetime RAF Officer, and Anne (Carter), teacher;

Education: Beechwood Park School, Markyate, Herts; Merchant Taylors' School, Northwood, Middx; St John's College, Oxford (President of the Union); Harvard University (Kennedy Scholar);

Occupation: Oil Trader (as Harcourt Consultants), "trading crude oil and refined petroleum products across the world" recently on his own account; quotes his own worth at a modest £2m; "I purchase oil from the Middle East and supply it to surrounding countries that are not oil producers"; "Korean companies have a major share of the construction business in Libya; they used to be paid in crude oil, which I purchased, sold in the market and converted to dollars to pay them"; on oil matters is a Consultant to the Vitol Group of companies; he served as "a Consultant to the Ahmed Mannai Group of Qatar and as an Adviser to the the Pakistani Goverment; it was in this capacity tht he made a killing himself during the Gulf War", "by being able to supply some tankers to Pakistan when her regular supplier, Kuwait, had been out of action" (PRIVATE EYE) '89-; Director: Ripponden Group Ltd (of which crashed Innovisions Ltd was a subsidiary) '89-; Shareholder, in Sigma Motors (Pvt) Ltd '95?-; ex: Chairman and Half-Owner (with 46%), of Innovisions Ltd (originally a Manchester-based corporate video production company, which went into receivership '93 with a deficiency of £178,847; creditors were owed £109,000) '89-93; Trader, in Marc Rich and Company, "an independent commodity trading company" owned by Marc Rich, a fugitive in extradition-free Switzerland from the US Internal Revenue, which sought £33m in back taxes from him; "Duncan was sent to the Far East to run Rich's Singapore office"; "Duncan received a generous salary (taxed at advantageous Singaporean levels)" '81-87; was with Shell International Petroleum '79-81;

Traits: Tiny, slim, dapper; "elfin". "strutting", ('Black Dog' MAIL ON SUNDAY); "small, slim and expensively dressed", "a sort of Bonsai Heseltine"; "a hawk light enough to rest on [Ann Widdecombe's] wrist were she to wear a leather falconer's gauntlet" (Matthew Parris, TIMES); he demanded £1,000 in damages for his paint-spattered suit; "Mr Duncan is a connoisseur of the arts, who recently immortalised his neat features in a work by the fashionable portraitist of today, Diccon Swan" (MAIL ON SUNDAY); fly fisherman; water-skier; skier; hockey-player; "millionaire" (EVENING STANDARD); was cox on first eight of St John's, Oxford and of a heavyweight crew at Harvard; a talented mimic who once did an imitation of John Major in the Commons Tearoom only to find Major standing behind him (Quentin Letts, DAILY TELEGRAPH); on hearing that he had donated £100 toward trapping the alleged 'Rutland Panther', a constituent allegedly said, "it must be the first time Alan's chased any kind of pussy" (PRIVATE EYE);

Address: House of Commons, Westminster, London SW1A 0AA;

Telephone: 0171 219 5204 (H of C); 0941 147704 (pager);

(George) Iain DUNCAN-SMITH Conservative **CHINGFORD & WOODFORD GREEN '97-**

Majority: 5,714 (12.9%) over Labour 4-way;
Description: An Essex lower-middle-class white dormitory and Tory stronghold, squeezed between the River Lea and Epping Forest in the Northern half of Waltham Forest; 80% owner-occupied, partly by successful East Enders; in '95 the old Chingford seat was altered by adding Monkhams and Church End wards from dismantled Wanstead and Woodford and moving Chapel End ward into Walthamstow;
Former Seat: Chingford '92-97
Position: Social Security Spokesman '97-; Chairman, Conservative MPs' Social Security Committee '97-; ex: on Select Committees: on Members' Interests '95-97, Standards and Privileges '95-97, Administration 94-95, Health '93-95; Secretary, Conservative MPs' Foreign and Commonwealth Committee '92-97; Vice Chairman, Fulham Conservative Association '91-;
Outlook: The Rightwing Tory Eurosceptics' belatedly-promoted top sane intellectual; "brainiest Shadow Cabinet member" (MAIL ON SUNDAY); "fastidious" (Michael White, GUARDIAN); allegedly refused repeated offers of jobs from John Major's Whips to call off his anti-Maastricht campaign; also rejected £2,500 election campaign offer from Europhobe Paul Sykes; "the sea-greeen incorruptible of the Conservative Party" (John Bercow MP); the personal and social antithesis of his predecessor, Norman Tebbit; instead of an East End street-fighter, a representative of the political squirearchy of "High Tories who can boast of generations of service in the party" (SUNDAY TIMES); a classic Rightwing Tory intellectual in the Thatcherite 'No Turning Back' group, bone-dry on the economy, strong on defence, anti-Nolan and a Eurosceptic; "one of the most original minds on the backbenches in the last Parliament" (TIMES); a "super-bright Europhobe" (MAIL ON SUNDAY); opposed over-deep Bosnian involvement; has "integrity and the courage of his convictions" (Dominic Lawson, SPECTATOR); "someone with Mr Duncan-Smith's qualities of integrity and honesty is the sort of person no government can do without indefinitely" (Simon Heffer, EVENING STANDARD); an Edinburgh-born publisher and former Captain in the Scots Guards;
History: "I could have chosen the well-trodden route to Westminster; I could have gone to Oxford and then the City, like so many others; but I didn't want that label; I come from a family with a history of service; my father was a fighter pilot in the second world war; I joined the Scots Guards and saw active service in Northern Ireland before becoming assistant to General Sir John Ackland during the Rhodesian negotiations"; the Conservative victory had a major political influence on him '79; joined the Conservative Party '81; was chosen to fight marginal Bradford West against Max Madden MP Jan '86; lost the seat by 7,551 votes, double the 1983 majority, despite increasing the Tory vote by over 2,000 June '87; was selected for Chingford in wake of Norman Tebbit's announced retirement Mar '91; co-signed letter from Tory candidates to DAILY TELEGRAPH expressing "scepticism about both a single currency and [European] political union" Nov '91; retained seat with majority of 14,938, down from 17,955, a swing to Labour of 6.3% Apr '92; in his Maiden, made clear his aversion for Maastricht's plan to for "a continuing progression toward a European superstate", not merely because of the Italian attempts to use the EC to regulate the size of condoms made by the London Rubber Company in his constitueny; ridiculed the Major-Hurd effort to eliminate the

f-word from the treaty; "a bite from a rottweiler hurts just as much even if we insist on calling it a pekinese"; Britons, accustomed to common law rather than Continental law, did not appreciate the power of the preambles to the Treaty of Rome, the Single European Act and Maastricht which, executed by the European Commission and interpreted by the Eurpopean Court, set Europe on a rachet towards a European super-state; urged the EC be refashioned into "a group of nation-states determined to seek co-operation on a defined but limited number of areas"; he was the only Tory new boy not to vote with the Government; he abstained May '92; signed the Euro-sceptic motion which, after the Danish referendum 'no', urged a "fresh start" on Maastricht June '92; urged Northern Ireland Secretary Sir Patrick Mayhew to push on to "strand three" of Northern Ireland talks, recalling that when he served there sixteen years before, in '76, there had been signboards saying "seven years was too much" June '92; was one of 26 Tory MPs who voted against the Government on Maastricht Nov '92; won SPECTATOR award for 'New Member of the Year' for the "integrity and the courage of his [anti-Maastricht] convictions" Nov '92; was invited to meet ex-President Richard Nixon by his biographer, Jonathan Aitken MP Dec '92; expressed concern about increase in asylum seekers, because so many settled in his constituency Nov '92; having congratulated the PM for rejecting Maastricht's social chapter, he now concluded "the treaty covers a series of open doors through which the social chapter may well be introduced" to avoid the UK becoming too competitive as "a low-cost country with much simpler worker-management relationships" Jan '93; expressed concern about murder by Burmese military of the brother of a constituent Mar '93; with 25 other Maastricht rebels, helped defeat Government over Maastricht by 22 votes Mar '93; said "I am a great supporter of contracting out through compulsory competitive tendering" which was opposed by his local, Labour-led Waltham Forest council Apr '93; pointed out, "clearly and incisively" (Sir Russell Johnston MP) that "even if the social chapter were not signed, competition policy would result in our arriving at the same destination" May '93; was one of 41 Maastricht rebels who voted against its 3rd Reading May '93; was rated as one of the most active Maastricht rebels, with 11 dissenting votes, 47 abstentions and only 4 votes for the Bill May '93; visited Azerbaijan as guest of BP May-June '93; enthused about "the successful management buy-out at Leyland DAF" backed by Michael Heseltine June '93; blamed the eruption in ex-Yugoslavia on "Germany's rush to recognise Bosnia and Croatia, against our better judgement" June '93; avoiding a pincer movement by Peter Lilley and Michael Howard, voted with Opposition in favour of Government-opposed social chapter July '93; claimed "the sale of bus companies", as in Oxford, was "good for employees" July '93; complained that Whitfiield School in his constituency was suffering 4% cuts (instead of 2.5%) because it was moving toward becoming grant-maintained July '93; insisted it was necessary to cut the £80b spent on social security "because the current rate of expenditure will result in a cycle of higher spending and higher taxes which will lead to higher inflation and will distort the labour market" July '93; repeated this in No Turning Back pamphlet, 'Who Benefits?' Aug '93; visited Taiwan as guest of its government Sep '93; pointed out that Britain's defence expenditure had already been cut from 5% of GDP to 3.2% in eight years and it still needed first-class equipment in an uncertain world Oct '93; voted for full deregulation of Sunday trading Dec '93; was named to the Select Committee on Administration Jan '94; again warned against defence cuts Jan '94; claimed it was a "criminal breach" for pressmen to have been supplied with copies of the District Auditor's Tory-damaging report on Westminster Council Jan '94; again blamed the failure of his Labour-run Waltham Forest local council on its dragging its heels on competitive tendering Feb '94; urged full deregulation, aligning himself with Neil Hamilton Feb '94; voted to restore capital punishment, especially for cop-killers Feb '94; raised the question of passport fraud on the basis of birth certificates retained by the Passport Office Feb '94; voted to reduce the age of homosexual consent to 18, not 16, Feb '94;

again demanded a free market in the EC, with slashed CAP and end of subsidies to Continental steel industries, which required renegotiating Maastricht Feb '94; co-authored No Turning Back pamphlet, 'A Conservative Europe', demanding a gurantee that Britain would not return to the ERM or subscribe to a single European currency Feb '94; claimed his local Labour-led authority, Waltham Forest, was "about to be investigated for maladministration by the Ombudsman" Mar '94; said women were inevitably securing equality but did not need the backing of European law to make women part-times wholly equal to male full-timers Mar '94; urged Douglas Hurd to stand his ground against the federalists in Brussels Mar '94; complained that mammoth social security spending was creating a dependency culture Apr '94; again complained that Waltham Forest's Labour-led council, backed by the Liberal Democrats, had set too high a council tax Apr '94; wrote 'Social Security, the Way Forward' for Conservative Way Forward, the Thatcherite think tank formed by Lord (Cecil) Parkinson; this urged the abolition of Child Benefit and State Earnings-Related Pensions and curbs on housing and invalidity benefits Apr '94; insisted "the Common Agricultural Policy is in huge need of revitalisation and reform" not least because "only 40% of the money ends up with farmers" with bureaucrats swallowing much of the rest, costing an unnecessary extra £1,000 a year for each British family May '94; protested the Football Association's monopolistic opposition to his constituent's mini-football game, Futbolito June '94; in the face of proposed EU expansion, urged repatriation of CAP and cut in European commissioners "to make the Community a workable one of nation states" July '94; urged reform of European Court of Justice July '94; said Tory backbenchers were "deeply cynical" about Foreign Secretary Douglas Hurd after his call fo a "common European defence" Oct '94; co-signed TIMES letter opposing higher contribution to EU Budget Oct '94; urged root-and-branch reform of fraud-ridden EU structures Dec '94; initiated debate on Private Clegg, imprisoned for shooting a civilian in Northern Ireland Jan '95; urged change of Northern Ireland rules of engagement to avoid risking prosecution of soldiers Feb '95;co-signed Ken Baker's Eurosceptics' motion congratulating PM John Major opposing signing up with the Euro in '97, Feb '95; co-wrote DAILY TELEGRAPH letter opposing signing up with Euro since those most likely to sign up - France, Germany and Benelux - accounted for only 28% of UK's foreign trade Feb '95; opposed Tory Eurosceptics circulating his speeches as a diagnostic test of sitting Tory MPs as getting "between an MP and his association" Feb '95; opposed making WEU into the European pillar of NATO as undermining the US role Mar '95; was named to Select Committee on Members' Interests Mar '95; said, "if we possess nuclear weapons we must make clear we are prepared to use them, otherwise we might as well not possess them" May '95; claimed British troops in Bosnia were "serving less and less purpose" there, backing their withdrawal May '95; opposed use of "some passing judge" to vet MPs' misdeeds May '95; said Tories were trailing in polls because they were not Tory enough June '95; urged wider rented housing market to increase labour mobility June '95; backed Redwood candidacy in TIMES article June '95; was named to new post-Nolan Standards and Privileges Select Committee July '95; was one of six named by Chairman Brian Mawhinney to plan election July '95; urged reduction of public spending from mid-40s to "mid-30s" Nov '95; urging an interest rate cut to help the economy, complained that National Lottery was siphoning off spending money from high-street trade Dec '95; with ten others, urged an end to "gang warfare" on Europe within the Conservative Party Dec '95; having found "the life of an MP a financial disaster", insisted a ban on consultancies would require higher pay for MPs Jan '96; urged a "structured and disciplined environment" in primary schools and publication of league tables to "help reverse the remaining facets of the socialist experiment that failed" Jan '96; raised the spectre of a return of fascism in Germany if Kohl's quest for a federal European superstate were not realised, in pamphlet co-authored with Bill Cash Feb '96; co-sponsored Labour MP Don

Touhig's Bill - opposed by Major Government - to protect staff blowing the whistle on crimes at work Mar '96; attacked European Court of Justice after its ruling favouring Spanish fishermen Mar '96; his Bill curbing the European Court of Justice was defeated by 83 to 77, Apr '96; spoke up for colleague Barry Legg over latter's involvement in Westminster's "homes for votes" scandal May '96; attacked Channel 4 series on poverty as a "two-week party political broadcast on behalf of the Labour Party" June '96; voted for Bill Cash's European Referendum Bill June '96; the Tories' spoof manifesto 'New Labour, New Dangers' was based on his idea July '96; voted against 3% cap on MPs' pay rise July '96; opposed EU working directive on 48-hour week July '96; urged rethink on higher funds for Scotland if devolution went ahead Oct '96; clashed with Commons Leader Tony Newton over latter's refusal to debate Euro Nov '96; tried to help embattled David Willetts in his rough interrogation by Quentin Davies before Standards and Privileges by suggesting he was an over-eager new Whip Nov '96; insisted Conservatives could either bar the Euro or commit suicide Dec '96; joined 16 other Tory Eurosceptics voting against EU fishing policy, calling for 200-mile British exclusion zone Dec '96; was listed as one of 13 Tory MPs whose manifestos would oppose ever joining the Euro Dec '96; voted to restore caning Jan '97; voted to dis-assemble target pistols, instead of banning them Feb '97; was mistakenly alleged to be one of the anti-Euro Tory candidates willing to accept £2,500 in election money from Paul Sykes; in fact, he refused it Mar '97; retained his altered and renamed seat by much-reduced majority of 5,714, on a pro-Labour notional swing of 13.8%, as one of only 11 Tory survivors in Greater London May '97; proposed John Redwood for Leader and managed his campaign May-June '97; finally voted, after hesitation, for Hague on final ballot June '97; was unexpectedly named Chief Spokesman on Social Security a leap from the back benches June '97; claimed Labour's welfare-to-work programme would prompt £300m in "collusion and fraud" June '97; attacked Labour for U-turn on council cuts in war pension tax disregards Aug '97; with David Heathcoat-Amory, threatened to leave the Shadow Cabinet unless Hague hardened his line on the Euro to banning it for a decade Oct '97; again opposed reducing age of homosexual consent below 18 as "sending out the wrong message" Oct '97; claimed Social Security was "rudderless" and the Social Security Bill "redistributive" Feb '98; accused PM Tony Blair of gagging his Minister, Frank Field Mar '98;

Born: 9 April 1954, Edinburgh

Family: Son, Group Captain W G G Duncan Smith, RAF and business, and Pamela Mary (Summers) ballet dancer; m '82 Elizabeth/'Betsy' Wynne (Fremantle) secretary; 2s Edward St Alban '87, Harry Alasdair St John '90, 2d Alicia Cecilia '89, Rosanna Tatiana '93;

Education: Various primary schools; H M Conway, Anglesey; Universita di Perugia; RMA, Sandhurst; Dunchurch College of Management;

Occupation: Journalism, broadcasting, lecturing '92-; Novelist: spent four years on thriller on an art fraud '93-97; ex: Publisher: Consultant '92-95, Director '89-92, Janes Information Group (part of Thomson International Corporation) '89-95; Director: Bellwinch Plc (property) '88-89; Executive, in GEC-Marconi ("I...was involved in manufacturing industry") '81-88; Captain '79-81, Lieutenant '75-79, in Scots Guards;

Traits: Dark, greying, retreating hair; "wild, penetrating eyes"; "a sub-Tebbit snarl, a populist turn of phrase, and a very good brain"; "with his high forehead, shark-like smile and penetrating stare could be mistaken for a Superintendent in the Stepney and Shoreditch police" (Matthew Parris, TIMES); sports waistcoats; "wears a pinstripe well, but the only thing about him much softer than Norman [Tebbit] [are] his vowels" (Charles Nevin, INDEPENDENT ON SUNDAY); "cerebral" (Patrick Wintour, GUARDIAN); thoughtful; eloquent; Rugby-player (on '94 Commons-Lords team against Irish Dail);

Address: House of Commons, Westminster, SW1A 0AA; c/o Scott Chapman, James Yard,

480 Larkshall Road, Chingford, E4 9UA;
Telephone: 0171 219 3574/2664 (H of C); 0181 524 4344 (constituency office);

Gwyneth (Patricia) DUNWOODY   **Labour**   **CREWE & NANTWICH '83-**

Majority: 15,798 (31.2%) over Conservative 4-way;
Description: The formerly-marginal seat including Crewe, the working class island in Cheshire (with Rolls-Royce and, formerly, railway workshops), plus affluent Nantwich market town and nearby commuter villages; made safer for Labour in '95 by the removal of Tory-leaning villages to Eddisbury and the acquisition of Haslington from Congleton;
Former Seat: Crewe '74-83; Exeter '66-70;
Position: Co-Chairman, Select Committee on Environment, Transport and Regional Affairs '97-; on Liaison Committee '97-; on Chairmen's Panel '92-; President '93-, Chairman 88-93 Labour Friends of Israel; Chairman, all-party Action on Smoking and Health (ASH) Group '80-; Vice Chairman, all-party British-Taiwan Parliamentary Group '97-; Secretary, all-party Opera Group '97-; ex: on Transport Select Committee '87-97; on Labour's National Executive '81-88; Parliamentary Secretary, Board of Trade '67-70; Spokesman: Transport '84-85, Party Campaigning '83-84, Health '81-83; Deputy Spokesman, on Foreign Affairs (Europe and Third World) '79-80; Delegate, to European Assembly '75-79; Chairman: Labour Solidarity '87-88, Vice President, Women's Executive of the Socialist International '86-92;
Outlook: A brave, bouncy, Centre-Right radical; "feisty, Rightwing Old Labour" (Matthew Parris, TIMES); Labour's longest-serving woman MP; a Shore-style opponent of Brussels; also against Trotskyists, tokenism for women, and smoking; tends to make up with strident verbal handbagging for lightness of preparation; has satirised herself as "the epitome of the gentle, calm and flexible politician" (GD); was the battered hammer of the hard Left on the NEC '81-88 when she was still the chubby pin-up girl of traditional trade union leaders - possibly partly for her father's sake; a multilateralist; pro: abortion, black African rights, the Commonwealth, furs (especially those trapped by Canadian Indians), Israel; anti: Militant, EC/EU, Japanese imports, devolution, bill collectors, lying pressmen; "a tremendous campaigner; she is a solid, reliable ally, one of the few people prepared to stand up under fire and expose an unpopular cause" - like Israel (Greville (later Lord) Janner); "I found her arrogant and insensitive; she covers up her lack of knowledge by a hectoring attitude" (Peter Snape MP): was RMT-sponsored;
History: She was expelled from the Fulham League of Youth '46; joined Labour Party '47; was selected for Exeter '61; was elected to Totnes Borough Council '63; was narrowly defeated for Exeter Oct '64; was elected for Exeter, ousting Sir Rolf Dudley-Williams Mar '66; strongly supported David Steel's Abortion Act '67; was appointed Parliamentary Secretary at Board of Trade, with responsibility for industrial development certificates and films Aug '67; lost Exeter June '70; was elected for Crewe Feb '74; stood for Shadow Cabinet, running last with five votes Apr '74; favoured Fourth Channel as a mixed service '74; was named delegate to European Assembly '75; forced apology from Travel Trade Gazette for alleging that she had criticised ABTA at instigation of its former Chairman Apr '75; stood for Women's section of

NEC, gaining 855,000 votes Oct '76; as a counter-devolutionary voted against guillotine of pro-devolution Bill Feb '77; stood for Women's Section of NEC, garnering 792,000 votes Oct '77; introduced Bill to give people (especially her late father, Morgan Phillips) libel protection for 50 years after their deaths July '78; opposed Japanese investment in UK Nov '78; co-sponsored Pavitt Bill to control tobacco advertising Dec '78; again opposed Japanese investment in UK June '79; battled against abortion curbs of John Corrie's Bill July '79-Mar '80; favoured import controls on Japanese motor cars Oct '80; first won seat on NEC with 3.7m votes Sep '81; was elected to bottom place in Shadow Cabinet Oct '81; was named Health Spokesman Nov '81; ousted Leftwinger Joan Maynard from Chairmanship of NEC's Local Government Committee Nov '81; opposed endorsement of homosexual Leftwinger Peter Tatchell as candidate for Bermondsey (which he lost) Dec '81; backed inquiry into Militant Dec '81; opposed endorsement of Militant-backed Pat Wall Feb '82; backed acceptance of hostile Militant Tendency Report by NEC June '82; claimed Tories would have demolished NHS had it not been popular with Tory voters Sep '82; was jeered by Leftwing feminists when she rejected, on behalf of NEC, motion to place a woman on every shortlist Sep '82; tied for second bottom place on Shadow Cabinet Nov '82; defeated Leftwinger Frank Allaun for Chairman of NEC Press Committee Nov '82; attacked common pension age of 63 as a "con" Dec '82; during the election claimed that Tory victory would mean dismantling of NHS May '83; urged Labour rethink June '83; attacked drug company overpricing June '83; stood for Deputy Leader as running mate for equally anti-Brussels Peter Shore June-Oct '83; ran third with 1.3% Oct '83; was re-elected to the NEC with 3.99m votes Oct '83; in Shadow Cabinet election, ran twelfth with 73 votes Oct '83; in effort to keep her Health portfolio, turned down four other posts offered her by Kinnock, settling for a non-frontbench Party Campaigning portfolio Nov '83; voted to expel six Blackburn Militants Apr '84; won 4,667,000 votes to stay on NEC Oct '84; voted against Dennis Skinner for Vice Chairman of the Labour Party Oct '84; on the NEC voted to delete full-scale sanctions from resolution on Apartheid Oct '84; on the Solidarity slate, came tenth with 88 votes for Shadow Cabinet Oct '84; led a CPA delegation to Botswana and Lesotho July-Aug '85; won 4,586,000 votes to stay on NEC Sep '85; on the Solidarity slate, failed to make it on to the Shadow Cabinet with 70 votes, the fourth runner-up; "my colleagues in the Parliamentary Labour Party clearly felt that there were too many women in the Shadow Cabinet" - of which she had been the only woman member Oct '85; won 3,820,000 votes to stay on NEC Sep '86; her local party executive complained about her connection with the British Fur Trade Association ("the episode left a very sour taste in our mouths") although she explained she needed the money to sort out her financial difficulties Apr '86; denied wanting to join Jonathan Aitken's anti-Channel-Tunnel group, her sponsoring union, the NUR, being strongly in favour of the Channel Tunnel Jan '87; with Ian Mikardo tried to talk out the Obscene Publications Bill because "one man's morality is another man's prudishness" Apr '87; voted for the removal of half-black Trotskyist, Sharon Atkin, as a candidate Apr '87; trebled her tiny majority June '87; received only 31 votes for the Shadow Cabinet, the twenty-fourth runner-up July '87; complained about her constituency being used as a trial ground for Availability for Work Test July '87; backed railway strikers July '87; warned annual conference against betraying Labour voters: "the Labour Party is too important to be left to the [hard Left] clowns" Sep '87; retained her NEC seat with 3,997,000 votes Sep '87; complained that the BREL workshop in Crewe had been modernised, then starved of orders, to make it ripe for privatiation Nov '87; the CND complained about her being on the Labour Party's International and Defence Study Group Dec '87; speculation about her being disqualified as a bankrupt emerged when the MAIL ON SUNDAY alleged that Barclays Bank was suing for debts of over £100,000 and Nationwide was starting proceedings for repossession of her Crewe home; Mrs Dunwoody vehemently denied its accuracy but refused to correct the report, insisting that the truth never catches up with a newspaper libel, even when a libel action is won, as in her father's case Mar '88; as a Consultant to the British Fur Trade Association, backed the labelling of furs from animals caught in leghold traps, allegedly on behalf of "indigenous peoples throughout the world" Apr-May '88; complained of elderly being pushed into private retirement homes May '88; asked Environment Secretary "would he like to live in a cardboard box under Waterloo Bridge?" May '88; asked for labelling "for leather goods manufactured from fur-bearing animals which he has identified as being commonly caught in leg-hold traps" June '88; announced the dissolution of the Solidarity Group of Labour MPs, its membership having sunk from a top of 40 to 25, July '88; received an insufficient 3,823,000 votes for Women's Section of Labour's NEC Oct '88; claimed midwives in North Middlesex Hospital were resigning wholesale, despite Health Secretary Kenneth Clarke's claim that satisfactory regrading was being conducted Nov '88; warned against NHS "partnership" deals with unknown new companies, like her local authority was trying with Bioplan Jan '89; complained that if balancing the books in transport was the only issue, you ended up with the current dirty dangerous and unattractive public transport system Feb '89; asked how many prosecutions had taken the place for the illegal importation of seal skins Feb '89; was accused by PA's Political Editor, Chris Moncrieff, of belabouring him physically for his "reactionary outpourings" Feb '89; "defended" Mrs Thatcher against the charge that she had not known what she was doing, as a Euro-sceptic, in pushing through the centralising Single European Act with the help of Tory Whips May '89; asked an embarrassed Sir Geoffrey Howe whether he supported Chancellor Nigel Lawson on going into the European Monetary System or PM Margaret Thartcher in staying out June '89; complained about "total chaos" in outdated air traffic control system July '89; contested Women's Section of Labour's NEC Aug '89; received 1,716,000 votes as the third runner-up Oct '89; her £180,000 constituency home was sold ten months after she was barred from it for falling behind on her £50,000 mortgage Oct '89; asked a series of questions about sexual abuse of children Oct-Nov '89; attacked Kenneth Clarke for further inflaming the ambulance strike Nov '89; attended Lisbon socialist conference with John Hume Nov '89; described Kenneth Clarke's National Health Service and Community Care Bill as "spawned in dislike, produced out of ignorance and apparently being pushed with malice" Dec '89; complained, in Broadcasting Bill, that children's TV often meant "cartoon films imported from America" Dec '89; her call for a publlicity campaign specifically aimed at insructing children how to protect themselves against abuse was turned down Dec '89; complained of sloppy security on airlines other than El Al Jan '90; in retaliation for Leftwing Labour MPs' attack on Tory consultancies, Tory MPs asked what she earned from the British Fur Trade Association Feb '90; a Paddington travel firm, Skytrek Travel Centre, sued her for £1,300 for services provided 17 months before Feb '90; voted with Eurosceptics on EC Agriculture Feb '90; was said to face an inquiry over her failure to register her connection with Channel Communications, a Kent-based company campaigning againt the high-speed rail link; its Director said "we have only ever used Gwyneth for clients that were particularly interested in transport; we paid her for six consultancies; it was a very small amount" Mar '90; while a Consultant to the British Fur Trade Association, asked for reduction of Japanese tariffs on leather and an end to their quota system Mar '90; deplored failure of Government to spend any signficant money on research or statistics on child abuse June '90; claimed the absence of a balanced railway policy was bringing London "quietly grinding to a halt" June '90; objected to pro-Arabs' linking of Israel with invasion of Kuwait by Iraq Nov '90; visited Namibia with other women from Socialist International Dec '90; complained about underfunding of hospitals Dec '90; was nominated for European Standing Committee A Jan '91; sought to adjourn Commons to protest loss of 1,200 jobs at Crewe's BR Engineering Ltd Feb '91; when Dr

Rhodes Boyson suggested a "work test" for the unemployed, she asked whether the cat-o-nine tails might also help Feb '91; visited Poland with the all-party Parliamentary Committee for East European Jewry, as a guest of the all-party Committee and the Inter-Parliamentary Council against Anti-Semitism May '91; co-sponsored an anti-Maastricht motion headed by Peter Shore Nov '91; warned against Maastricht's intention of shifting economic and political power from Westminster to Brussels Dec '91; retained seat with her majority up from 1,092 to 2,695, a swing to Labour of 1.25% Apr '92; seconded nomination of Betty Boothroyd for Speaker Apr '92; told Dennis Skinner he was being churlish for objecting to departing Speaker Weatherill being rewarded with a seat in the Lords May '92; with Allan Rogers, was eliminated in first round of contest for chairmanship of the Parliaemntary Labour Party July '92; was re-named to the Transport Select Committee July '92; urged targets in health, particularly against smoking which was accounting for one in six of the fatalities in her constituency Oct '92; deplored bankrupcy of Transport Secretary John McGregor's plan to semi-privatise BR Oct '92; introduced a Private Member's Bill to prohibit the use of age limits in job appointments, training schemes, promotions and advertising of jobs, the Bill her late mother, Baroness Phillips, had introduced in the Lords at 82, Nov '92; resisted extension of Brussels power, complaining that, within the EC, Britain was unable to defend its films as did the French, using "every known barrier to protect French films" Jan '93; said the unwillingness of Labour frontbench to vote for a probing amendment moved by Tony Blair to delete citizenship provisions of Maastricht Bill was "shaming" Feb '93; was named an additional Chairman of Standing Committee B in respect of the Railways Bill Feb '93; was clocked as having voted against the Maastricht Bill seven times already Feb '93; complained about "underfunding" of local Leighton Hospital Apr '93; attacked Virgina Bottomley's "incompetent, overweeningly arrogant behaviour", including giving rich contracts to private computer companies but depriving hospitals of "the software in their expensive computers to run the contracts that the Secretary of State tells us are the purpose behind the way in which wants to operate the NHS" May '93; voted against 3rd Reading of Maastricht Bill May '93; with nine other Labour women, wrote letter to GUARDIAN praising one-member one-vote for its contribution to party and union democracy June '93; backed right of public transport to lease rolling stock June '93; told Under Secretary Tom Sackville that his justification of the artificial marriage of two unwilling health authorities was "the greatest load of claptrap that even he has ever uttered" July '93; with Llin Golding MP, Irene Adams MP and Ann Carlton, wife of Denzil Davies MP, formed 'Labour Supporters of Real Equality' to oppose official quotas for women July '93; deplored distribution of book blaming World War II on the Jews Aug '93; received 82 votes -with 107 needed - in contest for Labour's 'Shadow Cabinet', perhaps half from 40 MCPs who also gave hard-Left Mildred Gordon 81 votes; Dunwoody accepted this was a protest against "certain, very particular, women who were of the opinion that they had a God-given right to be amongst the chosen" Oct '93; co-sponsored Andrew Mackinlay's Bill to pardon disgraced and executed soldiers of World War I, Oct '93; voted with Eurosceptics against EC-EFTA link Oct '93; backed right of Northern Irish to join Labour Party Oct '93; launched new campaign to save her local Leighton Hospital from underfunding Nov '93; backed Peter Shore's amendment criticising Maastricht's "deflationary" policies Dec '93; complained about further local hospital cuts Jan '94; complained about inability of local hospitals to act promptly enough in life-threatening situations like breast cancer Mar '94; demanded protection for Commonwealth bananas: "consumer want bananas that taste like bananas; Central American bananas taste like soap" May '94; co-sponsored Bill to prohibit collaboration on trade boycotts of Israel July '94; highlighted low safety standards of mini-buses July '94; voted for John Prescott for Leader and Deputy Leader July '94; co-signed SUNDAY TIMES letter urging Labour to organise in Northern Ireland Sep '94; introduced

Bill to regulate private residential care homes Nov '94; complained of Tories' "deliberate murder" of the railway industry and the "agony of the destruction of the BR works" at Crewe Dec '94; urged PM John Major to empower Commons European Committees to amend Ministers' suggestions, with results decided in the Commons Dec '94; challenged light prison sentences for men who killed constituent by dousing him with paint-stripper and setting him alight Jan '95; piloted through Commons Lord (David) Stoddart's Bill to restore single-sex hospital wards Feb '95; opposed abolition of union sponsorship of Labour MPs, claiming RMT had supplied her with important information June '95; again attacked rail privatisation: "all the Government care about is the money they can raise before the next election" Oct '95; deplored the suicide-causing Child Support Agency, "set up in haste and created in chaos" Oct '95; with other "Awkward Squaddies" voted against Commons procedural reforms as reducing MPs to "walk-ons" Nov '95; assailed Government encouragement of private health care as a "deliberate plan to run down the Health Service" Nov '95; joined in hostile questioning of Prisons Minister Anne Widdecombe defending manacling of a pregnant woman prisoner Jan '96; was rated among the most assiduous committee attenders, with 82 attendances in '94-95, Mar '96; warned PM John Major her farmers felt he was "wiping out the beef industry" May '96; attacked the pro-European FCO for not putting "enough money or energy into supporting the Commonwealth" June '96; voted against 3% cap on MPs' pay rise, for a pension based on £43,000 (up £9,000), and for cuts in MPs' mileage allowances July '96; alleged "real problems of racial discrimination and sexism" in the civil service July '96; claimed Government had wasted £435m on rail privatisation consultants which could have been used to modernise the railways Aug '96; was listed as one of "Blair's Bastards" in Hull University research because, since '92, she had voted 23 times against the party leadership Sep '96; worried about the safety implications of rail privatisation Nov '96; with 14 others was cleared by Sir Gordon Downey, in her case of receiving £250 from Tory lobbyist Ian Greer in '92 election contribution Mar '97; retained her altered, previously-marginal seat with enhanced majority of 15,798 on a notional pro-Labour swing of 11.3% May '97; uttered the first words in the new Parliament - "Sir Edward [Heath], this is a truly beautiful day" - launching the re-election of her friend Betty Boothroyd as Speaker; in a veiled barb at New Labour "babes", said Betty, "unlike some here, got here only after five attempts" May '97; visited Colombia to study human rights abuses as guest of Avianca and BP May-June '97; on her return, urged strengthening of Customs as a barrier against drugs June '97; was named, as its Co-Chairman, to the new Select Committee on Environment, Transport and Regional Affairs, taking charge of Transport July '97; also to the Liaison Committee (of Committee Chairmen) July '97; she deplored Vickers flogging off the ownership of local Rolls-Royce to German owners Dec '97; demanded the return from the New York Public Library, after 70 years, of Christopher Robin Milne's original toys as "part of our national heritage" Feb '98; attacked Parliamentary sketchwriters for "very cheerfully written but wholly inaccurate reports" Feb '98; her Select Committee urged a strategic rail authority to manage the existing franchise and to contemplate the partial renationalisation of Railtrack and failed operating companies Mar '98; as a veteran, resisted the "potentially dangerous situation" of the over-enthusiastic efforts of the Modernisation Committee, spurred on by new Labour MPs June '98; was one of 24 Labour rebels who voted against Murdoch-style predatory pricing of newspapers July '98;
Born: 12 December 1930, Fulham, London
Family: Daughter, the late Morgan Phillips, General Secretary of the Labour Party, and late Baroness (Nora) Phillips; m '54 Dr John Dunwoody, physician/health administrator and former Falmouth MP; divorced '75; 2s David, Gareth, 1d Tamsin (active in Newport, Pembrokeshire Labour Party);
Education: Fulham County Secondary School; Notre Dame Convent;

Occupation: Ex: Sponsored, by RMT (ex-NUR; 25% of agent's salary, 80% of election costs) '74-95; Director, of St David's Care in the Community, St David's, Pembrokeshire (school for mentally-handicapped children) '93-97; ex: Director, Dunwoody Computer Services (owned 99 shares of 100-share company started with £8,000 but which never made a profit; John Rice, who designed its logo complained he was unpaid after a year; it stopped trading in '89) '85-88; Consultant: British Fur Trade Association (at £4,000 p a) '85-91, Channel Communications (Kent-based company lobbying against route for high-speed rail link) '89, to the Association of Independent Cinemas '8?-8?; Director, of Film Production Association of Great Britain (resigned after unauthorised expenses were queried) '70-74; Actress; Scriptwriter, for Radio Netherlands; Journalist, on local Fulham paper, on leaving school '46;

Traits: Rotund ("the Battling Butterball"); "everything I've got is a suit or jacket and skirt; I'm not employed for my dress sense"; a "tough-minded woman in a rug-like jacket, looking as though she had not so much dressed as rolled herself up in the bedroom carpet and rolled in to work"; "a battling blonde lady from Crewe whose very glance could slice a banana at fifty paces" (Matthew Parris, TIMES); lively; punchy; vivid speaking style; "stentorian tone"; didactic; "I am a totally emotional politician" (GD); "all the charm and finesse of a sledgehammer" (Andrew Alexander, DAILY MAIL); "Madame Defarge" (did tapestry embroidery during NEC inquiry into Militant); "Gunboats"; multilingual (Dutch/French/Italian); over-generous with hospitality (she was threatened with legal proceedings to secure £1,000 owed to Commons' MPs' Restaurant Mar '88); narrowly escaped eviction proceedings from Barbican flat by paying £5,000 in rent arrears Apr '86, bailiffs seized her furniture over arrears of £7,000 May '87, was again threatened in Mar '88;

Address: House of Commons, Westminster, London SW1A 0AA; 13 Cromwell Tower, Beech Street, London EC2Y 6DD;

Telephone: 0171 219 3490/4616 (H of C); 0171 588 2615 (London home);

TRACKING SCANDALS

By noting the warts in our portraits of MPs, we have long tracked their scandals. Sometimes we have been the first to notice a wart. In the Profumo scandal, we were the first to publish, in 1963, his letter to Christine Keeler in our newsletter, WESTMINSTER CONFIDENTIAL. We pushed another hole in the dam holding back disclosure about the corrupt lobbying activities of the Ian Greer organisation when, in 1989, our PARLIAMENTARY PROFILES volume published, in its profile of Michael Grylls, the fact that he was accepting from Ian Greer an unregistered percentage of all the business referred to Greer's firm. Press Gallery colleagues declined to report this disclosure after Grylls pretended that he was going to sue us for libel. The story seemed to die for a long time until Greer and Neil Hamilton, with the full support of the Major Government, threatened to sue the GUARDIAN. In the preparation for that trial-which-never-happened, it was discovered that Ian Greer changed his whole accounting system when faced with our publication of his secret relationship with Grylls, giving the game away to the GUARDIAN lawyers.
